CANADIAN EDITION

ELEMENTARY AND MIDDLE SCHOOL MATHEMATICS

TEACHING DEVELOPMENTALLY

John A. Van De Walle
Virginia Commonwealth University

Sandra Folk
University of Toronto

PEARSON

Toronto

National Library of Canada Cataloguing in Publication

Van de Walle, John A.
    Elementary and middle school mathematics : teaching developmentally / John A. Van de Walle,
Sandra Folk. — Canadian ed.

Includes bibliographical references and index.
ISBN 0-205-42077-X

1. Mathematics—Study and teaching (Elementary) 2. Mathematics—Study and teaching (Middle school)
I. Folk, Sandra II. Title.

QA135.6.V35 2005   372.7'044   C2003-906303-8

ISBN 0-205-42077-X

Vice-President, Editorial Director: Michael J. Young
Acquisitions Editor: Christine Cozens
Marketing Manager: Ryan St. Peters
Signing Representative: Shannon Phillips
Senior Developmental Editor: Martina van de Velde
Production Editor: Charlotte Morrison-Reed
Copy Editor: Nadia Halim
Proofreader: Freya Godard
Production Manager: Wendy Moran
Page Layout: Carolyn E. Sebestyn
Art Director: Mary Opper
Cover and Interior Design: Lisa Lapointe

2 3 4 5   09 08 07 06 05

Printed and bound in the United States of America.

Contents

Preface

Children will become confident "doers" of mathematics only if mathematics makes sense to them and if they believe in their ability to make sense of it.

Trafton and Claus (1994, p. 21)

What is basic about mathematics is that "it makes sense." Every child, in her or his own way, should come to believe that mathematics makes sense and that she or he is capable of making sense of it. All children should leave school with the confidence of knowing that they understand mathematics and that they are able to do it.

The main goal of *Elementary and Middle School Mathematics* is to help you and your students come to believe that mathematics indeed does make sense and that you are capable of making sense of it. But your students will need to develop this knowledge themselves. As students engage in the doing of mathematics, you will find that their understanding and confidence will grow.

The subtitle of this book, *Teaching Developmentally*, requires that you engage students where you find them (rather than where you think they are) so that they can create or develop new ideas that they can use and understand-so that they can see through their own eyes that mathematics makes sense. They will believe it because they can do it!

The same is true for you as the teacher of these children. When you believe that mathematics makes sense and that you are capable of making sense of it, you will be in the best position to help your students do mathematics with understanding and confidence.

A continuing spirit of positive change has pervaded mathematics education now for well over a decade. More and more teachers are working to adapt newer ways to help children learn and this book is written to reflect the best of that change and to help you become a part of it.

As you work through this book you will find that most ideas and activities are referenced according to the grade level(s) for which they are appropriate, rather than by school division (i.e. elementary or middle school). The reason is that, in Canada, the term middle school varies in its determination depending on the jurisdiction in which you teach. For example, in one province it might include grades 5 and 6, whereas in another it refers to grades 6-8.

What You Will Find in This Book

Each of the three sections of this book plays an important role in helping you become an effective teacher of mathematics. Together, they form both a resource and a reference for teaching mathematics.

Section 1: Foundations Consistently, in our work with teachers we find that those who possess the best understanding of how children learn and the best knowledge of how to create a problem-solving environment are the ones who are most effective. From this perspective, the two most important chapters in the book are Chapters 3 and 4. Here you will learn about a constructivist view of learning, how that applies to the learning of mathematics, and how to teach mathematics through problem solving. Chapter 5 discusses the integration of assessment and instruction so that planning and evaluation are conducted in a way that most effectively aids student learning.

A body of critical thinking regarding how to help children learn mathematics is reflected in these core ideas. We have worked hard to ensure that these ideas are clearly and consistently represented throughout the second section of the book.

It is important to know the direction in which mathematics is moving and why so that you will know how to play a professional role in that endeavour. As well, it is necessary to have a feel for the discipline-to know what it means, "to do mathematics". The first two chapters address these issues.

Section 2: Concepts and Procedures Chapters 6 through 20 focus on the specific mathematics topics of the K–8 curricula. Every major topic is addressed in depth. Each chapter provides a perspective on the mathematical content, how children best learn that content, and numerous suggestions for problem-based activities to engage children in the process of doing mathematics.

Many classroom teachers use this text as a resource and consult it as they plan each new unit. They frequently talk about how this book is a valuable resource assisting them with the content of mathematics and how children learn this content. The problem-based tasks for students are integrated with the text, rather than being an "add on."

As you reflect on the activities you read, it will help you think about the mathematics from the perspective of the child. Every activity requires that students be mentally engaged: to figure something out, to search for a pattern, to explain a reason for an idea—in short, to do mathematics as a problem-solving endeavour.

The activities are also there for you. Read them along with the text, not as an aside. After all, you are constructing new knowledge yourself—knowledge about teaching mathematics to children. Like your students, you must become actively engaged in *your own learning* about *children learning* mathematics. By actually doing the activities as you read through the book, you can get an idea of how children might react to or learn from each activity.

Section 3: Issues and Perspectives As the foundational chapters of Section 1 provide a framework for the teaching of mathematics, the chapters in this section, which build on this foundation, offer perspectives on the challenging task of helping children learn mathematics.

Chapter 21 builds on the general principles for the design of effective lessons developed in Chapter 4 offering further practical information on topics such as forming cooperative learning groups, the value of drill and practice, homework, and other issues.

In Chapter 22 you will read about working with children whose needs are special whether they are children with learning problems, children of different cultural backgrounds, or children who are mathematically talented. Gender issues are also addressed. Chapter 23 provides perspectives on the issues surrounding technology in the teaching of mathematics. A strong case is made for the use of calculators in all grades. Guidance is also offered for the selection and use of computer software, and suggestions are made to help you find valuable resources on the Internet.

Special Features of This Text

The Canadian edition of *Elementary and Middle School Mathematics* retains many of the features that have helped make all of the American editions so successful. The overall intent is to make the book as useful for you as possible. Here are 11 things to look for.

Big Ideas Much of the literature espousing a student-centred approach suggests that teachers plan their instruction around "big ideas" rather than tiny skills or concepts. Identifying a big idea is not always easy. To help you develop an understanding of what is meant by "big ideas" you will find a list of the key mathematical ideas and concepts at the beginning of each chapter in Section 2. Teachers find these lists helpful for quickly getting a picture of the mathematics they are teaching.

Activities A variety of activities for developing important mathematical concepts are presented in each chapter in Section 2. They help to make this book a resource as well as a textbook. Most are clearly framed in a box with a title. Other ideas are described directly in the text or in the illustrations. Every activity, as described in Chapter 4, is a problem-based task. Some new activities have been added and some modified or discarded. Each one is designed to engage students in doing mathematics.

Assessment Notes Near the end of most chapters in Section 2, you will find a short Assessment Notes section. These sections are designed to build on the general themes of assessment established in Chapter 5. These notes can assist you in making assessment an integral part of instruction.

Literature Connections Children's literature is one of the most inviting ways to actively involve children in doing mathematics. Many of the chapters in Section 2 contain a Literature Connections section. In most of these sections, at least three children's literature titles are suggested, with a brief description of how the mathematics of the chapter can be profitably built on the stories. Though certainly not a comprehensive listing of potential literature, these sections will get you started using this exciting vehicle for teaching mathematics.

Technology Notes In each chapter of section 2 you will find one or more Technology Note sections. There you will find a general discussion of how computer software may be used profitably (or not) to help with the content just discussed. Descriptions of specific software titles (with special attention to available Canadian software) are provided. Even if you do not have the same software, the comments will help you look at similar software with an objective eye to judge its potential effectiveness. Inclusion of any software title in these Notes should not be considered an endorsement.

The computer icon marking the Technology Notes section, as well as certain activities and appropriate paragraphs, in the text is intended to identify the use of computer technology.

Calculators Calculator activities are found in every appropriate chapter. They are identified with a small calculator icon, which is intended to indicate the calculator's applicability for the particular topic. Because of their gradually increasing use in grades 6, 7, and 8, you will also find references to graphing calculators.

Writing to Learn To draw your attention to the important pedagogical ideas, a list of focusing questions is found at the end of every chapter under the heading Reflections on the Chapter: Writing to Learn. These study questions are designed to help you reflect on the main points of the chapter. Actually writing out the answers to these questions in your own words is one of the best ways for you to develop your understanding of each chapter's main ideas.

For Discussion and Exploration Following the Writing to Learn list are a few additional questions that ask you to explore an issue, reflect on observations in a classroom, compare text ideas with those found in traditional curriculum materials, or perhaps take a position on a controversial issue. There are rarely "right" answers to these questions, but they will certainly stimulate thought and spirited conversation. Discuss these with your peer group or with teachers in the classroom.

Recommendations for Further Reading The end of each chapter contains a bibliography of useful articles and books to augment the information found in the chapter. Usually these are taken from NCTM journals, yearbooks, and other professional resources that are targeted for the classroom teacher. Three or four of the selections that we feel are especially important or useful are offered with a short annotation under the heading "Highly Recommended." It would have been nice to annotate the whole list, however space does not permit. (Note that all sources *cited in the text proper* appear in the References at the back of the book.)

NCTM Principles and Standards   The spirit of the NCTM's *Principles and Standards for School Mathematics* is reflected throughout the book, particularly in Chapter 1. The six Assessment Standards and the four Purposes of Assessment from the *Assessment Standards for School Mathematics* are presented in Chapter 5. In Appendix A, you will find a list of the five content standards and specific expectations for grade bands pre-K–2, 3–5, 6–8, and 9–12. Appendix B contains the six Standards for Teaching Mathematics from the *Professional Standards for Teaching Mathematics*.

Blackline Masters   The Blackline Masters section at the end of the book offers an extensive collection of masters and directions for making important instructional materials. Suggestions for the use of these materials are found throughout the book. You are encouraged to copy these pages and duplicate them for classroom activities.

Features of the Canadian Edition

This Canadian Edition represents a substantial revision designed to make the content current, relevant, and of increased interest to Canadian faculty students and teachers. No chapter was left untouched. In particular, chapters 1, 15, 18, 19, and 22 have undergone considerable alteration. At the same time though, the best features of the American edition have been maintained throughout. The following are features and highlights of chapter changes to the new Canadian Edition:

- Current Canadian-based student assessment and evaluation data
- Canadian perspectives on the challenging task of helping *all* children learn mathematics
- Content and activities that fit with provincial and territorial curriculum expectations
- A focus on Canadian computer software
- Discussion of the latest Canadian studies and educational issues
- New metric examples and problems
- A thorough yet concise enhanced text of 23 chapters (reduced from 24 chapters)

Highlights of Changes to the Canadian Edition

Section 1: The Foundations Chapters
- Canadian data on national and international studies
- A Canadian perspective on reform in mathematics education, and explanation of links with the National Council of Teachers of Mathematics
- Change in the *before, during, after* model of lesson planning
- A Canadian perspective on traditional and reform curricula
- Canadian perspectives on assessment and evaluation
- Provincial-based references

Section 2: Development of Mathematical Concepts and Procedures Chapters
- Canadian computer software references and descriptions for number operations, estimation with whole numbers and fractional concepts
- Hundred chart activities replace 0-99 chart activities
- Metric problems and measurement activities
- Metric-based concept development
- Activities for the TI-15 and T-108 calculators, and for the TI-73 and TI-73 Explorer
- Canadian based data on students' TIMSS results
- New ratio problems adapted from Saskatchewan Education Middle Level 6-9 Curriculum
- A Canadian perspective on proportionality
- Canadian website references
- Canadian-based data for very large numbers
- Canadian sports data for developing the concept of integers

Section 3: Issues and Perspectives
- Canadian-based resources for strategies for effective instruction
- Substantial data and research on Inclusive education in Canada
- Multicultural, social equity, and gender issues
- Education for the gifted and talented and those with learning disabilities
- Examples of effective instruction
- Canadian Internet resources accessible to teachers and students

Companion Web Site (www.pearsoned.ca/vandewalle/)
This online course companion provides a wealth of resources for both students and instructors. Students will find chapter summaries, interactive Web activities, a complete guide to conducting research on the Internet, and more. Instructors will have protected access to the *Instructor's Manual* and teaching links.

Notes to the Instructor

No other book offers your students as much as this one does. Most importantly, it provides a strong theoretical perspective on children's learning of mathematics—not just a casual overview. This perspective is reflected consistently throughout the book. Second, no other book of this type develops so clearly the strong position articulated by Hiebert et al. (1996, 1997), that the best approach to teaching mathematics is to teach with problem-based tasks. Third, teachers find the book to be a valuable resource that almost all carry into the classroom rather than sell back to the bookstore. Many school divisions, principals, and classroom teachers buy the book for the same purpose. It has become a standard reference for K–8 teachers. Teachers and supervisors continually talk about how readable and valuable they find the book.

It is a large book! It is not a book to "cover" but a book to use. It is not intended that you teach the content of the entire book in a single year. In fact, the best approach is to cover fewer topics with time spent developing the spirit of Chapters 3 and 4. As you explore the content topics you do select, let your class be a model for the instruction you want for all topics. Teaching with problem-based tasks and classroom discourse is a complete shift from the experiences of most faculty students and teachers.

By providing your students with the detail and information found in this book, you send with them into the classroom the specifics you were unable to cover in class. And you can be assured that the spirit of what you do cover will also be evident in the chapters you did not cover.

There are many different styles of methods courses. Yet all who have used this book seem to find their own best strategies for their class. For this reason, we hesitate to dictate a course but are proud to offer this text. We wish you and your students much success and excitement as you explore good mathematics with children.

Acknowledgments

Many intelligent and talented people have contributed to the success of this Canadian edition of the book and we are deeply grateful to those who have assisted us along the way. There were people from faculties of education, ministries of education, teachers' associations, and other organizations across Canada. They generously took the time to answer e-mails and phone calls, and provided us with educational materials and software to assist us.

Without the success of the American editions, there certainly would not be a Canadian edition. Regardless of the number of editions that this text may see we will always be most sincerely indebted to Warren Crown (Rutgers), John Dossey (Illinois State University), Bob Gilbert (Florida International University), and Steven Willoughby (University of Arizona), who gave time and great care in offering detailed comments on the original manuscript. Few mathematics educators of their stature would devote the time and effort they gave to this endeavour.

In preparing this Canadian edition, we have received thoughtful input from the following educators, who offered comments on the manuscript:

Jerry Ameis, University of Winnipeg
Lynda Colgan, Queen's University
Ralph Connelly, Brock University

Doug Franks, Nipissing University
Lynn Gordon Calvert, University of Alberta
Wendy Klassen, Okanagan University College
Peter Liljedahl, Simon Fraser University
Craig Loewen, University of Lethbridge
Jim Montgomery, Malaspina University College
Arsalan Wares, University of Manitoba

Each review challenged us to think through important issues and ideas concerning our writing. Many of their suggestions have found their way into this book. These professionals have our utmost thanks and appreciation.

A very special thanks to Martina van de Velde, Senior Developmental Editor at Pearson Education Canada, who is always there to answer questions and prod us on to the next task—all in a very gentle and friendly manner. Our many e-mails and phone calls ensured that we were able to get this manuscript into shape.

A Personal Note

Many people contribute to the countless details that go into the production of this book. However, my wife is the one who continues to give the most. In a real sense, she is a part of this book. Her belief in me and her daily support and encouragement with each edition make this effort possible. She helps me believe and persevere. She has always been my strongest ally and my closest friend. I love you, Sharon.

On October 24, 2000, our daughter, Gretchen, brought into our world a beautiful ray of sunshine in the form of her very special daughter. This one's for you, Aidan!

John A. Van de Walle

A number of people generously contributed to the production of this Canadian Edition, many having done so without even realizing it. However, I want to extend some special notes of appreciation and gratitude. One is to my good friend Rich Cornwall, a talented mathematics teacher and kind and generous human being. He never hesitated to help me when I needed to bounce an idea around. Melissa and Jelena, my two research assistants, are two others I want to acknowledge. They were always there to carry out my requests at the drop of hat when I required assistance with my research.

The person to whom I owe my greatest note of thanks is my husband, Marshall. He is and has always been there for me in all that I undertake to do, both personally and professionally. His support is invaluable and his encouragement never-ending. I am most fortunate to have him as my life's partner.

Sandy Folk

Section 1

Foundations of Teaching Mathematics

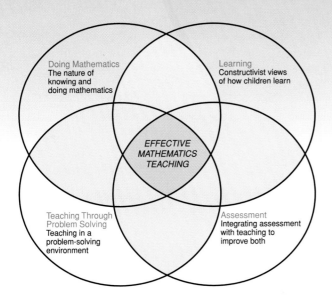

Doing Mathematics
The nature of knowing and doing mathematics

Learning
Constructivist views of how children learn

EFFECTIVE MATHEMATICS TEACHING

Teaching Through Problem Solving
Teaching in a problem-solving environment

Assessment
Integrating assessment with teaching to improve both

Truly effective teaching requires a bringing together of four basic components: (1) an appreciation of the discipline of mathematics itself—what it means to "do mathematics," (2) an understanding of how students learn and construct ideas, (3) an ability to design and select tasks so that students learn mathematics in a problem-solving environment, and (4) the ability to integrate assessment with the teaching process in order to enhance learning and improve daily instruction.

These four ideas are best understood in the context of reform in mathematics, which began in 1989 when the National Council of Teachers of Mathematics published its groundbreaking document, the *Curriculum and Evaluation Standards for School Mathematics*. This movement for reform, along with other important developments, is discussed in Chapter 1.

Chapters 2 through 5 each develop one of the four components of effective teaching. These chapters are in many ways the most important portion of the book. They lay out the foundational ideas on which effective teaching is built at any grade level.

Teaching Mathematics in the Context of the Reform Movement

In this changing world, those who understand and can do mathematics will have significantly enhanced opportunities and options for shaping their futures. Mathematical competence opens doors to productive futures. A lack of mathematical competence keeps those doors closed ... All students should have the opportunity and the support necessary to learn significant mathematics with depth and understanding. There is no conflict between equity and excellence.

—NCTM (2000, p. 5)

You are reading this book because you are interested in learning how to teach mathematics—to help children learn mathematics. What images and emotions does that bring to mind?

Pause now and reflect on your own ideas about the *topic* of mathematics. What does it mean to "do mathematics"? What parts of the subject seem most important? Where do calculators and computers fit in? Write down three or four of your strongest thoughts about mathematics. Compare your thoughts with those of others.

Next, focus on the teaching part. Someday soon you will find yourself in front of a class of students, or perhaps you are already teaching. What general ideas will guide how you teach mathematics? Do children learn mathematics differently from other topics? How can you make it interesting and enjoyable? If mathematics is not exactly your favourite subject, do you think that has anything to do with the way you were taught? How can you help children enjoy the subject more than you do? Add your written thoughts on these questions to those about mathematics.

It is very likely that the ideas in the next four chapters will challenge some of your beliefs and cause you to rethink what you have just written. Save these ideas and revisit them after you have finished the first five chapters of this text.

This is an important, perhaps pivotal, moment in the history of mathematics education, and you—the teachers who help children learn—will ultimately be the ones who shape mathematics for the children you touch.

This chapter explores the ongoing transformation in mathematics education. Also, it provides a window through which you can best understand the four components of effective mathematics teaching as discussed in the opening to this section of the book.

The Reform Movement

Several notable shifts in the direction of mathematics education have had an impact on our schools. It is useful to place these shifts and movements within the context of the forces that have shaped them. The reform movement stands out as one of the more dominant forces that have influenced mathematics education.

A Brief History of Reform

The momentum for reform in mathematics education began in the early 1980s. Educators were responding to a reaction to the "new math" of the 1960s, which consisted of fundamental principles of logical deduction and formal notation. Little attention was paid to the practical uses of mathematics and more to its abstract nature. Following the disillusionment with the "new math" came the fallout from the back-to-basics movement of the 1970s, with its emphasis on rote memorization. This time, the focus was on learning basic facts and ideas in order to build a solid foundation for thinking and problem solving (Barb & Larson Quinn, 1997). The 1980s were marked by a growing interest in making problem solving a focus of the mathematics curriculum. The work of Piaget and other developmental psychologists was shifting the focus of mathematics educators from mathematics content to how children can best learn mathematics. This shift brought with it a change in approach from an emphasis on teaching as telling to one that promoted meaning and understanding.

Reform and the National Council of Teachers of Mathematics

As the voice of reform, the National Council of Teachers of Mathematics (NCTM), a professional, nonprofit organization with over 125 000 members, consisting of K–12 teachers, consultants, administrators, researchers, etc. in the United States and Canada, has led the way. In 1989, the NCTM published the *Curriculum and Evaluation Standards for School Mathematics*. This influential document has had an enormous effect on school mathematics both in the United States and Canada. Since the publication of this document we have been caught up in a transformation in mathematics education—a transformation that is more positive, more pervasive, and more widely accepted that any change previously experienced.

In 1991, the NCTM published the *Professional Standards for Teaching Mathematics*. The *Professional Standards* articulates a vision of teaching mathematics and builds on the notion found in the *Curriculum and Evaluation Standards* that good and significant mathematics is a vision for all children, not just a few. The NCTM completed the package with the *Assessment Standards for School Mathematics* in 1995. The *Assessment Standards* shows clearly the necessity of integrating assessment with instruction, and indicates the key role that assessment plays in implementing change. From 1989 to 2000, these three documents have guided the reform movement in mathematics education in North America. Yet, there are other countries, such as Japan and China (Stevenson & Stigler, 1992), where mathematics instruction more closely resembles the principles of the NCTM *Standards* than it does in North America.

The NCTM leadership has always recognized the ongoing need to examine its standards and to make adjustments in light of new knowledge from research and practice, the new demands of a changing society, and the continued impact of improved and readily available technology. In 1998, a draft of an updated version of the *Standards* was released for a full year of discussion and feedback. Reviews

of the draft were secured from various professional organizations, from a range of selected experts, and from the membership of the NCTM. The review effort was designed, not to achieve consensus, but to be sure that the writers were aware of all important viewpoints as they articulated an updated version of the direction of mathematics. In April 2000, at its annual conference, the NCTM released the new updated *Standards* document, *The Principles and Standards for School Mathematics*. With this important document, the Council continued to guide a revolutionary reform movement in mathematics education, not just in the United States and Canada, but throughout the world.

Principles and Standards for School Mathematics

The new *Principles and Standards for School Mathematics* should be regarded as a replacement for the 1989 *Curriculum and Evaluation Standards,* in that it updates what was written 11 years earlier. It also builds on the major elements of the other two documents. Thus, the *Principles and Standards* addresses issues of teaching and assessment, advancing the ideas found in the *Professional Standards* and the *Assessment Standards*. It is useful to think of these as a coordinated trio of NCTM *Standards* documents, the main document being the new *Principles and Standards for School Mathematics,* which, along with the two supporting documents, clearly articulates the best vision for teaching and assessment in mathematics. It is important to note that these documents have played a role in shaping the philosophy and outcomes of documents such as *The Western Canadian Protocol Common Curriculum Framework for K–12 Mathematics* (1995), and the *Foundation for the Atlantic Canada Mathematics Curriculum,* as well as other provincial curricula.

Goals for Students

Principles and Standards begins with an ambitious vision of a mathematics classroom, one we have barely begun to realize. At the heart of this vision are the same five goals set forth in the 1989 *Standards*. These goals state that *all* students should:

1. Learn to value mathematics
2. Become confident in their ability to do mathematics
3. Become mathematical problem solvers
4. Learn to communicate mathematics
5. Learn to reason mathematically

Virtually every job in today's society requires mathematics and, more importantly, mathematical thinking and reasoning. Today's employers are searching for people with the ability and the confidence to solve problems that have never been encountered before. Children need to see themselves learning to reason and learning to solve problems, not just learning skills.

Taking pride in one's mathematical thinking power is all-important. It is no longer fashionable to announce, "I never was any good at math." Children must, from the earliest grades and throughout their school experiences, be made to feel the importance of personal success in solving problems, figuring things out, and making sense of mathematics. It is difficult to develop confidence in your mathematical abilities if all you do in that domain is follow unfathomable rules that seem handed down arbitrarily from on high.

In the last chapter of *Principles and Standards,* the authors describe the necessary support required at every level to bring the vision of Chapter 1 to reality. To do so will require effort and responsible action by teachers, students, supervisors and principals, administrators at the province level, teacher educators, and also families and other caregivers.

A Pre-K–to–12 Perspective

As shown in Figure 1.1, *Principles and Standards* is designed to help teachers and other leaders see the development of mathematics content and processes over the span of pre-K–12. The largest portion of the document is devoted to a discussion of ten standards: five content standards and five process standards. Chapter 3 provides an overview of these ten standards, showing how they are developed across the 14 years of schooling.

Chapters 4 through 7 examine the standards more specifically for each of the four grade bands: pre-K–2, 3–5, 6–8, and 9–12. These four chapters provide specific "expectations" for each of the five content standards (see Appendix A). Here you will find examples of activities and student work to help you envision how the standards might look if enacted in your own classroom. You should understand, however, that *Principles and Standards* was never intended as a curriculum or a resource guide.

Six Principles of High-Quality Mathematics Programs

One of the most important features of *Principles and Standards for School Mathematics* is the articulation of six principles fundamental to high-quality mathematics education:

- Equity
- Curriculum
- Teaching
- Learning
- Assessment
- Technology

Principles and Standards for School Mathematics

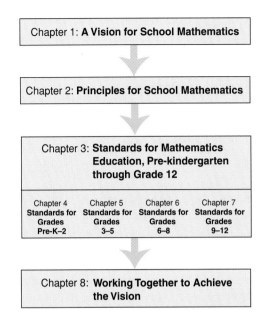

FIGURE 1.1 The structure of *Principles and Standards for School Mathematics* emphasizes the continuity of mathematics across all 14 years of school.

According to *Principles and Standards,* these principles must be "deeply intertwined with school mathematics programs. They can influence the development of curriculum frameworks, the selection of curriculum materials, the planning of instructional units or lessons, the design of assessments, the assignment of teachers and students to classes, instructional decisions in the classroom, and the establishment of supportive professional development programs for teachers" (NCTM, 2000, p. 12). The principles make it clear that excellence in mathematics education involves much more than simply listing content objectives.

The Equity Principle

Excellence in mathematics education requires equity—high expectations and strong support for all students.

(NCTM, 2000, p. 12)

The strong message of the Equity Principle is high expectations for all students. All students must have the opportunity and adequate support to learn mathematics, "regardless of personal characteristics, backgrounds, or physical challenges" (p. 12). The message of high expectations for all is intertwined with every other principle and the document as a whole.

Teachers and schools must communicate in their every action that they believe in the ability of *all* students to learn mathematics. High expectations for all must be accompanied by adequate support for both high- and low-achieving students. Teachers must be given the training and the resources to provide the best mathematics for every child.

The Curriculum Principle

A curriculum is more than a collection of activities: it must be coherent, focused on important mathematics, and well articulated across the grades.

(NCTM, 2000, p. 14)

Coherence speaks to the importance of building instruction around "big ideas" both in the curriculum and in daily classroom instruction. Students must be helped to see that mathematics is an integrated whole, not a list of isolated bits and pieces.

Mathematical ideas are "important" if they are useful in the development of other ideas, if they link ideas one to another, or if they serve to illustrate the discipline of mathematics as a human endeavour. This does not imply a single "best" configuration of the curriculum or a curriculum that is unchanging over time.

Articulation across the grades is explicit in this principle and is a significant feature of the entire *Principles and Standards* document. It is important that teachers and curriculum developers alike see how each of the strands of mathematics builds over the years. Without careful articulation across grades, duplication and gaps are inevitable.

The Teaching Principle

Effective mathematics teaching requires understanding what students know and need to learn and then challenging and supporting them to learn it well.

(NCTM, 2000, p. 16)

What students learn is almost entirely dependent on the experiences that teachers provide every day in the classroom. To provide high-quality mathematics education, teachers must (1) understand deeply the mathematics they are teaching; (2) understand how children learn mathematics, and develop a keen awareness of the individual mathematical development of their own students; and (3) select instructional tasks and strategies that will enhance learning. "Teachers' actions are what encourage students to think, question, solve problems, and discuss their ideas, strategies, and solutions" (p. 18).

Teachers and school districts must be committed to the continual development of teaching. Teachers must have ongoing opportunities to reflect on their practice and improve their understanding of pedagogical strategies, student learning, and mathematics content. Professional development cannot end with the pre-service training program.

The Learning Principle

Students must learn mathematics with understanding, actively building new knowledge from experience and prior knowledge.

(NCTM, 2000, p. 20)

This principle is based on two fundamental ideas. First, learning mathematics with understanding is essential. Mathematics today requires not only computational skills but also the ability to think and reason mathematically in order to solve the new problems and learn the new ideas that students will face in the future.

Second, the principle states quite clearly that students *can* learn mathematics with understanding. Learning is enhanced in classrooms where students are required to evaluate their own ideas and those of others, are encouraged to make mathematical conjectures and test them, and develop their reasoning skills. Learning, as envisioned in this principle, is clearly an active endeavor of students that takes place best in an environment that stresses problem solving, reasoning, and thoughtful interaction among students.

The Assessment Principle

Assessment should support the learning of important mathematics and furnish useful information to both teachers and students.

(NCTM, 2000, p. 22)

In the authors' words, "Assessment should not merely be done *to* students; rather, it should also be done *for* students, to guide and enhance their learning" (p. 22). Ongoing assessment conveys to students that mathematics is important. Assessment that includes ongoing observation and student interaction encourages students to articulate and thus clarify their ideas. Feedback from daily assessment helps students establish goals and become more independent learners.

Assessment should also be a major factor in making instructional decisions. By continually gathering information about student growth and understanding, teachers can better make the daily decisions that support student learning. For assessment to be effective, teachers must use a variety of assessment techniques, understand their mathematical goals deeply, and have a good idea of how their students are thinking about the mathematics that is being developed.

The Technology Principle

Technology is essential in teaching and learning mathematics; it influences the mathematics that is taught and enhances students' learning.

(NCTM, 2000, p. 24)

Calculators and computers should be seen as essential tools for doing and learning mathematics in the classroom. Technology permits students to focus on mathematical ideas, to reason, and to solve problems in ways that are often impossible without these tools. Technology enhances the learning of mathematics by allowing for increased exploration and enhanced representation of ideas. It extends the range of problems that can be accessed. It also allows students with special needs to bypass less important procedures so that important mathematics can be considered.

Far from being a crutch, technology actually enhances active involvement in the learning process. Students can explore ideas in a variety of modes—numeric, graphical, symbolic—and the teacher is better able to see how students are thinking about new ideas.

Technology is not a substitute for teaching, nor is it a replacement for important by-hand and mental skills. Rather, technology makes it possible to add to the curriculum important ideas that were previously unavailable to students. Realistic numbers and data sets are accessible by young children. Geometric software allows for the manipulation of figures and investigations of relationships impossible even with physical objects. Graphing technologies make realistic exploration of significant algebraic concepts possible.

The Five Content Standards

The *Principles and Standards* document describes five content standards or strands of mathematics:

- Number and Operations
- Algebra
- Geometry
- Measurement
- Data Analysis and Probability

(See Appendix A for the statement of the standards and the grade-band elaboration for grades pre-K–2, 3–5, 6–8, and 9–12.)

The *Standards* authors never intended that the five content strands would have equal weight or value across the four grade bands. Number and Operations is the largest strand from pre-K to grade 5 and continues to be important in middle school. That emphasis is reflected in this text, with Chapters 6 through 15 addressing content found in the Number and Operations standard.

The emphasis on Number and Operations should not diminish the importance of the other strands. Note that Geometry and Measurement are separate strands, suggesting the unique importance of each of these two areas.

Principles and Standards clearly defines Algebra as a strand for all grades. Almost certainly this was not the case when you were in school. This strand is an important

aspect of elementary school mathematics, and is becoming increasingly more prominent in curriculum objective lists. In this text, Chapters 19 and 20 address this strand.

The Five Process Standards

Following the five content standards, *Principles and Standards* lists five process standards:

- Problem Solving
- Reasoning and Proof
- Communication
- Connections
- Representation

Although they were never labelled or set apart in any way, the 1989 *Standards* began each grade band with the same four standards: the first four listed above. Those four standards have been cited in countless speeches and articles, used to define objectives and to guide performance assessments, and held up as a goal for all instruction. In short, they defined the original *Standards* document and the reform movement it heralded.

In *Principles and Standards for School Mathematics*, the writers updated those original four, added Representation, and officially labelled them "process standards," referring to the mathematical process through which students should acquire and use mathematical knowledge. The five process standards should not be regarded as separate strands in the mathematics curriculum. Rather, they direct the methods or processes of doing all mathematics and therefore should be seen as integral components of all mathematics learning and teaching.

To teach in a way that reflects these process standards is one of the best definitions of what it means to teach "according to the *Standards*."

Problem Solving

Problem solving has been the focus of school mathematics for more than two decades. Problem solving is much more than finding answers to word problems and exercises labelled "problem solving." The Problem Solving standard says that all students should "build new mathematical knowledge through problem solving" (NCTM, 2000, p. 52). This statement clearly indicates that problem solving is to be viewed as the vehicle through which children develop mathematical ideas. Learning and doing mathematics *as you solve problems* is probably the most significant difference between what the *Standards* indicate and the way you most likely experienced mathematics. As will be discussed in depth in Chapter 4, problem solving requires that students be mentally active and that they reflect on the ideas they already possess to build new ideas and increase understanding.

The Problem Solving standard also talks about developing students' disposition to work with problematic situations, to develop strategies for solving problems, and to learn to monitor and reflect on their mathematical thinking (metacognition).

Reasoning and Proof

Reasoning is at the heart of the shift from memorizing rules to doing mathematics. Without reasoning, mathematics is reduced to a set of mindless skills that seem mysterious and useless in the real world. If problem solving is the focus of mathematics, reasoning is the logical thinking that helps us solve problems and decide if and why our answers make sense. Students need to develop the habit of providing an argument or a rationale as an integral part of every answer. Children can and do learn that the reasons for their answers are at least as important as the answers themselves. The habit of providing reasons for answers is best started in kindergarten. However, it is never too late to learn the satisfaction and the value of defending ideas through logical argument.

Communication

The Communication standard points to the importance of being able to talk about, write about, describe, and explain mathematical ideas. Learning to communicate in mathematics fosters interaction and exploration of ideas in the classroom, as students learn in an active, verbal environment. It also makes accessible the world of mathematics beyond the classroom. Each day should include discussion or writing about the mathematical thinking that is going on in the classroom. No better way exists for wrestling with an idea than to attempt to articulate it to others. Mathematical expression, therefore, is part of the process and not an end in itself.

Connections

The Connections standard has two separate thrusts. First, the standard refers to connections within and among mathematical ideas. For example, addition and subtraction are intimately related; the idea of fractional parts of a whole is connected to concepts of decimals and percentages. Students should be helped to see how mathematical concepts build on one another in a useful network of connected ideas. Mathematics is not a laundry list of isolated rules and formulas.

Second, mathematics should be connected to the real world and to other disciplines. Children should see that mathematics plays a significant role in art, science, and social studies. This suggests that mathematics should frequently be integrated with other discipline areas and that applications of mathematics in the real world should be explored.

Representation

One of the aspects of mathematics that make it so powerful is the way ideas can be expressed with symbols, charts, graphs, and diagrams. Students need to understand that these are useful ways of communicating mathematical ideas to other people. Along with concrete representations such as counters or fraction "pie pieces," these visuals are also important learning tools. They permit students to manipulate abstract ideas in a form they can see. Moving from one representation to another is an important way to add understanding to an idea. For example, an algebraic equation leads to a chart of values and to a graph, both of which add a new dimension to the relationship. A story problem is often better understood when modelled with simple counters. As teachers help develop flexibility with a variety of representations for mathematical ideas, students not only add to their own understanding but also acquire skill in applying mathematical ideas to new areas and communicating ideas to others.

The *Professional Standards for Teaching Mathematics*

Although *Principles and Standards* incorporates principles of teaching and assessment, the emphasis is on curriculum. The *Professional Standards for Teaching Mathematics* focuses on teaching and is as important today as when it was released in 1991. The *Professional Standards* asserts that teachers are the key agents of change in the classroom. If the revolution is to continue, teachers must shift from a teacher-centred to a child-centred approach in their instruction. Research in cognitive psychology and mathematics education suggests that students actively construct their own meanings through mentally engaging experiences. They do not simply absorb knowledge delivered to them by the teacher or text. The *Professional Standards* describes teaching in ways that are reflective of this constructivist approach. Through extended vignettes of real teachers, the document articulates the careful reflective work that must go into teaching. Effective teaching engages students in problem solving and promotes valuable reflective student discourse about important mathematical ideas.

Five Shifts in Classroom Environment

The introduction to the *Professional Standards* lists five major shifts in the environment of the mathematics classroom that will be necessary to allow students to develop mathematical power. Teachers need to shift

- toward classrooms as mathematics communities and away from classrooms as simply a collection of individuals

- toward logic and mathematical evidence as verification and away from the teacher as the sole authority for right answers
- toward mathematical reasoning and away from mere memorizing procedures
- toward conjecturing, inventing, and problem solving and away from an emphasis on the mechanistic finding of answers
- toward connecting mathematics, its ideas, and its applications and away from treating mathematics as a body of isolated concepts and procedures

The Teaching Standards

The *Professional Standards for Teaching Mathematics* contains chapters on teaching, the evaluation of teaching, professional development, and necessary support for teaching. The teaching section is extraordinarily useful. It offers six standards for the teaching of mathematics, arranged in four categories: providing worthwhile mathematical tasks, encouraging discourse among students and between students and teacher, providing for an environment in which learning will be enhanced, and continually analyzing both teaching and learning. Chapter 4 of this text describes teaching through problem solving—a process involving these same ideas. A listing of the six teaching standards can be found in Appendix B.

The *Assessment Standards for School Mathematics*

The *Assessment Standards for School Mathematics* was published in 1995. It rounds out the trio of NCTM standards documents and is important reading for anyone interested in understanding the reform movement in mathematics education.

The *Assessment Standards* is not a how-to guide but a statement of philosophy and purpose, a book to provide guidance without prescription. It consists of six standards for assessment: Mathematics, Learning, Equity, Openness, Inferences, and Coherence. Further, it describes in some detail four purposes of assessment: to monitor the progress of students, to help make instructional decisions, to evaluate students' achievement, and to evaluate programs. All are aimed at the improvement of student learning.

The inescapable message of the *Assessment Standards* is that assessment and instruction are not separate activities but are intimately intertwined in improving the learning of mathematics. Chapter 5 of this text describes the six assessment standards and discusses the four purposes. There you will find suggestions for making assessment an integral component of instruction, an essential factor in being a *Standards*-oriented teacher.

Canadian Reform Initiatives

The NCTM has played a role in Canadian efforts to reform mathematics education (Anderson & Poirier, 1999). These efforts are reflected in a variety of initiatives undertaken at different government and school board levels. The Common Curriculum Framework for Mathematics K–12 of The Western Canada Protocol for Basic Education (WCP, www.wcp.ca, a consortium created in 1995 by the Ministers of Education of the western provinces and the territories) incorporates the principles and concepts of the NCTM *Standards*. As well, British Columbia and Saskatchewan, which have chosen to develop curricula independently of the WCP, have done so with the views of the NCTM in mind. Similarly, the Atlantic Provinces Education Foundation (APEF, www.apef-fepa.org), a creation of the Ministers of Education of the four Atlantic provinces, designed a framework whose outcomes and philosophy for curriculum development matched firmly with those articulated in the NCTM *Curriculum and Evaluation Standards for School Mathematics*, 1989. Ontario's curriculum, updated in 1997, is aligned with the reform perspective of the NCTM, as is Quebec's curriculum, which was recently updated. NCTM *Standards* also figure prominently in the development of national assessment programs, such as the School Achievement Indicators Program and provincially based testing.

Additional efforts to promote a mathematics that is different from the tradition that students still experience are thriving in Canada. The National Mathematics Education Institute, dedicated to the reform of Canadian education (Flewelling, Higginson, Roulet & Taylor, 1997), is responsible for the development of vision statements for mathematics education for this country. In 1996, *Tomorrow's Mathematics Classroom*, a series of brochures containing one-page vision statements outlining what mathematics from a reform-based perspective should look like in classrooms, were developed for distribution. The more recent *Handbook on Rich Learning Tasks* (Flewelling & Higginson, 2000) is closely aligned with the vision statements, and also promotes principles of reform-based learning.

As children engage in tasks that integrate mathematics with real life, they are challenged to problem-solve, reason, and find solutions through inquiry. A very recent project of the British Columbia Ministry of Education, the Early Numeracy Project (British Columbia Ministry of Education, 2003), assesses and builds on children's knowledge to improve outcomes. A key component of this project—the instructional package—well reflects the principles of the current spirit of reform. The Cognitively

Guided Instruction (CGI) project, based on the principles of Cognitively Guided Instruction (Carpenter et al., 1996) is another example of teachers in a school district (Langley School District, British Columbia) working to incorporate the principles of reform into their teaching.

Influences and Pressures on Reform

The NCTM has provided the major leadership and vision for the reform movement in mathematics education. However, there are other forces that interact to push and pull at the mathematics classroom in ways that are often more powerful than the NCTM. National and international comparisons of student performances make headlines and provoke public reaction. This reaction puts pressure on school boards and districts to show that their schools are all "above average." Results of provincial testing increase the pressure. But the most direct influence in the classroom is the textbook. Mainstream publishers are primarily influenced by the classroom teacher and provincial guidelines. Teachers are pressured by the need to cover curriculum and the demands of provincial test results. No single factor controls the direction of change.

National and International Studies

Large-scale studies that tell the Canadian public how the nation's children are doing in mathematics receive a lot of attention. They influence political decisions and provide useful data for mathematics education researchers. The most recently conducted studies are The School Achievement Indicators Program (SAIP) 2001, the Third International Mathematics and Science Study (TIMSS) 1995, and the Third International Mathematics and Science Study—Repeat (TIMSS-R) 1999.

The School Achievement Indicators Program

The School Achievement Indicators Program (SAIP) is a cyclical program of pan-Canadian assessments, which measures student performance in mathematics, reading and writing, and science. The Council of Ministers of Education (CMEC) (www.cmec.ca), the voice of education in Canada, is responsible for the design and implementation of this program. They have been carrying out these criterion-referenced assessments with 13- and 16-year-old students since 1993. The results, which are published and made available to participating schools, students, parents, and the public, provide us with reliable statistical information (Council of Ministers of Education, 1998) about the development of students' knowledge and skills.

Of the three disciplines, mathematics is the only area that has been assessed for the third time; the most recent

test was held in the spring of 2001. A representative sample of about 41 000 13- and 16-year-old English- and French-speaking students took part in the Mathematics III testing. It is important to note that, like the previous tests, the Mathematics III test reflects principles of the NCTM Standards. As in earlier tests, half the students responded to a mathematics content assessment and half responded to a problem-solving assessment. In order to compare students' progress, the assessment instruments in the 2001 test consisted of a mix of anchor questions drawn from the previous (1997) mathematics assessments, along with newly developed items reflecting current pedagogical practices and curricular content. Achievement is described according to five levels representing a continuum of mathematics knowledge and problem-solving skills acquired by students over the entire elementary and secondary school experience.

The good news is that a majority of 13-year-olds showed improvement in both problem-solving and mathematics content. However, fewer 16-year-olds reached the target level set by the test designers, even though there was a strong improvement in problem solving. It is suggested that 13-year-olds' longer exposure to reform-oriented curricula in elementary school might have played a role in their improvement.

The Third International Mathematics and Science Study

In 1995 and 1996, 41 nations participated in the Third International Mathematics and Science Study (TIMSS), the largest and most ambitious study of mathematics and science education ever conducted. The study was designed to compare and contrast the teaching and learning of mathematics and science at the elementary and secondary school levels around the world, so that educators might learn more about the kinds of exemplary practices and curricula that contribute to high levels of student achievement. Data for this study were gathered in grades 4, 8, and 12 from more than half a million students and teachers.

Canada's participation in the TIMSS was limited to five provinces: British Columbia, Alberta, Ontario, New Brunswick (English-speaking schools), and Newfoundland and two territories (Yukon and the Northwest Territories). Generally, Canada's results were higher than the international mean. Of the 10 countries whose students had significantly higher scores than Canada, four were from Asia, three from Western Europe, and three from Eastern or Central Europe. (See Table 1.1.)

Canadian grade 8 students attained a mean of 59 percent in mathematics, four percentage points higher than the international mean. The average score in British Columbia was 63 percent, placing students amongst the highest scoring in mathematics. Alberta students scored 61 percent; Newfoundland, 56 percent; Ontario, 54 percent; and New Brunswick, 54 percent; placing them significantly lower than the overall Canadian scores.

For Singapore, the country that ranked the highest overall, 45 percent of Grade 8 students were in the top 10 percent internationally, 75 percent in the top quarter, and 95 percent in the top half. In Canada, 7 percent were in the top tenth, 25 percent in the top quarter, and 60 percent in the top half internationally.

The achievement of Canadian grade 4 students was slightly above the international mean in mathematics. They did as well as or better than students from 17 other countries, and not as well as those from the following eight: Korea, Singapore, Japan, Hong Kong, the Netherlands, the Czech Republic, Austria, and Slovenia. The scores for the participating five provinces, unlike those for grade 8, were not significantly different from the national mean or from one another.

Impact of the Third International Mathematics and Science Study

Canadian responses to TIMSS findings varied. Changes that occurred in curriculum design and assessment practices seemed to have had a greater effect at the provincial and territorial levels than nationwide (due in part to the fact that there is no pan-Canadian curriculum). Even though review and revision of curricula and program assessment in mathematics are cyclical, TIMSS did not appear to have an effect on the content or emphasis of British Columbia's mathematics curriculum. However, the study did have an impact on the makeup of the province's mathematics assessment for grades 4 and 7; approximately half the achievement questions used were drawn from TIMSS. Alberta found that results in TIMSS helped to reinforce reforms that had recently been implemented. The publication of results at the time of curriculum revision in Ontario offered some direction for the process. In fact, instructional materials were developed as a direct outcome of TIMSS. Yet, in some instances, as in New Brunswick and Newfoundland, TIMSS results did not appear to affect change (Robitaille, Beaton & Plomp, 2000).

In the United States, a serious commitment was made at all levels—national, state, and local—to improving mathematics learning and to professional development. Increased attention was given to making mathematics curricula more ambitious, particularly in the middle school years. One such example is the Math Initiative, an ongoing joint effort by the Department of Education and the National Science Foundation initiated in 1998 as a response to TIMSS assessment results. This project was designed to help states, local school districts, and schools

Table 1.1: **Student Performance in Mathematics, by Population, Grade 8, TIMSS**

Country/Province	% Correct	Country/Province	% Correct
Singapore	79	**Newfoundland**	**56**
Japan	73	Sweden	56
Korea	72	**International Average**	**55**
Hong Kong	70	**New Brunswick (Anglophone)**	**54**
Belgium (Flemish)*	66	**Ontario**	**54**
Czech Republic	66	Germany**	54
British Columbia	**63**	New Zealand	54
Slovak Republic	62	Norway	54
Switzerland*	62	England*	53
Austria**	62	United States*	53
Hungary	62	Denmark**	52
France	61	Scotland**	52
Slovenia**	61	Latvia*	51
Alberta	**61**	Spain	51
Russian Federation	60	Iceland	50
Netherlands**	60	Greece**	49
Bulgaria**	60	Romania**	49
CANADA	**59**	Lithuania*	48
Ireland	59	Cyprus	48
Belgium (French)**	59	Portugal	43
Australia**	58	Iran, Islamic Rep.	38
Thailand**	57	Kuwait**	30
Israel**	57	Colombia**	29
		South Africa**	24

* Replacement schools, or less than the whole population sampled.
** Did not meet all sampling requirements.

Source: *TIMSS Canada Report*, Volume 1: Grade 8 (www.edu.gov.nf.ca/erp/reports/gradout/k12doc/tab2-9-3.htm).

improve teaching, upgrade curriculum, and integrate technology and high-quality instructional materials into the classroom, and to motivate students and help them understand how mathematics concepts are applied in the real world (Robitaille, Beaton & Plomp, 2000).

TIMSS results have stimulated considerable activity worldwide. Numerous articles have been published in journals, newsletters, magazines and newspapers. Participating countries have written reports analyzing findings. One of the most interesting developments of TIMSS is the grade 8 video study conducted in the United States, Germany, and Japan (U.S. Department of Education's Office of Educational Research and Improvement, 1997). The video (which is part of a kit that contains other TIMMS-related materials) shows mathematics being taught in an elementary classroom in each of these countries. This provides us with a basis for comparison and learning. The video reveals stark contrasts between instructional practices in Japan and the United States. "The typical goal of a U.S. eighth-grade mathematics teacher is to teach students how to do something. The typical goal of a Japanese teacher is to help students understand mathematical concepts" (U.S. Department of Education, 1997a, p. 33). Although 95 percent of U.S. teachers in the study said they were aware of the current reform ideas, in responses to questions about what constituted reform teaching, over 80 percent referred to something other than a focus on thinking. They pointed instead to cooperative learning or hands-on activities, which are strategies that can and do go on without any emphasis on thinking. In Japan, researchers found that 83 percent of the topics in grade 8 lessons were developed rather than stated. By contrast in the United States, only 22 percent of the topics were developed; 78 percent were stated (U.S. Department of Education, 1996). "The videotape study found that, in many ways, Japanese teaching resembled the recommendations of the U.S reform movement more closely than did American teaching" (p. 47).

The TIMSS data and the many reports and documents that have been produced about the study provide much more information than can be summarized easily in these pages. A wealth of information, including the U.S Department of Education's TIMSS Resource Kit, TIMSS test items, and numerous reports, can be found on the Web at http://ustimss.msu.edu. Canadian information about TIMSS is available at the following website: http://www.cust.educ.ubc.ca/wprojects/timss/.

The Third International Mathematics and Science Study—Repeat

In 1999 a partial replication of the 1995 TIMSS study was conducted for grade 8 only. (See Table 1.2.) Thirty-eight countries took part in TIMSS-99 (TIMSS-R). Twenty-six of these countries had also participated in

TIMSS-95. Nearly 9000 students from Alberta, British Columbia, Newfoundland, Ontario, and Quebec wrote the test. The good news is that Canada was only one of two countries in which students showed significant improvement from 1995 to 1999. According to David Robitaille, Canadian director of the TIMSS-99, these results are important because changes of such magnitude do not usually occur in a time span as short as four years (2000, December 5, TIMSS-99 Press Release). Canada had significantly higher scores than students from more than half the study's participating countries, including the United States and New Zealand.

Quebec students did particularly well in mathematics. Their overall score placed them within the group of the top six countries with scores significantly higher than the Canadian average. Their curriculum is focused on students' learning to explain their mathematical thinking through problem solving (www.mathematicallysane. com). Although Ontario showed marked improvement, scores for Alberta, British Columbia, and Ontario were not significantly different from the Canadian average. The average score in Newfoundland was significantly lower than the Canadian average. Canada's improvement in performance, particularly in Ontario, suggests that reform efforts and a focus on assessment are making a difference.

Provincial Assessment Programs

Province-wide testing programs are another way that Canadian students' knowledge of curriculum is evaluated. Unlike national and international assessments, these tests generally provide information regarding the achievement of individual students. In some provinces, such as Ontario and Alberta, testing is carried out yearly at key transitional stages (grades 3, 6, 9) in elementary and high school. In others, such as Manitoba, only one particular grade (grade 3) in elementary is tested in mathematics yearly. Classroom teachers generally play an important role in the development of these programs. The direct link of these tests with regional curriculum documents accounts for their strong influence on school board policy and instructional decision-making. The focus on assessment and accountability explains the popularity of provincial testing and the pressure on teachers to ensure favourable test results.

Curriculum

Mathematics curricula may differ from one part of the country to another, yet a high degree of congruency exists in many of the different areas. Most jurisdictions in Canada have recently renewed their curricula or are in the process of doing so. Although renewal initiatives have been

Table 1.2: Summary of Results of Mathematics Portion of TIMSS-99

For each participating country or province, the tables shows the mean scale score, the standard error of the mean, and the average age of the students in that country or province at the time they wrote the test.

Results Significantly Higher than Canada's				Results as Good as Canada's				Results Significantly Lower than Canada's			
Country	**Mean**	**s.e.**	**Age**	**Country**	**Mean**	**s.e.**	**Age**	**Country**	**Mean**	**s.e.**	**Age**
Singapore	60	(0.6)	14.4	Netherlands	54	(0.7)	14.2	Latvia	51	(0.3)	14.5
Korea	59	(0.2)	14.4	Slovak Republic	53	(0.4)	14.3	**Newfoundland**	**50**	**(0.6)**	**14.0**
Taiwan	59	(0.4)	14.2	Hungary	53	(0.4)	14.4	United States	50	(0.4)	14.2
Hong Kong	58	(0.4)	14.2	**CANADA**	**53**	**(0.3)**	**14.0**	England	50	(0.4)	14.2
Japan	58	(0.2)	14.4	Slovenia	53	(0.3)	14.8	New Zealand	49	(0.5)	14.0
Quebec	**57**	**(0.5)**	**14.3**	**Alberta**	**53**	**(0.4)**	**13.9**	Lithuania	48	(0.4)	15.2
Belgium (Flemish)	56	(0.3)	14.1	Russia	53	(0.6)	14.1	Italy	48	(0.4)	14.0
				Australia	53	(0.5)	14.3	Cyprus	48	(0.2)	13.8
				British Columbia	**52**	**(0.6)**	**13.9**	Romania	47	(0.6)	14.8
				Finland	52	(0.3)	13.8	Moldova	47	(0.4)	14.4
				Czech Republic	52	(0.4)	14.4	Thailand	47	(0.5)	14.5
				Malaysia	52	(0.4)	14.4	Israel	47	(0.4)	14.1
				Ontario	**52**	**(0.3)**	**13.9**	Tunisia	45	(0.2)	14.8
				Bulgaria	51	(0.6)	14.8	Macedonia	45	(0.4)	14.6
								Turkey	43	(0.4)	14.2
								Jordan	43	(0.4)	14.0
								Iran	42	(0.3)	14.6
								Indonesia	40	(0.5)	14.6
								Chile	39	(0.4)	14.4
								Philippines	35	(0.6)	14.1
								Morocco	34	(0.3)	14.2
								South Africa	28	(0.7)	15.5

Note: The numbers shown above have been rounded and should not be used for determining significance levels.

Source: TIMSS-Canada Report: Executive Summary (http://www.curricstudies.educ.ubc.ca/wprojects/TIMSS/TIMSS99.pdf)

designed with the spirit of reform in mind, outcomes do not always reflect intentions. The extensive list of what teachers are expected to cover in class often means that they are pressured to move quickly through the curriculum, detracting from a meaningful approach to instruction. The need to meet test expectations can be another deterrent.

The situation is further complicated because in most classrooms, the textbook is the single most influential factor determining *what* actually gets taught and *how*. Publishers employ author teams that always include excellent mathematics researchers and educators as well as teachers, yet the tendency is to produce very large textbooks so they can attend to a variety of agendas (Schmidt et al., 1996). Teachers need to be selective about how they use the textbook. When planning instruction, remember to always begin with your regional curriculum document; then consult the textbook or textbooks along with other teacher-based resources to support your objectives for students' learning. There are some excellent materials that promote teaching and learning from a reform-based perspective.

Reform Curricula

At present, there are elementary and middle-school programs commonly recognized as reform curricula* which

are now commercially available. A hallmark of these reform programs is student engagement. Children are challenged to make sense of new mathematical ideas through explorations and projects, often in real contexts. Most programs do not have textbooks but are supported with activity guides, teacher resources, and consumable materials for students. Teacher training is generally seen as important if not essential for district-wide implementation, a fact that adds to the already high cost of most reform programs.

Data concerning the effectiveness of reform curricula as measured by conventional testing programs continue to be gathered. It is safe to say that students in reform programs perform much better on problem-solving measures, and at least as well on traditional skills, compared to students in conventional programs (Bell, 1998; Boaler, 1998; Reys, Robinson, Sconiers & Mark, 1999; Stein, Grover, & Hennigsen, 1996; Stein & Lane, 1996; Wood & Sellers, 1996, 1997). Comparing any of these with a corresponding

---

*A listing of eight reform curricula—the developers, publishers, and Internet contacts—can be found at the end of this chapter. These programs have been included to provide you with examples and an opportunity to learn more about what it means to do mathematics from a reform-based perspective. You will also be able to see how these programs compare with the way you learned mathematics.

traditional publisher-developed textbook would be an effective way to understand what reform or *Standards*-based mathematics is all about.

Opposition to Reform

As we begin a new century it must be admitted that the vision of the NCTM *Standards* has not been realized. However, progress has been made. In Canada, as in the United States, change is visible, albeit slow and incremental. Controversy continues between advocates of reform and those favouring a more traditional approach to mathematics teaching. Vocal groups of parents and mathematicians who have acquired political clout are becoming more and more influential in calling for a return to the "basics." But, despite the slow pace of change in long-held beliefs about school mathematics, the revolution continues. This is not a pendulum that we can permit to swing backward.

An Invitation to Learn and Grow

The mathematics education described in the *Standards* is almost certainly not the same as the mathematics and the mathematics teaching you experienced from K through grade 8. Along the way, you may have had excellent teachers who really did reflect the current reform spirit. Examples of good reform curriculum have been around since the early

1990s, and you may have benefited from one of those. But for the most part, with the reform movement well into its second decade, its goals have yet to be realized in the large majority of school boards and districts in North America.

As a practicing or prospective teacher facing the challenge of teaching from a reform perspective, you may need to confront some of your personal beliefs—about what it means to *do mathematics*, how one goes about *learning mathematics*, how to *teach mathematics through problem solving*, and what it means to *assess mathematics* integrated with instruction. The next four chapters of this book will help you develop these four foundational ideas.

Section 2 of the book examines the teaching and learning of specific topics in mathematics. The chapters in the second section are designed not only as text materials but also as a source of instructional tasks for your future or current teaching. Section 3 covers other topics that influence mathematics teaching across all the strands and grade levels: planning and related classroom issues, reaching all children in mathematics, and the role of technology. The chapters in this section may be read at any time.

New directions in mathematics education have opened a world of exciting investigations and opportunities to all students. Mathematics can no longer be equated with mundane computational skills. Teaching mathematics can be an exciting adventure. Perhaps the most exciting part is that you grow and learn along with your students. Enjoy the journey.

Reflections **on** *Chapter 1*

Writing to Learn

At the end of each chapter of this book, you will find a series of questions under this same heading. The questions are designed to help you reflect on the most important ideas of the chapter. Writing (or talking aloud with a peer) is an excellent way to explore new ideas and incorporate them into your own knowledge base. The writing (or discussion) will help make the ideas your own. After you have written your responses in your own words, return to the text to compare what you have written with the book. Make changes, if necessary, or discuss differences with your instructor.

1. How is the new NCTM document *Principles and Standards for School Mathematics* related to the 1989 document *Curriculum and Evaluation Standards for School Mathematics*?
2. What are the five goals for all students that were described originally in the 1989 *Curriculum Standards* and reflected again in the *Principles and Standards* document? Pick two of these goals that you think are the most important, and explain what they mean to you.
3. Give a brief description of each of the six principles in *Principles and Standards* (Equity, Curriculum, Teaching,

Learning, Assessment, and Technology). Explain the importance of each principle to the teaching and learning of mathematics.
4. What are the five content strands (standards) defined by *Principles and Standards*?
5. What is meant by a *process,* as referenced in the *Principles and Standards* process standards? Give a brief description of each of the five process standards.
6. Among the ideas in the *Professional Standards* are five shifts in the classroom environment, from traditional approaches to a *Standards*-oriented approach. Examine these five shifts, and describe in a few sentences what aspects of each shift seem most significant to you.
7. Describe at least two results derived from SAIP data. What are the implications?
8. Describe at least two results derived from TIMSS data. What are the implications?
9. Describe the influences of province-wide assessment programs on classroom mathematics education.
10. Discuss the difference between traditional textbooks and reform curricula.

For Discussion and Exploration

1. As the last decade of the century ended, the outcry for "basics" arose again from a loud and very political minority. The debate over reform or the basics is both important and interesting. For an engaging discussion of the reform movement in light of the "back to basics" reaction, read one or more of the first five articles in the February 1999 issue of the *Phi Delta Kappan*. Where do you stand on the issue of reform versus the basics?

2. Examine a textbook currently in use in your school district, at a grade level of your choice. If possible, use a teacher's edition. Flip through any chapter, and look for signs of the five process standards. To what extent are children who are being taught from this book likely to be doing and learning mathematics in ways described by those processes? What would you have to do to change the general approach to this text?

3. Examine your provincial mathematics curriculum document to see how well it reflects the NCTM vision of reform, especially the five process standards. What is your view on how well the curriculum reflects the vision of reform?

4. Review the sample videos from the grade 8 TIMSS video study (they can be found on the web at http://ustimss.msu.edu., and they are probably also available at your faculty library). They show a geometry lesson and an algebra lesson from a typical grade 8 classroom in each of Germany, Japan, and the United States. What elements of the reform movement do you see in each of these lessons?

Recommendations for Further Reading

Highly Recommended

Mathematical Sciences Education Board, National Research Council. (1989). *Everybody counts: A report to the nation on the future of mathematics education.* Washington, DC: National Academy Press.

This little booklet, readable in a single evening, provides a compelling rationale for reform in both the mathematics we teach and how it is taught. Here you will find the description of mathematics as "the science of pattern and order" used throughout this text. Myths concerning the nature of mathematics, how it is learned, and by whom are challenged from an angle that is difficult to dispute. More than a decade after its publication, this remains a must-read for anyone who wishes to understand why reform is so necessary.

National Council of Teachers of Mathematics. (2000). *Principles and standards for school mathematics.* Reston, VA: Author.

This update to the 1989 document that signalled the beginning of the revolution in mathematics education is one of the most important books that you could read in order to understand the current directions in mathematics education. Every teacher and pre-service teacher should read the sections on Principles (Chapter 2), the K–12 overview (Chapter 3), and the standards for his or her grade band of interest. If you can, add this book to your professional library.

Stigler, J. W., & Hiebert, J. C. (1999). *The teaching gap: Best ideas from the world's teachers for improving education in the classroom.* New York: Free Press.

Certainly you have heard how U.S. students are constantly being compared to students in other countries, most notably Japan. The authors of this book have looked carefully at teaching practices in Japan, Germany, and the United States through the lens of the TIMSS video study. Their purpose was to improve education in the U.S. by providing a thoughtful study in contrasts of teaching in three distinctly different cultures.

Teppo, A. R. (Ed.). (1999). *Reflecting on practice in elementary school mathematics: Readings from NCTM's school-based journals and other publications.* Reston, VA: National Council of Teachers of Mathematics.

Frequently, NCTM publishes books of selected readings from its journals. In this instance, more than 60 articles provide perspective on the reform movement, organized according to major areas of the curriculum. If you seek to establish a resource of short, easily read articles on a wide variety of topics, this is an excellent book with which to begin.

Trafton, P. R., & Claus, A. S. (1994). A changing curriculum for a changing age. In C. A. Thornton & N. S. Bley (Eds.), *Windows of opportunity: Mathematics for students with special needs* (pp. 19–39). Reston, VA: National Council of Teachers of Mathematics.

Paul Trafton has long been a recognized leader in mathematics education, especially in the area of reform. With Claus, he describes in one chapter the vision of the 1989 *Standards* and the challenges that vision presents to teachers. The chapter ends with a vignette from a grade 2 classroom that vividly brings home the meaning of reform.

Other Suggestions

Anderson, A., Poirier, L. (1999). Elementary mathematics. In J. Grant McLoughlin (Ed.), *Proceedings of the Canadian Mathematics Education Study Group,* 91–95.

Battista, M. T. (1999). The mathematical miseducation of America's youth: Ignoring research and scientific study in education. *Phi Delta Kappan, 80,* 424–433.

Billstein, R. (1998). Middle grades math thematics: The STEM project—a look at developing a middle school mathematics curriculum. In L. Leutzinger (Ed.), *Mathematics in the Middle* (pp. 93–106). Reston, VA: National Council of Teachers of Mathematics.

Boaler, J. (1998). Open and closed mathematics: Student experiences and understandings. *Journal for Research in Mathematics Education, 29,* 41–62.

Burns, M. (1998). *Math: Facing an American phobia.* Sausalito, CA: Math Solutions Publications.

Burrill, G. (1998). Changes in your classroom: From the past to the present to the future. *Teaching Children Mathematics, 5,* 202–209.

Carpenter, T.P., Fennema, E., Franke, M.L., Levi, L, Empson, S.B., (1996). Cognitively guided instruction: a knowledge base for reform in primary mathematics instruction. *Elementary School Journal, 97* (1), 3–20.

Council of Ministers of Education, Canada, (1998). *School achievement indicators program (SAIP). Report on Mathematics Assessment 1997.* Toronto: Council of Ministers of Education, Canada.

Curcio, F.R. (1999). Dispelling myths about reform in school mathematics. *Mathematics Teaching in the Middle School, 4,* 282–284.

Early numeracy project (2003). British Columbia: Ministry of Education, British Columbia.

Ferrini-Mundy, J., Graham, K., Johnson, L., & Mills, G. (Eds.). (1998). *Making change in mathematics education: Learning from the field.* Reston, VA: National Council of Teachers of Mathematics.

Flewelling, G., Higginson, W. (2000). *Realizing a vision of tomorrow's mathematics classroom: A handbook on rich learning tasks.* Kingston, Ontario: Centre for Mathematics, Science and Technology Education, Queen's University.

Flewelling, G., Higginson, W., Roulet, G., & Taylor, P. (1997). Tomorrow's mathematics classroom: A vision of mathematics education, In Y.M. Pothier (Ed.), *Proceedings of the Canadian Mathematics Education Study Group,* 151–152.

Goldsmith, L.T., & Mark, J. (1999). What is a standards-based mathematics curriculum? *Educational Leadership, 57*(3), 40–44.

Jones, M.G., Jones, B.D., Hardin, B., Chapman, L., Yarbrough, T., & Davis, M. (1999). The impact of high-stakes testing on teachers and students in North Carolina. *Phi Delta Kappan, 81,* 199–203.

Lappan, G. (1999). Revitalizing and refocusing our efforts. *Teaching Children Mathematics, 6,* 104–109.

Lappan, G., & Phillips, E. (1998). Teaching and learning in the Connected Mathematics Project. In L. Leutzinger (Ed.), *Mathematics in the middle* (pp. 83-92). Reston, VA: National Council of Teachers of Mathematics.

National Council of Teachers of Mathematics. (1991). *Professional standards for teaching mathematics.* Reston, VA: Author.

National Council of Teachers of Mathematics. (1995). *Assessment standards for school mathematics.* Reston, VA: Author.

O'Brien, T.C. (1999). Parrot math. *Phi Delta Kappan, 80,* 434–438.

Popham, W.J. (1999). Why standardized tests don't measure educational quality. *Educational Leadership, 56*(6), 8–15.

Reys, B.J., Robinson, E., Sconiers, S., & Mark, J. (1999). Mathematics curricula based on rigorous national standards: What, why, and how? *Phi Delta Kappan, 80,* 454–456.

Reys, R.E., Reys, B.J., Barnes, D. E., Beem, J.K., Lapan, R.T., & Papick, I.J. (1998). Standards-based middle school mathematics curricula: What do students think? In L.P. Leutzinger (Ed.), *Mathematics in the middle* (pp. 153–157). Reston, VA: National Council of Teachers of Mathematics.

Robitaille, D.F., Beaton, A.E., & Plomp, T. (2000). *The impact of TIMSS on the teaching and learning of mathematics and science.* Vancouver: Pacific Educational Press.

Schoen, H.L., Fey, J.T., Hirsch, C.R., & Coxford, A.F. (1999). Issues and options in the math wars. *Phi Delta Kappan, 80,* 444–453.

Stevenson, H.W., & Stigler, J.W., (1992). *The learning gap.* New York: Simon & Schuster.

Stigler, J.W., & Hiebert, J.C.(1997). Understanding and improving classroom mathematics instruction: An overview of the TIMSS video study. *Phi Delta Kappan, 79,* 14–21.

Tsuruda, G. (1998). Middle school mathematics reform: Form versus spirit. In L. Leutzinger (Ed.), *Mathematics in the middle* (pp. 3–9). Reston, VA: National Council of Teachers of Mathematics.

U.S. Department of Education Office of Educational Research and Improvement. (1997). *Attaining excellence: A TIMSS resource kit.* Washington, DC: United States Department of Education.

Van Boening, L. (1999). Growth through change. *Mathematics Teaching in the Middle School, 5,* 27–33.

Willoughby, S.S. (1996). The *Standards:* Some second thoughts. *Mathematics Teaching in the Middle School, 2,* 8–11.

Reform Curricula

Elementary Programs

Information about the elementary programs can be obtained from the ARC Center:

> E-mail: arccenter@mail.comap.com
> URL: www.arccenter.comap.com

UCSMP Elementary: Everyday Mathematics (K–6)
Developer: University of Chicago School Mathematics Project
Publisher: Everyday Learning

> E-mail: aisaacs@midway.uchicago.edu

Investigations in Number, Data, and Space (K–5)
Developer: TERC
Publisher: Scott, Foresman

> URL: www.terc.edu/investigations/index.html

Math Trailblazers: A Mathematical Journey Using Science and Language Arts (K-5)
Developer: Institute for Math and Science Education, University of Illinois, Chicago
Publisher: Kendall/Hunt

> URL: www.math.uic.edu/IMSE

Middle School Programs

Information about the middle school programs can be obtained from the Show-Me Center:

> E-mail: Center@showme.missouri.edu
> URL: www.showmecenter.missouri.edu

Connected Mathematics (CMP) (6–8)
Developer: Michigan State University
Publisher: Prentice Hall

> URL: www.msu.edu/cmp

Mathematics in Context (MIC) (5–8)
Developer: University of Wisconsin-Madison
Publisher: Encyclopaedia Britannica

> URL: www.ebmic.com

MathScape (6–8)
Developer: Educational Development Center
Publisher: Creative Publications

> URL: www.edc.org/mathscape

Middle School Mathematics Through Applications Project (MMAP) (6–8)
Developer: Institute for Research on Learning
Publisher: Voyager Expanded Learning

> URL: www.imvoyager.com

Middle Grades Math Thematics (STEM) (6–8)
Developer: University of Montana
Publisher: McDougal/Littell

> URL: www.mlmath.com

Chapter 2

Exploring What It Means to Do Mathematics

As a practical matter, mathematics is a science of pattern and order. Its domain is not molecules or cells, but numbers, chance, form, algorithms, and change. As a science of abstract objects, mathematics relies on logic rather than on observation as its standard of truth, yet employs observation, simulation, and even experimentation as means of discovering truth.

Mathematical Sciences Education Board (1989, p. 31)

How would you describe what you are doing when you are *doing mathematics?* Stop for a moment and write a few sentences about what it means to know and do mathematics, based on your own experiences. Then put your paper aside until you have finished this chapter.

The description of doing mathematics you will read about here may not match your personal experiences. That's okay! It is okay to come to this point with whatever beliefs were developed in your previous mathematics experiences. However, it is not okay to accept outdated ideas about mathematics if you expect to be a quality teacher. Your obligation and your challenge as you read this chapter and this book are to rethink your own understanding of what it means to know and do mathematics so that the children with whom you work will have an exciting and accurate vision of mathematics.

Changing Perceptions of School Mathematics

Much change has taken place since 1989, when NCTM set a vision for change in mathematics classrooms. More teachers are beginning to use what might be called a reform-based approach: more emphasis on concept development and problem solving, more cooperative learning, and a greater tolerance for and use of calculators. Often these changes are superficial and do not really affect the nature of what children do and how they think in the mathematics classroom. Even though current provincial and territorial assessments are designed with a reform approach in mind, the pressures of test scores tend to bring out a teach-to-the-test, "drill and kill" approach. It is well known that such methods have proven consistently to be ineffective. Fortunately, wonderful exceptions are to be found everywhere.

Traditional Views of School Mathematics

In the traditional classroom, the teacher represents the source of all that is to be known in mathematics. After reviewing material covered the day before or checking homework, the teacher typically moves on to an explanation of whatever idea is on the next page of the text. Instruction generally consists of showing the children how they are to do the assigned exercises. Even with a hands-on activity using some form of manipulative, the traditional teacher is guiding the children, telling them exactly how to use the materials in a prescribed way. In this environment, the students' attention is necessarily on the teacher's directions, not on mathematical ideas. The focus of the lesson is primarily on getting answers. The students rely on the teacher to determine if their answers are correct.

Children emerge from these experiences with a view that mathematics is a series of arbitrary rules, handed down by the teacher, who in turn got them from some very smart source. The students' role in this exercise is largely passive. They accept what they are told and attempt to master each new rule. It is no wonder that students feel they must check with the teacher to see if an answer is correct.

When children are neither asked nor required to understand rules or evaluate their own answers, they are being told loudly and clearly, "You are not capable of understanding these ideas." By grade 5 or 6, many children simply refuse to attempt a problem that has not first been explained: "You haven't shown us how to do this." Children accept that every problem must have a predetermined solution, that there is only one way to solve any problem, and that they should not even expect to solve a problem unless they have been given a solution method ahead of time.

This follow-the-rules, computation-dominated, answer-oriented view of mathematics is a gross distortion of what mathematics is really about. It cannot be very exciting. A few children are good at learning rules and thrive on the ensuing good grades. But these are not necessarily the best thinkers in the room. The traditional system rewards the learning of rules but offers little opportunity to actually do mathematics.

Mathematics as a Science of Pattern and Order

Mathematics is the science of pattern and order. This wonderfully simple description of mathematics is found in the thought-provoking publication *Everybody Counts* (MSEB, 1989; see also Schoenfeld, 1992). This definition challenges the popular social view of mathematics as a discipline dominated by computation and rules without reasons. Science is a process of figuring things out or making sense of things. It begins with problematic situations. Although you may never have thought of it in quite this way, mathematics is a science of things that have a pattern of regularity and logical order. Finding and exploring this regularity or order and then making sense of it is what doing mathematics is all about.

Even the youngest schoolchildren can and should be involved in the science of pattern and order. Have you ever noticed that 6 + 7 is the same as 5 + 8 and 4 + 9? What is the pattern? What are the relationships? When two odd numbers are multiplied, the result is also odd, but if the same numbers are added or subtracted, the result is even. There is logic behind simple results such as these—an order, a pattern.

Consider the study of algebra. One can learn to graph the equation of a parabola by simply following rules and plotting points. Now calculators are readily available to do that as well, and with a speed and precision we could never hope to achieve. But understanding why certain forms of equations always produce parabolic graphs involves a search for patterns in the way numbers behave. Discovering what types of real-world relationships are represented by parabolic graphs (for example, a pendulum swing related to the length of the pendulum) is even more interesting and scientific—and infinitely more valuable—than the ability to plot the curve when someone else provides the equation.

Pattern is not just in numbers and equations; it is in everything around us. The world is full of pattern and order: in nature, in art, in buildings, in music. Pattern and order are found in commerce, science, medicine, manufacturing, and sociology. Mathematics discovers this order, makes sense of it, and uses it in a multitude of fascinating ways, improving our lives and expanding our knowledge. School must begin to help children with this process of discovery.

What Does It Mean to Do Mathematics?

Engaging in the science of pattern and order—in doing mathematics—is effortful and often takes time. There are a lot of ideas to learn. Often these ideas show up on lists of "basic skills." For example, children should be able to count accurately, know their basic facts for addition and multiplication, have efficient methods of computing whole numbers, fractions, and decimals, know measurement facts such as the number of centimetres in a metre or grams in a kilogram, know the names of geometric shapes, and so on. But to master these bits and pieces is no more doing mathematics than playing scales on the piano is making music.

Documents like *The Principles and Standards,* as well as your regional curriculum document, make it very clear that there is a time and a place for drill and practice. However, that drill should *never* come before understanding. Repetitive drill of the bits and pieces is not doing mathematics and will never result in understanding. Drill may produce short-term results on traditional tests, but the long-term result has been a nation of citizens happy to admit they can't do mathematics. The bits and pieces that are important are the result of actually doing mathematics. Mere mastery of skills is not doing mathematics.

The Verbs of Doing Mathematics

Envision for a moment an elementary mathematics class where students are doing mathematics. What verbs would you use to describe the activity in this classroom? Stop for a moment and make a short list before reading further.

Children in traditional mathematics classes often describe mathematics as "work" or "getting answers." They talk about "plussing" and "doing times" (multiplication).

In contrast, the following collection of verbs can be found in most of the literature describing the reform in mathematics education, and all are used in documents such as *The Principles and Standards for School Mathematics*:

explore	represent	develop
investigate	explain	construct
conjecture	formulate	describe
solve	predict	verify
justify	discover	use

These are science verbs, verbs indicating the process of "making sense" and "figuring out." When children are engaged in the kinds of activities suggested by this list, it is virtually impossible for them to be passive observers. They will necessarily be actively thinking about the mathematical ideas that are involved.

In classrooms where doing mathematics this way is a daily occurrence, the students are getting an empowering message: "You are capable of making sense of this—you are capable of *doing mathematics!*" The Math Science Investigations: Structures Program (Weininger, 1991), a program in which primary-age children learn mathematics concepts as they build with blocks and other manipulative materials, reflects this approach to mathematics. The Math Connections program, an extracurricular program for parents and children between the ages of 8 and 14 (Simmt, 1998, 1996) is another example.

What Is Basic in Mathematics?

In a climate where "basics" or "back to basics" is once again a matter of public discussion, it is useful to ask: what is basic in mathematics? The position of this text is as follows:

> **The most basic idea in mathematics is that mathematics makes sense!**
>
> ■ *Every day, students must experience that mathematics makes sense.*
>
> ■ *Students must come to believe that they are capable of making sense of mathematics.*
>
> ■ *Teachers must stop teaching by telling and start letting students make sense of the mathematics they are learning.*
>
> ■ *To this end, teachers must believe in their students—all of them!*

Every idea introduced in the mathematics classroom can and should be completely understood by *every* child. *There are no exceptions!* There is absolutely no excuse for children to learn any aspect of mathematics without com-

pletely understanding it. All children are capable of learning all of the mathematics we want them to learn, and they can do so in a meaningful manner, in a way that makes sense to them.

An Environment for Doing Mathematics

Look again at the verbs of doing mathematics. They are action verbs. They require reaching out, taking risks, putting out ideas where others can see them. Contrast these with verbs that might reflect the traditional mathematics classroom: *listen, copy, memorize, drill.* These are passive activities. They involve no risk and little initiative. Doing mathematics takes effort and initiative.

Though thinking, reasoning, and sense-making can be fun, it can nevertheless be a bit frightening to stick out your neck when no one tells you exactly what to do. The classroom must be an environment where doing mathematics is not threatening, where every student is respected for his or her ideas. Students should feel comfortable taking risks, knowing that they will not be ridiculed.

The teacher's role is to create a spirit of inquiry, trust, and expectation. Within that environment, students are invited to do mathematics. Problems are posed; students wrestle with ideas as they move toward solutions. The focus is on students actively figuring things out, testing ideas and making conjectures, developing reasons and offering explanations. Students work in groups, in pairs, or individually, but they are always sharing and discussing. Reasoning is celebrated as students defend their methods and justify their solutions.

An Invitation to Do Mathematics

If you are to create a classroom environment where children are truly doing mathematics, it is important that you have a personal feel for doing mathematics in this manner. It is quite likely that your experiences in mathematics classes have been quite different. The purpose of this portion of the chapter is to provide you with opportunities to engage in the science of pattern and order—to do some mathematics. Although the tasks or problems are appropriate for students in grades 5–8, you should not be at all concerned now with how children might approach these problems. Rather, get personally involved in the problems as an adult and discover as much as you can in the process. If possible, find one or two friends to work together with you. Get some paper to scribble ideas on. Try not to be shy about your ideas. Respect and listen to the ideas of your friends. You can and should challenge their ideas, but don't belittle them.

The text will provide hints and suggestions, but this is a poor substitute for interaction with a teacher. Don't read too much at once. Stop and do as much as you can until you and your group are stuck—really stuck; then read a bit more.

Let's Do Some Mathematics!

We will explore four different problems. Each is independent of the others. None requires any sophisticated mathematics, not even algebra. Don't be passive! Try your ideas out. Have fun!

START AND JUMP NUMBERS: SEARCHING FOR PATTERNS

You will need to make a list of numbers that begin with a "start number" and increase by a fixed amount we will call the "jump number." First try 3 as the start number and 5 as the jump number. Write the start number at the top of your list, then 8, 13, and so on, "jumping" by 5 each time until your list extends to about 130.

Your task is to examine this list of numbers and find as many patterns as you possibly can. Share your ideas with the group, and write down every pattern you agree really is a pattern.

 Get to work before reading further. Keep looking for patterns until you simply cannot think of any more.

A Few Ideas. Here are some kinds of things you may already have thought of:

- There is at least one alternating pattern.
- Have you looked at odd and even numbers?
- What can you say about the number in the tens place?
- How did you think about the first two numbers with no tens-place digits?
- What happens when the numbers go above 100? (There are two ways to think about that.)
- Have you tried doing any adding with the numbers? Numbers in the list? Digits in the numbers?

 If there is an idea in this list you haven't tried, try that now.

Remember to think about what happens to your patterns after the numbers go over 100. How are you thinking about 113? One way you might think of it is: 1 hundred, 1 ten, and 3 ones. Of course it could also be "eleventy-three," or eleven tens and three, where the hundreds has changed to ten tens and the tens digit has gone from 9 to 10 to 11. How do these different perspectives affect your patterns? What would happen after 999?

When you added the *digits* in the numbers, the sums are 3, 8, 4, 9, 5, 10, 6, 11, 7, 12, 8,... Did you look at every other number in this string? And what is the sum for 113? Is it 5 or is it 14? (There is no "right" answer here. But it is interesting to consider different possibilities.)

Next Steps. Sometimes, when you have discovered some patterns in mathematics, it is a good idea to make some changes and see how the changes affect the patterns. What changes might you make in this problem?

 Try some ideas now before going on.

Your changes may be even more interesting than the following suggestions. But here are some ideas that seem a bit more obvious than others:

- Change the start number but keep the jump number equal to 5. What is the same and what is different?
- Try keeping the start number the same, and examine different jump numbers. You will find out that changing jump numbers really "messes things up" a lot compared to changing the start numbers.
- If you have patterns for several different jump numbers, what can you figure out about how a jump number affects the patterns? For example, when the jump number was 5, the ones-digit pattern repeated every two numbers—it had a "pattern length" of two. Yet, when the jump number is 3, the length of the ones-digit pattern is ten! Do other jump numbers create different lengths?
- For a jump number of 3, how is the ones-digit pattern related to the circle of numbers in Figure 2.1? Are there other circles of numbers for other jump numbers?

Looking Back. You may want to explore this idea even further—or perhaps you've had enough of jump numbers. There are more ideas than have been suggested here.

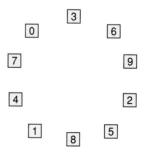

FIGURE 2.1 For jumps of 3, the cycle of digits will occur in the ones place.

A calculator can be used to make the list generation easy for young children or to work with big jump numbers, like 25 or 36. Most simple calculators have an automatic constant feature that will add the same number successively. For example, if you press 3 ⊞ 5 ⊟ and then keep pressing ⊟ , you will get the first sequence of numbers you wrote. (The calculator "stores" the last operation of +5 and repeats the operation on the display for each press the ⊟ . This also works for the other three operations.)

TWO MACHINES, ONE JOB

Ron's Recycle Shop was started when Ron bought a used paper-shredding machine. Business was good, so Ron bought a new shredding machine. The old machine could shred a truckload of paper in 4 hours. The new machine could shred the same truckload in only 2 hours. How long will it take to shred a truckload of paper if Ron runs both shredders at the same time?

Get Started. Sometimes you just have to jump in and do something. Before reading any of the ideas that follow, go ahead and work on this until you either get an answer or get stuck. If you get an answer, try to decide how you can establish that it is correct. If you get stuck, be absolutely certain you are stuck. Write down everything you know, and examine every idea you have had.

 Work before reading on.

Stuck? Are you overlooking any assumptions made in the problem? Do the machines run simultaneously? The problem says "at the same time." Do they run just as fast when working together as when they work alone?

 If this gives you an idea, pursue it before reading more.

Have you tried to predict approximately how much time you think it should take the two machines? Just make an estimate in round numbers. For example, will it be closer to 1 hour or closer to 4 hours? What causes you to answer as you have? Can you tell if your "guesstimate" makes sense or is at least in the ballpark? Checking a guess in this way sometimes leads to a new insight.

Some people draw pictures to solve problems. Others like to use something they can move or change. For example, you might draw a rectangle or a line segment to stand for the truckload of paper, or you might get some counters (chips, plastic cubes, pennies) and make a collection that stands for the truckload.

 Go back and try some more.

Consider Solutions of Others. Here are solutions of three elementary school teachers who worked on this problem. (The examples are adapted from Schifter & Fosnot, 1993, pp. 24-27.) Brigit teaches grade 6. Here is Brigit's solution:

> Brigit holds up a bar of plastic cubes. "Let's say these 16 cubes are the truckload of paper. In 1 hour, the new machine shreds 8 cubes and the old machine 4 cubes." Brigit breaks off 8 cubes and then 4 cubes. "That leaves these 4 cubes. If the new machine did 8 cubes' worth in 1 hour, it can do 2 cubes' worth in 15 minutes. The old machine does half as much, or 1 cube." As she says this, she breaks off 3 more cubes. "That is 1 hour and 15 minutes, and we still have 1 cube left." Long pause. "Well, the new machine did 2 cubes in 15 minutes, so it will do this cube in $7\frac{1}{2}$ minutes. Add that onto the 1 hour and 15 minutes. The total time will be 1 hour $22\frac{1}{2}$ minutes." (See Figure 2.2.)

Cora teaches grade 4. She disagrees with Brigit. Here is Cora's proposal:

> "This rectangle [see Figure 2.3] stands for the whole truckload. In 1 hour, the new machine will do half of this." The rectangle is divided in half. "In 1 hour, the old machine could do $\frac{1}{4}$ of the paper." The rectangle is divided accordingly. "So in 1 hour, the two machines have done $\frac{3}{4}$ of the truck, and there is $\frac{1}{4}$ left. What is left is one-third as much as what they already did, so it should take the two machines one-third as long to do that part as it took to do the first part. One-third of an hour is 20 minutes. That means it takes 1 hour and 20 minutes to do it all."

Sylvia teaches grade 3. She and her partner have these thoughts:

> "At first, we solved the problem by averaging. We decided that it would take 3 hours because that's the average. Then Deborah asked how we knew to average. We thought we had a reason, but then Deborah asked how Ron would feel if his two machines together took longer than just the new one that could do the job in only 2 hours. So we can see that 3 hours doesn't make sense. So we still don't know whether it's 1 hour and 20 minutes or 1 hour and $22\frac{1}{2}$ minutes."

At the Summer Math Institute where these teachers were participants, they were not told the solution to this problem. This caused some disturbance. However, there is little value in seeing a solution from a book or from a teacher. You end up feeling that the teacher is very smart and you are not. No solution is provided here either.

If you have a solution, a good thing is to see first why you think you are correct and try to articulate that. Then, see if you can find a different way to solve the problem than the way you did it the first time. (What would be the value of two different solutions that both lead to the same answer?)

FIGURE 2.2 Brigit's solution to the paper-shredding problem.

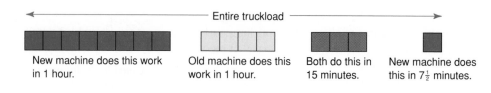

Entire truckload

New machine does this work in 1 hour.

Old machine does this work in 1 hour.

Both do this in 15 minutes.

New machine does this in 7½ minutes.

FIGURE 2.3 Cora's solution to the paper-shredding problem.

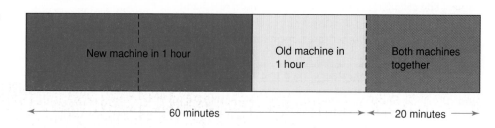

New machine in 1 hour

Old machine in 1 hour

Both machines together

60 minutes

20 minutes

WHAT CAN YOU FIND OUT ABOUT THIS?

An excellent exploration for young children to help them begin to see how facts are related is to confront them with this observation:

Add two numbers. When you make the first number 1 more and the second number 1 less, you get the same answer:

⇑ ⇓

7 + 7 = 14 is the same as 8 + 6 = 14

It works for 5 + 5 too

⇑ ⇓

5 + 5 = 10 is the same as 6 + 4 = 10

What can you find out about this?

Your task here is to examine what happens when you change addition to multiplication in this exploration. What can you find out about that? (7 × 7 = 49 and 8 × 6 = 48)? What other products should you examine?

STOP Explore until you have developed some ideas. Write down whatever ideas you discover.

Try Using a Physical Model. You have probably found some interesting patterns. Can you tell why these patterns work? In the case of addition, it is fairly easy to see that when you take from one number and give to the other, the total stays the same. That is not exactly the way multiplication works. One way to explore this is to make rectangles for each product and see how they change when you adjust one factor up and the other down (see Figure 2.4a).

You may prefer to think of multiplication as equal sets. For example, 7 × 7 means seven sets with seven things in each. You increase the number of sets and decrease the number in each set (or the other way around; see Figure 2.4b).

STOP Work with one or both of these approaches to see if you get any insights.

Things to Examine. There are a few ways to go with this exploration. Here are a couple of suggestions. Your exploring might take you in a different direction. That is fine!

FIGURE 2.4 Two physical ways to think about multiplication that might help in the exploration.

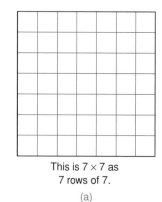

This is 7 × 7 as 7 rows of 7.

(a)

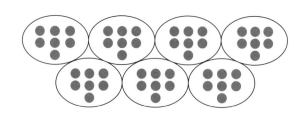

This is 7 × 7 as 7 sets of 7.

(b)

What happens when you change one of these to show 6 × 8?

The idea in this problem is to conduct your own exploration—to see what you can find out.

- Have you looked at how the first two numbers are related? For example, 7×7, 5×5, and 9×9 are all products with like factors. How do those results differ when the two factors are 1 apart (7×8 or 12×13)? What about when the factors differ by 2 or by 3?
- Maybe you have adjusted the factors up and down by 1. What if you go from 7×7 to 9×5? Try making adjustments by other numbers.
- Does it make any difference in the results if you use big numbers instead of small ones?
- What if *both* factors increase?

This exploration has many answers, but the questions to answer are the ones *you* ask. When the problem is really yours and it is not apparent that the teacher already knows the answer, students feel more ownership and interest. Problem ownership shifts the situation from "What do you want me to do?" to "I think I am going to..." (Baker & Baker, 1990). The questions offered here were presented as a list of suggestions because this is a textbook. In a classroom, the teacher can select challenges and offer ideas when necessary. The teacher can also help students make their own conjectures and observations. Frequently, children will pursue a completely different tack than the one anticipated. Scientists explore new ideas that strike them as interesting and promising, rather than blindly following the direction of others. Mathematics is a science.

THE BEST CHANCE OF PURPLE

Three students are spinning to "get purple" with two spinners (either by spinning first red and then blue or first blue and then red; see Figure 2.5). They may choose to spin each spinner once or one of the spinners twice. Mary chooses to spin twice on spinner A; John chooses to spin twice on spinner B; and Susan chooses to spin first on spinner A and then on spinner B. Who has the best chance of getting a red and a blue? (Lappan & Even, 1989, p. 17)

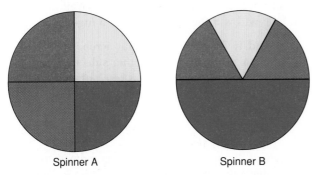

FIGURE 2.5 You may spin A twice, B twice, or A then B. Which option gives you the best chance of spinning a red and a blue?

 As with the other problems, begin by thinking over what you know about the problem, and then try something that gives you some help. Before reading the suggestions, see what you can come up with.

Try It Out. Sometimes it is tough to get a feel for problems that seem too abstract to think about. One thing that can be done in situations involving chance is to find a way to create the chance and see what happens. For this problem, you can easily make spinners using a freehand drawing on paper, a paper clip, and a pencil. Put your pencil point through the loop of the clip; then place it, point down, on the centre of your spinner. Now you can spin the paper clip with a flick of your fingers. Try at least 20 pairs of spins for each choice, and keep track of what happens.

- For Susan's choice (A then B), would it matter if she spun B first and then A? Why or why not?
- Try to describe why you think purple is more or less likely in one of the three cases compared to the other two. It sometimes helps to talk through what you have observed as a way of coming up with some more precise reasoning.

Try these suggestions before reading on.

Try Tree Diagrams. On spinner A, each of the four colours has the same chance of coming up. You could make a tree diagram for A with four branches, and all the branches would have the same chance (see Figure 2.6). On spinner B, what is the relationship between the blue region and each of the others? How could you make a tree diagram for B with each branch having the same chance?

How can you add to the diagram for spinner A so that it shows that A has been spun twice in succession? Why does your tree diagram make sense? What branches on your diagram represent getting purple?

How could you make tree diagrams to show John's and Susan's choices? Why do they make sense?

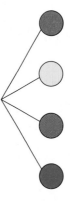

FIGURE 2.6 A tree diagram for spinner A in Figure 2.5.

You should test whatever idea you came up with on paper by actually spinning the spinners.

Tree diagrams are only one way to approach this. You may have a different way. As long as your way seems to be getting you somewhere, stick with it. There is one more suggestion to follow, but don't read further if you have an idea on which to work.

Using Grids. Suppose that you had a square that represented all the possible outcomes for spinner A and a similar square for spinner B. There are many ways to divide a square into four equal parts. However, someone figured out that if you use lines all going in the same direction, you could compare all the outcomes of one event (one whole square) with the outcomes of another event (drawn in a different square). When the second event (here the second spin) follows the first event, make the lines in the second square go in the opposite direction from the lines in the first square. Then, make a tracing of one square in Figure 2.7, and place it on the other. You will end up with 24 little sections.

Why are there six subdivisions for the square that represents spinner B? What does each of the 24 little rectangles stand for? What sections represent purple? In any other method you have been trying, did 24 come into play when spinner A was followed by B?

No-Answer Book

If you have worked hard on any or all of the four tasks just presented, you still may not have answers, or you may not have found the same patterns and ideas that someone else found. If you really gave it some effort and took some risks sharing whatever ideas you had, you are on the right track. The science of pattern and order sometimes takes a little time and nearly always requires effort.

No answers or solutions are given in this text. How do you feel about that? What about the "right" answers? Are your answers correct? What makes the solution to any investigation "correct"?

In the classroom, the ready availability of the answer book, or the willingness of the teacher to provide the solution or verify the answer as correct, sends a clear message to children about doing mathematics: "Your job is to find the answers that the teacher already has." In the real world of problem solving outside the classroom, there are no teachers with answers and no answer books. Doing mathematics includes deciding if an answer is correct and understanding why.

Some More Explorations

Here are four more explorations. For these tasks, there are no hints or discussions, only the problems. The first two you could try with grade 4 or grade 5 children. All four would be useful in grades 7 and 8. The main purpose of presenting them here is to give you an opportunity to do some more mathematics and to begin to experience what that means and feels like.

FOUR CONSECUTIVE NUMBERS

Some people say that to add four consecutive numbers, you add the first and the last numbers and multiply by 2. What can you find out about that?

Here is an example: 4, 5, 6, and 7 are four consecutive numbers. The sum is 22. Also $4 + 7 = 11$ and $11 \times 2 = 22$. The problem is taken from *Natural Learning and Mathematics* (Stoessiger & Edmunds, 1992). The authors use this task to provide a wonderful illustration of how 11- and 12-year-olds can generate ideas and make them grow. The book is highly recommended.

ACROBATS, GRANDMAS, AND IVAN

The problem is to use the information given to figure out who will win the third round of a tug-of-war.

Round 1: On one side are four acrobats, each of equal strength. On the other side are five neighbourhood grandmas, each of equal strength. The result is dead even.

Round 2: On one side is Ivan, the dog. Ivan is pitted against two of the grandmas and one acrobat. Again, it's a draw.

Round 3: Ivan and three of the grandmas are on one side, and the four acrobats are on the other.

Who will win the third round?

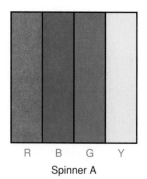
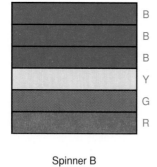

R B G Y
Spinner A   Spinner B

FIGURE 2.7 A square shows the chance of obtaining each colour for the spinners in Figure 2.5.

This problem was originally called "A Mathematical Tug-of-War" and is found in *Math for Smarty Pants* by Marilyn Burns (1982). For a discussion of how grade 5 students approached the problem, see *50 Problem-Solving Lessons: Grades 1-6* (Burns, 1996). Silver, Smith, and Nelson (1995) discuss solutions offered by grade 8 students.

PIZZAS: SMALL, MEDIUM, AND LARGE

Pizzas are often sold in small, medium, and large sizes—usually measured by the diameter of the circular pie. Of course, the prices are different for the three sizes. Do you think a large pizza is usually the best buy?

Pappa Mio's Pizzeria sells small, medium, and large pizzas. A small pizza is 23 cm in diameter, a medium one is 30 cm in diameter, and a large one is 38 cm in diameter. For a plain cheese small pizza, Pappa Mio's charges $6; for a medium pizza, it charges $9; for a large pizza, it charges $12. Are these fair prices?

■ **Which measures—circumference, area, radius, diameter—should be most closely related to the prices charged? Why?**

■ **Use your results to write a report on the fairness of Pappa Mio's pizza prices.**

This problem (adapted from Lappan & Briars, 1995, p. 139) has a number of characteristics worth noting. First, it is contextual; it is a very realistic problem that might interest students in grades 7 and 8. Second, the teacher can predict with some certainty what mathematics students will encounter in this problem (measurement and relationships in the geometry of circles). There are a lot of ideas involving the measurement of circles. This would be a good problem to use *before* the children have developed a collection of formulas. Students have many ways to get at the circle measurements, including measuring some actual circles. Formulas are not necessary. There is also a nice opportunity to discuss rate as a type of ratio in this problem.

TRAPEZOIDS

A trapezoid is a four-sided figure that has two parallel sides. Draw a trapezoid that has an area of 36 units.

If a teacher or a text gives you a formula for the area of a trapezoid, this is not a very interesting task. But there are some nice possibilities for discovering patterns and learning about area, perhaps even developing a formula, that can come from this. One suggestion is to get some grid paper and draw some trapezoids. (Blackline Masters are provided at the back of the book.)

Helping Students Do Mathematics

If you have worked on some of the problems in this chapter, you have most likely been trying to make sense of the situations or tasks with which you were confronted. You were involved in the science of pattern and order. You were *doing mathematics*.

In the best of situations, you did this science, this mathematics, with others. Perhaps you shared your ideas, right or wrong, and tried to defend them. You listened to your peers and tried to make sense of their ideas. Together you tried to come up with a solution. Then you had to decide, without looking in an answer book or asking the teacher, if your answer was correct.

When students do mathematics like this on a daily basis in an environment that encourages risk and expects participation, it becomes an exciting endeavour. Students who are more comfortable in an environment that is not answer-oriented and teacher-directed begin to develop confidence. They talk more, share more ideas, offer suggestions, and challenge or defend the solutions of others.

Being the teacher responsible for creating this environment may sound overwhelming. You may have envisioned teaching mathematics as relatively easy—just demonstrate the rules and manage practice. Creating a classroom culture and environment in which children are *doing* mathematics is not easy. There is no reason to believe that you will be an expert from the start.

NCTM's *Professional Standards for Teaching Mathematics* (1991) offers important guidelines and examples of teachers making changes toward this vision of doing mathematics. As noted in Chapter 1, the first of the major shifts envisioned by the *Professional Standards* is "toward classrooms as mathematical communities" and "away from classrooms as simply a collection of individuals" (p. 3). To create this mathematical community, you next need to understand how children develop mathematical ideas. That is what you will encounter in Chapter 3. In Chapter 4, we will build on the vision of what it means to do mathematics and on an understanding of how children learn. There you will find strategies for teaching with tasks or problems. It is an exciting venture!

Reflections **on Chapter 2**

Writing to Learn

1. Explain what is meant by "mathematics is a science of pattern and order." Contrast this view with traditional school mathematics.
2. How would you describe what it means to "do mathematics"?
3. Why is doing pencil-and-paper computation not "doing mathematics"?
4. What features of a classroom environment are important in order for students to be engaged in doing mathematics?
5. How can students come to believe that they are capable of making sense of mathematics?

For Discussion and Exploration

1. Explore the teacher's edition of any current basal textbook series for any grade level of your interest. Pick one chapter, and identify lessons or activities that promote doing mathematics as a science of pattern and order. In general, would you say that the flavour of the chapter you selected is in the spirit of mathematics as a science of pattern and order?
2. Talk to some teachers you know and find a program in which children are engaged in a hands-on approach to mathematics. Identify the features of this program that make it impossible for children to be passive observers.

Recommendations for Further Reading

Highly Recommended

Lampert, M. (1990). When the problem is not the question and the solution is not the answer: Mathematical knowing and teaching. *American Educational Research Journal, 27,* 29–63.

Magdalene Lampert is one of mathematics education's most articulate voices for making shifts toward classrooms as communities where children do mathematics. In this article, she clearly articulates the spirit of the traditional classroom and how it adversely affects the concept of mathematics held by children and teachers.

Malloy, C.E. (1999). Developing mathematical reasoning in the middle grades. In L.V. Stiff (Ed.), *Developing mathematical reasoning in grades K–12* (pp. 13–21). Reston, VA: National Council of Teachers of Mathematics.

Russell, S.J. (1999). Mathematical reasoning in the elementary grades. In L.V. Stiff (Ed.), *Developing mathematical reasoning in grades K–12* (pp. 1–12). Reston, VA: National Council of Teachers of Mathematics.

These two articles are the lead chapters in the 1999 NCTM yearbook on reasoning. Both authors provide excellent perspectives on the importance of helping children engage in the logical solution of problems. Russell's chapter begins with this: "Mathematical reasoning must stand at the center of mathematics learning." Malloy makes the point that even in a diverse classroom, different reasoning styles can be engaged to make learning happen.

Mokros, J., Russell, S.J., & Economopoulos, K. (1995). *Beyond arithmetic: Changing mathematics in the elementary classroom.* White Plains, NY: Cuisenaire-Dale Seymour.

These three author-researchers from TERC use numerous examples from the elementary classroom to develop a realistic image of teaching mathematics from a problem-solving perspective. In looking at teaching, curriculum, and assessment, the importance of problem solving as a way of learning mathematics is quite clear. If you want a realistic look at reform mathematics and children solving problems, this is a useful, accessible book to consider.

National Council of Teachers of Mathematics. (2000). Children as Mathematicians [Focus Issue]. *Teaching Children Mathematics, 6(6).*

Can young children do mathematics in the spirit described in this chapter? This focus issue of *TCM* provides ample evidence that children really can be engaged in doing mathematics. The articles provide numerous examples and suggest activities. A variety of content areas are explored, including counting, place value, geometry, measurement, and computation. Authors also address issues of developing a community of learners and tips for engaging students in discussion. This is a worthwhile focus issue.

Schifter, D., & Fosnot, C.T. (1993). *Reconstructing mathematics education: Stories of teachers meeting the challenge of reform.* New York: Teachers College Press.

The authors describe real teachers confronting their own concepts of mathematics by doing real mathematics themselves. There are also many insights into the classrooms to which these teachers return. It is in this book that Betsy and Cora solve the paper-shredder problem (the context was changed). If you feel a bit threatened by the call for change, this is a book that can make you realize you are not alone.

Other Suggestions

Artzt, A.F., & Yaloz-Femia, S. (1999). Mathematical reasoning during small-group problem solving. In L.V. Stiff (Ed.), *Developing mathematical reasoning in grades K–12* (pp. 115–126). Reston, VA: National Council of Teachers of Mathematics.

Backhouse, J., Haggarty, L., Pirie, S., & Stratton, J. (1992). *Improving the learning of mathematics.* Portsmouth, NH: Heinemann.

Baker, D., Semple, C., & Stead, T. (1990). *How big is the moon?* Portsmouth, NH: Heinemann.

Baker, J., & Baker, A. (1990). *Mathematics in process.* Portsmouth, NH: Heinemann.

Ball, D.L. (1991). Improving, not standardizing, teaching. *Arithmetic Teacher, 39(1),* 18–22.

Ball, D.L. (1991). What's all this talk about discourse? *Arithmetic Teacher, 39(2),* 44–48.

Borasi, R. (1990). The invisible hand operating in mathematics instruction: Students' conceptions and expectations. In T.J. Cooney (Ed.), *Teaching and learning mathematics in the 1990s* (pp. 174–182). Reston, VA: National Council of Teachers of Mathematics.

Bosangue, M.V., Gannon, G.E., & Watson, K.L. (2000). The wonderful world of digital sums. *Teaching Children Mathematics, 6,* 310–313, 318–320.

Cantlon, D. (1998). Kids + conjecture = mathematics power. *Teaching Children Mathematics, 5,* 108–112.

Cobb, P., & Merkel, B. (1989). Thinking strategies: Teaching arithmetic through problem solving. In P.R. Trafton (Ed.), *New directions for elementary school mathematics* (pp. 70–81). Reston, VA: National Council of Teachers of Mathematics.

Corwin, R.B. (1993). Doing mathematics together: Creating a mathematical culture. *Arithmetic Teacher, 40,* 338–341.

Curcio, F.R., & Schwartz, S.L. (1998). There are no algorithms for teaching algorithms. *Teaching Children Mathematics, 5,* 26–30.

Garofalo, J., & Durant, K. (1991). Where did that come from? A frequent response to mathematics instruction. *School Science and Mathematics, 91,* 318–321.

Karp, K.S., & Niemi, R.C. (2000). The math club for girls and other problem solvers. *Mathematics Teaching in the Middle Grades, 5,* 426–432.

Koehler, M.S., & Prior, M. (1993). Classroom interactions: The heartbeat of the teaching/learning process. In D.T. Owens (Ed.), *Research ideas for the classroom: Middle grades mathematics* (pp. 280–298). Old Tappan, NJ: Macmillan.

Schoenfeld, A.H. (1989). Problem solving in context(s). In R.I. Charles & E.A. Silver (Eds.), *The teaching and assessing of mathematical problem solving* (pp. 82–92). Reston, VA: National Council of Teachers of Mathematics.

Simmt, E. (1998). Reflections on an extracurricular parent-child mathematics program. *delta-K, 35* (1), 56–60.

Simmt, E. (1996). {Parents} {children} {mathematics}: researching the intersection. In Y.M. Pothier (Ed.), *Proceedings of the Canadian Mathematics Educational Study Group,* 99–109.

Smith, S.Z., Smith, M.E., & Romberg, T.A. (1993). What the NCTM standards look like in one classroom. *Educational Leadership, 50*(8), 4–7.

Steele, D.F. (2000). Enthusiastic voices from young mathematicians. *Teaching Children Mathematics, 6,* 464–468.

Stoessiger, R., & Edmunds, J. (1992). *Natural learning and mathematics.* Portsmouth, NH: Heinemann.

Weininger, O. (1991). *Third-R structures: The math research program in primary grades.* Toronto: The Ontario Institute for Studies in Education.

Whitin, D.J. (1989). The power of mathematical investigations. In P.R. Trafton (Ed.), *New directions for elementary school mathematics* (pp. 183–195). Reston, VA: National Council of Teachers of Mathematics.

Chapter 3

Developing Understanding in Mathematics

If the creation of the conceptual networks that constitute each individual's map of reality—including her mathematical understanding—is the product of constructive and interpretive activity, then it follows that no matter how lucidly and patiently teachers explain to their students, they cannot understand for their students.

Schifter and Fosnot (1993, p. 9)

It is a commonly accepted goal among mathematics educators that students should understand mathematics (Hiebert & Carpenter, 1992; Pirie & Kieren, 1992, 1994). The most widely accepted theory, known as *constructivism*, suggests that children must be active participants in the development of their own understanding. Constructivism provides us with insights concerning how children learn mathematics and guides us to use instructional strategies that begin with children rather than with ourselves. In the view of many educators and researchers, this theoretical perspective has become, in the past 10 years, the "watchword" for good teaching (Pirie & Kieren, 1992).

A Constructivist View of Learning

Constructivism is firmly rooted in the cognitive school of psychology and the theories of Piaget, dating back at least as far as 1960. This view of learning rejects the notion that children are blank slates who absorb ideas as teachers present them. Rather, the belief is that children are creators of their own knowledge.

The Construction of Ideas

The basic tenet of constructivism is simply this: *Children construct their own knowledge* (Pirie & Kieren, 1992). In fact, not just children, but all people, all of the time, construct or give meaning to things they perceive or think about. As you read these words, you are giving meaning to them. You are constructing ideas.

To construct or build something in the physical world requires tools, materials, and effort. How we construct ideas can be viewed in an analogous manner. The tools we use to build understanding are our existing ideas, the knowledge that we already possess. The materials we act on to build understanding may be things we see, hear, or touch—elements of our physical surroundings. Sometimes the materials are our own thoughts and ideas. The effort that must be supplied is active and reflective thought. If minds are not actively thinking, nothing happens (Janvier, 1987; Schroeder & Lester, 1989).

The diagram in Figure 3.1 is meant as a metaphor for the construction of ideas. Consider the picture to be a small section of our cognitive makeup. The blue dots represent existing ideas. The lines joining the ideas represent our logical connections, or relationships that have developed between and among ideas. The red dot is an emerging idea, one that is being constructed. Whatever existing ideas (dots) are used in the construction will necessarily be connected to the new idea because those were the ideas that gave meaning to it. If a potentially relevant idea that would add better meaning to the new idea is either not present in the learner's mind or is not actively engaged, then that potential connection to the new idea simply will not be made. Obviously, learners will vary in the number of connections between a new idea and existing ideas. Different learners will use different ideas to give

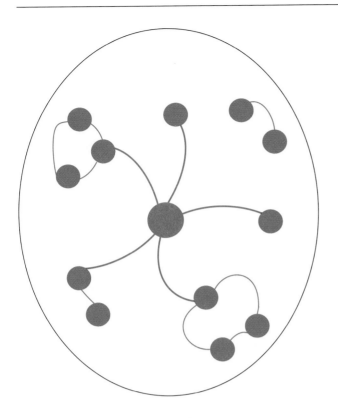

FIGURE 3.1 We use the ideas we already have (blue dots) to construct a new idea (red dot), developing in the process a network of connections between ideas. The more ideas used and the more connections made, the better we understand.

idea requires actively thinking about it. "How does this idea fit with what I already know?" "How can I understand this idea in the face of what I currently understand about it?" Mathematical ideas cannot be "poured into" a passive learner. Children must be mentally active for learning to take place. In classrooms, children must be encouraged to wrestle with new ideas, to work at fitting them into existing networks, and to challenge their own ideas and those of others. Put simply, constructing knowledge requires *reflective thought*—actively thinking about or mentally working on an idea. Reflective thought means sifting through existing ideas in order to find those that seem to be the most useful in giving meaning to the new idea.

Integrated networks, or *cognitive schemas,* are both the product of constructing knowledge and the tools with which additional new knowledge can be constructed. As learning occurs, the networks are rearranged, added to, or otherwise modified. When there is active, reflective thought, schemas are constantly being modified or changed so that ideas fit better with what is already known.

Examples of Constructed Learning

Consider the solution methods of two grade 4 children from schools where a highly constructivist approach to mathematics had been in place for several years. The "dots" these children had at their disposal included the meanings of the basic operations and a good understanding of place-value concepts. They were asked to solve the following problem: "Four children had 3 bags of M&Ms. They decided to open all 3 bags of candy and share the M&Ms fairly. There were 52 M&M candies in each bag. How many M&M candies did each child get?" (Campbell & Johnson, 1995, pp. 35–36). Their solutions are shown in Figure 3.2.

Both children were able to determine the product 3×52 mentally. The two children used different cognitive tools to

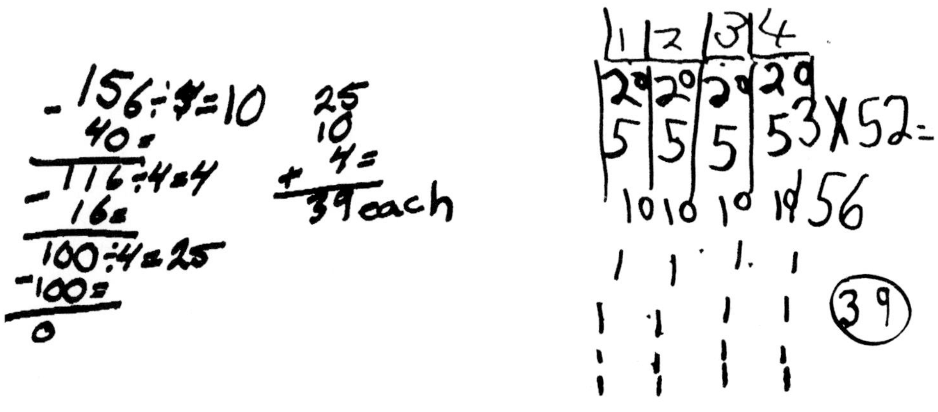

meaning to the same new idea. What is significant is that the construction of an idea is almost certainly going to be different for every learner, even within the same environment or classroom.

Constructing knowledge is an extremely active endeavour on the part of the learner (Pirie & Kieren, 1992; von Glasersfeld, 1990). To construct and understand a new

FIGURE 3.2 Two grade 4 children construct unique solutions to a computation.
Source: Campbell & Johnson (1995). Used with permission.

Myka's Solution

Harjit's Solution

solve the problem of 156 ÷ 4. Myka interpreted the task as "How many sets of 4 can be made from 156?" She first used facts that were either easy or available to her: 10 × 4 and 4 × 4. These totals she subtracted from 156 until she arrived at 100. This seemed to cue her to use 25 fours. Myka did not hesitate to add the number of sets of 4 that she found in 156 and knew the answer was 39 candies for each child.

Harjit's approach was more directly related to the sharing context of the problem. He formed four columns and distributed amounts to each, accumulating the amounts mentally and orally as he wrote the numbers. Like Myka, Harjit used numbers that were either easy or available to him; first 20 to each, then 5, then 10, and then a series of ones. He added one of the columns without hesitation (Rowan, 1995).

If computational speed and proficiency were your goal, you might be tempted to argue that the children need further instruction. However, both children clearly constructed ideas about the computation that had meaning for them. They demonstrated confidence, understanding, and a belief that they could solve the problem.

In contrast to these two children, consider a grade 3 child in a traditional classroom. She has made a quite common error in subtraction, as shown in Figure 3.3. The class had been doing subtraction with "borrowing," more appropriately known as trading or regrouping, and the problem appeared on a mathematics worksheet. The context narrowed the choices of ways to give meaning to the situation (the "dots" she would likely use). But this problem was a little different from the child's existing ideas about "borrowing." The next column contained a 0. How could she take 1 from the 0? That part was different, creating a situation that for her was problematic. The child decided that "the next column" must mean the next one that has something in it. She therefore believed that she had to "borrow" from the 6 and ignore the 0. The child used her existing ideas to give her own meaning to the rule "borrow from the next column."

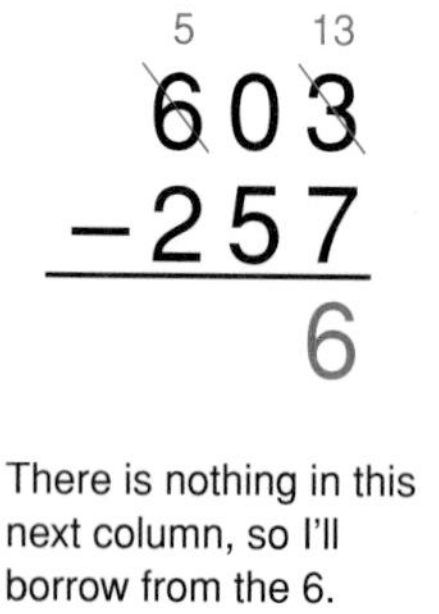

$$
\begin{array}{r}
^{5}\ \ ^{13} \\
6\,0\,3 \\
-\,2\,5\,7 \\
\hline
6
\end{array}
$$

There is nothing in this next column, so I'll borrow from the 6.

FIGURE 3.3 Children sometimes invent incorrect meanings by extending poorly understood rules.

Children rarely give random responses (Ginsburg, 1977; Labinowicz, 1985). Their answers tend to make sense in terms of their personal perspective or in terms of the knowledge they are using to give meaning to the situation. In many instances, children's existing knowledge is incomplete or inaccurate, or perhaps the knowledge we assume to be there simply is not. In such situations, as in the present example, new knowledge may be constructed inaccurately.

Construction in Rote Learning

Constructivism is a theory about how we learn. If it is correct, then it describes how *all* learning takes place, regardless of how we teach. We cannot choose to have children learn constructively on some days and not others. Even rote learning is a construction. But what tools or ideas are used for construction in rote learning? To what is knowledge learned by rote connected?

Children searching for a way to remember 7 × 8 = 56 might note that the numbers 5, 6 and 7, 8 go in order. Or they may connect the number 56 to that "hard fact" since 56 is unique in the multiplication table. (But then so is 54.) Repetition of a routine procedure may be connected to some mantra-type recitation of the rule, as in "Divide, multiply, subtract, and bring down." This sequence has even been related to the mnemonic "Dirty monkeys smell bad." New ideas learned like this are not connected to anything that can be called mathematical. Nor are they part of networks of ideas. Each newly learned bit is essentially isolated. Rote knowledge will almost never contribute to a useful network of ideas. Rote learning can be thought of as a "weak construction" (Noddings, 1993).

When mathematical ideas are used to create new mathematical ideas, useful cognitive networks are formed. Returning to 7 × 8, imagine a class where children discuss and share clever ways to figure out the product. One child might think of 5 eights and then 2 more eights. Another may have learned 7 × 7 and noted that this is just one more seven. Still another might look at a list of 8 sevens and take half of them (4 × 7) and double that. This may lead to the notion that double 7 is 14, and double that is 28, and double that is 56. Not every child will construct 7 × 8 using all of these approaches. However, the class discussion brings to the fore a wide range of useful mathematical "dots" so that the potential is there for profitable constructions.

Understanding

It is possible to say that we know something, but we might not necessarily understand it. Knowledge is something that we either have or don't have. Understanding is another matter. For example, how did you learn 7 × 8? If you learned it by rote, as most adults did, you may never have thought about the other ideas just discussed. Is your understanding of 7×8 just the same as that of a person who has connected some of these other ideas to that fact?

Understanding is never an all-or-nothing proposition. It depends on the existence of appropriate ideas and on the creation of new connections (Backhouse, Haggarty, Pirie & Stratton, 1992; Hiebert & Carpenter, 1992). It can be defined as a measure of the quality and quantity of connections that a new idea has with existing ideas.

One way we can think about an individual's understanding is to imagine it along a continuum (see Figure 3.4). At one extreme is a very rich set of connections. The understood idea is associated with many other existing ideas in a meaningful network of concepts and procedures. Hiebert and Carpenter (1992) refer to "webs" of interrelated ideas. Understanding at this rich interconnected end of the continuum will be referred to as *relational understanding,* borrowing a term made popular by Skemp (1978). At the other end of the continuum, ideas are largely or completely isolated. At this end, we have what we will call *instrumental understanding,* again borrowing from Skemp. Knowledge that is learned by rote is almost always understood instrumentally.

Examples of Understanding

If we accept the notion that understanding has both qualitative and quantitative differences, the question "Does she know it?" must be replaced with "How does she understand it? What ideas does she connect with it?" In the following examples, you will see how different children may well develop varied ideas about the same concept and thus have dissimilar understandings.

Computation in Two Classrooms

Schifter and Fosnot (1993) describe a grade 3 class where several children are discussing the problem of sharing 90 jelly beans among four children. They decide to use base-ten models (ones and tens). They distribute 2 tens to each group and trade a ten for 10 ones.

Next, they distribute 2 ones to each group. Then, there is a discussion of what to do with the 2 leftover ones and how to write down what they have done. One child suggests "$22\frac{1}{2}$" and another "22 R 2." They decide that the best answer for any division depends on the situation and what you want to do with the leftovers.

In a more traditional class, another grade 3 student was quite confident in her ability to do long divisions such as $24\,682 \div 5$. When asked what the "R 2" meant when she computed $32 \div 5$, she could only identify 2 as the remainder. Asked to demonstrate $32 \div 5$ with the base ten blocks, she began but then decided it couldn't be done. The child was at a loss to explain "R 2" in terms of the leftover counters (Schifter & Fosnot, 1993). These children all have different understandings of division. Some are very rich understandings; some are very limited.

Connections with Early Number Concepts

Consider the concept of "seven" as constructed by a child in grade 1. Seven for a first grader is most likely connected to the counting procedure and the construct of "more than" and is probably understood as less than 10 and more than 2. What else will this child eventually connect to the concept of seven as it now exists? Seven is 1 more than 6; it includes those numbers less than itself; it is 2 less than 9; it is the combination of 3 and 4 or 2 and 5; it is odd; it is small compared to 73; it is the number of days in a week; and so on. The web of ideas connected to a number can grow large and involved, depending on the level of the child's understanding.

A Web of Ideas Involving Ratio

A clear example of the potential for rich relational understanding is found in the many ideas that can be associated with the concept of "ratio" (see Figure 3.5). Unfortunately, many children learn only meaningless rules connected with ratio, such as, "Given one ratio, how do you find an equivalent ratio?"

Benefits of Relational Understanding

To teach for a rich or relational understanding requires a lot of work and effort. Concepts and connections develop over time, not in a day. Tasks must be selected. Instructional materials must be made. The classroom needs to be organized for group work and maximum interaction with and among the children. The important benefits to be derived from relational understanding make the effort not just worthwhile, but essential.

Relational Understanding

Instrumental Understanding

Continuum of Understanding

FIGURE 3.4 **Understanding is a measure of the quality and quantity of connections that a new idea has with existing ideas. The greater the number of connections to a network of ideas, the better the understanding.**

FIGURE 3.5 Potential web of associations that could contribute to the understanding of "ratio."

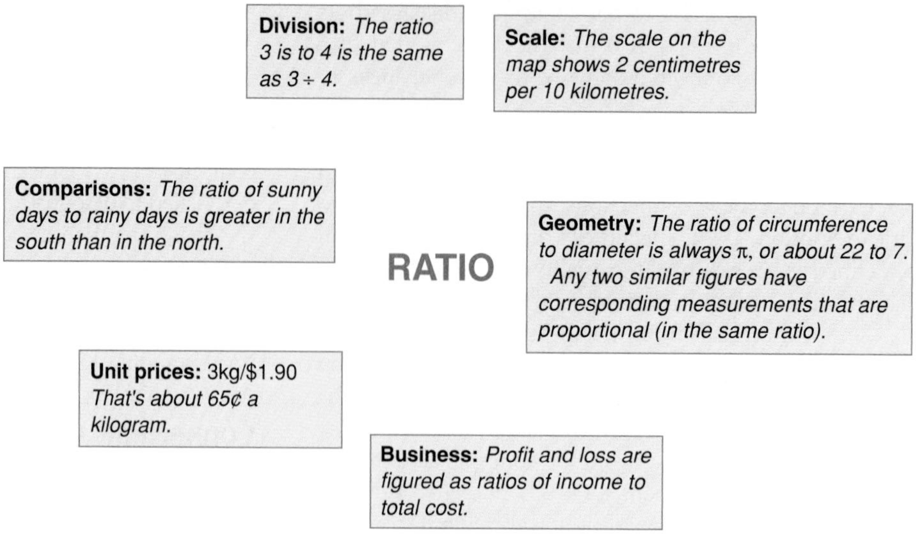

Division: *The ratio 3 is to 4 is the same as 3 ÷ 4.*

Scale: *The scale on the map shows 2 centimetres per 10 kilometres.*

Comparisons: *The ratio of sunny days to rainy days is greater in the south than in the north.*

Geometry: *The ratio of circumference to diameter is always π, or about 22 to 7. Any two similar figures have corresponding measurements that are proportional (in the same ratio).*

RATIO

Unit prices: 3kg/$1.90 *That's about 65¢ a kilogram.*

Business: *Profit and loss are figured as ratios of income to total cost.*

It Is Intrinsically Rewarding

Nearly all people, and certainly children, enjoy learning. This is especially true when new information connects with ideas already possessed. The new knowledge makes sense; it fits; it feels good. Children who learn by rote must be motivated by external means: for the sake of a test, to please a parent, from fear of failure, or to receive some reward. Such learning is distasteful. Rewards of an extra recess or a star on a chart may be effective in the short run but do nothing to encourage a love of the subject when the rewards are removed.

It Enhances Memory

Memory is a process of retrieving information. When learning in mathematics establishes a rich set of connections, there is much less chance that the information will deteriorate; connected information is more likely than disconnected information to be retained over time. It is also easier to retrieve. Connected information provides an entire web of ideas for which a learner can reach. If what you need to recall seems distant, reflecting on related ideas will, in most instances, eventually lead to the desired idea. Attempting to retrieve disconnected information is more like looking for a needle in a haystack.

A large portion of instructional time in schools is devoted to re-teaching and review. If teaching focused more on developing relational rather than instrumental understanding, much less review time would be needed.

There Is Less to Remember

Traditional approaches have tended to fragment mathematics into seemingly endless lists of isolated skills, concepts, rules, and symbols. The lists are so lengthy that teachers and students become overwhelmed. Constructivists, for their part, talk about teaching "big ideas" (Brooks & Brooks, 1993; Hiebert et al., 1996; Schifter & Fosnot, 1993). Big ideas are really just large networks of interrelated concepts. Ideas are learned relationally when they are integrated into a larger web of information, a big idea. Frequently, the network is so well constructed that whole chunks of information are stored and retrieved as single entities rather than isolated bits. For example, knowledge of place value subsumes rules about lining up decimal points, ordering decimal numbers, moving decimal points to the right or left in decimal-percent conversions, rounding and estimating, and a host of other ideas. Similarly, knowledge of equivalent fractions ties together rules concerning common denominators, reducing fractions, and changing between mixed numbers and whole numbers.

It Helps with Learning New Concepts and Procedures

An idea fully understood in mathematics is easily extended when a new idea is learned. Understanding of number concepts and relationships helps with mastery of basic facts. Fraction knowledge and place-value knowledge come together to make decimal learning easier, and decimal concepts directly enhance an understanding of percentage concepts and procedures. Many of the ideas of elementary arithmetic become the model for understanding ideas in algebra. Reducing fractions by finding common prime factors is the same thing as dividing out common factors.

Without these connections, children will need to learn each new piece of information they encounter as a separate, unrelated idea.

It Improves Problem-Solving Abilities

The solution of novel problems requires transferring ideas learned in one context to new situations. When concepts are embedded in a rich network, transferability is significantly enhanced and, thus, so is problem solving (Schoenfeld, 1992). The most recent results of the School Achievement Indicators Program (SAIP) for mathematics, the third assessment of its type, demonstrated that significantly more 13-year-old Canadian students improved (compared to results of the previous assessment) in problem solving, as well as in mathematics content. It is suggested that exposure to reform-oriented curricula, with their emphasis on understanding, may have played a role in students' improvement (Council of Ministers of Education, 2001).

It Is Self-Generative

"Inventions that operate on understandings can generate new understandings, suggesting a kind of snowball effect. As networks grow and become more structured, they increase the potential for invention" (Hiebert & Carpenter, 1992, p. 74). Skemp (1978) noted that when gaining knowledge is found to be pleasurable, people who have had that experience of pleasure are likely to seek or invent new ideas on their own, especially when confronting problematic situations.

It Improves Attitudes and Beliefs

Relational understanding has an affective as well as a cognitive effect on the learner. When relational learning occurs, the learner tends to be more positive about his or her ability to learn and understand mathematics. There is a definite sense of "I can do this! I understand!" There is no reason to fear or be in awe of knowledge learned relationally. Mathematics then makes sense. It is not some mysterious world that only "smart people" dare to enter. At the other end of the continuum, instrumental understanding may produce mathematics anxiety, a real phenomenon that involves fear and avoidance behaviour.

Relational understanding also promotes a positive view of mathematics itself. Sensing the connectedness and logic of mathematics, students are more likely to gravitate toward it or to describe the discipline in positive terms.

Types of Mathematical Knowledge

All knowledge, mathematical or otherwise, consists of internal or mental representations of ideas that the mind has constructed. For some time now, mathematics educators have found it useful to distinguish between two types of mathematical knowledge: conceptual knowledge and procedural knowledge (Hiebert & Lindquist, 1990).

Conceptual Knowledge of Mathematics

Conceptual knowledge of mathematics consists of logical relationships constructed internally and existing in the mind as a part of a network of ideas. It is the type of knowledge Piaget referred to as logico-mathematical knowledge (Kamii, 1985, 1989; Labinowicz, 1985). By its very nature, conceptual knowledge is knowledge that is understood (Hiebert & Carpenter, 1992).

Ideas such as seven, rectangle, ones/tens/hundreds (as in place value), sum, product, equivalent, ratio, and negative are all examples of mathematical relationships or concepts.

Figure 3.6 shows three different types of Dienes' Base-Ten Multibase Arithmetic Blocks, commonly used to represent ones, tens, and hundreds. (The blocks were designed by Zoltan Dienes, a mathematics educator whose experience extends to a number of Canadian provinces.) By the middle of grade 2, most children have seen pictures of these or have used the actual blocks. It is quite common for these children to be able to identify the rod as the "ten" piece and the large square block, the flat, as the "hundred" piece. Does this mean that they have constructed the concepts of ten and a hundred? All that is known for sure is that they have learned the names for these objects, the conventional names of the base ten blocks. The mathematical concept of a ten is that *a ten is the same as ten ones*. Ten is not a rod. The concept is the relationship between the rod and the small cube. It is not the rod or a bundle of ten sticks or any other model of a ten. It is this relationship called "ten" that children must create in their own minds.

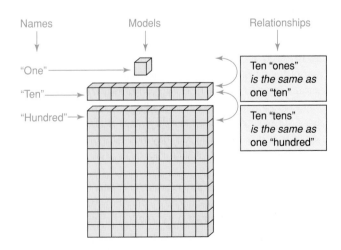

FIGURE 3.6 Objects and names of objects are not the same as relationships between objects.

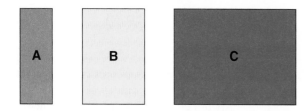

FIGURE 3.7 Three shapes, different relationships.

In Figure 3.7, the shape labelled A is a rectangle. But if we call shape B "one" or a "whole," then we might refer to shape A as "one-half." The idea of "half" is the *relationship* between shapes A and B, a relationship that must be constructed in our mind. It is not in either rectangle. In fact, if we decide to call shape C the whole, shape A becomes "one-fourth." The actual rectangle did not change in any way. The concepts of "half" and "fourth" are not in rectangle A; we construct them in our mind. The rectangles help us "see" the relationships, but what we see are rectangles, not concepts.

Procedural Knowledge of Mathematics

Procedural knowledge of mathematics is knowledge of the rules and the procedures that one uses in carrying out routine mathematical tasks, and of the symbolism that is used to represent mathematics. Knowledge of mathematics consists of more than concepts. Step-by-step procedures exist for performing tasks such as multiplying 47×68. Concepts are represented by special words and mathematical symbols. These procedures and symbols can be connected to or supported by concepts, but very few cognitive relationships are needed to have knowledge of a procedure.

Procedures are the step-by-step routines learned to accomplish a task. "To add two three-digit numbers, first add the numbers in the right-hand column. If the answer is 10 or more, put the 1 above the second column, and write the other digit under the first column. Proceed in a similar manner for the next two columns in order." We can say that someone who can accomplish a task such as this has knowledge of that procedure. Again, the conceptual understanding that may or may not support this procedural knowledge can vary considerably from one student to the next.

Some procedures are very simple and may even be confused with conceptual knowledge. For example, grade 7 children may be shown how to add the integers ⁻7 and ⁺4 by combining 7 red "negative" counters with 4 yellow "positive" counters. Pairs consisting of 1 red and 1 yellow counter are removed, and the result is noted. In this example, there would be 3 red negative counters remaining,

and the students would record ⁻3 as the sum. This might be called a manipulative or physical procedure. Notice that it is conceivable that a student could master a procedure such as this with very little understanding, or it could be integrated with a conceptual web related to integers and thus be well understood.

Symbolism includes expressions such as $(9 - 5) \times 2 = 8$, π, $\leq$, $\geq$, and $\neq$. The meaning attached to this symbolic knowledge depends on how it is understood—what concepts and other ideas the individual connects to the symbols. Symbolism is part of procedural knowledge, whether it is understood or not.

Procedural Knowledge and Doing Mathematics

Procedural knowledge of mathematics plays a very important role both in learning and in doing mathematics. Algorithmic procedures help us do routine tasks easily and thus free our minds to concentrate on more important tasks. Symbolism is a powerful mechanism for conveying mathematical ideas to others and for "doodling around" with an idea as we do mathematics. But even the most skillful use of a procedure will not help develop conceptual knowledge that is related to that procedure (Hiebert, 1990). Doing endless long-division exercises will not help a child understand the meaning of division. In fact, students who become skillful with a particular procedure are very reluctant, after the fact, to attach meaning to it.

From the perspective of learning mathematics, the question of how procedures and conceptual ideas can be linked is much more important than the usefulness of the procedure itself (Hiebert & Carpenter, 1992). Recall the two children who used their own invented procedure to solve $156 \div 4$ (see Figure 3.2, p. 29). Clearly, there was an active and useful interaction between the procedures the children invented and the ideas they were constructing about division.

It is generally accepted that procedural rules should never be learned in the absence of a concept. Unfortunately, that happens far too often.

The Role of Models In Developing Understanding

It has become a cliché that good teachers use a "hands-on" approach to teach mathematics. Manipulatives, or physical materials used to model mathematical concepts, are certainly important tools available for helping children learn mathematics. But they are not the panacea that some educators seem to believe them to be. It is important that you have the appropriate perspective on how manipulatives can help or fail to help children construct ideas.

Models for Mathematical Concepts

Return for a moment to the idea of a mathematical concept as a relationship, a logical idea. There are no physical embodiments of mathematical concepts in the physical world. The concept of "hundred," for example, is a quantity relationship that exists between a group of 100 items and a single item of the same type. We can talk of 100 people, 100 dollars, or 100 acts of kindness. None of those sets *is* a hundred. Hundred is only a relationship that the group has with one thing like those in the group. It is impossible to imagine "hundred" without first understanding "one."

A *model for a mathematical concept* refers to any object, picture, or drawing that represents the concept, or onto which the relationship for that concept can be imposed. In this sense, any group of 100 objects can be a model of the concept "hundred" because we can impose the 100-to-1 relationship on the group, and on a single element of the group.

It is incorrect to say that a model "illustrates" a concept. To illustrate implies showing. That would mean that when you look at the model, you would see an example of the concept. Technically, all that you actually see with your eyes is the object; only your mind can impose the mathematical relationship on the object (Thompson, 1994). If a person does not yet possess the relationship, the model does not illustrate the concept *for that person*.

Examples of Models

As noted, physical materials have become enormously popular as tools for teaching mathematics. They can run the gamut from common objects, such as lima beans for counters, to commercially produced materials, such as wooden rods or plastic geometric shapes. Figure 3.8 shows six common examples of models for six different concepts. Consider each of the concepts and the corresponding model. Try to separate the physical model from the relationship that you must impose on it in order to "see" the concept.

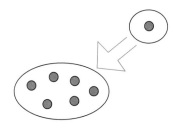

Countable objects can be used to model "number" and related ideas such as "one more than."

(a)

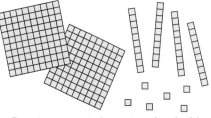

Base-ten concepts (ones, tens, hundreds) are frequently modelled with strips and squares. Sticks and bundles of sticks are also commonly used.

(d)

"Length" involves a comparison of the length attribute of different objects. Rods can be used to measure length.

(b)

"Chance" can be modelled by comparing outcomes of a spinner.

(e)

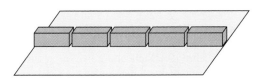

"Rectangles" can be modelled on a dot grid. They involve length and spatial relationships.

(c)

"Positive" and "negative" integers can be modelled with arrows with different lengths and directions.

(f)

FIGURE 3.8 **Examples of models to illustrate mathematics concepts.**

For the examples in Figure 3.8:

(a) The concept of "six" is a relationship between sets that can be matched to the words *one, two, three, four, five, six*. Changing a set of counters by adding one alters the relationship. The difference between the set of 6 and the set of 7 is the relationship of "one more than."

(b) The concept of "length" could not be developed without making comparisons of the length attribute of different objects. The length measure of an object is a comparison relationship between the length of the object and the length of the unit.

(c) The concept of "rectangle" is a combination of spatial and length relationships. By drawing on dot paper, the relationships of opposite sides that are equal in length and parallel, and the adjacent sides' meeting at right angles, can be illustrated.

(d) The concept of "hundred" is not in the larger square but in the relationship of that square to the strip ("ten") and to the little square ("one").

(e) "Chance" is a relationship between the frequency of an event's occurrence compared with all possible outcomes. The spinner can be used to create relative frequencies. These can be predicted by observing relationships of sectors of the spinner. Note how chance and probability are integrated with ideas of fractions and ratio.

(f) The concept of a "negative integer" is based on the relationship "is the opposite of." Negative quantities exist only in relation to positive quantities. Arrows on the number line are not themselves negative quantities but model the "opposite of" relationship in terms of direction and size, or magnitude in terms of length.

Staying with integers for a moment, this concept is often modelled with counters in two colours, perhaps red for negative quantities and yellow for positive. The "opposite" aspect of integers can be imposed on the two colours. The "magnitude" aspect is found in the quantities of red and yellow counters. Although coloured counters and arrows are physically very different, the same relationships can be imposed on each. Children must construct relationships in order to "see" positive and negative integers in either model.

It is important to include calculators in any list of common models. The calculator models a wide variety of numerical relationships by quickly and easily demonstrating the effects of these ideas. For example, if the calculator is made to count by increments of 0.01 (press ⊞ 0.01 ⊟), the relationship of one-hundredth to one whole is illustrated. Press 3 ⊞ 0.01. How many presses of ⊟ are required to get from 3 to 4? Doing the required 100 presses and observing how the display changes along the way is quite impressive. Especially note what happens after 3.19, 3.29, and so on.

Models and Constructing Mathematics

In order to "see" in a model the concept that it represents, you must already have that concept—that relationship—in your mind. If you do not, then you would have no relationship to impose on the model. This is precisely why models are often more meaningful to the teacher than to the students. The teacher already has the concept and can see it in the model. A student without the concept sees only the physical object.

Thus a child needs to know the relationship before imposing it on the model. If the concept does not come *from* the model—and it does not—how does the model help the child get it?

Mathematical concepts that children are in the process of constructing are not the well-formed ideas conceived by adults. New ideas are formulated little by little over time. As children actively reflect on their new ideas, they test them out through as many different avenues as we might provide. For example, this is where the value of student discussions and group work comes in. Talking through an idea, arguing for a viewpoint, listening to others, and describing and explaining are all mentally active ways of testing an emerging idea against external reality. As this testing process goes on, the developing idea gets modified and elaborated and further integrated with existing ideas. When there is a good fit with external reality, the likelihood of a concept being formed correctly is good.

Models can also play the role of a testing ground for emerging ideas. They can be thought of as "thinker toys," "tester toys," and "talker toys."* It is difficult for students (of all ages) to talk about and test out abstract relationships using words alone. Hence, models give learners something to think about, explore with, talk about, and reason with.

Expanding the Idea of a Model

Lesh, Post, and Behr (1987) talk about five "representations" for concepts, two of which are manipulative models and pictures (see Figure 3.9). In their research, they also consider written symbolism, oral language, and real-world situations as representations or models of concepts. Their research has demonstrated that children who have difficulty translating a concept from one representation to another also have difficulty solving problems and understanding computations. Strengthening children's ability to move between and among these representations improves their conceptual growth.

The five representations illustrated in Figure 3.9 are simply an expansion of the model concept. The more ways that children are given to think about and test out an

---

*The term *thinker* toy is taken from Seymour Papert's book *Mindstorms* (1980), in which the inventor of the Logo computer language describes the computer as a powerful and flexible device that encourages learners to play with ideas and work through problems. "Tester toys" and "talker toys" were suggested in the current context by Laura Domalik, a grade 1 teacher.

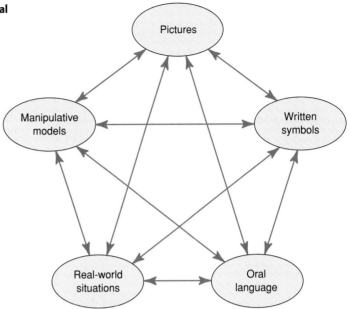

FIGURE 3.9 Five different representations of mathematical ideas. Translations between and within each can help develop new concepts.

emerging idea, the better chance the idea has of being formed correctly and integrated into a rich web of ideas and relational understanding.

Using Models in the Classroom

If we think of models as thinker toys or talker toys, we can identify three related uses for them in a developmental approach to teaching:

1. To help children develop new concepts or relationships
2. To help children make connections between concepts and symbols
3. To help educators assess children's understanding

Developing New Concepts

Models help children as they think and reflect on new ideas. Students should be encouraged to select and use materials to help them work through a problem or explain an idea to their group. To that end, a variety of models should be available to students so that they may use them freely when thinking through an important idea. Students should be free to select those models that make sense to them and not be forced to use a particular model.

You will undoubtedly encounter situations in which you use a model that you think clearly illustrates an idea, but the child just doesn't get it. Remember that you already possess the well-formed concept, so you are able to impose it on the model. Children are often able to see connections and relationships between concepts and models that we as adults miss because of our own well-formed concepts. Always encourage children to share their ideas with one another.

A child in the process of creating a concept may use a model to test an emerging idea. Your job is to get children to think with models, to work actively at the test-revise-test-revise process until the new concept fits with the physical model you have offered. It is not possible to show mathematics with models. You can only provide models on which mathematical relationships or concepts can be imposed. When the child's concept fits the model, the child sees the concept. When the concept does not seem to fit, the child cannot see it in the model. The child's concept is different from the one that you impose on the model and so must undergo further construction or revision.

Connecting Symbols and Concepts

Teachers will say, "But when they try to do it without manipulatives, they can't." Yet it is unrealistic to expect children automatically to transfer newly formed ideas to symbolic procedures without some guidance. Models can serve as a link between concepts and symbols as well as a means for developing concepts.

A general approach is to have students write down how they have used the models. "Write an equation to tell what you just did." "I see how you did that problem with the blocks. How would you go about recording what you did?" When children see written mathematics as expressions or recordings of ideas that they have already developed, the written or symbolic form is more likely to make sense.

Assessing Children's Understanding

When children in the classroom use models in ways that make sense to them (rather than following your directions), the manner in which they are used provides a wonderful window into their minds. Classroom observation of your students then becomes a student-by-student assessment.

If you want more detailed information about the understanding children have constructed, have them use manipulative materials to explain their ideas. The models give children the words they need to express themselves when abstract ideas prove difficult for them to explain. This might be done in a diagnostic setting, where you sit down, one-on-one, with a child and try to find out what he or she is thinking. Remember that drawings are also models. When students write explanations for their answers or describe their ideas in writing, always encourage them to draw pictures to help show what they are thinking. (Assessment is discussed in depth in Chapter 5.)

Incorrect Use of Models

The most widespread misuse of manipulative materials occurs when the teacher tells students, "Do as I do." There is a natural temptation to get out the materials and show children exactly how to use them. Children will blindly follow the teacher's directions, and it may even look as if they understand. It is just as possible to get students to move blocks around mindlessly as it is to teach them to "invert and multiply" mindlessly. Neither promotes thinking or aids in the development of concepts (Ball, 1992; Clements & Battista, 1990).

A natural result of overly directing the use of models is that children begin to use them as "answer-getting" devices rather than as thinker toys. When getting answers rather than solving problems becomes the focus of a lesson, children will gravitate to the easiest method available to get the answers. For example, if you have carefully shown and explained to children how to get an answer with a set of counters, then an imitation of that method is what they will most likely select. By strictly following your directions, little or no reflective thought will go into exploring the concepts involved. When an activity is not reflective, little real growth occurs, and little understanding is constructed.

Teaching Developmentally

Teaching involves decision-making. Decisions are made as you plan lessons. *What is the best task to propose tomorrow? Considering what happened today, what will move the children forward?* And decisions are made minute to minute in the classroom. *How should I respond? Should they struggle some more, or should I intervene? Is progress being made? How can I help Suzy move in the correct direction without discouraging her?*

The ideas that have been discussed in this chapter provide a theoretical foundation for making those decisions.

Foundations of a Developmental Approach

Following is a summary of the major implications of the theory that has been discussed. A teacher who keeps these ideas in mind can be said to be basing his or her instruction on a constructivist view of learning or, in the terminology of this book, a *developmental approach*.

1. *Children construct their own knowledge and understanding; we cannot transmit ideas to passive learners.* Each child comes to us with a unique but rich collection of ideas. These ideas are the tools that will be used to construct new concepts and procedures as students wrestle with ideas, discuss solutions, challenge their own and others' conjectures, explain their methods, and solve engaging problems. Ideas cannot be poured into children as if they were empty vessels.

2. *Knowledge and understanding are unique for each learner.* Each child's network of ideas is different from that of the next child. As new ideas are formed, they will be integrated into that web of ideas in a unique way as well. We should not try to make all children the same.

3. *Reflective thinking is the single most important ingredient for effective learning.* In order to create new ideas and to connect them in a rich web of interrelated ideas, children must be mentally engaged. They must find the relevant ideas they possess and bring them to bear on the development of new ideas and the solutions to new problems. Only by being mentally engaged with the task at hand can relational understanding of new ideas ever develop. "Passive learning" is an oxymoron!

4. *Effective teaching is a child-centred activity.* In a constructivist classroom, the emphasis is on learning rather than teaching. Students are given the task of learning. The role of the teacher is to engage the students by posing good problems and creating a classroom atmosphere of exploration and sense-making. The source of mathematical truth is found in the reasoning carried out by the class. The teacher is not the arbiter of what is mathematically correct.

Strategies for Effective Teaching

How can we structure lessons to promote appropriate reflective thought? Purposeful mental engagement or reflective thought about the ideas we want students to develop is the single most important key to effective teaching. Without active thinking about the important concepts of the lesson, learning will not happen. How can we make it happen? Here are seven suggestions based on the perspectives of this chapter. Perhaps you will be able to add to the list.

1. Create a mathematical environment.
2. Pose worthwhile mathematical tasks.
3. Use cooperative learning groups.
4. Use models and calculators as thinking tools.
5. Encourage discourse and writing.
6. Require justification of student responses.
7. Listen actively.

Creating a Mathematical Environment

In a mathematical environment, students feel comfortable trying out ideas, sharing insights, challenging others, seeking advice from other students and the teacher, explaining their thinking, and taking risks. No one is permitted to be a passive observer. An environment with these features is built around expectations, respect, and the belief that *all* children can learn. Learning takes effort, and children need to know that as a class, their task is to work at doing mathematics. The interactions of a mathematical environment require students and teachers alike to respect one another, to listen attentively, and to learn to disagree without offending.

We cannot simply tell children how to think or what habits to acquire. Processes and habits of thought are developed over time within a community where such processes and thinking are the norm. In a community of mathematical discourse, students evaluate their own assumptions and those of others and argue about what is mathematically true (Corwin, 1996; Lampert, 1990; Nova Scotia Department of Education and Culture, 1993). The goal is to let all students believe that they are the authors of mathematical ideas and logical arguments. In this environment, reasoning and mathematical argument—not the teacher—are the sources of an idea's legitimacy. "Doing mathematics is an act of sense-making" (Schoenfeld, 1994, p. 60). The classroom environment should be a place where figuring it out and "sense-making" are common practices, not just for individuals, but for the class as a whole.

In an urban school in Montreal, a class of grade 5 students was observed during a discussion about the meaning of area. As one child wrote on the blackboard, "area is P = l × w = 2 + 2," another said, "I disagree with Andre. I think area is something different." Another child commented, "I would like to add to what Marcel just said." All students faced the speaker and listened attentively as he spoke. In another classroom nearby, grade 2 students raised their hands with their index finger pointing up to indicate "a point of interest," a polite way to disagree. In both classrooms, it was clear that teachers had spent time and effort developing this atmosphere of respect. "Creating contexts where students can safely express their own

mathematical ideas is a central teaching task and a step toward developing students' mathematical power" (Smith, 1996, p. 397).

Posing Worthwhile Mathematical Tasks

The single most important principle for reform in mathematics is to allow students to make the subject of mathematics problematic (Hiebert et al., 1996). By problematic, these authors mean "allowing students to wonder why things are, to inquire, to search for solutions, and to resolve incongruities. It means that both curriculum and instruction should begin with problems, dilemmas, and questions for students" (p. 12). When students are actively looking for relationships, analyzing patterns, finding out which methods work and which don't, justifying results, or evaluating and challenging the thoughts of others, they are necessarily and optimally engaging in reflective thought about the ideas involved.

Tasks or problems must be designed to engage students in the concepts of the curriculum. The tasks given a class should be based on the students' knowledge of the mathematical content and an informed guess about the concepts they bring to the task (Fennema, Carpenter, Franke, & Carey, 1993; Flewelling & Higginson, 2000; Simon, 1995). Time must be given to permit students to wrestle with these tasks individually or in groups and also to discuss solutions and strategies with the class as a whole.

The selection of good tasks requires listening each day to the way students are thinking about whatever mathematics is currently being discussed. The next day's task should be chosen to help students reflect on the new ideas you want them to develop. Look for explorations that embody the big ideas of the chapter. As students wrestle with these problems, the tiny skills and ideas of the traditional curriculum will emerge. In a good task, students will "bump into" the important mathematics you have in mind for them to learn (Lappan & Briars, 1995).

Using Cooperative Learning Groups

Placing children in cooperative groups of three or four to work on a problem is an extremely useful strategy for encouraging the discourse and interaction envisioned in a mathematical community. A classroom arranged in small cooperative groups has much more interaction and discussion going on than can be accomplished in a full-class setting. It also encourages greater accountability on the part of the students. Frequently, a simple pairing of students is all that is necessary. In groups or pairs, children are much more willing and able to speak out, explore ideas, explain things to their peers, question and learn from one another, pose arguments, and have their own ideas challenged in a friendly atmosphere of learning. Children are more willing, within a small group, to take risks that they would never dream of taking in front of an entire class. Groups should usually be heterogeneous in ability so that all students are exposed to good thinking and reasoning (Bennett, Rolheiser-Bennett, & Stevahn, 1991).

While the groups are at work, the teacher has the opportunity to listen actively to six or more different discussions. Time should always be allotted for full-class discussions so that group members can share their group's ideas and the teacher can focus attention on important ideas. (See Chapter 21 for a more detailed discussion of cooperative groups.)

Using Models and Calculators as Thinking Tools

The use of models has already been thoroughly discussed, but it is worth repeating that models help children as they explore ideas and attempt to make sense of them. Many good explorations can be initiated with the use of concrete materials. For example, "Try to find different ways to make the number 437 using ones, tens, and hundreds pieces. What patterns can you find? What else do you notice about the ways you can make 437?" Here the model is the focus of the problem, rather than a means of exploring a different task.

Manipulatives and calculators should always be readily available for student use as a regular part of your classroom environment—a recommendation that is just as true for middle school classrooms as for kindergarten.

Encouraging Discourse and Writing

To explain an idea orally or in written form forces us to wrestle with that idea until it is really ours and we personally understand it. The more we try to explain something or argue reasonably about it, the more connections we will search for and use in our explanation or in our argument. Talking gets the talker involved.

When children are asked to respond to and critique others, they are similarly forced to attend to and assimilate what is being said into personal mental schemes. Frequently, when we get involved verbally with an idea, we find ourselves changing or modifying the idea in midstream. The reflective thought required to make an explanation or argue a point is a true learning experience in itself (Corwin, 1996; Whitin & Wilde, 1995; Yackel, Cobb, Wood, Wheatley, & Merkel, 1990).

Writing can be a part of nearly every problem posed. It can include journals, formal essays, and reports. It is also a useful tool for assessment of students' progress (Marks-Krpan, 2001). Not only does writing help children structure their thoughts, it obliges them to commit to an idea and to rehearse an explanation or defence in preparation for a class discussion. Countryman (1992) states, "The writer reflects on, returns to, and builds upon what has gone before" (p. 59).

Requiring Justification of Student Responses

Requiring children to explain their ideas in detail or to defend their responses has a positive effect on how they view mathematics and their own mathematical abilities. It communicates that mathematics is not mysterious or unfathomable, and that the teacher is not necessarily the source of all mathematical truth. It also promotes confidence and self-worth.

Having to justify responses forces students to think reflectively. It also eliminates guessing or responses based on rote learning. Thus, having children explain their answers is another excellent mechanism for achieving the same benefits as from discourse and writing.

Listening Actively

To promote reflective thinking requires teaching to be child-centred, not teacher-centred. By focusing on children's thoughts instead of our own, we encourage children to do more thinking and hence to search for and strengthen more internal connections—in short, to develop understanding. When children respond to questions or make an observation in class, an interested but nonevaluative response from the teacher is a way to have them elaborate their ideas or provide additional information: "Tell me more about that, Karen" or "I see. Why do you think that?" Even a simple "Um-hmm" followed by silence is very effective, as it permits the child and others to continue their thinking.

Active listening requires that we believe in children's ideas. Waiting 45 seconds, a minute, or even longer for a child to find a response or formulate even a simple idea is much easier when we believe that whatever the child says reflects a unique and valuable understanding. When you believe in children, they sense it and respond accordingly.

Reflections *on Chapter 3*

Writing to Learn

1. Describe in your own words what it means to say *we construct our own knowledge* as opposed to *we absorb knowledge*.
2. Explain why we should assume that each child's knowledge and understanding of an idea is unique for that child.
3. What is reflective thought? Why is it so important to promote reflective thinking in the classroom?
4. Contrast knowing an idea with understanding an idea. What do we mean when we say that there are degrees of understanding from relational to instrumental? Give an example of a concept, and explain how it might be understood by a learner according to these different stages of understanding.
5. Examine the seven benefits of relational understanding. Select the ones that you think are most important. Describe each benefit and why you personally believe it is significant.
6. Describe and contrast conceptual and procedural knowledge of mathematics. Provide examples of each.

For Discussion and Exploration

1. Discuss the meaning and validity of the following statement from Labinowicz (1985): "We see what we understand rather than understand what we see" (p. 7).
2. Consider your most recent classroom experience when mathematics was being taught. Compare and contrast this experience with the suggestions for developmental teaching given in this chapter. Would you say that the teaching reflected a constructivist view of learning? Why or why not?
3. Not every educator believes in constructivism. A common argument goes something like this: There is not enough time to let children discover everything. Basic facts and ideas are more efficiently taught through careful, well-planned, and meaningful explanations. Students should not have to "reinvent the wheel." How would you respond to someone with this perception of school and learning?

Recommendations for Further Reading

Highly Recommended

Ball, D.L. (1997). From the general to the particular: Knowing our own students as learners of mathematics. *Mathematics Teacher, 90,* 732–737.

> Don't be fooled because this article is in *Mathematics Teacher.* Deborah Ball, one of the leading advocates for classroom discourse and listening to children, offers a thought-provoking example of grade 3 thinking about fractions while raising our awareness of how difficult it is to see into the minds of children. She makes the point that understanding is not an all-or-nothing idea. Trying to know what students know is not an easy task. Ball provides us with useful food for thought.

Flewelling, G., & Higginson, W. (2000). *Realizing a vision of tomorrow's mathematics classroom: A handbook on rich learning tasks.* Kingston, ON: Queen's University.

> This handbook, produced at the Centre for Mathematics, Science and Technology at Queen's University, promotes a reform-based approach to learning mathematics. The tasks are intended to stimulate discourse and discussion and promote critical thinking. Through a process of exploration, interaction, and reflection, students engage in rich learning situations that link with pertinent concepts of the curriculum.

Fosnot, C.T. (Ed.). (1996). *Constructivism: Theory, perspectives, and practice.* New York: Teachers College Press.

> The first section of this book develops the theory of constructivism in three readable chapters. The next five chapters examine the application of constructivist theory in different disciplines. Deborah Schifter provides the perspective on teaching mathematics. The final section includes four chapters on classroom practice. You will not find Fosnot's book overly theoretical or difficult; at the same time, it is not exactly a light read. You will be challenged and rewarded.

Schifter, D. (Ed.). (1996). *What's happening in math class? Envisioning new practices through teacher narratives* (Vol. 1). New York: Teachers College Press.

> In each of the five chapters of this book, three or four teachers share their personal struggles with becoming more constructivist in approach. Noted mathematics educators then offer their personal perspectives on what the teachers have so candidly shared. This is a book about constructivism in practice. The teacher-authors each work in quite different schools and represent a range of grades. However, the common threads among all of them help us understand why constructivism is such a popular theory in education today.

Other Suggestions

Ball, D.L. (1996). Teacher learning and the mathematics reforms: What we think we know and what we need to learn. *Phi Delta Kappan, 77,* 500–508.

Brandt, R. (1994). On making sense: A conversation with Magdalene Lampert. *Educational Leadership, 55*(5), 26–30.

Brooks, J.G., & Brooks, M.G. (1993). *In search of understanding: The case for the constructivist classroom.* Alexandria, VA: Association for Supervision and Curriculum Development.

Brooks, M.G., & Brooks, G.B. (1999). The courage to be constructivist. *Educational Leadership, 57*(3), 18–24.

Campbell, P.F., & Johnson, M.L. (1995). How primary students think and learn. In I.M. Carl (Ed.), *Seventy-five years of progress: Prospects for school mathematics* (pp. 21–42). Reston, VA: National Council of Teachers of Mathematics.

Clements, D.H. (1997). (Mis?)constructing constructivism. *Teaching Children Mathematics, 4,* 198–200.

Cobb, P., & Bauersfeld, H. (Eds.). (1995). *The emergence of mathematical meaning: Interaction in classroom cultures.* Mahwah, NJ: Erlbaum.

Cobb, P., Wood, T., Yackel, E., & McNeal, E. (1993). Mathematics as procedural instructions and mathematics as meaningful activity: The reality of teaching for understanding. In R.B. Davis & C.A. Maher (Eds.), *School, mathematics, and the world of reality* (pp. 119–133). Needham Heights, MA: Allyn & Bacon.

Council of Ministers of Education (2001). *School achievement indicators program (SAIP). Mathematics 2001 assessment.* Toronto: Council of Ministers of Education.

Fennema, E., Carpenter, T.P., Franke, M.L., & Carey, D.A. (1993). Learning to use children's mathematics thinking: A case study. In R.B. Davis & C.A. Maher (Eds.), *School, mathematics, and the world of reality* (pp. 93–117). Needham Heights, MA: Allyn & Bacon.

Ginsburg, H.P., & Baron, J. (1993). Cognition: Young children's construction of mathematics. In R. J. Jensen (Ed.), *Research ideas for the classroom: Early childhood mathematics* (pp. 3–21). Old Tappan, NJ: Macmillan.

Greenes, C. (1999). Ready to learn: Developing young children's mathematical powers. In J.V. Copley (Ed.), *Mathematics in the early years* (pp. 39–47). Reston, VA: National Council of Teachers of Mathematics.

Hiebert, J.C. (1990). The role of routine procedures in the development of mathematical competence. In T.J. Cooney (Ed.), *Teaching and learning mathematics in the 1990s* (pp. 31–40). Reston, VA: National Council of Teachers of Mathematics.

Labinowicz, E. (1985). *Learning from children: New beginnings for teaching numerical thinking.* Menlo Park, CA: AWL Supplemental.

Marks-Krpan, C. (2001). *The write math: writing about math in the classroom.* Parsippany, NJ: Dale Seymour Publications.

Noddings, N. (1993). Constructivism and caring. In R. B. Davis & C. A. Maher (Eds.), *School, mathematics, and the world of reality* (pp. 35–50). Needham Heights, MA: Allyn & Bacon.

Perkins, D. (1999). The many faces of constructivism. *Educational Leadership, 57*(3), 6–11.

Pirie, S., & Kieren, T. (1994). Growth in mathematical understanding: how can we characterize it and how can we represent it? *Educational Studies in Mathematics, 26,* 165-190.

Pirie, S., & Kieren, T. (1992). Creating constructivist environments and constructing creative mathematics. *Educational Studies in Mathematics, 23,* 505-528.

Russell, S.J., & Corwin, R.B. (1993). Talking mathematics: "Going slow" and "letting go." *Phi Delta Kappan, 74,* 555–558.

Schifter, D. (1996). A constructivist perspective on teaching and learning mathematics. *Phi Delta Kappan, 77,* 492–499.

Smith, J.P., III. (1996). Efficacy and teaching mathematics by telling: A challenge for reform. *Journal for Research in Mathematics Education, 27,* 387–402.

Thompson, P.W. (1994). Concrete materials and teaching for mathematical understanding. *Arithmetic Teacher, 41,* 556–558.

Whitin, D.J. (1993). Number sense and the importance of asking "why?" In S. Brown & M. Walter (Eds.), *Problem posing: Reflections and applications* (pp. 121–129). Mahwah, NJ: Erlbaum.

Wiske, M.S. (1994). How teaching for understanding changes the rules in the classroom. *Educational Leadership, 51*(5), 18–21.

Wood, T. (1995). An emerging practice of teaching. In P. Cobb & H. Bauersfeld (Eds.), *The emergence of mathematical meaning: Interaction in classroom cultures* (pp. 203–227). Mahwah, NJ: Erlbaum.

Chapter 4

Teaching through Problem Solving

We believe that if we want students to understand mathematics, it is more helpful to think of understanding as something that results from solving problems, rather than something we can teach directly.

Hiebert et al. (1997, p. 25)

There is no other decision that teachers make that has a greater impact on students' opportunity to learn and on their perceptions about what mathematics is than the selection or creation of the tasks with which the teacher engages the students in studying mathematics.

Lappan and Briars (1995, p. 138)

In 1989, the NCTM *Curriculum and Evaluation Standards* said that problem solving should be "a primary goal of all mathematics instruction and an integral part of all mathematical activity" (p. 23) and that students should "use problem-solving approaches to investigate and understand mathematical content" (p. 75). This recommendation played an important role, and still does today, in the design and development of Canadian regional curriculum documents and other instructional materials. Over the next 10 years, evidence continued to mount that problem solving was a powerful and effective vehicle for learning. In 2000, NCTM's *Principles and Standards* document made the case in even stronger language:

> Solving problems is not only a goal of learning mathematics but also a major means of doing so. Problem solving is an integral part of all mathematics learning, and so it should not be an isolated part of the math-

ematics program. Problem solving in mathematics should involve all the five content areas described in these Standards... Good problems will integrate multiple topics and will involve significant mathematics. (p. 52)

This vision is far from being realized. However, in classrooms where teachers have adopted this approach, teacher and student excitement is high and no one wants to return to traditional instruction.

Problem Solving as a Principal Instructional Strategy

The following statement is a major thesis of this chapter. It is a clear reflection of the *Principles and Standards* document, as well as the *Foundation for the Atlantic Canada Mathematics Curriculum*, the *Common Curriculum Framework of the Western Canadian Protocol*, and other regional documents. Moreover, it represents the current thinking of a wide segment of mathematics education researchers.

> *Most, if not all, important mathematics concepts and procedures can best be taught through problem solving. That is, tasks or problems can and should be posed that engage students in thinking about and developing the important mathematics they need to learn.*

This proposition may strike some as extreme or unrealistic. Rather than accept it blindly or reject it, let's first consider why it may make sense.

Starting Where the Students Are: A Shift in Thinking about Mathematics Instruction

Traditionally, the teacher taught the mathematics, the students practised it for a while, and then they were expected to use the new skills or ideas in solving problems. This approach, strongly ingrained in our culture, rarely works well. First, it begins where the teacher is rather than where the children are, and ignores what the children may or may not bring to the lesson. It assumes that wonderful explanations, perhaps enhanced by hands-on materials, will produce understanding. Although this approach sometimes succeeds with some children, showing and telling depends on passive absorption of ideas and leaves most students believing that mathematics is mysterious and beyond understanding.

The second difficulty with the teach-then-solve paradigm is that problem solving is separated from the learning process. Children who have come to expect the teacher to tell them the rules are unlikely to solve problems for which solution methods have not been provided. When teaching is separated from problem solving, learning mathematics is separated from doing mathematics. This simply does not make sense.

Effective lessons begin where the students are, not where we are. That is, teaching should begin with the ideas that children already have, the ideas they will use to create new ones. To engage students requires tasks or activities that are problematic and require thought. Students learn mathematics as a *result* of solving problems. Mathematical ideas are the *outcomes* of the problem-solving experience, rather than elements that must be taught before problem solving (Hiebert et al., 1996, 1997). In this way the process of solving problems is completely interwoven with the learning; children are *learning* mathematics by *doing* mathematics!

An Illustration

Suppose that you are teaching a class of grade 5 children and the topic is comparison of fractions—given two fractions, tell which is greater. The teach-by-telling approach provides a rule: Get common denominators, and compare the numerators. You accompany the rule with a conceptual explanation and pictures so that students will see the concept. However, students are aware of the exercises to come and how to do them. The explanation is of little value since the rule is all that is necessary to get through the day. As your students find the common denominators and complete the exercises, they are doing little more than grade 3 multiplication. They are not thinking about fraction concepts at all.

In contrast, at the 1999 NCTM annual conference, Marilyn Burns shared these two solutions given by fifth graders who were asked to compare $\frac{6}{8}$ and $\frac{4}{5}$. No rules or procedures had been provided.

I know that $\frac{4}{5}$ is the same as $\frac{8}{10}$ and $\frac{8}{10}$ is two-tenths away from a whole. I know that $\frac{6}{8}$ is two-eighths away from a whole. And since tenths are smaller than eighths, $\frac{8}{10}$ must be closer to the whole and so $\frac{4}{5}$ is larger.

I know that $\frac{6}{8}$ is the same as $\frac{12}{16}$ and $\frac{4}{5}$ is the same as $\frac{12}{15}$. Since fifteenths are bigger than sixteenths, $\frac{4}{5}$ must be larger.

These students were concentrating on the meaning of fractions and the size of fractional parts. The second student actually used a common *numerator* approach that is never taught in schools but is completely reasonable. These students and the others in their class almost certainly learned more than if they had blindly followed rules.

The Value of Teaching with Problems

There is no doubt that teaching with problems is challenging. Tasks must be designed or selected each day. You must also take into consideration the current understanding of the students and the needs of the curriculum. It is often difficult to plan more than a few days in advance. If your textbook is not a good source for problem solving, modifications will need to be made. Yet there are good reasons to go to this effort.

■ *Problem solving places the focus of the students' attention on ideas and sense making.* When solving problems, students are necessarily reflecting on the ideas that are inherent in the problems. Developing ideas are more likely to be integrated with existing ones, thereby improving understanding. By contrast, when a teacher provides explanations and directions, no matter how skillfully this is done, students will be attending to "doing it right" or following the directions the teacher has provided.

■ *Problem solving develops "mathematical power."* Students solving problems in class will be engaged in all five of the process standards described by the *Principles and Standards* document: problem solving, reasoning, communication, connections, and representation. These are the processes of doing mathematics and go well beyond the content understanding that is developed.

■ *Problem solving develops the belief in students that they are capable of doing mathematics and that mathematics makes sense.* Every time you pose a problematic task and expect a solution, you say to students, "I believe you can do this." Every time the class solves a problem and students develop their understanding, confidence and self-worth are developed.

■ *Problem solving provides ongoing assessment data that can be used to make instructional decisions, help students succeed, and inform parents.* Students engaging in problem solving will be discussing ideas, drawing pictures or using manipulatives, defending their solutions and evaluating others', and writing reports or explanations. This activity provides you with a steady stream of valuable information for planning the next lesson, helping individual students, evaluating their progress, and communicating with parents.

■ *It is a lot of fun!* Teachers who try teaching in this manner never return to a teach-by-telling mode. The excitement of watching students develop understanding through their own reasoning is worth all the effort. And of course it is fun for the students.

Problems and Tasks for Learning Mathematics

We have been talking about using problems to teach mathematics, without having clearly defined what we mean by a problem. In the context of this discussion, the concept of "problem" is quite broad. The main point is that the problem, task, or activity must engage students in making sense of the key ideas you want them to learn.

A Description of Tasks or Problems

A *problem* is defined here as any task or activity for which the students have no prescribed or memorized rules or methods, and no perception that there is a specific "correct" solution method (Hiebert et al., 1997).

A problem for learning mathematics also has these features:

■ *It must begin where the students are.* The design or selection of the task must take into consideration the current understanding of the students. They should have the appropriate ideas to engage and solve the problem and yet still find it challenging and interesting. They should see the task as something to make sense of.

■ *The problematic or engaging aspect of the problem must be due to the mathematics that the students are to learn.* Although it is acceptable and even desirable to have contexts or external conditions for problems that make them interesting, these aspects should not be the focus of the activity. In solving the problem or doing the activity, students should be concerned primarily with making sense of the mathematics involved and thereby developing their understanding of those ideas.

■ *It must require justifications and explanations for answers and methods.* Students should understand that the responsibility for determining whether answers are correct and the reason why rests with them. Students should also expect to explain their solution methods.

Problems may be posed for individual students, pairs, or groups. They may involve hands-on materials or drawings. At other times, the work may involve pencil-and-paper tasks or be strictly mental. Calculators may or may not be used.

It is important to understand that mathematics is to be taught *through* problem solving. That is, problematic tasks or activities are the vehicle by which the desired curriculum is developed. The learning is an outcome of the problem-solving process.

Examples of Problematic Tasks

In Chapter 3, you saw that mathematical knowledge could be categorized as conceptual or procedural. Both types of knowledge can be learned through problematic activities. Here are some examples in each category.

Problems Promoting Conceptual Knowledge

The following problem may be used for different purposes, depending on the students.

Think about the number 6 broken into two different amounts. Draw a picture to show how six things can be in two parts. Think up a story to go with your picture.

At the kindergarten or grade 1 level, the teacher may want students simply to think about different parts of 6 and to connect these ideas into a context. In grades 1 or 2, the teacher may challenge children to find all of the combinations rather than focus on the story or context. There is a nice relationship and pattern to be constructed. In a class discussion following work on the task, students are likely to develop an orderly process for listing all of the combinations: As one part grows from 0 to 6, the other part begins at 6 and shrinks by ones to 0. There are seven combinations for 6.

The following task might be used in grades 3–6 as part of the development of fraction concepts.

Place an X on the number line about where $\frac{11}{8}$ would be. Explain why you put your X where you did. Perhaps you will want to draw and label other points on the line to help explain your answer.

Note that the task includes a suggestion for how to respond but does not specify exactly what must be done. Students are able to use their own level of reasoning and understanding to justify their answers. In the follow-up discussion, the teacher may well expect to see a variety of justifications from which to help the class refine ideas about fractions that are greater than 1.

I used two identical shapes to make a rectangle. What might they have been? (Baker & Baker, 1991)

This task, appropriate for grades 3–8, is very open-ended. There is a good potential for students to learn about congruent shapes and rotations. (When two congruent shapes form a rectangle, one can be rotated around the centre of the rectangle to match the other.) With this problem, everyone will be able to contribute some ideas and will be ready to reflect on the ideas of others.

Use your graphing calculator to find the intersection of the lines for $y = 3x - 6$ and $y = 2x + 4$. What do the coordinates of the point of intersection have to do with the two equations? Explain.

Students in grade 8 could use a variety of methods to find the point of intersection (graphing calculator, tables, graphs sketched on paper). They would find that the coordinates are solutions to both equations. This problem is a good example of a significant relationship. Students can best understand it by figuring it out on their own, rather than having it explained to them by the teacher or reading about it in the text.

Procedures and Processes

Critics of the problem-solving approach often point to the need for students to learn basic skills, saying that these must be taught through direct instruction. In reality, students can develop procedures via a problem-solving approach. Imagine a class of grade 2 students who had never been taught to add two-digit numbers in the conventional manner. They are challenged to find the sum of 48 and 25. In one grade 2 classroom, students offered at least seven different solutions. Two of the students employed two different counting techniques using a hundreds chart for assistance. Here are solutions of some of the others:

4$\boxed{8}$ + 2$\boxed{5}$ (Boxed digits help "hold" them.)
40 + 20 = 60
       $\boxed{3}$ (The 3 is left from the 5.)
8 + 2 = 10
60 + 10 = 70
70 + 3 = 73

---

40 + 20 = 60
60 + 8 = 68
68 + 5 = 73

---

48 + 20 = 68
68 + 2 ("from the 5") = 70
"Then I still have that 3 from the 5."
70 + 3 = 73

---

25 + 25 = 50 $\boxed{23}$
50 + 23 = 73
Teacher: Where does the 23 come from?
"It's sort of from the 48."
How did you split up the 48?
"20 and 20 and I split the 8 into 5 and 3."

---

48 − 3 = 45 $\boxed{3}$
45 + 25 = 70
70 + 3 = 73

In this class (reported by Russell, 1997), the students show a variety of levels of thinking and many interesting techniques. They had learned from each other the trick of placing numbers in "hold boxes," although not everyone used it. The children who are counting on the chart are showing that they may not yet have developed adequate place-value tools to understand these more sophisticated methods. On the other hand, the class discussion may help them activate those ideas or "dots" they simply had not considered. One question is this: Are these invented methods efficient or adequate? Regardless of how you feel about it, these children are at least minimally prepared to consider a variety of methods because they are developing meaningful ideas about the process. One option is to offer students an efficient way of adding two-digit numbers, and then ask them to figure out why it works and to decide if it will work every time.

Imagine for yourself what might happen if grade 5 students were asked to add 3.72 + 1.6 before being told about lining up decimal points. Many students would do it incorrectly, perhaps aligning the 2 and 6 or the 3 and 1. The decimal might be placed in a variety of places. But students attempting to defend their solutions will need to confront the size of the answer and the meaning of the digits in each position. A class of problem solvers will soon develop a good method for adding decimals.

Gary Tsuruda is a grades 7 and 8 teacher. His classes frequently work in small groups to solve problems. Figure 4.1 (p. 47) shows one example. Notice that the initial questions bring the requisite ideas needed for the task to the students' conscious level. Next they are asked to do some exploration and look for patterns. From these explorations the group must come up with a formula, test it, describe how it was developed, and illustrate its use.

Tsuruda (1994) reports that every group was able to produce a formula. "Not all the formulas looked like the typical textbook formula, but they were all correct, and more importantly, each formula made sense according to the way the students in that group had constructed the knowledge from the data they themselves had generated" (p. 6).

In all of these examples, the students are very much engaged in the processes of doing mathematics—figuring out procedures, not accepting them blindly. What is abundantly clear is that the more problem solving students do, the more willing they are to solve problems and the more methods they develop for attacking problems (Campbell, 1996; Lester, 1994; Rowan & Bourne, 1994; Schifter & Fosnot, 1993; Silver, Smith, & Nelson, 1995; Silver & Stein, 1996; Wood, Cobb, Yackel, & Dillon, 1993).

TRAPEZOID AREA

GOAL: *Find an easy way to determine the area of any trapezoid.*

Be sure that you understand the answers to each of these questions:

1. What does "area" mean?
2. What is a trapezoid?
3. How do you find the area of other polygons?
   Show as many different ways as you can.

Now see if your group can find an easy way to determine the area of any trapezoid.

HINTS:

1. Draw several trapezoids on dot paper and find their areas. Look for patterns.
2. Consider how you find the area of other polygons. Are any of the key ideas similar?
3. You might try cutting out trapezoids and piecing them together.
4. If you find a way to determine the area, make sure it is as easy as you can make it and that it works for *any* trapezoid.

WRITE-UP:

1. Explain your answers to the first three questions in detail. Tell how your group reached agreement on the answers.
2. Tell what you did to get your formula for the area of any trapezoid. Did you use any of the hints? How did they help you?
3. Show your formula and give an illustration of how it works.

FIGURE 4.1 A middle-school example in which students are required to construct a formula.

Source: From *Putting It Together: Middle School Math in Transition* (p. 7), by G. Tsuruda, 1994 Portsmouth, NH: Heinemann, a division of Reed Elsevier Inc. Reprinted by permission of Gary Tsuruda.

A Three-Part Lesson Format

It is safe to say that Canadian teachers, like their American counterparts, typically spend a small portion of a lesson explaining or reviewing an idea and then go into "production mode," where students wade through a list of exercises. Lessons set up in this explain-then-practise pattern condition students to focus on procedures so that they can get through the exercises. Teachers find themselves going from desk to desk re-teaching and explaining to individuals. This is in significant contrast to a lesson built around a single problem (Sawada, 1999, 1997), an approach that is fairly typical in Asian classrooms (see Figure 4.2). Much more learning occurs, and much more assessment information is available when a class works on a single problem and engages in discourse about the validity of the solution.

The emphasis on understanding is evident in the steps typical of Japanese grade 8 mathematics lessons:

- Teacher poses a complex thought-provoking problem.
- Students struggle with the problem.
- Various students present ideas or solutions to the class.
- Class discusses the various solution methods.
- The teacher summarizes the class's conclusions.
- Students practise similar problems.

In contrast, the emphasis on skill acquisition is evident in the steps common to most U.S. and German math lessons:

- Teacher instructs students in a concept or skill.
- Teacher solves example problems with class.
- Students practise on their own while the teacher assists individual students.

FIGURE 4.2 Comparison of the steps typical of grade 8 mathematics lessons in Japan, the United States, and Germany.

Source: Unpublished tabulations from the Third International Mathematics and Science Study, Videotape Classroom Study, University of California, Los Angeles, 1996. Used with permission.

Introduction, Development, and Follow-up

Teaching through problem solving does not mean simply providing a problem or task, sitting back, and waiting for magic to happen. The teacher is responsible for creating the atmosphere and making the lesson work. To this end, think of a lesson as consisting of three main parts: *introduction*, *development*, and *follow-up*. Each portion carries specific agendas and requires specific teacher actions to make the lesson effective (see Figure 4.3).

■ *Introduction.* The agenda in this part of the lesson is to get students mentally prepared to work on the problem and start them thinking about the kinds of ideas that will help them the most. You want to be sure they understand the task. You want to be sure they understand their responsibilities. At the end of this portion of the lesson, there should be no questions regarding the task or what is to be done. Students are ready to go to work.

■ *Development.* The first agenda item here is to *let go!* Give students a chance to work without your constant guidance. Give them the opportunity to use *their* ideas and not simply follow directions. Have faith in their abilities. The second point is to *listen.* Find out how different children or groups are thinking, what ideas they are using, and how they are approaching the problem.

■ *Follow-up.* In this portion of the lesson, you want to engage the class in productive discourse and help students begin to work as a community of learners. *Do not evaluate.* Students must learn to both contribute to and participate in these discussions. They must listen to others and help decide which approaches and solutions make the most sense and why. Thinking must not stop when the problem is solved. Now is the time to encourage reflection on solutions, methods, and extensions.

If you allot time for each segment, it is quite easy to devote a full period to one seemingly simple problem. As long as the problematic feature of the task is the mathematics you want students to learn, a lot of good learning will result from engaging students in only one problem. The same three-part structure can be applied to small tasks, resulting in a 10- to 20-minute mini-lesson (common in kindergarten). There are also times when the development and follow-up portions extend into the next day or even longer.

Teacher Actions in the Introduction Phase

The kinds of things you do in the introduction will vary with the task. Some tasks you can begin with immediately. More likely, however, you will first engage students in some form of activity directly related to the problem in order to get them prepared. Consider the following "introductory actions."

Begin with a Simple Version of the Task

Suppose that you are interested in developing some ideas about area and perimeter with grade 4 or 5 children, and this is the task you plan to present (Lappan & Even, 1989).

Assume that the edge of a square is 1 unit. Add squares to this shape so that it has a perimeter of 18 units.

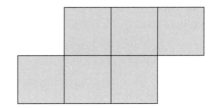

Instead of beginning your lesson with this problem, you might consider one of the following simpler tasks:

■ Draw a 3-by-5 rectangle of squares on the board, and let students tell things they know about the shape. (It's a rectangle. It has squares. There are 15 squares. There are three rows of five.) If no one mentions the words *area* and *perimeter,* you could write those two words on the board and ask if those words can be used in talking about this figure.

■ Provide students with some square tiles or grid paper. "I want everyone to make a shape that has a perimeter of 12 units. After you make your shape, find out what its area is." After a short time, have several students share their shapes.

Each of these "warm-ups" gets out in the open the vocabulary you will need for your exploration. The second activity suggests the tiles as a possible model that students

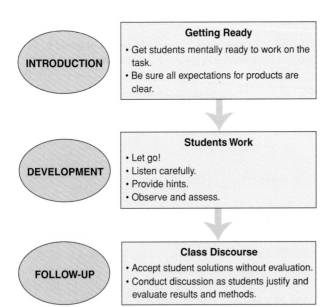

FIGURE 4.3 Teaching through problem solving suggests a simple three-part structure for lessons.

may choose to use. It has the added benefit of hinting that there are different figures with the same perimeter.

Dad says it is 403 km to the ski hills in Mont Ste-Anne. When we stopped for gas, we had gone 167 km. How much farther do we have to drive?

This problem is designed to help children develop an add-on method of subtraction. Before presenting this problem, have students supply the missing part of 100 after you supply one part. Try numbers like 80 or 30 at first; then try 47 or 62. After presenting the actual task, you might ask students if the answer to the problem is more or less than 200.

Brainstorm

If an activity or task involves presenting a new concept, or if a problem is relatively complex, a preliminary brainstorming session may help get students on the right track before they get too lost in doing the problem.

A grade 3 teacher in an urban school was planning an initial discussion of fractions. She needed to find out just what ideas her students had before she could decide exactly what to do next. On the overhead projector, she drew a simple square with both diagonals (see Figure 4.4). "Today we are going to begin talking about fractions. I want to find out what you know. Look at the figure on the screen, and think of one thing you can say about it." She used a "think-pair-share" strategy, suggesting that after they had thought of an idea, they should talk about their ideas with a partner. This gave all students the opportunity to put their ideas into words before having to share with the full class. Then, when she began calling on children to share their ideas, most children were ready. All ideas were written on the overhead without comment or judgment: "There is an X." "It is a fraction." "All the triangles are equal." The full list of ideas covered the board. Acceptance of the ideas gave all students a sense of confidence and involvement.

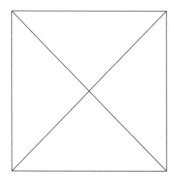

FIGURE 4.4 This figure was used to initiate a brainstorming session with grade 2 students to find out whether they knew about fractions.

When the brainstorming had aired all the children's ideas, the teacher focused on the comment about the triangles all being equal. "In your groups, I want you to talk about this: Does it matter that the pieces are equal in size?" The resulting discussion helped develop the idea of fair shares for fractions and also connected with some ideas about symmetry on which the students had been working earlier.

Often you can have students suggest solutions or strategies. Their suggestions will not solve the problem for others because students must still work out the solution and an explanation. The following problem for grade 7 and 8 students is designed to address the ideas of ratio and proportion as well as data analysis. Since this is not a straightforward task, brainstorming will likely produce a variety of approaches, resulting in more profitable solutions by more students.

A school collected the following data about its students:

	Number of Students	
	In School	*In Class 8B*
Number of siblings		
None	36	5
One	89	7
Two	134	12
More than two	103	8
Country of Birth		
India	23	2
Hong Kong	95	10
Taiwan	107	9
Italy	28	0
Canada	109	11
Travel-to-School Method		
Walk	205	20
Bus	145	12
Other	12	0

If someone asked you how your class 8B was of the rest of the school, how would you answer? Write an explanation for your answer. Include one or more charts or graphs that you think would support your conclusion.

Estimate or Use Mental Computation

When the task is aimed at the development of a computational procedure, a useful introductory action is to have students actually do the computation mentally or suggest a ballpark answer. Have students independently think of an estimate or compute mentally, and then list these "pre-answers" on the board. You may even have students explain their reasoning. Again, this process will not spoil the problem for the class.

This technique would be useful with the earlier problem concerning how many kilometres to the ski hills. The following task is another example where preliminary estimates or mental computations would be useful.

How many small squares (ones or units) will fit in a rectangle that is 54 units long and 36 units wide? Use base-ten pieces to help you with your solution.

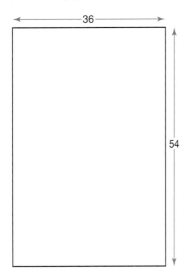

Make a plan for figuring out the total number of pieces without doing too much counting. Explain how your plan would work with a rectangle that is 27 units by 42 units.

Prior to estimation or mental computation for this problem, several simpler problems will also help. For example, rectangles such as 30 by 8 or 40 by 60 could be explored, or these may be given as problems in earlier days.

Be Sure the Task Is Understood

You must always be sure that students understand the problem before setting them to work. Remember that their perspective is different from yours.

Consider the task of mastering the multiplication facts. The most difficult facts can each be connected or related to an easier fact already learned.

Use a fact you already know to help you solve each of these facts: 4×6, 6×8, 7×6, 3×8.

For this task, it is essential that students understand the idea of using a helping fact. They have most likely used helping facts in addition. You can build on this by asking, "When you were learning addition facts, how could knowing $6 + 6$ help you figure out $6 + 7$?" You may also need to help students understand what is meant by a fact they

know—a fact they have mastered and know without counting.

When using a word problem, it is useful in the lower grades to ask a series of direct questions that can be answered just by looking at the problem.

The local convenience store purchases chocolate bars in cartons that each hold 12 boxes. The price paid for one carton was $42.50. Each box contains 8 chocolate bars that the store plans to sell individually. What is the convenience store's cost for each chocolate bar?

"What did the convenience store do? What is in a carton? What is in a box? What is the price of one carton? What does that mean when it says 'each box'?" The last question here is to identify vocabulary that may be misunderstood. It is also useful to be sure students can explain to you what the problem is asking. Rereading a problem does little good, but having students restate the problem in their own words forces them to think about what is being asked.

Establish Expectations

Students need to be clearly told what is expected of them beyond an answer. It is always a good idea to have students write out an explanation for their solution. There is a significant difference between "Show how you got your answer" and "Explain why you think your answer is correct." With the former direction, students may simply record their steps ("First we did..., and then we...") or present their work as self-evident. You can't expect students to explain their mental processes unless you ask for an explanation. In Figure 4.5, the work of two students illustrates the contrast.

When students are working in cooperative groups, only one written explanation should come from the group. Everyone in the group must understand what is written, and be prepared to make an oral presentation. Also, all group members should put their names on the written work.

It is never too early to begin written explanations, even in kindergarten (Marks Krpan, 2000). There the writing may be in the form of drawings and numbers, but this early form of written communication is just as important. Figure 4.6 shows one student's solution for ways to make 5.

The written explanations may be in a journal or on a separate sheet of paper. Sometimes a group report can be prepared on a large sheet of newsprint. This technique is useful when students are going to make a presentation.

There may be occasions when you will not require written work. A very simple yet useful technique is to have students share their ideas with a partner; then have the two of them select the best approach to present. This obliges students to defend their ideas to a peer and prepares them to talk to the class.

Then I divided by 2. I then added the 4 that was left to that answer. Then I added those 2 #'s.

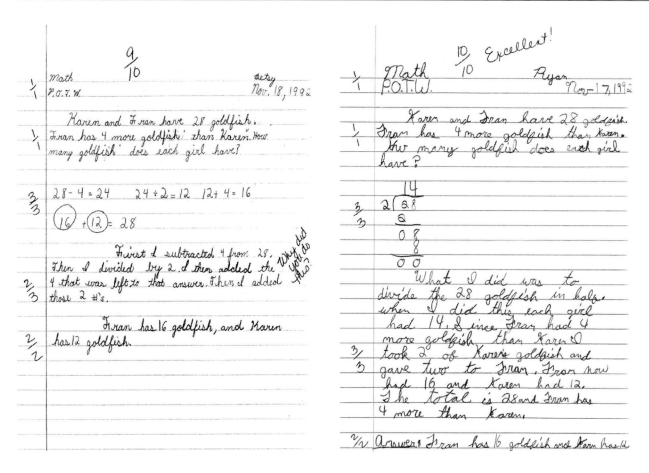

FIGURE 4.5 Betsy tells each step in her solution but provides no explanation. In contrast, Ryan's work includes reasons for his steps.

Kindergarten
How many ways can you show what 5 means?

FIGURE 4.6 A kindergarten student shows her thinking about ways to make 5.

Students preparing to explain and defend their answers will spend time reflecting on the validity of their results and will often make revisions even before sharing them. They will have a greater interest in the class discussion because they will want to compare their solution with others'. They will have "rehearsed" for the class discussion and be ready to participate. Even when students fail to solve a problem, they should be expected to show the ideas and the work that they have considered.

Teacher Actions in the Development Phase

Once you are comfortable that students are ready to work on the task, it is time to let go. You must demonstrate confidence and respect for your students' abilities. Set them to work with the expectation that they will solve the problem. You *must* let go!

Students should get in the habit of working in cooperative groups so that there is no lost time in moving from the full-class discussion to the small groups. Groups of three or at most four work well, but pairs of students are often best. (Chapter 21 includes a detailed discussion of cooperative group work.) Your role now shifts to that of facilitator and active listener. You might sit down with a group, listen for a while, have the students explain what they are doing, or just take notes.

Provide Hints and Suggestions

Knowing how much help to give students is always going to be challenging. Do you let them stumble down the wrong path? How much direction do you provide? Do you correct errors you see?

If a group is searching for a place to begin, a hint may be appropriate. You might suggest that the students try using a particular manipulative or draw a picture, if that seems appropriate.

In Leon's Furniture Store, all furniture is priced at 20 percent above wholesale. In preparation for a sale, Leon tells his staff to cut the regular price on all furniture by 10 percent. Will Leon be making a profit of 10 percent, less than 10 percent, or more than 10 percent? Explain your answer.

For this problem, consider the following hints:

- Try drawing a picture or a diagram of something that shows what 10 percent off means.
- Try drawing a picture or a diagram that shows what 20 percent more means.
- Maybe you could pick a price of something and see what happens.
- Let's try a simpler problem. Suppose that you had 8 blocks and got 25 percent more. Then you lost 25 percent of the new collection.

Encourage Testing of Ideas

Students will look to you for approval of their results or ideas. Avoid being the source of "truth" or of right and wrong. When asked if a result or method is correct, ask, "How can you decide?" or "Why do you think that might be right?" or "I see what you have done. How can you check that?" Even if you are not asked for an opinion, asking, "How can we tell if that makes sense?" reminds students that answers without reasons are not acceptable.

Suggest Extensions or Generalizations

A lot of good problems are simple on the surface. It is the extensions that make them more thought-provoking. The area and perimeter task is a case in point. Many students will quickly come up with one or two solutions. "I see you

found one way to do this. Are there any other solutions? Are any of the solutions different or more interesting than others? Which of the shapes you found with a perimeter of 18 is the largest and which is the smallest? Does the perimeter always change when you add another tile?"

What can you find out about that? This general question is at the very heart of mathematics as a science of pattern and order. It asks students to look for something interesting, to generalize. For example, in the area and perimeter problem, squares can be added to a shape to create three different situations: If a new square touches the old shape on only one side, the perimeter increases by 2. If it touches on two sides, there is no increase. If it fits into a "U" and touches on three sides, the perimeter actually decreases by 2.

Questions that begin "What if you tried... ?" or "Would that same idea work for... ?" are also ways to generate different extensions. For example, "Suppose you tried to find all the shapes possible with a perimeter of 18. What could you find out about the areas?"

Find a Second Method

The value of students' solving a problem in more than one way cannot be overestimated. It shifts the value system in the classroom from answers to processes and thinking. It is a good way for students to make new and different connections.

For example, consider this grade 6 problem.

The dress Grace purchased for her party was 25 percent off the regular price. If the regular price was $90, how much did it cost?

This is an example of a straightforward problem with a single answer. Many students will solve it by multiplying by 0.25 and subtracting the result from $90. Suggesting that they find another way may be all you need to do. Some classes may require specific directions: "How would you do it with fractions instead of decimals?" "Draw me a diagram that explains what you did." "How could this be done in just one step?" "Think of a way that you could do this mentally."

Grade 2 students will frequently solve the next problem by counting or using addition.

On Monday Maxine had $9 saved from doing chores around the house. The following day, she received her allowance. She then had $12. How much allowance did she get?

"How would you do that on a calculator?" and "Can you write an equation that tells what you did?" are ways of encouraging children to connect 9 plus ? = 12 with 12 − 9.

Solving a problem in a second way can help students who have made an error find their own mistake. Perhaps a student has used a symbolic method of her own invention and has made an error in reasoning. Suggesting that she try to do the problem only with concrete models ("so that I can understand what you did") may be all that is necessary for her to correct her own solution.

Teacher Actions in the Follow-up Phase

Be certain to plan ample time for this portion. Often this is when the best learning will take place. Twenty minutes or more is not at all unreasonable for a good class discussion and sharing of ideas. This is not a time for checking answers, but for the class to share ideas. Over time, you will develop your class into a community of learners who together are involved in making sense of mathematics. This atmosphere will not develop easily or quickly. You must inform your students about your expectations for this part of the lesson and teach them how to interact with their peers.

Engage the Class in Discussion

You may want simply to list answers from all of the groups and put them on the board without comment. Following that, you can return to one or more students to get explanations for their solutions or accounts of their processes. At other times, you may choose to call on groups or individuals that you noticed earlier doing something interesting or something of special value. The discussion should not be restricted to correct solutions.

When there are different answers, the full class should be involved in the discourse concerning which answers are correct. Allow those responsible for the answers to defend them, and then open the discussion to the class. "Who has an idea about this? Ravi, I noticed that you got a different answer than Tomeka. What do you think of her explanation?" Resist with every fibre in you the temptation to judge the correctness of an answer. Even when the class fails to come to a conclusion, rather than provide your solution, suggest that perhaps you will need to return to this later. Follow-up should take place when students have gained some additional insights to help them.

One of your functions is to make sure that all students participate, that all listen, and that all understand what is being said. Moving along too quickly cheats students who are not quite able to keep up with those children who come up with explanations more quickly. Encourage students to ask questions. "Emile, did you understand how they did that? Do you want to ask Aline a question?"

Identify Rules, Hypotheses, and Future Problems

When you are satisfied with the discussion about the answer and the solution, summarize the main points of the discussion, and make sure that all students understand what has been agreed on. When a problem involves creating a procedure, the class may decide on one or more methods for finding the solution, and these may be written on the board. For example, suppose that the task involved finding clever methods of adding when one of the addends is a 9 (e.g., 5 + 9 or 9 + 3). Some students may have devised a method of taking 1 off the smaller number and putting it with the 9. This might be listed as Maggie's rule: *Shift 1 from the little number to make 10; 5 + 9 becomes 4 + 10.* Other students may have added 10 to the smaller number and subtracted 1. Yolanda's rule might be written: *Add 10 instead of 9 and then take off 1; 5 + 9 is 5 + 10 − 1.* When students invent procedures for computation or measurement formulas, you may want to help them find a good way to write them down, but do not change the students' basic ideas. No student should be required to use the ideas of others; however, all students should try to understand each other's ideas.

Often someone will make a generalization or an observation that he or she strongly believes in but cannot completely justify. Everyone needs to listen to these ideas with interest, even if they are incorrect. Untested ideas can be written on the board as "Elana's Hypothesis." Explain the meaning of *hypothesis* as an idea that may or may not be true. Testing the hypothesis may become the problem for another day, or the hypothesis may simply be kept on the board until additional evidence comes up that either supports or disproves it. For example, when comparing fractions, suppose that a group makes this generalization and you write it on the board: *When deciding which fraction is larger, the fraction in which the bottom number is closer to the top number is the larger fraction. Example: $\frac{4}{7}$ is not as big as $\frac{7}{8}$ because 7 is only 1 from 8 but 4 is 3 away from 7.* This is not an unusual conclusion, but it is not correct in all instances. A problem for a subsequent day would be to decide if the hypothesis is always right, or to find fractions for which it is not right (counter-examples.)

Even when students have not suggested hypotheses, discussions will often turn up interesting questions that can profitably be used for tasks to help clarify an emerging idea.

Use Praise Cautiously

Be an attentive listener to both good and not so good ideas. Support and praise effort and risk taking, and concomitantly *expect* students to do good work. Praise offered for correct solutions or excitement over interesting ideas suggests that the students did something unusual or unexpected. Although this is positive, it can also be negative feedback for those students who do not receive praise. Comments such as "Good job!" and "Super work!" roll off the tongue easily. We use these statements to help children feel good about themselves. But there is evidence to suggest that we should be cautious when using expressions of praise, especially with respect to student products and solutions (Schwartz, 1996). Praise supports students' feelings, but it also evaluates. "Good job!" says, "Yes, you did that correctly." "Nice work" can establish an expectation for others that products must be neat or beautiful in order to have value. This can make students who do excellent mathematical science hide their efforts if they appear sloppy or poorly presented.

Rather than employ praise that is judgmental, Schwartz (1996) suggests comments of interest and extension: "I wonder what would happen if you tried..." or "Please tell me how you figured that out." Notice that these phrases show that you value the child's thinking. They can and should be used regardless of the validity of the responses.

Engage *All* Class Members

In most Canadian classrooms there is a wide range of academic diversity. But the belief that all children can learn the mathematics of the regular curriculum is clearly expressed in the NCTM *Standards* documents, as well as in Canadian curricular documents including the *Common Curriculum Framework for Mathematics: The Western Canadian Protocol*, and the *Foundation for the Atlantic Canada Mathematics Curriculum*. This view is also supported by a number of prominent mathematics educators who have worked extensively with at-risk populations (Campbell, 1996; Silver & Stein, 1996; Trafton & Claus, 1994).

Because the needs and abilities of children are different, conducting large group discussion that is balanced and includes all students requires skill and practice. Rowan and Bourne (1994) offer some excellent suggestions based on their work in an urban, multicultural, multi-ethnic, low-socioeconomic school district. They emphasize that the most important factor is to be clear about the purpose of group discussion—that is, to share and explore the variety of strategies, ideas, and solutions generated by the class and to learn to communicate these ideas in rich mathematical discourse. Every class has a handful of students who are always ready to respond. Other children learn to be passive or do not participate. So rule number one is that participating in the discussion is more important than stating an answer.

A second suggestion is to begin discussions by calling first on the children who tend to be shy or lack the ability to express themselves well. Rowan and Bourne (1994) note that the more obvious ideas are generally given at the outset of a discussion. When asked to participate early and given sufficient time to formulate their thoughts, these reticent children can more easily participate and thus feel valued.

Make it a habit to ask for explanations to accompany *all* answers. Soon the request for an explanation will not signal an incorrect response, as children initially believe. Many incorrect answers are the result of small errors in the context of otherwise excellent thinking. Likewise, many correct answers may not represent the insightful thinking you might have assumed. A child who has given an incorrect answer is very likely to see the error and correct it during the explanation. Try to support children's thinking without evaluating responses. "Does someone have a different idea or want to comment on what Janelle just said?" All children should hear the same teacher reactions that only the "smart kids" are used to hearing.

Many times a student will get stuck in the middle of an explanation. The silence can be difficult, and there is a temptation to call on someone else to "help out" or to suggest that the child seek assistance from a classmate. Though well intentioned, the message this sends to the child is that he is not capable on his own. Children must learn that they will be given time and that their classmates trust and believe in them. This attitude conveys a sense of support and confidence and is usually all that is necessary to get a quality response.

There will, of course, be times when a response is simply not forthcoming. When this occurs, you might suggest that the child take some time to get thoughts together or to work out the idea with some materials. Promise to return to the child later, and be *certain* to do so to hear what she figured out.

Designing and Selecting Effective Tasks

A task is effective when it helps students learn the ideas you anticipated it would. It must be the mathematics in the task that makes it problematic for the students so that mathematical ideas are their primary concern. Therefore, the first and most important consideration for selecting any task for your class must be the mathematics. That said, where do you look for tasks?

Your Textbook

Most teachers rely on the textbook for their day-to-day curriculum. But when teachers let the text determine the next lesson, they tend to assume that children have learned what was intended from each page. Avoid the "myth of coverage": If we covered it, they must have learned it. Good teachers use the teacher's guide that accompanies the textbook as a resource to support their curriculum guidelines. In the face of the current pressures from provincial assessments, the curriculum guideline is extremely important.

Using Traditional Textbooks

Traditional textbooks, in contrast to the approach you have been reading about, are designed to be used in teacher-directed instruction. But they should not be discarded. Much thought went into the content and the pedagogical ideas. If the textbook you are using is traditional, it can still be used as a prime resource if you are thinking about translating units and lessons to a problem-oriented approach.

Adopt a *unit perspective*. Avoid the idea that every lesson and idea in the unit requires modification. Examine a chapter or unit from beginning to end, and identify the two to four *big ideas*, the essential mathematics in the chapter. (Big ideas are listed at the start of each chapter in Section 2 of this book. These may be helpful as a reference.) Temporarily ignore the smaller sub-ideas that often take up a full lesson.

With the big ideas of the unit in mind, you can do two things: (1) adapt the best or most important lessons in the chapter to a problem-solving format, and (2) create or find tasks in the teacher's guide book and other resources that address the big ideas. This will almost certainly provide you with an ample supply of tasks.

Adapting a Traditional Textbook Lesson

Figure 4.7 shows a page from a grade 3 book. The lesson is about subtracting tens without trading. The use of pictorial representations of the base ten blocks to illustrate the steps for subtraction is a positive aspect of this lesson.

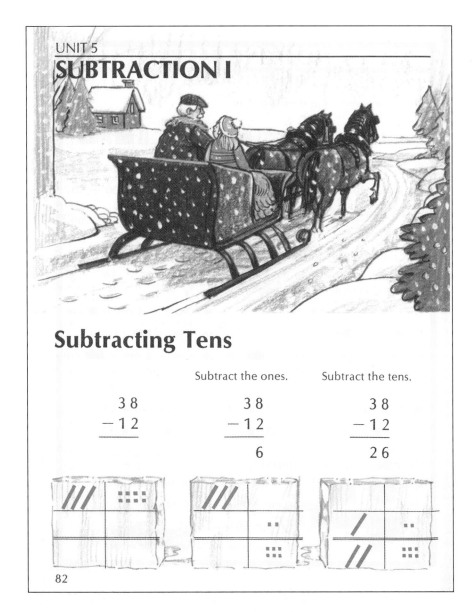

FIGURE 4.7 A Grade 3 lesson from a traditional textbook.

Source: From *Houghton Mifflin Mathematics Grade 3* (p. 82), by D. Super, F.K. Carlson, I.K. Burbank, and W. Klassen. Markham: Houghton Mifflin Canada Ltd., 1988. Reprinted with permission.

It helps the student "see" what subtracting with tens looks like. As is typical of traditional texts, the mechanics of subtraction are presented in a disconnected manner, independent of subtraction with trading. Also, in the exercise that follows on the adjacent page, the student is required to complete 27 questions in order to practise the procedure. Imagine how this lesson might be converted so that it is problem-based, offering a richer learning experience for students. You might want to try this before reading on.

One idea is to create a scenario for this problem and link it to the illustration (possibly a new illustration that would work better for the concept). Using the illustration you might work with the idea of Christmas presents to be delivered. Grandpa Sam and Natasha had 38 presents to deliver. They have already delivered 12. How many presents still need to be delivered? You might also include subtraction with trading (students in grade 3 have already been introduced to this concept in grade 2). Use the same problem but

change the number of presents that have already been delivered to 19. Then you could ask students to solve the problem in small groups. Offer them the base ten blocks, along with other materials. The students' task would be to write solutions that tell what they did to solve the problem. They should also describe how they used the materials.

Another thought is to have students create their own story problems and illustrate them in two ways, symbolically and with the materials. You will soon learn, depending on the questions students design, who understands subtraction with trading and who does not. Using this approach will avoid having students do 27 questions where the mechanics of subtraction are practised devoid of meaning.

Figure 4.8 is a geometry lesson from a grade 6 book. The lesson focuses on classifying triangles according to their side measures. Brief mention is made of how we identify equal sides of geometric figures. The lesson can

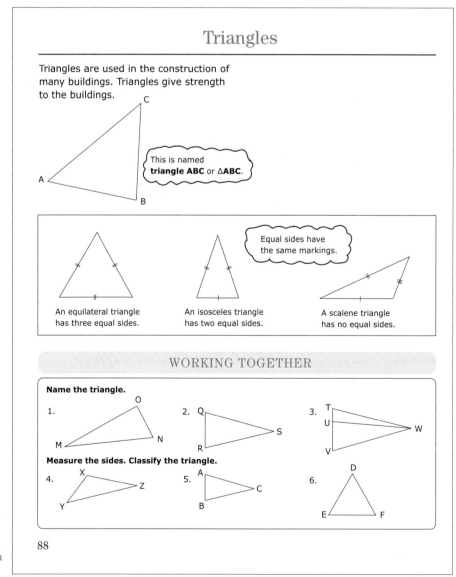

FIGURE 4.8 A Grade 6 lesson from a traditional textbook.

Source: From *Journeys in Math 6* (p. 88), by R. Connelly, Marsh, Sarkissian, Calkins, Hope, O'Shea, Sharp, Taschuk, and Tossell. Toronto: Ginn & Co., 1987. Reprinted with permission.

easily be made more problematic. Consider what *you* might do before reading on.

To make this lesson more problem-oriented and comprehensive, you might have included the idea of classifying triangles by their angle measure too. In so doing you would provide students with triangles in all six categories (three classified by their side measure and three by their angle measure), with two or three triangles per category. You might prepare a set of triangles, reproduce them, and have students cut them out. Geoboards could be used if they are available. (These and other ideas are discussed in Chapter 17.) Given a set of triangles, the task is to find two ways to sort the triangles into three separate piles. You could let students develop their own classification schemes. In the development portion, you might want to provide hints that will help ensure that some students create the categories you want. After students have created the categories, you can provide the appropriate vocabulary.

Using "Reform-Oriented" Programs

If your school is using a "reform-oriented" textbook series (e.g., *Quest 2000*, *Interactions*), then you will likely find that most lessons are problem-oriented. Your main difficulty may be assuring yourself that all of the skills and concepts of your local curriculum are appropriately emphasized. Some units may need additional activities or modifications based on the needs of your students, and others you may decide to skip. Some teachers use these programs as a resource, selecting only a few units or activities to augment the program they already have in place.

Children's Literature

The use of children's literature as a source of problems is sufficiently important that it deserves separate attention. Children's stories can be used in numerous ways to create reflective tasks at all grade levels, and there are many excellent books to help you in this area (Bresser, 1995; Burns, 1992a; Sheffield, 1995; Theissen, Matthias, & Smith, 1998; Welchman-Tischler, 1992; Whitin & Wilde, 1992, 1995).

By way of example, a very popular children's book, *The Doorbell Rang* (Hutchins, 1986), can be used with different agendas at various grade levels. The story is a sequential tale of children sharing 12 cookies. On each page, more children come to the kitchen, and the 12 cookies must be redistributed. This simple yet engaging story can lead K–2 children to explore ways to make equal parts of almost any number. It can serve as a springboard for multiplication and division for grades 3–4 children. It can also be used to explore fraction concepts in grades 4–6.

Most of the chapters in Section 2 of this text include a section titled "Literature Connection" that offers suggestions for using literature to explore the mathematics of that chapter. Literature ideas can also be found in NCTM journals and in provincial mathematics association periodicals. It is an exciting approach to developing lessons.

Other Resources

You will never compile a perfect set of tasks for your class; every class is different. As already noted, your textbook is a good place to begin, and children's literature should always be considered. Here are some additional options to consider:

- Read the NCTM journals regularly: *Teaching Children Mathematics* (for grades K–6) or *Mathematics Teaching in the Middle School* (for grades 5–8). You should copy and file articles you can use with each chapter of your text, or each section of your curriculum. Don't wait until you need an idea to begin flipping through journals.
- Check the periodicals of local mathematics associations. Articles in these periodicals contain a variety of ideas that can also be used to supplement your lessons. Copy and file them for future use.
- Begin to develop your personal professional library of resource books. Check out NCTM publications. The Addenda Series books are an excellent place to begin. As well, the NCTM's catalogue has many resources. Remember the book you have in your hands right now! Many teachers use it as their first resource. There are also commercial publishers and distributors who specialize in materials for teaching mathematics, which include teacher resource books, student activity books and manipulatives.
- Surf the web. There are numerous websites that offer help and teaching ideas for teachers. Many include complete lesson plans. One caution: Just because it's on the web doesn't mean it's good. The things you find will range widely in quality. Good sites to get you started are noted in Chapter 23.

A Task Selection Guide

Throughout this book, and in every student textbook, in every article you read and in-service workshop you attend, you will hear and read about suggestions for activities, problems, tasks, or explorations that someone believes are effective in helping children learn some aspect of mathematics. Selecting activities or tasks is, as Lappan and Briars (1995) contend, the most significant decision affecting your students' learning. In the accompanying box (p. 58) is a four-step guide you can use when considering a new activity for your students.

Activity Evaluation and Selection Guide

STEP 1: How is the Activity Done?

Actually do the activity. Try to get "inside" the task or activity to see how it is done and what thinking might go on.

How would *children* do the activity or solve the problem? (They don't know what you do!)

• What materials are needed?

• What is written down or recorded?

STEP 2: What is the Purpose of the Activity?

What *mathematical ideas* will the activity develop?

• Are the ideas concepts or procedural skills?

• Will there be connections to other related ideas?

STEP 3: Will the Activity Accomplish Its Purpose?

What is *problematic* about the activity? Is the problematic aspect related to the mathematics you identified in the purpose?

What must children reflect on or think about to complete the activity? (Don't rely on wishful thinking.)

Is it possible to complete the activity without much reflective thought? If so, can it be modified so that students will be required to think about the mathematics?

STEP 4: What Must You Do?

What will you need to do in the *introductory* portion of your lesson?

• How will you prepare students for this task?

• What will be the students' responsibilities?

What difficulties might you anticipate seeing in the *development* portion of your lesson?

What will you want to focus on in the *follow-up* portion of your lesson?

To evaluate the effectiveness of a task or activity you think may be good, begin by actually doing the activity yourself, trying to think of the ways children in your class might do it. Consider the information and skills *they* will bring to the activity.

The second step requires that you focus on what ideas and what mathematics the activity is likely to help children develop. Beware! The author's stated objective is not always an accurate indication of the mathematics in the task.

The third step is the most important point in determining if an activity will or will not accomplish its purpose. What is problematic about the activity? What will improve the chances that the children will be mentally active, reflecting on and constructing the ideas you identified in step 2? Try to predict what students will do with the activ-

ity. Think about how students might have difficulty with the task. Difficulties are usually the best opportunities for learning, but you should anticipate them if possible.

The fourth step in the guide focuses your attention on implementation issues. Consider possible introductory, development, and follow-up actions of a lesson that are built on the task to add to its effectiveness.

Throughout this book, practise using this guide with the activities you encounter. Work toward thinking about tasks or activities from the perspective of what is likely to happen in children's minds, not just what they are doing with their hands. Good tasks are minds-on, not just hands-on activities.

Teaching Tips and Questions

The ideas expressed here have been gathered from elementary and middle-school teachers who have been working hard at developing a problem-solving approach in their classrooms, and from the research literature on teaching via problem solving.

Four Suggestions

1. *Predict! Don't hope.* When planning a task, it is not sufficient to think about how it will work if everything goes well. Think about your students—all of them. Predict their likely responses, and be prepared to deal with them. Things rarely go as you hope they will.

2. *Be clear in your own mind about the purpose of the task or activity.* Don't select problems simply because they are interesting. Always ask, "What *mathematics* will students develop by working on this task?" The purpose of an activity is not the same as what the students are asked to do. For example, students don't use base ten blocks or graphing calculators in order to learn about base ten blocks or graphing calculators.

3. *Recognize that there is much more to a problem than the answer.* Often the most learning occurs during the class discussion. Children's social interaction is at least as important as their independent reflection. Discussing various paths to the solution and, most importantly, deciding why an answer is right or wrong are learning opportunities that should not be passed up. When children discover that they can determine the validity of answers, they learn that mathematics makes sense.

4. *Do not confuse open-ended problem solving with encouraging creativity.* Open-ended solutions are not the same as creative stories, artistic drawings, or students' supplying their own numbers for a problem.

These latter approaches often detract from the mathematics of the task, as students spend time colouring or writing stories. An "expensive" task is one in which students spend 50 percent or more of their time involved with context, materials, "cut and paste," and similar tasks with no mathematics being addressed.

How Much to Tell and Not to Tell

When teaching through problem solving, one of the most perplexing dilemmas is how much to tell. On the one hand, telling diminishes student reflection. Students who sense that the teacher has a preferred method or approach are extremely reluctant to use their own strategies. They tend not to develop self-confidence and problem-solving abilities by following the teacher's directions. On the other hand, to tell too little can sometimes leave students floundering and waste precious class time.

Researchers connected with four different constructivist programs, although they note that there will never be a simple solution to this dilemma, offer the following guidance: Teachers should feel free to share relevant information as long as the mathematics in the task remains problematic for the students (Hiebert et al., 1997). That is, "information can and should be shared as long as it does not solve the problem [and] does not take away the need for students to reflect on the situation and develop solution methods they understand" (p. 36).

They go on to suggest three types of information that teachers should provide for their students:

■ *Mathematical conventions.* The social conventions of symbolism and terminology that are important in mathematics will never be developed through reflective thought. For example, representing "three and five equals eight" as "3 + 5 = 8" is a convention. Definitions and labels are also conventions. What is important is to offer these symbols and words only when students need them or will find them useful. As a rule of thumb, symbolism and terminology should only be introduced *after* concepts have been developed and then specifically as a means of expressing or labelling ideas. They should rarely be presented solely as things to be memorized.

■ *Alternative methods.* You can, with care, suggest to students an alternative method or approach for consideration. You may also suggest more efficient recording procedures for student-invented computational methods. A teacher must be cautious in not conveying to students that their ideas are second-best. Nor should students ever be forced to adopt a teacher's suggestion over their own approach. The rule of thumb here is that the value of a procedure should always be a judgment of the students, not a dictate of the teacher. In this spirit, students can learn to appraise a teacher's suggestion without feeling obligated to use it.

■ *Clarification of students' methods.* You should help students clarify or interpret their ideas, even point out related ideas. A student may add 38 and 5 by noting that 38 and 2 more is 40, with 3 more making 43. This strategy can be related to the make-ten strategy used to add 8 + 3. The selection of 40 as a midpoint in this procedure is an important place-value concept. Such clarifications are reinforcing for the students who have the ideas. Discussion or clarification of students' ideas focuses attention on ideas you want the class to learn. Care must be taken that attention to one student's ideas does not diminish those of other students. Neither should teacher attention to one method imply that it is the preferred approach.

Frequently Asked Questions

The following are questions teachers have asked about a problem-solving approach to teaching mathematics.

1. *How can I teach all the basic skills I have to teach?* Many teachers resort to rote drill and practise to teach "basic skills." There is a tendency to believe that mastery of the basics is incompatible with a problem-solving approach. However, the evidence strongly suggests otherwise. First, drill-oriented approaches have consistently produced poor results (Battista, 1999; Kamii & Dominick, 1998; O'Brien, 1999). Short-term gains on low-level skills may possibly result from drill, but more is required if students are to be successful, as results of current testing programs such as TIMSS 99 (TIMSS-R) and the SAIP demonstrated.

    Second, research data indicate that students in constructivist-based programs that employ a problem-solving approach do as well or nearly as well as students in traditional programs on basic skills as measured by standardized tests (Campbell, 1995; Carpenter, Franke, Jacobs, Fennema, & Empson, 1998; Hiebert & Wearne, 1996; Silver & Stein, 1996). Any deficit in skill development is more than outweighed by strength in conceptual knowledge and problem-solving ability.

    Finally, skills such as basic fact mastery and computation can be effectively taught in a problem-solving approach (for example, see Campbell, Rowan, & Suarez, 1998; Huinker, 1998).

2. *Why is it OK for students to "tell" or "explain," but not for me?* There are two answers to this question. First,

students will question their peers when an explanation does not make sense to them, whereas explanations from the teacher are usually accepted without scrutiny (and hence without understanding). Second, when students are responsible for explaining, the class members develop a sense of pride and confidence that *they* can figure things out and make sense of mathematics. *They* have power and ability.

3. *Where can I find the time to cover everything?* Mathematics is much more connected and integrated than the itemized list of outcomes found in many provincial and territorial curriculum documents. To deal with coverage, the first suggestion is to teach with a goal of developing the "big ideas," the main concepts in a unit or chapter. Most of the skills and ideas on your list of objectives will be addressed as you progress. If you focus separately on each item on the list, big ideas and connections, the essence of understanding, are unlikely to develop. Second, we spend far too much time reteaching because students don't retain ideas. Time spent up front to help students develop meaningful networks of ideas drastically reduces the need for reteaching, thus creating time in the long term.

4. *Is there any place for drill and practice?* Absolutely! The tragic error is to believe that drill is a method of developing ideas. Drill is only appropriate when (a) the desired concepts have been meaningfully developed, (b) flexible and useful procedures have been developed, *and* (c) speed and accuracy are needed. Watch children who are counting on their fingers or using some other inefficient method as they drill the basic facts. What they may be improving is their ability to count quickly. They are not learning their facts. Too many children are still counting in middle school because drill has not helped them develop efficient strategies. When you accept that drill does not produce understanding, you find there are really not many topics, aside from basic fact mastery, that should ever require drill.

5. *What do I do when a task bombs?* It will happen, although not as often as you think, that students just will not know what to do with a problem you pose, no matter how many hints and suggestions you offer. Do not give in to the temptation to "tell 'em." Set it aside for the moment. Ask yourself why it bombed. Did the students have the ideas they needed? Was the task too advanced? Often we need to regroup and offer students a simpler related task that gets them prepared for the one that proved difficult. When you sense that a task is not going anywhere, regroup! Don't spend days just hoping that something wonderful might happen. If you listen to your students, you will know where to go next.

Developing Effective Problem Solvers—Teaching about Problem Solving

How to teach using a problem-solving approach has obviously been a theme of this chapter. In order to develop effective problem solvers, however, more is needed. The standard on problem solving in *Principles and Standards*, which echoes the views of George Polya (the mathematician best know for his conceptualization of mathematics as problem solving), speaks to the need to develop problem-solving *strategies and processes, metacognitive habits* of monitoring and regulating problem-solving activity, and a *positive disposition* toward mathematical problem solving. Each area suggests objectives or goals for the development of good problem solvers.

Strategies and Processes

Strategies for solving problems are identifiable methods for approaching a task. Polya saw these as general suggestions that help one to understand a problem better or to make progress toward its solution (Barb & Larson Quinn, 1997). Strategies are completely independent of the specific topic or subject matter, and strategy goals play a part in all phases of the problem-solving process: understand the problem, solve the problem, and reflect on the answer and solution. It is Polya's four-stage model (Polya, 1957) that forms a framework for the phases identified in this book.

Strategy and Process Goals

- *Develop problem analysis skills*—to improve students' ability to analyze an unfamiliar problem, identify wanted and needed information, ignore nonessential information, and clearly state the goal of the problem or task
- *Develop and select strategies*—to help students acquire a collection of problem-solving strategies that are useful in a variety of problem-solving settings and to select and use those strategies appropriately
- *Justify solutions*—to improve students' ability to assess the validity of answers
- *Extend or generalize problems*—to help students learn to go beyond the solution to problems; to consider results or processes applied in other situations or used to form rules or general procedures

Metacognition

Metacognition refers to conscious monitoring (being aware of how and why you are doing something) and regulation (choosing to do something or deciding to make changes) of your own thought process. Good problem solvers monitor their thinking regularly and automatically. They recognize when they are stuck or do not fully understand. They make conscious decisions to switch strategies, rethink the problem, search for related content knowledge that may help, or simply start afresh (Schoenfeld, 1992).

There is evidence that metacognitive behaviour can be learned (Campione, Brown, & Connell, 1989; Garofalo, 1987; Lester, 1989, Williamson, 1991). Further, students who learn to monitor and regulate their own problem-solving behaviours do show improvement in problem solving.

Metacognitive Goal

■ *Monitor and regulate actions*—to help students develop the habit and ability to monitor and regulate their strategies and progress as they solve problems

Disposition

Disposition refers to the attitudes and beliefs that students possess about mathematics. Students' beliefs concerning their abilities to do mathematics and to understand the nature of mathematics have a significant effect on how they approach problems and, ultimately, on how well they succeed.

Students' attitudes (likes, dislikes, and preferences) about mathematics are nearly as important as their beliefs. Children who enjoy solving problems and feel satisfaction or pleasure at conquering a perplexing problem are much more likely to persevere, make second and third attempts, and even search out new problems. Negative attitudes have just the opposite effect.

Attitudinal Goals

■ *Gain confidence and belief in abilities*—to develop students' confidence in their ability to do mathematics and to confront unfamiliar tasks
■ *Be willing to try and to persevere*—to improve students' willingness to attempt unfamiliar problems and to develop their perseverance in solving problems without being discouraged by initial setbacks
■ *Enjoy doing mathematics*—to help students learn to enjoy and derive personal reward from the process of thinking, searching for patterns, and solving problems

Working toward Problem-Solving Goals While Students Learn

All of the goals of problem solving can and will be attained in classrooms that employ a problem-solving approach to the regular curriculum on a daily basis. A separate problem-solving strand is neither desirable nor necessary. It is important that the teacher be clearly aware of the goals of problem solving and focus attention on them regularly.

Developing Problem-Solving Strategies

Problem-solving strategies and processes are not so much taught as *modelled*. Your task as teacher is to suggest appropriate strategies and to point them out to students in class discussions as important ways of doing mathematics.

Strategies for Understanding the Problem

Your actions in the introductory portion of your lesson should provide a daily model of problem analysis skills. By entertaining a discussion of what is known, needed, and asked for or expected in the task, children will begin to understand that this is part of what solving problems is about. Soon you can say, "Before we get started, what should we do first?" Let students articulate strategies that demonstrate a good understanding of how to solve a problem such as "Tell what we know" in their own language. Eventually, you can put students in groups and present problems or tasks without having to provide such explicit guidance. Give the responsibility to the students to do the things that you have modelled.

Plan-and-Carry-Out Strategies

The follow-up portion of your lesson will inevitably include a discussion of methods that were used. When important or especially useful strategies crop up, they should be identified, highlighted, and discussed. Labelling a strategy provides a useful means for students to talk about their methods and for you to provide hints and suggestions. Hints or suggestions about a particular strategy may be appropriate in the introductory or development phases of your lesson.

In the 1980s and early 1990s, it was popular to select problems for the purpose of teaching a particular strategy or heuristic (Polya, 1957). The following strategies, which are closely linked with Polya's list of suggestions, are just a few of those that became popular during that period.

These strategies are most likely to appear in lessons where mathematical content is the main objective.

- *Draw a picture, act it out, use a model.* This is the strategy of using models as "thinker toys" as described in Chapter 3. "Act it out" extends the idea of modelling problems to include enactments of the problem situation.
- *Look for a pattern.* Pattern searching is at the heart of many activities, especially in the algebraic reasoning strand. Patterns in number and in operations play a major role in helping students learn about and master basic facts, and continue to be a key factor into the middle- and high-school years.
- *Make a table or chart.* Charts of data, function tables, tables for operations, and tables involving ratios or measurements are a major form of analysis and communication within mathematics. The use of a chart is often combined with pattern-searching as a means of solving problems or constructing new ideas.
- *Try a simpler form of the problem.* Here the general idea is to modify or simplify the quantities in a problem so that the resulting task is easier to understand and analyze. By solving the easier problem, the students may gain insights that can then be used to solve the original, more complex problem.
- *Guess and check.* This might be called "try and see what you can find out." A good way to work on a task that has you stumped is to *do something*. Make an attempt! Reflection even on a failed attempt can lead to a better idea. Another form of this strategy is to make an educated or reasoned guess at the solution and then see how the guess fits the conditions.
- *Make an organized list.* This strategy involves systematically accounting for all possible outcomes in a situation, either to find out how many possibilities there are or to be sure that all possible outcomes have been accounted for. One area where organized lists are very important is in probability.

Looking-Back Strategies

Looking-back strategies are the things that should always be done after a solution has been found: justify the answer, consider how the problem was solved, and look for possible extensions or generalizations. These are developed as you follow the teacher actions in the follow-up portion of a lesson. Students in the upper grades should begin to accept responsibility for doing these things themselves without your leading every discussion. Help students understand that post-problem reflection is not just something one does in school, but something that should be done whenever a problem is solved.

Developing Metacognitive Habits

We know that it is important to help students learn to monitor and control their own progress in problem solving. A simple formula that can be employed consists of three questions: *What* are you doing? *Why* are you doing it? *How* does it help you?

Though the exact form of the three questions is not significant, the idea is to be persistent with this reflective questioning as students work through problems or explorations. You can ask the questions as you sit down to listen to any group. By joining the group, you model questioning that you want the students eventually to do on their own. In the upper grades, each group will soon be able to designate a member to be the monitor. The monitor's job is to play the role of reflective questioner, as you have modelled it when working with the group.

Students can also be helped to develop self-monitoring habits that are used after the problem-solving activity is over. A brief discussion after a problem is over can focus on what types of things were done in solving the problem. "What did you do that helped you understand the problem? Did you find any numbers or information you didn't need? How did you decide what to do? Did you think about your answer after you got it? How did you decide your answer was right?"

This type of questioning tells students that all of these things are important. If they know you are going to be asking such questions, students will think about them ahead of time. Oral discussions with the class will be most helpful with younger children.

Attending to Attitudinal Goals

A classroom environment built on high expectations for all students and respect for each student's thoughts will go a long way toward achieving the attitudinal goals. Here are some additional ideas to help with these goals for all students.

- *Build in success.* At the beginning of the year, plan problems that you are confident your students can solve. Avoid creating a false success that depends on your showing the way at every step and curve.
- *Praise efforts and risk taking.* Students need to hear frequently that they are "good thinkers" capable of good, productive thought. When students volunteer ideas, be sure to listen carefully and actively to each idea, and give credit for the thinking and the risk that children take by venturing to speak out. Be careful to focus praise on the risk or effort and not the products of that effort, regardless of the quality of the ideas. Children whose weak or incorrect ideas are slighted or ignored develop a low sense of self-worth: "I'm no good. I can't think of good ideas." The same negative

message comes through when praise is reserved only for the "best" ideas.

■ *Listen to all students.* Avoid ending a discussion with the first correct answer. As you make non-evaluative responses, you will find many children repeating the same idea. Were they just copying a known leader? Perhaps, but more likely they were busy thinking and did not even hear what had already been said by those who were a bit faster. If 10 hands go up, 10 children may have been doing good thinking. Don't forget the suggestion made earlier to call on less secure students early in a discussion, so that the most obvious ideas are not taken by the more aggressive students.

■ *Provide special successes for special children.* Not all children will develop the same problem-solving abilities, but all have abilities and can contribute. This must be something you truly believe because it is difficult to fake. One way to provide success for students who are slower or not as strong is to involve them in groups with strong and supportive children. All children can be made to feel that they are a part of the group's success.

Reflections *on Chapter 4*

Writing to Learn

1. Explain the difference between teaching that begins where the teacher is and teaching that begins where the students are.
2. Discuss each of the benefits of teaching with problems.
3. Describe, as outlined in this chapter, what is meant by tasks or problems that can be used for teaching mathematics. Be sure to include the three important features that are required to make this method effective.
4. What is the teacher's purpose or agenda in each of the three parts—introduction, development, and follow-up—of a lesson?
5. Describe the kinds of actions or things that a teacher should be doing in each of these three parts of a lesson. (Note that not all of these would be done in every lesson.)
6. Select an activity from any chapter in Section 2 of this text. How can the activity be used as a problem or task for the purpose of instruction, as described in this chapter? If you were using this activity in the classroom, what specifically would you do during the "introduction" part of the lesson?
7. The first of the four suggestions for teaching through problem solving is to predict rather than hope. Explain what this means. How should good predictions affect your lesson planning?
8. Goals for the development of good problem solving were separated under the headings of "Strategies and Processes," "Meta-cognition," and "Disposition." Describe what is meant by each of these goals.
9. Describe how a teacher can help students develop the goals for problem solving in the "introduction," "development, " and "follow-up" phases of a lesson.

For Discussion and Exploration

1. If you were to begin teaching a class of students who had never experienced learning mathematics in a problem-solving environment, they might not be familiar with how to work at solving problems, how to do so with a partner, or how to engage in discussion about the process. How would you begin to deal with these and similar challenges so that students would develop an understanding of their role in such a classroom?
2. Find a traditional basal textbook for any grade level. Look through a chapter, and find at least one lesson that you could convert to a problem-solving lesson without drastic alterations. Is there any content in the chapter, other than conventions, that you do not feel you could teach through problem solving?
3. Select a lesson from a "reform-oriented" textbook series (see Chapter 1 for a list). Determine how the general structure of the lesson you selected compares with the problem-solving approach to teaching described in this chapter.

Recommendations for Further Reading

Highly Recommended

Borasi, R. (1992). *Learning mathematics through inquiry*. Portsmouth, NH: Heinemann.

Borasi describes in great detail a 10-lesson "mini-course" on mathematical definitions conducted with two 16-year-old girls. It includes insights into the girls' thoughts as they change their perceptions of doing and learning mathematics. As well, Borasi discusses her unique perspectives on mathematics as a humanistic discipline and learning as meaning-making. The topics are slightly above the middle-grades level, but the discussion, as a reflection of the current chapter, is worth reading by all who teach mathematics.

Burns, M. (1996). *50 problem-solving lessons: Grades 1–6*. Sausalito, CA: Math Solutions Publications.

The 50 lessons each reflect the spirit of teaching through problem solving. The content strands include number, geometry, measurement, statistics, probability, patterns and functions, algebra, and logic. Each is described in a few pages with ample examples of children's work, all in the spirit of this master teacher of mathematics. It is not just a good resource but a good model.

Corwin, R.B. (1996). *Talking mathematics: Supporting children's voices*. Portsmouth, NH: Heinemann.

It is rare to find a book that explains the value of discourse and the struggles that constructivist teachers encounter, while also providing practical suggestions for making mathematical talk happen in the classroom. Corwin's little book comes as close as any. It is based on a project that involved teachers exploring how to create classrooms that valued and supported mathematical discourse. It is written in simple terms that inform and inspire. Included are eight related readings from other sources.

Flewelling, G., & Higginson, W. (2000). *Realizing a vision of tomorrow's mathematics classroom: A handbook on rich learning tasks.* Kingston, ON: Centre for Mathematics, Science and Technology Education.

This handbook gives educators an understanding of the nature and assessment of rich learning tasks and of new ways to nourish the teaching and learning process. It provides teachers with sample tasks, along with accompanying rubrics that reflect the type of problem solving recommended in this chapter.

Hiebert, J.C., Carpenter, T.P., Fennema, E., Fuson, K.C., Wearne, D., Murray, H.G., Olivier, A.I., & Human, P.G. (1997). *Making sense: Teaching and learning mathematics with understanding.* Portsmouth, NH: Heinemann.

The authors of this highly readable and significant book are connected to four problem-based, long-term research projects. They make one of the best cases currently in print for developing mathematics via problematic tasks. After reviewing features of the general approach and the supporting theory, they present a vignette from each project and discuss it in detail. *Making Sense* and the companion article by the same authors in *The Educational Researcher* (see "Other Suggestions") have guided our revision of Chapter 4 in this text.

Other Suggestions

Arvold, B., Turner, P., & Cooney, T.J. (1996). Analyzing teaching and learning: The art of listening. *Mathematics Teacher, 89,* 326–329.

Baker, A., & Baker, J. (1991). *Maths in the mind: A process approach to mental strategies.* Portsmouth, NH: Heinemann.

Baker, J., & Baker, A. (1990). *Mathematics in process.* Portsmouth, NH: Heinemann.

Ball, D.L. (1996). Connecting to mathematics as part of learning to teach. In D. Schifter (Ed.), *What's happening in math class? Reconstructing professional identities* (Vol. 2, pp. 36–45). New York: Teachers College Press.

Barb, C., & Larson Quinn, A. (1997). Problem solving does not have to be a problem. *The Mathematics Teacher, 90* (7), 536–542.

Bickmore-Brand, J. (Ed.). (1990). *Language in mathematics.* Portsmouth, NH: Heinemann.

Brown, S.L., & Walter, M.I. (1990). *The art of problem posing* (2nd ed.). Mahwah, NJ: Erlbaum.

Brownell, W.A., & Chazal, C.B. (1935). The effects of premature drill in third-grade arithmetic. *Journal of Educational Research, 29,* 17–28.

Campbell, P.F. (1996). Empowering children and teachers in the elementary mathematics classrooms of urban schools. *Urban Education, 30,* 449–475.

Chambers, D.L. (1995). Improving instruction by listening to children. *Teaching Children Mathematics, 1,* 378–380.

Dacey, L.S., & Eston, R. (1999). *Growing mathematical ideas in kindergarten.* Sausalito, CA: Math Solutions Publications.

English, L.D., Cudmore, D., & Tilley, D. (1998). Problem posing and critiquing: How it can happen in your classroom. *Mathematics Teaching in the Middle School, 4,* 124–129.

Henningsen, M., & Stein, M.K. (1997). Mathematical tasks and student cognition: Classroom-based factors that support and inhibit high-level mathematical thinking and reasoning. *Journal for Research in Mathematics Education, 28,* 524–549.

Hiebert, J.C., Carpenter, T.P., Fennema, E., Fuson, K.C., Human, P.G., Murray, H.G., Olivier, A.I., & Wearne, D. (1996). Problem solving as a basis for reform in curriculum and instruction: The case of mathematics. *Educational Researcher, 25,* 12–21.

Hiebert, J.C., & Wearne, D. (1993). Instructional tasks, classroom discourse, and students' learning in second-grade arithmetic. *American Educational Research Journal, 30,* 393–425.

Hyde, A.A., & Hyde, P.R. (1991). *Mathwise: Teaching mathematical thinking and problem solving.* Portsmouth, NH: Heinemann.

Lappan, G., & Briars, D. (1995). How should mathematics be taught? In I.M. Carl (Ed.), *Seventy-five years of progress: Prospects for school mathematics* (pp. 115–156). Reston, VA: National Council of Teachers of Mathematics.

Liedtke, W. (1999). *Teacher-centred projects: Risk taking and flexible thinking.* Proceedings of a faculty conference, Connections '98, Victoria, BC.

Lubienski, S.T. (1999). Problem-centered mathematics teaching. *Mathematics Teaching in the Middle School, 5,* 250–255.

Manouchehri, A., & Enderson, M.C. (1999). Promoting mathematical discourse: Learning from classroom examples. *Mathematics Teaching in the Middle School, 4,* 216–222.

McNeal, B. (1995). Learning not to think in a textbook-based mathematics class. *Journal of Mathematical Behavior, 14,* 205–234.

Mokros, J., Russell, S.J., & Economopoulos, K. (1995). *Beyond arithmetic: Changing mathematics in the elementary classroom.* White Plains, NY: Cuisenaire–Dale Seymour.

Parker, R.E. (1993). *Mathematical power: Lessons from a classroom.* Portsmouth, NH: Heinemann.

Polya, G. (1957). *How to solve it.* Princeton, NJ: Princeton University Press.

Reys, B.J., & Long, V.M. (1995). Teacher as architect of mathematical tasks. *Teaching Children Mathematics, 1,* 296–299.

Ritchhart, R. (1999). Generative topics: Building a curriculum around big ideas. *Teaching Children Mathematics, 5,* 462–468.

Romagnano, L. (1994). *Wrestling with change: The dilemmas of teaching real mathematics.* Portsmouth, NH: Heinemann.

Rowan, T.E., & Bourne, B. (1994). *Thinking like mathematicians: Putting the K–4 Standards into practice.* Portsmouth, NH: Heinemann.

Rowan, T.E., & Robles, J. (1998). Using questions to help children build mathematical power. *Teaching Children Mathematics, 4,* 504–509.

Sawada, D. (1997). Mathematics as reasoning: Episodes from Japan. *Mathematics Teaching in the Middle School, 2,* 416–421.

Sawada, D. (1999). Mathematics as problem solving: A Japanese way. *Teaching Children Mathematics, 6,* 54–58.

Schifter, D., & Fosnot, C.T. (1993). *Reconstructing mathematics education: Stories of teachers meeting the challenge of reform.* New York: Teachers College Press.

Schwartz, S.L. (1996). Hidden messages in teacher talk: Praise and empowerment. *Teaching Children Mathematics, 2,* 396–401.

Schweitzer, K. (1996). The search for the perfect resource. In D. Schifter (Ed.), *What's happening in math class? Reconstructing professional identities* (Vol. 2, pp. 47–65). New York: Teachers College Press.

Silver, E.A., & Smith, M.S. (1996). Building discourse communities in mathematics classrooms: A worthwhile but challenging journey. In P.C. Elliott (Ed.), *Communication in mathematics, K–12 and beyond* (pp. 20–28). Reston, VA: National Council of Teachers of Mathematics.

Smith, J.P., III. (1996). Efficacy and teaching mathematics by telling: A challenge for reform. *Journal for Research in Mathematics Education, 27,* 387–402.

Smith, M.S., & Stein, M.K. (1998). Selecting and creating mathematical tasks: From research to practice. *Mathematics Teaching in the Middle School, 3,* 344–350.

Stein, M.K., & Smith, M.S. (1998). Mathematical tasks as a framework for reflection: From research to practice. *Mathematics Teaching in the Middle School, 3,* 268–275.

Stigler, J.W., & Hiebert, J.C. (1999). *The teaching gap: Best ideas from the world's teachers for improving education in the classroom.* New York: Free Press.

Tsuruda, G. (1994). *Putting it together: Middle school math in transition.* Portsmouth, NH: Heinemann.

Williamson, M.E. (1991). Implementing metacognitive processing in the mathematics classroom. Unpublished master's thesis, Vancouver: University of British Columbia.

Wood, T. (1999). Creating a context for argument in mathematics class. *Journal for Research in Mathematics Education, 30,* 171–191.

Wood, T., & Sellers, P. (1996). Assessment of a problem-centered mathematics program: Third grade. *Journal for Research in Mathematics Education, 27,* 337–353.

Yackel, E. (1995). Children's talk in inquiry mathematics classrooms. In P. Cobb & H. Bauersfeld (Eds.), *The emergence of mathematical meaning: Interaction in classroom cultures* (pp. 131–162). Mahwah, NJ: Erlbaum.

Chapter 5

Building Assessment into Instruction

Assessment should be the servant of teaching and learning. Without information about their students' skills, understanding, and individual approaches to mathematics, teachers have nothing to guide their work.

Mokros, Russell, and Economopoulos (1995, p. 84)

It is not surprising that assessment plays an important role in Canadian education. It is at the heart of educational reform initiatives worldwide and is a key component of the agenda for improving student learning. In terms of expressed goals for students, assessment has always been a central feature of schooling (Earl & Katz, 2000). Moreover, assessment is one of the six principles of *Principles and Standards for School Mathematics*.

Appropriate assessment practices, integral to the instructional process, can inform teaching so that student learning is improved. As teachers, it is important to rethink what mathematics instruction means, and to re-evaluate the process of assessment. Chapter-end tests and reliance on formal testing programs are simply inadequate in a truly student-centred, problem-oriented classroom. The challenge for Canadian teachers in this first decade of the 21st century is to develop and rely on quality assessment strategies and not to be overwhelmed by the pressures of testing from outside the classroom.

What Is Assessment?

The NCTM *Assessment Standards* for School Mathematics defines assessment as "the process of gathering evidence about a student's knowledge of, ability to use, and disposition toward mathematics and of making inferences from that evidence for a variety of purposes" (NCTM, 1995,

p. 3). It is important to note, though, that assessment is not at all the same as testing, measurement, or evaluation. These latter terms include the elements of value or worth. Although assessment focuses on data collection, assessment data are certainly used in the evaluation of both students and programs. There are multiple ways to collect and use these data, but only one of the four uses of data described in the *Assessment Standards* is related to assigning evaluative grades.

As illustrated in Figure 5.1, assessment should be seen as an ongoing but very deliberate process. Assessments must be planned and then data gathered in the classroom. The evidence is then interpreted and is used to design instruction and inform students. This leads to planning the next assessment, and the cycle continues.

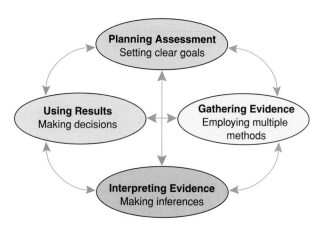

FIGURE 5.1 Assessment involves four stages that usually operate in a cycle.

Source: Reprinted with permission from *Principles and Standards for School Mathematics*. Copyright © 2000 by the National Council of Teachers of Mathematics. All rights reserved.

The Assessment Standards

In 1995, NCTM's *Assessment Standards for School Mathematics* called for a shift away from "assessing only students' knowledge of specific facts and isolated skills" toward "assessing students' full mathematical power" (NCTM, 1995, p. 83). Unlike traditional testing, which focuses on what students *do not know* (tallying wrong answers), the general spirit of the *Assessment Standards* is to find out what students *do know*. The document contains six standards for assessment and details four purposes that assessment practices should serve. *Assessment Standards* is consistent with the Principles for Fair Student Assessment Practices for Education in Canada (Joint Advisory Committee, 1993) and provides a basis for provincial assessment programs designed to determine students' progress and knowledge of regional curricula. A full description of assessment practices of the different jurisdictions can be found in *Student Assessment in Canada* (Taylor & Tubianosa, 2001) or by contacting your local ministry or department of education.

Six Assessment Standards

The six assessment standards are statements against which assessment practices can be judged. They are not prescriptions for how to create assessments. The classroom teacher should periodically reflect on his or her assessment methods using the standards as a benchmark.

1. The Mathematics Standard

Assessment should reflect the mathematics that all students need to know and be able to do. (NCTM, 1995, p. 11)

Principles and Standards provides teachers with a broad perspective of the five content strands that outline what students should know and be able to use as they progress through school. Further, there are the five process standards that reflect students' mathematical power. Assessment practices should reflect these 10 standards, as well as the expectations of regional curriculum guidelines as they provide a finer description of required mathematical content. When the pressures of testing accompany these expectations, there is a danger of focusing on tests and low-level skills rather than on the broader view of doing mathematics. This does not, however, exclude appropriate attention to computational skills and traditional basics.

2. The Learning Standard

Assessment should enhance mathematics learning. (NCTM, 1995, p. 13)

The Learning standard suggests that the main purpose of assessment is to improve performance, not merely to audit it. Classroom assessment practices should communicate to students *during* the learning process, guiding students to improve their learning and letting them know what is valued.

In like manner, assessment should guide teachers in their design of instruction by providing a constant stream of information with which decisions can be made during a unit, rather than after instruction is finished.

For assessment to support and enhance learning, it must be viewed and designed as an integral part of instruction, not as an addendum or an interruption.

3. The Equity Standard

Assessment should promote equity. (NCTM, 1995, p. 15)

Equitable assessment respects the unique qualities, experiences, and expertise of each student. Equity in assessment sets high mathematical standards for all students, including those with special needs. This standard is reflected in the equity principle of *Principles and Standards,* which says that we must hold high expectations for all students while recognizing that students need different forms of instructional support. Equity aims directly at finding out what all students *do* know, rather than establishing a high hurdle that too often screens students from further mathematics or implies only that they have failed to achieve.

4. The Openness Standard

Assessment should be an open process. (NCTM, 1995, p. 17)

Students need to know what is expected of them and how they can demonstrate what they have learned. The criteria for quality performance must also be clear to students. Reasoning, communication, and problem solving must be integrated with content knowledge. Performance should be viewed in a holistic manner, based on much more than correct answers. Students need to be involved in setting the criteria and even using the criteria to assess their own performance. Openness also means that parents and other teachers are aware of the methods and criteria that are valued in the classroom.

5. The Inferences Standard

Assessment should promote valid inferences about mathematics learning. (NCTM, 1995, p. 19)

The question that teachers in a developmental approach to instruction must constantly ask is "What does this performance tell me about this student's understanding or reasoning?" Assessments are based on students' doing mathematics—communicating, reasoning, justifying results, testing hypotheses, looking for patterns. An examination of the number of correct exercises provides only a shallow glimpse into a student's understanding. No objectively scored test can determine the workings of children's thought processes or individual understandings.

This standard requires that teachers reflect seriously and honestly on what students are revealing about what they know. The use of multiple assessment techniques is one way that teachers can improve the validity of their inferences. Lessons developed around problems using the three-part format described in Chapter 4 will provide ample data for valid assessments.

6. The Coherence Standard

Assessment should be a coherent process. (NCTM, 1995, p. 21)

This assessment cycle (Figure 5.1) must be in complete accord with the objectives of instruction—what you want students to learn—as well as the methods of instruction. There must be a balance of assessment methods that reflect conceptual and procedural understanding as well as mathematical processes. Traditional paper-and-pencil tests alone will not be sufficient. The Coherence standard also suggests an alignment of assessment methods with the methods of instruction. That is, students should be evaluated using the same methods, materials, and approaches with which they learned.

Purposes of Assessment

Even a cursory glance at the six assessment standards suggests a complete integration of assessment and instruction. The *Assessment Standards* outlines four specific purposes of assessment as depicted in Figure 5.2. For each purpose, the adjacent rectangle indicates a corresponding result.

Monitoring Student Progress

As a teacher, you need to establish high goals for your students. Assessment should provide teacher, students, and parents with ongoing feedback concerning progress toward those goals. Assessment should inform each individual student and the teacher about growth toward mathematical power and problem-solving ability, not just mastery of procedural skills. Furthermore, the feedback should be received during instruction, not at the end of the unit, when it is perhaps too late to promote student learning.

Making Instructional Decisions

Teachers planning tasks each day to develop student understanding must have current information about how their students are thinking and what ideas they are using and developing. When teaching with problems and tasks, this information is readily available, especially in the development and follow-up stages of a lesson. Daily problem solving and discussion provide a much richer and more useful array of data than can ever be gathered from a chapter test. The information comes at a time when you can formulate plans to help students develop ideas, rather than having to remediate after the fact. Thus, daily assessment data are essential to the effective design of instruction.

Evaluating Student Achievement

Assessment differs from evaluation. *Assessment* is the collection of data; *evaluation* is "the process of determining the

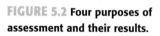

FIGURE 5.2 Four purposes of assessment and their results.
Source: Adapted from NCTM (1995, p. 25). Used with permission.

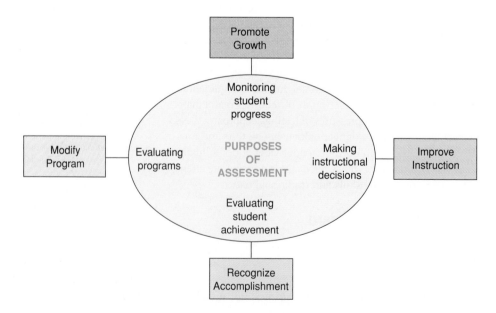

worth of, or assigning a value to, something on the basis of careful examination and judgment" (NCTM, 1995, p. 3). Evaluation involves a teacher's judgment about a student's demonstrated understanding. It may include test data but should take into account a wide variety of sources and types of information gathered during the course of instruction. Most importantly, evaluation should reflect performance criteria about what students know and understand; it should not be used to compare one student with another.

Traditional evaluation was nearly synonymous with the end-of-unit test. There was a clear line between instruction and evaluation. The *Assessment Standards* approach to appropriate assessment, reiterated in *Principles and Standards,* is to eradicate that line by gathering assessment data continuously in informal ways, and frequently in more structured ways, and by including these data in evaluation. (A more complete discussion of grading can be found near the end of this chapter.)

Evaluating Programs

Assessment data should be used as one significant component in answering the question "How well did this program work to achieve my goals?" In this context, *program* refers to any organized unit of study and need not be restricted to school or district or board decisions, such as which textbook should be adopted. For the classroom teacher, program includes such things as self-designed units of instruction, a chapter from a resource book or text, or even a particular strategy for cooperative group learning or for learning centres. In evaluation of these as well as larger curricular programs, students' knowledge, understanding, processes, and disposition—based on multiple sources of information—should all be taken into account.

What Should Be Assessed?

A quality assessment program will not only include the specific concepts and skills of your current unit but will also attend to the processes of doing mathematics. You can and should develop a general framework within which you can assess information concerning all content and processes.

Concepts and Procedures

Recall that understanding occurs on a continuum determined by the number and quality of connections that an individual has made. A good assessment strategy will provide opportunities for students to demonstrate how they themselves understand the concepts under discussion. The traditional test generally targets only one way to know an idea: that of the test designer. If you collect information from students as they complete an activity, discuss an idea,

or justify results—in short, as they do mathematics—you will gain information that provides insight into the nature of the students' understanding of that idea.

Procedural knowledge, including skill proficiency, should be included, although it should not be considered more important than conceptual understanding. If your curricular objectives emphasize skills, be careful to ensure that the conceptual foundations are there as well. If a student can compute with fractions, but has no idea of why she needs a common denominator for addition but not for multiplication, then the rules that have been "mastered" have little connection to meaning. This situation would indicate only the tenuous presence of a skill. Whereas a routine skill such as mastering addition with regrouping can easily be checked with a traditional test, the desired conceptual connections require assessment of a different nature.

Mathematical Processes

Guidelines for defining the specifics of mathematical power can be found in the five process standards of *Principles and Standards.* Be aware that it is not reasonable to try to assess all of these processes at the same time, especially not every day. For each grade band, *Principles and Standards* describes what the process standards might look like at that level. Use these descriptions along with local guidelines to craft statements about doing mathematics that your students can understand. Here are a few examples, but you should write your own or use those provided by your school system.

Problem Solving

- Works at understanding a problem before beginning work.
- Uses drawings, graphs, and physical models to help solve problems.
- Has and uses appropriate strategies for solving problems.
- Assesses the validity of answers.

Reasoning

- Justifies solution methods and results.
- Makes conjectures based on reasoning.
- Observes and uses patterns in mathematics.

Communication

- Explains ideas in writing.
- Communicates ideas clearly in class discussions.

These statements should be discussed with your students, to help clarify the ideas and to let students know that you value their feedback. Periodically, use the statements to rate students' mathematical processes based on their individual work, on group work, and on participation in class discussions. If you use portfolios, which look at work developed and collected over time, process assessment should almost certainly be considered. Processes must also be used in your grading or evaluation scheme, or students will not take them seriously.

Disposition

You will recall that attitudinal goals were a separate component of the objectives of problem solving. It is important to make occasional efforts to collect data on students' confidence and beliefs in their own mathematical abilities, as well as on their likes and dislikes about mathematics. This information is easily obtained with self-reported checklists and journal writing. Information on your students' perseverance and willingness to attempt problems is available to you every day in a problem-solving approach. These too are data that you must make an effort to collect, perhaps with anecdotal notes or a checklist attached to an observation scheme.

Combining Instruction and Assessment

Real change in the classroom cannot be achieved without integrating instruction with assessment. If your instruction becomes more problem-based but your assessment methods focus on recall and closed-response items, the instruction is doomed to failure. Students quickly learn that what is valued is getting answers. Older students tune out or even refuse to participate in the tasks provided. "Just show us how to get the answer," is what they will think. Assessment strategies must reflect our values in exactly the same manner as our instruction.

The reverse situation—to engage in "traditional," teacher-directed instruction with open-ended, problem-solving tasks for assessment—asks children to demonstrate mathematical power without ever having experienced it. Students who are accustomed to being told how to do everything in the mathematics classroom, when faced with novel, problem-solving tasks, will understandably complain, "You've never told us how to do this!" Teachers who have tried various "alternative assessments" without significantly altering their instruction find that these assessments are difficult or impossible for their students, and all involved become frustrated.

Quality instruction and appropriate assessment need not be different activities. Assessment and instruction should be nearly indistinguishable. We can assess as we provide opportunities for learning. The search for quality assessment tasks is simultaneously a search for quality learning tasks. They are one and the same!

Performance Tasks

Recall from Chapter 4 that a problem was any task or activity for which the students have no prescribed or memorized rules or specific "correct" solution method. The same definition should be used for performance tasks. The assessment literature often refers to "performance assessment tasks" or "alternative assessments," but those expressions imply tasks that are in some way different from those used in instruction. They are not different.

Problems for instruction also have three features that should be revisited in the context of assessment.

First, a problem must *begin where the students are.* Good tasks should permit every student in the class, regardless of mathematical prowess, to demonstrate some knowledge, skill, or understanding. Lower-ability students should be encouraged to use the ideas they possess to work on a problem even if they are not the same skills or strategies used by others in the room. A forgotten computational procedure should not preclude a student from working on a performance task. At the same time as we consider accessibility, we should strive to select or design tasks that are sufficiently rich to challenge the thinking and reasoning ability of all students.

Second, the *problematic or engaging aspect of the problem must be tied to the mathematics that the students are to learn.* Too often what has been promoted as "alternative assessment " focuses on the real-world or authentic context of problems. We must remember that what we should be assessing is students' understanding of mathematics, not the non-mathematical aspects of the task. Although contextual situations are often nice, how a student completes a task and justifies the solution should inform us about his or her understanding.

Third, problems must *require justifications and explanations for answers and methods.* The justifications, even those given orally, will almost certainly provide more information than the answers alone. Perhaps no better method exists for getting at student understanding.

The unfortunate separation of learning and assessment tasks is partly due to our lengthy history of equating assessment with summative, evaluative testing. There may be times when you do decide to use a task as a summative evaluation and choose not to interact with students as they are working. In these instances, you will have already provided students with an opportunity to access and develop content that is essential to the task. Remember that the task should not be identical to a previous learning experience. If it is, then the students will simply be following an earlier example, not *doing* mathematics. Using a task as a summative assessment simply changes its purpose and intent. The task should still look the same (exactly like a learning task) even when used in an evaluative context.

Selecting Tasks for Assessment

Anne is a grade 3 teacher. Over the course of an academic year, she was one of a group of teachers learning to use appropriate assessment techniques in mathematics. Anne used the following task with her class working together in groups of three or four.

Find ways to add consecutive numbers in order to reach sums between 1 and 15. For example, 3 + 4 + 5 = 12, and 3, 4, and 5 are consecutive numbers.

Anne reports:

I wanted to assess my student to find out if they were able to both estimate and solve math facts mentally. I also wanted to assess how far my students had come in cooperative learning. I developed a checklist to use when making my observations. Some items on the list included "able to recall basic facts," "able to add mentally," "adds by counting up on fingers," "interacts with peers positively," and "participates with the group." The task was long enough and engaging enough that I was able to spend time with each group listening to the interaction and questioning the members about their thinking.

By thinking of her objective ahead of time, Anne, knowing what she was looking for, was able to listen actively to her students. Anne stated her objectives in procedural terms: "able to recall," "able to add mentally." Alternatively, she might have focused on how children connect facts. For example, do children see that 4 + 5, 5 + 6, and 6 + 7 are odd sums or are each 2 apart? Do those who are still counting use one fact, say, 4 + 5, to arrive at 3 + 4 + 5? By focusing on behaviours, Anne forgot to plan a discussion that would have allowed her to see the ideas students may have constructed. However, she did use this opportunity to assess some group skills.

When selecting a task for assessment purposes, it is most important to be very clear about what you want to assess. In this example, there were a number of things on which Anne could have focused. The essential content of this task was addition and number relationships. Yet the focus could have been on either procedural or conceptual knowledge, and may or may not have included attention to problem solving or other skills. Anne also had a written report from each group that she could have taken home and reflected on in order to evaluate their communication skills. Had she entertained a class discussion after the task, she would have opened the door for whatever thoughts students may have had. There would have been an opportunity to wonder how many sums were possible for different numbers. "Do all numbers have consecutive sums? How do we know? What else do you notice?"

Examples of Problems for Assessment

Each of the following tasks provides ample opportunity for students to learn. At the same time, it provides data for the teacher to use in assessment. Notice that these are not elaborate tasks. Along with a discussion, each could engage students for most of a session. As you read each task, think about the following questions to decide what specific information might be assessed:

- What is the essential conceptual content in the task?
- What problem-solving processes might be observed?
- What opportunity might there be to observe communication skills?
- What about reasoning (if-then thinking)?
- Are there opportunities for students to connect the content with other content either in or outside of mathematics?
- Is the task accessible in some way to a range of students?

SHARES (GRADES K–3)

Leila has 6 gumdrops, Darlene has 2, and Melissa has 4. They want to share them equally. How will they do it? Draw a picture to help explain your answer.

In grade 2 or 3, the numbers in this "shares" problem would probably be larger. What would happen if the problem were about cookies and the total number of cookies were 14?

SUBTRACTION (GRADES 1–2)

If you did not know the answer to 12–7, what are some ways you could find the answer?

HOW MUCH? (GRADES 1–2)

Jelena has saved $15 to buy a game that she wants. The game costs $23. How much money does Jelena still need?

These two problems are similar in that they involve subtraction and allow the teacher to see what strategies a student might use. In the second problem, the context increases the chances that students will use an "add-on" approach (15 and how much more to make 23?). Without context, you get a better chance to see what strategies students are using most regularly.

BROKEN KEYS (GRADES 2–4)

If the 5 key on your calculator was broken, how could you do this problem: 458 + 548 + 354? Is there more than one way? Which way do you like the best? Why?

"Broken Keys" is a good example of a task with many solutions. As students are working, you will be able to assess how easily students arrive at different approaches.

THE WHOLE SET (GRADES 3–5)

When Fabio counted the leftover cupcakes from the batch that his mother made for the picnic, there were 15. "We've already eaten two-fifths of these," he noted. How many cupcakes did his mother bake?

This last problem could easily have been posed without any context. What is the value of context in tasks such as these?

TOP AND BOTTOM (GRADES 4–6)

In the fraction $\frac{3}{4}$, how would you explain the meaning of the top number (numerator) to a grade 3 student? Do the same for the bottom number (denominator). Use two different ways to explain each.

A great source of problem solving is to have students explain ideas that have been developed in class. Explanations for these ideas could be presented, as in "Top and Bottom," to students in another grade level, or to a fictional peer who missed yesterday's lesson. Here the task tells you how effective the previous lesson was.

In the following task, students are asked to judge the performance of other students. Analysis of student performance is another good way to create tasks.

DECIMALS (GRADES 4–6)

Lee Cheng tried to make a decimal number as close to 50 as she could using the digits 1, 4, 5, and 9. She arranged them in this order: 51.49. Natasha thinks she can arrange the same digits to get a number that is even closer to 50. Do you agree or disagree? Explain.

MENTAL MATH (GRADES 4–8)

Explain two different ways to multiply 4×276 in your head. Which way is easier to use? Would you use a different way to multiply 5×98? Explain why you would use the same or different methods.

Mental computation tasks should be done frequently at all grade levels beginning around grade 2. As students share their explanations for their computations, others will pick up their methods. The explanations will also provide a lot of information about students' conceptual knowledge and the types of strategies they have already acquired. This information can be recorded in a variety of ways over time.

TWO TRIANGLES (GRADES 4–8)

Tell everything you can about these two triangles.

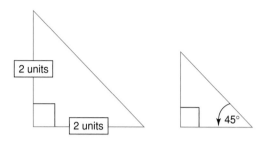

This task is a good example of a very open-ended assessment. Consider how much more valuable this task is than asking for the angle measure in the left-hand triangle.

PROBABILITY (GRADES 7–8)

In the "Rolling Cube" dice game that Chantal and Omar are playing, two cubes with the numbers 1–6 on them are rolled. What is the possibility of getting a total greater than 9?

This task requires knowing the number of possible combinations that can be obtained for each of the numbers when the cubes are rolled, and applying this knowledge to solve the problem. Observing the strategies students use allows you to assess what they know.

More Thoughts about Assessment Tasks

In some instances, the real value of the task, or the useful data about students, will come only in the discussion that follows the work. For others, the information will be in the written report. In many of Marilyn Burns's books, you will see the phrase "We think the answer is... We think this because..." Students must develop the habit of listening to justifications, then adding to their own explanations. If this is not a regular practice in your classroom, do not expect students to be able to offer good explanations during either written or oral assessment.

Much of the assessment literature has placed a significant value on situational, or realistic, problems and open-ended problems. You might want to consult the *Handbook on Rich Learning Tasks* (Flewelling & Higginson, 2000) to which we alluded in Chapter 1. It provides some excellent examples of tasks that, while they are realistic problems, are also excellent assessment tasks. There is no doubt that such problems have an important place in the mathematics classroom. However, "open-endedness" or real-world contexts do not necessarily guarantee that students will be engaged in constructing mathematics. Neither do these features make for quality assessment. There are open-ended, real-life problems that can be interesting and engaging, but that are also mathematically trivial. For example, tasks involving spending money from a fast-food menu or a catalogue are rarely more than glorified addition exercises. *Keep your focus on the mathematics.* As the *Handbook of Rich Learning Tasks* demonstrates, the inclusion of real-life connections and open-ended tasks is possible without sacrificing the mathematics.

Many activities have no written component and no set "answer" or result. For example, students may play a game where dice or dominoes are being used. A teacher who sits in on the game will see the variety of ways that children use numbers. Some will count every dot on the card or domino. Others will use a counting-on strategy. Some will recognize certain patterns without counting. Others may be unsure if 13 beats 11. This information significantly differentiates students relative to their understanding of number concepts. Data gathered from listening to a pair of children work on a simple activity or an extended project provide considerably greater insight into students' thinking than almost any written test we could devise. Data from student conversations and from observations of their behaviour can be recorded and used for the same purposes as written data, or for evaluation or grading. It is important, especially in the case of grading, to keep dated, written notes that can be used for later reference.

If you have been helping children develop a computational procedure, a formula, or some other routine procedure, you may be tempted to restrict assessment to use of the procedure to get answers. A conceptual understanding must also be assessed. Assessment can be achieved by asking students to explain a particular step (*What does this little "1" stand for up on the top of the tens column?*) or by asking them to find and correct, with an appropriate explanation, an error made by a fictional student.

Rubrics and Performance Indicators

A rubric is a comprehensive scoring guide that is used to assess student performance of high-level skills, techniques, and processes in an authentic way. These scoring tools can be designed or adapted by the teacher for a particular group of students or for a particular mathematical task. Rubrics guide both teachers and students, in that they help to distinguish acceptable from unacceptable responses, identify qualitative differences in responses, and make sense of what a score value means (Colgan, 2000). While making it easier for the teacher to rate the quality of a student's finished product, rubrics also act as instructional resources for students. As students see examples of exemplary work they begin to raise their own standards.

Note that a rubric is a scale to judge performance on a single task, rather than a count of how many items are correct or incorrect on a series of exercises. Typically rubrics are used for written work, where you can consider thoughtfully each student's performance. They are just as valuable as tools for observation as they are for judgment of oral performance by students, and can make your recording schemes more meaningful and easier to use.

Simple Rubrics

The following simple four-point rubric (designed to assess performance in language arts) was developed by the Saskatchewan Professional Development Unit as one of a number of tools for assessing children in multi-level classrooms.

This rubric, created to measure depths of student understanding, allows a teacher to rate performance using the criteria illustrated in Table 5.1. The relatively simple scale and general nature of the categories makes this rating scale a good starting point for working with rubrics. It can easily be adapted to mathematics.

Table 5.1 Example of a Four-Point Rubric

Powerful	The response is personalized and thoughtful. The student integrates previous experience and includes specific references to the text. The ideas expressed go beyond the text, describe the comparisons or metaphors, and indicate a relatively deep and sophisticated understanding of the selection.
Competent	The response is consistent and logical, features some integration of previous experience, and includes text references. The student may focus on one aspect of the poem, or may describe the metaphor or deal with the idea on a surface level.
Partial	Some inconsistencies are apparent, suggesting a partial or incomplete understanding of the poem. Typically the student makes less frequent use of images, emotions, and specific text references.
Undeveloped	The response is inconsistent or illogical. The student may offer broad general statements without explanation. If any references are included, they may be inappropriate or illogical.

Source: Saskatchewan Professional Development Unit. (1997). *Learning Together in Multi-Level Classrooms.* Regina, SK: Author, p. 48.

Performance Indicators

For any given task or process, it is usually helpful to create performance indicators. These task-specific statements describe what performance looks like at each level of the rubric. In so doing, they establish criteria for acceptable performance. The language used should clearly describe each level of performance (Rolheiser, Bower, & Stevahn,

2000). Indicators that are well designed reflect appropriate levels of student work for different ages and abilities. They also help students to see how performance at each level varies and to distinguish between acceptable and unacceptable performance (Horsman, 1997). Notice how the language at each level of the four-point problem-solving rubric in Table 5.2 describes for students what performance should look like. As well, the descriptions at each consecutive level on the scale form a continuum.

A rubric and its performance indicators should direct you and your students towards your goals and away from the self-limiting question "How many can you miss and still get an A?" Like athletes who continually strive for better performances rather than "good enough," students should always see the possibility to excel. When you take into account the total performance (processes, answers, justifications, extension, and so on), it is always possible to "go beyond."

Deciding on Performance Indicators

It may be difficult to predict what performances at different levels of your rubric will, or should, look like. Much depends on your experience with children at that grade level, your past experiences with students working on the same task, and your insights about the task itself and the ideas that it embodies or that children may use as they work on it.

If possible, it is good to write out indicators of "proficient" or "on target" performances before you use the task in class. This is an excellent self-check to ensure that the task is likely to accomplish its original purpose. Think about your process goals as well as your content goals. Think about how children are likely to approach the activity. Remember, *pre-*

Table 5.2 Problem-Solving Rubric

The student:

	Level 1	Level 2	Level 3	Level 4
Understanding the Problem	• requires teacher assistance to understand the problem	• shows partial understanding of the problem, needs teacher assistance to clarify	• shows complete understanding of the problem	• shows complete understanding of the problem and has insights beyond the problem
Formulating a Plan	• needs assistance to choose an appropriate strategy • applies a strategy such as Guess and Check in a random fashion	• shows evidence of plans and use of a strategy, which may or may not be applied effectively	• independently chooses and applies appropriate strategies, and applies them effectively	• develops sophisticated strategies and applies them within an effective plan
Solving the Problem	• gives incorrect solution even with direction • makes major mathematical errors	• makes a minor mathematical error leading to a wrong answer or incomplete solution	• independently provides a correct and complete solution	• provides a correct and complete solution • may show more than one way to solve the problem
Looking Back	• requires prompting and assistance to determine the reasonableness of a solution	• judges the reasonableness of a solution when directed or encouraged to do so	• independently judges the reasonableness of a solution and verifies the answer	• continually monitors the reasonableness of the selected strategies and the progress towards a solution • considers variations and extensions of the problem
Communicating the Solution	• explains reasoning in a disorganized fashion that is difficult to follow	• gives an answer and begins to elaborate upon explanations with teacher assistance	• independently explains reasoning in a well-organized fashion with justifications	• explains reasoning with clarity, coherence and insight

Source: Ontario Association for Mathematics Education (1998). *Linking Assessment and Instruction in Mathematics: Junior Years* (Revised Edition). London, ON: Author, p. 34. Reproduced with permission.

dict; don't hope. Consider different materials that might be used, different ways to describe the results, and ways the product might be explained or the answer justified.

Remember that rubrics are applied to performance on a single task, even though the task may have multiple components. If you find yourself writing performance indicators in terms of number of correct responses, you are most likely looking at drill exercises and not tasks for which a rubric is appropriate.

If you are clear in your mind what performance that meets your goals looks like, then you will easily recognize performance that goes beyond, and that which is marginal.

Unexpected methods and solutions happen. Don't box students into demonstrating their understanding only as you thought or hoped they would when there is evidence that they are accomplishing your objectives in different ways.

Student Involvement with Rubrics

When mathematics consisted primarily of arithmetic, students knew that correct computation was the goal—the only goal. Today, not only is the curriculum significantly broader than computation, but the focus is on *doing mathematics* and all that it entails. Students need information about what doing good mathematics looks like, and they need to know what your expectations are for acceptable and exceptional performance. This is part of the Openness standard for assessment.

At the beginning of the year, discuss your general rubric with the class. Post it prominently. Many teachers use the same rubric for all subjects; others prefer to use a special rubric for mathematics. In your discussion, let students know that as they do activities and solve problems in class, you will look at their work, listen to their explanations, and provide them with feedback in terms of the rubric, rather than as a letter grade or a percentage.

When students start to understand what the rubric really means, they begin to discuss performance on tasks in terms of the general rubric. You might have students rate their own work according to the general rubric and explain their reasons for the rating. Older students can do this in written form, and you can respond in writing. For all students, you can have class discussions about a task that has been done and what might constitute good and exceptional performance.

More Examples of Rubrics

The four-point scale in Table 5.2 is an example of a *holistic scale,* a single scale used to rate a complete task as a whole while possibly covering many subtopics and agendas. One rating on the scale summarizes the full performance. A single grade on a report card is also a holistic rating.

Suppose that you wanted to provide feedback to students concerning one or more aspects of their work. You may be interested in separating out one or more of the following: procedural skill, conceptual understanding, problem-solving processes, communication skills, or reasoning. It is never reasonable to rate any given task for every one of these features, but you may want to focus on two or three. It is possible to add several dimensions to your scale or rubric. A scale that rates a performance separately on each of two or more traits is known as an *analytic scale.*

The analytic scale in Figure 5.3 focuses on different aspects of students' problem-solving skills. For the most part, the scale is used to rate written performance on a problem-solving task. Unlike the holistic scoring scale in Table 5.2, performance is rated separately on each of the traits. An interesting feature of the scale is the differential weighting used. On this scale, a score of 3, 6, 3 would mean something quite different from a score of 6, 6, 0, although both scores total 12 points. The point total becomes a holistic rating based on an analytic process.

Analytic Scoring Scale

Understanding the Problem	0 – Complete misunderstanding of the problem
	3 – Part of the problem misunderstood or misinterpreted
	6 – Complete understanding of the problem
Planning a Solution	0 – No attempt, or totally inappropriate plan
	3 – Partially correct plan based on correct interpretation of part of the problem
	6 – Plan could lead to a correct solution if implemented properly
Getting an Answer	0 – No answer, or wrong answer based on an inappropriate plan
	1 – Copying error, computational error, or partial answer for a problem with multiple answers
	2 – Incorrect answer although this answer follows logically from an incorrect plan
	3 – Correct answer and correct label for the answer

FIGURE 5.3 An analytic scale for problem solving with differential weightings.

Source: Adapted from *How to Evaluate Progress in Problem Solving,* by R.I. Charles, F.K. Lester Jr., & P. O'Daffer, 1987, Reston, VA: National Council of Teachers of Mathematics, as presented in "Cooperative Problem Solving: But What about Grades?" by D.L. Kroll, J.O. Masingila, & S.T. Mau, 1992, *Arithmetic Teacher 39*(6), p. 18. Reprinted by permission of the National Council of Teachers of Mathematics.

Using Observation in Assessment

All teachers learn useful bits of information about their students every day. When the three-part lesson format suggested in Chapter 4 is used, the flow of data increases dramatically, especially in the development and follow-up portions of lessons. If you have a systematic plan for gathering this information while observing and listening to students, at least two very valuable things occur. First, you will likely gather a lot more information. Suddenly, important information that may have gone unnoticed is visible. Second, observation data gathered systematically can be added to other data and used in planning lessons, providing feedback to students, conducting parent conferences, and determining grades.

Observation can provide information about students' attitudes toward mathematics, their feelings about themselves as learners, their preferred learning styles, their areas of interest, work habits, and social development, and their ability to use mathematical language and concepts (*Manitoba Curriculum Framework of Outcomes and Grade 3 Standards, 1995*). Depending on what information you may be trying to gather, a single observation scheme may may take from several days to two weeks to implement. Long-term goals can be observed over a full marking period. Shorter periods of observation will focus on a particular cluster of concepts or skills. Over longer periods, you can note growth in various aspects of mathematical power, such as particular problem-solving skills or communication skills. To use observation effectively as a means of gathering assessment data from performance tasks, you should take seriously the following maxim: *Do not attempt to observe every student in a single class period.*

No single format for recording observation will serve all purposes. Formats and methods of gathering observation data will be influenced by your individual teaching style and habits. Further, observation methods will vary with the purposes for which they are used.

Anecdotal Notes

A simple system for recording observations is to write short notes either during or immediately after a lesson in a brief narrative style. One possibility is to have a card for each student. Some teachers keep the cards on a clipboard, with each taped at the top edge (see Figure 5.4). Each card can then be accessed quickly. Another option is to select cards for about five students a day, focusing your observations on those five. On another day, different students are selected. The students selected may be members of one or two cooperative groups. An alternative to cards is the use of large peel-off file labels with student names that can be preprinted on your computer. The labelled notes are then moved to a more permanent notebook, which has a page for each student.

An Observation Rubric

Another possibility is to use your three- or four-point general rubric on a reusable form as in Figure 5.5. Include space for content-specific descriptors and another space to jot down names of students. A quick note or comment may be amended to a name when appropriate. This method is especially useful for planning purposes.

FIGURE 5.4 Cards for observation notes can be taped to a clipboard or folder for quick access.

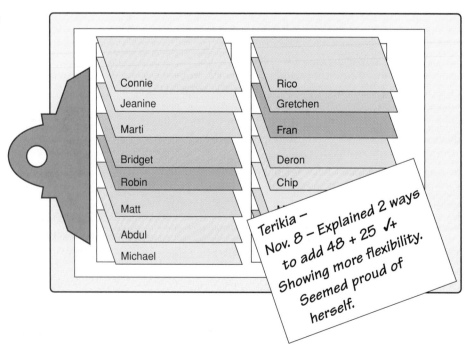

Making Whole Given Fraction Part	(3/17)
Super Clear understanding. Communicates concept in multiple representations. Shows evidence of using idea without prompting. *Fraction whole made from part in rods and in sets. Explains easily.*	Sally ✓ Latania ✓+ Greg Zal
On Target Understands or is developing well. Uses designated models. *Can make whole in either rod or set format (note). Hesitant. Needs prompt to get unit fraction.*	Lavant Tanisha Julie Lee George J.B. Maria John H.
Not Yet Some confusion or misunderstands. Only models idea with help. *Needs help to do activity. No confidence.*	John S. Mary

FIGURE 5.5 Record names in a rubric during an activity or for a single topic over several days.

Checklists or Forms for Individuals

To cut down on writing and to help focus your attention, a small form with several specific processes or content areas of interest can be devised and duplicated for each student (see Figure 5.6). Some teachers have found methods of printing these on their computer, perhaps on adhesive labels. Once a computer format is worked out, it is easy to change the items on the checklist without retyping all the student names. Regardless of the checklist form, a place for comments should be included.

Checklists for Full Classes

Another format involves listing all students in a class on a single page, or not more than three pages (see Figure 5.7). Across the top of the page are specific things for which to look. Pluses and minuses, checks, or codes corresponding to your general rubric can be entered in the grid. A space left for comments is useful. A full-class checklist is more likely to be used for long-term objectives. Topics that might be appropriate for this format include problem-solving processes, communication skills, and such skills as basic facts or estimation. Dating entries or noting specific activities you observed is also helpful.

NAME: *Sharon V.* FRACTIONS	NOT YET	OK	SUPER	COMMENTS
Understands numerator/denominator		✓		
Area models		✓		
Set models	✓			
Uses fractions in real contexts	✓			
Estimates fraction quantities		✓		*getting better*
PROBLEM SOLVING				
Understands problem before beginning work		✓		*this is good*
Is willing to take risks	✓			*problem area*
Justifies results				

FIGURE 5.6 A focused checklist and rubric can be printed for each student with the help of a computer.

Topic: Mental Computation + of 2 — dig. nos. Names	Not Yet Can't do mentally	On Target Has at least one strategy	Wow! Uses different methods with different numbers	Comments
Lalie		✓ 3-18 -21		
Gideon	✓ 3-20			Needs place value help
Amara			3-12 ✓+	Super
Lakeshia		✓		Good
George		✓		
Pam	✓			Close — getting a tens first idea
Maria			✓ 3-24	Finally!

FIGURE 5.7 A full-class observation checklist can be used for longer-term objectives or for several days to cover a short-term objective.

Journals and Writing

Having students write in mathematics is a natural and very important way to help them reflect on what they are learning. Some teachers have students write explanations and justifications for every problem or task. Writing as a form of communication is a major objective for mathematics instruction. Though many children have difficulty writing in mathematics initially, persistence pays off.

Writing has some real advantages over oral communication. Written expression is usually preceded by time spent organizing one's thoughts, whereas oral responses are immediate and irretrievable. Writing can be revised or edited by scratching out and writing over. It can include pictures, graphs, and symbols—powerful communication tools that are not available orally. Finally, written expression can be organized so that it is a private communication between teacher and student. In this way students can learn to put trust in your respect for what they write. You can develop trust through your thoughtful, helpful responses and respect for students' privacy.

Journals

Writing can of course be done on a single sheet of paper and turned in separately, but the use of a journal has real value. A journal may take the form of a composition booklet, or folded writing paper stapled within a construction-paper cover for K–1 children. Binders and spiral notebooks are other options, but teachers find these bulky, and students are more likely to remove unwanted pages.

Journals are a way to make written communication a regular part of doing mathematics. Journals help you

abandon the mistaken, counterproductive myth "If they write it, I must grade it." Journals offer students an opportunity to respond, practise, record, gain awareness of themselves as writers, make observations and predictions, collect information, and share with others (Stiles, 1992). They also are a place for students to write about such things as:

- Their conceptual understandings and problem solving, including descriptions of ideas, solutions, and justifications of problems, graphs, charts, and observations
- Their questions concerning the current topic, an idea that they may need help with, or an area they don't quite understand
- Their feelings about aspects of mathematics, their confidence in their understanding, or their fears of being wrong

Even if you have students write in their journals nearly every day, be sure that these journals are special places for writing about mathematics. Drill and practice, for example, should not be done in a journal. Lengthy projects done over several days should be kept separate from journals and given a special presentation. A performance task you plan to use primarily for evaluation purposes should probably not be in a journal. But the work for many of your performance tasks can and should go in the journal as part of doing mathematics. In this way, you communicate that the work is important and you do want to see it, but you are not going to grade it.

Journals are vehicles for communication, not evaluation. To grade journal writing defeats its purpose as a way to learn about students' ideas and to provide them with valuable feedback and direction. Graded journals communicate that there is a specific "right" response you are seeking, and that would change the flavour of the communication. However, it is essential that you read and respond to journal writing. One form of response that you might use in a journal for a performance task is the classroom's general rubric along with a helpful comment. It is another way to distinguish between rubrics and grades and still provide feedback.

On a regular basis, it is manageable to read and respond to about five journals a night. Following an especially interesting lesson, you might want to read the journal entry of every student in the class. Allow students to flag entries for which they want your special attention or response. If you do not read and respond to journals, students will quickly come to regard them as busywork and conclude that you do not value their efforts. Teachers whose students have learned to communicate honestly through their journals find them a key element in their assessment program, prized above all other sources of information for their usefulness in improving learning and instruction.

Writing Prompts and Ideas

Students should always have a clear, well-defined purpose for writing in their journals. They need to know exactly what to write about and who the audience is (you, an imaginary friend, a student in a lower grade, an adult, a Martian). They should also be given a definite time frame within which to write. Journal writing that is completely open-ended, without goal or purpose, will be a waste of time. Here are some suggestions for prompts to get you thinking; the possibilities are endless.

Concepts and Problem Solving

- "I think the answer is... I think this because..." (The journal can be used to solve and explain any problem. Always be sure to include the problem. Some teachers duplicate the problem and have students tape it into the journal to save time and effort.)
- Write an explanation for other students (or for students in a lower grade) of why 4×7 is the same as 7×4 and why this works for 6×49 and 49×6.
- Draw four different quadrilaterals that are alike in some way. Tell why they are alike. Draw one that is different. Tell why it is different.
- Explain to a student in grade X (or who was absent today) what you learned about decimals today.
- Write about the work we did today. What was easy? What was hard? What do you still have questions about?
- If you got stuck today in solving a problem, where did you get stuck? Why do you think you had trouble there? If you did not get stuck, what idea helped you solve the problem?
- After you got the answer to today's problem, what did you do that convinced you your answer was correct? How sure are you that you got the correct answer?
- How can addition help you complete subtraction facts like $12 - 4$ and $15 - 6$?
- Write a story problem that goes with this picture (this graph, this diagram, this equation).

Affective Ideas

- "What I like most (or least) about mathematics is..."
- Write a mathematics autobiography. Tell about your experiences in mathematics outside of school and how you feel about the subject.
- "Mathematics is like a... because..."
- Write to an imaginary friend who is the same age as you, telling how you feel about what we did in mathematics this week.

Journals for Early Learners

If you are interested in working with K–1 children, these writing suggestions may seem discouraging, because it is difficult for pre-writers and beginning writers to express ideas like these. There are specific techniques for journals in kindergarten and grade one that have been used successfully.

The Giant Journal

To begin the development of the writing-in-mathematics process, one kindergarten teacher uses a language experience approach. After an activity, she writes the heading "Giant Journal" and a topic or prompt on a large flip chart. Students respond to the prompt, and she writes their ideas, adding the contributor's name and even drawings when appropriate, as in Figure 5.8.

Drawings and Early Writing

All students can draw pictures of some sort to describe what they have done. Dots can represent counters or blocks. Shapes and special figures can be cut out from duplicated sheets and pasted onto the journal page.

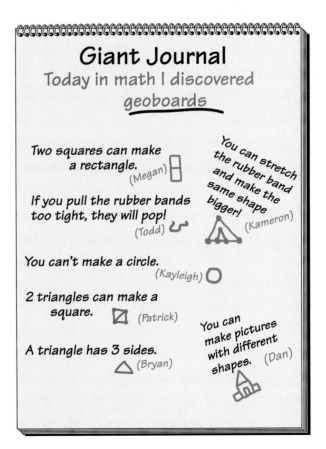

FIGURE 5.8 A journal in kindergarten may be a class product on a flip chart.

It is important for the "writing" to be a record of something the student has just done and with which he is comfortable. Do not be concerned about invented spellings to communicate ideas. But do have the students read their papers to you. Figure 5.9 shows problems solved in grades 1 and 2.

Brainstorming

Young children have difficulty translating what they say and think into written form. One way to help is to use discussion time to help children think about their journal entries. As students contribute their ideas, record them on the board. For kindergarten and grade one, use very simple abbreviated versions of what they say. For children in grades 2 and 3, you may limit your recording to key phrases and special words. In this manner, the ideas that have been generated are recorded for students to incorporate into their own writing. When a student says, "I don't know what to write," have him tell you about his task or idea. Then have him write what he has just told you.

Grade 1
Read the problem. Think and use "stuff" to help you solve it.

There were 7 owls.
They found some mice in the woods to eat. Each owl got 5 mice.
How many mice did they find? How do you know?
Use pictures and words to show how you solved the problem.

Grade 2
The farmer saw five cows and four chickens. How many legs and tails in all did he see?

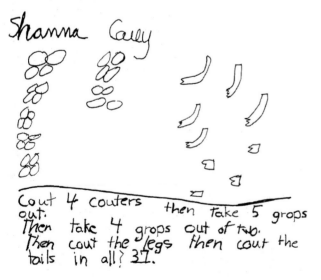

FIGURE 5.9 **Journal entries of early-grades children.**

Student Self-Assessment and Reflection

Stenmark (1989) notes that "the capability and willingness to assess their own progress and learning is one of the greatest gifts students can develop.... Mathematical power comes with knowing how much we know and what to do to learn more" (p. 26).

In a self-assessment, students may tell you

- how well they think they understand a piece of content
- what they believe or how they feel about some aspect of mathematics, perhaps what you are covering right now
- how well they perceive they are working in class or in their group

It is important to see that this is not your measure of their learning, disposition, or behaviour but rather a record of how *they perceive* these things.

In each of these three possible areas for student self-assessment (content, disposition, and behaviour), there is potential for interesting and useful input into your instructional program. What are the implications when a student feels she knows content better than (or not as well as) she actually does? How do you react to positive attitudes from a poorly performing student or negative attitudes from a generally strong student? How can you use students' assessment of their group behaviours as a tool for improving group behaviour? These and similar questions are aimed at getting you to think about why you might want to use periodic self-assessments in your class. It is important to consider how you want the assessment to help you as a teacher before you begin collecting the data. Tell your students why you are having them do this activity. Encourage them to be honest and candid. Though it may seem like fun to collect class information early in the year on a topic such as "why I like mathematics," do not assign a self-assessment activity just to make yourself feel good about your students.

You can gather self-assessment data in several ways. A common method is to use some form of a questionnaire to which students respond. These can have open-ended questions, response choices (e.g., *seldom, sometimes, often; disagree, don't care, agree*), mind maps, drawings, and so on. Many such instruments appear in the literature, and many textbook publishers provide examples. Whenever you use a form or questionnaire that someone else has devised, be certain that it serves the purpose you intend. Often these forms are too long or include questions in which you have little interest. Modify them to suit your purposes. The fact that a form was professionally prepared or accompanies your text does not necessarily make it appropriate or useful to you.

An open-ended writing prompt such as was suggested for journals is one method of getting self-assessment data:

- How well do you think you understand the work on fractions we have been doing the last few days? If there is something that is causing you difficulty with fractions, please tell me what it is.
- Write one thing you liked and one thing you did not like about math class today (or this week).
- How well do you think you have followed the rules about helping others in your group? About asking for ideas from others? About keeping the group on task?

These questions indicate how an open-ended writing prompt can be directed at any of the three areas of self-assessment. You may find that a simple prompt can become familiar to students if you use it on a regular basis. For example, midway through a unit, prompt students to tell you what elements of the material they feel they know and do not know. As students learn that you will react in some way that is helpful to them, they will be more apt to provide you with candid, useful information.

Attitude Inventories

Students may find it difficult to write about attitudes and beliefs. An inventory where they can respond "yes," "maybe," or "no" to a series of statements is another approach. Encourage students to comment further on an item if they wish. Here are some items you could use to build such an inventory:

- I feel sure of myself when I get an answer to a problem.
- I sometimes just put down anything so I can get it over with.
- I like to work on really hard math problems.
- Math class makes me feel nervous.
- If I get stuck, I usually just quit or go to another problem.
- I am not as good in math as most of the other students in this class.
- Mathematics is my favourite subject.
- I do not like to work at problems that are hard to understand.
- Memorizing rules is the only way I know to learn mathematics.
- I will work a long time at a problem until I think I've solved it.

Another technique is to ask students to write a sentence at the end of any work they do in mathematics class saying how that activity made them feel. Young children can draw a face on each page to tell you about their feelings.

Frequency of Self-Assessments

How often should self-assessment data be gathered? The answer varies with the type of assessment and the purpose. You should always have a clear purpose for asking students for information, and that purpose should be tied directly to helping students learn. There should never be any grades attached to affective assessments, nor should students be asked to spend time and effort if the information is not serving a real purpose.

Finding out about student attitudes, or likes and dislikes, can help you get to know your students early in a new year. Periodic follow-up assessments throughout the year can help you gauge how well you are connecting with your students. Once per grading period is probably often enough. Discuss the results with your students, or find other ways to let them know you value their thoughtful responses. Do not collect affective data simply to make yourself feel good.

Some teachers have students rate every written performance as "easy," "OK," or "difficult." Lack of confidence suggests a potential problem. Statements made in class will also need to be evaluated. In most instances, you will want to give students feedback individually. If there is a consensus in the class, you might let students know that you are ready to "raise the bar" or, alternatively, to spend more time on an area of discomfort.

Self-evaluation of group work should also be conducted periodically. As discussed in Chapter 21, cooperative group behaviour needs to be an ongoing objective. As you focus on various specific group behaviours, group self-assessment may be in order.

Tests

Tests will always be a part of assessment and evaluation, no matter how adept we become at blending assessment with instruction. But tests need not be a collection of low-level skill exercises. Although simple tests of computational skills may have a role in your classroom, their use should be limited. Like all other forms of assessment, tests should reflect the goals of your instruction. Tests can be designed to find out what concepts students have acquired and how ideas are connected. Tests of procedural knowledge should challenge students to go beyond just knowing how to perform an algorithm. They should allow and oblige students to demonstrate a conceptual basis for the process. The examples that follow illustrate these ideas.

1. Write a multiplication problem that has an answer between the answers to these two problems:

$$
\begin{array}{cc}
49 & 45 \\
\times 25 & \times 30 \\
\end{array}
$$

2. a. In this division exercise, what number tells how many tens were shared among the 6 sets?
    b. Instead of writing the remainder as "R 2," Elaine writes "$\frac{1}{3}$". Explain the difference between these two ways of handling the leftover part.

$$
\begin{array}{cc}
49\,R2 & 49\frac{1}{3} \\
6\overline{)296} & 6\overline{)296} \\
\end{array}
$$

3. On the grid, draw two figures with the same area but different perimeters. List the area and perimeter of each.
4. For each subtraction fact, write an addition fact that helps you think of the answer to the subtraction.

$$
\begin{array}{cccc}
12 & 9 & 9 & 14 \\
-3 & +3 & -4 & -7 \\
\hline
9 & 12 & & \\
\end{array}
$$

5. Draw pictures of arrows to show why $^-3 + {}^-4$ is the same as $^-3 - {}^+4$.

Much more information than simply the number of correct or incorrect answers can be gleaned from a well-constructed test. Here are some things to think about when constructing a test:

1. *Permit calculators all the time.* Except for tests of computational skills, the calculator allows students to focus on what you really want to test. It also communicates a positive attitude about calculator use to your students.
2. *Use manipulatives and drawings.* Students can use appropriate models to work on test questions especially when those same models have been used to develop concepts. (Note the use of drawings in example 5 above.) Simple drawings can be used to represent counters, base-ten pieces, fraction pieces, and the like (see Figure 5.10). Be sure to provide examples in class of how to draw the models before you ask students to draw them on a test.
3. Include opportunities for explanations.
4. *Assess affective factors on the test.* One idea is to have students rate their personal confidence level on each question as A (high), B (moderate), or C (low).

Another idea is to have students draw a face showing how they feel about the question or the test in general. Ask students to complete a sentence that begins "I liked this test because..." or "I did not like this test because..."

5. *Avoid "pre-answered" tests.* These are tests where questions have only one correct answer, whether it is a calculation, a multiple-choice, or a fill-in-the-blank. Tests of this type tend to fragment what children have learned and hide most of what they know. Rather, construct tests that allow students the opportunity to show what they know.

Dealing with Standardized Testing

Standardized tests are firmly in place in school systems throughout Canada. These external tests (originating from outside the classroom) are usually referred to as standardized because the same tests are given to large numbers of students. These tests are a legitimate concern for teachers, who feel that they are often evaluated in terms of their students' performance. It is important to be informed about

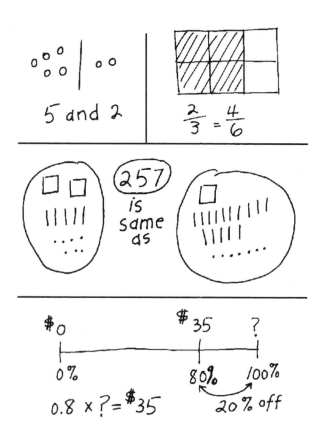

FIGURE 5.10 Students can use drawings to illustrate concepts on tests.

the nature of these high-stakes tests and how you can help your students perform well on them.

Standardized Curriculum-Based Testing

As noted in Chapter 1, curriculum-based provincial and territorial tests are designed to provide information regarding the achievement of individual students in the different school districts or boards of a province or territory. While assessment practices may differ somewhat among provinces, testing is designed to assess students' knowledge of curriculum expectations and provide feedback to teachers, parents, students, and the general public. In some provinces, such as Ontario and Alberta, testing is carried out at key transitional stages (grades 3 and 6) in elementary school. In others, such as Saskatchewan, province-wide testing is carried out biannually. In Nova Scotia testing is done every two years in grades 5 and 8. Results of curriculum-based testing play an important role in school-board or -district policy and instructional decision-making. They form the basis of school improvement plans. They are used to develop plans for identifying students' individual needs and developing intervention strategies for improvement, amongst a variety of other purposes.

Teachers and Standardized Testing

The consequences of low scores on curriculum-based tests are almost certainly going to cause teachers to be anxious and concerned. Regardless of the province or the territory, the tests, or the consequences of the tests, the best advice is to teach to the big ideas in the mathematics curriculum. Students who have a strong, relational understanding of the main ideas in mathematics and who have good mathematics process skills will always do well on standardized tests. When teachers try to teach to the test or gear their teaching specifically to a list of expectations, they tend to leave their students with an array of isolated bits of information. The dots will simply not be well connected. This does not mean you ignore these lists; rather, you identify broad concepts on which specific expectations can be built. To obsess over tests and ignore big ideas and conceptual understanding will almost certainly be counterproductive.

Improving Performance on High-Stakes Tests

There is no doubt that your students can benefit from a bit of test "savvy" and test preparation. Here are some strategies you can use to help them improve performance:

- *Ensure they have an opportunity to learn the content.* Plan your year so that you teach the big ideas for most or all of the curriculum objectives before the test is given.

- *Provide ongoing review and practice.* For skills such as computation, mental computation, estimation, use of formulas, and other procedural ideas, short, regularly spaced reviews are much more effective than a massive practice effort the week before the test.
- *Provide experience with different question formats.* If you have information about the different question formats that the standardized tests employ, be sure to use these regularly (not exclusively) in class.
- *Teach test-taking strategies.* Students are often not very efficient test takers, so helping them learn to take tests can have some benefits. Here are some teachable strategies:

   Read questions carefully. Practise identifying what the questions are asking, and what information they give that can be used to get the answers.

   Estimate the answer before spending time with computation. On multiple-choice test items, estimation and good number sense are often all that is needed to select the correct answer.

   Eliminate unreasonable choices. Look at the available options. Does a choice make sense? Can looking at the ones digit eliminate answers?

   Work backward from an answer.

Caution! Test-taking strategies require good concepts, skills, and number sense. Without good understanding, test strategies will do little good. Invest most of your efforts teaching mathematics rather than test skills.

Portfolios in the Assessment Plan

A *portfolio* is a systematic collection of a variety of student work, designed to provide a holistic view of mathematical learning that may not be evident from examination of any single entry. It is an excellent form of communication between student and teacher, student and parent, and parent and teacher. A portfolio should demonstrate and help students reflect on their mathematical power and what that really means. It may also be used to focus on progress and growth, understandings, or problem-solving processes. Clarifying your goals and identifying your reasons for portfolio assessment will help to determine the type of portfolio that will best suit your needs (Rolheiser, Bower, & Stevahn, 2000).

Portfolio Content Suggestions

A portfolio should be more than a folder of student papers. It should tell a story that goes beyond the individual entries. Both student and teacher input should have an influence on what material goes into a portfolio. These materials, selected over time, may include assignments, projects, reports, student writing, worksheets from texts or other sources, comments by teachers, observations from interviews, and self-evaluations of group and individual efforts.

Your own portfolio program should be carried out to serve the particular goals you have in mind and to communicate achievement of these goals to students and parents. These plans and goals should be discussed with your students from the outset and revisited periodically, so that the students are fully involved in the process.

Table 5.3 is from a superb NCTM booklet, *Mathematics Assessment: Myths, Models, Good Questions, and Practical Suggestions* (Stenmark, 1991). It provides ideas for the types of entries that could be included to correspond to different goals. Any given portfolio will include only a sampling of these ideas and may contain only eight to ten entries.

Teachers who have used portfolios have noted that students begin to take more pride in their work and make extra efforts. Portfolios can add a sense of importance to daily work.

Portfolio Management

At first, the idea of keeping a portfolio for every child is a bit daunting. Included in this section are some ideas found in Rolheiser, Bower, & Stevahn (2000) and Stenmark (1991).

A Working Portfolio

Set up folders for each student, and keep them where students can easily get to them. The constraints and realities of your particular setting will influence your decision regarding storage. These folders serve as working portfolios and will hold students' potential portfolio entries. Encourage students to revise or correct work on special projects, but always keep the original versions to be able to track progress. The working portfolio is also the place where your observation notes or other items that originate with you can be kept. When groups turn in reports or projects, make copies for each group member's work portfolio.

Assembling the Portfolio

At the end of the unit or grading period, or whenever it is time to assemble the final portfolio, students select and clip together the items from the working portfolio that they want to be included in their final portfolio. Have a class discussion about how to select items and what the items should show. Remember, "the learner needs to take primary responsibility for the selection process" (Rolheiser, Bower, & Stevahn, 2000, p. 25). Encourage

children to pick things that tell about themselves in mathematics: their strengths, weaknesses, points of pride, places they need help, and progress made over the period. Students should write a few sentences explaining each selection and why it was included. You should designate two or three items as "must include," usually the same ones for the whole class.

Students then review their portfolios and write a cover letter that discusses the content as a whole and gives their personal perspective on such things as problem-solving skills, confidence, attitudes, and growth in understanding, depending on the goals you and your class have established. This portfolio is now ready for evaluation and subsequent sharing with parents.

Portfolio Evaluation

You will probably have made comments on most or all of the materials as they were completed. Now you are looking at the portfolio as a whole. It is very important to provide feedback. It is an excellent way to encourage students, and to build confidence and communicate perspective about mathematics. Your comments should be made with this in mind. If you plan to include the portfolio in your grading scheme, a rubric will be useful, as it will help all parties (students, teacher, peers, and parents) by clarifying criteria, expectations, and standards of performance.

Diagnostic Interviews

An interview is simply a one-on-one discussion with a child to help you see how she is thinking about a particular subject, the processes she uses in solving problems, or the attitudes and beliefs she may have. A structured interview may be as short as five to ten minutes. More open-ended or exploratory interviews may last as long as half an hour.

Reasons to Consider an Interview

There are several reasons why it may occasionally be well worth the time and effort to conduct interviews. The most obvious reason is that you need more information concerning a particular child and how he or she is constructing concepts or using a procedure. You might want to conduct at least one interview a week, changing the topic and the children you interview. Remediation will almost always be more successful if you can pinpoint *why* a student is having difficulty before you try to fix the problem.

A second reason for conducting an interview is to get information either to plan or to assess the effectiveness of your instruction. For example, are you sure that your students have a good understanding of equivalent fractions, or are they just doing the exercises in a rote manner

Table 5.3 Goals and Suggested Portfolio Contents

Goal	Evidence, Examples, and Comments
Positive mathematical disposition Motivation Curiosity Perseverance Risk taking Flexibility Self-responsibility Self-confidence	• Journal entries depicting enthusiasm for mathematics • Photographs of large, colourful mathematics graphics by students • Problem solution with an added paragraph beginning with "On the other hand..." or "What if..." • Log of a week's or month's work showing a single important problem or investigation worked on over a period of time • Homework paper with a description of several approaches to a problem • Student-written planning calendar outlining work to be done • Mathematics autobiography
Growth in mathematical understanding Concept development Problem-solving skills Communication skills Construction of mathematics Reflection on approaches and solutions to problems or tasks	• Similar items collected at regular intervals from the beginning of the year • Written explanation of why an algorithm works • Diagram, table, or similar organized representation that clarifies a problem situation • Solution that defines assumptions, includes counterexamples • Photographs of a mathematics project • Journal entries delineating solution justifications and variations in strategies • Student identification of papers that need more work, with reasons • A paper that starts with "Today in math class I learned..." • Inclusion of drafts as well as finished work
Mathematical reasoning in a variety of mathematical topics Estimation, number sense, number operations, and computation Measurement, geometry, and spatial sense Statistics and probability Fractions and decimals Patterns and relationships	• Report on an investigation (e.g., number patterns in sums of sequential numbers) • Student-planned statistical survey, with accompanying graphic designs • Written report of a probability experiment and accompanying theoretical design • Response to an open-ended question regarding measurement of geometric shapes • Student explanation of what $\frac{1}{2}$ minus $\frac{1}{3}$ means • Diagram examples of multiplication using a number line, a rectangular array, and repeated groups of physical objects • Annotated drawing illustrating the Pythagorean theorem • Representation of an area model solution for a statistical problem
Mathematical connections Connecting a mathematical idea to other mathematical topics, to other subject areas, and to real-world situations	• Papers that show authentic use of mathematics in other curricular areas such as science or social studies • Student reflections on how mathematics is meaningful as it is used in the adult world • Examples from nature of occurrences of Pascal's triangle number patterns • A report on the relationship among arithmetic, algebra, and geometry with demonstrative examples on a coordinate grid • Student-constructed table of equivalent fractions, decimal numbers, and percentages, with examples of where each type of number is used • Mathematical art project • Report about a historical figure or personal friend, acquaintance, or family member who contributed to mathematics
Group problem solving Development of skills in working with others Communication	• A task design or plan • Group paper that includes the names of the members of the group and the tasks each did • Group self-assessment sheet • Videotape or audiotape of group working on problems or making oral reports • Group-work report of trying a second or third strategy when the first one didn't work
Use of tools Integration of technology—use of calculators and computers and so on Use of manipulatives	• Computer-generated statistical analysis of a problem • Frequent mention of use of calculators on open-ended problems • Diagrams representing use of manipulative material
Teacher and parent involvement Communication between teacher and parent and between parent and student Parental understanding of educational objectives and values	• Consistency of program demonstrated by items from every grading period • Anecdotal report • Informal assessment sheet • Interview of student • Teacher- or parent-written comments • Assessment by teacher of student work • Student presentation of portfolio to parent during parent-teacher conference

Source: National Council of Teachers of Mathematics © 1991. In J. K. Stenmark (Ed.), *Mathematics Assessment.* Reprinted by permission.

according to rules? At the end of Chapter 9, a collection of tasks is suggested to get at students' understanding of place value. Conceptual tasks such as these might be used in interviews conducted at the beginning of a unit to see what ideas you need to work on with your students. They can also be used later in the unit or at the end to assess growth or retention of ideas.

A third reason is to learn more about the way children learn and think, which contributes to your growth as a teacher. In addition to increasing your knowledge of children, you will also grow in your ability to conduct good interviews.

Planning an Interview

There is no magic right way to plan or structure an interview. In fact, flexibility is a key ingredient. You should, however, have some overall game plan before you begin, and be prepared with key questions and materials. Begin an interview with questions that are easy or closest to what the child is likely to be able to do, usually some form of procedural exercise. For numeration or computation topics, you might, for example, begin with a pencil-and-paper task such as a computation, writing or comparing numerals, or a simple translation problem. When the opening task has been completed, ask the child to explain what was done. "How would you explain this to a grade 2 student (or your younger sister)?" "What does this (point to something on the paper) stand for?" "Tell me about why you did it that way." At this point, you may try a similar task but with a different feature; for example, after doing 372 − 54, try 403 − 37. The second problem has a zero in the tens place, a possible source of difficulty.

The next phase in the interview involves the use of models or drawings that the child can use to demonstrate understanding of the earlier procedural task. Computations can be done with base-ten materials, blocks or counters can be used, number lines explored, grid paper used for drawing, and so on. Be careful not to interject or teach. The temptation to do so is sometimes overwhelming. Watch and listen. Next, explore connections between what was done with models and what was done with pencil and paper. Many children will do the very same task and get two different answers. Does it matter to the child? How does she explain the discrepancy? Can she connect actions using models to what was written or explained earlier?

Alternative approaches for beginning an interview include making an estimate for the answer to a computation or a word problem, doing a computation mentally, or trying to predict the solution to a given task. Notice that an interview does not generally proceed in the same way as instruction does. In an interview, the conceptual explanations and discussions generally come after the proce-

dural activity. Your goal is not to use the interview to teach; rather, it is to determine where the child is in terms of her conceptual and procedural understanding.

Suggestions for Effective Interviews

The following suggestions have been adapted from excellent discussions on interviewing children by Labinowicz (1985, 1987), and Liedtke (1988):

■ *Be accepting and neutral as you listen to the child.* Smiles, frowns, or other body language can make the child think that the answer he or she gave is right or wrong. Develop neutral responses such as "Uh-huh," "I see," or even a silent nod of the head.

■ *Avoid cueing or leading the child.* "Are you sure about that?" "Now look again closely at what you just did." "Wait. Is that what you mean?" These responses will indicate to children that they have made some mistake and cause them to change their responses. Doing so can mask what they really think and understand. A similar form of leading is asking a series of easily answered questions that direct the student to a correct response. That is teaching, not interviewing.

■ *Wait silently.* Give the student plenty of time before you ask a different question or probe. After the child responds, wait again! This second wait time is even more important because it allows and encourages the child to elaborate on the initial thought and provides you with more information. Wait even when the response is correct. Waiting can also give you a bit more time to think about the direction you want the interview to take. Your wait time will almost never be as long as you imagine it is.

■ *Do not interrupt.* Let children's thoughts flow freely. Encourage children to use their own words and ways of writing things down. Interjecting questions or correcting language can be distracting to the child's thinking.

■ *Use imperatives rather than questions.* Say, "show me," "tell me," "do," or "try," rather than "Can you...?" or "Will you...?" In response to a question, the child can simply say no, leaving you in a vacuum.

■ *Avoid confirming a request for validation.* Students frequently follow answers or actions with "Is that right?" This query can easily be answered, whether the answer is right or wrong, with a neutral, "That's fine," or "You're doing OK."

Interviewing is not an easy thing to do well. Many teachers are timid about it and fail to take the time. But not much damage is possible, and the rewards of listening to children, both for you and your students, are so great that you really do not want to pass it up.

Grading

Myth: A grade is an average of a series of scores on tests and quizzes. The accuracy of the grade depends primarily on the accuracy of the computational technique used to calculate the final numeric grade.

Reality: A grade is a statistic that is used to communicate to others the achievement level that a student has attained in a particular area of study. The accuracy or validity of the grade is dependent on the information that is used in preparing the grade, the professional judgment of the teacher, and the alignment of the assessments with the true goals and objectives of the course.

Confronting the Myth

Most experienced teachers will tell you that they know a great deal about their students. They can identify what the students know, how they perform in different situations, their attitudes and beliefs, and their various levels of skill attainment. Good teachers have always been engaged in ongoing performance assessment, albeit informally and usually with no recording. However, even good teachers have relied on test scores to determine grades, essentially forcing themselves to ignore a wealth of information that would have reflected a more realistic picture of their children.

The myth of grading by statistical number crunching is so firmly ingrained in schooling at all levels that you may find it hard to abandon. If one thing is clear from the discussions in this chapter, it should be that it is quite possible to gather a wide variety of rich information about students' understanding, problem-solving processes, and attitudes and beliefs. To ignore all of this information in favour of a handful of numbers based on tests that usually focus on low-level skills is unfair to students, to parents, and to you as the teacher.

Grading Issues

For effective use of the assessment information gathered from problems, tasks, and other appropriate methods for assigning grades, some hard decisions are inevitable. Some are philosophical, some require school or district agreement about grades, and all oblige us to examine what we value and the objectives we communicate to students and parents.

Values

In contrast to the many myths of grading, one thing is undeniably true: *What gets graded is what gets valued.* When rubrics are used to provide feedback and to encourage a pursuit of excellence, they must also relate to grades.

However, "converting four out of five to 80 percent or three out of four to a grade of C can destroy the entire purpose of alternative assessment and the use of scoring rubrics" (Kulm, 1994, p. 99). Kulm explains that directly translating rubrics to grades focuses attention on grades and away from the purpose of every good problem-solving activity: to strive for an excellent performance. When papers are returned with less than top ratings, the purpose is to help students know what is necessary to achieve at a higher level. Early on, there should be opportunities to improve one's performance based on feedback. When a grade of 60 percent or a C– is returned, all the student knows is that he or she did poorly. If, for example, a student's ability to justify her own answers and solutions has improved, should she be penalized in the process of averaging of numbers by a weaker performance early in the marking period?

Grading must be based on the performance tasks and the other activities to which you assigned rubric ratings; otherwise, students will soon realize that these scores are not important. These ratings need not be added or averaged in any numerical manner. A grade at the end of a marking period should reflect a holistic view of where the student is at that time relative to your goals and your value system. That value system should be clearly reflected in your framework for rating tasks.

Alignment

The grades you assign should reflect your objectives for learning. A multi-dimensional reporting system is a big help. If you can assign several grades for mathematics and not one, reporting to parents will be more meaningful. Even if the school's report card does not permit multiple grades, you can devise a supplementary form with several ratings to represent different objectives. A place for comments will also be helpful. This form can then be shared with students periodically during a grading period and can easily accompany a report card.

If you are restricted to assigning a single grade for mathematics, you will need to decide what weight or value different factors will have in making up the grade. Procedural skills remain important but should be weighted in proportion to the goals of your value system. Student X may be fantastic at reasoning and truly love mathematics, yet may be weak in traditional skills. Student Y may be mediocre in problem solving but possess good communication skills. How much weight should you give to cooperation in groups, to written versus oral reports, to computational skills? There are no simple answers to these questions. However, they should be addressed at the beginning of the grading period and not the night you set out to assign grades.

You can always involve students and parents in a discussion of a multi-dimensional approach to determining a grade based on rubric ratings for different components of your program. Traditional test averaging has always used this approach. Not every test covers the same thing, and various scores (quizzes, homework, exams) are often assigned different weights. This subjective, "teacher-decision" approach can be used with rubric scores without computing numerical averages.

Reflections *on* Chapter 5

Writing to Learn

1. Describe the four purposes of assessment outlined in the *Assessment Standards*. How do these purposes relate to your work as a teacher?
2. What should we look for if we are trying to assess "mathematical power"?
3. In looking at procedural knowledge, what should be assessed in addition to skill proficiency? Why?
4. Describe the characteristics of a quality assessment program that would be integrated with a problem-based approach to instruction.
5. How can a learning task or problem be an assessment task? Why should these be the same thing?
6. Describe the essential features of a rubric. What are performance indicators? What is the difference between a rubric and a performance indicator? What is the difference between a holistic rubric and an analytic rubric?
7. How can students be involved in understanding and using rubrics to help with their learning?

For Discussion and Exploration

1. Examine a few chapter-end tests in various textbooks. How well do the tests reflect what is important in the chapter (e.g., concepts and understanding, mathematical power)?
2. Select any good performance task for a grade level in which you are interested. Try to answer the six questions on page 71, just above the examples of problems for assessment. If possible, get some other people to do the same for the same task. Compare your ideas.
3. Pick a topic and a grade level. Try to write three good test questions for that topic.
4. The pressures of mandated provincial testing cause teachers to take time out from their instructional routine and spend, in some cases, inordinate amounts of class time preparing students for these tests, rather than carrying on with their regular program. What is your view regarding this practice? What are the pros and cons?

Recommendations for Further Reading

Highly Recommended

Kulm, G. (1994). *Mathematics assessment: What works in the classroom.* San Francisco: Jossey-Bass.

Kulm has excellent credentials in the area of both mathematics and science assessment. This book provides perspective, detailed guidance, and models that can be copied for direct use in the classroom. This is one of the best books available on assessment in mathematics.

Lambdin, D.V., Kehle, P.E., & Preston, R.V. (Eds.). (1996). *Emphasis on assessment: Readings from NCTM's school-based journals.* Reston, VA: National Council of Teachers of Mathematics.

A collection of 30 articles on assessment taken from NCTM's various journals and organized in four categories: rationale for change, testing and grading, alternative assessment options, and evaluation of teacher effectiveness. At the end of the book are three annotated bibliographies—one for elementary and middle-grade teachers, a second for high school teachers, and a third from the *Journal for Research in Mathematics Education.*

Munby, H., Locke, C.L. (2000). Changing assessment practices in the classroom: A study of one teacher's challenge. *Alberta Journal of Educational Research, 46*(3), 267–279.

This article is well worth reading, as it considers the interrelatedness of assessment with other instructional practices. The research discussed reveals the importance of links between planning, instruction, and assessment, as Munby and Locke show how George's (the subject of this study) beliefs about teaching and learning constrained him from practising new methods of assessment.

Rolheiser, C., Bower, B., & Stevahn, L. (2000). *The Portfolio Organizer.* Alexandria, VA: Association for Supervision and Curriculum Development.

This book provides teachers with a flexible framework to guide decision-making for effective and efficient use of portfolios in the classroom. It is an excellent resource on portfolios as one form of performance assessment.

Stenmark, J.K. (Ed.). (1991). *Mathematics assessment: Myths, models, good questions, and practical suggestions.* Reston, VA: National Council of Teachers of Mathematics.

If you want a comprehensive look at new directions in assessment with examples, alternatives, ideas, and formats, this book is indispensable. Since its publication, it has been one of NCTM's most popular books. The author is associated with the EQUALS project and has written extensively on assessment. You'll find this an excellent resource.

Taylor, A.R.& Tubianosa, T.S. (2001). *Student assessment in Canada.* Kelowna, BC: Society for the Advancement of Excellence in Education.

This publication examines many important facets of student evaluation in Canada. It analyses and compares provincial and national assessment systems. The role of testing and measurement in teaching and learning, emerging assessment technologies, and online testing are explored. Recommendations for a balanced model of assessment designed to improve teaching and learning are also included.

Other Suggestions

Billstein, R. (1998). Assessment: The STEM model. *Mathematics Teaching in the Middle School, 3,* 282–286, 294–296.

Brown-Herbst, K. (1999). So math isn't just answers. *Mathematics Teaching in the Middle School, 4,* 448–455.

Burns, M. (1995). *Writing in math class.* Sausalito, CA: Math Solutions Publications.

Cai, J., Lane, S., & Jakabcsin, M.S. (1996). The role of open-ended tasks and holistic scoring rubrics: Assessing students' mathematical reasoning and communication. In P.C. Elliott (Ed.), *Communication in mathematics, K–12 and beyond* (pp. 137–145). Reston, VA: National Council of Teachers of Mathematics.

Cai, J., Magone, M.E., Wang, N., & Lane, S. (1996). Describing student performance qualitatively. *Mathematics Teaching in the Middle School, 1,* 828–835.

Cole, K.A. (1999). Walking around: Getting more from informal assessment. *Mathematics Teaching in the Middle School, 4,* 224–227.

Colgan, L.E. (2000). Testing the big ideas in mathematics. *Orbit, 30*(4), 54–57.

Earl, L., Katz, S. (2000). The paradox of classroom assessment. *Orbit, 30*(4) 8–10.

Flewelling, G. Lind, S., Sauer, R. (1999) *Mathematics assessment activities 3. Teacher's resource book.* Vancouver: Gage Educational Publishing Company. Note: Resource books in this series are available for the different elementary grades.

Helton, S.M. (1995). I thik the citanre will hoder lase: Journal keeping in mathematics class. *Teaching Children Mathematics, 1,* 336–340.

Horsman, H. *Learning together in multi-level classrooms.* (1997). Regina: Saskatchewan Instructional Development and Research Unit.

Huinker, D.M., & Laughlin, C. (1996). Talk your way into writing. In P.C. Elliott (Ed.), *Communication in mathematics, K–12 and beyond* (pp. 81–88). Reston, VA: National Council of Teachers of Mathematics.

Karp, K.S., & Huinker, D.M. (1997). Portfolios as agents of change. *Teaching Children Mathematics, 3,* 224–228.

Moon, J. (1997). *Developing judgment: Assessing children's work in mathematics.* Portsmouth, NH: Heinemann.

National Council of Teachers of Mathematics. (1995). *Assessment standards for school mathematics.* Reston, VA: Author.

Newman, V. (1994). *Math journals: Tools for authentic assessment.* San Leandro, CA: Watten/Poe Teaching Resource Center.

O'Brien, D.C. (1996). Math journals: First attempts in third grade. In D. Schifter (Ed.), *What's happening in math class? Reconstructing professional identities* (Vol. 2, pp. 146–157). New York: Teachers College Press.

Ontario Association for Mathematics Education. (1998). *Linking assessment and instruction in mathematics: Junior Years* (Revised Edition). London, ON: Author.

Peressini, D., & Bassett, J. (1996). Mathematical communication in students' responses to a performance-assessment task. In P.C. Elliott (Ed.), *Communication in mathematics, K–12 and beyond* (pp. 146–158). Reston, VA: National Council of Teachers of Mathematics.

Popham, W.J. (1999). Why standardized tests don't measure educational quality. *Educational Leadership, 56*(6), 8–15.

Reys, B.J., & Long, V.M. (1995). Teacher as architect of mathematical tasks. *Teaching Children Mathematics, 1,* 296–299.

Stiles, C. (1992). Journals as a tool for assessment. *Research Forum, 9,* 20–22.

Vincent, M.L., & Wilson, L. (1996). Informal assessment: A story from the classroom. *Mathematics Teacher, 89,* 248–250.

Zawojewski, J.S. (1996). Polishing a data task: Seeking better assessment. *Teaching Children Mathematics, 2,* 372–378.

Zazkis, R., & Hazzan, O. (1999). Interviewing in mathematics education research: Choosing the questions. *Journal of Mathematical Behavior, 17,* 429–439.

Development of Mathematical Concepts and Procedures

The K-8 mathematics curriculum encompasses a large number of concepts and procedures. It is not realistic to expect that teachers will become experts on every one of these ideas. For this reason, the foundational ideas of the first five chapters are most important. Each of the 15 chapters in this section provides specific instructional ideas that are built on those foundations. Moreover, each chapter serves as a source of ideas for nearly all topics covered from kindergarten to grade 8.

At any grade level, there are overarching mathematical ideas that tie together the endless list of objectives often mandated by provincial and territorial curricula. To address these expectations, it is often useful to focus on larger mathematical ideas of a unit or chapter. In this section, each chapter begins with a listing of "Big Ideas," which are the mathematical concepts that form an umbrella for the smaller ideas discussed in the chapter. This list can help you focus on the big ideas of a corresponding unit of study in the classroom. Numerous activities, along with ideas for incorporating children's literature, technology, and assessment, are built into every chapter in this section.

Chapter 6

Developing Early Number Concepts and Number Sense

Number is a complex and multi-faceted concept. A rich understanding of number, often referred to as a relational understanding, involves many different ideas, relationships, and skills. Experience suggests that these relationships do not develop automatically, and it is our job to provide children with a wide assortment of activities that will help them construct these many ideas of number.

BIG IDEAS

1. Counting tells how many things are in the set.
2. Numbers are linked to each other through a wide variety of relationships.
3. Numbers have different values when connected to real objects and measures: 5 elephants is a big amount, but 5 crayons is a small amount even though the quantity is the same; 12 minutes is not much more than 10 minutes, but it is a lot more than 30 seconds.

Early Number Sense

Howden (1989) described number sense as a "good intuition about numbers and their relationships. It develops gradually as a result of exploring numbers, visualizing them in a variety of contexts, and relating them in ways that are not limited by traditional algorithms" (p. 11). More than a decade later, this definition may still be the best. *Principles and Standards* calls for pre-K–2 students to understand numbers and to have ways of representing them and exploring relationships among them. As larger numbers, fractions, decimals, and percentages are added to students' repertoire of number ideas, they still need to continue to develop flexible thinking with numbers throughout their school years. It is also important that

number sense development begin in kindergarten, as it forms the foundation of number-related ideas that will be accumulated throughout students' school years.

In this chapter, we will focus on a small yet important piece of number sense: relationships for numbers up to about 20. The focus is on helping children construct a variety of important relationships with these numbers and on their connections to the real world. These are the relationships on which all further numerical thinking and number sense development will be built.

Number Development in Pre-K and Kindergarten

Parents help children count their fingers, toys, people at the table, and other small sets of objects. Questions like "Who has more?" or "Are there enough?" are part of the daily life of children as young as two or three. Considerable evidence indicates that these children have some understanding of the concepts of number and counting (Baroody, 1987; Fuson & Hall, 1983; Gelman & Gallistel, 1978; Gelman & Meck, 1986; Ginsburg, 1977).

In school, conceptual knowledge of numbers is developed alongside the related procedural skills of counting, number recognition, and number writing. Procedural skills become tools that children use to refine their understanding of number concepts.

The Relationships of More, Less, and Same

The concepts of "more," "less," and "same" are basic relationships contributing to the overall concept of number.

Children begin to develop these ideas before they start school. On entering kindergarten, a child can almost always choose the set that is *more* if presented with two sets that are obviously different in number. In fact, Baroody (1987) states, "A child unable to use 'more' in this intuitive manner is at considerable educational risk" (p. 29). It is important that classroom activities help children build on this basic notion and refine it.

Though the concept of less is logically related to the concept of more (selecting the set with more is the same as *not* selecting the set with less), the word *less* proves to be more difficult for children than *more*. A possible explanation is that children have many opportunities to use the word *more* but have limited exposure to the word *less*. To help children with the concept of less, frequently pair it with the word *more* and make a conscious effort to ask "Which is less?" questions as well as "Which is more?" questions. For example, suppose that your class has correctly selected the set that has more from two that are given. Immediately follow with the question "Which is less?" In this way, the less familiar idea can be connected with the one that is better-known.

For all three concepts (more, less, and same), children should construct sets using counters, and also make comparisons or choices between two given sets. The activities described here include both types. These activities should be conducted in a spirit of inquiry, followed whenever possible with requests for explanations. "Why do you think this set has less?"

ACTIVITY 6.1

Make Sets of More/Less/Same

At a workstation or table, provide about eight cards with sets of 4 to 12 objects, a set of small counters or blocks, and some word cards labelled "More," "Less," and "Same." Next to each card, have students make three collections of counters: a set that is more, one that is less, and one that is the same. The appropriate labels are placed on the sets (see Figure 6.1).

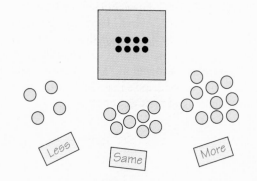

FIGURE 6.1 **Making sets that are more, less, and the same.**

In Activity 6.1, students create a set with counters; this activity gives them the opportunity to reflect on the sets and adjust them as they work. The next activity is done without counters. Although it addresses the same basic ideas, it provides a different problem situation.

ACTIVITY 6.2

Find the Same Amount

Give children a collection of cards with sets on them. Dot cards are one possibility (see the Blackline Masters at the back of this book). Have the children pick up any card in the collection and then find another card with the same number to form a pair. Children continue to find other pairs until all the cards have been played.

Activity 6.2 can be altered to have children find dot cards that are "less" or "more."

Watch how children do this task. Those children whose number ideas are completely tied to counting and nothing more will select cards at random and count each dot. Those who instead begin by selecting a card that appears to have about the same number of dots are at a significantly higher level of understanding. Also observe how the dots are counted. Are the counts made accurately? Is each counted only once? Another milestone for children occurs when they begin recognizing small patterned sets without counting.

The same concepts of more, less, and same are developed in the following game of "More and Less War."

Early Counting

Meaningful counting activities can begin in preschool. Generally, children at mid-year in kindergarten should have a fair understanding of counting, but they must construct this idea on their own. It cannot be forced. The *meaning* attached to counting is the key conceptual idea on which all other number concepts are developed. Only the counting sequence is a rote procedure.

The Development of Counting Skills

Counting involves at least two separate skills. First, one must be able to produce the standard list of counting words in order: "One, two, three, four,..." Second, one must be able to connect this sequence in a one-to-one manner with the items in the set being counted. Each item must get one and only one count.

There are a variety of factors that play a role in the development of these counting skills. Experience and guidance are the major ones. Many children come to

ACTIVITY 6.3

More and Less War

The familiar game of "War" can be played with the dot cards or any cards that have sets on them; it can also be played with dominoes. In this version, children spin a more/less spinner before each turn (see Figure 6.2). If the spinner shows "Less," the player with less wins, and vice versa.

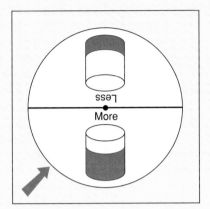

FIGURE 6.2 **A more/less spinner.**

kindergarten able to count sets of ten or beyond. At the same time, there are children from low-income inner-city communities who have not had these opportunities. Their intuitive knowledge of number may be one and a half to two years below the expected level (Griffin, 1998). As a result, they may require considerable practice to make up their experience deficit.

The size of the set is also a factor related to success in counting. Obviously, longer number strings present a greater challenge and require more practice to learn. The first 12 counts involve no pattern or repetition, and many children are unable to recognize patterns in the teens.

There seems to be little advantage in making counting tasks difficult. Therefore, children still learning the skills of counting—that is, matching oral number words with objects—should be given sets of blocks or counters that they can move or pictures of sets that are arranged for easy counting. A set of objects that can be moved as they are counted is easier to count than objects that cannot be moved or touched. A set that is ordered in some way, such as in a string of dots or other pattern, is easier to count than a randomly displayed set.

Meaning Attached to Counting

There is a difference between being able to count (as just described) and knowing what the counting conveys (Bialystok & Codd, 2000). When we count a set, the last number word used represents the magnitude or the *cardinality* of the set. Though very young children seem to have

some concept of quantity, they do not necessarily connect this concept with the act of counting. When children understand that the last count word names the quantity of the set, they are said to have the *cardinality principle*. Most children have made this connection by age four and a half (Fuson & Hall, 1983).

To determine if children have the cardinality rule, they can be given a set of objects and asked, "How many?" If they repeat or emphasize the last count word, it can be inferred that their understanding has switched from a count use to a cardinality use. For example, "One, two, three, four, five, six. There are six." If this cardinal usage is not clear, the "How many?" question can be repeated. If the child then announces the total without counting, it is clear that he or she is using the cardinal meaning of the counting word. However, a recount of the entire set would indicate that the question "How many?" was interpreted by the child as a command to count rather than a request for the quantity in the set.

In the classroom, you can help students develop a deeper sense of cardinality through almost any counting activity. The following two activities can also provide you with some insight into children's current development.

ACTIVITY 6.4

Counting Sets

Have children count several sets where the number of objects is the same but the objects are very different in size. Discuss how they are alike and different. "Were you surprised that they were the same amount? Why or why not?"

ACTIVITY 6.5

Count and Rearrange

Have students count a set of objects. Then rearrange the objects and ask, "How many now?" If they see no need to count over, you can infer that they have connected the cardinality to the set regardless of its arrangement. If they choose to count again, discuss why they think the answer is the same.

Number Writing and Recognition

Helping children read and write single-digit numbers is similar to teaching them to read and write letters of the alphabet. Traditionally, instruction has involved various forms of repetitive practice. Children trace over pages of numbers, repeatedly write the numbers from 0 to 10, make the numbers from clay, trace them in sand, write them on the chalkboard or in the air, and so on. The principle has been that number formation is a rote activity that can best be learned through practice.

Baroody (1987) argues convincingly that while some practice writing numbers is clearly necessary, much time can be saved by focusing on the defining characteristics of each number and on a motor plan for forming them. These characteristics should be articulated and discussed. For example, 1, 4, and 7 are made up of straight lines, whereas 2 and 5 are a mix of straight and curved. Numbers with similar characteristics should be taught together in order to focus on the properties that they share and those that distinguish them from each other. For example, the numbers 6 and 9 are distinguished from all other numbers by a closed loop on a stick. But the loop for the 6 at the bottom, and the loop for the 9 at the top, are features that differentiate one number from the other. The calculator is also a good instructional tool for number recognition. In addition to aiding children with number recognition, early activities can help develop familiarity with the calculator and prepare them for more complex ones to come.

ACTIVITY 6.6
Find and Press

Every child should have a calculator. Always begin by having the children press the clear key. Then you say a number, and the children press that number on the calculator. If you have an overhead calculator, you can then show the children the correct key so that they can confirm their responses, or you can write the number on the board for children to check. Begin with single-digit numbers, then progress to two or three numbers called in succession. For example, call, "Three, seven, one" (not "Three hundred seventy-one"). Children press the complete string of numbers as called.

Perhaps the most common kindergarten textbook exercises have children match sets of objects with numbers. In these exercises, the children are given sets of pictures and asked to write or match them with the number that tells how many. Alternatively, they may be given a number and requested to make or draw a set with that many objects. Many teacher resource books also include appealing learning-centre activities where children are required, for example, to put a number 1 with the correct-size set—frogs (with dots) on numbered lily pads. It is important to note that these frequently overworked activities involve only the skills of counting sets, of number recognition, or of number writing. When children are successful with these activities, little is gained by having them continue to do them.

Technology Note

Computer software that allows children to create sets on the screen with the click of a mouse is quite common. *Unifix Software* (Hickey, 1996) is an electronic version of the popular Unifix cubes, plastic cubes that snap together to make bars. The software allows the teacher to add features to counting activities that are not available with the cubes alone. In its most basic form, the software lets children make bars of cubes in any colour, break the bars, move them around, add sounds to each cube, and more. The teacher can choose to have a number appear on each bar showing the total number of cubes. One to four loops can also be created, with the loop total another option. Not only can students count these specified numbers and have them appear on the screen for reinforcement, they can informally begin to explore the idea that two quantities can form a larger amount.

Do not let these computer tools become play toys. It is important to keep tasks problematic. For example, in early kindergarten, students could make a set of single blocks to form a bar in one loop that is just as many as (or more, or less than) the bar the teacher has made in the first loop. (Files can be prepared ahead of time.) Later, students can explore different combinations where two bars equal a third.

Other software titles that can assist with early number development include *Number Meanings and Counting* (Tenth Planet, 1998c), *MathKeys: Unlocking Whole Numbers, Grades K–2* (MECC, 1996b). Two other programs that have been developed in Canada are Mathville Kidway (Courseware Solutions, 2000) and Math Trek 1,2,3 (Nectar Foundation, 1999). ■■

Counting On and Counting Back

Although the forward sequence of numbers is relatively familiar to most young children, counting on and counting back are difficult skills for many. Frequent short practice drills are recommended.

ACTIVITY 6.7

Up and Back Counting

Counting up to and back from a target number in a rhythmic fashion is an important counting exercise. For example, line up five children and five chairs in front of the class. As the whole class counts from 1 to 5, the children sit down

one at a time. When the target number, 5, is reached, it is repeated; the child who sat on 5 now stands, and the count goes back to 1. As the count goes back, the children stand up one at a time, and so on, "1, 2, 3, 4, 5, 5, 4, 3, 2, 1, 1, 2,..." Kindergarten and grade 1 children find exercises such as this both fun and challenging. Any movement (clapping, turning around, doing jumping jacks) can be used as the count goes up and back in a rhythmic manner.

A variation of Activity 6.7 is to count up and back between two numbers. For example, start with 4 and count to 11 and back to 4, and so on. Keep a rhythm as in the other exercises. Counting on the calculator is an excellent exercise for young children because they see the numbers as they count.

ACTIVITY 6.8

Calculator Up and Back

Have each child press ⊞ 1 ⊟ ⊟ ⊟ ⊟ ⊟. The display will go from 1 to 5 with each ⊟ press. Counting should be done out loud in a rhythm as in the other exercises. To start over, press the clear key and repeat the activity. Counting up and back is also possible, but the end numbers will not be repeated. The following illustrates the key presses and what the children would say in rhythm:

3 ⊞ 1   ⊟ ⊟ ⊟ ⊟   ⊟ 1   ⊟ ⊟ ⊟ ⊟
⊞ 1 ⊟ ⊟ …

"3 plus 1, 4, 5, 6, 7, minus 1, 6, 5, 4, 3, plus 1, 4, 5,..."

As not all calculators work in this way, ensure students' calculators are appropriate. For some calculators, press 0 ⊟ before beginning this activity. The last two activities, although not easy for young students, are designed only to help them become fluent with the number words in both forward and reverse order and to begin counts with numbers other than 1. They do not address counting on or counting back in a meaningful manner. However, the next two activities are designed for that purpose.

ACTIVITY 6.9

Counting On with Counters

Give each child a collection of 10 or 12 small counters that they line up left to right on their desks. Tell them to count four counters and push

them under their left hands (see Figure 6.3). Then say, "Point to your hand. How many are there?" (Four.) "So let's count like this: four (pointing to their hand), five, six,..." Repeat the activity with other numbers.

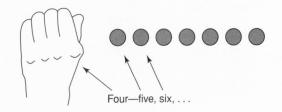

Four—five, six, . . .

FIGURE 6.3 Counting on: "Hide four. Count, starting from the number of counters hidden."

The following activity addresses the same concept but in a more problematic manner.

ACTIVITY 6.10

Real Counting On

Cover some counters on the overhead with a card before the light is turned on and place additional counters to the side of the card, as in Figure 6.4. Point to the card, and tell students how many are hidden. Ask how many counters there are in all.

How students respond is a good assessment of where they are in the development of this important idea. Do they repeat the count of the first set? Is it necessary for them to see the covered set? Or can they count on meaningfully and confidently? Do not forget to challenge their responses. "Why do you think there are 12?"

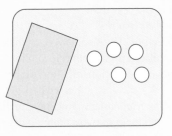

FIGURE 6.4 "There are four under the card. How many are there altogether? Count."

Applying counting-back skills is more difficult for children but can be developed in a manner similar to counting on. To learn about counting back, the children first count out a set as they did in the counting-on activities. The set is covered. As the children point to the set, they say the number that represents the covered counters. Then, the backward count is made as counters are removed one at a time. As a possible problem, count and cover a set. Remove a few counters, then ask how many still remain covered.

Relationships among Numbers One to Ten

Counting activities such as matching sets with numbers are vitally important to number development. However, they focus only on the basic meaning of number and on accurate counting skills. Once children have acquired the concept of cardinality and can meaningfully use their counting skills, little more is to be gained from the kinds of counting activities described so far. More relationships must be created for children in order to develop their number sense, a flexible concept of number not completely tied to counting.

A Collection of Number Relationships

Figure 6.5 illustrates the four different types of number relationships that children can and should develop:

- *Spatial relationships:* Children need to learn to recognize sets of objects in patterned arrangements and tell how many there are without counting. For most numbers, there are several common patterns. Also, two or more simpler patterns for smaller numbers can be combined to make a new pattern.
- *One and two more, one and two less:* The two-more-than and two-less-than relationships involve more than just the ability to count on two or count back two. Children should know that 7, for example, is 1 more than 6 and also 2 less than 9.
- *Anchors or "benchmarks" of 5 and 10:* Our number system is based on 10. Also, two fives make up a 10. Since five and ten are important anchors, it is very useful to develop relationships for numbers from 1 to 10.
- *Part-part-whole relationships:* To conceptualize a number as being made up of two or more parts is the most important relationship that can be developed about numbers. For example, 7 can be thought of as a set of 3 and a set of 4 or a set of 2 and a set of 5.

The traditional number curriculum places almost no emphasis on these part-part-whole relationships. Once children have learned to count and to read and write numbers, unfortunately, the next step is to begin addition

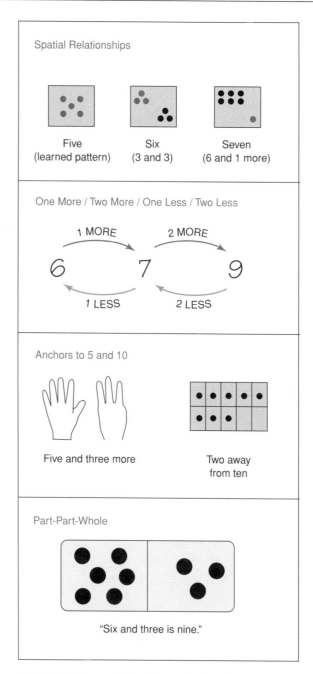

FIGURE 6.5 Four relationships to be developed involving small numbers.

and subtraction. The development of these relationships requires many months' work at the kindergarten and grade 1 levels. Initially, you will notice a lot of counting, the principal tool that is used in this development. You may wonder if you are making progress. Have patience! Counting will become less and less necessary as children construct these new relationships and begin to use these more powerful ideas.

Spatial Relationships: Patterned Set Recognition

Many children learn to recognize the dot arrangements on standard dice because of the many games they play with them. Similar instant set recognition can be developed for other patterns as well. The patterns represent more than an abstract symbol for the number of dots. Much repetitive counting goes into learning to recognize the patterns, which is intimately connected to knowledge of the particular number concept. Quantities up to 10 can be known and named without the routine of counting, which can then aid in counting on (from a known patterned set) or learning combinations of numbers (seeing a pattern of two known smaller patterns). In general, the idea then is to help children access real quantities and be free of the tedium of counting. The activities suggested here not only promote set recognition, they encourage reflective thinking about the patterns so that relationships will be constructed.

A good set of materials to use in pattern recognition activities is a set of dot plates. These can be made using small paper plates and the peel-off dots commonly available in stationery stores. A reasonable collection of patterns is shown in Figure 6.6. Note that some patterns are combinations of two smaller patterns or a pattern with one or two additional dots. These should be made in two colours. Keep the patterns compact. If the dots are spread out, the patterns are hard to see.

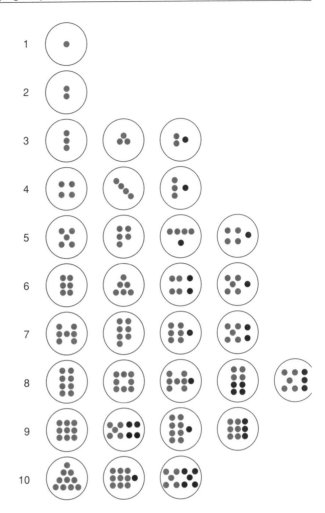

FIGURE 6.6 A useful collection of dot patterns for "dot plates."

ACTIVITY 6.11

Learning Patterns

To introduce the patterns, provide each student with about 10 counters and a piece of construction paper as a mat. Hold up a dot plate for about 3 seconds. "Make the pattern you saw using the counters on the mat. How many dots did you see? How did you see them?" Spend some time discussing the configuration of the pattern and how many dots. Do this with a few new patterns each day.

ACTIVITY 6.12

Dot Plate Flash

Hold up a dot plate for only 1 to 3 seconds. "How many? Describe what you saw." Children like to see how quickly they can recognize and say how many dots. Include a lot of easy patterns and a few with more dots as you build their confidence. Students can also flash the dot plates to each other as a workstation activity.

ACTIVITY 6.13

Dominoes

Make a set of dominoes out of poster board and put a dot pattern on each end. The dominoes can be about 5 cm by 10 cm. Have different pairs of patterns, but include a lot of the same. Let the children play dominoes in the regular way, matching up the ends. As a speed activity, spread out all of the dominoes and see how fast the children are able to play all of the dominoes or play until it is not possible to play any more. Regular dominoes could also be used, but there would not be as many patterns.

The dot plates and patterned sets, as we will see, can easily be used in many other activities. There is value in using them in any primary grade at all times of year. However, the instant recognition activities with the plates are exciting and can be done in five minutes at any time of day or between lessons.

One and Two More, One and Two Less

When young children count, they do not reflect on the way one number is related to another. Their goal is only to match number words with objects until they reach the end of their count. To learn that 6 and 8 are related by the twin relationships of "two more than" and "two less than" they must reflect on these ideas as they engage in tasks that permit counting. Counting on (or back) one or two counts is useful in constructing these ideas.

ACTIVITY 6.14

One-Less-Than Dominoes

Use the dot-pattern dominoes or a standard set to play "one-less-than" dominoes. Play in the usual way, but instead of adding a domino if the ends match (the number of dots are the same), a new domino is added if the number of dots on the end is one less than the number of dots on the end on the board. A similar game can be played for two less, one more, or two more.

The following activities can be done for any of the four different types of relationships that children can and should develop with numbers. Each activity will be described for only one.

ACTIVITY 6.15

Make a Two-More-Than Set

Provide students with about six dot cards. Their task is to construct a set of counters that is two more than the set shown on each card. Similarly, spread out eight to 10 dot cards, and find another card for each that is two less than the card shown. (Omit the 1 and 2 cards for two less than, and so on.)

In activities where children find a set or make a set, they add a number card (a small card with a number written on it) to all of the sets involved. They should be encouraged to take turns reading a number sentence to their partner. If, for example, a set has been made that is

two more than a set of four, the child can read this by saying the number sentence "Two more than four is six."

The following activities involve numbers and sets together or just numbers. These are especially important in late grade 1 through grade 3.

ACTIVITY 6.16

One-More-Than Response Cards

Provide each child with six to eight number cards about the size of index cards. (Children can cut up paper and make their own.) On the cards, put the numbers you will need for the day (e.g., 5 through 10). Now flash a dot plate and have students hold up the card that is one more than the plate. Nothing is said out loud as all students respond. Similarly, you can hold up a number card or say a number orally, and they respond with their number cards.

The calculator can be an exciting device to practice the relationships of one more than, two more than, one less than, and two less than. Ensure student's calculators are appropriate as not all calculators work in this way.

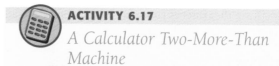

ACTIVITY 6.17

A Calculator Two-More-Than Machine

Teach children how to make a two-more-than machine. Press 0 ⊞ 2 ⊟ . This procedure makes the calculator a two-more-than machine. Now press any number—for example, 5. Children hold their finger over the ⊟ key and predict the number that is two more than 5. Then they press ⊟ to confirm. If they do not press any of the operation keys (+, −, ×, ÷) the "machine" will continue to perform in this way.

What is really happening in the two-more-than machine is that the calculator "remembers" or stores the last operation, in this case "+2," and adds that to whatever number is in the window when the ⊟ key is pressed. If the child continues to press ⊟ , the calculator will count by twos. At any time, a new number can be pressed followed by the equal key. To make a two-less-than machine, press 2 ⊟ 2 ⊟ . (The first press of 2 is to avoid a negative number.) At first, students forget and press operation keys, which change what their calculator is doing. Soon they get the hang of using the calculator as a machine.

Anchoring Numbers to 5 and 10

Here again, we want to help children relate a given number to other numbers, specifically 5 and 10. These relationships are especially useful in thinking about various combinations of numbers. For example, in each of the following, consider how the knowledge of 8 as "5 and 3 more" and as "2 away from 10" can play a role: 5 + 3, 8 + 6, 8 − 2, 8 − 3, 8 − 4, 13 − 8. (It may be worth stopping here to consider the role of 5 and 10 in each of these examples.) Later, similar relationships can be used in the development of mental computation skills on larger numbers such as 68 + 7.

The most common and perhaps most important model for this relationship is the ten-frame. The ten-frame is simply a 2 × 5 array in which counters or dots are placed to illustrate numbers (see Figure 6.7). Ten-frames can be drawn simply on a full sheet of construction paper (or use the Blackline Master). Nothing fancy is required, and each child can have one. The ten-frame has been incorporated into a variety of activities in this book and is popular in standard textbooks for children.

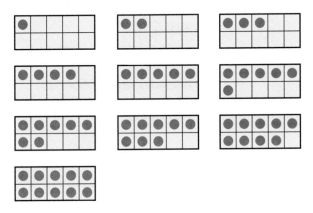

FIGURE 6.7 Ten-frames.

For children in kindergarten or early grade 1 who have not yet explored a ten-frame, it is a good idea to begin with a five-frame. This row of five sections is also drawn on a sheet of construction paper (or use the Blackline Master). Provide children with about 10 counters that will fit in the five-frame sections, and conduct the following activity.

ACTIVITY 6.18

Five-Frame Tell-About

Explain that only one counter is permitted in each section of the five-frame. No other counters are allowed on the five-frame mat. Have the children show 3 on their five-frame. "What can you tell us about 3 from looking at your mat?" After hearing from several children, try other numbers from 0 to 5. Children may place their counters on the five-frame in any manner. What they observe will differ a great deal from child to child. For example, with four counters, a child with two on each end may say, "It has a space in the middle" or "It's two and two." There are no wrong answers. Focus attention on how many more counters are needed to make 5 or how far away from 5 a number is. Next try numbers between 5 and 10. The rule of one counter per section still holds, but don't explain how to do this. As shown in Figure 6.8, numbers greater than 5 are shown with a full five-frame and additional counters on the mat, not in the frame. In discussion, focus attention on these larger numbers as 5 and some more: "Eight is 5 and 3 more."

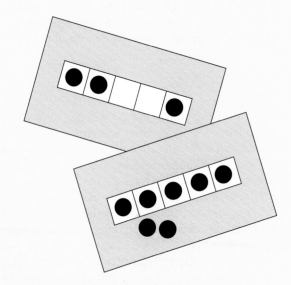

FIGURE 6.8 A five-frame focuses on the 5 anchor. Counters are placed one to a section, and students tell how they see their number in the frame.

Notice that the five-frame really focuses on the relationship of 5 as an anchor for numbers, not 10. When five-frames have been used for a week or so, introduce ten-frames. You may want to play a ten-frame version of a "Five-Frame Tell-About." Soon after, introduce the following rule for showing numbers on the ten-frame: *Always fill the top row first, starting on the left, the same way you read. When the top row is full, counters can be placed in the bottom row, also starting from the left.* This will produce the "standard" way to show numbers on the ten-frame as in Figure 6.7.

For a while, many children will count every counter on their ten-frame. Some will take all counters off and begin each number from a blank frame. Others will soon learn to adjust numbers by adding on or taking off only what is required, often capitalizing on a row of five without counting. Do not pressure students. With continued practice, all students will grow. How they are using the ten-frame provides insight into their current number concept development.

ACTIVITY 6.19

Crazy Mixed-Up Numbers

This activity is adapted from *Mathematics Their Way* (Baratta-Lorton, 1976). All children make their ten-frame show the same number as the teacher calls out random numbers between 0 and 10. After each number, the children change their ten-frames to show the new number. Children can play this game independently by preparing lists of about 15 "crazy mixed-up numbers." One child plays "teacher," and the rest use the ten-frames. Children like to make up their own number lists.

"Crazy Mixed-Up Numbers" is much more of a problem than it first appears. How do you decide to change your ten-frame? Some children will wipe off the entire frame and start over with each number. Others will already know what each number looks like. To add another dimension, have the children tell, *before changing their ten-frames,* how many more counters need to be added ("plus") or removed ("minus"). They then call out plus or minus whatever amount is appropriate. If, for example, the frames showed 6, and the teacher called out "four," the children would respond, "Minus two!" and then change their ten-frames accordingly. A discussion of how they know what to do is valuable.

ACTIVITY 6.20

Ten-Frame Translation

Give students a number in a form other than a ten-frame. You could show them a dot card, hold up fingers, show some counters on the overhead, hold up a number card, or simply say a number out loud. Then, have them show the number on their ten frames. The activity could also be done independently at a workstation by placing the number cards or sets along with the ten-frames and counters at a table on which the children

work. Worksheets could be prepared for independent seatwork, as shown in Figure 6.9. The children would use an actual ten-frame and then record the result on the paper.

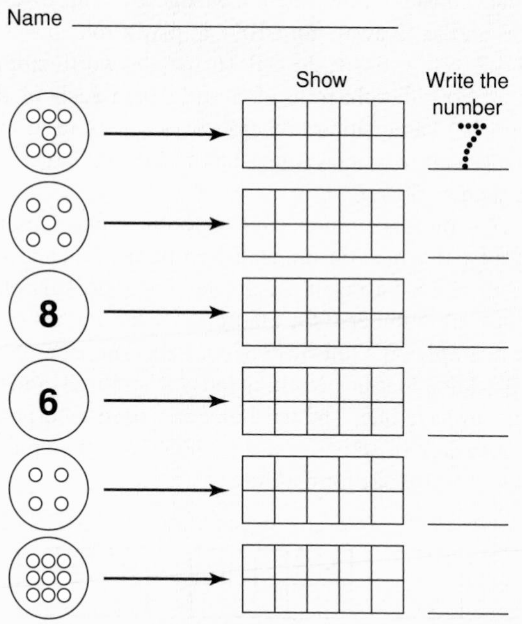

FIGURE 6.9 A ten-frame record sheet. Children can use a large ten-frame with counters and then draw dots in the ten-frames on the worksheet.

Ten-frame flash cards are an important variation of ten-frames. Make cards about the size of a small index card from poster board, each with a ten-frame and dots drawn in the frames. A set of 20 cards consists of a 0 card, a 10 card, and two each of the numbers 1 to 9. The cards allow for simple drill activities to reinforce the 5 and 10 anchors.

ACTIVITY 6.21

Ten-Frame Flash

Flash ten-frame cards to the class or the group, and see how fast the children can tell how many dots are shown. This activity is fast-paced, takes only a few minutes, can be done at any time, and is a lot of fun if you encourage speed.

Important variations of "Ten-Frame Flash" include

■ Saying the number of spaces on the card instead of the number of dots

- Saying one more than the number of dots (or two more, and also less than)
- Saying the "ten fact"—for example, "Six and four make ten"

After students have become familiar with the ten-frame, simply having a large blank ten-frame drawn on the board can have a valuable influence on children's thinking about 5 and 10 as they do number activities or discuss numbers at any time. Try looking at a ten-frame while doing the following two activities.

ACTIVITY 6.22

Five-And

In "Five-And," the teacher calls out numbers between 5 and 10. The children respond "Five and _____" using the appropriate number. For example, if you say, "Eight!" the children respond, "Five and three."

ACTIVITY 6.23

Make-Ten

Call out numbers between 0 and 10. The children respond by saying how many more are needed to make 10. This is most effective with numbers between 5 and 10.

Ten-frame tasks are surprisingly problematic for students. Even in the drill activities just described, students must reflect on the two rows of five, the spaces remaining, and how a particular number of dots is so much more or less than 5. Discussing how numbers are seen on the five-frames or ten-frames is a good brief follow-up activity in which students learn from one another.

Part-Part-Whole Relationships

Consider what you think about when you count a set of seven objects. What you do *not* think about is significant. Counting a set is unlikely to make you think about the fact that it could be made up of two parts, or what the size of those parts might be. Without activities that focus on these characteristics of number, many children simply continue to use counting as their principal means of accessing quantity. A noted researcher in children's number concepts, Lauren Resnick (1983), states:

> *Probably the major conceptual achievement of the early school years is the interpretation of numbers in terms of part and whole relationships. With the application of a Part-Whole schema to quantity, it*

becomes possible for children to think about numbers as compositions of other numbers. This enrichment of number understanding permits forms of mathematical problem solving and interpretation that are not available to younger children. (p. 114)

A study of kindergarten children examined the effects of part-part-whole activities on number concepts (Fischer, 1990). With only 20 days of instruction to develop the part-part-whole structure, children showed significantly higher achievement than the control group on number concepts, word problems, and place-value concepts.

Basic Ingredients of Part-Part-Whole Activities

Most part-part-whole activities focus on a single number for the entire activity. Thus a child or group of children working together might work on the number 7 throughout the activity. Either the children build the designated quantity in two or more parts, using a wide variety of materials and formats, or else they start with the full amount and separate it into two or more parts. A group of two or three children may work on one number in one activity for 5 to 20 minutes. Kindergarten children will usually begin these activities working on the number 4 or 5. As concepts develop, the children can extend their work to numbers 6 to 12. It is not unusual to find children in grade 2 who have not developed firm part-part-whole constructs for numbers that range from 7 to 12.

When children do these activities, have them say or "read" the parts aloud or write them down on some form of recording sheet (or do both). Reading or writing the combinations encourages reflective thought that focuses on the part-whole relationship. Writing can be in the form of drawings, numbers written in blanks (_____ and _____), or addition equations if these have been introduced ($3 + 5 = 8$). There is a clear connection between part-part-whole concepts and addition and subtraction ideas.

A special and important variation of part-part-whole activities is referred to as a *missing-part* activity. In a missing-part activity, children know the whole amount and use their already developed knowledge of the parts of that whole to try to tell what the covered or hidden part is. If they do not know or are unsure, they simply uncover the unknown part and say the full combination as they would normally. These activities should never be conducted as "problems" or "tests" with right and wrong answers. They are simply learning activities where children try to think of a part of a number that they cannot see. Missing-part activities provide maximum reflection on the combinations for a number. They also serve as the forerunner to subtraction concepts. With a whole of 8 and only 3 showing, the child can later learn to write "$8 - 3 = 5$."

In most of the part-part-whole activities that involve materials, children will display sets with the designated number of objects in two or more parts. It is reasonable to have children show a number with one set of materials in at least eight different ways. Each number display can be placed on a small mat or piece of construction paper. Two or three children working together may have quite a large number of displays, all using the same materials and all representing the same quantity in two or more parts. As you come around to observe, ask individuals to "read a number sentence" to go with their representations. Also encourage them to read their designs to each other.

ACTIVITY 6.24

Build It in Parts

The ideas here are illustrated in Figure 6.10.

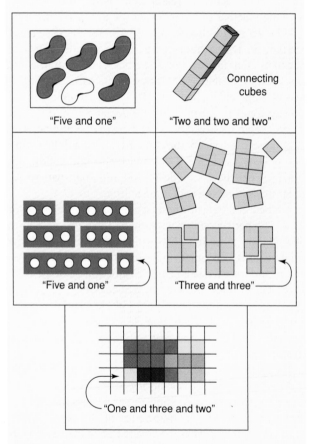

FIGURE 6.10 Assorted materials for building parts of 6.

■ Make sets with "two-colour counters" such as lima beans spray-painted on one side.
■ Make bars of interlocking cubes or other connecting cubes. Use two colours for each bar.
■ Colour rows of squares on 2-cm grid paper.
■ Make combinations with "dot strips," which are simply strips of poster board with dots on

them. Make a lot of strips with one to four dots on them and some with five to ten dots. The strips should only be as long as the row of dots that is on them. (Punch holes in the dots to make a set for the overhead projector.)
■ Make combinations with two-column strips. Cut these strips from tag-board that is ruled in 2-centimetre squares. Except for the single square, all numbers are cut from two columns of squares. Odd numbers will have an odd square on one end. (Punch holes in the centre of the squares to make a set for the overhead projector.)

Part-Part-Whole Activities

As a variation of "Build It in Parts," have students make patterns with different materials. Each pattern should have the same prescribed number of objects. When talking with the children, ask them to explain how they see their pattern as two or three parts.

■ Make arrangements with wooden cubes.
■ Make designs with pattern blocks. It is a good idea to use only one or two shapes at a time.
■ Make designs with flat toothpicks. These can be dipped in white glue and placed on small squares of construction paper to create a permanent record.
■ Make designs with squares or triangles that touch. Cut a large supply of small squares or triangles out of construction paper. These can also be pasted down.

It is both fun and useful to challenge children to see their designs in different ways, thus producing different number combinations. In Figure 6.11, think about how children look at the designs to get the combinations listed under each. Ensure students understand that adding 0 does not change a number.

ACTIVITY 6.25

Two Out of Three

Make lists of three numbers, two of which total the number on which children are focusing. An example for the number 5 follows:

2—3—4
5—0—2
1—3—2
3—1—4
2—2—3
4—3—1

With the lists on the board or overhead, children can take turns selecting the two numbers that make up the whole. As with all problem-solving activities, children should be challenged to justify their answers. The same activity can be used in a worksheet format, but the real value lies in the discussion and justification.

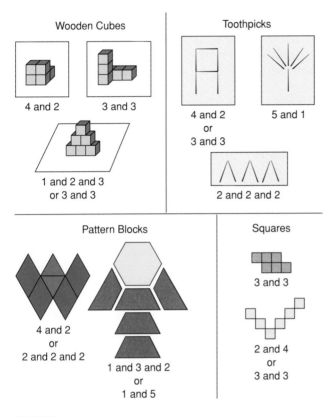

Wooden Cubes

4 and 2

3 and 3

1 and 2 and 3
or 3 and 3

Toothpicks

4 and 2
or
3 and 3

5 and 1

2 and 2 and 2

Pattern Blocks

4 and 2
or
2 and 2 and 2

1 and 3 and 2
or
1 and 5

Squares

3 and 3

2 and 4
or
3 and 3

FIGURE 6.11 Designs for 6.

Missing-Part Activities

Missing-part activities require some way for a part to be hidden or unknown. Usually this is done with two children working together, but it can also be done with the class in a teacher-directed manner. Again, the focus of the activity is on a single designated quantity as the whole.

ACTIVITY 6.26

Covered Parts

A set of counters equal to the target amount is counted out, and the rest are put aside. One child places the counters under a margarine tub or piece of tag-board. The child then pulls some out into view. (This amount could be none, all, or

any amount in between.) For example, if 6 is the whole and 4 are showing, the other child says, "Four and two are six." If the child hesitates or is unable to determine how many are under the tub, then what is hidden is shown immediately. Remember, the focus is on learning and thinking, not on testing and anxiety.

ACTIVITY 6.27

Missing-Part Cards

For each number from 4 to 10, make missing-part cards on strips of 7-cm-by-22-cm tag-board. Each card has a number representing the whole, which is visible, and two sets of dots with one set covered by a flap. For the number 8, you need nine cards with the visible part ranging from 0 to 8 dots. Students use the cards as in "Covered Parts," saying, "Four and two are six" for a card showing four dots and hiding two (see Figure 6.12).

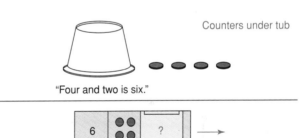

Counters under tub

"Four and two is six."

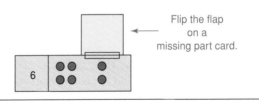

"Six minus four is two" or "Four and two is six."

Flip the flap
on a
missing part card.

"I Wish I Had 6."

I have

(You need 3 more.)

I have

(You need 1 more.)

FIGURE 6.12 Missing-part activities.

ACTIVITY 6.28

I Wish I Had

Hold out a bar of interlocking cubes, a dot strip, a two-column strip, or a dot plate showing 6 or less. Say, "I wish I had six." The children respond with the part that is needed to make 6. Counting on can be used to check (refer to Activities 6.9 and 6.10). The game can focus on a single whole, or the "I wish I had" number can change each time.

The following are also missing-part activities but are completely symbolic.

ACTIVITY 6.29

Calculator Parts of 8 Machine

With an appropriate calculator, make a parts of 8 machine by pressing 8 ⊟ 8 ⊜. Now if any number from 0 to 8 is pressed followed by ⊜, the display shows the other part. (The second part will show as a negative number. Tell students this is how they can tell it is the second part.) Children should try to say the other part before they press ⊜. Though this is basically a drill activity, a discussion with any child concerning his or her reasoning returns it to a problem orientation. Machines can be made for other numbers in the same way.

Technology Note

There are many ways you can use computer software to create part-part-whole activities. All that is needed is a program that permits students to create sets of objects on the screen. *Unifix Software* (Hickey, 1996) is especially useful for this purpose. One approach is to have students create two-part bars to match a single bar that you specify. Students could make many bars, all for the same number. Alternatively, students could put counters in two set loops they form on the computer. As always, the computer should offer more than a hands-on simple manipulative. In this instance, the advantage is that you have the ability to control the type of feedback provided as students work through the activity. Options include showing the total in a bar, the total in a loop, and the total of all blocks on the screen. For example, a student can make a bar of two cubes and a bar of six cubes with a number showing on each. When the bars are snapped together, the new bar total of eight appears.

Combining and Breaking Apart Numbers (Tenth Planet, 1998a) is specifically designed for part-part-whole activities. Although the early activities in this package are fairly passive and slow, the "Through" or last section makes the mathematics reasonably problematic. In various animated settings, children attempt to make a number either in two parts or by adding two groups and then removing one or two groups. This is an example of software that requires some teacher guidance to create good problems, without which students will not stay engaged. The printed support material includes suggestions for corresponding off-line activities that make this a worthwhile program. ■

Dot Card Activities

Many good number development activities involve more than one of the relationships discussed so far. As children learn about ten-frames, patterned sets, and other relationships, the dot cards in the Blackline Masters at the back of this book provide a wealth of activities (see Figure 6.13). The cards contain dot patterns, patterns that require counting, combinations of two and three simple patterns, and ten-frames with both "standard" and unusual placements of dots. When children use these cards for almost any activity that involves number concepts, the cards make them think about numbers in many different ways. The dot cards add another dimension to many of the activities already described and can be used effectively in the following activities.

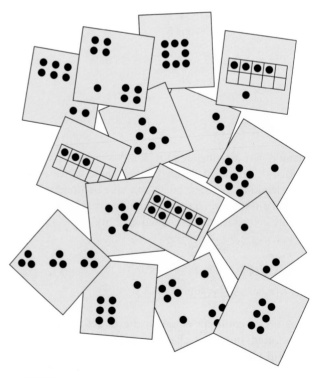

FIGURE 6.13 Dot cards can be made using the Blackline Masters at the back of this book.

ACTIVITY 6.30

Double War

The game of "Double War" (Kamii, 1985) is played like "War," but on each play, both players turn up two cards instead of one. The winner is the one with the larger total number. Children playing the game can use many different number relationships to determine the winner without actually finding the total number of dots.

ACTIVITY 6.31

Dot-Card Trains

Make a long row of dot cards from 0 to 9, then go back again to 1, then up, and so on. Alternatively, begin with 0 or 1 and make a two-more/two-less train.

ACTIVITY 6.32

Difference War

Besides dealing out the cards to the two players as in regular "War," prepare a pile of about 50 counters. On each play, the players turn over their cards as usual. The player with the greater number of dots wins as many counters from the pile as the difference between the two cards. The players keep their cards. The game is over when the counter pile runs out. The player with the most counters wins the game.

ACTIVITY 6.33

Missing-Part Combos

Select a number between 5 and 12, and find combinations of two cards that total the number. When students have found a number of combinations, one student can then turn one card in each group face down. The next challenge is to name the card that was turned down. ("Before you check, why do you think you are right?")

Relationships for Numbers 10 to 20

Every day, children in kindergarten, grade 1, and grade 2 experience numbers up to 20 and beyond. These numbers play a big part in many simple counting activities, in basic facts, and in much of what we do with mental computation. Do not assume that the children will automatically extend the set of relationships they have developed for numbers less than 10 to those beyond 10. Relationships with these numbers are just as important as relationships involving the numbers through 10.

A Pre-Place-Value Relationship with 10

Sets of 10 should play a major role in children's initial understanding of numbers between 10 and 20. When children see a set of six with a set of 10, they should know without counting that the total is 16. Remember, though, it is not appropriate to discuss place-value concepts while working on the numbers between 10 and 20. Children should not be asked or expected to explain that the one in 16 represents "one 10" prior to a more complete development of place-value concepts (appropriate for grade 2 and beyond). (Stop for a moment and ask yourself: "One 10. What would this mean to a 5-year-old?" Think about it! Ten is a lot more than one. How can it be one? Initially, this is a strange idea for the child.) The inappropriate nature of this discussion, "one 10 and six ones" (what's a one?) does not mean that a set of 10 should not figure prominently in a conversation about numbers in the teens. The following activity illustrates this idea.

ACTIVITY 6.34

Ten and Some More

Use a simple two-part mat and have children count out 10 counters on one side. Next have them put five counters on the other side. Together count all of the counters by ones. Then together with the children, chant the combination: "Ten and five is 15." Turn the mat around: "Five and 10 is 15." Without changing the 10 side of the mat, repeat the process using other numbers, randomly selected.

Activity 6.34 is designed to teach new number names, so it requires a certain amount of direct teaching. Following this activity, explore numbers to 20 in a more open-ended manner. Provide each child with two ten-frames, drawn one under the other on a construction paper mat. In random order, have children show numbers to 20 on their mats. There is no preferred way to do this as long as the number of counters is correct. What is interesting is to discuss how the counters can be placed on the mat so that it is easy to see how many there are. Have children share their ideas. Not every child will use a full set of 10. As the idea becomes more popular, the notion that 10 and some more is an amount in the teens will soon be developed. Do not forget to include numbers less than 10 as well. As you listen to your children, you may want to begin challenging them to find ways to show 26 counters or even more.

Extending More and Less Relationships

Relationships of one more than, two more than, one less than, and two less than a number are important for all numbers. These ideas build on, or are connected to, the same concepts for numbers less than 10. The fact that 17 is one less than 18 is connected to the idea that 7 is one less than 8. Consider that children may need help in making these connections.

ACTIVITY 6.35

More and Less Extended

On the overhead, show 7 counters, and ask what is two more, or one less, and so on. Now add a filled ten-frame to the display (or 10 in any pattern), and repeat the questions. Pair up questions by covering and uncovering the ten-frame as illustrated in Figure 6.14.

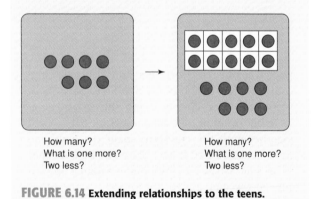

How many?
What is one more?
Two less?

How many?
What is one more?
Two less?

FIGURE 6.14 Extending relationships to the teens.

Double and Near-Double Relationships

The use of doubles (double 6 is 12) and near-doubles (13 is double 6 and 1 more) is generally considered a strategy for memorizing basic addition facts. There is no reason why children should not begin to develop these relationships long before they are concerned with memorizing basic facts. Doubles and near-doubles are simply special cases of the general part-part-whole construct.

Relate the doubles to special images. Thornton (1982) helped grade 1 students connect doubles to these visual ideas:

Double 3 is the bug double: three legs on each side.

Double 4 is the spider double: four legs on each side.

Double 5 is the hand double: two hands.

Double 6 is the egg carton double: two rows of six eggs.

Double 7 is the two-week double: two weeks on the calendar.

Double 8 is the crayon double: two rows of eight crayons in a box.

Double 9 is the 18-wheeler double: two sides, nine wheels on each side.

Children can draw pictures or make posters that illustrate the doubles for each number. There is no reason that the images need be restricted to those listed here. Any images that are strong ideas for your children will be good for them.

Periodically conduct oral exercises in which students double the number you say. Ask children to explain how they knew a particular double. Many will not use the pictures.

ACTIVITY 6.36

The Double Maker

Some calculators can be made into a "double maker" by pressing 2 ⊠ ⊟. Now a press of any digit followed by ⊟ will produce the double of that number. Children can work in pairs or individually to try to beat the calculator.

As a related oral task, say a number that is the sum of a double; then ask students to tell what double it is. "What is fourteen?" (Double 7!) When students can do this well, use any number up to 20. "What is seventeen?" (Double 8 and 1 more.)

Number Sense and the Real World

So far we have discussed the development of number meanings and some specific relationships involving numbers. These ideas are very much a part of what is meant by number sense. Here, we examine ways to broaden children's early knowledge of numbers even further. Relationships of numbers to real-world quantities and measures and the use of numbers in simple estimations can help children develop the flexible, intuitive ideas about numbers that are most desirable.

Estimation and Measuring

One of the best ways for children to think of real quantities is to associate numbers with measures of things. In the early grades, measures of length, mass, and time are good places to begin. Just measuring and recording results will not be very effective, since there is no reason for children to be interested in or think about the results. To help children think about or reflect a bit on what number might tell how long the desk is or how heavy the book is, it would be good if they could first write down or tell you an estimate. However, producing an estimate is a very difficult task for young children. They do not understand the concept of "estimate" or "about." For example, suppose that you have cut out of poster board an ample supply of very large footprints, say, about 36 centimetres long. All are exactly the same size. You would like to ask the class, "About how many footprints will it take to measure the distance across the rug in our reading corner?" The key word here is *about,* and it is one which you will need to spend a lot of time helping children understand. The request for an estimate needs to be done in ways that help develop understanding of the concept of "about," while still permitting children to respond.

The following estimation questions can be used with most early estimation activities:

- *More or less than _____?* Will it be more or less than 10 footprints? Will the mass of the apple be equal to more or less than 20 wooden blocks? Are there more or less than 15 connecting cubes in this long bar?
- *Closer to _____ or to _____?* Will it be closer to 5 footprints or closer to 20 footprints? Will the mass of the apple be closer to 10 blocks or closer to 30 blocks? Does this bar have closer to 10 cubes or closer to 50 cubes?
- *Less than _____, between _____ and _____, or more than _____?* Will it take less than 10, between 10 and 20, or more than 20 footprints? Will the mass of the apple be less than 5 blocks, between 5 and 15 blocks, or more than 15 blocks? Are there less than 20, between 20 and 50, or more than 50 cubes in this bar?
- *About _____.* Use one of these numbers: 5, 10, 15, 20, 25, 30, 35, 40,... About how many footprints? About how many blocks will the mass of the apple be? About how many cubes are in this bar?

This list of estimation question formats is arranged from the easiest to the most difficult. Notice that each clearly indicates to the children that they need not come up with an exact amount or number. Asking for estimates using these formats helps children learn what you mean by "about." Every child can make an estimate without having to pull a number out of the air.

For almost all estimation measurement activities at the K–2 level, it's a good idea to use informal (non-standard) units of measure, instead of standard units such as centimetres, kilograms, or litres. Doing so helps children gain familiarity with the different units. If, however, you want them to learn about a particular unit of measure, say, the metre, then by all means include it in these exercises.

Another suggestion is to estimate several things in succession using the same unit. This will help children develop an understanding of relative measures. For example, suppose that you are estimating and measuring "around things" using a string. In order to measure, the string is wrapped around the object; then it is compared with some unit such as a popsicle stick. After measuring the distance around Cheng Lee's head, estimate the distance around the wastebasket or around the globe or around Amar's wrist. Each successive measure helps children with the new estimates.

An alternative approach is to estimate and measure the same item successively with different-sized units. Don't be surprised when young children guess that the measure is larger when the unit gets larger. The idea that smaller units produce larger measurements and large units produce small measurements is a difficult relationship for children to construct. (See Chapter 16 for a more complete discussion of measurement.)

More Connections

Here are some additional activities that can help children connect numbers to real situations.

ACTIVITY 6.37

Add a Unit to Your Number

Write a number on the board. Now suggest some units to go with it, and ask the children what they can think of that fits. For example, suppose the number is 9. "What do you think of when I say 9 *dollars?* 9 *hours?* 9 *cars?* 9 *kids?* 9 *metres?* 9 *o'clock?* 9 *hand spans?* 9 *litres?*" Spend some time discussing each example. Let children suggest units as well. Be prepared to explore some of the ideas either immediately or as projects or tasks to share with parents at home.

ACTIVITY 6.38

Is It Reasonable?

Select a number and a unit—for example, 5 metres. Could the teacher be 5 metres tall? Could your living room be 5 metres wide? Can a

man jump 5 metres high? Could three children standing side-by-side stretch their arms 5 metres with their hands touching? Pick any number, large or small, and a unit with which children are familiar. Then make up a series of questions such as these.

Once children are familiar with Activity 6.38, have them select the number and the unit or things (10 kids, 20 bananas, ...), and see what kinds of questions they construct. When a difference of opinion develops, capitalize on the opportunity to explore their thinking. Resist the temptation to supply your adult-level knowledge. Rather, say, "Well, how can we find out if it is or is not reasonable? Who has an idea about what we could do?"

ACTIVITY 6.39

Things That Are Seven

Pick any number (7 is used here as an example), and have groups of children find ways to tell about that number. Seven might be the days in a week, the number of people in Mandy's family, or the number of kittens in Inky's litter. Other children might want to show 7 in some measurement way, such as a stack of 7 books, 7 glasses of water in a jug, 7 long giant steps, the length of 7 children lying down head to toe, or how many times they can hop in 7 seconds. Groups can present their ideas orally, make a written report, contribute a page to put on the bulletin board, or present a demonstration.

These activities are real problems in the truest sense. There are no clear answers. Children can easily begin to pose their own questions and explore number in a way that is most interesting to them. Children will not have these real-world connections when you begin, and you may be disappointed in their limited ideas about number. Howden (1989) writes about a grade 1 teacher whose children came from very impoverished backgrounds. Resources were scarce but, she told Howden, "They all have fingers, the school grounds are strewn with lots of pebbles and leaves, and pinto beans are cheap. So we count, sort, compare, and talk about such objects. We've measured and weighed almost everything in this room and almost everything the children can drag in" (p. 6). This teacher's children had produced a wonderfully rich and long list of responses to the question "What comes to your mind when I say twenty-four?" In another school in a professional community where test scores were high, the same question brought almost no response from a class of grade 3 students. It can be a very rewarding effort to help children connect their number ideas to the real world.

Graphs

Graphing activities are another good way to connect the child's world with number. Chapter 18 discusses ways to make graphs with children in K–2. Graphs can be quickly made of almost any data that can be gathered from the students: favourite ice cream flavour, favourite colour, favourite sports team; number of sisters and brothers; children who ride different buses; types of shoes; number of pets you have; and so on. Graphs can be connected to content in other areas. A unit on sea life might lead to a graph of favourite sea animals.

Once a simple bar graph is made, it is very important to take a few minutes to ask as many number questions as is appropriate for the graph. In the early stages of number development (K–1), the use of graphs for teaching number relationships and for connecting numbers to real quantities in the children's environment is more important than the building of the graphs themselves. The graphs focus attention on counting of real things. Equally important, bar graphs clearly illustrate comparisons between and among numbers that are rarely evident when only one number or quantity is considered at a time. See Figure 6.15 for an example of a graph and questions that can be asked. At first, children will have trouble with the questions involving differences, but repeated exposure to these ideas in a bar graph format will improve their understanding. These comparison concepts add considerably to children's understanding of number.

 Literature Connections

Children's literature abounds with wonderful counting books. Involving children in books in different ways connects number to reality, makes it a personal experience, and provides ample opportunities for problem solving. Be sure to go beyond simply reading a counting book or a number-related book and looking at the pictures. Find a way to connect the book to the children's world. Create problems related to the story. Have children write a similar story. Extend the numbers and see what happens. Create a mural, graphs, or posters. The ideas are as plentiful as the books. Here are a few ideas for making literature connections to number concepts and number sense.

Anno's Counting House
(Anno, 1982)

In the beautiful style of Anno, this book shows 10 children in various parts of a house. As the pages are turned, the front of the house covers the children in it, so only a few are visible through cut-out windows. A second house is on the opposite page. As you move through the book, the children move one at a time to the second house, creating the potential for a 10–0, 9–1, 8–2, ..., 0–10 pattern of

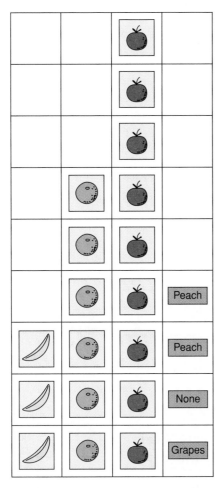

Class graph showing fruit brought for snack. Paper cut-outs for bananas, oranges, and apples, and cards for "others."

- — Which bar (or refer to what the graph represents) is most, least?
- — Which are more (less) than 7 (or some other number)?
- — Which is three less (more) than this bar?
- — How much more is _____ than _____? (Follow this question immediately by reversing the order and asking how much less.)
- — How much less is _____ than _____? (Reverse this question after receiving an answer.)
- — How much difference is there between _____ and _____ ?
- — Which two bars together are the same as _____ ?

FIGURE 6.15 Relationships and number sense in a bar graph.

pairs. As each page shows part of the group of children through the window, there is an opportunity to discuss how many are in the missing part. Have children use counters to model the story as you "read" it the second or third time.

The following are some questions you might ask the children: What if the children moved in pairs instead of one at a time? What if there were three houses? What if there were more children? What else could be in the house to count? How many rooms, pictures, windows? What about your house? What about two classrooms or two buses instead of houses?

The Very Hungry Caterpillar
(Carle, 1969)

This is a predictable-progression counting book about a caterpillar that first eats one thing, then two, and so on. Children can create their own eating stories and illustrate them. What if more than one type of thing were eaten at each stop? What combinations for each number are there? Are seven little things more or less than three very large things? What is the mass of all of this stuff? How many things are eaten altogether?

Two Ways to Count to Ten
(Dee, 1988)

This Liberian folktale is about King Leopard in search of the best animal to marry his daughter. The task devised involves throwing a spear and counting to 10 before the spear lands. Many animals try and fail. Counting by ones proves too lengthy. Finally, the antelope succeeds by counting "2, 4, 6, 8, 10."

The story is a perfect lead-in to skip counting. Can you count to 10 by threes? How else can you count to 10? How many ways can you count to 48? What numbers can you reach if you count by fives? The size of the numbers you investigate is limited only by the children's ability. A hundred board or counters are useful thinker toys to help with these problems. Be sure to have children write about what they discover in their investigations.

Another amusing book to use is *The King's Commissioners* (Friedman, 1994), a hilarious tale that also opens up opportunities to count using different groupings or skip counting. ▪▪

Extensions to Early Mental Mathematics

Teachers in grades 2 and 3 can capitalize on some of the early number relationships and extend them to numbers up to 100. A useful set of materials to help with these relationships is the group of little ten-frames found in the Blackline Masters. Each child should have a set of 10 tens and a set of frames for each number from 1 to 9, with an extra 5.

The following three ideas are illustrated with the little ten-frames in Figure 6.16. First are the relationships of one more than and one less than. If you understand that one more than 6 is 7, then in a similar manner, ten more than 60 is 70 (that is, one more ten). The second idea really looks ahead to fact strategies. If a child has learned to think about adding on to 8 or 9 by first adding up to 10 and then adding the rest, the extension to similar two-digit numbers is quite simple; see Figure 6.16(b). Finally, the most powerful idea for small numbers is thinking of them in parts. It is a very useful idea (though not one found in textbooks) to take apart larger numbers and to begin to develop some flexibility in the same way. Children can

begin by thinking of ways to take apart a multiple of 10 such as 80. Once they do it with tens, the challenge can be to think of ways to take apart 80 when one part has a 5 in it, such as 25 or 35.

More will be said about early mental computation in Chapter 10. The point to be made here is that early number relationships have a greater impact on what children know than may be apparent at first. Even teachers in the upper grades can profit from the use of ten-frames and part-part-whole activities.

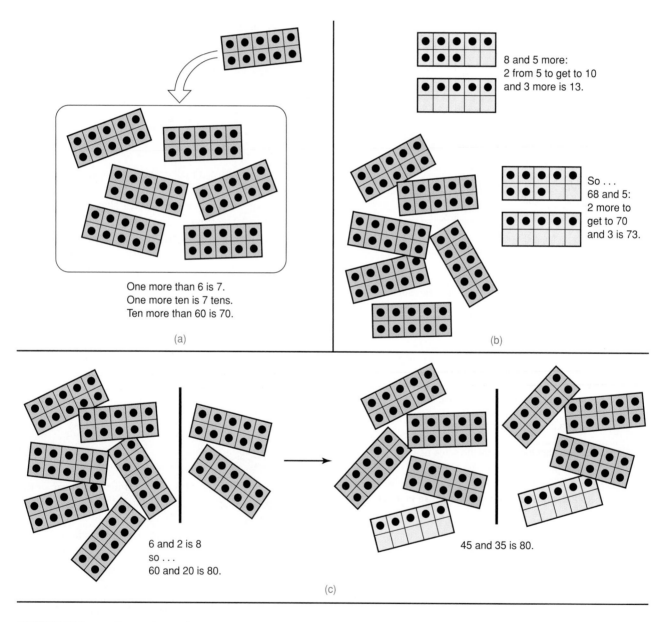

One more than 6 is 7.
One more ten is 7 tens.
Ten more than 60 is 70.

(a)

8 and 5 more:
2 from 5 to get to 10
and 3 more is 13.

So . . .
68 and 5:
2 more to
get to 70
and 3 is 73.

(b)

6 and 2 is 8
so . . .
60 and 20 is 80.

45 and 35 is 80.

(c)

FIGURE 6.16 Extending early number relationships to mental computation activities.

Reflections on Chapter 6

Writing to Learn

1. When children are counting, how can you tell whether they are attaching meaning to the activity?
2. Describe a "set-to-number matching" activity. What understandings must a child have in place in order to do the activity meaningfully and correctly?
3. What are the four types of relationships for small numbers that children need to develop at the kindergarten and grade 1 levels? Explain briefly what each of these means, and suggest at least one activity for each.
4. Describe a missing-part activity. What could you do if a child who was trying to give the missing part did not know it?
5. a. How can a calculator be used for developing early counting ideas?
   b. How can a calculator be used to help a child practise number relationships such as part-part-whole or one less than?
6. For numbers between 10 and 20, describe how to develop each of these ideas:
   a. The idea of the teens as a set of 10 and some more.
   b. Extension of the one-more/one-less concept to the teens.
7. Describe briefly your idea of number sense.
8. What are three ways that we can help children connect numbers to real-world ideas?
9. Give two examples of how early number relationships can be used to develop early mental computation skills.

For Discussion and Exploration

1. Examine a textbook series for K–2. Compare the treatment of counting and number concept development with that presented in this chapter. What ideas are stressed? What ideas are missed altogether? If you were teaching one of these grades, how would you plan your number concept development program? What part would the text play?
2. Many teachers above grade 2 find that their children do not possess the number relationships discussed in this chapter; they still rely heavily on counting. Given the pressures to cover other content areas at these grades, how much effort should be made to re-mediate these number concept deficiencies?

Recommendations for Further Reading

Highly Recommended

Burton, G. (1993). *Number sense and operations: Addenda series, grades K–6.* Reston, VA: National Council of Teachers of Mathematics.

For developing number concepts, either this book or the *Number Sense and Operations* book in the Addenda Series for your grade level is a must. The activities are developed in sufficient detail to give you clear guidance, yet allow considerable flexibility.

Early math strategy: The report of the expert panel on early math in Ontario. (2003). Queen's Printer for Ontario.

This document summarizes the findings of an expert panel of researchers and educators regarding best practices for the teaching and learning of mathematics in the early grades. It includes a list of appropriate materials that should be used in the primary classroom along with the concepts and skills with which they should be employed. There are also some suggestions for instruction and assessment strategies.

There is also a very useful parent's guide, *Helping your child learn Math: A parent's guide* (2002), which suggests simple activities that parents can do with their children to explore math at home. The guide is most useful for parents of children in junior kindergarten through grade 3.

A technical guide for teachers, which provides, in detail, strategies for instruction and assessment is being prepared. It will be available in the fall of 2003.

Kelleher, H. Nicol, C., Anderson, A., Martin, L., Ercikan, K. (2000). *Early Numeracy Project*, Ministry of Education, BC.

This project, funded by the Ministry of Education, is designed to assess the numeracy skills and develop instructional strategies for K–3 children, particularly those at risk in mathematics. In conjunction with assessment work, instructional resource packages will be available for teachers along with a companion program for parents.

Van de Walle, J.A., & Watkins, K.B. (1993). Early development of number sense. In R.J. Jensen (Ed.), *Research ideas for the classroom: Early childhood mathematics* (pp. 127–150). Old Tappan, NJ: Macmillan.

This chapter includes a discussion of many of the K–2 topics covered in this text as well as a broader discussion of number sense, including mental computation and estimation. It provides a good mix of practical ideas with ample references to the research literature.

Other Suggestions

Baroody, A.J., & Wilkins, J.L.M. (1999). The development of informal counting, number, and arithmetic skills and concepts. In J.V. Copley (Ed.), *Mathematics in the early years* (pp. 48–65). Reston, VA: National Council of Teachers of Mathematics.

Bialystok, E., Codd, J. (2000). Representing quantity beyond whole numbers: some, none and part. *Canadian Journal of Experimental Psychology, 54*(2), 117–128.

Bresser, R., & Holtzman, C. (1999). *Developing number sense.* Sausalito, CA: Math Solutions Publications.

Clements, D.H. (1999). Subitizing: What is it? Why teach it? *Teaching Children Mathematics, 5,* 400–405.

Fuson, K.C. (1989). *Children's counting and concepts of number.* New York: Springer-Verlag.

Greenes, C., Schulman, L., & Spungin, R. (1993). Developing sense about numbers. *Arithmetic Teacher, 40,* 279–284.

Griffin, S. (1998). Math readiness: How can families make sure kids will have it? *Transition Magazine, 28*(1), 1–5.

Leutzinger, L.P., & Bertheau, M. (1989). Making sense of numbers. In P.R. Trafton (Ed.), *New directions for elementary school mathematics* (pp. 111–122). Reston, VA: National Council of Teachers of Mathematics.

Liedtke, W. (1996-97). Fostering the development of conceptual knowledge: The basic addition facts. *Prime Areas, 93*(1), 42–51.

Liedtke, W., & Kallio, P. (1992-93). Promoting the development of number sense in the early years. *Prime Areas*, 35 (1), 43–45.

McClain, K., & Cobb, P. (1999). Supporting students' ways of reasoning about patterns and partitions. In J.V. Copley (Ed.), *Mathematics in the early years* (pp. 112–118). Reston, VA: National Council of Teachers of Mathematics.

McIntosh, A., Reys, B.J., & Reys, R.E. (1997). *Number SENSE: Simple effective number sense experiences* [Grades 1–2]. White Plains, NY: Cuisenaire–Dale Seymour.

National Council of Teachers of Mathematics. (1990). *Number sense now! Reaching the NCTM Standards* [Video and teacher's guide]. Reston, VA: Author.

Phillips, E. (1992–93). A selection of math games and activities for early primary. *Prime Areas, 35*(3), 8–10.

Schwartz, S.L. (1995). Enchanting, fascinating, useful number. *Teaching Children Mathematics, 1,* 486–491.

Tenth Planet. (1998). *Combining and breaking apart numbers* [Computer Software]. Pleasantville, NY: Sunburst Communications.

Tenth Planet. (1998). *Number meanings and counting* [Computer Software]. Pleasantville, NY: Sunburst Communications.

Van de Walle, J.A. (1990). Concepts of number. In J.N. Payne (Ed.), *Mathematics for the young child* (pp. 63–87). Reston, VA: National Council of Teachers of Mathematics.

Varney, S. (1992–93). Using calculators in the early primary classroom. *Prime Areas, 35*(3), 17–21.

Weinberg, S. (1996). Going beyond ten black dots. *Teaching Children Mathematics, 2,* 432–435.

Whitin, D.J., Mills, H., & O'Keefe, T. (1994). Exploring subject areas with a counting book. *Teaching Children Mathematics, 1,* 170–174.

Whitin, D.J., & Wilde, S. (1995). *It's the story that counts: More children's books for mathematical learning, K–6.* Portsmouth, NH: Heinemann.

Wicket, M.S. (1997). Serving up number sense and problem solving: *Dinner at the panda palace. Teaching Children Mathematics, 3,* 476–480.

Chapter 7

Developing Meanings for the Operations

This chapter is about helping children connect different meanings, interpretations, and relationships to the four operations of addition, subtraction, multiplication, and division so that they can effectively use these operations in real-world settings.

The main thrust of this chapter is helping children develop what might be termed *operation sense,* a highly integrated understanding of the four operations and the many different but related meanings these operations take on in real contexts. As children solve simple word problems, they learn about the operations. While doing so, they are constructing new number relationships and thinking strategies that will help them master basic facts.

 BIG IDEAS

1. Addition and subtraction are connected. Addition names the whole in terms of the parts, and subtraction names a missing part.
2. Multiplication involves counting groups of equal size and determining how many are in all (multiplicative thinking).
3. Multiplication and division are related. Division names a missing factor in terms of the known factor and the product.
4. Models, both concrete and pictorial, can be used to solve contextual problems for all operations and to figure out what operation is involved in a problem regardless of the size of the numbers.

Two Sources for Developing Operational Meaning

Word problems and models, both concrete (e.g., sets of counters) and pictorial (e.g., number lines) are the two

basic tools teachers have to help students develop conceptual understanding for the four operations (addition, subtraction, multiplication and division). As you will see, each of the four operations is a little more complex than you may have thought. For example, there are as many as 14 different types of word problems identified for addition and subtraction.

Constructing Operational Meaning from Word Problems

The most important way in which children construct meaning for the operations is by solving word problems. Word problems provide an opportunity for examining a diverse set of meanings for each operation. They can and should be handled in a spirit of inquiry, allowing children to use their own methods and justify their solutions.

We know from research that children can and do solve story problems as early as kindergarten—information that is not commonly acknowledged in traditional textbooks. However, the problems that young children are asked to solve must be suited to their ability. Otherwise, those children who have not yet learned to grasp the meaning of numbers in a story problem and to perform the required operation will be unduly challenged. They will be forced to think very hard, possibly becoming frustrated. As long as the numbers are kept relatively simple, the children will usually be able to solve these problems by directly modelling the meaning of the problem with counters. In the process, many children will develop new and more efficient counting strategies.

Basic Meanings Developed with Models

A variety of models such as movable objects (counters, interlocking cubes, pattern blocks), pictures of sets in various arrangements, arrays (things arranged in rows and columns), and variations of these basic ideas can be used to help children develop meaning for the operations. Number lines are also good at the upper grade levels, but can be more confusing than helpful at the primary level.

It is important that models be used appropriately. An activity with only models and no problem to solve is of little value. As well, the teacher must provide direction and explain what is to be done. For example, children could do something with a model (arrange, separate, join, draw arrows on the number line, count rows and lengths of rows, and so on) and then write number sentences (equations) that mean the same thing as the model. The purpose here is to associate or connect a new symbolic language (the equation and operation sign) with the concept of the operation as seen in the model.

Models can also serve both as a thinker toy for analyzing the structure of a story problem and as a connection between the meaning in the story problem and the symbolic equation. Your knowledge of different ways that models can represent operations can assist children in the process. Often a suggestion from you can help children clarify their own thought processes. Concrete models and drawings used in the follow-up portion of a lesson can also help communicate to other children ideas that may otherwise be difficult to explain. There is evidence to suggest that models, both concrete and pictorial, often help make the underlying structure of a story problem more apparent to the students.

As much as possible, modelling of ideas should flow from the students and not be imposed artificially. Your suggestions should be kept as close to the children's thought processes as possible. Never impose a "correct" model, forcing students to "do as you show them." Models should not become the objective of a lesson. There is no reason to have students "learn a model" (Gutstein & Romberg, 1995).

Teaching Symbolism for the Operations

The symbols we use for the operations and the equal sign are all conventions; you have to show students how to use this symbolism to express their ideas. This is best done in the development portion of a lesson, once students have solved a word problem. You can show them how to write an appropriate equation for the problem just solved.

As you will soon see, each of the operations has many different meanings. Care must be taken to help students see that the same symbol can have multiple meanings. For example, the minus sign (–), which is often narrowly defined as "take away," has a broader meaning.

Carla was at Chudleigh's Apple Orchard picking apples. The first time she counted how many apples she had in her bag, there were 7. The next time she counted, there were 11 apples. How many more apples did she pick?

In this problem of 7 apples, picking some more, and ending up with 11 apples, the action is "put together," yet it is solved as a subtraction problem. One child may write 7 + 4 = 11 and another 11 – 7 = 4. A discussion will help children see that both make sense and that they are actually equivalent equations. Forcing children to write exactly the equation we have in mind, or to solve a problem as we would solve it, may be a waste of precious classroom time. The time may be better spent allowing children to solve problems and write equations in ways that make the most sense to them, and then discussing their solutions in order to share and develop a rich array of ideas (Gutstein & Romberg, 1995).

Using Models to Learn about Symbolism

Because symbolism for the operations is an arbitrary convention that children must learn from us, the use of more directed activities is appropriate, even in a problem-oriented classroom. In a models-only activity, the activity begins with a model, then a full equation is written that tells about the model. For example, a model could tell something about 12 – 8 = 4 and how this equation relates the quantities 12, 8, and 4. As children use similar models to solve other word problems, they can be expected to select an appropriate equation based on how they understood the problem and also how they represented it. The model becomes an intermediate linkage between the meaning of the operation and the symbolism. It is important to note that one model can be used to represent various meanings for an operation. In this way models make it possible for students to see how one operational symbol can represent all the different meanings.

Connecting Operations

You have often heard that subtraction is the "inverse of addition" or that division is the "inverse of multiplication." Although this is technically correct, saying it to children is not very helpful to them. The concept of "inverse operation" is fairly sophisticated. However, it is very important to connect addition and subtraction, and multiplication and division. As you will see, models make that connection much more effectively than words. The models for subtraction are precisely the same as those for addition. Similarly, the models for multiplication and division are alike. It is only a matter of which numbers are unknown in the problem.

When students have modelled an operation and have written an equation to go with it, it is often useful to ask what other equation can be written for the same model. Doing so will not only help students see how the inverse operations are connected but also will help them with the connection between multiplication and division.

Translations: Models, Words, and Symbols

It is useful to think of models, word problems, and symbolic equations as three separate languages. Each language can be used to express the relationships involved in one of the operations. Given these three languages, a powerful approach to helping children develop operational meaning is to have them make translations from one language to another. Once children develop a familiarity with an assortment of models and drawings and gain exposure to a variety of meanings through word problems, they can begin to make translations from any one language to the other two, as shown in Figure 7.1. Note that Figure 7.1 is actually a simplification of the five representations discussed in Chapter 3 (see Figure 3.9, p. 37).

In a translation exercise, students are provided with an expression in one of the three languages: a model (usually in the form of a drawing), a word problem, or an equation. They are then asked to come up with expressions in each of the other two languages that represent the same relationships. For example, students could be asked to make up a story problem to go with the equation 4 × 7 = 28 and to illustrate the meaning with a drawing. Since different cooperative groups or individuals will devise different ideas, the results provide a wonderful basis for discussion.

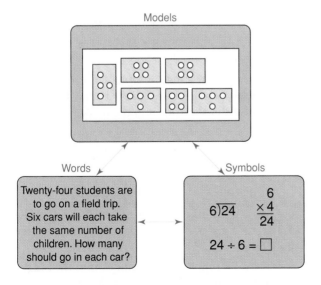

FIGURE 7.1 Translations from any one language to the others help develop students' concepts of the operators.

Word Problems for Addition and Subtraction

Researchers have sorted addition and subtraction problems into categories based on the kinds of relationships involved. These include *join* problems, *separate* problems, *part-part-whole* problems, and *compare* problems (Carpenter & Moser, 1983; Gutstein & Romberg, 1995; Fennema, Carpenter, Levi, Franke, & Empson, 1997). The basic structure for each of these four types of problems is illustrated in Figure 7.2. Different problems can be made by changing which of the three quantities in the structure is unknown.

Examples of Problems for Each Structure

The number family 4, 8, 12 is used in each of the story problems that follow. For each problem, refer to the structure in Figure 7.2, and determine which of the three elements is the unknown. Note that the drawings are not intended for children but to help you as a teacher consider the different structures. Also note that the problems are described in terms of their structure and not as addition or subtraction problems. Joining action does not always mean addition, nor does separate or remove always mean subtraction.

Join Problems

There are three quantities involved for the action of joining: an initial amount, a change amount (the part being added or joined), and the resulting amount (the amount after the action is over).

JOIN: RESULT UNKNOWN

Phillippa had 8 pennies. George gave her 4 more. How many pennies does Phillippa have altogether?

JOIN: CHANGE UNKNOWN

Phillippa had 8 pennies. George gave her some more. Now Phillippa has 12 pennies. How many did George give her?

JOIN: INITIAL UNKNOWN

Phillippa had some pennies. George gave her 4 more. Now Phillippa has 12 pennies. How many pennies did Phillippa have to begin with?

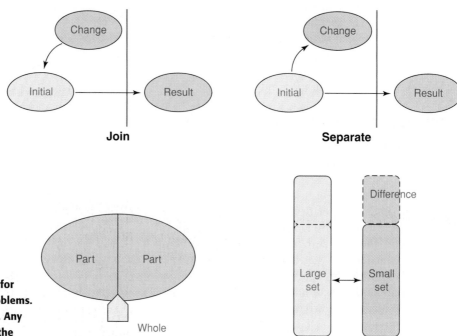

FIGURE 7.2 Four basic structures for addition and subtraction story problems. Each structure has three numbers. Any one of the three numbers can be the unknown in a story problem.

Separate Problems

Notice that in the separate problems, the initial amount is the whole or the largest amount, whereas in the join problems, the result was the whole. Again, refer to Figure 7.2 as you consider these problems. Be sure you can identify which quantities are the initial, the change, and the resultant amounts.

SEPARATE: RESULT UNKNOWN

Phillippa had 12 pennies. She gave 4 pennies to George. How many pennies does Phillippa have now?

SEPARATE: CHANGE UNKNOWN

Phillippa had 12 pennies. She gave some to George. Now she has 8 pennies. How many did she give to George?

SEPARATE: INITIAL UNKNOWN

Phillippa had some pennies. She gave 4 to George. Now Phillippa has 8 pennies left. How many pennies did Phillippa have to begin with?

Part-Part-Whole Problems

Part-part-whole problems involve two parts that are combined into one whole. The combining may be a physical action, or it may be a mental one where the parts are not combined physically.

There are only two kinds of part-part-whole problems, instead of three as with the other structures. There is no meaningful distinction between the two parts in a part-part-whole situation, so there is no need to have a different problem for each part as the unknown. For each possibility (whole unknown and part unknown), two problems are given here. The first is a mental combination where there is no action. The second problem involves a physical action.

PART-PART-WHOLE: WHOLE UNKNOWN

George has 4 pennies and 8 nickels. How many coins does he have?

George has 4 pennies and Phillippa has 8 pennies. They put their pennies into a piggy bank. How many pennies did they put into the bank altogether?

PART-PART-WHOLE: PART UNKNOWN

George has 12 coins. Eight of his coins are pennies, and the rest are nickels. How many nickels does George have?

George and Phillippa put 12 pennies into the piggy bank. George put in 4 pennies. How many pennies did Phillippa put in?

Compare Problems

Compare problems involve the comparison of two quantities. The third amount is not actually present but is the difference between the two amounts. There are three types of compare problems, corresponding to which quantity is unknown (smaller, larger, or difference). For each of these, two examples are given: one problem where the difference is stated in terms of more and another in terms of less.

COMPARE: DIFFERENCE UNKNOWN

George has 12 pennies and Phillippa has 8 pennies. How many more pennies does George have than Phillippa?

George has 12 pennies. Phillippa has 8 pennies. How many fewer pennies does Phillippa have than George?

COMPARE: LARGER UNKNOWN

Phillippa has 8 pennies. George has 4 more pennies than Phillippa. How many pennies does George have?

Phillippa has 4 fewer pennies than George. She has 8 pennies. How many pennies does George have?

COMPARE: SMALLER UNKNOWN

George has 4 more pennies than Phillippa. George has 12 pennies. How many pennies does Phillippa have?

George has 12 pennies. Phillippa has 4 fewer pennies than George. How many pennies does Phillippa have?

An exercise to help you, the teacher, grasp these problem structures is to match the numbers in each problem with the components of the structures in Figure 7.2. For each problem, do two additional things. First, use a set of counters to model (solve) the problem as you think children in the primary grades might. Second, write an equation, either addition or subtraction, that best represents each problem.

Reflections on the Four Structures

In many curricula, the emphasis tends to be on the easier join and separate problems with the result unknown. These become the de facto definitions of addition and subtraction. Addition is "put together" and subtraction is "take away." The fact is, these are *not* the definitions of addition and subtraction. When students develop these limited put-together and take-away definitions for addition and subtraction, they often have difficulty later, when addition or subtraction is called for and the structure is other than these two forms. It is important that children be exposed to all forms within these structures.

Computational and Semantic Forms of Equations

If you wrote an equation for each of the problems just suggested, you may have written some equations where the unknown quantity is not isolated on one side of the equal sign. For example, a likely equation for the join problem with initial part unknown is $\boxed{8} + 4 = 12$. This is referred to as the *semantic* equation for the problem, since the numbers are listed in the order that follows the meaning of the problem. When the semantic form does not isolate the unknown, an equivalent equation can be written for the same problem. In this case, the equation $12 - 4 = \boxed{8}$ is referred to as the *computational* form of the equation; it isolates the unknown. For some of the problems, the computational form and the semantic form are the same. When they are not the same, children must eventually come to see the equivalence of these equations.

Problem Difficulty

The various types of problems are not all equal in difficulty for children (Thompson & Hendrickson, 1986). The change problems where the initial part is unknown are among the most difficult, probably because children do not know how many counters to put down in the beginning. Problems where the change amounts are unknown are also difficult.

Compare problems are significantly different because they do not exactly match up with the part-part-whole model. When a child models a problem with the difference unknown, there is a good chance that the two quantities will be represented. The tendency is to see the two amounts and put them together. This is even more likely to happen when children try to solve compare problems without using a model.

Many children will solve these compare problems as part-part-whole problems without making separate sets of counters for the two amounts. The whole is used as the large amount, one part for the small amount and the second part for the difference. There is absolutely no reason this should be discouraged as long as children are clear about what they are doing. Again, the best value of these problems is in the discussion of the approaches different children use to solve them.

Using Addition and Subtraction Word Problems in the Classroom

No one is suggesting that children should be taught the four structures of word problems as illustrated in Figure 7.2. These are presented for your understanding so that you can create and discuss story problems with children. When making up your own problems, a good idea is first to think of a context (Martians, shopping, a magic tree that grows doughnuts and a child who comes to eat them, a car going down the road and how many kilometres it has travelled). Use the context to provide a storyline, then put some numbers into the various structures and create problems. The examples presented here have been very sterile to allow you to focus on the meaning. It is much better to embellish your problems when you work with children. Put them in contexts that relate to their own lives; use students' names, add unnecessary information, or leave out a number. Use problems related to literature that you are reading. Let children make up problems, but supply a context to inspire them. Unless children are exposed to all of these types of problems, the problems they make up will most likely be result-unknown.

The important goal here is to analyze relationships and discuss approaches. Children should have access to a variety of familiar materials with which to work as they think about a problem. Present a problem orally as well as in written form. If children work in pairs or small groups, they can discuss their ideas and come to some common agreement. It is almost always a good idea to request a written explanation of how they solved the problem, including a picture if that is helpful. A full-sentence answer should always be required: "Now George has 12 cents."

The task for an entire class period can be one or two problems. Remember to leave time for discussion. Have children explain how they solved the problem. If children are ready—if they have been exposed to the necessary symbolism—have them include an equation that "goes with the solution." Some teachers have children circle the number in the equation that was the answer to the problem. Trial equations can be "written" with number and symbol cards so that changes can be made easily. The tendency is to have students solve a lot of problems or do a lot of exercises in a single class period. However, it is more effective, as is done in Japan, if a complete lesson revolves around one or two problems and the related discussion (Reys & Reys, 1995).

Even though your text is unlikely to include this wide variety of problem types, all of these problems should be presented to children, even at the K–1 level. By grade 2, begin to put numbers like 56 and 39 in the problems, or even numbers in the hundreds. These problems, even when presented before children learn to compute, will challenge them to invent ways to work with the larger numbers. As well, it will move students to the computational form of the equations. Of course, calculators should always be available.

Technology Note

The *Fizz & Martina* series (Tom Snyder Productions, 1998) embeds problems in the "real-life" adventures of Fizz and Martina. Available in videotape, videodisc, and CD formats, the stories require students to pay attention and take notes. A story is stopped when the problem is posed, and students work in groups without the video or computer. Printed support material is included. This model fits nicely with the setting the stage, development, and follow-up format of a problem-solving lesson.

Math Trek 1, 2, 3 (Nectar Foundation, 2000), a Canadian software program (mentioned in Chapter 6), has children solve problems involving the operations in the context of a toy store. However, the problems are of the exercise type, not the varied types found in this chapter.

At present, few software products offer addition and subtraction word problems with the variety of problem types we have just explored. However, there are two other ways that you can take advantage of your classroom computers and almost any basic software tool you might have. First, you can use your word processor, or any program that allows shapes to be easily drawn and words to be typed, to design your own problems. An example of the latter type is *Kid Pix* (Brøderbund, 1996a). Open a new file, and write a word problem in an appropriate space. Students may use counters before they use the computer. But the advantage of the computer is its increased recording capabilities. Students open the file and use the drawing capabilities to record their solution. The students' work is either not saved or is renamed, so that your file remains as an activity. Children can also write on the page before printing their solutions.

These same programs can be used to reverse the process. Bridget Phipps, a grade 1 teacher, notes that her children were much better at writing story problems on the computer than by hand, and she often had students write problems for pictures she created. A program such as *MathKeys: Unlocking Whole Numbers* (MECC, 1995b, 1996b) has a large variety of stamps to create counters and a readily available writing space beneath the pictures. Make a file with a drawing involving counters in two parts or with a whole specified and one part showing. Students write and solve a story problem on the computer to go with the drawing. ■■

Model-Based Problems for Addition And Subtraction

The model is a thinking tool. It can help children understand what is happening in the problem, and also keep track of the numbers and the process of solving the problem. Problems can also be posed using models when there is no context involved. The part-part-whole concept discussed in Chapter 6 is a good way to help students think about addition and subtraction when they are focused on models.

As noted earlier, some of the more directed activities with models are useful to help children learn the conventions of the symbols +, −, and = and to serve as linkages between equations and the richer meanings of addition and subtraction word problems.

Addition

When the parts of a set are known, addition is used to name the whole in terms of the parts. This simple, albeit sterile, definition of addition serves both action situations (join and separate) and static or non-action situations.

As noted earlier, an activity in which children *do* something with manipulatives, then *write* a designated equation that tells what they did, is really not a problem to solve. At this time children simply need to be told that it is a convention to write equations with plus signs and equal signs to stand for these meanings. There is an opportunity, though, for reflection and discussion, as children use different models for the same equation and begin to see the same idea in different contexts.

Each of the part-part-whole models shown in Figure 7.3 is a model for 5 + 3 = 8. Some of these are the result of a definite put-together or joining action; some are not. Notice that in every example, both of the parts are distinct, even after the parts are joined. If counters are used, the two parts should be kept in separate piles or sections of a mat, or should be in two distinct colours. For children to see a relationship between the two parts and the whole, the image of the 5 and 3 must be kept as two separate sets. This helps children reflect on the action after it has taken place. "These red chips are the ones I started with. Then I added these five blue ones, and now I have eight altogether."

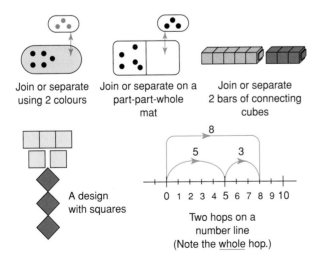

Join or separate using 2 colours

Join or separate on a part-part-whole mat

Join or separate 2 bars of connecting cubes

A design with squares

8

5   3

0 1 2 3 4 5 6 7 8 9 10

Two hops on a number line
(Note the whole hop.)

FIGURE 7.3 Part-part-whole models for 5 + 3 = 8 and 8 − 3 = 5.

A number line measures distances from zero the same way a ruler does. Its use as a model for grade 1 and 2 students is not generally recommended as it presents some real conceptual difficulties. In the early grades, children focus on the dots or numbers instead of the spaces. They think of numbers in terms of sets and objects, not lengths. However, if arrows (hops) are drawn from one unit to the next to represent each number in an exercise, the length concept is illustrated more clearly. To model the part-part-whole concept of 5 + 3, start by drawing an arrow from 0 to 5, indicating, "This much is five." Do not point to the dot for 5, saying, "This is five;" rather, draw attention to the distance covered.

Two children can work together, do something with a model, say the combination, and together write the equation. The children can vary the total amounts they construct each time—within appropriate limits, of course. Remember, what makes "Equations with Number Patterns" problem-based is the challenge to find different combinations for a number.

Subtraction

In a part-part-whole model, when the whole and one of the parts are known, subtraction names the other part. This definition fits with the drastically overused language of "take away." If you start with a whole set of 8 and remove a set of 3, the two sets that you know are the sets of 8 and 3. The expression 8 − 3, read "eight minus three," names the five that remains. Therefore, eight minus three is five. Notice that the models in Figure 7.3 are models for subtraction as well as addition (except for the action). Helping children see that they are using the same models or pictures assists them in connecting the two operations.

Directed activities for part-part-whole subtraction concepts are similar to those for addition, except for two important differences:

1. The amount left (for action situations) or the unknown part (for non-action situations) should ini-

tially be covered. In this way the child is encouraged to "think addition": "What goes with this part to make the whole amount?"

2. Two equations should almost always be written for the model. That is, if the whole amount, 9, and 3 are showing, the child first writes "9 – 3 = 6." Then the unknown part is uncovered, and the corresponding addition equation is written as well. The single model for both equations serves as a way of helping the child construct the relationship between addition and subtraction.

ACTIVITY 7.2

Missing-Part Subtraction

A fixed number of counters are placed on a mat. One child separates the counters into two parts while the other child hides her or his eyes. The first child covers one of the two parts with a sheet of tag-board, revealing only the other part (see Figure 7.4). The second child says the subtraction sentence, for example, "Nine minus four [the visible part] is five [the covered part]." The covered part can be revealed, if necessary, for the child to say how many there are. Both the subtraction equation and the addition equation can then be written.

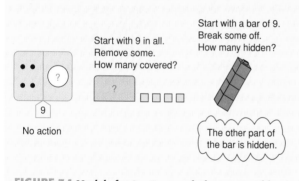

Start with 9 in all. Remove some. How many covered?

Start with a bar of 9. Break some off. How many hidden?

9

No action

The other part of the bar is hidden.

FIGURE 7.4 Models for 9 – 4 as a missing-part problem.

"Missing-Part Subtraction," where one part of the whole is hidden, can be played with any materials.

Subtraction as Think-Addition

Note that in Activity 7.2, the situation ends with two parts clearly distinct, even when there is a "remove" action. The part that is removed remains on the mat as a model for an addition equation to be written after the subtraction equation has been written. A discussion of how two equations can be written for the same model is an important opportunity to connect addition and subtraction. This is significantly better than the traditional worksheet activity of "fact fam-

ilies" in which children are given a family of numbers such as 3, 5, and 8 and are told to write two "plus" equations and two "minus" equations. Very quickly this becomes a matter of dropping the numbers into the various slots.

The previously modelled activity for subtraction has further value that is extremely significant for later learning and for mastery of subtraction facts. Because the counters for the remaining or unknown part are left hidden under the cover, when children do these activities, they are encouraged to think about the hidden part: "What goes with the part I see to make the whole?" For example, if the total or whole number of counters is 9, and 6 are removed from under the cover, the child is likely to think in terms of "6 and what makes 9?" or "What goes with 6 to make 9?" The mental activity is "think-addition" instead of a "count what's left" approach. Later, when working on subtraction facts, a subtraction fact such as 9 – 6 = □ should trigger the same thought pattern: "6 and what makes 9?" However, this relationship between addition and subtraction must be constructed by the children. A more traditional approach to subtraction facts has no hope of inspiring children to think about addition and connecting a known addition fact to subtraction. The traditional approach with counters for 9 – 6 = □ is: first count out 9, next count and take away 6, and then count what is left. The 6 that are removed are just that—removed. They do not form the other part in the part-part-whole model.

Comparison Models

Comparison situations involve two distinct sets or quantities and the difference between them. Several ways of modelling the difference relationship are shown in Figure 7.5. The same kind of model can be used whether the unknown element is the difference, or one of the two quantities.

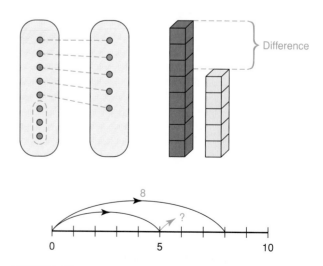

Difference

8

0   5   10

FIGURE 7.5 Models for the difference between 8 and 5.

Children modelling comparison word problems will frequently use a model like those in the figure to solve the problem. Note that it is not immediately clear how to associate either the addition or subtraction operations with a comparison situation. This is another reason why this is a difficult type of problem. From an adult vantage point, you can see that if you match part of the larger amount with the smaller amount, the large set is now a part-part-whole model that can solve the problem. In fact, many children do model compare problems in just this manner. But that is a very difficult idea to show children, unless they construct it themselves.

To approach the model and comparison idea as a problem situation, have children make two amounts, perhaps with two bars of connecting cubes. Discuss the difference between the two bars to generate the third number. For example, if the children make a bar of 10 and a bar of 6, the difference is 4. "What equations can we make with these three numbers?" Have children make up story problems that involve two amounts of 10 and 6. Discuss which equations go with the problems that are created.

The Order Property and the Zero Property

Put simply, the *order* property (or *commutative* property) for addition says that it makes no difference in which order two numbers are added. Most children have little difficulty with this idea. Since it is quite useful in problem solving, mastering basic facts, and mental mathematics, there is value in spending some time helping children construct this relationship. The name of the property is not important, but the idea is.

Show a set on a two-part mat on the overhead projector. Ask the children to say the addition name for how much is shown—for example, "Eight plus four." Now draw careful attention to the mat as you turn it around completely. Again request the addition name, "Four plus eight." Discuss which is more, 8 plus 4 or 4 plus 8. "Will this work for other numbers? What if we had really big numbers like 432 on one side and 189 on the other?" A discussion similar to this will very likely generate the order property. Notice that the rule is not arbitrary but comes from the students and the model.

Many children have difficulty with addition and subtraction when zero is involved. Zero as a number is probably not understood as early as other numbers. Also, there is an intuitive idea that addition "makes numbers bigger" and subtraction "makes numbers smaller." Avoid providing arbitrary-sounding "rules" about zero. Rather, use and model story problems involving addition and subtraction with zero and make a special effort to discuss ways to make sense of these with your students. What you do not want to do is make a statement such as "Whenever you add zero, you get the same number back." That may make sense to you, but it sounds like an arbitrary rule to a child. It is always better to have a good discussion using a story problem and concrete and pictorial models. Have faith. Children can figure these things out.

Word Problems for Multiplication and Division

Most researchers identify four different classes of multiplicative structures (Greer, 1992). Of these, the two described in Figure 7.6, *equal groups* (*repeated addition, rates*) and *multiplicative comparison,* are by far the most prevalent in the elementary school. Problems matching these structures can be modelled with sets of counters, number lines, or arrays. They represent a large percentage of the multiplicative problems in the real world. (The term *multiplicative* is used here to describe all problems that involve multiplication and division structure.)

The two other types of problems, *combinations* (*Cartesian products*) and *product-of-measures* problems (e.g., length times width equals area), are also important but receive much less attention in school. These problems will be described in terms of real-world contexts instead of a general structure.

The diagrams of the two basic structures are presented here for you as a teacher to organize your thoughts. Children do not consciously recognize the structures. Do not attempt to teach the abstract structures of these problems to the children.

Examples of Problems for Each Structure

Multiplicative problems differ from additive problems in that the numbers involved represent different kinds of things. One number or *factor* informs how many sets, groups, or parts of equal size are involved. The other factor tells the size of each set or part. These two factors have traditionally been referred to as the *multiplier* (number of parts) and the *multiplicand* (size of each part). These terms are not particularly useful to children and will not be used here unless needed for clarity. The third number in each of these two structures is the *whole* or *product* and is the total of all of the parts. The parts and wholes terminology is useful in making the connection to addition.

Equal-Group Problems

When the number and size of groups are known, the problem is a multiplication situation. When either the number or the size of sets is unknown, division results. But note that these latter two situations are not alike. Problems

FIGURE 7.6 Two of the four basic structures for multiplication and division story problems. Each structure has three numbers. Any one of the three numbers can be the unknown in a story problem.

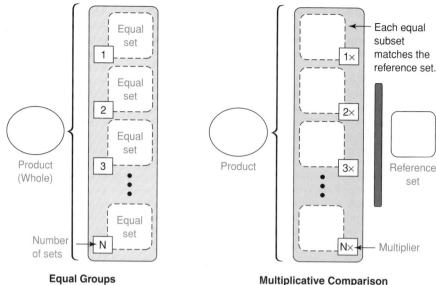

Equal Groups

Multiplicative Comparison

where the size of the sets is unknown are called *fair-sharing* or *partition* problems. The whole is shared or distributed among a known number of sets to determine the size of each. If the number of sets is unknown but the size of the equal sets is known, the problems are called *measurement* or sometimes *repeated-subtraction* problems. The whole is "measured off" in sets of a given size. These terms are used with the examples to follow. Keep in mind the structure in Figure 7.6 to see which numbers are given and which are unknown.

There is also a subtle difference between problems that might be termed *repeated-addition* problems (If 3 children have 4 apples each, how many apples are there?) and those that might be termed *rate* problems (If there are 4 apples per child, how many apples would 3 children have?). For each category, two examples of rate problems are provided.

EQUAL GROUPS: WHOLE UNKNOWN (MULTIPLICATION)

Mark has 4 bags of apples. There are 6 apples in each bag. How many apples does Mark have altogether?

If apples cost 32 cents each, how much did Jill have to pay for 5 apples? (*rate*)

Peter walked for 3 hours at 6 kilometres per hour. How far did he walk? (*rate*)

EQUAL GROUPS: SIZE OF GROUPS UNKNOWN (PARTITION DIVISION)

Mark has 24 apples. He wants to share them equally among his 4 friends. How many apples will each friend receive?

Jill paid 96 cents for 3 apples. What was the cost of 1 apple? (*rate*)

Peter walked 18 kilometres in 3 hours. How many kilometres per hour (how fast) did he walk? (*rate*)

EQUAL GROUPS: NUMBER OF GROUPS UNKNOWN (MEASUREMENT DIVISION)

Mark has 24 apples. He put them into bags containing 6 apples each. How many bags did Mark use?

Jill bought apples that cost 32 cents each. The total cost of her apples was 96 cents. How many apples did Jill buy? (*rate*)

Peter walked 18 kilometres at a rate of 6 kilometres per hour. How many hours did it take Peter to walk the 18 kilometres? (*rate*)

Multiplicative Comparison Problems

In multiplicative comparison problems, there are really two different sets, as there are with comparison situations for addition and subtraction. One set consists of multiple copies of the other. Two examples of each possibility are provided here. It may be useful for you to consider the distinction between additive comparisons and multiplicative comparisons. In the former, the comparison is an amount or quantity difference. In multiplicative situations, the comparison is based on one set being a particular multiple of the other.

COMPARISON: PRODUCT UNKNOWN (MULTIPLICATION)

Jill picked 6 apples. Mark picked 4 times as many apples as Jill. How many apples did Mark pick?

This month Mark saved 5 times as much money as he did last month. Last month he saved $15. How much money did Mark save this month?

COMPARISON: SET SIZE UNKNOWN (PARTITION DIVISION)

Mark picked 24 apples. He picked 4 times as many apples as Jill. How many apples did Jill pick?

This month Mark saved 5 times as much money as he did last month. If he saved $75 this month, how much did he save last month?

COMPARISON: MULTIPLIER UNKNOWN (MEASUREMENT DIVISION)

Mark picked 24 apples, and Jill picked only 6. How many times as many apples did Mark pick as Jill did?

This month Mark saved $75. Last month he saved $15. How many times as much money did he save this month as last?

Combinations Problems

Combinations problems involve counting the number of possible pairings that can be made between two sets. The product consists of *pairs* of things; one member of each pair is taken from each of the two given sets. The two factors in these problems each represent the size of a set, so there is no reason to distinguish between two division situations.

COMBINATIONS: PRODUCT UNKNOWN

Samson bought 4 pairs of pants and 3 jackets. They all can be worn interchangeably . How many different outfits consisting of a pair of pants and a jacket does Samson have?

You want to make a set of attribute pieces that have 3 colours and 6 different shapes. If you want your set to have exactly one piece for every possible combination of shape and colour, how many pieces will you need to make?

An experiment involves tossing a coin and rolling a die. How many different possible results or outcomes can this experiment have?

COMBINATIONS: SIZE OF A SET UNKNOWN

Samson bought some new pants and jackets. He has a total of 12 different outfits. If he bought 4 pairs of pants, how many jackets did Samson buy?

Your set of attribute materials consists of 18 different pieces. There are 3 colours, and each colour comes in different shapes. How many different shapes are in the set?

In the experiment of tossing a coin and rolling a die, there are 12 possible outcomes. Of course, the coin has two sides. How many sides does the die have?

Note that in the last "outfits" example, if the unknown were the number of pairs of pants instead of the number of jackets, the problem would be the same structurally. A similar observation could be made of the other two problems.

There are different ways to model these problems: indicate pairings using lines, model all pairs concretely, or use an array. Figure 7.7 (p. 126) provides examples of all of these possibilities.

Combinations problems can have more than two quantities. For example, Samson may also have six different ties ($4 \times 3 \times 6$), the attribute pieces could include two sizes and have one, two, or three holes in each piece ($3 \times 6 \times 2 \times 3$), and the experiment may include two coins instead of one ($2 \times 2 \times 6$). Modelling combinations for three or more sets is possible but quickly becomes tedious. The lower-right example in Figure 7.7 shows a three-dimensional array. (A line drawing or pairings could also have been used.) In the upper grades, it is worthwhile exploring such combinations with small numbers so students can see that this concept of multiplication can be extended to any number of sets. As students become more familiar with probability and finite mathematics, experiences with combinations problems will gain importance for them.

Product-of-Measures Problems

What distinguishes product-of-measures problems from the others is that the product is literally a different type of thing from the other two factors. In a rectangle, the product of two lengths (length × width) yields an area measure in square units. Figure 7.8 (p. 126) illustrates how different the square units are from each of the two factors of length: 4 metres multiplied by 7 metres is not 28 metres but 28 *square* metres. The factors are each one-dimensional entities, but the product consists of *two*-dimensional units. If the area of the rectangle and the length of one side were given, division would be used to determine the length of the unknown side.

Two other fairly common examples in this category are number of workers × hours worked = worker hours and kilowatts × hours = kilowatt hours.

FIGURE 7.7 Models for combinations situations.

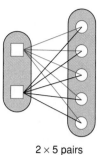

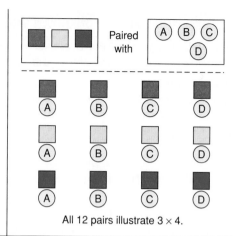

2 × 5 pairs

Each line indicates a possible pair.

All 12 pairs illustrate 3 × 4.

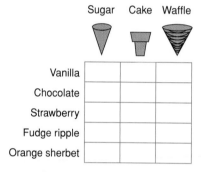

5 × 3 possible ice cream cones

Each section is one combination of a flavour and a type of cone.

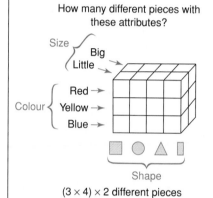

How many different pieces with these attributes?

(3 × 4) × 2 different pieces (concept extended to 3 factors)

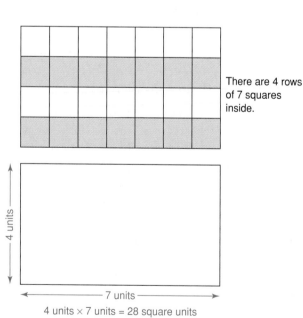

There are 4 rows of 7 squares inside.

4 units × 7 units = 28 square units

FIGURE 7.8 Length times length equals area.

Reflections on Multiplicative Problems

The remainder of this chapter will focus on equal-group and multiplicative comparison problems. These are the most common multiplication and division problems found in the elementary and middle grades.

Extensive research on children's multiplicative thinking suggests that children are slow to think of sets of objects as singular items to be counted (Clark & Kamii, 1996; Kouba, 1989; Steffe, 1988). However, there is also evidence that kindergarten and grade 1 children are quite successful at solving multiplication and division problems, even division involving remainders (Carpenter, Ansell, Franke, Fennema, & Weisbeck, 1993; Carpenter, Carey, & Kouba, 1990; Fennema et al., 1997). Based on their own research and that of others, Mulligan and Mitchelmore (1997) strongly argue that students should be exposed to all four operations from the first year of school and that multiplication and division should be much more closely linked in the curriculum. (Generally, multiplication is taught prior to, and separately from, division.) In the early years, the strategies students use may not reflect multiplicative thinking, but exposure will improve understanding of all four operations and lead to an earlier development of multiplicative strategies.

Notation and Language

In most books, the convention is that the first factor in a product indicates the number of sets and the second the size of the sets. Thus 4 × 8 refers to four sets of eight, not eight sets of four. There is no reason to be rigid about this convention, but it will be useful for communication and for textbook work to establish it in your classroom. Introduction of this convention and the operation symbols × and ÷ is best done as students solve multiplicative problems. In the development portion of a lesson, you can simply explain that these are symbols used to represent the ideas in the problems.

Unfortunately, there are two commonly used symbols for division: 24 ÷ 6 and $6\overline{)24}$. The second form is the computational form. It would probably not exist if there were no pencil-and-paper computational procedure that made use of it. (For the other three operations, the vertical format is the computational form.)

These two forms cause trouble that is worth noting. First, the order of the numbers is reversed. To read them both as "24 divided by 6," one must be read from left to right and the other from right to left. Compounding this difficulty is the meaningless but traditional statement, "6 goes into 24," which probably originated with the question, "How many 6's are in 24?" The "goes into" terminology is so ingrained in our society that most adults continue to use it as if it carried some clear meaning. This statement is generally not used in student textbooks. Perhaps it would help if we realized that "goes into" is language connected to our tradition and our understanding but not to children's. If "goes into" is in your vernacular, and it probably is, try not to use it in the classroom.

Remainders

More often than not, division does not result in a simple whole number. For example, problems with 6 as a divisor will "come out even" only one time out of six. In the absence of a word-problem context, a remainder can be dealt with in only two ways: It can either remain a quantity left over or be partitioned into fractions. In Figure 7.9, the problem 11 ÷ 4 is modelled to show fractions.

In real contexts, remainders sometimes have three additional effects on answers:

The remainder is discarded, leaving a smaller whole-
number answer.

Partition $11 \div 4 = 2\frac{3}{4}$
$2\frac{3}{4}$ in each of the 4 sets
(each leftover divided in fourths)

Measurement $11 \div 4 = 2\frac{3}{4}$
$2\frac{3}{4}$ sets of 4
(2 full sets and $\frac{3}{4}$ of a set)

FIGURE 7.9 Remainders expressed as fractions.

The remainder can "force" the answer to the next highest whole number.

The answer is rounded to the nearest whole number for an approximate result.

The following problems illustrate all five possibilities.

You have 30 pieces of candy to share fairly with 7 children. How many pieces of candy will each child receive?
Answer: 4 pieces of candy and 2 left over. (*left over*)

Each jar holds 4 litres of liquid. If there are 37 litres in the barrel, how many jars will that be?
Answer: 9 and $\frac{1}{4}$ jars. (*partitioned as a fraction*)

The rope is 25 metres long. How many 2-metre skipping ropes can be made?
Answer: 12 skipping ropes. (*discarded*)

The ferry can hold 8 cars. How many trips will it have to make to carry 25 cars across the river?
Answer: 4 trips. (*forced to next whole number*)

Six children are planning to share a bag of 50 pieces of bubble gum. About how many pieces will each child get?
Answer: About 8 pieces for each child. (*rounded, approximate result*)

Students should not just think of remainders as "R 3" or "left over." Remainders should be put in context and dealt with accordingly. It is useful for you to make up problems in different contexts. Include continuous quantities such as length, time, and volume. See if you can come up with problems in each division category for equal-group and comparison problems that would have remainders dealt with as fractions or as results that are rounded up or rounded down.

Using Multiplication and Division Word Problems in the Classroom

Multiplication and division word problems are excellent examples of tasks that should be used to structure a lesson using the introduction, development, and follow-up format described in Chapter 4. If you are teaching in K–2, you may need to make up your own problems. By grade 3, most textbooks will have good problems from which to select. However, a traditional textbook lesson will likely have a short illustration of some multiplication idea followed by a series of problems to solve. The need to complete many problems encourages children to pull out the numbers and perform an operation, rather than to take their time and think about the problem they are solving. If instead you structure a lesson around one to three problems and include a full discussion of strategies, models, and reasoning, students will have a much greater opportunity to develop multiplicative thinking. Also, presenting division and multiplication problems in pairs will give you an opportunity to focus on the relationships between the two operations.

The numbers in multiplicative problems are generally larger than in additive problems. They are somewhat tedious to model with counters or drawings. Fairly early in grade 3, you will want to move to problems involving 14 × 8 or even larger numbers. Children encouraged to wrestle with large numbers can and will invent a variety of methods for doing the computation in these problems. An alternative is to encourage the use of the calculator. However, children should be able to defend anything they do on the calculator. For example, if they do not know what 14 × 8 means or why they are using the multiplication key instead of ⊞ or ⊟, they have not solved the problem.

As has been noted, with division problems, the numbers involved frequently do not produce answers that "come out even." Textbooks are especially notorious about shielding children from remainders in division. The result is that many children believe their answers must be wrong when the division doesn't work out evenly. However, in the real world, division situations rarely result in whole-number answers. The emphasis in your word problems at all grade levels should therefore be on realistic numbers.

There is a lot of value in discussing with children how to interpret these results.

Technology Note

The *Fizz & Martina* series (Tom Snyder Productions, 1998) was mentioned earlier as a vehicle for embedding story problems into real contexts. For the upper grades, the problems are both one- and two-step, involving a wider range of mathematical concepts than have been discussed here. Many teachers like the ease of use that a video format allows.

A few other programs that use word problems, developed in Canada, are *Math Trek* (Nectar Foundation, 2000) and *Mathville* (Courseware Solutions, 2000), These software programs are aimed at grades 1–8. *Word Problem Square Off* (Gamco, 1994) and *Math for the Real World* (Davidson) are two examples that are not Canadian. Both are designed for grade 3 and higher, with *Square Off* available in three grade levels. ▪▬

Model-Based Problems for Multiplication and Division

In the beginning, children will be able to use the same models—sets and number lines—for all four operations. A model not generally used for addition but extremely important and widely used for multiplication and division is the array. An *array* is any arrangement of things in rows and columns, such as a rectangle of square tiles or blocks.

To make clear the connection to addition, early multiplication activities should also include writing an addition sentence for the particular model. A variety of models is shown in Figure 7.10. Notice that the products are not included: only the addition and multiplication "names" are written—another way to avoid the tedious counting of large sets. An alternative approach is to write one sentence that expresses both concepts at once, for example, 9 + 9 + 9 + 9 = 4 × 9. Note again that the first factor, 4, tells the number of sets and the second factor, 9, the size of the sets.

Multiplication and Division Activities

As was the case with additive problems, children can benefit from a few activities with models and no context. Activities such as these focus on the meaning of the operation and the associated symbolism. Activity 7.3 effectively reflects the spirit of problem solving. The language you use depends on what you have used with your children in the past.

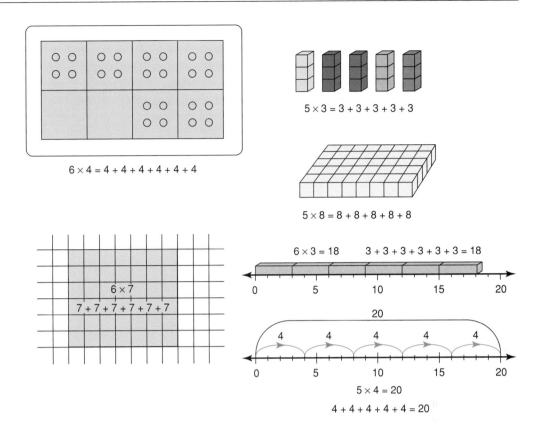

$$6 \times 4 = 4 + 4 + 4 + 4 + 4 + 4$$

$$5 \times 3 = 3 + 3 + 3 + 3 + 3$$

$$5 \times 8 = 8 + 8 + 8 + 8 + 8$$

$$6 \times 7$$
$$7 + 7 + 7 + 7 + 7 + 7$$

$$6 \times 3 = 18 \qquad 3 + 3 + 3 + 3 + 3 + 3 = 18$$

$$5 \times 4 = 20$$
$$4 + 4 + 4 + 4 + 4 = 20$$

FIGURE 7.10 **Models for equal-group multiplication.**

ACTIVITY 7.3

Finding Factors

Start by assigning a number that has several factors—for example, 12, 18, 24, 30, or 36. Have students find multiplication expressions for their assigned number. If using counters, students attempt to find a way to separate the counters into equal subsets. With arrays (perhaps made from square tiles or cubes or drawn on grid paper), students try to build different rectangles for the given number of squares. For each arrangement of sets or rectangles, both an addition and a multiplication equation are written.

Consider for a moment how you would go about doing each of the following tasks: First, take 18 counters and find out how many sets of 6 counters you can make. Draw a picture of the result. Write a simple story problem that fits with what you just did. Second, take 18 counters and separate them into 6 equal sets. Draw another picture, and write a story problem that fits with what you did. Now look at your pictures. What is interesting is that each picture illustrates a different multiplication situation.

For the first task, you should have made 3 sets of 6. That is a model for $\boxed{3} \times 6 = 18$. The second time you cre-

ated 6 sets of 3 each. That is a model for $6 \times \boxed{3} = 18$. Division involves finding a missing factor. It is related to multiplication in the same way that subtraction is related to addition.

Your first word problem should have been a measurement problem involving measuring out *groups of 6*. The second word problem should be a partition problem. You partitioned or shared the 18 among *6 sets*. It is important that as a teacher you be able to create problems that fit the measurement and partition concepts.

Activity 7.3 can also include division concepts. When children have learned that 3 and 6 are factors of 18, they can write the equations $18 \div 3 = 6$ and $18 \div 6 = 3$ along with $3 \times 6 = 18$ and $6 + 6 + 6 = 18$ (assuming that three sets of six were modelled). A variation of activity 7.3, focusing on division, follows. Another excellent extension of this activity is to have children create word problems. Have children explain how their story problems fit with what they did with the counters.

ACTIVITY 7.4

Learning about Division

Provide children with an ample supply of counters and a way to organize them into small groups. Small paper cups work well. Have children count out a number of counters to represent

the whole or total set. They record this number: "Start with thirty-one." Next, specify either the number of equal sets to be made or the size of the sets to be made: "Separate your counters into four equal-sized sets," or "Make as many sets of four as possible." Then have the children write a multiplication equation that corresponds to what their materials show; under that, have them write a division equation.

Be sure to include both types of exercises: number of equal sets and size of sets. Discuss with the class how, although these two are different, each is related to multiplication and each is written as a division equation. You can show both ways to write division equations at this time. Do Activity 7.4 several times. Start with whole quantities that are multiples of the divisor (no remainders), but soon introduce situations with remainders. (Note that it is technically incorrect to write 31 ÷ 4 = 7 R 3. However, in the beginning, that form may be the most appropriate to use.)

You can vary the activity by changing the model that is used. Have children build arrays using square tiles or blocks or have them draw arrays on centimetre grid paper. Present the exercises by specifying how many squares are to be in the array. You can then specify the number of rows that should be made (partition) or the length of each row (measurement). How could children model fractional answers using drawings of arrays on grid paper?

ACTIVITY 7.5

The Broken Multiplication Key

The calculator is a good way to relate multiplication to addition. Students can be told to find various products on the calculator without using the × key. For example, 6 × 4 can be found by pressing ⊞ 4 ⊟ ⊟ ⊟ ⊟ ⊟ ⊟ . (Successive presses of = add 4 to the display each time. You began with zero and added 4 six times.) Students can be challenged to demonstrate their result with sets of counters. But note that this same technique can be used to determine products such as 23 × 459 (⊞ 459 and then 23 presses of ⊟). Students will want to compare to the same product using the ⊠ key.

Note: "The Broken Multiplication Key" activity can profitably be followed by "The Broken Division Key."

ACTIVITY 7.6

The Broken Division Key

Have children work in groups to find methods of using the calculator to solve division exercises without using the divide key. The problems can be posed without a story context. "Find at least two ways to figure out 61 ÷ 14 without pressing the divide key." If the problem is put in a story context, one method may actually match the problem better than another. Good discussions may follow different solutions with the same answers. Are they both correct? Why or why not?

There is no reason ever to show children how to do Activity 7.6. However, it would be a good idea for *you* to see if you can find *three* ways to solve 61 ÷ 14 on a calculator without using the divide key. For a hint, see the footnote.*

Useful Multiplication and Division Properties

As with addition and subtraction, multiplication has some properties that are useful and thus worthy of attention. The emphasis should be on the ideas and not the terminology or the definitions.

The Order Property in Multiplication

Because the two factors in a multiplication expression carry different meanings, it is not intuitively obvious that 3 × 8 is the same as 8 × 3 or that, in general, the order of the numbers makes no difference (the *order* or *commutative* property). A picture of 3 sets of 8 objects cannot immediately be seen as 8 piles of 3 objects. Eight hops of 3 lands at 24, but it is not clear that 3 hops of 8 will land at the same point.

The array, by contrast, is quite powerful for illustrating the order property, as shown in Figure 7.11. Children should draw or build arrays and use them to demonstrate why each array represents two different multiplications with the same product.

The Role of Zero and One in Multiplication

Zero and, to a lesser extent, 1 as factors often cause difficulty for children. In one grade 3 text (Charles et al., 1998), a lesson on factors 0 and 1 has children use a calculator to examine a wide range of products involving multiplication with 0 or 1 (423 × 0, 0 × 28, 1536 × 1, etc.) and look for patterns. A pattern suggests the rules for mul-

---

*There are two measurement approaches or two ways to find out how many 14s are in 61. A third way is essentially related to partitioning or finding 14 times what number is close to 61.

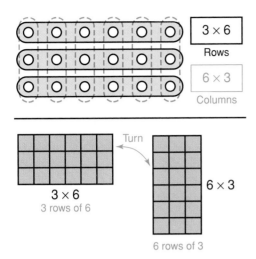

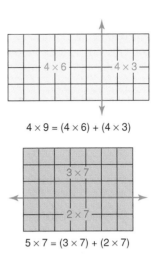

FIGURE 7.11 Two ways an array can be used to illustrate the order (commutative) property for multiplication.

FIGURE 7.12 Models for the distributive property.

tiplication with factors 0 and 1, but not a reason. In the same lesson, a word problem asks how many grams of fat there are in 7 servings of celery with 0 grams of fat in each serving. This approach is far preferable to an arbitrary rule, since it provides a context and asks students to reason. Make up interesting word problems involving 0 or 1, and discuss the results. Problems with 0 as a first factor are really strange for children. Note that on a number line, 5 hops of 0 land at 0 (5×0). What would 0 hops of 5 be? Another amusing activity is to try to model 6×0 or 0×8 with an array. (Try it!) Arrays for factors of 1 are also worth investigating.

The Distributive Property

It may not be essential for young children to know the *distributive* property in the form $a \times (b + c) = (a \times b) + (a \times c)$. But the concept involved is very useful in relating one basic fact to another, and it is also involved in the development of two-digit computation for multiplication. Figure 7.12 illustrates how the array model can be used to illustrate that a product can be broken up into two parts. Children could be asked to draw specific rectangles, slice them into two parts, and write the corresponding equation.

Why Not Division by Zero?

Some children are simply told "Division by zero is not allowed." Though this fact is quite important, children do not always understand it. To avoid an arbitrary rule, pose problems that involve modelling with zero: "Take 30 counters. How many sets of zero can be made?" or "Put 12 blocks in zero equal groups. How many in each group?" Even if children think they have a result that makes sense, suggest that they write the corresponding multiplication equations as they have done for other exercises.

Contextual Problems in the Upper Grades

So far in this chapter, we have discussed the meanings of the operations and looked at simple one-step problems that amplify those meanings. The word problems have been relatively simple, and the numbers involved have been relatively small. The value of these problems is that they allow children to use simple models to analyze the problems. By grade 4 and beyond, most children have developed meaning for the operations. The problems they encounter at that point include problems with large numbers with decimals and fractions, problems with data that are embedded in charts or tables, problems involving more data than necessary, and problems that have two or sometimes even three steps. Here we will discuss how the methods that have been used in this chapter can be applied to help children analyze these more complex situations.

Analyzing Context Problems with Large Numbers

Consider the following problem:

In order to build a road through a subdivision, a low section in the land had to be filled in with dirt hauled in by trucks. The complete fill required 638 truckloads of dirt. The average truck carried $4\frac{3}{4}$ cubic metres of dirt, with a mass of 15.6 tonnes. How many tonnes of dirt were used for the fill?

Typically, in grade 6 to grade 8 books, problems of this type are found as part of a series of problems revolving around a single context or theme. Data may be found in a graph or chart or perhaps in a short news item or story. Most likely the problems will include all four of the operations. Students have difficulty deciding on the correct operation and even finding the appropriate data for the problem. Many students will find two numbers in the problem and guess at the correct operation. These children simply do not have any tools for analyzing problems. At least two strategies can be taught that are very helpful: Think about the answer before solving the problem, or solve a simpler problem that is just like this one.

Think about the Answer before Solving the Problem

Poor problem solvers fail to spend adequate time thinking about the problem and what it is about. They rush in and begin doing calculations, believing that "number crunching" is what solves problems. They need to be encouraged to instead spend time talking about (later, thinking about) what the answer might look like. For our sample problem, it might go as follows:

What is happening in this problem? Some trucks were bringing dirt to fill up a hole.

What will the answer tell us? How many tonnes of dirt were needed in the fill.

Will that be a small number of tonnes or a large number of tonnes? Well, each truck carried 15.6 tonnes of dirt, but there were a lot of trucks, not just one. It's probably going to be a lot of tonnes.

About how many do you think it will be? It's going to be a lot. If there were just 100 trucks, it would be 1560 tonnes. It might be close to 2000 tonnes. That's a lot of tonnes!

In this type of discussion, two things are happening. First, the students are asked to focus on the problem and the meaning of the answer instead of on numbers only. The numbers are not significant when thinking about the structure of the problem. Second, the thinking leads to a rough estimate of the answer. Sometimes, for everyday things, this can simply be based on common sense. In any event, thinking about what the answer tells us and about how large it might be is a useful first step. When a final answer is reached, it should be given in a full sentence and compared with the early ballpark estimate.

Work a Simpler Problem

The reason that models are rarely used with problems such as the dirt problem is that the numbers are impossible to model easily. Dollars and cents, distances in thousands of kilometres, and time in minutes and seconds are all examples of data likely to be found in the upper grades, and all are difficult to model. The general problem-solving strategy

of "try a simpler problem" can almost always be applied to problems with unwieldy numbers.

A simple strategy has the following steps:

1. Substitute small whole numbers for all relevant numbers in the problem.
2. Model the problem concretely or pictorially (counters, drawings, number lines, arrays) using the new numbers.
3. Write an equation that solves the small-number version of the problem.
4. Write the corresponding equation using the original numbers where the small-number substitutes were used.
5. Use a calculator to do the computation.
6. Write the answer in a complete sentence, and decide if it makes sense.

A good rule of thumb is to substitute numbers between 3 and 25. Avoid the use of 1 and 2, as relationships might be obscured. Figure 7.13 shows what might be done for the dirt problem. It also shows an alternative in which only one of the numbers is made smaller and the other number is illustrated symbolically. Both methods are effective. The use of symbols in a conceptual drawing is a powerful strategy in itself.

The idea is to provide students with a tool they can use to analyze a problem, so that they don't have to guess at what computation to do. It is much more useful to have students do a few problems where they must use a model of a drawing to justify their solution than to give them a lot of problems where they guess at a solution and do not know if their guess is correct.

Two-Step Problems

Students often have difficulty with multi-step problems. If your students are going to work with multi-step problems, be sure they can analyze one-step problems in the way that we have discussed. The following ideas, adapted from suggestions by DeAnn Huinker (1994), are designed to help children see how two problems can be linked together.

1. Give students a one-step problem, and have them solve it. Before discussing the answer, have each student or group make up a second problem that uses the answer to the first problem. The rest of the class can then use the answer to the first problem to solve each student's or group's second problem. Here is an example:

Given problem: **It took $3\frac{1}{3}$ hours for the Mercier family to drive the 312 km to Quebec City. What was their average speed?**

Second problem: **The Mercier children remember passing the turkey farm at about 10:30, or 2 hours after they left home. About how far from home is the turkey farm?**

FIGURE 7.13 Working a simpler problem: two possibilities.

2. Make a "hidden question." Repeat the first exercise by beginning with a one-step problem. You might give different problems to different groups. This time, have students write out both problems as before. Then write a single related problem that leaves out the question from the first problem. That question from the first problem is the "hidden question." Here is a simple example:

Given problem: **Tony bought three dozen cookies at the bakery outlet for 89 cents a dozen. How much was the bill?**

Second problem: **How much change did Tony get back from $5?**

Hidden-question problem: **Tony bought three dozen cookies for 89 cents a dozen. How much change did Tony get back from $5?**

Have other students identify the hidden question. Since all students are working on a similar task but with different problems (be sure to mix the operations), they will be more likely to understand what is meant by a hidden question.

3. Pose standard two-step problems, and have the students identify and answer the hidden question. Consider the following problem:

Willard Sales decides to add CDs to its line of sale items. To begin with, Willard bought 275 CDs wholesale for $5.69 each. In the first month, the company sold 205 CDs at $7.99 each. How much did Willard make or lose on the CDs? Do you think Willard Sales should continue to sell CDs?

Begin by considering the questions that were suggested earlier: "What's happening in this problem?"

(Something is being bought at one price and sold at another.) "What will the answer tell us?" (How much profit or loss there was.) These questions will get you started. If students are stuck, you can ask, "Is there a hidden question in this problem?"

Assessment Notes

Simple one- and two-step word problems are excellent assessment tasks. Because similar tasks can be provided on different days, observation data can easily be gathered over time. The problems should lend themselves to both group and independent work. All children, even the youngest, can produce a written report of their work providing evidence to keep—evidence of their written communication skills.

Not only does the use of story problems make data gathering easy, it also provides you with a wonderful opportunity to assess a wide range of data about your students. The obvious information is conceptual understanding of the operations involved, connections between related operations, connections with the symbolic form for the operations (equations), and connections with real-world information.

Another aspect of conceptual knowledge and understanding is number sense. After students have decided what computation to perform in a problem, it is useful to see how they go about doing it. There are programs, most notably *Cognitively Guided Instruction* (CGI) (Fennema et al., 1997; Hankes, 1996), that rely almost entirely on solutions to word problems for the development of basic fact mastery and the invention of computational procedures. Regardless of how computational methods are developed in your class, children will exhibit their most spontaneous and personal approaches to computation when solving realistic story problems.

Finally, all aspects of problem solving, including metacognitive and affective components, can be observed as children work on simple story problems.

The message is that using a few story problems each week at all grade levels (including kindergarten and the middle grades) is an excellent way to help children construct meaning for the operations and provide you with a wealth of ongoing feedback that is crucial to your overall assessment program.

 ## Literature Connections

Finding an exciting and entertaining way to use literature to develop or expand understanding of the operations is extremely easy. There are many books with stories or pictures concerning sets of things, buying things, measures, and so on, that can be used to pose problems or, better, to stimulate children to invent their own problems. Perhaps the most widely mentioned book in this context is *The Doorbell Rang* by Pat Hutchins (1986). You can check that one out yourself. Here are three additional suggestions.

How Many Snails?
(Giganti, 1988)

Appropriate for the K–2 set, this book includes a variety of pictures where the objects belonging to one collection have various sub-collections (parts and wholes). For example, a sky full of clouds has various types of clouds. The text asks, "How many clouds are there? How many clouds are big and fluffy? How many clouds are big and fluffy and gray?" These pages lead directly to addition and subtraction situations matching the part-part-whole concepts. Of special note is the opportunity to have missing-part thinking for subtraction. Children can think of collections that they would like to draw so that sub-collections have a variety of attributes. They can then pose their own questions about the drawing and add appropriate number sentences. In discussion, children could explain why they selected the particular equation and how it fits the picture.

More Than One
(Hoban, 1981)

The wonderful black and white photos in this book are designed to introduce group words such as a *crowd* of people, a *herd* of elephants, or a *bundle* of wood. A discussion of group words (animal groups fit nicely with science—*flock, pride, covey,* etc.) beyond those that are in the book can be interesting in and of themselves. Do different groups typically contain different numbers of things? Is it likely that there would be two elephants in a herd? Could there be 50? What is typical? These grouping words provide a real opportunity for children to develop *group* as a single entity, but with separate things inside. Now suppose that there are many groups (herds, flocks, crowds). If we know the size of one, and we know how many herds, do we know how many elephants in all? Imagine a situation where that was always the case—all groups with group names have the same number of things. If there are 87 pieces of wood in 3 bundles, how many in a bundle? Clever one- and two-step multiplication and division stories can be generated.

Each Orange Had 8 Slices
(Giganti, 1992)

Each two-page spread shows objects grouped in three ways. For example, one spread has four trees, three bird's nests in each tree, and two eggs in each nest. The author asks three questions: "How many trees? How many nests? How many eggs?" The three questions with each picture extend multiplication to a three-factor product. In the case of the trees, nests, and eggs, the product is $4 \times 3 \times 2$. After children get a handle on the predictable arrangement of the book's pictures, they can not only write multiplication stories that go with the pictures but also make up situations of their own. What similar situations can be found in the classroom? Perhaps desks, books, and pages or bookshelves, shelves, and books. There is no need to restrict the discussion to three nestings of objects. The same idea is present in measurements: kilometres, metres, centimetres, kilograms, grams, etc. New problems can be posed that require division. What if there were some boxes with 6 cartons in each? Each carton has 4 CDs. If there are 72 CDs, how many boxes are there?

Reflections on Chapter 7

Writing to Learn

1. Make up a context for some story problems, and make up six different join-and-separate problems: three with a join action and three with a separate action. For all six problems, use the same number family: 9, 4, 13.
2. Make up a comparison word problem. Next, change the problem to provide examples of all six different possibilities for comparison problems.
3. Make up multiplication word problems to illustrate the difference between equal groups and multiplicative comparison. Can you create problems involving rates or continuous quantities?
4. Make up two different word problems for 36 ÷ 9. For one, the modelling should result in four sets of nine, and for the other, the modelling should result in nine sets of four. Which is which? Which of your problems is a measurement problem, and which is a partition problem?
5. Make up realistic measurement and partition division problems where the remainder is dealt with in each of these three ways: (a) it is discarded (but not left over); (b) it is made into a fraction; (c) it forces the answer to the next whole number.
6. Use three different models to illustrate what 3 × 7 means in terms of repeated addition. What is the meaning of each factor? What is the meaning of 3 × 7 in the combination concept? Make a drawing to illustrate what you mean.
7. Explain how to help students analyze problems when the numbers are not small whole numbers but rather are large or are fractions or decimals that do not lend themselves to using counters.
8. What roles can story problems play in your assessment scheme? What will you have to do in the classroom to make the most of story problems as assessment opportunities?

For Discussion and Exploration

1. In the article "Whole Math: Exploring the Possibilities" (Wisnia and Rutherford, 1993–94), the authors discuss how they began to change their classroom practice to reflect a more holistic approach to mathematics. Read the article and discuss how the authors made mathematics more meaningful for their students. What are some of the strategies that you might use in your classroom to make mathematics "real" for students?
2. Examine a student textbook at one or more grade levels. Identify how, and in what chapters, the meanings for the operations are developed. Discuss the relative focus on meanings of the operations with one-step story problems, use of models, and mastery of basic facts.
3. See how many different types of story problems you can find in a student textbook. In the primary grades, look for join, remove, part-part-whole, and compare problems. For grades 4 and up, look for the four multiplicative types. (Look in the multiplication and division chapters and also at special problem-solving lessons.) Are the various types of problems well represented?

Recommendations for Further Reading
Highly Recommended

Fennema, E., Carpenter, T.P., Levi, L., Franke, M.L., & Empson, S. (1997). *Cognitively guided instruction: Professional development in primary mathematics.* Madison: Wisconsin Center for Education Research.

Although this book is designed for leaders of in-service or preservice workshops, it is a valuable and affordable reference for any teacher wanting to understand the CGI approach to instruction. In particular, the classifications of word problems for all operations, as discussed in this chapter, are explained in detail, along with methods for using these problems. With the book come six videotapes that detail children's strategies for solving problems and provide a look at several CGI classrooms.

There are also many excellent articles in journals of the NCTM that talk about Cognitively Guided Instruction, which are well worth reading. You should be able to find them in your faculty library.

Gutstein, E., & Romberg, T.A. (1995). Teaching children to add and subtract. *Journal of Mathematical Behavior, 14,* 283–324.

A bit more research-oriented than Carpenter et al. (1990) and yet very worthwhile reading for a teacher who wants to have a clear understanding of how children develop addition and subtraction concepts. The article explores several research programs that have investigated different strategies for teaching addition and subtraction. It extends beyond operation meaning to the development of computational strategies.

Kouba, V.L., & Franklin, K. (1993). Multiplication and division: Sense making and meaning. In R.J. Jensen (Ed.), *Research ideas for the classroom: Early childhood mathematics* (pp. 103–126). Old Tappan, NJ: Macmillan.

This chapter, which seeks to help teachers understand the intricacies of multiplicative concepts, is complete and readable, providing teachers at the 3–4 level with a good perspective without being too technical.

Schifter, D., Bastable, V., & Russell, S.J. (1999). *Developing mathematical ideas: Numbers and operations, Part 2: Making meaning for operations* (Casebook). White Plains, NY: Cuisenaire–Dale Seymour.

In this casebook, teachers in K–7 share their stories of working with children as they develop meanings for the four operations. The teachers discuss the kinds of actions and situations that students use as they come to understand the operations. This is a companion book to an extended in-service guide. There is also a video available to augment the series. However, the casebook is worthwhile by itself.

Other Suggestions

Baroody, A.J., & Standifer, J.D. (1993). Addition and subtraction in the primary grades. In R.J. Jensen (Ed.), *Research ideas for the classroom: Early childhood mathematics* (pp. 72–102). Old Tappan, NJ: Macmillan.

Burns, M. (1992). *About teaching mathematics: A K–8 resource.* Sausalito, CA: Math Solutions Publications.

Burns, M. (1995). *Math by all means: Multiplication, grade 3.* Sausalito, CA: Math Solutions Publications.

Carey, D.A. (1991). Number sentences: Linking addition and subtraction word problems and symbols. *Journal for Research in Mathematics Education, 22,* 266–280.

Carpenter, T.P., Carey, D.A., & Kouba, V.L. (1990). A problem-solving approach to the operations. In J.N. Payne (Ed.), *Mathematics for the young child* (pp. 111–131). Reston, VA: National Council of Teachers of Mathematics.

Clark, F.B., & Kamii, C.K. (1996). Identification of multiplicative thinking in children in grades 1–5. *Journal for Research in Mathematics Education, 27,* 41–51.

Frketich, D., Tomlinson, M. (1996-97). Problem solving + communication = successful, confident math students. *Prime Areas, 39*(1), 18–23.

Hankes, J.E. (1996). An alternative to basic-skills remediation. *Teaching Children Mathematics, 2,* 452–457.

Kamii, C.K. (1994). *Young children continue to reinvent arithmetic: 3rd grade.* New York: Teachers College Press.

Kouba, V.L., Zawojewski, J.S., & Strutchens, M.E. (1997). What do students know about numbers and operations? In P.A. Kenney & E.A. Silver (Eds.), *Results from the sixth mathematics assessment of the National Assessment of Educational Progress* (pp. 87–140). Reston, VA: National Council of Teachers of Mathematics.

Ohanian, S., & Burns, M. (1995). *Math by all means: Division, grades 3–4.* Sausalito, CA: Math Solutions Publications.

Payne, W. (1992-93). Whole math and the computer: Beyond drill and practice. *Prime Areas, 35*(3), 71–72.

Rathmell, E.C., & Huinker, D.M. (1989). Using "part-whole" language to help children represent and solve word problems. In P.R. Trafton (Ed.), *New directions for elementary school mathematics* (pp. 99–110). Reston, VA: National Council of Teachers of Mathematics.

Schwartz, S.L., & Curcio, F.R. (1995). Learning mathematics in meaningful contexts: An action-based approach in the primary grades. In P.A. House (Ed.), *Connecting mathematics across the curriculum* (pp. 116–123). Reston, VA: National Council of Teachers of Mathematics.

Wisnia, L., Rutherford, S. (1993–94). Whole math: exploring the possibilities. *Prime Areas, 36*(1), 76–82.

Chapter 8

Helping Children Master the Basic Facts

asic facts for addition and multiplication refer to combinations where both addends or both factors are less than 10. Subtraction and division facts correspond to addition and multiplication facts. Thus, $15 - 8 = 7$ is a subtraction fact, because both parts are less than 10.

Mastery of a basic fact means that a child can give a quick response (in less than three seconds) without resorting to non-efficient means, such as counting. Work toward mastery of addition and subtraction facts typically begins in grade 1. Most books include all addition and subtraction facts for mastery in grade 2, although much additional drill is usually required in grade 3 and beyond. Multiplication and division facts are generally targeted for mastery in grade 3, with more practice required in grades 4 and 5. Unfortunately, many children in grade 8 and above do not have a complete command of the basic facts.

The use of calculators in no way diminishes the importance of basic fact mastery; quite the contrary. With the shift in emphasis from pencil-and-paper computation to mental computation and estimation skills, command of the basic facts is more important than ever. Further, it is true that *all* children are able to master the basic facts—including children with learning disabilities and slow learners. Children simply need to construct efficient mental tools that will help them. This chapter is about helping children develop those tools.

BIG IDEAS

1. Number relationships can be used to help remember basic facts.
2. For subtraction facts, the concept "think addition" is the most important idea.

3. There are patterns and relationships in basic facts. You can figure out new or unknown facts from the ones you already know.
4. All the facts can be learned with the help of efficient strategies.

A Three-Step Approach to Fact Mastery

Every teacher of grades 4 to 10 knows children who are still counting on their fingers, making marks in the margins to do their counting, or simply guessing at answers. These children have certainly been given more than adequate opportunity to practise their facts over their school years. They have not mastered their facts because they have not developed efficient methods of producing a fact answer. Drill of inefficient methods does not produce mastery!

Fortunately, we know quite a bit about helping children develop fact mastery, and it has little to do with quantity of drill or drill techniques. Three components or steps to this end can be identified:

1. Help children develop a strong understanding of the operations and of number relationships.
2. Develop efficient strategies for fact retrieval.
3. Then provide practice in the use and selection of those strategies.

The Role of Number and Operation Concepts

Number relationships play a significant role in fact mastery. For example, an efficient mental strategy for $8 + 5$ is to think "8 and 2 more is 10. That leaves 3. 10 and 3 is 13." This requires the relationship between 8 and 10 (8 is 2 away from 10), the part-part-whole knowledge of 5 (2 and 3 more makes 5), and the fact that 10 and 3 is 13. For 6 × 7, it is efficient to think "5 times 7 and 7 more." For many children, the efficiency of this approach is lost because they need to count on 7 to get from 35 to 42. With an extension of the number relationships just noted, it is possible to think "35 and 5 more is 40, and 2 more is 42." Every relationship discussed in Chapter 6 can contribute to fact mastery.

The meanings of the operations also play a role in the construction of efficient strategies. The ability to relate 6 × 7 to "5 times 7 and 7 more" is based on an understanding of the meanings of the first and second factors. To relate 13 − 7 to "7 and what makes 13" requires an understanding of how addition and subtraction are related. The commutative or "turn-around" property for addition and multiplication reduces the number of addition and multiplication facts from 100 each to 55. These are just a few examples of the role that operation sense plays in the mastery of basic facts.

Teachers in the upper grades with students who have not mastered basic facts will do well to investigate what command of number relationships and operations they do have. Without these relationships and concepts, the strategies discussed throughout this chapter will necessarily be learned in an instrumental (rote) manner. The results will not be nearly as effective as they would if these basic ideas had been established first.

Development of Efficient Strategies

An efficient strategy is one that can be done mentally and quickly. The emphasis is on *efficient*. Counting is not efficient. If drill is undertaken when counting is the only strategy available, all you provide is practice in counting.

The use of strategies is not at all a new idea. Brownell and Chazal (1935) recognized that children use different thought processes with different facts. Since the mid-1970s, there has been a strong interest among mathematics educators in the idea of directly teaching strategies to children (e.g., Baroody, 1985; Bley & Thornton, 1995; Fuson, 1984, 1992; Steinberg, 1985; Thornton & Toohey, 1984). Many of the ideas that appear in this chapter have been adapted from the work of these researchers.

What Is a Strategy?

We have already seen some efficient strategies: the use of building up through 10 in adding 8 + 5 and the use of the related fact 5 × 7 to help with 6 × 7. Consider for a moment how you think about 6 + 6. What about 9 + 5? You may think that you just "know" these. What is more likely is that you used some ideas similar to double six (for 6 + 6) and 10

and 4 more (for 9 + 5). Your response may be so automatic by now that you are not reflecting on the use of these relationships or ideas. That is one of the features of efficient mental processes—they become automatic with use.

Many children have learned basic facts without being taught efficient strategies. They develop or learn many of these methods in spite of the drill they may have endured. With an understanding of numbers and operations, many children invent their own strategies, usually without conscious thought. The challenge for teachers is to devise lessons in which all children will develop strategies that are useful. A strategy is most useful to students when it is theirs, built on and connected to concepts and relationships they already own.

For your students to develop effective strategies, you yourself need to have a command of as many good strategies as possible, even if you have never used them. This will help you recognize your students' invented strategies and capitalize on their ideas.

Two Basic Approaches

You need to plan lessons in which specific strategies are likely to be developed. There are two basic types of lessons suggested for this purpose. The first uses simple story problems designed in such a manner that students are likely to develop strategies as they solve them. As you discuss the solutions, you can focus attention on the methods that are most useful. You can also have students try the methods others have developed. Often, suggesting an idea is all that is necessary. A second possible approach is a bit more direct. A lesson may revolve around a special collection of facts for which a particular type of strategy is appropriate. You can discuss how these facts might all be alike in some way, or you might suggest an approach and see if students are able to use it on similar facts. There is a huge temptation simply to tell students about a strategy and then have them practise it. Although this can be effective for some students, many others will not personally relate to your ideas or may not be ready for them. Continue to discuss strategies invented in your class and plan lessons that encourage their development, but do not force them on your students.

Drill of Efficient Methods and Strategy Selection

Drill plays a significant role in fact mastery, and the use of old-fashioned methods such as flash cards and fact games can be effective if used wisely.

Avoid Premature Drill

Many activities suggested in this chapter involve drill using simple flash cards. However, it is critical that you not introduce or suggest such drill too soon. Suppose that a child does not know the 9 + 5 fact and has no way to deal with it other than to count fingers or use counters, which are inefficient methods. Premature drill introduces no new information, and encourages no new connections. It is both a waste of time and a frustration to the child.

As you read through this chapter you may feel that the strategies for some facts, especially the ones for the more challenging multiplication facts, do not seem at all efficient. As long as the strategy has been firmly developed, and does not rely on the use of a model, picture, or tedious counting, repeated use of the strategy will almost certainly render it automatic. Thus, the strategy provides a mental path from fact to answer. The fact and the answer are soon "connected" as use of the strategy becomes an almost unconscious response.

The discussion in this chapter focuses on one strategy at a time. It is not unreasonable for students to be engaged in drill activities with one strategy before they have developed (via practice or problem-based activities) strategies for other facts.

Many of the activities are simple drills—flash cards, matching games, dice, or spinner activities—in which the objective is quick response. Do not misinterpret these activities as ways to introduce or develop strategies. Drill should only be used when an efficient strategy is in place.

Practise Strategy Selection or Strategy Retrieval

Strategy selection or *strategy retrieval* is the process of deciding which strategy in your personal repertoire is appropriate for a particular fact. If you have not thought of using a strategy, then you probably won't use it. Many teachers who have tried teaching fact strategies report that the method works well while the children are focused on the particular strategy on which they are working. They also acknowledge that children can learn and use strategies. But when the facts are all mixed up or the child is not in "fact practice" mode, old counting habits return. Not only do students need to know how to use the strategy, they also need to know how to select the appropriate strategy when required. This selection or retrieval of a strategy from a personal repertoire is as important a part of fact strategy instruction as the strategies themselves.

For example, suppose that your children have been practising the near-doubles facts for addition: Use the better-known double, 7 + 7, to derive the unknown 8 + 7. Children become quite skilled at doubling the smaller addend and adding 1. This model is then selected to fit all of the facts they are practising. On other days, they learn and practise other strategies. Later, on a worksheet or in a mental math exercise, the children are presented with a mixture of facts. In a single exercise, they might see

$$\begin{array}{cccc} 7 & 4 & 2 & 8 \\ +\ 6 & +\ 9 & +\ 6 & +\ 5 \end{array}$$

but there is no mindset or reminder to use different processes for each. If the children are used to counting to get answers, they will very likely revert to it and ignore the efficient methods they recently practised. When they were drilling the strategy, there was no need to decide what strategy might be useful. All of the facts in the near-doubles practise were near-doubles, and the strategy worked. Later, however, there is no one to suggest the strategy.

A simple activity that is useful is to prepare a list of facts selected from two or more strategies; then, one fact at a time, ask children to name a strategy that would work for that fact. Once again, the strategies a particular child uses may not be the same as those you emphasized in class. Regardless, children should explain why they picked that strategy and demonstrate its use. They still need to develop the habit of using the relationships they have constructed and avoid falling back on inefficient methods. This type of activity draws attention to the features of a fact that lend it to this or that strategy.

Overview of the Approach

For each particular strategy, from development to eventual drill when the strategy is well understood, the general approach for instruction is very similar.

Make Strategies Explicit in the Classroom

As has been discussed, your students will develop strategies as they solve word problems or as they investigate a category of facts you present. When a student suggests a new strategy, be certain that everyone else in the room understands how it is used. Suppose that Sara explains how she figured out 3×7 by starting with double 7 (14) and then adding 7 more. She knew that 6 more added on to 14 is 20 and one more is 21. You can ask another student to explain what Sara just shared. Doing so requires students to attend to ideas that come from their classmates. Now explore with the class to see what other facts would work with Sara's strategy. This discussion may go in a variety of directions. Some may notice that all of the facts with a 3 in them will work. Others may say that you can always add one more set on if you know the smaller fact. For example, for 6×8 you can start with 5×8 and add 8.

Don't expect that once a strategy is introduced, it will be understood with just one word problem or one exposure. Try on several successive days to solve problems in which the same type of strategy might be used. Children need many opportunities to make a strategy their own. Many children will simply not be ready to use an idea for the first few days, and then all of a sudden something will click and a useful idea will be theirs.

It is a good idea to write new strategies on the board or make a poster with strategies students develop. Give the strategies names that make sense. (*Double and add one more set. Sara's idea. Use with 3s.*)

Your task is to get students to think about different strategies and to try them out. No student should be forced to adopt someone else's strategy, but every student should be required to understand strategies that are brought to the discussion.

Drill Established Strategies

When you observe that children are able to use a strategy without recourse to physical models and that they are beginning to use it mentally, it is time to practise it. It is a good idea to have as many as 10 different activities for each strategy or group of facts. They can be designed as file folder or boxed activities and used by children individually, in pairs, or even in small groups. With a large number of activities, children can either work on strategies they understand or on the facts they need the most.

Flash cards are among the most useful approaches for practising fact strategies. For each strategy, make several sets of flash cards using all of the facts that fit. Label the strategy or use drawings or cues to remind the children of the strategy. Examples appear throughout the chapter.

Other activities involve the use of special dice made from wooden cubes, teacher-made spinners, activities where a helping fact or a relationship is matched with the new fact being learned, and all sorts of games. Almost any existing game involving fact drill can be modified to drill only one strategy or one collection of facts. A child or group of children may even want to make their own flash cards or drill games to match their own newly invented ideas.

Individualize

To some extent you want to individualize drills so that the students are using their own preferred strategies. This is not as difficult as it may seem at first. Different students will likely invent or adopt different strategies for the same collection of facts. For example, there are several methods or strategies that use 10 when adding 8 or 9. Therefore, a drill that includes all of the addition facts with an 8 or 9 can accommodate any child who has a strategy for the collection. Two children can play a spinner drill game using different strategies.

It is imperative that you listen to your students. Keep track of the strategies that different students are using, and note which students still need to develop an efficient strategy for one or more collection of facts.

This will also help when you want to create groups that will benefit from the same drills. If you are not sure which facts students know, work with them in small groups so that you can give them a diagnostic test: a sim-ple fact test with facts randomly mixed. Explain that you want them first to answer only those facts they "know" without any counting. Then they should go back and attempt facts with which they are unfamiliar. As they do this, listen to find out what strategies they employ.

Practise Strategy Selection

After children have worked on two or three strategies, strategy selection drills are very important. These can be conducted quickly with the full class or with a group. Independent games and activities can also be prepared. Examples are described toward the end of the chapter.

Strategies for Addition Facts

The strategies for addition facts are directly related to one or more number relationships. In Chapter 6, numerous activities for developing these relationships were suggested. When the class is working on addition facts, the number relationship activities can and should be included with those described here. The teaching task is to help children connect these number relationships to the basic facts.

One-More-Than and Two-More-Than Facts

Each of the 36 facts highlighted in the chart has at least one addend of 1 or 2. These facts are a direct application of the one-more-than and two-more-than relationships.

+	0	1	2	3	4	5	6	7	8	9
0		1	2							
1	1	2	3	4	5	6	7	8	9	10
2	2	3	4	5	6	7	8	9	10	11
3		4	5							
4		5	6							
5		6	7							
6		7	8							
7		8	9							
8		9	10							
9		10	11							

Join or part-part-whole problems in which one of the addends is a 1 or a 2 are easy to make up. For example, *When Mario was at the circus, he saw 8 clowns come out in a little car. Then 2 more clowns came out on bicycles. How many clowns did Mario see in all?* Ask different students to explain how they got the answer of 10. Some will count on from 8. Some may still need to count 8 and 2 and then count all. Others will say they knew that 2 more than 8 is 10. The last response gives you an opportunity to talk about facts where you can use the two-more-than idea.

The different responses will provide you with a lot of information about students' number sense. As students become ready to use the two-more-than idea without counting all, they can begin to practise with activities such as the following.

One-/Two-More-Than Dice

Make a die labelled +1, +2, +1, +2, "one more," and "two more." Use with another die labelled 4, 5, 6, 7, 8, and 9. After each roll of the dice, children should say the complete fact: "Four and two is six."

One-/Two-More-Than Match

In a matching activity, children can begin with a number, match that with the one that is two more, and then connect that with the corresponding basic fact.

Lotto for +1/+2

A lotto-type board can be made on a file folder. Small fact cards can be matched to the numbers on the board. The back of each fact card can have an answer, written in small script, to use as a check.

Figure 8.1 illustrates some of these activities and shows several possibilities for flash cards. Notice that activities such as dice or spinner games and lotto-type activities can be modified for almost all of the strategies in the chapter. These activities are not repeated for each strategy.

Facts with Zero

Nineteen facts have zero as one of the addends. Though such problems are generally easy, some children tend to over-generalize the idea that answers to addition are bigger. Word problems involving zero will be especially helpful. In the discussion, use drawings that show two parts with one part empty.

+	0	1	2	3	4	5	6	7	8	9
0	0	1	2	3	4	5	6	7	8	9
1	1									
2	2									
3	3									
4	4									
5	5									
6	6									
7	7									
8	8									
9	9									

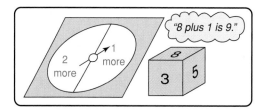

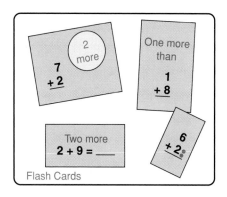

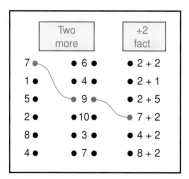

FIGURE 8.1 One-more and two-more facts.

What's Alike? Zero Facts

Write about 10 zero facts on the board, some with the zero first and some with the zero second. Discuss how all of these facts are alike. Have children use counters and a part-part-whole mat to model the facts at their seats.

Figure 8.2 suggests some practice ideas.

Doubles

There are only ten doubles facts from 0 + 0 to 9 + 9, as shown here. These 10 facts are relatively easy to learn and become a powerful way to learn the near-doubles

FIGURE 8.2 Facts with zero.

(addends one apart). Some children use them as anchors for other facts as well.

+	0	1	2	3	4	5	6	7	8	9
0	0									
1		2								
2			4							
3				6						
4					8					
5						10				
6							12			
7								14		
8									16	
9										18

ACTIVITY 8.5

Double Images

Have students make picture cards for each of the doubles, and include the basic fact on the card as shown in Figure 8.3.

Word problems can focus on pairs of like addends. *Alex and Zack each found 7 seashells at the beach. How many did they find altogether?*

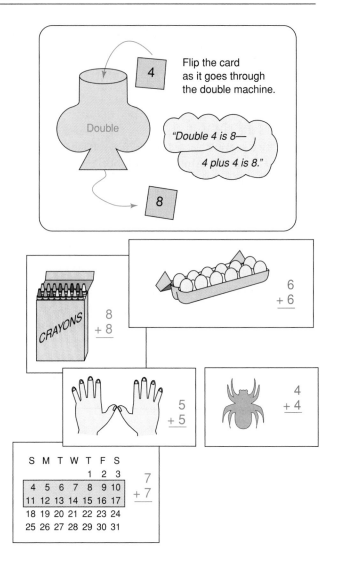

FIGURE 8.3 Doubles facts.

ACTIVITY 8.6

Calculator Doubles

Use the calculator and enter the "double maker" (2 ⊠ ⊟). Let one child say, for example, "Seven plus seven." The child with the calculator should press 7, try to give the double (14), and then press ⊟ to see the correct double on the display. (Note that the calculator is also a good way to practise +1 and +2 facts.) Check that students' calculators work in this way.

Near-Doubles

Near-doubles are also called the "doubles plus one" facts and include all combinations where one addend is one more than the other. The strategy is to double the smaller number and add 1. Be sure students know the doubles facts before you focus on this strategy.

+	0	1	2	3	4	5	6	7	8	9
0		1								
1	1		3							
2		3		5						
3			5		7					
4				7		9				
5					9		11			
6						11		13		
7							13		15	
8								15		17
9									17	

After discussing the strategy with the class, write 10 or 15 near-doubles facts on the board. Use vertical and horizontal formats, and vary which addend is smaller. Quickly go through the facts. First have students identify only the number to be doubled. The next time through, have students name the double that will be used. The third time, have students say the double, then the near-double.

Before using the following activity or the two shown in Figure 8.4, be sure to try word problems involving near-doubles. The discussion will give you a good idea of who is ready to practise this strategy.

ACTIVITY 8.7

Double Dice plus One

Roll a single die with numbers or dot sets, and say the complete double-plus-one fact. For example, for 7, students should say, "Seven plus eight is fifteen."

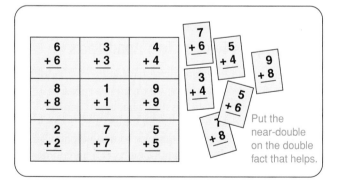

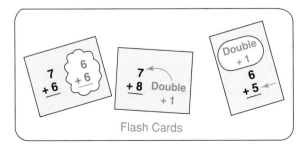

Flash Cards

FIGURE 8.4 Near-doubles facts.

Make-Ten Facts

These facts all have at least one addend of 8 or 9. One strategy for these facts is to build on the 8 or 9 to make 10; then add on the rest. For 6 + 8, start with 8, then 2 more makes 10, and that leaves 4 more for 14.

+	0	1	2	3	4	5	6	7	8	9
0										
1										10
2									10	11
3									11	12
4									12	13
5									13	14
6									14	15
7									15	16
8		10	11	12	13	14	15	16	17	
9	10	11	12	13	14	15	16	17	18	

Before using this strategy, be sure that children have learned to think of the numbers 11 to 18 as 10 and some more. Many grade 2 and 3 children have not constructed this relationship. (Refer to "Relationships for Numbers 10 to 20" in Chapter 6, pp. 107–108.)

Provide a lot of time with the make-ten activity. Encourage discussion and exploration of "easy ways" to think about adding two numbers when one of them is 8 or 9. Perhaps discuss why this is not a useful idea for a fact such as 6 + 5 where neither number is near 10. Note that children will have many other ways of using 10 to add with 8 or 9. For example, with the fact 9 + 5, some will add 10 + 5 and subtract 1. This is a perfectly good strategy, and it uses 10. You may want to give efficient strategies unique names determined by the children and discuss which ones seem especially useful.

When children seem to have the make-ten idea, try the same activity without counters. Use the little ten-frame cards found in the Blackline Masters. Make a transparency set for the overhead. Show an 8 (or 9) card on the overhead. Place other cards beneath it one at a time. Suggest *mentally* "moving" two dots into the ten-frame with 8. Have students say what they are doing. For 8 + 4, they might say, "Take 2 from the 4 and put it with 8 to make 10. Then 10 and 2 left over is 12." The activity can be done independently with the little ten-frame cards.

Make flash cards with either one or two ten-frames, with reminders to "make ten" out of the 8 or the 9.

Other Strategies and the Last Six Facts

To appreciate the power of strategies for fact learning, consider the following. We have discussed only five ideas or strategies (one or two more than, zeros, doubles, near-doubles, and make-ten), yet these ideas have covered 88 of the 100 addition facts! Further, these ideas are not really new but rather the application of important relationships.

ACTIVITY 8.8

Make 10 on the Ten-Frame

Give students a mat with two ten-frames (see Figure 8.5). Place flash cards next to the ten-frames, or give facts orally. The students should first model each fact number in the ten-frames, then decide on the easiest way to show (without counting) what the total is. The obvious (but not the only) choice is to move counters into the frame showing either 8 or 9. Get students to explain what they did. Focus especially on the idea that 1 (or 2) can be taken from the other number and put with the 9 (or 8) to make 10. Then you have 10 and whatever is left.

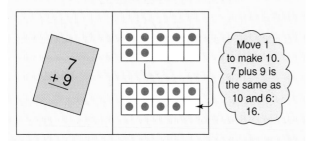

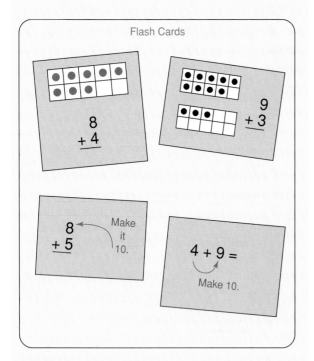

FIGURE 8.5 Make-ten facts.

The 12 remaining facts are really only six facts and their respective turnarounds, as shown on the chart.

+	0	1	2	3	4	5	6	7	8	9
0										
1										
2										
3						8	9	10		
4							10	11		
5				8				12		
6				9	10					
7				10	11	12				
8										
9										

Before trying to develop any particular strategies for these facts, spend several days with word problems where these facts are the addends. Listen carefully to the ideas that students use in figuring out the answers. If no strategies seem to emerge, try the following activity with any of these facts.

ACTIVITY 8.9

If You Didn't Know

Pose the following task to the class: If you did not know the answer to 7 + 5 (or any fact on which you want to work), what are some clever ways you can think of to get the answer?

The value of this activity is the same as the word problem but focuses attention on the development of a strategy. In the event that no one comes up with a practical strategy, you can offer one that a fictional friend shared with you—perhaps a student you heard about in another school. Then provide one of the strategies discussed here, and ask students what they think of it.

Doubles plus Two, or Two-Apart Facts

Of the six remaining facts, three have addends that differ by 2: 3 + 5, 4 + 6, and 5 + 7. There are two possible relationships that might be useful here; each depends on knowledge of doubles. Some children find it easy to extend the idea of the near-doubles to double plus 2. For example, 4 + 6 is double 4 and 2 more. A different idea is to take 1 from the larger addend and give it to the smaller. Using this idea, the 5 + 3 fact is transformed into the double 4 fact—*double the number in between.*

Make-Ten Extended

Three of the six facts have 7 as one of the addends. The make-ten strategy is frequently extended to these facts as well. For 7 + 4, the idea is *7 and 3 more makes 10 and 1 left is 11.* You may decide to suggest this idea at the same time that you initially introduce the make-ten strategy. It is interesting to note that in Japan, mainland China, Korea, and Taiwan, not only is the addition strategy of building through 10 taught, it is taught in grade 1.

Counting On

Counting on is the most widely promoted strategy. It is generally taught as a strategy for all facts that have 1, 2, or 3 as one of the addends, and thus includes the one- and two-more-than facts. For the fact 3 + 8, the child starts with 8 and counts on three more: *9, 10, 11.* There are several reasons this approach is downplayed in this text. First, it is frequently applied to facts where it is not efficient, such as 8 + 5. It is difficult to explain to young children that they should count for some facts but not others. Second, it is much more procedural than conceptual. Finally, if other strategies are used, it is not necessary.

Ten-Frame Facts

If you have been keeping track, you'll see that all of the remaining six facts have been covered by the discussion so far, and a few have been touched on by two different thought patterns. The ten-frame model is so valuable for seeing certain number relationships that these ideas cannot be passed by when thinking about facts. The ten-frame helps children learn the combinations that make 10. Ten-frames immediately model all of the facts from 5 + 1 to 5 + 5 and their respective turnarounds. Even 5 + 6, 5 + 7, and 5 + 8 are quickly seen as two fives and some more when depicted with these powerful models (see Figure 8.6).

A good idea might be to group the facts shown in the chart here and practise them using one or two ten-frames as a cue to prompt the thought process.

+	0	1	2	3	4	5	6	7	8	9
0						5				
1						6				10
2						7		10		
3						8	10			
4						9	10			
5	5	6	7	8	9	10	11	12	13	14
6					10	11				
7			10			12				
8		10				13				
9	10					14				

The next two activities indicate the type of relationship that can be developed.

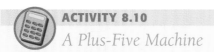

ACTIVITY 8.10

A Plus-Five Machine

Use the calculator to practise adding five. Enter ⊞ 5 ⊟. Next enter any number, and say the sum of that number plus 5 before pressing ⊟.

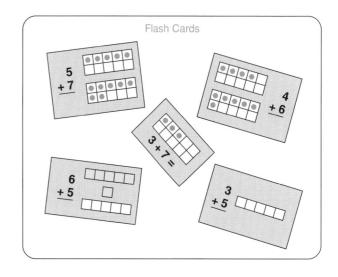

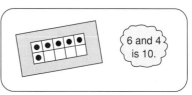

FIGURE 8.6 Ten-frame facts.

Continue with other numbers. (The ⊞ 5 ⊟ need not be repeated.) If a ten-frame is present, the potential for strengthening the 5 and 10 relationships is heightened.

Obviously, the calculator can be made into a machine for adding any number and is a powerful drill device.

ACTIVITY 8.11

Say the Ten Fact

Hold up a ten-frame card, and have children say the "ten fact." For a card with 7 dots, the response is "seven and three is ten." Later, with a blank ten-frame drawn on the board, say a number less than 10. Children start with that number and complete the "ten fact." If you say, "four," they say, "Four plus six is ten." Use the same activities for independent or small group practice.

Strategies for Subtraction Facts

Subtraction facts prove to be more difficult than addition. This is especially true when children have been taught subtraction through a "count-count-count" approach; for

13 – 5, *count* 13, *count* off 5, *count* what's left. There is little evidence that anyone who has mastered subtraction facts has found this approach helpful. Unfortunately, many grade 6, 7, and 8 students are still counting.

Subtraction as Think-Addition

In Figure 8.7, subtraction is modelled in a way that encourages students to think, "What goes with this part to make the total?" When subtraction is done in this *think-addition* manner, the child uses known addition facts to produce the unknown quantity or part. (You might want to revisit missing-part activities in Chapter 6 and part-part-whole subtraction concepts in Chapter 7.) If this important relationship between parts and wholes—between addition and subtraction—can be made, subtraction facts can be much easier. When children see 9 – 4, you want them to think spontaneously, "Four and *what* makes nine?" By contrast, observe a grade 3 child who struggles with this fact. The idea of thinking addition never occurs to the child. Instead, the child begins to count either back from 9 or up from 4. The value of think-addition cannot be overstated.

Word problems that promote think-addition are those that sound like addition but have a missing addend: *join, initial part unknown; join, change unknown;* and *part-part-whole, part unknown* (see Chapter 7). Consider this problem: *Elitha had 5 fish in her aquarium. Grandma gave her some more fish. Then she had 12 fish. How many fish did Grandma give Elitha?* Notice that the action is join and thus suggests addition. There is a high probability that students will think *5 and how many more makes 12.* In the discussion in which you use problems such as this, your task is to connect this thought process with the subtraction fact, 12 – 5.

Subtraction Facts with Sums to 10

Think-addition is most applicable to subtraction facts with sums of 10 or less. These are generally introduced with a goal of mastery in grade 1. Sixty-four of the 100 subtraction facts fall into this category.

If think-addition is to be used effectively, it is essential that addition facts be mastered first. Evidence suggests that children learn very few, if any, subtraction facts without first mastering the corresponding addition facts. In other words, mastery of 3 + 5 can be thought of as prerequisite knowledge for learning the facts 8 – 3 and 8 – 5.

Even though there are 64 subtraction facts that are easily learned with a think-addition strategy, it is useful to consider breaking these down into groups that match the corresponding addition facts. For example, children are more likely to use a think-addition strategy for 8 – 4 and 6 – 3 because these are "doubles." Actually, it is the corresponding addition fact that is the double. With this idea on the floor, you can ask, "How could we use an idea like this with these facts: 9 – 4 or 7 – 3?" Here the related think-addition fact is a near-double. All of the facts with a sum of 10 (10 – 3, 10 – 4, etc.) are also nicely clustered for think-addition with a ten-frame. A group of these facts could be written on the board. The task might be to find an easy way to use the ten-frame to get the answers. Similarly, facts involving minus 5 (8 – 5, 9 – 5, etc.) are also related to the ten-frame in a think-addition manner.

Children will solve facts involving 0, 1, and 2 in many different ways, including with think-addition. These facts are closely related to important basic number relationships. If children experience difficulties with facts such as 8 – 0 or 7 – 2, it would be a good idea to investigate their number concepts. A child who says that 7 – 0 is 6 may have over-generalized the idea that subtraction makes the number smaller.

The 36 "Hard" Subtraction Facts: Sums Greater than 10

Before reading further, look at the three subtraction facts shown here, and try to reflect on what thought process you use to get the answers. Even if you "just know them," think about what a likely process might be.

$$\begin{array}{ccc} 14 & 12 & 15 \\ -\ 9 & -\ 6 & -\ 6 \end{array}$$

Many people will use a different strategy for each of these facts. For 14 – 9, it is easy to start with 9 and work up through 10: *9 and 1 more is 10, and 4 more makes 5.* For

Connecting Subtraction to Addition Knowledge

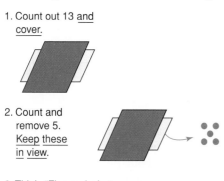

1. Count out 13 <u>and</u> cover.

2. Count and remove 5. Keep <u>these</u> in <u>view</u>.

3. Think: "Five and what makes thirteen?" 8! 8 left. 13 minus 5 is 8.

4. Uncover.

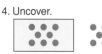

8 and 5 is 13.

FIGURE 8.7 Using a think-addition model for subtraction.

the 12 − 6 fact, it is quite common to hear "double 6," a think-addition approach. For the last fact, 15 − 6, 10 is used again but probably by working backward from 15—a take-away process: *Take away 5 to get 10, and 1 more leaves 9*. We could call these three approaches, respectively, build up through 10, think-addition, and back down through 10. Each of the remaining 36 facts with sums of 11 or more can be learned using one or more of these strategies. Figure 8.8 shows how these facts, in three overlapping groups, correspond to these three strategies. Keep in mind that these are not required strategies. Some children may use a think-addition method for all. Others may have a completely different strategy for some or all of these. The three approaches suggested here are based on ideas already developed: the relationship between addition and subtraction and the power of 10 as a reference point.

11	11	11	11	11	11	11	11
−2	−3	−4	−5	−6	−7	−8	−9

12	12	12	12	12	12	12
−3	−4	−5	−6	−7	−8	−9

13	13	13	13	13	13
−4	−5	−6	−7	−8	−9

14	14	14	14	14
−5	−6	−7	−8	−9

15	15	15	15
−6	−7	−8	−9

16	16	16
−7	−8	−9

17	17
−8	−9

18
−9

Build up through 10

Back down through 10

Think-addition (any fact)

FIGURE 8.8 The 36 "hard" subtraction facts.

Build Up through 10

This group includes all facts where the part or subtracted number is either 8 or 9. Examples are 13 − 9 and 15 − 8.

ACTIVITY 8.12

Build Up through the Ten-Frame

On the board or overhead, draw a ten-frame with 9 dots. Discuss how you can build numbers

between 11 and 18, starting with 9 in the ten-frame. Stress the idea of *one more to get to 10* and then the rest of the number. Repeat for a ten-frame showing 8. Next, with either the 8 or 9 ten-frame in view, call out numbers from 11 to 18, and have students explain how they can figure out the difference between that number and the one on the ten-frame. Later, use the same approach, but show fact cards to connect this idea with the symbolic subtraction fact (see Figure 8.9).

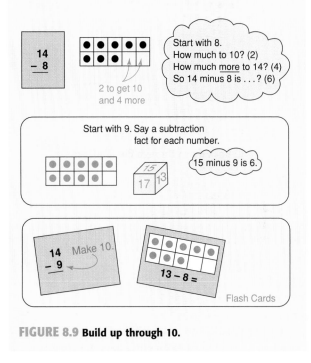

FIGURE 8.9 Build up through 10.

Back Down through 10

Here is one strategy that is really take-away and not think-addition. It is useful for all facts that have a difference of 8 or 9, such as 15 − 6 or 13 − 5. For example, with 15 − 6, you start with the total of 15 and take off 5. That gets you down to 10. Then take off 1 more to get 9. For 14 − 6, just take off 4 and then take off 2 more to get 8. Here we are working backward with 10 as a "bridge."

ACTIVITY 8.13

Back Down through the Ten-Frame

Start with two ten-frames on the overhead, one filled completely and the other partially filled, as in Figure 8.10. For 13, for example, discuss what is the easiest way to think about taking off 4 counters or 5 counters. Repeat with other numbers between 11 and 18. Have students write or say the corresponding fact.

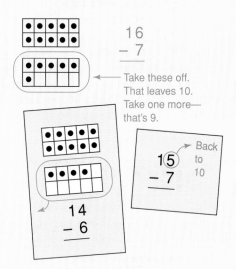

FIGURE 8.10 **Back down through the ten-frame 10.**

Extend Think-Addition

Think-addition remains one of the most powerful ways to think about subtraction facts. When the think-addition concept of subtraction is well developed, many children will use this approach for all subtraction facts. (Notice that virtually everyone uses a think-multiplication approach for division. Why?)

It is vital to listen to children's thinking as they attempt to answer subtraction facts that they have not yet mastered. If they are not using one of the three ideas suggested here, it is a good bet that they are counting—an inefficient method. Work hard at the think-addition concept. Return to missing-part activities as found in Chapter 6. Use wholes greater than 10, and have the students write both an addition and subtraction fact for each. Perhaps most importantly, continue lessons built around word problems—*join, initial or change unknown,* and *part-part-whole, part unknown.* The following activities are also effective.

The activities that follow are all of the think-addition variety. There is of course no reason why these activities could not be used for all of the subtraction facts. They need not be limited to the "hard facts."

Missing-Number Cards

Show children, without explanation, families of numbers with the sum circled as in Figure 8.11(a). Ask why they think the numbers go together and

why one number is circled. When this number family idea is fairly well understood, show some families with one number replaced by a question mark, as in Figure 8.11(b), and ask what number is missing. When students understand this activity, explain that you have made some missing-number cards based on this idea. Each card has two of the three numbers that go together in the same way. Sometimes the circled number is missing (the sum), and sometimes one of the other numbers is missing (a part) (see figure 8.11(c)). The cards can be made both vertically and horizontally with the sum appearing in different positions. The object is to name the missing number.

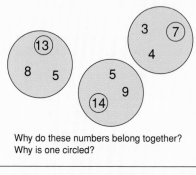

(a) Why do these numbers belong together? Why is one circled?

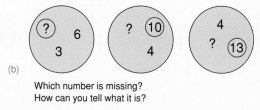

(b) Which number is missing? How can you tell what it is?

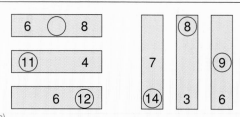

(c) These missing-number cards are just like the number families. Say the missing number.

FIGURE 8.11 **Introducing missing-number cards.**

Missing-Number Worksheets

Make copies of the blank form found in the Blackline Masters to make a wide variety of drill exercises. In a row of 13 "cards," assemble all of the combinations from two families with different numbers missing, some parts and some wholes. Put blanks in different positions. An example is shown in Figure 8.12. After filling in numbers, run off the sheet and have students fill in the missing numbers. Another idea is to group facts from one strategy or number relation, or perhaps mix facts from two strategies on one page. Have students write an addition fact and a subtraction fact to go with each missing-number card. This is an important step, because many children are able to give the missing part in a family but are not able to connect this knowledge with subtraction.

ACTIVITY 8.16

Find a Plus Fact to Help

Select a group of subtraction facts that you wish to practise. Divide a sheet of paper into small cards, about 10 or 12 to a sheet. For each subtraction fact, write the corresponding addition fact on one of the cards. Two subtraction facts can be related to each addition fact. Duplicate the sheet, and have students cut the cards apart. Now write one of the subtraction facts on the board. Rather than call out answers, students find the addition fact that helps with the subtraction fact. On your signal, each student holds up the appropriate fact. For 12 − 4 or 12 − 8, the students would select 4 + 8. The same activity can be made into a matching card game.

Strategies for Multiplication Facts

Multiplication facts can also be mastered by relating new facts to existing knowledge. For example, the fact 4 × 7 can be found from double 7 and then double again. Rote memory is not required.

Since the first and second factors in multiplication stand for different things (7 × 3 is 7 threes and 3 × 7 is 3 sevens), it is imperative that students completely understand the commutative property (go back and review Figure 7.11, p. 131). For example, 2 × 8 is related to the addition fact double 8. But the same relationship also applies to 8 × 2. Most of the fact strategies are more obvious when the factors are in one order rather than in the other, but turnaround facts should always be learned together.

Of the five groups or strategies discussed next, the first four strategies are generally easier and cover 75 of the

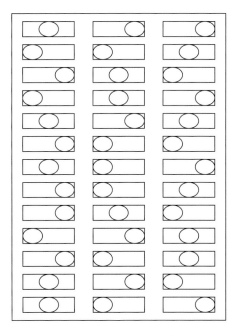

FIGURE 8.12 Missing-part worksheets. The blank version can be filled in with any sets of facts you wish to emphasize (see Blackline Masters).

100 multiplication facts. Remember throughout that these strategies are suggestions, not rules, and that the most general approach is to have children discuss ways that *they* can use to think of facts easily.

Doubles

Facts that have 2 as a factor are equivalent to the addition doubles and should already be known by students who know their addition facts. The major problem is to realize that not only is 2×7 double 7, but so is 7×2. Try word problems where 2 is the number of sets. Later, use problems where 2 is the size of the sets.

×	0	1	2	3	4	5	6	7	8	9
0			0							
1			2							
2	0	2	4	6	8	10	12	14	16	18
3			6							
4			8							
5			10							
6			12							
7			14							
8			16							
9			18							

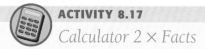

ACTIVITY 8.17

Calculator 2 × Facts

Review the concept of doubles from addition. Play "Say the Double." You say a number, and the children say the double of that number. Use the calculator to practise doubles (press 2 ⊠ ▭).

Make and use flash cards with the related addition fact or word *double* as a cue (see Figure 8.13).

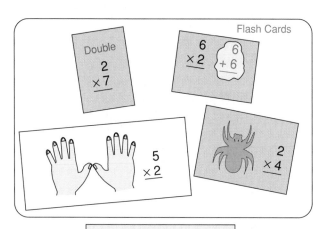

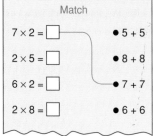

FIGURE 8.13 Multiplication doubles.

Fives Facts

This group consists of all facts with 5 as the first or second factor, as shown here.

×	0	1	2	3	4	5	6	7	8	9
0						0				
1						5				
2						10				
3						15				
4						20				
5	0	5	10	15	20	25	30	35	40	45
6						30				
7						35				
8						40				
9						45				

Practise counting by fives to at least 45. Connect counting by fives with rows of 5 dots. Point out that six rows is a model for 6×5, eight rows is 8×5, and so on.

ACTIVITY 8.18

Clock Facts

Focus on the minute hand of the clock. When it points to a number, how many minutes after the hour is it? Draw a large clock, and point to numbers 1 to 9 in random order. Students respond by telling the number of minutes after the hour. Now connect this idea to the multiplication facts with 5. Hold up a flash card, and then point to the number on the clock corresponding to the other factor. In this way, the fives facts become the "clock facts."

Include the clock idea for making flash cards or for matching activities (see Figure 8.14).

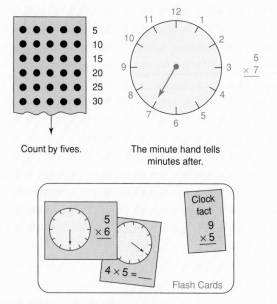

FIGURE 8.14 Fives facts.

Zeros and Ones

Thirty-six facts have at least one factor that is either 0 or 1. These facts, though apparently easy, tend to get confused with "rules" that some children learned for addition. The fact 6 + 0 stays the same, but 6 × 0 is always zero. The 1 + 4 fact is a one-more idea, but 1 × 4 stays the same. Make flash cards and games that reflect a conceptual approach to these facts. The concepts behind these facts can be developed through discussion and story problems. Above all else, avoid rules that sound arbitrary and without reason, such as "Any number multiplied by zero is zero." Though true, it is an idea that should come from the children and should never be generalized unless they can explain why it is so.

×	0	1	2	3	4	5	6	7	8	9
0	0	0	0	0	0	0	0	0	0	0
1	0	1	2	3	4	5	6	7	8	9
2	0	2								
3	0	3								
4	0	4								
5	0	5								
6	0	6								
7	0	7								
8	0	8								
9	0	9								

Nifty Nines

Facts with a factor of 9 include the largest products but can be among the easiest to learn. The table of nine facts includes some nice patterns that are fun to discover. Two of these patterns are useful for mastering the nines: (1) The tens digit of the product is always one less than the "other" factor that is not 9, and (2) the sum of the two digits in the product is always 9. So these two ideas can be used together to get any nine fact quickly. For 7 × 9, *1 less than 7 is 6, 6 and 3 make 9, so the answer is 63.*

×	0	1	2	3	4	5	6	7	8	9
0										0
1										9
2										18
3										27
4										36
5										45
6										54
7										63
8										72
9	0	9	18	27	36	45	54	63	72	81

Children are not likely to invent this strategy simply by solving word problems involving a factor of 9. Therefore, consider building a lesson around the following task.

Once children have invented a strategy for the nines, practice activities such as those shown in Figure 8.15 are

Patterns in the Nines Facts

In column form, write the nines table on the board (9 × 1 = 9, 9 × 2 = 18, ..., 9 × 9 = 81). The task is to find as many patterns as possible in the table. As you listen to the students work on this task, be sure that somewhere in the class the two patterns necessary for the strategy have been found. After discussing all the patterns, a follow-up task is to use the patterns to think of a clever way to figure out a nine fact you didn't know. (Note that even for students who know their nines facts, this remains a valid task.)

appropriate. Also consider word problems with a factor of 9 and check to see if the strategy is used.

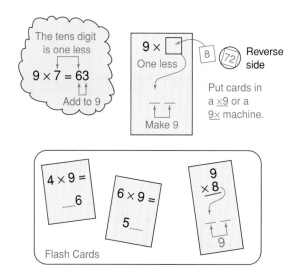

FIGURE 8.15 *"Nifty nines" rule.*

Warning: Although the nines strategy can be highly successful, it can also cause confusion. Because two separate rules are involved and a conceptual basis is not apparent, children may confuse the two rules or attempt to apply the idea to other facts. It is not, however, a "rule without reason." It is an idea based on a very interesting pattern that exists in the base-ten numeration system. One of the values of patterns in mathematics is that they help us do seemingly difficult things quite easily. The nifty-nine pattern illustrates clearly one of the values of pattern and regularity in mathematics.

An alternative strategy for the nines is almost as easy to use. Notice that 7 × 9 is the same as 7 × 10 less one set of 7, or 70 − 7. This can easily be modelled by displaying rows of 10 cubes, with the last one a different colour, as in Figure 8.16. For students who can easily subtract 4 from 40, 5 from 50, and so on, this strategy may be preferable.

$4 \times 10 = 40$

4×9 is 4 less,

36

FIGURE 8.16 Another way to think of the nines.

Helping Facts

The chart shows the remaining 25 multiplication facts. It is worth pointing out to children that there are actually only 15 facts remaining to master, because 20 of them consist of 10 pairs of turnarounds.

×	0	1	2	3	4	5	6	7	8	9
0										
1										
2										
3				9	12		18	21	24	
4				12	16		24	28	32	
5										
6				18	24		36	42	48	
7				21	28		42	49	56	
8				24	32		48	56	64	
9										

These 25 facts can be learned by relating each one to a *helping* fact. For example, 3 × 8 is connected to 2 × 8 (double 8 and 8 more). The 6 × 7 fact can be related to either 5 × 7 (5 sevens and 7 more) or to 3 × 7 (double 3 × 7). The helping fact must already be known, and the ability to do the mental addition must also be there. For example, to go from 5 × 7 is 35 and then add 7 for 6 × 7, a student must be able to add 35 and 7. If you see finger counting at that stage, the idea of make-ten can be extended: 35 and 5 more is 40 and 2 left makes 42.

How to find a helping fact that is useful varies with different facts and sometimes depends on which factor you focus on. Figure 8.17 illustrates models for four overlapping groups of facts and the thought process associated with each.

The *double and double again* approach is applicable to all facts with 4 as one of the factors. Remind children that the idea works when 4 is the second factor as well as when it is the first. For 4 × 8, double 16 is also a difficult fact.

Help children with this by noting, for example, that 15 + 15 is 30, 16 + 16 is two more, or 32. Adding 16 + 16 on paper defeats the purpose.

Double and one more set is a way to think of facts with one factor of 3. With an array or a set picture, the double part can be circled, and it is clear that there is one more set. Two facts in this group involve difficult mental additions.

If either factor is even, a *half then double* approach can be used. Select the even factor, and cut it in half. If the smaller fact is known, that product is doubled to get the new fact. For 6 × 7, half of 6 is 3. 3 times 7 is 21. Double

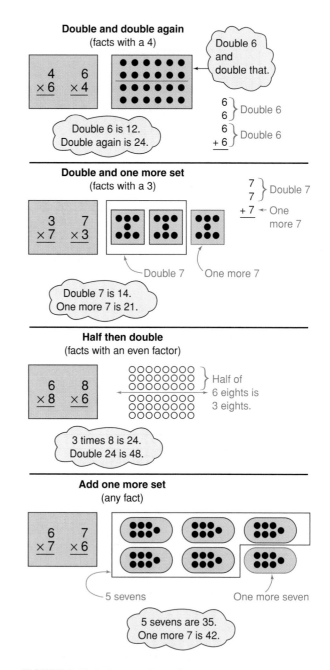

FIGURE 8.17 Finding a helping fact.

21 is 42. For 8 × 7, the double of 28 may be hard, but it remains an effective approach to that traditionally hard fact. (Double 25 is 50 + 2 times 3 is 56.)

Many children prefer to go to a fact that is "close" and then *add one more set* to this known fact. For example, think of 6 × 7 as 6 sevens. Five sevens is close: That's 35. Six sevens is one more seven, or 42. When using 5 × 8 to help with 6 × 8, the set language "6 eights" is very helpful for remembering to add 8 more and not 6 more. Admittedly difficult, this approach is used by many children, and it becomes the best way to think of one or two particularly difficult facts. "What is seven times eight? Oh, that's 49 and 7 more—56." The process can become almost automatic.

The relationships between easy and hard facts are fertile ground for good problem-based tasks. Rather than tell students what helping facts to use and how to use them, select a fact from one of the strategies. Use the same formulation as in Activity 8.9, "If You Didn't Know" (p. 144). For example, "If you didn't know what 6 × 8 is, how could you figure it out by using something that you do know?" Students should be challenged to find as many interesting and useful ways as possible to answer a hard multiplication fact.

Since arrays are a powerful thinking tool for these strategies, provide students with copies of the ten-by-ten dot array (Figure 8.18, also in Blackline Masters). An L-shaped tag-board is used to outline specific array products. The intersecting lines in the array make counting the dots easier and often suggest the use of the easier five facts as helpers. For example, 7 × 7 is 5 × 7 plus double 7 $\longrightarrow$ 35 + 14.

Remember to use word problems as a vehicle for developing the more challenging facts. Consider this problem: *Lauren gathered all of her old crayons and put them into bags, with 7 crayons in each. She was able to fill 8 bags with 3 crayons left over. How many crayons did she have?* As students work to get an answer, they may use many of the strategies just discussed. There is also the added value of assessment you will gain as you listen to the methods different children bring to a situation that does not look like a fact drill.

Word problems can also be structured to prompt the use of a strategy. *Carlos and Jose kept their baseball cards in albums. On each page there were 6 cards. Carlos filled 4 pages and Jose filled 8. How many cards did each boy have?* (Do you see the half-then-double strategy?)

As with other strategies, drill activities can be devised that reflect the strategies that students invent (see Figure 8.19).

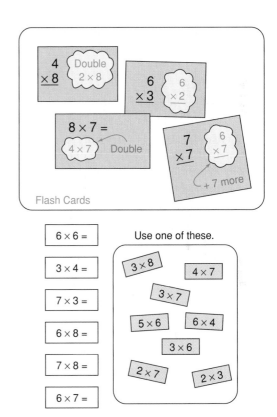

FIGURE 8.19 Practise thinking of a helping fact.

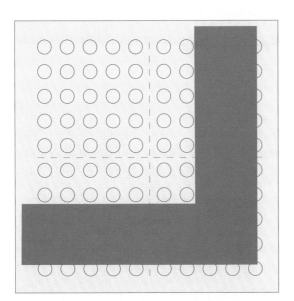

FIGURE 8.18 An array is a useful model for developing strategies for the hard multiplication facts. (A Blackline Master is in the back of the book.)

Division Facts and "Near Facts"

Children are likely to use the corresponding multiplication fact to think of a division fact. If we are trying to think of 36 ÷ 9, we tend to think, "Nine times what is thirty-six?"

For most, 42 ÷ 6 is not a separate fact but is closely tied to 6 × 7. (Wouldn't it be wonderful if subtraction were so closely related to addition? It can be!)

An interesting question to ask is, "When children are working on a page of division facts, are they only practising division or are they doing multiplication too?" There is undoubtedly some value in practice that is limited to division facts. However, mastering multiplication facts and connecting multiplication with division are the key elements for mastery of division facts. Word problems continue to be an important tool for creating this connection.

Exercises such as 50 ÷ 6 might be called "near facts." Divisions such as these that do not come out evenly are much more prevalent in computations and in real situations than division facts or division without remainders. To determine the answer to 50 ÷ 6, most people run through a short sequence of the multiplication facts, comparing each product to 50: "6 times 7 (low), 6 times 8 (close), 6 times 9 (high). Must be 8. That's 48 and 2 left over." This process can and should be practised. Children should be able to do problems with one-digit divisors and one-digit answers with remainders mentally and with reasonable speed.

ACTIVITY 8.20

How Close Can You Get?

To practise "near facts," try this exercise. As illustrated, the idea is to find the one-digit factor that yields a product as close as possible to the target without going over. Help children develop the process of going through the multiplication facts as just described. A list prepared for the overhead can be a drill with the full class, or it can be a worksheet activity.

> Find the largest factor without going over the target number.

$4 \times \boxed{} \longrightarrow 23, \boxed{}$ left over

$7 \times \boxed{} \longrightarrow 52, \boxed{}$ left over

$6 \times \boxed{} \longrightarrow 27, \boxed{}$ left over

$9 \times \boxed{} \longrightarrow 60, \boxed{}$ left over

Effective Drill

There is little doubt that the development of strategies and general number sense (number relationships and operation meanings) are the best contributors to fact mastery. Drill in the absence of these factors has repeatedly been demonstrated as ineffective. But the positive value of practice should not be completely ignored. Practice of nearly any mental activity strengthens memory and retrieval capabilities (Ashcraft & Christy, 1995).

When and How to Drill

Teachers and parents hold tenaciously to their belief in drill. Undoubtedly, far too much time is devoted to inefficient drill of basic facts, often with a negative impact on students' attitudes toward mathematics and beliefs in their abilities.

Avoid Inefficient Practice

Adopt this simple rule and stick with it: *Do not subject any student to fact drills unless the student has developed an efficient strategy for the facts included in the drill.* Drill can strengthen strategies with which children feel comfortable—ones they "own"—and will help to make these strategies increasingly automatic. Therefore, drill of strategies such as those discussed in this chapter will allow students to use them with increased efficiency, even to the point of recalling the fact without being conscious of the strategy they used. Counting on fingers and making marks on paper can never result in automatic fact recall, regardless of the amount of drill. Drill without an efficient strategy offers no assistance. Short-term gains from inefficient drill are almost certain to be lost over time. Drill prior to development of efficient methods is simply a waste of precious instructional time.

It is worth mentioning that the preceding statement applies equally to students in the upper elementary grades who have not yet mastered facts. Because the curriculum for these grades does not include expectations for the development of strategies, drill is generally the only approach that is offered.

Individualize Drill

It is unreasonable to expect every student in your class to develop and be comfortable with the same strategies. As you have seen, there are multiple paths to most facts. Different students will bring different number tools to the task and will develop strategies at different rates. For this reason, few drills are likely to be useful to the whole class at any one time. This is why so many of the suggested activities are designed as flash cards, games, or simple repeatable worksheets. By creating a large number of drill activities that promote different strategies and address different collections of facts, you will be able to direct students to the activities that are most appropriate for them.

By grade 3, students will be able to help you with the process of individualizing learning by keeping their own chart of facts they have mastered and those yet to be mastered. If games and drill activities are well labelled, students can even select the activities on which they are ready to work.

It is also important to listen carefully to the strategies different students use as they work. For example, if a student tends to solve multiplication facts with 9 by multiplying by 10 and subtracting the number being multiplied, it is not useful to suggest the "nifty nines" strategy. A student who has not mastered addition facts is not ready for subtraction practice.

Drill for Strategy Retrieval

When a fact is presented without a reminder of a strategy, students need to select from memory the method that works best for that fact. Drills can be devised that help students look at a fact and recall a strategy that works. The next two activities suggest how.

ACTIVITY 8.21

Circle the Strategy

On a worksheet, have students circle the facts that belong to a strategy on which they have been working and answer only those facts. The same approach can be used with two or three strategies on one sheet.

ACTIVITY 8.22

Sort Them As You Do Them

Mix ordinary flash cards from two or more strategies into a single packet. Prepare simple pictures or labels for the strategies in the packet. Students first match a card with a strategy and then use the strategy to answer that fact.

Both of these activities can be tailored to match the strategies on which an individual student is working. Talk with the students, and have them help you put the activity together.

 Technology Note

Although there is an abundance of software programs that offer drill and practice of basic facts, few are developed in Canada. Nearly all of these fact programs offer games or exercises at various levels of difficulty. Unfortunately, there does not seem to be any program that organizes facts the way they are organized in this chapter. Of course, computerized fact practice should be used only after students have developed some strategies.

A few representative programs are described here. *Mathville* (Courseware Solutions, 2000) is a Canadian-developed program. There are eight different components in the series, each geared to match curriculum expectations for a particular grade level from K-8. Activities are fast-paced, theme-based and motivating. The program is best suited for use in applying or reinforcing concepts that have been developed in class.

Math Trek (Nectar Foundation, 2000) is another Canadian courseware program. It consists of three different components, *Math Trek 1, 2, 3*, *Math Trek 4, 5, 6*, and *Math Trek 7, 8, 9*, which fit with the elementary curriculum expectations. Each component offers an interactive mathematical tutorial, which teaches a concept. The user then can engage in an activity to reinforce the learning. There is also a practice and a test section.

In *Math Munchers Deluxe* (MECC, 1995d), students move their muncher in a 3-D grid format. By answering questions, they can avoid six Troggles that chase the muncher and try to eat it. Like many programs, *Math Munchers* encourages speed and is highly motivating. It is aimed at grades 3 to 6 and could profitably provide practice up through grade 8.

Mega Math Blaster (Davidson) promotes speed through an arcade format. There are children who are attracted to this approach, but there are also many who are not. For some, the formats of fancy, high-paced programs distract from the mathematical thinking you want to promote. Like most programs, *Mega Math Blaster* includes drills for more than just facts. It is not uncommon to see drill with multidigit computation, decimals, fractions, percentages, estimation, and other topics, all in the same format.

One aspect of a program you should be aware of is how it allows answers to be entered. For fact practice, numbers are usually typed left to right. But in the same program, multi-digit computation may be entered beginning with the ones place, or right to left. In *Gold Medal Mathematics* (EdVenture Software, 1997), responses are always in multiple-choice format. This is not uncommon, especially for programs designed for younger children.

Teasers by Tobs (O'Brien) uses a 3 × 3 operational grid for either addition or multiplication. Addends or factors appear on two sides of the grid, sums or products on the inside. Interestingly, blank spaces are sometimes inside the grid (sums or products) and sometimes on the sides. In this way, subtraction and division are implicitly linked to addition and multiplication. (This is similar to the missing-number worksheets in Figure 8.12, p. 149).

Many (not all) programs automatically keep performance records of individual students. Others offer teachers the option of customizing the difficulty level in some way. *Performance Mathematics* (Jazz Interactive) drills only basic facts. However, the program presents facts in small increments of increasing difficulty and keeps track of which facts are "mastered" (determined by correct responses within a fixed time). New sets of facts are tailored to the progress of the individual student, including a number of mastered facts and a few new facts. ■

What about Timed Tests?

Teachers who use timed tests believe that the tests help children learn basic facts. This perspective makes no instructional sense. Children who perform well under time pressure display their skills. Children who have difficulty with skills or who work more slowly run the risk of reinforcing wrong practices under pressure. Also, they can become fearful about and negative toward their mathematics learning. (Burns, 1995a, p. 408)

Think about this statement whenever you are tempted to give a timed test: *"Reasoning and pattern searching are never facilitated by restricting time."* Some children simply cannot work well under pressure or in situations that provoke stress.

Speed tests have been most popular for assessment of basic facts. Although speed may encourage children to memorize facts, it is effective only for students who are goal-oriented and who can perform under pressure. Speed in a testing situation is debilitating for many and provides no positive benefits.

The problems with speed drills or timed tests as a learning tool can be summed up as follows:

Time tests

- cannot promote reasoned approaches to fact mastery;
- will produce few long-lasting results;
- reward a few;
- punish many; and
- should generally be avoided.

If there is a defensible purpose for a timed test of basic facts it may be for diagnosis—to determine which combinations are mastered and which remain to be learned. Even for diagnostic purposes, there is little reason for a timed test more than once every couple of months.

Fact Remediation with Upper-Grade Students

Children who have not mastered their basic facts by grade 6 or 7 need something other than more practice. Certainly, they have seen and practised facts countless times over the years. There is no reason to believe that the drills *you* provide will somehow be more effective than last year's. These students need something more appropriate. The following key ideas can guide your efforts to help these older students.

1. *Recognize that more drill will not work.* Students' difficulties with facts are due to their failure to develop or to connect concepts and relationships such as those discussed in this chapter, not a lack of drill. At best, more drill will provide temporary results. At worst, it will cause negative attitudes about mathematics.

2. Conduct an *inventory of known and unknown facts for each student in need.* Find out from each student which facts they know, with which facts they are comfortable, and with which they are not. Middle-grade students can assist you with the diagnosis. Provide sheets of all facts for one operation in random order. Have the students circle those about which they are hesitant, then answer all others. Suggest that finger counting or making marks in the margin is not permitted.

3. *Diagnose strengths and weaknesses.* Find out what students do when they encounter a fact that is unknown. Do they count on their fingers? Add up numbers in the margins? Guess? Try to use a related fact? Write down times tables? Are they able to use any of the relationships that might be helpful, as suggested in this chapter? You may be able to accomplish some of this by having students write reflective papers about two or three specific facts. More efficiently, you should conduct a 15-minute diagnostic interview with each student in need. Simply pose unknown facts and ask the student how he/she would approach them. Try an idea from this chapter, and see what connections are already there. Don't try to teach; just find out.

4. *Provide hope.* Children who have experienced difficulty with fact mastery often believe that they cannot learn facts or that they are doomed to finger counting forever. Let these children know that you will help them and that you will provide some new ideas that they will be able to use. Take that burden off them and spare them the prospect of more defeat.

5. *Build in success.* As you begin a well-designed fact program for a child who has experienced failure, be sure that successes come quickly and easily. Begin with easy strategies, and introduce only a few new facts at a time. Even with pure rote drill, repetitive practice with five facts in three days will provide more success than introducing 15 facts in a week. Success builds success! With strategies as an added assist, success comes even more quickly. Point out to children how one idea, one strategy, is all that is required to learn many facts. Use fact charts to show what set of facts you are working on. It is surprising how the chart quickly fills up with facts that have been mastered. Keep reviewing newly learned facts and those that are already known. This is success. It feels good, and failures will not be as apparent. Short practice exercises can be designed as homework. Explain strategies and build them into exercises. At the end of the exercises, have students write about which ideas are helpful and which are not. Use this information to design the next exercise.

Your extra effort beyond class time can help motivate a student to make some personal effort on her or his own time. During class, these students should continue to work with all students on the regular curriculum. You must believe and communicate to these students that their being a little slower at mastering basic facts is not a reflection of their ability. With efficient strategies and individual effort, success will come. Believe!

Facts: No Barrier to Good Mathematics

Students who have total command of basic facts do not necessarily *reason better* than those who, for whatever reason, have not yet mastered the facts. Today, mathematics is not about computation, especially pencil-and-paper computation. Mathematics is about reasoning and patterns and making sense of things. Mathematics is problem solving. There is no reason that a child who has not yet mastered all the basic facts should be excluded from real mathematical experiences.

The most obvious alternative is the calculator. It should be on the desk every day for all students. There is absolutely no evidence that the presence of a calculator will impede basic fact mastery. On the contrary, the more students use the calculator, the more proficient they will be with it. This will make many of the calculator fact drills more effective and provide students with ready access to electronic flash cards. In a classroom climate where most students do know their facts, where students help one another and share thinking strategies, very few of them will rely on the calculator for any prolonged period.

Students who are relegated to drill of facts when the rest of the class is engaged in meaningful experiences will soon feel stupid and incapable of doing "real" mathematics. By contrast, when students who have not mastered facts are engaged in exciting and meaningful experiences, they will have real motivation to learn the facts and real opportunities to develop relationships that can aid in that endeavour. Do not allow students who are behind in fact mastery to fall behind in mathematics.

Reflections *on Chapter 8*

Writing to Learn

1. Explain briefly each part of the three-step approach to fact mastery.
2. Explain how a teacher can use word problems to help students construct strategies for the basic facts. What type of word problem would you use for subtraction fact strategies? Explain.
3. For each addition fact strategy:
   a. List at least three facts for which the strategy can be used.
   b. Explain the thinking process or concepts that are involved in using the strategy. Use a specific fact as an illustration.
4. What is meant by subtraction as "think-addition"? How can you help children develop a think-addition thought pattern for subtraction?
5. For subtraction facts with sums greater than 10, it is reasonable that as many as three different thought patterns or strategies might be used. Describe each of those suggested in the text.
6. Why is the turnaround property (commutative property) more important in multiplication fact mastery than in addition?
7. For each multiplication strategy, except "use a helping fact," answer the items in question 3.
8. The "last 25" multiplication facts involve using a fact that has already been learned and working from that fact to the new or harder fact. Four different ways to make this con-

nection with a helping fact were described. Some are applicable only to certain facts. Describe each of these approaches, and list the facts for which the approach is applicable.
9. Describe when it is appropriate to use drill and how it can help. What is "premature" drill?
10. Why should you not use speed drills to learn facts?
11. How do you help children who have been drilled in the basic facts for years and still have not mastered them?

For Discussion and Exploration

1. Explore a computer software program that drills basic facts. What features of the program are good? Not so good? Explain. In general, do you think these programs are effective? How would you use software such as this in a classroom with only one or two available computers?
2. One view of thinking strategies is that they are little more than a collection of tricks for kids to memorize. Discuss the question "Is teaching children thinking strategies for basic fact mastery in keeping with a constructivist view of teaching mathematics?" Carole Thornton (1990), a leading researcher in the area of basic-fact strategies, suggests a fairly direct approach to teaching strategies.
3. Examine a recently published grade 2, 3, or 4 textbook to determine how thinking strategies for the basic facts have been developed. Compare what you find with the way that facts are grouped in this chapter. How would you use the text effectively in your program?

Recommendations for Further Reading

Highly Recommended

Fennema, E., Carpenter, T.P., Levi, L., Franke, M.L., & Empson, S. (1997). *Cognitively guided instruction: Professional development in primary mathematics.* Madison: Wisconsin Center for Education Research.

The CGI program is based on the belief that students develop their own strategies for mastering the basic facts. They are helped in this process by solving well-selected story problems. Teachers listen carefully to students' emerging processes and encourage increasingly efficient methods. This book provides detailed explanations. (See also the annotation for this book in Chapter 7, p. 135.)

Hope, J.A., Leutzinger, L.P., Reys, B.J., & Reys, R.E. (1988). *Mental math in the primary grades.* White Plains, NY: Cuisenaire–Dale Seymour.

This is the first book in a series of three on mental mathematics. Roughly half of it is devoted to the development of basic facts using strategies similar to those found in this chapter. The lessons include transparency masters as well as activity sheets for children. They also encourage the appropriate use of manipulatives such as ten-frames.

Thornton, C.A. (1990). Strategies for the basic facts. In J.N. Payne (Ed.), *Mathematics for the young child* (pp. 133–151). Reston, VA: National Council of Teachers of Mathematics.

Carole Thornton was one of the first researchers to test the effectiveness of basic-fact strategies. She has co-authored two series of Blackline Masters for fact development and has done research in both the United States and Australia. This article is a good supplement to what you have read in this chapter.

Other Suggestions

Baroody, A.J. (1985). Mastery of the basic number combinations: Internalization of relationships or facts? *Journal for Research in Mathematics Education, 16,* 83–98.

Baroody, A.J., & Standifer, D.J. (1993). Addition and subtraction in the primary grades. In R.J. Jensen (Ed.), *Research ideas for the classroom: Early childhood mathematics* (pp. 72–102). Old Tappan, NJ: Macmillan.

Brownell, W.A., & Chazal, C.B. (1935). The effects of premature drill in third-grade arithmetic. *Journal of Educational Research, 29,* 17–28.

Burns, M. (1995). Timed tests. *Teaching Children Mathematics, 1,* 408–409.

Carpenter, T.P., Carey, D.A., & Kouba, V.L. (1990). A problem-solving approach to the operations. In J.N. Payne (Ed.), *Mathematics for the young child* (pp. 111–131). Reston, VA: National Council of Teachers of Mathematics.

Kamii, C.K., Lewis, B.A., & Booker, B.M. (1998). Instead of teaching missing addends. *Teaching Children Mathematics, 4,* 458–461.

Labinowicz, E. (1985). *Learning from children: New beginnings for teaching numerical thinking.* Menlo Park, CA: AWL Supplemental.

Leutzinger, L.P. (1999). Developing thinking strategies for addition facts. *Teaching Children Mathematics, 6,* 14–18.

Leutzinger, L.P. (1999). *Facts that last: A balanced approach to memorization* [one volume for each operation]. Chicago: Creative Publications.

Rightsel, P.S., & Thornton, C.A. (1985). 72 addition facts can be mastered by mid-grade 1. *Arithmetic Teacher, 33*(3), 8–10.

Steinberg, R.M. (1985). Instruction on derived facts strategies in addition and subtraction. *Journal for Research in Mathematics Education, 16,* 337–355.

Thornton, C.A., & Jones, G.A. (1994). Computation sense. In C.A. Thornton & N.S. Bley (Eds.), *Windows of opportunity: Mathematics for students with special needs* (pp. 205–227). Reston, VA: National Council of Teachers of Mathematics.

Thornton, C.A., & Smith, P. (1988). Action research: Strategies for learning subtraction facts. *Arithmetic Teacher, 35*(8), 8–12.

Thornton, C.A., & Toohey, M.A. (1984). *A matter of facts: Addition, subtraction, multiplication, division.* Mountain View, CA: Creative Publications.

Chapter 9

Whole-Number Place-Value Development

A complete understanding of place value includes a complex array of ideas and relationships that develop over the K–6 grade span. In most jurisdictions in Canada, children begin learning in kindergarten to count to 100. By grade 2, they are talking about tens and ones and are using these ideas in many ways. By grade 4, students are working with numbers involving four or more digits. They are experiencing numbers in computations, on calculators, in mental calculations and estimations, and in connection with real-world quantities and measures. In grades 4 and 5, the idea of place value with whole numbers is extended to decimals.

In addition to number meaning, students should begin in the early grades to develop number sense for large numbers and should continue to do so throughout the elementary years. Number sense for whole numbers refers to the following concepts:

- A sense of the relative size of numbers (185 is large compared to 15, small compared to 1219, and about the same as 179)
- A connection to real-world concepts (estimation of quantities, knowing what would be reasonable numbers for the capacity of a football stadium or school cafeteria, the dollars required to purchase a sweatshirt or a TV or a car, or the mass of an adult)
- A flexible use of numbers when estimating (using 250 instead of 243 in a computation because "four 250s" is easy to work with; thinking about 1296 as "about thirteen hundred")
- A knowledge of the effect of operating with large numbers (adding 1000 increases 3472 by less than a third; 1000 times 3472 will be over 3 million; division by 1000 will produce a very small result)

The view of the NCTM, reflected in regional curricular documents, is that computation is as important as ever. However, the emphasis should be on multiple methods of computation, including mental computation, estimation strategies, and paper methods that may differ from the traditional procedures of the past. All computational methods are intimately connected with an understanding of place value. Neither number sense nor computational understanding can possibly be developed without a firm understanding of place value.

 BIG IDEAS

1. Sets of ten (and tens of tens) must be perceived as single entities. These sets can then be used to describe how many. This is the main principle of base-ten numeration.
2. The positions of digits in numbers determine what they represent, i.e., which size group they count. This is the main principle of place-value numeration.
3. There are patterns to the way numbers are formed.
4. The groupings of ones, tens, and hundreds can be taken apart in different ways. For example, 256 can be 1 hundred, 14 tens, and 16 ones.
5. "Really big" numbers are best understood in terms of familiar real-world referents.

Pre-Base-Ten Concepts

Base-ten concepts are not at all trivial for children to develop. It is important for teachers to understand how these new and complex concepts must be built on and connected to children's initial concepts of quantity.

It is tempting to think that children know a lot about numbers with two digits (10 to 99) even as early as kindergarten. After all, most kindergarten children can and should learn to count to 100, even to count out sets of things that may have 20 or 30 objects in them. They do daily calendar activities, count children in the room, turn to specified page numbers in their books, and so on. However, their understanding is quite different from yours. It is based on a one-more-than or count-by-ones approach to quantity.

Children's Pre-Base-Ten View of Number

Ask grade 1 or grade 2 children to count out 53 tiles, and most will be able to do so or will make only careless errors. It is a tedious but not formidable task. If you watch closely, you will note that the children count out the tiles one at a time and put them into the pile without using any type of grouping. Have the children write the number that tells how many tiles they just counted. Most will be able to do so. You will find that some may write "35" instead of "53," a simple reversal.

So far, so good. Now ask the children to write the number that is 10 more than the number they just wrote. Most will begin to count, either starting from 1 or from 53. Those counting on from 53 will find it necessary to keep track of the counts, probably on their fingers. Many, if not most, children in grade 1 and in early grade 2 will not be successful at this task, and almost none will know immediately that 10 more than 53 is 63. Asking for the number that is 10 less will be even more problematic.

Finally, show a large collection of cards, each with a ten-frame drawn on it. Explain that the cards each have 10 spaces that will hold 10 tiles. Demonstrate putting tiles on the cards by filling up one of the ten-frames with 10 tiles. Now ask, "How many cards like this do you think it will take if we want to put all of these tiles [to show the 53 that were already counted out] on the cards?" A usual response is "53." Other children will say they do not know, and a few will try to put the tiles on the cards to figure it out.

Quantity Tied to Counts by Ones

The children just described know that there are 53 tiles "because I counted them." Writing the number and saying the number are usually done correctly, but this procedural knowledge is connected to the count-by-ones approach. With minimal instruction, children can tell you that the 5 is in the tens place or that there are 3 ones. It is likely that this is simply a naming of the positions with little understanding of the place value of the digits. If children have been exposed to base-ten materials, they may name a rod of ten cubes as a "ten" and a single cube as a "one." However, these same children may not be readily able to tell how many ones are required to make a ten. It is easy to attach words to both materials and groups without realizing what the materials or symbols represent.

Children do know that 53 is "a lot" and that it's more than 47 (because you count past 47 to get to 53). They often think of the "53" they are writing as a single number. Moreover, they do not realize that the 5 represents five groups of ten things and the 3 three single things (Fuson et al., 1997; Ross, 1989). Fuson and her colleagues refer to children's pre-base-ten understanding of number as "unitary," that is, there are no groupings of ten, even though a two-digit number is associated with the quantity. They rely on unitary counts to understand quantities.

Basic Ideas of Place Value

Place-value understanding requires an integration of the difficult-to-construct concept of grouping by tens (the base-ten concept) with procedural knowledge of how groups are recorded in our place-value scheme, how numbers are written, and how they are spoken.

Integration of Base-Ten Groupings with Counts-by-Ones

Recognizing that children can count out by ones a set of 53, we want to help them see that making groupings of tens with leftovers is a way of counting that same quantity. Each of the groups in Figure 9.1 has 53 tiles. We want children to construct the idea that all of these representations are the same, in that they all stand for the number 53. Also, their sameness is evident by virtue of their groupings.

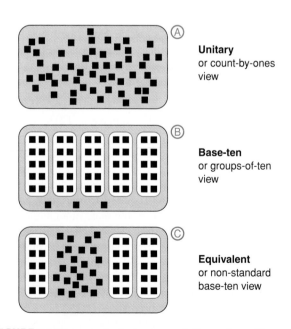

Ⓐ **Unitary** or count-by-ones view

Ⓑ **Base-ten** or groups-of-ten view

Ⓒ **Equivalent** or non-standard base-ten view

FIGURE 9.1 Three equivalent representations of 53 objects. Group A is 53 because "I counted them (by ones)." Group B has 5 tens and 3 more. Group C is the same as B, but now some groups are broken into singles.

There is a subtle yet profound difference between those children who know that group B is 53 because they understand the idea that 5 groups of 10 and 3 more is the same as 53 counted by ones, and those who simply say, "It's 53," because they have been told that when things are grouped this way, it's called 53. The latter group may not be sure how many they will get if they counted the tiles in set B by ones, or whether there would still be 53 objects if they were "ungrouped.". The children who understand will see no need to count set B by ones. They understand the "fifty-threeness" of sets A and B to be the same.

 You will need to understand the ideas in the preceding paragraph in order to make sense of the activities discussed later. Spend some time with these ideas before reading further.

Recognition of the equivalence of groups B and C is another step in children's conceptual development. Groupings with fewer than the maximum number of tens can be referred to as *equivalent groupings* or *equivalent representations*. With an understanding of the equivalence of B and C, grouping by tens is not just a rule that is followed; any grouping by tens, including all or some of the singles, can help tell how many.

The Role of Counting in Constructing Base-Ten Ideas

Not only is counting the vehicle with which children construct ideas about small numbers up to 10, but it also plays a key role in the construction of base-ten ideas about quantity and the connection of these concepts to symbols and oral names for numbers.

Children can count sets such as those in Figure 9.1 in three different ways. Each way helps children think about the quantities in a different way (Thompson, 1990).

1. *Counting by ones.* This is the method with which children begin to count. Initially, counting by ones is the only way they are able to name a quantity or "tell how many." All three sets in Figure 9.1 can be counted by ones. Before base-ten ideas develop, this method is the only way children can be convinced that all three sets are the same.
2. *Counting by groups and singles.* In group B in Figure 9.1, counting by groups and singles would go like this: "One, two, three, four, five bunches of 10, and one, two, three singles." Consider how novel this method would be for a child who had never thought about counting a group of things as a single item. Also notice how this counting does not tell directly how many items there are. This counting must be coordinated with a count by ones before it can be a means of telling "how many."
3. *Counting by tens and ones.* This is the way adults would probably count group B and perhaps group

C: "Ten, twenty, thirty, forty, fifty, fifty-one, fifty-two, fifty-three." While this count ends by saying the number that is there, it is not as explicit as the second method in counting the number of groups. Nor will it convey a personal understanding of "how many" unless it is coordinated with the more meaningful count by ones.

Regardless of the specific activity that you may be doing with children, helping them integrate the grouping-by-tens concept with what they know about number from counting by ones should be your foremost objective. Children should frequently have the opportunity to count sets of objects in several ways. If they first count by ones, the question might be, "What will happen if we count these by groups and singles (or by tens and ones)?" If a set has been grouped into tens and singles and counted accordingly, "How can we be really certain that there are 53 things here?" or "What do you think we will get if we count by ones?" It is inadequate to *tell* children that these counts will all be the same. It is a relationship they must construct themselves through reflective thought, not because the teacher says it works that way.

Integration of Groupings with Words

The way we say a number such as "fifty-three" must also be connected with the grouping-by-tens concept. The counting methods provide a connecting mechanism. The count by tens and ones results in saying the number of groups and singles separately: "five tens and three." This is an acceptable, albeit non-standard, way of naming this quantity. Saying the number of tens and singles separately in this fashion can be described as *base-ten language* for a number. Children can associate the base-ten language with the conventional language: "five tens and three—fifty-three."

Notice that base-ten language has several variations for 53: 5 tens and 3; 5 tens and 3 ones; 5 groups of 10 and 3 leftovers; 5 tens and 3 singles; and so on. Each may be used interchangeably with the standard name, "fifty-three." The same flexibility is available for three-digit numbers; for example, 230 can be 23 tens, or 2 hundreds and 3 tens. It can easily be argued that base-ten language should be used throughout grade 2, even in preference to standard oral names.

Integration of Groupings with Place-Value Notation

In like manner, the symbolic scheme that we use for writing numbers (ones on the right, tens to the left of ones, and so on) must be coordinated with the grouping scheme. Activities can be designed so that children physically associate groupings by tens and ones with the correct representations for the individual digits, as Figure 9.2 indicates.

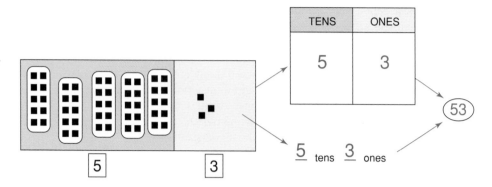

FIGURE 9.2 Groupings by 10 are matched with numerical representations, coordinated with the correct labelled places, and eventually written in standard form.

Language again plays a key role in making these connections. The explicit count by groups and singles matches the individual digits as the number is written in the usual left-to-right manner.

A similar coordination is necessary for hundreds.

Relational Understanding

Figure 9.3 summarizes the ideas that have been discussed so far.

■ The conceptual knowledge of place value is based on the grouping ideas.

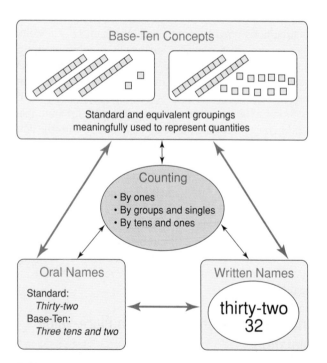

FIGURE 9.3 Relational understanding of place value integrates three components, shown as the corners of the triangle: base-ten concepts, oral names for numbers, and written names for numbers. Counting is a key activity by which children can construct and integrate these three ideas and connect them to the pre-place-value concepts of number with which they begin.

For example, a collection of objects can be grouped in sets of 10 and some leftover singles.

■ There can be equivalent representations with fewer than the maximum quantity of groupings (and a greater number of ones) for any number.
■ The base-ten grouping ideas must be integrated with oral and written names for numbers.
■ In addition to counting by ones, children use two other ways of counting: by groups and singles separately and by tens and ones. All three methods of counting are coordinated as the principal method of integrating the concepts, the written names, and the oral names.

Remember that these ideas are built on a count-by-ones understanding of number. The notion of sets of 10 as single entities must be constructed as a completely new way of thinking about number. Simply showing children groups of 10 and telling them that "10 ones is the same as 1 ten" will not construct that idea for them.

The idea of grouping is the conceptual knowledge of place value, whereas counting, oral names, and written names fall under the category of procedural knowledge. A relational understanding of place value integrates all of these ideas.

Models for Place Value

Physical models for base-ten concepts can play a key role in helping children develop the idea of "a ten" as both a single entity and as a set of 10 units. Remember, though, that the models do not "show" the concept to the children. The children must construct the concept and impose it on the model.

Base-Ten Models and the Ten-Makes-One Relationship

A good base-ten model for ones, tens, and hundreds is *proportional*. That means there is a one-to-one ratio and the ten model is physically ten times larger than the model for one, and a hundred model is ten times larger than the ten model. Base-ten models can be categorized as *"groupable"* and *"pre-grouped."*

Groupable Models

Models that most clearly reflect the relationships of ones, tens, and hundreds are those for which the ten can actually be made or grouped from the singles, and the hundred from the tens. When you bundle 10 Popsicle sticks, the bundle of 10 literally *is the same as* the 10 ones from which it was made. Examples of these "groupable" models are shown in Figure 9.4(a). These could also be called "put-together-take-apart" models.

Of the "groupable" models, beans or counters in cups are the cheapest and easiest for children to use. (Plastic portion cups can be purchased from restaurant supply houses.) Plastic connecting cubes are attractive and provide a good transition to pre-grouped tens sticks. Plastic chain links in ten-link chains are another popular model. Bundles of Popsicle sticks are perhaps the best-known base-ten model, but small hands have trouble with rubber bands and making the bundles. With most "groupable" materials, hundreds are possible but not as practical.

As children become more and more familiar with these models, collections of tens can be made in advance by the children and kept as ready-made tens. Lids can be purchased for the plastic portion cups, and the connecting cubes or the links can be left pre-bundled. This is a good transition into the "pre-grouped" models described next.

Pre-grouped or Trading Models

At some point, you will need to represent hundreds. Models that are pre-grouped must be introduced. As with all base-ten models, the ten piece is physically equivalent to 10 ones and a hundred piece is equivalent to 10 tens, as in Figure 9.4(b). When 10 single pieces are accumulated, they are exchanged or *traded* for a group of ten, and likewise, 10 tens are traded for a group of a hundred. Note that there are some base-ten materials where the tens and hundreds can actually be taken apart and put together. There are others where the tens and hundreds cannot be separated.

The chief advantage of these models is they can be used easily and efficiently to represent large numbers. The disadvantage is the potential for children to use them without reflecting on the ten-to-one relationships. For example, if children are told to trade 10 ones for a ten, it is quite possible for them to make this exchange without attending to the "tenness" of the piece they call a ten. Similarly, children can learn to make the number 42 with 4 tens and 2 ones pieces without realizing that 42 can also be represented as 42 individual pieces.

Though no model, either "groupable" or "pre-grouped," will guarantee that children reflect on the ten-to-one relationships of the materials, it is important with pre-grouped models to make an extra effort to ensure that children understand that a ten piece really is the same as

(a) Groupable Base-Ten Models

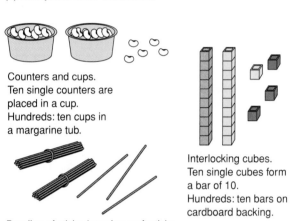

Counters and cups.
Ten single counters are placed in a cup.
Hundreds: ten cups in a margarine tub.

Bundles of sticks (wooden craft sticks, coffee stirrers). (If bundles are left intact, these are a pre-grouped model.)
Hundreds: ten bundles in a big bundle.

Interlocking cubes.
Ten single cubes form a bar of 10.
Hundreds: ten bars on cardboard backing.

(b) Pre-grouped Base-Ten Models

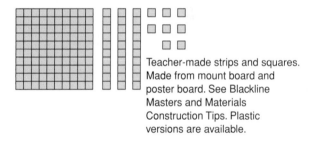

Teacher-made strips and squares. Made from mount board and poster board. See Blackline Masters and Materials Construction Tips. Plastic versions are available.

Wooden or plastic units, longs, flats, and cubes. Also known as Dienes blocks or base-ten blocks. Expensive, durable, easily handled, the only model with 1000.

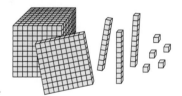

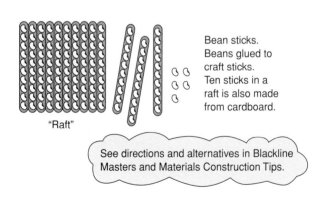

"Raft"

Bean sticks.
Beans glued to craft sticks.
Ten sticks in a raft is also made from cardboard.

See directions and alternatives in Blackline Masters and Materials Construction Tips.

FIGURE 9.4 Groupable and pre-grouped base-ten models.

10 ones. (See the Blackline Masters and Materials Construction Tips for making base-ten strips and squares and the bean sticks.)

Non-proportional Materials

Materials such as coloured counters, abacuses, and money are considered non-proportional. In this text, they are not regarded as models for base-ten ideas because they do not develop physical relationships amongst the numbers. With an abacus like the ones shown in Figure 9.5, ten beads in one column are exchanged for one bead in the column to the left. This is more or less arbitrary; there is nothing in the representation that illustrates a relationship between the 10 beads and the single bead to the left. A stack of number cards from 0 to 9 could easily replace the beads in each position of the abacus without affecting its representational value. Non-proportional materials can keep track of numbers, but they do not illuminate an understanding of them in the same manner as proportional materials do.

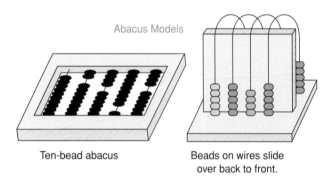

Abacus Models

Ten-bead abacus   Beads on wires slide
                         over back to front.

FIGURE 9.5 Abacus models are non-proportional.

Teachers and textbooks frequently use money to model place value. If the children already understand that a dime is worth 10 pennies and a dollar is worth 10 dimes, then the money is an effective base-ten model for place value. But if the teacher must explain or impose this understanding, the relationship between the pennies and dimes and the dimes and dollars is simply a "rule of the game" from the children's view. They can learn to obey the rule, but the model is not helping them see why 10 ones is the same as 1 ten. The relationship should be in the model.

The pivotal question may be, "Why not just use proportional models?"

Developing Place-Value Concepts and Procedures

Now that you have some idea of what we want to accomplish, we can look at some activities designed to help build children's understanding. This is one area of mathematics where the conceptual and procedural knowledge are developed in an integrated or coordinated manner. While a particular activity may focus on grouping or on oral or written names, all activities involve models that add to the complete coordination of concepts, oral names, and written symbols as depicted in Figure 9.3.

Grouping Activities

Because children start their development of base-ten concepts with a count-by-ones idea of number, you must begin there. You cannot arbitrarily impose grouping by 10 on children. At the same time, we ask, why groups of 10 and not groups of some other number? The decision to use 10 as the base of our number system is certainly arbitrary. It most likely stems from the fact that humans have ten fingers. So we want children to experiment with showing amounts in groups of equal size and possibly come to some agreement that 10 is a very useful size to use. The following activity could be done in late grade 1 or in grade 2 and is designed as an example of a first effort at developing grouping concepts.

ACTIVITY 9.1

Counting in Groups

Find a collection of things that children might be interested in counting—perhaps the number of eyes in the classroom, or the number of shoes, a mystery jar of buttons or cubes, a long chain of plastic links, or the number of crayons in the crayon box. The quantity should be countable, somewhere between 25 and 100. Pose the question, "How could we count our shoes in a way that would be easier than counting by ones?" Whatever suggestions you get, try to implement them. After trying several methods, you can have a discussion of what worked well and what did not. If no one suggests counting by tens, you might casually suggest that as possibly another idea.

One teacher found a good way to count all the interlocking cubes that he had given his grade 2 students to hold in their pockets. The first suggestion was to count by sevens. They tried that, but it did not work very well because none of the children in this grade 2 class could count by sevens. In search of a faster way, the next suggestion was to count by twos. This did not seem to be much better than counting by ones. Finally, they settled on counting by tens and realized that this was a pretty good method, although counting by fives worked pretty well also.

This activity and similar ones provide you with the opportunity to suggest to your students that materials could be arranged into groups of tens before the "fast" way of counting is begun. Remember that children may count "ten, twenty, thirty, thirty-one, thirty-two" but not fully realize the "thirty-two-ness" of the quantity. To connect the count-by-tens method with their understood method of counting by ones, the children need to count both ways and discuss why they get the same result.

The idea in the next activity is for children to make groupings of 10 and record or say the amounts. Number words are used so that children will not mechanically match tens and ones with individual digits. It is important that children confront the actual quantity in a manner meaningful to them.

ACTIVITY 9.2

Groups of 10

Prepare bags of different types of counters such as toothpicks, buttons, beans, plastic chips, connecting cubes, craft sticks, or other items. Children are given a recording sheet similar to the top example in Figure 9.6. The bags are either placed at stations around the room, or one bag is given to each pair of children. The children dump out and count the contents of the bag and record the amount as a number word. Then the counters are grouped in as many tens as possible and the groupings are recorded on the sheet. Bags are traded, or children move to another station after they return all their counters to the bag.

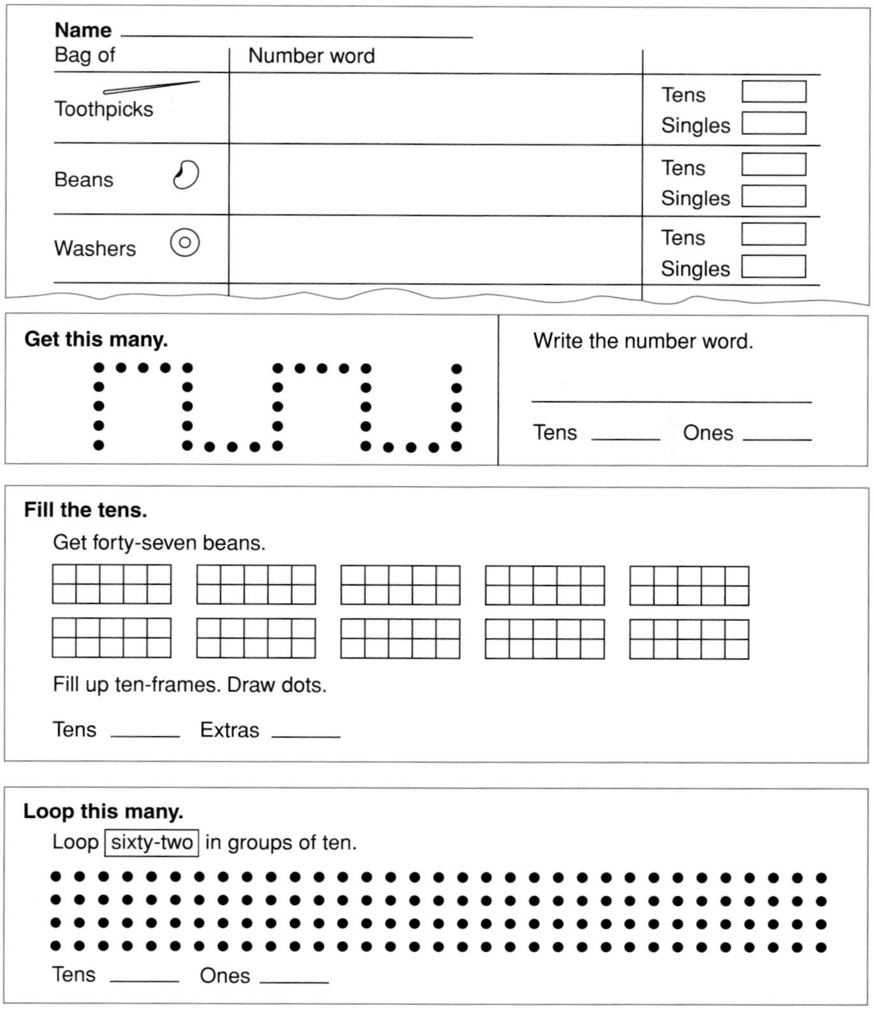

FIGURE 9.6 Number words and making groups of 10.

Number Words		
eleven	ten	one
twelve	twenty	two
thirteen	thirty	three
fourteen	forty	four
fifteen	fifty	five
sixteen	sixty	six
seventeen	seventy	seven
eighteen	eighty	eight
nineteen	ninety	nine

FIGURE 9.7 A chart to help children write number words.

If children have difficulty writing the number words, a chart can be displayed from which they can copy the words (see Figure 9.7).

Variations of the "Groups of 10" activity can be derived from the other record sheets in Figure 9.6. In "Get This Many," the children count the dots and then count out the corresponding number of counters. Small cups in which to put the groups of 10 should be provided. Notice that the activity requires students to address quantities in a way they understand, record the amount in words, and then make the groupings.

The activity starts at where the students are and develops the idea of groups. Make various countable designs with the dots. "Fill the Tens" and "Loop This Many" each begin with a verbal name (number word), and students must count the indicated amount and then make groups. As you watch children doing these activities, you will be able to learn a lot about their base-ten concept development. For example, how do children count out the objects? Do they make groupings of 10 as they go? Do they count to 10 and then start again at 1? Children who do that are already using the base-ten structure. What you are more likely to see early on is children counting a full set without stopping at ten and without any effort to group the materi-

Estimating Groups of Tens and Ones

Show students a distance they are going to measure—for example, the length of a student lying down or the distance around a sheet of newspaper. At one end, line up 10 units (e.g., 10 cubes in a bar, 10 toothpicks, 10 rods, or 10 blocks) that will be used for measuring. On a recording sheet (see Figure 9.8), students write down their guess of how many groups of 10 and leftovers they think will fit the length being measured. Next they find the actual measure, placing units along the full distance. These units are counted by ones and also grouped in tens. Both results are recorded.

als in piles. A grade 2 teacher had her students count a jar of small beans. After they had recorded the number, they were to ask for plastic cups in which to make groups of 10. Several children, when asked how many cups they thought they might need, had no idea or made random guesses.

The following activity is another variant but includes an estimation component that adds interest, makes the activity more problematic, and contributes to number sense. It is helpful to add estimation to these early counting and grouping activities. Estimation encourages children to think about total quantities. Listening to students' estimates is also a useful assessment opportunity that tells you a lot about their concept of numbers in the context of your current activities.

Notice that all place-value components are included in Activity 9.3. Children can work in pairs to measure several lengths around the room. A similar estimation approach could be added to "Groups of 10" (Activity 9.2), where students first estimate then count out the quantity of objects in the bags. Estimation requires reflective thought concerning the quantities expressed in groups.

FIGURE 9.8 Record sheet for estimating groups of tens and ones.

NAME _Jessica_____

OBJECT	ESTIMATE	ACTUAL
_desk_____	_5_ TENS _6_ SINGLES	_3_ TENS _2_ SINGLES
		_ThirTy-TWO_____
		Number Word
_____	___ TENS ___ SINGLES	___ TENS ___ SINGLES
		_____
		Number Word

Technology Note

Unifix Software (Hickey, 1996) allows you to create useful grouping activities on the computer. As many as 100 individual cubes can be "stamped" onto the screen. The cubes can then be easily snapped into rods. With the "bar total" option on, the size of each rod can be printed on it. A single cube would show "1." You might wish to prepare a file with, say, 78 cubes and have students estimate how many tens. This could be done with or without displaying the total number of cubes on the screen. With both amounts displayed (rod and screen totals), students will note that the total does not change when cubes are made into bars of 10 or when bars are broken into singles. Another option is to turn off all totals, and ask students to show a specific number of bars. Will students use bars of 10 to keep track of counts?

Grouping and Place Value (Tenth Planet, 1997) offers three animated grouping tasks: Balls are packed by a machine in groups of tens and then 10 tens form a hundred; a "space money" scenario has children match hundreds, tens, and ones "coins" to specified amounts; and children try to find which of four collections of objects matches a given number. Children have little control over the ball-packing task, but the animation is catchy. The money task involves more interaction but is symbolic. The last task is perhaps the best. Children select a gadget that groups objects by twos, fives, or tens, thereby providing three grouping possibilities. After grouping, the counting is not done for the students as it is in the warm-up exercises. As with other Tenth Planet products, the print material offers excellent suggestions for using the software as well as related off-computer tasks. ■■

The Strangeness of Ones, Tens, and Hundreds

As students begin to make groupings of 10, the language of these groupings must also be introduced. At the start, language such as "groups of 10 and leftovers" or "bunches of tens and singles" is most meaningful. For tens, use whatever terminology fits: bars of 10, cups of 10, bundles of 10. Eventually you can abbreviate this simply to "ten." There is no hurry to use the word "ones" for the leftovers. Language such as "four tens and seven" works very well.

Reflect for a moment on how strange it must sound to say "seven ones." Certainly children have never said they were "seven ones" years old. The use of the word *ten* as a singular group name is even more mysterious. Consider the phrase "Ten ones makes one ten." The first *ten* carries the usual meaning of 10 things, the amount that is 1 more than 9 things. But the other *ten* is a singular noun, one thing. How can something the child has known for years as the name for a lot of things suddenly become one thing?

Bunches, bundles, cups, and groups of 10 make more sense in the beginning than "a ten."

The word *hundred* is equally strange, yet usually gets less attention. It must be understood in three ways: as 100 single objects, as 10 tens, and as a singular thing. These names are not as simple as they seem.

Equivalent Representations

An important variation of the grouping activities is aimed at the equivalent representations of numbers. (See Figure 9.3, p. 162.) For example, with children who have just completed the "Groups of 10" activity with a bag of counters, ask, "What is another way you can show your 42 besides 4 groups of ten and 2 singles? Let's see how many ways you can find." Interestingly, most children will go next to 42 singles. The following activities are also directed at the idea of equivalent representations.

ACTIVITY 9.4

Odd Groupings

Show a collection of materials partly grouped in sets of 10. For example, you may have 5 chains of 10 links and 17 additional links. Be sure the children understand that each group has 10 items. Count the number of groups, and also count the singles. Let the children use whatever method they wish to count. Ask, "How many links in all?" Record and discuss all responses. Next change the number of groupings of ten (make a ten from the singles, or break apart one of the tens) without changing the total number of links. Repeat the questions and the discussion. Once students begin to understand that the total does not change, only the number of groupings, ask in what other ways the items could be grouped if you use tens and singles.

The next activity is similar but is done using pregrouped materials.

ACTIVITY 9.5

Three Other Ways

Students work in groups or pairs. First they show "four hundred and sixty-three" on their desks with strips and squares in the standard representation. Next they find and record at least three other ways to show this number.

A variation of "Three Other Ways" is to challenge students to find a way to show an amount with a specific number of pieces. "Can you show 463 with 31 pieces?" (There is more than one way to do this.) Students in grades 4 or 5 can get quite involved with finding all the ways to show a three-digit number.

After children have had sufficient experiences with pre-grouped materials, a "dot, stick, and square" notation can be used for recording ones, tens, and hundreds. By grade 3, children can use small squares for hundreds, as shown in Figure 9.9. Use the drawings as a means of telling the children what pieces to get out of their own place-value kits and as a way for children to record results.

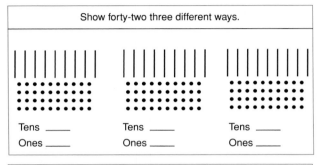

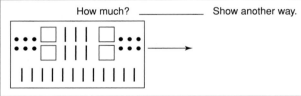

FIGURE 9.9 Equivalent representation exercises using square-stick-dot pictures.

The next activity begins to incorporate oral language with equivalent representation ideas.

ACTIVITY 9.6

Base-Ten Riddles

Base-ten riddles can be presented orally or in written form. In either case, children should use base-ten materials to help solve them. The examples here illustrate a variety of possibilities with different levels of difficulty.

  I have 23 ones and 4 tens. Who am I?
  I have 4 hundreds, 12 tens, and 6 ones. Who am I?
  I have 30 ones and 3 hundreds. Who am I?
  I am 45. I have 25 ones. How many tens do I have?

I am 341. I have 22 tens. How many hundreds do I have?
I have 13 tens, 2 hundreds, and 21 ones. Who am I?
If you put 3 more tens with me, I would be 115. Who am I?
I have 17 ones. I am between 40 and 50. Who am I?
I have 17 ones. I am between 40 and 50. How many tens do I have?

Oral Names for Numbers

The standard name for the collection in Figure 9.10 is "forty-seven." A more explicit terminology is "four tens and seven ones." When children use this base-ten language as they work with base-ten materials, it encourages them to think in terms of groups instead of a large pile of singles.

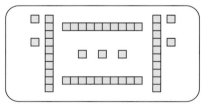

"Four tens and seven ones—forty-seven"

FIGURE 9.10 Mixed model of 47.

Two-Digit Number Names

In grades 1 and 2, children need to connect the base-ten concepts with the oral number names they have used many times. They know the words but have not thought of them in terms of tens and ones.

Almost always use base-ten models while teaching oral names. Use base-ten language paired with standard notation. Emphasize the teens as exceptions. Acknowledge that they are formed "backwards" and do not fit the patterns.

ACTIVITY 9.7

Counting Rows of 10

Use a 10 × 10 array of dots on the overhead projector. Cover up all but two rows, as shown in Figure 9.11(a). "How many tens? (2.) Two tens is called *twenty*." Have the class repeat. Show

another row. "Three tens is called *thirty*. Four tens is *forty*. Five tens should have been *fivety*, but we call it *fifty*." The names *sixty, seventy, eighty,* and *ninety* all fit the pattern. Slide the cover up and down the array, asking how many tens are showing and the name for that amount. Use the same 10×10 array to work on names for tens and ones. Show, for example, four full lines—"forty." Next expose one dot in the fifth row. "Four tens and one. Forty-one." Add more dots one at a time. "Four tens and two. Forty-two." "Four tens and three. Forty-three." This is shown in Figure 9.11(b). When that pattern is established, repeat with other decades from twenty through ninety.

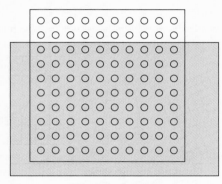

(a)   "Two tens—twenty"

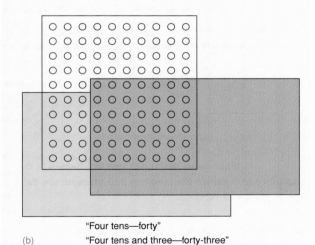

(b)   "Four tens—forty"
          "Four tens and three—forty-three"

FIGURE 9.11 10×10 **dot arrays are used to model sets of 10 and singles.**

Repeat this basic approach with other base-ten models. The next activity shows how this might be done.

ACTIVITY 9.8

Counting with Base-Ten Models

Show some tens pieces on the overhead. Ask how many tens. Ask for the usual name. Add a ten or remove a ten, and repeat the questions. Next add some ones. Always have children give the base-ten name and the standard name. Continue to make changes in the materials displayed by adding or removing 1 or 2 tens and by adding and removing ones. For this activity, show the tens and ones pieces in different arrangements rather than the standard left-to-right order for tens and ones. The idea is to connect the names to the quantities, not the order in which they are.

Reverse the activity by having children use base-ten pieces at their desks. For example, you say, "Make 63." The children make the number with the models and then give the base-ten name.

Note that Activities 9.7 and 9.8 will be much enhanced by discussion. Have children explain their thinking. If you don't require children to reflect on these responses, they soon learn how to give the response you want, matching number words to models, without actually thinking about the total quantities.

ACTIVITY 9.9

Tens, Ones, and Fingers

Ask your class, "How can you show 37 fingers?" (It is fun to precede this question by asking for different ways to show 6 fingers, 8 fingers, and other amounts less than 10.) Soon children will figure out that four children are required. Line up four children, and have three hold up 10 fingers and the last child 7 fingers. Have the class count the fingers by tens and ones. Ask for other children to show different numbers. Emphasize the number of sets of 10 fingers and the single fingers (base-ten language) and pair this with the standard form.

In the last three activities, it is important occasionally to count an entire representation by ones. Remember that the count by ones is the young child's principal linkage with the concept of quantity. For example, suppose you have just had children use interlocking cubes to make 42. Try asking, "Do you think there really are 42 cubes there?" Many children are not convinced, and the count by ones is very significant.

The language pattern for two-digit numbers is best developed and connected with models using numbers 20 and higher. Teens can and should appear in the activities, but should be noted as exceptions to the oral rules you are developing.

One approach to the teen numbers is to "back into them." Show, for example, 6 tens and 5 ones. Get the standard and base-ten names from the children as before. Remove groups of tens one at a time, each time asking for both names for the amount shown. The switch from 2 tens and 5 ("twenty-five") to 1 ten and 5 ("fifteen") is a dramatic demonstration of the "backward" name for a number in the teens. Take the opportunity to point it out as an exception. Count the materials out by ones and name them in both languages. Then add tens to get to numbers that follow the rules. Return to a teen number and repeat the process. Continue to contrast the teens with the numbers 20 and above.

Three-Digit Number Names

The approach to three-digit number names is essentially the same as for two-digit names. Show mixed arrangements of base-ten materials. Have children give the base-ten name and the standard name. Vary the arrangement from one example to the next by adding or removing only ones or only tens or only hundreds.

Similarly, have children model at their desks numbers that you give to them orally using the standard names. By the time children are ready for three-digit numbers, the two-digit number names, including the difficult teens, usually will have been mastered. The major difficulty will be with numbers that have no tens, such as 702. As noted earlier, the use of base-ten language is quite helpful here. The zero tens difficulty is more pronounced when the numbers are written. Children frequently write 7002 for "seven hundred and two." However, the emphasis on meaning in the oral base-ten language form will be a significant help.

Written Symbols

The discussion so far has stressed the ideas of groups of 10 and the connection of these base-ten concepts with oral number names. No one would expect that written numbers be completely absent during this development. At the same time, it is correct to focus on the ideas of base-ten concepts before emphasizing the written numbers.

Place-Value Mats

Place-value mats are mats that are divided into two or three sections to hold ones and tens pieces or ones, tens, and hundreds pieces as shown in Figure 9.12. You can explain to your students that the mats are a good way to organize their materials when working with base-ten

pieces. Also point out that the standard way to use a place-value mat is to put the ones in the space that is farthest on the right. The tens are to the left of the ones and the hundreds to the left of the tens.

Though it's not strictly necessary to print anything on the mats, it is strongly recommended that two ten-frames be drawn in the ones place as shown. (See Blackline Masters and Materials Construction Tips for directions for making the mats.) That way, the number of ones on the ten-frames is always evident, eliminating the need for frequent and tedious counting (Thompson & Van de Walle, 1984). The ten-frame also makes it obvious how many additional counters would be needed to make the next set of 10. If children are modelling two numbers at the same time, one ten-frame can be used for each number. Most illustrations of place-value mats in this book will show two ten-frames, even though that feature is not commonly seen in standard texts.

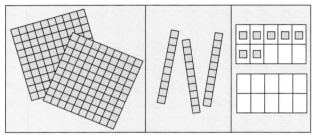
Strips and squares show
237 on three-place mat.

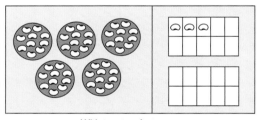
With two ten-frames,
cups and beans show 53.

FIGURE 9.12 Place-value mats with two ten-frames in the ones place to organize the counters and promote the concept of groups of 10.

As children use their place-value mats, they can be shown how numbers are written according to the left-to-right order of the pieces. In this way the place-value mat becomes a link between the base-ten models and the written form of the numbers. Once again, be aware of how easy it would be for a child to show a number on a mat using tens and ones pieces, then learn to write the number, without developing any understanding of what it represents. Grade 1 and 2 textbooks often show a model and have children record numbers in this manner:

___7___ tens and ___3___ ones is ___73___ in all.

It is all too easy to copy down the number of sticks and single blocks and rewrite these digits in a single number such as 73 without thinking about what these symbols mean.

1	2	3	4	5	6	7	8	9	10
11	12	13	14	15	16	17	18	19	20
21	22	23	24	25	26	27	28	29	30
31	32	33	34	35	36	37	38	39	40
41	42	43	44	45	46	47	48	49	50
51	52	53	54	55	56	57	58	59	60
61	62	63	64	65	66	67	68	69	70
71	72	73	74	75	76	77	78	79	80
81	82	83	84	85	86	87	88	89	90
91	92	93	94	95	96	97	98	99	100

FIGURE 9.13 **A 100 chart.**

The Hundreds Chart

The hundreds chart (see Figure 9.13) is such an important tool in the development of place value concepts that it deserves special attention. K-2 classrooms should have a hundreds chart prominently displayed.

An extremely useful version of the chart has transparent pockets into which the 100 number cards can be inserted. You can hide a number by inserting a blank card in front of a number pocket. Coloured pieces of paper can also be inserted into the slots to highlight various number patterns. You can have students remove number cards which are out of order, and replace them in the correct slots. A plastic desk-sized chart with number tiles works well for individual use.

An overhead transparency of a hundreds chart is almost as flexible as the pocket-chart version. You can hide numbers by placing opaque counters on them. Patterns can be marked with a pen or with transparent counters. A transparency of a blank 10 × 10 grid serves as an empty hundreds chart on which you can write numbers. These transparencies can be made from the Blackline Masters

and are also commercially available. (A set of four smaller charts on one page is also available in the Blackline Masters and is useful for many kindergarten activities.)

At the kindergarten level, students can be helped to count and recognize two-digit numbers with the hundreds chart. There are many useful hundreds-chart activities for the K–2 level.

ACTIVITY 9.10

Patterns on the Hundreds Chart

Have children work in pairs to find patterns on the chart. Solicit ideas orally from the class. Have children explain patterns found by others to be sure that all understand the suggested ideas.

There are many different patterns on the hundreds chart. In a discussion, different children will describe the same pattern in various ways. Accept all ideas. Here are some of the patterns they may point out:

- The numbers in a column all end with the same number (the same ones digit), which is the same as the number at the top.
- In a row the "second number" (the ones digit) goes up by ones (0, 1, 2, 3, …, 9), but the "first number" (tens digit) stays the same. However, this is not true for the last number in the row.
- In a column, the first "number" (tens digit) counts or goes up by ones.
- You can count by tens going down the right-hand column.
- The numbers under the 2 are all even numbers. (Every other number is even.)
- If you count by fives, you get two columns: the last column and the 5 column.

For children, these patterns are not at all obvious or trivial. For example, one child may notice the pattern in the column under 4: every number ends in a 4. Two minutes later another child will "discover" the parallel pattern in the column under 7. It may not be completely obvious that actually there is a pattern like this in every column.

Other patterns you might have students explore include numbers that have a seven in them, numbers where the digits add up to four, and various skip-count patterns.

ACTIVITY 9.11

Skip-Count Patterns

As a class activity have students skip count by twos, threes, fours, and so on. Then have them

record a specific skip-count pattern on their own copy of a hundreds chart, colouring in each number they count. Every skip count will produce an interesting pattern. Discuss the patterns in the numbers too. For example, when you skip-count by fours, you only land on numbers that you get when you count by twos. Which counts make columnar patterns, and which make diagonal ones?

In the beginning, skip counting may be quite difficult for children. As they become more comfortable with skip counting, you can challenge them to skip-count without the aid of the hundreds chart. Skip-counting skills show a readiness for multiplication combinations and also help children begin to look for interesting and useful patterns in numbers.

ACTIVITY 9.12

Missing Numbers

Provide students with a hundreds chart from which some of the number cards have been removed. (Use the classroom pocket chart or the plastic desktop charts.) The students' task is to replace the missing numbers in the chart. At first, remove only a random selection of individual numbers. Later, remove sequences of numbers from three or four rows. Finally, remove all but one or two rows or columns. Eventually, challenge the children to replace all the numbers when the chart is blank.

Replacing the number cards or tiles from a blank chart is a good station activity on which two students can work together. As you listen to the way that they go about finding the correct places for the numbers, you will learn a lot about how well they have constructed an understanding of the 1–100 sequence.

ACTIVITY 9.13

More and Less on the Hundreds Chart

In a similar manner to "Missing Numbers," begin with a blank or nearly blank chart. Circle a particular missing number. Students are then required to fill in the designated number and its "neighbours" (the numbers to the left, right, above and below). You can do this

activity on the overhead with the full class, or distribute worksheets with a blank hundreds chart or 10 × 10 grid. After the students become comfortable naming the neighbours of a number, ask what they notice about the neighbouring numbers. The numbers to the left and right are one more and one less than the given number. Those above and below are 10 less or 10 more, respectively. Discussing these relationships on the chart will allow students to see how the sequence of numbers is related to the numerical relationships in the numbers.

Notice that children first use the hundreds chart to learn about patterns in the sequence of numbers. Many, especially at the kindergarten or grade 1 level, will not understand the corresponding numerical relationships, such as those discussed in the last activity. In the following activity, base-ten models are used to make number relationships on the chart more explicit.

ACTIVITY 9.14

Models with the Hundreds Chart

This activity has several variations that can be conducted with the whole class, or it can be an activity in which students work in pairs to explore an idea and write about what they have discovered. Use any concrete model for two-digit numbers with which the students are familiar.

■ Give students one or more numbers to make with the models; then have them find the numbers on the hundreds chart. Use groups of two or three numbers that are in the same column or the same row.

■ Have students make all the numbers in a row or column. How are the numbers in the row (or column) alike? How they different? What happens at the end of the row?

■ Indicate a number on the chart. What would you have to change to make each of its neighbours (the numbers to the left, right, above, and below)?

It is becoming more and more popular to have a chart that extends to 200, even in grade 1. Perhaps a more powerful idea is to extend the hundreds chart to 1000, even in grade 2.

ACTIVITY 9.15

The Thousands Chart

Provide students with several sheets of blank hundreds charts from the Blackline Masters. Assign groups of three or four students the task of creating a 1–1000 chart. Make the chart by taping ten charts together in a long strip. Students should decide how they will divide up the task and who will work on the different parts of the chart.

The thousands chart should be discussed by the whole class to examine how numbers change as you count from one hundred to the next number, what the patterns are, and so on. In fact, the earlier hundreds-chart activities can be extended to the thousands chart. You may want to make a blank thousands chart (clearly indicating each 100-square). Use the students' charts for other discussions.

 Technology Note

Several software packages include hundreds charts that allow students to explore patterns. In *MathKeys: Unlocking Whole Numbers* (MECC, 1995b, 1996b), the number chart offers very little in the way of problematic tasks. Students select a pattern from a menu (multiples, primes, odds, etc.), and the computer fills in all the corresponding numbers. Patterns can be combined so that even multiples of three would be coloured in.

Math and More 3: Patterns on Lattices (EduQuest, 1994) allows the chart to scroll to 1000. Both programs focus on finding and describing patterns on the chart. Here is a situation where the computer does not seem to improve on the overhead projector. ◼

More Connections with Numbers

The next three activities are designed to help children make connections among all three representations: models, oral language, and written forms. They can be done with two- or three-digit numbers in grades 1–4.

 **ACTIVITY 9.16**

Say It/Press It

Display some ones and tens (and hundreds) so that the class can see. (Use the overhead projector or magnetized pieces on the board, or simply draw using the square-stick-dot method.)

Arrange the materials in a mixed design, not in the standard left-to-right format. Students say the amount shown in base-ten language ("four hundreds, one ten, and five") and then in standard language ("four hundred and fifteen"); finally, they enter it on their calculators. Have someone share his or her display and defend it. Change the materials and repeat.

"Say It/Press It" is especially good for helping with teens (note the example in the activity description) and for three-digit numbers with zero tens. If you show 7 hundreds and 4 ones, the class says "seven hundreds, zero tens, and four—seven hundred (*slight pause*) and four." The pause and the base-ten language suggest the correct three-digit number to press on the calculator or write. Many students have trouble with this example and write "7004," writing exactly what they hear in the standard name. Similarly, grade 1 and 2 children often write "504" for fifty-four. This activity will help. The next two activities simply change the representation that is presented first to the students.

 **ACTIVITY 9.17**

Show It/Press It

Say the standard name for a number (with either two or three digits). At their desks, students use their own base-ten models to show that number and input it on their calculators (or write it). Again, pay special attention to the teens and the case of zero tens.

 **ACTIVITY 9.18**

Write It/Say It

In this variant, you silently write a number (or input it on your overhead calculator), and the students show it at their desk with their models. On cue, all say the amount in unison.

In Activities 9.17 and 9.18, you could have students record each example on paper using the square-stick-dot notation. Students who are having difficulties should lay materials on a place-value mat. Worksheet activities can combine all three forms for numbers. Figure 9.14 shows two variations. A third variation would be to give the numeral and have children supply the number and draw the model.

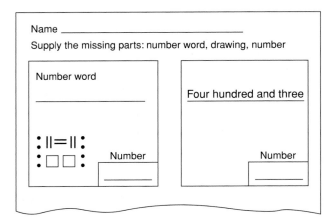

FIGURE 9.14 Connecting language, models, and numbers.

Number-Sense Development

The discussion so far has addressed three key components of place-value understanding: the integration of base-ten groupings, oral names for numbers, and written names. But students need to expand these ideas beyond basic numeration concepts and reading and writing numbers in order to develop number sense. Even though this section highlights number-sense activities, number sense is not a new or separate curriculum topic. These activities should be an ongoing feature of your instruction.

Relative Magnitude

Relative magnitude refers to the size relationship one number has with another—is it much larger, much smaller, close, or about the same? There are several quick activities that can be done with a number line sketched on the board. The number line can help children see how one number is related to another.

ACTIVITY 9.19

Who Am I?

Sketch a line labelled with 0 and 100 at opposite ends. Mark a point that corresponds to your secret number. (Estimate the position the best you can.) Students try to guess your secret number. For each guess, place and label a mark on the line. Continue marking each guess until your secret number is discovered. As a variation, the endpoints can be other than 0 and 100. For example, try 0 and 1000, 200 and 300, or 500 and 800.

ACTIVITY 9.20

Squeeze

Label only the end points of the number line, but subdivide the line into 10 equal segments. Have a student stand at each end with a marker card. As the students try to guess your secret number, announce that the guess is either too high or too low. If the guess is too high, the student on the high end moves in to mark the guess by holding the marker card at the appropriate place. When the guess is too low, the student at the other end moves in and marks that number in a similar manner. Guessing continues as the ends squeeze in on the secret number.

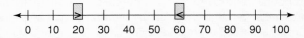

ACTIVITY 9.21

Who Could They Be?

Label two points on a number line (not necessarily the ends).

Ask students what numbers they think different points already labelled with letters might be, and have them give reasons for their choices. In the example shown here, B and C are less than 100 but probably more than 60. E could be about 180. You could also ask where 75 might be, or 400. About how far apart are A and D? Why do you think D is more than 100?

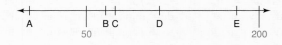

In the next activity, some of the same ideas are discussed without the benefit of a number line.

ACTIVITY 9.22

Close, Far, and in Between

Put any three numbers on the board. If appropriate, use two-digit numbers.

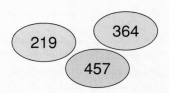

With these three numbers as referents, ask questions such as the following, and encourage discussion of all responses:

Which two are closest? Why?

Which is closest to 300? to 250?

Name a number between 457 and 364.

Name a multiple of 25 between 219 and 364.

Name a number that is more than all of these.

About how far apart are 219 and 500? 219 and 5000?

If these are "big numbers," what are some small numbers? Numbers about the same size? Numbers that make these seem small?

Connections to Real-World Ideas

We should not permit children to study place-value concepts without encouraging them to see number in the world about them. You do not need a prescribed activity to bring real numbers into the classroom.

Children in grade 2 should be thinking about numbers under 100 first and, soon after, numbers up to 1000. Quantities larger than that are difficult for them to think about. Where do you find numbers like this? Around your school: the number of children in each class, the number of children on the school buses, the number of minutes devoted to mathematics each day and each week, the numbers on the calendar (days in a week, month, year), the number of days since school has started. And then there are measurements, numbers at home, numbers on a field trip, and so on.

What do you do with these numbers? Turn them into interesting graphs, write stories using them, make up problems, devise contests.

As children get a bit older, the interest in numbers can expand beyond the school and classroom. All sorts of things can and should be measured to create graphs, draw inferences, and make comparisons. For example, what numbers are associated with the "average" grade 5 student? Height, mass, arm span, age in months, number of siblings, number of grandparents, distance from home to school, length of standing broad jump, number of pets, hours spent watching TV in a week. How can you find the average for these or other numbers that may be of interest to the students in your room? Is anyone really average?

The particular way you bring number and the real world together in your class is up to you. But do not underestimate the value of connecting the real world to the classroom.

Approximate Numbers and Rounding

In our number system, some numbers are considered "nice" because they are easy to think about and to work with. What makes a "nice" number is sort of fuzzy. However, numbers such as 100, 500, and 750 are easier to use than 94, 517, and 762. Multiples of 100 are very nice, and multiples of 10 are not bad either. Multiples of 25 (50, 75, 425, 675, etc.) are nice because they combine into 100s and 50s rather easily, and we can mentally place those between multiples of 100s. Multiples of 5 are a little easier to work with than other numbers.

Flexible thinking about numbers and estimation skills is related to the ability to substitute a nice number for one that is not so nice. The substitution may be used to make a mental computation easier, to compare it to a familiar referent, or simply to store the number in memory more easily.

The choice of a nice number to substitute for a less manageable one is never completely clear-cut. There is no "correct" or "best" substitute for $327.99 or 57 grams. The choice depends on the need for clarity and accuracy and how the substitute will be used. Nice substitutes for $327.99 might be $300, $325, $328, $330, or even $350. In a given situation, there may be more than one good choice for a substitute. For example, $325 might be used in combination with other prices "rounded" to the nearest $5. An amount like $325 lends itself easily to multiplication. For instance, for 7 times $325, we might think 7 × 300 is $2100 plus 7 × $25 is $175 (four 25s is 100, and three more is 75). Note that $350 is also not a nearest ten or hundred but the nearest 50, which makes a nice round number that allows a little extra in an estimation situation. "Our vacation expenses were approximately $350."

In the past, students were taught rules for rounding numbers to the nearest 10 or nearest 100. Unfortunately, the emphasis was placed on applying the rule correctly. (If the next digit is 5 or more, round up; otherwise, leave the number alone.) A context to suggest *why* they might want to round numbers was usually a lesser consideration.

The activities here are designed to help students recognize what nice numbers are and to identify a nice-number substitute. (*Note:* The term *nice number* is not found in standard textbooks. It is John's invention. There is no commonly accepted definition.)

 **ACTIVITY 9.23**

Nice-Number Skip Counts

Count by 5s, 10s, 25s, and 50s with your students. The 5s and 10s are fairly easy, but the skill is certainly worth practising. Counting by 25s or 50s may at first cause hesitation. Students can use a calculator to assist with their counting and connect the counts with numbers (press ⊞ 25⊟ ⊟ ⊟...). At first, start all counts at zero. Later, start at a multiple of the number with which you have been skip counting. For example, begin at 275 and count by 25s. Counting by 10s should also begin at numbers ending in 5 as well as multiples of 10. Also, count backward using these same amounts (press 650 ⊟ 50 ⊟ ⊟ ⊟...).

For children in grades 1 and 2, a hundreds chart can be used for skip counting with 5s and 10s. Older children should count to at least 1000 and should discuss the patterns that they see in these counts.

Counting Money

Too often children are expected to count coins without any preparation or background. It is not that money is hard for children to work with; rather, it is skip counting by different amounts that is difficult. The next activity extends "Nice-Number Skip Counts" by shifting from one skip count to another in preparation for counting money.

ACTIVITY 9.24

Money Counts

Explain to the students that they will start counting by one number and at your signal they will shift to a count by a different number. Begin with only two different amounts, say, 25 and 10. Write these numbers on the board. Point to the larger number (25), and have students begin to count. After three or more counts, raise your hand to indicate a pause in the counting. Then lower your hand and point to the smaller number (10). Children continue the count from where they left off, but now count by 10s. Use any two of these numbers: 100, 50, 25, 10, 5, 1. Always start with the larger. Later, try three numbers, still in descending order.

Note that the counts in "Money Counts" are the same as those used when counting coins or money. These skills can be applied to work with bills and coins. Also, plastic money is available for use on the overhead and is an effective substitute.

Rounding

To round a number simply means to substitute a nice number that is close, so that computation can be done more easily. The close number can be any nice number

and need not be a multiple of 10 or 100, as traditionally taught. It should be whatever makes the computation or estimation easier or simplifies numbers sufficiently in a story, chart, or conversation. You might say, "Last night it took me 57 minutes to do my homework" or "Last night it took me about one hour to do my homework." The first expression is more precise; the second substitutes a rounded number for better communication.

ACTIVITY 9.25

Near and Nice

The idea is to say or write a number and have students select a close nice-number substitute. Begin by requesting a close multiple of 50. Explain that these are the numbers that you get when you count by 50s. It is a good idea to include a real-world measurement as well. For example, "Instead of 243 centimetres, let's use _____ centimetres." Pause at the blank, and students fill in an appropriate number, here 250 centimetres. Finding the nearest 25 is sometimes difficult. For example, is 463 kilometres closer to 450 or 475 kilometres? Actually, either is a good substitute. In fact, place your emphasis on selecting a close nice number rather than the closest or best nice number.

A number line with nice numbers highlighted can be useful in helping children select near nice numbers. A number line that is not labelled, like the one shown in Figure 9.15, can be made using three strips of poster board taped end to end. Labels are written below the line on the chalkboard. The ends can be labelled 0 and 100, 100 and 200, ..., 900 and 1000. The other markings then show multiples of 25, 10, and 5. Indicate a number below the line that you want to round. Discuss the marks (nice numbers) that are close.

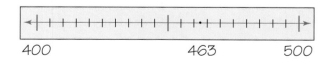

FIGURE 9.15 A blank number line can be labelled in different ways to help students with near and nice numbers.

Numbers beyond 1000

For children to have good concepts of numbers beyond 1000, the conceptual ideas that have been carefully developed must be extended. This is sometimes difficult to do because physical models for thousands are not commonly available. At the same time, number-sense ideas must also be developed. In many ways, it is these informal ideas about very large numbers that are the most important.

Extending the Place-Value System

Two important ideas developed for three-digit numbers should be carefully extended to larger numbers. First, the grouping idea should be generalized. That is, when you reach 10 in any position it makes a single group in the next position, and the single group becomes ten again when you move the opposite way. Second, the oral and written patterns for numbers in three digits are duplicated in a clever way for every three digits to the left. These two related ideas are not as easy for children to understand as adults seem to believe. Because models for large numbers are so difficult to have or picture, textbooks must deal with these ideas in a predominantly symbolic manner. That is not sufficient!

ACTIVITY 9.26

What Comes Next?

Have a "What Comes Next?" discussion using base-ten strips and squares. The unit or ones piece is a 1-centimetre (cm) square. The tens piece is a 10 × 1 strip. The hundreds piece is a square, 10 cm × 10 cm. What is next? Ten hundreds is called a thousand. What shape? It could be a strip made of 10 hundred squares. Tape 10 hundreds together. What is next? (Reinforce the idea of "ten making one" that has progressed to this point.) Ten one-thousand strips would make a square measuring 1 metre (m) on each side. Once the class has figured out the shape of the thousands piece, the question is, "What comes next?" Let small groups work on the dimensions of a ten-thousands piece.

If your students become interested in seeing the big pieces from "What Comes Next?", engage them in laying the pieces out on paper. Ten ten-thousand squares (10 000) go together to make a huge strip. Draw this strip on a long sheet of butcher paper, and mark off the 10 squares that make it up. Your strip will reach out into the hall!

How far you want to extend this square, strip, square, strip sequence depends on your class. The idea that "10 in one place makes 1 in the next" can be brought home dramatically. It is quite possible with older children to make the next 10 m × 10 m square using masking tape on the cafeteria floor or chalk lines on the playground. The next

strip is 100 m × 10 m. This can be measured out on a large playground with kids marking the corners. At this point, the payoff includes an appreciation of the increase in size of each successive amount as well as the "ten-makes-one" progression. The 10 m × 10 m square models 1 million, and the 100 m × 10 m strip is the model for 10 million. The difference between 1 million and 10 million is dramatic. Even the concept of 1 million tiny centimetre squares is dramatic.

The three-dimensional wooden or plastic base-ten materials (Dienes blocks) are all available with a model for thousands, which is a 10-cm cube. Although these models are more costly than base-ten materials we can make ourselves, they are worth having for showing and talking about base-ten concepts.

Try the "What Comes Next?" discussion in the context of these three-dimensional models. The first three shapes are a *cube* (which is one unit), a *long* (which is ten), and a *flat* (which is a hundred). What comes next? Stack 10 flats (which is a thousand) and they make a cube, the same shape as the first one only 1000 times larger. (See Figure 9.16.) What comes next? Ten 1000 *cubes* make a *long*. What comes next? Ten big *longs* make a big *flat*. The first three shapes have now been repeated! Ten big flats will make an even bigger cube, and the triplet of shapes begins again.

The first cube is a *unit*, the next is a *thousand,* the next a *million*, then a *billion*, and so on. Each long is 10 cubes: 10 units, 10 thousands, 10 millions. Similarly, each flat is 100 cubes.

To read large numbers, group the digits in threes starting from the right. (See Figure 9.17). Note that the last grouping on the left might have fewer than three digits. Beginning at the left the grouped digits are then read, stopping at the end of each triple to name the unit (or cube shape) for it. Leading zeros are ignored. If students can learn to read numbers like 059 (fifty-nine) or 009 (nine), they should be able to read any number. To write a number,

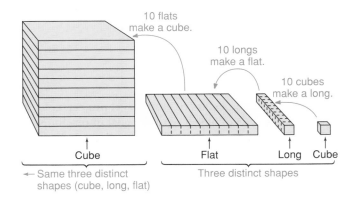

10 flats make a cube.

10 longs make a flat.

10 cubes make a long.

Cube   Flat   Long   Cube

← Same three distinct shapes (cube, long, flat)   Three distinct shapes

FIGURE 9.16 With every three places, the shapes repeat. Each cube represents a 1, each long represents a 10, and each flat represents a 100.

FIGURE 9.17 The triples system for naming large numbers.

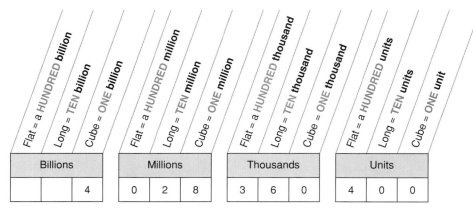

"Four billion twenty-eight million three hundred and sixty thousand four hundred."

use the same scheme. If first mastered orally, the system is quite easy.

It is important for children to realize that our number system does have a logical structure, is not totally arbitrary, and can be understood.

Conceptualizing Large Numbers

The ideas just discussed are only partially helpful in thinking about the actual quantities involved in very large numbers. For example, in extending the square-strip-square-strip sequence, some appreciation for the quantities of 1000 or of 100 000 is included. But it is hard for anyone to translate quantities of small squares into quantities of other items, distances, or time.

Creating References for Special Big Numbers

In these activities, numbers like 1000, 10 000, or even 1 million are translated literally or imaginatively into something that is easy or fun to think about. Interesting quantities become lasting reference points or benchmarks for large numbers and thereby add meaning to numbers encountered in real life.

ACTIVITY 9.27

Collecting 10 000

Collections. For a class or grade-level project, collect some type of object with the goal of reaching some specific quantity—for example, 1000 or 10 000 buttons, walnuts, old pencils, jar lids, or pieces of junk mail. If you begin aiming for 100 000 or 1 million, be sure to think it through. One teacher spent nearly 10 years with her classes before amassing a million bottle caps. It takes a small dump truck to hold that many!

ACTIVITY 9.28

Showing 10 000

Illustrations. Sometimes it is easier to create large amounts. For example, start a project where students draw 100 or 200 or even 500 dots on a sheet of paper. Each week, different students contribute a specified number. Another idea is to cut up newspaper into pieces the same size as five-dollar bills to see what a large quantity would look like. Paper chain links can be constructed over time and hung down the hallways with special numbers marked. Let the school be aware of the ultimate goal.

ACTIVITY 9.29

How Long?/How Far?

Real and imagined distances. How long is a million baby steps? Other ideas that address length: toothpicks or chocolate bars end to end; children holding hands in a line; blocks or bricks stacked up; children lying down head to toe. Real measures can also be used: centimetres, metres.

 **ACTIVITY 9.30**

A Long Time

Time. How long is 1000 seconds? How long is a million seconds? A billion? How long would it take to count to 10 000 or 1 million? (To make the counts all the same, use your calculator to do the counting. Just press the ⊟ .) How long would it take to do some task like buttoning a button 1000 times?

Estimating Large Quantities

Activities 9.27 through 9.30 focus on a specific number. The reverse idea is to select a large quantity and find some way to measure, count, or estimate how many.

ACTIVITY 9.31

Really Large Quantities

Ask how many

    Chocolate bars would cover the floor of your room

    Steps an ant would take to walk around the school building

    Grains of rice would fill a container that holds a litre or 25 litres

    Quarters could be stacked in one stack from floor to ceiling

    Pennies can be laid side by side down an entire block

    Pieces of notebook paper would cover the gym floor

    Seconds you have lived

Big-number projects need not take up large amounts of class time. They can be explored over several weeks as take-home projects or group projects or, perhaps best of all, they can be translated into great school-wide estimation contests. The many children's books that examine large numbers in inventive ways are among the best tools to motivate large-number projects. A few suggestions follow.

 Literature Connections

Books that emphasize groups of things, even simple counting books, are a good beginning to the notion of 10 things in a single group. Many books wonderfully explore large quantities and the ways that they can be combined and separated.

Moira's Birthday
(Munsch, 1987)

As Moira plans her birthday party, she invites more and more children until she has invited all the children in the kindergarten and grades 1, 2, 3, 4, 5, and 6. Then she needs to order food. She orders 200 cakes and 200 pizzas. Bedlam ensues brilliantly as the food and the children all arrive at the party. A grade 2 teacher, Diane Oppedal (1995), used this story as a background for the question "How can you show 200 things in different ways?" As children work on this or similar projects, they can be encouraged to use some form of grouping to keep track of their collections.

The same book can also be used to motivate a variety of computation situations that could be used prior to structured computation instruction. "How many children are in 3 classrooms?" "What if everyone at the party got 2 pieces of pizza?" "Moira gave 37 of her 94 presents back to the children who helped her clean up. How many presents did she have left?"

How to Count like a Martian
(St. John, 1975)

This book explores number systems from different ancient cultures (Chinese, Roman, Egyptian, etc.) and so has a cultural as well as a mathematical connection. The contrast of the different systems, most of which are not base-ten systems, can be a good way for children in grades 4 and 5 to appreciate and discuss the base-ten place-value system. Most other numeration systems do not have a zero, for example. Several numeration systems use the same symbol repeatedly to express multiples of a certain quantity. Children could write numbers in different systems, try to compute in another system, or discuss how they might make up a system of their own. Why is it that most of the world has adopted the system we use?

The King's Commissioners
(Friedman, 1994)

The king has so many commissioners, he can't keep track of how many there are. In a hilarious tale, the commissioners are marched into the throne room to be counted. One person tries to count them by twos and another by fives. The princess convinces the king that there are many other excellent ways to count. The story is a natural background for place-value concepts, including grouping and different counting methods, large numbers, and informal early computation challenges. Stephanie Sheffield (1995) offers specific suggestions for using this story with children at about the grade 2 level.

Can You Count to a Googol?
(Wells, 2000)

If you're looking for a book that focuses on large numbers and is entertaining at the same time, this is an excellent choice. As you read through the book, the author provides you with a variety of amusing situations, which demonstrate how you can make numbers grow exponentially by powers of ten until you reach a googol. You can also use the book to support your work with place value. The illustrations are humorous and connect to real life.

A Million Fish... More or Less
(McKissack, 1992)

This story, which takes place in lower Louisiana, is a tall tale of a boy who catches three fish ... and then a million more. The story is full of exaggerations, such as a turkey that weighs 500 pounds and a skipping-rope contest (using a snake) where the story's hero wins by skipping 5553 times. "Could these things really be? How long would it take to skip 5553 times? Could Hugh put a million fish in his wagon? How do you write half of a million?" Rusty Bresser (1995) suggests a number of excellent ways this tale can be used to investigate large numbers and how they are written. The connections to real things and real ideas are just the ticket to add number sense to an upper-grade unit on place value.

(Note: If you do use this book, you will want to change any imperial measurements to metric.)

Many other excellent books investigate very large numbers in interesting contexts. *How Much Is a Million?* (1985) and *If You Made a Million* (1989), both by David Schwartz, have become very popular. Wanda Gag's *Millions of Cats* (1928) is a classic that is still worth the time to investigate. Just one more of many possibilities is *Six Dogs, Twenty-Three Cats, Forty-Five Mice, and One Hundred Sixteen Spiders* (Chalmers, 1986). The imagination that these books inspire can lead children into fascinating investigations of large numbers, and with a bit of guidance, good place-value concepts can be visited along the way.

 ## Assessment Notes

Ongoing Assessment

Most of the activities suggested in this chapter provide opportunities to find out what children know and understand about place value. They are performance tasks. A lot of the assessment information you will need will come from watching and listening as children do these tasks.

- How do children count or estimate quantities? Do they spontaneously use sets of tens?

- When materials are already arranged in groups of 10 (counters in cups, dots in ten-frames) or in groups of 100, do the children use these structures to tell how many?

- How flexible are children in their thinking about numbers? Can they take them apart and combine them in ways that reflect an understanding of ones, tens, and hundreds?

- How well are they able to relate numbers appropriate for their age to real quantities, measures, and events?

The following activity is frequently used in interviews with individual students but could easily be a task posed to the whole class or a small group for discussion. As you listen to how children solve these problems, you will realize that there is much more to learn about their thinking beyond simply getting the answer correct. ■■

 ### ACTIVITY 9.32
Mystery Mats

First, show a mat or board that has some base-ten pieces covered and some showing. Tell the child how many pieces are hidden under the cover, and ask her or him to figure out how much is on the board altogether, as in Figure 9.18(a). After that, show a board partially covered as before. Tell the child how many pieces are on the board altogether, and ask how many are hidden, as in Figure 9.18(b).

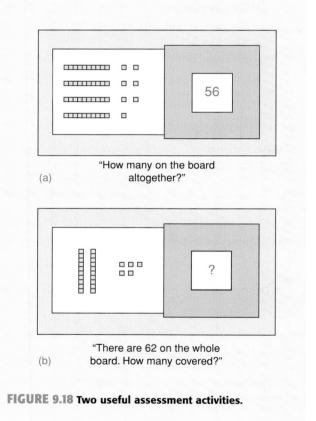

FIGURE 9.18 Two useful assessment activities.

Activity 9.32 could also involve hundreds. The previous amounts could be given in written form instead of orally.

Diagnosis of Place-Value Concepts

Much information can be gleaned from observation and discussion. But you may still be curious to know exactly what level of understanding a few particular children may have about place-value concepts. This is one reason to conduct a diagnostic consultation. Often children are able to disguise their lack of understanding by following directions, using the tens and ones pieces in prescribed ways, and using the language of place value.

Another reason for a short diagnostic interview with some students might be to confirm the validity of the assessments you have made through observation.

The diagnostic tasks presented here are designed to help you look more closely at children's understanding of place value. They are not suggested as definitive tests but as a means of obtaining information for the thoughtful teacher. These tasks have been used by several researchers and are adapted primarily from Labinowicz (1985) and Ross (1986). The tasks are designed for one-on-one settings. They should not be used as instructional activities.

Counting Skills

A variety of oral counting tasks provide insight into the counting sequence.

- ■ Count forward for me, starting at 77.
- ■ Count backward, starting at 55.
- ■ Count by tens.
- ■ Count by tens, starting at 34.
- ■ Count backward by tens, starting at 130.

In the tasks that follow, the manner in which the child responds is as important as the answers. For example, counting individual squares on tens pieces (longs) that are known to the child as "tens" will produce correct answers, but indicates that the structure of tens is not being used.

One More and Ten More, One Less and Ten Less

Write the number 342. Have the child read the number. Then have the child write the number that is 1 more than 342. Next ask for the number that is 10 more than 342. You may wish to explore further with models. One less and 10 less can be checked the same way.

Digit Correspondence

Dump out 36 cubes. Ask the child to count the cubes; then write the number that tells how many there are. Circle the 6 in 36 and ask, "Does this part of your 36 have anything to do with how many cubes there are?" Then circle the 3 and repeat the question in the same way. Do not give clues. Based on responses to the task, Ross (1989) has identified five distinct levels of understanding of place value:

1. *Single number.* The child writes 36 but views it as a single number. The individual digits 3 and 6 have no meaning by themselves.
2. *Position names.* The child identifies correctly the tens and ones positions but still makes no connection between the individual digits and the cubes.
3. *Face value.* The child matches 6 cubes with the 6, and 3 cubes with the 3.
4. *Transition to place value.* The 6 is matched with 6 cubes and the 3 with the remaining 30 cubes, but not as 3 groups of 10.
5. *Full understanding.* The 3 is correlated with 3 groups of 10 cubes, and the 6 with 6 single cubes.

Using Tens

Dump out 47 counters, and have the child count them. Next show the child at least 10 cards, each with a ten-frame drawn on it. Ask, "If we wanted to put these counters in the spaces on these cards, how many cards could we fill up?" (If the ten-frame has been used in class to model sets of 10, use a different frame such as a 10-pin arrangement of circles. Be sure the child knows there are 10 spaces on each card.)

Using Groups of 10

Prepare cards with beans or other counters glued to them in an obvious arrangement of 10. Provide at least 10 such cards, and a large supply of loose beans. After you are sure that the child has counted several cards with beans and knows there are 10 on each, say, "Show me 34 beans." (Does the child count individual beans or use the cards of 10?) This activity can also be done with hundreds.

Reflections *on Chapter 9*

Writing to Learn

1. Explain how a child who has not yet developed base-ten concepts understands quantities as large as, say, 85. Contrast this with a child who understands these same quantities in terms of base-ten groupings.
2. What is meant by *equivalent representations?*
3. Explain the three ways one can count a set of objects and how these methods of counting can be used to coordinate concepts and oral and written names for numbers.
4. Name and describe the two types of concrete models that are used to represent base-ten concepts. What is significant about the difference between these two types of models? Why is an abacus not considered a model for place value?
5. Describe an activity for developing base-ten grouping concepts, and reflect on how the activity encourages children to construct base-ten concepts.
6. How do children learn to write two- and three-digit numbers in a way that is connected to the base-ten meanings of ones and tens or ones, tens, and hundreds?
7. How would you describe good place-value number sense? There are varied aspects to number sense with large numbers. Describe activities that will help to develop these different features of good number sense with larger numbers.
8. What are two different ideas that you would want children to know about very large numbers (beyond 1000)? Describe one or two activities that could be used to promote each of these.

For Discussion and Exploration

1. On the basis of the suggestions toward the end of this chapter and on the content of a standard basal textbook, design a diagnostic interview for a child at a particular grade level, and conduct the interview. It is a good idea to take a friend to act as an observer or to use a tape recorder or video camera to keep track of how the interview went.
2. A popular collection of activities, commonly known as "trading activities," are done with base-ten models. In all of these activities, children have a place-value mat on which they accumulate materials or from which they remove materials. The activities generally take the form of a game. Perhaps a die is rolled and the die tells the child how many ones are to be placed on the mat or how many may be removed. Whenever 10 pieces in one section are accumulated, a trade is made for a single piece in the next place: 10 ones for a ten, 10 tens for a hundred. Similarly, in the process of removing pieces, trades are made in the reverse manner: 1 ten for 10 ones.

Do these trading activities contribute any new connections or ideas to place-value understanding? If so, what are they? Are trading activities problematic? Are there any activities in this chapter that get at the same ideas?

Recommendations for Further Reading

Highly Recommended

Burns, M. (1994). *Math by all means: Place value, grade 2.* Sausalito, CA: Math Solutions Publications.

Burns provides 25 days of very detailed lessons in place value for grade 2 children. As in her other books, she provides numerous examples of children's written work and descriptions of interactions that took place in the classroom. It is possible to take issue with the claims Burns makes for the complete development resulting from these lessons, but that does not detract from the value of most of the activities. Perhaps most important is the way that Burns brings you into the classroom to get a feel for how these activities will work with children.

Hiebert, J.C., & Wearne, D. (1992). Links between teaching and learning place value with understanding in grade 1. *Journal for Research in Mathematics Education, 23,* 98–122.

This study compares four grade 1 classrooms where a highly conceptual approach to place value was used with two classrooms where the teachers followed a traditional textbook. The article provides an excellent, objective description of a constructivist approach to this complex topic in grade 1 and shows the stark contrast of this method with the traditional text-based methods. For example, a major difference was found between materials used to "work through an idea" and materials used to "show."

Richardson, K. (1990). *A look at children's thinking: Video II and study guide.* Norman, OK: Educational Enrichment.

This tape showing diagnostic interviews is essential viewing for anyone interested in how children develop number concepts, especially place value. Richardson poses the same series of questions to several children at different stages of development. Her commentary clearly explains why the questions are asked and what she is looking for, and includes an analysis of the students' responses. You cannot watch this tape and not fully appreciate the complexity of place-value concepts and the difficulty children have developing them.

Schifter, D., Bastable, V., & Russell, S.J. (1999). *Developing mathematical ideas: Numbers and operations, Part 1: Building a system of tens* (Casebook). White Plains, NY: Cuisenaire–Dale Seymour.

Schifter and her colleagues at TERC have compiled in this book a wonderful collection of cases, each written by a classroom teacher, in which the complexities of place-value development truly come to light. Although this is intended as a companion book to an in-service program, the cases by themselves are worth reading. They will provide useful insights into children's thinking and useful points of discussion. The book contains 29 different cases from grades 1 to 6 and covers situations involving invented computations and decimals as well as whole-number meanings.

Other Suggestions

Bove, S.P. (1995). Place value: A vertical perspective. *Teaching Children Mathematics, 1,* 542–546.

Fuson, K.C., Wearne, D., Hiebert, J.C., Murray, H.G., Human, P.G., Olivier, A.I., Carpenter, T.P., & Fennema, E. (1997). Children's conceptual structures for multidigit numbers and methods of multidigit addition and subtraction. *Journal for Research in Mathematics Education, 28,* 130–162.

Kamii, C.K. (1986). Place value: An explanation of its difficulty and educational implications for the primary grades. *Journal of Research in Childhood Education, 1,* 75–86.

Labinowicz, E. (1985). *Learning from children: New beginnings for teaching numerical thinking.* Menlo Park, CA: AWL Supplemental.

Larsen, N. (1996). Making cents. *Teaching Children Mathematics, 2,* 520–522.

Little, C. (1999). Counting grass. *Mathematics Teaching in the Middle School, 5,* 7–10.

Nagel, N.G., & Swingen C.C. (1998). Students' explanations of place value in addition and subtraction. *Teaching Children Mathematics, 5,* 164–170.

O'Connell, S.R. (1995). Newspapers: Connecting the mathematics classroom to the world. *Teaching Children Mathematics, 1,* 268–274.

Oppedal, D.C. (1995). Mathematics is something good. *Teaching Children Mathematics, 2,* 36–40.

Payne, J.N., & Huinker, D.M. (1993). Early number and numeration. In R.J. Jensen (Ed.), *Research ideas for the classroom: Early childhood mathematics* (pp. 43–71). Old Tappan, NJ: Macmillan.

Reys, B.J. (1991). *Developing number sense in the middle grades: Addenda series, grades 5–8.* Reston, VA: National Council of Teachers of Mathematics.

Ross, S.H. (1989). Parts, wholes, and place value: A developmental perspective. *Arithmetic Teacher, 36*(6), 47–51.

Schwartz, S.L., & Curcio, F.R. (1995). Learning mathematics in meaningful contexts: An action-based approach in the primary grades. In P.A. House (Ed.), *Connecting mathematics across the curriculum* (pp. 116–123). Reston, VA: National Council of Teachers of Mathematics.

Thompson, C.S. (1990). Place value and larger numbers. In J.N. Payne (Ed.), *Mathematics for the young child* (pp. 89–108). Reston, VA: National Council of Teachers of Mathematics.

Whitin, D.J. (1995). Connecting literature and mathematics. In P.A. House (Ed.), *Connecting mathematics across the curriculum* (pp. 134–141). Reston, VA: National Council of Teachers of Mathematics.

Chapter 10

Strategies for Whole-Number Computation

In the context of Canadian efforts to reform mathematics (Anderson & Poirier, 1999) and the public's push for accountability and testable standards, computation is a major issue. In the past, only one method of computing was developed for each operation. Before calculators became common, it was important to have an efficient method of computing, applicable to all situations, regardless of the size of the numbers. With today's technology, the need for doing tedious computations by hand has essentially disappeared. At the same time, we know that there are numerous methods of computation that can be handled either mentally or with pencil-and-paper support. In most everyday instances, these alternative strategies for computing are easy and fast, can often be done mentally, and contribute to our overall number sense. It is important to note that traditional algorithms (procedures for computation) do not have these benefits.

BIG IDEAS

1. Flexible methods of computation involve taking apart and combining numbers in a wide variety of ways, most depending on place value.

2. Invented strategies, mental computation, estimation, and the traditional algorithms are all based on place-value concepts and an understanding of the different meanings of the operations and how they are related.

3. Each of the traditional algorithms is simply a clever way to record an operation for a single place value with transitions (trades, "borrows," or "carries") to an adjacent position. As such, traditional algorithms have a digit orientation.

Invented Strategies

In the past two decades, a number of research projects have focused attention on how children handle computational situations when they have not been taught a specific algorithm or strategy.* The three elementary reform curricula each base the development of computational methods on student-invented strategies. "There is mounting evidence that children both in and out of school can construct methods for adding and subtracting multi-digit numbers without explicit instruction" (Carpenter, Franke, Jacobs, Fennema, & Empson, 1998, p. 4). Data supporting students' ability to construct useful methods for multiplication and division have also been gathered (Baek, 1998; Kamii & Dominick, 1997; Schifter, Bastable, & Russell, 1999b).

Try solving the following problem using a method other than the usual algorithm you were taught in school. Can you do it mentally? Can you do it in more than one way?

Talia's photo album can hold 114 photographs. So far she has 89 photos in the album. How many more photos can she put in before the album is full?

---

*The Cognitively Guided Instruction Project (CGI), directed by Carpenter, Fennema, and Franke at the University of Wisconsin; the Conceptually Based Instruction project (CBI), directed by Hiebert and Wearne at the University of Delaware; the Problem Centered Mathematics Project (PCMP), directed by Human, Murray, and Olivier at the University of Stellenbosch, South Africa; the Supporting Ten-Structured Thinking project (STST), directed by Fuson at Northwest University; and ongoing research by Kamii at the University of Alabama are all examples of efforts that have informed thinking about strategies for computation.

Here are just four of many methods that have been used by students in the primary grades to solve the problem:

89 + 11 is 100. 11 + 14 is 25.

90 + 10 is 100 and 14 more is 24 plus 1 is 25.

Take away 14, then take away 11 more. That is 25 in all.

89, 99, 109 (that's 20), 110, 111, 112, 113, 114

$\longrightarrow$ 25 (keep track on fingers).

Strategies such as these that can be done mentally are generally faster than traditional algorithms and make sense to the person using them. Every day, students and adults resort to traditional strategies when more meaningful methods would be faster and less susceptible to error. Flexibility with a variety of computational strategies is an important tool for successful daily living. It is time to broaden our perspective of what it means to compute.

Carpenter et al. (1998) use the term *invented strategy* to refer to any strategy other than the traditional algorithm that does not involve using physical materials such as base-ten blocks or drawings. (The terms *flexible* and *personal* might also be appropriate.) The developmental step that usually leads to the creation of an invented strategy is known as *direct modelling:* the use of manipulatives or drawings to represent directly the meaning of the operation or story problem (see Figure 10.1). Invented strategies are often but not always done mentally. For example, 75 + 19 can be done mentally (75 and 20 is 95, less 1 is 94). For 847 + 256, some students may write down intermediate steps to help them remember. In the classroom, some written support is often used as strategies develop. For some students, these methods will gradually become entirely mental.

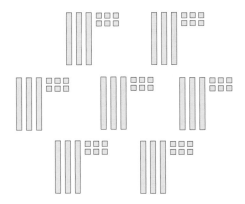

FIGURE 10.1 A possible direct modelling of 36 $\times$ 7 using base-ten models.

Not all students invent their own strategies. Strategies invented by class members are shared, explored, and tried out by others. However, no student should be permitted to use any strategy without understanding it (Campbell, Rowan, & Suarez, 1998).

Contrasts with Traditional Algorithms

There are significant differences between invented strategies and traditional algorithms.

1. *Invented strategies are number-oriented rather than digit-oriented.* For example, an invented strategy for 68 $\times$ 7 begins 7 $\times$ 60 is 420 and 56 more is 476. The first product is 7 times *sixty,* not the digit 6, as would be the case in the traditional algorithm. Using the traditional algorithm for 45 + 32, children never think of 40 and 30 but rather 4 + 3. Kamii, long a crusader against standard algorithms, claims that they "unteach" place value (Kamii & Dominick, 1998).

2. *Invented strategies are left-handed rather than right-handed.* Invented strategies begin with the largest parts of numbers, those represented by the leftmost digits. For 26 $\times$ 47, invented strategies will begin with 20 $\times$ 40 is 800, providing some sense of the size of the eventual answer in just one step. The traditional algorithm begins with 7 $\times$ 6 is 42. By beginning on the right with a digit orientation, traditional methods hide the result until the end. Long division is an exception.

3. *Invented strategies are flexible rather than rigid.* Invented strategies tend to change with the numbers involved in order to make the computation easier. Try each of these mentally: 465 + 230 and 526 + 98. Did you use the same method? The traditional algorithm uses the same tool on all problems. The traditional algorithm for 7000 – 25 typically leads to student errors, yet a mental strategy is relatively simple (Carroll & Porter, 1997).

Benefits of Invented Strategies

The development of invented strategies delivers more than computational facility. Both their development and their regular use have positive benefits that are difficult to ignore, as the following indicate.

- *Base-ten concepts are enhanced.* There is a definite interaction between the development of base-ten concepts and the process of inventing computational strategies (Carpenter et al., 1998). "Invented strategies demonstrate a hallmark characteristic of understanding" (p. 16). The development of invented strategies should be integrated with the development of base-ten concepts as early as grade 1.

- *Invented strategies are built on student understanding.* Because invented strategies are so dependent on base-ten concepts and are developed in a problem-solving atmosphere, students rarely use an invented strategy they do not understand. In contrast, students frequently use traditional algorithms without being able to explain why they work (Carroll & Porter, 1997).

- *Students make fewer errors with invented strategies.* Data collected by Kamii and Dominick (1997) provide some hard evidence for this claim. With traditional algorithms, students tend to develop systematic errors or "buggy algorithms" that they fall into again and again. Careless errors often result from confusion with digits that are carried, or column alignment. Systematic errors are not typical of invented strategies.

■ *Use of invented strategies promotes mathematical thinking.* Invented strategies grow out of students' thinking, guided by the teacher. Sense-making is a hallmark of their development. Students use invented strategies in meaningful ways. Thus the development and use of these strategies is an example of *doing mathematics.* In contrast, the traditional algorithms are often accepted on faith because the teacher says, "This is how you are to do it."

■ *Invented strategies serve students at least as well on standard tests.* Evidence from reform programs suggests that students who are not taught traditional algorithms fare about as well in computation on standardized tests as students in traditional programs (Campbell, 1996; Carroll, 1996, 1997; Chambers, 1996). As an added bonus, students tend to do quite well with word problems, since they are the principal vehicle for developing invented strategies. The pressures of external testing do not dictate a focus on the traditional algorithms.

Development of Invented Strategies: A General Approach

Students do not spontaneously invent wonderful computational methods while the teacher sits back and watches. In different experimental programs, students tended to develop or gravitate toward different strategies, suggesting that teachers and programs do have an effect on which methods students develop (Fuson et al., 1997). This section discusses general pedagogical methods for helping children develop invented strategies.

Use Story Problems Frequently

When computational tasks are embedded in simple contexts, students seem to be more engaged than they are with mere computation. Furthermore, the choice of story problems influences the strategies students use to solve them. Consider these problems:

Max had already saved 68 cents when his mother gave him some money for running an errand. Now Max has 93 cents. How much did Max earn for his errand?

Kiam took 93 cents to the store. He spent 68 cents. How much does he have left?

The computation 93 − 68 solves both problems, but the first is more likely than the second to be solved by an add-on method. In a similar manner, fair-share division problems are more likely to encourage a share strategy than problems involving measurement or repeated subtraction.

Problems need not be elaborate but should involve themes and topics of interest to the students. Use the students themselves in the problems. Build problems around sets of data collected in the class or literature that you've been reading. Use the measurements from your measurement unit to create problems.

Not every task need be a story problem. Especially when students are engaged in figuring out a new strategy, straightforward arithmetic problems are quite adequate.

Use the Three-Part Lesson Format

The three-part lesson format described in Chapter 4 is a good structure for an invented-strategy lesson. The task can be one or two story problems or even a mere computation, always with the expectation that the method of solution will be discussed. Sometimes you can meet individual needs by providing variations with different numbers to different groups.

In the introduction section, some teachers solicit estimates or solutions done mentally and record these on the board. This is a way to get everyone thinking before setting students free to work in pairs or independently (Lester, 1996). Familiar materials such as base-ten models and counters should be readily available but never required for a solution. It is often useful to have students write or use pictures to explain their methods (Whitin & Whitin, 1998).

Allow plenty of time to solve a problem. Listen to the different strategies students are using, but do not interject with your own. Challenge able students to find a second method, solve a problem without models, or improve on a written explanation. Encourage slower children using even the simplest counting methods. Students who finish quickly may share their methods with others before sharing with the class.

The most important portion of the lesson comes when students explain their solutions. Avoid focusing on the same students each time. Help students write their explanations on the board or overhead. Encourage students to ask questions of their classmates. Occasionally have the class try a particular method with different numbers to see how it works. When students find an idea worthwhile, record it on a "strategies chart." Remember, not every student will invent strategies. However, students can and will try strategies that they have seen and that make sense to them. Make it a firm rule that *no one may use a strategy that he or she does not understand.*

Allow for a Range of Methods

Virtually all methods can be separated into three categories: *direct modelling, invented strategies,* and *traditional algorithms* (see Figure 10.2). Many teachers who hope to develop invented strategies are disappointed when students rely on very primitive and tedious counting methods. Another frustration occurs when children use a traditional algorithm, even if the teacher has never introduced it before. It is important to view all methods that students use from their perspective, in terms of what they know and understand.

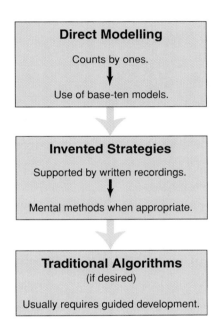

FIGURE 10.2 The typical progress of computational strategies.

Direct Modelling

Direct modelling methods generally fall into one of two categories: those that involve a count-by-ones method with no evidence of base-ten concepts being used, and those in which students use their knowledge of tens and hundreds to model more efficiently.

Students who consistently count by ones most likely have not developed base-ten grouping concepts. This does not mean that they should not continue to solve problems involving two-digit numbers. As you work with these children, suggest (don't force) that they group counters by tens as they count. Perhaps, instead of making large piles, they might make bars of ten from interlocking cubes, or organize counters by tens in cups. Some students will use the ten-stick (base ten materials) as a counting device to keep track of the number of tens, even though they are counting each segment of the stick by ones.

If you feel students are capable of more sophisticated strategies, perhaps the counters should mysteriously "disappear" for a few days, or you might challenge students to find a more clever way to solve a problem.

When children have plenty of experience with base-ten concepts and models, they will begin to use these ideas in the direct modelling of the problems. Also remember the power of drawing squares, sticks, and dots for hundreds, tens, and ones. Some students will find such drawings more useful than the actual blocks. Even when students use base-ten materials, they will find many different ways to solve problems.

Progression to Invented Strategies

Direct modelling involving tens and ones can and will lead eventually to invented strategies, methods that rely solely on mental processes. These methods can also be supported by pencil and paper. However, students do tend to stick with strategies with which they are comfortable, and may need to be encouraged to move away from the direct modelling process. Here are some ideas that could be used to encourage them:

- Record students' verbal explanations on the board in ways that they and others can model. Have the class follow the recorded method using different numbers.
- Ask students to see if they can solve in their heads a problem they have just solved.
- Pose a problem to the class, then ask students if they are able to solve it mentally.
- Ask children to record numerically what they did when they solved the problem with models. Ask them to try to use the same method on a new problem.

Unsolicited Introduction of Traditional Algorithms

You probably cannot keep the traditional algorithms out of your classroom. Children pick up these algorithms from older siblings, last year's teacher, well-meaning parents ("My dad showed me an easy way"). Traditional algorithms are in no way evil, so to forbid their use is somewhat capricious. However, students who latch on to a traditional method often resist the invention of more flexible strategies. What do you do then?

First and foremost, apply the same rule to traditional algorithms that you use for all strategies: *If you use it, you must understand why it works and be able to explain it.* In an atmosphere that says, "Let's figure out why this works," students can profit from making sense of these algorithms just like any other. But the responsibility should be theirs, not yours.

Accept a traditional algorithm (once it is understood) as one more strategy to put in the class "tool box" of methods.

But reinforce the idea that, like the other strategies, it may be more useful in some instances than in others. Pose problems such as 504 − 498 or 75 × 4 where using a mental strategy would be effective. Follow with a discussion regarding which method seemed to work best. Point out that for a problem such as 4568 + 12 813, the traditional algorithm has some advantages. However, in the real world, most people do these computations on a calculator.

Invented Strategies for Addition and Subtraction

Research has demonstrated that children will invent a lot of different strategies for addition and subtraction. Your goal might be for each of your children to develop at least one or two methods that are reasonably efficient, mathematically correct, and useful with a lot of different numbers. Expect different children to settle on different strategies.

Many of the techniques for addition and subtraction are easily done mentally, without recording. It is not at all unreasonable to expect students to be able to add and subtract two-digit numbers mentally by grade 3. Recording strategies daily on the board not only helps communicate ideas, it also helps those children who need assistance with their short-term memory of intermediate steps.

Adding and Subtracting Single Digits

Children can easily extend addition and subtraction facts to higher decades.

On Wednesday, Jade was on page 47 of her book. She read 8 more pages that day. How many pages did she read altogether?

If students are simply counting on by ones, an activity in which students solve a series of problems may be useful. Consider the following activity. It is an extension of the make-ten strategy for addition facts.

ACTIVITY 10.1

Ten-Frame Adding and Subtracting

Quickly review the make-ten idea from addition facts using two ten-frames. (Add on to get up to 10 and then add the rest.) Challenge children to use the same idea to add on to a two-digit number as shown in Figure 10.3. Students can work together in pairs. First, they make a specified two-digit number with the little ten-frame cards.

Then they stack up all of the less-than-10 cards and turn them over one at a time. Together they talk about how to get the total quickly.

The same approach is used for subtraction. For instance, for 53 − 7, take off 3 to get to 50, then 4 more is 46.

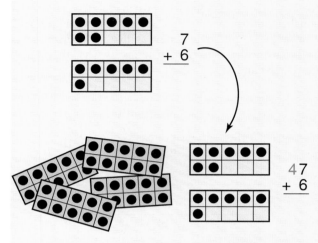

FIGURE 10.3 Little ten-frame cards can help children extend the make-ten idea to larger numbers.

Adding and Subtracting Tens and Hundreds

Sums and differences involving multiples of 10 or 100 are easily computed mentally. Write a problem such as the following on the board:

$$300 + 500 + 20$$

Challenge children to solve it mentally. Ask them to share how they did it. Look for ways to use place-value words: "3 *hundred* and 5 *hundred* is 8 *hundred,* and 20 is 820."

Use base-ten models to help children begin to think in terms of tens and hundreds. Early examples should not include any trades. The exercise 420 + 300 involves no trades, whereas 70 + 80 may be more difficult.

Adding Two-Digit Numbers

For the examples that follow, a possible recording method is offered. These are intended to be suggestions, not prescriptions. Children have difficulty inventing recording techniques. If you write the children's ideas on the board as they explain them, you are helping them develop their recording techniques. You may even discuss methods of recording, individually or with the whole class, to decide on a form that seems to work well. Horizontal formats encourage students to think in terms of numbers instead of digits. A horizontal format is also less likely to encourage use of the traditional algorithms.

Students will often use a count-by-tens-and-ones technique with some of these methods. That is, instead of "46 + 30 is 76," they may count "46 $\longrightarrow$ 56, 66, 76." To help students keep track of these counts, they can be written down as they are said. Eventually, students should move toward a more efficient approach.

Figure 10.4 illustrates four different strategies for addition of two two-digit numbers. Here is a story problem you might use.

The school's junior and senior choirs went on a field trip to the National Arts Centre in Ottawa. There were 46 students in the junior choir and 38 in the senior choir. How many students went on the trip?

The *move to make ten using compensation* strategy is helpful when one of the numbers ends in 8 or 9. To promote this technique, present problems with addends like 39 or 58. Note that it is necessary to adjust only one of the two numbers.

Subtracting by Counting Up

This is an amazingly powerful way to subtract. Most of us have never thought of using it since traditionally, subtraction as take-away predominates. Students working on the *think-addition* strategy for their basic facts can also solve problems with larger numbers. The concept is the same. It is important to use *join with, change unknown,* or *missing-part* problems to encourage the counting-up strategy. Here is an example of each.

Sam had 46 baseball cards. He went to a card show and bought some more cards for his collection. Now he has 73 cards. How many cards did Sam buy at the card show?

Juanita counted all of her markers. She had 73 in all. Some had dried up and were not working. Forty-six were working. How many markers were not working?

The numbers in these problems are used in the strategies illustrated in Figure 10.5.

FIGURE 10.4 **Four different invented strategies for adding two two-digit numbers.**

Invented Strategies for Addition with Two-Digit Numbers

Add Tens, Add Ones, Then Combine

46 + 38
40 and 30 is 70.
6 and 8 is 14.
70 and 14 is 84.

$$\begin{array}{r} 46 \\ +38 \\ \hline 70 \\ 14 \\ \hline 84 \end{array}$$

Add On Tens, Then Add Ones

46 + 38
46 and 30 more is 76.
Then I added on the other 8.
76 and 4 is 80 and 4 is 84.

$46 + 30 \rightarrow$
$76 + 8 \rightarrow 80, 84$

Move Some to Make Tens

46 + 38
Take 2 from the 46 and put it with the 38 to make 40. Now you have 44 and 40 more is 84.

$46 + 38$
$44 + 40$
84

Use a Nice Number and Compensate

46 + 38
46 and 40 is 86.
That's 2 extra, so it's 84.

$46 + 38$
$46 + 40 \rightarrow$
$86 - 2 \rightarrow 84$

FIGURE 10.5 **Subtraction by counting up is a powerful method.**

Invented Strategies for Subtraction by Counting Up

Add Tens to Get Close, then Ones

73 − 46
46 and 20 is 66.
  (30 more is too much.)
Then 4 more is 70 and 3 is 73.
That's 20 and 7 or 27.

$\begin{array}{r} 46 > 20 \\ 66 > 4 \\ 70 > 3 \\ 73 \overline{} \\ 27 \end{array}$

Add Tens to Overshoot, then Come Back

73 − 46
46 and 30 is 76.
That's 3 too much,
so it's 27.

$73 - 46$
$46 + 30 \rightarrow 76 - 3 \rightarrow 73$
$30 - 3 = 27$

Add Ones to Make a Ten, Then Tens and Ones

73 − 46
46 and 4 is 50.
50 and 20 is 70 and 3 more is 73. The 4 and 3 is 7 and 20 is 27.

$73 - 46$
$46 + 4 \rightarrow 50$
$+20 \rightarrow 70$
$+3 \rightarrow 73$
$\overline{27}$

Similarly,
46 and 4 is 50.
50 and 23 is 73.
23 and 4 is 27.

$46 + 4 \rightarrow 50$
$50 + 23 \rightarrow 73$
$23 + 4 = 27$

Take-Away Subtraction

Take-away is considerably more difficult to do mentally. However, take-away strategies are common, probably because traditional textbooks emphasize take-away as the meaning of subtraction. Four different strategies are shown in Figure 10.6.

There were 73 children on the playground. After the bell rang, 46 grade 2 students came in. How many children were still outside?

The two methods that begin by taking tens from tens are reflective of what most students do with base-ten pieces (Madell, 1985). The other two methods leave one of the numbers intact and subtract from it. Try 83 – 29 in your head by first taking away 30 then adding 1 back. This is a good mental method when subtracting a number that is close to a multiple of ten.

Sometimes we need to be reminded of what comes naturally to children. Campbell (1997) tested over 2000 students in Baltimore who had not been taught the traditional algorithm for subtraction. Not one student began with the ones place!

Extensions and Challenges

Each of the examples in the preceding sections involve sums less than 100 and all involve *bridging a ten;* that is, if done with a traditional algorithm, they require carrying or borrowing. Bridging, the size of the numbers, and the potential for doing problems mentally are all issues to consider.

Bridging

For most of the strategies, it is easier to add or subtract when bridging is not required. Try each strategy with 34 + 52 or 68 – 24 to see how it works. Easier problems instill confidence and permit you to challenge your students with a "harder one." There is also the issue of bridging 100 or 1000. Try 58 + 67 with different strategies. Bridging across 100 is also an issue for subtraction. Problems such as 128 – 50 or 128 – 45 are more difficult than ones that do not bridge 100.

Larger Numbers

Most provincial and territorial curricula will expect grade 3 students to add and subtract three-digit numbers. Your curriculum may even require working with four-digit numbers. Try seeing how *you* would do these without using the traditional algorithms: 487 + 235 and 623 – 247. For subtraction, a counting-up strategy is usually the easiest. Occasionally, other strategies appear with larger numbers. For example, "chunking off" multiples of 50 or 25 is often a useful method. For 462 + 257, pull out 450 and 250 to make 700. That leaves 12 and 7 more $\longrightarrow$ 719.

Pencil or Mental Strategies

You may want to be sure that by grade 3 every student has a pencil-and-paper method that is adequate for most purposes. This need not be the traditional algorithm. Many invented strategies will work quite satisfactorily for large numbers and later for decimals. A single invented strategy will generally not be sufficient for dealing with all problems. Often the heart of the matter is in devising a recording strategy that will work for larger numbers.

FIGURE 10.6 Take-away strategies work reasonably well for two-digit problems. They are a bit more difficult with three digits.

Invented Strategies for Take-Away Subtraction	
Take Tens from the Tens, then Subtract Ones	**Take Away Tens, then Ones**
73 – 46	73 – 46
70 minus 40 is 30. $73 - 46$	73 minus 40 is 33. $73 - 40 \rightarrow 33 - 3$
Take away 6 more $70 - 40 \rightarrow 30 - 6 \rightarrow$	Then take away 6: $30 - 3 \rightarrow 27$
is 24.	3 makes 30 and
Now add in the $24 + 3 \rightarrow 27$	3 more is 27.
3 ones $\longrightarrow$ 27.	
	Take Extra Tens, then Add Back
	73 – 46
Or	73 take away 50 is 23. $73 - 50 \rightarrow 23 + 4$
70 minus 40 is 30. 7̶3̶	That's 4 too many. 27
I can take those 3 away, -46	23 and 4 is 27.
but I need 3 more $\overline{30}$	
from the 30 to make 27. -3	**Add to the Whole if Necessary**
$\overline{27}$	73 – 46
	Give 3 to 73 to make 76. $+3$
	76 take away 46 is 30. $73 - 46$
	Now give 3 back $\longrightarrow$ 27. $76 - 46 \rightarrow 30$
	$-3 \rightarrow 27$

As students develop invented strategies, they (and you) will find that doing mental addition and subtraction is actually fairly easy, even with three-digit numbers. Try it! Every once in a while, have a "no-paper day" when all computations are to be done mentally.

Traditional Algorithms for Addition and Subtraction

It can easily be argued that students no longer need the traditional algorithms for addition and subtraction. However, for various reasons, you may feel that your students should learn them. The traditional algorithms require an understanding of *regrouping,* exchanging 10 of the number value in one place for 1 in the position to the left—or the reverse, exchanging 1 of the number value for 10 in the position to the right. The corresponding terms *carrying* and *borrowing* are obsolete and conceptually misleading. The word *regroup* also has little meaning for young children. A preferable term is *trade*. Ten ones are *traded* for a ten. A hundred is *traded* for 10 tens. It is a serious error to work for mastery of problems that do not require grouping before tackling those that require regrouping. Keeping these problems separate has been the documented source of many error patterns. Teaching problems that do not require grouping first causes bad habits that children must later unlearn.

If you develop traditional algorithms in a problem-solving manner, there is no reason why your students should not be expected to understand them!

The Addition Algorithm

Explain to the students that they are going to learn a method of adding that most "big people" learned when they were in school. It is not the only way or even the best way; it is just a method you want them to learn.

Begin with Models Only

In the beginning, avoid any written work except, possibly, for the recording of an answer. Provide children with place-value mats and base-ten models. The mat with two ten-frames in the ones place (Blackline Masters) is suggested.

Have students make one number at the top of the mat and a second beneath it as shown in the top portion of Figure 10.7. If children are still developing their base-ten concepts, a "groupable" model such as counters in cups is most helpful.

Explain this rule: *You begin in the ones column.* "This is a way that people came up with a long time ago, and it worked for them." Let students solve the problem on their own. Provide plenty of time, and then have students

explain what they did and why. Let students use overhead models or magnetic pieces to help with their explanations.

One or two problems in a lesson with much discussion will be more productive than a lot of problems based on rules children don't understand.

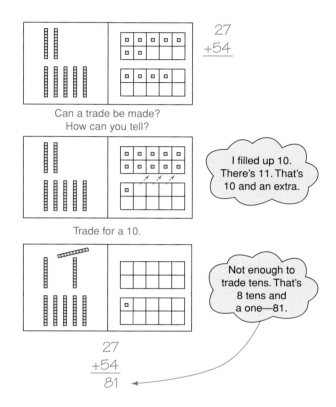

FIGURE 10.7 Working from right to left in addition.

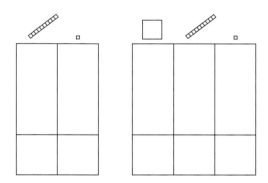

FIGURE 10.8 Blank recording charts are helpful (see Blackline Masters).

Develop the Written Record

Reproduce pages with simple place-value charts similar to those shown in Figure 10.8. The charts will help young children with the recording of numbers in columns. The general idea is to have children record on these pages each step of the procedure with the base-ten models *as it is done*. The first few times you do this, guide each step carefully, as illustrated in Figure 10.9. A similar approach would be used for three-digit problems.

One way to approach this is to have children work in pairs. One child is responsible for the models and the other for recording the steps. Children reverse roles with each problem.

Figure 10.10 shows a variation of the traditional recording scheme that is quite reasonable, at least for up to three digits. It avoids the little "carried ones" and focuses attention on the value of the digits. If students were permitted to start adding on the left as they are inclined to do, this recording procedure would be the same as that shown for the invented strategy "Add tens, add ones, then combine" (Figure 10.4, p. 189). Why not let students start on the left and use this method of recording?

The Subtraction Algorithm

The general approach to developing the subtraction algorithm is the same as for addition. Once the procedure is completely understood with models, a do-and-write approach connects it with a written form.

Begin with Models Only

Start by having children model the top number in a subtraction problem on the top half of their place-value mats. For the amount to be subtracted, have children write each digit on a small piece of paper and place these pieces near the bottom of their mats in the respective columns, as in Figure 10.11. To avoid inadvertent errors, suggest making all trades first. That way, the full amount on the paper slip can be taken off at once. Also explain to children that they are to begin working with the ones column first, as they did with addition.

FIGURE 10.9 Help students record on paper each step they do on their mats as they do it.

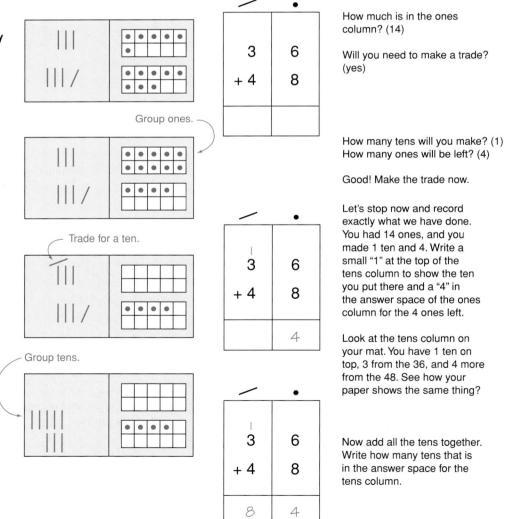

How much is in the ones column? (14)

Will you need to make a trade? (yes)

How many tens will you make? (1) How many ones will be left? (4)

Good! Make the trade now.

Let's stop now and record exactly what we have done. You had 14 ones, and you made 1 ten and 4. Write a small "1" at the top of the tens column to show the ten you put there and a "4" in the answer space of the ones column for the 4 ones left.

Look at the tens column on your mat. You have 1 ten on top, 3 from the 36, and 4 more from the 48. See how your paper shows the same thing?

Now add all the tens together. Write how many tens that is in the answer space for the tens column.

$$
\begin{array}{r}
358 \\
+276 \\
\hline
500 \\
120 \\
14 \\
\hline
634
\end{array}
$$

FIGURE 10.10 **An alternative recording scheme for addition. Notice that this can be used from left to right as well as from right to left.**

Anticipate Difficulties with Zeros

Exercises in which zeros are involved anywhere in the problem tend to cause special difficulties. Give extra attention to these cases while still using models. A zero in the ones or tens place of the bottom number means there is nothing to take away and leaves some children wondering what they are supposed to do. Zeros in the top number mean there are no materials in that column, which presents an unusual situation.

The very common error of "borrowing across zero" is best addressed at the modelling stage. For example, in 403 − 138, children must make a double trade, exchanging a hundreds piece for 10 tens and then one of the tens for 10 ones.

Develop the Written Record

The process of recording each step as it is done is the same as was suggested for addition. The same recording sheets (Figure 10.8) are also recommended.

When a problem has been solved and recorded, children should be able to explain the meaning of all the markings at the top of the problem in relation to the base-ten materials. The ability to explain the symbolic form indicates that children are ready to move on to a completely symbolic level. Again, be attentive to problems with zeros.

If students are permitted to follow their natural instincts and begin with the big pieces (working from the left instead of the right), recording schemes similar to that shown in Figure 10.12 are possible. The trades are made from the pieces remaining *after* the subtraction in the column to the left has been done. However, a "borrow across zero" difficulty will still occur in problems like this: 462 − 168. Try it.

Invented Strategies for Multiplication

Computation strategies for multiplication are considerably more complex than for addition and subtraction. Often,

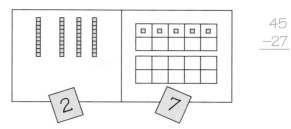

45
−27

Not enough ones to take off 7.
Trade a ten for 10 ones.

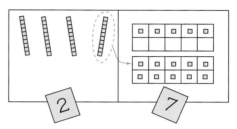

Now there are 15 ones.
I can take 7 off easily.

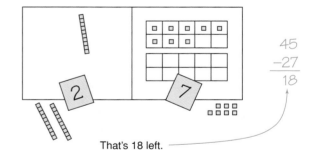

It does not matter which ones come off. Put the leftovers together.

And now I can take off 2 tens.

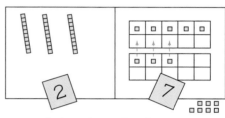

45
−27
18

That's 18 left.

FIGURE 10.11 **Two-place subtraction with models.**

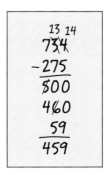

$$
\begin{array}{r}
^{13\ 14} \\
7\cancel{3}\cancel{4} \\
-275 \\
\hline
\cancel{5}00 \\
4\cancel{6}0 \\
59 \\
\hline
459
\end{array}
$$

FIGURE 10.12 **A left-hand recording scheme for subtraction. Other methods can also be devised.**

but by no means always, the strategies that students invent are very similar to the traditional algorithm. The big difference is that students think about numbers, not digits. They always begin with the large or left-hand numbers.

For multiplication, the ability to break numbers apart in flexible ways is even more important than in addition or subtraction. The distributive property is an important concept for computation with multiplication. For example, to multiply 43 × 5, one might think about breaking 43 into 40 and 3, multiplying each by 5, and then adding the results. Children should have ample opportunities to develop these concepts as they attempt to make sense of their own ideas and those of their classmates.

Useful Representations

The problem 34 × 6 may be represented in a number of ways, as illustrated in Figure 10.13. Often the choice of a model is influenced by a story problem. To determine how many Easter eggs 34 children will need if each colours 6 eggs, children may model 6 sets of 34 (or possibly 34 sets

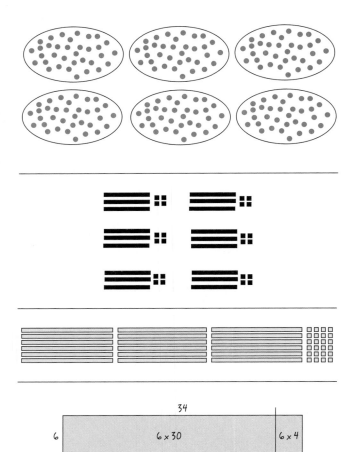

FIGURE 10.13 Different ways to model 34 × 6 may support different computational strategies.

of 6). If the problem is about the area of a rectangle that is 34 cm by 6 cm, then some form of an array is likely. But each representation is appropriate for thinking about 34 × 6 regardless of the context, and students should get to a point where they select ways to think about multiplication that are meaningful to them.

Children should represent a product in a way that fits with their method for determining the answer. The groups of 34 might suggest repeated addition—perhaps taking the sets two at a time. Double 34 is 68 and there are three of them, so 68 + 68 + 68. From there a variety of methods are possible.

The 6 sets of base-ten pieces might suggest breaking the numbers into tens and ones: 6 times 3 tens or 6 × 30 and 6 × 4. Some children might use the tens individually: 6 tens make 60. So that's 60 and 60 and 60 (180). Then add on the 24 to make 204.

It is not uncommon for children to arrange the base-ten pieces in a nice array, even if the story problem does not suggest it. The area model is very much like an arrangement of the base-ten pieces.

All of these ideas should be part of students' repertoire of models for multi-digit multiplication. Introduce (one at a time) different representations as ways to explore multiplication until you are confident that the class has a collection of useful ideas. At the same time, do not force students who reason very well without drawings or manipulatives to use models when they are not needed.

Multiplication by a Single-Digit Multiplier

As with addition and subtraction, it is helpful to place multiplication tasks in the context of story problems. Let students model the problems in ways that make sense to them. Do not be concerned about mixing of factors (6 sets of 34 or 34 sets of 6). Nor should you be timid about the numbers you use. The problem 3 × 24 may be easier than 7 × 65, but the latter provides a greater challenge. The types of strategies that students use for multiplication are much more varied than for addition and subtraction. The following are three categories that current research has identified.

Complete-Number Strategies

Children who are not yet comfortable using tens and ones to break numbers into parts will approach the numbers in the sets as single groups. Figure 10.14 illustrates two methods that students who think this way may use. These children will benefit from listening to others who use base-ten models. They may also need more work with base-ten grouping activities where they take numbers apart in different ways.

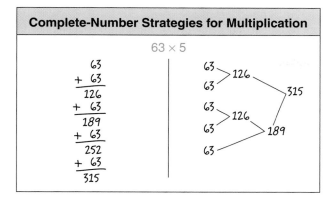

Complete-Number Strategies for Multiplication

63×5

FIGURE 10.14 **Children who use a complete-number strategy do not break numbers apart into decades or tens and ones.**

Partitioning Strategies

Children break numbers up in a variety of ways that reflect their understanding of base-ten concepts. At least four are illustrated in Figure 10.15. The "Partitioning By Decades" approach is the same as the standard algorithm except that students always begin with the large values. It extends easily to three digits and is very powerful as a mental math strategy. Another valuable strategy for mental methods is found in the "Other Partitions" example. It is easy to compute mentally with multiples of 25 and 50 and then add or subtract to make a small adjustment. It should be noted that all partitioning strategies rely on the distributive property.

Compensation Strategies

Children look for ways to manipulate numbers so that the calculations are easy. In Figure 10.16, the problem 27×4 is changed to an easier one, and then an adjustment or compensation is made. In the second example, one factor is cut in half and the other doubled. This is often used when a 5 or a 50 is involved. Because these strategies depend so much on the numbers involved, they can't be used for all computations. However, they are powerful strategies, especially for mental math and estimation.

Using Multiples of 10 and 100

There is value in exposing students early to products involving multiples of 10 and 100.

The Eagle boy scouts troop wanted to make up 400 first-aid kits for a fund-raising project. If each kit has 12 gauze bandages, how many gauze bandages will the scouts need?

Children will use $4 \times 12 = 48$ to figure out that 400×12 is 4800. There will be discussion about how to say and write "forty-eight hundred." Be aware of students who simply tack on zeros without understanding why. Try problems such as 30×60 or 210×40 where tens are multiplied by tens.

Some teachers suggest using "cluster problems," which consist of a list of simpler but related products that can be used to solve the larger task. For 210×40, a cluster of simple products might be

4×2 4×21 4×10 4×20 40×20
40×200 40×21

Students discuss which problems in the cluster could be used to help solve the larger problem. Initially the teacher suggests the cluster problems, but later on students can create their own (Schifter et al., 1999b).

FIGURE 10.15 **Numbers can be broken apart in different ways to make easier partial products, which are then combined. Partitioning by decades is useful for mental computation and is very close to the standard algorithm.**

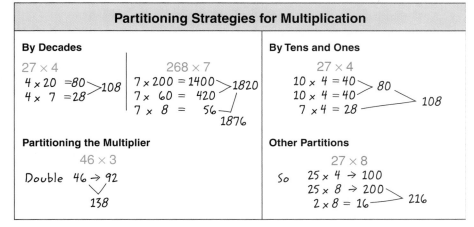

Partitioning Strategies for Multiplication

By Decades

27×4

268×7

By Tens and Ones

27×4

Partitioning the Multiplier

46×3

Other Partitions

27×8

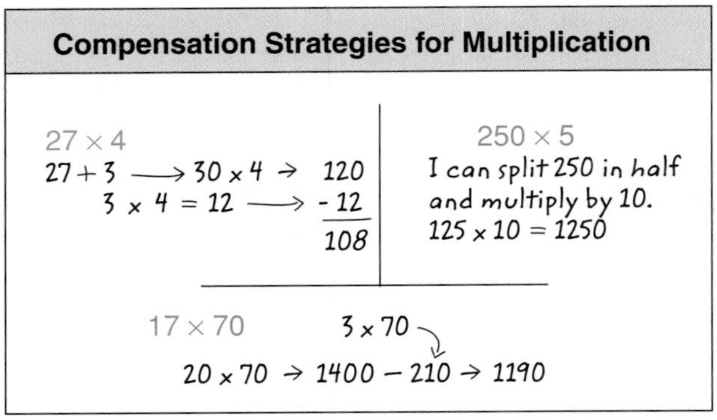

Compensation Strategies for Multiplication

27 × 4
27 + 3 ⟶ 30 × 4 → 120
3 × 4 = 12 ⟶ − 12
‾‾‾‾‾
108

250 × 5
I can split 250 in half
and multiply by 10.
125 × 10 = 1250

17 × 70   3 × 70
20 × 70 → 1400 − 210 → 1190

FIGURE 10.16 Compensation methods use a product related to the original. A compensation is made in the answer, or one factor is changed to compensate for a change in the other factors.

Two-Digit Multipliers: The Area Model

A problem such as this one can be solved in many different ways:

There were 23 clowns in the parade. Each clown carried 18 balloons. How many balloons were there altogether?

Some children look for smaller products such as 6 × 23 and then add that result three times. Another method is to do 20 × 23 and then subtract 2 × 23. Others will calculate four separate partial products: 10 × 20 = 200, 8 × 20 = 160, 10 × 3 = 30, and 8 × 3 = 24. And still others may add up a string of 23s. Two-digit multiplication is both complex and challenging. But children can solve these problems in a variety of interesting ways, many of which will contribute to the development of the traditional algorithm or one that is just as efficient. Time devoted to working on these tasks in grades 4 through 6 is well spent.

A valuable exploration is to prepare large rectangles for each group of two or three students. The rectangles, with dimensions between 25 cm and 60 cm, drawn accurately with square corners (use the corner of a piece of poster board for a guide), should be measured carefully. The students' task is to determine how many of the ones pieces (base-ten materials) will fit inside. Wooden or plastic base-ten pieces are best, but cardboard strips and squares will also work. Alternatively, rectangles can be drawn on base-ten grid paper (see Blackline Masters), or students can be given the task verbally: *What is the area of a rectangle that is 47 cm by 36 cm?*

Most children will fill the rectangle first with as many hundreds pieces as possible. One obvious approach is to

put the 12 hundreds in one corner. This will leave narrow regions on two sides that can be filled with tens pieces and a final small rectangle that will hold ones. Especially if students have had earlier experiences with finding products in arrays, figuring out the size of each sub-rectangle is not terribly difficult. The sketch in Figure 10.17 shows the four regions. If you did not already know the algorithm, how would you determine the size of the rectangle? Use your method on a rectangle that measures 68 cm by 24 cm. Make a sketch to explain your work.

As you will see in the discussion of the traditional algorithm, the area model leads to a fairly reasonable approach to multiplying numbers, even if your students never "carry" digits.

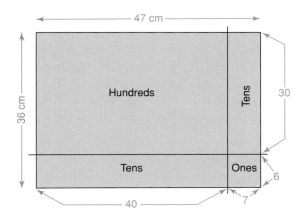

FIGURE 10.17 Ones, tens, and hundreds pieces fit exactly into the four sections of this 47 × 36 rectangle. Figure out the size of each section to determine the size of the whole rectangle.

The Traditional Algorithm for Multiplication

The traditional multiplication algorithm is probably the most difficult of the four algorithms if students have not had plenty of opportunities to explore their own strategies. Without understanding, children put numbers in wrong columns, add in "carried" digits before they multiply, and make a host of other errors. When children are recording methods that make sense to them, these errors are much less likely to occur.

The multiplication algorithm can be meaningfully developed using either a repeated addition model or an area model. For single-digit multipliers, the difference is minimal. When you move to two-digit multipliers, the area model has some advantages. For that reason, the discussion here will use the area model.

One-Digit Multipliers

As with other algorithms, as much time as possible should be devoted to the conceptual development of the algorithm, with the recording or written part coming later.

Begin with Models

Give students a drawing of a rectangle, which is 47 cm by 6 cm. *How many small square centimetre pieces will fit in the rectangle?* (What is the area of the rectangle in square centimetres?) Let students solve the problem in groups before discussing it as a class.

As shown in Figure 10.18, the rectangle can be "sliced" or separated into two parts so that one part will be 6 ones by 7 ones, or 42 ones, and the other will be 6 ones by 4 tens, or 24 tens. Notice that the base-ten language "6 ones times 4 tens is 24 tens" tells how many *pieces* (sticks of 10) are in the big section. To say "6 times 40 is 240" is also correct and tells how many units or square centimetres are in the section. Each section is referred to as a *partial product.* By adding the two partial products, you get the total product or area of the rectangle.

To avoid the tedium of drawing large rectangles and arranging base-ten pieces, use the base-ten grid paper found in the Blackline Masters. On the grid paper, students can easily draw accurate rectangles showing all of the pieces. Check to be sure students understand that for a product such as 74 × 8, there are two partial products,

70 × 8 = 560 and 4 × 8 = 32, and the sum of these is the product. Do not force any recording technique on students until they understand how to use the two dimensions of a rectangle to get a product.

Develop the Written Record

To help with a recording scheme, provide sheets with base-ten columns on which students can record problems. When the two partial products are written separately as in Figure 10.19(a), there is little new to learn. Students simply record the products and add them together. As illustrated, it is possible to teach students how to write the first product with a "carried" digit so that the combined product is written on one line. This traditional recording scheme is known to be problematic. The little "carried" digit is often the source of difficulty—it gets added in before the second multiplication is carried out, or it is simply forgotten.

There is absolutely no practical reason why students can't be allowed to record both partial products and avoid the errors related to the "carried" digit. When you accept that, it makes no difference in which order the products are written. Why not simply permit students to do written multiplication as shown in Figure 10.19(b)? When the factors are in a word problem, chart, or other format, all that is really necessary is to write down all the partial products and add. Furthermore, that is precisely how it is done mentally. It is time to make this change!

FIGURE 10.18 A rectangle filled with base-ten pieces is a useful model for two-digit-by-one-digit multiplication.

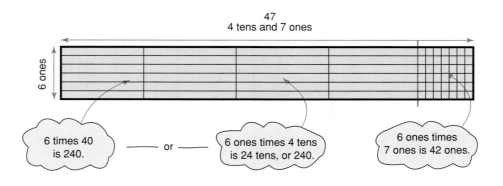

FIGURE 10.19 (a) In the standard form, the product of ones is recorded first. The tens digit of this first product can be written as a "carried" digit above the tens column. (b) It is quite reasonable to abandon the carried digit and permit the partial products to be recorded in any order.

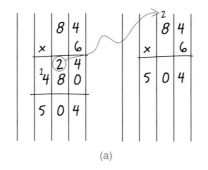

(a)   (b)

Most standard curricula progress from two digits to three digits with a single-digit multiplier. Students can make this progression easily. They still should be permitted to write all three partial products separately, without having to "carry."

Two-Digit Multipliers

With the area model, the progression to a two-digit multiplier is relatively straightforward. Rectangles can be drawn on base-ten grid paper, or full-sized rectangles can be filled in with base-ten pieces. There will be four partial products, corresponding to four different sections of the rectangle.

Several variations in language might be used. Consider the product 47 × 36 as illustrated in Figure 10.20. In the partial product 40 × 30, if base-ten language

is used—*4 tens times 3 tens is 12 hundreds*—the result tells how many hundreds pieces are in that section. In standard form, the product "forty times thirty" is formidable. Try to avoid "four times three," which promotes thinking about digits rather than numbers. It is well worth stressing the idea that in all cases, a product of *tens times tens is in the hundreds.*

Figure 10.20 also shows the recording of four partial products in the traditional order and how these can be collapsed into two lines if "carried" digits are used. Here, the second "carry" technically belongs in the hundreds column but is rarely written there. Often it gets confused with the first and is thus an additional source of error. The lower left of the figure shows the same computation with all four products written in a different order. This is an acceptable algorithm. In the rare instance when someone

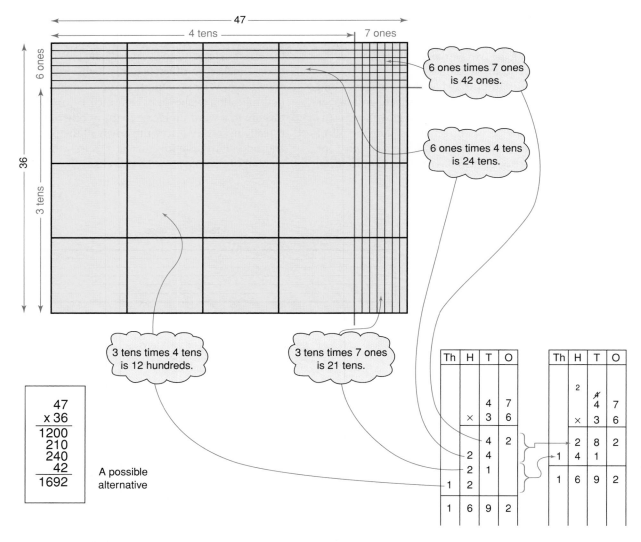

FIGURE 10.20 A 47 × 36 rectangle filled with base-ten pieces. Base-ten language connects the four partial products to the traditional written format. Note the possibility of recording the products in some other order.

multiplies numbers such as 538 × 29 with pencil and paper, there would be six partial products. But far fewer errors would occur, requiring less instructional time and much less remediation.

Invented Strategies for Division

Even though many adults think division is the most onerous of the computational operations, it can be considerably easier than multiplication. Conceptual methods are easily developed through the use of simple story problems. It is appropriate to begin thinking about computation with division in grade 4.

Recall that there are two concepts of division. First there is the partition or fair-sharing idea, illustrated by this story problem:

There are 783 jelly beans in the bag. Mohani and her four friends want to share them equally. How many jelly beans will Mohani and each of her friends get?

Then there is the measurement or repeated subtraction concept:

Jumbo the elephant loves peanuts. His trainer has 625 peanuts. If he gives Jumbo 20 peanuts each day, how many days will the peanuts last?

Students should be challenged to solve both types of problems. However, the fair-share problems are often easier to solve with base-ten pieces. Furthermore, the traditional algorithm is built on this idea. Eventually, students will develop strategies that they will apply to both types of problem, even when the process does not match the action of the story.

Figure 10.21 shows some strategies that grade 4 children have used to solve division problems. The first example illustrates 92 ÷ 4 using the base-ten pieces with a sharing process. A ten is traded for 10 ones when there are no longer enough tens to be shared equally. Then the 12 ones are distributed, resulting in 23 in each set. This direct modelling approach with base-ten pieces is quite easy to understand and use.

In the second example, the student sets out the base-ten pieces and draws a "bar graph" with 6 columns. After noting that there are not enough hundreds for each child, he splits the 3 hundreds in half, putting 50 in each column. That leaves 1 hundred, 5 tens, and 3 ones. After trading the hundred for 10 tens (now 15 tens), the student gives 20 to each, recording 2 tens in each bar. Now he is left with 3 tens and 3 ones, or 33. He knows that 5 × 6 is 30, so he gives each child 5, leaving him with 3. He splits these in half and writes $\frac{1}{2}$ in each column.

The child in the third example is solving a sharing problem but tries to do it as a measurement process. She

wants to find out how many 8s are in 143. Initially she guesses. By multiplying 8 first by 10, then by 20, and then by 14, she knows the answer is more than 14 and less than 20. After some more work (not shown), she rethinks the problem as "how many 8s in 100?" and "how many in 40?"

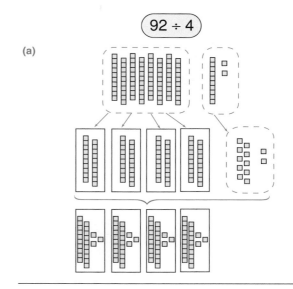

(a)

$92 \div 4$

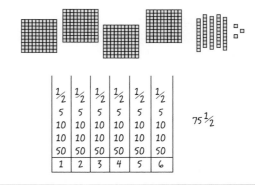

(b)   **453 ÷ 6**
(share with 6 kids)

$\frac{1}{2}$	$\frac{1}{2}$	$\frac{1}{2}$	$\frac{1}{2}$	$\frac{1}{2}$	$\frac{1}{2}$
5	5	5	5	5	5
10	10	10	10	10	10
10	10	10	10	10	10
50	50	50	50	50	50
1	2	3	4	5	6

$75\frac{1}{2}$

(c)   **143 jelly beans shared with 8 kids**

Try 14 × 8 → 112
12 groups of 8 is 96.
12 groups in 100 leaves 4.
 5 groups of 8 in 40.
And 3 more left over.
12 + 5 is 17 with 7 left.

FIGURE 10.21 Students use both models and symbols to solve division tasks.

Source: Adapted from *Developing Mathematical Ideas: Numbers and Operations, Part I: Building a System of Tens Casebook*, by D. Schifter, V. Bastable, & S. J. Russell. Copyright ©1999 by the Educational Development Center, Inc. Published by Dale Seymour Publications, an imprint of Pearson Learning. Used by permission.

The Traditional Algorithm for Division

Long division is the one traditional algorithm that starts with the left-hand or big pieces. The conceptual basis for the algorithm most often taught in textbooks is the partition or fair-share method.

One-Digit Divisors

Typically, the division algorithm with one-digit divisors is introduced in grade 4. If done well, it should not have to be re-taught, and it should provide the basis for two-digit divisors. Students in the upper grades who are having difficulty with the algorithm would also benefit from a conceptual development of division.

Begin with Models

Traditionally, if we were to do a problem such as $4\overline{)583}$, we might say "4 goes into 5 one time." This is quite mysterious to children. How can you just ignore the "83" and keep changing the problem? Preferably, you want students to think of the 583 as 5 hundreds, 8 tens, and 3 ones, not as three disconnected digits 5, 8 and 3. One idea is to use a context such as candy bundled in boxes of ten with 10 boxes to a carton. Then the problem becomes *We have 5 boxes, 8 cartons, and 3 pieces of candy to share evenly amongst 4 schools.* In this context, it is reasonable to share the cartons first until no more can be shared. The remaining boxes are then "unpacked" and shared, and so on. Money ($100, $10, and $1) can be used in a similar manner. Figure 10.22 shows the process in detail. Make up a three-digit problem, and try this yourself using base-ten pieces.

The task is to share these 5 hundreds, 8 tens, and 3 ones among these four sets so that each set gets the same amount.

I'll begin with the hundreds pieces. There are enough so that each set can get 1 hundred. That leaves 1 hundred left that cannot be shared.

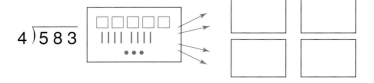

I can trade the hundred for 10 tens. That gives me a total of 18 tens. With 18 I can put 4 tens in each of the four sets and have 2 tens left. Two is not enough to go around to all four sets.

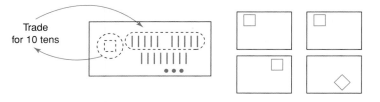

I can trade the 2 tens for 10 ones each or a total of 20 ones. With the 3 ones I already had, that gives me 23 ones. I can put 5 ones in each of the four sets. That leaves me with only 3 ones left over as a remainder.

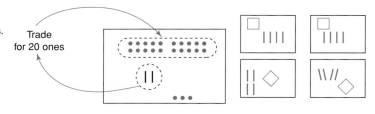

Each set got 145. I record that on the top of the problem in the right place-value columns. The answer tells how much went to each set.

If I added up how much they got altogether, that would be 4 × 145 or 580. The remainder of 3 makes the 583 I started with.

FIGURE 10.22 Sharing pieces within each place and trading leftovers for the next place to the right is the entire conceptual basis for the long-division algorithm.

Develop the Written Record

The recording scheme for the long-division algorithm is not completely intuitive. You will need to be quite directive in helping children learn to record fair sharing with models. There are essentially four steps:

1. *Share* and record the number of pieces put in each group.
2. *Record* the number of pieces shared in all. Multiply to find this number.
3. *Record* the number of pieces remaining. Subtract to find this number.
4. *Trade* (if necessary) for smaller pieces, and combine with any that are there already. Record the new total number in the next column.

When students model problems with a one-digit divisor, steps 2 and 3 seem unnecessary. Explain that these steps really help when you don't have the pieces there to count.

Record Explicit Trades

Figure 10.23 (p. 202) details each step of the recording process just described. On the left, you see the traditional algorithm. To the right is a suggestion that matches the actual action with the models that explicitly record the trades. Instead of the somewhat mysterious "bring-down" procedure, the traded pieces are crossed out, as is the number of existing pieces in the next column. The combined number of pieces is written in this column using a two-digit number. In the example, 2 hundreds are traded for 20 tens, and combined with the 6 that were already there, making a total of 26 tens. Therefore the 26 is written in the tens column.

Students who are required to make sense of the long-division procedure find the explicit-trade method easier to follow. Blank division charts with wide place-value columns are highly recommended. These can be found in the Blackline Masters. Without the charts, it is important to spread out the digits in the dividend when writing down the problem. (The explicit-trade method is John's invention and is not found in textbooks. It has been used successfully in grades 3 to 8.)

Both the explicit-trade method and the use of place-value columns will help with the problem of leaving out a middle zero in a problem (see Figure 10.24, p. 203).

Two-Digit Divisors

There is almost no point in having children master division with two-digit divisors. On only a few occasions in any adult's life will an exact result for such a computation be required without a calculator being available. In some grade 5 and 6 classrooms, large chunks of time are still being spent on this outdated skill. The costs in time and the negative effect on students' attitudes toward mathematics are enormous. If you can possibly encourage the removal of this outdated skill from your school's curriculum, we encourage you to do so.

With a two-digit divisor, it is hard to come up with the right amount to share at each step along the way. A guess that is too high or too low will necessitate erasing and starting all over.

An Intuitive Idea

Suppose that you were sharing a large pile of candies with 36 friends. Instead of passing them out one at a time, you conservatively estimate that each person could get at least 6 pieces. So you give 6 to each of your friends. Now you find there are more than 36 pieces left. Do you have everyone give back the 6 pieces so you can then give them 7 or 8? That would be silly! You simply pass out more.

The candy example gives us two good ideas for sharing in long division. First, always underestimate how much can be shared. Second, if there is enough left to share some more, just do it! To avoid overestimating, always pretend there are more sets or "friends" among which to share than there really are. For example, if you are dividing 312 by 43 (sharing among 43 sets or "friends"), pretend you have 50 sets instead. Round *up* to the next multiple of 10. You can easily determine that 6 pieces can be shared among 50 sets because 6 × 50 is an easy product. Since there are really only 43 sets, clearly you can give *at least* 6 to each. Always consider a larger divisor. If you underestimate and you have more to share, simply pass out some more.

Using the Idea Symbolically

These ideas are used in Figure 10.25 (p. 203). Both the traditional method and the explicit-trade method of recording are illustrated. The rounded-up divisor, 70, is written in a little "think bubble" above the real divisor. Rounding up has another advantage: it is easy to run through the multiples of 70 and compare them to 374. Think about sharing base-ten pieces (thousands, hundreds, tens, and ones). Work through the problem one step at a time, saying exactly what each recorded step stands for.

This approach has proven successful with children in grade 4 learning division for the first time, and with children in grades 6 to 8 who are in need of remediation. It reduces the mental strain of making choices and essentially eliminates the need to erase. If an estimate is too low, that's okay. And if you always round up, the estimate will never be too high. Nor is there ever any reason to change to the more familiar approach. It is just as good for adults as for children. The same is true of the explicit-trade notation. It is certainly an idea to consider.

FIGURE 10.23 The traditional and explicit trade methods are connected to each step of the division process. Every step can and should make sense.

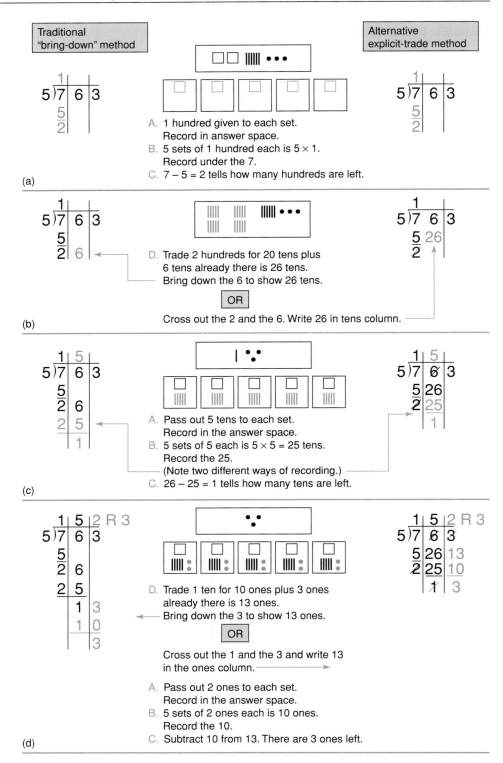

(a)

A. 1 hundred given to each set. Record in answer space.
B. 5 sets of 1 hundred each is 5 × 1. Record under the 7.
C. 7 − 5 = 2 tells how many hundreds are left.

(b)

D. Trade 2 hundreds for 20 tens plus 6 tens already there is 26 tens. Bring down the 6 to show 26 tens.

OR

Cross out the 2 and the 6. Write 26 in tens column.

(c)

A. Pass out 5 tens to each set. Record in the answer space.
B. 5 sets of 5 each is 5 × 5 = 25 tens. Record the 25. (Note two different ways of recording.)
C. 26 − 25 = 1 tells how many tens are left.

(d)

D. Trade 1 ten for 10 ones plus 3 ones already there is 13 ones. Bring down the 3 to show 13 ones.

OR

Cross out the 1 and the 3 and write 13 in the ones column.

A. Pass out 2 ones to each set. Record in the answer space.
B. 5 sets of 2 ones each is 10 ones. Record the 10.
C. Subtract 10 from 13. There are 3 ones left.

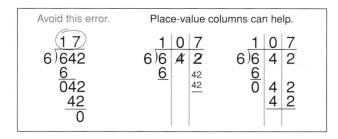

FIGURE 10.24 Using lines to mark place-value columns can help a student remember to record zeros.

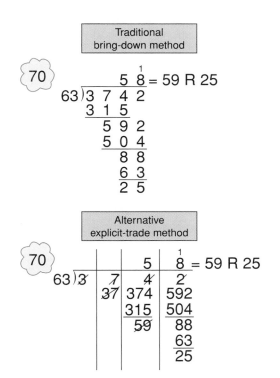

FIGURE 10.25 To help your thinking, round the divisor up to 70, but multiply what you share by 63. In the ones column, share 8 with each set. Oops! 88 left over. Just give 1 more to each set.

 Technology Note

Most software programs that provide drill of any sort will also provide drill in multi-digit computation. They mostly provide problems at different levels and evaluate answers. These programs have limited advantages for the teacher. In *Gold Medal Mathematics* (EdVenture Software, 1997), for example, students are first "warmed up" with fact practice. Then, in a practice setting, students continue to solve problems until they complete 10 in a row correctly. The challenge round encourages speed. Somewhat unusual is the fact that all answers are in multiple-choice format. This permits students to use any strategy, encourages mental computation, and may be good practice for standardized tests. The program includes two-digit addition and subtraction as well as multiplication and division.

Some programs provide base-ten blocks on the screen that students can manipulate to help solve problems. Before purchasing these programs, see how much freedom is allowed, and ask what the computer program does that could not be accomplished at least as well with physical materials. *MathKeys* (MECC, 1995a, 1996b), for example, includes very attractive screen graphics that permit the modelling of numbers into the thousands. However, the computer forces trading and always updates totals. This may provide the user with an explanation of what has been done, but there is no problem-solving spirit to this program.

 Literature Connections

Children's literature can play a very useful role in helping you develop problems for your invented strategies and mental computation lessons. Simple story problems every day may be great, but children deserve a change. Turn to children's books. There are a great many fascinating books that involve large numbers and opportunities to compute. Some are about real data, and others are fictional.

Cookies
(Jaspersohn, 1993)

This is the true story of Wally Amos and his Famous Amos Chocolate Chip Cookies. (Are you interested already?) The text includes a large number of colour and black-and-white photos that show the production and distribution of Famous Amos cookies. Because it is filled with facts about the cookies—numbers sold, number the average person eats in a year, and so on—you can easily pose questions that require computation and that children will find interesting. Although actual computations can be done on a calculator, this context clearly suggests that estimates and rounded numbers make more sense. As you discuss ideas generated by the book, some computations can be done mentally to determine exact answers. Other computations will be estimates. Students can extend the story to a project to research cookie consumption in their own homes, or gather data from grocery stores about other cookies, or the number of trucks required, or kilometres travelled to get cookies to market. The possibilities are endless. During these projects, suggest that students take note of the times when an estimate makes more sense than an exact computation. As they are working on their projects, find out if there are situations where they made a quick mental estimate or did a mental computation.

Is a Blue Whale the Biggest Thing There Is?
(Wells, 1993)

This is one of the most intriguing books you will find about large things and large distances. Blue whales look small next to Mount Everest, which in turn looks small next to the earth. The data in the book allow children to make other comparisons, such as the number of grade 4 students that would have the same mass or volume as a blue whale or would fill the gymnasium. As with the Famous Amos data, these comparisons are the perfect opportunity for estimations and discussions about how much accuracy is necessary to make a meaningful comparison. Bresser (1995) provides excellent insights into the use of this story with grade 4, 5, and 6 students.

 Assessment Notes

Parents are perhaps more interested in their children's computational skills than in any other area. It is quite easy to give a test of computation like those provided in traditional textbooks. When students do well on these tests, parents are pleased. But what do you know about students when they do not do well? At best, you can make inferences based on their results. You can look for basic-fact errors and carelessness, or perhaps find a systematic error in an algorithm. What you do not know is how children are solving these problems and what ideas and strategies they have developed that are useful or need further development.

Ongoing Assessment

When computational strategies and algorithms are developed in the manner suggested in this chapter, every day you are presented with a wealth of assessment data about the individual children in your class. The important thing is to gather, record, and use these data the same as you would with tests and quizzes. A simple chart something like the one in Figure 10.26 may be all you need. Note that the third column includes a mini-rubric or a three-point scale. Students' names can be arranged in groups, or by how they sit in the room, or alphabetically, or … any way that makes them easy to find.

As you walk around the class in the development portion of your lessons, and also in the follow-up part when children explain their computational strategies and reasoning, you can make notes on the chart. Make a new chart each week, but keep the old ones to provide evidence of growth over time. These charts can be useful for evaluation and for parent conferences. There is no harm in giving an occasional quiz or test of computational skills. But avoid giving more value to tests simply because they are objective. Compare the results with the information you have gathered through observation. Did you get any new information? Were the results consistent? If not, why weren't they?

Occasional Interviews

It is not always easy to tell what concepts or thought processes individual students are using. For example, some students may get overly attached to a particular approach and may not be flexible enough to switch to a more efficient method when the numbers call for it. Some children do not provide as much information in class as you need because they are shy or not very verbal. You may need to find out more about underlying conceptual understanding of base-ten concepts. For these and many other reasons, it is often useful to stop and listen more carefully to a single child. A little interview may take five to 10 minutes. Perhaps you can do it while others are working on a

FIGURE 10.26 A checklist with space for comments or notes lets you record daily observations of students' direct modelling and invented strategies.

Topic: Mental addition and subtraction Student	Adds 2-digit + 1-digit numbers	Adds 2-digit + 2-digit numbers; note methods	Flexibility in choosing a method: 1, 2, 3	Comments
Lalie				
Pete				
Amara				
Lakeshia				

problem you have posed, or maybe you will find a time outside of the lesson.

The interview format is similar to the lessons that have been described. Pose a word problem or computation, and ask the student to "think out loud" while she works. Explain that you want to find out how she is thinking. Avoid any teaching at this time. Do not make evaluative comments. Show your interest in the student's thinking. Ask questions to clarify thinking that may not be clear.

If a child is making errors with symbolic techniques, ask if she can show you how to do the same task with counters or base-ten models. Similarly, a student who seems to rely heavily on physical models can be challenged in an interview to try a problem without models.

Some children will give you a much clearer picture of their abilities and understanding in an interview than when they feel inhibited by the pressure of trying to talk in a full-class setting. ▪▪

Reflections on Chapter 10

Writing to Learn

1. What is the difference between solving a problem with direct modelling and solving a problem with an invented strategy? What is a traditional algorithm?

2. How are traditional algorithms different from invented strategies? Explain the benefits of invented strategies over traditional algorithms.

3. When a problem has been solved, how do you manage all of the different methods that students may propose, and what should you do about students who propose no ideas of their own?

4. What do you do when someone brings a traditional algorithm into the classroom before you have introduced it? What if you never plan to teach the traditional algorithm but students want to use it anyway?

5. Explain how strategies for problems such as 58 + 6 or 72 − 5 are similar to the make-ten strategies for basic facts. How can you help children extend their basic fact strategies to these larger numbers?

6. Illustrate three different strategies for adding 46 + 39. Which ones are easy to do mentally? Is there a strategy that is easier because 39 is close to 40? What strategies work well for sums such as 538 + 243? For each strategy with which you work, think about how you could record it on the board so that other students will be able to follow what is being done.

7. Use two different adding-up strategies for 93 − 27 and for 545 − 267. Make up a story problem that would encourage an adding-up strategy.

8. Describe how you would go about developing the traditional algorithms for addition and subtraction. How would you deal with the issue of beginning on the right with the ones place when students' natural tendency is to begin on the left? Use 385 + 128 to illustrate a reasonable written algorithm that begins on the left instead of the right. Do the same for 453 − 278.

9. Draw pictures showing how 57 × 4 could be modelled in the following ways: with counters, with base-ten pieces, with rectangles or arrays on base-ten grids.

10. How might you help a student who is using a complete-number strategy for multiplication?

11. Try to develop some skill using an invented strategy for multiplying by single-digit numbers. Can you do 327 × 6 mentally? How would you record the steps on the chalkboard if a student gave them to you the way you did it?

12. Use a compensation strategy for these: 68 × 20, 5 × 46, 25 × 480.

13. Draw a rectangle for 28 × 57, and explain how it could be used to compute the product.

14. Which division concept, measurement or partition, is easier for direct modelling and is also the one used to develop the usual long-division algorithm? Make up an appropriate word story using that concept for 735 ÷ 6.

15. Use the traditional algorithm for 735 ÷ 6, and then repeat the process using our suggested method of recording trades explicitly. With the two algorithms side by side, explain every recorded number in terms of what it stands for when sharing base-ten pieces.

16. To avoid erasures in long division, a rounded-up divisor can be used to make estimates of the quotient in each place value. Show how this method works and avoids erasures using the problem 4589 ÷ 62.

For Discussion and Exploration

1. Select any grade between 2 and 6, and discuss what you feel is an appropriate skill level for whole-number computation at that grade. Should these skills be taught at that grade or earlier? How do your views compare with the treatment given whole-number computation in a traditional textbook for that grade level? How does the textbook treatment compare with the general position offered in this chapter?

2. Examine your regional curriculum document. How is whole-number computation developed? How does it compare with the ideas regarding invented strategies offered in this chapter?

Recommendations for Further Reading
Highly Recommended

Campbell, P.F., & Johnson, M.L. (1995). How primary students think and learn. In I.M. Carl (Ed.), *Prospects for school mathematics* (pp. 21–42). Reston, VA: National Council of Teachers of Mathematics.

Campbell and Johnson describe a project in an urban school system that is completely based in a constructivist paradigm. Their purpose is to describe how children are able to construct their own ideas. Interestingly, most of the examples provided involve computation and student-invented methods. Absolutely worth reading.

Fosnot, C.T. & Dolk, M. (2001). *Young mathematicians at work: Constructing multiplication and division.* Portsmouth, NH: Heinemann.

Fosnot, C.T. & Dolk, M. (2001). *Young mathematicians at work: Constructing number sense, addition, and subtraction.* Portsmouth, NH: Heinemann.

These are two in a series of three books that are the product of Fosnot (a U.S. mathematics educator and expert in constructivism) and Dolk (a mathematics educator at the Freudenthal Institute in the Netherlands). The books are products of a collaborative effort (begun in 1988) that focused on working with teachers, examining how children learn, and looking for ways to support that learning. They show children constructing ideas about number, operations, and computation in ways not found elsewhere. The authors talk about the "landscape of learning" and ideas "on the horizon"—the places where children are working and the ideas toward which they are working. Refreshing, thoughtful, and informative. (Their third book is on fractions and decimals.)

Morrow, L. (Ed.). (1998). *The teaching and learning of algorithms in school mathematics.* Reston, VA: National Council of Teachers of Mathematics.

Mastery of algorithms is and always has been a topic that anti-reformers choose to attack, usually because they believe that reform means an end to teaching computation. This NCTM yearbook offers well-articulated perspectives on the issue. More importantly, it contains numerous articles with practical teaching suggestions at the elementary, middle, and secondary levels.

Schifter, D., Bastable, V., & Russell, S.J. (1999). *Developing mathematical ideas: Numbers and operations, Part 1: Building a system of tens* (Casebook). White Plains, NY: Cuisenaire–Dale Seymour.

The cases in this book clearly demonstrate the interaction between children's place-value understanding and their invented strategies for computation. It is from this book and its companion in-service guide that much of the information in this chapter regarding invented strategies was derived. For any teacher seriously interested in the development of student-invented methods of computation, this book provides practical insights.

Other Suggestions

Baek, J. (1998). Children's invented algorithms for multi-digit multiplication problems. In L.J. Morrow (Ed.), *The teaching and learning of algorithms in school mathematics* (pp. 151–160). Reston, VA: National Council of Teachers of Mathematics.

Bresser, R., & Holtzman, C. (1999). *Developing number sense: Grades 3–6.* Sausalito, CA: Math Solutions Publications.

Burns, M. (1992). *About teaching mathematics: A K–8 Resource.* Sausalito, CA: Math Solutions Publications.

Campbell, P.F., Rowan, T.E., & Suarez, A.R. (1998). What criteria for student-invented algorithms? In L.J. Morrow (Ed.), *The teaching and learning of algorithms in school mathematics* (pp. 49–55). Reston, VA: National Council of Teachers of Mathematics.

Carpenter, T.P., Franke, M.L., Jacobs, V.R., Fennema, E., & Empson, S.B. (1998). A longitudinal study of invention and understanding in children's multidigit addition and subtraction. *Journal for Research in Mathematics Education, 29,* 3–20.

Carroll, W.M. (1996). Use of invented algorithms by second graders in a reform mathematics curriculum. *Journal of Mathematical Behavior, 15,* 137–150.

Carroll, W.M., & Porter, D. (1997). Invented strategies can develop meaningful mathematical procedures. *Teaching Children Mathematics, 3,* 370–374.

Chambers, D. (1996). Direct modeling and invented procedures: Building on students' informal strategies. *Teaching Children Mathematics, 3,* 92–95.

Hiebert, J.C., & Wearne, D. (1996). Instruction, understanding, and skill in multidigit addition and subtraction. *Cognition and Instruction, 14,* 251–283.

Irvine, R., & Walker, K. (1996). *Smart arithmetic: A thinking approach to computation, grades 1–3.* Mountain View, CA: Creative Publications.

Irvine, R., & Walker, K. (1996). *Smart arithmetic: A thinking approach to computation, grades 4–6.* Mountain View, CA: Creative Publications.

Kamii, C.K. (1989). *Double-column addition: A teacher uses Piaget's theory* [Videotape]. New York: Teachers College Press.

Kamii, C.K. (1994). *Young children continue to reinvent arithmetic: 3rd grade.* New York: Teachers College Press.

Kamii, C.K., & Dominick, A. (1997). To teach or not to teach algorithms. *Journal of Mathematical Behavior, 16,* 51–61.

Kamii, C.K., & Lewis, B.A. (1993). The harmful effects of algorithms in primary arithmetic. *Teaching K–8, 23*(5), 36–38.

Reys, B.J., & Reys, R.E. (1999). Computation in the elementary curriculum: Shifting the emphasis. *Teaching Children Mathematics, 5,* 236–241.

Reys, R.E., & Nohda, N. (Eds). (1994). *Computational alternatives for the twenty-first century: Cross-cultural perspectives from Japan and the United States.* Reston, VA: National Council of Teachers of Mathematics.

Reys, R.E., Reys, B.J., Nohda, N., & Emori, H. (1995). Mental computation performance and strategy use of Japanese students in grades 2, 4, 6, and 8. *Journal for Research in Mathematics Education, 26,* 304–326.

Silver, E.A., Shapiro, L.J., & Deutsch, A. (1993). Sense making and the solution of division problems involving remainders: An examination of middle school students' solution processes and their interpretations of solutions. *Journal for Research in Mathematics Education, 24,* 117–135.

Skinner, P. (1999). *It all adds up! Engaging 8-to-12-year-olds in math investigations.* Sausalito, CA: Math Solutions Publications.

Thornton, C.A., & Jones, G.A. (1994). Computation sense. In C.A. Thornton & N.S. Bley (Eds.), *Windows of opportunity: Mathematics for students with special needs* (pp. 205–227). Reston, VA: National Council of Teachers of Mathematics.

Trafton, P.R., & Hartman, C.L. (1997). Developing number sense and computational strategies in problem-centered classrooms. *Teaching Children Mathematics, 4,* 230–233.

Chapter 11

Number Sense and Estimation with Whole Numbers

All of the topics related to whole numbers are intimately connected. Number meanings and relationships (Chapter 6) are connected to the way students understand the operations (Chapter 7), and these ideas collectively contribute to basic fact mastery (Chapter 8). As children solve story problems, the numbers begin to get larger, and they use the ideas of place value (Chapter 9) to invent a variety of computational strategies (Chapter 10).

The ideas discussed in this chapter are part of the full development of flexible and fluent thinking with whole numbers. The number-sense activities will help children build relationships specifically related to computation. The skills of estimation, started as early as grade 3 and later extended to already developed mental math strategies, can be employed to deal with real-world situations that do not demand exact answers.

 BIG IDEAS

1. Multi-digit numbers can be represented in a wide variety of ways: with decades (36 is 30 and 6), with place-value concepts (36 is 2 tens and 16 ones), and with other multiples (480 is 500 less 20 or 475 and 5). They can easily be recombined when these parts are recognized.

2. Nearly all estimation involves replacing or substituting difficult-to-handle numbers with close "nice" numbers so that the resulting computation can be done mentally.

Number Sense for Whole-Number Computation

Number sense has been a part of every topic discussed so far in this text. It refers to flexible thinking and intuitive ideas about number. Here we examine only a small slice of number sense: the ability to represent numbers, to take them apart, and combine them in flexible ways. It's extremely important that students develop this flexibility with multi-digit numbers if they are to improve their use of invented strategies and algorithms for whole numbers.

Working with Tens and Hundreds

Most invented strategies for whole-number computation grow out of children's work with direct modelling. Because they are in the process of developing the strategies they will be using, students must support their thinking by writing the steps they use on paper. It is not reasonable to expect them to operate only mentally. However, many invented strategies will eventually become automatic. When this happens, students can begin to use them without resorting to pencil and paper. This is somewhat analogous to mastering the basic facts. Efficient strategies for the facts are developed using assorted models, and children appear to be very slow and deliberate about something as simple as adding 6 + 8. But soon these strategies become so ingrained that students can quickly respond to basic facts. The activities here will help students gain greater flexibility with numbers, and therefore become more efficient with their invented computational strategies.

ACTIVITY 11.1

Arrow Math

In front of the class, write a number on a hundreds chart followed by one or more arrows. The arrow can point up, down, left, right, or diagonally. Each arrow represents a move of one square on the board.

63 ↓ ↓ →
Read: "63, 73, 83, 84"

45 ↑ ↑ ↖ ← ←
Read: "45, 35, 25, 14, 13, 12"

After students become adept at "Arrow Math," talk about what each arrow means. The left and right arrows are one-less and one-more arrows. The up and down arrows are the same as 10 less and 10 more. What do each of the four possible diagonal arrows represent? (adapted from Hope, Leutzinger, Reys, & Reys, 1988).

The possibility of a 1–1000 chart can be discussed with your class, and you may even want to make one. Show a hundreds chart, and draw a second 10 × 10 grid below it. "What number would go in these squares?" (101 to 200) "And if we had some more charts below this one, what numbers would be in each of them?" Each new grid represents the next 100 numbers: 201 to 300, 301 to 400, and so on.

With an extended chart idea, the "Arrow Math" activity can be extended to include "super arrows."

426 ⇓ ⇓ ↓ → →
Read: "426, 526, 626, 636, 637, 638"

In the next example, note how three "super up arrows" and a regular down arrow are actually a good way to subtract 290.

674 ⇑ ⇑ ⇑ ↓
"674 minus 300 is 374, plus 10 is 384"

"Arrow Math" is only mildly problematic, and there is some evidence that the activity does not directly contribute to computation strategies (Cobb, 1995). However, the following activity connects arrows on the chart more directly to computation.

ACTIVITY 11.2

More Arrow Math

Begin with an arrow math task as before. For example:

56 ↓ ↓ →

After getting a result, ask, "How much did we add?" (21) "Now write an equation to go with this arrow problem." (56 + 21 = 77)

This works well in a similar manner for up and then left arrows for subtraction:

81 ↑ ↑ ↑ ↑ ← ←
81 − 43 = 38

That is, one way to subtract 43 from 81 is first to subtract 40 and then to subtract 3 more. The next two examples offer another twist.

64 ↓ ↓ ↓ ← and 72 ↑ ↑ ↑ →

In the first example, you add 20 and then subtract 1, a nice way of adding 19. In the second example, 30 is subtracted and then 1 added—a good way to subtract 29.

"More Arrow Math" certainly requires more than four examples. After a few straightforward tasks like the first two, introduce the equations, and have students write and complete the arrow problem: For 27 + 34, you first go down 3 (add 30) and then right 4 (add 4). How would you do 457 − 238? When adding or subtracting a number ending in 8 or 9, a good strategy, as indicated in "More Arrow Math," is to add or subtract a close multiple of 10 and then compensate.

 Technology Note

Math and More 3: Patterns on Lattices (EduQuest, 1994) allows students to create a wide variety of arrow paths on a number chart that scrolls as high as 999. The software is only a tool, providing the number chart and arrows. Unfortunately, the start and end numbers are always visible. Still, the software is well designed to explore this idea, and the teacher support material provides good explanations. It is also important to ask yourself: Does using the computer add something of value to the task of doing and engaging in mathematics that you wouldn't have without it? ▪

 ACTIVITY 11.3

Calculator Tens and Hundreds

Students work in pairs with one calculator. They press ⊞ 10 ⊜ to make a "+10 machine." One child enters any number. The other student says or writes the number that is 10 more. The = is pressed for confirmation. The roles are then reversed. The same activity can be done using any multiple of 10 or multiple of 100. The student whose turn it is to challenge can select what kind of "machine" to use. For example, she may first press 0 ⊞ 300 ⊜ and then press 572. The other student would say or write 872 and then press ⊜ for confirmation. This game can also be played using ⊟ instead of ⊞ to practise mentally subtracting tens or hundreds.

As with all calculator exercises, ensure students have calculators that work in this way.

As described, "Calculator Tens and Hundreds" is very similar to "Arrow Math" without the hundreds chart. Students doing these activities will soon discover that it is fairly easy to add and subtract hundreds and tens mentally. In "Calculator Tens and Hundreds," students could easily begin to add or subtract numbers such as 240 or 73. Every student who has not been taught to add and subtract in the traditional pencil-and-paper manner will begin these tasks mentally, starting with the largest amounts, just as in "Arrow Math."

Many of the skills and concepts developed so far also appear in the next activity, which combines symbolism with base-ten representations. In all of these activities, class discussions should be held so children can explain how they did the exercises or how they thought about them.

ACTIVITY 11.4

Numbers, Squares, Sticks, and Dots

As illustrated in Figure 11.1, prepare a worksheet or overhead transparency on which a number and some base-ten pieces are shown. Use small squares, sticks, and dots for base-ten pieces to keep drawings simple. Students write the totals that they compute mentally.

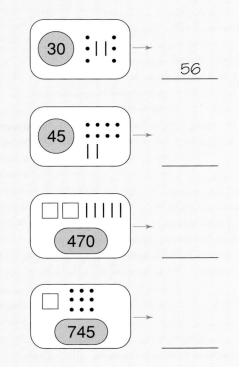

FIGURE 11.1 Flexible counting on or addition using both models and numbers.

Figure 11.2 is a take-away version of the same activity. As shown, the amount removed can be either the number or the squares and sticks. Try it both ways.

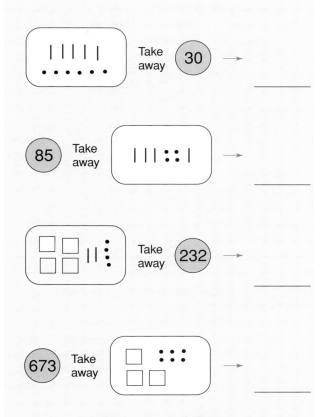

FIGURE 11.2 Counting back or subtraction using both models and numbers.

Notice how many ideas related to invented strategies and counting money are included in Activity 11.4. The next two activities encourage the same thinking with less dependence on models.

ACTIVITY 11.5

Moving Models Mentally

Display on the overhead a number with the tens and hundreds base-ten pieces. Students say the number shown. Next tell how much will be added or subtracted, as in "minus 300," and have students say the result. Build another number and repeat. Finally, move to examples with trades. Show 820. "Minus 50." (Think: "Minus 20 is 800, and 30 more is 770.")

ACTIVITY 11.6

The Chain Game

Each student has one or more cards with numbers written on them. After naming a start number, the teacher calls out, for example, "Plus 300" or "Minus 70." The student holding the result card calls out the result. Then the teacher reads the next change, and the chain continues. If the cards are prepared so that some numbers occur more than once, all students must remain alert even after their numbers have been called. Figure 11.3 illustrates the ideas with only seven cards.

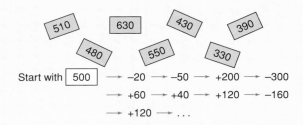

Start with [500] ⟶ –20 ⟶ –50 ⟶ +200 ⟶ –300
⟶ +60 ⟶ +40 ⟶ +120 ⟶ –160
⟶ +120 ⟶ . . .

FIGURE 11.3 A chain game for adding and subtracting tens and hundreds.

Thinking about Parts of Numbers

The activities in the previous section had children counting on or counting back in various ways. The next few activities focus on taking numbers apart.

ACTIVITY 11.7

Break It in Two Parts

Pick any two-digit or three-digit number. The task is to find ways to make the number in two parts. For example, 375 can be 300 and 75 or 215 and 160. Children should be permitted to use base-ten pieces or other models if they wish.

Potential problems may arise from the previous activity. Treat them as opportunities for learning. For example, children who do not have good place-value concepts may write 3 and 75 for 375. It may be unintentional, or it may be a signal of a larger problem. Suggest modelling the number with base-ten pieces, and see how the child connects the pieces and the digits.

Some children may see an easy pattern: 374 and 1373 and 2372 and 3, and so on. Compliment the nice pattern. Then ask, "What would the other part be if one part is 120? Would you have to continue your pattern all the way to 120?"

The next activity is similar but focuses on parts of important "nice" numbers such as 50, 100, or 300.

ACTIVITY 11.8

The Other Part of 100

Give students a number, say, 28, and have them determine "the other part of 100" (72). Discuss strategies. If students have difficulty with this, try using the little ten-frame cards (Blackline Masters). Show the given part of 100 with the little ten-frame cards as in Figure 11.4. When students become more adept at determining the other part of the number, they can practise with a calculator, either by themselves or with a partner. They make the calculator into a "parts of 100 Machine" by pressing 100 ⊟ 100 ⊟ . Now when they press any number less than 100 followed by ⊟ , the calculator will give the other part of 100 (with a minus sign).

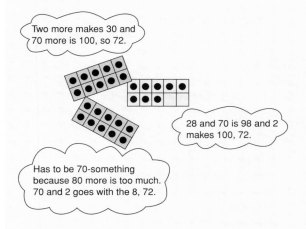

Two more makes 30 and 70 more is 100, so 72.

28 and 70 is 98 and 2 makes 100, 72.

Has to be 70-something because 80 more is too much. 70 and 2 goes with the 8, 72.

FIGURE 11.4 Using little ten-frames to help think about the "other part of 100."

Students can play "The Other Part" of 50 or 200 or 450 or any rounded number; 50 is probably the best number with which to begin. In the following activity, the nice number is seen as a part of another number. Often in computations, it is useful to recognize a nice part of a number, work with that part, and then deal with the rest.

ACTIVITY 11.9

50 and Some More

Say a number between 50 and 100. Students respond with "50 and ___." For 63, the response is "50 and 13." Use other numbers that end in 50, such as "450 and Some More."

Compatible numbers for addition and subtraction are numbers that go together easily to make nice numbers. Numbers that make tens or hundreds are the most common examples. Compatible sums also include numbers that end in 5, 25, 50, or 75, since these numbers are easy to work with as well. The teaching task is to get students accustomed to looking for combinations that work together, then encourage them to look for these combinations in computational situations.

ACTIVITY 11.10

Compatible Pairs

Searching for compatible pairs can be done as an individualized worksheet activity, or with the full class, using the overhead projector. Prepare a transparency, or duplicate a page with a search task. Five possible levels of difficulty are shown in Figure 11.5. Students call out or connect the compatible pairs as they see them.

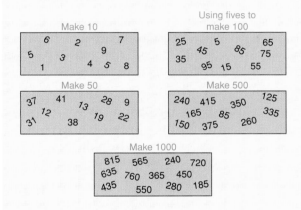

FIGURE 11.5 Compatible-pair searchers.

ACTIVITY 11.11

Compatible Calculations

Present strings of numbers that use compatibles:

$$30 + 80 + 40 + 50 + 10$$
$$25 + 125 + 75 + 250 + 50$$
$$95 + 15 + 35 + 5 + 65$$

Strings such as these can be approached in two ways, and each should be practised. One way is to search out compatible combinations, such as 5 and 95 in the third example. The other way is simply to add one addend at a time, saying the result as you go. For the first example, that would be "30, 110, 150, 200, 210."

Change some of the operations to subtraction for a good variation.

Flexible Thinking

Students may approach the following activities in a variety of ways. While they are good for work-station activities, it is often useful to have a class discussion regarding the strategies students are using.

ACTIVITY 11.12

Calculator Challenge Counting

Students press any number on the calculator (e.g., 17), then ⊞ 8. They say the sum before they press ⊟. Then they continue to add 8 mentally, challenging themselves to say the number before they press ⊟. They should see how far they are able to go before making a mistake.

The constant addend in "Challenge Counting" can be any number, even a two- or three-digit number. Try 20 or 25. Try 40, then 48. As an added challenge, after a student has progressed eight or ten counts, have the student reverse the process by pressing ⊟ followed by the same number and then ⊟ repeatedly. Discuss patterns that appear.

ACTIVITY 11.13

Little Ten-Frame Addition and Subtraction

Provide a set of little ten-frame cards for each student. Working in pairs, each student makes a number with her or his cards. When both have their number ready, they lay it down so both can see. Then they try to be the first to tell the total. For the subtraction version, one student makes a number greater than 50 with her or his cards and the other writes a number on paper that is less than 50. The number on the paper is subtracted from the modelled number. Students should be encouraged to share strategies to see how fast they can become.

Assessment Notes

The activities presented so far in this chapter not only develop appropriate number-sense skills, they also provide clues about students who is having difficulty going beyond counting by ones when solving multi-digit story problems. Students who exhibit difficulty with any of these activities will also have difficulty with almost any type of invented computation and certainly with the estimation activities to come. For example, how do students go about the exercises in Activity 11.4, "Numbers, Squares, Sticks, and Dots" (p. 209)? This activity demands that children have sufficient understanding of base-ten concepts and the ability to use them for meaningful counts. If students are counting by ones on their fingers, more practice with these activities may be inappropriate. Consider additional counting and grouping activities (Chapter 9) where students have the opportunity to see the value of groups of ten. In Activity 11.7, "Break It in Two Parts" (p. 210), look for the types of numbers children use. Could they be encouraged to use parts that are nice, or rounded numbers? When they select one part, how do they go about finding the other part? Perhaps the task should be modified to use numbers such as 20 or 30 so that you can see what number concepts are being employed.

These are just two examples of how the activities in this section can be used in a diagnostic manner. Consider thinking about other activities in this way. Build them into a brief interview with students about whom you need more information. ■■

Introducing Computational Estimation

The long-term goal of computational estimation is to be able to produce quickly an approximate result for a computation that will be adequate for the situation. In everyday life, estimation skills are valuable time savers. Many situations do not require an exact answer, so reaching for a calculator or a pencil is not necessary if one has good estimation skills.

Good estimators tend to employ a variety of computational strategies they have developed over time. Teaching these strategies to children has become a regular part of the curriculum. Beginning about grade 3, we can help children develop an understanding of what it means to estimate a computation and start to develop some early strategies that may be useful. From then on through middle school, children should continue to develop and add to their estimation strategies and skills.

Understanding the Concept of an Estimate

Estimation of measures and quantities is a significant part of the measurement strand. Students estimate length, mass, and other attributes as a practical skill and a means to develop unit familiarity. Students also estimate quantities: How many jelly beans in the jar?

Computational estimation is a significantly different skill. There are no physical materials; it is not a visual task.

Computational estimation is not a guess. Since it is based on computation, which has always meant "get the correct answer exactly," how can there be different estimates for the same problem? The answer, of course, is that the estimate depends on the strategy used and the kinds of adjustments made to the numbers. Estimates also tend to vary according to the purpose of the estimate. Estimating the amount and cost of gas for a family trip is quite different from trying to decide if your last $5 will cover the three items you need at the Hasty Mart. These are new and difficult ideas for young students.

Suggestions for Estimation Instruction

Here are some general principles that are worth keeping in mind as you help your students to develop estimation skills.

Find Real Examples of Estimation

Discuss situations where computational estimations are used in real life. Some simple examples include figuring the relationship of litres of gas to kilometres travelled on a family trip, dealing with grocery store situations (doing comparative shopping, determining if there is enough to pay the bill), determining approximate yearly or monthly totals of all sorts of things (school supplies, haircuts, lawnmowing income, time spent watching TV), and figuring the cost of going to a sporting event or show, including transportation, tickets, and snacks. Help children see how each of these involves a computation (as opposed to a measurement). You could sit down with a calculator or pencil and paper and compute an exact answer. Discuss why exact answers are not necessary in some instances and why they are in others. Look in a newspaper or magazine to find examples of numbers that are estimates and numbers that are the result of exact computations.

Use the Language of Estimation

Words and phrases such as *about, close, just about, a little more* (or *less*) *than,* and *between* are part of the language of estimation. Students should understand that they are trying to come as close as possible using quick and easy methods, but there is no "exact" estimate. Language can help convey that idea.

Build on Related Skills and Concepts

Estimation skills are related to number sense and to mental computation skills. Most estimation strategies are based on the idea of using nice numbers that are close to the numbers in the computation. The nice-number substitutes lend themselves to mental computation that is not possible with the actual numbers.

A real-world sense of number is also important. Is $2.10, $21, or $210 most reasonable for 30 69-cent soft drinks? It is much easier to focus on 7 × 3 and use a result that makes sense than to compute 0.69 × 30 and try to place the decimal correctly. Similar assists come from knowing if the cost of a car would likely be $950 or $9500. Could attendance at the school play be 30 or 300 or 3000? A simple computation can provide the important digits, with number sense providing the rest.

Accept a Range of Estimates

What estimate would you give for 27 × 325? If you use 20 × 300, you might say 6000. Or you might use 25 for the 27, noting that four 25s make 100. Since 325 ÷ 4 is about 81, it would make 8100. If you use 30 × 300, your estimate is 9000, and 30 × 320 gives an estimate of 9600. Are any of these "right"?

By listing the estimates of many students and letting the class discuss how and why different estimates resulted, students can begin to see that estimates generally fall in a range around the exact answer. Different approaches provide different results. And don't forget the context. Some situations call for more careful estimates than others.

Beginning Formats for Estimation

Consider the point of view of a grade 3 student when you ask for an estimate of the sum $349.29 + $85.99 + $175.25. The requirement is to come up with *a number.* Even textbooks, in an attempt to teach a particular estimation strategy, will lead students through a process of rounding and adding to come up with a singular answer. This is contrary to the idea of what an estimate really is: producing answers that are "good enough" for the purpose. The purpose often determines what we need to know. For the three prices, the question "About how much?" is quite different from "Is it more than $600?" How would you answer each of those questions?

Each activity that follows suggests a strategy for estimation when an exact numerical response is not required.

ACTIVITY 11.14

Over or Under?

Prepare several estimation exercises on a transparency. With each, provide an "over or under number." In Figure 11.6, each is either over or under $1.50, but the number need not be the same for each task.

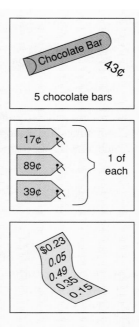

FIGURE 11.6 "Over or Under?" is a good beginning estimation activity.

ACTIVITY 11.15

Which One's Closest?

Make a transparency of a page of drill-and-practice computations (see Figure 11.7). Have students focus on a single row or other collection of five to eight problems. Ask them to find the one with an answer that is closest to some rounded number that you provide. One transparency could provide a week's worth of five-minute drills.

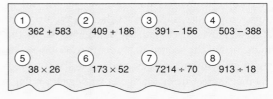

Which of these is closest to 600? To 1000? To 100?

FIGURE 11.7 A textbook drill page can be a good source of estimation exercises.

ACTIVITY 11.16

Best Choice

For any single estimation task, offer three or four possible estimates.

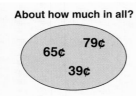

About how much in all?

65¢   79¢

39¢

How close the choices are will determine the difficulty of the task. Sometimes it is a good idea to use multiples of 10, such as $21, $210, and $2100.

Even with these multiple-choice tasks, the three-part lesson format remains useful. Present the exercise, have students quickly write their choice on paper (this commits them to an answer), then discuss why they made that choice. All three parts may take only five or 10 minutes. In the discussion, a wide variety of estimates and estimation methods will be shared. This will help students see that estimates fall in a range and that there is no single correct estimate or method.

Computational Estimation Strategies

Estimation strategies are specific algorithms that produce approximate results rather than exact results. The strategies discussed in this section are the ones good estimators use.

It is always a good idea to begin by simply presenting an estimation task and seeing what strategies and ideas students use. However, it is likely that you will soon need to be more instructive and suggest at least some of these strategies. After introducing a strategy, you could have students practise it so that it is clearly understood.

After a variety of strategies have been presented to students, stop specifying which one to use. Instead, provide students with a task, then let them come up with an estimate using whatever strategy makes sense to them. Even in groups of three or four, students can each make an estimate, then compare their estimates and their strategies. This lets them select from a range of strategies, and allows for a range of answers.

Front-End Methods

Front-end methods focus on the leading or leftmost digits in numbers and ignore the rest. Estimates are made on the basis of only these front-end digits. Adjustments can then be made to the smaller parts of the quantity.

Front-End Addition and Subtraction

Front-end is a good beginning strategy for addition or subtraction. This approach is reasonable when all or most of

the numbers have the same number of digits. Figure 11.8 illustrates the idea. Notice that when a number has fewer digits than the rest, that number is ignored completely.

After adding or subtracting the front digits, an adjustment is made to compensate for the digits or numbers that were ignored. Making an adjustment is actually a separate skill. For young children, just practise at first using the front digits. Pay special attention to numbers, not in column format, that do not have the same number of digits.

When teaching this front-end strategy, present additions or subtractions in column form, and cover all but the leading digits. Remember to use these digits as you discuss the estimates for the sum or difference. Is it more or less than the actual amount? Is the estimate off by a little or a lot? Later, show numbers written in horizontal form or numbers on price tags that are not lined up. What numbers should be added?

The leading-digit strategy is easy to use and easy to teach because it does not require rounding or changing numbers. The numbers used are visible, so children can see with what they are working. It is a good first strategy for children as early as grade 3.

Front-End Multiplication and Division

For multiplication and division, the front-end method uses the first digit in each factor. The computation is then done using zeros in the other positions. For example, a front-end estimation of 48×7 is 40 times 7, or 280. When

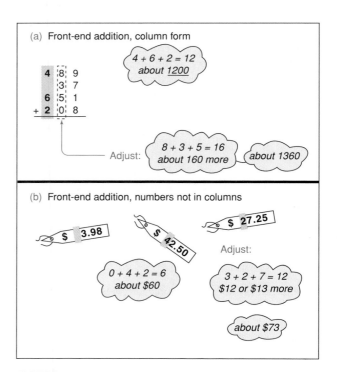

FIGURE 11.8 Front-end estimation in addition.

both numbers have more than one digit, the front ends of both are used. For 452 × 23, consider 400 × 20, or 8000.

Division with pencil and paper is almost a front-end strategy already. First determine in which column the first digit of the quotient belongs. For 7)3482 , the first digit is a 4 and belongs in the hundreds column, over the 4. Therefore, the front-end estimate is 400. This method always produces a low estimate, as students will quickly figure out. In this particular example, the answer is clearly much closer to 500, so 480 or 490 is a good adjustment.

Rounding Methods

Rounding is the most familiar form of estimation. Rounding the numbers in a problem is a way of changing the problem to one that is easier to work with mentally. Good estimators follow mental computation with an adjustment to compensate for the rounding. To be useful, rounding should be flexible and well understood conceptually.

Rounding in Addition and Subtraction

When a lot of numbers are to be added, it is usually a good idea to round them to the same place value. Keep a running sum as you round each number. In Figure 11.9, the same total is estimated two ways using rounding. A combination of the two is also possible.

For subtraction, as for addition with two addends, there are only two numbers with which to deal. Generally, it is necessary to round only one of the two numbers. In subtraction situations, round only the number being subtracted. For 6724 – 1863, round 1863 to 2000. Then it is easy: 6724 – 2000 is 4724. Now adjust. You took away a bigger number, so the result must be too small. Adjust to about 4800. For 627 + 385, you might round 627 to 625 because multiples of 25 are almost as easy to work with as multiples of 10 or 100. After substituting 625 for 627, you may or may not want to round 385 to 375 or 400. The

point is that there are no rigid rules. Choices depend on the relationships held by the estimator, on how quickly the estimate is needed, and on how accurate an estimate is required. The more adjusting and "playing around" you do with the numbers, the more accurate you are likely to be. After a while, you should reach for the calculator.

Rounding in Multiplication and Division

The rounding strategy for multiplication is no different from that for other operations. However, the error involved can be significant, especially when both factors are rounded. In Figure 11.10, several multiplication situations are illustrated, and rounding is used to estimate each.

If one number can be rounded to 10, 100, or 1000, the resulting product is easy to determine without adjusting the other factor.

When one factor is a single digit, examine the other factor. Consider the product 7 × 836. If 836 is rounded to 800, the estimate is relatively easy and is low if 36 is multiplied by 7. If a more accurate result is required, round 836 to 840, and add two partial products (7 × 800 and 7 × 40). Then the estimate is 5600 plus 280, or 5880.

If possible, round only one factor—select the larger one if it is significantly larger. (Why?) For example, in 47 × 7821, 47 × 8000 is 376 000, but 50 × 8000 is 400 000. The actual product is 367 587.

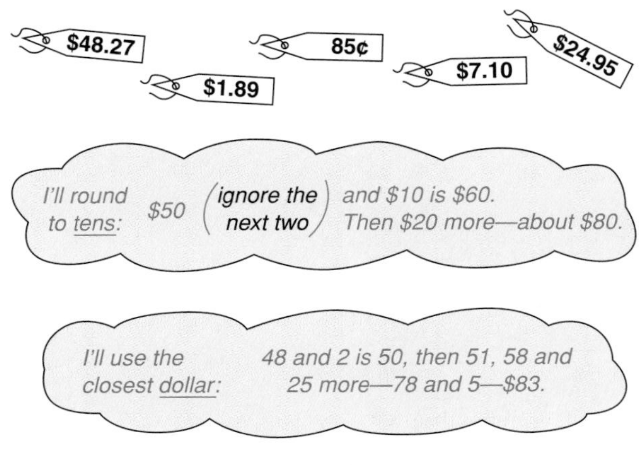

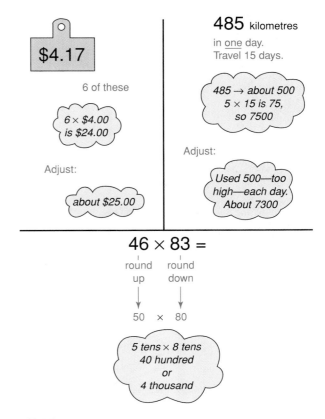

FIGURE 11.9 Rounding in addition.

FIGURE 11.10 Rounding in multiplication.

Another good rule of thumb with multiplication is to round one factor up and the other down (even if that is not the closest rounded number). When estimating 86 × 28, 86 is between 80 and 90, but 28 is very close to 30. Try rounding 86 down to 80 and 28 up to 30. The actual product is 2408, only 8 off from the 80 × 30 estimate. If both numbers were rounded to the nearest 10, the estimate would be based on 90 × 30, with an error of nearly 300.

With one-digit divisors, it is almost always best to search for a compatible dividend rather than to round off. For example, 7)4325 is best estimated by using the close compatible number, 4200, to yield an estimate of 600. Rounding would suggest a dividend of 4000 or 4300, neither of which is very helpful.

When the divisor is a two-digit number, rounding it to tens or hundreds makes looking for a missing factor much easier. For example, for 42)3890, round the divisor to 40. Then think: 40 multiplied by *what* is close to 3890?

Using Compatible Numbers

When adding a long list of numbers, it is sometimes useful to look for two or three numbers that can be grouped to make 10 or 100. If there are numbers that can be adjusted

slightly to produce these groups, it will make finding an estimate easier. This approach is illustrated in Figure 11.11.

In subtraction, as illustrated in Figure 11.12, it is often possible to adjust only one number to produce an easily observed difference.

Frequently in the real world, an estimate is needed for a large list of addends that are relatively close. This might happen with a series of prices of similar items, attendance at a series of events in the same arena, cars passing a point on successive days, or other similar data. In these cases, as illustrated in Figure 11.13, a nice number can be selected to represent each addend, and multiplication used to determine the total. This is more of an *averaging technique* than a compatible-numbers strategy.

One of the best uses of the compatible-numbers strategy is in division. The two exercises shown in Figure 11.14 illustrate adjusting the divisor or dividend (or both) to create a division that comes out even and is therefore easy to do mentally. Many percent, fraction, and rate situations involve division, and the compatible-numbers strategy, as shown in Figure 11.15, is quite useful.

Estimation Exercises

The ideas presented so far illustrate some of the types of estimation and thought patterns you want to suggest to your students. But making up examples and putting them

FIGURE 11.12 **Compatibles can mean an adjustment that produces easy difference.**

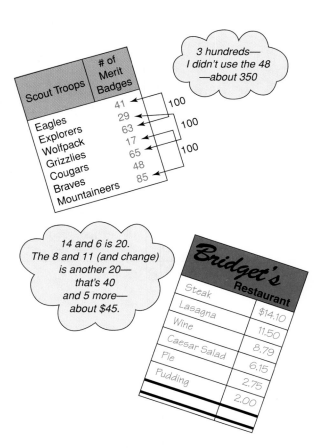

FIGURE 11.11 Compatibles used in addition.

Cookies Sold Class 7A	
1. Marcie	___ 68
2. Sally	___ 42
3. Chris	___ 81
4. Yvonne	___ 35
5. Yolanda	___ 57
6. Andrea	___ 60
7. Meggan	___ 71
8. Jo Ann	___ 63

Looks like about 60 each— 8 × 60 is 480

FIGURE 11.13 Estimating sums using averaging.

FIGURE 11.14 **Adjusting to simplify division.**

Source: From *GUESS (Guide to Using Estimation Skills and Strategies)* (box II, cards 2 and 3), by B. J. Reys and R. E. Reys, 1983, White Plains, NY: Dale Seymour Publications. Copyright 1983 by Dale Seymour Publications. Reprinted by permission of Dale Seymour Publications.

FIGURE 11.15 **Using compatible numbers in division.**

into a realistic context is not easy and is very time-consuming. Fortunately, good estimation material is now being included in virtually all textbooks. However, exposure to this material is only a part of the kind of ongoing, intensive program that is necessary for developing estimation skills. Try supplementing the textbook with one or more of the many good teacher resource materials that are available commercially. Some of these are listed at the end of the chapter.

The examples presented here are not designed to teach estimation strategies, only to offer useful formats for providing your students with practice as they develop their skills. These examples are a good addition to any estimation program.

Calculator Activities

The calculator is not only a good source of estimation activities but also one of the reasons estimation is so important. In the real world, we frequently hit a wrong key, leave off a zero or a decimal, or simply enter numbers

incorrectly. An estimate of the expected result alerts us to these errors. The calculator as a tool for teaching estimation provides students with an opportunity to work independently or in pairs in a challenging, fun way without fear of embarrassment. Some of the activities described here work very well with an overhead projector calculator and a whole class.

ACTIVITY 11.17
The Range Game

This is an estimation game for any of the four operations. First pick a start number and an operation. The start number and operation are stored in the calculator. Students then take turns entering a number and pressing ▱ to try to make the result land in the target range. The following example for multiplication illustrates the activity: Suppose that a start number of 17 and a range of 800 to 830 are chosen. Press 17 ☒ ▱ to store

17 as a factor. Note that the number 289, which is 17 ⊠ 17, will appear on the display. Press a number and then ⊟. Perhaps you try 25. (Press 25 ⊟.) The result is 425. That is about half the target. Try 50. The result is 850—maybe 2 or 3 too high. Try 48. The result is 816—in the target range! Figure 11.16 gives examples for all four operations. Prepare a list of start numbers and target ranges. Let students play in pairs to see who can hit the most targets on the list (Wheatley & Hersberger, 1986).

After entering the setup with the start # as shown, players take turns pressing a number, then ⊟ to try to get a result in the target range.

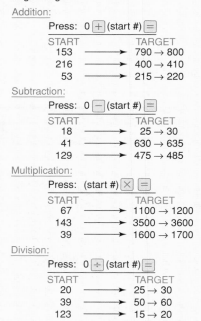

Addition:
Press: 0 ⊞ (start #) ⊟

START		TARGET
153	⟶	790 → 800
216	⟶	400 → 410
53	⟶	215 → 220

Subtraction:
Press: 0 ⊟ (start #) ⊟

START		TARGET
18	⟶	25 → 30
41	⟶	630 → 635
129	⟶	475 → 485

Multiplication:
Press: (start #) ⊠ ⊟

START		TARGET
67	⟶	1100 → 1200
143	⟶	3500 → 3600
39	⟶	1600 → 1700

Division:
Press: 0 ÷ (start #) ⊟

START		TARGET
20	⟶	25 → 30
39	⟶	50 → 60
123	⟶	15 → 20

FIGURE 11.16 "The Range Game"—a calculator game.

"The Range Game" can be played by the whole class with an overhead calculator, by an individual, or by two or three children with calculators who can race one another. The speed element is important. The extent of the range and the type of numbers used can all be adjusted to suit the level of the class.

ACTIVITY 11.18
Secret Sum

This calculator activity uses the memory feature. A target number is selected—for example, 100. Students take turns entering a number and pressing the M⊞ key. Each of the numbers is accumulated in the memory, but the sum is never displayed on the screen. If one player thinks that the other player has made the sum go beyond the target, he or she announces "over," and the MRC (memory return) key is pressed to check. If a player is able to hit the target exactly, bonus points can be awarded. Interesting strategies quickly develop.

"Secret Sum" can also be played with the M⊟ key. First enter a total amount in the memory. Each player's number is followed by a press of M⊟ and is subtracted from the memory. Here, the first to announce correctly that the other player has made the memory go negative is the winner.

ACTIVITY 11.19
The Range Game: Sequential Versions

Select a target range as before. Next enter the starting number in the calculator, and hand it to the first player. For addition and subtraction, the first player then presses either ⊞ or ⊟, followed by a number, and then ⊟. The next player begins his or her turn by entering ⊞ or ⊟ and an appropriate number, operating on the previous result. If the target is 423 to 425, a sequence of turns might go like this:

Start with 119.

⊞ 350 ⊟ ⟶ 469 (too high)

⊟ 42 ⊟ ⟶ 427 (a little over)

⊟ 3 ⊟ ⟶ 424 (success)

For multiplication or division, only one operation is used through the whole game. After the first or second turn, decimal factors are usually required. This variation allows students to develop an excellent understanding of multiplication or division by decimals. A sequence for a target of 262 to 265 might be like this:

Start with 63.

⊠ 5 ⊟ ⟶ 315 (too high)

⊠ 0.7 ⊟ ⟶ 220.5 (too low)

⊠ 1.3 ⊟ ⟶ 286.65 (too high)

⊠ 0.9 ⊟ ⟶ 257.985 (too low)

⊠ 1.03 ⊟ ⟶ 265.72455 (very close!)

(What would you press next?)

Try a target of 76 to 80, begin with 495, and use only division.

Technology Note

Estimation skills are often embedded in software drill-and-practice packages, although very few are designed for estimation skills alone. *Mathville* (Courseware Solutions, 2000) and *Math Trek* (Nectar Foundation, 2000) are two Canadian software programs that offer practice with estimation. *Mathville Jungleway*, one of the seven products in the series, is recommended for use in grade 2, but can also be used in grades 1 and 3. The program has two activities in particular that provide practice with estimation. *Hummer Race* asks children to round numbers to the nearest 10. For *Bubble Fish,* they are required to estimate sums and differences. The activities are fast-paced and motivating. *Mathville VIP*, which is geared to grade 7, also provides practice with estimating. The interactive tutorial in *Math Trek 4, 5, 6*, one of the components of the *Math Trek* program, teaches students about estimating and rounding. Tools such as the number line are used to help students. Rounding extends to large numbers, decimals and extensions. The program also includes *Math Trek 1, 2, 3* and *Math Trek 7, 8, 9.*

Mega Math Blaster (Davidson), *Power Rangers ZEO: Power Active Math* (MacWarehouse, 1996), and *CornerStone Mathematics, Grades 3–8* (SkillsBank, 1996) are some computer software programs that have been developed outside Canada. *Power Rangers* has six levels for each of its skills, including one called "estimation," which proves to be exercises in rounding. The estimation activities in *Mega Math Blaster* are in an arcade format. This adds the useful element of speed, but may be a turn-off for students who do not care for the context. *CornerStone Math* has test materials both in software and in paper form that are useful for evaluation and practice in test taking.

The *Blue Falls Elementary* title in *Fizz & Martina's Math Adventures* (Tom Snyder Productions, 1998) includes three estimation problems in each of the four episodes. (The *Fizz & Martina* programs are each built around adventure stories with group problem solving in a realistic context.) Students are encouraged to estimate and then explain the strategy they have used. At least one strategy is provided. ■■

Activities for the Overhead Projector

The overhead projector offers several advantages. You can prepare the computational exercises ahead of time. You can control how long a particular computation is viewed by the students. There is no need to prepare handouts. Commercial materials such as GUESS cards (Figure 11.14, p. 217) can be copied onto transparencies for instructional purposes.

ACTIVITY 11.20

What Was Your Method?

Select any single computational estimation problem, and put it on the board or overhead. Allow 10 seconds for each class member to make an estimate. Discuss briefly the various estimation techniques that were used. As a variation, prepare a problem and provide one estimation. For example, 139×43 might be estimated as 6000. Ask questions concerning this estimate: "How do you think that estimate was arrived at? Was that a good approach? How should it be adjusted? Why might someone select 150 instead of 140 as a substitute for 139?" Almost every estimate can involve different choices and methods. Alternatives make for good discussion, helping students to see different methods and learn that there is no single correct estimate.

ACTIVITY 11.21

In the Ballpark

Using a page of problems from a workbook, write in answers to six or seven problems. On one or two problems, make a significant error that can be caught by estimation. For example, write $5408 \div 26 = 28$ (instead of 208) or $36 \times 17 = 342$ (instead of 612). Other answers should be correct. Encourage the class to estimate each problem to find errors "not even in the ballpark."

Estimating with Fractions, Decimals, and Percentages

Fractions, decimals, and percentages are three different notations for rational numbers. Many real-world situations that call for computational estimation involve the part-to-whole relationships of rational numbers. To estimate with such numbers first requires an ability to estimate with whole numbers. Beyond this, it involves an understanding of fractions and decimals and what these two types of numbers mean. Calculations with percentages are generally done as fractions or as decimals. The key is to be able to use an appropriate fraction or decimal. The examples in this chapter have not included fractions, decimals, or percentages. A few examples are suggested here:

SALE! $51.99. Marked one-fourth (one-quarter) off.

What was the original price?

About 62 percent of the 834 students bought their lunch last Wednesday. How many students bought lunch?

Tickets sold for $1.25. If attendance was 3124, about how much was the total amount collected?

I drove 464 km on 48.63 litres of gas. How many kilometres per litre did my car get?

In the first example, one approach is, if $51.99 (or $52) is the result of one-fourth (one-quarter) off, it means $52 is three-fourths (three-quarters) of the total. So one-fourth (one-quarter) is a third of $52, or a little less than $18. Thus about $52 + $18 = $70, or about $69, seems a fair estimate of the original cost. Notice that conceptualization of this problem requires an understanding of fractions, but the estimation skill involves only whole numbers. This is the case for almost all problems involving fractions, decimals, or percentages.

From a developmental perspective, it is important to realize that the skills of estimation and the conceptualization of rational numbers are separate from each other. It would be a mistake to work on the difficult process of estimation using fractions or percentages if concepts for those numbers were poorly developed. In later chapters, where rational numbers are discussed, it will be demonstrated that an ability to estimate can contribute to increased flexibility of number sense with fractions, decimals, and percentages.

 ## Literature Connections

Interesting literature often provides a diversionary context in which the mathematics may be a bit more fun and possibly more realistic. Even if the realism of these two books is a bit stretched, the context makes a welcome change of pace.

The Twelve Circus Rings
(Chwast, 1993)

Based on the same pattern as "The Twelve Days of Christmas," the 12 circus rings each contain more animals or more acts: "six acrobats, five dogs a-barking, four aerialists zooming, three monkeys playing, two elephants, and a daredevil on high wire." The colourful illustrations add to the excitement of the circus and the growing number of performers. After 12 days, how many aerialists are zooming? Remember that there are four aerialists not only in ring 4 but also in rings 5 through 12. The story lends itself to some early estimation but can easily be extended to create some fun questions. "About how much do the bows cost for all the dogs a-barking if each bow costs $1.29?"

Both you and your students can make up estimation questions that challenge the skills you've been developing. In addition to the potential for both estimation and mental computation, the author also considers patterns as another extension.

The 329th Friend
(Sharmat, 1979)

This book not only offers the opportunity to examine mental math strategies and practice in the context of the story, but is also about friendship and the need to be liked. The story is about Emery Raccoon, who has no friends. Because he is lonely, Emery invites 328 strangers to lunch to make new friends. There are considerations about the number of dishes, knives, forks, and spoons that suggest multiplying 329 by small numbers in various different ways. The story is easily expanded into other similar number questions. At the end, Emery discovers that although his guests ignored him, there was one friend that was there all along—himself.

 ## Assessment Notes

Since estimation involves an element of speed, teachers often wonder how they can test it so that students are not computing on paper and then rounding the answer to look like an estimate. One method is to prepare a short list of about three estimation exercises on a transparency. You can use straightforward computations. Students have paper and pencils ready as you briefly show one exercise at a time on the overhead, perhaps for 20 seconds each, depending on the task. Students immediately write their estimate, indicating whether they think it is "low" or "high"—that is, lower or higher than the exact computation. They do not do any written computation. Continue until you are finished. Then show all the exercises, and have students write down how they did each estimate. They should also indicate if they think the estimate was a good estimate or not so good and why. By doing only a few estimates but having the students reflect on them in this way, you actually receive more information than you would with just the answers to a longer list.

A theme of these assessment notes is that you receive a lot of information each day about your students, and all you have to do is record it. Information can be gathered from your daily estimation activities in much the same way as for invented strategy computations, by using a recording sheet for your observations (see Chapter 10). ■■

Reflections on Chapter 11

Writing to Learn

1. Describe specific examples where number sense plays a direct role in the development of invented computational strategies, mental computation, and estimation.
2. Why might the idea of an estimate for a computation be a difficult concept?
3. Describe each of the general strategies that were offered for conducting estimation activities.
4. Young children often find it difficult to come up with an estimate. What techniques are suggested where students are required to estimate but not to actually produce an estimate?
5. Describe each of the following estimation strategies. Make up a good example for each and include it in your explanation.
   a. Front-end addition and subtraction.
   b. Front-end multiplication.
   c. Rounding in addition.
   d. Rounding in subtraction.
   e. Rounding in multiplication.
   f. Compatible numbers in addition and subtraction.
   g. Compatible numbers in division.
6. How could the calculator be used to practice estimation strategies?

For Discussion and Exploration

1. In the past, the computation component of the curriculum focused only on traditional algorithms. There was only one way to compute. How much emphasis should be given to each of the forms of computation that have been discussed (invented strategies both mental and with pencil and paper, traditional algorithms and variations, and finally estimation) in today's elementary curriculum? Try to support your argument on the basis of real-world use.
2. Examine your regional mathematics curriculum document. Does the curriculum require that computational estimation and mental computation be taught? For "straightforward computation," is there any requirement that a particular algorithm or method of computation be used? How do guidelines for computation influence what computation methods are taught in school? Do you agree with what is required?

Recommendations for Further Reading

Highly Recommended

Bresser, R., & Holtzman, C. (1999). *Developing number sense: Grades 3–6.* Sausalito, CA: Math Solutions Publications.

Bresser and Holtzman are classroom teachers who have compiled 13 worthwhile number-sense activities covering a range of topics including mental computation, number meanings, and estimation. With each activity, the authors provide pages of extensions, practical suggestions, and answers to questions about using the activity in the classroom. Most activities include examples of students' work.

Reys, R.E., & Nohda, N. (Eds.). (1994). *Computational alternatives for the twenty-first century: Cross-cultural perspectives from Japan and the United States.* Reston, VA: National Council of Teachers of Mathematics.

This book addresses similarities and differences in computation in the United States and Japan. Divided into three sections, the articles discuss mental computation, estimation, and the use of calculators in the two countries. Respected researchers from both countries have contributed to this work. Although not designed as a resource book, the thoughtful teacher will find practical ideas as well as interesting perspectives.

Other Suggestions

Auriemma, S.H. (1999). How huge is a hundred? *Teaching Children Mathematics, 6,* 154–159.

Hunting, R.P. (1999). Rational-number learning in the early years: What is possible? In J.V. Copley (Ed.), *Mathematics in the early years* (pp. 80–87). Reston, VA: National Council of Teachers of Mathematics.

Lemaire, P., Lechacheur, M., & Farioli, F. (2000). Children's strategy use in computational estimation. *Canadian Journal of Experimental Psychology, 54*(2), 141–148.

Leutzinger, L.P., Rathmell, E.C., & Urbatsch, T.D. (1986). Developing estimation skills in the primary grades. In H.L. Schoen (Ed.), *Estimation and mental computation* (pp. 82–92). Reston, VA: National Council of Teachers of Mathematics.

McIntosh, A., Reys, B.J., & Reys, R.E. (1997). *Number SENSE: Simple effective number sense experiences, grades 3–4.* White Plains, NY: Cuisenaire–Dale Seymour.

McIntosh, A., Reys, B.J., & Reys, R.E. (1997). *Number SENSE: Simple effective number sense experiences, grades 4–6.* White Plains, NY: Cuisenaire–Dale Seymour.

McIntosh, A., Reys, B.J., & Reys, R.E. (1997). *Number SENSE: Simple effective number sense experiences, grades 6–8.* White Plains, NY: Cuisenaire–Dale Seymour.

Reys, B.J. (1986). Teaching computational estimation: Concepts and strategies. In H. L. Schoen (Ed.), *Estimation and mental computation* (pp. 31–44). Reston, VA: National Council of Teachers of Mathematics.

Reys, R.E. (1998). Computation versus number sense. *Mathematics Teaching in the Middle School, 4,* 110–112.

Reys, R.E., Trafton, P.R., Reys, B.J., & Zawojewski, J.S. (1987). *Computational estimation (grades 6, 7, 8).* White Plains, NY: Cuisenaire–Dale Seymour.

Reys, R.E., & Yang, D. (1998). Relationship between computational performance and number sense among sixth- and eighth-grade students in Taiwan. *Journal for Research in Mathematics Education, 29,* 225–237.

Sowder, J.T., & Kelin, J. (1993). Number sense and related topics. In D. T. Owens (Ed.), *Research ideas for the classroom: Middle grades mathematics* (pp. 41–57). Old Tappan, NJ: Macmillan.

Sowder, J.T., & Wheeler, M.M. (1989). The development of concepts and strategies used in computational estimation. *Journal for Research in Mathematics Education, 20,* 130–146.

Thornton, C.A., Jones, G.A., & Neal, J.L. (1995). The 100s chart: A stepping stone to mental mathematics. *Teaching Children Mathematics, 1,* 480–483.

Trafton, P.R. (1986). Teaching computational estimation: Establishing an estimation mind-set. In H.L. Schoen (Ed.), *Estimation and mental computation* (pp. 16–30). Reston, VA: National Council of Teachers of Mathematics.

Van de Walle, J.A., & Watkins, K.B. (1993). Early development of number sense. In R.J. Jensen (Ed.), *Research ideas for the classroom: Early childhood mathematics* (pp. 127–150). Old Tappan, NJ: Macmillan.

Chapter 12

Developing Fractional Concepts

Fractions have always represented a considerable challenge for students, even into the middle grades. But most programs teach some fractional ideas in grade 1 or 2 and have a full development of fractional concepts in grades 3 and 4.

A fraction is an expression of a relationship between a part and a whole. Helping children construct that relationship and connect it meaningfully to symbolism is the topic of this chapter.*

 BIG IDEAS

1. Fractional parts are equal shares or equal-sized portions of a whole or unit. The unit, counted as 1, can be an object or collection of things.

2. Fractional parts have special names that tell how many equal parts of that size are needed to make a whole. For example, *thirds* require three equal parts to make a whole.

3. The more parts needed to make the whole, the smaller the parts.

4. The numerator of a fraction tells how many parts are being considered. The denominator indicates the kind or size of the equal parts the numerator counts.

5. Two equivalent fractions represent two ways of describing the same amount using different-sized fractional parts.

---

*Technically, the relationship between a part and a whole is a rational number, and a fraction is one type of symbolism used to represent a rational number. This distinction between number and symbol is ignored in this book, primarily because it is not meaningful to children before approximately grade 8. The context will generally make the intent clear.

Three Categories of Fractional Models

There is substantial evidence to suggest that the use of models in fractional tasks is important (Cramer & Henry, 2002). Unfortunately, many teachers in the upper grades, where manipulative materials are not as common, fail to use models for the development of fractions. Models should be used at all grade levels to develop fractional concepts (and other mathematical concepts) as they help students clarify ideas that are often confused when working symbolically. Children should have experiences with a wide assortment of models. A change in the model usually marks a significant change in the activity from the viewpoint of the children. As you examine the ideas in this chapter, consider how the same activity could be done using different models. Three categories of models are presented here: area or region models, length models, and sets models.

Area or Region Models

In region models, a surface or area is subdivided into smaller parts. Each part can be compared with the whole. This is a good place to begin when working with fractions and is almost essential when doing sharing tasks with students. Figure 12.1 shows a variety of models in this category.

Circular (pie) regions and rectangular models can be duplicated on tag-board or construction paper, laminated, and cut into fraction kits to be kept in plastic bags. Be aware that rectangles allow for almost any piece to be designated as the whole so that other pieces change accordingly in fractional value. There are some excellent com-

FIGURE 12.1 Area or region models for fractions.

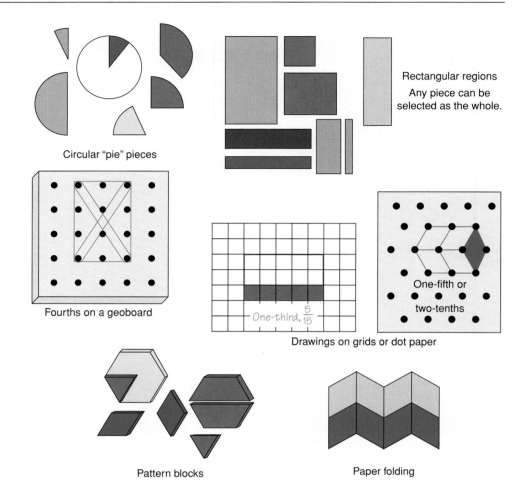

Circular "pie" pieces

Rectangular regions
Any piece can be selected as the whole.

Fourths on a geoboard

One-third, $\frac{5}{15}$

One-fifth or two-tenths

Drawings on grids or dot paper

Pattern blocks

Paper folding

mercially produced plastic area models in rectangular and other shapes, where colour facilitates identification of the fractional parts. Pattern blocks, geoboards, and grid paper also provide the same flexibility as the above-mentioned models. With grid paper or dot paper, children can easily draw pictures to explore fractional ideas. Paper folding is another model that is available to everyone.

Length or Measurement Models

With measurement models, length instead of area is compared. Either lines are drawn and subdivided, or physical materials are compared on the basis of length, as shown in Figure 12.2. Manipulative versions provide more opportunity for trial and error and for exploration.

Fraction pieces can be an effective model for length or measurement. The piece model provides the most flexibility while still having separate pieces for comparison. (A master for Fraction Pieces is included in the "Blackline Masters and Materials Construction Tips.") The strips have pieces that are in lengths of one to 10, measured in terms of the smallest strip. Each length can be coloured differ-

ently for ease of identification. As an alternative, strips of construction paper or adding-machine tape can be folded to produce equal-sized subparts.

The number line is significantly more abstract as a measurement model than the strip model. From a child's vantage point, there is a real difference between putting a number on a number line and comparing one length to another. Each number on a line denotes the distance of the labelled point from zero. Place the numbers $\frac{2}{3}$ and $\frac{3}{4}$ on a number line, and consider how a child would think about these numbers in the context of that model.

Set Models

In set models, the whole is understood to be a set of objects, and subsets of the whole make up fractional parts. For example, three objects are one-fourth of a set of 12 objects. The set of 12, in this example, represents the whole or one. It is the idea of referring to a collection of counters as a single entity that makes set models difficult not only for primary, but also for older children. However, the set model helps establish important connections with many real-world uses of fractions and with ratio concepts. Figure 12.3 illustrates several set models for fractions.

Any type of counter can be used to model fractional parts of sets, including hand-drawn Xs and Os. However, if the counters are coloured in two colours on opposite sides, they can easily be flipped to change their colour to

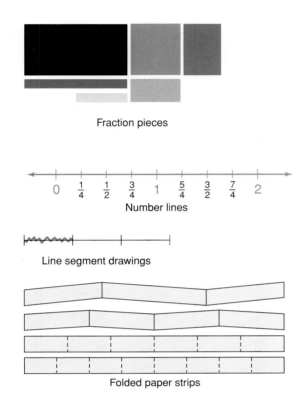

Fraction pieces

Number lines

Line segment drawings

Folded paper strips

FIGURE 12.2 Length or measurement models for fractions.

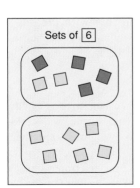

Sets of 6

Two-colour counters in loops drawn on paper.

Shows $1\frac{2}{6}$.

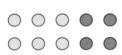

Two-colour counters in arrays. Rows and columns help show parts. Each array makes a whole. Here $\frac{3}{5} = \frac{9}{15}$.

Drawings using Xs and Os.

Shows $\frac{2}{3} = \frac{10}{15}$.

FIGURE 12.3 Set models for fractions.

model various fractional parts of a whole set. Two-sided counters can be purchased, or coloured picture-mount board can be cut into 2-cm squares.

Developing the Concept of Fractional Parts

Fractions are the first phenomenon in children's experiences where a number represents something other than a count. The notion of a fractional part is completely relative to the whole and may be represented in some instances by one piece or object and in others by many pieces or objects. Helping children develop a firm understanding of fractional parts and of all the related nuances is critical if they are to have any number sense with fractions.

Constructing Fractional Parts

The first goal in the development of fractions is to help children construct the idea of *fractional parts of the whole*—the parts that result when the whole has been partitioned into *equal-sized portions* or *fair shares*.

The one idea that young children do bring to the concept of fractions is the notion of partitioning or sharing. Children seem to understand the idea of separating a quantity into two or more parts to be shared among friends. This concept of sharing is therefore a good place to begin the discussion of fractional parts.

Two Requirements for Fractional Parts

In Figure 12.4, some of the regions are divided into fourths, and some are not. (To have fourths, you need four equal parts to make up the whole.) Examine those that are not fourths. Why are they not fourths? Are they cut into *equal* or *fair shares*? (The parts are not fair shares or equal parts.)

For any particular fractional part, children need to reflect on two aspects or components:

1. The whole must be made up of the *correct number* of parts or shares.
2. Each of the parts must be *equal* or *fair shares;* they must be the same size.

The *names* of fractional parts are determined by the number of equal or fair shares making up the whole: *halves,* two equal or fair shares; *thirds,* three equal or fair shares; *fourths,* four equal or fair shares; and so on.

Note that the equal parts need not be the same shape. Congruence is not necessary to have fractional parts. Nor should the concept of "part" be considered a singular entity. The term *share* may be more appropriate. For example, a pizza cut into 12 equal slices can be partitioned into four equal shares or parts. Each share would consist of three

FIGURE 12.4 Find correct examples of fourths. Why are the non-examples wrong?

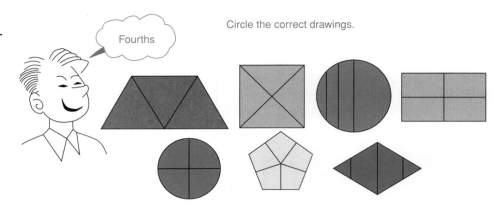

Circle the correct drawings.

Fourths

pieces. The fact that the individual slices are also fractional parts (twelfths) in no way negates the fact that three of them make up one-fourth of the pizza.

We are in the habit of saying "four equal parts" when talking about fourths. The phrase comes out so quickly that the emphasis on the two requirements of four parts and fair shares may be lost.

Children can generalize the notion of fractional parts right from the beginning. Yet a mistake that is frequently made is to assume that halves, thirds, and fourths are somehow easier for children in the early grades than sixths, eighths, or twelfths. Restricting children's learning to one-half, one-third, and one-fourth defeats the development of more general relationships. Once the notion of fractional parts is introduced and fractions other than halves, thirds and fourths are made available, children will have more to explore and discuss.

Activities with Fractional Parts and Fraction Words

Fractional parts should be explored using all available models. The terminology of *the whole* or *one whole* or simply *one* should also be introduced informally at the same time. In all activities, the *fractional words—halves, thirds, fourths, fifths,* and so on—should be used orally and written out. The early emphasis is on the halves, thirds, fourths, fifths and not on one-half, one-third and so on. These fractional parts or equal shares are the nouns, things, or objects of fractions. They are the building blocks of virtually all fraction concepts.

ACTIVITY 12.1

Correct Shares

As in Figure 12.4, show examples and non-examples of specified fractional parts. Have students identify the wholes that are correctly divided into fractional parts as requested, and those that

are not. For each response, have students explain their reasoning. The activity should be done with a variety of models, including length and set models.

The most important part of the "Correct Shares" activity is the discussion of the non-examples. The wholes were already divided, either correctly or incorrectly, and the children were not involved in the partitioning. It is also useful to give children a whole and have them create designated equal shares, as they are asked to do in the next activity.

ACTIVITY 12.2

Finding Fair Shares

Give students models, and have them find fifths or eighths or other fractional parts using the models. (The models should never have the fractions written on them.) The activity is especially interesting when the same fractional parts are represented by different wholes, or the same whole is divided to make different fractional parts. That way, a given fractional part does not get identified with a special shape or colour but with the relationship of the part to the designated whole. Some ideas are suggested in Figure 12.5.

Folding paper is another good way to involve children in the construction of fractional parts. As a paper is folded into halves, then fourths, followed by eighths, students see how the same whole can be divided to make different fractional parts as in Activity 12.2. These fractional parts are also the easiest with which to work because they make successive halves. With some help, children can fold strips into three parts and from these thirds fold sixths.

Having children draw slices to subdivide a circle or even a rectangle is very difficult and is not recommended. Frequently, children will draw four lines in a rectangle to show fourths; then realize they have made five parts. Others will construct three nice equal parts—then the last one is far too large to illustrate fourths. These drawbacks and other difficulties with eye-hand coordination get in the way of concept development. Try to keep the focus on the number and fairness of the shares and less on the ability to draw them.

Notice that children frequently confuse the number of counters in a share with the name of the share when sets are partitioned. In the last example in Figure 12.5, the 12 counters are partitioned into four sets—*fourths.* Each share or part has 3 counters. However, it is the number of shares, not the number of counters in each share that makes the partition show *fourths.*

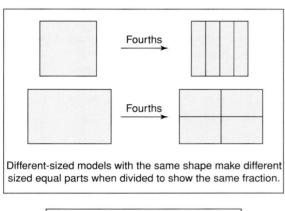

Different-sized models with the same shape make different sized equal parts when divided to show the same fraction.

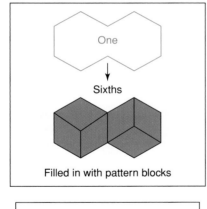

One

↓

Sixths

Filled in with pattern blocks

Fraction Pieces

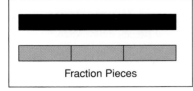

Eighths

Line segments

Fourths

Counters

FIGURE 12.5 **Given a whole, find fractional parts.**

Counting Fractional Parts

Counting fractional parts to see how multiple parts compare to the whole creates a foundation for the two conceptual elements of a fraction. Students should come to think of counting fractional parts in much the same way that they might count apples or any other objects. If you know the kind of part you are counting, you can tell when you get to one, when you get to two, and so on. Students who understand fractional parts should not need to arrange pie pieces into a circle to know that four fourths make a whole.

Counting Fractional Parts

Once students have identified fourths, for example, count fourths. Show five or six fourths on the overhead. "How many fourths? Let's count: *one*-fourth, *two*-fourths, *three*-fourths, *four*-fourths, *five*-fourths, *six*-fourths." Count other collections of fourths. Ask if a collection that has been counted is more or less than a whole or more or less than two wholes. As shown in Figure 12.6, make informal comparisons among different counts. "Why did we get almost two wholes with seven-fourths, and yet we don't even have one whole with seven-twelfths? What is another way we could say seven-thirds?" (Two wholes and one-third or one whole and four-thirds.)

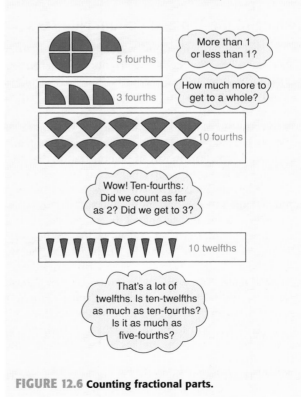

FIGURE 12.6 **Counting fractional parts.**

By counting fractional parts, we can help children develop a completely generalized system for naming fractions before they learn about fractional symbolism. The oral names then can easily be connected to the fractional notation.

Counting fractional parts can lay the groundwork for several important ideas. The idea that eighths are smaller than thirds, for example, is an elusive idea. Counting different-sized parts and discussing how many parts it takes to make one whole is one way to help children begin to reflect on this idea. "Count three-fourths and then count three-twelfths. Which is more? Why?"

Counts should frequently include sets such as 5 thirds or 11 fourths or other sets greater than one whole. When counting reaches one whole (3 thirds or 4 fourths), stop and discuss other names for that amount. Such counts will dispel the notion that a fraction is something less than 1. With older children, counts can also be stopped when equivalent fractions are evident, for example 6 twelfths (1 half) or 9 sixths (1 whole and 1 half). Discussions such as these will serve as useful forerunners for work with equivalent fractions and mixed fractions.

Connecting Concepts with Symbolism

Fractional symbolism should be delayed as long as possible. The first three activities can all be done orally, and written fraction words such as *7 fourths* or *3 eighths* can be used. Eventually, the standard symbolic form must be used.

Meaning of the Top and Bottom Numbers

The way that we write fractions, with a top and a bottom number and a bar between, is a convention—an arbitrary agreement for how to represent fractions. (Remember, always write fractions with a horizontal bar, not a slanted one. Write $\frac{3}{4}$ not 3/4.)

As a convention, it falls into the category of things that you simply tell students. However, a good idea is to make the convention so clear by way of demonstration that students will tell you what the top and bottom numbers stand for. The following procedure will help students develop meaning for the top and bottom numbers of fractions.

Display several collections of fractional parts, and have children count each set and write the count using fractional words such as "3 fourths." Explain that you are going to show how these words can be written more easily. For each collection, write the standard fractional form next to the word. Display some other collections, and ask students if they can tell you how to write the fraction. Talk about the written form using the language already developed while working with the models and when writing the fraction symbols.

Next have children count by fourths as you write the fractions on the board. Repeat for other fractional parts.

$$\frac{1}{4}, \frac{2}{4}, \frac{3}{4}, \frac{4}{4}, \frac{5}{4}, \frac{6}{4}, \frac{7}{4}, \frac{8}{4}, \frac{9}{4}$$

$$\frac{1}{6}, \frac{2}{6}, \frac{3}{6}, \frac{4}{6}, \frac{5}{6}, \frac{6}{6}, \frac{7}{6}, \frac{8}{6}, \frac{9}{6}$$

$$\frac{1}{8}, \frac{2}{8}, \frac{3}{8}, \frac{4}{8}, \frac{5}{8}, \frac{6}{8}, \frac{7}{8}, \frac{8}{8}, \frac{9}{8}$$

Discuss each row. How are the fractions alike? How are they different? What part of each row looks like counting? Why does the bottom number stay the same as you count fourths or sixths or eighths? Finally, ask:

What does the top number in a fraction tell you?

What does the bottom number in a fraction tell you?

Answer those two questions yourself. Think in terms of fractional parts and what we have covered up to this point. Write your explanations for the meanings of the top and bottom numbers using your own words. Explore several ways of saying each. Your meaning should not be tied to a particular model.

Here are some reasonable explanations for the top and bottom numbers.

▪ *Top number:* This part of the fraction is the counting number. It tells how many shares or parts we have. It tells how many have been counted. It tells how many parts we are talking about. It counts the parts or shares.

▪ *Bottom number:* This part of the fraction tells what is being counted. It tells what fractional part is being counted. If it is a 4, it means we are counting *fourths*; if it is a 6, we are counting *sixths*; and so on.

This formulation of the meanings of the top and bottom numbers may seem unusual to you. It is often said that the top number tells "how many" (this phrase seems unfinished) and the bottom tells "how many parts it takes to make a whole." This may be correct but can be misleading. For example, a piece that is $\frac{1}{6}$ in size is often cut from a cake without making any slices in the remaining $\frac{5}{6}$ of the cake. The fact that the cake is only divided into two pieces does not change that the piece taken is $\frac{1}{6}$. If a pizza is cut in 12 pieces, 2 pieces still make $\frac{1}{6}$ of the pizza. In neither of these instances does the bottom number tell how many pieces make a whole.

There is evidence that an iterative notion of fractions, one that views a fraction such as $\frac{3}{4}$ as a count of three things called *fourths*, is an important idea for children to develop (Post, Wachsmuth, Lesh, & Behr, 1985; Tzur, 1999). The iterative concept is most clear when focusing on these two ideas about fraction symbols:

▪ The top number *counts.*

▪ The bottom number tells *what is being counted.*

The *what* of fractions are the fractional parts that can be counted. Fractional symbols are just a shorthand for saying *how many* and *what.*

Numerator and *Denominator*

To count a set is to *enumerate* it. *Enumeration* is the process of counting. The common name for the top number in a fraction is the *numerator.*

A $5 bill, a $10 bill, and a $20 bill are said to be bills of different denominations. Similarly, the word *denomination* is used to differentiate among the ranks of playing cards within a suit, the branches of religions, and so on. A denomination is the name of a class or type of thing. The common name for the bottom number in a fraction is the *denominator.*

Up to this point, the terms *numerator* and *denominator* have not been used, as is the case in much of the remainder of the chapter. Why? No child in grade 3 would mistake the designations *top number* and *bottom number.* However, the words *numerator* and *denominator* have no common reference for children. Using these words will not necessarily help young children understand their meaning.

Mixed Numbers and Improper Fractions

Many children use mindless rules they have been taught while working with mixed numbers and improper fractions that are in fact relatively easy to construct. If you have been counting fractional parts beyond a whole, your students already know how to write $\frac{13}{6}$ or $\frac{11}{3}$. Ask, "What is another way that you could say 13 *sixths?*" Students may suggest "two wholes and one-sixth more," or "two plus one-sixth." Explain that these are correct and that $2 + \frac{1}{6}$ is usually written as $2\frac{1}{6}$ and is called a *mixed number.* You will need to explain to children that this is a symbolism convention. What is not at all necessary is to teach a rule for converting mixed numbers to common fractions (multiply the whole number by the denominator and add the numerator) and the reverse (divide the numerator by the denominator, then write the answer as a whole number and the remainder as a fraction). Rather, consider the following task.

ACTIVITY 12.4

Mixed-Number Names

Give students a mixed number such as $3\frac{2}{3}$. Their task is to find a single fraction that names the same amount. They may use any familiar materials (pattern blocks work well for this activity) or make drawings, but they must be able to give an explanation for their result. Similarly, give students a fraction greater than 1, such as $\frac{17}{6}$, and have them determine the mixed number and provide a justification for their result.

Repeat the "Mixed-Number Names" task several times with different fractions. After a while, challenge students to

figure out the new fraction name without the use of models. A good explanation for $3\frac{1}{4}$ might be that there are 4 fourths in one whole, so there are 8 fourths in two wholes and 12 fourths in three wholes. The extra fourth makes 13 fourths in all, or $\frac{13}{4}$. (Note the iteration concept playing a role.)

There is absolutely no reason ever to provide a rule about multiplying the whole number by the bottom number and adding the top number. Nor should students need a rule about dividing the bottom number into the top to convert fractions to mixed numbers. The materials will help the children "see" the relationship between the mixed numbers and improper fractions. They will not need the rules and will readily develop a complete understanding, in their own words.

ACTIVITY 12.5

Calculator Fraction Counting

Calculators that permit fraction entries and displays are quite common in schools. Texas Instrument's TI-108 (more commonly used for primary-grade children) and TI-15 (more commonly used for junior- and intermediate-grade children) are two excellent examples. The TI-15 can be an effective educational tool for helping children understand fractional symbolism and the relationship between mixed numbers and improper fractions. Counting by fourths, for example, can be done by pressing ⊞ 1, ⧄ 4, ▤. The display will show $\frac{1}{4}$ on the bottom left corner and the symbol above it. Students could have models for fourths to manipulate as they count. When they add successive fourths to the pile, they press ▤ for each piece. At 4 fourths, the calculator shows 1. Continued presses simply add on $\frac{1}{4}$ showing mixed number values. To see the corresponding improper fractions, press the ▣ key. Since the calculator does not reduce the fraction automatically unless set to do so, the count agrees with the physical models.

Calculators with fraction functions, such as the TI-15, provide an exciting and powerful way to help children develop fractional symbolism. A variation on Activity 12.5 is to show children a mixed number such as $3\frac{1}{8}$ and ask how many inputs of $\frac{1}{8}$ on the calculator it will take to count that high. The students should record their count (25) ($\frac{28}{5}$) before pressing ▣ + **1**.

Parts-and-Wholes Tasks

The exercises presented here can help children develop their understanding of fractional parts as well as the meanings of the top and bottom numbers in a fraction. Models are used to represent wholes and parts of wholes. Written or oral fractional names represent the relationship between the parts and their wholes. Given any two of these—whole, part, and fraction—the students can use their models to determine the third.

Any type of model can be used as long as different sizes can represent the whole. For region and area models, it is also necessary that single regions or lengths be used to represent non-unit fractions. Traditional pie-shaped pieces do not work because the whole is always the circle, and all the pieces are *unit fractions*. (A *unit fraction* is a single fractional part. The fractions $\frac{1}{3}$ and $\frac{1}{8}$ are unit fractions.)

Examples of each type of exercise are provided in Figure 12.7, Figure 12.8, and Figure 12.9. Each figure includes examples with a region model (freely drawn rectangles), a length model (fraction pieces), and a set model. It would be a good idea to work through these exercises before reading on. For the rectangular models, simply sketch a similar rectangle on paper. For the length model, use fraction pieces. Lengths are not given in the figures so that you will not be tempted to use an adult-type numerical approach. If you do not have access to the pieces, just draw lines on paper. The questions that ask for the fraction when given the whole and part require much trial and error and can be quite frustrating for young students. Be sure that appropriate fractional parts are available for the region and length versions of these questions.

Two or three challenging parts-and-whole questions in which the tasks are presented in the same format as in Figures 12.7, 12.8, and 12.9 can make for an excellent lesson. Remember that concrete models are often the best way to present the tasks so students can use a trial-and-

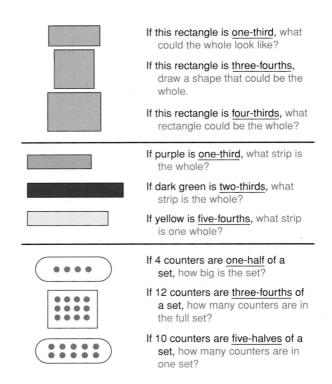

If this rectangle is <u>one-third</u>, what could the whole look like?

If this rectangle is <u>three-fourths</u>, draw a shape that could be the whole.

If this rectangle is <u>four-thirds</u>, what rectangle could be the whole?

If purple is <u>one-third</u>, what strip is the whole?

If dark green is <u>two-thirds</u>, what strip is the whole?

If yellow is <u>five-fourths</u>, what strip is one whole?

If 4 counters are <u>one-half</u> of a set, how big is the set?

If 12 counters are <u>three-fourths</u> of a set, how many counters are in the full set?

If 10 counters are <u>five-halves</u> of a set, how many counters are in one set?

FIGURE 12.8 Given the part and the fraction, find the whole.

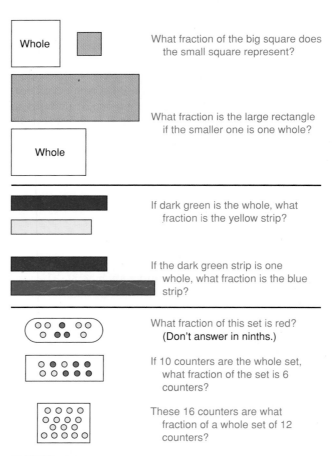

What fraction of the big square does the small square represent?

What fraction is the large rectangle if the smaller one is one whole?

If dark green is the whole, what fraction is the yellow strip?

If the dark green strip is one whole, what fraction is the blue strip?

What fraction of this set is red? (Don't answer in ninths.)

If 10 counters are the whole set, what fraction of the set is 6 counters?

These 16 counters are what fraction of a whole set of 12 counters?

FIGURE 12.9 Given the whole and the part, find the fraction.

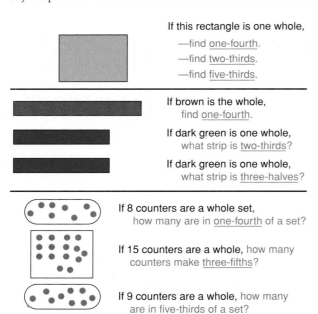

If this rectangle is one whole,
—find <u>one-fourth</u>.
—find <u>two-thirds</u>.
—find <u>five-thirds</u>.

If brown is the whole, find <u>one-fourth</u>.

If dark green is one whole, what strip is <u>two-thirds</u>?

If dark green is one whole, what strip is <u>three-halves</u>?

If 8 counters are a whole set, how many are in <u>one-fourth</u> of a set?

If 15 counters are a whole, how many counters make <u>three-fifths</u>?

If 9 counters are a whole, how many are in <u>five-thirds</u> of a set?

FIGURE 12.7 Given the whole and the fraction, find the part.

error approach to determine their results. As with all tasks, it should be clear that an explanation is required to justify each answer. For each task, let several students supply answers and explanations.

Sometimes it is a good idea to create simple story problems that ask the same questions.

Mr. Samuels has finished $\frac{3}{4}$ of his patio. It looks like this:

Draw a picture that might be the shape of the finished patio.

The problems can also involve numbers instead of models:

If the swimming team sold 400 raffle tickets, it would have enough money to pay for new team shirts. So far the swimmers have $\frac{5}{8}$ of the necessary raffle tickets sold. How many more tickets do they need to sell?

In the second problem, the number 400 is easily divisible by 8. If the total or whole had been given as 500, for example, you could ask "about" how many more tickets are necessary. The first problem asks for the whole, given the part and fraction. The second problem asks for the part, given the whole and fraction. Make up a story problem where the whole and part are given and students are asked for the fraction.

With some models, it is necessary to be certain that the answer exists within the model. For example, if you were using fraction pieces, you could ask, "If the blue piece (9) is the whole, what piece is two-thirds?" The answer is the 6 or dark green piece. You could not ask students to find "three-fourths of the blue piece" because each fourth of 9 would be $2\frac{1}{4}$ units, and no piece has that length. Similar caution must be taken with rectangular pieces.

Questions involving unit fractions are generally the easiest. The hardest questions usually involve fractions greater than 1. For example, "If 15 chips are five-thirds of one whole set, how many chips are in a whole?" However, in every question, the unit fraction plays a significant role. If you have $\frac{5}{3}$ and want the whole, you first need to find $\frac{1}{3}$.

Avoid being the answer book for your students. Empower students by making them responsible for determining the validity of their own answers. In these exercises, the results can always be confirmed by what is given. Students will learn that they can understand these ideas, and that there are no obscure rules. Everything makes sense!

Fraction Number Sense

The focus on fractional parts is an important beginning in developing students' number sense because it helps them reflect on the meaning of the part-to-whole relationship and the corresponding top and bottom numbers. But number sense with fractions demands more—it requires that students have some intuitive feel for fractions. They should know "about" how big a particular fraction is and be able to tell easily which of two fractions is larger. These ideas require building further on the relationships already discussed.

Flexibility with Fractional Parts

Since children have a tremendously strong mindset about numbers, they tend to have difficulties with the relative sizes of fractions. In their experience, larger numbers mean "more" and the tendency is to transfer this whole-number concept to fractions: Seven is more than four, so sevenths should be bigger than fourths (Mack, 1995). The inverse relationship between the number of parts and the size of the parts cannot be told to students. It must be a creation of each student's own thought process.

ACTIVITY 12.6

Ordering Unit Fractions

List a set of unit fractions such as $\frac{1}{3}$, $\frac{1}{8}$, $\frac{1}{5}$, and $\frac{1}{10}$. Ask children to put the fractions in order from least to greatest. Challenge children to defend the way they ordered the fractions. The first few times you do this activity, have them explain their ideas using models. Encourage the language of sharing—the more shares in one whole, the smaller each share will be.

This idea is so basic to the understanding of fractions that arbitrary rules—"the larger the bottom number (the denominator), the smaller the fraction"—are not only inappropriate, they are also dangerous. Come back to this basic idea periodically. Children will seem to understand one day and then revert to their more comfortable ideas about big numbers a day or two later.

Another way to help students think about fractional parts in a flexible manner is to consider the way we help younger children think about small whole numbers: Take them apart.

ACTIVITY 12.7

Taking Fractions Apart

Assign a fraction to work with. For example, consider $1\frac{1}{4}$. The task is to find ways to write the

fraction in terms of two parts. $1\frac{1}{4}$ is clearly 1 and $\frac{1}{4}$. But what are some other ways to think about this fraction in two parts? Have children make lists and see what they can find out. You will probably want to let them use a physical model, perhaps one of their own choosing. Or you may suggest that they do the activity without a model as a means of stretching themselves.

How children approach Activity 12.7 will vary a lot with age and experience. The activity could be done at any grade from 3 to 8. Consider just a few possibilities for $1\frac{1}{4}$:

All ways using fourths: $\frac{1}{4}$ and $\frac{4}{4}$, $\frac{2}{4}$ and $\frac{3}{4}$,...

All ways using another denominator: $\frac{1}{8}$ and $\frac{9}{8}$, $\frac{2}{8}$ and $\frac{8}{8}$, $\frac{3}{8}$ and $\frac{7}{8}$,...

Using two or more different fractions: $\frac{1}{2}$ and $\frac{3}{4}$, $\frac{1}{3}$ and $\frac{2}{3}$ and $\frac{1}{4}$, or $\frac{1}{3}$ and $\frac{11}{12}$

Thinking in terms of money or decimals: 75 cents and 50 cents, 0.8 and 0.45

With this activity there is ample opportunity to develop patterns and relationships among fractions. As a variation, you could supply one part and ask children for one or more ways to determine what the other part is. Children will not necessarily think about this as subtraction; they will use their own concepts and ideas to come up with solutions. This activity serves as a good assessment of how children are thinking about fractions.

Benchmarks of Zero, One-Half, and One

The most important reference points or benchmarks for fractions are 0, $\frac{1}{2}$, and 1. For fractions less than 1, a simple comparison to these three numbers gives quite a lot of information. For example, $\frac{1}{8}$ is small, close to 0, whereas $\frac{3}{4}$ is between $\frac{1}{2}$ and 1. The fraction $\frac{9}{10}$ is quite close to 1. Since any fraction greater than 1 is a whole number plus an amount less than 1, the same reference points are just as helpful: $3\frac{3}{7}$ is almost $3\frac{1}{2}$.

ACTIVITY 12.8

Zero, One-Half, or One

On the board or overhead, write a collection of 10 to 15 fractions. A few should be greater than 1 ($\frac{9}{8}$ or $\frac{11}{10}$), with the others ranging from 0 to 1. Let students sort the fractions into three groups: those close to 0, close to $\frac{1}{2}$, and close to 1. For the group close to $\frac{1}{2}$, have the students decide if each fraction is more or less than $\frac{1}{2}$. The difficul-

ty of this task depends largely on the fractions selected. The first time you try doing this activity, use fractions that are very close to the three benchmarks, such as $\frac{1}{20}$, $\frac{53}{100}$, or $\frac{9}{10}$. On subsequent days, use fractions with most of the denominators less than 20. You might include one or two fractions, such as $\frac{2}{8}$ or $\frac{3}{4}$, that are exactly in between the benchmarks. As usual, have students provide explanations for their choice for each fraction.

The next activity is also aimed at developing the same three reference points for fractions. In "Close Fractions," however, the students must come up with the fractions rather than sort them.

ACTIVITY 12.9

Close Fractions

Have your students name a fraction that is close to 1 but not more than 1. Next have them name another fraction that is even closer to 1. Then have them explain why they believe their second choice is closer to 1 than their previous one. Continue in the same manner for several fractions, each one being closer to 1 than the preceding fraction. Similarly, try the activity using close to 0 or close to $\frac{1}{2}$ (either under or over). The first several times you do this activity, let the students use models to help with their thinking. Later, see how well their explanations work when they cannot use models or drawings. Focus discussions on the relative size of fractional parts.

Understanding why a fraction is close to 0, $\frac{1}{2}$, or 1 is a good beginning for developing number sense with fractions. It draws attention to the size of fractions in an important yet simple manner. The next activity also helps students reflect on fraction size.

ACTIVITY 12.10

About How Much?

Draw a picture like one of those in Figure 12.10 (or prepare some ahead of time for the overhead). Have each student write down a fraction that he or she thinks is a good estimate of the amount shown (or the indicated mark on the number line). Listen without judgment to the ideas of several students, and discuss with them why any particular estimate might be a good one.

There is no single correct answer, but estimates should be "in the ballpark." If children have difficulty coming up with an estimate, ask if they think the amount is closer to $0, \frac{1}{2}$, or 1.

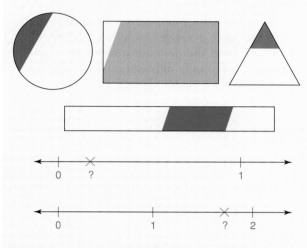

FIGURE 12.10 **About how much? Name a fraction for each drawing, and explain why you chose that fraction.**

Thinking about Which Is More

The ability to tell which of two fractions is greater is another aspect of number sense with fractions. This ability is built around a conceptual understanding of fractions, not on an algorithmic skill or on symbolic tricks.

Concepts, Not Rules

You have probably learned rules or algorithms for comparing two fractions. The usual approaches are finding common denominators and using cross-multiplication. These rules can be effective in getting correct answers but require no thought about the size of the fractions. This is especially true of the cross-multiplication procedure. If children are taught these rules before they have had the opportunity to think about the relative size of various fractions, there is little chance that they will develop any familiarity with, or number sense about, the size of fractions. Comparison activities (Which fraction is more?) can play a significant role in helping children develop concepts about the relative size of fractions. But keep in mind that reflective thought is the goal, not an algorithmic method of choosing the correct answer.

Before reading further, try the following exercise. Assume for a moment that you know nothing about equivalent fractions or common denominators or cross-multiplication. Assume that you are a grade 4 or grade 5 student who was never taught these procedures. Now examine the pairs of fractions in Figure 12.11 and select from each the fraction that is larger. Write down or explain in each case one or more reasons for your choice.

Which fraction in each pair is greater?
Give one or more reasons. Try not to use drawings or models.
Do not use common denominators or cross-multiplication.
Rely on concepts.

A. $\frac{4}{5}$ or $\frac{4}{9}$ G. $\frac{7}{12}$ or $\frac{5}{12}$

B. $\frac{4}{7}$ or $\frac{5}{7}$ H. $\frac{3}{5}$ or $\frac{3}{7}$

C. $\frac{3}{8}$ or $\frac{4}{10}$ I. $\frac{5}{8}$ or $\frac{6}{10}$

D. $\frac{5}{3}$ or $\frac{5}{8}$ J. $\frac{9}{8}$ or $\frac{4}{3}$

E. $\frac{3}{4}$ or $\frac{9}{10}$ K. $\frac{4}{6}$ or $\frac{7}{12}$

F. $\frac{3}{8}$ or $\frac{4}{7}$ L. $\frac{8}{9}$ or $\frac{7}{8}$

FIGURE 12.11 **Comparing fractions using concepts.**

Conceptual Thought Patterns for Comparison

The first two comparison schemes listed here rely on the meanings of the top and bottom numbers in fractions and on the relative sizes of unit fractional parts. The third and fourth use the additional ideas of $0, \frac{1}{2}$, and 1 as convenient anchors or benchmarks for thinking about the size of fractions.

1. *More of the same-size parts.* To compare $\frac{3}{8}$ and $\frac{5}{8}$, it is easy to think about having 3 of something and also 5 of the same thing. When the fractions are given orally, the comparison is almost trivial. When given in written form, it is possible for children to choose $\frac{5}{8}$ as larger simply because 5 is more than 3 and the bottom numbers are the same; right choice, wrong reason. Comparing $\frac{3}{8}$ and $\frac{5}{8}$ should be like comparing 3 apples and 5 apples.

2. *Same number of parts, but parts are different in size.* Consider the case of $\frac{3}{4}$ and $\frac{3}{7}$. If a whole is divided into 7 equal parts, the parts will certainly be smaller than if divided into only 4 equal parts. Many children will select $\frac{3}{7}$ as larger because 7 is more than 4 and the top numbers (the numerators) are the same. This approach yields correct choices when the equal parts (the denominators) are the same size, but in this case it causes problems. It is like comparing 3 apples with 3 melons. You have the same number of things, but melons are larger.

3. *More and less than one-half or one whole.* The fractional pairs $\frac{3}{7}$ versus $\frac{5}{8}$ and $\frac{5}{4}$ versus $\frac{7}{8}$ do not lend themselves to either of the previous thought processes. In the first pair, $\frac{3}{7}$ is less than half of the number of sevenths needed to make a whole, and so $\frac{3}{7}$ is less than a half. Similarly, $\frac{5}{8}$ is more than a half. Therefore, $\frac{5}{8}$ is the larger fraction. The second pair is

determined by noting that one fraction is less than 1 and the other is greater than 1. The benchmark numbers of $\frac{1}{2}$ and 1 are useful when making judgments about size.

4. *Distance from one-half or one whole.* Why is $\frac{9}{10}$ greater than $\frac{3}{4}$? Not because the 9 and 10 are big numbers, although you will find that to be a common student response. Each is one fractional part away from one whole, and tenths are smaller than fourths. Similarly, notice that $\frac{5}{8}$ is smaller than $\frac{4}{6}$ because it is only one-eighth more than a half, while $\frac{4}{6}$ is a sixth more than a half. Can you use this basic idea to compare $\frac{3}{5}$ and $\frac{5}{9}$? (*Hint:* Each fraction is half of a fractional part more than $\frac{1}{2}$.)

How did your reasons for choosing fractions in Figure 12.11 compare to these ideas?

Classroom activities should help children develop informal ideas like those just explained for comparing fractions. However, the ideas should come from student experiences and discussions. To teach "the four ways to compare fractions" would be nearly as self-defeating as teaching cross-multiplication.

ACTIVITY 12.11

Compare and Test

Provide students with a familiar fraction model. Present a pair of fractions for comparison. (They should be fractions that can be illustrated with the model.) Have the students think about which is more (compare), write down their choice, and then test their selection with the models. Be sure they make a commitment first, before they use the models.

When students begin to do well with the "Compare and Test" activity, see if they can give reasons without the use of models. Be sure you include fractional pairs that cover all of the possibilities discussed earlier.

ACTIVITY 12.12

Why Is It More?

Give students a pair of fractions to compare. The task is to find as many good explanations for their choice as possible. Explanations should be written down and then discussed as a full class. The same exercise is a very good homework assignment and is also a good assessment activity.

ACTIVITY 12.13

Line 'Em Up

Have students put four or five fractions in order from least to greatest. In this way, a variety of methods for making comparisons can be included in the same exercise. As with all conceptual activities, limit the denominators to reasonable numbers. It is rarely necessary to consider fractions with denominators greater than 12.

A word of caution is needed when approaching the following situation. Krishana is offered the choice of a third of a pizza or a half of a pizza. Since she is hungry and likes pizza, she chooses the half. Her friend, Yonette, gets a third of a pizza but ends up with more than Krishana. How can that be? Figure 12.12 illustrates how Krishana erred in her choice. The point of the "pizza fallacy" is that whenever two or more fractions are discussed in the same context, the assumption (such as the one Krishana made in choosing a half of the pizza) is that the fractions being compared are all parts of the same whole.

Comparisons with any model can be made only if both fractions are parts of the same whole. For example, $\frac{2}{3}$ of a light green strip cannot be compared to $\frac{2}{3}$ of an orange strip if the strips represent different-sized wholes.

Other Methods of Comparison

Conceptual approaches, already discussed, cannot always be relied on for comparing fractions. Most adults would be hard-pressed to compare $\frac{2}{3}$ and $\frac{3}{5}$ without some other methods.

When simple logical methods do not work, more sophisticated and usually more complex methods are required. The most common approach is to convert a fraction to another form. When knowledge of equivalent fractions is well developed, one or both of the fractions can be rewritten so that they have the same denominator. Although finding a common denominator is the method most often taught, why not use finding a common numerator? Another way is to translate the fraction to a different

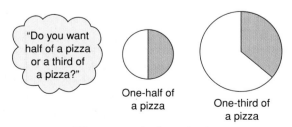

FIGURE 12.12 The "pizza fallacy."

notation—decimals or percentages. Many decimal and percentage equivalents can and should become second nature and require no computation.

With good fractional concept development, you can easily argue that there is never a need to teach an algorithm for comparing two fractions. Repeated application of rules hampers students from thinking about the size of fractions. When students have a good understanding of equivalent fractions and their equivalent decimal and percent representations, they will have plenty of meaningful tools to compare fractions. Marilyn Burns (1999) tells of grade 5 students comparing $\frac{6}{8}$ to $\frac{4}{5}$. One child changed the $\frac{4}{5}$ to $\frac{8}{10}$ so that both fractions would be two parts away from a whole. Since tenths are smaller than eighths, he concluded that $\frac{4}{5}$ was larger. Another child used common numerators. When percentages are connected to fractions, these two fractions might quickly be seen as 75 percent and 80 percent and compared that way.

Remember, restrict comparison exercises with fractions to denominators of 12 or less.

 Technology Note

Math Trek 4, 5, 6 (Nectar Foundation, 2000) is Canadian software that offers a range of challenges for the development of fractions. *In Search of Reptiles*, one of the interactive activities in the Number Sense and Numeration component, offers students an opportunity to apply their knowledge of fractions. There are four levels of difficulty from which students may choose to work as they order and compare simple fractions, mixed numbers, and improper fractions. Tasks are designed so that students work at a symbolic level without the aid of visual representations.

In the *Math Trek* tutorials, ideas and concepts about fractions are presented using a variety of models. Students are able to work independently through a series of tasks to reinforce learning. Using a pizza model, students explore fractions by slicing the whole into equal parts. Strip models are employed for comparing unit fractions, and sets models for introducing improper fractions.

The *Mathville* series (Courseware Solutions, 2000) is also Canadian software that provides students with an opportunity to engage in activities to reinforce their knowledge of fractions. Activities, which are presented in a visually appealing context at levels as early as grade 2 (*Mathville Jungleway*), are fast-paced, highly motivating, and creative, allowing students to work in a non-linear, non-hierarchical manner. However, this environment can also be quite challenging for those students who require the benefit of the models discussed earlier.

Representing Fractions (Tenth Planet, 1998d) is software that offers a range of challenges for fraction development. In two of the four activities, students build given fractions using models of unit fractions. Though not open-ended, these activities may reinforce the iterative concept of fractions. The computer orally counts to the fraction target when a solution is offered: "One-fourth, two-fourths, three-fourths." Another task area requires students to build a whole based on a given fractional part. This activity is similar to building a whole with fraction strips, given the fraction and the part as described earlier in this chapter. "Open-Ended Build and Play" is a component of *Representing Fractions* in which the user can slice up squares, circles, or triangles by connecting equally spaced dots on the edges. Parts can then be cut into even smaller pieces. The individual pieces can be painted different colours and dragged to any part of the screen. This open-ended model provides teachers or students with a tool that is more flexible than any physical model. Note that this is a pure model or tool. No fraction symbols are provided, nor are any problems posed. The computer does no evaluation. The teacher can pose tasks and let students use the program to work on solutions. Alternatively, students can devise their own challenges for each other using the drawing tool. As with all Tenth Planet activities, a journal permits students to copy a picture of their work, write about it, and even record a short message.

Fizz & Martina's Math Adventures: Lights, Camera, Fractions (Tom Snyder Productions, 1998) is software supposedly designed for grades 5 and 6. However, the concepts and presentation are closer to grade 4. Fraction problems are embedded in an elaborate cartoon video involving Fizz and Martina. The software is designed to be shown to a full class and stopped at appropriate times to let students work in groups to solve the problem and write on the journal sheets provided. Multiple-solution strategies are encouraged. The problems are good, but the story line is a bit corny and very time-intensive. Most tasks involve finding fractional parts of amounts ($\frac{1}{4}$ of 120 words, $\frac{2}{3}$ of $180). The ideas and the support material are good, and the program is designed in the same spirit as the three-part lesson format described in this text. Since each episode involves only a few problems, the program is somewhat limited in its use. ■■

Estimation

A frequently quoted result from the Second National Assessment (Post, 1981) concerns the following item:

Estimate the answer to $\frac{12}{13} + \frac{7}{8}$. You will not have time to solve the problem using paper and pencil.

Here is how 13-year-olds answered:

Response	Percentage of 13-Year-Olds
1	7
2	24
19	28
21	27
Don't know	14

This result vividly demonstrates that a good understanding of fractions is more significant for estimation purposes than mastery of the pencil-and-paper procedures. Knowing if a fraction is closer to 0, $\frac{1}{2}$, or 1 proves useful. Numbers can be rounded to the nearest whole or nearest half and then added easily. For example, $2\frac{1}{8} + \frac{4}{9}$ is about the same as $2 + \frac{1}{2}$. A front-end approach is also possible: Deal with the whole numbers, then look at the fractions, using estimates to the nearest half to make an adjustment. The following activities are useful for developing these ideas for estimating with fractions.

ACTIVITY 12.14

Pick the Best

Flash sums or differences of proper fractions. Response options can vary with the age and experience of the students. One possibility is more than 1 or less than 1. Closer to 0, 1, or 2 is also an easy option. A more sophisticated option is for students to give the result to the nearest half: 0, $\frac{1}{2}$, 1, $1\frac{1}{2}$, or 2.

ACTIVITY 12.15

Speed Estimates

Provide short speed drills for estimating sums and differences with mixed numbers, as illustrated in Figure 12.13.

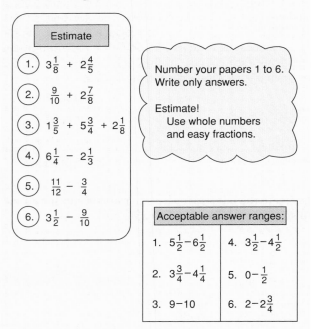

Estimate

1. $3\frac{1}{8} + 2\frac{4}{5}$
2. $\frac{9}{10} + 2\frac{7}{8}$
3. $1\frac{3}{5} + 5\frac{3}{4} + 2\frac{1}{8}$
4. $6\frac{1}{4} - 2\frac{1}{3}$
5. $\frac{11}{12} - \frac{3}{4}$
6. $3\frac{1}{2} - \frac{9}{10}$

Number your papers 1 to 6. Write only answers.

Estimate!
    Use whole numbers
    and easy fractions.

Acceptable answer ranges:	
1. $5\frac{1}{2} - 6\frac{1}{2}$	4. $3\frac{1}{2} - 4\frac{1}{2}$
2. $3\frac{3}{4} - 4\frac{1}{4}$	5. $0 - \frac{1}{2}$
3. $9 - 10$	6. $2 - 2\frac{3}{4}$

FIGURE 12.13 Fraction estimation drill.

When more than two addends are involved, an acceptable range may be a bit wider. Encourage students to give whole-number estimates at first; later, practise refining estimates to the nearest half. Discuss both front-end and rounding techniques.

Equivalent-Fraction Concepts

How do you know that $\frac{4}{6} = \frac{2}{3}$? Before reading further, think of at least two different explanations.

Concepts versus Rules

Here are some possible answers to the question just posed:

1. They are the same because you can reduce $\frac{4}{6}$ and get $\frac{2}{3}$.
2. If you have a set of 6 things and you take 4 of them, it would be $\frac{4}{6}$. But you can make the 6 into groups of 2. Then there would be 3 groups, and the 4 would be 2 groups out of the 3 groups, which means it's $\frac{2}{3}$.

3. If you start with $\frac{2}{3}$, you can multiply the top and the bottom numbers by 2, which will give you $\frac{4}{6}$, so they are equal.
4. If you cut a square into 3 parts and you shaded 2 parts, it would be $\frac{2}{3}$ shaded. If you cut all 3 of these parts in half, it would be 4 parts shaded and 6 parts in all. That's $\frac{4}{6}$, and it would be the same amount.

These answers, which are all correct, exemplify the distinction between conceptual and procedural knowledge. Responses 2 and 4 are conceptual in their explanation, though not efficient. Responses 1 and 3 are quite efficient but indicate no conceptual knowledge. All students should eventually know how to write an equivalent fraction for a given fraction. At the same time, the rules should never be taught or used until the students understand what the result means.

Concept: Two fractions are equivalent if they are representations for the same amount or quantity—if they represent the same number.

Rule: To make an equivalent fraction, multiply (or divide) the top and bottom numbers by the same non-zero number.

The rule or algorithm for equivalent fractions has no intuitive connection with the concept. As a result, students can easily learn and use the rule in exercises such as "List the first four equivalent fractions for $\frac{3}{5}$" without any idea of how the fractions in the list are related. It becomes an exercise in multiplication. A developmental approach suggests that students should be led to see that the algorithm is a meaningful and efficient way to find equivalent fractions.

Finding Different Names for Fractions

The general approach to helping students create a conceptual understanding of equivalent fractions is to have them use a variety of models to generate different names for fractions. Consider that this is the first time in their experience that a fixed quantity can have multiple names (actually an infinite number).

Area or Region Models

Examples of equivalent fraction representations using area models are illustrated in Figure 12.14.

ACTIVITY 12.16

Different Fillers

Using the area models that students have, draw the outline of several fractions on paper, and duplicate them. For example, if the model is rectangles, you might draw an outline (no subdivisions) of a rectangle for $\frac{2}{3}$, $\frac{1}{2}$, and perhaps $\frac{5}{4}$. Have children try to fill in the outlines with various unit fraction pieces to determine as many simple fractional names as possible for the regions. In class discussion, see if students can go beyond the actual models they have. For example, if the model has no tenths, it would be interesting to ask what other names could be generated if tenths were available. An easier question involves pieces that can be derived from existing pieces. "You found out that $\frac{5}{4}$ and $\frac{10}{8}$ and $\frac{15}{12}$ are all the same. What if we had some sixteenths pieces? Could we cover this same region with those? How many? How can you decide?"

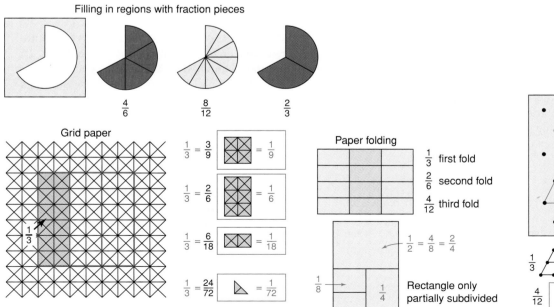

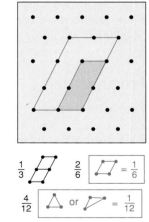

FIGURE 12.14 Area models for equivalent fractions.

ACTIVITY 12.17

Folding and Refolding

Paper folding effectively models the equivalent fraction concept. Have students fold a sheet of paper into halves or thirds. Unfold and colour a fraction of the paper. Write the fraction. Now refold and add one more fold. Before opening, it is fun to discuss with the students how many sections will be in the whole sheet and how many of them will be coloured. Then, open and discuss what fractional names can now be given to the shaded region. Is it still the same? Why? Repeat until the paper cannot be folded any more.

ACTIVITY 12.18

Dot Paper Equivalencies

Use grid paper or dot paper so that regions can easily be subdivided into many smaller parts. Have students draw a model for a whole, then shade in part to show a fraction that can be determined by using the lines or dots on the paper. Now see how many different names for the shaded part they can find with the aid of the smaller regions in the drawing (see Figure 12.14). Have a transparency of a grid or dot pattern so you can do this exercise with the full class. Teams or individuals can take turns explaining different names for the shaded part.

Although subdivided regions illustrate why there are multiple names for one fractional part, students should be aware that these subdivisions are not required. Half of a rectangle is still $\frac{2}{4}$, even if no subdivisions are present and even if the other half is divided into three parts. Work toward this understanding by drawing models for fractions, then erasing the subdivision lines. "Is this $\frac{2}{3}$ still $\frac{4}{6}$?"

Length Models

Equivalent fractions are modelled with length models in much the same way as area models. One fraction is modelled; then different lengths are used to determine other names for the fraction. Some examples are shown in Figure 12.15.

Set Models

The general concept of equivalent fractions is the same with set models as with length and area models, although

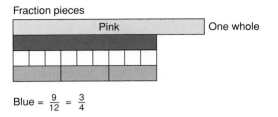

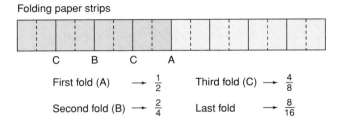

Blue $= \frac{9}{12} = \frac{3}{4}$

Folding paper strips

	C	B	C	A

First fold (A) $\longrightarrow \frac{1}{2}$ Third fold (C) $\longrightarrow \frac{4}{8}$

Second fold (B) $\longrightarrow \frac{2}{4}$ Last fold $\longrightarrow \frac{8}{16}$

FIGURE 12.15 Length models for equivalent fractions.

there are more limitations to how a particular set can be partitioned. For example, if $\frac{2}{3}$ is modelled with 8 out of 12 counters, that particular representation can also be seen as $\frac{4}{6}$ and $\frac{8}{12}$ but not as $\frac{6}{9}$ or $\frac{10}{15}$. As shown in Figure 12.16, a given number of counters in two colours can be arranged in different subgroups to illustrate equivalent fractions.

ACTIVITY 12.19

Group the Counters, Find the Names

Have students set out a specific number of counters in two colours—for example 24 counters, 16 of them red and 8 yellow. These 24 counters represent the whole. The task is to have students arrange them into different subgroups according to colour and find as many fractional names as they can for each subgroup. For example, the 16 red counters can be arranged into 4 rows of 4 ($\frac{4}{6}$) and the 8 yellow counters can be arranged into 2 rows of 4 ($\frac{2}{6}$). This would make $\frac{4}{6}$ and $\frac{2}{6}$. Students should record the different groupings and explain how they found the fractional names. Xs and Os can be used to represent the counters.

In the activities so far, there has only been a hint of a rule for finding equivalent fractions. The following activity moves a bit closer but should be done before development of a rule.

ACTIVITY 12.20

Missing-Number Equivalencies

Give students an equation expressing equivalence between two fractions. Leave out one of the numbers. Here are four different examples:

$$\frac{5}{3} = \frac{\square}{6} \qquad \frac{2}{3} = \frac{6}{\square} \qquad \frac{8}{12} = \frac{\square}{3} \qquad \frac{12}{8} = \frac{3}{\square}$$

The missing number can be either a numerator or a denominator. Furthermore, the missing number can be either larger or smaller than the corresponding part of the equivalent fraction. (All four of these possibilities are represented in the examples.) The task is to find the missing number and to explain your solution.

When doing "Missing-Number Equivalencies" you may want to specify a particular model, such as sets or pie pieces. Alternatively, you can allow students to select whatever methods they wish to solve these problems. One or two equivalencies followed by a discussion is sufficient for a good lesson. This activity is surprisingly challenging, especially if students are required to use a set model.

Before continuing with development of an algorithm for equivalent fractions with your class, you should revisit the comparison tasks, as children begin to realize that they can change the names of fractions in order to help reason about which fraction is greater.

Developing an Equivalent-Fraction Algorithm

Kamii and Clark (1995) argue that undue reliance on physical models does not help children construct equivalence schemes. When children eventually understand that fractions can have different names, they should be challenged to develop a method for finding equivalent names. It might also be argued that students who are experienced at looking for patterns and developing schemes for doing things can invent an algorithm for equivalent fractions without further assistance. However, the following approach will certainly improve the chances of that happening.

An Area-Model Approach

Your goal is to help students see that if they multiply both the top and the bottom numbers of a fraction by the same given number, they will always get an equivalent fraction. The approach suggested here is to look for a pattern in the

FIGURE 12.16 Set models for equivalent fractions.

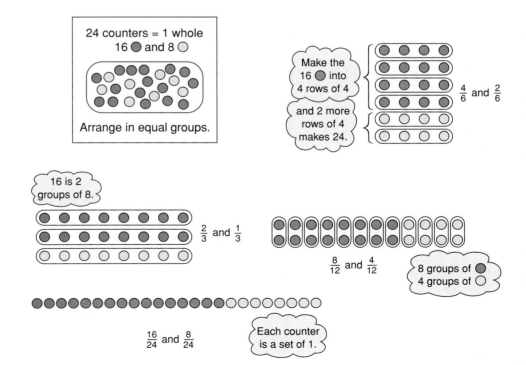

way that the fractional parts in both the part and the whole are counted. Activity 12.21 is a good beginning, but a good class discussion following the activity is required.

Slicing Squares

Give students a worksheet with four squares, each about 3 cm on each side. Have them shade in the same fraction in each square using vertical subdividing lines. For example, slice each square into fourths and shade in three fourths as in Figure 12.17. Next tell students to slice each square into an equal number of horizontal slices. Each square is divided vertically into a different number of slices, anywhere from one to eight. An equation showing the equivalent fraction that represents it should be written for each square. Then have the students examine the four equations and the accompanying drawings. Challenge them to discover any patterns in what they have done. You may want them to repeat this activity with four more squares and a different fraction.

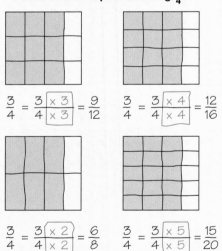

Start with each square showing $\frac{3}{4}$.

$$\frac{3}{4} = \frac{3 \times 3}{4 \times 3} = \frac{9}{12} \qquad \frac{3}{4} = \frac{3 \times 4}{4 \times 4} = \frac{12}{16}$$

$$\frac{3}{4} = \frac{3 \times 2}{4 \times 2} = \frac{6}{8} \qquad \frac{3}{4} = \frac{3 \times 5}{4 \times 5} = \frac{15}{20}$$

What <u>fraction</u> tells how many parts are shaded?

What <u>fraction</u> tells how many parts in the whole?

Notice that the same factor is used for both part and whole.

FIGURE 12.17 A model for the equivalent-fraction algorithm.

Examine examples of equivalent fractions that have been generated with other models, and see if the rule of multiplying the top and the bottom numbers by the same number holds there also. If the rule is correct, how can $\frac{6}{8}$ and $\frac{9}{12}$ be equivalent? What about fractions like $2\frac{1}{4}$? How could it be demonstrated that $\frac{9}{4}$ is the same as $\frac{27}{12}$?

Writing Fractions in Simplest Terms

The multiplication scheme for equivalent fractions produces fractions with larger denominators. To write a fraction in *simplest terms* means to write it so that both numerator and denominator have no common whole number factors, other than one. (Some texts use the name *lowest terms* instead of *simplest terms*.) One meaningful approach to this task of finding simplest terms is to reverse the earlier process, as illustrated in Figure 12.18. Try to devise a problematic task that will help students develop this reverse idea.

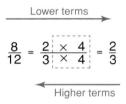

Lower terms ⟶

$$\frac{8}{12} = \frac{2 \times 4}{3 \times 4} = \frac{2}{3}$$

⟵ Higher terms

FIGURE 12.18 Using the equivalent-fraction algorithm to write fractions in simplest terms.

Of course, finding and eliminating a common factor of the numerator and denominator is the same as dividing both top and bottom by the same number. The search for a common factor keeps the process of writing an equivalent fraction to one rule: Multiply the top and bottom numbers of a fraction by the same non-zero number. There is no need for a different rule for rewriting fractions in lowest terms.

Two additional notes:

1. Notice that the phrase "reducing fractions" was not used. This unfortunate terminology implies making a fraction smaller and is not often used anymore in textbooks.

2. Many teachers seem to believe that answers to a fraction problem are incorrect if they are not in simplest or lowest terms. This belief is also unfortunate. When students add $\frac{1}{6} + \frac{1}{2}$ and get $\frac{4}{6}$, they have added correctly and have found the answer. Having students rewrite $\frac{4}{6}$ as $\frac{2}{3}$ is a separate issue.

Multiplying by One

Many middle-school textbooks use a strictly symbolic approach to equivalent fractions. It is based on the multiplication identity property of rational numbers that says that any number multiplied by 1 remains unchanged. Any fraction of the form *n/n* can be used as the identity element. Therefore, $\frac{3}{4} = \frac{3}{4} \times 1 = \frac{3}{4} \times \frac{2}{2} = \frac{6}{8}$. Furthermore, the numerator and denominator of the identity element can also be fractions. In this way, $\frac{6}{12} = \frac{6}{12} \times (\frac{1/6}{1/6}) = \frac{1}{2}$.

This explanation relies on an understanding of the multiplicative identity property, which most students in grades 4 to 6 do not fully appreciate. It also relies on the procedure for multiplying two fractions. Finally, the argument uses solely deductive reasoning based on an axiom of the rational number system. It does not lend itself to intuitive modelling. A reasonable conclusion is to delay this important explanation until at least grade 7 or 8 in an appropriate pre-algebra context, and avoid using it as a method or a rationale for producing equivalent fractions.

 ## Technology Note

Math Trek (Nectar Foundation, 2000) tutorials offer students an opportunity to reinforce learning about equivalent fractions and related concepts. Models, such as pizza pies, rectangles, and circles, are used effectively but terms such as reducing fractions do appear. There also seems to be an emphasis on employing the multiplication and division rule for making fractions equivalent rather than on promoting the development of understanding. In the tutorials for the upper elementary grades, cross-multiplication is also employed as a strategy for making fractions equivalent.

Much of the American computer software seems to be better at providing a high-tech model to illustrate equivalent fractions than it does at creating a problem-solving mode where students can think through an equivalent fraction task.

MathKeys: Unlocking Fractions and Decimals, Grades 3–5 (MECC, 1996a) provides a counter model, a bar model, and a circle model for fractions. Using circles, two fractions can be modelled side-by-side, subdivided, and shaded in up to 16 sections. However, the symbolic fractions are never in lowest terms, and the symbols for each model are always present with the relation symbol ($<, >, =$) placed between them. The graphics are easy to manipulate and are quite good. However, this is an example of software that allows students to use a model to solve a problem without reflecting on the process. The symbolic form is always correct, with no student input. Programs such as this would be best used as a class demonstration tool.

CampOS Math (Pierian Spring Software, 1996) is a multi-concept package with at least two fractional components. Both use circular pie models to help students learn concepts. Although presented in a much more intriguing manner than in *MathKeys*, the models in *CampOS Math* provide so much help that students may not connect the

model with the fraction symbolism. The "Fractionator" component permits changing numerator and denominator to create circular region models, including fractions greater than 1. When the computer "locks" either the numerator or the denominator, the student is challenged to create a given fraction in an equivalent form. A non-model drill of equivalent fractions is provided.

 ## Literature Connections

Fractional concepts in textbooks, even the activities in this chapter, are often presented devoid of context. Yet context takes children away from rules and encourages them to explore ideas in a more open and informal manner. The way that children approach fractional concepts in these contexts may surprise you.

The Doorbell Rang
(Hutchins, 1986)

Often used to investigate whole-number operations of multiplication and division, this book is also an excellent early introduction to fractions. The story is a simple tale of two children preparing to share a plate of 12 cookies. Just as they have figured out how to share the cookies, the doorbell rings and more children arrive. This continues until there are more children than cookies, but Grandma saves the day. Change the number of children to create an uneven division, and ask your students to figure out how to divide the remaining cookies fairly. Using drawings of circles for cookies, students can try to figure out how to share four cookies among six children, discovering in the process a variety of ways to solve fractional problems, and discussing the need for fractional parts consisting of equal shares.

Gator Pie
(Mathews, 1979)

Appropriate even for grades 5 and 6, this delightful book has Alvin, Alice, and other alligators sharing a pie they find in the woods. As more and more gators arrive, the pie must be cut into more and more pieces until finally it is divided in hundredths, making a nice connection between decimals and fractions. An interesting exploration involves cutting a pie (or a rectangle) into halves or thirds, and then deciding how to share these slices among a larger number. To go from halves to sixths is reasonably easy, but may surprise you. What if the pie is cut in thirds and then we want to share it in tenths?

The Man Who Counted: A Collection of Mathematical Adventures
(Tahan, 1993)

This book contains a story, "Beasts of Burden," about a wise mathematician, Beremiz, and the narrator, who are travelling together on one camel. They are asked by three brothers to solve an argument. Their father has left them 35 camels to divide among them: half to one brother, one-third to another, and one-ninth to the third. The story provides an excellent context for discussing fractional parts of sets and how fractional parts change as the whole changes. However, if the whole is changed

from 35 to, say, 36 or 34, the problem of the indicated shares remains unresolved. The sum of $\frac{1}{2}$, $\frac{1}{3}$, and $\frac{1}{9}$ will never be one whole, no matter how many camels are involved. Bresser (1995) describes three full days of wonderful discussions with his grade 5 students, who proposed a wide range of solutions. Bresser's suggestions are worth considering. ▪▪

Reflections on Chapter 12

Writing to Learn

1. Give examples of three categories of fractional models. What real models have you used that correspond to each of these?

2. Why are set models more difficult for children to understand?

3. What are the two distinct requirements of fractional parts? Explain how children's concepts of partitioning need to be refined to produce a concept of fractional parts.

4. What are children learning in activities in which they are asked to count fractional parts? How can these types of activities help children learn to write fractions meaningfully?

5. Give a grade 4 explanation for the meaning of the top and the bottom numbers in a fraction.

6. Using a length model, make up part-and-whole questions for each of the following cases:
   a. Given a part and a non-unit fraction less than 1, find the whole.
   b. Given a part and a non-unit fraction greater than 1, find the whole.
   c. Given a whole and a non-unit fraction less than 1, find the part.
   d. Given a whole and a non-unit fraction greater than 1, find the part.

   Once you have finished, have a friend try answering your questions. Then change each question to a set model. Be sure that a unit fraction never represents a single counter. For example, if the question is about fourths, use 8 or 12 objects to represent the whole set.

7. Describe several ideas that illustrate what is meant by number sense with fractions; include an activity for each.

8. Create pairs of fractions that can be compared ("Select the larger") without the use of an algorithm. See if you can make up examples using the four different ideas that were suggested for comparing fractions.

9. Explain the difference between understanding the concept of equivalent fractions and knowing the algorithm for making an equivalent fraction.

10. Describe some activities that will help children develop the concept of equivalent fractions..

11. How could you help children develop the algorithm for equivalent fractions?

For Discussion and Exploration

1. A common error that children make is to write $\frac{3}{5}$ for the fraction represented here:

   Why do you think that they do this? In this chapter, the notation of fractional parts and counting by unit fractions were introduced before any symbols. How could this help avoid the type of thinking that is involved in this common error?

2. Experiment with bars of interlocking cubes as a model for fractions. For example, if a bar of 12 cubes is a whole, then bars of 3 cubes would be fourths. Since the bars can be taken apart and put together and the individual cubes can be counted, there are some significant differences between this model and those suggested in the text. Is the bar a length model or a set model?

3. In an editorial in *Mathematics Teaching in the Middle School*, Patrick Groff (1996) questions the importance of teaching fractions in the upper-elementary and middle grades. His arguments are based in part on the difficulty of learning fractional ideas at this level, the decreased use of fractions in everyday life, and the pressure for space in the curriculum from other topics that have been introduced. His opinion is rebutted in the "Readers Write" section of the September-October 1996 issue by a former physicist and by a current teacher. The discussion has merit. Which side of this argument makes more sense? Why?

Recommendations for Further Reading

Highly Recommended

Payne, J.N., Towsley, A.E., & Huinker, D.M. (1990). Fractions and decimals. In J.N. Payne (Ed.), *Mathematics for the young child* (pp. 175–200). Reston, VA: National Council of Teachers of Mathematics.

These authors explore many of the ideas covered in this chapter, provide additional activities or variations on those found here, and show how the early development of fractions can be connected to decimal concepts. Do not be put off by the date; this resource will be timely for many years to come.

Pirie, S. & Kieren, T. (1992). Creating constructivist environments and constructing creative classrooms. *Educational Studies in Mathematics, 23,* 505-528.

This article focuses on the constructivist nature of teaching and learning mathematics in the elementary classroom, and also describes children's work with fractions. A series of episodes show how teachers attempt to teach fractional concepts for understanding. Both the narrative and the accompanying illustrations reinforce the concept development in this chapter in a unique manner.

Reys, B.J., Kim, O., & Bay, J.M. (1999). Establishing fraction benchmarks. *Mathematics Teaching in the Middle School, 4,* 530–532.

This short article describes a simple three-question interview administered to 20 grade 5 students. The results are both sad and surprising. A significant conclusion is that the teaching of benchmarks for fractions, specifically 0, H, and 1, is generally neglected in the standard curriculum. The questions used in the interview can profitably be used with children in grades 4–7.

Tzur, R. (1999). An integrated study of children's construction of improper fractions and the teacher's role in promoting learning. *Journal for Research in Mathematics Education, 30,* 390–416.

Tzur's teaching experiment is described in detail, providing the reader with a real understanding of the construction of fraction concepts at the grade 4 level.

Watanabe, T. (1996). Ben's understanding of one-half. *Teaching Children Mathematics, 2,* 460–464.

This provocative article examines three very interesting tasks that were presented to a grade 2 child. Even if you are interested in the upper grades, this is a worthwhile article. Not only are the tasks (or variations of them) quite interesting for all children, but the implications are also worth considering. Listening carefully to children informs us best.

Other Suggestions

Armstrong, B.E., & Larson, C.N. (1995). Students' use of part-whole and direct comparison strategies for comparing partitioned rectangles. *Journal for Research in Mathematics Education, 26,* 2–19.

Bezuk, N.S., & Bieck, M. (1993). Current research on rational numbers and common fractions: Summary and implications for teachers. In D.T. Owens (Ed.), *Research ideas for the classroom: Middle grades mathematics* (pp. 118–136). Old Tappan, NJ: Macmillan.

Dorgan, K. (1994). What textbooks offer for instruction in fraction concepts. *Teaching Children Mathematics, 1,* 150–155.

Groff, P. (1996). It is time to question fraction teaching. *Mathematics Teaching in the Middle School, 1,* 604–607.

Kieren, T. (1984). Helping children understand rational numbers. *Arithmetic Teacher, 31* (6), 3.

Kieren, T., Davis, B., & Mason, R. (1996). Fraction flags: Learning from children to help children learn. *Mathematics Teaching in the Middle School, 2,* 14–19.

Langford, K., & Sarullo, A. (1993). Introductory common and decimal fraction concepts. In R. J. Jensen (Ed.), *Research ideas for the classroom: Early childhood mathematics* (pp. 223–247). Old Tappan, NJ: Macmillan.

Mack, N.K. (1995). Confounding whole-number and fraction concepts when building on informal knowledge. *Journal for Research in Mathematics Education, 26,* 422–441.

Middleton, J.A., van den Heuvel-Panhuizen, M., & Shew, J.A. (1997). Using bar representations as a model for connecting concepts of rational number. *Mathematics Teaching in the Middle School, 3,* 302–312.

Moss, J., & Case, R. (1999). Developing children's understanding of the rational numbers: A new model and an experimental curriculum. *Journal for Research in Mathematics Education, 30.* 122–147.

Pothier, Y., & Sawada, D. (1983). Partitioning: The emergence of rational number ideas in young children. *Journal for Research in Mathematics Education, 14,* 307–317.

Reys, B.J. (1991). *Developing number sense in the middle grades: Addenda series, grades 5–8.* Reston, VA: National Council of Teachers of Mathematics.

Saenz-Ludlow, A. (1994). Michael's fraction schemes. *Journal for Research in Mathematics Education, 25,* 50–85.

Schifter, D., Bastable, V., & Russell, S.J. (1999). *Developing mathematical ideas: Numbers and operations, Part 2: Making meaning for operations* (Casebook). White Plains, NY: Cuisenaire–Dale Seymour.

Chapter 13

Computation with Fractions

Like the *Principles and Standards for School Mathematics*, provincial and territorial curricula are explicit about what fractional computational skills should be taught and when. Even though specific learning outcomes may vary in the different regions across Canada, students are usually expected to develop strategies for addition and subtraction of decimal numbers and fractions between grades 5 and 8. Instruction typically begins with a variety of concrete and pictorial methods, continuing until students are able to demonstrate proficiency in operations with fractions. (Of course, the grade level at which students begin to learn about the operations will have an influence on proficiency.) *Principles and Standards* calls for students in grades 6–8 to extend their understanding of the operations to include fractions and decimals. All methods of fractional computation (mental, estimation, paper-and-pencil, and calculator) are recommended (NCTM, 2000).

 BIG IDEAS

1. The same ideas developed for operations with whole numbers should apply to operations with fractions. Operations with fractions should begin by applying these same ideas to fractional parts.

2. Estimation of computation with fractions is an integral part of student's computation development. It helps computation with fractions make sense. As well, many fractional computations can be done mentally without relying on formal algorithms.

Number Sense and Fraction Algorithms

Despite the recommendations of the *Principles and Standards* and provincial and territorial curricula, too often there is a rush to develop computational proficien-cy. This limits the all-important conceptual development time for the fundamental ideas discussed in Chapter 12. Moreover, traditional textbooks do not always encourage the development of number sense and an understanding of operations with fractions. The result, therefore, is usually a collection of procedures that students do not fully understand.

The Dangerous Rush to Rules

It is important to give students ample opportunity to develop fractional number sense as described in the previous chapter, rather than starting immediately to teach them about common denominators and other rules of computation.

Premature attention to rules for fractional computation has a number of serious drawbacks. None of the rules help students think about the operations and what they mean. Armed only with rules, students have no means of assessing their results to see if they make sense. Surface mastery of rules in the short term is quickly lost. When mixed together, the myriad rules of fractional computation soon become a meaningless jumble. When adding fractions, students will ask, "Do I need a common denominator, or do you just add the bottom numbers like in multiplication?" Frequently confused when dividing fractions, they will wonder, "Which one do you invert, the first or the second number?" The algorithm rules do not immediately apply to mixed numbers. More rules! This approach to mathematics is immensely defeating to children.

A Problem-Based, Number-Sense Approach

Without a firm understanding of fractional concepts, the development of computational algorithms for fractions can quickly become superficial, rule-oriented, and perplexing. This is why this chapter was written separately from the preceding one—to place more emphasis on fractional concepts. You are advised to delay rushing to algorithmic procedures until it is clear that students are ready. Students can become adequately proficient using informal methods they invent themselves and understand.

The following guidelines should be kept in mind when developing computational strategies for fractions:

1. *Begin with simple contextual tasks.* Huinker (1998) makes an excellent case for the use of contextual problems and for letting students develop their own methods of computation with fractions. Problems or contexts need not be elaborate or themselves problematic. What you want is a context for both the meaning of the operation and the fractions involved.

2. *Connect the meaning of fractional computation with whole-number computation.* When considering what $2\frac{1}{2} \times \frac{3}{4}$ might mean, we could think about a whole number example such as 2×3 and ask ourselves, "What does 2×3 mean?" (It could mean 2 groups of 3.) In a similar manner, $2\frac{1}{2} \times \frac{3}{4}$ could mean $2\frac{1}{2}$ groups of $\frac{3}{4}$. The concepts in each situation, then, are the same. Thus, it is beneficial to connect these ideas.

3. *Let estimation and informal methods play a significant role in the development of strategies.* "Should $2\frac{1}{2} \times \frac{3}{4}$ be more or less than 1? More or less than 3?" Estimation helps to focus on the meaning of the numbers and the operations, encourages reflective thinking, and assists in building informal number sense with fractions. For many computations, there is no need for a standard algorithm, and children can find interesting ways to get answers, if they are asked to try. Here is a simple example: $\frac{7}{8} + \frac{1}{2}$ is $1\frac{1}{2}$ less $\frac{1}{8}$, and I know that $\frac{1}{2}$ is the same as $\frac{4}{8}$, so it is $1\frac{3}{8}$.

4. *Explore each of the operations using models.* Use a variety of models. Have students defend their solutions using the models. You will find that sometimes it is possible to get answers with models using approaches that do not seem to work as effectively with pencil and paper. One example is with division of fractions. When we show students with models why 9 divided by $\frac{1}{3}$ is 27, it helps them better understand why division makes "larger." The ideas will help children learn to think about the fractions and the operations, contribute to mental methods, and provide a useful background when you eventually do get to the standard algorithms.

In the discussions that follow, informal exploration is encouraged for each operation. There is also a guided development for each traditional algorithm.

Addition and Subtraction

The idea of beginning with contextual problems to develop invented strategies for fractions is similar to the approach described in Chapter 10 for whole-number computation. As with whole numbers, expect that students will use a variety of methods and that their methods will vary widely with the fractions encountered in the problems.

No attempt is made in this chapter to describe all of the solution strategies that students might develop. Students will continue to find ways to solve problems with fractions, and their informal approaches will contribute to the development of more standard methods (Huinker, 1998; Lappan & Mouck, 1998; Schifter, Bastable, & Russell, 1999c).

Informal Exploration

Consider the following simple context:

Paul and his brother were each eating the same kind of chocolate bar. Paul still had $\frac{3}{4}$ of his chocolate bar left. His brother had $\frac{1}{2}$ of his. How much chocolate do the two boys now have together?

This is an example of the type of task you can pose to students from the very beginning of their exploration with fractional computation. Most of your problems should involve simple fractions with denominators of 12 or smaller. Avoid a focus on traditional categories such as like and unlike denominators or mixed and common fractions. Rather, include a mix of problem types so that artificial rules do not develop that must be unlearned later.

Encourage students to use drawings or models of their choice. However, there should be a clear connection between the context of the problem, the models, and the symbolism used. When using flexible models like strips or counters, students will first need to decide on a representation of the whole so that both fractions can be modelled correctly. (Recall the pizza fallacy from Figure 12.12, p. 234). For example, in the chocolate bar problem, students might incorrectly draw two different-sized rectangles or use a set of 4 for fourths and a set of 8 for eighths. When such errors occur, let students work through the ensuing difficulties in class discussions.

Figure 13.1 illustrates how three different models might be used to solve simple addition tasks. Many other strategies are possible. For example, can you find at least two ways to solve the chocolate bar problem?

Subtraction of two fractions with models is a similar process, as shown in Figure 13.2. Notice that it is sometimes possible to find the sum or difference of two fractions without subdividing either one. Instead, you can

Find a piece for a whole that allows both fractions to be modelled.

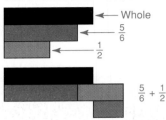

The sum is 1 whole and a green piece more than a whole.

So $\frac{5}{6} + \frac{1}{2} = 1\frac{1}{3}$.

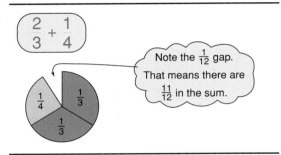

What set size can be used for the whole? The smallest is a set of 15.

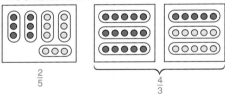

Combine (add) the fractions.
$\frac{2}{5}$ is 6 counters, and $\frac{4}{3}$ is 20 counters.
In sets of 15, that is $\frac{26}{15}$, or $1\frac{11}{15}$.

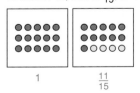

FIGURE 13.1 Using models to add fractions.

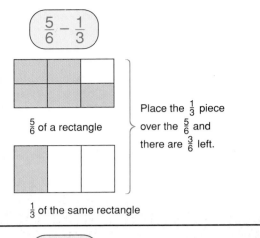

Place the $\frac{1}{3}$ piece over the $\frac{5}{6}$ and there are $\frac{3}{6}$ left.

$\frac{1}{3}$ of the same rectangle

Find a piece that can be broken into eighths and halves: brown.

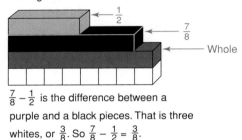

$\frac{7}{8} - \frac{1}{2}$ is the difference between a purple and a black pieces. That is three whites, or $\frac{3}{8}$. So $\frac{7}{8} - \frac{1}{2} = \frac{3}{8}$.

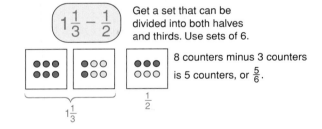

Get a set that can be divided into both halves and thirds. Use sets of 6.

8 counters minus 3 counters is 5 counters, or $\frac{5}{6}$.

FIGURE 13.2 Using models to subtract fractions.

focus on the size of a leftover part. When area models are used for addition and subtraction, common denominators are frequently not involved at all. Selecting a length that permits modelling of two fractions is mathematically the same as finding a common denominator. (Why?)

When making up addition and subtraction exercises to be done with models, do not be afraid of difficult problems. Include exercises with unlike denominators, fractions greater than 1, and mixed numbers. For subtraction, explore problems such as $3\frac{1}{8} - 1\frac{1}{4}$, where a trade of wholes for eighths might occur. At this stage, avoid directing students with a completely formulated method. The problem-solving approach, combined with the use of models, will help students develop relationships.

The Myth of Common Denominators

Teachers commonly tell students, "In order to add or subtract fractions, you must first get common denominators." The explanation usually goes something like, "After all, you can't add apples and oranges." This well-intentioned statement is essentially false. A correct statement might be, "In order *to use the standard algorithm* to add or subtract fractions, you must first get common denominators." And the explanation is then, "The algorithm is designed to work only with common denominators."

If students have spent adequate time solving contextual and non-contextual addition and subtraction problems using their own invented strategies, you will find that many correct solutions are found without ever getting a common denominator, especially when a concrete model is used. Consider these sums and differences:

$$\frac{3}{4} + \frac{1}{8} \qquad \frac{1}{2} - \frac{1}{8} \qquad \frac{2}{3} + \frac{1}{2} \qquad 1\frac{1}{2} - \frac{3}{4} \qquad 1\frac{2}{3} + \frac{3}{4}$$

Working with the ways different fractional parts are related to one another often provides solutions without finding common denominators. For example, how are halves, fourths, and eighths related? Also, picture three-thirds making up a whole, either in a circle or on a line segment. Have you ever noticed that one-half of the whole is one-and-a-half thirds? That is, the difference between a half and a third is half of a third, or one-sixth. Similarly, the difference between a third and a fourth is a twelfth. With relationships such as these, many fractional computations can be solved without first getting common denominators.

Developing the Algorithm

The foregoing notwithstanding, it is important to develop algorithms for addition and subtraction so that students have different ways, including those that are conventional, for solving computations. However, they will likely need some guidance to get to that stage. At the same time, though, they will easily be able to build on their informal explorations and see that the common-denominator approach is meaningful.

Like Denominators

Generally, most lists of objectives first specify addition and subtraction with like denominators. This is both unfortunate and unnecessary! If students have a good foundation with fractional concepts, they should be able to add or subtract like fractions immediately. Students who are not confident solving problems such as $\frac{3}{4} + \frac{2}{4}$ or $3\frac{7}{8} - 1\frac{3}{8}$ almost certainly do not have good fractional concepts and will be lost in any further development. The idea that the top number counts and the bottom number tells what is being counted makes addition and subtraction of like fractions the same as adding and subtracting whole numbers.

Unlike Denominators

To get students to move to common denominators, consider a task such as $\frac{5}{8} + \frac{2}{4}$. Let students use pie pieces to get the result of $1\frac{1}{8}$ using any approach. Many will note that the models for the two fractions make one whole and there is $\frac{1}{8}$ extra. The key question to ask at this point is, "How can we change this problem into one that is just like the easy ones where the parts are the same?" For this example, it is relatively easy to see that fourths could be changed into eighths. Have students use models to show the original problem and also the converted problem. The main idea is to see that $\frac{5}{8} + \frac{2}{4}$ is exactly the same problem as $\frac{5}{8} + \frac{4}{8}$.

Next try some examples where both fractions need to be changed—for example, $\frac{2}{3} + \frac{1}{4}$. Again, focus attention on *rewriting the problem* so that the bottom parts of each fraction are the same, which makes it like "adding apples and apples." As students discuss their solutions, be sure they clearly understand that the new form of the problem is still the same problem. This can and should be demonstrated with models. If your students express any doubt about the equivalence of the two expressions ("Is $\frac{11}{12}$ really the answer to $\frac{2}{3} + \frac{1}{4}$?"), this indicates that the concept of equivalent fractions (Chapter 12, p. 236) is not well understood.

As a result of modelling and renaming fractions to make the problems easy, students should come to understand that the process of getting a common denominator is really one of looking for a way of rewriting the *statement* of the problem without changing the problem itself. These ideas are illustrated in Figure 13.3.

Subtraction of two simple fractions follows exactly the same approach.

Common Multiples

Many students have trouble with finding common denominators because they are not able to come up with common multiples of the denominators quickly. It is a skill that can be practised. But it also depends to a large degree on having *a good command of the basic facts* for multiplication. Without this, fraction computation can be frustrating for students. Here are two activities aimed at the skill of finding least common multiples or common denominators.

ACTIVITY 13.1

Running through the Multiples

For this oral drill, give students a number between 2 and 16 (likely denominators), and have them list the multiples in order. At first, writing the multiples may be helpful. But work toward doing this exercise orally and quickly. You should find that students will be able to list the multiples to about 30 with ease.

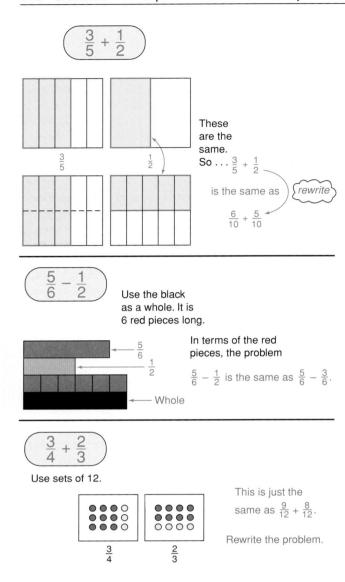

FIGURE 13.3 Rewriting addition and subtraction problems involving fractions.

LCM (Least Common Multiple) Flash Cards

Make flash cards with pairs of numbers that are potential denominators. Most should be less than 16, as before. For each card, students try to give the least common multiple (LCM; see Figure 13.4). Be sure to include pairs of numbers that are prime, such as 9 and 5; pairs in which one is a multiple of the other, such as 2 and 8; and pairs that have a common divisor, such as 8 and 12.

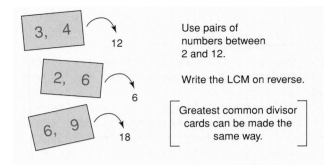

FIGURE 13.4 Least common multiple (LCM) flash cards.

Mixed Numbers

A separate algorithm for mixed numbers in addition and subtraction is not necessary, even though mixed numbers are often treated as separate topics in traditional textbooks and in some lists of objectives. Avoid layering fractions with yet another rule. Include mixed numbers in all of your activities with addition and subtraction, and let students solve these problems in ways that make sense to them. It is almost certain that students will add the whole numbers first and then deal with the fractions, using the algorithm or whatever method makes sense.

For subtraction, dealing with the whole numbers first still makes sense. Consider this problem: $5\frac{1}{8} - 3\frac{5}{8}$. After subtracting 3 from 5, students will need to deal with the $\frac{5}{8}$. Some will take $\frac{5}{8}$ from the whole part, 2, leaving $1\frac{3}{8}$, and then $\frac{1}{8}$ more is $1\frac{4}{8}$. Others may take away the $\frac{1}{8}$ that is there and then $\frac{4}{8}$ from the remaining 2. A third but inefficient method that you might have learned is to change mixed numbers into improper fractions before subtracting. Another, somewhat unlikely, method is to trade one of the wholes for $\frac{8}{8}$, add it to the $\frac{1}{8}$, and then take $\frac{5}{8}$ from the resulting $\frac{9}{8}$. This last method is the same as the traditional decomposition algorithm for subtracting fractions.

Estimation and Simple Methods

Almost all computation with fractions, even on standardized tests, will involve small denominators. Occasionally, the need for a common denominator might require sixteenths or twentieths. Even that is rare. With denominators of 16 or less, estimation using "nice" fractions such as halves and fourths is usually possible and should be encouraged. Estimation also leads to informal methods that are often easier than traditional algorithms for getting exact answers.

Consider $7\frac{1}{8} - 2\frac{3}{4}$. Ignoring the fractions, a first estimate might be 5. Will it be more or less than 5? Others may begin by thinking $7\frac{1}{8}$ is close to 7 and $2\frac{3}{4}$ is close to 3 → about 4, maybe a little more. Once students begin to think in these terms, a meaningful method for an exact answer is often possible without using an algorithm.

Examine the fraction exercises for addition and subtraction in a middle-grades textbook. See how many of them you can do without pencil and paper. Challenge students to do the same.

Multiplication

When working with whole numbers, we would say that 3×5 means "3 sets of 5." The first factor tells how much of the second factor you have or want. *Billy bought 3 packages of 5 balloons.* Here Billy bought whole sets of things that were also whole numbers. This is a good place to begin. Simple story problems are a significant help in the development of multiplication of fractions.

Informal Exploration

The story problems that you use to pose multiplication tasks to children need not be elaborate, but it is important to think about the numbers that you use in the problems. A possible progression of problem difficulty is developed in the sections that follow.

Beginning Concepts

Consider these two problems as good starting tasks:

There are 15 cars in Michael's toy car collection. Two-thirds of the cars are red. How many red cars does Michael have?

Suzanne has 11 cookies. She wants to share them with her 3 friends. How many cookies will Suzanne and each of her friends get?

In both of these problems, the task is to find a fractional part of a whole number. Notice that in the first problem, the 15 cars can be easily divided into thirds. Students will first need to find thirds and then take two of those. In the second problem, a type of unit that can be subdivided (cookies) is used because 11 cannot be broken into fourths. Students will solve this problem in different ways, as illustrated in Figure 13.5.

Problems in which the first factor is a whole number are also important.

Wayne filled 5 glasses with $\frac{2}{3}$ litre of juice in each. How much juice in all did Wayne use?

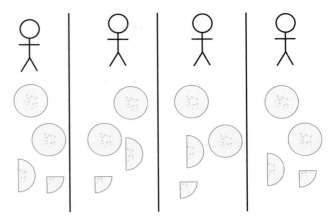

Pass out whole cookies. Cut 2 cookies in half.
Cut last cookie in fourths. Each child gets $2 + \frac{1}{2} + \frac{1}{4}$ or $2\frac{3}{4}$.

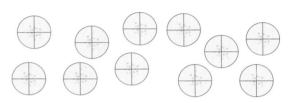

Cut all 11 cookies in fourths. Give a fourth of each cookie to each girl. Each will get $\frac{11}{4}$ or $2\frac{3}{4}$ cookies

FIGURE 13.5 Two ways to solve the problem of sharing 11 cookies among four children.

This problem may be solved in different ways. Some children will put the thirds together, making wholes as they go. Others will count all of the thirds and then find out how many whole litres are in 10 thirds.

In this last problem, replace $\frac{2}{3}$ litre with $\frac{2}{7}$ litre. Initially, attention is on the number of parts in each glass (2). Because there are 5 glasses, there are 10 unit parts altogether, just as in the original problem. Then the focus changes to the size of the parts to determine the number of wholes. That is, in the first problem the size of the parts is thirds, while in the second problem the size of the parts is sevenths.

Unit Parts without Subdivisions

To expand on the ideas just presented, consider these three problems:

You have $\frac{3}{4}$ of a pizza left. If you give $\frac{1}{3}$ of the leftover pizza to your brother, how much of a whole pizza will your brother get?

Someone ate $\frac{1}{10}$ of the cake, leaving only $\frac{9}{10}$. If you eat $\frac{2}{3}$ of the cake that is left, how much of a whole cake will you have eaten?

Kate made $2\frac{1}{2}$ pitchers of punch for the family picnic. If she used $\frac{4}{5}$ of a litre of ginger ale for each pitcher, how many litres of ginger ale did she need for the punch?

Notice that the units or fractional parts in these problems do not need to be subdivided further. The first problem is $\frac{1}{3}$ of 3 things, the second is $\frac{2}{3}$ of 9 things, and the last is $2\frac{1}{2}$ of 4 things. The focus remains on the number of unit parts in all, and then the size of the parts determines the number of wholes. Figure 13.6 shows how problems of this type might be modelled. However, it is very important to let students model and solve these problems in their own way, using whatever models or drawings they choose. Require only that they be able to explain their reasoning.

Subdividing the Unit Parts

When the pieces must be subdivided into smaller unit parts, the problems become more challenging.

Zack had $\frac{2}{3}$ of the lawn left to cut. After lunch, he cut $\frac{3}{4}$ of the part that was left. How much of the entire lawn did Zack cut after lunch?

The zookeeper had a huge bottle of Zoo Cola, the animals' favourite liquid treat. The monkey drank $\frac{1}{5}$ of the bottle. The zebra drank $\frac{2}{3}$ of what was left. How much Zoo Cola did the zebra drink?

Stop for a moment and figure out how you would solve each of these problems. Draw pictures to help you, but do not use a computational algorithm.

In Zack's lawn problem, it is necessary to find fourths of 2 things, the 2 *thirds* of the grass left to cut. In the Zoo Cola problem, you need thirds of 4 things, the 4 *fifths* of the cola that remain. Again, the concepts of the top num-

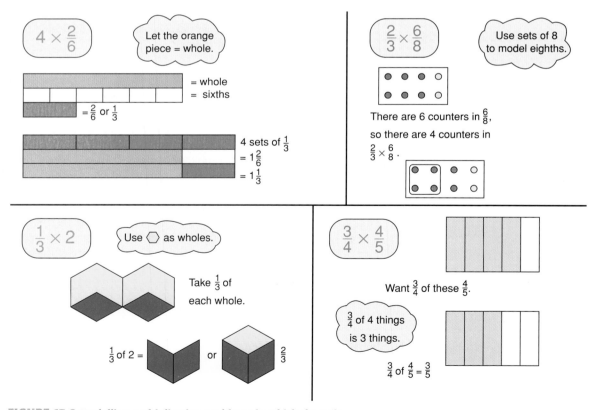

FIGURE 13.6 Modelling multiplication problems in which the unit pieces do not require further subdivision.

ber counting and the bottom number naming what is being counted play an important role.

Often story problems that go along with fraction products are contrived or not realistic. At the same time, though, they help to provide a model or visual for students. Probably no one would actually need to determine in fractional form how much Zoo Cola is drunk; however, using models can help us better understand the concept. Figure 13.7 shows two possible solutions for Zack's lawn problem. Similar approaches can be used for the Zoo Cola problem. You may use different drawings, but the ideas should be the same.

If students use counters to model problems where the units require subdivision, an added difficulty arises. Figure 13.8 illustrates what might happen solving the problem $\frac{3}{5} \times \frac{2}{3}$. (*Three-fifths of $\frac{2}{3}$ of a whole is how much of a whole?*) The typical way to show $\frac{2}{3}$ is with 2 out of 3 counters. But the thirds need to be divided into 5 parts in order to get 3 fifths of them. Here the representation of a whole must be changed so that the thirds can be subdivided. Do not discourage students from using counters, but be prepared to help them find ways to show thirds using larger sets.

The problem in Figure 13.8 offers another possible twist worth mentioning. Since there is no context for the problem, why not use the commutative property (the order property)? Turn the factors around and consider $\frac{2}{3}$ of $\frac{3}{5}$. Wow! Do you see almost immediately that the answer is $\frac{2}{5}$?

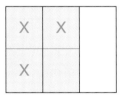

How much is $\frac{3}{4}$ of $\frac{2}{3}$?

Cut each third in half, and take 3 parts.

Half of a third is a sixth, so it's $\frac{3}{6}$.

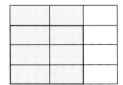

Cut all 3 thirds into 4 parts. Each part is $\frac{1}{12}$.

Three-fourths of the 8 twelfths of the grass

left to cut is $\frac{6}{12}$.

FIGURE 13.7 Solutions to fraction products when the unit parts must be subdivided.

Developing the Algorithm

If you have spent adequate time exploring multiplication of fractions as just described, the traditional multiplication algorithm is relatively simple to develop. A square or any other rectangle to represent the whole is the most commonly used model for developing the algorithm.

A Beginning Task

To develop the algorithm in a problem context, provide students with a drawing of $\frac{3}{4}$ of a square as shown in Figure 13.9. The task is to use the drawing to determine the product $\frac{3}{5} \times \frac{3}{4}$ (three-fifths of three-fourths of a whole) and explain the result.

Drawn as shown, the easiest way to get $\frac{3}{4}$ of the shaded region is to divide it into fourths. To take $\frac{3}{5}$ of $\frac{3}{4}$, draw lines in the opposite direction dividing the $\frac{3}{4}$ into fifths. Now shade in 3 of those fifths. Now, the problem is to determine what types of unit pieces these are. The product of the denominators tells how many pieces are in the whole (the kind of unit), and the product of the numerators tells the number of pieces in the product.

Begin with problems where the units must be subdivided, as in this example. If you were to use $\frac{3}{4} \times \frac{4}{5}$ instead of $\frac{3}{5} \times \frac{3}{4}$, there would be no reason to subdivide the unit pieces, and thus no reason to multiply the numerators and denominators.

Avoid pushing students to formalize the rule or algorithm of multiplying the tops and bottoms of the fractions. Many students will simply count each small part in the drawing and not notice that the number of rows and columns is actually the two numerators and the two denominators, respectively. You might steer students in

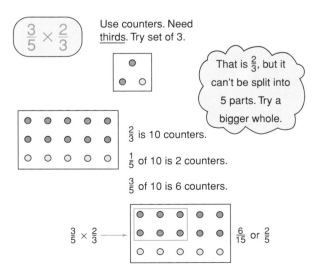

FIGURE 13.8 Modelling multiplication of fraction with counters.

FIGURE 13.9 Development of the algorithm for multiplication of fractions.

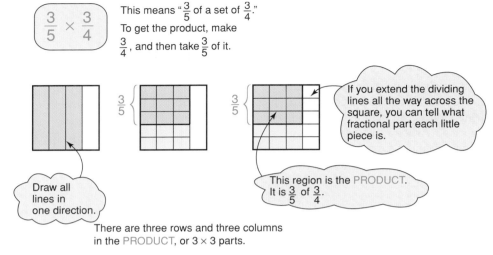

This means "$\frac{3}{5}$ of a set of $\frac{3}{4}$."
To get the product, make $\frac{3}{4}$, and then take $\frac{3}{5}$ of it.

If you extend the dividing lines all the way across the square, you can tell what fractional part each little piece is.

Draw all lines in one direction.

This region is the PRODUCT. It is $\frac{3}{5}$ of $\frac{3}{4}$.

There are three rows and three columns in the PRODUCT, or 3×3 parts.

The WHOLE is now five rows and four columns, so there are 5×4 parts in the whole.

$$\text{PRODUCT} = \frac{3}{5} \times \frac{3}{4} = \frac{\boxed{\text{Number}}\text{ of parts in product}}{\boxed{\text{Kind}}\text{ of parts}} = \frac{3 \times 3}{5 \times 4} = \frac{9}{20}$$

this direction by posing a problem with the initial sketch, asking them to determine the product without additional drawing. Try this with $\frac{7}{8} \times \frac{4}{5}$, where the numbers make it almost mandatory that you multiply.

A cautionary note: Many texts make this "sliced-square" approach so mechanical that it actually becomes a meaningless algorithm in itself. Students are told to shade a square one way for the first factor and the opposite way for the second factor. Without a rationale, they are told that the product is the region that has double shading. You might as well give students the rule and forget about explanations.

Factors Greater than 1

Once students have explored products where both factors are less than 1, it may be challenging to have them explore fractions where either or both factors are greater than 1. Presenting the task in a problem context can make it a significant and worthwhile challenge. There is no need to explain how to do this.

It is useful to have students explore products with fractions greater than 1 as area problems. For example, the task might be: *Find the area of a rectangular patio that is $3\frac{1}{5}$ metres by $5\frac{1}{2}$ metres* (see Figure 13.10). In this context, students may approach the task in a manner very similar to two-digit multiplication of whole numbers. There are four different sections to the rectangle, just as with whole numbers. The size of each can be determined by figuring out a partial product. The largest part is the product of the two

whole numbers, 3×5. The smallest part is the product of the two fractions, $\frac{1}{5} \times \frac{1}{2}$. The other two parts are products of $3 \times \frac{1}{2}$ and $\frac{1}{5} \times 5$.

This area context is advantageous for connecting mathematical ideas. Not only is it the same approach that is used for a product such as 36×48, it can also be used for decimals (3.5×2.4). The same concept is used again in algebra for products such as $(2x + 3)(x + 4)$. You may have learned this as the "FOIL" method: *First, Outer, Inner,* and *Last,* which is the same as the four partial products found in all of these examples.

A Disadvantage of the Algorithm

Interestingly, the multiplication algorithm *always* subdivides the parts, even when it is not necessary. For example, $\frac{3}{4} \times \frac{8}{5}$ results in $\frac{24}{20}$ when the algorithm is used. However, a student with a good understanding might say, "Three-fourths of 8 is 6, so it's 6 fifths, or $1\frac{1}{5}$." Like most algorithms, this one can sometimes steer us away from simple solutions that can be handled mentally. The simpler, less complicated solutions always involve smaller denominators and are often more useful.

More Mental Techniques

In the real world, there are many instances when the product of a whole number and a fraction is required, and a mental estimate or even an exact answer is quite useful. For example, sale items are frequently listed as "$\frac{1}{4}$ off," or

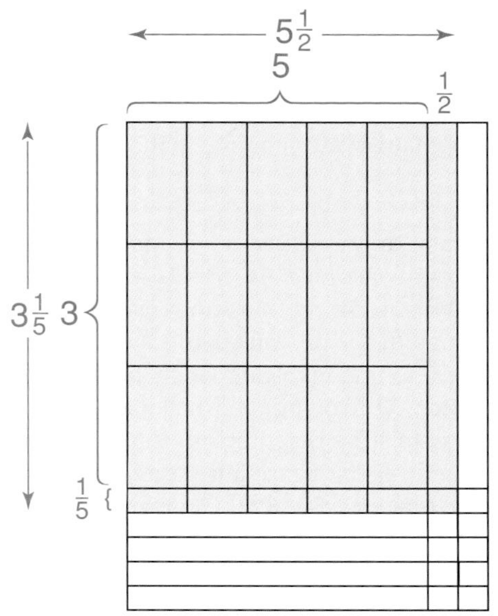

$$5\tfrac{1}{2} \times \tfrac{1}{5} = (1)\ 3 \times 5$$
$$(2)\ \tfrac{1}{5} \times 5$$
$$(3)\ 3 \times \tfrac{1}{2}$$
$$(4)\ \tfrac{1}{5} \times \tfrac{1}{2}$$

FIGURE 13.10 The product of two mixed numbers as four partial products.

we read of a "$\tfrac{1}{3}$ increase" in the population of urban communities in Ontario. Fractions are excellent substitutes for percentages, as you will see in the next chapter. To get an estimate of 60 percent of $36.69, it is useful to think of 60 percent as $\tfrac{3}{5}$ or a little less than $\tfrac{2}{3}$, because we know that 66 percent is approximately $\tfrac{2}{3}$.

These products of fractions with large whole numbers can be calculated mentally by thinking of the meanings of the top and bottom numbers. For example, $\tfrac{3}{5}$ is 3 *one*-fifths. So if you want $\tfrac{3}{5}$ of 350, for example, first think about *one*-fifth of 350, or 70. If *one*-fifth is 70, then *three*-fifths is 3×70, or 210. Although this example has very accommodating numbers, it illustrates a process for mentally multiplying a large number by a fraction: First determine the unit fractional part, and then multiply by the number of parts you want. Once again, you can see the importance of the fractional-part concept and the meanings of the top and bottom numbers.

When numbers are not so nice, encourage students to use compatible numbers. To estimate $\tfrac{3}{5}$ of $36.69, a useful compatible is $35. One-fifth of 35 is 7, so three-fifths is 3×7, or 21. Now adjust a bit—perhaps add an additional 50 cents, for an estimate of $21.50.

Students should practise estimating multiplication of fractions with whole numbers in various real-life contexts: a 6.75-kilogram turkey at $4.95 a kilogram, or $\tfrac{7}{8}$ of the

476 students who attended Friday's volleyball game. These skills will be revisited when working with decimals and percentages, and once again mathematics will seem more connected than disconnected.

Division

"Invert the divisor and multiply" is probably one of the most mysterious rules in elementary mathematics. We want to avoid this mystery at all costs. It makes sense to examine division with fractions from a more familiar perspective. It is also important to note that division with fractions is not introduced before grade 8 in most jurisdictions in Canada.

As with the other operations, go back to the meaning of division with whole numbers. Recall that there are two meanings of division: partition and measurement, and repeated subtraction (a useful way for conceptualizing division, just as repeated addition is for multiplication). We will review each briefly for division of a fraction by a whole number or its opposite, and look at some story problems that involve fractions. (Can you make up a word problem right now that would go with the computation $2 \div \tfrac{1}{4}$?)

You should have students explore both measurement and partition problems. Here we will discuss each type of problem separately for the purpose of clarity. In the classroom, the types of problems should probably be mixed. As with multiplication, the way in which the numbers in the problems relate to each other tends to affect the difficulty.

Informal Exploration: Partition Concept

Too often we think of partition problems strictly as sharing problems: 24 hockey cards are to be shared among 4 friends. How many will each friend get? This same share structure also applies to rate problems. If you run 10 kilometres in 48 minutes, how many kilometres per minute can you run? Both of these problems, in fact all partition problems, ask the question, "How much is one?"

24 cards is the amount for 4 friends. "How much is the amount for 1 friend?"

10 kilometres is the amount for 48 minutes. "How many kilometres in 1 minute?"

In the partition concept for $13 \div 3$, the task is to share 13 things among 3 sets and determine the amount in 1 set. Since partition problems involving fractional divisors are often about rates, put this whole-number situation in a rate context: *If 3 CDs cost $13, how much does one CD cost? That is, what is the price per CD?*

Working with Whole Numbers

Almost any fair-share problem can involve sharing a fractional amount.

Kavita has $4\frac{4}{5}$ metres of ribbon to make 3 bows for birthday packages. How much ribbon should she use for each bow if she wants to use the same length of ribbon for each?

In this problem, the idea of sharing equally is clear. When the $4\frac{4}{5}$ is thought of as fractional parts, there are 24 fifths to share, or 8 fifths for each ribbon. Alternatively, one might think of 1 metre per bow, leaving $1\frac{4}{5}$, or 9 fifths. These 9 fifths are then shared, 3 fifths per bow, for a total of $1\frac{3}{5}$ metres for each bow. Regardless of the particular process, the unit parts required no further subdivision in order to do the division. In the following problem, the parts must be split into smaller parts.

Sasha found out that if she walks fast during her morning exercise, she can cover 4 kilometres in $\frac{3}{4}$ of an hour. She wondered how fast she is walking in kilometres per hour.

With Sasha, the task is to distribute the kilometres over each of the 3 equal *fourths* of an hour, and then determine the number of kilometres in 1 hour. What makes this problem a bit different is that 4 kilometres will first need to be broken into smaller units so they can be distributed evenly across the 3 fourths. Think about the different subunits into which the whole can be divided. Draw pictures or use models to solve this problem.

Informal Exploration: Measurement Concept

Almost all division explorations with fractions found in the elementary curriculum involve the measurement concept. To review, $13 \div 3$ means "How many sets of 3 are in 13?" Here is a contextual setting: *If you have 13 litres of lemonade, how many jugs holding 2 litres each can you fill?* A key idea to get from this example involves how to deal with that last litre after filling the first 6 jugs. If you continue to fill a seventh jug, it will get only 1 litre. It will be only one-half full. So one answer is $6\frac{1}{2}$ *jugs.*

Since this concept of division is almost always seen in textbooks and is used to develop an algorithm for dividing fractions, it is important for students to explore this idea in contextual situations.

Working with Whole Numbers

Students readily understand problems such as the following:

Mr. Walker bought 6 metres of cotton fabric for the wall hangings that his class would be making for their art projects. If it takes $\frac{3}{4}$ of a metre to make each wall hanging, how many wall hangings will the class be able to make?

Students typically draw pictures of 6 things divided into fourths and count out how many sets of $\frac{3}{4}$ can be found. The difficulty is in seeing this as $6 \div \frac{3}{4}$, which will require some direct guidance on your part. One idea is to compare the problem to one involving whole numbers (6 metres, 2 metres per wall hanging) and make a comparison. An effective way to solve this problem is to use a linear model, using the units on a fraction piece or number line to represent the 6 metres. Students can mark off every 1 metre to find out how many wall hangings could be made.

Here is another problem:

Krishana offered to make fruit punch for the year-end party at her school. Fruit punch concentrate comes in 2-litre containers. If it takes $\frac{1}{3}$ litre of concentrate to make a large bowl of punch, how many bowls of punch could she make?

Try solving this problem yourself. Use any model or drawing you wish to help explain what you are doing. Notice that you are trying to find out *How many sets of $\frac{1}{3}$ are in 2?* Your answer should be 6 bowls (not 2 thirds).

Here is another problem to try:

To earn some extra money after a winter snow storm, Nunzio decided to shovel walks in his neighbourhood. He found that it took him about $\frac{3}{5}$ hour to shovel a walk. If he spent 6 hours shovelling, how many walks did he shovel?

In this problem the quantity is the whole number, 6, and the divisor is in fifths. Since you want to measure off "sets" of $\frac{3}{5}$, someplace in the solution you will need to use fifths. Of course, this problem could also be solved by converting $\frac{3}{5}$ hour to 36 minutes.

Developing the Algorithms

There are two different algorithms for division of fractions. Methods of teaching both algorithms are discussed here.

The Common-Denominator Algorithm

The common-denominator algorithm relies on the measurement or repeated subtraction concept of division. Consider the problem "5 divided by $\frac{1}{2}$." As shown in

Figure 13.11, once each number is expressed in terms of the same fractional part, the answer is exactly the same as the whole-number problem 10 ÷ 2. The name of the fractional part (the denominator) is no longer important, and the problem is one of dividing the numerators. The resulting rule or algorithm, therefore, is as follows: *To divide fractions, first get common denominators, and then divide numerators.* $5 \div \frac{1}{2} = \frac{10}{2} \div \frac{1}{2} = 10 \div 1 = 1$.

The Invert-and-Multiply Algorithm

The more traditional algorithm for division by a fraction is to invert the divisor and multiply. This may be one of the most poorly understood procedures in the elementary curriculum. (Do you know why "invert and multiply" works?) It is possible to develop this algorithm by exploring the partition concept of division. There is very little research to support such an approach. The usual development of the invert-and-multiply approach relies on a symbolic rationale, as is outlined in Figure 13.12.

Curricular Decisions

Which of these two division algorithms for fractions would you select to teach your students? Each of the algorithms has value. Regardless of which algorithm you choose, you are strongly advised to build on informal work with story problems. It matters little how students do operations, only that they can do them in a meaningful way, accurately, and in a reasonably efficient manner.

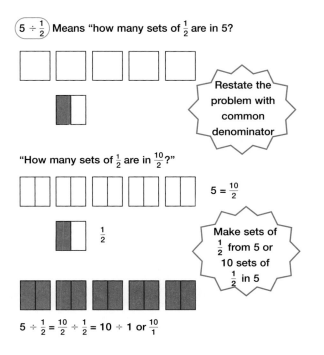

FIGURE 13.11 Models for the common-denominator method for division with fractions.

$$\frac{3}{4} \div 6 = \boxed{} \text{ or } \frac{3}{4} \div \frac{6}{1} = \boxed{}$$

Write the equation in an equivalent form as a product with a missing factor.

$$\frac{3}{4} = \boxed{} \times \frac{6}{1}$$

Multiply both sides by $\frac{1}{6}$. ($\frac{1}{6}$ is the inverse of $\frac{6}{1}$.)

$$\frac{3}{4} \times \frac{1}{6} = \boxed{} \times (\frac{6}{1} \times \frac{1}{6})$$
$$\frac{3}{4} \times \frac{1}{6} = \boxed{} \times 1$$
$$\frac{3}{4} \times \frac{1}{6} = \boxed{}$$

But $\frac{3}{4} \div \frac{6}{1} = \boxed{}$ also.

Therefore,
$$\frac{3}{4} \div \frac{6}{1} = \frac{3}{4} \times \frac{1}{6} = \boxed{}$$

In general,
$$\frac{a}{b} \div \frac{c}{d} = \frac{a}{b} \times \frac{d}{c}$$

FIGURE 13.12 To divide, invert the divisor and multiply.

If students are able to understand the symbolic explanation of the invert-and-multiply approach, it is certainly much more quickly explained, with no ambiguities or special cases to consider. For some students in grade 8, this may be a very appropriate approach.

"Invert and multiply" is generally the algorithm taught in algebra, although the common-denominator algorithm works in algebra almost as well.

 Technology Note

Very few software programs adequately address the four operations with fractions. *Math Trek 4, 5, 6* tutorials (Nectar Foundation, 2000), although algorithm-based with a focus on rule development, provide detailed guided instruction for performing the four operations with fractions. One tutorial focuses on addition and subtraction, the other on multiplication and division. For addition and subtraction, pie-shape models are used together with the symbolic form to demonstrate operations with like and unlike denominators. In contrast to the ideas promoted in this chapter, cross-multiplication is encouraged for finding common denominators and "reducing" for answers not in lowest terms. Pictorial illustrations are again paired with the symbolic form for multiplication and division. Both the regions and sets models are employed. Yet the development focuses on "the invert and multiply" rule for division and the procedure of multiplying numerator with numerator and denominator with denominator for multiplication.

Mathville VIP (Courseware Solutions, 2000), which is designated for grade 7, can also be used, according to its creators, for grades 6 through 9. Unlike the Math Trek tutorials, it offers students an opportunity to apply their knowledge of the operations with fractions in a dynamic and fast-paced context. Students must determine which operation they need to use in the various scenarios with which they are presented. However, only practice with addition and subtraction in the work component and some multiplication in the clothing store are provided.

Tenth Planet's *Fraction Operations* (1998b) is one of the better programs in this arena. All Tenth Planet packages have three sections called "Into," "Through," and "Beyond." In *Fraction Operations,* the "Through" section focuses entirely on finding common denominators. Students will see that common denominators are the same as common subdivisions. The software cleverly helps find them in a visual manner. However, as is true with this entire program, there is nothing in the presentation that will help students develop an independent or symbolic method of finding common denominators. The program finds a common subdivision but does not relate this to a common multiple of the denominators.

The "Beyond" section has four components, one for each of the four operations. In each, a contextual setting remains fixed, with different problems randomly generated for that context. For addition, two bars shown end to end (segments of a carpeted path into the castle) must be "added" so that a single red carpet can replace them, permitting the royal family to enter the castle. A measuring tool makes it easy to find a common subdivision for each bar and, thus, a common denominator to complete the addition. The subtraction component is similar. A fractional amount designates the length of a gap in a railway bridge. One fraction bar is in place. The task is to find the length of the missing bar to complete the bridge. The measuring tool is again used..

For multiplication, a square model, the floor plan of a house, is used. Part of the floor is shaded in vertical segments. The student is told what fraction of the shaded por-

tion is to be his or her bedroom. The task is to find what fraction of the whole house the bedroom will be. The graphics are wonderful and are identical to the approach described in Figure 13.9 (p. 252). Interestingly, it is possible, but not required, to extend the horizontal lines subdividing the shaded region across the entire square.

The division model starts with an amount of liquid shown in a vertical cylinder. The setting is a laboratory, and the liquid must be transferred into a number of smaller beakers. The size of the smaller beakers represents the divisor. Both the dividend and the divisor are always amounts less than 1. A problem might be to transfer $\frac{2}{3}$ of a litre of liquid to beakers that hold $\frac{1}{5}$ of a litre each. A measuring device helps determine the fractional amount in the final beaker. Only the final beaker can be subdivided, so the common-denominator method is not likely to evolve.

Each of these four components in the "Beyond" section illustrates a concept very nicely and correctly. The development of the harder concepts of multiplication and division (measurement concept) are especially well designed. The downside is that there is nothing in the program to promote reflective thinking or problem solving. The clever graphics and audio information provide all the directions. The measurement tools even make finding the common denominators and fractional parts nearly mechanical.

How can each of the packages in the program be used profitably? One idea is to use them to pose problems to the class. With numbers randomly generated, it is easy to flip through problems until you find one you would like students to solve. The essential parts of the graphics are easy to sketch on paper. Students can solve the problems themselves, pose solutions, and discuss as usual. Student solutions and methods can then be compared with the computer solutions.

Students who need special help with concepts can work independently. Remember, it is not likely that students will develop an independent strategy working with this program. ■

Reflections on *Chapter 13*

Writing to Learn

1. Make up an example, and use pie pieces (or draw pictures) to show how two fractions with unlike denominators can be added without first getting a common denominator. In your example, did you get your answer by looking at the part that was more than a whole, or by looking at the missing part that was less than a whole? Explain both of these ideas.

2. Suppose that you used pie pieces to show $\frac{2}{3} + \frac{1}{2}$ and, through some informal means, your students are now convinced that the sum is $1\frac{1}{6}$. Suppose that you now substitute $\frac{16}{24}$ for the $\frac{2}{3}$ and $\frac{7}{14}$ for the $\frac{1}{2}$. "What is this sum ($\frac{16}{24} + \frac{7}{14}$)?" Explain why you would want students to say *immediatly* that the sum was $1\frac{1}{6}$. Why is this idea important to the use of common denominators in addition and subtraction?

3. Explain why it is obvious, without using the algorithm and without first getting $\frac{24}{20}$, that $\frac{3}{4} \times \frac{8}{5} = \frac{6}{5}$.

4. Draw pictures of squares to represent the whole to illustrate these products. Provide an explanation for each:

$$3 \times \frac{2}{5} \qquad \frac{3}{4} \times \frac{2}{3} \qquad 2\frac{1}{2} \times \frac{2}{3}$$

5. Explain at least one mental method (estimation or mental computation) for each of these:

$$\frac{3}{4} \times 5\frac{1}{2} \qquad 1\frac{1}{8} \text{ of } 679$$

6. Make up a word problem with a fraction as a divisor. Is your problem a measurement problem or a partition problem? Make up a second word problem in which you use the other type (measurement or partition).

7. **a)** Use a set of counters to explain why $13 \div 5 = 2\frac{3}{5}$, using a measurement approach (that is, how many sets of 5 are in a set of 13?).

   b) Draw pictures to explain each of these divisions using a measurement approach:

$$7 \text{ divided by } \frac{1}{4} \qquad \frac{2}{3} \text{ divided by } 6$$

8. Use the problems you modelled in question 7 to explain a common-denominator algorithm for division. Use the same rationale to explain why $\frac{13}{79} \div \frac{5}{79} = 13 \div 5 = \frac{13}{5}$.

9. What is one sound reason for not teaching "invert and multiply"?

For Discussion and Exploration

1. Give two reasons why the following argument is flawed:

2. Examine a textbook series to determine where each of the fraction algorithms is first introduced. Does the presentation of the algorithm seem appropriate? How guided is the development? Will students develop an understanding of the rule, or will they simply apply it to the exercises?

3. As noted in the previous chapters, the TI-15 calculator does computations in both fractional and decimal forms. It will also give results in simplest terms. Discuss how this educational tool might be used to teach fractions, especially fractional computation. Since the TI-15 and other calculators like it can be used to compute operations with fractions, is it necessary to continue teaching fractional computation?

Recommendations for Further Reading

Highly Recommended

Huinker, D.M. (1998). Letting fraction algorithms emerge through problem solving. In L.J. Morrow (Ed.), *The teaching*

and learning of algorithms in school mathematics (pp. 170–182). Reston, VA: National Council of Teachers of Mathematics.

Huinker takes the idea of students inventing algorithms, as described for whole numbers in Chapter 10, and applies it to problems involving fractions. With examples of children's work, this article makes a good case for avoiding rules and letting students work with ideas that make sense. As always, Huinker is worth reading.

Kamii, C.K., & Warrington, M.A. (1999). Teaching fractions: Fostering children's own reasoning. In L.V. Stiff (Ed.), *Developing mathematical reasoning in grades K–12* (pp. 82–92). Reston, VA: National Council of Teachers of Mathematics.

Kamii begins with a quick review of Piagetian constructivism but quickly moves to apply this theory to the development of operations with fractions. As always, Kamii avoids the use of models and relies on carefully selected word problems. All four operations are discussed.

Kieren, T., Davis, B., & Mason, R. (1996). Fraction flags: Learning from children to help children learn. *Mathematics Teaching in the Middle School, 2,* 14–19.

The authors began with a simple area model involving rectangular pieces cut from a standard sheet of paper. When smaller pieces were placed on larger pieces with spaces in between, the results looked like flags and presented interesting problematic tasks for the students. These researchers have a long history of work with fractions, and this article offers useful insights, as well as a suggestion for an easily made model.

Other Suggestions

Behr, M.J., Wachsmuth, I., & Post, T.R. (1985). Construct a sum: A measure of children's understanding of fraction size. *Journal for Research in Mathematics education, 16,* 120–131.

Bezuk, N.S., & Bieck, M. (1993). Current research on rational numbers and common fractions: Summary and implications for teachers. In D.T. Owens (Ed.), *Research ideas for the classroom: Middle grades mathematics* (pp. 118–136). Old Tappan, NJ: Macmillan.

Graeber, A.O., & Tanenhaus, E. (1993). Multiplication and division: From whole numbers to rational numbers. In D.T. Owens (Ed.), *Research ideas for the classroom: Middle grades mathematics* (pp. 99–117). Old Tappan, NJ: Macmillan.

Groff, P. (1996). It is time to question fraction teaching. *Mathematics Teaching in the Middle School, 1,* 604–607.

Mack, N.K. (1998). Building a foundation for understanding the multiplication of fractions. *Teaching Children Mathematics, 5,* 34–38.

Nowlin, D. (1996). Division with fractions. *Mathematics Teaching in the Middle School, 2,* 116–119.

Post, T.R., Wachsmuth, I., Lesh, R.A., & Behr, M.J. (1985). Order and equivalence of rational numbers: A cognitive analysis. *Journal for Research in Mathematics Education, 16,* 18–36.

Warrington, M.A., & Kamii, C.K. (1998). Multiplication with fractions: A Piagetian, constructivist approach. *Mathematics Teaching in the Middle School, 3,* 339–343.

Chapter 14

Decimal and Percent Concepts and Decimal Computation

In most Canadian mathematics programs, fractions receive earlier attention than decimals, which are typically introduced in grade 3. When decimal concepts are developed, they need to be closely linked with fractions and the connections between these two ideas must be made explicit. Most of this chapter focuses on theese connections.

BIG IDEAS

1. Decimal numbers are simply another way of writing fractions. Connections between fraction and decimal symbolism can help in understanding both.

2. The base-ten place-value system extends infinitely in two directions: to very tiny values as well as to large values.

3. The decimal point indicates the position of the digits.

4. Percentages are another way of representing hundredths, and as such are a third way of writing fractions and decimals.

Connecting Two Different Representational Systems

The symbols 3.75 and $3\frac{3}{4}$ represent the same quantity, yet on the surface the two appear quite different. For children especially, the world of fractions and the world of decimals are very distinct. Even adults tend to think of fractions as sets or regions (three-fourths *of* something), whereas we think of decimals as being more like numbers. The reality is that fractions and decimals are two different ways that have been developed to represent the same idea. When we tell children that 0.75 is the same as

$\frac{3}{4}$, it can be especially confusing. Even though different ways of writing the numbers have been invented, the numbers themselves represent the same amount. A significant goal of instruction with decimal and fraction numeration should be to help students see that both systems represent the same concepts.

For example, in many contexts, it is easier to think about $\frac{3}{4}$ than 75 hundredths or 0.75. Conversely, the decimal system makes it easy to use numbers that are close to $\frac{3}{4}$, such as 0.73 or 0.78. An obvious application of the decimal system is in digital equipment such as calculators, computers, and electronic meters.

To help students see the connection between fractions and decimals, we can do three things. First, we can use familiar fractional concepts and models to explore rational numbers that are easily represented by decimals: tenths, hundredths, and thousandths. Second, we can extend the base-ten decimal system to include numbers less than 1 as well as large numbers. Third, we can help children use models to make meaningful translations between fractions and decimals. These three components are discussed here in turn.

Base-Ten Fractions

Fractions that have denominators of 10, 100, 1000, and so on will be referred to as *base-ten fractions* in this chapter. This is simply a convenient label and is not one commonly found in the literature. Fractions such as $\frac{7}{10}$ or $\frac{63}{100}$ are examples of base-ten fractions.

Base-Ten Fraction Models

Most of the common models for fractions are somewhat limited for the purpose of depicting base-ten fractions.

FIGURE 14.1 A hundredths disk for modelling base-ten fractions.

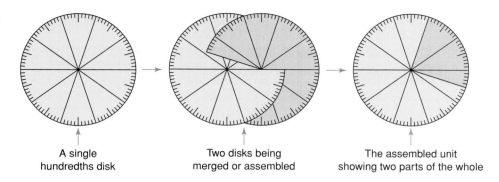

A single
hundredths disk

Two disks being
merged or assembled

The assembled unit
showing two parts of the whole

Generally, the familiar fractional models cannot show hundredths or thousandths. It is important to provide models for these fractions using the same conceptual approaches that were used for smaller fractions such as thirds and fourths.

Two very important region models can be used to model base-ten fractions. First, to model tenths and hundredths, circular disks such as the one shown in Figure 14.1 can be printed on tag-board (see Blackline Masters). Each disk is marked with 100 equal intervals around the edge and is cut along one radius. Two disks of different colours, slipped together as shown, can be used to model any fraction less than 1. Fractions modelled on this hundredths disk, reminiscent of the traditional pie model, can be read as base-ten fractions by noting the spaces around the edge.

The most common model for base-ten fractions is a 10 × 10 square. Squares, representing one whole, can be run off on paper so that students can shade in various fractions (see Figure 14.2 and Blackline Masters). Another important model, fashioned after the Dienes blocks (see Chapter 9, page 163), is the base-ten place-value model using strips and squares. Although this variation of the model is better than working without models, the Dienes blocks themselves are preferable. As a fractional model, the 10-cm square used to represent one hundred when whole numbers were being studied is now the whole or 1. Each strip is thus 1 tenth, and each small square is 1 hundredth. The *Decimal Squares* materials (Bennett, 1982) include squares in which each hundredth is again partitioned into ten smaller sections. Shading in portions of the square permits modelling of thousandths. One more step is provided in the Blackline Masters, where a large square is subdivided into 10 000 tiny squares. When shown on an overhead projector, individual squares or ten-thousandths can easily be identified and shaded in with a pen on the transparency.

One of the best length models is a metre stick. Each decimetre is one-tenth of the whole stick, each centimetre is one-hundredth, and each millimetre is one-thousandth. Any number-line model broken into 100 subparts is likewise a useful model for hundredths.

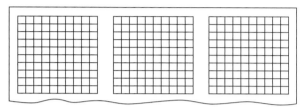

10 × 10 squares on paper. Each square is one whole.
Students shade fractional parts.

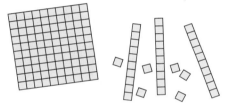

Base-ten strips and squares can be used to model base-ten fractions. Instead of shading in the large square, strips and small squares are placed on it to show a fractional part.

FIGURE 14.2 10 × 10 squares model base-ten fractions.

Many teachers use money as a model for decimals, and to some extent this is helpful. However, for children, money is mostly a two-place system: Numbers like 3.2 or 12.1389 do not relate to money. Children's initial contact with decimals should be more flexible, and so money is not recommended as a decimal model. However, money is certainly an important *application* of decimals. It is well suited for reinforcing, clarifying, and consolidating what children are learning about decimals.

Multiple Names and Formats

Early work with base-ten fractions is designed primarily to acquaint students with the models, to help them begin to think of quantities in terms of tenths and hundredths, and to help them learn to read and write base-ten fractions in different ways.

Have students show a base-ten fraction using any base-ten fractional model. Once a fraction, say, $\frac{65}{100}$, is modelled, the following ideas can be explored:

■ Is this fraction more or less than $\frac{1}{2}$? than $\frac{2}{3}$? than $\frac{3}{4}$? Some familiarity with these fractions can be developed by comparing them with fractions that are easy to think about.

■ Using tenths and hundredths, what are some different ways to say this fraction? ("6 tenths and 5 hundredths," "65 hundredths") Include thousandths when appropriate.

■ Show two different ways to write this fraction ($\frac{65}{100}$ or $\frac{6}{10} + \frac{5}{100}$).

The last two questions are very important. When base-ten fractions are later written as decimals, they should be read as a single fraction. That is, 0.65 should be read as "sixty-five hundredths." However, to understand the number in terms of its place value, it needs to be thought of as 6 tenths and 5 hundredths. The decimal number 5.13 should be read the same way as the mixed number $5\frac{13}{100}$ "five and thirteen-hundredths." For purposes of place value, it should also be understood as $5 + \frac{1}{10} + \frac{3}{100}$. Special attention should also be given to numbers such as the following:

$$0.030 = \frac{0}{10} + \frac{3}{100} + \frac{0}{1000} = \frac{30}{1000}$$

$$0.70 = \frac{7}{10} + \frac{0}{100} = \frac{70}{100}$$

The expanded forms will be helpful in translating these decimal numbers to fractions. Sometimes, fractions or decimal numbers with trailing zeros are used in oral form to indicate a higher level of precision. Even though seven-tenths is the same in value as 70 hundredths, the latter conveys precision to the nearest hundredth, instead of to the nearest tenth.

Exercises at this introductory level should include all possible connections between models, and various oral and written forms. Given a model or an oral or written form for a fraction, students should be able to give the other two forms, including equivalent forms where appropriate.

Extending the Place-Value System

Before considering decimal numbers with students, it is advisable to review some whole-number place-value ideas. One of the most basic ideas is the 10-to-1 relationship between the digits in any two adjacent positions in a number. This means that each time you move from right to left for any number, the value of the place you are in increases by a factor of ten. Conversely, as you move from left to right, the value of the place you are in decreases by a factor of ten. In terms of a base-ten model such as strips and squares, 10 of any one piece is equal to 1 of the next larger piece, and vice versa.

A Two-Way Relationship

The 10-to-1 rule can be extended to larger pieces or positional values. This concept is fun to explore when you consider how large the strips and squares will actually be if you move six or eight places in either direction. If you are using the strips-and-squares model, the shapes alternate in an infinite progression as they become larger and larger. Once you have established the progression for larger pieces, concentrate on the idea that each piece to the right in this string decreases by one-tenth. The critical question then becomes, "Is there ever a smallest piece?" In the students' experience, the smallest piece is the centimetre square or unit piece. Couldn't that piece be divided into 10 small strips? And couldn't these small strips be divided into 10 smaller squares, and so on? Hence, in the mind's eye, there is no smallest strip or smallest square.

The goal of this discussion is to help students see that a 10-to-1 relationship could extend *infinitely in two directions*. There is no smallest piece and no largest piece. The relationship between two adjacent pieces is the same regardless of which two pieces are being considered. Figure 14.3 illustrates this idea.

The Role of the Decimal Point

An important idea to realize in this discussion is that any one position could be chosen to be the unit, or ones position. There is no built-in reason why this could not happen. In terms of strips and squares, for example, which piece is the ones piece? Is it the small centimetre square? Why? Why not a larger or a smaller square? Why not a strip? *Any piece could effectively be chosen as the ones piece.*

When a number such as 1624 is written, the assumption is that the 4 is in the units or ones position. But if a position to the left of the 4 is selected as the ones position, some method of designating that position must be devised. Enter the decimal point. As shown in Figure 14.4, the same amount can be written in different ways, depending on the choice of the unit. The decimal point is situated between two positions, with the convention that the place to the left of the decimal point is the units or ones place. Thus, the role of the decimal point is *to designate the units place,* and it does so by sitting just to the right of it.

A fitting caricature of the decimal point is shown in Figure 14.5. The "eyes" of the decimal point always focus up toward the name of the units or ones. A tag-board disk of this decimal-point face can be used between two adjacent base-ten models or on a place-value chart (found with the hundredths disk in the Blackline Masters). If such a decimal point were placed between the squares and strips

FIGURE 14.3 Theoretically, the strips and squares extend infinitely in both directions.

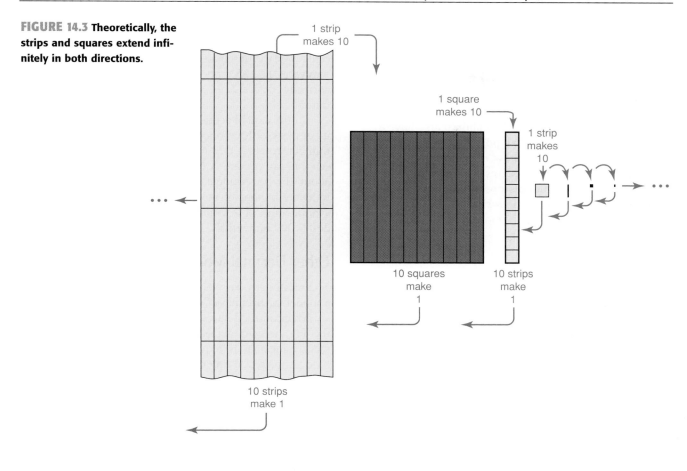

FIGURE 14.4 The decimal point indicates which position is the units.

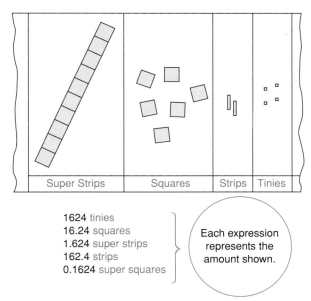

Super Strips	Squares	Strips	Tinies

1624 tinies
16.24 squares
1.624 super strips
162.4 strips
0.1624 super squares

Each expression represents the amount shown.

in Figure 14.4, the squares would then be designated as the units, and 16.24 would be the correct written form for the model.

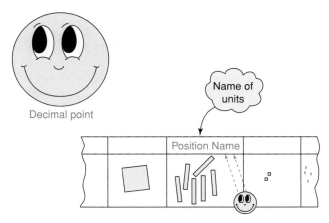

Decimal point

Name of units

Position Name

FIGURE 14.5 The decimal point always "looks up at" the name of the units position.

The Decimal Names the Unit

Have students display on their desks a given amount in base-ten pieces. For example, put out

3 squares, 7 strips, and 4 tinies. Refer to the pieces as "squares," "strips," and "tinies," and reach an agreement on names for both the smaller and larger theoretical pieces. To the right of tinies can be "tiny strips" and "tiny squares." To the left of squares can be "super strips" and "super squares." Each student should also have a tag-board smiley decimal point. Now ask students to write and say how many squares they have, how many super strips, and so on, as in Figure 14.4. The students position their decimal point accordingly and write and say the amounts.

Activity 14.1 illustrates that the decimal point dictates the name and value of a unit. (Depending on its position, the decimal point can change the value of a unit without changing the original quantity, as Figure 14.4 illustrates.)

A related discussion could involve multiplication or division of a quantity by powers of 10. If the display shows, for example, 3.74 squares, what would 10 times this amount be? Ten times 3.74 squares is 37.4 squares. Here the decimal remains to the right of the units, since 10 times 3.74 squares will still be squares. But 37.4 squares is also the same as 3 super strips, 7 squares and 4 strips.

The Decimal with Measurement and Monetary Units

The convention that the place to the left of the decimal point is the units or ones place can be useful in a variety of contexts. For example, in Figure 14.6, as shown with linear measure, the decimal point can be used to designate any of the seven places as the unit without changing the actual length. Our monetary system is also a decimal system. For the amount $172.95, the decimal point designates the dollars position as the unit. This amount of money consists of 1 hundred, 7 tens, 2 singles, 9 dimes, and 5 pennies or cents regardless of how it is written. If cents were the designated unit, the same amount would be written as 17 295 cents or 17 295.0 cents. It could just as correctly be 0.17295 thousands of dollars or 1729.5 dimes.

In the case of actual measures for length, area, capacity or mass, or for money, the unit name is written after the number. You may be 1.62 metres tall, but it does not make sense to say you are "1.62 tall." In the paper, we may read about the government spending $7.3 billion. Here the units are billions of dollars, not dollars. A city may have a population of 2.4 million people. That is the same as 2 400 000 individuals.

Other Decimal Models

Technically, any base-ten place-value model can be used as a model for decimals. With the strips-and-squares model, students can each have a set of materials at their desks. If the kit includes a tag-board smiley decimal point, no place-value mat is required. Students can arrange their base-ten pieces in order and put the decimal point to the right of the designated unit piece. Usually, the 10-cm square is selected. This allows students to model decimal fractions to hundredths. Some teachers even cut wooden toothpicks into 1-cm lengths to represent the next smaller strip, the thousandths. These show up very nicely on an overhead projector.

Dienes blocks (see Chapter 9) have four different pieces. If the 10-cm cube or "block" is designated as 1, then the flats, longs, and small cubes can be used to model decimals to three places.

Any base-ten fraction model is also a decimal model since decimals and fractions are simply two different ways to represent the same amounts. Three-fourths is shown on the hundredths disk as 7 tenths and 5 hundredths. If these pieces could be cut up and put on a place-value chart, they would be shown as 0.75, with the decimal point between the circles (ones) and tenths place, as in Figure 14.7.

FIGURE 14.6 Each place-value position for metric measure has a name. The decimal point designates which length is the unit length.

kilometre	hectometre	decametre	metre	decimetre	centimetre	millimetre	
		4	3	8	5		

4 decametres, 3 metres, 8 decimetres, and 5 centimetres =

43.85	metres
43850	millimetres
0.04385	kilometres
4385	centimetres

Unit names

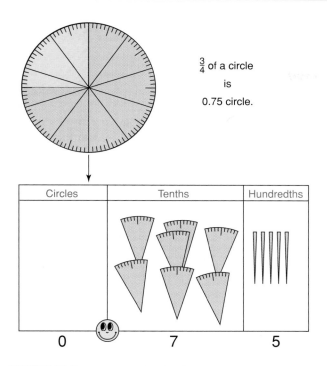

$\frac{3}{4}$ of a circle

is

0.75 circle.

FIGURE 14.7 Fraction models could be decimal models.

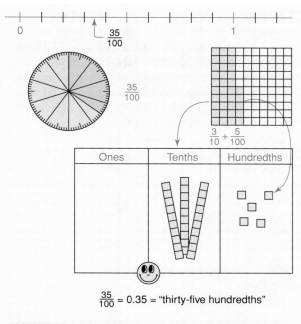

$\frac{35}{100}$ = 0.35 = "thirty-five hundredths"

FIGURE 14.8 Translation of a base-ten fraction to a decimal.

Making the Fraction-Decimal Connection

To connect the two numeration systems, fractions and decimals, students need to make concept-oriented translations. The purpose of such activities has less to do with the skill of converting a fraction to a decimal than with constructing the concept that both systems express the same ideas.

ACTIVITY 14.2

Base-Ten Fractions to Decimals

Start with a base-ten fraction, such as $\frac{35}{100}$ or $\frac{28}{10}$. Have students use their place-value strips and squares. Agree that the large square will represent one. Then have students cover the square using their strips and tinies to represent a base-ten fractional amount. Whole numbers will require additional squares. The task for students is to write the fraction they have shown as a decimal number, pointing out the connection using the materials (see Figure. 14.8).

Once a fraction is modelled and written as both a fraction and a decimal, both symbolisms should be read. The oral language for both fraction and decimal should be the same.

Activity 14.2 starts with a fraction and ends with a decimal. The reverse activity is equally important: Begin with a decimal number; have students use several models to represent it. Then have them read and write it as a fraction. As long as the fractions are restricted to base-ten fractions, the conversions are straightforward.

The calculator can also play a significant role in decimal concept development.

ACTIVITY 14.3

Calculator Decimal Counting

This activity works well with the TI-15 calculator. Review how to make the calculator "count" by pressing 1 ⊞ , then ⊟ repeatedly. Have students press 0.1 ⊞ , then continue to press ⊟ until the display shows 0.9. Now, stop and discuss what this means and what the display will look like with the next press. Many students will predict 0.10 (thinking that 10 comes after 9). This challenge is even more interesting if, with each press, the students have been accumulating base-ten strips as models for tenths. One more press would mean one more strip, or 10 strips. Why should the calculator not show 0.10? When the tenth press produces a display of 1 (calculators do not usually display trailing zeros to the right of the decimal), the discussion should revolve around trading 10 strips for a square.

Continue to count to 4 or 5 by tenths. How many presses to get from one whole number to the next? Try counting by 0.01 or by 0.001. These counts illustrate dramatically how small one-hundredth and one-thousandth really are. It requires 10 counts by 0.001 to get to 0.01 and 1000 counts to reach 1. This activity may work differently with other calculators.

Activity 14.3 provides an excellent opportunity for class discussion. Never cite the calculator as the reason for any result or as a source of truth. The fact that the calculator counts 0.8, 0.9, 1., 1.1 instead of 0.8, 0.9, 0.10, 0.11 should give rise to the question "Does this make sense? If so, why?" After all, experts made the calculator this way. Did they do it right? Why did they make it this way?

ACTIVITY 14.4
Double Calculator Counting

A fascinating variation of Activity 14.3 is to use two calculators side by side: the TI-15, which displays fractions, and a calculator that does not (such as the TI-108). On the fraction calculator, enter ⊞ 1, then ⊟, 10, and ⊟ again. On the standard calculator, enter ⊞ 0.1⊟. Repeatedly press ⊟ on the standard calculator and ⊟ on the fraction calculator simultaneously. At 10 presses, both calculators show 1. With continued increments, the fraction calculator numerator will show $\frac{11}{10}$, and so on. If the ⬛ key is pressed, the mixed number is displayed. The display can be made to toggle back and forth among the mixed number, the improper fraction, and the decimal equivalent by pressing ⬛. If models are also coordinated with the counting, the activity helps relate two symbol systems and a conceptual model in a powerful illustration.

Activities such as "Calculator Decimal Counting" and "Double Calculator Counting" are enhanced with the TI-15 because of the mode choices, because both calculation and results are displayed for successive counts, and because fractions are nicely displayed with a horizontal fraction bar. This educational device also has the most flexible fraction and decimal displays available. It can be set to automatically simplify fractions to lowest terms or to permit "manual" simplification, letting the user select a common factor. In the manual simplify mode, the key converts 0.25 to ↓25/100. The down arrow indicates that lower terms are possible. In the simplify mode, 0.25 is converted to $\frac{1}{4}$. Results will be either mixed or improper fractions, depending on mode choice.

Developing Decimal Number Sense

So far, the discussion has revolved around the connection of decimals with base-ten fractions. Number sense implies more. It means having intuition about, or a friendly understanding of, numbers. To this end, it is useful to connect decimals to the fractions with which children are familiar, to be able to compare and order decimals readily, and to approximate decimals with useful familiar numbers.

Familiar Fractions Connected to Decimals

Chapter 12 showed how to help students develop a conceptual familiarity with simple fractions, especially halves, thirds, fourths, fifths, and eighths. We should extend this familiarity to the same concepts expressed as decimals. One way to do this is to have students translate familiar fractions to decimals by means of a base-ten model.

The purpose of the following activity is to help students think of decimals in terms of familiar fractional equivalents and to make the connection in a conceptual manner.

ACTIVITY 14.5
Friendly Decimal Fractions

Have students shade in familiar fractions on a 10 × 10 grid. Because the grid effectively translates any fraction to a base-ten fraction, the fractions can then easily be written as decimals. Under each shaded figure, write the fraction in familiar form, then as a base-ten fraction, and finally as a decimal, as shown in Figure 14.9.

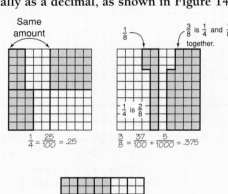

FIGURE 14.9 Familiar fractions converted to decimals using a 10 × 10 square.

Begin with halves and fifths, since these can be shown with strips of 10 squares. Next explore fourths. Many students will shade $\frac{1}{4}$ by shading in a 5×5 square of the grid. See if they can then shade the same amount using ten strips only. You might ask them how they can show an amount that requires fewer than the 10 small squares of a ten strip. Repeat for other fourths, such as $\frac{3}{4}$ or $\frac{7}{4}$. You might want to try eighths, but they will present an interesting challenge. Thirds are best done as a special activity.

ACTIVITY 14.6

Dual Counts with Friendly Fractions

Repeat Activity 14.4, "Double Calculator Counting," but this time begin with a familiar or friendly fraction such as $\frac{1}{5}$ or $\frac{1}{4}$ on the fraction calculator and the corresponding decimal on the other calculator. Again, explore counts beyond 1 or 2 wholes, and also switch between mixed and improper fractions. Notice also that while the F↔D **key changes a fraction to a decimal, when changing a decimal to a fraction it uses a base-ten fraction. Thus 2.6 is changed to $2\frac{6}{10}$. The** Simp **key can then be used to find the fraction $2\frac{3}{5}$ with which you are working.**

Results of the U.S. based National Assessment of Educational Progress (NAEP) examinations consistently reveal that students have difficulties with fraction-decimal equivalences. Kouba et al. (1988a) note that students could express proper fractions as decimals, findings which are substantiated by Canadian test results (SAIP, 1993, 1997, 2001) for 13-year-old students. Yet only 40 percent of grade 7 students who participated in the fourth NAEP could give a decimal equivalent for a mixed number. In the sixth NAEP, students had difficulty placing decimal numbers on a number line where the subdivisions were fractions (Kouba, Zawojewski, & Strutchens, 1997). These results suggest that students may be memorizing equivalences without thinking about the conceptual relationships. Learning to explain a decimal equivalent for a mixed number such as $4\frac{2}{3}$ or a fraction equivalent for $8\frac{3}{4}$ is much more important than mastering a rule for conversion. Division of the numerator by the denominator may be a means of converting fractions to decimals, but it contributes nothing to understanding its equivalent result. Note that this method has not been and will not be suggested in this chapter.

Approximation with a Nice Fraction

In the real world, decimal numbers rarely have exact equivalents of nice fractions. What fraction would you say approximates the decimal 0.52? In the sixth NAEP exam in the United States, only 51 percent of grade 8 students selected $\frac{1}{2}$. The other choices were $\frac{1}{50}$ (29 percent), $\frac{1}{5}$ (11 percent), $\frac{1}{4}$ (6 percent), and $\frac{1}{3}$ (4 percent) (Kouba et al., 1997). Again, the most plausible explanation for this performance is a reliance on rules. The less-than-satisfactory results achieved by Canadians (as well as international students) on the Third International Mathematics and Science Study (TIMSS) suggests that more time needs to be spent developing conceptual understanding of decimals, rather than relying on rules (Robitaille, Taylor, Orpwood, 1996). Students need to wrestle with the size of decimal numbers and begin to develop a sense of familiarity with them. And this must extend to all decimal numbers, not just those such as 0.75 that have exact equivalents.

As with fractions, the first benchmarks that should be developed are 0, $\frac{1}{2}$, and 1. For example, is 7.3962 closer to 7 or 8? Why? (Would you accept this response: "Closer to 7 because 3 is less than 5"?) Is it closer to 7 or $7\frac{1}{2}$? Often the 0, $\frac{1}{2}$, or 1 benchmarks are good enough to make sense of a situation. If a closer approximation is required, students should be encouraged to consider the other friendly fractions (thirds, fourths, fifths, and eighths). In this example, 7.3962 is close to 7.4, which is $7\frac{2}{5}$. A good number sense with decimals would grant the ability to think quickly of a meaningful fraction that is a close substitute for almost any number.

To develop this type of familiarity with decimals, children do not need new concepts or skills. They need the opportunity to apply and discuss the related concepts of fractions, place value, and decimals in activities such as the following.

ACTIVITY 14.7

Close to a Friendly Fraction

Make a list of decimal numbers that do not have nice fractional equivalents. Have students suggest a nearby decimal number that does have a nice equivalent. Try this yourself with this list:

24.8025   6.59   0.9003   124.356

Different students may select different fractions for these numbers. Having them explain the rationale for their choices presents an excellent opportunity for discussion.

ACTIVITY 14.8

Best Match

On the board, list a scattered arrangement of four familiar fractions and at least four decimals that are close to the fractions but not exact. Students are to pair each fraction with the decimal that best matches it. Figure 14.10 is an example. The difficulty is determined by how close the various fractions are one to another.

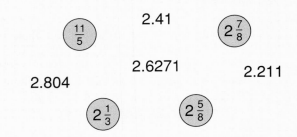

FIGURE 14.10 Match the decimal numbers with the closest fraction expression.

In Activities 14.7 and 14.8, students will have a variety of reasons for their answers. Sharing their thinking with the class provides a valuable opportunity for all to learn. Do not focus on the answers but on the rationales.

Ordering Decimal Numbers

Putting a list of decimal numbers in order from least to greatest is a skill closely related to the one just discussed. The most common error is to select numbers with more digits, which is an incorrect application of whole-number ideas. However, there are some students who later pick up the idea that the digits far to the right actually represent very small number values. They then incorrectly identify numbers with more digits as always being smaller. Both errors reflect a lack of conceptual understanding of how decimal numbers are constructed, as findings from TIMSS suggest (Robitaille, Taylor, Orpwood, 1996). The following activities can help promote discussion about the relative size of decimal numbers.

ACTIVITY 14.9

The Larger Decimal Number

Present two decimal numbers, and have students use models to explain which is larger. A metre stick or a 10 × 10 square is useful for this purpose.

ACTIVITY 14.10

Close "Nice" Numbers

Write a four-digit decimal on the board—3.0917, for example. Start with the whole number: "Is it closer to 3 or 4?" Then go to the tenths: "Is it closer to 3.0 or 3.1?" Repeat with hundredths and thousandths. At each answer, challenge students to defend their choices with the use of a model or other conceptual explanation. Including a decimal number such as 2.49 should lead to some interesting discussion regarding how numbers like this should be rounded (Is 2.49 closer to 2 or 3?) A large number line without numbers, shown in Figure 14.11, is useful.

Too often, the process of rounding numbers is taught as an algorithm without any reflection on why the algorithm makes sense. Children come to believe that to "round" a number means to do something to it or change it in some way. In reality, to *round* a number means that you *substitute* a "nice" number as an approximation for the cumbersome original number. In this sense, we can also round decimal numbers to "nice fractions" and not just to tenths and hundredths. For example, instead of rounding 6.73 to the nearest tenth, from a number sense perspective rounding it to the nearest quarter (6.75 or $6\frac{3}{4}$) or to the nearest third (6.67 or $6\frac{2}{3}$) is suggested.

ACTIVITY 14.11

Line 'Em Up

Prepare a list of four or five decimal numbers that students might have difficulty putting in order. They should all be between the same two consecutive whole numbers. Have students first predict the order of the numbers, from least to greatest. Next, have them place each number on a number line with 100 subdivisions, as in Figure 14.11. As an alternative, have students shade in the fractional part of each number on a separate 10 × 10 grid using estimates for the thousandths and ten-thousandths. In either case, it quickly becomes obvious which digits contribute the most to the size of a decimal number.

 Technology Note

The key to making the connection between fractions and decimals is ample class discussion of comparisons and

FIGURE 14.11 A decimal number line.

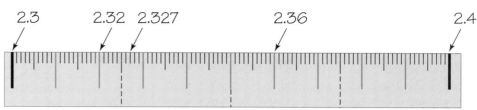

Cut four strips of poster board measuring 15 × 70 centimetres. Tape end to end. Place on chalk tray. Write on board above. Endpoints can be any interval of 1, $\frac{1}{10}$, $\frac{1}{100}$.

equivalent expressions, as in the activities already described. Although discussion is not the focus of the *Math Trek* software (Nectar Foundation, 2000), it does reinforce the connection between decimals and their fractional equivalents. The interactive tutorial in *Math Trek 4, 5, 6* (Nectar Foundation, 2000), a subsection of the component comparing decimals and fractions, uses the number line and the 10 × 10 square to illustrate the connection between the two numeration systems. When a button is clicked a portion of a 10 × 10 square is coloured to show its fractional, decimal, and symbolic equivalents. The same technique is used with rectangles to demonstrate fractions to the thousandths place. Opportunities for practice are available. In the lesson component of *Math Trek 7, 8, 9* (Nectar Foundation, 2000), money is used as a starting point to illustrate the conversion of decimals to their fractional equivalents. A pictorial representation is also used as part of the lesson. Both base-ten fractions and those whose denominators are not factors of 100 are included. Contrary to the ideas for converting fractions to their decimal equivalents promoted in the chapter, the software provides only one method: dividing the numerator by the denominator.

MathKeys: Unlocking Fractions and Decimals (MECC, 1996a) has one decimal component that you may find useful. The software permits easy "stamping" of squares for wholes, strips for tenths, and small squares for hundredths. When the addition mode is selected, two numbers can be made side by side, one in red and the other in yellow. The decimal numbers are shown in an addition equation. The two numbers can then be compared visually. Clicking on the button unfortunately combines the two models automatically and displays the sum in both horizontal and vertical format, with no student input.

The drill program *Math Munchers Deluxe* (MECC, 1995d) provides useful practice in decimal-fraction equivalence in a format students seem to like. An array of 25 fractions, decimals, fraction region models, percents, and ratios is presented. The student is to find all instances that are equivalent to a given decimal number; the settings can also be changed so that the goal is to find quantities less than or greater than the given number. The 17 levels of difficulty provide ample challenge. This is a good example of worthwhile drill. However, it must come after conceptual ideas are well developed. The program offers no feedback or conceptual assistance. ■

Other Fraction-Decimal Equivalents

So far, fraction-decimal equivalents have been discussed for the nice fractions: halves, thirds, fourths, fifths, and eighths. Also, any base-ten fraction is easily converted to a decimal. Working with these fractions and their decimal equivalents will provide a significant degree of number-sense development with decimal numbers. The major component of decimal instruction should be a conceptual focus on these ideas.

At times, however, other fractions must be expressed as a decimal. Remember that in any fraction the denominator is a divisor and the numerator is a multiplier. (The indicated division is one of at least five meanings of fractions.) For example, $\frac{3}{4}$ means the same as $3 \times 1 \div 4 = 3 \div 4$. So how do you express $\frac{3}{4}$ on simple four-function calculator? Simply enter $3 \div 4$. The display will read 0.75. Now see what happens with the fraction $\frac{3}{7}$. The answer is based on the fact that $\frac{3}{7}$ is also an expression for $3 \div 7$. If this division is carried out on paper, an infinite but repeating decimal will result. The ninths also have very interesting decimal equivalents, and looking for a pattern is a worthwhile activity (try $1 \div 9$, $2 \div 9$,..., on your calculator). The division process should also be checked out for familiar fractional equivalents. If students have constructed a good understanding of familiar fractions and their decimal equivalents, what they know will confirm the division result. If the division $4 \div 5$ is the only explanation students have for why $\frac{4}{5} = 0.8$, there is likely a significant lack of understanding of the conceptual linkage between fractions and decimals.

In grades 7 or 8, students are frequently taught to convert a repeating decimal to a fraction. These conversions demonstrate that every repeating decimal can also be represented as a fraction and therefore as a rational number. This important theoretical result is useful primarily for distinguishing between rational and irrational numbers. However, the contribution such tedious activities make to number sense is minimal.

Introducing Percentages

Textbooks have traditionally treated percent as a separate topic from fractions and decimals, or included it in a chapter on ratios. The concept of percent is so closely tied to fractions and decimals that it makes better sense to discuss percents as students begin to understand the fraction-decimal relationship.

A Third Operator System

When children have made a strong connection between the concepts of fractions and decimals, the topic of percents can be introduced. Rather than approach percents as a new idea, children should see that percents are simply a different way to record ideas they have already developed about fractions and decimals.

Another Name for Hundredths

The term *percent* is simply another name for *hundredths*. If students can express common fractions and simple decimal numbers as hundredths, the term *percent* can be substituted for the term *hundredth*. Consider the fraction $\frac{3}{4}$. As a fraction expressed in hundredths, it is $\frac{75}{100}$. When $\frac{3}{4}$ is written in decimal form, it is 0.75. Both 0.75 and $\frac{75}{100}$ are read in exactly the same way, "seventy-five hundredths." As a percent, $\frac{3}{4}$ is the same as 0.75 or 75 percent. Thus percent is merely a new notation and terminology, not a new concept.

Models provide the main link amongst fractions, decimals, and percents, as shown in Figure 14.12. Base-ten

fraction models are suitable for fractions, decimals, and percents, since they all represent the same idea.

Another helpful approach to the terminology of percent is through the role of the decimal point. Recall that the decimal identifies the units. When the unit is ones, a number such as 0.659 means a little more than 6 tenths of 1. The word *ones* is understood (6 tenths of 1 *one*). But 0.659 is also 6.59 tenths and 65.9 hundredths and 659 thousandths. In each case, the name of the unit must be explicitly identified, or else it would be assumed to be ones. In 6.59 tenths, the interpretation is 6 and 59 hundredths *of the things called tenths*. Since *percent* is another name for *hundredths*, when the decimal identifies the hundredths position as the units, the word *percent* can be specified as a synonym for *hundredths*. Thus 0.659 (of some whole or 1) is 65.9 hundredths or 65.9 percent of that same whole. As illustrated in Figure 14.13, the notion of placing the decimal point *to identify the percent position* is conceptually more meaningful than the apparently arbitrary rule: "To change a decimal to a percent, move the decimal two places to the right." A better idea is to equate hundredths with percent both orally and in notation.

Using Percent with Familiar Fractions

Students should use base-ten models for percents in much the same way as they would for decimals. The disk with 100 markings around the edge is now a model for percent as well as a fraction model for hundredths. The same is true of a 10 × 10 square. Each tiny square inside is 1 percent of the square. Each row or strip of 10 squares is not only a tenth but also 10 percent of the square.

Similarly, the familiar fractions (halves, thirds, fourths, fifths, and eighths) should become familiar in terms of percents as well as decimals. Three-fifths, for example, is 60 percent as well as 0.6. One-third of an amount is frequently expressed as $33\frac{1}{3}$ percent instead of 33.3333 ... percent. Likewise, $\frac{1}{8}$ of a quantity is $12\frac{1}{2}$ percent or 12.5 percent of the quantity. These ideas should be explored with base-ten models and not as rules about moving decimal points.

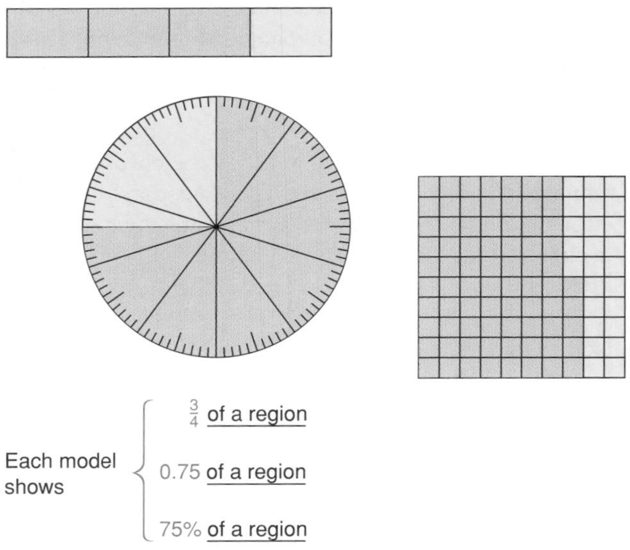

Each model shows
$\frac{3}{4}$ of a region
0.75 of a region
75% of a region

FIGURE 14.12 Models connect three different notations.

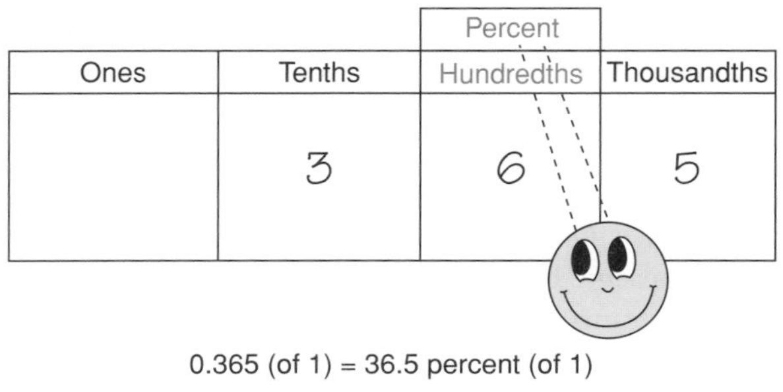

Ones	Tenths	Percent	
		Hundredths	Thousandths
3	6		5

0.365 (of 1) = 36.5 percent (of 1)

FIGURE 14.13 Hundredths are also known as percents.

Realistic Percent Problems

The Three Percent Problems

Frequently, senior grade teachers talk about "the three percent problems." The sentence "_____ is _____ percent of _____" has three spaces for numbers; for example, "20 is 25 percent of 80." The classic three percent problems come from this sterile expression: two of the numbers are given, and the students are asked to produce the third. Students learn very quickly that you either multiply or divide the two given numbers, and sometimes you have to move a decimal point. But they have no way of determining when to do what, which numbers to divide, or which way to shift the decimal. As a result, performance on percentage problems is very poor. Furthermore, commonly encountered expressions using percent terminology, such as sales figures, taxes, census data, political information, and economic trends, are almost never in the "_____ is _____ percent of _____" format. So when asked to solve a realistic percent problem, students are frequently at a loss.

Chapter 12 explored three types of exercises with fractions in which one element—part, whole, or fraction—was unknown. Students used models and simple fraction relationships in those exercises. Those three types of exercises are precisely the same as the three percent problems. Developmentally, then, it makes sense to help students make the connection between the exercises done with fractions and those done with percents. How? Use the same types of models and the same terminology of parts, wholes, and fractions. The only thing that is different is that the word *percent* is used instead of *fraction*. In Figure 14.14, three exercises from Chapter 12 have been changed to the corresponding percent terminology. A good idea for

early work with percents would be to review (or explore for the first time) all three types of exercises in terms of percents. The same three types of models can be used (refer to Figures 12.7, 12.8, and 12.9 on p. 230).

Realistic Percent Problems and Nice Numbers

Though students must have some experience with the non-contextual situations in Figure 14.14, it is important to have them explore these relationships in real-life contexts. Find or make up percent problems, and present them in the same way that they appear in newspapers, on television, and in other real contexts. In addition to realistic problems and formats, follow these maxims for your unit on percents:

- Limit the percents to familiar fractions (halves, thirds, fourths, fifths, and eighths) or easy percents ($\frac{1}{10}$, $\frac{1}{100}$), and use numbers compatible with these fractions. The focus of these exercises is the relationships involved, not the complex computational skills.
- Do not suggest any rules or procedures for different types of problems. Do not categorize or label problem types.
- Use the terms *part, whole,* and *percent* (or *fraction*). *Fraction* and *percent* should be interchangeable. Help students see these percent exercises as the same types of exercises they did with simple fractions.
- Students should be obliged to use models or drawings to explain their solutions. It is better to assign three problems that require a drawing and an explanation than to give 15 problems needing only computation and answers. Remember that the purpose is the exploration of relationships, not computational skill.
- Encourage mental computation.

The following sample problems meet these criteria for easy fractions and numbers. Try solving each problem, identifying each number as a part, a whole, or a fraction. Draw length or area models to explain or work through your thought process. Examples of this informal reasoning are illustrated with additional problems in Figure 14.15.

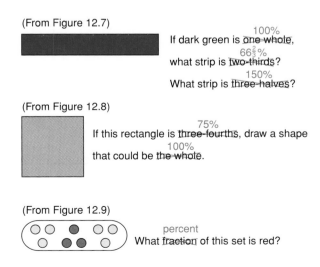

(From Figure 12.7)

If dark green is ~~one whole~~ 100%, what strip is ~~two-thirds~~ 66⅔%? What strip is ~~three-halves~~ 150%?

(From Figure 12.8)

If this rectangle is ~~three-fourths~~ 75%, draw a shape that could be ~~the whole~~ 100%.

(From Figure 12.9)

What ~~fraction~~ percent of this set is red?

FIGURE 14.14 **Part-whole-fraction exercises can be translated into percent exercises.**

1. **The Parent Advisory Council reported that 75 percent of the total number of families was represented at the meeting last night. If children from 320 families go to the school, how many were represented at the meeting?**

2. **The baseball team won 80 percent of the 25 games it played this year. How many games were lost?**

3. **In Mrs. Carter's class, 20 students, or $66\frac{2}{3}$ percent, were on the honour roll. How many students were in her class?**

4. Freda bought her new computer at a $12\frac{1}{2}$ percent discount. She paid $1200. How many dollars did she save by buying it at a discount?

5. If Alicia has read 60 of the 180 pages in her library book, what percent of the book has she read so far?

6. The hardware store bought machine bolts at 80 cents each and sold them for $1 each. What percent did the store mark up the price of each bolt?

Estimation in Percent Problems

Of course, not all real percent problems have nice numbers. Frequently in real life, an approximation or estimate in percent situations is all that is required, or is enough to help one think through the situation. Even if a calculator were used to get an exact answer, an estimate based on an understanding of the relationship could confirm that a correct operation was performed, or that the decimal was positioned correctly.

To help students with estimation in percent situations, two ideas that have already been discussed can be applied. First, when the percent is not a "nice" one, substitute a close percent that is easy to work with. Second, select

numbers that are compatible with the percent involved in order to make the calculation easy to do mentally. In essence, convert the not-nice percent problem into one that is nice. Here are some examples. Try your hand at estimating each.

1. The 83 000-seat stadium was 73 percent full. How many people were at the game?

2. The treasurer reported that 68.3 percent of the dues had been collected, for a total of $385. How much more money could the club expect to collect if all dues are paid?

3. Max McStrike had 217 hits in 842 turns at bat. What was his batting average?

Possible Estimates

1. (Use $\frac{3}{4}$ and 80 000) $\longrightarrow$ about 60 000
2. (Use $\frac{2}{3}$ and $380; will collect $\frac{1}{3}$ more) $\longrightarrow$ about $190
3. ($4 \times 217 > 842$; $\frac{1}{4}$ is 25 percent, or 0.250) $\longrightarrow$ a bit more than 0.250

The following activities are also useful in helping students with estimation in percent situations.

FIGURE 14.15 Real percent problems with nice numbers. Simple drawings help with reasoning.

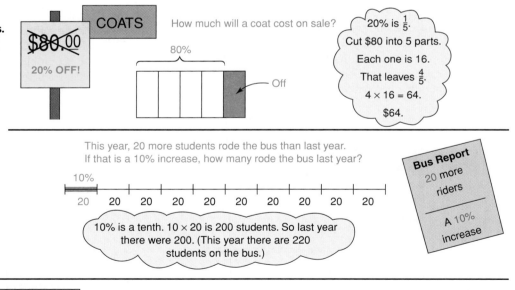

ACTIVITY 14.12

Percents as Nice Fractions

Choose the closest nice fraction. For example, which fraction is closest to 78 percent: $\frac{1}{2}$, $\frac{2}{3}$, or $\frac{4}{5}$? Multiple-choice exercises such as this one can be done with a full class or can be made into worksheet exercises. Later, the multiple-choice element can be dropped and students can be asked to come up with a nice fraction that is close to the percent. Have students justify their answers.

ACTIVITY 14.13

Easy Percents

Work with "easy percents," especially 1 percent and 10 percent. Begin with exercises where students give 1 percent and 10 percent of numbers. Then show them how to use these easy percents to get other percentages, either exact or approximate. For example, to get 15 percent of $349, think that 10 percent is about $35.00 and 5 percent is half of that, or $17.50. So 15 percent is $35.00 + $17.50, or $52.50. Similar reasoning can be used to adjust an estimate by 1 percent or 2 percent. To find 82 percent of $400, it is easy to think of $\frac{4}{5}$ (80 percent) as $4 \times \frac{1}{5}$ of 400, or $4 \times $80, which is $320. Since each 1 percent is $4, add on $8.

Sometimes an exact result, and therefore some calculation, is required. But the emphasis on conceptual thinking, nice fractions, and the estimation of results will all help to make finding an exact result easier. The use of an estimate will determine if the result is in the ballpark or if it makes sense. Frequently, this same estimation process will dictate the computation required so that the problem can be entered on a calculator.

Computation with Decimals

In 1989, the NCTM *Standards* said, "It is no longer necessary or useful to devote large portions of instructional time to performing routine computations by hand. Other mathematical experiences for middle school students deserve far more emphasis" (p. 94). The NCTM's call for less emphasis on computation has been misinterpreted and often criticized as a "watering down" of mathematics. The issue is especially significant in the area of decimal computation. There is a tendency to have students learn traditional computational algorithms, even though provincial and territorial curricula encourage the development of a conceptual understanding of operations with decimal numbers. The focus on rules that are often learned without a firm rationale frequently results in re-teaching of skills and processes learned in grade 5. Practices such as this consume a great deal of scarce instructional time. The *Principles and Standards* document calls only for *estimation* of computations with decimal numbers in grades 3–5. The 6–8 band says that students should "understand the meaning and effects of arithmetic operations with fractions, decimals, and integers" (NCTM, 2000, p. 214). According to *Principles and Standards,* students in grades 6–8 should develop "the ability to compute efficiently and accurately" with these numbers by the time they leave middle school (p. 220). These statements stop short of specifying levels of computational proficiency with decimals. For example, it is reasonable for students to compute 2.7×25, and they should be able to estimate this product as a bit less than 75. However, one should question the value of devoting time to tedious exercises such as 3.78×24.62 or $16.51 \div 2.54$. Anyone needing an exact answer to such computations should use a calculator.

Due to requirements of their prescribed curricula, some teachers undoubtedly feel compelled to teach more decimal computation or teach it earlier than is suggested by the NCTM. Even so, the operations on decimal numbers can be developed as extensions of students' understanding of whole-number computation. Students can develop algorithms that they understand. Estimation can and should play a significant role in this development. There is no reason to revert to mindless rules of "lining up decimal points" or "counting decimal places."

The Role of Estimation

Students should learn to estimate decimal computations before they learn to compute with pencil and paper. For many decimal computations, rough estimates can be made easily by rounding the numbers to nice whole numbers or simple base-ten fractions. In almost all cases, a minimum goal for your students should be to have the estimate contain the correct number of digits to the left of the decimal—the whole-number part. Select problems for which estimates are not terribly difficult. Before going on, try making easy whole-number estimates of the following computations. Do not spend time on fine adjustments in your estimates.

1. $4.907 + 123.01 + 56.1234$
2. $459.8 - 12.345$
3. 24.67×1.84
4. $514.67 \div 3.59$

Your estimates might be similar to the following:

1. Between 175 and 200
2. More than 400, or about 425 to 450
3. More than 25, closer to 50 (1.84 is more than 1 and close to 2)
4. More than 125, less than 200 (500 ÷ 4 = 125 and 600 ÷ 3 = 200)

In these examples, an understanding of decimal numeration and some simple whole-number estimation skills can produce rough estimates. When estimating, thinking should focus on the meaning of the numbers and the operations and not on counting decimal places. However, students who are taught to focus primarily on the pencil-and-paper algorithms for decimals may find even simple estimation difficult.

Therefore, a good place to begin decimal computation is with estimation. Not only is it a highly practical skill, it also helps children to look at answers in terms of their ballpark estimates. As well, it acts as a check for pencil-and-paper computation, and provides an alternative method for determining the placement of the decimal in multiplication and division.

A good time to begin computation with decimal numbers is as soon as a conceptual background in decimal numeration has been developed. Learning the pencil-and-paper algorithms will do little or nothing to help students understand decimal numeration.

Addition and Subtraction

Consider this problem:

Max and Moe each timed their own half-kilometre run with a stopwatch. Max said that he ran the half-kilometre in 135.5 seconds. Moe was more accurate. He reported his run as 141.34 seconds. How many seconds faster did Max run than Moe?

Students who understand decimal numeration should first of all be able to tell approximately what the difference is—close to 6 seconds. With an estimate as a beginning, students should then be challenged to figure out the exact difference. The estimate will help them avoid the typical error of lining up the 5 under the 4. A variety of strategies are possible. For example, students might note that 135.4 and 6 is 141.4, then figure out how much extra that is. Others may count on from 135.5 by adding 0.5 and then 5 more seconds to get to 141 seconds, and then add on the remaining 0.34 seconds. These and other strategies will help students deal with the difference between the one-place decimal (.5) and the two-place decimal (.34). Drawing on their understanding of place value will also help them to resolve this issue. Similar story problems for

addition and subtraction, some involving different numbers of decimal places, will also help develop students' understanding of these two operations. It is always best, then, to request an estimate prior to computation.

If you want to work toward a more typical algorithm, you might suggest writing the numbers on a place-value chart. This simple suggestion focuses attention on the idea of adding or subtracting like place values (see Figure 14.16). It also separates the whole-number and decimal parts of the problem. Students may first work from the left, computing the whole-number portion, then the decimal part.

Multiplication

Estimation should play a significant role in developing an algorithm for multiplication. As a beginning point, consider this problem:

Farmer Daniela sells apple cider in plastic jugs. She fills each jug with 3.7 litres of cider. If you buy 4 jugs when you visit her apple orchard, how many litres of cider is that?

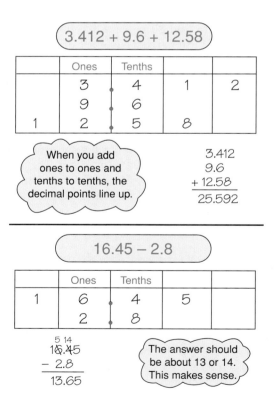

FIGURE 14.16 Using a place-value chart to develop rules for adding and subtracting decimals.

Begin with an estimate. It is more than 12 litres. What is the most it could be? Could it be 16 litres? Once an estimate of the result is decided on, let students use their own methods for determining an exact answer. Many will use repeated addition: 3.7 + 3.7 + 3.7 + 3.7. Others may begin by multiplying 3 × 4 and then adding up 0.7 four times. Eventually, students will agree on the exact result of 14.8 litres. Explore other problems involving whole-number multipliers. Multipliers such as 3.5 or 8.25 that involve nice fractional parts—here, one-half and one-fourth—are also reasonable.

As a next step, have students compare a decimal product with one involving the same digits but no decimal. For example, how are 23.4 × 6.5 and 234 × 65 alike? Interestingly, both products have exactly the same digits: 15210. (The zero may be missing from the decimal product.) Using a calculator, have students explore other products that are alike except for the decimals involved. The digits in the answer are always alike. Try multiplying each of these numbers by 2.6: 347 and 3.47. The first product is 902.2 and the second is 9.022. This result leads to the following task:

If the numbers turn out the same except for the decimal point, how can we use this idea to figure out 83.48 × 0.35?

The result is actually a very good algorithm for multiplication: *Ignore the decimal points, and do the computation as if all numbers were whole numbers. When finished, place the decimal point according to your estimation.* See Figure 14.17 for an example.

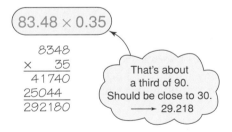

FIGURE 14.17 Using estimation to place decimals.

Division

Division can be extended in a similar manner.

In 8 days, Max ran a total of 33.5 kilometres. What was his average distance per day?

This is a partition problem that calls for sharing the 33.5 kilometres equally across 8 days. The algorithm developed for whole numbers extends to problems of this kind very nicely, as shown in Figure 14.18. The 5 extra in the ones column are traded 1 for 10 to the next column, just as with whole numbers. The explicit-trade method (see Chapter 10, p. 201) makes this quite clear.

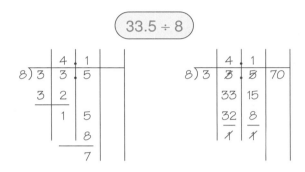

Trade 3 tens for 30 ones, making 33 ones.
Put 4 ones in each group, or 32 in all.
That leaves 1 one.

Trade 1 one for 1 tenth, making 1 tenth.
Put 1 tenth in each group, or 8 in all.

Trade the 7 tenths for 70 hundredths.

(Continue trading for smaller pieces as long as you wish.)

FIGURE 14.18 Extension of the division algorithm.

As with multiplication, compare two divisions of numbers with and without decimal points—for example, 14.6 ÷ 8 = 1.825 and 146 ÷ 8 = 18.25. Both have the same digits. Have students try this with other quotients using a calculator. The only difference is the placement of the decimal point! Therefore, the algorithm for multiplication can also be used for division: *Ignore the decimal points, and do the computation as if all numbers were whole numbers. When finished, place the decimal point according to your estimation.*

Outside the classroom, it is unusual for ordinary people to perform divisions with decimal divisors using pencil and paper. This is not to say that such computation cannot be taught meaningfully. It simply means that this is not a productive use of school time.

 Literature **Connections**

In the daily papers and weekly magazines, you will find endless real-world situations in which decimals and percentages play a role. One issue with percents in news stories is the frequent omission of the base amount, or the whole on which the percent is determined. "March sales of widgets were reported to be up 3.6 percent." Does that mean an increase over February or over March of the previous year? Increase and decrease by percents are interesting to project over several years. If the consumer price index rises 3 percent a year, how much will an $85 basket of groceries cost by the time your students are 21 years old?

The Phantom Tollbooth
(Juster, 1961)

Few interesting stories inspire exploration of decimals and percents for children in grade 5 and higher. One notable exception is *The Phantom Tollbooth,* a story that should not be missed regardless of its mathematical significance.

References to mathematical ideas abound throughout this book. Milo enters a world of crazy places and imaginative creatures after driving his toy car through a model of a turnpike tollbooth. Several chapters involve adventures in Digitopolis, where everything is number-oriented. In Digitopolis, Milo meets a boy who is only half of a boy. Only the left half, cut top-to-bottom, appears in the drawing. As it turns out, the boy is actually 0.58 since he is a member of the average family: a mother, father, and 2.58 children. The boy is the 0.58. One advantage, he explains, is that he is the only one who can drive the 3/10 of a car, the average family owning 1.3 cars. This section of the tale could be used to start a great discussion of averages that come out in decimal numbers.

One obvious extension of the story is to explore averages of things that are interesting to the students (average number of siblings, average arm span, etc.) and see where these odd decimal parts come from. In the case of measures of length, for example, an average length can be a real length even if no one has it. But an average number of things like cars or sisters can be very humorous, as discussed in the story. It would also be interesting to compare present-day statistical information from Statistics Canada with averages listed in the book. For example, the number of children in the average North American family today could be compared with the data in the book. Also, where else are fractions and decimals used to explore information in this way?

 ### Assessment Notes

The real danger in teaching the topics discussed in this chapter is in emphasizing skills instead of the concepts and big ideas. Traditional tests will focus on children's ability to round numbers, order decimals, compute with pencil and paper, and solve sterile percent problems. These assessments are far too skill-oriented.

The activities described in this chapter will involve discussion and explanations. For example, Activity 14.7, "Close to a Friendly Fraction" (p. 265), will very likely produce an array of answers as your students select a "nice" decimal and fractional equivalent. How did they make that choice? Which seems "best"? Is there always a best answer? When students use a 10×10 square to find a decimal equivalent for $\frac{3}{8}$ or $\frac{2}{3}$, there will be lots of discussion if you are not overly directive. From these discussions, you can gather data about your students' understanding of concepts.

So as not to rely totally on listening to discussions, you can and should have students write out explanations and draw pictures to support their answers to many of the activities. Here are two questions that could serve as assessments or as instructional tasks:

1. **Consider these two computations: $3\frac{1}{2} \times 2\frac{1}{4}$ and 2.276×3.18. Without doing the calculations, which do you think is larger? Provide a reason for your answer that could be understood by someone else in this class.**

2. **How much larger is 0.76×5 than 0.75×5? How can you tell without doing the computation? (Kulm, 1994)**

Realistic percent problems are still the best way to assess a student's understanding of percent. Assign one or two, and have students explain why they think their answer makes sense. You might take a realistic percent problem and substitute fractions for percents (e.g., use $\frac{1}{8}$ instead of 12.5 percent) to see how students handle these problems with fractions compared to decimal numbers.

If you focus on reasoning and justification rather than on the number of correct solutions, you will be able to collect all the information you need. ■■

Reflections *on Chapter 14*

Writing to Learn

1. Describe three different base-ten models for fractions and decimals, and use each to illustrate how base-ten fractions can easily be represented.
2. Explain why the place-value system extends infinitely in two directions. How can this idea be developed with students in grade 5 or grade 6?
3. Use an example involving base-ten blocks to explain the role of the decimal point in identifying the units position. Relate this idea to changing units of measurement with money or with linear measure.
4. What are the suggested "familiar fractions"? How can these fractions be connected to their decimal equivalents in a conceptual manner?
5. What should be emphasized if you want children to have good number sense with decimals?
6. Describe one or two ways in which a calculator can be used to develop number ideas with decimals.
7. What does rounding mean? How can we round numbers other than rounding them to the nearest tenth or hundredth? Explain how a number line can be used in rounding.
8. Make up three realistic percent problems in which the percents are actually nice fractions and the numbers involved are compatible with the fractions. One problem should ask for the part, given the whole and the percent. One should ask for the percent, given the whole and the part. The third should ask for the whole, given the part and the percent. Model each, and show how each can be solved using fraction ideas.
9. Why should we not spend a lot of time with pencil-and-paper computation with decimals?
10. For addition and subtraction, the rule for lining up the decimals can reasonably be taught without much trouble. Explain.
11. Using an example explain how, in most multiplication and division problems with decimals, the rule for placement of the decimal point can be replaced with estimation and whole-number methods.

For Discussion and Exploration

1. For each of the four operations with decimals, discuss what computational skill children need to have. For example, if you believe that division with decimal numbers is important, what is the most tedious problem you would consider having students master? What alternatives to traditional pencil-and-paper computation do you think should be included in the curriculum?
2. One way to order a series of decimal numbers is to annex zeros to each number so that all numbers have the same number of places to the right of the decimal. For example, rewrite

0.34		0.3400
0.3004	as	0.3004
0.059		0.0590

Now ignore the decimal points and any leading zeros, and order the resulting whole numbers. Discuss the merits of teaching this approach to children.
3. Talk individually with some grade 7 or 8 students. First find out if they can do simple fraction exercises that ask for the part, the whole, or the fraction given the other two forms (as in Chapter 12). Encourage them to make drawings and give explanations. Next, ask them to solve simple percent word problems, with simple fractions and compatible numbers, that require using the same type of reasoning. Compare students' abilities for both of these mathematically identical problems.

Recommendations for Further Reading

Highly Recommended

Bennett, A.B., Jr., & Nelson, L.T. (1994). A conceptual model for solving percent problems. *Mathematics Teaching in the Middle School, 1,* 20–25.

This article introduces a practical twist on the use of the 10 × 10 grid for understanding percent. The authors provide a series of increasingly difficult tasks that can easily be used in a constructivist environment to challenge a range of students. Realistic percent problems are used throughout.

McIntosh, A., Reys, B.J., & Reys, R.E. (1997). *Number SENSE: Simple effective number sense experiences* (3 vols.: grades 3–4; 4–6, with J. Hope; and 6–8). White Plains, NY: Cuisenaire–Dale Seymour.

These three activity resource books provide Blackline Masters that are designed to help students develop a wide range of useful number relationships. Of special note are activities that use benchmarks of 0, H, and 1 for fractions and for decimals. There are also good activities for connecting fractions and decimals. The pages can be used individually or with a full class as overhead transparencies.

Moss, J., & Case, R. (1999). Developing children's understanding of the rational numbers: A new model and an experimental curriculum. *Journal for Research in Mathematics Education, 30,* 122–147.

These authors devised and taught a grade 4 sequence that began with percents, moved to decimals, and lastly covered fractions—the exact opposite of the sequence suggested in this text. A linear model was the main representation used. Although their approach is non-traditional, much can be learned from this study by two thoughtful researchers who have done considerable work in the area of fraction and decimal conceptual development.

Owens, D.T., & Super, D.B. (1993). Teaching and learning decimal fractions. In D.T. Owens (Ed.), *Research ideas for the classroom: Middle grades mathematics* (pp. 137–158). Old Tappan, NJ: Macmillan.

Owens and Super offer insights from research on how children develop decimal concepts and the difficulties involved. The chapter also provides a variety of useful activities for decimal concept development. The authors have also included results of NAEP testing that give some perspective on "typical" student development.

Other Suggestions

Allinger, G.D., & Payne, J.N. (1986). Estimation and mental arithmetic with percent. In H.L. Schoen (Ed.), *Estimation and mental computation* (pp. 141–155). Reston, VA: National Council of Teachers of Mathematics.

Chappell, M.F., & Thompson, D.R. (1999). Modifying our questions to assess students' thinking. *Mathematics Teaching in the Middle School, 4,* 470–474.

Hiebert, J.C., Wearne, D., & Taber, S. (1991). Fourth graders' gradual construction of decimal fractions during instruction using different physical representations. *Elementary School Journal, 91,* 321–341.

Huinker, D.M. (1992). Decimals and calculators make sense! In J.T. Fey (Ed.), *Calculators in mathematics education* (pp. 56–64). Reston, VA: National Council of Teachers of Mathematics.

Langford, K., & Sarullo, A. (1993). Introductory common and decimal fraction concepts. In R.J. Jensen (Ed.), *Research ideas for the classroom: Early childhood mathematics* (pp. 223–247). Old Tappan, NJ: Macmillan.

Lembke, L.O., & Reys, B.J. (1994). The development of, and interaction between, intuitive and school-taught ideas about percent. *Journal for Research in School Mathematics, 25,* 237–259.

Oppenheimer, L., & Hunting, R.P. (1999). Relating fractions and decimals: Listening to students talk. *Mathematics Teaching in the Middle School, 4,* 318–321.

Reys, B.J. (1991). *Developing number sense in the middle grades: Addenda series, grades 5–8.* Reston, VA: National Council of Teachers of Mathematics.

Robitaille, D.F., Taylor, A.R., Orpwood, G. (1996). *The TIMMS-Canada Report, Volume 1: Grade 8.* Vancouver: University of British Columbia.

Robitaille, D.F., Taylor, A.R., Orpwood, G. (1996). *The TIMMS-Canada Report, Volume 2: Grade 4.* Vancouver: University of British Columbia.

Thompson, C.S., & Walker, V. (1996). Connecting decimals and other mathematical content. *Teaching Children Mathematics, 2,* 496–502.

Wearne, D., Hiebert, J.C., & Taber, S. (1991). Fourth graders' gradual construction of decimal fractions during instruction using different physical representations. *Elementary School Journal, 91,* 321–341.

Williams, S.E., & Copley, J.V. (1994). Promoting classroom dialogue: Using calculators to discover patterns in dividing decimals. *Mathematics Teaching in the Middle School, 1,* 72–75.

Chapter 15

Developing Concepts of Ratio and Proportion

Ratio and proportion are important topics in mathematics because of their wide application. Within the discipline they are connected to measurement and geometry. They are also relevant in geography, music, art and science. In real-world situations ratio and proportion are related to pricing (Which is the better buy?), mixing of ingredients for recipes and other substances (e.g. gasoline is mixed with 2-cycle engine oil in the ratio of 40:1 to run outboard motors), distance and rate of travel, etc. (Saskatchewan Education, 1996). The importance of developing an understanding of proportional reasoning cannot be overstated.

Proportional reasoning has been referred to as the capstone of the elementary curriculum and the cornerstone of algebra and beyond (Lesh, Post, & Behr, 1987). The ability to reason proportionally was a hallmark of Piaget's distinction between concrete levels of thought and formal operational thought. It represents the ability to begin to understand multiplicative relationships, while most arithmetic concepts are additive in nature. In 1989, the *Curriculum Standards* noted that proportional reasoning was "of such great importance that it merits whatever time and effort must be expended to assure its careful development" (NCTM, 1989, p. 82). *Principles and Standards* suggests that the topic should be addressed in grades 6–8 with "a strong intuitive basis" (NCTM, 2000, p. 221). In an era of ever-increasing pressure to cover curriculum, the tendency is to focus more on the development of rules for solving routine problems. However, the rush to rules, where proportional reasoning is concerned, is a serious error. Time must be allowed for development of intuitive ideas, as the *Standards* suggests.

BIG IDEAS

1. A ratio is a comparison of two quantities. A milestone in a student's development is the ability to begin thinking of a ratio as distinctly different from the two related measures that it represents.

2. Proportions involve multiplicative rather than additive comparisons. Equal ratios result from multiplication or division, rather than from addition or subtraction.

3. Proportional reasoning is developed through activities that involve comparing and determining the equivalence of two ratios. Solving proportions in a wide variety of problem-based contexts and situations without relying on rules and formulas is also helpful.

Proportional Reasoning

To create a common ground for the reading of this chapter, several exercises have been provided for your exploration. Each typifies the relationships that make up the concepts of ratio and proportion. It does not matter what your personal acquaintance with ratio actually is. Try each of the following exercises; then discuss and explore them in a group or with a friend.

THE FRENCH CONNECTION

Mr. Boulanger sells imported French sourdough bread in his specialty food shop. According to his price chart, as shown in Figure 15.1, small loaves 24 cm in length sell for $2.00 each. The larger ones sell for $5.00 each. Based on the same pricing scale, what is the size of the larger loaves?

FIGURE 15.1 The "French Connection" problem.

LAPS

Yesterday, Beth counted the number of laps she ran and recorded the amount of time it took. Today she ran fewer laps in more time than yesterday. Did she run faster, slower, or at about the same speed today— or can't you tell? What if she had run more laps in more time?

SIMILAR SHAPES

Place a piece of paper over the dot grid in Figure 15.2. Using the dots as a guide, draw a shape that is *like* the one shown but larger. How many different shapes that are like the given shape can you draw and still stay within the grid provided?

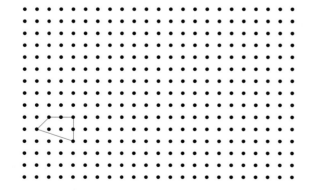

FIGURE 15.2 Draw some shapes just like this, only larger.

COLLECTION

Jesse bought a new collection of baseball cards. The collection has 8 Hall of Fame players and 12 others who are only rookies. His mother says that he has to share part of the collection with his younger brother, Matty. She also insists that Jesse include a fair number of valuable cards. If Jesse gives Matty 2 of the Hall of Famers, how many of the other cards should he give his brother if the mix of valuable and ordinary cards is to be the same as in the original set?

Examples of Ratios in Different Contexts

A *ratio* is an ordered pair of numbers or measurements that express a comparison between the numbers or the measures. This definition covers a wide range of situations. To students, ratios in different settings or contexts may present very different ideas and different difficulties.

Part-to-Whole Ratios

Ratios can express comparisons of a part to a whole. For example, the ratio of girls to all students in Ms. Angelo's class is a part-to-whole ratio, because the number of girls is being compared to the number of students that make up the whole class. Fractions are part-to-whole ratios. For example, in the fraction $\frac{3}{4}$, 3 parts are compared to the 4 parts that make up the whole. Both the whole and the part are measured in fourths. Similarly, percentages are ratios and are sometimes used to express these ratios. Probabilities are also ratios because a part of a sample space is being compared to the whole sample space.

Part-to-Part Ratios

A ratio can also compare one part of a whole to another part of the whole. For example, the number of girls in Ms. Angelo's class can be compared to the number of boys. In the "Collection" exercise, there were 8 of one kind of card and 12 of the other. The ratio of valuable cards to the whole set is 8 to 20. But you can also compare the two kinds of cards (valuable to less valuable) to each other instead of one part of the set to the total. A comparison such as this is a ratio of a part to a part. The valuable and less valuable cards are in the ratio of 8 to 12, or 2 to 3. For other examples of part-to-part ratios, consider yellow Labrador retriever dogs compared to chocolate Labrador retriever dogs, and sailboats to speedboats. The probability of an event (the number of favourable outcomes compared to the number of possible outcomes) is a part-to-whole ratio. However, the odds of an event happening—the ratio of the number of ways that an event can happen to the number of ways it cannot happen—is a part-to-part ratio.

Rates as Ratios

Both part-to-whole and part-to-part ratios compare two measures of the same type of thing. A ratio can also be a *rate*. A rate is a comparison of the measures of two different things or quantities in which the measuring unit is different for each value.

In the "French Connection" exercise, centimetres are compared to money, an example of a rate. The "Laps" exercise involves a comparison of time to distance, another example of rate. There are no numbers involved in this exercise, so the reasoning is qualitative rather than quantitative, but the ratio concept is basically the same. All rates of speed are comparisons of time and distance: for example, driving at 90 kilometres per hour (time to distance) or jogging at 4.8 minutes per kilometre (distance to time).

Other rates that we may not think of as ratios are kilometres per litre, square metres of coverage per litres of paint, centimetres of tape per roll, passengers per busload, and roses per bouquet. Relationships between two units of measure are also rates or ratios: for example, millilitres per litre, and grams per kilogram. The distance scale on a map is another example of a ratio that is a rate.

Other Examples of Ratio

In geometry, the ratios of corresponding parts of similar geometric figures, as in the "Similar Shapes" exercise, are always the same. The Greek letter π (pi) is the symbol that represents the ratio of the circumference of a circle to the diameter. The diagonal of a square is always $\sqrt{2}$ times a side. The slope of a line or of a roof is a ratio of rise for each unit of horizontal distance or run.

The chances of rolling a sum of 7 with two dice are 6 in 36, or 1 in 6. Probabilities are part-to-whole ratios: the number of favourable outcomes compared to the total number of possible outcomes.

In nature, the ratio known as the *golden ratio* is found in many spirals, from nautilus shells to the swirls of a pine cone or a pineapple. Artists and architects use the same ratio in creating structures and works of art that are naturally pleasing to the eye.

Proportions

As students begin to reflect on a variety of examples of ratios, they will also begin to see comparisons that are in the *same ratio*. In the "Similar Shapes" exercise, the ratio of any two sides of a small shape is the same as the ratio of the corresponding sides of a larger but similar shape. In the "Collection" exercise, the ratios of valuable to less valuable cards in Jesse's set of 15 cards, in Matty's set of 5 cards, and in the original set of 20 cards can be seen as the same even though there are different numbers in each situation.

A *proportion* is a statement of equality between two ratios. Different notations for proportions can be used, for example:

$$3 : 9 = 4 : 12 \qquad \text{or} \qquad \frac{3}{9} = \frac{4}{12}$$

These might be read "3 is to 9 as 4 is to 12" or "3 and 9 are in the same ratio as 4 and 12."

A ratio that is a rate usually includes the units of measure when written, for example:

$$\frac{\$12.50}{1 \text{ kilogram}} = \frac{\$37.50}{3 \text{ kilograms}}$$

Similarly, 1000 metres per kilometre is the same as 3000 metres per 3 kilometres.

There is a distinction between a proportion and the idea of equivalent fractions. Equivalent fractions are different symbols for the same quantity or amount; they represent the same rational number in different forms. In a proportion, the quantities that the symbols represent may vary, yet the ratios still remain equivalent. If there are 3 red and 9 white balls in one bag and 4 red and 12 white in another bag, the number of red balls in each bag is different. However, the ratios of red to white and red to total—the comparisons of these quantities—is the same for both bags.

Finding one number in a proportion when given the other three is called *solving* a proportion.

Proportional Reasoning and Children

Not only does *proportional reasoning* include an understanding of ratio, it requires the ability to compare ratios and to predict or produce equivalent ratios. It entails the ability to make comparisons, not just of the quantities involved but also of the relationships between quantities. As the exercises have shown, proportional reasoning is a quantitative as well as a qualitative process. According to Lamon (1999), the following are a few of the characteristics of proportional thinkers.

- Proportional thinkers have a sense of co-variation. That is, they understand relationships in which two quantities vary and they are able to see how the variation in one coincides with the variation in the other.
- Proportional thinkers recognize, in real-world contexts, proportional relationships as distinct from nonproportional relationships.
- Proportional thinkers develop a wide variety of strategies for solving proportions or comparing ratios, most

of which are based on informal thinking rather than on prescribed algorithms.

■ Proportional thinkers understand ratios as distinct entities representing a relationship that is different from the quantities they compare.

A Developmental Perspective

Research to find out how children reason on various proportionality tasks, and to determine if developmental or instructional factors are related to proportional reasoning (for example, see Karplus, Pulos, & Stage, 1983; Lamon, 1993; Lo & Watanabe, 1997; Noelting, 1980; and Post, Behr, & Lesh, 1988), indicates that proportional reasoning is not necessarily a function of natural growth and development. It does suggest, though, that instruction can have an effect, especially if rules and algorithms for fractional computation, for comparing ratios, and for solving problems are delayed (Lamon, 1999). It is thought that as much as three years' experience reasoning with multiplicative situations is required in order for students to adequately develop their proportional reasoning skills. The premature use of rules only encourages the application of rules, often without the development of proportional reasoning.

The research also offers direction for how to help children develop proportional thought processes. Some of these ideas are outlined here.

1. Provide ratio and proportion tasks in a wide range of contexts. These might include situations involving measurements, prices, geometric and other visual contexts, and rates of all sorts.

2. Encourage discussion and experimentation in predicting and comparing ratios. Help children distinguish between proportional and non-proportional comparisons by providing examples of each and discussing the differences.

3. Help children relate proportional reasoning to existing processes. The concept of unit fractions is very similar to unit rates. Research indicates that the use of a unit rate for comparing ratios and solving proportions is the most common approach among junior high students, even when cross-product methods have been taught.

4. Recognize that symbolic or mechanical methods for solving proportions, such as the cross-product algorithm, do not develop proportional reasoning and should not be introduced until students have had many experiences with intuitive and conceptual methods. "The cross-product algorithm is efficient but often has little meaning" (Saskatchewan Education, 1996).

It takes considerable class time to provide students with experiences that permit intuitive thought and reflec-

tion. Situations that are very different on the surface must be explored before commonalities show through. Contextual and numerical differences in problems play a significant role in how children approach proportional tasks and how difficult they are to solve (Lamon, 1993; Thompson & Thompson, 1994). A focus on procedures does not help students think about relationships in any global manner.

Time can be found for exciting activities in grades 6 to 8 and procedural knowledge can easily be connected to the resulting concepts.

No one method for solving a proportion should be favoured over another, and none should be taught in a rote manner. In the beginning, activities should focus on the development of understanding rather than on efficient strategies (Saskatchewan Education, 1996). Activities and guided discussions should help students learn to think proportionally in a variety of ways and contexts.

Informal Activities to Develop Proportional Reasoning

Four categories of activities are suggested here: selection of equivalent ratios, comparison of ratios, scaling or table activities, and construction and measurement activities. Each provides a different opportunity for the development of proportional reasoning. The activities are not in any definitive sequence, nor are they designed to teach specific methods for solving proportions. Some activities can be modified or repeated using different numbers or contexts to produce more or less challenging situations or to suggest different thought processes.

Equivalent Ratio Selections

In selection activities, a ratio is presented, and students select an equivalent ratio from a range of others. The focus should be on an intuitive rationale for why the pairs selected are in the same ratio. Sometimes numerical values will play a part, helping students develop numerical methods to explain their reasoning. In later activities, students will be asked to construct an equivalent ratio without choices being provided.

It is extremely useful in these activities to include pairs of ratios that are not proportional but have a common difference. For example, $\frac{5}{8}$ and $\frac{9}{12}$ are not equivalent ratios, but the corresponding differences are the same: $8 - 5 = 12 - 9$. Students who focus on this additive relationship are not seeing the multiplicative relationship of proportionality.

Look-Alike Rectangles

Draw a collection of 13 rectangles on one sheet of paper. Use a sheet of centimetre grid paper, and trace the rectangles using whole-number measures for the dimensions of each rectangle. Make four rectangles with sides in the ratio of 1 to 4, four in the ratio of 2 to 5, four in the ratio of 5 to 8, and one square about midsize to the other 12 rectangles. Label the rectangles A to M in a mixed order.

With the students working in small groups, the task is to group the rectangles into three sets of four that "look alike" with one "oddball." Do not tell them that the oddball is the square. When they have decided on their groupings, stop and discuss the reasons they classified the rectangles as they did. Be prepared for some students to try to match sides or look for rectangles that have the same amount of difference between them. Do not evaluate any rationale offered. Next, have them measure and record the sides of each rectangle and calculate the ratios of the short to long sides for each. You may want to prepare a little worksheet as shown in Figure 15.3. Discuss these results, and ask students to offer explanations. If the rectangles within each of the groups are proportional (similar), their ratios will be the same.

If you laminate the rectangles before cutting them out, they can be used from year to year.

Look-Alike Rectangles

Group 1

Rectangle	Short Side	Long Side	Short ÷ Long

Group 2

Rectangle	Short Side	Long Side	Short ÷ Long

FIGURE 15.3 A recording sheet for "Look-Alike Rectangles"

The "Look-Alike Rectangles" are actually groups of similar figures. The same activity can be done with triangles or any sets of shapes with groups of similar figures.

The focus in this activity is on observing like ratios. From a geometric perspective, this activity is about similarity. The two concepts—proportionality and similarity—are closely connected.

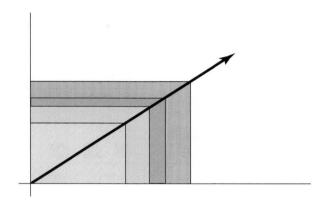

FIGURE 15.4 The line made by the straightedge will pass through the origin when the rectangles are placed with the common corner on it

Another feature of proportional rectangles can be observed by stacking like rectangles aligned at one corner, as in Figure 15.4. Place a straightedge across the diagonals, and you will see that opposite corners also line up. If the rectangles are placed on a coordinate axis with the common corner at the origin, the line made by the straightedge will pass through the origin.

Different Objects, Same Ratios

Prepare cards showing groups of distinctly different objects, as shown in Figure 15.5. Given one card, students then select another card or cards where the ratios of the two types of objects match. This task moves students to a numerical approach rather than a visual one and introduces the notion of ratios as rates. A unit rate (when one term of the rate is one) is depicted on a card that shows exactly one of either of the two types of objects. For example, the card with three boxes and one truck illustrates a unit rate. However, there is no unit rate shown for the other ratio. If it were, what would it be? Pairing objects with coins or bills is a way to introduce price as a ratio.

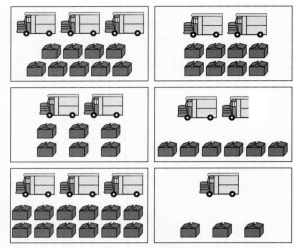

On which cards is the ratio of trucks to boxes the same?
Also, compare trucks to trucks and boxes to boxes.

FIGURE 15.5 Rate cards: Match cards with the same rate of boxes per truck.

Comparing Ratios

An understanding of proportional situations includes being able to distinguish between two ratios as well as to identify those ratios that are equivalent. Consider the following problem:

Two boy-scout troops, the Bears and the Raccoons, were having pizza parties. The Bears' leader ordered enough pizza so that every 3 scouts would have 2 pizzas. The Raccoons' leader ordered 3 pizzas for every 5 scouts. Who had more pizza to eat, the Bears or the Raccoons?

Before reading further, solve the problem without using any numerical algorithms such as cross-products. You may want to draw pictures or use counters. There is no prescribed method to use.

Figure 15.6 shows two different possibilities for informal methods.

When the pizzas are sliced into fractional parts (Figure 15.6a), the approach is to look for a unit rate—pizzas per boy scout. A sharing approach has been used for each ratio just as described for fractions in Chapter 12. Notice that this problem does not say that the troops have only 3 and 5 boy scouts, respectively. Any multiples of 2 to 3 (2:3) and 3 to 5 (3:5) can be used to make the appropriate comparison. This is the approach used in Figure 15.6b. Three "clones" of the 2-to-3 ratio and two "clones" of the 3-to-5 ratio are made so that a like number of boy scouts getting pizza can be compared. This is like getting common numerators in fractions. Because there are more

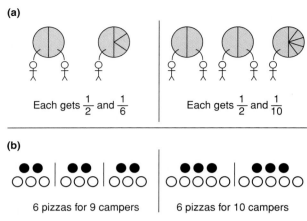

Each gets $\frac{1}{2}$ and $\frac{1}{6}$ Each gets $\frac{1}{2}$ and $\frac{1}{10}$

6 pizzas for 9 campers   6 pizzas for 10 campers

FIGURE 15.6 Two informal methods for comparing two ratios.

boy scouts in the Raccoon ratio (larger denominator), there is less pizza for each of them.

The following activity suggests some similar comparison tasks.

Comparing Ratios

Pose problems to students that are similar to the following. Allow them to solve the problems in any manner they wish as long as they can explain why their answer makes sense. Do not allow any algorithms that the students cannot defend in the context of the problem.

a. **Terry can run 4 laps in 12 minutes. Susan can run 2 laps in 5 minutes. Who is the faster runner?**

b. **Jack and Jill were picking strawberries at the Pick Your Own Berry Farm. Jack "sampled" 5 berries every 25 minutes. Jill ate 3 berries every 10 minutes. If they both picked at about the same speed, who took home more berries?**

c. **Some of the hens in Farmer Joan's chicken farm lay brown eggs and the others lay white eggs. In her large hen house she was able to collect about 4 brown eggs for every 10 white eggs. The ratio in the smaller house was 1 to 3 (1:3). In which house do the hens lay more brown eggs?**

d. **The Good Deal Phone Company charges 70 cents for every 15 minutes. The Super Saver Company charges $1.00 for 20 minutes. Which company is offering the better rate?**

e. Which rectangle is "fatter": a 3 × 5 rectangle or an 8 × 14 rectangle?

f. Arrange the prices below in order, from most expensive to least expensive. Explain how you know which is least expensive. (By permission of Saskatchewan Education.)

Alaskan Pollock fillets 69 cents/100 grams
Pacific Sole $3.90/ kilogram
Manitoba Whitefish $0.32/100 grams

The suggested problems in Activity 15.3 are simply to provide you with some ideas. You can easily make up your own. You can also change the numbers to make the tasks more challenging.

Scaling Activities

Scaling activities involve filling in charts or tables that show how two variable quantities are related. Other formats can also be used. Some examples of scaling are: finding distances with a map using the given scale, scaling a recipe up or down according to a given ratio, and making a scale enlargement or reduction of a drawing. Scaling up is a matter of providing entries with larger numbers, and scaling down is entering smaller numbers. The following are examples of scaling up:

1 metre	⟶ 100 centimetres	1 can of juice	⟶ $0.85
2 metres	⟶ 200 centimetres	2 cans of juice	⟶ $1.70
3 metres	⟶ ? centimetres	3 cans of juice	⟶ $?

Items in charts can be related measures such as time (minutes to hours), money (nickels to quarters), and mass (grams to kilograms), or common pairings such as crayons to boxes, hands to fingers, or wheels to tricycles. They can also be arbitrary ratios, such as a man who eats three bagels for every two bananas.

In a scaling-down activity, one or two larger entries in a list or ratio table are given, and students are asked to provide smaller entries:

28 days	⟶ 4 weeks	12 baskets	⟶ 24 apples
21 days	⟶ 3 weeks	11 baskets	⟶ 22 apples
? days	⟶ 2 weeks	10 baskets	⟶ ? apples

Be careful not to make these exercises too long or tedious. Allow students to use repeated addition or subtraction as well as multiplication and division. Also be sure to permit the use of calculators to make computation easy.

Notice that in the examples so far, the unit ratio is easy to determine without the use of fractions. These easier scaling activities can be done at an early grade. Later, fractions

and decimals can be used. Students can scale down with one division to get a unit ratio and then multiply to get the requested quantity, as in the following example:

3 boxes for $2.25 → 5 boxes for ? 1 box is $0.75 (unit ratio), so 5 boxes is 5 × $0.75 = $3.75.

Scaling can also be done up or down without using a unit ratio:

Minutes:	5	?	15	20	25	30	35
Bagels made:	?	14	21	?	?	?	?

The next activity relates scaling to ratio tables.

ACTIVITY 15.4

Using Ratio Tables

Given a situation like one of the following, the task is to build a table and use it to answer the questions.

a. Gisele makes orange paint with 5 parts yellow to every 2 parts red. If she used 6 parts red, how many parts yellow would she need?

b. Sanjay reads 26 pages in 2 hours. At that rate, how many pages would he read in 5 hours?

c. If 5 pens cost $5.50, what would 7 pens cost?

d. At Pineway Elementary School, 5 out of every 8 students eat their lunch at school. How many of the 30 students in Mr. Gladstone's class are likely to eat their lunch at school?

(Tasks are adapted from Saskatchewan Education, *Mathematics 6–9: A Curriculum Guide for the Middle Level*, 1996.)

The following Jupiter problem, adapted from Lamon (1999), is a typical "solve the proportion" task. One ratio and part of a second are given, with the task being to find the fourth number. Tasks such as these should come long before any formal approach is suggested. Further, note that in no case is it easy to simply add or subtract to get to the desired entry. Rather, the student should use a ratio table to solve the problem. Figure 15.7 shows three different ways to solve the Jupiter problem using ratio tables. The format of these tables is not essential to solving the problem. You may find that some students will not use a table format at all, but will draw arrows and explain in words how they got from one ratio to another.

Graphs provide another way of thinking about proportions and they connect proportional thought to algebraic interpretation. All graphs of equivalent ratios fall

(a)

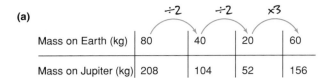

(b)

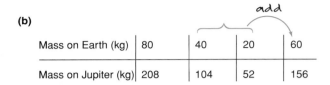

(c)

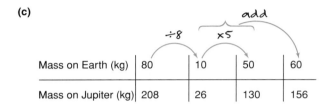

FIGURE 15.7 A person whose mass is 80 kilograms on Earth will weigh 208 kilograms on the planet Jupiter. How much will a person whose mass is 60 kilograms on Earth weigh on Jupiter?

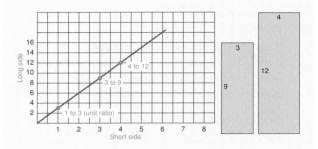

FIGURE 15.8 Graphs showing ratios of sides in similar rectangles.

Construction and Measurement Activities

In these activities, measurements are made to construct physical or visual models of equivalent ratios in order to provide a tangible example of a proportion and a look at numerical relationships.

ACTIVITY 15.6

Different Units, Equal Ratios

Cut strips of adding machine tape all the same length, and give one strip to each group in your class. Each group is to measure the strip using a different unit. Possible units include interlocking cubes, a piece of chalk, a pencil, the edge of a book or index card, or standard units such as centi- metres or centi-cubes. When every group has measured their strip, ask for one of the groups' measurements. At the same time, display the unit of measure the group used. Next, hold up the unit of measure used by another group, and have the class compare it with the first one. See if the class can estimate the measurement that the second group found. The ratio of the measuring units should be the inverse of the measurements made with those units. For example, if two measuring units are in a ratio of 2 to 3, the respective meas- urements will be in a ratio of 3 to 2. Examine measurements made with other units. Finally, present a unit that no group has used, and see if the class can predict what the measurement will be when made with that unit.

along a straight line that passes through the origin. Consider the following activity.

ACTIVITY 15.5

Graphs Showing Ratios

Have students make a graph of the data from a collection of equal ratios that they have scaled or discussed. The graph in Figure 15.8 repre- sents the ratios of two sides of similar rectan- gles. If only a few ratios have actually been computed, the graph can be drawn carefully and then used to determine other equivalent ratios. This is especially interesting when there is a physical model to coincide with the ratio. In the rectangle example, students can draw rectangles with sides determined by the graph and compare them to the original rectangles. A unit ratio can be found by locating the point on the line that is directly above or to the right of the number 1 on the graph. (There are actually two unit ratios for every ratio. Why?) Students can then use the unit ratio to scale up to other values and check to see that they are on the graph as well.

Activity 15.6 can be profitably extended by providing each group with an identical set of four strips of quite dif- ferent lengths. Good lengths might be 20, 50, 80, and 120 cm. As before, each group measures the strips using a dif- ferent length.

ACTIVITY 15.7
Density Ratios

This activity involves mass and density ratios. Provide each group with four small containers of different sizes. The four containers must be the same for each group. Have each group fill its containers with different fillers. Select fillers that vary greatly in density—for example, dry oatmeal, rice, sand, and small metal washers. Each group weighs the contents of its containers (not including the containers) to the nearest gram. Use a chart or table to record the results and compare ratios of the different masses of the fillers. The different densities of the fillers will have different masses.

ACTIVITY 15.8
Scale Drawings

On grid or dot paper (see the Blackline Masters), have students draw a simple shape using straight lines lining up the vertices on the dots. After one shape is complete, students draw a larger or smaller shape that is the same as or similar to the first. This can be done on the same size grid or a different size one, as shown in Figure 15.9. After completing two or three pictures of varying sizes, the ratios of the lengths of the different sides can be compared.

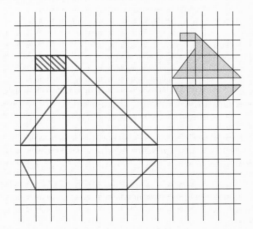

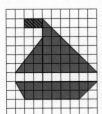

Use a metric ruler
- Choose two lengths on one boat and form a ratio (use a calculator). Compare to the ratio of the same parts of the other boats.
- Choose two boats. Measure the same part of each boat, and form a ratio. Compare with the ratios of another part.
- Compare the areas of the big sails with the lengths of the bottom sides.

FIGURE 15.9 Comparing similar figures drawn on grids.

Corresponding sides of one figure to the next should be in the same ratio. Also, the ratio of two sides of one figure should match with the ratio of the corresponding two sides in another. This activity connects the geometric idea of similarity with the numerical concept of ratio.

ACTIVITY 15.9
Length, Surface, and Volume Ratios (Three-Dimensional Scaling)

A three-dimensional version of Activity 15.8 can be done with blocks or cubes, as shown in Figure 15.10. Using 2-cm wooden blocks or interlocking cubes, begin with a simple "building." Then make a similar but larger building, and compare measurements. A different size can also be made using different-sized blocks. To measure buildings made with different blocks or cubes, use a standard unit such as centimetres. (Notice that volumes and surface areas do not vary proportionally with the edges of solids. However, these are relationships that are interesting to observe.)

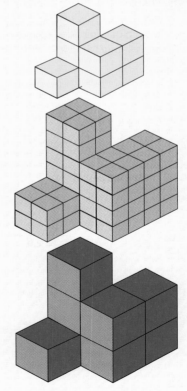

Similar "buildings" can be made by changing the number of blocks in each dimension or by using different-sized blocks.

FIGURE 15.10 Similar constructions

Activities 15.8 and 15.9 involve area and volume as well as length. Comparisons of corresponding lengths, areas, and volumes in proportional figures lead to some interesting ratios. If two figures are proportional (similar), any two linear dimensions you measure on each will be in the same ratio, for example, 1 to k. Corresponding areas will be in the ratio of 1 to k^2, and corresponding volumes in the ratio of 1 to k^3. Try this with some constructions of your own.

As a means of contrasting proportional situations with additive ones, try starting with a figure on a grid or a building made with blocks or cubes and adding two units to every dimension in the figure. The result will be larger but will not look at all the same. Try this with a simple rectangle that is 1 cm by 15 cm. The new rectangle will be twice as "thick" (2 cm), but only a bit longer. It will not appear to be the same shape as the original.

Dynamic geometry software such as *The Geometer's Sketchpad* (Key Curriculum Press, 1995) offers a very effective method of exploring the idea of ratio. In Figure 15.11, two line segments are drawn on a grid using the "snap-to-grid" option. The line segments are measured, then altered, and the two ratios are computed. As the length of either line segment is changed, the measures and ratios are instantly updated. A screen similar to this could be used to discuss, with the whole class, length ratios as well as inverse ratios. Notice that in this example the difference between the second pair of lines is the same as the first, but the ratios are not. A similar drawing could be prepared

for the overhead on a transparency of a centimetre dot grid, if software were not available.

Activity 15.10 is a useful follow-up to the discussion of equal ratios of line segments. Measures and ratios can be turned on or off, so the information the student receives can change the activity considerably.

ACTIVITY 15.10

Match the Ratios

Create a sketch like the one shown in Figure 15.12 using *The Geometer's Sketchpad*. The lengths of each of the four segments can be adjusted by dragging the right endpoints along the dotted-line rays. If the top pair of segments (AB and CD) is set, the students' task is to adjust segments EF and GH so that they are in the same ratio as AB:CD. Segment EF can be preset, or students can be free to change it as well. In the figure, all measurements and ratios are shown. The Hide and Show buttons turn the indicated information on or off. The ratio EF:GH should be hidden for use as a check when students feel they have the two pairs of lines in the same ratio. If measurements and ratios are hidden, the task is purely visual. If the ratio of AB:CD or the measurements of segments are shown, the task changes considerably. All modes should be explored.

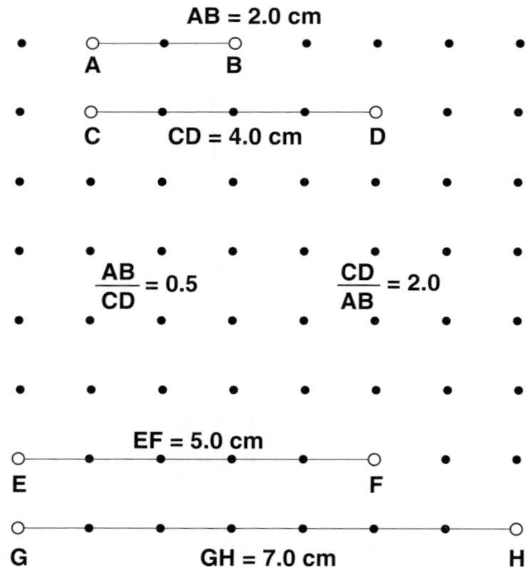

FIGURE 15.11 Dynamic geometry software or just a centimetre grid can be used to discuss ratios of two lengths.

Source: From *The Geometer's Sketchpad*. Key Curriculum Press, 1150 65th Street, Emeryville, CA 94608; (800)995-MATH. Used by permission.

Solving Proportions

The activities to this point have been designed to lead students to an intuitive concept of ratio and proportion, to help in the development of proportional reasoning.

One practical application of proportional reasoning is to use observed proportions to find unknown values. Knowledge of one ratio can often be used to find a value in the other. Comparison pricing, using scales on maps, and solving percentage problems are just a few everyday instances where solving proportions is required. Students need to learn to set up proportions symbolically and to solve them.

An Informal Approach

There are textbooks that show students how to set up two ratio equations involving an unknown, "cross-multiply," then solve for the unknown. Doing so can be very mechanical and will almost certainly lead to confusion and error. Although you may wish eventually to cover the

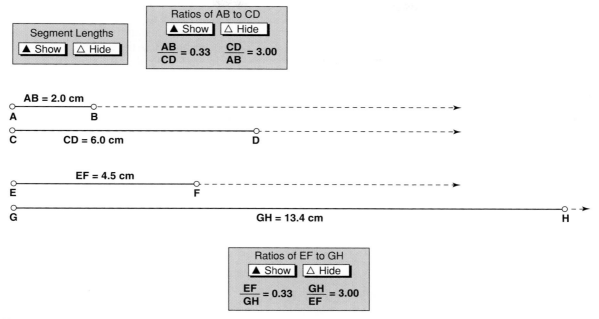

Drag the right-hand endpoints to change the lengths of the segments. Set AB and CD first. Then adjust EF and GH so that those two segments are in the same ratio.

FIGURE 15.12 **This activity was created with** ***The Geometer's Sketchpad.*** **The task is to adjust segments EF and GH so they are in the same ratio as AB and CD. To change the difficulty, the measures and ratios can be hidden by clicking on the Hide and Show buttons.**

Source: From *The Geometer's Sketchpad.* Key Curriculum Press, 1150 65th Street, Emeryville, CA 94608; (800) 995-MATH. Used by permission.

cross-product algorithm, allowing students to find ways to solve proportions using their own ideas first will be well worth the class time. If you have been exploring proportions in various activities, students will have a good foundation on which to build their own approaches.

Have students solve each of the following two problems using their own methods. To help them, you might suggest they use a simple picture (as shown earlier with the boy scout problem). Do not use cross-multiplication.

At the Office Super Store, you can buy plain #2 pencils, priced at 4 for 59 cents. The store also sells the same pencils in a large box of 5 dozen for $7.79. How much do you save if you buy the large box?

A box of 2 dozen chocolate bars is $4.80. Yonette wants to buy only 5 chocolate bars. How much will she have to pay?

To solve the pencil problem you might notice that the ratio of pencils to pencils is 4 to 60, or 1 to 15. If you multiply the 59 cents by 15 you will get the price of the box of

60 if the pencils were sold at the same price. In the chocolate bar problem ($\frac{24}{4.80}$), the ratio of 24 to $4.80 is easy to use to get the unit rate of 20 cents per chocolate bar. But what do you do if the numbers don't "come out nicely" like they do in these problems?

Try solving the same problems with new numbers that do not work out so easily. If you are having difficulty with the new problems, discuss them with a friend.

Finally, try the following problem. Use a technique you have figured out yourself. (Do this now before reading on.)

Brian can run 4 km in 18.4 minutes. If he keeps on running at the same speed, how far can he run in 23 minutes?

You might want to make a little sketch of the first situation, Brian's 4-km run and the time that it took him (18.4 minutes). The second situation is the unknown distance and 23 minutes. There are at least two things you might consider in solving this problem, and one is no easier than the other. You could look at the ratio of minutes to minutes. That is, what do you multiply 18.4 by to get 23? On the calculator, compute 23 ÷ 18.4 to get 1.25. Now 4 km × 1.25 is 5 km.

The second possibility is to get a unit rate for the 4 km and multiply by 23. That would mean divide $\frac{4}{18.4}$ by $\frac{18.4}{18.4}$ (like finding a fraction in lowest terms, with a denominator of 1). The calculator yields 0.2173913043, or about 0.22 km per minute. Multiply this unit rate by 23 minutes and you get 4.999993 km. In both cases, the longer distance is 5 km.

What is important here is to see how to use multiplication to solve a proportional situation. The sketch of the two ratios should help keep things straight and avoid ambiguous cross-multiplying.

The Cross-Product Algorithm

The methods just described come close to being well-defined algorithms, though they are a bit more flexible than cross-product methods. The computations involved are, in fact, exactly the same as in cross-multiplication, yet some teachers may still want to teach cross-multiplication.

Draw a Simple Model

Given a ratio word problem, the greatest difficulty students have is setting up a correct proportion or equation of two ratios, one of which includes the missing value. "Which fractions do I make? Where does the *x* go?"

Rather than drill and drill in the hope that they will somehow eventually get it, you might want to show students how to sketch a simple picture that will help them determine what parts are related. In Figure 15.13, a simple model is drawn for a typical rate or price problem. The two equations in the figure come from setting up the ratios.

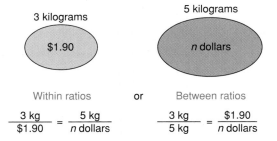

Apples are 3 kilograms for $1.90. How much should you pay for 5 kilograms?

3 kilograms

5 kilograms

$1.90

n dollars

Within ratios   or   Between ratios

$$\frac{3 \text{ kg}}{\$1.90} = \frac{5 \text{ kg}}{n \text{ dollars}} \qquad \frac{3 \text{ kg}}{5 \text{ kg}} = \frac{\$1.90}{n \text{ dollars}}$$

FIGURE 15.13 **A simple drawing helps in a price-to-ratio problem.**

Solve the Proportion

Examine the left ratios in the same way as for Brian's 5-km race: Find out what to multiply the left fraction by to get

the right. To do this, we would divide 5 by 3, then multiply that result by $1.90:

$$\frac{5}{3} \times 1.90$$

Looking at the same left equation in Figure 15.13, we could also determine the unit price, or the price for 1 kilogram of apples, by dividing the $1.90 by 3 and then multiplying this result by 5 to determine the price of 5 kilograms:

$$\frac{1.90}{3} \times 5$$

Now look what happens if we cross-multiply in the original equation:

$$3n = 5 \times 1.90$$

$$n = \frac{5 \times 1.90}{3}$$

This equation can be solved by dividing the 5 by 3 and multiplying by 1.90, or by dividing 1.90 by 3 and multiplying by 5. These are exactly the two devices we employed in our more intuitive approach. If you cross-multiply the ratios in the second example, you get exactly the same result. Furthermore, you would get the same result if you had written the two ratios so they were inverted, that is, with the reciprocals of each fraction. Try it!

So if you want to develop a cross-product algorithm, it is not unreasonable to do problems like these and encourage students to use their own methods. If you write out the computations involved, a very small amount of direct teaching can develop the cross-product approach. But why hurry?

In Figure 15.14, a problem involving rates of speed is modelled with simple line segments representing the two distances. The distance and the time for each run is represented by the same line segment. You cannot see time, but

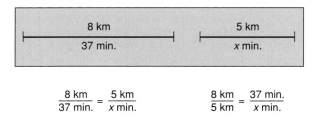

Brian can run an 8-km race in 37 minutes. If he runs at the same rate, how long should it take him to run a 5-km race?

8 km

37 min.

5 km

x min.

$$\frac{8 \text{ km}}{37 \text{ min.}} = \frac{5 \text{ km}}{x \text{ min.}} \qquad \frac{8 \text{ km}}{5 \text{ km}} = \frac{37 \text{ min.}}{x \text{ min.}}$$

FIGURE 15.14 **Line segments can be used to model both time and distance.**

it fits into the distance covered. All equal-rates-of-speed problems can be modelled this way. There really is no significant difference from the drawing used for the apples problem. Students need not worry which number goes on top. As long as the numbers of the ratios are written in the same order, it is equally acceptable. The models will help with this difficulty.

Activities Involving Proportions

In the preceding discussion, simple rate problems were used to help students develop a technique for solving proportions. The next two activities illustrate other common uses of proportional reasoning.

ACTIVITY 15.11

Scale Drawings

Provide students with a drawing of a simple geometric figure, with its dimensions labelled. The task is to create a new drawing that is either larger or smaller than the given one. One dimension of the new drawing is specified (see Figure 15.15 for an example). Students can set up ratios and determine the other dimensions by solving the proportion.

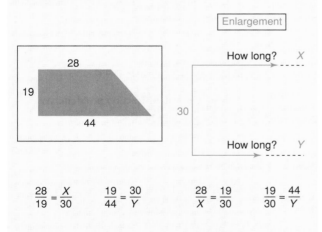

FIGURE 15.15 Pictures help in establishing equal ratios.

This activity is somewhat simplistic, but it provides students with the essential ideas for solving proportions in more realistic situations such as these:

- If you wanted to make a scale model of the solar system and use a ping-pong ball for the Earth, how far away should the sun be? How large a ball would you need?
- What scale should be used to draw a scale map of your city (or some interesting region) so that it will fit nicely onto a standard piece of poster board?

- Use the scale on a map to estimate the distance and travel time between two points of interest.
- Your little sister wants a table and chairs for her doll. Her doll is 35 centimetres tall. How big should you make the table?
- Determine the various distances that a 10-speed bike travels in one turn of the pedals. You will need to count the sprocket teeth on the front and back gears.

Have you ever wondered how scientists estimate the number of bass in a lake or the number of monarch butterflies that migrate each year to Mexico? One method often used is a capture-recapture technique modelled in the next activity.

ACTIVITY 15.12

Capture-Recapture

Prepare a shoebox full of some uniform small object such as centi-cubes or plastic chips. You could also use a larger box filled with Styrofoam packing "peanuts." If the box is your lake and the objects are the fish you want to count, how can you estimate the number without actually counting them? Remember, if they were fish, you couldn't even see them! Have a student reach into the box and "capture" a representative sample of the "fish." For a large box, you may want to capture more than a handful. "Tag" each fish by marking it in some way—marking pen or sticky dot. Count and record the number tagged, and then return them to the box. The assumption of the scientist is that tagged animals will mix uniformly with the larger population, so mix them thoroughly. Next, have five to 10 students carry out a recapture of fish from the box. Each student counts the total captured, and notes how many of these are tagged. The data are accumulated.

**   The task now is to use all of the information to estimate the number of fish in the lake. The recapture data provide an estimate of the ratio of tagged to untagged fish. The number tagged to the total population should be in the same ratio. After solving the proportion, have students count the actual items in the box to see how close their estimate was.**

For a more detailed description of the "Capture-Recapture" activity, see the NCTM Addenda Series book *Understanding Rational Numbers and Proportions* (Curcio & Bezuk, 1994).

Percent Problems as Proportions

Percent has traditionally been included as a topic with ratio and proportion, because percent is one form of a ratio: a part-to-whole ratio. In Chapter 14, it was shown that percent problems can be connected to fractional concepts. Here, the same part-to-whole fractional concept of percent will be extended to ratio and proportion concepts. Ideally, all of these ideas (fractions, decimals, ratio, proportion, and percent) should be integrated conceptually. The better students get at connecting these ideas, the more flexible and useful their reasoning and problem-solving skills will be.

Equivalent Fractions as Proportions

First consider how equivalent fractions can be interpreted as a proportion using the same simple models already used. In Figure 15.16, a line segment is partitioned in two different ways: in fourths on one side and in twelfths on the other. In the previous examples, proportions were established based on two amounts of apples, two different distances or runs, and two different sizes of drawings. Here only one thing is measured—the part of a whole—but it is measured or partitioned two ways: in fourths and in twelfths.

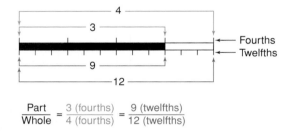

$$\frac{\text{Part}}{\text{Whole}} = \frac{3 \text{ (fourths)}}{4 \text{ (fourths)}} = \frac{9 \text{ (twelfths)}}{12 \text{ (twelfths)}}$$

FIGURE 15.16 Equivalent Fractions as Proportions.

The ratios of part to whole within each measurement result in the usual equivalent fraction equation, $\frac{3}{4} = \frac{9}{12}$ (3 fourths are to 4 fourths as 9 twelfths are to 12 twelfths). Also, the proportion equates a part-to-part ratio with a whole-to-whole ratio, or $\frac{3}{9} = \frac{4}{12}$ (3 fourths are to 9 twelfths as 4 fourths are to 12 twelfths).

A simple line-segment illustration, similar to the one in Figure 15.16, could be drawn to set up a proportion to solve any equivalent-fraction problem, even ones that do not result in whole-number numerators or denominators. Two examples are shown in Figure 15.17.

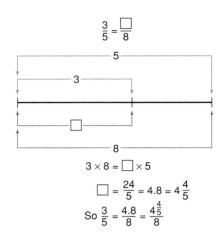

$$\frac{3}{5} = \frac{\square}{8}$$

$$3 \times 8 = \square \times 5$$

$$\square = \frac{24}{5} = 4.8 = 4\frac{4}{5}$$

$$\text{So } \frac{3}{5} = \frac{4.8}{8} = \frac{4\frac{4}{5}}{8}$$

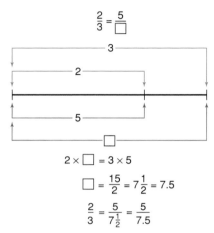

$$\frac{2}{3} = \frac{5}{\square}$$

$$2 \times \square = 3 \times 5$$

$$\square = \frac{15}{2} = 7\frac{1}{2} = 7.5$$

$$\frac{2}{3} = \frac{5}{7\frac{1}{2}} = \frac{5}{7.5}$$

Can you interpret these fractions?

FIGURE 15.17 Solving equivalent-fraction problems as equivalent ratios using cross-products.

Percent Problems

All percent problems can be treated in exactly the same way as the equivalent-fraction examples. They involve a part and a whole measured in some unit and the same part and whole measured in hundredths—that is, in percents. A simple line-segment drawing can be used for each of the three types of percent problems. Using this model as a guide, a proportion can be written and solved by the cross-product algorithm. Examples of each type of problem are shown in Figure 15.18.

It is tempting to teach all percent problems in this one way. Developmentally, such an approach is not recommended. Even though the approach is conceptual, it does not translate easily to intuitive ideas, mental arithmetic, or estimation as discussed in Chapter 14. The modelling and proportion approach of Figure 15.18 is suggested only as a way to help students analyze problems that may verbally present some difficulty. The approach of Chapter 14,

On any given day, the total number of passengers travelling on VIA Rail end-to-end from Montreal to Toronto could be 300. If there were 25% fewer passengers travelling on the train last Thursday, how many passengers were there?

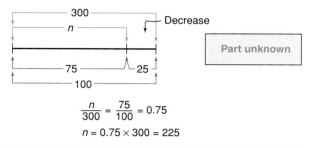

$$\frac{n}{300} = \frac{75}{100} = 0.75$$
$$n = 0.75 \times 300 = 225$$

Janice put $25.00 down on a portable CD player she wanted to buy. If the price of the CD player is $200.00, what percent of the price is her down payment?

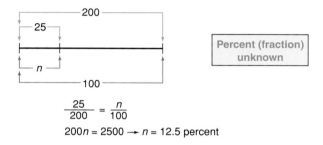

$$\frac{25}{200} = \frac{n}{100}$$
$$200n = 2500 \rightarrow n = 12.5 \text{ percent}$$

60% of all salmon caught in Canada comes from British Columbia. If this represents 500 tonnes, about how much salmon was caught in Canada last year?

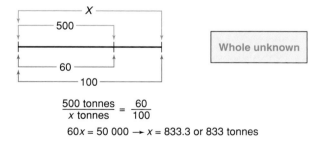

$$\frac{500 \text{ tonnes}}{x \text{ tonnes}} = \frac{60}{100}$$
$$60x = 50\,000 \rightarrow x = 833.3 \text{ or } 833 \text{ tonnes}$$

FIGURE 15.18 **The three percentage problems solved by setting up a proportion using a simple line-segment model.**

which relates percent to part-whole fractional concepts, should probably receive more emphasis.

Literature Connections

Literature brings an exciting dimension to the exploration of proportional reasoning. Many books and stories discuss comparative sizes; concepts of scale as in maps; giants and miniature people who are proportional to regular people; comparative rates, especially rates of speed; and so on. A book may not appear to explore proportions, and the author may not have had that in mind at all, but comparisons are the stuff of many excellent stories and are at the heart of proportional ideas. The suggestions here are intended to give you an idea of what you might look for.

If You Hopped like a Frog
(Schwartz, 1999)

David Schwartz, the author of *How Much Is a Million?* and *If You Made a Million*, has used some wonderful mathematics in nature in this book. Here Schwartz uses proportional reasoning to determine what it would be like if we possessed the powers or dimensions of familiar animals. "If you hopped like a frog, you could jump from home plate to first base in one mighty leap." This short picture book contains 12 of these fascinating proportions: if you were as strong as an ant, if you flicked your tongue like a chameleon, and so on. At the end of the book, Schwartz provides some factual data on which the proportions are based. The book could be read at least twice at the start of a lesson, and students could find their own comparisons to calculate. This is a wonderful way to make the connection to science. There is no reason the comparisons need be limited to animals and humans, as in this book. Students could be encouraged to explore many other ratios, such as the ratio of a toy car to a real car, using this delightful book as a springboard.

Counting on Frank
(Clement, 2000)

We will refer to this wonderful book again when we discuss measurement in Chapter 16. It is hard to imagine that so much mathematics could spring from 24 pages mostly covered with pictures. But the ideas appeal to all ages, and the potential for good investigations is clearly there for older children. The narrator and his pet dog, Frank, estimate, figure, and ponder interesting facts, usually about large numbers in odd settings (enough green peas to be level with the kitchen tabletop). Three spreads of the book are wonderful fantasies of proportions that could easily inspire an entire unit of proportional reasoning projects.

> "If I had grown at the same speed as the gum tree—about two metres per year—I'd now be almost 16 metres tall!" How fast do we grow? What if we kept growing at the same rate? How old is the narrator? How old would he be when he was 23 metres tall?
>
> If the mosquito that bothers him were 4 million times bigger ... What would any common object be like if it were a million times bigger?
>
> If the toaster that shoots toast about a metre in the air were as big as the house....

Frank also notes that the average ballpoint pen can produce a line that is 2060 metres long. The ratio of a line drawn by a ballpoint pen compared to a pencil is about 1:18 (Saskatchewan Ministry of Education, 1996).

As another activity, students could figure out how many kilometres long the pencil line would be. They could then use this information as the basis for figuring out other interesting data.

 ## Assessment Notes

Proportional reasoning is a way of thinking that includes the ability to understand and compare ratios. It is one of the hallmarks of Piaget's formal operational stage of development, acquired around adolescence. But this form of reasoning may not develop in people who have not had ample opportunities to reflect on proportional situations.

As you work with your students in solving proportional reasoning tasks, it will be useful for you to think about the type of reasoning that students are using.

- Do they distinguish between proportional situations and additive or non-proportional ones?

- Are they flexible in the way that they attempt to solve proportions? A non-flexible or algorithmic approach, even if correct, may signal that a student is simply following rules.

- Are there differences in thinking about different types of proportional situations? For example, discrete (countable) items in a proportion are sometimes easier to deal with than continuous quantities such as time, distance, or volume.

- Do students seem to understand rates (kilometres per hour, centimetres per metre, dollars per kilogram) as ratios? How students deal with these ideas reflects the development of their proportional thinking.

Keep in mind that proportional reasoning develops slowly over grades 6–8. A first unit of two or three weeks' duration in grade 6 (if your curriculum requires you to teach it) may not be enough for many children to develop true proportional thought. It will be useful to collect anecdotal evidence related to the questions just listed. If most of your students seem to be at the beginning levels of proportional thought, activities involving selection of equal ratios, constructions, and scaling will be more useful than harder proportional problems. Using numbers that lend themselves to creating relationships that are not as complex will make it easier for students to describe different methods for solving proportion tasks. ■◗

Reflections *on Chapter 15*

Writing to Learn

1. Describe the idea of a ratio in your own words. Explain how your idea fits with each of the following statements:
   a. A fraction is a ratio.
   b. Ratios can compare things that are not at all alike.
   c. Ratios can compare two parts of the same whole.
   d. Rates such as prices or speeds are ratios.

2. What is a proportion? For each of the statements in item 1, give an example of a proportion. Also give an example of a comparison that is additive rather than proportional.

3. Make up a realistic proportional situation that can be solved by a unit-rate approach. Include an explanation with it.

4. Much of this chapter is about activities that help students observe ratios and develop proportional reasoning abilities. These activities were placed in four groups:
   a. Selection of equivalent ratios
   b. Comparing ratios
   c. Scaling activities
   d. Construction and measurement activities

   For each group, pick one activity presented in the text that you did not do as part of class experiences. Do the activity, and describe briefly how you think the activity would contribute to students' proportional reasoning.

5. Consider this problem: If 12 metres of material costs $56.95, how much can be purchased for $100? Draw a sketch to illustrate the proportion, and set up the equation in two different ways. One equation should equate within ratios and the other between ratios.

6. Make up a realistic percentage problem, and set up a proportion. Draw a model to help explain why the proportion makes sense. Illustrate how this method could be used for any of the three types of percentage problems.

For Discussion and Exploration

1. Examine a teacher's edition of a basal textbook for grade 6, 7, or 8. How is the topic of ratio developed? What is the emphasis? Select one lesson, and write a lesson plan that extends and actively involves the ideas found in the students' edition.

2. In Chapter 14, the three percent problems were developed around the theme of which element was missing—the part, the whole, or the fraction that related the two. In this chapter, percent is related to proportion: an equality of two ratios with one of the ratios a comparison to 100. How are these two approaches alike? Do you prefer one or the other?

Recommendations for Further Reading

Highly Recommended

Lamon, S.J. (1999). *Teaching fractions and ratios for understanding: Essential content knowledge and instructional strategies for teachers.* Mahwah, NJ: Lawrence Erlbaum.

Lamon is one of the most prolific researchers and writers on the subject of fractions, ratios, and proportional reasoning. Her work is full of specific practical examples of activities and is freely illustrated with children's work. At the same time this is a serious, research-based, and thought-provoking book. Many of the ideas found in this chapter are adapted from this book and other works by Lamon. Anyone seriously interested in the development of proportional reasoning needs to have this book. There is a companion volume with additional examples that elaborate on the ideas found here. (See the other suggested examples that follow.)

Langrall, C.W., Swafford, J. (2000). Three balloons for two dollars. *Mathematics Teaching in the Middle School, 6,* 254–261.

If you cannot find the Lamon book just mentioned and would like to see an overview of her ideas in a short article, then try this one. The author describes and gives examples from the classroom. A good article on a difficult topic.

Miller, J.L., & Fey, J.T. (2000). Proportional reasoning. *Mathematics Teaching in the Middle School, 5,* 310–313.

This short article, one of very few recently published on this topic, describes three proportionality tasks with a total of seven questions that were posed to middle-grade students. The results from students learning within a reform curriculum are compared to results from those learning within a traditional curriculum. The interesting tasks are quite reproducible. The discussion is also valuable.

Other Suggestions

Alcaro, P., Alston, A., & Katims, N. (2000). Fractions attack! Children thinking and talking mathematically. *Teaching Children Mathematics, 6,* 562–565.

Ben-Chaim, D., Fey, J.T., Fitzgerald, W.M., Benedetto, C., & Miller, J.L. (1998). Proportional reasoning among 7th grade students with different curricular experiences. *Educational Studies in Mathematics, 36,* 247–273.

Cramer, K., & Post, T.R. (1993). Making connections: A case for proportionality. *Arithmetic Teacher, 40,* 342–346.

Cramer, K., Post, T.R., & Currier, S. (1993). Learning and teaching ratio and proportion: Research implications. In D.T. Owens (Ed.), *Research ideas for the classroom: Middle grades mathematics* (pp. 159–178). Old Tappan, NJ: Macmillan.

Haubner, M.A. (1992). Percents: Developing meaning through models. *Arithmetic Teacher, 40,* 232–234.

Hoffer, A.R., & Hoffer, S.A.K. (1992). Ratios and proportional thinking. In T.R. Post (Ed.), *Teaching mathematics in grades K–8: Research-based methods* (2nd ed., pp. 303–330). Needham Heights, MA: Allyn & Bacon.

Kenney, P.A., Lindquist, M.M., & Hefferman, C.L. (2002). Butterflies and caterpillars: Multiplicative and proportional reasoning in the early grades. In B. Litwiller (Ed.), *Making sense of fractions, ratios, and proportions* (pp. 87–99). Reston, VA: National Council of Teachers of Mathematics.

Lamon, S.J. (1993). Ratio and proportion: Connecting content and children's thinking. *Journal for Research in Mathematics Education, 24,* 41–61.

Lo, J., & Watanabe, T. (1997). Developing ratio and proportion schemes: A story of a fifth grader. *Journal for Research in Mathematics Education, 28,* 216–236.

Middleton, J.A., & van den Heuvel–Panhuizen, M. (1995). The ratio table. *Mathematics Teaching in the Middle School, 1,* 283–287.

Moss, J. (2002). Percents and proportions in the center: Altering the teaching sequence for rational number. In B. Litwiller (Ed.), *Making sense of fractions, ratios, and proportions* (pp. 109-120). Reston, VA: National Council of Teachers of Mathematics.

Smith, J.P. III. (2002). The development of students' knowledge of fractions and ratios. In B. Litwiller (Ed.), *Making sense of fractions, ratios, and proportions* (pp. 3–17). Reston, VA: National Council of Teachers of Mathematics.

Teach Magazine (2002). Curricula: The math-art project. [Incorporating nautilus fossils]. Pines Senior Public School, Clarke Township.

Thompson, D.R., Austin, R.A., & Beckmann, C.E. (2002). Using literature as a vehicle to explore proportional reasoning. In B. Litwiller (Ed.), *Making sense of fractions, ratios, and proportions* (pp. 130–137). Reston, VA: National Council of Teachers of Mathematics.

Chapter 16

Developing Measurement Concepts

Although provincial and territorial curricula vary in the way that concepts are presented, all include measurement as a key area of concentration. It is significant that measurement is one of only five standards (each spanning K–12) around which the NCTM chose to organize the content in the *Principles and Standards*. In this highly influential document, the authors note the pervasiveness of measurement in our lives and the opportunities this provides for learning. They also point out that measurement can be applied to most other mathematical concepts, and can enhance or contribute to the study of number, geometry, statistics, and functions.

That measurement was given its own standard in *Principles and Standards* is indicative of its complexity. Between kindergarten and grade 8, students must learn the attributes that they will be measuring (length, capacity, mass, and so on); what it means to measure, including an understanding of units of measure and how unit size affects measures; the selection and use of measurement instruments; and formulas that can be used for determining measurements. Measurement is far more complex than we often realize.

BIG IDEAS

1. Measurement involves a comparison of an item that is being measured with a unit that has the same attribute (area, length, volume, etc.). To measure anything meaningfully, the attribute to be measured must be understood.

2. Meaningful measurement and estimation of measurements depend on a personal familiarity with the unit of measure being used.

3. Measurement instruments are devices that replace the need for actual measurement units in making comparisons.

4. Area and volume formulas rely on measures of length, not of units of area or volume, in order to calculate the area or volume of an object.

The Meaning and Process of Measuring

Suppose that you were asked to measure an empty bucket. The first thing you would need to know is *what* attributes of the bucket are to be measured. Various lengths could be measured: height or depth, diameter (distance across), circumference (distance around). The surface area of the side could be determined. A bucket also has volume and mass. Each of these *aspects that can be measured* is an *attribute* of the bucket.

Once you determine the attribute to be measured, you can choose a unit of measure. The unit must have the attribute that is being measured. Length is measured with linear units (units that have length), volume with cubic units (units that have volume), and so on.

Technically, a *measurement* is the number that indicates a comparison between the attribute of the object being measured and the same attribute of a given unit of measure. We commonly use small units of measure to determine in some way a numerical relationship (the measurement) between what is measured and the unit. For example, to measure a length, the comparison can be done by lining up copies of the unit directly against the length being measured. If you used your hand to measure the height of the bucket (your hand would serve as the unit of measure in this case), you would start at either the top or bottom and place one hand next to the other repeatedly until you reached the opposite end. This is what you do when you use a ruler or tape measure. To measure the mass of an object, you would first attach the object to a spring scale. Then a comparison is made between the mass of the object and the number of units of mass required to produce the effect on the spring. In either case, the number of units is the measure of the object.

For most of the attributes that students explore in school, we can say that *to measure* means to "fill," "cover," or "match" the attribute being measured with a unit of measure for that attribute (as illustrated in Figure 16.1). This concept of measurement will adequately serve the purposes of this chapter and is a good way to discuss with children what a measurement is. It is appropriate, then, to say that the measure of an attribute is a count of how many units are needed to fill, cover, or match the attribute of the object being measured.

In summary, to measure something, one must perform three steps:

1. Decide on the attribute to be measured.
2. Select a unit that has that attribute.
3. Compare the units with the attribute of the object being measured, by filling, covering, matching, etc. the object.

Measuring instruments such as rulers, scales, protractors, and clocks are devices that make the filling, covering, or matching process easier. A ruler lines up units of length and numbers them. A protractor lines up angular units and numbers them. A clock lines up units of time and marks them off.

Developing Measurement Concepts and Skills

A typical group of grade 1 children measures the length of their classroom using informal (non-standard) units. They lay paper strips of equal size end to end. But the strips sometimes overlap, and the line weaves in a snakelike fashion around the desks. Do they understand the concept of length as an attribute of the classroom? Do they understand that each strip has this attribute of length? Do they understand that their task is to fill the longer unit of length with smaller ones? What they most likely understand is that they are supposed to be making a line of strips stretching from wall to wall (and from their vantage point, they are doing quite well). They are performing a procedure instrumentally, without a conceptual basis.

A General Plan of Instruction

A basic understanding of measurement will help children develop their conceptual knowledge as summarized in the following table.

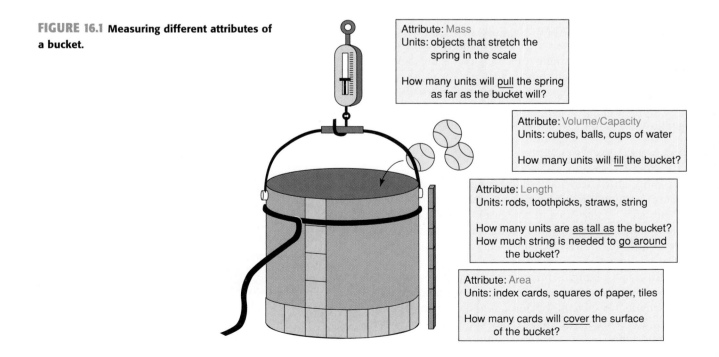

FIGURE 16.1 Measuring different attributes of a bucket.

Attribute: Mass
Units: objects that stretch the spring in the scale

How many units will <u>pull</u> the spring as far as the bucket will?

Attribute: Volume/Capacity
Units: cubes, balls, cups of water

How many units will <u>fill</u> the bucket?

Attribute: Length
Units: rods, toothpicks, straws, string

How many units are <u>as tall as</u> the bucket?
How much string is needed to <u>go around</u> the bucket?

Attribute: Area
Units: index cards, squares of paper, tiles

How many cards will <u>cover</u> the surface of the bucket?

Conceptual Knowledge to Develop	Type of Activity to Use
1. Understand the attribute being measured.	1. Make comparisons based on the attribute.
2. Understand how filling, covering, matching, or making other comparisons of an attribute with units produces what is known as a measure.	2. Use physical models of measurement units to fill, cover, match, or make the desired comparison of the attribute with the unit.
3. Understand the way measuring instruments work.	3. Take measuring instruments and use them along with actual unit models to compare how each works.

Let's briefly discuss each of these instructional activities.

Making Comparisons

When students compare objects on the basis of some measurable attribute, that attribute becomes the focus of the activity. For example, is the capacity of one box more than, less than, or about the same as the capacity of another? No measurement is required, but some manner of comparing one volume to the other must be devised. The attribute of "capacity" (how much a container can hold) is inescapable.

Many attributes can be compared directly; for example, one length can be placed next to another. In the case of volume or capacity, some indirect method is probably required, such as filling one box with beans and then pouring the beans into the other box. Using a string to compare the height of a wastebasket to its circumference is another example of an indirect comparison. The string is the intermediary. It is impossible to compare these two lengths directly.

Constructing or making something that is the same in terms of a measurable attribute is another type of comparison activity—for example, "Cut the straw to be just as long as this piece of chalk" or "Draw a rectangle that is about the same size (has the same area) as this triangle."

Using Models of Units

For most attributes that are measured in elementary school, it is possible to have physical models of the units of measure. Time and temperature are exceptions. (Many other attributes not commonly measured in school also do not have physical units of measure. Light intensity, speed, loudness, viscosity, and radioactivity are just a few examples.) Unit models can be found for both informal (non-standard) units and standard units. For length, for example, drinking straws or tag-board strips 25 centimetres long might be used as non-standard units.

The concept of a unit is most easily understood when as many copies of the unit as needed are used to fill or match the attribute being measured. For example, to measure the area of a desktop using an index card as a non-standard unit of measure, you actually need to cover the entire desk with index cards. It is somewhat more difficult, especially for younger children, if a single copy of the unit is used with an iteration process—in other words, if the same desktop area is measured by moving the single index card from position to position. This procedure requires keeping track of which parts the card has covered.

It is important for students to measure the same object with different-sized units. Doing so will help them come to understand that the unit used is as important as the attribute being measured. The fact that smaller units produce larger numerical measures, and vice versa, is hard for young children to understand. This inverse relationship can only be constructed by having students reflect on measurements with varying-sized units. Results should be predicted in advance and discussed afterward; this will add to the reflective nature of the activities.

Making and Using Measuring Instruments

In the sixth National Assessment of Educational Progress in the United States (Kenney & Kouba, 1997), only 24 percent of grade 4 students and 62 percent of grade 8 students could give the correct measure of an object that was not aligned with the end of a ruler, as in Figure 16.2. These results point to the difference between using a measuring device and understanding how it works. Students also experienced difficulty when the increments on a measuring device were other than one unit.

If students actually make simple measuring instruments using unit models with which they are familiar, it is more likely that they will understand how an instrument works. A ruler is a good example. If students line up physical units along a strip of tag-board and mark them off, they can see that it is the *spaces (the distance between two units)* on the ruler and not the marks or numbers that are important. It is essential that measurement with actual unit models (strips or squares of paper, interlocking cubes, and so on) be compared with measurement using an instrument. Without this comparison, students may not understand that these two methods are really two means to the same end. Always have students explain how the ruler, scale, or other device compares to using actual units.

FIGURE 16.2 "How long is this segment?"

A discussion of student-made measuring instruments for each attribute is provided in the text that follows. Of course, children should also use standard, ready-made instruments, such as rulers and scales, and should compare the use of these devices with the use of the corresponding unit models.

Informal (Non-Standard) Units and Standard Units: Reasons for Using Each

It is common in primary grades to use non-standard or informal units to measure length and sometimes area. Unfortunately, measurement activities in the upper grades, where additional attributes are measured, often do not begin with informal (non-standard) units. The use of informal units for beginning measurement activities is beneficial at all grade levels.

- Informal (non-standard) units, such as paper strips, pencils, paper clips, and squares, make it easier to focus directly on the attribute being measured. For example, instead of using square centimetres to measure area, an assortment of different-sized area units, some of which are not square, can be used. Doing so will help build understanding of the essential features of area and its required units of measure.
- By selecting units carefully, the numerical measure in early measurements can be kept reasonable. For example, the measures of length for grade 1 students can be kept to less than 20 units, even when measuring long distances. Angular units much larger than a degree are significantly easier for a grade 6 student to use, because degrees are such small units of measure.
- Using informal units in a beginning lesson can avoid conflicting objectives. Is your lesson about what it means to measure area, or about understanding square centimetres? Learning about measurement is different from learning about the standard units used for measuring.
- Working with informal units first provides a good rationale for work with standard units. A discussion of the need for a standard unit can have more meaning after groups in your class have measured the same objects using their own informal units.

Using informal units can be fun and meaningful. However, the use of standard units is an important part of your measurement program at any grade level.

- Knowledge of standard units is a necessary objective of any measurement program and must be addressed. Students must not only develop a familiarity with standard units, they must also understand the appropriate relationships between them.
- Once a measuring concept is fairly well developed, it is often just as easy to use standard units. If there is no

good instructional reason for using informal units, why not use standard units and expose students to them?

There is no simple rule regarding when to use standard or informal units. Initial measurement of any attribute should probably begin with informal units and progress over time to the use of standard units and standard measuring tools. The amount of time that should be spent using informal unit models varies with the age of the child and the attribute being measured. Grade 1 children need a lot of experience with a variety of informal units of length, mass, and capacity. Informal units will likely be used at this level all year. Conversely, the benefits of non-standard measuring units may last only two or three days for measurements of mass or capacity at the middle-school level.

The Role of Estimation in Learning Measurement

It is very important to have students estimate a measurement before actually making it. This applies to both non-standard and standard units. There are three reasons for including estimation in measurement activities:

- Estimation helps students focus on the attribute being measured and the measuring process. Think how you would estimate the area of the front of this book with standard playing cards as the unit. To do so, you have to think about what area is and how the units might fit on to the cover.
- Estimation offers intrinsic motivation for measuring. It is fun to see how close you can come in your estimate or if your team can make a better estimate than the other teams in your class.
- When standard units are used, estimation helps develop familiarity with the unit. If you estimate the height of the door in metres before measuring, you have to devise some way to think about the size of a metre.

Helping Children with Measurement Estimates

Having said that estimation should be included in most measurement activities, there remains the problem of how to go about doing so. Later we will discuss teaching children specific estimating strategies that can be used throughout life. Until these strategies are developed, children will have difficulty making estimates. Here are three ways to ask for estimates without asking children to come up with an actual number.

1. Ask for a comparison estimate rather than a measure. For example, is the teacher's height more than,

less than, or about the same as 2 metres? Is the mass of the book more than, less than, or about the same as 500 grams? The same can be done with informal units: Is the area of the desktop more than, less than, or about the same as 20 index cards?

2. Ask to which of two or more suggested measures an actual measure is closer. For example, is the angle measure closer to 15, 60, or 90 degrees? Is the capacity of the box closer to 1 litre or 3 litres?

3. Provide an actual unit or set of units for comparison. The children can make an initial estimate privately on paper. Then show the unit or set of 10 or 100 units, and let them adjust their first estimate accordingly. Sets of 10 or 100 are suggested for reasons of place value. The use of the set of units allows students to mentally mark off or compare their estimate with it in some way. Being able to estimate first adds a bit of interest. For example, after seeing a bar of 10 cubes placed at one end of the chalkboard, the children can count by tens as they visually mark off these bars along the board. For larger units such as a metre or a kilogram, one copy of the unit can be placed directly alongside the object being estimated. Of course, to estimate an attribute such as mass, the children need to handle the unit as well as the object.

Notice the progression of the specificity of the estimating in the previous three ideas. Use this progression as you develop children's estimation skills.

The Approximate Nature of Measurement

In all measuring activities, emphasize the use of approximate language. The desk is *about* 15 orange strips long. The chair is *a little less than* 4 straws high. The use of approximate language is especially appropriate for younger children because many measurements do not come out exact. Older children will begin to search for smaller units or will use fractional units as they try to measure exactly. Here is an opportunity to develop the idea that all measurements include some error. Each smaller unit or subdivision does produce a greater degree of precision. For example, a length measure can never be more than one-half unit in error. But since there is mathematically no "smallest unit," there is always some error involved.

The notion of precision as related to the size of the unit is an important idea with all measuring tasks. Sometimes precision is not required, in which case a larger unit is much easier to deal with. At other times, precision is significant, and smaller units become important. For example, measuring a pane of glass for a window requires a different precision than measuring a wall to decide how many posters can fit on it. Awareness of precision in unit size and the degree of need for it in different

situations is an important aspect of measurement, especially at the upper grades.

Suggested Measurement Sequence

For each attribute that we measure, we can employ the three types of activities that have been discussed. Comparison activities should generally precede the use of units, informal (non-standard) units should precede standard ones, and measuring instruments should come last. Within each of these categories, there is also a rough guideline of progression that can be considered:

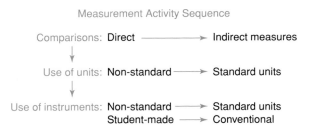

Measurement Activity Sequence

Almost all activities should include an estimation component. Familiarity with standard units is a separate but important objective. In the discussions that follow, the focus is on activities for comparison, use of units, and use of instruments for each attribute. Separate discussions for standard units and estimation are also provided.

Measuring Length

Length is usually the first attribute students learn to measure. Be aware that linear (length) measure is not immediately understood by young children.

Comparison Activities

At the kindergarten level, children should begin with direct comparisons of two or more lengths.

It is important to compare lengths that are curved.

ACTIVITY 16.1

Longer, Shorter, Same

Make a sort-by-length station at which students sort objects as longer than, shorter than, or about the same as a specified object. It is easy to have several such stations in your room. The reference object can be changed occasionally to produce different sorts. A similar task is to put objects in order from shortest to longest.

ACTIVITY 16.2

Length Hunt

Give pairs of students a strip of tag-board, a stick, a length of rope, or some other object in which length is an obvious dimension. The task on one day might be to find five things in the room that are shorter than or longer than or about the same as their object of choice. They can draw pictures or write the names of the things they find.

One way to do this is with string or rope. Students can wrap string around objects as they search for things that are, for example, the same distance around as the distance from the floor to their belly button, or the distance around one's head or waist. Body measures are always fun.

Indirect comparisons are a next step in comparing length.

ACTIVITY 16.3

Crooked Paths

Make some crooked or curved paths on the floor with masking tape. The task is to determine which path is the longest, the next-longest, and so on. The students should find a way to make straight paths that are equal in length to the crooked paths so that they can be compared easily. (You may or may not wish to offer this suggestion.) Provide each pair of students with a long piece of rope. The task is easier if the rope is longer than the crooked paths. The students can draw their straight paths on the board, mark them with tape on the floor, or use some other method that you devise. Have students explain how they solved the problem. (This is a good outdoor activity also.)

The "Crooked Paths" activity can also be done with shorter distances at students' desks. A simple worksheet like the one in Figure 16.3 might be prepared. Instead of crooked paths, students can make straight paths that are as long as the distance around simple shapes (their perimeters).

Using Units of Length

Students can use a variety of informal units to begin measuring length, for example:

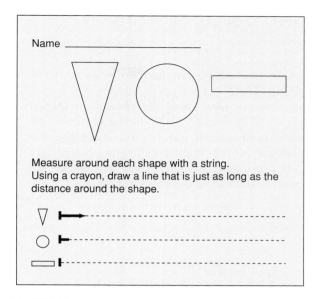

FIGURE 16.3 Making a straight path just as long as a crooked path.

Giant footprints: Make about 20 copies of a large footprint about 50 to 60 centimetres long, cut out of poster board.

Measuring strips: Cut strips of poster board about 5 centimetres wide. Several sets with different lengths can be made to provide different units of measure. Some can be long, some short, and a third set about 30 centimetres long. Make each set a different colour.

Measuring ropes: Cut cotton clothesline into lengths of 1 metre. These are useful for measuring curved lines and the circumference of large objects such as the teacher's desk.

Plastic straws: Drinking straws are inexpensive and provide a useful unit in large quantities. The straws can be easily cut into smaller units. You can link the straw units together with a long string. A string of straws is an excellent bridge to a ruler or measuring tape.

Short units: Toothpicks, interlocking cubes, wooden cubes, and paper clips are all useful units for measuring shorter lengths. Paper clips can readily be made into chains.

For young children, initial measurements should be done along lines or edges. If different teams of students measure the same distances and get different results, then discuss the differences. The discussion can help focus on why units need to be lined up end to end in a straight line, and why measuring tools such as ropes must be stretched to their full length.

Guess and Measure

Make lists of things in the room to measure (see Figure 16.4). For younger children, run a piece of masking tape along the dimension of each object to be measured. On the list, designate the units to be used. Remember to include distances that are curved. Include estimating before actually measuring. Young children will not be very good at estimating distances at first.

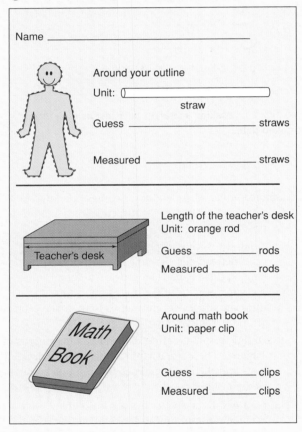

FIGURE 16.4 **Record sheet for measuring with informal (non-standard) units of length.**

ACTIVITY 16.5

Changing Units

Have students measure a distance with one unit, then provide them with a different unit and see if they can predict the measure with the new unit. Students should write down their predictions and explanations of how they were made. Then have them make the actual measurement. Going over the predictions and explanations in the class discussions that follow will be the most educational part of the activity. The first few times you do this activity, the larger unit should be a simple multiple of the smaller unit. If the two units are not related by a whole-number multiple, the task becomes difficult numerically.

Two Units and Fractional Parts of Units

As children develop a need for more precision, two units can be used at the same time. The second unit should be a sub-unit of the first. For example, with interlocking cubes, the first unit could be a bar 10 cubes long. The second unit could be an individual cube. Cut plastic straws so that an even number of paper clips is equal to one straw. With measuring strips, make sub-units that are one-fourth or one-tenth as long as the longer strip. You could also use a different colour for the sub-unit. Have children measure with the larger unit until no more of that unit will fit, and then add on sufficient smaller sub-units to fill up the distance (see Figure 16.5). Report measures in two parts: "8 straws and 3 clips long." For older students, smaller units can simply be fractional parts of longer units.

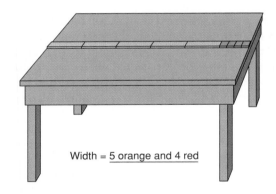

Width = 5 orange and 4 red

FIGURE 16.5 **Using two units to measure length.**

After a measurement with two related units has been made and recorded, have students figure out how to report the same measurement in terms of either unit—for example, $5\frac{3}{4}$ orange strips or 23 red strips. This is a readiness exercise for standard units. For example, in standard measure, 1 metre 20 centimetres could be reported as 120 centimetres or 1.2 metres. The use of two units also provides readiness for subdivision marks on a ruler.

Making and Using Rulers

Rulers or tape measures can be made for almost any unit of measure. It is important that students have used the actual unit models before making the rulers.

Ruler construction should be connected to a measuring experience with a unit that is small, but not less than 5 centimetres. Rulers can be made on long strips of tag-board about 5 centimetres wide. If you precut narrow strips of construction paper, students can cut these into shorter pieces, using their unit model as a guide. Discuss how the paper strips could be used for measuring just as well as the actual units. Next, students can paste the paper units along the edge of the tag-board. Use two contrasting colors, and alternate them as shown in Figure 16.6.

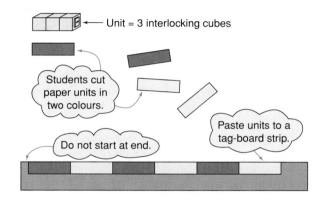

FIGURE 16.6 **Making a simple ruler.**

Pasting down copies of the units on a ruler maximizes the connection between the spaces on the ruler and the actual units. Older children can make rulers by using a real unit to make marks along a tag-board strip; then they can colour in the spaces. Children should not be encouraged to use the end of a ruler as a starting point, as most real rulers are not made that way. If the first unit on a ruler does not coincide with the end of the ruler, the student will be forced to attend to aligning the units on the ruler with the object measured.

Students should eventually put numbers on their homemade rulers, as shown in Figure 16.7. For young children, numbers can be written in the centre of each unit to make it clear that the numbers are a way of pre-counting the units. When numbers are written in the standard way, at the ends of the units, the ruler becomes a number line. This format is more sophisticated and should be carefully discussed with children.

Assessment Note

Although Figure 16.7 illustrates a developmental progression, children should be encouraged to make and number their rulers in ways that make sense to them. Having students make their own rulers, in their own way, and explain the measures they obtained using their rulers, will provide you with an enormous amount of assessment data regarding how well they understand the measurement process. On the other hand, if you carefully direct how children

First rulers: Students count units.

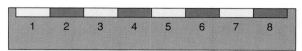

Second rulers: Numbers help to count.
Numbers in centre of units.

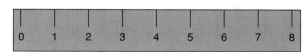

Standard rulers: Numbers are at ends of
units. Notice where 0 is.

FIGURE 16.7 **Give meaning to numbers on rulers.**

should construct and use their rulers, they may very well use the rulers mechanically, without understanding what they are doing.

Putting measurement tasks into problem-solving exercises will provide you with increased information. For example, how could you explain in a letter to a class in another city or country just how large your classroom is, or the size of the model of a blue whale you have been building? Let different groups decide how to do this making their own measurements. Then compare results and see if each solution actually conveys the meaning intended.

Using Rulers and Tape Measures

It is important to use the rulers students have made. In addition to the estimate-and-measure activities mentioned earlier, have teams measure items once with a ruler and a second time with actual unit models. Although the results should be the same, inaccuracies or incorrect use of the ruler may produce differences that are important to discuss. Also, use the ruler to measure lengths that are longer than the ruler. To do this you will need to show the students how to take the ruler and place the beginning of it where the last measure ended.

ACTIVITY 16.6

More Than One Way

Challenge students to find different ways to measure an identical length with the same ruler. (Measure the object starting at opposite ends of the ruler; start at a point not at the end; measure different parts of the object, then add the results.)

Tape measures, especially useful for measuring around objects, can be made in a variety of ways employing the same approach as with the rulers. With longer units such as metres, a clothesline can be marked with a piece of masking tape or a marking pen at the end of each metre. Grosgrain ribbon is easily marked with a ballpoint pen. Even adding-machine tape can be used to make a tape measure.

After working with simple rulers and tape measures, have students make rulers with sub-units or fractional units. Much of the value of student-made rulers can be lost if you do not transfer this knowledge to standard rulers. Give children a standard ruler, and discuss the similarities with and differences from the ones they have made. What are the units? Could you make a ruler with paper units the same as this? Could you make some cardboard units and measure the same way as with the ruler? What do the numbers mean? What are the other marks for? Where do the units begin?

Measuring Area

Data from the sixth National Assessment of Educational Progress suggest that grade 4 and grade 8 U.S. students have an incomplete understanding of area (Kenney & Kouba, 1997). Results from the Third International Mathematics and Science Study (TIMSS) reveal similar findings for grade 4 and particularly grade 8 Canadian students (Robitaille, Taylor, Orpwood, 1996).

Comparison Activities

When comparing two areas, there is the added consideration of shape, not present when measuring lengths, and this frequently causes difficulty. One of the purposes of early comparison activities with areas is to help students distinguish between size (or area) and shape, length, and other features. A long, skinny rectangle may have a smaller area than a triangle with shorter sides. This is an especially difficult concept for young children to understand. Piagetian experiments indicate that many 8- or 9-year-olds (even older children) do not understand that rearranging areas into different shapes does not affect the area.

Direct comparison of two areas is almost always impossible, except when the shapes involved have some common dimension or property. For example, two rectangles with the same width can be compared directly, as can any two circles. But comparison of these special shapes does not adequately deal with the attribute of area. Instead, activities in which one area is rearranged should be employed. By cutting a shape into two parts and reassembling it into a different shape you can show that the before and after shapes, even though they are different,

have the same area. This idea is not at all obvious to primary children.

ACTIVITY 16.7

Two-Piece Shapes

With the children working in small groups, give each child a rectangle of construction paper. Have the children fold and cut the paper on the diagonal, making two identical triangles. Next, have them rearrange the triangles into different shapes, including the original rectangle. The rule is that only sides that have the same length can be matched up. Have each group find all the shapes that can be made; then have them paste the triangles on paper as a record of the shapes they made (see Figure 16.8). Discuss the size and shape of the different results. Is one shape bigger than the rest? How is it bigger? Did one take more paper to make, or do they all have the same amount of paper? Help children come to the understanding that although each figure has a different shape, all of them have the same *area*. (In this context, with very young children, size is a useful substitute for *area* even though it does not mean exactly the same thing.)

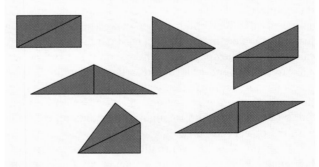

FIGURE 16.8 Different shapes, same size.

A tangram is a very old and popular set of puzzle shapes that can be used in a similar way. The standard set of seven tangram pieces is cut from a square, as shown in Figure 16.9. The two small triangles can be used to make the parallelogram, the square, and the medium triangle. Although their shapes vary, each of these figures has the same size (area). Four small triangles can also be used to make the large triangle, thus permitting a similar discussion about the pieces having the same size (area) but different shapes. (Tangram pieces can be found in the Blackline Masters.)

The following activities suggest methods for comparing areas without measuring.

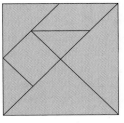
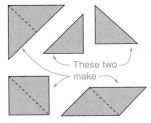

7 tangram pieces

The 2 small triangles make each of the medium shapes.

These two make

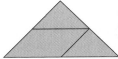

Two small triangles with the parallelogram will make the large triangle.

FIGURE 16.9 Tangrams provide a nice opportunity to investigate concepts of size and shape.

ACTIVITY 16.8

Tangram Areas

Use the tangram pieces to draw the outline of several shapes as in Figure 16.10. Then let students use their tangram pieces to figure out which shapes are equal in size, which ones are larger than the others, and which ones are smaller. The shapes can be duplicated on paper so children can work in groups. Let students explain how they came to their conclusions. There are several different approaches to this task, and it is best if students determine their own solutions rather than blindly follow your directions. You might want to stop here, get a set of tangram pieces, and make the area comparisons suggested in Figure 16.10.

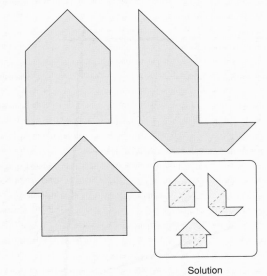

Solution

FIGURE 16.10 Compare shapes made of tangram pieces.

ACTIVITY 16.9

Cover and Compare

Draw two or three shapes on a piece of paper and duplicate them. The shapes can be irregular blobs or more familiar shapes such as triangles, circles, or rectangles. In pairs or small groups, have students decide, simply by observation, which shape is the largest and which is the smallest. Then have them find a way to figure out if their original estimates are correct. You can suggest methods of comparison, or you can leave the methods completely to the students' invention.

Activity 16.9 allows you to observe what kinds of ideas your children bring to the concept of area. You might suggest a wide variety of "tools" from which they may choose, or let them select their own methods of determining which shape is largest. For example, you could provide scissors, plastic squares (such as Colour Tiles), lima beans, string, centimetre grid paper, tangrams, or any other type of counter or tile. By not prescribing the method of comparison, you will be able to see what it is that the children understand about area.

One method of comparison involves covering one shape with counters and then moving these same counters to a second shape to see if it takes more or fewer counters to fill its interior. Another possibility is to cut out the shapes and place one on top of the other. Some children may think of cutting a shape into two or more pieces so that it can be rearranged to compare with another. Shapes may be traced onto grid paper to count the interior squares. String is not really useful for comparing areas. However, if someone does use string to compare the boundaries of the shapes, a discussion of what was actually compared can be very helpful.

Using Units of Area

Although squares are very nice units of area (and the most commonly used), any tile that conveniently fills up a plane region can be used. It is important that children understand that finding area is all about filling a region with a particular area unit of measure. Even covering a region with lima beans provides a useful idea of what it means to measure area. Here are some suggestions for area units that are easy to gather or make in the large quantities you will need.

Cut squares or triangles (by cutting on the diagonals of the squares) from cardboard. (Use a paper cutter.) Large squares or triangles (about 20 cm on a side) work well for large areas. Smaller units should be about 5 to 10 cm on a side.

Sheets of newspaper make excellent units for very large areas.

Poster board can easily be cut into large quantities of congruent tiles for smaller units. Include rectangles, equilateral triangles, and right triangles as well as squares. These tiles can be about 2 to 5 cm on a side.

Pattern blocks can also be used as units. There are six different shapes, and the yellow hexagon, red trapezoid, blue rhombus, and green triangle are all related to each other, similar to the way that the tangram pieces are.

Playing cards, index cards, or old business cards make good medium-sized units.

Children can use units to measure surfaces in the room such as desktops, bulletin boards, or books. Large regions can be outlined with masking tape on the floor. Use the gym or hallway for very large areas. Small regions can be duplicated on paper so that students can work at their desks. Odd shapes and curved surfaces provide more challenge and interest. The surfaces of a watermelon or a wastebasket provide useful challenges.

When measuring length, it is only the last unit that may not completely fit the surface being measured. With area measurements, there may be a number of units that only partially fit. However, you may wish to begin with shapes in which the units do fit exactly. You can do so by first building a shape with units, and drawing the outline. By grade 3 or 4, students should begin to wrestle with partial units and be able to mentally put together two or more partial units to count as one (see Figure 16.11).

Your objective in the beginning is to develop the idea that area is a *measure of finding how many units will cover a particular surface*. Do not introduce formulas. Simply have the students cover the shapes and count the units. Be sure to have them estimate before measuring (this process is significantly more difficult for area than for length), use the language of approximation, and relate precision to the size of the units in the same manner as with length. Groups are very likely to come up with different measures for the same region. Discuss these differences with the children, and point to the difficulties involved in making estimates around the edges. Avoid the idea that there is a "right" answer. Discussions such as these should ultimately lead students to recognize the need for a standard unit.

The following activity is similar to Activity 16.9, "Cover and Compare." What is different is that you are now asking students not only to make comparisons but also to use a measurement of some sort to order the shapes by size.

ACTIVITY 16.10

Smaller to Larger

Present a series of different shapes with only slightly different areas. Students first predict the order of the shapes from smallest to largest and record their prediction. Then the task is to determine the correct order using any methods and units they wish. The determination of the "correct" order is left to the students; this can lead to a profitable class discussion about different methods.

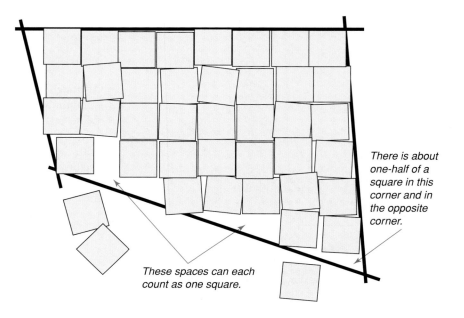

FIGURE 16.11 Measuring the area of a large shape made with tape on the floor. Units are pieces of tag-board all cut to the same shape.

There is about one-half of a square in this corner and in the opposite corner.

These spaces can each count as one square.

The next activity requires an application of ideas about area developed so far.

ACTIVITY 16.11

Same-Size Rectangle

This activity works best when students work in small groups. It can be done before the formula for area has been introduced. The activity can be done with small shapes that can be drawn on paper or very large shapes on the floor made with tape or chalk. Using whatever materials they wish, have students make a rectangle that has the same size as a shape that you have given them. All groups in the class should be given the same shape with which to work but no direction as to how to design their rectangle. The given shape may be a blob or some other irregular shape, or it may be a triangle or even a rectangle. Even if all groups have very good solutions, they will almost certainly come up with rectangles that have different dimensions. Each group must explain why they believe their rectangle has the same area as the given shape.

Using Grids

With the exception of computer drafting equipment, there really are no instruments designed for measuring area. However, there are various types of grids that can be thought of as a kind of "area ruler." A grid of squares does exactly what a ruler does: It lays out the units for you. Square grids are available in the Blackline Masters. Note that triangular grids can also be used. Make transparencies of any grid paper. Have students place the grid over a region to be measured and count the units inside. An alternative method is to trace around a region on a paper grid.

ACTIVITY 16.12

Floor Grids

For larger regions on the floor, make two lines with tape in an L shape, as shown in Figure 16.12. On the tape, mark off appropriate units of length. Explain that the two lines are the edges of a grid and can be used to help visualize imaginary squares without drawing them. To demonstrate, large shapes cut from butcher paper or other flat items can be positioned in the corners of the L.

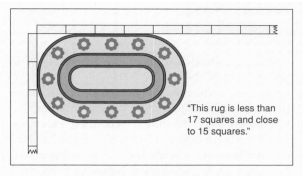

"This rug is less than 17 squares and close to 15 squares."

FIGURE 16.12 Two masking-tape rulers on the floor make an imaginary grid for measuring the area of large shapes.

Since most standard units of area are squares derived from standard units of length (square centimetres, square metres, etc.), the most useful grid is one made of squares. As children use square grids to determine areas of rectangular shapes, many will begin to see that the product of the number of rows times the number of columns is an easy way to count the squares. The L approach (which can also be used for small shapes on paper) hints at how the lengths of the sides of a region are used to determine areas.

Measuring Volume and Capacity

Volume and *capacity* are both terms for measures of the "size" of three-dimensional regions. Standard units of volume, frequently regarded in terms of their linear measure, are expressed in cubic centimetres, cubic metres, etc. Capacity units are generally used for measuring liquids or the containers that hold those liquids. Standard capacity units include litres, millilitres, etc.

Comparison Activities

Most solid shapes and containers must be compared indirectly. By far the easiest comparisons are made between containers that can be filled with some substance, which is then poured from one container to the other.

Young children should have many experiences directly comparing the capacities of different containers. Collect a large assortment of cans, small boxes, and plastic containers. Gather as many different shapes as possible. Also gather some plastic scoops. Cut a plastic 2-litre bottle in half, and use the top portion as a funnel. Rice or dried beans are good fillers to use. Sand and water are both considerably messier.

Capacity Sort

Provide a collection of labelled containers, with one marked as the "target." The students' task is to sort the collection into those that hold more than, less than, or about the same amount as the target container. Provide a recording sheet on which each container is listed and a place to circle "holds more," "holds less," and "holds about the same." List the choices twice for each container. The first choice is to record an estimate made by observation. The second is to record "what was found." Provide some filler material (such as beans or rice), scoops, and funnels. Avoid explicit directions, but later discuss students' ideas for solving the task.

Volume Lineup

Given a series of five or six labelled containers of different size and shape, the task is to order them from least to greatest volume. This can be quite challenging. Do not provide answers. Let students work in groups to come up with a solution and explain how they arrived at it.

The volume of solids such as a rock, a ball, a block, an apple, or an eggplant can also be compared, but it is a bit more difficult. Some method of displacement must be used. One approach is to use a container that will hold each of the items. Begin by placing an object in the container and fill with rice to a level that is above the object. Mark this level on the container. Then remove the object and mark the new level. Repeat the procedure for the other objects. For consistency it is important that you use the same level of rice used for the first object each time a new object is placed in the container for measuring. The problem-solving nature of the activity is enhanced if students are challenged to devise their own methods.

Using Units of Volume

Two types of units can be used to measure volume and capacity: solid units and containers. Solid units, such as wooden cubes or old tennis balls, are objects that can be used to fill a container being measured. Small containers, filled and emptied repeatedly into a container being measured, are the other type of unit. The following are a few examples of units you might want to collect.

Thimbles, plastic caps, and liquid medicine cups are all good examples of very small units.

Plastic jars and containers of almost any size can also serve as units for measuring capacity.

Wooden cubes or blocks of any shape can be used as units, as long as you have enough of the same size.

Styrofoam packing chips, walnuts, or even marbles can be used. Even though they do not pack perfectly, they still produce conceptual measures of volume.

Measuring activities for volume and capacity are similar to those for length and area. On the other hand, estimating volume is considerably more challenging than estimating length or area, so it would be more enjoyable to do it as a class activity. Finding ways to measure containers such as large cardboard cartons in relation to a relatively small container-type unit can be an excellent challenge for groups of grade 4 or 5 students. These activities can be done long before volume formulas are developed.

When measuring with solid units such as cubes or balls, it is difficult to use only one object with repeated iterations, as can be done when working with length or area. A worthwhile challenge, though, is to determine the volumes of containers when there are only enough units to cover the bottom. Do not forget very large volumes, such as your room. How many cubic metres will the room hold? Be sure to design these projects so that groups devise their own methods along with written explanations and drawings.

Making and Using Measuring Cups

Instruments for measuring capacity are generally used for small amounts of liquids or materials that can be poured, such as rice or water. These tools are commonly found in kitchens and laboratories. As with other instruments, if children make their own, they are likely to develop a better understanding of the units and the approach to the measuring process.

A measuring cup can be made using a smaller container as the unit of measure. Select a large, transparent container for the measuring cup and a smaller one for the unit. Fill the smaller one (the unit) with beans or rice, empty it into the large container, and mark the level. Repeat until the large container is nearly full. If the unit container is small, then it may only be necessary to mark the large container after every 5 fillings. It is not necessary to write numbers for every marking on the container. Students frequently have difficulty reading scales when the gradations represent more than one unit or when not every mark is labelled. Therefore, this activity is an opportunity to help them understand how to interpret lines on a real measuring cup.

Students should use their measuring cups and compare their results with those made when the container is filled directly from the unit. It is likely that their measuring cups will produce errors due to inaccurate markings. This is an opportunity to point out that measuring instruments themselves can also be a source of error. The more accurate the instrument is, and the finer its calibration, the less the chance of error from that source. (The ultimate measuring cup you can use to avoid error is a cube-shaped cup for standard measurement. It is marked with 10 intervals, each exactly one centimetre high, and it has the capacity to hold one base-ten thousands block.)

Measuring Mass

Mass is the amount of matter in an object and a measure of the force needed to accelerate it. Weight, on the other hand, is a measure of the pull or force of gravity on an object. On the moon, where gravity is much less than on Earth, an object has a smaller weight but the identical mass as on Earth. For purposes of metric measure we will talk about mass.

Making Comparisons

The most conceptual way to compare the mass of two objects is to hold one in each hand, extend your arms, and experience the relative downward pull on each—effectively communicating to a young child what "heavier" means. This personal experience can then be transferred to one of two basic types of scales—balances and spring scales. Figure 16.13 (p. 308) shows a homemade version of each. Simple scales of each type are available through school-supply catalogues.

Children should first use their hands to estimate which of two objects is heavier. When they then place the objects in the two pans of a balance, the pan that goes down can be understood to hold the heavier object. Even a relatively simple balance will detect small differences. If two objects are placed one at a time in a spring scale, the heavier object pulls the pan down farther. Both balances and spring scales have real value in the classroom. Sorting and ordering tasks are possible with either scale.

Using Units of Mass

Any collection of uniform objects can be used as informal units of mass. For very light objects, wooden or plastic cubes work well. Large metal washers found in hardware stores are effective for finding the mass of slightly heavier objects. You will need to rely on units as heavy as a kilogram or more in order to find the mass of larger objects.

Place an object to be measured in one pan of a balance scale and enough of the object that is being used as the unit of measure, e.g. plastic cubes, washers and so on, in the other until the two pans are equal. Then, place the object being measured on a spring scale. Mark the position of the pan on a piece of paper, which is taped behind the pan. Remove the object. Then place just enough of the units of measure in the pan to pull it down to the same level that it reached when it held the object being measured. Discuss how different objects of equal mass will pull the spring or rubber band with the same amount of force.

While the concept of heavier and lighter is learned rather early, the notion of units of mass is a bit more challenging. At any grade level, even a brief experience with informal units of mass is good preparation for standard units and scales.

Making and Using a Scale

Most scales that we use in our daily lives produce a number when an object is placed on or in them. There are no visible units of mass. How does the scale produce the right number? By making a scale that gives a numerical result without recourse to units, children can see how scales work.

Students can use informal units and calibrate a simple rubber-band scale like the one in Figure 16.13. Mount the scale with a piece of paper behind it, and place units of mass in the pan. After every five units, make a mark on the paper. These marks correspond to the markings on the dial of a standard scale. The pan serves as the pointer. If we had a dial scale, the downward movement of the pan would cause the dial to turn mechanically. The value of this activity is that students see how scales are made. Even digital readout scales are based on the same principle.

Measuring Angles

Angle measurement causes difficulty for two reasons: The attribute of angle size is often misunderstood, and protractors are introduced and used without students' understanding how they work.

Comparing Angles

The attribute of angle size might be referred to as the "spread of the angle's rays," or the amount of rotation. Angles are composed of two rays whose lengths are infinite. The only difference in their size is how widely or narrowly spread apart the two rays are.

Some authors have students think of how much one ray has rotated in either direction away from the other. Two rulers held together near the ends can be used to demonstrate this idea. As one ruler is rotated in either direction, the size of the angle is seen to increase. However, when we see angles, the rays have already been

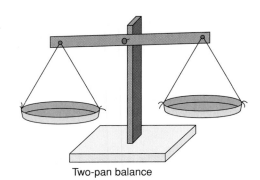

Two-pan balance

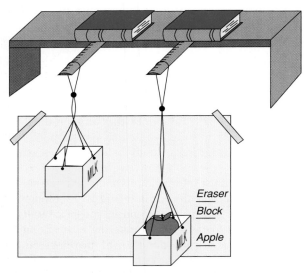

Rubber-band (spring) scales
Marks show where different objects
pulled the scale.

FIGURE 16.13 Two simple scales.

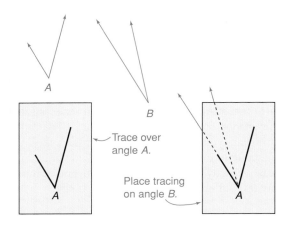

FIGURE 16.14 Which angle is larger? Trace one angle and use it to compare.

spread—no rotation is visible. Do you think of the angles in a triangle as the result of one side being rotated away from the other?

To help children conceptualize the attribute of the spread of the rays, two angles can be compared directly by tracing one and placing it over the other, as in Figure 16.14. Be sure to have students compare angles whose rays vary in length. A wide angle constructed of short rays may seem smaller than a narrow angle constructed of long rays. This is a common misconception among students. As soon as students can tell the difference between a large angle and a small one, regardless of the length of the rays, you can move on to measuring angles.

Using Units of Angular Measure

A unit for measuring an angle must involve a measure of rotation in some way. Nothing else has the same attribute

of spread or rotation that we want to measure. (Contrary to popular opinion, you do not need to use degrees to measure angles.)

ACTIVITY 16.15

An Angle Unit

Give each student an index card or a small piece of tag-board. Have students draw a narrow angle on the tag-board using a straightedge and then cut it out. This angle can now be used as an informal unit of angular measure by counting the number that will fit in a given angle. Pass out a worksheet with assorted angles on it, and have students use their angle unit to measure them. Because students made their own angular units, the results will differ and can be discussed in terms of their size.

Activity 16.15 illustrates that measuring an angle is similar to measuring length or area. Angular units are used to fill or cover the spread of an angle just as linear units are used to cover a length. Once this concept is well understood, you can move on to using measuring instruments.

Making a Protractor

The protractor is one of the most poorly understood measuring instruments found in schools. Part of the difficulty arises because the units of measure (degrees) are so very small. It would be physically impossible to cut out a single degree and use it in, say, Activity 16.15. Another problem is that there are no visible angles showing; there are only little marks around the outside edge of the protractor. Finally, the numbering that appears on most protractors runs both clockwise and counterclockwise along the marked edges. "Which numbers do I use?" By making a protractor with a large angle unit, all of these mysterious features can be understood. A careful comparison with this student-made instrument will then allow for the standard protractor to be used with understanding.

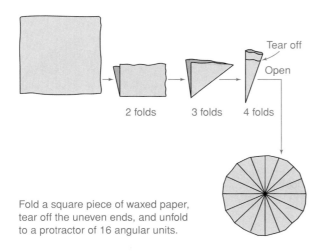

Fold a square piece of waxed paper, tear off the uneven ends, and unfold to a protractor of 16 angular units.

FIGURE 16.15 **Making a waxed-paper protractor.**

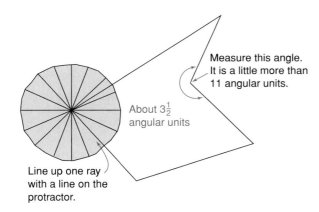

Measure this angle. It is a little more than 11 angular units.

About $3\frac{1}{2}$ angular units

Line up one ray with a line on the protractor.

FIGURE 16.16 **Measuring angles in a polygon using a waxed-paper protractor.**

Tear off about 30 centimetres of ordinary waxed paper for each student. Have the students fold the paper in half and crease the fold sharply. Fold in half again so that the folded edges match. Repeat this two more times, each time bringing the folded edges together and creasing sharply. Now, cut or tear off the end of the resulting wedge shape about 10 centimetres from the vertex and unfold. If done correctly, there will be 16 angles surrounding the centre, as in Figure 16.15. This serves as an excellent protractor with an angle unit that is one-eighth of a straight angle (about 20 degrees). It is sufficiently transparent that it can be placed

over an angle on paper, on the blackboard, or on the overhead projector to measure angles, as shown in Figure 16.16. Reasonable estimates of angle measures can be made with a waxed-paper protractor as small as the one in Figure 16.16. In that figure, one angle of a free-form polygon is measured for you. Use a waxed-paper protractor to measure as carefully as possible the other four angles in this polygon. Use fractional estimates. Your sum for all five interior angles should be very close to 24 angular units. There are two possible ways to get the measure of the angle indicated with the arrow. How would you measure that angle if your protractor were only a half circle instead of a full circle?

The waxed-paper protractor makes it quite clear how a protractor fits informal angular units into a given angle for measurement. When measuring angles, students can easily estimate halves, thirds, or fourths of an angle unit. This is sufficiently accurate to measure, for example, the interior angles of a polygon and discover the usual relationship between the number of sides and the sum of the interior angles. Figure 16.17 illustrates how a tag-board semicircle can be made into a protractor to measure angles using informal angular units. This tag-board version is a bit closer to a standard protractor, since the rays that denote the units do not extend down to the vertex, and they are numbered in two directions. The only difference between this protractor and a standard one is the size of the unit. The standard unit for measuring angles is the *degree,* which is simply a very small angle. A standard protractor by itself is not very helpful in teaching the meaning of a degree. But an analogy between an informal angular unit of measure and degrees and between these two protractors is a very effective approach.

Introducing Standard Units

As pointed out earlier, there are a number of reasons for teaching measurement using non-standard units. However, measurement sense demands that children be familiar with the common units of measurement and that they be able to make estimates in terms of these units. It also requires that they be able to meaningfully interpret measures depicted with standard units.

Perhaps the biggest error that occurs with instruction in measurement is the failure to recognize and distinguish between two objectives: first, that students understand the meaning and technique of measuring a particular attribute, and second, that they learn about the standard units commonly used to measure that attribute. These two objectives should be developed separately. When both are attempted together, there is likely to be confusion. Reread the list of reasons for using non-standard units (p. 297), and be very clear about why you would use them. Only when students are comfortable with the idea of measurement of an attribute can they focus on standard units of

FIGURE 16.17 Comparisons of protractors and angular units.

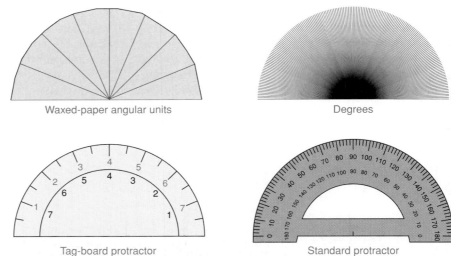

Waxed-paper angular units

Degrees

Tag-board protractor

Standard protractor

The marks on the tag-board wedge protractor are the rays on the waxed-paper version.
The marks on a plastic protractor are the rays of *degrees*. A degree is just a very small angle.

measurement and have a feel for them. Though both domains of knowledge (non-standard and standard) are important, it may be useful to keep the objectives separate when planning your lessons.

Instructional Goals

Three broad goals for standard units of measure can be identified:

1. *Familiarity with the unit.* Familiarity means that students should have a basic idea of the size of commonly used units and what they measure. Without this familiarity, measurement sense is impossible. It is more important to know about how much 1 litre of water is, or to be able to estimate a shelf as $1\frac{1}{2}$ metres long, than to have the ability to measure either of these accurately.

2. *Ability to select an appropriate unit.* Related to unit familiarity is understanding what a reasonable unit of measure is in a given situation. The choice of an appropriate unit is also a matter of required precision. (Would you measure your lawn with the same precision when purchasing grass seed as you would when measuring a window to buy a pane of glass?) In addition to precision, practicality is important when selecting an appropriate unit. For example, when measuring the dimensions of a room, it makes more sense and is more practical to use metres as a unit of measure than centimetres or millimetres. Students need practice using common sense when selecting the appropriate standard units.

3. *Knowledge of a few important relationships between units.* The emphasis should be on relationships that

are commonly used, such as those between centimetres, metres, and kilometres; grams and kilograms; or millilitres and litres. Tedious conversion exercises do little to enhance measurement sense. The goal of unit relationships is the least important of all measurement objectives.

Students also need to know the meanings of the prefixes—kilo, centi, milli, etc.—used with metric measurement, and be aware that the same prefixes are used for linear measurement, volume, capacity, mass and so on.

Developing Unit Familiarity

Familiarity with standard units of measure, particularly those units most popularly used, should be the principal focus of almost all instruction. The average adult develops a "feel" for units, metres, centimetres, litres, grams, and kilograms throughout life. Two types of activities that can help students develop familiarity with the most frequently used units of measure are (1) comparisons that focus on a single unit, and (2) activities that develop personal referents or benchmarks for single units or easy multiples of units.

ACTIVITY 16.16

About One Unit

Give students a model of a standard unit, and have them search for things that measure about the same as that one unit. For example, to develop familiarity with the metre, give students a piece of rope 1 metre long. Have them make lists of things that are about 1 metre. Keep separate lists for things that are a little less (or more) or twice as long (or half as long). Encourage students to find familiar items in their daily lives. In the case of lengths, be sure to include circular lengths. Later, students can try to predict if a given object is more than, less than, or close to 1 metre.

The same activity can be done with other unit lengths. Parents can be enlisted to help students find familiar distances that are about 1 kilometre. Suggest in a letter that they check distances around the neighbourhood, to the school or shopping centre, or along other frequently travelled paths.

For capacity units such as litres or millilitres, students need a container that holds or has a marking for a single unit. They should then find other containers at home and at school that hold about as much as, more than, or less than the given container. Remember that the shape of a container can be very deceptive when estimating its capacity.

For standard measures of mass—grams or kilograms—students can compare objects on a two-pan balance with single copies of these units. It may be more effective to work with 10 grams. Students can be encouraged to bring in familiar objects from home to compare on the classroom scale.

Standard area units such as square centimetres or square metres are reported in terms of their linear units, so familiarity with length is important. Familiarity with a single degree is not as important as having some idea of what 30, 45, 60, and 90 degrees might look like. The second approach to unit familiarity is to begin with very familiar items and use their measures as references or benchmarks. A doorway is a bit more than 2 metres. A bag of flour is a good reference for about 5 kilograms. Your bedroom may be about 3 metres long. A paper clip weighs about a gram and is about 1 centimetre wide.

ACTIVITY 16.17

Familiar References

For each unit of measure on which you wish to focus, have students make a list of at least five familiar things and measure them using that unit. For length, encourage them to include both long and short things; for mass, both light and heavy things; and so on. The measures should be rounded off to nice whole numbers. Discuss lists in class so that different ideas are shared.

Benchmarks found on the body are of special interest for length. These become quite familiar over time and can be used as approximate rulers in many situations. Even though young children grow quite rapidly, it is useful for them to know the approximate lengths that they carry around with them.

ACTIVITY 16.18

Personal Benchmarks

Measure your body. About how long is your foot, your stride, your hand span (with fingers stretched and together), the width of your finger, your arm span (finger to finger and finger to nose), the distance around your wrist and around your waist, and your height to waist, to shoulder, and to head? Perhaps you cannot remember all of these, but some may prove to be useful benchmarks, and some may be excellent models for single units. (The average child's fingernail width is about 1 cm, and most people can find a 10-cm length somewhere on their hands.)

To help remember these references, they must be used in activities where length, volume, and so on are compared to the benchmarks when estimating measurements.

Choosing Appropriate Units

Should the room be measured in metres or centimetres? Should the concrete blocks be weighed in grams or kilograms? The answers to questions such as these involve more than simply knowing how big the units are, although that is certainly required. Another consideration is the need for precision. If you were measuring your wall to ensure that a piece of molding or woodwork you were cutting would fit, you would need to measure it very precisely. The smallest unit would be a centimetre, and you would also use small fractional parts. But if you were determining how many molding strips to buy, the nearest centimetre would probably be sufficient.

ACTIVITY 16.19

Guess the Unit

Find examples of measurements of all types in newspapers, on signs, or in other everyday situations. Present the context and measurements, without their units. The task is to predict what units of measure were used. Have students discuss their choices.

Developing Relationships between Units

Before students have developed a full understanding of decimal notation, there is little advantage in teaching the very nice relationships that exist in the metric system that allow a single type of unit to be used to describe a measurement. For example, a length can be recorded as "235 cm" instead of "2.35 m" or "2 m and 35 cm." As children begin to appreciate the structure of decimal notation, the metric system can and should be developed with all seven places: three prefixes for smaller units (*deci-, centi- milli-*) and three for larger units (*deca-, hecto-, kilo*). With decimal knowledge and familiarity with the basic and popularly used units, the complete metric system is easy to learn.

Perhaps one of the worst errors in teaching metric measurement prior to a complete development of decimal notation is to have students "move the decimal point" when converting from one metric unit to another. Confusion will only lead to children memorizing rules about moving decimals so many places to the right or left. Rather than a conceptual understanding of how to convert from one unit to another, the focus then becomes rules and right answers. Yet the number of centimetres in a metre or kilometre, or of grams in a kilogram, is the type of information that must be eventually committed to memory. Practice with conversion lends itself well to pencil-and-paper work. But this procedural aspect of unit familiarity has been overworked in the curriculum, largely due to the ease of testing rather than the need to know. Many students may know that there are 100 centimetres in a metre, but when they try to determine how many metres are equivalent to 85 centimetres or how many grams are equivalent to 1.4 kilograms, they get confused over which operation to use. This is partly a matter of understanding the meaning of the operation to be carried out. Common sense can help. In the first example, since metres are larger than centimetres, it is reasonable to end up with fewer metres than centimetres. In the second example, it would make sense that there would be more grams because grams are so much smaller than kilograms.

Making conversions within the metric system can be approached in two related ways. As we saw in Figure 14.6 in Chapter 14 (p. 262), a place-value chart gives a metric name to each of seven consecutive places. If it is understood that the decimal point always identifies the units position, then, in any metric measurement, each digit is in a position with a metric name. The decimal point can be repositioned if the name of the unit is changed. In the measure 17.238 kg, the decimal indicates that the 7 is in the units position. The label "kg" indicates that the name of the position is kilograms. Therefore, the 2 is in the hectogram position, the 3 in the decagram position, and the 8 in the gram position. Repositioning the decimal to indicate grams as the units makes the same measure read 17 238 g.

An alternative rationale is to think of decimal point shifting as multiplying or dividing by powers of 10. In our example, since there are 1000 grams in a kilogram, change to grams by multiplying by 1000, or shift the decimal three places to the right.

Although unit conversion is not the most important part of learning the metric system, it is regularly used in areas such as the sciences, technology, engineering, and so on.

Estimating Measures

Estimation in measurement is the process of using mental and visual information to measure or make comparisons without the use of a measuring instrument. It is a practical skill. Almost every day, we make estimates of measures. Do I have enough sugar to make the cookies? Will the car fit in that space? How far can you throw the ball? Is the mass of this suitcase over the acceptable limit? About how long is the fence? Will this paper cover the box? Each of these involves estimation.

Besides its value outside the classroom, estimation in measurement activities helps students focus on the attribute being measured, adds intrinsic motivation, and helps develop familiarity with standard units. Consequently, estimation improves measurement instruction at the same time that it develops a valuable life skill.

Techniques for Estimating with Measurement

Just as with computational estimation, specific strategies exist for estimating measurements. Four of these can be taught:

1. *Develop and use benchmarks or referents for important units.* (This strategy was also mentioned as a way to develop familiarity with units.) Students should have good referents for single units and for useful multiples of the standard units. Referents or benchmarks for 1, 5, 10, and perhaps 100 kilograms might be useful. A referent for 500 millilitres is very useful. These benchmarks can then be compared mentally to objects being estimated: "That tree is about as tall as four doorways, or between 8 and 9 metres tall."

2. *Use "chunking" when appropriate.* Figure 16.18 is an example. It may be easier to estimate the shorter chunks along the wall than to estimate the whole length as one. The mass of a stack of books is easier if some estimate is given of an "average" book.

3. *Use subdivisions.* This is a similar strategy to chunking, with the chunks imposed on the object by the estimator. For example, if the wall length to be estimated has no useful chunks, it can be mentally

divided in half, then in fourths or even eighths by repeated halving in order to arrive at a more manageable length. Length, volume, and area measurements all lend themselves to this technique.

4. *Iterate a unit mentally or physically.* For length, area, and volume, it is sometimes easy to mark off single units visually. You might use your hands or make marks or folds to keep track as you go. For length, it is especially useful to use a body measure as a unit and iterate with that. If you know, for example, that your stride is about $\frac{3}{4}$ metre, you can walk off a length and then multiply to get an estimate. Hand and finger widths are useful for shorter measures.

Tips for Teaching Estimation

Each of the four strategies just listed should be taught and discussed with students. But the best approach to improving students' estimation skills is to have them practise a lot, keeping the following tips in mind:

1. Help students learn strategies by having them use a specified approach. Later activities should permit students to choose whatever techniques they wish.

2. Periodically, discuss how different students made their estimates. This practice will help students understand that there is no single right way to estimate. It will also remind them of different approaches that are useful.

3. Accept a range of estimates. Think in relative terms about what is a good estimate. Within 10 percent for length is quite good. Even 30 percent off may be reasonable for mass or volume.

4. Sometimes have students give a range of measures that they believe includes the actual measure. Not only is this a practical approach in real life, it also helps focus on the approximate nature of estimation.

5. Let students measure to check estimates. However, if the focus is on estimating, it is necessary for only one or two students or one team to do the actual measuring. If all students are expected to follow estimates with actual measurements, they may justifiably wonder why they bothered estimating.

6. Make estimation in measurement an ongoing activity. A daily measurement to be estimated can be posted on the bulletin board. Students can turn in their estimates on paper and discuss them in a 5-minute period. In the higher grades, the task of making up measurements to estimate can be assigned to a team of students each week.

7. Make an effort to include estimations of all attributes. It is easy to get carried away with length and forget about area, volume, mass, and angles.

Estimation Activities for Measurement

Estimation activities need not be elaborate. Any measurement activity can have an "estimate first" component. To increase the emphasis on the process itself, simply think of things that students can estimate; then have them do it. Here are a few suggestions.

ACTIVITY 16.20

Estimation Quickie

Select a single object such as a box, a watermelon, or a jar. Each day, select a different attribute or dimension to estimate. For a watermelon, for example, students can estimate its length, girth, mass, and surface area.

FIGURE 16.18 Estimating measurements by chunking.

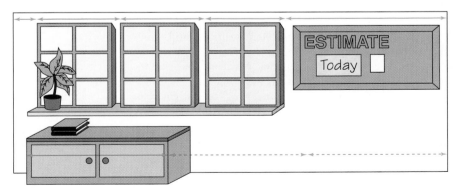

Estimate the room length.
Use: windows, bulletin board, and spaces between as "chunks."
Use: cabinet length—looks like about three cabinets will fit into the room—plus a little bit.

ACTIVITY 16.21

Estimation Scavenger Hunt

Conduct measurement scavenger hunts. Give teams a list of measurements, and have them find things whose measurements are close to those on the list. Have them do this without measuring instruments. A list might include the following items:

A length of 3.5 m

Something with a mass of more than 1 kg but less than 2 kg

A container that holds about 200 ml

Let students suggest how accuracy of results should be judged.

ACTIVITY 16.22

E-M-E Sequences

Use an estimate-measure-estimate sequence (Lindquist, 1987a). Select pairs of objects that are somehow related, or that are close in measure but not the same, to estimate. Have students estimate the measurement of the first object, then actually check by measuring. Follow by having them estimate the measure of the second object. Here are some examples of pairs:

Width of a window, compared with width of a wall

Capacity of a coffee mug, compared with capacity of a pitcher

Distance between the eyes, compared with width of the head

Mass of a handful of marbles, compared with mass of a bag of marbles

Activity 16.22 can help students understand how benchmarks are used in estimation.

Developing Formulas

In some textbooks measurement and geometry are presented together. The relationship between these two areas of mathematics is most evident in the development of formulas for measures of geometric figures. Formulas help us by allowing us to use easily made measurements to determine some other measurement that cannot be found as effortlessly. For example, it is easier to measure the dimensions of a box with a ruler to find its volume than to actually measure the number of cubic units of the box. Using the formula, the volume can easily be determined from the length measures.

Children should never use formulas without taking part in their development. They should participate actively in developing formulas for area and volume. Doing so will help them see how these attributes are connected and interrelated. This is significantly more important than blindly plugging numbers into formulas, which is primarily computational tedium.

Common Difficulties

Many children become so encumbered with the use of formulas and rules that an understanding of what these formulas are all about is completely lost.

Overemphasizing Formulas

Children often have difficulty applying area measurement formulas. As well, they often confuse formulas for area and perimeter. For example, they will illustrate the formula for perimeter as $(l \times w) \times 2$, multiplying the length by the width, then multiplying this product by 2. Or they might add when they need to multiply. The most likely explanation is a premature emphasis on formulas with little effort to develop an understanding of why they work.

The tasks in Figure 16.19 cannot be solved with simple formulas; they require an understanding of concepts and how formulas work. "Length times width" is not a definition of area that works.

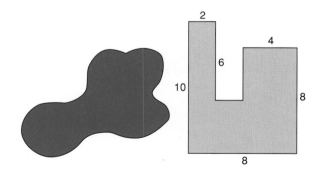

"How would you determine the areas of these shapes?"

Note: Many children believe that such shapes do not have areas or that the areas are impossible to determine because there are no formulas.

FIGURE 16.19 Understanding the attribute of area.

Height or Side

Another error that is common when students use formulas comes from their lack of understanding of height in both two- and three-dimensional geometric figures. The shapes in Figure 16.20 each have a given slanted side and a given height. Students tend to confuse these two. Any side of a 2-dimensional figure, or flat surface of a 3-dimensional figure, can be called a *base* of the figure. For each base that a figure has, there is a corresponding height. If the figure were to slide into a room on its base, the *height* would be the height of the shortest door it could pass through without bending over—that is, the perpendicular distance to the base. Children have a lot of early experiences with the length-multiplied-by-the-width formula for rectangles, where the height is actually the same as the length of a side. Perhaps this is the source of the confusion.

Before formulas involving heights are discussed, children need to be able to identify from where a height could be measured for the base of any figure.

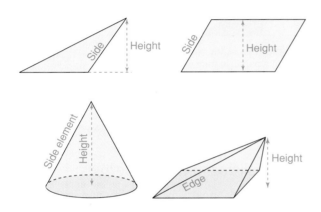

FIGURE 16.20 Heights of figures are not always measured along an edge or a surface.

The Area of Rectangles, Parallelograms, Triangles, and Trapezoids

The development of area formulas is a fantastic opportunity to follow the spirit of the NCTM *Principles and Standards*. First, a problem-solving approach can meaningfully involve students and help them see that mathematics is a sense-making endeavour. Second, the connectedness of mathematics is evident. Here you will see that all of the standard area formulas are intimately related and can be developed and learned as an integrated whole, rather than as a collection of isolated facts.

Rectangles

The formula for the area of a rectangle is one of the first that is developed and is usually given as $A = L \times W$, "area equals length multiplied by width." Looking forward to

other area formulas, an equivalent but more unifying idea might be $A = b \times h$, "area equals *base* multiplied by *height*." (In this case *base* refers to the length of a side.) The base-multiplied-by-height formulation can be generalized to all parallelograms and is useful in developing the area formulas for triangles and trapezoids. Furthermore, the same approach can be extended to three dimensions, where volumes of cylinders are given in terms of the *area of the base* multiplied by the height (here, *base* refers to a flat surface, "the bottom"). Base multiplied by height, then, helps connect a large family of formulas that otherwise must be mastered independently.

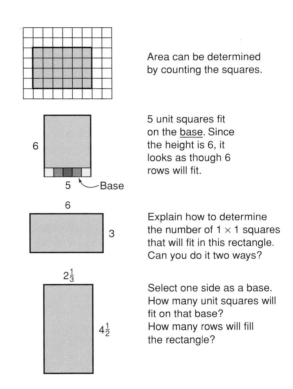

FIGURE 16.21 Determining the area of a rectangle.

The following sequence of exercises to develop the area formula for a rectangle is illustrated in Figure 16.21. Approaching each step of this sequence with a problem-solving spirit, how can we figure this formula out?

1. Have students determine the areas of rectangles drawn on square grids or on geoboards. You might also have students draw rectangles that have specified areas (do not give the dimensions.). Some may count every square; others may multiply to find the total number of squares.

2. Examine rectangles (not on a grid) given only their whole-number dimensions. Designate one side as the base, and line unit squares along this side. How many such rows can fit into the rectangle? On the

same rectangle, repeat this approach using the other side as the base.

3. Give students rectangles providing only their dimensions, and have them determine the area. Oblige them to justify their results. Encourage approaches similar to those in step 2.

4. Examine rectangles with dimensions that are not whole numbers. If the base is $4\frac{1}{2}$ units, then $4\frac{1}{2}$ square units will fit along the base. If the height is $2\frac{1}{4}$ units, then there are $2\frac{1}{4}$ rows with $4\frac{1}{2}$ squares in each, or $2\frac{1}{4}$ sets of $4\frac{1}{2}$.

From Rectangles to Parallelograms

Once students understand the base-times-height formula for rectangles, the next challenge is to determine the area of parallelograms. Do not provide a formula or other explanation. Rather, give students a rectangle drawn on a grid or on a plain sheet of paper. Their task is to develop a method for finding the area of the parallelogram that they can use with any parallelogram, not just the one with which they are working. If students are stuck, ask them to examine ways that the parallelogram is like a rectangle or how it can be changed into a rectangle. As shown in Figure 16.22, a parallelogram can always be transformed into a rectangle with the same base, the same height, and the same area. Thus, the formula for the area of a parallelogram is exactly the same as for a rectangle: base multiplied by height (the perpendicular distance from the base to the opposite side as shown in Figure 16.22).

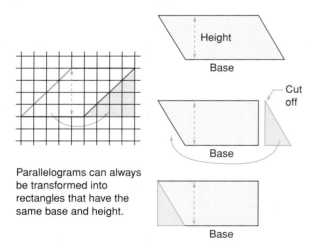

Parallelograms can always be transformed into rectangles that have the same base and height.

FIGURE 16.22 Area of a parallelogram.

From Parallelograms to Triangles

It is very important for students to understand the parallelogram formula before exploring triangle area. With that background, the area of a triangle is relatively simple.

As with parallelograms, students should be challenged to figure the area of a triangle in such a manner that

the method applies to all triangles. They can explore the areas of triangles on grids or geo-boards, just as with parallelograms. As a hint toward a formula, have students fold a piece of paper in half on the diagonal, and cut it out, making two identical copies of a triangle. Suggest that they try using the two triangles to construct a figure for which they have an area formula.

As shown in Figure 16.23, two congruent triangles can always be arranged to form a parallelogram with the same base and height as each of the triangles. The area of each triangle will therefore be one-half as much as the area of the parallelogram. Have students further explore all three possible parallelograms, one for each side of the triangle serving as the base. Will the computed areas always be the same?

Two copies of any triangle will always form a parallelogram with the same base and height; therefore, the triangle has an area of half of the parallelogram, $A = \frac{1}{2}$(base × height).

FIGURE 16.23 Two triangles always make a parallelogram.

From Parallelograms to Trapezoids

After developing formulas for parallelograms and triangles, your students may be interested in tackling trapezoids without any further assistance. (See Figure 4.1, p. 47, for an example of a completely open challenge.) There are several methods of arriving at a formula for trapezoids, each related to the area of parallelograms or rectangles. One of the nicest methods uses the same general approach that was used for triangles. Suggest that students try working with two trapezoids that are identical, just as they did with triangles. Figure 16.24 shows how this method results in the formula. Now, not only are all of these formulas connected, but similar methods were used to develop them.

(Do you think that a special formula for the area of squares should be taught? What about formulas for perimeters?)

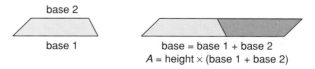

Two trapezoids always make a parallelogram with the same height and a base equal to the sum of the bases in the trapezoid. Therefore,

$$A = \frac{1}{2} \times \text{height} \times (\text{base 1} + \text{base 2})$$

FIGURE 16.24 Two trapezoids always form a parallelogram.

Technology Note

The relationship among the areas of rectangles, parallelograms, and triangles can be dramatically illustrated using a dynamic geometry program such as *The Geometer's Sketchpad* (Key Curriculum Press, 1995). Draw two congruent segments on two parallel lines, as shown in Figure 16.25. Then connect the endpoints of the segments to form a parallelogram and two triangles. A segment between the parallel lines and perpendicular to each indicates the height. Either of the two line segments can be dragged left or right to "sheer" the parallelogram and triangle without changing the base or height. All area measures remain fixed! ▨

Circle Formulas

The relationship between the *circumference* of a circle (the distance around) and the length of the *diameter* (a line through the centre joining two points on the circle) is one of the most interesting that children can discover. The circumference of every circle is about 3.14 times as long as the diameter. That exact ratio is an irrational number close to 3.14 and is represented by the Greek letter π. So $\pi = C/D$, the circumference divided by the diameter. In a slightly different form, $C = \pi D$. Half the diameter is the radius (r), so the same equation can be written $C = 2\pi r$. (Chapter 17 will discuss in detail the concept of pi and how students can discover this important ratio.)

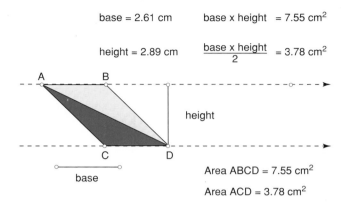

Explore the area of parallelograms and triangles.

base = 2.61 cm   base x height = 7.55 cm²

height = 2.89 cm $\dfrac{\text{base x height}}{2}$ = 3.78 cm²

Area ABCD = 7.55 cm²

Area ACD = 3.78 cm²

FIGURE 16.25 Dynamic geometry software shows that figures with the same base and height maintain the same area.

Even young children can start to develop, by exploration or discovery, a sense of the relationships in a circle. They can use wool or string to measure the distance around and across circular objects and compare them. Sufficient practice with different objects should eventually lead them to discover that the distance around a circle is approximately 3 times greater than the distance across it.

Figure 16.26 presents an argument for the area formula $A = \pi r^2$. This development is one commonly found in textbooks. Another informal proof is based on the

FIGURE 16.26 Development of the formula for the area of a circle.

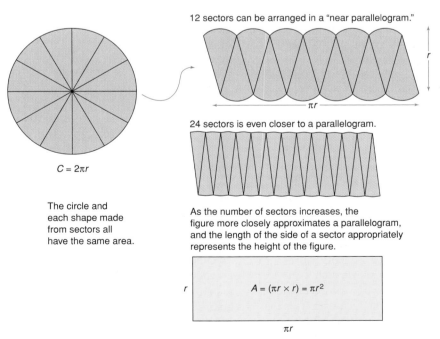

$C = 2\pi r$

The circle and each shape made from sectors all have the same area.

12 sectors can be arranged in a "near parallelogram."

24 sectors is even closer to a parallelogram.

As the number of sectors increases, the figure more closely approximates a parallelogram, and the length of the side of a sector appropriately represents the height of the figure.

$A = (\pi r \times r) = \pi r^2$

Students can cut a circle into 12 sectors or more and rearrange them to form a near rectangle with one dimension being half the circumference and the other the radius.

notion that the area of a polygon inscribed in a circle gets closer and closer to the area of the circle as the number of sides increases.

Regardless of the approach you use to develop the area formula for a circle, students should be challenged to figure it out on their own. You might show students how to arrange 12 sectors of a circle into an approximation of a parallelogram. Their task then should be to use this as a hint toward developing an area formula for the circle. You may need to help them notice that the arrangement of sectors is an approximation of a parallelogram and that the smaller the sectors, the closer the arrangement approaches a rectangle. But the complete argument for the formula should come from your students.

Technology Note

The lesson component of the geometry unit in *Math Trek 7, 8, 9* (Nectar Foundation, 2000) develops the relationship between the circumference and the diameter of a circle, in a sequential, but interactive manner. The lesson begins by defining circle, circumference, diameter, and radius. Through a series of steps, the area formula, similar to the one used in this book, is developed for the student. Practice questions are provided in the lesson and in the practice component of the program. ▪▪

Volumes of Common Solid Shapes

The relationships between the formulas for volume are completely analogous to those for area. As you read, notice the similarities between rectangles and prisms, between parallelograms and "sheered" (oblique) prisms, and between triangles and pyramids. Not only are the formulas related, but the process for development of the formulas is similar.

Volumes of Cylinders

A *cylinder* is a solid with two congruent parallel bases and sides with parallel elements. There are several special classes of cylinders, including *prisms* (with polygons for bases), *right prisms, rectangular prisms,* and *cubes* (see Chapter 17). Interestingly, all of these solids have the same volume formula, and the formula is analogous to the area formula for parallelograms.

Provide students with some wooden cubes and square grid paper that matches the face of the cubes. Have students draw a 3 × 5 rectangle on the paper, and place 15 cubes on the rectangle. This makes a box with a height of 1 unit. The volume of this box is 1 multiplied by the area of the base. Now place a second layer of cubes on the first. What is the height? The volume? Continue to add layers up to 5 or 6 (see Figure 16.27). For each new layer that is

added, notice that the total number is the number of cubes on the bottom layer multiplied by the number of layers. The number on the bottom layer (or any layer) is the area of the base. The number of layers is the height. Therefore, the volume of the solid is $V = A \times h$, *the area of the base multiplied by the height.*

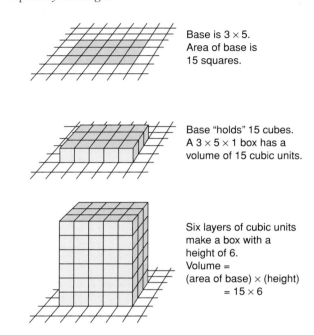

Base is 3 × 5.
Area of base is
15 squares.

Base "holds" 15 cubes.
A 3 × 5 × 1 box has a
volume of 15 cubic units.

Six layers of cubic units
make a box with a
height of 6.
Volume =
(area of base) × (height)
= 15 × 6

FIGURE 16.27 Volume of a prism.

Recall how the area formula for rectangles was developed (see Figure 16.21, p. 315), and notice how that development is like the one for volume. Instead of *length* of the base × height (for *area* of rectangles), in three dimensions, the *volume* formula for the corresponding figure is *area* of the base × height.

Recall that a parallelogram can be thought of as a "sheered" rectangle, as was illustrated with the dynamic geometry software (Figure 16.25). Show students a stack of three or four decks of playing cards (or a stack of books or paper). When stacked straight, they form a rectangular solid. The volume, as just discussed, is $V = A \times h$, with *A* equal to the area of one card. Now if the stack is sheered or slanted to one side as shown in Figure 16.28, what will the volume of this new figure be? Students should be able to argue that this figure has the same volume (and same volume formula) as the original stack.

What if the cards in this activity were some other shape? If they were circular, the volume would still be the area of the base multiplied by the height; if they were triangular, it would still be the same. The conclusion is that the volume of *any* cylinder is equal to the *area of the base* times the *height*.

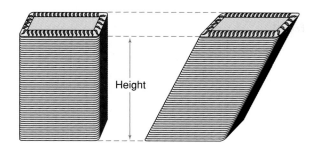

FIGURE 16.28 **Two cylinders with the same base and height have the same volume.**

Measuring Time

Time is measured in the same way that other attributes are measured: A unit of time is selected and used to "fill" the time to be measured. *Time* can be thought of as the duration of an event from its beginning to its end. An informal unit of time might be the duration of a pendulum swing, the steady drip of a tap, or the movement of the sun's shadow between two fixed points (as on a sundial). To measure time, the units of time are started at the same time as the activity being measured ("timed") and counted until the activity is finished. Thus, the pendulum swings, for example, are "fitted into" the duration of time that it takes the child to print his or her name. Young children enjoy timing events with informal units. Older children can appreciate the measurement of time as a process similar to the measurement of other attributes and thus see the commonality in all measuring.

Clock Reading

Telling time has little to do conceptually with the measurement of time. The skills of clock reading are related to the skills of reading any meter that uses pointers on a numbered scale. Clock reading is a difficult skill to teach in the early grades, yet nearly everyone learns to tell time by middle school.

Some Difficulties

Young children's problems with clock reading may be caused by the way in which concepts are presented in the curriculum. Usually children are taught to read clocks to the hour first, then to the half and quarter hours, and finally to 5- and 1-minute intervals. In the early stages of this sequence, children are shown clocks set exactly to the hour or half-hour. Many children who can read a clock at 7:00 or 2:30 have no idea what time it is at 6:58 or 2:33.

Digital clocks permit students to read times easily but do not necessarily promote the concept of time very well.

To understand that a digital reading of 7:58 is nearly 8 o'clock, the child must know that there are 60 minutes in an hour, that 58 is close to 60, and that 2 minutes is not a very long time. Most grade 2 and many grade 3 children have not yet developed these concepts. The analogue clock (with hands) allows a child to see that the time is close to the hour, without the need for understanding larger numbers or even knowing how many minutes are in an hour.

It is important in clock reading not to ignore the distinctly different actions and functions of the two hands: the little hand indicates broad, approximate time (nearest hour), while the big hand indicates time (minutes) before or beyond an hour. Frequently, when we look at the hour hand, we focus only on where it is pointing. With the minute hand, the focus is generally on the distance that it has gone around the clock or the distance it has yet to go to get back to the top.

Suggested Approach

The following suggestions can help students better understand and read analogue clocks.

1. Begin with a one-handed clock. A clock with only an hour hand can be read with reasonable accuracy. As much as possible, use language that signifies approximation: "It's about 7 o'clock." "It's a little past 9 o'clock." "It's halfway between 2 o'clock and 3 o'clock" (see Figure 16.29).

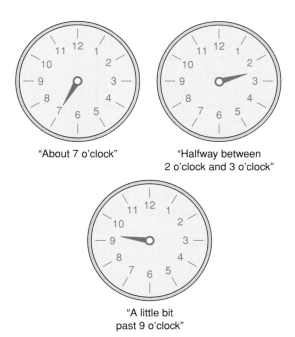

FIGURE 16.29 **Approximate time with one-handed clocks.**

2. Discuss what happens to the big hand as the little hand goes from one hour to the next. When the big

hand is at 12, the hour hand is pointing exactly to a number. If the hour hand is about halfway between numbers, about where would the minute hand be? If the hour hand were a little past or before an hour (10 to 15 minutes), about where would the minute hand be?

3. Use two real clocks, one with only an hour hand and one with two hands. (Break off the minute hand from an old clock.) Cover the two-handed clock. Periodically, during the day, direct attention to the one-handed clock. Discuss the time using the language of approximation. Have students predict where the minute hand should be. Uncover the other clock and check.

4. Teach time after the hour in 5-minute intervals. After step 3 has begun, count by fives going around the clock. Instead of predicting that the minute hand is pointing at the 4, encourage students to say it is about 20 minutes after the hour. As skills develop, suggest that students always look first at the little or hour hand to learn approximately what time it is and then focus on the minute hand for precision.

5. Predict the reading on a digital clock when shown an analogue clock, and vice versa. Set an analogue clock to match the time shown on a digital clock. This can be done with both one-handed and two-handed clocks.

A Teaching Clock

A simple clock for use on the overhead projector can be made easily with three sheets of acetate. On one, draw a simple clock face but leave off the hands. Cut a small hole in the centre, and insert a brass fastener from the back. Leave the fastener sticking straight up; do not spread the prongs. Cut two circles from the other sheets. The radius of the circles should be the same as the minute and hour hands of the clock. Cut small holes in the centre of these circles, and draw a clock hand on each that extends from the centre to the edge of the circle. If you slip just the smaller hour hand over the brass fastener, you have a very nice one-handed clock. For a clock with two hands, place the larger circle on first.

Use your overhead clock to practise one-handed clock reading, emphasizing approximate language. Set the little hand at various places on the clock, and have children suggest how to read it. Let students set the hour hand at times like half-past 5 or a little before 8 o'clock.

Related Concepts

Students also need to learn about seconds, minutes, and hours and develop some concept of how long these units are. You can help by making a conscious effort to note the duration of short and long events during the day. Timing

small events of half a minute to two minutes is fun and useful. TV shows and commercials are a good standard. Have students time familiar events in their daily lives: brushing teeth, eating dinner, riding to school, time spent in the reading group.

As students learn more about two-digit numbers, the time after the hour can also be related to time remaining before the next hour. This is helpful not only for telling time but for number sense as well. Note that in the sequence suggested, time after the hour is stressed almost exclusively. Time before or until the hour can come later.

Problem-solving exercises such as "If it was 7:30 when Bill left home and the trip took 8 hours, what time did he arrive?" are important. Even middle-school students have difficulty with these ideas. Adding and subtracting time involves understanding the relationships between minutes and hours and the connection between the two 12-hour cycles in a day.

 ### Assessment Notes

Gathering useful assessment data in the area of measurement requires open-ended activities that permit students to demonstrate their understanding of measurement concepts. Traditional test approaches tend to focus on prescriptive, procedural skills, such as conversion of units from centimetres to metres, or the use of a formula. Ask yourself if they really tell you what you want to know about your students' knowledge and understanding of measurement.

Focus on Ideas

As you progress through your measurement unit, think about what students really need to know in order to develop an understanding of measurement of any given attribute.

How well do students understand the attribute being measured? Observing how students do with comparison activities ("Which of these regions is the largest? How can you tell?") will provide you with information you need to know. Be wary of being overly instructive with students. Make sure the ideas you observe are theirs, not yours. Rather than directing students to measure something the way you prescribe, have them select their own methods and explain what they did and why they made the choices they did. If their explanations seem reasonable, ask them to find more than one way to measure the same object.

Do students use measuring tools meaningfully? Rulers, protractors, and clocks are often poorly understood. Ask students to find two different ways to measure with a ruler, or have them react to the technique used by another student. ("Monique measured the width of her locker. She lined up the 10 cm mark on one side. The other side of the locker was lined up between the 42 and 43 cm marks. Monique was confused. Without measuring the locker again, how would you help Monique?") Another technique is to have students explain how a ruler or protractor is used for making measurements. To help with their explanations, have them compare a student-made device, such as the waxed-paper protractor, with the standard device.

Standard Units

Again, the danger is the traditional focus on conversion of units, rather than on familiarity with the units. Consider these two tasks:

1. 427 centimetres = _____ metres
2. Estimate the length of this rope in centimetres and in metres. What ideas did you use to help make your estimate?

Both tasks relate centimetres to metres. The second task requires that a student have unit familiarity as well. Does the student make use of the metre-centimetre relationship or make two independent estimates? How are the estimates made? Are familiar benchmarks for the unit used? Feedback is provided as children work through the second task, not the first. As with all assessment, the information can guide your instruction or can be used for evaluation.

Formulas

Plugging numbers into formulas, even requiring students to memorize the formulas, does very little to develop understanding in measurement. Spend more time on the conceptual development of formulas and less on practising their use. ▨

 Literature Connections

Various fantasy books about giants, strange lands, or unusual occurrences prompt comparisons of measures with our everyday world. There are also a large number of "concept books" for measurement, books that are designed to help children explore interesting aspects of measurement. The selections here are offered as examples.

How Big Is a Foot?
(Myller, 1990)

The story in this concept book is very attractive to younger children. The king, wishing to have a bed made for his queen, asks her to lie on the floor and then measures her (crown included) with his own big feet. He then has his Prime Minister summon the Chief Carpenter, and commissions a bed three feet wide by six feet long. The Chief Carpenter's apprentice, who is very small, makes the bed according to his own foot size. The bed is delivered to the king, who presents it to his wife. Alas, it is too small, and

the apprentice is thrown in jail for displeasing the king. The problems, of course, give rise to the need for standard units. Children are also motivated to use their own measuring methods for different purposes. Lubinski and Thiessen (1996) show how students can create a "ruler" with footprints linked together, and share activities conducted in a grade 1 class.

Jim and the Beanstalk
(Briggs, 1970)

In this variation on the classic tale of *Jack and the Beanstalk*, Jim (not Jack, as the author notes) helps the giant, who is growing quite old. First, Jim has a giant-sized pair of glasses made for the giant so he is able to read. He then measures the giant for false teeth and a wig and has these made for the giant. When Jim pays the oculist, the dentist, and the wig-maker each with a "giant" gold coin for the item purchased, they can hardly believe their eyes. Children will be intrigued with the notion of how big these giant things would be and will enjoy discussing other large things that would fit in the story.

A similar story is Jonathan Swift's classic, *Gulliver's Travels*. Students can create drawings and use measurements to explore the lands in Gulliver's journey. The land of the Brobdingnag is a place where objects are about 10 times normal size.

Counting on Frank
(Clement, 1991)

The dog, Frank, and his young master, the narrator of the story, engage in a series of estimations of everyday things: the length of a line that can be drawn by the average ball-point pen, the number of Franks that would fit in the bedroom, or the time it would take to fill the entire bathroom with water if the tap were left on. These fanciful ideas and hilarious drawings easily motivate students to make their own estimates. Young children may not be able to go further than a guess. By grade 3, students may investigate how well their estimate agrees with reality. This book can lead children to investigate length, mass, volume, area, and time and connect each of these concepts to their personal world. "If I filled my room with stuffed duffel bags, I estimate it would take 3000 bags. Altogether the mass of these bags would be more than 6000 kilograms. If the duffel bags were each as big as my dad's car, they would take up a space as big as a football stadium." Ideas such as this are fun to imagine but can also be tested against reality through measurement and calculation. One idea is to have class members contribute to their very own Frank book and provide an appendix that explains their estimates.

8,000 Stones
(Wolkstein, 1972)

This is an interesting folktale concerning the Supreme Governor of China, who wishes to find a method of weighing an elephant that has been received as a gift. The emperor's son solves the problem by putting the elephant in a boat and noticing the water level on the side. The weight required to produce the same effect is that of the elephant. This is a wonderful introduction to indirect methods of measurement for middle-grade students. Not only can students explore the same method for determining the mass of an object, but they could also research other measurements and find out how they work. For example, how do we measure temperature with a mercury thermometer, and how is it done with a bimetal thermometer, the kind that causes a dial to rotate? ■■

Reflections *on Chapter 16*

Writing to Learn

1. Explain what it means to *measure* something. Does your explanation work equally well for length, area, mass, volume, and time?

2. A general instructional plan for measurement has three parts. Explain how the type of activity that would be used with each part accomplishes the instructional goal.

3. Five reasons were offered for using informal (non-standard) units instead of standard units in instructional activities. Which of these seem most important to you, and why?

4. For each of the following attributes, describe a comparison activity, one or two possible informal units, and a group activity that includes an estimation component:
    a. Length
    b. Area
    c. Volume
    d. Mass
    e. Capacity

5. With a straightedge, draw a triangle, a quadrilateral, and a five-sided figure. Make each about as large as a sheet of notebook paper. Make a waxed-paper protractor. Estimate the sum of the interior angles of each figure; then measure them and find their sum. Did the sum of the angles for each figure come close to what was predicted?

6. What is a degree? How would you help children learn what a degree is?

7. What do students need to know about standard units? Of these, which is the most and least important?

8. Develop in a connected way the area formulas for rectangles, parallelograms, triangles, and trapezoids. Draw pictures and provide explanations.

9. Explain how the volume formula for a right rectangular prism can be developed in an analogous manner to the area formula for a rectangle.

10. Explain how the area of a circle can be determined using the basic formula for the area of a parallelogram. (If you have a set of fraction "pie pieces," these can be used as sectors of a circle.)

11. Describe the differences between a typical approach for teaching clock reading and the one-handed approach discussed in this chapter.

For Discussion and Exploration

1. Make your own measuring instrument for an informal unit of measure. Use your instrument to measure, and then make the same measurement directly with a unit model. What are the values and limitations of each method? Can you see the importance of having children do this both ways?

2. Get a teacher's edition of a basal textbook for any grade level, and look at the chapters on measurement. Based on the ideas developed in the chapters, how well does the book cover measurement ideas? How would you modify or expand on the lessons found in the book?

3. Read Chapter 10, "Foot Activities," in *A Collection of Math Lessons from Grades 3 through 6* (Burns, 1987). Identify two good ideas in the sequence of lessons. Modify the activities to suit your own needs, and try them out with a class of children.

Recommendations for Further Reading
Highly Recommended

Nitabach, E., & Lehrer, R. (1996). Developing spatial sense through area measurement. *Teaching Children Mathematics, 2,* 473–476.

This is a superb article. The authors describe six principles of measurement, giving special attention to area measurement. They then proceed to describe some nice activities with grade 1 and 2 students, and the children's responses. Too often we take simple measurement ideas for granted. This article provides a research-based view of reality.

Rubenstein, R.N., Lappan, G., Phillips, E., & Fitzgerald, W.M. (1993). Angle sense: A valuable connector. *Arithmetic Teacher, 40,* 352–358.

This is an important article for the middle-grade teacher. The authors describe a series of investigations of angles in various polygons, using pattern blocks and an angle-measuring device called a *goniometer.* Among other interesting ideas is a discussion of the question "Why are there 360 degrees in a circle?" and a graphical exposition of the interior angles of polygons that goes beyond the usual.

Wilson, P.S., & Rowland, R.E. (1993). Teaching measurement. In R.J. Jensen (Ed.), *Research ideas for the classroom: Early childhood mathematics* (pp. 171–194). Old Tappan, NJ: Macmillan.

There is an interesting research-based idea for every teacher in this well-written review of measurement in the classroom. All areas of measurement are discussed, with clear descriptions of some of the difficulties children experience. The chapter contains great activities as well.

Other Suggestions

Battista, M.T. (1999). Fifth graders' enumeration of cubes in 3D arrays: Conceptual progress in an inquiry-based classroom. *Journal for Research in Mathematics Education, 30,* 417–448.

Clopton, E.L. (1991). Area and perimeter are independent. *Mathematics Teacher, 84,* 33–35.

Coburn, T.G., & Shulte, A.P. (1986). Estimation in measurement. In H.L. Schoen (Ed.), *Estimation and mental computation* (pp. 195–203). Reston, VA: National Council of Teachers of Mathematics.

Corwin, R.B., & Russell, S.J. (1990). *Measuring: From paces to feet* (Unit of study for grades 3–5 from *Used numbers: Real data in the classroom*). White Plains, NY: Cuisenaire–Dale Seymour.

Friederwitzer, F.J., & Berman, B. (1999). The language of time. *Teaching Children Mathematics, 6,* 254–259.

Gerver, R. (1990). Discovering pi: Two approaches. *Arithmetic Teacher, 37*(8), 18–22.

Kenney, P.A., & Kouba, V.L. (1997). What do students know about measurement? In P.A. Kenney & E.A. Silver (Eds.), *Results from the sixth mathematics assessment of the National Assessment of Educational Progress* (pp. 141–163). Reston, VA: National Council of Teachers of Mathematics.

Liedtke, W.W. (1990). Measurement. In J.N. Payne (Ed.), *Mathematics for the young child* (pp. 229–249). Reston, VA: National Council of Teachers of Mathematics.

McClain, K., Cobb, P., Gravemeijer, K., & Estes, B. (1999). Developing mathematical reasoning within the context of measurement. In L.V. Stiff (Ed.), *Developing mathematical reasoning in grades K–12* (pp. 93–106). Reston, VA: National Council of Teachers of Mathematics.

Rectanus, C. (1998). *Math by all means: Area and perimeter, grades 5–6.* Sausalito, CA: Math Solutions Publications.

Reynolds, A., & Wheatley, G.H. (1997). Third-grade students engage in a playground measuring activity. *Teaching Children Mathematics, 4,* 166–170.

Rhone, L. (1995). Measurement in a primary-grade integrated curriculum. In P.A. House (Ed.), *Connecting mathematics across the curriculum* (pp. 124–133). Reston, VA: National Council of Teachers of Mathematics.

Richardson, K. (1997). Too easy for kindergarten and just right for first grade. *Teaching Children Mathematics, 3,* 432–437.

Robitaille, D.F., Taylor, A.R., Orpwood, G. (1996). *The TIMMS-Canada Report, Volume 1: Grade 8.* Vancouver, BC: University of British Columbia.

Robitaille, D.F., Taylor, A.R., Orpwood, G. (1996). *The TIMMS-Canada Report, Volume 2: Grade 4.* Vancouver, BC: University of British Columbia.

Shaw, J.M., & Cliatt, M.J.P. (1989). Developing measurement sense. In P.R. Trafton (Ed.), *New directions for elementary school mathematics* (pp. 149–155). Reston, VA: National Council of Teachers of Mathematics.

Whitin, D.J. (1994). Exploring estimation through children's literature. *Arithmetic Teacher, 41,* 436–441.

Wilson, P.S. (1990). Understanding angles: Wedges to degrees. *Mathematics Teacher, 83,* 294–300.

Wilson, P.S., & Adams, V.M. (1992). A dynamic way to teach angle and angle measure. *Arithmetic Teacher, 39*(5), 6–13.

Chapter 17

Geometric Thinking and Geometric Concepts

The geometry curriculum in K–8 should provide students with an opportunity to experience shapes in as many different forms as possible. These should include shapes built with blocks, sticks, or tiles; shapes drawn on paper or with a computer; and shapes observed in art, nature, and architecture. Hands-on, reflective, and interactive experiences are at the heart of good geometry activities at the elementary and middle-school levels. The goal of the geometry curriculum should be to develop geometric reasoning and spatial sense. The three Big Ideas for geometry parallel the three levels of thinking that characterize development over the K–8 school years.

 BIG IDEAS

1. Both two- and three-dimensional shapes exist in great variety. There are many different ways to see and describe their similarities and differences. The more ways that one can classify and discriminate amongst these shapes, the better one understands them.
2. Shapes have properties—e.g., similarity or congruency, line symmetry or rotational symmetry, parallel or perpendicular sides—that can be used when describing and analyzing them. These properties can be explored and analyzed in a variety of ways. Awareness of these properties helps us appreciate shapes in our world.
3. An analysis of geometric properties leads to deductive reasoning in the context of geometry.

Three Exploratory Activities

To provide some common view of the nature of elementary and middle-school geometry and how young chil-

dren approach geometric concepts, three simple activities are offered here for you to do. The activities will provide some idea of the spirit of informal geometry as well as background for a discussion of children's geometric thinking. All you will need is a pencil, several pieces of paper, scissors, and 15 to 20 minutes.

DIFFERENT TRIANGLES

Draw a series of at least five triangles. After the first triangle, each new one should be different in some way from those already drawn. Write down why you think each is different.

SHAPES WITH TRIANGLES

Make a few copies of the 2-cm isometric grid found in the Blackline Masters, or simply place a sheet of paper over the grid. Draw three or four different figures by following the grid lines. Construct each figure so that it has an area of 10 triangles. Find the distance around each figure (the perimeter), and record it next to each drawing. Check your results for any ideas you may have noticed. Did you find shapes with different perimeters? What makes a shape have a larger or smaller perimeter? Explore these ideas and any others you might have by drawing additional figures.

A TILING PATTERN

First make at least eight copies of any shape in Figure 17.1. An easy way to do this is to fold a piece of paper so there are eight layers. Trace the shape onto the top section, then cut through all the layers at once to make eight copies of the shape. Think of these shapes as tiles. The task is to use the shapes to make a regular tiling pattern. A tiling pattern made with one shape has two basic properties. First, there are no holes or gaps and the tiles must fit together so there is no overlapping or spaces. Secondly, the tiles must be in a repeating pattern that could extend indefinitely. That is, if you were to tile a floor that went on endlessly, the design in one section of the floor would be the same as that in any other section. Several different tiling patterns are possible for each of the three tiles in Figure 17.1. Experiment to decide on a pattern that you like.

Notice that each of the shapes in Figure 17.1 is made up of triangles and can be drawn on a triangle grid such as the 2-cm isometric grid or on the 1-cm isometric dot grid, found in the Blackline Masters. When you have decided on a tiling pattern, place a sheet of tracing paper over one of these two grids and draw your tiling pattern, using the grid as a guide. Cover most of the grid with your pattern.

Finally, suppose that your tiles came in two colours. With a pen or pencil, shade in some of the tiles to make a regular two-colour pattern.

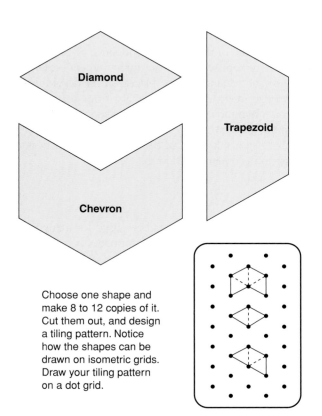

Choose one shape and make 8 to 12 copies of it. Cut them out, and design a tiling pattern. Notice how the shapes can be drawn on isometric grids. Draw your tiling pattern on a dot grid.

FIGURE 17.1 Three tile patterns.

Reflections on the Activities

The following observations apply to all geometry activities, as well as to the activities you have just completed.

Different People Think about Geometric Ideas in Different Ways

Compare your response to the three exploration activities with those of your peers. Are there qualitative differences as well as objective differences? How would primary-age children's approaches to these activities compare to those of grade 8 students? Figure 17.2 shows how two students, one in grade 5 and one in grade 8, responded to the triangle task. Research indicates that age is not the major criterion for how students think geometrically. The kinds of experiences that a child has with geometry may be a more significant factor. What might this suggest about supposed gender differences in spatial reasoning?

Explorations Can Help Develop Relationships

The more you play around with the ideas in any of these activities, the more relationships you will discover. You might be able to extend each of these activities to develop the ideas beyond the obvious. For example:

FOR "DIFFERENT TRIANGLES"

How many different ways can two triangles be different? Could you draw five or more *quadrilaterals* that are different from each other?

FOR "SHAPES WITH TRIANGLES"

What did you notice about the shapes that had smaller perimeters, compared to those with the larger perimeters? If you tried the same activity with rectangles on a square grid, what would the shapes with the largest and smallest perimeters look like? What about three-dimensional boxes? If you were to build different boxes with the same number of cubes, what could you say about the surface areas?

FOR "A TILING PATTERN"

How many different tiling patterns are there for the shape? Can you use any shape to tile with? Are there any larger shapes within your pattern?

Notice that it takes more than just doing an activity to learn or create a new idea. The greatest learning occurs when you stop and reflect on what you did, and begin to ask questions or make observations. Like all mathematics, geometry is best developed in a spirit of problem solving.

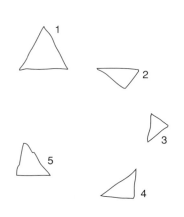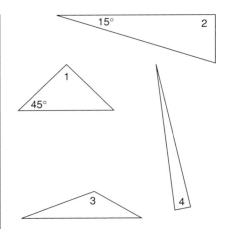

Bud, Grade 5
Triangle 1 was "straight up."
Triangle 2 was "upside down."
Triangle 3 was "pointing way down."
Triangle 4 was "pointing way to the left."
Triangle 5 "has crooked lines."

Amy, Grade 8
"Triangle 2 has a smaller angle than triangle 1."
"Triangle 1 has a 45-degree angle."
"Triangle 2 has a 15-degree angle."
"Triangle 3 has a wider angle than triangles 1 and 2."
"Triangle 4 has a 90-degree angle and a really small angle."

FIGURE 17.2 Two children show markedly different responses to the task of drawing a series of different triangles.

Source: From "Characterization of the van Hiele Levels of Development in Geometry," by W. F. Burger and J. M. Shaughnessy, 1986, *Journal for Research in Mathematics Education*, 17(1), pp. 38–39. Reprinted by permission of the National Council of Teachers of Mathematics.

Geometry Activities and Hands-On Materials

The best geometry activities involve hands-on materials. Even the simple paper tiles used in "A Tiling Pattern" gave you the opportunity to explore spatial relationships and search for patterns much more easily than it would have been to do this in your head. Activities on the dot grid in "Shapes with Triangles" are a second-best alternative to real objects. The same area and perimeter activity is much more effective with a collection of cardboard triangles that can be rearranged to form different shapes. The first activity is the least enticing of the three, but at least you can freely draw pictures. Virtually *every activity* that lends itself to easy spatial explorations and that is appropriate for K–8 geometry should involve some form of hands-on materials or models—at a minimum, graph paper or dot paper.

Informal Geometry and Spatial Sense

In *Principles and Standards for School Mathematics,* the authors chose only five broad content standards, and

Geometry is one of them. The prominence of this strand, appropriately kept separate from measurement, speaks to the importance that should be placed on the development of geometric ideas at all grade levels. Prior to the 1989 *Standards* document, geometry received only limited attention in most curricula. Now, in an effort to ensure that students do not fall short in this area, there is a heavier emphasis on geometry than in the past.

Informal Geometry

The term *informal geometry* has been used for many years to refer to geometric activities appropriate for students in elementary and middle school. Informal geometry activities provide children with the opportunity to explore, to feel and see, to build and take apart, and to make observations about shape in the world around them, as well as in the world they create with drawings, models, and computers. Activities involve constructing, visualizing, comparing, transforming, and classifying geometric figures. The experiences and explorations can take place at different levels of sophistication: from shapes and their appearances, to properties of shapes, to relationships among properties. The spirit of informal geometry is one of exploration, almost always in a hands-on, engaging activity.

Spatial Sense

Just as a good definition of *number sense* is an intuition about numbers and their relationships, *spatial sense* can be defined as an intuition about shapes and the relationships among shapes. It is the ability to visualize objects and spatial relationships—to turn things around in your mind. It includes a comfort with geometric descriptions of objects and position. People with spatial sense appreciate geometric form in art, nature, and architecture. They are able to use geometric ideas to describe and analyze their world.

Many people say they aren't very good with shape, or they have poor spatial sense. The typical belief is that you are either born with spatial sense or not. This simply is not true! We now know that when rich experiences with shape and spatial relationships are provided consistently over time, children can and do develop spatial sense. Without geometric experiences, most people do not grow in the development of their spatial sense or spatial reasoning. Between 1990 and 1996, American-based NAEP data indicated a significant improvement in students' geometric reasoning at all three grades tested, 4, 8, and 12 (Martin & Strutchens, 2000). It's unlikely that students suddenly just got smarter. What is more likely is that the improvement is due to an increasing emphasis on geometry at all grades.

Results from the *Third International Mathematics and Science Study (TIMSS)* (Robitaille,Taylor, Orpwood, 1996) for Canadian students appear to corroborate these American findings. Grade 8 and grade 4 students, especially, tested above the international mean in geometry. But more recent results from the national SAIP test (2001) reveal that the majority of Canadian 13-year-olds achieved a lower average score in the Geometry strand than in 1997. It is evident that there is still more to be done in geometry.

The Importance of Geometry

Most elementary and middle-grade teachers have spent less time in the past on geometry than on other areas of the curriculum. This may be due to a discomfort with the topic, or a belief that the topic is not important. Also, traditional norm-referenced tests have placed little weight on geometric thinking. Thanks to the increased emphasis of provincial and territorial standards and the NCTM, more geometry is being taught. Still, it is fair to ask, "Why study geometry?" Here are a few reasons that come to mind.

1. Geometry can provide a more complete appreciation of the world. Geometry can be found in the structure of the solar system, in geological formations, in rocks and crystals, in plants and flowers, even in animals. It is also a major part of our synthetic universe: art, architecture, cars, machines, and virtually everything that humans create have elements of geometric form.

2. Geometric explorations can develop problem-solving skills. Spatial reasoning is an important form of problem solving, and problem solving is one of the major reasons for studying mathematics.

3. Geometry plays a key role in the study of other areas of mathematics. For example, fractional concepts are related to geometric part-to-whole constructs. Ratio and proportion are directly related to the geometric concept of similarity. Measurement and geometry are clearly related.

4. Geometry is used daily by many people. Scientists, architects, artists, engineers, and land developers are just a few of the professionals who use geometry regularly. At home, geometry helps in building a fence, designing a dog-house, planning a garden, or arranging a living room.

5. Geometry is enjoyable. If geometry increases students' fondness for mathematics, that makes the effort worthwhile.

The Development of Geometric Thinking

The work of two Dutch educators, Pierre van Hiele and Dina van Hiele-Geldof, provides a foundation for the principles regarding geometric thinking that have influenced provincial and territorial curricula. Although the van Hieles' work immediately attracted much attention in the Soviet Union when they began in 1959, it took much longer to be recognized in North America. However, the impact of their work is significant and has become the most influential factor in the design of geometry instruction and curriculum.

The van Hiele Levels of Geometric Thought

The van Hieles developed a model of geometric thinking, the most prominent feature of which is a five-level hierarchy of ways of understanding spatial ideas. Each of the five levels describes the thinking processes used in geometric contexts. The levels describe how one thinks and what types of geometric ideas one thinks about, rather than how much knowledge one has. As one progresses from one level to the next, the object of one's geometric thinking changes.

Level 0: Visualization

The objects of thought at level 0 are shapes and what they "look like."

Students recognize and name figures based on their global, visual characteristics—a Gestalt-like approach to shape. Students operating at this level are able to make measurements and even talk about properties of shapes, but are unable to be explicit in their thinking about these properties. It is the appearance of the shape that defines it for the student. A square is a square "because it looks like a square," not because it has the characteristics of a square. Because appearance is dominant at this level, appearances can overpower the properties of a shape. For example, a square that has been rotated so that all sides are at a 45°; angle to the vertical plane may not appear to be a square for a level 0 thinker. Students at this level will sort and classify shapes based on their appearances—"I put these together because they are all pointy" (or "fat," or "look like a house," or are "dented in sort of, " and so on.) With a focus on the appearances of shapes, students are able to see how shapes are alike and different. As a result, students at this level can create and begin to understand classifications of shapes.

The products of thought at level 0 are classes or groupings of shapes that seem to be "alike."

Level 1: Analysis

The objects of thought at level 1 are classes of shapes rather than individual shapes.

Students at the analysis level are able to consider all shapes within a class rather than a single shape. Instead of talking about *this* rectangle, it is possible to talk about *all* rectangles. By focusing on a class of shapes, students are able to think about what makes a rectangle a rectangle (four sides, opposite sides parallel, opposite sides same length, four right angles, congruent diagonals, etc.). The irrelevant features (e.g., size or orientation) fade into the background. At this level, students begin to appreciate that a collection of shapes goes together because of properties the shapes possess. Ideas about an individual shape can now be generalized to all shapes that fit that class. If a shape belongs to a particular class such as cubes, it has the corresponding properties of that class. "All cubes have six congruent faces, and each of those faces is a square." These properties were only implicit at level 0. Students operating at level 1 may be able to list all the properties of squares, rectangles, and parallelograms, but not see that these are subclasses of one another, that all squares can be classified as rectangles and all rectangles can be classified as parallelograms. In defining a shape, level 1 thinkers are likely to list as many properties of a shape as they know.

The products of thought at level 1 are the properties of shapes.

Level 2: Informal Deduction

The objects of thought at level 2 are the properties of shapes.

As students begin to be able to think about properties of geometric objects without the constraints of a particular object, they are able to develop relationships between and amongst these properties. "If all four angles are right angles, the shape must be a rectangle. If it is a square, all angles are right angles. If it is a square, it can also be a rectangle." With greater ability to engage in "if-then" reasoning, they can classify shapes using only minimum characteristics. For example, four congruent sides and at least one right angle can be sufficient to define a square. Rectangles are also parallelograms with a right angle. Observations go beyond properties themselves and begin to focus on logical arguments *about* the properties. Students at level 2 will be able to follow and appreciate an informal deductive argument about shapes and their properties. "Proofs" may be more intuitive than rigorously deductive. However, there is an appreciation that a logical argument is compelling, and the axiomatic structure of a formal deductive system remains under the surface.

The products of thought at level 2 are relationships among properties of geometric objects.

Level 3: Deduction

The objects of thought at level 3 are relationships among properties of geometric objects.

At level 3, students are able to examine more than just the properties of shapes. Their earlier thinking has produced conjectures concerning relationships among properties. Are these conjectures correct? Are they "true"? As this analysis of the informal arguments takes place, the structure of a system, complete with axioms, definitions, theorems, corollaries, and postulates, begins to develop and can be appreciated as the necessary means of establishing geometric truth. At this level, students begin to appreciate the need for a system of logic that rests on a minimum set of assumptions and from which other truths can be derived. The student at this level is able to work with abstract statements about geometric properties and make conclusions based more on logic than intuition. This is the level of the traditional high school geometry course. A student operating at level 3 can clearly observe that the diagonals of a rectangle bisect each other, just as a student at a lower level of thought can. However, at level 3, there is an appreciation of the need to prove this from a series of deductive arguments. By contrast, the level 2 thinker follows the argument but fails to appreciate the need.

The products of thought at level 3 are deductive axiomatic systems for geometry.

Level 4: Rigor

The objects of thought at level 4 are deductive axiomatic systems for geometry.

At the highest level of the van Hiele hierarchy, the object of attention is axiomatic systems themselves, not just the deductions within a system. There is an appreciation of the distinctions and relationships between different axiomatic systems. This is generally the level of university mathematics majors who are studying geometry as a branch of mathematical science.

> *The products of thought at level 4 are comparisons and contrasts among different axiomatic systems of geometry.*

Characteristics of the van Hiele Levels

You no doubt noticed that the products of thought at each level are the same as the objects of thought at the next. This object-product relationship between levels of the van Hiele theory is illustrated in Figure 17.3. The objects (ideas) must be created at one level so that relationships among these objects can become the focus of the next level. In addition to this key concept of the theory, four related characteristics of the levels of thought merit special attention.

1. The levels are sequential. To arrive at any level above level 0, students must move through all prior levels. To move through a level means that one has experienced geometric thinking appropriate for that level and has created in one's own mind the types of objects or relationships that are the focus of thought at the next level. Skipping a level rarely occurs.
2. The levels are not age-dependent in the sense of the developmental stages of Piaget. A grade 3 or a high school student could be at level 0. Indeed, some students and adults remain forever at level 0, and a significant number of adults never reach level 2. But

age is certainly related to the amount and types of geometric experiences that we have. Therefore, it is reasonable for all children in the K–2 range to be at level 0, as well as the majority of children in grades 3 and 4.

3. Geometric experience is the greatest single factor influencing advancement through the levels. Activities that permit children to explore, talk about, and interact with content at the next level, while increasing their experiences at their current level, are most likely to advance the level of thought for those children.
4. When instruction or language is at a level higher than that of the student, there will be a lack of communication. Students required to wrestle with objects of thought that have not been constructed at the earlier level may be forced into rote learning and achieve only temporary and superficial success. For example, a student could memorize that all squares can be classified as rectangles without having constructed that relationship. A student may memorize a geometric proof but fail to create the steps or understand the rationale involved (Fuys, Geddes, & Tischler, 1988; Geddes & Fortunato, 1993).

Implications for Instruction

The van Hiele theory does not tell us what content to teach, but it does provide the thoughtful teacher with a framework within which to conduct geometric activities. Your regional curriculum document, along with other programmatic materials developed by your school board or district, will prescribe the specific content. You will also need to be clear about the content goals and the goals implicit in the van Hiele theory.

The van Hiele Theory of Geometric Thought

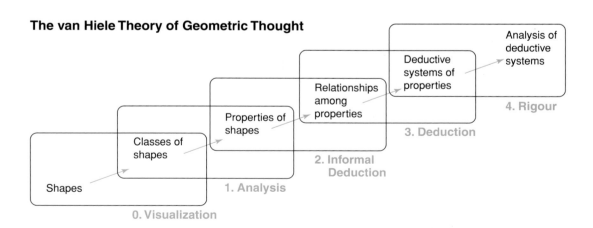

FIGURE 17.3 At each level of geometric thought, the ideas created become the focus or object of thought at the next level.

Instructional Goals: Content and Levels of Thought

The Geometry standard in *Principles and Standards* focuses on process as well as content. Verbs such as *describe, compare, relate, represent, investigate, sort, reason, analyze, predict, test* (conjectures), and *critique* (arguments) are all used in the description of the standard (see Appendix A). The goals are much broader than a collection of facts and bits of knowledge about geometric ideas. The standard is best summed up by the term *spatial sense*. The van Hiele theory fits well with a *Principles and Standards* view of geometry. It focuses our attention on how students think in geometric contexts and on the object of their thinking: shapes $\longrightarrow$ properties $\longrightarrow$ informal logic $\longrightarrow$ deductive principles. If the van Hiele theory is correct—and there is much evidence to support it—then a major goal of the K–8 curriculum must be to advance students' level of geometric thought. If students are to be adequately prepared for the deductive geometry curriculum of high school, their thinking needs to have advanced at least to level 2.

Not every teacher will be able to move children to the next level. However, all teachers should be aware that the experiences they provide are the single most important factor in moving children up this developmental ladder. Every teacher should be able to see some growth in geometric thinking over the course of a year.

Teaching at the Student's Level of Thought

The van Hiele theory and the developmental perspective of this book highlight the necessity of teaching at the child's level of thought. However, almost any activity can be modified to span two levels of thinking, even within the same classroom. For many activities, the way we interact with individual children will adapt the activity to their levels and encourage them or challenge them to operate at the next higher level.

The following sections contain descriptions of the types of activity and questioning that are appropriate for each of the first three van Hiele levels of thinking. Apply these descriptors to the tasks that you pose to students, and use them to guide your interaction with students. The use of concrete materials, drawings and computer models are important at every level.

Instruction at Level 0

Instructional activities in geometry appropriate for level 0 should:

■ Involve a lot of sorting and classifying. Seeing how shapes are alike and different is the primary focus of level 0. As students learn more content, the types of things that they notice will become more sophisticated. At an early stage they may talk about very non-geometric-sounding attributes of shape, calling shapes "skinny" or "fat" or even focusing on the colour of the pieces. When properties such as symmetry and numbers of sides and corners are introduced, students should be challenged to use these features to classify shapes.

■ Include a sufficient variety of examples of shapes so that irrelevant features do not become important. Students need ample opportunities to draw, build, make, put together, and take apart shapes in both two and three dimensions. These activities should be built around specific characteristics of properties, so that students develop an understanding of geometric properties and begin to use them naturally.

To help students move from level 0 to level 1, they should be challenged to test ideas about shapes for a variety of examples from a particular category. Say to them, "Let's see if that is true for other rectangles," or "Can you draw a triangle that does *not* have a right angle?" In general, students should be challenged to see if observations made about a particular shape apply to other shapes of a similar kind.

Instruction at Level 1

Instructional activities in geometry appropriate for level 1 should:

■ Focus more on the properties of figures than on simple identification. Define, measure, observe, and change properties with the use of models. As new geometric concepts are learned, the number of properties that figures have can be expanded.

■ Apply ideas to entire classes of figures (e.g., *all* rectangles, *all* prisms) rather than to individual models. Analyze classes of figures to determine new properties. For example, find ways to sort all possible triangles into groups. From these groups, define types of triangles. Dynamic geometry software such as *The Geometer's Sketchpad* is especially useful for exploring many examples of a class of shapes.

To assist students in moving from level 1 to level 2, challenge them by asking "Why?" and other questions that involve some reasoning. For example, "If the sides of a four-sided shape are all congruent, will you always have a square?" and "Can you find a counterexample?"

Instruction at Level 2

Instructional activities in geometry appropriate for level 2 should:

■ Encourage the making and testing of hypotheses or conjectures: "Do you think that will work all the time?" "Is that true for all triangles or just equilateral ones?"

■ Examine properties of shapes to determine necessary and sufficient conditions for different shapes or concepts: "What properties of diagonals do you think will guarantee that you have a square?"

■ Use the language of informal deduction: *all, some, none, if… then, what if,* and so on.

■ Encourage students to attempt informal proofs. As an alternative, require them to make sense of informal proofs that other students or you have suggested.

Task Selection and Level of Thought

If you teach at the K-3 level, nearly all of your students will be at level 0. By at least grade 3, you will certainly want to begin to challenge students who seem able. In the upper grades you may have children at two or even three different levels within the same classroom. How do you discover the level of each student? Once you know, how will you select the right activities to match your students' levels?

No simple test exists to pigeonhole students at a certain level. However, you can examine the descriptors for the first two levels. As you conduct an activity, listen to the types of observations that students make. Can they talk about shapes as classes? Do they refer, for example, to "rectangles" rather than basing discussion around a particular rectangle? Do they generalize that certain properties are attributable to a type of shape, or simply the shape at hand? Do they understand that shapes do not change when the orientation changes? With simple observations such as these, you will soon be able to distinguish between levels 0 and 1.

At the upper grades, attempt to push students from level 1 to level 2. If students are not able to follow or appreciate logical arguments, and are not comfortable with conjectures and if-then reasoning, these students are likely still at level 1 or below.

The remainder of this chapter offers a sampling of activities organized broadly around the first three van Hiele levels. An activity found at one level can easily be adapted to an adjacent level simply by adjusting the way it is presented to the students.

The intent here is to illustrate the wide variety of things that can be done. Find ideas that you like, and develop them fully. Search out additional resource books to help you.

Informal Geometry Activities: Level 0

The emphasis at level 0 is on shapes that students can observe, feel, build, take apart, and perceive in many ways. The goal is to explore the ways in which shapes are alike and different, and use these ideas to create classes of shapes (both physically and mentally). Some of these classes of shapes have names—rectangles, triangles, prisms, cylinders, and so on. Properties of shapes, such as parallel lines, symmetry, right angles, and so on, are included at this level, but only in an informal, observational manner.

Remember that *level 0* is not a synonym for *primary*. If you teach in the upper grades, you will almost certainly have students who need to begin with activities similar to these.

Exploring Shapes and Properties

Children need experiences with a rich variety of both two- and three-dimensional shapes. Triangles should be more than just equilateral. Shapes should have curved sides, straight sides, and combinations of these. Along the way, the names of shapes and their properties can be introduced casually.

The activities here all begin with shapes already made or drawn, which students work with in various ways. The shapes may be two- or three-dimensional. Some activities can be done equally well with two-dimensional shapes or solid shapes.

Sorting and Classifying Shapes

At level 0, perhaps the most important type of activity you can do is to have students work with a wide variety of shapes to find similarities and differences. As the young students work at classification of the shapes, be prepared for them to notice features that you do not consider to be "real" geometric attributes, such as "curvy" or "looks like a rocket." Children at this level will also attribute to shapes ideas that are not part of the shape, such as "points up" or "has a side that is the same as the edge of the board."

ACTIVITY 17.1

Shape Sort

Make collections of a wide variety of shapes by running them off on card stock, laminating them, and cutting them out. Figure 17.4 provides some ideas, but you will want many more shapes than those shown. Have students select a shape at random and then find other shapes that are like it in some way. All shapes should be alike in the same way. By finding only one set at a time, you avoid the problem of trying to put every shape into a category. Students should describe, either orally or in writing, what makes their set of shapes alike. Challenge them to draw a new shape that fits the category and explain why it belongs.

If your set of shapes has five or six examples of a commonly named shape (for example, rectangle or rhombus), it is likely that some students will sort these out. You can also ask them to find other shapes that are "like" the special shape that you selected. In this way, the concept of that particular class of shapes is being formed without any definition from you. You can then label the concept or provide the proper name for the shape. Names of shapes should always come after the concept of the shape has been developed. Figure 17.5 indicates some concepts that can be explored this way.

Shape sorts can be done with three-dimensional shapes. Wooden or plastic collections are available as one option. Another is to make some solids from tag-board or modelling clay. Real objects such as cans, boxes, balls, or Styrofoam shapes are another source for three-dimensional models. Figure 17.6 illustrates some classifications of solids.

Matching Shapes

ACTIVITY 17.2

Feel-It Match

Prepare two identical collections of shapes. Place one set in the children's view. Out of the children's sight, place a shape from the other set in a box or bag. Have children reach into the box, feel a shape without looking, and attempt to find the matching shape from those that are displayed. The activity can be done with either two-dimensional tag-board shapes or three-dimensional solids. The shapes in the collection determine the ideas that might develop and the

Shapes with curved edges

Opposite sides "go the same way"—parallelograms

Three sides—triangles

Shapes with a "square corner"—right angle

These all "dent in"—concave

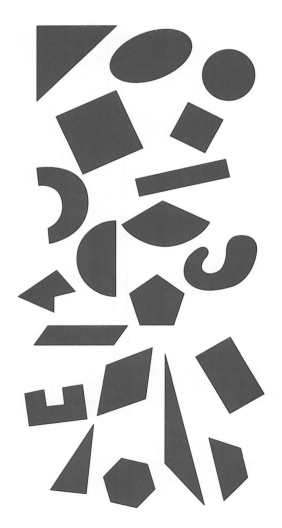

FIGURE 17.4 An assortment of shapes for sorting.

FIGURE 17.5 By sorting shapes, students begin to recognize properties.

level of difficulty of the activity. For example, all shapes may have a different number of sides or faces, or all shapes may be different but still belong to the same category, such as quadrilaterals, triangles, pyramids, prisms, curved surfaces, or curved edges.

The following matching activity is similar but can be done with the entire class. It provides more opportunity for informal discussion of shapes and their properties.

ACTIVITY 17.3

What's like This?

Display a collection of shapes (either two- or three-dimensional) for all to see. Show the class a "target" shape that has something in common with one or more of the shapes in the collection. Students are to select a shape that is like the target shape in some way and explain their choice. There may be excellent choices and reasons that you did not even think about. Figure 17.7 illustrates only a few of the many possibilities for this activity.

Matching activities can also match solids with copies of the faces. "Face cards" can be made by tracing around the different faces of a solid, as in Figure 17.8.

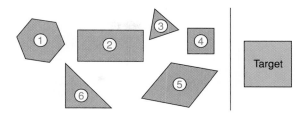

Like ④ – Both are squares.
Like ⑤ – All four sides same, squeezed in a little.
Like ⑥ – Has the same kind of corner.
     – Looks like half of it.
Like ② – Same except it's longer.

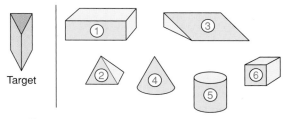

Like ③ – Both are wedges.
     – Both have two triangles.
Like ①, ③, and ⑥ – All have a rectangle face.
Like ①, ⑤, and ⑥ – All have a "flat top"
          (i.e., two parallel faces—so does ③).
Like ② and ③ – Have triangles.

FIGURE 17.7 Playing "What's like This?" involves finding a shape that's like the target. There are usually many good solutions.

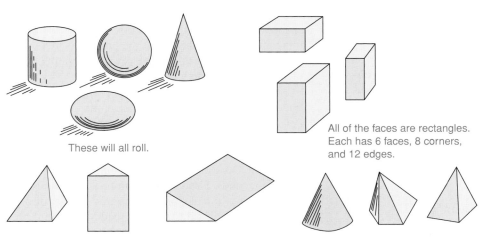

These will all roll.

All of the faces are rectangles. Each has 6 faces, 8 corners, and 12 edges.

These all have a triangle.

These all have a "point."

FIGURE 17.6 Early classifications of three-dimensional shapes.

FIGURE 17.8 Matching face cards with solid shapes.

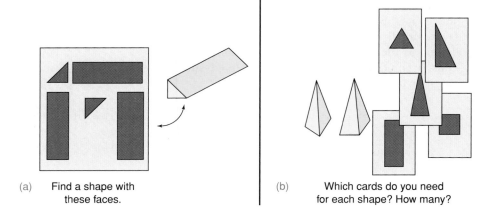

(a)   Find a shape with these faces.

(b)   Which cards do you need for each shape? How many?

ACTIVITY 17.4

Face Match

Two different matching activities can be done with face cards. Given a face card, find the solid, or given a solid, find the face card. If cards are made with only one face per card, students can select from a larger collection those faces that belong with a particular shape. Another variation is to show only one face at a time as clues.

Going on a "shape hunt" is a well-worn but still worthwhile activity. The activity can be modified to accommodate level 0 and level 1 thought within the same classroom by altering what children are searching for. Discussions of objects in the environment contribute to the geometric experiences of all students.

ACTIVITY 17.5

Shape Hunt

Have students search not just for triangles, circles, squares, and rectangles but also for properties of shapes. A shape hunt will be much more successful if you let students look for either one thing or a specific list. Different groups can hunt for different things, for example:

Parallel lines (lines "going in the same direction")

Right angles ("square corners")

Curved surfaces or curved lines

Two or more shapes that make another shape

Circles inside each other (concentric)

Shapes with "dents" (concave) or without dents (convex)

Shapes used over and over in a pattern (brick wall, chain link fence)

Solids that are somehow like a box, a cylinder (tube), a pyramid, a cone

Five shapes that are alike somehow (specify solid or flat)

Shapes that are symmetrical

Constructing Shapes

These activities have children building, drawing, or constructing shapes in some way. It is good to begin by giving students the freedom to make whatever shapes or designs they wish. Doing so permits children to gain experience with the new materials. Prepared activities can then go beyond this free-play level and challenge children to build shapes that have a particular feature. These challenges promote reflective thinking about the properties involved and are a good way to encourage level 1 thinking without pushing children too hard.

Several commercial materials permit fairly creative building of geometric solids (for example, 3D Geo-shapes, Polydrons, and the Zome System). Pattern blocks, colour tiles, and tangrams are among the most popular sets of "tiles." In addition to commercial products, all sorts of other materials can be used. Modelling clay is an obvious choice for solids. Plastic straws can be fastened together in different ways to make skeletal models. Special tiles, such as a collection of right triangles made by cutting on the diagonal of a rectangle, can be constructed from poster board. Geo-boards and various grid papers provide excellent opportunities for children to make drawings of shapes.

Using Tiles to Make Shapes

A good way to explore shapes at level 0 is to use smaller shapes or tiles to create larger shapes. Among the best materials for this purpose are pattern blocks, but many teacher-made materials can be used too. A variety of shapes are suggested in Figure 17.9. Refer to the Tangrams and Five Easy Pieces Blackline Master. Class sets can be cut from poster board and placed in plastic bags for individual or group use. Some of the activities that follow can be repeated using a different set of tiles to provide not only variety but also a different perspective.

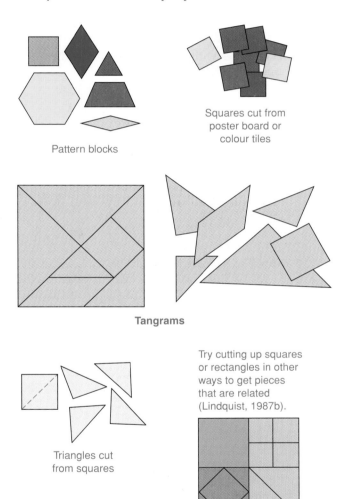

Pattern blocks

Squares cut from poster board or colour tiles

Tangrams

Triangles cut from squares

Try cutting up squares or rectangles in other ways to get pieces that are related (Lindquist, 1987b).

FIGURE 17.9 Activities with tiles can involve an assortment of shapes or can be designed with just one shape.

Geo-board Explorations

The geo-board is one of the best tools for creating two-dimensional shapes. Here are just a few of many activities for use with geo-boards at a beginning level.

ACTIVITY 17.6

Geo-board Copy

Copy shapes, designs, and patterns from pre-pared cards onto geo-boards, as in Figure 17.10. Begin with designs shown with dots, as on a geo-board. Later, have students copy designs that are drawn without dots.

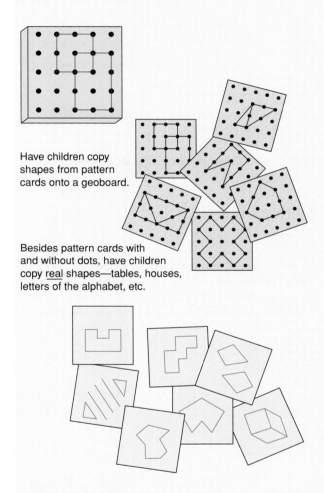

Have children copy shapes from pattern cards onto a geoboard.

Besides pattern cards with and without dots, have children copy <u>real</u> shapes—tables, houses, letters of the alphabet, etc.

FIGURE 17.10 Shapes on geo-boards.

ACTIVITY 17.7

Geo-board Tiles

Challenge the students to create a shape on the geo-board from a smaller shape shown on a shape card. Use the smaller shape as if it were a tile (Figure 17.11). Cards can be prepared with smaller shapes to direct the activity.

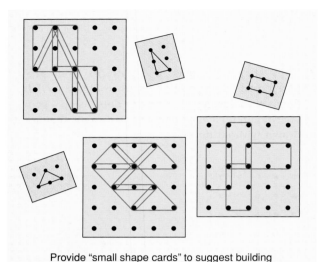

Provide "small shape cards" to suggest building blocks to students.

FIGURE 17.11 Bigger shapes from small shapes.

ACTIVITY 17.8

Congruent Parts

Copy a shape from a card, and have students subdivide or cut it into smaller shapes. Specify the number of smaller shapes. Also specify whether they are all to be congruent or simply of the same type, as shown in Figure 17.12.

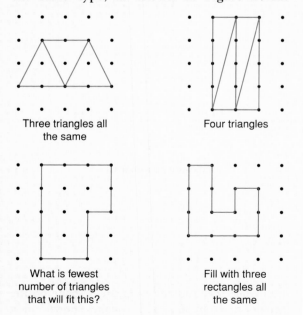

Three triangles all the same

Four triangles

What is fewest number of triangles that will fit this?

Fill with three rectangles all the same

Start with a shape, and cut it into smaller shapes. Add special conditions to make the activity challenging.

FIGURE 17.12 Subdividing shapes.

Depending on the shapes involved, this activity can be made relatively easy or challenging.

ACTIVITY 17.9

Geo-board Challenges

Challenge students to see how many different shapes of a specific type or with a particular property they can make. (Very young children will feel more comfortable searching for three or four shapes rather than "many" shapes.) Here are some appropriate ideas for level 0:

Make shapes with five sides (or some other number of sides).

Make shapes with all square corners. Can you make one with three sides? Four sides? Six, seven, eight sides?

Make some trapezoids that are all different (or suggest any other shape that students can identify).

Make a shape that has a line of symmetry. Check it with a mirror.

Two practical comments should be made about the use of geo-boards. First, have a lot of them available in the classroom. It is better for two or three children to have 10 or 12 boards at a station than for each to have only one. That way, a variety of shapes can be made and compared before they are changed.

This leads to the second point. Teach students from the very beginning to copy their geo-board designs onto paper. Paper copies allow students to create complete sets of drawings that fulfill a particular task. Drawings can be placed on the bulletin board for classification and discussion, made into booklets illustrating a new idea that is being discussed, and sent home to show parents what is happening in geometry.

Younger students can use paper with a single large geo-board on each sheet. Later, a paper board about 10 centimetres square is adequate. Older children can use centimetre dot paper or a page of small boards, each about five centimetres square (see the Blackline Masters).

In the very early grades, children will have some difficulty copying geo-board designs onto paper, especially designs with slanted lines. To help, suggest that they first mark the corners of their shape ("Second row, end peg") on the dots. With the corners identified, it is much easier for them to draw lines to make the shape.

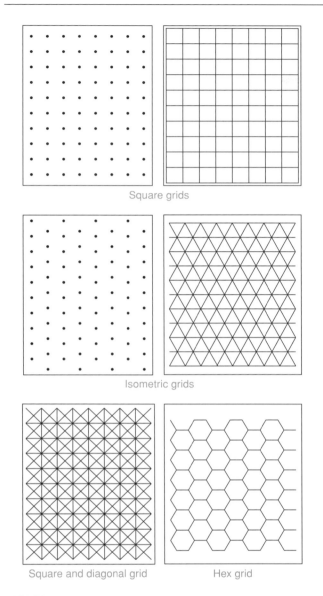

Square grids

Isometric grids

Square and diagonal grid   Hex grid

FIGURE 17.13 **Dot and grid paper of various types and sizes can be used for many geometric explorations.**

Dot and Grid Paper Explorations

The ease with which figures and designs can be constructed and changed makes geo-boards an excellent tool for exploring geometric concepts. But they do have limitations in terms of size, arrangement, and number of pegs. Assorted dot and grid papers provide an alternative. Virtually all of the activities suggested for tiles and geo-boards can be done on dot or grid paper. Changing the type of paper changes the activity and provides new opportunity for insight and discovery. Figure 17.13 shows several possibilities for dot and grid papers, all found in the Blackline Masters.

Here are some additional ideas that lend themselves particularly well to dot and grid paper.

ACTIVITY 17.10

Three-Dimensional Drawings

Isometric dot paper is effective for illustrating structures built with cubes. Square dot paper can be used to draw side and top views, as shown in Figure 17.14. Building a simple structure with cubes, then drawing plan and perspective views is an excellent activity for students in grades 6–8. Doing so will help with perspective and visual perception. (See Winter, Lappan, Phillips, & Fitzgerald, 1986, for a series of excellent activities.)

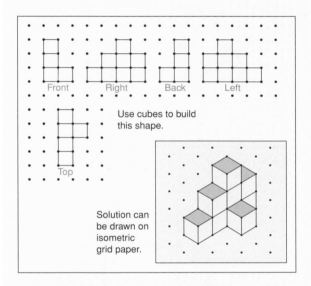

FIGURE 17.14 **Develop perspective and visual perception with cubes and plain views. Draw block "buildings" on isometric grids.**

A slightly different idea is to reverse Activity 17.10. Provide students with a perspective drawing that you have made, and have them build the structure with blocks. Drawings can be prepared on worksheets, or you can develop a collection of cards for use at workstations. A top view, with the number of cubes indicated in each square, can be used as an answer key. However, it is best to let students work together to decide if they have made an accurate construction.

ACTIVITY 17.11

Slides, Flips, and Turns

Slides, flips, and turns can be investigated on any grid. Start with a simple shape. Draw the same shape flipped over, turned, or placed in a different orientation. Trace the original shape, and cut it out. This copy can be flipped or reoriented to test the drawings that are made (see Figure 17.15).

Slides, flips, and turns could also be investigated with tangram pieces. (A tangram is an ancient Chinese puzzle made up of seven pieces: five triangles of varying proportion, a square and a parallelogram.) You could start with the two large triangles and have the students slide or flip them to create patterns or other geometric shapes. This could also be done with the two small triangles, the square, or the parallelogram.

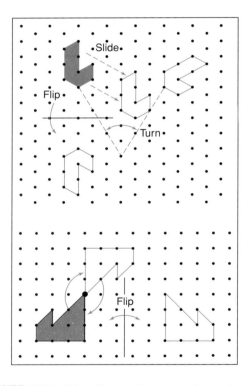

FIGURE 17.15: Slides, flips, and turns can be explored on almost any type of grid paper.

Building Solids

Building three-dimensional shapes is a little more difficult than building two-dimensional shapes, but possibly even more important. Building a model of a three-dimensional shape is an informal way to gain an intuitive understanding of a shape in terms of its component parts.

As noted earlier, commercial plastic building sets can be used to build a wide variety of solids. The pieces are all equilateral polygons (triangles, squares, pentagons, and hexagons) with edges all the same length. The resulting shapes are quite rigid.

Skeletal models, built using sticks of some sort, are representations of three-dimensional "solids." In addition to commercial materials such as the Zome System, the following two ideas are highly recommended.

- *Plastic drinking straws with flexible joints.* With scissors, cut the straws lengthwise from the top down to the flexible joint. These slit ends can then be inserted into the uncut bottom ends of other straws, making a strong but flexible joint. Three or more straws can be joined in this fashion to form two-dimensional polygons. To make skeletal solids, use tape or wire twist ties to join polygons side to side.

- *Rolled newspaper rods.* Fantastic "super-large" skeletons can be built using newspaper and masking tape. Roll three large sheets of newspaper on the diagonal to form a rod, approximately 1 metre long. The more tightly the paper is rolled, the less likely the rod is to bend. Secure the roll at the centre with a bit of tape. The ends of the rods are thin and flexible where there is less paper. Connect rods by bunching the thin part together and fastening with tape. Use tape freely, wrapping it several times around each joint. Additional rods can be added after two or three are already taped (see Figure 17.16).

Regardless of the method used for making structures, there should be an opportunity for students to compare and discuss the rigidity of a triangle with the lack of rigidity of polygons with more than three sides. Point out that because of their rigidity, triangles are used in many bridges, in the long booms of construction cranes, in gates, and in the structural parts of buildings. As children build large skeletal structures, they will find that they need to add diagonals that form triangles for support. The more triangles, the less likely their structure will collapse.

The newspaper rod method is exciting because the structures quickly become large. Let students work in groups of four or five. Soon they will discover what makes structures rigid as well as ideas related to balance and form. Primary-grade students can benefit from creating free-form structures. Older students can be challenged to make more well-defined shapes.

ACTIVITY 17.12

Unfolded Solids

Have students design nets for various solids. (A *net* **is a flat shape that will fold up to make a solid.) On a square centimetre grid, parallel lines and angles can be drawn without tedious measuring (see Figure 17.17). Nets made out of paper**

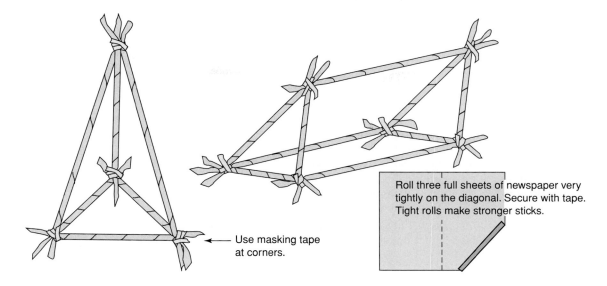

Roll three full sheets of newspaper very tightly on the diagonal. Secure with tape. Tight rolls make stronger sticks.

← Use masking tape at corners.

FIGURE 17.16 Large skeletal structures and special shapes can be built with tightly rolled newspaper. Young children can build free-form sculptures. Older children can be challenged to build shapes with specific properties. Overlap the ends by about 15 centimetres to ensure strength and fasten with tape.

can be traced or pasted onto tag-board for a sturdier solid. Cones can be easily made by cutting a sector from a circle. Experiment with different circle sizes and different sectors. Much of the value gained from folding up a solid is planning what shape the faces will be and where the faces can be connected. Encourage groups to solve these problems themselves, providing only as much help as necessary.

Plastic building sets, such as Polydrons, that can be unfolded into flat shapes provide a great way to explore nets. A net can be made by linking the desired faces together to form a flat array. If the array is actually a net, it will fold to make the desired shape. There is value in predicting whether a potential net will in fact create the specified shape. Doing so helps to develop spatial visualization. The activity can be reversed, and a shape can be unfolded to make its net. The potential challenges here are to predict in advance the shape of the net, or to try to find how many different nets there are for a shape. For example, how many different nets are there that form a simple cube? Is every arrangement of six squares a net of a cube? Since Polydrons and 3D Geo-shapes consist only of regular polygons (all sides and angles congruent), use two shapes for one face to add more variety to nets and solids.

Solids can also be built from blocks such as wooden cubes (2 cm). Plastic connecting cubes (for example, inter-

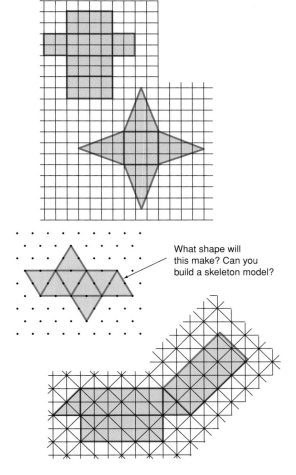

What shape will this make? Can you build a skeleton model?

FIGURE 17.17 Nets are easily drawn on grid paper. After making one net for a solid, try to find others that will fold up to make the same solid.

locking cubes or cube-a-links) can be linked on any side, then rearranged into other orientations. The following tasks can make such activities challenging.

ACTIVITY 17.13

Block Boxes

In groups, have students see how many different rectangular solids can be made using just 12 cubes each. (A rectangular solid has six faces, and each face is a rectangle.) Try other numbers of cubes. When are two rectangular solids congruent (exactly the same)? How would you have to turn one solid to give it the same orientation as another that has a matching shape?

ACTIVITY 17.14

Building Plans

As in Figure 17.18, create a task card with five views of a simple building you have constructed. Students use trial and error to try to construct the same building using the five views. Omitting the top view but giving the total number of cubes makes it slightly harder. This is a good exercise in spatial perception.

Challenges for Level 0

In many activities, the traditional content may be minimal but the problem-solving value is significant. These activities provide opportunity for growth in geometric thinking and spatial sense.

At level 0, geometric problems involve manipulating, drawing, and creating shapes of all types. The tasks revolve around considering the global features of shapes, rather than on analysis of properties or relationships between classes or figures. Many of the activities already suggested have a problem-solving orientation. The following are additional suggestions.

ACTIVITY 17.15

Tangram Puzzles

Tangrams have been popular geometric puzzles for many years. Figure 17.19 shows tangram puzzles of varying levels of difficulty. The easy ones are appropriate even for pre-school children. There are a number of different books and sets of activities for tangrams that can be purchased from your local educational supplier.

ACTIVITY 17.16

Pentominoes

A pentomino is a geometric shape that is formed by joining five squares. Each square must have at least one side in common with another. Squares cut from a grid or commercial squares may be used. Provide students with five square tiles and a sheet of square grid paper for recording. Challenge them to see how many different pentominoes they can find. (Each square in a shape can touch adjacent squares on one side only). Shapes that are flips or turns of other shapes are not considered different. Do not tell students how many pentominoes there are. Allowing students to decide whether some shapes are really different and whether all shapes have been found will lead to good discussions.

FIGURE 17.18 Views of a simple building.

| Top | Left | Front | Right | Back |

(Lines indicate different faces.)

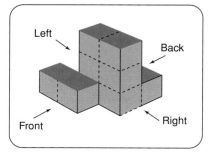

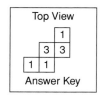

Given the five cards at the top, use wooden cubes to build the building. An answer key can be made by putting the numbers of cubes in each vertical stack on the top view. To make your own task cards, start by constructing a building, and then make the cards.

Once students have decided that there are just 12 pentominoes (see Figure 17.20), the 12 pieces can then be used in a variety of activities. Paste the grids with the children's pentominoes onto tag-board, then let them cut out the 12 shapes. These can be used in the next two activities.

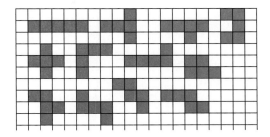

There are 12 pentominoes.

Finding all possible shapes made with five squares—or six squares (called "hexominoes") or six equilateral triangles and so on—is a good exercise in spatial problem solving.

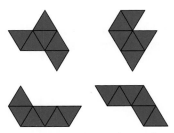

Four of the different shapes that six equilateral triangles will make.

Four of the different shapes that four "half-square" triangles will make.

FIGURE 17.20 Pentominoes and related shape challenges.

ACTIVITY 17.17

Pentomino Puzzles

A variety of puzzles can be made from the pentominoes. Students can make puzzles to challenge their classmates by selecting four or more pentominoes and putting them together to make a single shape. The outline of this shape is then drawn on grid paper. The challenge for students, not knowing which pieces were used, is to find a

---

Easy

Use

To make

Full-sized outlines

Fit in the tangram pieces.

Dog

Harder

Full-sized outlines

Fit all seven tangram pieces in this shape.

Hardest

Each of these shapes can be made using all seven pieces.

Outlines are to scale but much smaller.

FIGURE 17.19 Four types of tangram puzzles illustrate a range of difficulty levels.

way to create the shape. The more pieces there are, the more difficult the puzzle will be. Many puzzles will have more than one solution. A much more challenging version is to construct a rectangle using all 12 pieces. It is possible to make a 6×10, 5×12, and 4×15 rectangle using the 12 pieces.

ACTIVITY 17.18

Pentomino Squeeze

Play "Pentomino Squeeze" on an 8×8 grid of squares. Pieces are dealt out randomly to two players. The player with the cross shape places it on the board. In turn, players place their pieces on the board without overlapping any piece that is already placed. The last player to be able to play a piece is the winner. Smaller boards can be used to make the game more difficult.

An extended challenge is to find out how many *hexominoes* (shapes made from six squares) there are. It is also fun to explore the number of shapes that can be made from six equilateral triangles or from four isosceles right triangles (halves of squares). With the right triangles, the

sides that touch must be the same length. How many of each of these "ominoes" do you think there are?

Tessellations

A *tessellation* is a tiling of the plane with one or more shapes in a repeated pattern so there are no holes or gaps. The "Tiling Pattern" activity at the beginning of the chapter was a tessellation activity. Making tessellations is an artistic way for level 0 students from grade 1 to grade 8 to explore patterns in shapes and to see how shapes combine to form other shapes. One-shape or two-shape tessellation activities can vary considerably in difficulty and still remain level 0 activities.

Some shapes are easier to tessellate than others (see Figure 17.21). When the shapes can be put together in more than one pattern, both the problem-solving level and the creativity increase. Literally hundreds of shapes can be used as tiles for tessellations. Every one of the 12 pentominoes will tessellate. It is fun to create shapes on various grid papers and then test them to see if they can be used to tessellate.

Most children will benefit from using actual tiles to create patterns. Simple construction paper tiles can be cut quickly on a paper cutter. Other tiles can be traced onto construction paper, then several layers can be cut at once with scissors. Older children may be able to use dot or line grids and plan their tessellations with pencil and paper.

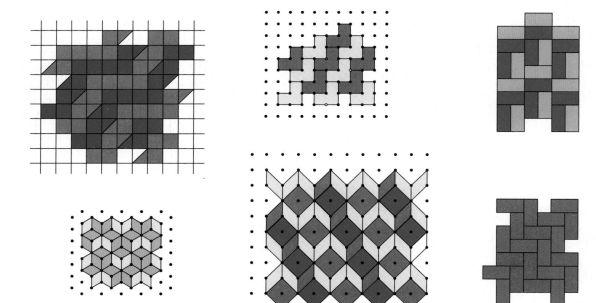

Tessellations can be drawn on grids or made of construction paper tiles. They are challenging and provide an opportunity for both artistic creativity and spatial reasoning.

FIGURE 17.21 Tessellations.

Spend one period with tiles or grids, letting children experiment with tiling patterns. To plan a tessellation, use only one colour so that the focus is on the spatial relationships. To complete an artistic-looking tessellation, add a colour design. With younger children you may use only two colours, and never more than four. Colour designs can also be repeated regularly over the tessellation.

Tessellations can be made by gluing paper tiles to large sheets of paper, by drawing them on dot or line grids, or by tracing around a poster board tile. Do not worry about the edges of tessellations. Work from the centre out, leaving ragged edges to indicate that the pattern goes on and on.

Technology Note: Level 0

Geometry is one area of the curriculum for which a variety of fascinating computer programs exist. Many programs allow students to "stamp" geometric shapes onto the screen and then manipulate them with the mouse. Other programs mimic geo-boards. These allow much more flexibility and ease of use than a physical geo-board. All of these programs have real value for level 0 thinkers. You can find software that is appropriate for all grade levels.

Shape and Geo-board Software

Shape Up (Sunburst, 1995) and *Shapes* (Clements & Sarama, 1995) are two good examples of computer versions of real tiles. Both programs include a pattern-block and tangram format in which students can stamp pieces onto a blank screen. Pieces are easily moved around, rotated, or flipped through either a vertical or horizontal line. In *Shapes,* two or more pieces can be "glued together" to create new shapes. The pattern blocks include a quarter circle that adds to the variability. Both programs allow shapes to be enlarged or reduced in size. Some puzzles are included with the packages, and new puzzles similar to those in Figure 17.19 are easily created. *Shape Up* has a third mode in which six regular shapes can be manipulated, and each can be cut into many smaller shapes and rearranged in endless ways.

The critical question to ask is, "What do these programs provide that cannot be accomplished with real objects?" Both modes are enticing to children, but the computer versions require more deliberate actions. For example, the rotate button must be clicked, and a shape must be rotated in incremental amounts. The ability to enlarge or shrink pieces is at least interesting and may help with the understanding of similarity. It is not clear that any greater geometric benefit is gained, but the environment and the experience are sufficiently different to warrant the use of this type of program along with real objects. Students who have difficulty with fine motor control are often unable to produce drawings or cut-and-paste recordings of their geometry activities. Since the computer permits students to print colourful copies of their work and include written journal entries, these students take real pride in the work they produce.

James Discovers Math (Brøderbund, 1995a) and *Millie's Math House* (Edmark, 1993) also have components in which shapes can be stamped and arranged. Designed for the three- to six-year-old set, these programs are much more limited than the others discussed here. *James Discovers Math* also has a feature in which any one of several tessellations can be coloured in to make wonderful shape patterns. Although students only colour in the shapes, the activity has plenty of spatial value for young children.

GeoComputer (Edmark, 1996) is an example of an electronic geo-board. This program shows a dot grid (geo-board) on which students can draw lines between points. Lines can be stretched over other pegs just like rubber bands on a geo-board. *GeoComputer* allows students to manipulate shapes by dragging their edges without changing the lengths. Regions can be shaded in with a palette of colours. Any shape can be flipped or rotated 90 degrees, moves that are not simple to accomplish on a real board. This program will also measure areas and perimeters of regions. *MathKeys: Geometry, Vol. 1* (MECC, 1995a) includes a similar geo-board, but without the measuring and reflection capabilities. A larger array of pegs, ease of shape manipulation, and the ability to save and print work are the major advantages of electronic geo-boards. As with shape programs, they should be used in tandem with hands-on versions. ■■

Informal Geometry Activities: Level 1

A significant difference between level 1 and level 0 is the object of students' thought. While students will continue to use models and drawings of shapes, they begin to see these as representative of class and shape. Their understanding of the properties of shapes, such as symmetry, perpendicular and parallel lines, and so on, continues to be refined.

Transitions to Level 1

Most of the materials in the suggested activities are the same as those for level 0, and many level 0 activities can easily be extended to level 1. For example, consider Activity 17.6, "Geo-board Copy" (p. 335). If students who seem to be ready for more challenging work have successfully copied a parallelogram, talk briefly with them about what makes that shape special. Can other shapes be made that also have sides that are parallel? Make at least five different parallelograms, and copy them onto dot paper. What is the same about all five? Now this activity is beginning to focus the attention on the *class* of *all* parallelograms and its properties.

It is quite reasonable to have several similar but related investigations proceeding in the classroom at the same time, with different groups pursuing tasks at different levels of the van Hiele model.

Classifying Shapes by Properties

Sorting activities for level 1 are grouped here in a manner similar to that used for level 0 activities. To promote the kind of thinking that is appropriate for this level, shapes are presented so that specific properties and categorizations are clearly evident. For example, the shapes used might be quadrilaterals or even a collection of two or three types of quadrilaterals. In other words, the children are looking at a class of shapes and generating ideas unique to this class—properties of the class and of all potential members of the class.

You may have to be more direct in pointing out particular properties or categories that students do not notice. When a classification for a set of shapes has been made and discussed, and is well understood, the appropriate name for the classification can be supplied.

Special Categories of Two-Dimensional Shapes

Table 17.1 lists some important categories of two-dimensional shapes. Examples of these shapes can be found in Figure 17.22.

In the classification of quadrilaterals and parallelograms, the subsets are not all disjoint sets. For example, a square can be classified as a rectangle and a rhombus. All parallelograms can be classified as trapezoids, but not all trapezoids can be classified as parallelograms. Children at level 1 have difficulty seeing these more subtle relationships. They may correctly list all the properties of a square, a rhombus, and a rectangle but still identify a square as a "non-rhombus" or a "non-rectangle." Is it wrong for students to refer to these subgroups as disjoint sets? By grade 4 or 5, it is inappropriate to encourage such thinking. Burger (1985) points out that upper elementary students correctly use classification schemes such as these in other contexts, which may be used as analogies. For example, if individual students in a class can belong to more than one club, then a square could be an example of a quadrilateral that belongs to two other clubs.

Several types of sorting activities can help students grow in their understanding of how shapes are related.

ACTIVITY 17.19

Shape Sort II

Sort shapes by naming their properties, not by the names of the shapes. When two or more properties are combined, sort shapes one property at a time. "Find all of the shapes that have opposite sides parallel." Once this is done, "Find all those that also have a right angle." (This group should include squares as well as rectangles that are not squares.) After sorting, discuss what the names of the shapes are. Also try sorting by the same combinations of properties but in a different order.

Table 17.1: Categories of Two-Dimensional Shapes

Shape	Description
Simple Closed Curves	
Concave, convex	An intuitive definition of *concave* might be "having a dent in it." If a simple closed curve is not concave, it is *convex*. A more precise definition of *concave* may be interesting to explore with older students.
Symmetrical, non-symmetrical	Shapes may have one or more lines of symmetry and may or may not have rotational symmetry. These concepts will require more detailed investigation.
Polygons Concave, convex Symmetrical, non-symmetrical	Simple closed curves with all straight sides.
Regular	All sides and all angles are congruent.
Triangles	
Triangles	Polygons with exactly three sides.
Classified by sides	
Equilateral	All sides are congruent.
Isosceles	At least two sides are congruent.
Scalene	No two sides are congruent.
Classified by angles	
Right	Has a right angle.
Acute	All angles are smaller than a right angle.
Obtuse	One angle is larger than a right angle.
Convex Quadrilaterals	
Convex quadrilaterals	Convex polygons with exactly four sides.
Kite	Two opposing pairs of congruent adjacent sides.
Trapezoid Isosceles trapezoid	At least one pair of parallel sides. A pair of opposite sides is congruent.
Parallelogram Rectangle Rhombus Square	Two pairs of parallel sides. Parallelogram with a right angle. Parallelogram with all sides congruent. Parallelogram with a right angle and all sides congruent.

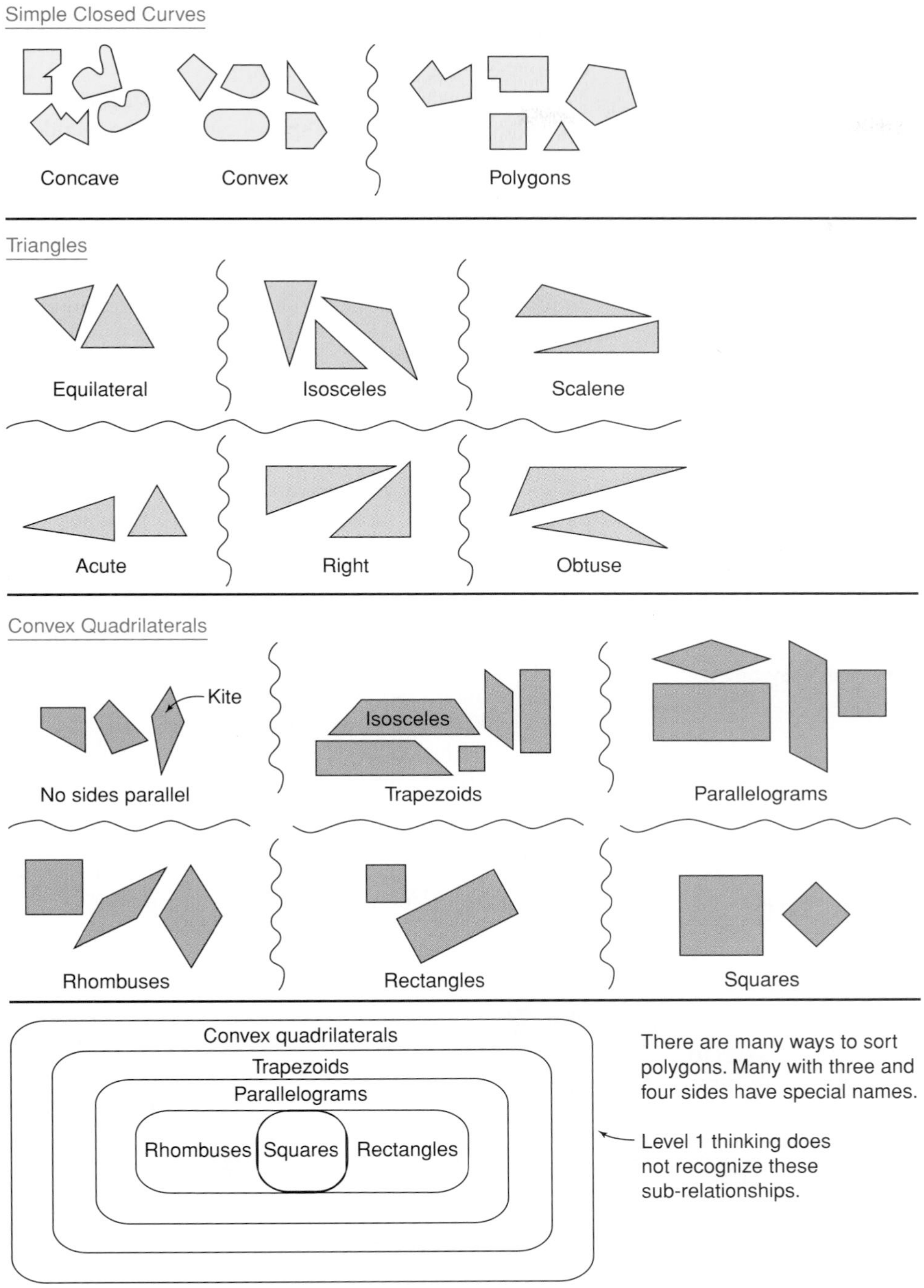
Simple Closed Curves
Concave
Convex
Polygons
Triangles
Equilateral
Isosceles
Scalene
Acute
Right
Obtuse
Convex Quadrilaterals
Kite
No sides parallel
Isosceles
Trapezoids
Parallelograms
Rhombuses
Rectangles
Squares
Convex quadrilaterals
Trapezoids
Parallelograms
Rhombuses
Squares
Rectangles
There are many ways to sort polygons. Many with three and four sides have special names.
Level 1 thinking does not recognize these sub-relationships.

FIGURE 17.22 Classification of two-dimensional shapes.

Use loops of string to keep track of shapes as you sort them. Lay two loops out on a flat surface. Have students put all of the shapes with four congruent sides in one loop and those with a right angle in the other. Where do squares go? Let them wrestle with this dilemma until they realize that the two loops must overlie each other, with the squares placed in the overlapping region.

ACTIVITY 17.20

Mystery Definition

Use an "all of these, none of these" type of activity as in Figure 17.23.

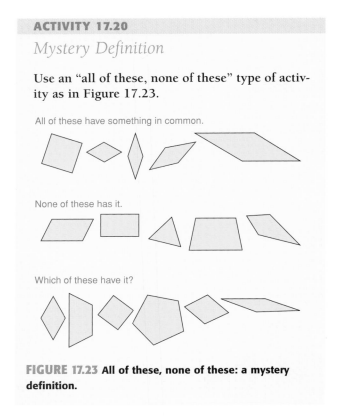

All of these have something in common.

None of these has it.

Which of these have it?

FIGURE 17.23 All of these, none of these: a mystery definition.

Special Categories of Three-Dimensional Shapes

Important and interesting shapes and relationships also exist in three dimensions. Some classifications of solids are given here. Three-dimensional solids can be sorted in a variety of ways without assigning them to classes with special names (see Table 17.2, p. 348). Figures 17.24 and 17.25 show examples of cylinders and prisms. Note that prisms are defined here as a special category of a cylinder—a cylinder with a polygon for a base. Figure 17.25 shows a similar grouping of cones and pyramids. Many textbooks define cylinders strictly as circular cylinders. These books do not have special names for other cylinders. Under that definition, the prism is not a special case of a cylinder. This points to the fact that definitions are conventions, and not all conventions are agreed upon universally.

Constructing and Measuring Shapes

Constructing shapes in two and three dimensions is one of the most profitable activities that can be done in geometry. As children begin to demonstrate level 1 thinking, construction activities can be posed as tasks. This way, students are given the properties of shapes rather than the characteristics of their appearance.

Measurements of shapes will help students recognize even more relationships. The area, perimeter, surface area, volume, angle, radius, and circumference of various shapes can be measured. For example, students who measure interior angles of various polygons will discover that when the number of sides of two polygons is the same, so is the sum of the measures of the interior angles. Direct comparisons, informal units, and simple student-made measuring devices are sufficient for exploring almost all interesting relationships involving measures.

FIGURE 17.24 Cylinders and prisms.

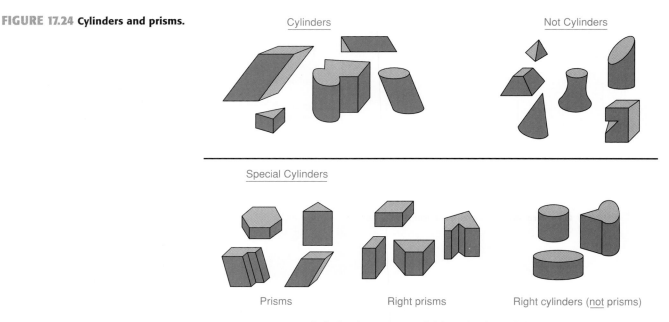

Cylinders

Not Cylinders

Special Cylinders

Prisms

Right prisms

Right cylinders (not prisms)

Cylinders have two parallel faces, and parallel lines join corresponding points on these faces. If the parallel faces are polygons, the cylinder can be called a prism.

FIGURE 17.25 Cones and pyramids.

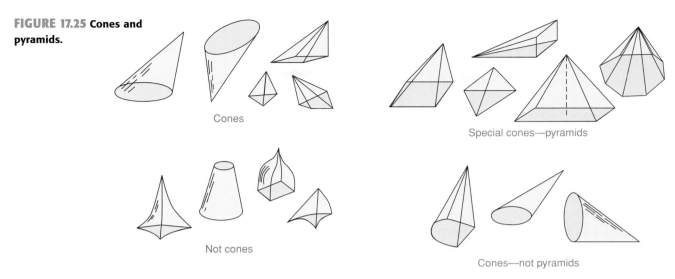

Cones

Special cones—pyramids

Not cones

Cones—not pyramids

Cones and cones with a polygon base (pyramids) all have straight-line elements joining every point of the base with the vertex. (Yes, a pyramid is just a special type of cone.)

Two-Dimensional Constructions

Tiles, geo-boards, dot paper, and grid paper are among the best materials for constructing two-dimensional shapes. On the computer, dynamic geometry programs such as *The Geometer's Sketchpad* (Key Curriculum Press, 1995), *Geometry Inventor* (LOGAL, 1994a), and *Cabri Geometry II* (Texas Instruments, 1994) are fantastic for students from about grade 6 and up.

The first activity here (adapted from the 5–8 section of NCTM's 1989 *Standards*) uses ordinary flat toothpicks to make triangles.

ACTIVITY 17.21

Toothpick Triangles

Provide children with a supply of toothpicks. They are to arrange the toothpicks in straight lines to make triangles. Begin with three toothpicks, then move to four, then five, and so on. For each number of toothpicks, the children first decide if any triangle is possible. If so, they sketch it (showing the arrangement of the toothpicks); then they see if there are other possible triangles that can be made with the same number of picks. For example, only one triangle is possible with three toothpicks, none are possible with four toothpicks, and two different triangles can be made with seven toothpicks.

"Toothpick Triangles" is an example of an opportunity to extend reasoning to level 2. If students are asked to explain why certain triangles are impossible ("Why is only one triangle possible with eight toothpicks?"), they may go beyond just looking at properties of triangles and begin to do some informal reasoning. The sum of any two sides of a triangle must be greater than the third side. (Why?)

ACTIVITY 17.22

Property Challenges

This activity can be done with almost any material that allows students to draw or construct shapes easily. List properties or relationships; then have students construct as many shapes as possible that possess those properties or exhibit those relationships. Compare the shapes made by different groups. Here are some examples:

Make a four-sided shape with two opposite sides the same length, but not parallel.

Make some six-sided shapes. Make some with one, two, and then three pairs of parallel sides and some with no parallel sides.

Make shapes with all square corners. Can you make one with three sides? Four sides? Five sides? Six, seven, or eight sides?

Make some six-sided shapes with square corners. Count how many squares are inside each. What is the distance around each square?

Make five different triangles. How are they different? (This is also good for four-, five-, or six-sided shapes.)

Make some triangles with two equal (congruent) sides.

Make some four-sided shapes with three congruent sides.

Try five-sided shapes with four congruent sides.

Make some quadrilaterals with all sides equal (or with two pairs of equal sides).

Make a shape with one or more lines of symmetry or with rotational symmetry. (A longer discussion of symmetry is provided later in the chapter.)

It is easy (and fun) to make up property challenges. Explore some of these, and make up others that suit your needs. One idea is to use combinations of previously explored concepts. Can you make a triangle with two right angles? Can you make a rhombus that has a right angle? Can you make a parallelogram that has only two equal sides?

Make a chart like the one shown here: Challenge children to draw or construct triangles that fit into each of the nine cells. Of the nine, two are impossible. (Can you tell which ones?)

	Equilateral	Isosceles	Scalene
Right			
Acute			
Obtuse			

Combination challenges can also include the notions of perpendicular, angle measurement, area, perimeter, similarity, concave and convex, regularity, and symmetry, to name just a few. Also encourage your students to come up with some of their own. Notice that some of the challenges in Activity 17.22 are not possible. Discovering that some combination of relationships is not possible—and why—is just as valuable as learning about the relationships themselves.

ACTIVITY 17.23

Measure Investigation

Ask students to make shapes according to special measurement requirements.

Make at least five different shapes with an area of _____ (approximate number for your materials). What is the perimeter of each?

Table 17.2: Categories of Three-Dimensional Shapes

Shape	Description
Sorted by Edges and Vertices Spheres and "egglike" shapes	Shapes with no *edges* and no *vertices* (corners). Shapes with *edges* but no *vertices* (e.g., a flying saucer). Shapes with *vertices* but no *edges* (e.g., a football).
Sorted by Faces and Surfaces Polyhedron	Shapes made of all faces (a *face* is a flat surface of a solid). If all surfaces are faces, all the edges will be straight lines. Some combination of faces and rounded surfaces (cylinders are examples, but this is not a definition of a cylinder). Shapes with all curved surfaces. Shapes with and without edges and with and without vertices. Faces can be parallel. Parallel faces lie in planes that never intersect.
Cylinders Cylinder	Two congruent, parallel faces called *bases.* Lines joining corresponding points on the two bases are always parallel. These parallel lines are called *elements* of the cylinder.

Shape	Description
Cylinders Right cylinder	A cylinder with elements perpendicular to the bases. A cylinder that is not a right cylinder is an *oblique cylinder.*
Prism	A cylinder with polygons for bases. All prisms are special cases of cylinders.
Rectangular prism	A cylinder with rectangles for bases.
Cube	A square prism with square sides.
Cones Cone	A solid with exactly one face and a vertex that is not on the face. Straight lines (elements) can be drawn from any point on the edge of the base to the vertex. The base may be any shape at all. The vertex need not be directly over the base.
Circular cone	Cone with a circular base.
Pyramid	Cone with a polygon for a base. All faces joining the vertex are triangles. Pyramids are named by the shape of the base: *triangular* pyramid, *square* pyramid, *octagonal* pyramid, and so on. All pyramids are special cases of cones.

Make shapes with a fixed perimeter, and examine the area of each.

Try to make the shape with the largest area for a given perimeter or the smallest perimeter for a given area. (For polygons, the largest area for a fixed perimeter is always regular. Try it.)

Angle and side specifications provide many opportunities to examine properties. Angles can usually be kept to multiples of 30 and 45, or informal units can be used.

Make several different triangles that all have one angle the same. Next make some different triangles with two angles the same (for example, 30 and 45 degrees). What do you notice?

Can you make a parallelogram with a 60-degree angle? Make several. Are they all alike? How? How are they different?

Make some parallelograms with a side of 5 and a side of 10. Are they all the same?

Draw some polygons with 4, 5, 6, 7, and 8 sides. Divide them all up into triangles, but do not let any lines cross or triangles overlap. What did you discover? Measure the angles inside each polygon.

Draw an assortment of rectangles, and draw the diagonals for each rectangle. Measure the angles that the diagonals make with each other. Measure each part of each diagonal. What did you notice? Try this exercise with squares, rhombuses, other parallelograms, and kites (quadrilaterals with two pairs of adjacent sides congruent).

Three-Dimensional Constructions

Students need to be able to identify and draw two-dimensional images of three-dimensional figures and to build three-dimensional figures from two-dimensional images. Activities often involve drawings of small "buildings" made of interlocking cubes.

ACTIVITY 17.24

Viewpoints

In the first version, students begin with a building and draw the left, right, front, and back direct views. In Figure 17.26, the building plan shows a top view of the building and the number

of cubes in each position. After students construct a building from a plan like this, their task is to draw the front, left, and back direct views as shown in the figure.

In the reverse version of the task, students are given a right and front view. The task is to construct the building that has those views. To record their solutions, students draw a building plan (top view with numbers).

Notice that the front and back direct views are symmetrical, as are the left and right views. That is why only one of each is given in the second part of the activity.

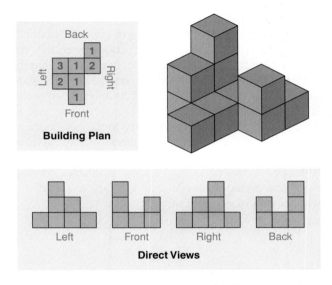

FIGURE 17.26 Tasks can begin with the Building Plan, or with the Direct View, or even with the building. Students give the other representations.

Another interesting connection between two and three dimensions is found by slicing solids in different ways. When a solid is sliced into two parts, the slice faces form a two-dimensional figure. Figure 17.27 shows a cube being sliced off at the corner, leaving a triangular face. Slices can be explored with clay sliced with a potter's wire as shown.

ACTIVITY 17.25

Clay Shapes and Slices

You can make almost any shape with modelling clay, then slice it to investigate the resulting faces. Use oil-based craft clay that will not dry out. An inexpensive tool called a *piano wire*, a wire with two handles, is used to cut the clay.

This works much better than a knife and can be purchased at an art supply store. Have students make cubes, cones, prisms, cylinders, a torus (doughnut shape), and other shapes. Precision is not important as long as the essential features are there.

Give students a solid and ask them to find a way to slice the shape to produce a face with a particular shape. For example, how could you slice a cube so that the resulting face is a trapezoid? Will it be isosceles? Always? Figure 17.27 suggests a few ways that different solids can be cut (Carroll, 1988).

If clay slicing presents a problem, plastic three-dimensional shapes can serve the same purpose. (For example, *Power Solids* from Cuisenaire are reasonably priced and include 12 shapes.) Pour a small amount of water into the hollow shape. The surface of the water is the same shape as a sliced face. By tilting the solid in different ways, different "slices" are formed. Students may have to add or remove a little water to get the shape in the right place.

Note that predicting ahead of time where to make the slice, or how it might be possible to get the desired shape, is the key to making this last activity profitable. With the water and plastic shapes, it is all too easy to experiment without a lot of reflective thought.

Slicing helps students see how a plane intersects with a solid shape. Another connection between two and three dimensions involves "generating" solids from a two-dimensional shape. Sliding (translating) or revolving a plane surface, as shown in Figure 17.28, can generate imaginary solids. Spinning a shape about an edge can make unusual as well as standard shapes.

ACTIVITY 17.26
Solid Generation Challenges

There are two similar types of challenges:

1. Start with a generator by providing students with a shape cut from tag-board. The task is to describe, draw, or make from clay all solids that can be generated from this one shape. The shape may be spun or translated in any way. Can some shapes be generated in more than one way?

2. Start with a solid. Give students a model of a solid, or describe one orally. Students are to draw and cut out one or more shapes that will generate the solid and describe how the generating will be done.

What solids cannot be generated in this way? What can you say about any solid generated by

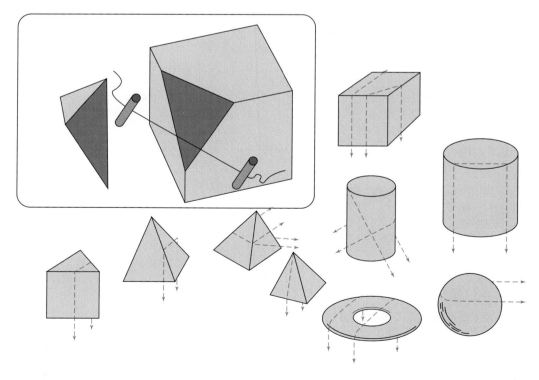

FIGURE 17.27 Predict the sliced face before you cut a clay model with a piano wire.

FIGURE 17.28 Generating imaginary solids.

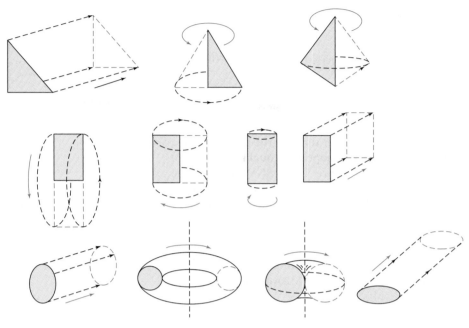

Use a poster board model of a flat shape to generate solids in the air. Slide or rotate the shape. Try to make your generated solid from clay.

sliding? How else can cylinders be generated? What about prisms? What types of cones can be generated and how?

Using cubes to build shapes was a suggestion for level 0. At level 1, it is interesting to examine rectangular prisms (box shapes) using cubes, because surface area and volume are easily determined in this format. These tasks are analogous to those in two dimensions involving area and perimeter.

ACTIVITY 17.27

Surface and Volume Inquiry

Working with 36 cubes, have students figure out how many boxes (rectangular prisms) they can make using all the cubes. For each box, they should list the dimensions and the total surface area. What can you say about boxes with larger surface areas? Smaller surface areas? Try 60 cubes and then 64 cubes. (Good numbers will have several factorizations into three factors.) Later, reverse the problem. Have students construct boxes that have a given surface area. Can boxes with the same surface area have different volumes? Try surface areas of 24, 54, or 96 squares.

One general conclusion from the "Surface and Volume Inquiry" activity is that boxes that are the closest to cubical will have the smallest surface areas. (Recall that the rectangles with the smallest perimeters were squares.) If the experiment could be carried out for boxes with more and more sides, you would see that shapes with the most volume and least surface area tend to get closer and closer to the shape of a sphere. (A cube is sort of a six-sided "sphere.") This explains why soap bubbles are spherical. The volume of air is fixed (trapped inside), and the soap film tends to contract. When the surface is minimal for the amount of air, the bubble is a sphere.

Exploring Special Properties and Relationships

Some geometric properties of shape merit special attention. Here you will recognize some of the traditional content of geometry. The activities are generally adaptable to several levels. Since the activities are designed to investigate properties, they are suitable for level 1 thinking. Students still at level 0 will be able to work at the activities but may not apply the properties to whole classes of shapes. Those ready for level 2 thinking can be challenged to see how properties are related, or what conditions give rise to particular properties.

Line Symmetry

Line symmetry (bilateral or mirror symmetry) is fun and challenging to explore using a variety of materials.

ACTIVITY 17.28

Symmetry on a Grid

On a geo-board or on dot or grid paper, make a line. Next, create a shape that touches the line on one side, as in Figure 17.29. Try to make the mirror or symmetrical image of the shape on the other side of the line. Then, try starting with two intersecting lines of symmetry. Make the shape between two of the rays formed by these lines. Reflect the shape across each line. Continue this process until further reflections produce no new images on your drawing. Mirrors can be used to test the results.

ACTIVITY 17.29

Line Symmetry Analysis

On a piece of dot paper, use the technique of Activity 17.28 to create a symmetrical drawing. Fold the paper on the mirror line, and notice how corresponding points on each side of the line match up. Open the paper, and connect several corresponding points with straight lines. Notice that the mirror line is the perpendicular bisector of the lines joining the points. Use this process to create a symmetrical drawing on plain paper. Draw the mirror line and half of the figure as before. From several critical points, draw perpendicular lines to the mirror line and extend them an equal distance beyond it (see Figure 17.30).

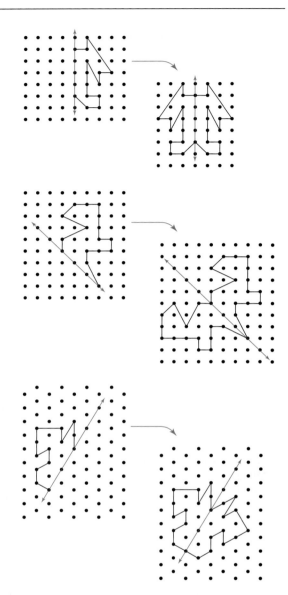

FIGURE 17.29 Exploring symmetry on dot grids.

A *flip* or *reflection* of a shape about a line is related to the concept of symmetry. If you plan to investigate *transformations* (slides, flips, and turns), Activities 17.28 and 17.29 are good beginnings.

A useful device for studying symmetry and transformations is the Mira, a piece of red transparent Plexiglas (see Figure 17.31) that stands perpendicular to the surface of a table. The Mira is essentially a transparent mirror. You can reach behind the Mira and draw the image that you see. Since you can see the original image as well as the reflected image, it is possible to match images with reflections and draw the mirror line at the base of the Mira. This feature of the Mira allows the user to draw perpendicular

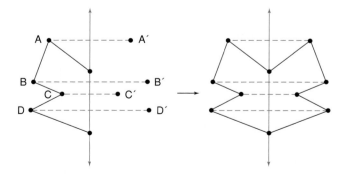

FIGURE 17.30 From points on one side, draw perpendicular lines to the mirror line, and extend them an equal distance beyond.

bisectors and angle bisectors, reflect images, and make a variety of constructions more easily than with a compass and straightedge, in a very meaningful manner.

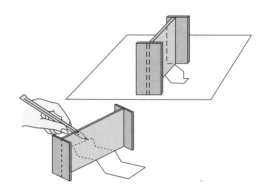

FIGURE 17.31 The Mira is a "see-through mirror" that allows you to draw the image that you see in the glass.

The following activity offers a slightly different view of symmetry. As well, it provides good preparation for rotational symmetry.

ACTIVITY 17.30

Flip into the Box

Cut out a small rectangle from paper or cardboard. Colour one side, and label the corners A, B, C, and D so that both sides have the same labels. Place the rectangle on a sheet of paper, and trace around it. Refer to this traced rectangle as a "box" for the cut-out rectangle. The question

is, "How many different ways can you flip the rectangle over so that it fits in the box?" Before each flip, place the rectangle in the box in the initial orientation. As shown in Figure 17.32, each flip into the box is a flip about a line, and these lines are also lines of symmetry. Students can discover that for a plane shape, there are as many lines of symmetry as there are ways to flip a figure over and still have it fit into its box. Try with other figures: square, rhombus, kite, parallelogram with unequal sides and angles, triangles, regular pentagons, and others.

Rotational Symmetry

One of the easiest introductions to rotational symmetry is to create a box for a shape by tracing around it, as in Activity 17.30. If a shape will fit into its box in more than one way without being flipped over, it has *rotational symmetry*. The *order of rotational symmetry* is the number of different ways it can fit into the box. Thus a square has rotational symmetry of order 4, as well as four flip lines or lines of symmetry. A parallelogram with unequal sides and angles has rotational symmetry of order 2 but no lines of symmetry (see Figure 17.33).

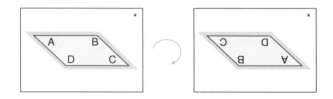

FIGURE 17.33 This parallelogram fits in its box two ways without being flipped over. Therefore, it has rotational symmetry of order 2.

FIGURE 17.32 There are at least two ways to flip this diamond into its box. Are there more? Cut one out and try it!

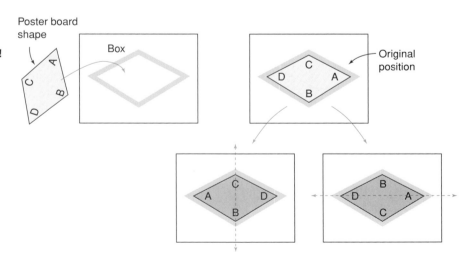

ACTIVITY 17.31

Building "Rotatable" Shapes

Use tiles, geo-boards, dot paper, or grid paper to create a shape that has rotational symmetry of a given order. Except for regular polygons, this can be quite challenging. To test a result, trace around it, and cut out a copy of the shape. Try to rotate it on the drawing.

Symmetries in Three-Dimensional Figures

A plane of symmetry in three dimensions is analogous to a line of symmetry in two dimensions. Each point in a symmetrical solid corresponds to a point on the other side. The plane of symmetry is the perpendicular bisector of the line segments joining each pair of points. Figure 17.34 illustrates a shape built with cubes that has a plane of symmetry.

ACTIVITY 17.32

Plane Symmetry Buildings

With cubes, construct a building that has a plane of symmetry. If the plane of symmetry should go between the cubes, separate the shape into two symmetrical parts. Try making shapes that have two or more planes of symmetry. Build various prisms. Do not forget that a plane can cut diagonally through the blocks. Try using clay to build solids with planes of symmetry, and slice through these planes with a piano wire.

Rotational symmetry in the plane has an analogous counterpart in three dimensions. Whereas a figure in a plane is rotated about a point, a three-dimensional figure is rotated about a line. Such a line is called an *axis of symmetry*. As a solid with rotational symmetry revolves around an axis of symmetry, it will occupy the same position in space (its box), but in different orientations. Although plane figures have only one centre of rotation, solids can have more than one axis of rotation. For each axis of symmetry, there is a corresponding order of rotational symmetry. A regular square pyramid has only one axis of symmetry, which runs through the vertex and the centre of the square. A cube, by contrast, has a total of 13 axes of symmetry: three (through opposite faces) of order 4, four (through diagonally opposite vertices) of order 3, and six (through midpoints of diagonally opposite edges) of order 2.

ACTIVITY 17.33

Find the Spin Lines

Give students a solid that has one or more axes of rotational symmetry. Colour or label each face of the solid to help keep track. The students' task is to find all axes of rotational symmetry (spin lines) and determine the order of rotational symmetry for each. Suggest that students use one finger of each hand to hold the solid at the two points where the axis of symmetry emerges. A partner can then slowly turn the solid, and both can decide when the solid is again "in its box"— that is, in the same space it was in originally (see Figure 17.35).

Diagonals of Quadrilaterals

The usual approach to analyzing quadrilaterals is in terms of their sides (parallel or not, congruent or not) and angles. Another way to analyze them is in terms of their *diagonals*. Consider the following relationships for diagonals of quadrilaterals:

Length: Either equal in length or not (two possibilities)

Angle of intersection: Either right angle or not (two possibilities)

Ratio of parts (from the corners to the intersection): One diagonal bisected, both bisected, neither bisected but parts proportional, or none of these (four possibilities)

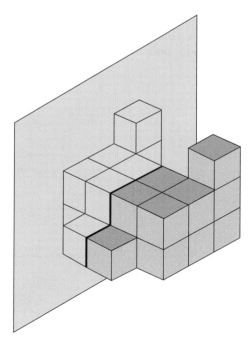

FIGURE 17.34 A block building with one plane of symmetry.

FIGURE 17.35 Rotations of a cube.

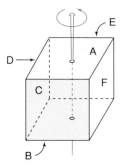

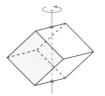

These two axes also have rotational symmetry of order 4.

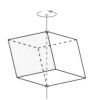

With A on top, the cube fits in its "box" four ways. Through this axis, the order of rotational symmetry is order 4.

Edge-to-edge axes each have symmetry of order 2. How many are there?

If the axis is from corner to opposite corner, what is the order of symmetry? How many of these axes are there?

ACTIVITY 17.34

Diagonal Investigation

Have students select a particular type of quadrilateral (say, parallelogram) and draw several different examples of it. Use dot or grid paper so drawing of parallel lines and congruent angles will be easy. For each example, students should draw the diagonals, making whatever measurements and calculations they desire. The goal is to discover the properties of the diagonals of that particular type of quadrilateral. Different groups of students can investigate different quadrilaterals, then information can be discussed and shared.

In Activity 17.34, the students begin with a quadrilateral and examine properties of the diagonals. A similar activity begins with the diagonals.

ACTIVITY 17.35

Diagonal Strips

For this activity, students need three strips of tagboard about 2 cm wide. Two should be the same length (about 30 cm) and the third somewhat shorter (about 20 cm). Punch nine holes, equally spaced, along a strip. (Punch a hole near each

end. Divide the distance between these two holes into 8.) Use a brass fastener to join two strips. Quadrilaterals can be formed by joining the four end holes, as shown in Figure 17.36. Move the brass fasteners to form other quadrilaterals. Provide students with the list of possible relationships for angles, lengths, and ratios of parts. Their task is to use the strips to determine the properties of diagonals that will produce different quadrilaterals. The strips are there to help in the exploration. Students may want to make additional drawings on dot grids to test their hypotheses.

Every type of quadrilateral can be uniquely described in terms of its diagonals using only the conditions of length, angle of intersection, and ratio of parts. Some students will work with the diagonal relationships to see what shapes can be made. Others will begin with examples of the shapes and observe the diagonal relationships. A dynamic geometry program such as *The Geometer's Sketchpad* is an excellent vehicle for this investigation.

Angles, Lines, and Planes

The relationships between angles within a figure can initially be explored by tracing angles for comparisons, by comparing angles to a square corner, and by using informal units. With only such simple techniques, students can begin to look at relationships such as the following:

FIGURE 17.36 Diagonals of quadrilaterals.

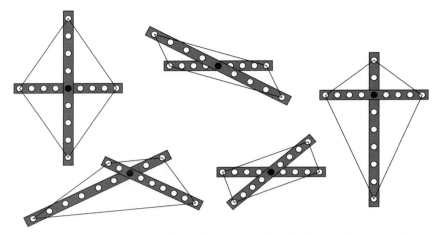

Quadrilaterals can be determined by their diagonals. Consider the length of each, where they cross, and the angles between them. What conditions will produce parallelograms? Rectangles? Rhombuses? Challenge: What properties will produce a non-isosceles trapezoid?

- The angles made by intersecting lines or by lines crossing two parallel lines: Which angles are equal? Which add up to a straight angle?
- The sum of the interior angles of polygons of different types: Is there a relationship between the number of sides and the sum of the angles? What if the shape is concave?
- The exterior angles of polygons: Extend each side of the polygon in the same direction (for example, clockwise), and observe the sum of the angles. How is the exterior angle related to the interior angle?

Similar Figures

In both two and three dimensions, two figures can be the same shape but be different sizes. At level 0, students can sort out shapes that look alike. At that level, the concept of "similar" is strictly visual and not likely to be precise. At level 1, students can begin to measure angles, lengths of sides, areas, and volumes (for solids) of shapes that are similar. By investigation, relationships between similar shapes can be observed. For example, students will find that all corresponding angles must be congruent, but other measures vary proportionately. If one side of a larger yet similar figure is triple that of the smaller figure, all linear dimensions will be triple those of the smaller figure. If the ratio of corresponding lengths is 1 to n, the ratio of areas will be 1 to n^2, and the ratio of volumes will be 1 to n^3.

All similar figures have proportional measurements. It only makes sense to combine this area of geometry with the study of proportional reasoning. In Chapter 15, similar rectangles were used to help students observe equal ratios. Recognition of similar figures and proportional rea-

soning are very much connected and are a good place to make connections in the mathematics curriculum.

A good first definition of *similar figures* is that they are figures that "look alike" but are different in size. To help with this, draw three rectangles on the board. Make two of them similar, say, with sides in the ratio of 1 to 2. The third rectangle should be very different, perhaps long and skinny with sides closer to a 1-to-10 ratio. "Which rectangles look most alike?" As in Chapter 15, this initial concept should be developed intuitively. Later a more precise definition of similarity can be provided: Two shapes are *similar* if all corresponding angles are congruent and all corresponding lengths are proportional; or two shapes are similar when one shape is a magnified or shrunk version of the other, and there are no distortions. The following activity could be done before students have been given this definition.

ACTIVITY 17.36

Build a Similar Figure

The initial task is to draw or construct at least three shapes similar to a shape you provide. (In two dimensions, rectangles, triangles, or circles are good shapes, but any polygon will work. In three dimensions, rectangular prisms or cylinders are good choices.) After making the shapes, students should measure at least three lengths on each shape. They should also compute the areas of each shape. In the case of three-dimensional shapes, they should compute areas of corresponding surfaces. For three-dimensional shapes, they should also measure or compute the volume of each shape. All measures should be entered into a table so that comparisons can be made. The follow-up task is to look for special relationships in the table of measurements. If necessary, suggest that students examine various ratios.

Figure 17.37 shows some measurements for similar rectangles and cylinders illustrating length, area, and volume ratios. Note how these three are related. Of course, the measurements your students make will probably not have nice whole numbers like these, so calculators or spreadsheets are indispensable. Once students determine that similar figures have proportional measurements, the more formal definition can be provided.

Circles

The circle is a simple shape encountered frequently in our world. Many interesting relationships can be observed between measures of different parts of the circle. Among the most astounding and important is the ratio between measures of the circumference and the diameter.

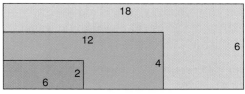

Similar rectangles

Compare the ratios of lengths
of sides and ratios of areas.

Example: Small to Large

Length	2 to	6	(1 to 3)
Area	12 to	108	(1 to 9)

Similar shapes have corresponding dimensions in predictable ratios. What measures stay the same? How do lengths, areas, and volumes change? Is that true of all shapes?

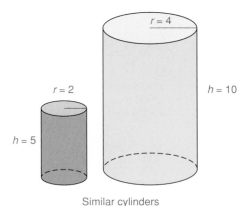

Similar cylinders

Height, radius, and circumference
are all in ratio 1 to 2.

Surface Areas:

Sides	20π to	80π	⎫
Tops	4π to	16π	⎬ 1 to 4
Volumes:	20π to	160π or 1 to 8	⎭

FIGURE 17.37 Similar solids.

ACTIVITY 17.37

Discovering Pi

Have groups of students carefully measure the circumference and diameter of many different circles. Each group should measure different circles.

Measure both the circumference and diameter of items such as jar lids, tubes, cans, and wastebaskets. To measure circumference, carefully wrap string once around the object and then measure that length of string.

Draw larger circles using a string, as shown in Figure 17.38. String can be used to measure the circumference. Also measure large circles marked on gym floors and playgrounds. Use a trundle wheel or rope to measure their circumference.

Measures of circumference and diameter should be collected from all groups and entered in a table. Ratios of the circumference to the diameter should also be computed for each circle. A scatter plot of the data should be made with the horizontal axis representing diameters and the vertical axis circumferences. If the data are entered on a spreadsheet or in a graphing calculator, the scatter plot can be generated easily and all ratios computed at once.

Most ratios should be in the neighbourhood of 3.1 or 3.2. The scatter plot should approximate a straight line through the origin. The slope of the line should also be close to 3.1. (Recall from Chapter 15 that graphs of equivalent ratios are always straight lines through the origin.) The exact ratio is an irrational number, about 3.14159, represented by the Greek letter π (pi).

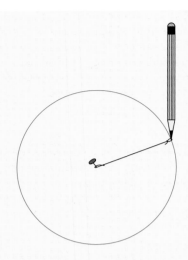

A string with two loops can be used to draw very large circles that are larger than those drawn with a compass. Two students working together will have better success than just one.

FIGURE 17.38 Drawing a circle.

What is most important in Activity 17.37 is that students develop a clear understanding of π as the ratio of circumference to diameter in any circle. The quantity π is not some strange number that appears in math formulas; it is a naturally occurring and universal ratio.

There are many other explorations that can be done with circles. For example, drawing circles with compasses and then drawing arcs with the same radius through the centre has delighted students for ages. Making three folds of a circular disk into the centre forms a very nice equilateral triangle, complete with flaps on each edge. These can then be glued together to make three of the five Platonic solids (to be discussed in connection with level 2). It is interesting to notice that all triangles drawn with two vertices on opposite ends of a diameter and the third at some other point on the circle have something in common.

Assorted Problem-Solving Activities

Problem solving continues to be an important feature of geometry activities at level 1. A few additional explorations are suggested here.

ACTIVITY 17.38

Triangle Communication

Draw any triangle. Choose exactly three measurements consisting of either angles or side lengths, and try to use these to tell a partner how to draw a triangle that is congruent to yours. What combinations of angles and sides will work?

ACTIVITY 17.39

Area Problems

Determine the areas of odd shapes and surfaces, such as those in Figure 17.39, for which there are no formulas or for which dimensions are not provided.

ACTIVITY 17.40

A Geometric Probability Problem

If a dart has an equal chance of landing at any point on a circular target, is it more likely to land closer to the centre or closer to the edge?

Tessellations Revisited

Either by using transformations or by combining compatible polygons, students at level 1 can create tessellations that are artistic and quite complex.

The Dutch artist M.C. Escher is well known for his tessellations, where the tiles are very intricate and usually take the shape of things like birds, horses, angels, or lizards. What Escher did was take a simple shape such as a triangle, parallelogram, or hexagon and perform transforma-

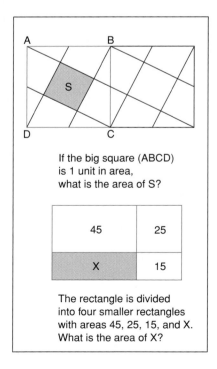

If the big square (ABCD) is 1 unit in area, what is the area of S?

45	25
X	15

The rectangle is divided into four smaller rectangles with areas 45, 25, 15, and X. What is the area of X?

FIGURE 17.39 Examples of area problems that require some analysis.

Source: Adapted from Milauskas (1987).

tions on the sides. For example, a curve drawn along one side might be translated (slid) to the opposite side. Another idea was to draw a curve from the midpoint of a side to the adjoining vertex. This curve was then rotated about the midpoint to form a totally new side of the tile. These two ideas are illustrated in part (a) of Figure 17.40. Dot paper is used to help draw the lines. *Escher-type tessellations,* as these have come to be known, are quite popular projects for students in grades 6–8. Once the tile has been designed, it can be cut from two different colours of construction paper instead of drawing the tessellation on a dot grid.

A *regular tessellation* is made of a single tile that is a regular polygon (all sides and angles congruent). Each vertex of a regular tessellation has the same number of tiles meeting at that point. A checkerboard is a simple example of a regular tessellation. A *semi-regular tessellation* is made of two or more tiles, each of which is a regular polygon. At each vertex of a semi-regular tessellation, the same collection of regular polygons comes together in the same order. A vertex (and therefore the complete semi-regular tessellation) can be described by the series of shapes that meet there. Under each example of these tessellations in part (b) of Figure 17.40, the vertex numbers are given. Students can figure out what polygons are possible at a vertex and design their own semi-regular tessellations.

Tessellations are very popular with teachers in grades 4 through 10. A number of excellent resource books from different educational publishers can be found.

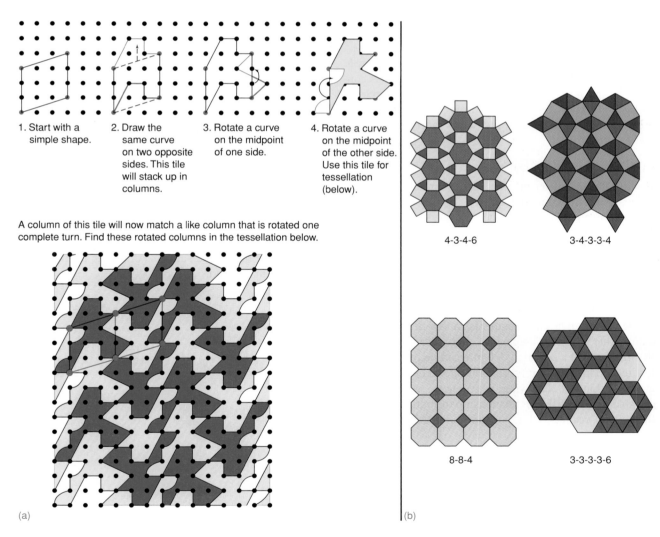

1. Start with a simple shape.

2. Draw the same curve on two opposite sides. This tile will stack up in columns.

3. Rotate a curve on the midpoint of one side.

4. Rotate a curve on the midpoint of the other side. Use this tile for tessellation (below).

A column of this tile will now match a like column that is rotated one complete turn. Find these rotated columns in the tessellation below.

4-3-4-6   3-4-3-3-4

8-8-4   3-3-3-3-6

(a)   (b)

FIGURE 17.40 **(a) One of many ways to create an Escher-type tessellation. (b) Example of semi-regular tessellations.**

Technology Note: Level 1

As students begin to do more than build with different "geometric" materials (tangrams, pattern blocks, grid drawing, etc.), the computer begins to offer powerful tools for explorations.

Math Trek, 4, 5, 6 (Nectar Foundation, 2000) provides students with an opportunity to work with transformations in different contexts. In the lesson component students learn in an interactive environment about slides, flips, and turns. A variety of real-life objects and two-dimensional figures are used to demonstrate the different motions. Students then participate in a number of different activities, trying out what they have learned. In the activities part of the program, students can apply what they have learned about transformations, sliding, flipping, and turning pentomino pieces to complete a puzzle. Both practice and test components are also included.

Mathville Starways (Courseware Solutions, 2000) and *Mathville VIP* (Courseware Solutions, 2000) also offer practice with slides, flips, and turns in a theme-based context. In Rocket Rotation, one of the many activities in *Mathville Starways*, students collect points if they rotate rockets correctly to hit the varied targets. In *Mathville VIP* students are engaged in sliding, flipping, and turning the pieces to solve the puzzles in the context of the hobby shop.

Dynamic Geometry Software

In a dynamic geometry program, points, lines, and geometric figures are drawn on the screen using only the computer mouse. Once drawn, the geometric objects can be moved about and manipulated in endless variety. Distances, lengths, areas, angles, and perimeters can be measured. When the figures are changed, the measurements update instantly.

Most significantly, geometric objects can be created with special relationships to other objects. For example, lines can be drawn perpendicular or parallel to other lines or segments. Angles and segments can be drawn congruent to other angles and segments. A point can be placed at the midpoint of a segment. A figure can be produced that is a reflection, rotation, or dilation of another figure. The amazing thing is that when a geometric object is constructed with a particular relationship to another, that relationship is maintained no matter how either object is moved or changed.

Three well-known dynamic geometry programs are *The Geometer's Sketchpad* (Key Curriculum Press, 1995), *Geometry Inventor* (LOGAL, 1994a), and *Cabri Geometry II* (Texas Instruments, 1994). *Cabri* and *Sketchpad* were originally designed for high-school students, whereas *Geometry Inventor* was designed for use in middle schools. *Inventor* and *Sketchpad* can be used profitably from grades 6–8. Of the three programs, *Geometer's Sketchpad*, approved by

provincial ministries of education, is more commonly used in schools across Canada. Although each of the programs operates somewhat differently, they are substantially alike. For this reason separate descriptions are not provided.

Dynamic Geometry Examples

To appreciate the potential (and the fun) of dynamic geometry software, you really need to try it out. In the meantime, two examples are offered here in an attempt to illustrate how these programs work.

Follow these steps in Figure 17.41 (the example uses *Sketchpad*):

1. Points A, B, and C were placed freely, and a segment was drawn between A and B.

2. A line was constructed through C parallel to AB.

3. A point D was placed on the line through C, and segments AD and DB were drawn.

   (At this time, the line through C can be moved, but it will remain parallel to AB. If A or B is moved, C remains fixed, but the line through C will rotate so that it remains parallel to AB. Through all of this, the point D will remain on the line, and triangle ABD will adjust accordingly.)

4. A segment is constructed (some steps are omitted here) so that it runs from D to a hidden line through AB and is always perpendicular to AB. This line is clearly the height of triangle ABD. *Sketchpad* permits labelling any way you wish.

5. Measurements of the height, AB, and the area of ABD are made. The formula $\frac{1}{2}$ AB × height is also calculated.

Now D can be dragged along line DC, and the height of ABD will remain constant, as will the length of AB. The area of the triangle remains fixed as long as the base and height remain fixed.

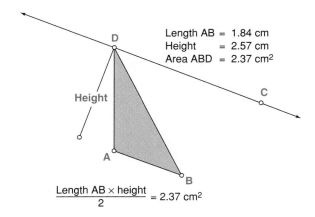

Length AB = 1.84 cm
Height = 2.57 cm
Area ABD = 2.37 cm²

$$\frac{\text{Length AB} \times \text{height}}{2} = 2.37 \text{ cm}^2$$

FIGURE 17.41 A *Geometer's Sketchpad* construction. When D is moved along the line DC, all measures are constant.

FIGURE 17.42 A *Geometer's Sketchpad* construction illustrating an interesting property of quadrilaterals.

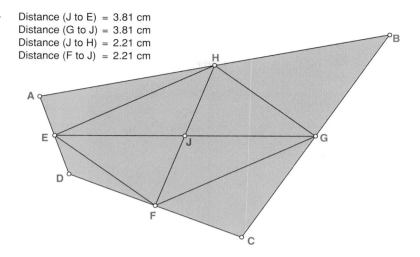

Distance (J to E) = 3.81 cm
Distance (G to J) = 3.81 cm
Distance (J to H) = 2.21 cm
Distance (F to J) = 2.21 cm

In Figure 17.42, the midpoints of a freely drawn quadrilateral ABCD have been joined. The diagonals of the resulting quadrilateral (EFGH) are also drawn and measured. No matter how the points A, B, C, and D are dragged around the screen, even if the quadrilateral is inverted, the other lines will maintain the same relationships (joining midpoints and diagonals), and the measurements will be instantly updated on the screen.

Remember that at level 1, the objects of thought are *classes* of shapes. In a dynamic geometry program, if a quadrilateral is drawn, only one shape is observed, as would be the case on paper or on a geo-board. But now that quadrilateral can be stretched and altered in endless ways. Students actually explore not one shape but an enormous number of examples from that class of shapes. If a property does not change when the figure changes, the property is attributable to the *class* of shapes rather than to any particular shape.

"Property Challenges" (Activity 17.22, p. 347), "Measure Investigation" (Activity 17.23, p. 348), all of the symmetry investigations (both line symmetry and rotational symmetry), "Diagonal Investigation" (Activity 17.34, p. 355), investigations of similarity, and "Discovering Pi" (Activity 17.37, p. 359) can all be explored profitably with dynamic geometry programs. The publishers of these programs provide excellent activities that are appropriate for level 1 investigations. Many activities are included with the software, and others are found in supplementary publications.

Tessellations on the Computer

TesselMania! (MECC, 1994) is a popular software program that makes it very easy to produce intricate tessellations that are similar in spirit to those of Escher. Using the mouse to alter one or more sides of a simple tile such as a parallelogram, square, diamond, or triangle produces the

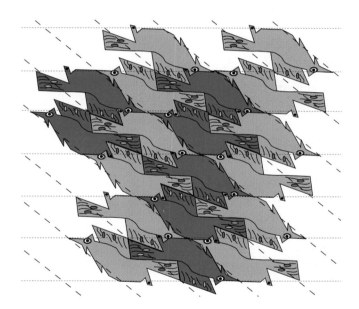

FIGURE 17.43 An example of a tessellation produced with *TesselMania! Deluxe*. Only complete tiles are shown. Notice the grid. The tile was created using the same types of transformations as illustrated in Figure 17.40.

tessellations. Select the type of pattern in advance, and the program automatically performs the necessary translations or rotations to the other sides of the tile. With a single click, the screen is filled with the resulting tessellation (see Figure 17.43). Colour and other visual properties can be added to the tiles to create results that are quite striking. This program must be used with care. It is so easy to create intricate results with no understanding of what has been done geometrically that it can quickly become an art tool rather than an opportunity to learn about transformations. But if a desired tessellation is carefully designed and planned away from the computer, the software can be used to do the tedious work of creating the finished product. Tessellations created with the program can also be analyzed to determine exactly what transformations were involved. ■■

Informal Geometry Activities: Level 2

The hallmark of level 2 activities is the inclusion of informal logical reasoning. By now, students should have developed an understanding of various properties of shapes. Now it is time to encourage conjecture and to wonder "Why?" or "What if?"

Students at this level are beginning to use informal deductive reasoning. That is, they can follow and use logical arguments, although they may have a difficult time constructing a proof of their own. Concrete models and drawings are still important, but for different reasons. Models become more a tool for thinking and verification than for exploration.

Many topics in the grade 7 and 8 curriculum lend themselves to projects that promote level 2 thinking. It is important to challenge students to reason through these topics and not just memorize formulas and procedures.

Definitions and Properties

Activities at level 2 can begin to focus on the definitions of shapes and how different classes of shapes are related. Students begin to engage in simple proofs and explore ideas that connect directly to algebra.

ACTIVITY 17.41

Minimal Defining Lists

Give each group of students a particular type of shape—for example, rectangles. The first task is to list all the possible properties for that shape that they can think of. It is useful to have students share their lists for different shapes with the class. Their classmates may have additional properties to include, or they may wish to challenge a property that they believe does not hold for all possible shapes of that type. A possible list for rectangles is offered here.

The next challenge is to find *minimal defining lists*, or MDLs, for each shape. An MDL is a subset of the properties for a shape that is "defining" and "minimal." Here, "defining" means that any shape that has all the properties on the MDL *must* be that shape. Thus, an MDL for a rectangle will guarantee that you have a rec-

tangle. "Minimal" means that if any single property is removed from the list, it is no longer defining. For example, one MDL for a rectangle is a quadrilateral with opposite sides parallel. Students should attempt to find at least two or three MDLs for their shape. A proposed list can be challenged as either not minimal or not defining. A list is not minimal if a property can be removed and the list still defines the shape. A list is not defining if a counter-example—a shape other than the one being described—can be produced using only the property list.

<u>Rectangle Properties</u>

> **Four sides**
> **Four right angles**
> **Opposite sides parallel**
> **Diagonals bisect each other**
> **Adjacent sides perpendicular**
> **Opposite sides equal in length**
> **Diagonals congruent**
> **Lines of symmetry through opposite sides**
> **Rotational symmetry of *at least* order 2**

Which properties are necessary for an MDL for a rectangle?

Creation of property lists is an important exercise for beginning level 2 thinkers. A parallelogram, rhombus, rectangle, and square each have at least four MDLs. One of the most interesting MDLS for each shape consists only of the properties of its diagonals. For example, a quadrilateral with diagonals that bisect each other and are perpendicular (intersect at right angles) is a rhombus. Several MDLs have only one property. For example, a parallelogram is a quadrilateral with rotational symmetry of at least order 2.

The MDL activity is worth further discussion. First, notice the logic component. "If a quadrilateral has these properties, *then* it must be a rectangle." Logic is also involved in disproving a faulty list. A second feature is the opportunity to discuss what constitutes a definition of the shape. In fact, any MDL could be the definition of the shape. The MDLs we usually use as definitions have probably been chosen because they are easy to understand. A quadrilateral with diagonals that bisect each other does not immediately call to mind a parallelogram. Recall that when students created their property lists, no definition was given, only a collection of shapes and a label. Theoretically, they could have created the lists without ever having heard of these shapes. Finally, notice that the object of students' thinking in this activity clearly has to do with properties, not shapes. The products of the activity are relationships amongst the properties.

Property lists and minimal property lists can be used in the logical arguments required in the next activity.

ACTIVITY 17.42

If-Then, True or False

Prepare statements using the following forms:

If it is a _____, then it is also a _____.

All _____ are _____.

Some_____ are_____.

A few examples are suggested here, but many possibilities exist.

> If it is a cylinder, then it is a prism.
>
> If it is a square, then it is a rhombus.
>
> All squares are rectangles.
>
> Some parallelograms are rectangles.
>
> All parallelograms have congruent diagonals.
>
> If it has exactly two lines of symmetry, it must be a quadrilateral.
>
> All prisms have a plane of symmetry.
>
> All pyramids have square bases. If a prism has a plane of symmetry, then it is a right prism.

The task is to decide if the statements are true or false and to present an argument to support the decision. Four or five true or false statements will make a good lesson. Once this format is understood, let students challenge each other by making their own lists of five statements. Each list should have at least one true statement and one false statement. The students' lists can be used in subsequent lessons.

Informal Proofs

Perhaps you think geometric proof seems a bit difficult for grade 7 or 8. That may be a result of your personal experience with proof in your high-school geometry. The typical high-school geometry proof is based on axioms, definitions, and theorems that have already been established. Each tiny statement must be defended.

What is quite possible in grades 7 and 8 is to have students build informal arguments that involve everyday logic. This can easily be done if students are given the opportunity to explore an idea and get a good feel for what is involved. Here are some simple examples.

ACTIVITY 17.43

Two Congruent Parts

"I have a rectangle that has been divided into two congruent parts. What could the parts be?"

There is no single answer to this question, and some answers depend on the specific rectangle in question. How students respond will depend somewhat on the materials you provide. If you suggest that students use a rectangular dot grid, you will likely get different answers than if you simply have them make sketches on plain paper.

What is interesting about "Two Congruent Parts" is the discussion that can surround any given answer. Many answers can be generalized to apply to any original rectangle or to a specific rectangle. A generalized answer is now a conjecture that can potentially be proven. You may want to explore this activity on your own for a while before reading further. Here are a few possible conjectures that are probable results of such an investigation:

1. The two shapes could be right triangles.
2. The two shapes could be squares.
3. The two shapes could be rectangles with one side the same as the given rectangle and the other half the length of the given rectangle.
4. The line dividing the rectangle will always go through the centre of the rectangle (the intersection of the diagonals).

Each of these statements is open to some scrutiny, even though most seem to be true on the surface. Consider statement 1. Here is a possible argument: If you draw a line from one corner to the opposite corner, there will be two triangles. Because the shape is a rectangle, the remaining two corners are right angles and are angles in the two triangles. Therefore, they are right triangles. The two shapes are congruent because all of the sides are congruent: One side is the same—the diagonal; the two legs of one triangle are adjacent sides of the rectangle. These sides match the opposite sides of the rectangle and are the legs of the second triangle.

Statement 2 is true only for a special class of rectangles but can be proven just as easily. Statement 4 is the toughest to prove but is certainly worth struggling with.

Another opportunity for proof is found in the next activity.

ACTIVITY 17.44

Two Polygons from One

Pose the following problem:

> Begin with a convex polygon with a given number of sides. Connect two points on the polygon with a line segment forming two new polygons. How many sides do the two resulting polygons have altogether?

Demonstrate with a few examples (see Figure 17.44). Have students explore by drawing polygons and slicing them. Encourage students to make a table showing the number of sides in the original polygon and the number of sides in the polygons that result. Students should first make conjectures about a general rule. When groups are comfortable with their conjectures, they should try to reason why their statement is correct—that is, prove the conjecture.

Obviously, the number of resulting sides depends on where the slice is made. With the exception of triangles, there are three possibilities. For each case, a clear argument can be made. The appropriate conjecture and proof are left to you. Trust that students working together can do this task.

Notice that in this task, as in others we have explored, the statements to be proved come from the students. If you write a theorem on the board and ask students to prove it, you have already told them that it is true. If, by contrast, a student makes a statement about a geometric situation the class is exploring, it can be written on the board with a question mark as a *conjecture*, a statement whose truth has not yet been determined. You can ask, "Is it true? Always? Can we prove it? Can we find a counter-example?" Reasonable deductive arguments can be forged out of discussions.

Other Topics for Level 2 Investigation

Here are some examples of topics that should be explored or extended in a way that challenges students to reason in a deductive manner. Some of these topics are new and will not have been covered before.

The Pythagorean Relationship

The *Pythagorean relationship* is so important that it deserves some special attention. In geometric terms, this relationship states that if a square is constructed on each side of a right triangle, the areas of the two smaller squares will together equal the area of the square on the longest side, the hypotenuse. To discover this relationship, consider the following activity.

ACTIVITY 17.45

The Pythagorean Relationship

Have students draw a right triangle on half-centimetre grid paper. Assign each student a different triangle, specifying the length of the two legs. Students draw a square on each leg and the hypotenuse, then find the area of all three squares. (For the square on the hypotenuse, the exact area can be found by making each of the sides the diagonal of a rectangle. [See Figure 17.45.]) Make a table for the area data (square on leg 1, square on leg 2, square on hypotenuse) and ask students to look for a relationship amongst the squares.

As an extension of the last activity, students can explore drawing other figures on the legs of right triangles and compute the areas. For example, draw semicircles or equilateral triangles instead of squares. The areas of any regular polygons drawn on the three sides of right triangles will have the same relationship.

FIGURE 17.44 Start with a polygon, and draw a segment to divide it into two polygons. How many sides will the two new polygons have?

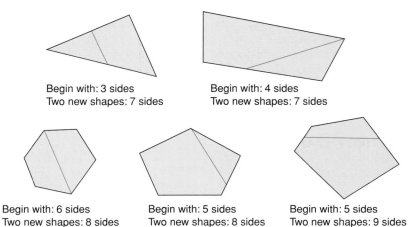

Begin with: 3 sides
Two new shapes: 7 sides

Begin with: 4 sides
Two new shapes: 7 sides

Begin with: 6 sides
Two new shapes: 8 sides

Begin with: 5 sides
Two new shapes: 8 sides

Begin with: 5 sides
Two new shapes: 9 sides

FIGURE 17.45 The Pythagorean relationship. Note that if drawn on a grid, the area of all squares is easily determined. Here, 4 + 16 = area of the square on the hypotenuse.

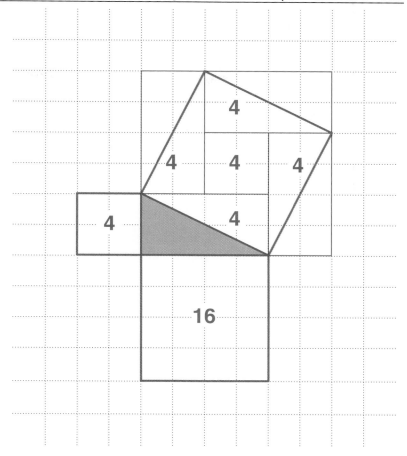

The Platonic Solids

A *polyhedron* is a three-dimensional shape with polygons for all faces. Amongst the various polyhedra, the Platonic solids are especially interesting. *Platonic solids* is the name given to the set of completely regular polyhedra. "Completely regular" means that each face is a regular polygon and every vertex has exactly the same number of faces joining at that point. An interesting visualization task for students at this level is to find and describe all of the Platonic solids. (There are five completely regular polyhedra)

ACTIVITY 17.46

Search for the Platonic Solids

Provide students with a supply of equilateral triangles, squares, regular pentagons, and regular hexagons. These can be cut from tag-board, but plastic construction kits such as Polydrons or Geoshapes are excellent for the purpose. (If you use tag-board shapes, an ample supply of tape will also be necessary.) Explain what a completely regular solid is. The task is to find as many different completely regular solids as possible.

One approach to conducting this activity is to simply present the task and allow students to tackle it on their own, with minimal additional guidance. Success will depend on their problem solving skills. Alternatively, you might suggest a systematic approach as follows: Since the smallest number of sides a face can have is three, begin with triangles, then squares, then pentagons, and so on. Furthermore, since every vertex must have the same number of faces, try three faces at a point, then four, and so on. (It is clearly impossible to have two faces at a point.)

With this plan, the students will find that, for example, they can have three, four, or five triangles coming to a point. For each of these, they can begin with a "tent" of triangles and then add more triangles so that each vertex has the same number. With three at a point, you get a four-sided solid called a *tetrahedron* (tetra = four). With four at each point you get an eight-sided solid called an *octahedron* (octa = eight). It is really exciting to build the shape with five triangles at each point. It will have 20 sides and is called an *icosahedron* (icosa = 20).

In a similar manner, students will find that there is only one solid made of squares—three at each point and six in all—a *hexahedron* (hex = six), also known as a cube. And there is only one solid with pentagons, three at each point, 12 in all. This is called a *dodecahedron* (dodeca = 12).

A fantastic skeletal icosahedron can be built out of the newspaper rods described earlier in the chapter. Start with five at a point, and join the other ends with five rods to form a pentagonal pyramid. Add two more rods at each vertex of the base, and continue from there. Keep in mind that you want five rods at each vertex and that all faces make triangles. The icosahedron will be about 1 metre in diameter and will be amazingly rigid.

Another way to make all of the Platonic solids in skeletal form is to use the bendable drinking straws described earlier. They are sufficiently rigid to work effectively.

Constructions

Too frequently, students are taught to perform constructions with a straightedge and compass but have no idea why the constructions work. In most instances, the constructions represent simple theorems that students can follow step by step, providing reasons for each step. An example of bisecting an angle is illustrated in Figure 17.46.

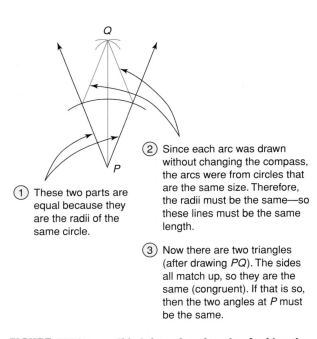

① These two parts are equal because they are the radii of the same circle.

② Since each arc was drawn without changing the compass, the arcs were from circles that are the same size. Therefore, the radii must be the same—so these lines must be the same length.

③ Now there are two triangles (after drawing *PQ*). The sides all match up, so they are the same (congruent). If that is so, then the two angles at *P* must be the same.

FIGURE 17.46 A possible informal explanation for bisecting an angle with compass and straightedge.

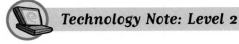

Technology Note: Level 2

Dynamic geometry software (*The Geometer's Sketchpad, Geometry Inventor,* and *Cabri*) was discussed in the context

of level 1 thinking. These programs allow students to explore an entire class of figures and observe properties or relationships that are attributable to that class. At level 2, however, the focus is on reasoning or deductive thinking. Can these computer programs help students develop deductive arguments, so that the relationships they come to believe are supported by inductive reasoning?

Consider the following situation: Suppose that you have students use a dynamic geometry program to draw a triangle, measure all of the angles, and add them up. As the triangle vertices are dragged around, the sum of the angles would remain steadfast at 180 degrees. Students can conjecture that the sum of the interior angles of a triangle is always 180 degrees, and they would be completely convinced of the truth of this conjecture based on this inductive experience. (Several activities that can be done without the computer will lead to the same conclusion.) As Michael de Villiers notes in his excellent book *Rethinking Proof with the Geometer's Sketchpad* (1999), "The observation that the sun rises every morning does not explain why this is true" (p. 24). De Villiers points out that the experience leading to the conjecture or truth should also help students develop a rationale for the result. In the case of interior angles of a triangle, the experience just described does not help students understand why it is so. Consider the following activity, which can be done easily with paper and scissors or quite dramatically with a dynamic geometry program.

ACTIVITY 17.47

Angle Sum in a Triangle

Have all students cut out three congruent triangles. (Stack three sheets of paper, and cut three shapes at one time.) Place one triangle on a line and the second directly next to it in the same orientation. Place the third triangle in the space between the triangles as shown in Figure 17.47(a). Based on this experience, what conjecture can you make about the sum of the angles of a triangle?

In a dynamic geometry program, the three triangles in Figure 17.47(a) can be drawn by starting with one triangle, translating it to the right the length of AC, and then rotating the same triangle around the midpoint of side BC. When vertices of the original triangle are dragged, the other triangles will change accordingly and remain congruent. We still do not know why the angle sum is always a straight angle, but this exploration allows students to see why it might be so. In the figure, there are lines parallel to each side of the original triangle. By using properties of angles formed by cutting two lines with a transverse line,

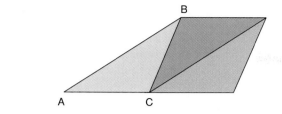

(a)

Three congruent triangles can be arranged to show that the sum of the interior angles will always be a straight angle or 180 degrees.

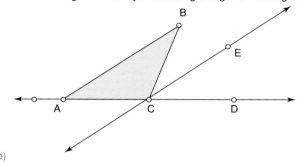

(b)

Draw CE parallel to AB. Why is angle BAC congruent to angle ECD? Why is angle ABC congruent to angle BCE?

FIGURE 17.47 Deductive, logical reasoning is necessary to prove relationships that appear true from observations.

it is easy to argue that the sum of the angles will always be a straight line [see Figure 17.47 (b); the proof is left to you]. By setting up the three triangles and focusing on parallel lines, students can develop the deductive argument or can follow an argument developed by the class.

Dynamic geometry software can be enormously powerful for helping students observe geometric relationships and make conjectures. The truth of the conjectures will often be obvious. At level 2, however, we must begin to ask why.

Defining Shapes

Some dynamic geometry programs come with built-in shapes. For example, in *Geometry Inventor,* selecting the correct icon and dragging the mouse will draw a square. The resulting shape will remain a square no matter how the vertices are dragged about the screen. Suppose that you did not have this capability.

ACTIVITY 17.48

Squares That Remain Square

Challenge students to find a way to use their dynamic geometry program (but without using a built-in capability) to create a square that will remain a square even when its sides or vertices are dragged about the screen.

There are numerous ways of solving the "Squares That Remain Square" task. Note that lines, circles, or points that may be necessary in the construction, but are not part of the square, can be hidden in the final drawing so that only the square remains. Different groups will come up with different methods. To solve the problem, reasoning must proceed from the properties to the square: If my shape maintains these relationships (properties), it must therefore remain a square. Students can be challenged to find efficient methods for creating a square. Solutions from different groups can be displayed and discussed. If a particularly interesting approach has not been used, challenge students to use that method. For example, can you make a square by using what you know about the diagonals?

The shape used in Activity 17.48 can easily be changed from a square to an equilateral triangle, an isosceles triangle, a rhombus, a kite, a trapezoid, a parallelogram, and so on. As students become more familiar with the workings of their dynamic geometry program, the possibilities for these constructions increase. For example, reflections and rotations are often useful. Even finding ways to draw a segment congruent to another segment involves valuable reasoning.

Shape Makers

If you begin with a collection of shapes that retain their properties, these can then be used to explore the relationships among classes of shapes. As a simple example, suppose you have a shape that remains a parallelogram and one that remains a rectangle. Is there a shape that can be made with the rectangle maker that cannot be made with the parallelogram maker? What about the reverse: Can the parallelogram maker make any rectangle shapes? What conjecture can you make based on these explorations?

Shape Makers: Developing Geometric Reasoning with the Geometer's Sketchpad (Battista, 1998) is a book of explorations based on this type of reasoning. The activities are appropriate for students in grades 6–8. The book includes a disk of files with all the shape makers already developed. The research-based explorations are designed to move students into level 2 thinking. With or without Battista's book, the idea of using shape makers to explore the relationships between shapes is very powerful. ■

 Assessment Notes

At the beginning of this chapter we talked about two kinds of goals for your students: goals of spatial sense and geometric thinking, and goals of content. This chapter has been organized to help you gain some perspective on these two agendas. By planning to assess geometric thinking as well as, and separately from, content, you can avoid the trap of teaching to content objectives in a superficial manner.

Activities that do not appear to directly match a content objective should at least have a level of growth objective. ■■

Clarifying Your Geometry Objectives

The greatest mistake that can be made is to take the fuzziness of geometry goals to mean that geometry is not important. You must clearly articulate the goals of your geometry program and find ways to assess them. You will then know when you are being successful, know how to defend or explain what you are doing in your geometry program, and be able to make well-documented evaluations of your students.

The most important geometric agenda for K–8 teachers is to provide experiences that move students from level 0 thinking to level 2 thinking by the end of the grade 8. Not every teacher will be able to move children to the next level. However, all teachers should be aware that the experiences they provide are the most important factor in moving children up this developmental ladder. Every teacher should be able to see some growth in geometric thinking over the course of the year.

A useful idea is to separate your objectives into those that deal with content and those that deal with general geometric growth. By attending to geometric growth in a general way, you can avoid the trap of teaching so specifically to content objectives that students are parroting back what you tell them without really developing their spatial sense.

Spatial Sense and van Hiele Objectives

In the early grades, when you can expect your students to be level 0 thinkers, you want to be sure that their thinking is increasing in its sophistication and is moving toward level 1. Here are some things you might look for:

- The child attends to a variety of characteristics of shapes in sorting and building activities.
- The child uses language that is descriptive of geometric shapes.
- The child shows evidence of geometric reasoning in solving puzzles, exploring shapes, creating designs, and analyzing shapes.
- The child recognizes shapes in the environment.
- The child solves spatial problems.

Each of these statements is indicative of either a level 0 thinker or a level 1 thinker. For example, at level 0, the types of characteristics that students are likely to pay attention to are not properties of general classes of shapes ("pointy," "fat," "has five sides," "goes up," etc.). Yet students here, as well as those at level 1, might also mention properties such as "parallel" or "symmetrical." The distinction between the two levels is found in what the properties are attributed to. At level 0, students are restricted in

thought to the shapes they are currently working with, while at level 1, students attribute properties to classes of shapes (*all* rectangles or *all* cylinders). Language, reasoning, shape recognition, and spatial problem solving can all be assessed as being appropriate for level 0 or level 1. By thinking in this manner, teachers can begin to get a sense of the geometric growth of their students beyond the specific content knowledge that may have been developed.

At the upper elementary grades, teachers can begin to think in terms of students being at level 1 or level 2 in their geometric thought. Before grade 6 or 7, very few students will have achieved level 2 thinking, but teachers need to be aware of progress in that direction. The following general indicators are more indicative of level 2 thinkers than level 1:

- The child shows improvement in spatial visualization skills.
- The child has an inclination to make and test conjectures in geometric situations.
- The child makes use of logical explanations in geometric problem solving.
- The child justifies conclusions in geometric contexts.
- The child assesses the validity of logical arguments in geometric situations.

Most of these indicators or objectives include elements of reasoning and logical sophistication that are not generally present in a level 1 thinker. As noted in the discussions of dynamic geometry software, a level 1 thinker is using inductive reasoning to discover relationships in shapes, whereas a level 2 thinker is, with guidance, beginning to develop arguments that explain why these relationships exist.

Geometric Concept Objectives

Helping students grow in geometric thought includes encouraging the development of specific concepts and ideas. As with concepts in other strands of mathematics, understanding of most ideas will vary considerably from one student to the next, and you will want to be aware of different levels of understanding.

Children should begin at level 0 and continue in level 1 to attach appropriate names to classifications of shapes that they readily recognize. It will be useful to see if the ideas are present even if the actual names are not. Shape recognition, however, should not be a major focus of your program and should not dominate your assessment agenda.

Rather than focus on mastery of definitions, be more aware of the appropriate use of terms in student activities. A student who can give you a memorized definition of a ray and an angle but shows little understanding when using these terms in an activity has not learned much of value. Similar statements can be made about a host of other geometric terms and relationships (*parallel, perpendicular, diameter, radius, skew, congruence, supplemental angles,* etc.).

For some larger concepts, understanding grows over the years as new connections and sophistication with the concepts develop. These include *line symmetry, rotational symmetry, similarity,* and *transformations (slides, flips, turns).* The concept of line symmetry, for example, may be introduced as early as grade 2 and continue to be developed through grade 8. It is not reasonable to say that Johnny "knows symmetry." It may be appropriate to note that Johnny can recognize line symmetry in simple geometric designs and can produce a symmetric image if given a simple design and a line of symmetry. But Johnny may not use or even recognize the relationship of corresponding elements in a symmetrical pattern, or know how symmetry and the reflection transformation are related. For the purpose of assessment, you need to make descriptive statements that indicate what a student does know about the concepts. You should also be descriptive in articulating your objectives.

Principles and Standards is extremely helpful for articulating growth in geometry across the grades (refer to Appendix A to see how the general standards for geometry are articulated for each grade band). These statements can help you decide on the level of sophistication that is appropriate for the particular topics you are teaching in your classroom.

Putting It All Together

In deciding what to assess and how, it is best to take a long-term view of geometry rather than a more traditional mastery-oriented approach. Two large perspectives have been suggested:

- Growth in spatial sense and geometric thought
- Understanding of geometric concepts and the corresponding terminology and notation

As a teacher, you should establish and articulate goals for your geometry program in each area. Share them with others at your grade level. Create checklists, observation schemes, and rubrics that reflect long-range objectives. In this way, you can gather data that will inform and support your geometry program. By thinking in terms of long-range objectives, you will be able to articulate the value of a pentomino activity or other geometric challenges. Furthermore, you will learn what things to look for and listen for during a geometry exploration. What a child "knows" is not just a list of terms committed to memory, but a way of thinking in a geometric context.

Reflections *on Chapter 17*

Writing to Learn

Note: There are many activities in this chapter. Rather than trying to become familiar with all the activities, pick some and start doing the same activities that are designed for students. Do not worry about being "right." What is right is to *do something,* to think about what you are doing, and to have fun. As your interest increases, you will begin to search for ideas and relationships, and you may even decide you want to do further reading. Good geometry resource books for teachers are plentiful, and articles in the journals *Teaching Children Mathematics* and *Mathematics Teaching in the Middle School* are often excellent. However, you would not go wrong by simply exploring activities from this chapter.

1. Describe what is meant by informal geometry. How is it different from the geometry usually taught in high school? How is it different from what you remember from school? What is spatial sense?

2. What do you think are the two best reasons for studying geometry? Explain.

3. Describe in your own words the first three van Hiele levels of geometric thought (levels 0, 1, and 2). Note in your description the object of thought and the product of thought. How do these ideas create a progression from one level to the next?

4. Describe the four characteristics of the van Hiele levels of thought. Reflect on why each characteristic might be important for teachers.

5. How would activities aimed at levels 0, 1, and 2 differ?

6. Select an activity from each level, and do it (perhaps with a friend). Describe your experiences. If you were a child operating at that level, describe how you might approach the activity.

7. What can you do when the students in your classroom are at different van Hiele levels of thought?

8. The use of computers was discussed at each of the three van Hiele levels. Describe at least one computer activity for each level, and explain why it is appropriate for that level rather than one that is higher or lower. If possible, try some geometric software, and consider its usefulness in relation to the van Hiele levels of thought.

9. How can a teacher assess students in terms of general geometric growth or spatial sense? Assuming that the van Hiele theory is correct, why is it important to understand where your students are in terms of that theory?

For Discussion and Exploration

1. How much emphasis should be placed on geometry in each of the different grade divisions in elementary school (e.g., primary, junior, intermediate or middle school)? For each of these divisions, consider the competing demands of other areas of the mathematics curriculum, and suggest how many weeks of the school year should be spent on geometry. What justification can you give for your position?

2. Examine the teacher's edition for any grade level of a current textbook series. Select any lesson on geometry. Remember that the authors of the student's edition are restricted to the printed page of the book. However, teachers are not so restricted. How would you teach this lesson so that it was an *effective* informal geometry lesson? Your lesson should include a hands-on activity and have a problem-solving spirit.

3. In any elementary program, computer software should be an important component of your instructional tools for teaching geometry. If you are not familiar with the types of software discussed in this chapter, find out which ones are available. Play with each program so that you learn what can be done with it. Consult the manual for teaching suggestions.

Recommendations for Further Reading

Highly Recommended

Bertheau, M. (1994). The most important thing is.... *Teaching Children Mathematics, 1,* 112–115.

This short article reminds us that children's literature is a wonderful springboard for mathematics, even if the book is not about mathematics. In addition to providing a nice idea for a good geometry lesson, the article contains suggestions for a discussion you might have with your students about shapes and what is important about them, which is a good activity to begin moving children from level 0 to level 1 thinking. It is also a good assessment activity for finding out what children know.

Del Grande, J. (1993). *Geometry and spatial sense: Addenda series, grades K–6.* Reston, VA: National Council of Teachers of Mathematics.

Findell, C.R., Small, M., Cavanagh, M., Dacey, L., Greenes, C.E., & Sheffield, L. (2001). *Navigating through geometry in pre-kindergarten–grade 2.* Reston, VA:National Council of Teachers of Mathematics.

Gavin, M.K., Sinelli, A.M., & St. Marie, J. (2001). *Navigating through geometry in grades 3–5.* Reston, VA: National Council of Teachers of Mathematics.

Geddes, D. (1992). *Geometry in the middle grades: Addenda series, grades 5–8.* Reston, VA: National Council of Teachers of Mathematics.

These two *Addenda* books are outstanding. Each provides a useful perspective on geometry for the particular grade span, and exciting activities. As with all the *Addenda Series* books, the activities are accompanied by discussions of how to "get into" the activity and develop the ideas with chil-

dren. Blackline Masters are provided when appropriate. The K–6 activities are also found in each of the elementary-grade-level *Addenda* books from NCTM.

Pugalee, D.K., Frykholm, J., Johnson, A., Slovin, H., Malloy, C., & Preston, R. (2002). *Navigating through geometry in grades 6–8.* Reston, VA: National Council of Teachers of Mathematics.

Each of these three excellent books from the *Navigation Series* provides both a perspective on the geometry standard and a collection of first-rate activities appropriate for the grade band of the book. Activities are organized under the four strands of the Geometry Standard. Each book includes a CD-ROM with the Blackline Masters, a small collection of applets, plus the full text of selected articles. Definitely a great resource.

National Council of Teachers of Mathematics. (1999). Geometry and geometric thinking [Focus Issue]. *Teaching Children Mathematics, 5(6).*

One of the best focus issues in recent years, this issue of *TCM* is full of practical ideas and useful perspectives on geometry for the early grades. Of special note is a wonderful article by Pierre van Hiele in which he describes a series of activities with a unique collection of shapes (the mosaic puzzle). This issue is a valuable resource for any teacher.

Wyat, K.W., Lawrence, A., & Foletta, G.M. (1998). *Geometry activities for middle school students with the Geometer's Sketchpad.* Emeryville, CA: Key Curriculum Press.

As noted in this chapter, dynamic geometry software belongs in the upper elementary grades. This book of explorations for the *Geometer's Sketchpad* can be used to introduce students (and you) to the software, even if you have never used *Sketchpad* before. The activities explore triangles, quadrilaterals, symmetry, transformations, and constructions. This book will convince you of the value of dynamic geometry in grades 4–8. (Also see Battista, 1998.)

Other Suggestions

Battista, M.T. (1998). *Shape makers: Developing geometric reasoning with the Geometer's Sketchpad.* Emeryville, CA: Key Curriculum Press.

Bennett, D. (1999). *Exploring geometry with the Geometer's Sketchpad* (2nd ed.). Emeryville, CA: Key Curriculum Press.

Brahier, D.J., & Speer, W.R. (1997). Worthwhile tasks: Exploring mathematical connections through geometric solids. *Mathematics Teaching in the Middle School, 3,* 20–28.

Bruni, J.V., & Seidenstein, R.B. (1990). Geometric concepts and spatial sense. In J.N. Payne (Ed.), *Mathematics for the young child* (pp. 203–207). Reston, VA: National Council of Teachers of Mathematics.

Carroll, W.M. (1998). Middle school students' reasoning about geometric situations. *Mathematics Teaching in the Middle School, 3,* 398–403.

Clements, D.H. (1999). Geometric and spatial thinking in young children. In J.V. Copley (Ed.), *Mathematics in the early years* (pp. 66–79). Reston, VA: National Council of Teachers of Mathematics.

Confer, C. (1994). *Math by all means: Geometry, grade 2.* Sausalito, CA: Math Solutions Publications.

Crowley, M.L. (1987). The van Hiele model of the development of geometric thought. In M.M. Lindquist (Ed.), *Learning and teaching geometry, K–12* (pp. 1–16). Reston, VA: National Council of Teachers of Mathematics.

Dana, M.E. (1987). Geometry: A square deal for elementary teachers. In M.M. Lindquist (Ed.), *Learning and teaching geometry, K–12* (pp. 113–125). Reston, VA: National Council of Teachers of Mathematics.

de Villiers, M.D. (1999). *Rethinking proof with the Geometer's Sketchpad.* Emeryville, CA: Key Curriculum Press.

Enderson, M.C., & Manouchehri, A. (1998). Technology-based geometric explorations for the middle grades. In L.P. Leutzinger (Ed.), *Mathematics in the middle* (pp. 193–200). Reston, VA: National Council of Teachers of Mathematics.

Ernie, K.T. (1995). Mathematics and quilting. In P.A. House (Ed.), *Connecting mathematics across the curriculum* (pp. 170–176). Reston, VA: National Council of Teachers of Mathematics.

Flores, A. (1993). Pythagoras meets van Hiele. *School Science and Mathematics, 93,* 152–157.

Fuys, D.J., & Liebov, A.K. (1993). Geometry and spatial sense. In R.J. Jensen (Ed.), *Research ideas for the classroom: Early childhood mathematics* (pp. 195–222). Old Tappan, NJ: Macmillan.

Geddes, D., & Fortunato, I. (1993). Geometry: Research and classroom activities. In D.T. Owens (Ed.), *Research ideas for the classroom: Middle grades mathematics* (pp. 199–222). Old Tappan, NJ: Macmillan.

Giganti, P., Jr., & Cittadino, M.J. (1990). The art of tessellation. *Arithmetic Teacher, 37*(7), 6–16.

Kleiman, G.M. (1995). Seeing and thinking mathematically in the middle school. In P.A. House (Ed.), *Connecting mathematics across the curriculum* (pp. 153–158). Reston, VA: National Council of Teachers of Mathematics.

Lehrer, R., & Curtis, C.L. (2000). Why are some solids perfect? Conjectures and experiments by third graders. *Teaching Children Mathematics, 6,* 324–329.

Malloy, C. (1999). Perimeter and area through the van Hiele model. *Mathematics Teaching in the Middle School, 5,* 87–90.

Manouchehri, A., Enderson, M.C., & Pugnucco, L.A. (1998). Exploring geometry with technology. *Mathematics Teaching in the Middle School, 3,* 436–442.

Mercer, S., & Henningsen, M.A. (1998). The pentomino project: Moving students from manipulatives to reasoning and thinking about mathematical ideas. In L.P. Leutzinger (Ed.), *Mathematics in the middle* (pp. 184–192). Reston, VA: National Council of Teachers of Mathematics.

Rectanus, C. (1994). *Math by all means: Geometry, grade 3.* Sausalito, CA: Math Solutions Publications.

Rubenstein, R.N., & Thompson, D.R. (1995). Making connections with transformations in grades K–8. In P.A. House (Ed.), *Connecting mathematics across the curriculum* (pp. 65–78). Reston, VA: National Council of Teachers of Mathematics.

Sandberg, S.E. (1998). A plethora of polyhedra. *Mathematics Teaching in the Middle School, 3,* 388–391.

Sconyers, J. M. (1995). Proof and the middle school mathematics student. *Mathematics Teaching in the Middle School, 1,* 516–518.

Senk, S.L., & Hirschhorn, D.B. (1990). Multiple approaches to geometry: Teaching similarity. *Mathematics Teacher, 83,* 274–280.

Serra, M. (1993). *Discovering geometry: An inductive approach.* Emeryville, CA: Key Curriculum Press.

Teppo, A. R. (1991). Van Hiele levels of geometric thought revisited. *Mathematics Teacher, 84,* 210–221.

Whiteley, W. (1999). Mathematics Lecture II: The decline and rise of geometry in 20th century North America. In J. Grant McLoughlin (Ed.), *Proceedings of the Canadian Mathematics Education Study Group,* (7-21).

Chapter 18

Exploring Concepts of Probability and Data Analysis

The related topics of probability and data analysis represent two of the most prominent uses of mathematics in our everyday lives. We hear about the possibility of contracting a particular disease, having twins, winning the lottery, or living to be 100. Simulations of complex situations are frequently based on simple probabilities and are then used in the design of highways, storm sewers, medical treatments, sales promotions, and spacecraft. Graphs and statistics bombard the public in advertising, opinion polls, reliability estimates, population trends, health risks, and the progress of students in schools and schools in school systems, to name only a few areas.

To deal with this information, students should have plenty of informal yet meaningful experiences throughout their school years with the basic concepts involved. The emphasis from elementary to high school should be placed on activities leading to intuitive understanding and conceptual knowledge, rather than on computations and formulas.

 BIG IDEAS

1. The possible occurrence of a future event, compared to all possible events, can be characterized along a continuum from impossible to certain—i.e., impossible, less likely, equally likely, more likely, or certain. To determine the likelihood of an event's occurrence along this continuum is to determine the probability of its happening. Assigning a number from 0 (impossible) to 1 (certain) to a future event is a measurement of the probability of that event.

2. Data sets can be analyzed in various ways to provide a sense of the shape of the data, including how spread out they are (range, variance) and how centred (mean, median, mode). Measures that describe data with numbers are called statistics. Data can be organized in various graphical forms to convey information visually.

3. A collection of objects with various attributes can be classified or sorted in different ways. A single object can belong to more than one class. Classification is the first step in the organization of data.

4. Data are organized to help with decision-making or inference-making, or the development of new ideas about situations or the populations from which the data are drawn.

Probability and Data Analysis in Schools

A number of factors have led to the inclusion and development of probability and data analysis instruction in elementary and middle schools in recent years:

Increased awareness of the importance of probability and data analysis concepts and methods

An emphasis on experimental or simulation-based approaches to probability (instead of rules and formulas)

The use of simplified yet powerful technology to describe data visually without complicated procedures

The use of calculators and computers, especially graphing calculators, to conduct thousands of random trials of experiments, from flipping coins to simulating baseball batting performances; to do the tedious work of constructing graphs; and to perform computations on large sets of numbers almost instantaneously

In 1989, the NCTM focused attention on the topics of probability and statistics when it included standards for specifically addressing these topics at all grade levels. With the *Principles and Standards for School Mathematics,* the NCTM expanded the emphasis on these topics by making Data Analysis and Probability one of the five content standards for all grades. These initiatives of the NCTM have significantly influenced the inclusion and development of Data Management as a key concept in Canadian curriculum documents for K-8.

Data analysis refers to the collection and organization of information for the purpose of analyzing it to answer questions or supply information about the population from which it was taken. *Statistics,* on the other hand, refers to methods of planning experiments for obtaining data and drawing conclusions or making decisions on the basis of available data (James & James, 1976). Statistics is also used in reference to the numbers that describe data, such as *mean* and *range.* So even kindergarten children can be involved in gathering data and making graphs to describe data—doing data analysis. As children move through school, the methods of data analysis become more sophisticated, with new graphing techniques and the use of statistics.

Similarly, concepts of chance can be developed long before sophisticated ideas of probability are introduced. Both provincial and territorial curricula and the *Principles and Standards* recognize that children need to begin these experiences in the earliest grades so that an intuitive understanding of probability, on which more traditional methods can be built, is developed.

Introduction to Probability

Let's first experiment with some basic ideas of probability before considering how to help children develop these ideas.

Two Experiments

Consider answering the following two questions by actually performing the experiments enough times to make a reasonable guess at the results.

TOSSING A CUP

Toss a small "portion" cup or other small cup once or twice, letting it land on the floor. Notice that there are three possible ways for the cup to land: upside down, right side up, or on its side. If the cup were tossed this way 100 times, about how many times do you think it would land in each position?

FLIPPING TWO COINS

If you were to flip one coin 100 times, you would expect that it would come up heads about as many times as tails. If two coins were tossed 100 times, about how many times do you think they would both come up heads?

A quick way to conduct these experiments is to work in groups. If 10 people each do 10 trials and pool their data, the time needed for 100 trials is not long. Twenty cups can be placed on a tray and tossed at one time. Even if you do not actually do the experiments, jot down your predictions now before reading on.

Theoretical versus Experimental Probability

In the cup toss, there is no practical way to determine the results before you start. However, once you had results for 100 flips, you would undoubtedly feel more confident in predicting the results of the next 100 flips. If you gathered data on that same cup for 1000 trials, you would feel even more confident in your prediction. Say that your cup lands on its side 78 times out of 100. You might choose a round figure of 75 or 80 for the 100 tosses. If, after 200 flips, there were 163 sideways landings, you would feel even more confident of the 4- to-5 ratio and predict about 800 sideways landings for 1000 tosses. The more flips that are made, the more confidence you gain in your predictions. You have determined an *experimental probability* of $\frac{4}{5}$, or 80 percent, for the cup to land on its side. It is experimental because it is based on the results of an experiment rather than a theoretical analysis of the cup.

In a one-coin toss, the prediction of about 50 percent heads, based on your understanding of a fair coin toss, could confidently be made before you flipped the coin. Your prediction for two heads in the two-coin version may be more difficult. It is quite common for people to observe that there are three types of outcomes: two heads, two tails, and one of each; so they predict that two heads will come up about one-third of the time. (What did you predict?) The prediction is based on their analysis of the experiment, not on experimental results. However, after conducting the experiment they are surprised to find that two heads come up only about one-fourth of the time. This experience might cause them to return to their original analysis and look for an error in their thinking.

There is only one way that two heads will occur and one way for two tails to occur, but there are *two* ways that a head and a tail could result: Either the first coin is heads and the second tails, or vice versa. As shown in Figure 18.1, that makes a total of four possible outcomes, not three. The assumption that each outcome is equally likely was correct. Each time you toss a coin you have one out of two chances that a head or a tail will result, when two coins are being tossed. Therefore, the correct probability of two heads is 1 out of 4, or $\frac{1}{4}$, not $\frac{1}{3}$. This *theoretical probability* is based on a logical analysis of the experiment, not on experimental results.

First Coin	Second Coin
Head	Head
Head	Tail
Tail	Head
Tail	Tail

FIGURE 18.1 Four possible outcomes of flipping two coins.

When we talk about probability, we are assigning some measure of chance to an experiment. An *experiment* is any activity that has two or more clearly discernible results or *outcomes*. Both tossing the cup and tossing the two coins were experiments. Observing tomorrow's weather and shooting 10 free throws on the basketball court are also experiments. The collection of all outcomes is generally referred to as the *sample space*. As you have already seen, the toss of two coins has four outcomes in the sample space. The set of possible outcomes for tomorrow's weather can be described in many ways: "precipitation or no precipitation," or "dry, rain, sleet, or snow." An *event* is any subset of the outcomes or any subset of the sample space. For the two-coin experiment, the event with which we were concerned was getting two heads. For the free-throw shoot, we might be interested in the event of getting five or more baskets out of the 10 possible tosses.

When all possible outcomes of a simple experiment are equally likely, the *theoretical probability* of an event is

$$\frac{\text{Number of outcomes in the event}}{\text{Number of possible outcomes}}$$

In real-world situations, outcomes are often not equally likely, as they are for coin flips or dice rolls. The cup-tossing experiment, though not a practical situation, is "muddy" and real. The outcomes are difficult to predict, and they are not equally likely. In situations like these, we can determine the observed relative frequency of the event by performing the experiment a lot of times. The *relative frequency* of an event is

$$\frac{\text{Number of observed occurrences of the event}}{\text{Total number of trials}}$$

It should be clear that the relative frequency is not a good predictor of the chance of the event's happening, unless the number of trials is very large. The *experimental probability* of an event is the ratio that the relative frequency approaches as the number of trials gets infinitely large. Because it is impossible to perform an infinite number of trials, we must be satisfied with some large number of trials. The more trials, the more confident we might be that the experimental probability is close to the actual probability.

Implications for Instruction

There are many reasons why an experimental approach to probability—actually conducting experiments and examining outcomes—is important in the classroom.

■ It is significantly more intuitive. Results begin to make sense, as they are not the product of some abstract rule.

■ It eliminates guessing at probabilities and wondering, "Did I get it right?" Counting or trying to determine the number of elements in a sample space can be very difficult without some intuitive background information.

■ It provides an experiential background for examining the theoretical model. When you begin to sense that the probability of two heads is $\frac{1}{4}$ instead of $\frac{1}{3}$, the analysis in Figure 18.1 seems more reasonable.

■ It helps students see how the ratio of a particular outcome to the total number of trials begins to converge toward (get closer and closer to) a fixed number. For an infinite number of trials, the relative frequency and theoretical probability would be the same.

■ It develops an appreciation for a simulation approach to solving problems. Many real-world problems are actually solved by conducting experiments or simulations.

■ It is a lot more fun and motivating than a rules-based approach! Even searching for a correct explanation in the theoretical model is more interesting.

So, try to use an experimental approach in the classroom, whenever possible. If a theoretical analysis (such as the two-coin experiment) is possible, it should also be examined, and the results compared. Rather than correcting a student error in an initial analysis, we can let experimental results guide and correct student thinking.

Developing Probability Concepts

When informal ideas about chance and probability are developed early, they provide the necessary background for concepts to be constructed later, at the middle and secondary levels.

Early Concepts of Chance

Children in kindergarten and the primary grades need to develop an intuitive concept of chance: the idea that some events, when compared with others, have a better or worse likelihood, or an approximately equal likelihood, of happening.

Many young children believe that an event will happen "because it's my favourite colour" or "because it's lucky" or "because it did it that way last time." Many games such as Candy Land or Snakes and Ladders are very exciting for young children, who do not comprehend that the outcomes are entirely random. When they finally learn that they have no control over the outcome, children begin to look for other games where there is some element of player determination.

ACTIVITY 18.1

Is It Likely?

Ask students to judge various events as *certain, impossible,* or *possible* ("might happen"). Consider these examples:

It will rain tomorrow.

Drop a rock in water, and it will sink.

Trees will talk to us in the afternoon.

The sun will rise tomorrow morning.

Three students will be absent tomorrow.

George will go to bed before 8:30 tonight.

You will have two birthdays this year.

Children describe or make up events that are certain, impossible, or possible. For each event, they should justify their estimate of likelihood.

ACTIVITY 18.2

Who Will Win?

Play simple games where the chance of one side winning can be controlled. Before the games are played, have students predict who will win and why. Afterward, discuss why they think things turned out as they did. For example, the hockey game in Figure 18.2 starts with a counter in the centre. Two players take turns spinning a spinner. After each spin the counter is moved one space toward the goal closest to the colour that came up on the spinner. Play the game with different spinners. As a variation, let students choose a spinner on each turn. Ask them to explain their choices.

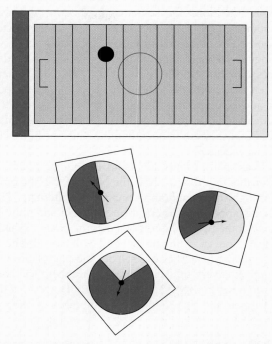

FIGURE 18.2 **A simple game of chance played with different spinners helps young children with basic concepts of chance.**

ACTIVITY 18.3

Predictions

Have students make predictions about the outcomes of simple experiments, using the terms *more, less, all,* and *none.* For example, show children how many red and yellow cubes you have in a bag. Then let children draw cubes one at a time without looking and put them back each time. "If we do this 10 times, will there be more reds, fewer reds, all reds, or no reds?" Change the number of each colour and repeat. The same activity can be done by spinning spinners, rolling dice, drawing cards, or using any random device that you can adjust. Include situations in which the outcomes are certain to occur, such as placing all yellow cubes in the bag.

Determining Probabilities for Simple Events

From a basic understanding that one event can be more or less likely to occur than another, students can begin to predict specific ratios of outcomes of simple events. If students have not yet worked with the concepts of ratio, you might want to use language such as "65 out of 100." A discussion of reasons for students' predictions is always important. The experiment should then be conducted, and the results compared with expected outcomes.

Figure 18.3 illustrates a number of simple random devices that can be used for experiments. To get large numbers, let groups of students conduct the same experiment and combine their results. Ask students to notice that the results for smaller numbers of trials are all different and that they are frequently quite different from what might be expected.

Occasionally, have students list the outcomes of their experiments in a row to show the order of the outcomes. Interestingly, truly random events do not alternate. They frequently appear in clusters or runs. If eight odd numbers in a row come up on the roll of a die, the chance remains exactly $\frac{1}{2}$ (1 out of 2) that the next roll will be odd. The die has no memory. The previous roll of a die cannot affect the next roll. It is very unlikely that even numbers will come up seven times in a row (1 chance in 128). However, if that does happen, the chance for an even number on the next roll is still $\frac{1}{2}$.

Experiments with Two or More Independent Events

Flipping two coins and observing the result of each is an example of an experiment with two independent events.

The flip of one coin has no effect on the other. The events are *independent*. Another example is that of drawing a card and spinning a spinner. Many interesting experiments involve two or more separate, independent events.

Determining the experimental probability of compound events is no different than for simple events. The experiment is performed numerous times, and the number of favourable results is compared, as before, to the total number of trials. The challenge comes in trying to reconcile experimental results with theoretical ones.

Suppose that a class is conducting an experiment to determine the probability of rolling a 7 with two dice. They might tally their results in a chart showing each sum from 2 to 12 as a single event, as in part (a) of Figure 18.4.

The results of their experiment will show clearly that these events are not equally likely and that in fact the sum of 7 has the best chance of occurring. To explain this, they might look for the combinations that make 7:1 and 6, 2 and 5, and 3 and 4. But there are also three combinations for 8. It seems as though 8 should be just as likely as 7, and yet it is not.

Now suppose that the experiment is repeated. For the sake of clarity, this time suggest that students roll two different-coloured dice and that they keep the tallies in a chart like the one in part (b) of Figure 18.4.

The results of a large number of rolls of the dice indicate what one would expect: namely, that all 36 cells of this chart are equally likely. But there are more cells with a sum of 7 than any other number. Therefore, students were really looking for the event that consists of any of the six ways, not three ways, that two dice can add up to 7. There

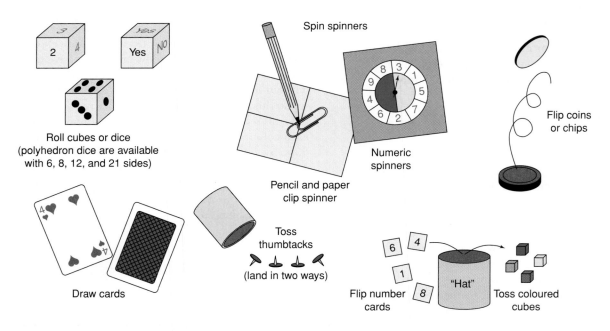

FIGURE 18.3 There are many simple ways to produce random outcomes.

are six outcomes out of a total of 36 in the desired event, for a probability of $\frac{6}{36}$, or $\frac{1}{6}$.

When investigating the theoretical probability of a compound event, it is helpful to use a chart or diagram that keeps the two independent events separate and illustrates the combinations. The matrix in Figure 18.4(b) is one good suggestion when there are only two events. A tree diagram (Figure 18.5) is another method that can be used with any number of events.

ACTIVITY 18.4

Compound Outcomes

The following are examples of compound events composed of independent events.

> Rolling an even sum with two dice
> Spinning blue and flipping a cup on end
> Getting two blues out of three spins (depends on spinner)
> Having a tack or a cup land right way up if each is tossed once
> Getting *at least* two heads from a toss of four coins

Have students first make and defend a prediction for the probability of an event. Then have them conduct an experiment with a large number of trials, comparing their results to their predicted probabilities. Finally, they should reconcile the differences. Where appropriate, students can try to determine the theoretical probability as part of their final analysis of the experiment.

Words and phrases such as *and, or, at least,* and *no more than* can also cause children some trouble. Of special note is the word *or,* since its everyday usage is generally not the same as its strict logical use in mathematics. In mathematics, *or* includes the case of *both.* So in the tack-and-cup example, the event includes tack right way up, cup right way up, and *both* tack *and* cup right way up. It is also worth noting that the word *and* has a somewhat different connotation in logical mathematical usage than it does in everyday common use. In mathematics, *and* limits the possible outcomes, resulting in the union of the two events, the tack right way up *and* the cup right way up.

Sum of Two Dice

2	卌 I
3	卌 卌
4	卌 卌 卌 IIII
5	卌 卌 卌 IIII
6	卌 卌 卌 卌 卌 IIII
7	卌 卌 卌 卌 卌 卌 卌 IIII
8	卌 卌 卌 卌 卌 卌 IIII
9	卌 卌 卌 卌 卌
10	卌 卌 卌 I
11	卌 II
12	卌 卌

(a)

Red Die

Green Die	1	2	3	4	5	6
1	卌	卌 I	卌 III	卌 II	卌 IIII	(卌 II)
2	卌 IIII	卌 III	卌 I	卌 卌	(卌 III)	卌 II
3	卌 卌	卌	卌 III	(卌 II)	卌 卌 II	卌 IIII
4	卌 II	卌 卌 II	(卌 IIII)	卌 卌	卌 卌 II	卌 III
5	卌 IIII	(卌 卌 II)	卌 卌	卌 III	卌	卌 IIII
6	(卌 III)	卌 IIII	卌 III	卌 II	卌 IIII	卌 II

There are six ways to get 7.

(b)

FIGURE 18.4 Tallies can account only for the total (a) or keep track of the individual dice (b).

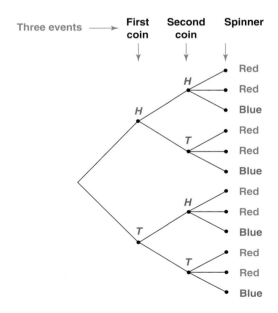

FIGURE 18.5 A tree diagram showing all possible outcomes for two coins and a spinner that is $\frac{2}{3}$ red.

Theoretical Probabilities with an Area Model

One way to determine the theoretical probability of a compound event is to list all possible outcomes and count those that are favourable, that is, those that make up the event. This is a useful and intuitive first approach. However, it has some limitations. First, what if the events are not all equally likely? For example, the spinner may be only $\frac{1}{4}$ blue. Second, it is difficult to move from that approach to even slightly more sophisticated methods. An area model approach has been used successfully with students in grade 5 and is quite helpful for some reasonably difficult problems.

Suppose that after many experiences, you have decided that your cup lands on its side 82 percent of the time. The experiment is to toss the cup and draw a card from a deck. What is the probability that the cup will land on its side *and* you will draw a spade? Draw a square to represent one whole. First partition the square to represent the cup toss, 82 percent and 18 percent, as in Figure 18.6(a). Now partition the square in the other direction to represent the four equal card suits. As shown in Figure 18.6(b), one region is the proportion of time that both events, sideways and spades, happen. The area of this region is $\frac{1}{4}$ of 82 percent, or 20.5 percent.

You can use the same drawing to determine the probability of other events in the same experiment. For

example, what is the probability of the cup landing on either end *or* drawing a red card? As shown in Figure 18.6(c), half of the area of the square represents the possibility of drawing a red card. Therefore, this section represents the case of drawing a red card *and* an end landing. The other half of the 18 percent end landings will occur when a red card is not drawn. Half of the 18 percent area is 9 percent. The total area for a red card *or* an end landing is 59 percent.

The area approach for experiments involving two independent events when the probability of each is known is easy for students to use and understand. For more than two independent events, further subdivision of each region is reasonable and necessary, and the use of *and* and *or* connectives can be dealt with easily. It is clear to students, without memorizing formulas, how probabilities can be combined.

Simulations

Simulation is a technique used for answering real-world questions or making decisions in complex situations where an element of chance is involved. To see what is likely to happen in the real event, a model must be designed that has the same probabilities as the real situation. For example, in designing a rocket, a large number of related systems all have some chance of failure. Various combinations of failures might cause serious problems with the rocket. Knowing the probability of serious failures will help determine if a redesign is necessary, or backup systems are required. It is not reasonable to make repeated tests of the actual rocket. Instead, a model that simulates all of the chance situations is designed and run repeatedly, most likely with the help of a computer. The computer model can simulate hundreds or even thousands of flights, and an estimate of the chance of failure can be made. Many real-world situations lend themselves to simulation analysis. Following is a series of steps (Gnanadeskian, Schaeffer, & Swift, 1987) that can serve as a useful guide for working through a simulation.

1. *Identify key components and assumptions of the problem.*
2. *Select a random device for the key components.* Any random device (e.g. spinners, computer software graphics showing a coin being flipped) can be selected that has outcomes with the same probability as the key component.
3. *Define a trial.* A trial consists of simulating a series of key components until the situation has been completely modeled one time.
4. *Conduct a large number of trials, and record the information.*
5. *Use the data to draw conclusions.*

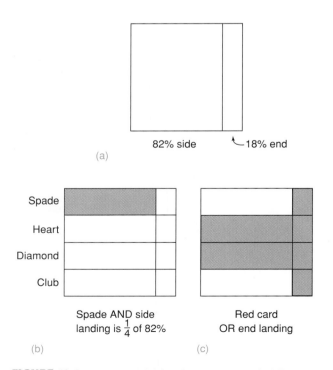

(a)

Spade
Heart
Diamond
Club

Spade AND side
landing is $\frac{1}{4}$ of 82%

(b)

Red card
OR end landing

(c)

FIGURE 18.6 An area model for determining probabilities.

Steps 4 and 5 are the same as solving a probability problem by experimental means. The interesting problem-solving aspects of simulation activities are in the first three steps, where the real-world situation is translated into a model. Translation of real-world information into models is the essence of applied mathematics.

Here are a few more examples of problems that can be solved by simulation and are easy enough to be tackled by middle-school students.

In a true-or-false test, what is the probability of getting 7 out of 10 questions correct by guessing alone? (*Key component:* answering a question. *Assumption:* Chance of getting it correct is $\frac{1}{2}$.) What if the test were multiple-choice, with 4 choices?

In a group of five people, what is the chance that two were born in the same month? (*Key component:* month of birth. *Assumption:* All 12 months are equally likely.)

Casey's batting average is .350. What is the chance he will go hitless in a complete nine-inning game? (*Key component:* getting a hit. *Assumptions:* Probability of a hit for each at-bat is .35. Casey will get to bat four times in the average game.)

Krunch-a-Munch cereal packs one of five games in each box. About how many boxes should you expect to buy before you get a complete set? (*Key component:* getting one game. *Assumption:* Each game has a $\frac{1}{5}$ chance. *Trial:* Use a $\frac{1}{5}$ random device repeatedly until all five outcomes appear; the average length of a trial is the answer to the question.) What is the chance of getting a set in eight or fewer boxes?

 ### *Technology Note*

Truly random events often occur in unexpected groups; a fair coin may turn up heads five times in a row. A 100-year flood may hit a town twice in 10 years. Hands-on random devices such as spinners, dice, or cubes drawn from a bag give students an intuitive feel for the imperfect distribution of randomness. Students believe in the unbiased outcomes of these devices. The downside is that the use of spinners and bags of cubes requires a lot of time to produce a large number of trials and keep track of the results. This is where technology can help enormously.

Electronic devices, including some relatively simple calculators and graphing calculators, are designed to produce random outcomes at the press of a button. Computer software is available that flips coins, spins spinners, or draws numbers from a hat. Calculators produce random numbers that can then be interpreted in terms of the desired device. As long as students accept the results generated by the technology as truly random or equivalent to the hands-on device, technology offer significant advantages for performing experiments.

Probability Software

Software for exploring probability concepts can generally be described as computer-animated random devices. Graphics show students the coins being flipped or the spinner being spun. Most allow different speeds. In a slow version, students may watch each spin of a spinner or coin flip. Faster speeds show the recording of each trial but omit the graphics. An even quicker mode simply shows the cumulative results. The number of trials can be set by the user. Volume 1 of MathKeys: Unlocking Probability (MECC, 1995c) includes options for a single coin, a single die, a choice of six different two-colour spinners, or two colours of marbles drawn from a bag. In Volume 2, compound experiments using multiple spinners, dice, or marble bags can be designed and run. As is typical of these programs, results are not only tallied but also shown on a bar graph for a visual display of outcome ratios. Both volumes include some interesting games that are problematic and permit students to apply their understanding of probability.

The Probability Constructor (LOGAL, 1994b), designed for students in the middle grades, is more sophisticated and offers many more options. Within each of six devices, the probability of the outcomes is adjustable. An area model allows for the exploration of compound events, and outcomes can be displayed in a variety of ways. The support materials include a complete series of lessons and useful teacher notes.

Math Trek (Nectar Foundation, 2000) provides students with an opportunity to engage in interactive tutorials and activities to expand their knowledge of probability. Experiments are not designed by students; rather, a series of structured activities are presented in a meaningful context. For primary children, Math Trek 1, 2, 3 looks at probability in the context of games found in a toy store. The games of chance involve spinning a spinner or rolling dice to find out if there is an equal chance of landing on a particular colour or getting a certain number. Results are then recorded in a graph. In Math Trek 4, 5, 6 students learn about concepts related to probability in the interactive tutorial. They are then given a chance to apply this learning as they engage in activities, which involve spinning spinners, rolling dice, and tossing coins.

Even with only one computer in the room, a good probability program is a worthwhile investment.

Probability with Calculators

Many relatively simple calculators include a key that will produce a random number. Examples are the Casio FX-55, or the recently introduced TI-34 Roman Numeral 2, and of course any graphing calculator such as the TI-73 and the newer TI-73 Explorer, designed for middle-school students. Usually, the random numbers generated are between 0 and 1. Students will need some direction in using these random-number generators to their advantage. Each number generated will likely have eight or more decimal places. A list of five numbers might look like this:

> 0.8904433368
>
> 0.0232028877
>
> 0.1669322714
>
> 0.1841957303
>
> 0.5523714952

How could a list of decimals like this replace flipping a coin or spinning a spinner? Suppose you multiplied each number by 2. The results would be between 0 and 2. If you focus only on the whole number part of these numbers, you would have a series of zeros and ones which could then be used to stand for heads and tails, boys and girls, true and false, or any other pair of equally likely outcomes. For three outcomes, the same as a $\frac{1}{4}$, $\frac{1}{4}$, $\frac{1}{2}$ spinner, you might decide to look at the first two digits of the number and assign values from 0 to 24 and from 25 to 49 to the two quarter portions and values 50 to 99 for the one-half portion. Alternatively, you could multiply each number by 4 and ignore the decimal part, which would produce random numbers 0, 1, 2, and 3. These numbers could then be assigned to the desired outcomes. In effect, random numbers can simulate any simple random device.

With graphing calculators, the random number generator can be used within a simple program that produces the numbers and stores them in a list. This list can be displayed graphically. Calculators such as the TI-73 or the TI-73 Explorer have built-in coin and dice functions that will graph the results of flipping a coin or rolling dice.

Although computer programs are much faster, allow for more variation, and include attractive graphics, the advantage of calculator approaches is availability. Every student can design and run an experiment individually. When computers are at a premium, this is a significant advantage. ■■

Gathering Data to Answer Questions

The first bullet in the Data Analysis and Probability standard of *Principles and Standards* says students should "formulate questions that can be addressed with data and collect, organize, and display relevant data to answer them" (NCTM, 2000, p. 48). The significant feature of this statement that has been missing in the past is that there should be a purpose for data collection—to answer a question, just as in the real world. In all grades, the agenda for analysis of data should be to increase the available information about some aspect of our world. This is what political pollsters, advertising agencies, market researchers, census takers, wildlife managers, and hosts of others do: gather data to answer questions. This means that the process of data analysis should begin with questions. Preferably, these questions should be about things of interest to the students.

When students formulate the questions they want to ask, the data they gather become more and more meaningful. In this way the manner in which they organize the data and the techniques they use for analyzing them have a purpose. For example, one class of students gathered data concerning which cafeteria foods were most often thrown in the garbage. As a result of these efforts, certain items were removed from the regular menu. The activity illustrated to students the power of organized data, and it helped them get food they liked better.

Ideas for Questions and Data

Often the need to gather data will come naturally in the course of class discussion or from questions that arise in other content areas. Science, of course, is full of measurements and thus abounds in data requiring analysis. Social studies is also full of opportunities for posing questions that require analysis of data. The next few sections offer some additional ideas.

Classroom Questions

Young children can learn about themselves, their families and pets, the animals in their neighbourhood, measurements such as their arm span or time required to get to school, their likes and dislikes, and so on. At the K–2 level, the easiest questions to deal with are those that can be answered by each class member's contribution of one piece of data. When there are lots of possibilities, suggest that students restrict the number of choices. Here are a few ideas:

Favourites: TV shows, fruit, season of the year, colour, hockey team, pet, ice cream flavour

Numbers: Number of pets, sisters, or brothers; hours watching TV or hours of sleep; birthdays (month or day of month); bedtime

Measures: Height, arm span, area of foot, long-jump distance, letters in name, time to button a sweater, daily temperature, weather, shadow length, rainfall

Beyond the Classroom

As children get older, they can begin to think about various populations and the differences between them. For example, how are grade 5 students similar to or different from grade 7 or 8 students? Students might examine questions concerning boys versus girls, adults or teachers versus students, or categories of workers or university graduates. These situations involve issues of sampling and making generalizations and comparisons.

The news media frequently report what the latest survey reveals about the "typical" family, business, teenager, or member of some other population or group. How did they survey everyone, and what does "typical" mean? Do the students in your classroom believe they are typical? Are they like those in the next classroom or the next grade level? Describing a group usually involves asking a variety of questions, and deciding which questions to ask is not nearly as easy as it may sound. How many questions should be asked? Should they be multiple choice? If not, how will the answers be handled? To describe a large group (say, the school), how many people should be surveyed? How should they be selected? Students should be involved in making these decisions as they formulate their questions and design surveys.

Other Sources of Information

It's important that students feel free to ask questions that can be answered by gathering the data themselves. Gathering data can also mean using information that has been collected by others. For example, newspapers, almanacs, sports record books, maps, and various government agencies such as Statistics Canada (www.statcan.ca) are sources of data that may be used to answer student questions. (Statistics Canada is an excellent source for a variety of real data that can easily be used by students in many different ways.) Students may be interested in facts about another country as a result of a social studies unit. Olympic records in various events over the years, or data related to space flight, are other examples of topics around which student questions may be formulated. For these and hundreds of other questions, data can be found on the World Wide Web. (See Chapter 23.)

The Shape of Data

The shape of any data is important conceptually to the process of data analysis. It gives a sense of how data are spread or grouped, what characteristics they have, and what they tell us in a global way about the population from which they are taken.

Each of the graphical techniques we will discuss gives a visual picture of the shape of data. Students should learn that different graphs provide different snapshots of the data. For the particular question being answered, graphs are chosen in relation to the shape of the data.

Statistical techniques provide a numerical picture of the shape of the data. The numbers can be considered as measures of the shape. For example, the median tells us where the centre is. The range tells about the spread of the data.

The better we can answer the question "What is the shape of the data?" the better we can answer the question that prompted the data to be gathered in the first place.

Classification and Data Analysis

Classification involves making decisions about how to categorize things. This basic activity is fundamental to data analysis. In order to formulate questions and decide how to represent data that have been gathered, decisions must be made regarding how different things should be categorized. Farm animals, for example, could be grouped by number of legs; by type of product they provide; by those that work, those that provide food, and those that are pets; by size or colour; by the type of food they eat; and so on. Each of these groupings is based on a different attribute of the animals.

Young children need experiences with categorizing things in different ways in order to learn to make sense of real-world data. Attribute activities are specifically designed to develop this flexible reasoning about the characteristics of data.

Attribute Materials

Attribute materials are sets of objects that lend themselves to being sorted and classified in different ways. *Unstructured* attribute materials include such things as seashells, leaves, the children themselves, or the set of the children's shoes. *Attributes* are characteristics of an object or thing that are used to determine the different ways that the objects can be sorted. For example, hair colour, height, and gender are attributes of children. Each attribute may have a number of different *values:* for example, blond, brown, or red (for the attribute of hair colour); tall or short (for height); male or female (for gender).

A *structured* set of attribute pieces has exactly one piece for every possible combination of attribute values. For example, commercial sets of plastic attribute blocks are designed so they vary according to four attributes: colour (red, yellow, blue), shape (circle, triangle, rectangle, square, hexagon), size (big, little), and thickness (thick, thin). In the set just described, there is exactly one large, thin, red triangle, just as there is one of each of all other combinations. However, the specific values, number of values, or number of attributes that a set may have is not important. Three teacher-made sets of structured attribute pieces are illustrated in Figure 18.7.

The value of using structured attribute materials is that the attributes and values are clearly identified and can be described easily by students. There is no confusion about what values a particular piece possesses, so you can focus your attention on the reasoning skills that the activities are meant to serve.

Activities with Attribute Materials

Most attribute activities with young children are best done with participants sitting on the floor in a large circle,

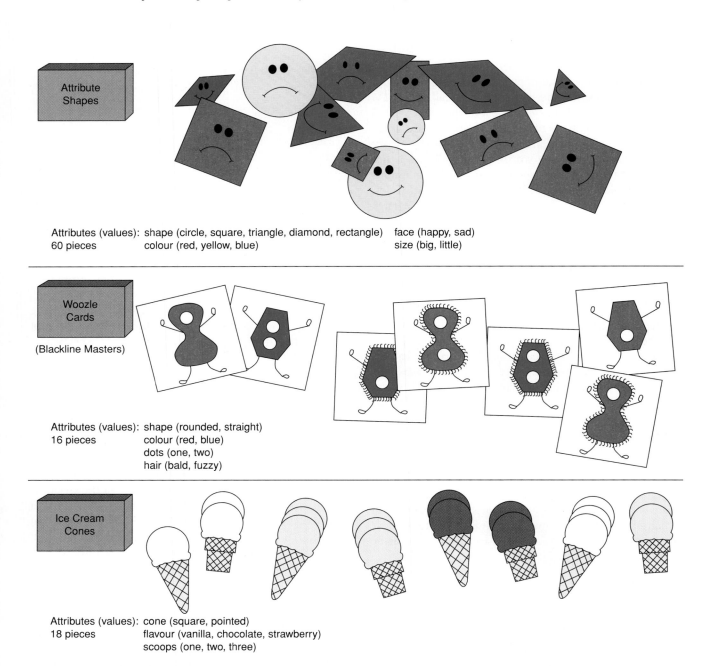

Attribute Shapes

Attributes (values): shape (circle, square, triangle, diamond, rectangle)   face (happy, sad)
60 pieces   colour (red, yellow, blue)   size (big, little)

Woozle Cards

(Blackline Masters)

Attributes (values): shape (rounded, straight)
16 pieces   colour (red, blue)
                   dots (one, two)
                   hair (bald, fuzzy)

Ice Cream Cones

Attributes (values): cone (square, pointed)
18 pieces   flavour (vanilla, chocolate, strawberry)
                   scoops (one, two, three)

FIGURE 18.7 **Three teacher-made attribute sets. Attribute shapes are made in large sizes from poster board and laminated. Woozle Cards can be duplicated on card stock, quickly coloured in two colours, laminated, and cut into cards (see Blackline Masters). The ice cream cones are made from construction paper and laminated. They could also be duplicated, coloured, and cut out by students.**

where all can see and have access to the materials. Older children can work in groups of four to six students, each with its own set of materials. With that format, problems can be addressed to the full class, and then groups can explore them independently. All activities should be conducted in an easygoing manner that encourages risk taking, clear thinking, attentiveness, and discussion of ideas.

Most of the activities here will be described using the geometric shapes in Figure 18.7. However, each could be done with any structured set, and some could be done with non-structured materials.

Learning Classification Schemes

Several attribute activities involve using overlapping loops (similar to Venn diagrams), each containing a designated class of materials, such as pieces that are "red" or "not square." Loops (like Venn diagrams) can be made of yarn or drawn on large sheets of paper. When two loops overlap, the common area is for the pieces that share both properties. Children as young as kindergarten can have fun with simple loop activities. With the use of words such as *and, or,* and *not,* the loop activities become quite challenging.

Loops or *Venn diagrams* should be thought of as a method of representing data. Loops are much easier for young children to use than bar graphs. Yet they permit students to show data in a powerful way.

Before children can use loops in a problem-solving activity, the scheme itself must be understood. A good way to develop this idea is to do a few activities that involve the loops. Children find these interesting and fun. After several days of working with these initial activities, you can move on to problem-solving activities involving the same formats.

ACTIVITY 18.5

The First Loops

Give children two large loops of yarn or string. Direct them to put all the red pieces inside one loop and all triangles inside the other. Let the children try to resolve the difficulty of what to do with the red triangles. When the notion of overlapping the loops to create an area common to both is clear, more challenging activities can be explored.

Later, "strings" or loops can be drawn on poster board or on large sheets of paper. If you happen to have a magnetic blackboard, try gluing small magnets to the backs of the pieces, and conduct full-class activities with these pieces on the board. Students can come to the board and place or arrange pieces inside loops drawn on the board with coloured chalk.

ACTIVITY 18.6

Labelled Loops

Label overlapping loops with cards indicating values of different attributes. Children take turns randomly selecting attribute pieces from the pile. The task is to decide in which region each piece belongs. Pieces that do not belong in either loop are placed outside. Allow other students to decide if the placement is correct, and occasionally have someone else provide an explanation. Do this even when the choice of regions is correct.

A significant variation of Activity 18.6 is to introduce negative attributes such as "not red" or "not small." Also important is the use of the *and* and *or* connectives, as in "red and square" or "big or happy." The use of *and, or,* and *not* significantly widens children's classification schemes. It also makes these activities more challenging for very young children. In Figure 18.8 a three-loop string activity illustrates some of these ideas.

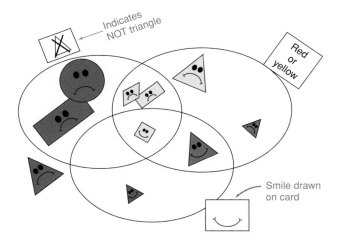

FIGURE 18.8 A three-loop activity with attribute pieces.

Solving Logic Problems

The activities described so far have students attempting to classify materials according to *our* schemes—the teacher creates a classification, and the children fit pieces into it. All that is required in these activities is an understanding of classification using the loop method, and the ability to discriminate the attributes. When the words *and, or,* and *not* are used, children gain experience with those logical connectives. However, very limited logical reasoning is involved. A more significant activity is to infer how things have been classified when the scheme is not clearly articulated. The following activities require students to make and test conjectures about how things are classified. These activities more directly prepare students to analyze their world, to formulate questions, and to do data analysis.

ACTIVITY 18.7

Guess My Rule

For this activity, try using the students instead of the shapes as attribute "pieces." Decide on an attribute such as "blue jeans" or "stripes on clothing" for grouping your students, but do not tell them your rule. Silently sort the children, one at a time, by moving each child to the left or right according to this attribute rule. After a number of students have been sorted, have the next child come up and ask students to predict to which group he or she belongs. Continue the activity for a while before the rule is articulated so that others in the class will have an opportunity to determine what it is. This same activity can be done with virtually any material that can be sorted. When unstructured materials such as students, students' shoes, shells, or buttons are used, the classifications may be quite obscure, thus providing an interesting challenge.

ACTIVITY 18.8

Hidden Labels

The same inference approach can be applied to "Labelled Loops" (Activity 18.6). Select label cards for the loops of string, and place them face down. Begin to sort pieces according to the labels that have been turned down. As you sort, have students try to determine what the labels for each of the loops are. Let students who think they have guessed the labels try to place a piece in the proper loop. Ask them not to guess the labels aloud. Students who think they know the correct labels can be asked to "play teacher" and respond to the guesses of others. Point out that one way to test an idea about the labels is to select pieces that you think might go in a particular section. Do not turn the cards up until most students have figured out the rule. Notice that some rules or labels are equivalent: "Not large" is the same as "small." With simple, one-value labels and only two loops, this activity can easily be played in

kindergarten. With the use of three loops and logical connectives, it can become challenging even for middle-school students.

ACTIVITY 18.9

Which One Doesn't Belong?

Select four pieces so that three of the pieces have some feature in common that the fourth doesn't. The students try to decide which piece is different. In Figure 18.9, there are two pieces that are each different from the other three. Frequently, there can be three or even four possible choices, each for a different reason. The students should explain their reasons, and classmates should decide if the reasons are good. Be sure to emphasize good reasoning and not right answers.

FIGURE 18.9 "One of these things is not like the others."

ACTIVITY 18.10

Sets of Four

Choose one value for each of two attributes, such as "happy triangles" or "large red pieces." Select any four pieces that share both values, and arrange them in a 2 × 2 array. The challenge is to make more arrays similar to or like the original one. To make new arrays, you must first decide how the pieces in the original array are alike, and then use those same attributes, with different values, to make the other arrays. Look at the example in Figure 18.10. The original array was all happy triangles: attributes of face and shape. The values of colour and size are mixed. Within each new array, face and shape values are the same. Corresponding pieces each match the original array in colour and size. If this activity is done with the Woozle Cards, where each of the attributes has exactly two values, all of the pieces will be used up in four arrays.

Be prepared to adjust the difficulty of these and similar activities according to the skills and interests of your children. Remember that children like to be challenged, but an activity that is either too easy or too difficult is likely to result in restlessness and discipline problems.

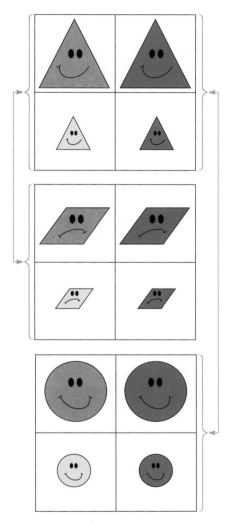

FIGURE 18.10 Making sets of four.

Difference Games

As an introduction to these activities, let each child select an attribute piece. Then, hold up one piece for all to see, and ask questions such as these:

Who has one that is like mine? How is it like mine?

Who has one that is different? Explain how it is different.

Look at your neighbour's piece. Tell how yours is like that one. Let your partner explain how your neighbour's piece is different from yours.

These same questions used with real objects (leaves, farm animals, students) help students think of categories for sorting. They will also help with the formulation of questions for data analysis.

Students will soon find that sometimes a piece differs in three or four ways, while other pieces differ in perhaps one or two ways. To focus attention on this, ask, "Who has a piece that is different in *just exactly one way* from mine? Who has a piece that is different in *exactly two ways?*" Notice that for a set with four attributes, a piece differing in three ways is alike in one way.

ACTIVITY 18.11

Difference Trains and Tracks

Place an attribute piece in the centre of a group of pieces. The first student finds a piece that is different in exactly one way from this attribute piece and places it beside it. Students take turns finding pieces that differ from the *preceding* piece in just one way, creating a "one-difference train." The train can be made as long as the students wish, or until pieces no longer fit the one-difference rule.

As a variation, draw a circular track divided into six to ten sections on a sheet of paper or poster board. Place the first piece in one of the sections. Subsequent pieces, which differ in one way from the adjacent piece, are then placed to the right or the left around the track. Placing the last piece may be difficult or even impossible, as it must differ in exactly one way from the piece on either side. A sample is shown in Figure 18.11.

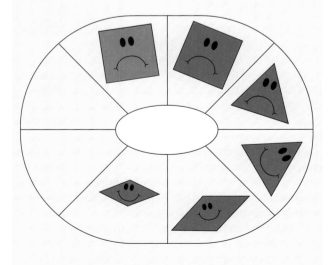

FIGURE 18.11 Can you finish this one-difference track?

Two-difference games are possible as well as one-difference games. These are not significantly more difficult, but add variety.

 ### *Technology Note*

Few computer programs address issues of classification. Attribute activities are actually quite effective without a computer. One of the most challenging and most interesting programs in this area is Logical Journey of the Zoombinis (Brøderbund, 1996b). Zoombinis are little creatures with variations in hair, eyes, nose, and feet. The program has 12 problems of increasing difficulty to solve, each in an adventure context involving the Zoombini creatures.

A bit closer to the issue of creating classification schemes and using loop diagrams is Tabletop, Jr. (Brøderbund, 1995b). This program can be used by individuals or the whole class. It provides a wide variety of objects that can be constructed with varying attributes. Various techniques for sorting are available, including the loop diagrams and the difference patterns seen in this chapter. Objects can also be sorted according to a hidden rule specified by a user—a computer version of "Guess My Rule," but with a lot of variation. Picture graphs can be constructed with the objects, thus providing a direct link to data graphing. ▪▪

Graphical Representations

Once data have been gathered, what are you going to do with them? Students should be involved in the decisions that go into answering this question. To whom do you want to communicate the information? What ideas in the data are most important, and what are some good ways to show these off?

Children who have little experience with the various ways of picturing data will not be aware of the many options that are available to them. Sometimes you can suggest new ways for displaying data and have children learn to construct that type of graph or chart. Once they have used the new technique, they can discuss its value. Did this graph (or chart or picture) tell about our data in a clear way? Compared to other ways of displaying data, how is this better?

The emphasis or goal of instruction should be to help children see that graphs and charts convey information, and that different types of representations tell different things about the same data. The value of having students actually construct their own graphs is not so much that they learn the techniques. Rather, it is that they are personally invested in the data and they are learning how a graph conveys information. Once a graph is constructed, the most important activity is discussing what it tells the people who see it, especially those who were not involved

in making the graph. Discussions about graphs of real data which the children have participated in gathering will help them interpret other graphs and charts that they see in newspapers and on TV.

What we should *not* do is get overly anxious about the tedious details of graph construction. Analysis and communication are your goals, and are much more important than the technique! In the real world, technology will take care of details.

There are two equally good possibilities you may consider when planning to have your students construct graphs or charts. First, you can simply encourage students to do their best, and to make charts and graphs that they feel make sense and communicate the information they wish to convey. This is not to say that children do not need guidance. They should see, and be involved in the construction of, various types of graphs and charts. This will provide them with some ideas from which to choose when constructing their own graphs. This informal approach may be best with younger students, because they will be more personally invested in their own work and not be distracted by the techniques of the technology. Care should be taken not to worry about fancy labelling or nice, neat pictures. The intent is to get the students involved in communicating a message about their data.

The second option is to use technology. The computer and graphing calculator provide us with different tools for constructing simple yet powerful representations. With the help of technology, it is possible to construct several varied pictures of the same data with very little effort. The discussion can then focus on the message or information that each format provides. Students can select their own graphs and justify their choice based on their intended purpose. As an example, Figure 18.12 shows four graphs produced by *The Graph Club* (Tom Snyder, 1993). When two or more graphs are created for the same data, it is possible to see how graphs change accordingly. How does a pie graph show information differently than a picture graph?

Bar Graphs

Bar graphs and tally charts are among the first ways to group and present data and are especially useful in grades K–3. At this early level, bar graphs should be made so that each bar represents countable things such as squares, objects, tallies, or pictures of objects. No numerical scale is necessary. Graphs should be simple and quickly constructed. Figure 18.13 illustrates a few techniques that can be used to make a graph quickly with the whole class.

A "real graph" uses the actual objects being graphed. Examples include types of shoes, seashells, and books. Each item can be placed in a square so that comparisons and counts are easily made.

FIGURE 18.12 **Four graphs produced with *Graph Club* software.**

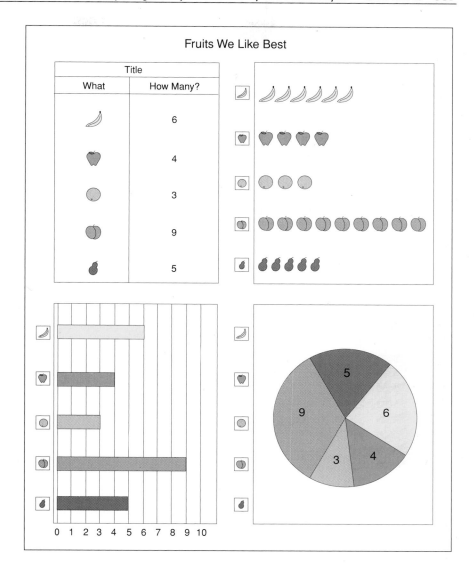

Picture graphs use a drawing of some sort that represents what is being graphed. Students can make their own drawings, or you can duplicate drawings to be coloured or cut out to suit particular needs.

Symbolic graphs use something like squares, blocks, tallies, or Xs to represent the things being counted. An easy idea is to use Post-it Notes as components of the graph. They can be attached directly to the chalkboard or to a chart and rearranged if needed.

To make a quick graph of class data, follow these steps:

1. Decide on what groups of data the different bars will represent. It is good to have two to six different bars in a graph.
2. Have each participant prepare a contribution for the graph before you begin. For real or picture graphs, the object or picture should be ready to be placed on the graph. For symbolic graphs, students should write down or mark their choice.
3. Have students, in small groups, quickly place or mark their entry on the graph. A graphing mat can be placed on the floor, or a chart can be prepared on the wall or chalkboard. If tape or pins are to be used, have these items ready.

A class of 25 to 30 students can make a graph in less than 10 minutes, leaving ample time for questions and observations.

Once a graph has been constructed, engage the class in a discussion regarding what information the graph tells or conveys. "What can you tell about our class by looking at this shoe graph?" Graphs convey factual information: "More people wear sneakers than any other kind of shoe."

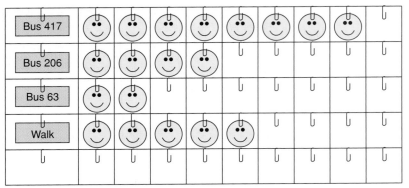

Clip paper pictures or symbols on a chart that
has a paper clip prepared in each square.

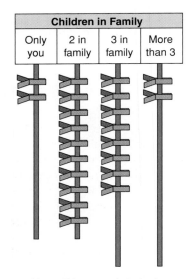

Hang ribbons, and students
clip on pinch-style clothespins

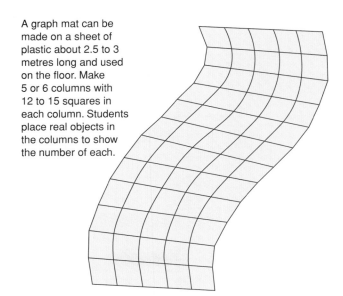

A graph mat can be
made on a sheet of
plastic about 2.5 to 3
metres long and used
on the floor. Make
5 or 6 columns with
12 to 15 squares in
each column. Students
place real objects in
the columns to show
the number of each.

FIGURE 18.13 **Some ideas for quick graphs that can be used again and again.**

They also provide opportunities for making inferences that are not directly observable in the graph: "Children in this class do not like to wear leather shoes." The difference between facts and inferences is an important idea in graph construction and is also an important idea in science. Older students can examine graphs found in newspapers or magazines and discuss the *facts* in the graphs and the *message* that may have been intended by the person who made the graph.

As children see different types of graphs, they can begin to make their own graphs of information gathered independently or by a group. A simple way to move graphing from the entire class to a small group is to assign different data collection tasks to different groups of children. The task is to gather the data, then decide on and make a graph that displays as clearly as possible the information found.

Stem-and-Leaf Plots

Stem-and-leaf plots are a popular form of bar graph where numerical data is plotted by using the actual numbers in the data to form the graph. By way of example, suppose that the American League baseball teams had posted the following record of wins over the past season:

Baltimore Orioles	45	Oakland As	101
Milwaukee Braves	91	Cleveland Indians	91
Boston Red Sox	94	Seattle Mariners	48
Minnesota Twins	98	Detroit Tigers	102
California Angels	85	Toronto Blue Jays	64
New York Yankees	100	Kansas City Royals	96
Chicago White Sox	72	Texas Rangers	65

If the data are to be grouped by tens, list the tens digits in order and draw a line to the right, as in Figure 18.14(a). These form the "stem" of the graph. Next, go through the list of scores, and write the ones digits next to the appropriate tens digit, as in Figure 18.14(b). These are the "leaves." The process of making the graph groups the data for you. Furthermore, every piece of data can be retrieved from the graph. (Notice that stem-and-leaf plots are best made on graph paper so that each digit takes up the same amount of space.)

To provide more information, the graph can be quickly rewritten, ordering each leaf from least to most, as in Figure 18.14(c). In this form, it may be useful to identify the number that belongs to a particular team, indicating its relative place within the grouped listing.

Stem-and-leaf graphs are not limited to two-digit data. For example, if the data ranged from 600 to 1300, the stem could be the numbers from 60 to 130 and the leaf values remain as one-digit. If the ones digit is not important, round the data to the nearest 10, using only the tens digit in the leaves.

Figure 18.15 illustrates two additional variations. When two sets of data are to be compared, the leaves can extend in opposite directions from the same stem. Notice that in the same sample the data are grouped by fives instead of tens. When plotting 62, the 2 is written next to the 6; for 67, the 7 is written next to the dot below the 6.

Stem-and-leaf plots are significantly easier for students to make than bar graphs. All of the data are maintained. They provide an efficient method for ordering data, and the individual elements can be identified.

Continuous Data Graphs

Bar graphs or picture graphs are useful for illustrating categories of data that have no numerical ordering—for example, colours or TV shows. When data are grouped along a continuous scale, it makes sense to represent them in that order and perhaps to show progressions from one point on the scale to the next. Examples of such information include temperatures that occur over time, height or mass over age, and percentages of test takers who score at different intervals along the scale of possible scores.

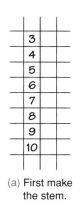

(a) First make the stem.

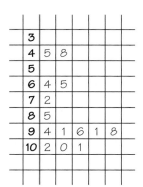

(b) Write in the leaves directly from the data.

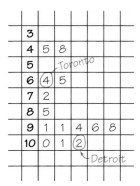

(c) It is easy to rewrite each leaf in numerical order. This puts all of the data in order.

FIGURE 18.14   Making a stem-and-leaf plot.

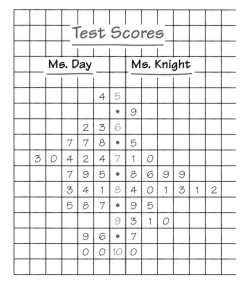

FIGURE 18.15 Stem-and-leaf plots can be used to compare two sets of data.

Line Plots

Line plots are useful *counts* of things along a numerical scale. To make a line plot, a number line is drawn and an X is made above the value on the line for every corresponding data element. One advantage of a line plot is that every piece of data is shown on the graph. It is also a very easy type of graph for students to make. It is essentially a bar graph with a potential bar for every possible value. A simple example is shown in Figure 18.16. (A stem-and-leaf plot is a lot like a line plot except that the data are grouped.)

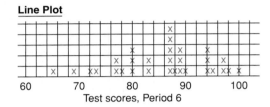

Line Plot

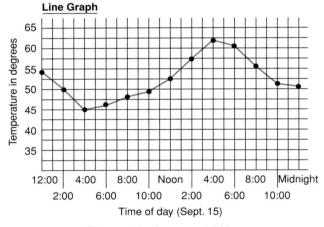

Line Graph

FIGURE 18.16 Two approaches to graphing data over continuous intervals. Notice that the horizontal scale must show some progression and is not just a grouping, as in a bar graph.

Histograms

A *histogram* is a form of bar graph in which the categories are consecutive equal intervals along a numerical scale. The height or length of each bar in the graph is determined by the number of data elements that fall into that particular interval. Histograms are not difficult in concept, but can cause problems for the students constructing them. What is the appropriate interval to use for the bar width? What is a good scale to use for the length of the bars? That all of the data must be grouped and counted

within each interval causes further difficulty. But technology helps us with all of these decisions, allowing children to focus on the graph and its message. A graphing calculator can produce a histogram without much difficulty, as it allows for the size of the interval to be specified and easily changed.

Line Graphs

A *line graph* is used when there is a numerical value associated with points equally spaced along a continuous number scale. The points are plotted to represent related pieces of data, and a line is drawn to connect these points. For example, a line graph might be used to show how the temperature changed from one hour to the next during the day. The horizontal scale would represent the time, and the vertical scale the temperature. Discrete points can be plotted and straight lines drawn to connect them. In the example Figure 18.16, the temperature changed continuously over 24 hours, as suggested by the graph.

Circle Graphs

A circle or pie graph is used when data have been partitioned into parts and the focus is on the ratio of each part to the whole. In Figure 18.17, each of the graphs shows the percentages of students with different numbers of siblings. One graph is based on classroom data and the other on school-wide data. Because pie graphs display ratios rather than quantities, the small set of class data can be compared to the large set of school data. That could not be done with bar graphs.

Easily Made Circle Graphs

You have already seen (in Figure 18.12, p. 387) a computer-generated circle graph (or pie graph) that can be used by children as early as grade 2. Nearly every spreadsheet program has circle graph capabilities.

Even without technology, there are a variety of ways that circle graphs can easily be made. Circle graphs of the students in your room can be made quickly and quite dramatically. Suppose, for example, that each student picked his or her favourite hockey team in the Stanley Cup semifinal playoffs (the Conference finals). Line up all of the students in the room so that students favouring the same team are together. Now form the entire group into a circle. Tape the ends of four long strings to the floor in the centre of the circle, and extend each string to a point along the circumference of the circle where the teams change. Voilà! Now you have a very nice pie graph with no measuring and no percentages. If you copy and cut out a hundredths disk (one is in the Blackline Masters) and place it on the centre of the circle, the strings will show approximate percentages for each part of your graph (see Figure 18.18).

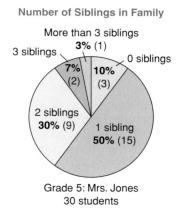

Grade 5: Mrs. Jones
30 students

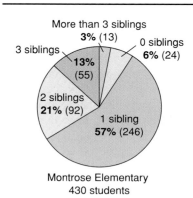

Montrose Elementary
430 students

FIGURE 18.17 **Circle graphs show ratios of part to whole and can be used to compare ratios.**

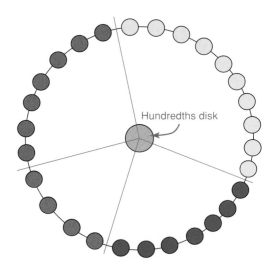

FIGURE 18.18 **A human pie graph: Students are arranged in a circle, with string stretched between them to show the divisions.**

Another easy approach to circle graphs is similar to the human pie graph. Begin by having students make a bar graph of the data. Cut out the bars themselves, and tape them together end to end. Next, tape the two ends together to form a circle. Estimate where the centre of the circle is, draw lines to the points where different bars meet, and trace around the full loop. The result is, again, a very meaningful circle graph. You can estimate percentages using the hundredths disk as before.

From Percentages to Pie Graphs

If students have experienced either of the two methods just described, using their own calculations to make pie graphs will make more sense. The numbers in each category are added to form the total or whole. (That's the same as taping all of the strips together, or lining up the students.) By dividing each of the parts by the whole with a calculator, numbers between 0 and 1 result—fractional parts of the whole. If rounded to hundredths, these numbers become percentages of the whole. (Check that the total is 1 whole, or 100 percent. Rounding may cause some error.) With a copy of the hundredths disk, students can easily make a pie chart and never have to mess with degrees and protractors. Trace around the disk to make the outline of the pie. Mark the centre through a small hole in the disk, and draw a line to the circle. Start from that point, and use the disk to measure hundredths around the outside.

Descriptive Statistics

Although graphs provide visual images of data, measures of the data are a different and important way to think about the shape of data. Numbers that describe data are *statistics,* measures that quantify some attribute of the data. The things that are most often described numerically about a set of data are the distance between the highest and lowest data values (the *range*), some measure of where the centre of the data is (an *average*), and how dispersed the data are within the range (the *variance* or *dispersion*). Students can get an idea of the importance of these statistics by exploring the ideas informally.

Averages

The term *average* is heard quite frequently in everyday usage. Sometimes it refers to an exact arithmetic average, as in "the average daily rainfall." Sometimes it is used quite loosely, as in "She is about average height." In either situation, an average is a single number or measure that represents a larger collection of numbers. If your test average is 92, it is assumed that somehow this number reflects all of your test scores. The *mean, median,* and *mode* are specific types of averages or *measures of central tendency.* The *mode* is the value that occurs most frequently in the data set. Of these three statistics, the mode is the least useful and could perhaps be ignored completely. Consider the following set of numbers:

1, 1, 3, 5, 6, 7, 8, 9

The mode of this set is 1. The mode is not a very good description of this set, and such is often the case. If the 8 in this string of numbers were a 9, there would be two modes. If one of the ones were a 2, there would be no mode at all. In short, the mode is a statistic that does not always exist, does not necessarily reflect the centre of the data, and can be highly unstable, changeable with very small movements in the data.

The *mean* is computed by adding all of the numbers in the set and dividing the sum by the number of elements added. This is the statistic that is sometimes referred to as the *average,* although the terms are not synonymous. The mean of our sample set is 40 ÷ 8, or 5. The mean is discussed in more detail later in this chapter.

The *median* is the middle value in an ordered set of data. Half of all values lie at or above the median and half below. For the eight numbers in our sample set, the median is between 5 and 6, or 5.5. The median is easier to understand and to compute and is not affected, as the mean is, by one or two extremely large or extremely small values outside the range of the rest of the data.

Box-and-Whisker Plots

Box-and-whisker plots (or just *box plots*) are an easy method for visually displaying not only the median statistic but also information about the range and distribution or variance of data. This is a topic that is included in few of the provincial and territorial curricula expectations for grade 8 students.

The ages in months for 27 grade 6 students are given in Figure 18.19, along with stem-and-leaf plots for the full class and for the boys and girls separately. Box-and-whisker plots are shown in Figure 18.20.

Each box-and-whisker plot has these three features:

1. A box that contains the "middle half" of the data, one-fourth to the left and right of the median. The ends of the box are at the *lower quartile,* the median of the lower half of the data, and the *upper quartile,* the median of the upper half of the data.
2. A line inside the box at the median of the data.
3. A line extending from the end of each box to the *lower extreme* and *upper extreme* of the data. Each line therefore covers the upper and lower fourths of the data.

Look at the information these box plots provide at a glance! The box and the lengths of the lines provide a quick indication of how the data are spread out or bunched together. Since the median is shown, this spreading or bunching can be determined for each quarter of the data. The entire class in this example is much more spread out in the upper half than the lower half. The girls are much more closely grouped in age than either the boys or the class as a whole. It is immediately obvious that at least three-fourths of the girls are younger than the median age of the boys. The *range* of the data (difference between upper and lower extremes) is represented by the length of the plot, and the extreme values can be read directly. It is easy to mark and label entries of particular interest. For example, Joe B. and Whitney might be the class officers.

Making box-and-whisker plots is quite simple. First, put the data in order. An easy and valuable method is to make a stem-and-leaf plot and order the leaves, providing another visual image as well. Next, find the median. Simply count the number of values and determine the middle one. This can be done directly on the stem-and-leaf plots, in Figure 18.19. To find the two quartiles, ignore the median itself, and find the medians of the upper and lower halves of the data. Mark the two extremes, the two quartiles, and the median above an appropriate number line. Draw the box and the lines. Box plots can also be drawn vertically.

Note that the means for the data in our example are each just slightly higher than the medians (class = 132.4; boys = 133.9; girls = 130.8). For this example, the means themselves do not provide nearly as much information as the box plots. In Figure 18.20, the means are shown with small marks extending above and below each box.

Graphing calculators and several computer programs draw box-and-whisker plots, making this relatively simple process even more accessible. The TI-73 calculator can draw box plots for up to three sets of data on the same axis. In Figure 18.21, the data for the top box plot are based on 23 items. The second plot has 122 items. The third plot has 48 items of data. When you compare both large and small sets of data in this manner, the spread or lack of spread of the data becomes much more obvious.

Box-and-whisker plots are pictures of statistics more than pictures of data. They show the range and the median and pictorially indicate a sense of the spread.

Understanding the Mean

Due to ease of computation and stability, the median has some advantages over the mean as a practical average. However, the mean will continue to be used in popular media and in books. For smaller sets of data such as your test scores, the mean is perhaps a more meaningful statistic. Finally, the mean is used in the computation of other statistics such as the standard deviation. Therefore, it remains important that students have a good concept of what the mean tells them about a set of numbers.

How do you describe the mean, other than by explaining how to compute it? There are actually two dif-

FIGURE 18.19 Ordered stem-and-leaf plots grouped by fives. Medians and upper and lower quartiles are found on the stem-and-leaf plots. Medians and quartiles are circled or are represented by a bar (I) if they fall between two elements.

The following numbers represent the ages in months of a class of grade 6 students.

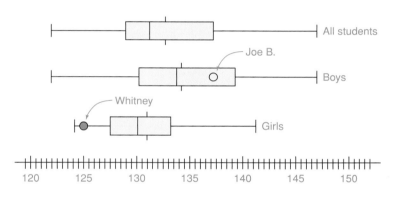

Boys		Girls	
132	122	140	131
140	130	129	128
133	134	141	131
142	125	134	132
134 *Joe B.*	147	124	130
(137) *Joe B.*	131	129 *Whitney*	127
139	129	(125) *Whitney*	

All students

12	2, 4
¥	5, 5, 7, 8, (9,) 9, 9,
13	0, 0, 1, 1, (1,) 2, 2, 3, 4, 4, 4
¥	(7,) 9
14	0, 0, 1, 2
¥	7

Boys

12	2
¥	5, 9
13	(0,) 1, 2, 3, (4, 4
¥	7, (9)
14	0, 2
¥	7

Girls

12	4
¥	5, 7, (8, 9, 9
13	(0,) 1, 1, 2, (4
¥	
14	0, 1
¥	

FIGURE 18.20 Box-and-whisker plots show a lot of information.

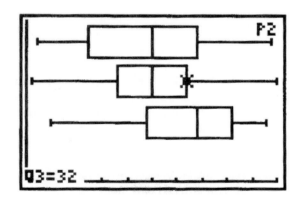

Age (months) of 27 grade 6 students

FIGURE 18.21 Three box plots of data falling between the values of 0 and 50. Twenty-three items are represented by the top plot, 122 by the middle plot, and 48 by the bottom plot. The cursor on the middle plot shows the third quartile is 32. What other information can be determined from this plot?

ferent ways to think about the mean. First, it is a number that represents what all of the data items would be if they were levelled out. In this sense, the mean represents all of the data items. Statisticians prefer to think of the mean as a central balance point. This concept of the mean is more in keeping with the notion of a measure of the "centre" of the data, or a measure of central tendency. Both concepts are discussed in the following sections.

A Levelling Concept of the Mean

When you say that the average score on your class math test was 92, one way to interpret that is as follows: If every student had received the same score, that score would be 92. Higher scores balance out lower scores. This concept of the mean is easy to understand and explain, and has the added benefit that it leads directly to the algorithm for computing the mean.

Levelling the Bars

Have students make a bar graph of some data using interlocking cubes (Unifix, or Cube-a-Links). Choose a situation with 5 or 6 bars with no more than 10 or 12 cubes in each. For example, the graph in Figure 18.22 shows prices for 6 toys. The task for students is to use the graph to determine how much each toy would cost if all of the toys were the same price, assuming that the total remained the same. Do not tell students that they are finding the average or mean, only that they are to find equal length bars. Students will use various techniques to rearrange the cubes in the graph and eventually will create six equal bars, possibly with some leftovers that could mentally be distributed in fractional amounts. (In the example, the total number of cubes is a multiple of 6.)

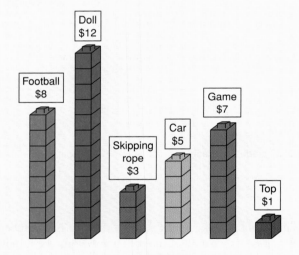

Bar graph made with plastic snap cubes

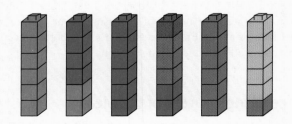

The same cubes rearranged into equal stacks.
Their height is the <u>mean</u> value of the bars above.

FIGURE 18.22 Understanding the mean as a levelling of the data.

On completion, focus attention on the methods students used to stack the bars and divide the whole stack into six parts. If no one has done that, create a new bar graph with the cubes, show it to the class, then stack all of the bars into one long bar. Pose this task: "How could we use this long bar to determine the size of the bars if they were all the same?" It is relatively easy to see that you should first figure out the length of the long bar (the total of all of the bars), then divide that by the number of bars with which you began.

The same levelling activity can be used with any bar graph that students have made on paper. Once the graph is made, have students cut the bars out and tape them together end to end. Ask them to use this long strip to determine the size the bars would be if they were all the same. The students can do this by folding the strip into as many equal parts as there are bars.

Numerical Levelling

Provide a set of about 15 varied numbers. They might be student heights in centimetres or any other meaningful data. Ask, "If the total was the same and the numbers were all alike, what might these numbers be?"

The last task more explicitly develops the add-up-and-divide algorithm. Once students see how to use this technique to determine a levelling number for a data set, it is time to tell them that this number they are finding is called the *mean*.

The next activity is a good follow-up to early discussions of the mean.

Over and Under the Mean

Duplicate a simple bar graph on grid paper and distribute one to each student. The task is to estimate the mean and draw a horizontal line across the graph at that point. No computation is to be done! Make a transparency of the graph to use for discussion. Draw a line on a second piece of acetate that can be placed on the graph as the estimated mean line. Have students say where they drew their lines and why (see Figure 18.23). What is likely to emerge from the discussion is that the total of the parts of the bars above the mean line must match the sum of all the spaces between the mean line and the bars below the line. That is, you should be able to cut off the

bars above the mean line and fit the pieces in the spaces below the mean line. After the discussion, use a calculator to compute the mean numerically and compare with the estimates.

A Balance Point Concept of the Mean

Statisticians think about the mean as a point on a number line where the data on either side of the point are balanced. To help think about the mean in this way, it is useful to think about the data as a line plot rather than as a bar graph. What is important is not how many pieces of data are on either side of the mean or balance point; it is the distances of data from the mean that must balance.

To illustrate, draw a number line on the board, and arrange eight Post-it Notes above the number 3 as shown in Figure 18.24(a). Each Post-it Note represents one family. The notes are positioned on the line to indicate how many pets each family owns. Stacked up like this, it appears that all families have the same number of pets. The mean is 3 pets. But different families are likely to have different numbers of pets. So we could think of 8 families with a range of numbers of pets. Some may have 0 pets,

and some may have as many as 10 or more. How could you change the number of pets for these 8 families so the mean remains at 3? Students will suggest moving the Post-it Notes in opposite directions along the horizontal axis, probably in pairs. This will result in a symmetrical arrangement. But what if one of the families has 8 pets, a move of 5 spaces from the 3? This might be balanced by moving 2 families to the left, one 3 spaces to 0 and one 2 spaces to 1. Figure 18.24(b) shows one way the families could be rearranged to maintain a mean of 3. You should stop here and find at least two other distributions for the families, each with a mean of 3.

Use the next activity to find the mean or balance point, given the data.

ACTIVITY 18.15

Finding the Balance Point

Have students draw a number line from 0 to 12 with about 2-3 centimetres between the numbers. Use 6 small Post-it Notes to represent the prices of 6 toys, as shown in Figure 18.25. Have students place a light pencil mark on the point where they think the mean might be. At this

FIGURE 18.23 Estimating the mean on a bar graph.

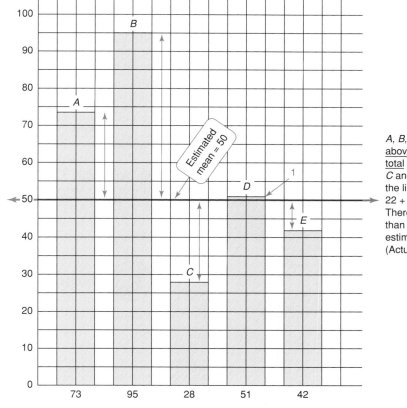

A, B, and D are <u>above</u> the line a <u>total</u> of 23 + 45 +1 = 69. C and E are <u>below</u> the line a total of 22 + 8 = 30. There is more ABOVE than BELOW. This estimate is <u>too low</u>. (Actual mean = 57.8)

Percentage of voters who voted in five ridings

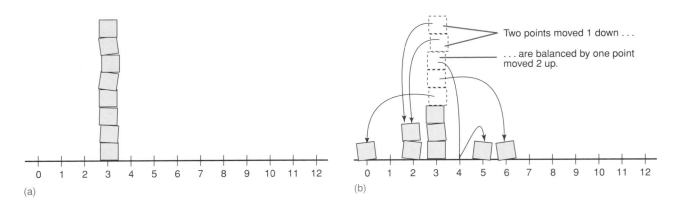

(a)

(b)

Two points moved 1 down . . .

. . . are balanced by one point moved 2 up.

FIGURE 18.24 **(a) If all data points are the same, the mean is that value. (b) By moving data points away from the mean in a balanced manner, different distributions can be found that have the same mean.**

point, avoid the add-up-and-divide computation. The task is to determine the actual mean by moving the Post-it Notes toward the "centre." In so doing, the students are finding out what price or point on the number line balances out the 6 prices. For each move of a Post-it® one space to the left (a toy with a lower price), a Post-it® must be moved one space to the right (a toy with a higher price). Eventually, all Post-it Notes should end up stacked above the same number: the balance point or mean.

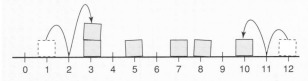

FIGURE 18.25 **Move data points in toward the centre or balance point without changing the balance around that point. When you have all points at the same value, that is, the balance or the mean.**

Stop now and try this exercise yourself. Notice that after any pair of moves that keep the distribution balanced, you actually have a new distribution of prices, but still the same mean. The same thing was true when you moved the Post-its® away from the mean when they were all stacked on the same point.

The balance concept does not lead to the add-up-and-divide algorithm for computing the mean. However, you can show that the computation will always produce the same value as determined by the balance.

Notice that the mean only defines the centre of a set of data, so by itself it is not a very useful description of the

shape of the data. The balance approach to the mean clearly illustrates that many different distributions can have the same mean.*

Changes in the Mean

Especially for small sets of data, the mean is significantly affected by extreme values. For example, suppose that another toy with a price of $20 is added to the six we have been using in the examples. How will that change the mean? If the $1 toy were removed, how would the mean be affected? Suppose that one new toy, that increases the mean from $6 to $7, is added. How much does the new toy cost? Students should be challenged with questions such as these, using small sets of data and either the balance or the levelling concept.

Technology provides an efficient method for exploring the mean as well as other statistics. Spreadsheets can be used when computing the range, mean, and median for any set of data. On a spreadsheet, these statistics update immediately when a number is changed or added to the data. This is a dynamic, albeit not very conceptual, way to explore how these measures of the data centre are affected by changes to the data.

   Technology Note

Throughout this discussion of data analysis, there have been references to graphing calculators, spreadsheets, and

---

*The balance concept of the mean is the one developed in the Connected Math Project, one of the three reform programs for the middle grades. It is also developed in the *Used Numbers* book *Statistics: Middles, Means, and In-Betweens* (Friel, Mokros, & Russell, 1992).

graphing software. This is an area of the curriculum where technology really changes the way we teach. In the past, the emphasis was on how to create the graph and how to compute the statistic. Students had to labour over graph paper, drawing scales, labelling axes, colouring the graphs, and so on. Today, the graphical techniques and statistics mentioned in this chapter are available in a variety of technologies. An exception may be stem-and-leaf plots. With the help of technology, the focus of instruction in data analysis can and should shift to the big ideas of using graphs and statistics: how to describe data, get a sense of the shape of data, answer questions with data, and communicate this information to others.

At the primary level, it is useful to have a software program into which children can enter data and select from a variety of graphical representations. *The Graph Club* (Tom Snyder, 1993), though not new, is an excellent example of software in this category. *Cruncher* (SRA/McGraw-Hill, 1996) is a slightly simplified spreadsheet suitable for students who are new to working with spreadsheets. Every popular spreadsheet will compute any statistic for columns or rows of data. If the data are changed, the statistics change instantly. Spreadsheets also make very nice bar graphs, line graphs, and circle graphs. Since spreadsheets are often bundled with the software that comes with computers, the software is almost as widely available as the computers themselves. Teachers should also check to see if the publishers of textbooks they are using offer graphing software.

Graphing calculators put data analysis technology in the hands of every student. The TI-73 calculator or the more recent TI-73 Explorer, designed for middle-grade students, will produce eight different kinds of plots or graphs, including pie charts, bar graphs, and picture graphs. An argument can be made for having students do some graphing and computing of statistics without technology. Appropriate methods have been suggested in this chapter. However, the intent of "by-hand" methods should always be to help understand the graphs or the statistics. Given today's readily available technology, there is no reason for repetitious exercises with tedious "by-hand" methods. Keep the emphasis on data interpretation by taking advantage of technology.

 Assessment Notes

When assessing probability and statistical ideas, care should be taken to distinguish between the use of related algorithms and techniques and the kind of knowledge that involves judgment and interpretation.

Probability

Skills that involve the computation of probability are easy to assess. Even young children should be able to tell if an event is possible or impossible, or very likely or not very likely. Older children should be able to determine probability in well-designed experiments such as those discussed in this chapter.

You also want to be aware of students' understanding of chance and probability. What does it mean that an event has a probability of 89 percent, or $\frac{2}{3}$? How many times should a simulation or an experiment be conducted before you can have confidence in the results? What does "confidence in the results" mean? Can knowing the probability of an event ever predict what will happen on the next trial? How are probability ideas used in the real world?

Students' progress with these more subtle ideas can be determined by having class discussions and listening to students' reasoning, and making efforts to monitor their understanding of the key concepts. You might use a four-point rubric to rate students quickly on their understanding. Middle-school students can write short reports about a situation that includes your main ideas, and you can have them specifically address the issues you want to assess.

Statistics

In the area of statistics and data analysis, the same distinction is important. Of course, you want your students to know how to make a stem-and-leaf plot and a box plot or find the mean and the median, but many students can learn to do these things without knowing how to interpret them. Choices and interpretation of graphs and statistics are more important than the ability to construct and compute.

Choice

Computers and calculators will construct graphs that might not suit your needs, so students must be able to select the graphs and statistics that best fit their purposes. It is important to pose situations with a real-life context and have students decide which statistics and which graphs would best fit the situation. Is a bar graph more appropriate than a line graph? Why? Which statistic is better in this situation, the mean or the median?

Interpretation

In a similar manner, making the graph or computing the mean does not necessarily help me understand what the graph is telling me about the data. There are a number of ways to get at interpretation. One is to present several graphs and statistics for the same situation. "Suppose you were a newspaper editor. Which of these statistics and graphs should you use in your story? Explain your selection. Are any of these statistics of no value to the message?" In this type of interpretation, several options are provided, and the choice is based on the intended audience and purpose. There is no need actually to compute the statistics or create the graphs.

Another idea is to provide graphs and statistics for two related situations: your class and the rest of the school, your province or territory and the rest of the country, hamburgers at McDonald's and hamburgers at Burger King. What can be determined for sure from these data? What inferences can be made? What would help you make a decision about _____ that you cannot determine from the information gathered? How could you use this information to argue in favour of _____? How could you use the same information to argue for the reverse side of the issue?

 ## Literature Connections

It may be difficult to find books that specifically address the concepts of probability or data analysis. The books suggested here will provide springboards for discussions of chance, classification, and comparisons.

Do You Wanna Bet? Your Chance to Find Out About Probability
(Cushman, 1991)

The two characters in this book, Danny and Brian, become involved in everyday situations both in and out of school. Each situation involves an element of probability. For example, two invitations to birthday parties are for the same day. What is the chance that two friends would have the same birthday? In another situation, Brian wonders if he should bother doing his homework, because the weather forecaster predicts a 60 percent chance that there will be enough snow to close the schools. When it doesn't snow at all, the question is: Was the forecaster wrong? Secret notes passed in class lead to the discussion of letter frequencies in our language. These and other situations, woven into an interesting story, can each lead to a probability experiment or discussion. Students might create simulations to examine some of the same ideas, or the story may provoke questions for exploration.

Frog and Toad Are Friends
(Lobal, 1970)

When Frog and Toad go walking, Frog loses a button. As they search to find the button, they find many buttons. Whenever one of Frog's friends asks, "Is this your button?" Frog responds (with a touch of anger), "No, that is not my button! That button is _____, but my button was _____." The phrase is repeated with each newly found button. It turns out that Frog did not lose the button on the walk but in his own home before they left. This situation adds value to the story, as Frog must find a way to make up for being so angry with his friends.

The approach to finding the button is very much like the game "One of These Things Is Not Like the Others." It is also a perfect lead-in to secret sorting activities as described in this chapter. Young students can model the story directly with sets of buttons, shells, attribute blocks, Woozle Cards, or other objects with a variety of attributes. With a highly varied set of geometric shapes, the children could play the game and explore geometric language and their perceptions of the geometric attributes.

Incredible Comparisons
(Ash, 1996)

Not a story but an amazing collection of facts and comparisons, Ash's book includes 23 topics for comparison, each graphically displayed. For example, different-sized squares are used to compare the size of the continents. Maps of major countries are layered on top of each other to indicate relative areas. Data about area and distances are also provided in different units of measure. The amount of time needed to travel the widths of countries is demonstrated as well. Data and drawings such as these can prompt students to find appropriate and clever ways to display the information, or to research similar information in other resources. Other topics include big buildings, animal speeds, growth and age, and population. ■■

Reflections on Chapter 18

Writing to Learn

1. Describe the difference between theoretical probability, relative frequency, and experimental probability.
2. Why is it a good idea to have students conduct experiments before trying to figure out probabilities?
3. What are the first ideas that young students should develop about the concept of chance? How can this be done?

4. What is the purpose of a simulation? Set up a simulation for at least one of the examples on page 379. Conduct a few trials.
5. Use an area model and a tree diagram to determine the theoretical probability for the following experiment:

   Dad puts a $10 bill and three $5 bills in the first box. In a second box, he puts another $10 bill but just one $5 bill. For washing the car, Junior gets to take one bill from the first box without looking and put it in the second box. After these have been well mixed, he then gets to take one from the second box without looking. What is the probability that he will get a $10 bill ?

6. Explain why attribute activities are important in the development of data analysis skills. Why would you use structured attribute materials for these activities instead of informal or unstructured materials such as buttons?

7. In initial loop activities, the teacher tells the students how to sort the attribute pieces. What is the purpose of these not-so-problematic activities? What are students learning in activities where the loop labels are not shown or the sorting rule is a secret?

8. How is a two-difference game played on an oval track? Draw a picture showing a two-difference solution for a track with seven spaces. Use attribute blocks or Woozle Cards.

9. Draw a picture of a line plot, a histogram, and a line graph. How are all of these alike?

10. Put at least 30 numbers in a stem-and-leaf plot, and use it to determine the median, the upper and lower quartiles, and the range, and to draw a box-and-whisker plot.

11. What are three ways to make a circle graph? What does a circle graph tell you that a bar graph does not? What does it not tell?

12. What are three different forms of averages? Which is the most stable? Explain.

13. Describe two different concepts of the mean. How can each be developed? Which idea leads to the method of computing the mean?

For Discussion and Exploration

1. Examine one of six books from the Used Numbers Project or the two *Teach-Stat Activities* books (see Recommendations for Further Reading). These books have some of the best statistics activities for elementary students. You might share an activity or idea in the book that excited you, react to a lesson described in the book, or share an idea in the book with a teacher and get his or her reaction.

2. How important is it, in your opinion, to teach probability concepts in the early grades (K–4)? What about in grades 5–8? Does your answer change if you substitute statistics for probability? Explain your position. Some experts have argued that the ability to understand probability and statistical ideas is so much more important than mastery of the related skills (such as the ability to compute probabilities and statistics, or to make graphs) that we could skip skills teaching in order to devote more time to reasoning in this area. What position would you take on this issue?

Recommendations for Further Reading

Highly Recommended

Currah, J., and Felling, J. (2001). *Deca dice vol. ix*. Edmonton: Box Cars & One-Eyed Jacks.

Currah, J., and Felling, J. (2001). *Stratedice*. Edmonton: Box Cars & One-Eyed Jacks.

These are just two of the many books of games developed by the authors under the award-winning name of Box Cars & One-Eyed Jacks. Using either dice or cards, students from K–9 can engage in games of chance and probability that fit with regional curriculum expectations. The games also cover expectations from other strands such as number sense and numeration, patterning, and problem solving.

National Council of Teachers of Mathematics. (1999). Data and chance in the middle school curriculum [Focus issue]. *Mathematics Teaching in the Middle School, 4*(6).

In keeping with the overall quality of this journal, this focus issue is a valuable resource for the twin topics of data and probability. The first article describes a fascinating activity involving data about killer bees, with a solid connection to biology. Other articles are equally useful.

University of North Carolina Mathematics and Science Education Network. (1997). *Teach-stat activities: Statistics investigations for grades 1–3*. White Plains, NY: Cuisenaire–Dale Seymour.

University of North Carolina Mathematics and Science Education Network. (1997). *Teach-stat activities: Statistics investigations for grades 3–6*. White Plains, NY: Cuisenaire–Dale Seymour.

These two books contain a wealth of superb data activities developed through a National Science Foundation grant under the direction of some of North Carolina's top mathematics educators. The activities are each designed to follow a four-stage model: pose the question, collect the data, analyze the data, and interpret the results. In other words, data are collected for the purpose of answering a question. The activities are each described in detail, with all necessary Blackline Masters included. A companion professional development manual is also available.

Used numbers: Real data in the classroom. White Plains, NY: Cuisenaire–Dale Seymour.

This set of six books, each covering two or three grades between kindergarten and grade 6, is a result of an NSF-supported project at Technical Education Research Centers (TERC) and Lesley College. The books are an excellent resource for elementary statistics activities. Each book is a unit of study, most with subtopics that can be used independently. The authors (authorship varies with each book) include ample detail to help you get a feel for what might happen in the classroom. The spirit of these activities is excellent! The suggestions are realistic and can all be implemented as suggested. Blackline Masters are included when needed. (All six titles are included under "Other Suggestions.")

Zawojewski, J.S. (1991). *Dealing with data and chance: Addenda series, grades 5–8*. Reston, VA: National Council of Teachers of Mathematics.

Middle-school teachers interested in teaching probability and statistics *must* have this book. It is not timid in its suggestions for challenging activities, yet all activities are appropriate for students in grades 5 to 8. The book is organized around the four theme standards of the *Curriculum Standards*.

Other Suggestions

Bright, G.W., & Hoeffner, K. (1993). Measurement probability, statistics, and graphing. In D.T. Owens (Ed.), *Research ideas for the classroom: Middle grades mathematics* (pp. 78–98). Old Tappan, NJ: Macmillan.

Burns, M. (1995). *Math by all means: Probability, grades 3–4.* Sausalito, CA: Math Solutions Publications.

Corwin, R.B., & Friel, S.N. (1990). *Statistics: Prediction and sampling* (Unit of study for grades 5–6 from *Used numbers: Real data in the classroom*). White Plains, NY: Cuisenaire–Dale Seymour.

Corwin, R.B., & Russell, S.J. (1990). *Measuring: From paces to feet* (Unit of study for grades 3–5 from *Used numbers: Real data in the classroom*). White Plains, NY: Cuisenaire–Dale Seymour.

Curcio, F.R., & Artzt, A.F. (1996). Assessing students' ability to analyze data: Reaching beyond computation. *Mathematics Teacher, 89,* 668–673.

Curcio, F.R., Nimerofsky, B., Perez, R., & Yaloz-Femia, S. (1998). Developing concepts in probability: Designing and analyzing games. In L.P. Leutzinger (Ed.), *Mathematics in the middle* (pp. 206–211). Reston, VA: National Council of Teachers of Mathematics.

Dessart, D.J. (1995). Randomness: A connection to reality. In P.A. House (Ed.), *Connecting mathematics across the curriculum* (pp. 177–181). Reston, VA: National Council of Teachers of Mathematics.

Elementary Quantitative Literacy Project. (1998). *Exploring statistics in the elementary grades: Book 1 (K–6).* White Plains, NY: Cuisenaire–Dale Seymour.

Friel, S.N., Mokros, J.R., & Russell, S.J. (1992). *Middles, means, and in-betweens* (Unit of study for grades 5–6 from *Used numbers: Real data in the classroom*). White Plains, NY: Cuisenaire–Dale Seymour.

Gnanadesikan, M., Schaeffer, R.L., & Swift, J. (1987). *The art and techniques of simulation: Quantitative literacy series.* White Plains, NY: Cuisenaire–Dale Seymour.

Haruta, M.E., Flaherty, M., McGivney, J., & McGivney, R.J. (1996). Coin tossing. *Mathematics Teacher, 89,* 642–645.

Jones, G.A., Thornton, C.A., Langrall, C.W., & Tarr, J.E. (1999). Understanding students' probabilistic reasoning. In L.V. Stiff (Ed.), *Developing mathematical reasoning in grades K–12* (pp. 146–155). Reston, VA: National Council of Teachers of Mathematics.

Karp, K.S. (1994). Telling tales: Creating graphs using multicultural literature. *Teaching Children Mathematics, 1,* 87–91.

Leutzinger, L.P. (1990). Graphical representation and probability. In J.N. Payne (Ed.), *Mathematics for the young child* (pp. 251–263). Reston, VA: National Council of Teachers of Mathematics.

Lindquist, M.M. (1992). *Making sense of data: Addenda series, grades K–6.* Reston, VA: National Council of Teachers of Mathematics.

Martin, H.M., & Zawojewski, J.S. (1993). Dealing with data and chance: An illustration from the middle school addendum to the standards. *Arithmetic Teacher, 41,* 220–223.

Russell, S.J., & Corwin, R.B. (1989). *Statistics: The shape of the data* (Unit of study for grades 4–6 from *Used numbers: Real data in the classroom*). White Plains, NY: Cuisenaire–Dale Seymour.

Russell, S.J., & Corwin, R.B. (1990). *Sorting: Groups and graphs* (Unit of study for grades 2–3 from *Used numbers: Real data in the classroom*). White Plains, NY: Cuisenaire–Dale Seymour.

Russell, S.J., & Friel, S.N. (1989). Collecting and analyzing real data in the elementary classroom. In P.R. Trafton (Ed.), *New directions for elementary school mathematics* (pp. 134–148). Reston, VA: National Council of Teachers of Mathematics.

Russell, S.J., & Stone, A. (1990). *Counting: Ourselves and our families* (Unit of study for grades K–1 from *Used numbers: Real data in the classroom*). White Plains, NY: Cuisenaire–Dale Seymour.

Shaughnessy, J.M., & Dick, T. (1991). Monty's dilemma: Should you stick or switch? *Mathematics Teacher, 84,* 252–256.

Uccellini, J.C. (1996). Teaching the mean meaningfully. *Mathematics Teaching in the Middle School, 2,* 112–115.

Zawojewski, J.S., & Heckman, D.S. (1997). What do students know about data analysis, statistics, and probability? In P.A. Kenney & E.A. Silver (Eds.), *Results from the sixth mathematics assessment of the National Assessment of Educational Progress* (pp. 195–224). Reston, VA: National Council of Teachers of Mathematics.

Chapter 19

Algebraic Reasoning, Functions, and Functional Relationships

It is significant that the authors of *Principles and Standards for School Mathematics* chose Algebra as one of the five content standards. Clearly, they are not talking about traditional grade 8 or high school algebra; they do not mean that every child should take a "course" in algebra. Rather, the *Principles and Standards* Algebra standard is about the development of algebraic thinking and algebraic concepts throughout K–12 curricula. The focus is on patterns, functions, and the ability to analyze situations with the help of symbols. A close look at provincial and territorial curricula reveals how these views have played a role in the development of algebra and patterning strands.

Algebraic reasoning involves representing, generalizing, and formalizing patterns and regularity in all aspects of mathematics. In this chapter, we will look specifically at activities that focus on this thinking and reasoning throughout the grades. As algebraic reasoning develops, so must the language and symbolism that have been developed to support and communicate that thinking—specifically equations, variables, and functions. Because of their importance to the development of algebraic reasoning, both the concept of function and functional notation are also examined in this chapter.

BIG IDEAS

1. Logical patterns exist and are a regular occurrence in mathematics. They can be recognized, extended, or generalized. The same pattern can be found in many different forms. Patterns are found in physical and geometric situations as well as in numbers.

2. Symbolism, especially that involving equations and variables, is used to express generalizations of patterns and relationships.

3. Variables are symbols that take the place of numbers or ranges of numbers. They have different meanings depending on whether they are being used as representations of quantities that vary or change, representations of specific unknown values, or place holders in a generalized expression or formula.

4. Equations and inequalities are used to express relationships between two quantities.

5. Functions are relationships or rules that uniquely associate members of one set with members of another set. These relationships can be expressed in real contexts, graphs, algebraic equations, tables, and words—different ways of expressing the same idea.

Repeating Patterns

Identifying and extending patterns is an important process in algebraic thinking. Simple patterns can be explored as early as kindergarten. Young children love to work with patterns such as those made with coloured blocks, connecting cubes, and buttons.

Using Materials in Patterning

When possible, patterning activities should involve some form of physical materials. This is especially true of repeating patterns in grades K–4. When patterns are built with materials, children are able to test the extension of a pattern and make changes without fear of being wrong.

Many kindergarten and grade 1 textbooks have pages where students are given a pattern such as a string of coloured beads. The task may be to colour the last bead or two in the string. There are two differences between this and the same activity done with actual materials.

First, when done by colouring on the page, the activity takes on an aura of right versus wrong. If a mistake is made, correction on the page is difficult and this can cause feelings of inadequacy. Materials allow a trial-and-error approach to be used. Second, patterning activities on worksheets prevent children from extending patterns beyond the few spaces provided by the page. Most children enjoy using materials such as coloured blocks, buttons, and interlocking cubes to extend their patterns indefinitely. Children are frequently observed continuing a pattern with materials halfway across the classroom floor. In doing so, they receive a great deal of satisfaction and positive feedback from the activity itself. "Hey, I understand this! I can do it really well. I feel good about how I solved my pattern problem."

Repeating-Pattern Activities

The concept of a repeating pattern and how a pattern is extended or continued can be introduced to the full class in several ways. One possibility is to draw simple shape patterns on the board and extend them in a class discussion. All children can join in when the class is working on oral patterns. For example, "do, mi, mi, do, mi, mi, ..." is a simple singing pattern. Up, down, and sideways arm positions provide three elements with which to make patterns: up, side, side, down, up, side, side, down, ... Boy-girl patterns or stand-sit-squat patterns are also fun. From these ideas, the youngest children quickly learn the concept of patterns. Students can begin to work more profitably in small groups or even independently once a general notion of patterning is developed.

ACTIVITY 19.1

Pattern Strips

Students can work independently or in groups of two or three to extend patterns made from simple materials: buttons, coloured blocks, interlocking cubes, toothpicks, geometric shapes—items you can gather easily. For each set of materials, draw *three* complete repetitions of a pattern on strips of tag-board about 5 cm by 30 cm. The students' task is to copy the pattern using actual materials, and extend it as far as they wish. Discussions with students will help them describe their patterns and uncover errors. Figure 19.1 illustrates possible patterns for a variety of materials. It is not necessary to have class-size sets of materials. Make 10 to 15 different pattern strips for each set of materials. With six to eight sets, your entire class can work at the same time, in small groups, with different patterns and a variety of materials.

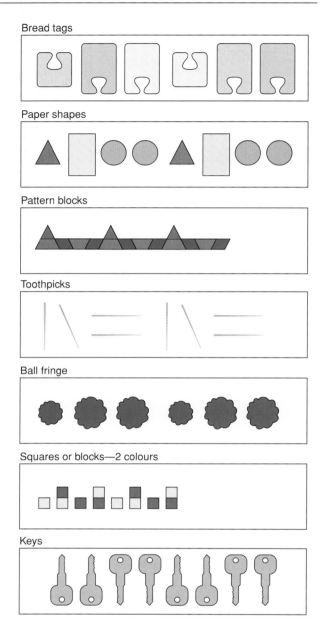

FIGURE 19.1 Examples of pattern cards drawn on tagboard. Each pattern repeats completely and does not split in the middle of a core.

The *core* of a repeating pattern is the shortest string of elements that repeats. Notice in Figure 19.1 that the core is always fully repeated and never only partially shown. If the core of a pattern is –oo, a card might have –oo–oo–oo (three repetitions of the core) It would be ambiguous if the card showed –oo–oo– or –oo–.

A significant step forward mathematically is to see that two patterns constructed with different materials are actually the same pattern. For example, the first pattern in Figure 19.1 and the first pattern in Figure 19.2 can both be "read" A-B-B-A-B-B-A-B-B- and the pattern below those in both figures is A-B-C-C-A-B-C-C-A-B-C-C. Challenging students to translate a pattern from one medium to another or to find two patterns that are alike, even though made with different materials, helps them focus on the relationships that are the essence of repeated patterns.

ACTIVITY 19.2
Pattern Match

Using the chalkboard or overhead projector, show six or seven patterns with different materials or pictures. Teach students to use an A, B, C method for articulating a pattern. Half of the class can close their eyes while the other half reads aloud, using the A, B, C scheme, the pattern to which you point. After hearing the pattern, the students who had their eyes closed

examine the patterns and try to decide which pattern was read. If two of the patterns in the list have the same structure, the discussion can be very interesting.

The following independent activity, which involves translation of a pattern from one medium to another, is another way of helping students separate the relationship in a pattern from the materials used to build it.

ACTIVITY 19.3
Same Pattern, Different Stuff

This activity can be set up so that sets of materials can be switched easily from one pattern strip to another. Provide students with a strip on which a set of materials illustrates a pattern.

FIGURE 19.2 More examples of repeating patterns.

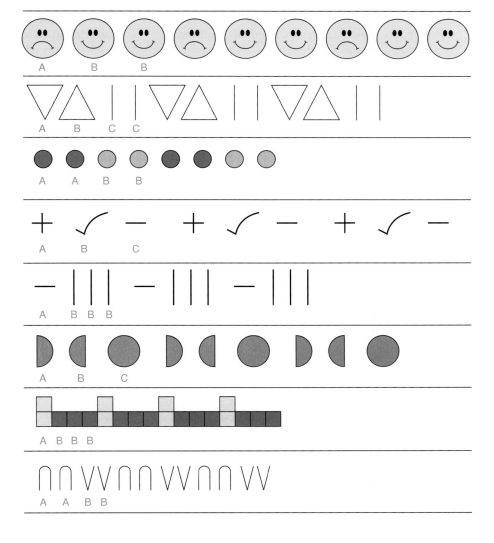

Have students make a pattern that resembles this pattern using a different set of materials. Compare to see if the two patterns match. A similar idea is to make pattern strips using four or five different sets of materials, then have students find strips that have the same pattern. Students can test to find out if two patterns are the same by translating each of the patterns into a third set of materials, or they can write down the A, B, C pattern for each of them.

The challenge in the next activity is a forerunner to looking at the function aspect of patterns.

ACTIVITY 19.4

Predict Down the Line

For most repeating patterns, the elements of the pattern can be numbered 1, 2, 3, and so on. Provide students with a pattern to extend. Before students begin to extend the pattern, have them predict exactly what element will be in, say, the fifteenth position. Students should be required to provide a reason for their prediction, preferably in writing. Students should then extend the pattern as before and check their prediction. If their prediction is incorrect, have them examine their reasoning and try to figure out why the prediction was off.

The prediction activity may be quite challenging for students prior to grade 2. Eventually, they will figure out the importance of the core to the design of the pattern. If you ask students what the hundredth or even the three-hundredth element might be, they will not be able to check their prediction by extending the pattern. Hence verification will focus on the rationale for their prediction. In some cases students may need to use a calculator to skip-count or multiply, but it is always the reasoning that is most important.

Growing Patterns

Beginning at about grade 4 or 5 and extending through to grade 8, students can explore patterns in which there is a progression from one element (step) to the next. In technical terms, these are called *sequences;* we will simply call them *growing patterns* because the elements increase as you move from one to the next. With these patterns, students not only extend a pattern, but they also look for a generalization or an algebraic relationship that will tell them

what the pattern will be at any point along the way. Growing patterns also demonstrate the concept of function and can be used as an entry point to this very important mathematical idea.

Figure 19.3 illustrates some growing patterns that are built with various materials or drawings. The patterns consist of a series of separate elements or *frames*. Each new frame is related to the previous one according to the pattern.

The first thing to do with patterns in the upper and middle grades is to get students comfortable with building them and talking about how they can be extended in a logical manner. Constructing patterns with physical materials such as tiles, counters, or flat toothpicks allows students to make changes if necessary, and to build on to one frame to make a new frame. It is also more fun and helpful!

ACTIVITY 19.5

Extend and Explain

As an introduction to growing patterns, show students the first three elements or frames of a pattern. Provide them with appropriate materials or grid paper, and have them extend the patterns and explain why they extended the patterns the way they did. There may be more than one way to extend a pattern. If, for example, you were to suggest only the first two elements of the block pattern at the top of Figure 19.3, students might well develop four or five patterns that are different from the stair steps shown in the figure. The purpose would simply be to explore the idea of progression from one frame, or part, to the next in a growing pattern.

When discussing a pattern, students should try to determine how each frame in the pattern differs from the preceding frame. If each new frame can be built by adding to, or changing the previous frame, the discussion should include how this can be done. For example, in Figure 19.3, each stair step can be made by adding a column of blocks to the preceding stair steps. In contrast, the pattern of red tiles involves a form of expansion rather than adding on.

Growing patterns also have a numerical component: the number of objects in each frame. As shown in Figure 19.4, a table can be made for any growing pattern. One row of the table or chart is for the frame number, and the other is for recording the number of objects in that frame. Frequently, a pattern grows so quickly and requires so many blocks or spaces that it is only reasonable to build or draw the first five or six frames. This leads to the following activity.

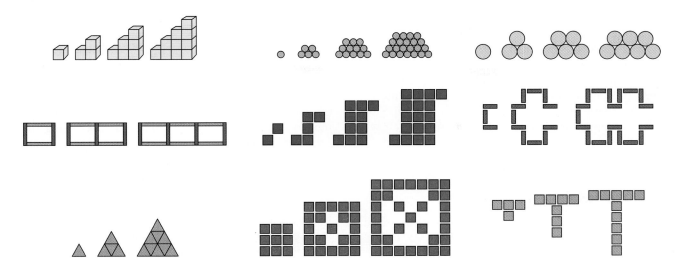

FIGURE 19.3 Growing patterns with materials or drawings.

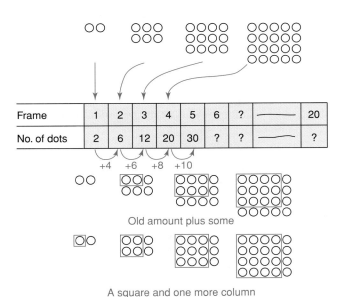

FIGURE 19.4 Two different relationships in a visual pattern.

ACTIVITY 19.6

Predict How Many

Have students begin to extend a growing pattern you provide. They should also make a table showing the number of items that are needed in each frame of the pattern. The task is to predict the number of items in the twentieth frame of the pattern. The challenge is to see if there is a way to do this without filling in the first 19 entries of

the table. Predictions should also be accompanied by an explanation.

Activity 19.6 is a natural progression from the earlier prediction activity with repeating patterns. Finding a way to determine the twentieth or even the hundredth entry in the table gets at the heart of how to find a relationship that students will later recognize as an example of a function. We next look at how to help students find these relationships.

Searching for Relationships

Once a table or chart is developed, students have two representations of the pattern: the one created with the drawing or materials, and the numerical version in the table. When looking for relationships, some students will focus on the table and others will focus on the concrete or pictorial pattern. It is important for students to see that any relationships they discover exist in both forms. So if a relationship is found in a table, challenge students to see how that plays out in the concrete or pictorial version.

Patterns from Frame to Frame: Recursive Relationships

For most students, it is easy to see the pattern developing from one frame to the next. When you have a chart constructed, the difference from one frame to the next can be written next to or below the chart, as in Figure 19.4. In that example, the numbers in each of the frames can be determined by adding successive even numbers to the numbers in the previous frame. The description that tells how a pattern changes from any given frame to the next is known as a *recursive relationship*.

Whenever there is a pattern in the table, see if students can find that same pattern in the physical version. In Figure 19.4, notice that for every frame, the picture or concrete pattern and the table are closely connected. This lets you examine the amount added. It also lets you see how the pattern of adding on even numbers is created.

Patterns from Frame Number to Frame: Functional Relationships

The recursive frame-to-frame pattern is almost certain to be the first that your students will observe. However, to find the entry for the hundredth frame, the only way a recursive pattern can help is to find all of the prior 99 entries in the table. If a rule or relationship can be discovered that connects the number of objects in a frame to the frame number, any entry in a table can be determined without having to build or calculate the intermediate entries. A rule that determines the number of elements in a frame from the frame number is an example of a *functional relationship*.

There is no single best method for finding the relationship between the frame number and the frame. Some students may get an insight by simply "playing around" with the numbers and asking, "How can I operate on the frame number to get the corresponding number in the table?" Most will benefit from examining the concrete or pictorial pattern for regularities. At the bottom of Figure 19.4, a square array is outlined for each frame. Each successive square increases by one row and one column of dots. What relationship might exist between this subset of

the pattern and the frame numbers? In this example, the side of each square has the same number of dots as the frame number. The row to the right of each square is also the same as the frame number. With that information, how would you describe the twentieth frame? Can you determine how many elements it would have without drawing the picture? At this point, a significant activity is to write a numerical expression for each frame number using the same pattern. For example, the first four frames in Figure 19.4 are $1^2 + 1$, $2^2 + 2$, $3^2 + 3$, and $4^2 + 4$.

It may take much searching and experimenting for students in groups or as a class to come up with an expression that is similar for each frame. Do not be upset if students have difficulty. Encourage the search for relationships to continue, even if it takes more than one day. The search for relationships is the most significant portion of these activities.

Moving from Patterns to Function and Variable

When students have discovered a numerical expression for each frame, enclose the frame numbers with brackets, as shown in Figure 19.5. If this results in a pattern, then only the numbers in the brackets will change from one frame to the next while the other numbers in the expressions remain the same. Now, if you replace the numbers in the brackets with a letter or variable, the result will be a general formula. This formula defines functional relationship between the frame number and the frame value.

Before reading further, explore each of the patterns in Figure 19.3 to see if you can find formulas (functional relationships) for each. You should be able to plug the

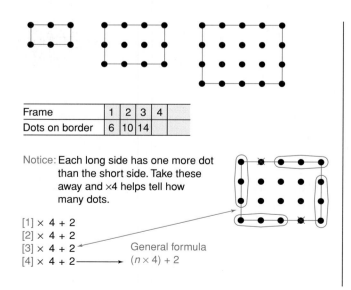

Frame	1	2	3	4	
Dots on border	6	10	14		

Notice: Each long side has one more dot than the short side. Take these away and ×4 helps tell how many dots.

[1] × 4 + 2
[2] × 4 + 2
[3] × 4 + 2
[4] × 4 + 2 ——→ General formula
                     (n × 4) + 2

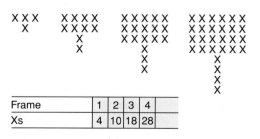

Frame	1	2	3	4	
Xs	4	10	18	28	

Notice: If the tail part is added to the side of the top part, there is always a square and three more columns.

[1] × [1] + (3 × [1])
[2] × [2] + (3 × [2])
[3] × [3] + (3 × [3])

⋮   General formula
$n \times n + 3n = n^2 + 3n$

FIGURE 19.5 Finding functional relationships in patterns.

frame numbers into your formula and get the value for that frame. Some are much harder than others.

The discussion to this point is summarized in the following activity, an elaboration of "Predict How Many." It is best to do this in groups so that ideas can be generated more freely.

ACTIVITY 19.7

Find the Function in the Pattern

Give students the beginning of a pattern. At least three frames is usual. Their tasks are as follows:

1. Extend the pattern by several more frames until they are sure they understand it. They should always look backward to the beginning of the pattern to see that their idea works for all frames. Record this in a drawing.

2. Make a table that shows the frame number and elements for every frame they have constructed.

3. Find and describe in writing as many patterns as possible found in the table and in the concrete or pictorial pattern. For each pattern found in the table, students should be able to see how it can be found in the concrete or pictorial pattern. The most important pattern to look for is the one that links frame number to frame—the functional relationship.

4. Write the frame-number-to-frame relationship as a formula in terms of the frame number. Show how the formula works for each part of the table already constructed. Use the formula to predict the next entry in the table. If possible, check this with the actual construction of the pattern. Use the formula to predict the twentieth entry in the table.

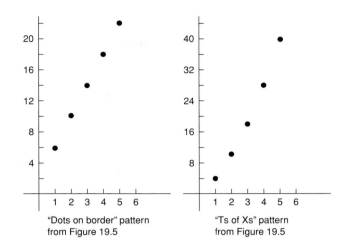

"Dots on border" pattern from Figure 19.5

"Ts of Xs" pattern from Figure 19.5

FIGURE 19.6   Graphs of growing patterns.

Other Patterns to Explore

It would be an error to leave the impression that repeated patterns and growing patterns, as discussed so far, are all that students need to know about patterns. Mathematicians continue to search for and discover new patterns and relationships. Applications of mathematical patterns have led to solutions of real-world problems that were once thought to be unsolvable. Patterns are powerful ideas.

Patterns on the Hundreds Chart

The hundreds chart is a rich field for exploring number relationships and should not be thought of solely as a device for teaching numeration.

ACTIVITY 19.8

Skip-Counting Patterns on a Hundreds Chart

Duplicate a lot of small copies of hundreds charts (see Blackline Masters). Let children pick a number from 2 to 10. Their task is to begin with 0 and skip-count using that number. For each count, they should colour in the corresponding number on their chart and look for patterns. When they have finished skip-counting and colouring all the way to 100, they should write a description of their pattern. The written report can then accompany the coloured pattern on the hundreds chart. See Figure 19.7 for two examples of patterns.

Graphing the Patterns

So far, concrete materials, drawings, charts, and symbolic rules have been used to represent growing patterns. A fourth way is a graph. The individual points in a pattern can be plotted even if the concrete or pictorial pattern has not been discovered. Figure 19.6 shows the graph for each of the two patterns in Figure 19.5. Notice that the first is a straight-line (linear) relationship and the other is a curved line that would make half of a parabola if the points were joined.

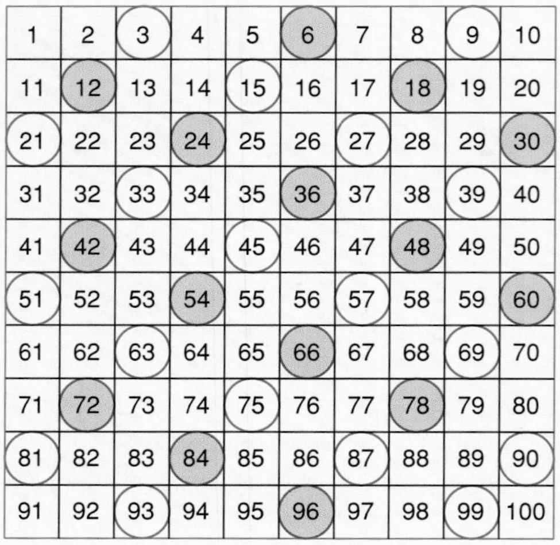

FIGURE 19.7 Skip-counting by sixes (coloured blue) and threes (circled with red).

Here are some possible follow-up problems to accompany Activity 19.8:

Which numbers make diagonal patterns? Which make columnar patterns?

Can you find two skip-counting patterns in which the same squares are coloured? That is, the pattern for one is on top of the pattern for the other. How are these two skip-counting numbers related? Are there others in which the patterns cover each other?

What patterns only have a few squares in common? On what numbers do the patterns cross? Can you tell without looking at the charts?

What happens to the patterns if you use the same skip-counting number but start with 1 or some other number instead of starting with 0?

Change the Charts, Change the Patterns

Have students make number charts with fewer than 10 numbers in a row. Use centimetre grid paper. Repeat the skip-counting tasks from Activity 19.8. The challenge is to discover which skip-counts will form diagonal patterns and which will form columnar patterns. The answer will vary, depending on the width of the chart. (See Figure 19.8 for two examples.)

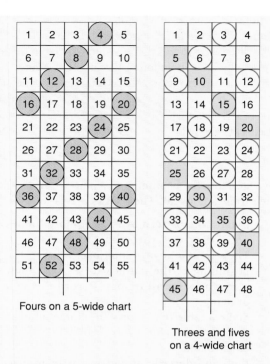

Fours on a 5-wide chart

Threes and fives on a 4-wide chart

FIGURE 19.8 Patterns on hundreds charts of different widths.

Have students look for relationships that involve the skip-counting number, the width of the chart, and the direction of the pattern. Is it diagonal or columnar?

Students will find that the same patterns occur as in the regular chart. However, patterns will occur in columns when skip-counting is done with a factor or a multiple of the chart width. For example, on a chart that is 9 squares wide, the multiples of 3 will make a columnar pattern and the multiples of 2 a diagonal one. What will a pattern for a multiple of 6 do on a chart, which is 9 squares wide? What if the number of squares in the width of the chart is equal to a prime number? You can also explore charts that are wider than 10 squares.

Number Patterns

Many worthwhile patterns can be observed with numbers alone. These can be simple repeating patterns such as 1, 2, 1, 2, … Even very young children can use numbers in patterns like these. Generally, however, numerical patterns involve some form of progression. The pattern 1, 2, 1, 3, 1, 4, 1, 5, … is a simple example that even young students can discover. Here are some more numerical patterns:

2, 4, 6, 8, 10, ...	(even numbers; add 2 each time)
1, 4, 7, 10, 13, ...	(start with 1; add 3 each time)
1, 4, 9, 16, ...	(squares: 1^2, 2^2, 3^2, etc.)
0, 1, 5, 14, 30, ...	(add the next square number)
2, 5, 11, 23, ...	(double the number and add 1)
2, 6, 12, 20, 30, ...	(multiply consecutive pairs of natural numbers)
3, 3, 6, 9, 15, 24, ...	(add the two preceding numbers —an example of a Fibonacci sequence)

The challenge in these sequences of numbers is not only to find and extend the pattern, but also to try to determine a general rule to produce the *n*th number in the sequence. Informal or exploratory approaches are similar to those described for growing patterns.

ACTIVITY 19.10

Pairs of Patterns: Alike and Different

Give students two patterns that are related in some way. To indicate that they understand the patterns, they should first extend each one by at least five more numbers. Next, they should write an explanation of how the two patterns are *alike* and how the two patterns are *different*. Here are some pairs to use:

2, 4, 6, 8, 10, ... and 3, 5, 7, 9, 11, ...
2, 4, 6, 8, 10, ... and 2, 4, 8, 16, 32, ...
3, 4, 3, 4, 3, 4, ... and 7, 9, 7, 9, 7, 9, ...
5, 10, 15, 20, 25, ... and 2, 7, 12, 17, 22, ...
10, 20, 30, 40, 50, ... and 50, 100, 150, 200, 250, ...

After solving several pairs of related number patterns, students can make up their own pairs of patterns and challenge other students to discover how they are alike and different.

The calculator is a powerful tool for approaching patterns. A few examples are presented here, but there are many more.

ACTIVITY 19.11

Skip-Counting Patterns

Choose a start number between 0 and 9, and add a constant (skip number) repeatedly to that number. Remember to use the automatic constant feature. For example, to start with 7 and add 4 repeatedly, you press 7 ⊞ 4 ⊟ ⊟ ⊟ .... What digits appear in the ones place? (1, 5, 9, 3, 7, 1, 5, 9, 3, 7, ...) How long is the pattern before it repeats? Are all patterns the same length? Are

there shorter ones? Can you find one that is six numbers in length? Why not? How does this change when the start number changes? How does it change when the skip number changes?

An extended discussion of this last activity can be found in Chapter 2, "Start and Jump Numbers" (p. 20).

ACTIVITY 19.12

Secret Function I

This game can be introduced using an overhead calculator with the full class, then pairs of children can play independently. Without the class looking, store a one-step operation (secret function) in the calculator. Here is an example for each operation:

Addition:	Secret ⊟ ⊞ 8	
	Press 0 ⊞ 8 ⊟ ± ⊟	
Subtraction:	Secret ⊟ ⊟ 24	
	Press 0 ⊟ 4 ⊟ ± ⊟	
Multiplication:	Secret ⊟ ⊠ 36	
	Press 6 ⊠ 0 ⊟	
Division:	Secret ⊟ ⊞ 3	
	Press 0 ⊞ 3 ⊟	

The display will show 0 after the function has been stored. After a secret function has been entered, students try to guess the secret rule or function. They can get up to three clues. To get the first clue, they enter any number and press ⊟ to see what the secret function does to the entered number. They can get a second clue to the secret by pressing ⊟ again and the third clue by pressing ⊟ a third time. After each clue, they should try to guess the secret function and predict the display after the next ⊟ press.

"Secret Function I" can be played at any grade level with addition and subtraction. Be prepared to talk about numbers less than zero. When division is used, decimals will appear. At the upper grade levels, the multiplication and division functions may be decimals or fractions. Consider the discussion when the rule is × 0.5 and a student guesses ÷ 2. As a variation, a different number can be entered each time before pressing ⊟ , instead of successively pressing ⊟ . If any of the operation keys are pressed, the function will no longer be stored. (Your calculator must have a sign-change key ± to enter addition or subtraction functions. Some calculators store the second rather than the first factor for multiplication. In that case, reverse the order in the hidden function.) As with all calculator activities, check your students' calculators before beginning.

ACTIVITY 19.13

Amazing Digits

Enter 9 ⊠ *n*, where *n* is any number from 1 to 9. Press ⊟ . Now press other numbers followed by ⊟ . Even if students know their 9 facts, this step will serve to clarify the process and illustrate that each new press of ⊟ multiplies the display by 9. Now enter 99 ⊠ *n* =. Try other values of *n* followed by ⊟ . What is the pattern? Try 999 ⊠ *n* and even 9999 or 99999 ⊠ *n*. Students should play with and explore this idea as long as they wish. Next try using repeating digits for *n* (3333 or 66). Instead of using nines for the multiplier, try using 0.009 or 99.9. Also experiment with other repeating-digit multipliers. If students are interested, the patterns with nines might be analyzed by looking at 999 as 1000 − 1 or as 9 × 111.

ACTIVITY 19.14

More Amazing Digits

Especially if students have shown interest in "Amazing Digits," try division by 9. Begin by just dividing single-digit numbers by 9. (The calculator remembers the last divisor, so after the first division, just enter the new number and press ⊟ .) After this, there are all sorts of variations to try:

a. Divide by 99, 999,...

b. Divide by 0.9, 0.09, 0.009,...

c. Divide by 9, but use two-digit dividends. Can you predict the results?

d. Try three-digit dividends and a divisor of 9.

e. Combine (a) or (b) with (c) or (d).

The patterns in "More Amazing Digits" are spectacular and interesting by themselves, but you may also want to try using a digit other than 9 in that exercise.

ACTIVITY 19.15

Consecutive Odd Numbers

Before doing this activity, you will need to explain what consecutive odd numbers are and how to add them on the calculator. Consecutive odd numbers are odd numbers whose counting order is sequential. Thus 1, 3, 5, 7 are consecutive odd numbers, as are 27, 29, 31. To add a string of these numbers, it might be helpful to some students to write the numbers down before adding them on the calculator. Young students are often confused when they have to add more than two numbers in a row. When they press ⊞ after the second addend, the display shows the sum as if ⊟ had been pressed.

Part 1

Have students use their calculators as they construct a chart that lists the sums of the first *n* consecutive odd numbers.

1	1
1 + 3	4
1 + 3 + 5	9
1 + 3 + 5 + 7	16

and so on.

The sums should look familiar. If students (around grades 5 to 8) do not recognize these as square numbers, suggest that they press the √ key after they get the sum. It would be a good idea for them to express the sums as squares (1^2, 2^2, 3^2, 4^2, ...). Can they predict the sum of the first 20 or first 50 consecutive odd numbers?

Part 2

If the consecutive odd numbers are written in a triangular list as shown here, and the sum of each horizontal row is recorded, there is an interesting result:

$$1$$
$$3 \quad 5$$
$$7 \quad 9 \quad 11$$
$$13 \quad 15 \quad 17 \quad 19$$

and so on.

As follow-up to the odd sum activity, students may want to examine consecutive even numbers or simply consecutive numbers. For example, what can you tell about the sum of any four consecutive numbers? Any five? Pick a number less than 100. Can you find a string of consecutive numbers that add up to your number? Can you find two different consecutive strings of numbers that have the same sum? (3 + 4 + 5 + 6 = 5 + 6 + 7). What numbers have only one sum?

The Fibonacci Sequence

For a growing pattern that is just a little bit different, see Figure 19.9. It begins with a little square. Each successive frame is formed by building a new and larger square onto the previous one. (Can you see how to continue drawing this pattern?) If the side of each of the first two little squares is 1, then the sides of each new square are the numbers of most interest in this pattern. For those squares shown in the figure, the sides are 1, 1, 2, 3, 5, 8, and 13. What would the side of the next square be? This series of numbers, known as the *Fibonacci sequence,* is named for the Italian mathematician Leonardo Fibonacci (c. 1180–1250). The sequence occurs in a variety of living things. For example, if you count the sets of spirals that go in opposite directions on a pineapple or the seeds of a sunflower, the two numbers will be adjacent numbers in the Fibonacci sequence, usually 8 and 13 for a pineapple and 55 and 89 for sunflowers.

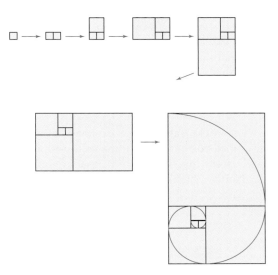

FIGURE 19.9 A growing pattern of squares: Each new rectangle is a little closer to a "golden rectangle."

Another interesting fact about the Fibonacci sequence is that the ratio of adjacent numbers in the sequence gets closer and closer to a single fixed number known as the *golden ratio,* a number very close to 1.618. Each larger rectangle in Figure 19.9 has sides in a ratio, which are a little closer to the golden ratio. A rectangle in that ratio is called a *golden rectangle.* Examples can be found in most of prominent ancient Greek architecture as well as in much art and architecture through the ages. The spiral in the last rectangle in Figure 19.9, made from quarter circles drawn in each square, is the same spiral found in the shell of the chambered nautilus.

The usual Fibonacci sequence begins with 1, 1. After these first two terms, the next term is found by adding the two preceding terms: 1 + 1 = 2, 1 + 2 = 3, 2 + 3 = 5, 3 + 5 = 8, and so on. What happens if you use the same rule for generating each new number but you begin with numbers other than 1 and 1? This is an interesting exploration. Among other things you may discover is that the ratio of successive pairs of terms also gets closer and closer to the

same golden ratio, 1.618 ..., as in the regular Fibonacci sequence. The Fibonacci sequence and the golden ratio are fascinating phenomena of mathematics. For those who would like to learn more about the connections of this sequence with nature, art, and mathematics, books by Runion (1990) and by Garland (1987) are highly recommended.

Variables and Equations

One of the most powerful ways we have of expressing the regularities found in mathematics is with variables. Variables enable us to use mathematical symbolism as a tool to better think about and understand mathematical ideas, in the same way we use concrete objects and drawings. But if variables are included with these other "thinker toys," it is important to help students develop an understanding of the various ways they are used.

Variables

A *variable* is a symbol that can stand for any one of a set of numbers or other objects. This simple-sounding definition has a variety of interpretations, depending on how the variables are used. A less-than-clear understanding can lead to a host of misinterpretations.

Misunderstandings about Variables

Even though students are exposed throughout the elementary years to boxes and letters in arithmetic expressions, studies indicate that most children have a very narrow understanding of the concept of "variable" (Booth, 1988; Chalouh & Herscovics; Lodholz, 1990).

Some students believe that there are different solutions for $7w + 22 = 109$ and $7n + 22 = 109$. Students readily accept L for length but have difficulty accepting another letter for the same quantity. Letters are sometimes taken to represent objects rather than numerical values. Converting the statement "John has three times as many apples as Mary" to symbols, we might use $3a$ for John's apples. Here, the a stands not for *apples,* but for the *number of apples.*

Conventions of notation also compound the difficulty. For example, we use ab to mean $a \times b$, but $3 \times 5 \neq 35$. Similarly, $ab = ba$, but $35 \neq 53$; and $4 + 0.75 = 4.75$, but $2x + y \neq 2xy$.

Different Uses of Variables

Meanings of variables change with the way they are used. Usiskin (1988) identified three uses of variables that are commonly encountered in school mathematics:

1. *As a specific unknown.* In the early grades, this is the use found in equations such as $8 + \square = 12$. Later, we

see exercises such as this: If $3x + 2 = 4x - 1$, solve for x.

2. *As a pattern generalizer.* Variables are used in statements that are true for all numbers. For example, $a \times b = b \times a$ for all real numbers. Formulas such as $A = L \times W$ also show a pattern.

3. *As quantities that vary in joint variation.* Joint variation occurs when change in one variable determines a change in another. In $y = 3x + 5$, as x changes or varies, so does y. Formulas are also an example of joint variation. In $C = 2\pi r$, as r, the radius, changes, so does C, the circumference.

Variables as Unknowns

The following activity is a reasonable way for students to experience the meaning of a variable as a placeholder.

ACTIVITY 19.16

Story Translations

Read a simple story problem to students, but omit the question. Their task is to write an equation that means the same thing. For example: *There are 3 full boxes of pencils and 5 extra pencils. There are 41 pencils in all.* ($3 \times \square + 5 = 41$) Be sure to include all meanings of all four operations as described in Chapter 7. The activity can be reversed by providing an equation with an unknown, and letting students make up a story to go with it. Once equations are agreed on, students should use whatever means they wish to find values that make the sentences true. Trial and error is a reasonable first strategy.

Sometimes students will write what may look like different equations. For example, *If Richveer has 12 cards and Sofia has 5, write the equation that tells how many more cards Richveer has.* Both of these equations might be written: $12 - 5 = \square$ and $5 + \square = 12$. Students should decide how these equations are alike and how they are different.

ACTIVITY 19.17

Number Tricks

Have students do the following sequence of operations:

Write down any number.

Add to it the number that comes after it.

Add 9.

Divide by 2.

Subtract the number with which you began.

Now you can "magically" read their minds. Everyone ended up with 5!

The challenge is to see if students can discover the secret to the trick. If students need a hint, suggest that instead of using an actual number, they use a box or a letter to begin with. Start with n. Add the next number: $n + (n + 1) = 2n + 1$. Adding 9 gives $2n + 10$. Dividing by 2 leaves $n + 5$. Now subtract the number with which you began, which leaves 5.

There are endless trick sequences like the one in this activity. Here are two more:

Pick a number between 1 and 9, multiply by 5, add 3, multiply by 2, add another number between 1 and 9, subtract 6. What do you see?

Pick a number, multiply by 6, add 12, take half of the result, subtract 6, divide by 3. What happens?

These tricks can also be explored with models by using a small box or a cube for the unknown. Figure 19.10 shows how the first of the two tricks above might be modelled. Notice the place-value component required to understand the result.

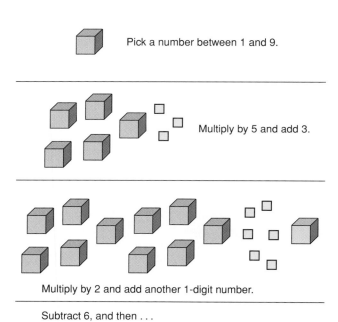

Pick a number between 1 and 9.

Multiply by 5 and add 3.

Multiply by 2 and add another 1-digit number.

Subtract 6, and then . . .

$10 \times \square + \square = \square\square$

(a 2-digit number)

FIGURE 19.10 Number tricks can be modelled using a block or a box for the unknown. Additional numbers are shown with counters or base-ten pieces.

Variables as Pattern Generators

Variables are often used to illustrate rules or regularities that exist in our number system. We often write down these rules using variables, without giving much thought to the fact that students may not understand the variables involved.

ACTIVITY 19.18

What's True for All Numbers?

Ask students how they know that 465 + 137 = 137 + 465 without doing the computation. Students' explanations should show evidence of understanding the commutative (order) property for addition, even though the name of the property is not important. How can this be written to show that it's a rule that is true for every number, even for fractions and decimals? If students do not suggest it, offer the idea that letters or shapes could be used like this:

$$\Delta + \square = \square + \Delta \quad \text{or} \quad n + m = m + n$$

Be sure students understand that the choice of letter or shape is totally arbitrary; each variable may stand for any number, but when the same letter or shape appears more than once in the same equation, it must represent the same value.

With this introduction, challenge students to find other statements that are true for all numbers.

Students may need some prodding to think up things that are always true, but it is best that they come up with the ideas themselves. One way to provide hints is to explore some specific examples. For example, draw a rectangle and divide it as shown in Figure 19.11. What are two ways to calculate the area? One way is to add 30 + 13, then multiply by 8: 8 (30 +13). Another way is to multiply 30 by 8 and 13 by 8, and add the two products: (8 x 30) + (8 x 13). These examples can lead students to the generalized version of the distributive property:

$a(b + c) = (a \times b) + (a \times c)$. In addition to properties of the number system, also think about definitions of exponents or rules for negative numbers, all of which can be expressed in a general form using variables.

ACTIVITY 19.19

Special Quantities

What numerical expression would tell the number of chair legs on 376 chairs? (376 × 4) What about 195 chairs? (195 × 4) How would you write the number of legs on any number of chairs? (n × 4) Using this as an example, challenge students to write expressions for other types of quantities: fingers on students, eggs in cartons, crayons in boxes, wheels on tractor trailers, hours in days, centimetres in a metre, grams in a kilogram, and so on. Similarly, use variables to express these special numbers: any odd number, any even number, any multiple of 7, a multiple of 3 plus a different multiple of 5, any two-digit number, any power of 2. Once students get the idea, have them make up their own special quantities and see if others can describe them verbally.

The way that variables are used in the "Special Quantities" activity is essentially the way variables are used in spreadsheets. In Figure 19.12, odd and even numbers are generated from the numbers in column A. These values are then used in the sums and products columns.

Formulas that relate two or more quantities also express generalizations. For example, the formula $A = b \times h$ shows the relationship between the area of a rectangle and the product of its base and height. $F = (\frac{9}{5})C + 32$ illustrates the relationship between Fahrenheit and Celsius temperatures. What equation would you use to indicate the relationship between hours and days? A common error would be to write $24h = d$. If you wished to find the number of hours in 2 days, you might substitute 2 for h—but in this formula, the result would be 48 days instead of 2 days. The difficulty is found in the syntax. Contrast "There are 24 hours in 1 day" with "The number of hours is 24 times the number of days." The variables stand for the *number* of hours and the *number* of days, not hours and days. Therefore, the correct relationship is h = 24d.

Variables as Quantities That Vary

"Joint variation is at the heart of understanding patterns and functions. As students grow in their ability to derive meaning for variables in contexts, they encounter variables that are changing in relation to each other" (Lappan, 1998,

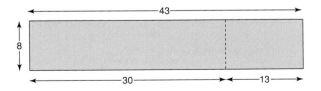

FIGURE 19.11 The distributive property is just one of many ideas that can be generalized using variables.

FIGURE 19.12 A spreadsheet formula uses variables to represent values in other cells. The expression in a cell is a pattern generalizer for that cell. The same spreadsheet is shown twice here, once with the formula in each cell and once with the cell values calculated. Note that any change in column A will produce changes in the entire row.

	A	B	C	D	E	F	G	H	I
1	**Exploring Odd and Even Numbers**								
2									
3	N	Even	Odd	E + E	E + O	O + O	E × E	E × O	O × O
4	1	2	3	4	5	6	4	6	9
5	2	4	5	8	9	10	16	20	25
6	7	14	15	28	29	30	196	210	225
7	10	20	21	40	41	42	400	420	441
8	15	30	31	60	61	62	900	930	961

	A	B	C	D	E	F	G	H	I
1	**Exploring Odd and Even Numbers**								
2									
3	N	Even	Odd	E + E	E + O	O + O	E × E	E × O	O × O
4	1	=2*A4	=2*A4+1	=B4+B4	=B4+C4	=C4+C4	=B4*B4	=B4*C4	=C4*C4
5	2	=2*A5	=2*A5+1	=B5+B5	=B5+C5	=C5+C5	=B5*B5	=B5*C5	=C5*C5
6	7	=2*A6	=2*A6+1	=B6+B6	=B6+C6	=C6+C6	=B6*B6	=B6*C6	=C6*C6
7	10	=2*A7	=2*A7+1	=B7+B7	=B7+C7	=C7+C7	=B7*B7	=B7*C7	=C7*C7
8	15	=2*A8	=2*A8+1	=B8+B8	=B8+C8	=C8+C8	=B8*B8	=B8*C8	=C8*C8

p. 57). Whenever students develop charts that list the corresponding values of two related quantities, they are exploring the idea of *joint variation;* the value in one row varies according to the value in the other row. Young children make charts showing the number of eyes for different numbers of students. In the study of ratio and proportion, slightly older students make charts relating cost to the number of units purchased, or relating kilometres driven to litres of gasoline used. In measurement, charts are made that relate circumference to diameter, or volume to the area of the base of a cylinder. In this chapter, we have seen that the study of growing patterns results in formulas that connect the frame number to the number of elements in that frame of the pattern.

All of these are examples of joint variation—one value changing in relation to another. They are also examples of functions, the rules that determine the way that the two variables are related. These are explored in more detail later.

Equations and Inequalities

In the expression $3b + 7 = b - c$, the equal sign means that the quantity on the left *is the same as* the quantity on the right. To understand expressions in this way, students must interpret simple arithmetic expressions such as $3 + 5$ or 4×87 as *single quantities*.

Unfortunately, students tend to look on expressions such as $3 + 5$ and 4×87 as commands or things to do. The = tells you to add, and students think of *add* as a verb or an operator button, like pressing = on a calculator. As students read left to right in an equation, the = tells them, "Now give the answer." Because of this "get an answer" view of operations and equal signs, students fail to think of $5 + 2$ as another way to write 7.

A Balance-Pan Approach to Equality

The following activities are ways to help students with the basic concepts needed to understand equations.

ACTIVITY 19.20

Names for Numbers

Challenge students to find different ways to express a particular number, say, 10. Give a few simple examples, such as 5 + 5 or 12 − 2. Encourage the use of two or more different operations. "How many names for 8 can you find using only numbers less than 10 and at least three operations?" In your discussion, emphasize that each expression is a way of representing or writing a number. Notice that there are no equal signs in this activity.

The next activity develops the concept of the equal sign. It begins with numbers only but is quickly extended to include variables.

Tilt or Balance

On the board, draw a simple two-pan balance. In each pan, write a numerical expression, and ask, "Will the two pans balance each other, or will one of them go down? If so, which one?" (see Figure 19.13). Challenge students to write expressions for each side of the scale to make it balance. For each, write a corresponding equation to illustrate the meaning of =. Note that when the scale "tilts," either a "greater than" or "less than" symbol (> or <) is used.

After a short time, add variables to the two-pan balance activity.

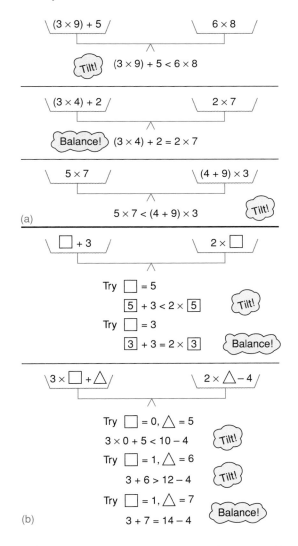

FIGURE 19.13 Using expressions and variables in equations and inequalities. The two-pan balance helps develop the meaning of =, <, and >.

Solving Equations

Variables and equations lead to the task of *solving equations*, which means finding values for the variables that make the equations true—or, in terms of the previous activity, that make the two pans balance evenly. Activities that use the two-pan balance idea help develop the concepts of equality and variable.

Variables in the Balance

Provide a drawing of a two-pan balance with three different shapes in the pans. For example, show two boxes, a triangle balancing a triangle, and a hexagon. Challenge students to find values for each of the shapes without tipping the scales. Explain that like shapes must represent the same number. This is true of variables in any equation. Students will generally use a guess-and-check approach, but you may see some begin to try other problem-solving approaches. For an equation with three variables, there will be many solutions.

Scales and More Scales

Provide pictures of balances or scales in which variables are represented by either shapes or letters. The task is to find values for the variables that will make all of the scales balance. Identical shapes or letters must represent the same values on all scales. Examples are shown in Figure 19.14. Notice that some scales are two-pan balances and others are spring scales that have a value showing. What students will quickly determine is that they can use the relationships between the shapes and the number on one scale to figure out the value of the variables on another scale, to help them arrive at a solution. Often there are multiple paths to the same result.

Encourage students to find methods other than guess-and-check to solve problems such as those in Figure 19.14. For example, can you tell how much greater the mass of one shape is than that of another ? What if you combine the amounts on two or more scales, either by adding or subtracting? Be sure to have students share their solution strategies so that all will hear different methods. Scale problems are easily designed by working backward from a solution. Assign values to the variables, and arrange them on the scales. For three variables, be sure to provide three scales.

Eventually, students will need more general techniques for solving simple equations in one variable. The following task challenges students to begin to develop these methods.

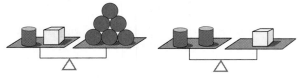

Which shape has the greatest mass? Explain.
Which shape has the least mass? Explain.

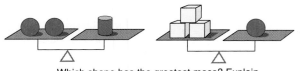

What will balance 2 spheres? Explain.

What is the mass of each shape? Explain.

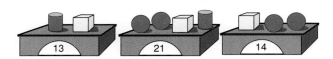

What is the mass of each shape? Explain.

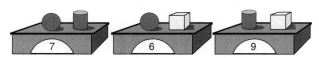

What is the mass of each shape? Explain.

FIGURE 19.14 Examples of problems with multiple scales (equations).

ACTIVITY 19.24

Adjust the Balance

Show a balance that has expressions on each side. Use only one variable. (See Figure 19.15a). Make the tasks such that finding a solution by guess and check is not reasonable. For example, the solution to $3x + 2 = 11 - x$ is not a whole number. Suggest that adjustments can be made

---

to the quantities in each pan as long as the balance is maintained. If you begin with simple equations such as $x - 17 = 31 - x$, students should be able to develop their skills and explain their rationale. Students should also be challenged to devise a method for proving that their solutions are correct. (Solutions can be tested by substitution in the original equation.)

Figure 19.15 shows solutions for two equations, one with a balance and the other without. Even after you have stopped using the balance, it is a good idea to refer to the scale- or balance pan concept of equality and the idea of keeping the scales balanced.

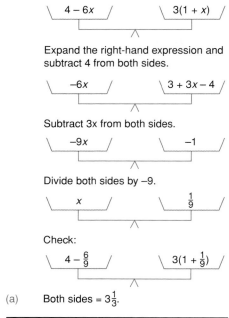

Expand the right-hand expression and subtract 4 from both sides.

Subtract 3x from both sides.

Divide both sides by −9.

Check:

(a) Both sides = $3\frac{1}{3}$.

$4.2n + 63 = \frac{n}{2}$

Subtract 63 from both sides.

$4.2n = \frac{n}{2} - 63$

Multiply both sides by 2.

$8.4n = n - 126$

Subtract n from both sides.

$7.4n = -126$

Divide both sides by 7.4. (Use a calculator!)

$n = -17.03$ (about)

(b)

FIGURE 19.15 Using a balance scale to think about solving equations.

Exploring Functions

A study of functions is a study of *joint variation*. It is a study of the way change in one variable affects change in another. Technically, a *function* is a rule of correspondence between two sets that uniquely associates elements of the first set with elements of the second. In other words, it is the rule that defines how the first variable affects the second. The variable representing elements from the first set is called the *independent* variable. Since the value of the second variable in the function depends on the value of the first, it is called the *dependent* variable. Though correct, these definitions are not very good starting points for students. The best way to develop functional relationships is to begin with meaningful situations in which functions can be found.

Developing Function Concepts in the Classroom

An investigation of meaningful contexts can result in the development and articulation of functional concepts in ways that make sense to students. To develop facility with functions, study should begin with a context, explore the relationships, and develop different representations to show what has been found.

Begin with Meaningful Contexts

The search for functional relationships is part of the science of pattern and order—the doing of mathematics. Some contexts can be tied to other strands of the curriculum, providing important connections within mathematics.

- Statistical explorations lead to collecting data and making scatter plots. A function (curve) is found to approximate the data.
- Patterns that grow (*sequences*) combine the direct search for pattern with the idea of functional relationships (see p. 405).
- Proportional situations can be graphed and tables made. This produces a special class of linear functions with all graphs passing through the origin (see Chapter 15).
- Geometry and measurement come together in an assortment of formulas that take on new meaning when expressed as functions. You have already seen how area and length can be related in a rectangle with a fixed perimeter.

Just as important as these mathematical connections are the connections to the real world. Our lives abound with situations that involve functional relationships. Making money, and the ideas related to profit and loss, are both realistic and interesting. Social studies provides many relationships. For example, populations of various regions may be analyzed in terms of health, income, production levels, education levels, death rates, and so on. Science offers another area of investigation. Pendulums can be swung to investigate period as a function of length. The distance a toy car will roll down a ramp can be compared to the angle of the ramp. Plant growth can be related to quantities of fertilizer or to the number of days since germination. These are just a few real contexts that can make the study of functions meaningful and accessible to students as early as grade 6.

Explore the Relationships

A function relationship may be developed simply by exploring and making sense of a context, as in the following hot-dog vendor example.

Brian is trying to make money to help pay for university by selling hot dogs from a hot-dog cart at the coliseum during major performances and ball games. He pays the cart owner $35 per night for the use of the cart. He sells hot dogs for $1.25 each. His costs for the hot dogs, condiments, napkins, and other paper products are about 60 cents per hot dog on average. The profit from a single hot dog is therefore 65 cents.

In the context of Brian's sales, a discussion can involve finding the number of hot dogs that need to be sold to make a given amount of money, and how much profit is made by selling a particular number of hot dogs. By examining and answering these questions, students are working with the joint variation between hot dogs sold and profit made. They are actually using a function before they have even been asked to worry about symbols and definitions.

Develop Different Representations

There are at least five different ways to interpret or represent the relationship or rule of correspondence. The most important idea is that for a given function, each of these representations illustrates the same relationship. The *context* provides an embodiment of the relationship outside the world of mathematics. *Language* helps express the relationship in a meaningful and useful manner. *Tables* explicitly match up selected elements that are paired by the function. The joint variation is implicit in the pairings of numbers. A *graph* translates the number pairs into a picture. Any point on the graph of a function has two coordinates. The function is the rule that relates the first coordinate to the second. An *equation* expresses the same functional relationship with the economy and power of mathematical symbolism. Figure 19.16 illustrates five representations for the relationship or rule of correspondence in the hot-dog vendor situation. The most important idea is to see that for a given function, each of these representations illustrates the same relationship.

Contextual Representation of a Function

This approach begins with a context: selling hot dogs and the resulting profit. We are interested in Brian's profit in terms of the number of hot dogs sold. The more hot dogs Brian sells, the more profit he will make. Brian does not begin to make a profit immediately, because he must pay the $35 rent on the vending cart. So Brian's profit is a function of the number of hot dogs he sells.

Table Representation of a Function

Brian, the hot-dog vendor, might well sit down and calculate some possible income figures based on hypothetical sales. This will give him some idea of how many hot dogs he must sell to break even, and what his profit might be for an evening. For example, if he sells no hot dogs, he will be $35 in the hole, or his profit will be negative $35. Selling 70 hot dogs would yield a profit of $70 \times 0.65 - 35 = 45.50 - 35$, or $10.50. See Figure 19.16 for a table of values.

The number of hot dogs shown in the table (see Figure 19.16) is purely a matter of choice. One could calculate the profit for 10 000 hot dogs (10 000 × 0.65 – 35), even though it is not reasonable to expect Brian to sell that many. One of the values of thinking about functions in real-life contexts is that it allows students to see that there is a risk that mathematical representations can ignore real-

ity. The person who interprets the table must take the context into consideration.

Language Expression for a Function

Functional relationships are dependent relationships or rules of correspondence. In the hot-dog vendor situation, Brian's profit depends on the number of hot dogs that are sold. In functional language, we can say, "Profit *is a function of* the number of hot dogs sold." The phrase "is a function of" expresses the dependent relationship. The profit *depends on*—is a function of—the hot-dog sales.

Graphical Representations of Functions

The old saying goes that a picture is worth a thousand words. This is certainly true of functions. One important way of representing a function is with a graph. In Figure 19.16, the horizontal axis represents the number of hot dogs sold, and the vertical axis, the profit. As we have already established, the profit goes up as the sales go up.

Equations to Represent Functions

Suppose that we pick a letter, say, *H,* to represent the number of hot dogs Brian sells. For each hot dog sold, his income is $1.25 \times H$ dollars. But to determine his profit, we have to subtract from his income the rental cost of the cart and 60-cent cost per hot dog. Therefore, Brian's profit is represented by $(1.25 \times H) - (0.60 \times H) - 35$, or $(0.65 \times H) - 35$. To make an equation, we can assign another letter to stand for profit: $P = (0.65 \times H) - 35$. This equation defines a mathematical relationship between two values or two variables: profit and hot dogs.

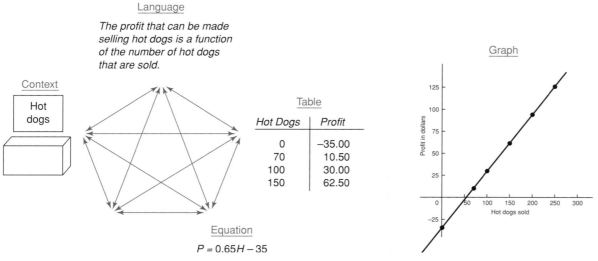

FIGURE 19.16 Five different representations of a function. For any given function, students can that all these representations are connected and illustrate the same relationship. Each representation provides a different perspective.

Use Function Machines

Another representation of a function has come into common use: the *function machine*. It can be thought of as a "black box" with input and output slots, as shown in Figure 19.17. Inside the box is the function rule—the rule of correspondence between the input numbers and the output numbers. This representation helps illustrate what makes a function a function. It highlights that a function is a rule of correspondence (the rule inside the box), that for any input there is a unique output value, that the elements the machine will accept are the elements for which the function is defined (also known as the *domain* of the function), and that the set of all possible outputs is the set known as the *range* of the function.

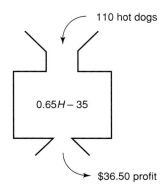

FIGURE 19.17 A function machine illustrates the idea that a single input value from the domain of the function produces a unique value in the range of the function. Each in-out pair corresponds to an entry in the function table and a point on the graph of the function.

These ideas tend to focus on generic aspects of functions and do little to illustrate the specific function that is "in the box." The function machine is most like the table representation of a function. In fact, a table is often generated by recording the inputs and outputs of a function machine. Notice that in a function machine, the input value is the independent variable and the output value is the dependent variable.

Functions from Patterns

Now that we have a more complete view of the function concept and the various representations of functions, let's explore one more example of a growing pattern and see how all of these ideas fit together in that context.

Students working at "Perimeter Patterns" should first develop a table by adding tiles to their string one at a time and recording the perimeters in a table as they go. A recur-

ACTIVITY 19.25

Perimeter Patterns

In this activity, students explore the perimeters of strings of regular polygons. Each string is made up of tiles of the same shape. Adjoining tiles share one side, as shown in Figure 19.18. For a given shape, the task is to develop a rule or formula for the perimeter of strings of any number of tiles. For example, if the tiles are square, the perimeter for one square is 4, for two squares 6, for three squares 8, and so on. What is a formula for the perimeter of a string of *n* squares? Figure 19.18 shows strings for three different shapes. Pattern blocks are an excellent manipulative for this task because all edges are 2.5 centimetres long except for the trapezoid, which has a long side of 5 centimetres.

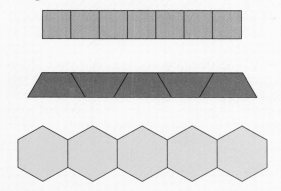

FIGURE 19.18 What is the perimeter of a string of *n* pattern blocks?

sive relationship is easy to determine. For hexagons, it is "add 4 to the preceding perimeter." A table for hexagons looks like this:

1	2	3	4	5	6	7	8	...	n
6	10	14	18	22	26	32	36	...	?

So now we have a table and a contextual situation. The next challenge is the most interesting: Find a rule or equation that tells the perimeter for *n* hexagons. What students come up with will depend on whether they focus on the table of numbers or the string of tiles. In either case, they are likely to have a variety of ideas. Before reading further, see if you can come up with at least two different formulas.

Here are five different-looking formulas:

$$4n + 2$$
$$2(2n + 1)$$
$$6 + (n - 1)\,4$$
$$(n - 2)4 + (2 \times 5)$$
$$2n + 2n + 2$$

Are your formulas in this list? Perhaps you found a different one. When students share different formulas for the same pattern, they might be challenged to see how others in the class arrived at their patterns. The following three ideas generate three of the five formulas given:

- *The first tile has a perimeter of 6. Each new tile adds 4 more.* (This idea can be found in the table as well as the block pattern.)
- Each tile has two edges on the top. Include the one extra edge on the left along with the top edges. The bottom edges plus the right edge are the same as this.
- Each tile has two edges on the top and two on the bottom plus the two end edges.

Match these three ways of thinking of the perimeter with three of the formulas. Then try to figure out what process of thinking could have led to the other two. Of course, all of these "different" formulas are equivalent, with the simplest form being $4n + 2$.

To add language to our representations, we can say, "The perimeter of a string of hexagons is a function of the number of hexagons in the string."

Next, a graph of the perimeter relationship provides the fifth representation. The points on the graph will lie along a straight line and go up 4 units for every added tile. The graphs for each of the other tile shapes will go up at different rates or with different *slopes* (see Figure 19.19).

The perimeter problem has an interesting extension. If different groups of students have been working on strings of shapes using different polygons, the resulting formulas will be similar. See if students can find an even more general formula with two variables: n representing the number of tiles and s representing the number of sides per tile. (This challenge is left to you.)

Real-world situations, such as the example of Brian selling hot dogs, can be explored with children by having them make tables of data using the information given. By computing several entries in the table, students will begin to see a pattern develop. Consider the following activity.

ACTIVITY 19.26

How Many Litres Left?

Present this situation to students: A car gets 9.7 kilometres per litre of gas. It has a gas tank that holds 76 litres. Suppose that you were on a trip and had filled the tank at the outset. Make a table showing the number of litres remaining in the tank for at least 3 different points on a trip of 550 kilometres. Plot the data on a graph. Show how you calculated each entry in your table, and be prepared to discuss with the class what you did.

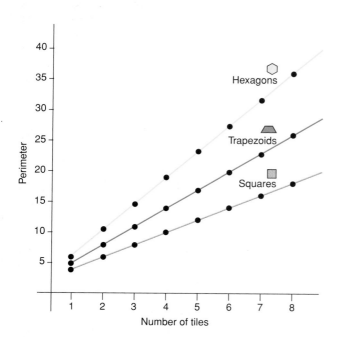

FIGURE 19.19 Graphs of the perimeters of three different pattern-block strings.

Notice that very little direction is given in this activity. However, the situation presented to the students is fairly clear. Some teachers may prefer to use numbers that would be easier to compute, but that takes much of the realism out of the situation. If a student decides to make a table entry for 50 kilometres, he or she will first have to figure out what to do. On a calculator, $50 \div 9.73 = 5.138746$. This amount should be subtracted from 76 to find out how many litres remain in the tank. Should you subtract 5 or 5.13 or 5.138746? This is a good example to use to discuss numbers in real contexts. Avoid being prescriptive; students should do their own thinking and not rely on your directions. Students are bound to make errors in reasoning as well as in computation. Class discussion will sort things out.

As part of the discussion, help students develop functional language to represent the situation. Here, the number of litres in the tank is dependent on how far the car has been driven, so the number of litres remaining *is a function of* the kilometres driven. Also, work toward student development of an equation that represents the relationship in the situation. In this case, one possible equation is $L = 76 - \frac{k}{97}$.

Students can draw a line through their plotted points, or they can enter the equation into a computer or graphing calculator and have technology do the graphing. In either case, use the graph to answer questions about the situation: "How can you tell from the graph how much gas will be left after driving 500 kilometres?" "How many kilometres can you drive before the gas tank has only 10 litres left?" "What will happen to the graph if the driver stops to fill the tank after driving 550 kilometres?" The *trace* feature on a graphing calculator is a great help for getting values from a graph.

 ## Literature Connections

Many teachers find pattern explorations sufficiently interesting that they may not think of using literature to provide a springboard for student explorations. However, here are three examples of books that are excellent beginnings for patterns and chart building.

Pattern
(Pluckrose, 1988)

This book brings pattern from the real world to the classroom in the form of brilliantly coloured photographs. Pattern is seen in the soles of tennis shoes, dishes, butterflies, leaves, and flowers. The book provides a jumping-off point for an exploration of pattern in the world around us. A photo collage could be made of patterns found by the children. Drawings of patterns, with explanations of their source and descriptions, can be assembled into a book. A display of patterns from your class activities and those found in nature, in the home, and in the neighbourhood would make an excellent show for parents.

Anno's Mysterious Multiplying Jar
(Anno & Anno, 1983)

Like all of the books illustrated by Mitsumasa Anno, this one is beautiful. It tells an imaginative story of a mysterious jar that contains a sea. On the sea is one island. The island has two mountains. Each mountain has three countries. Within each country are four walled kingdoms.... Finally, each of nine boxes contains ten jars. The illustrations help develop the quickly expanding numbers of factorials. After the story, the authors help conceptualize the size of each factorial with arrays of tiny stars and suggest other ways to explore this fascinating number pattern.

Children of almost any age are likely to be interested in exploring the factorial concept due to the large numbers. A simple idea is to create a multiplication story and illustrate it or collect objects to show how many items are involved. Another idea is to examine nested situations in the real world, even if they are not factorials. For example, talk to someone who works in a grocery store about how small items such as chewing gum are shipped to the store. There will likely be cartons in which there are smaller boxes. In each box there may be packages. Each package might contain several packs of gum, and then, finally, single sticks. How many in all is determined by the same multiplication process.

Anno's Magic Seeds
(Anno, 1994)

Another wonderful book by Mitsumasa Anno, *Magic Seeds* develops a pattern that changes throughout, becoming a bit more elaborate with each change. A wise man gives Jack two magic seeds. He is told to eat one and plant the other. The seed he eats will keep him from hunger for a whole year, and the planted seed will produce two new seeds by the following year. Several years later, Jack decides to plant both seeds rather than eat one. This new pattern continues until he marries, has a child, and starts to sell seeds.

At each stage of the story, there is an opportunity to develop a chart and extend the pattern into the future. Austin and Thompson (1997) outline in considerable detail how they used the story to develop patterns and charts with grade 6 and 7 students. Their article is worth looking up. However, you will have no problem developing good pattern lessons from this book without any assistance. ■■

 ## Assessment Notes

The main content of this chapter has to do with patterns (repeating, number, and growing) and the related ideas of variables, equations and functions. At any grade level, your curriculum will likely specify particular skills in these areas. To assess this specific knowledge is straightforward. Can your students recognize and extend patterns of the appropriate type for their grade level? Do they use variables in ways that suggest an understanding of the various uses and meanings of *variable*—again, commensurate with their grade level? Do they solve equations appropriate for their grade level? Do they see functional relationships in a variety of different situations—relationships where the change in one quantity has a predictable effect on the change in the other? And are they able to communicate these relationships in varied, but related, ways? Answers to these questions should be found in the way students respond to the activities you conduct in class, or in end-of-unit tests that assess these ideas directly.

More pervasive than these specific ideas, however, is the general notion of algebraic reasoning. It is appropriate to gather data that indicate the degree to which students make generalizations based on their mathematical experiences and use appropriate language and symbolism to represent these generalizations. Since pattern and regularity can be found in nearly all areas of mathematics, algebraic reasoning should be developed and assessed throughout the curriculum. Students who ask questions like "Will that work for any numbers?" or who observe similarities from one area of mathematics to another are using algebraic reasoning. Students who have difficulty seeing and expressing relationships such as the way two patterns are alike, or who have difficulty expressing rules and formulas, are not as strong in their algebraic reasoning.

Make a conscious effort to observe and keep anecdotal records of behaviours that are indicative of algebraic reasoning. It is quite likely that such records over time will give you useful insights into the mathematical talents of your students. ◼◼

Reflections *on Chapter 19*

Writing to Learn

1. Describe in your own words what algebraic reasoning means. At what grade level should algebraic reasoning begin?
2. Make up three pattern strips showing repeating patterns for some common objects that might be found in the classroom. Label each using an A, B, C scheme. No two schemes should be alike, but all should use the same materials. What is the core of each pattern? What will be the twenty-fifth element of each?
3. The following growing pattern consists of square borders. The elements of each frame are the number of squares or tiles that make up the border. Draw the fifth border and the tenth border in the sequence. Make a chart showing the number of tiles in each of the first 10 borders. Find a recursive relationship that permits you to get from one frame to the next. With attention to the drawings of this growing pattern, try to find one or more ways to express the general functional relationship that the pattern defines.

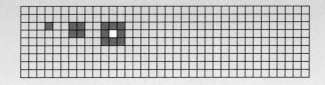

4. How can a hundreds chart be used to develop pattern ideas?
5. Show how a simple calculator can be used to play "Secret Function I" (p. 409) for all four operations.
6. Give an example of each of the three different uses of variables. For each use, describe at least one activity that addresses students' understanding of variables used in that manner.
7. Make up a scales problem involving three different variables. After you have made it up, show at least one way that it can be solved other than by guess-and-check.
8. What misconceptions do children have about expressions such as 4 + 8 and the equal sign that can cause difficulty working with equations?
10. Make up a real-world situation that defines a functional relationship. Use your example to do the following:
   a. Sketch a graph illustrating the relationship.
   b. State the relationship using the language of functions.
   c. Build a chart with numbers that might go with your relationship.
   d. Explain the graph and the chart as ways of presenting the same information in different forms.
   e. Explain how your example meets the formal definition of a function.

For Discussion and Exploration

1. The Reasoning standard in *Principles and Standards for School Mathematics* is meant to permeate all content areas. However, it has special significance for the types of activities found in this chapter. Read the Reasoning standard, either the overview found in Chapter 3 of *Principles and Standards* or the corresponding elaboration found in the grade band of most interest to you. Discuss how the inclusion of algebraic reasoning throughout the elementary and middle-school grades emphasizes the use of reasoning for all students.
2. The Disney film *Donald in Mathmagic Land* is a classic from the 1940s that is now available on videotape and is occasionally aired on the Disney Channel. The film explores pattern and several related beauties of mathematics in a timeless manner. Your mathematics education is not quite complete if you haven't seen it. It will intrigue children from grade 3 to high school, and a creative teacher can find many ways to follow up with explorations. View it if you can, and share an idea for using the film with children.
3. As a part of the *Third International Mathematics and Science Study* (TIMSS), a video study was done at grade 8. Tapes are available that show algebra lessons from grade 8 classes in the United States, Japan, and Germany. The lessons show marked differences in the focus and methods of instruction. If at all possible, view the tapes and discuss your reactions.

Recommendations for Further Reading
Highly Recommended

Coburn, T.G. (1993). *Patterns: Addenda series, grades K–6.* Reston, VA: National Council of Teachers of Mathematics.

This is one of the best resource books on patterns for the K–6 grades. Examples of virtually every type of pattern activity are included. As with other elementary *Addenda Series* books, the same activities are found in each of the grade-level books. What you get in this book are not only good activities but also a view of how pattern can easily progress from kindergarten to grade 6.

Moses, B. (Ed.). (1999). *Algebraic thinking, grades K–12: Readings from NCTM's school-based journals and other publications.* Reston, VA: National Council of Teachers of Mathematics.

In this collection, NCTM has assembled nearly 60 articles addressing the broad topic of algebraic thinking. After looking at definitions and issues surrounding the teaching of algebra at various levels, the book provides classroom activities from patterns to functions. Technology gets a special section, as does assessment. This is an excellent single source for a lot of information.

National Council of Teachers of Mathematics. (1997). Algebraic thinking [Focus Issue]. *Teaching Children Mathematics, 3*(6).

National Council of Teachers of Mathematics. (1997). Algebraic thinking: Opening the gates [Focus issue]. *Mathematics Teaching in the Middle School, 2*(4).

National Council of Teachers of Mathematics. (1997). Algebraic thinking [Focus issue]. *Mathematics Teacher, 90*(2).

In 1997, NCTM responded to the growing interest in algebraic reasoning by publishing focus issues on the topic in all three of its school-based journals. Together, these journals provide not just algebraic activities at all levels but also a long-range perspective on the growth of algebraic reasoning across the grades. These are especially valuable publications.

Phillips, E., Gardella, T., Kelly, C., & Stewart, J. (1991). *Patterns and functions: Addenda series, grades 5–8.* Reston, VA: National Council of Teachers of Mathematics.

It is hard to do better than this book for ideas related to function development. The first section involves students with a wide variety of functions in real contexts, including exponential decay, linear, quadratic, and cubic functions. Throughout the book, the concept of function grows out of pattern development in a variety of creative and interesting activities that connect many middle-school mathematics topics to a development of functions. This is an important contribution to the development of function concepts prior to algebra.

Other Suggestions

Bell, A. (1995). Purpose in school algebra. *Journal of Mathematical Behavior, 14,* 41–73.

Burns, M. (1992). *About teaching mathematics: A K–8 resource.* Sausalito, CA: Math Solutions Publications.

Day, R.P. (1995). Using functions to make mathematical connections. In P.A. House (Ed.), *Connecting mathematics across the curriculum* (pp. 54–64). Reston, VA: National Council of Teachers of Mathematics.

Day, R.P., & Jones, G.A. (1997). Building bridges to algebraic thinking. *Mathematics Teaching in the Middle School, 2,* 209–212.

Driscoll, M.J. (1999). *Fostering algebraic thinking: A guide for teachers, grades 6–10.* Portsmouth, NH: Heinemann.

English, L.D., & Warren, E.A. (1998). Introducing the variable through pattern exploration. *Mathematics Teacher, 91,* 166–172.

Esty, W.W., & Teppo, A.R. (1996). Algebraic thinking, language, and word problems. In P.C. Elliott (Ed.), *Communication in mathematics, K–12 and beyond* (pp. 45–53). Reston, VA: National Council of Teachers of Mathematics.

Falkner, K.P., Levi, L., & Carpenter, T.P. (1999). Children's understanding of equality: A foundation for algebra. *Teaching Children Mathematics, 6,* 232–236.

Feinberg-McBrian, C. (1996). The case of trapezoidal numbers. *Mathematics Teacher, 89,* 16–24.

Greenes, C., & Findell, C. (1999). Developing students' algebraic reasoning abilities. In L.V. Stiff (Ed.), *Developing mathematical reasoning in grades K–12* (pp. 127–137). Reston, VA: National Council of Teachers of Mathematics.

Greenes, C., & Findell, C. (1999). *Groundworks: Algebraic thinking* (3 vols.: grades 1, 2, and 3). Chicago: Creative Publications.

Greenes, C., & Findell, C. (1999). *Groundworks: Algebra puzzles and problems* (4 vols.: grades 4, 5, 6, and 7). Chicago: Creative Publications.

MacGregor, M., & Stacey, K. (1999). A flying start to algebra. *Teaching Children Mathematics, 6,* 78–85.

National Council of Teachers of Mathematics & Mathematical Sciences Education Board. (1998). *The nature and role of algebra in the K–14 curriculum: Proceedings of a national symposium, May 27 and 28, 1997.* Washington, DC: National Academy Press.

Phillips, E., Gardella, T., Kelly, C., & Stewart, J. (1991). *Patterns and functions: Addenda series, grades 5–8.* Reston, VA: National Council of Teachers of Mathematics.

Quinn, A.L., Koca, R.M., Jr., & Weening, F. (1999). Developing mathematical reasoning using attribute games. *Mathematics Teacher, 92,* 768–775.

Quinn, A.L., & Larson, K.R. (1996). When does a dog become older than its owner? *Mathematics Teacher, 89,* 734–737.

Rubenstein, R. (1996). The function game. *Mathematics Teaching in the Middle School, 2,* 74–78.

Schifter, D. (1999). Reasoning about operations: Early algebraic thinking in grades K–6. In L.V. Stiff (Ed.), *Developing mathematical reasoning in grades K–12* (pp. 62–81). Reston, VA: National Council of Teachers of Mathematics.

Speer, W.R., & Brahier, D.J. (1996). What comes next ? *Teaching Children Mathematics, 1,* 100–108.

Swafford, J.O., & Langrall, C.W. (2000). Grade 6 students' pre-instructional use of equations to describe and represent problem situations. *Journal for Research in Mathematics Education, 13,* 89–112.

Talbert, M.K., & Stallings-Roberts, V. (1994). Introducing prealgebra skills in an egg-citing way. *Mathematics Teaching in the Middle School, 1,* 198–202.

Vance, J.H. (1998). Number operations from an algebraic perspective. *Teaching Children Mathematics, 4,* 282–285.

Williams, S.E., & Copley, J.V. (1994). Promoting classroom dialogue: Using calculators to discover patterns in dividing decimals. *Mathematics Teaching in the Middle School, 1,* 72–75.

Zawojewski, J.S. (1992). *Dealing with data and chance: Addenda series, grades 5–8.* Reston, VA: National Council of Teachers of Mathematics.

Chapter 20

Developing Concepts of Exponents, Integers, and Real Numbers

Many of the topics of the middle-grades curriculum, including ratio and proportion, percent, probability, and algebraic reasoning, have been discussed in earlier chapters. Each of these topics has its initial development in earlier grades. But students in the upper elementary grades need to develop a more complete understanding of the number system—extending whole numbers to integers, starting to think of fractions as rational numbers (both positive and negative), and beginning to appreciate the completeness of the real number system.

 BIG IDEAS

1. Exponential notation is a powerful way to express repeated products of the same number. Specifically, powers of 10 express very large and very small numbers in an economical manner.

2. Integers add to number the idea of opposite, so that every number has both size and a positive or negative relationship to other numbers. A negative number is the opposite of the positive number of the same size.

3. Every fraction, both positive and negative, is a rational number. Furthermore, every rational number can be expressed as a fraction.

4. Many numbers are not rational and can be expressed only symbolically or approximately using a close rational number. For example, the square root of 2 is approximately equal to 1.41421... and π (pi) is approximately equal to 3.114159....

Large Numbers, Small Numbers, and Exponents

As numbers in our technological world get very large or very small, expressing them in standard form is cumbersome. Exponential notation is much more efficient for conveying numerical or quantitative information, especially for these numbers. Because negative exponents, used to express small numbers in exponential notation, are generally addressed in high school, they are not included in most provincial and territorial curricula for grade 8.

Exponents

Students often get confused in algebra when they try to remember the rules for exponents. For example, when you raise numbers to powers, do you add or multiply the exponents? Here is an example of procedural knowledge that is often learned without supporting conceptual knowledge. Students should have ample opportunity to explore working with exponents on whole numbers before working with letters or variables in algebra. In this way, they are able to deal directly with the concept and actually generate the rules themselves.

A *whole-number exponent* is simply shorthand for repeated multiplication of a number times itself, for example, $3^4 = 3 \times 3 \times 3 \times 3$. That is the only conceptual knowledge required.

Conventions of symbolism must also be learned. These are arbitrary rules with no conceptual basis. The first is that *an exponent applies to its immediate base.* For example, in the expression $2+5^3$, the exponent 3 applies only to the 5, so the expression is equal to $2 + (5 \times 5 \times 5)$. However, in the expression $(2 + 5)^3$, the 3 is an exponent of the quantity 2 + 5 and the expression is evaluated as (2 + 5) × (2 + 5) × (2 + 5), or 7 × 7 × 7.

The other convention involves the *order of operations*: Multiplication and division are always done before addition and subtraction. Since exponentiation is repeated multiplication, it also is done before addition and subtraction. In the expression 5 + 4 × 2 − 6 ÷ 3, 4 × 2 and 6 ÷ 3 are done first. Therefore, the expression is evaluated as 5 + 8 − 2 = 13 − 2 = 11. If done in left-to-right order, the result would be 4. Parentheses, or brackets, are used to group operations that are to be done first. Therefore, in (5 + 4) × 2 − 6 ÷ 3, the addition inside the parentheses can be done first, or the distributive property can be used, and the final result is 16. The phrase "**P**lease **E**xcuse **M**y **D**ear **A**unt **S**ally" is sometimes used to help students recall that operations inside **p**arentheses, or **b**rackets, are done first, followed by **e**xponentiation, then **m**ultiplication and **d**ivision (or **d**ivision and **m**ultiplication) before **a**ddition and **s**ubtraction. Also used in this way is the word "**BEDMAS**."

Calculators and Notation

Most scientific calculators employ "algebraic logic"—i.e., they have an algebraic operating system that will evaluate expressions correctly and also allow grouping with parentheses. The simple four-function calculators generally used in elementary school do not use algebraic logic. Operations are processed as they are entered. On calculators without algebraic logic, the following two keying sequences produce the same results:

Key: → 3 [+] 2 [×] 7 [=]
Display → 3   2 5 7 35

Key: → 3 [+] 2 [=] [×] 7 [=]
Display → 3   2 5   7 35

Whenever an operation sign is pressed, the effect is the same as pressing [=] and then the operation. Of course, neither result is correct for the expression 3 + 2 × 7, which should be evaluated as 3 + 14, or 17. Calculators designed for middle grades do use algebraic logic and include parenthesis keys, so that both 3 + 2 × 7 and (3 + 2) × 7 can be keyed in in the order that the symbols appear. Today, all of the major manufacturers offer calculators that show an entire expression in the window, including parentheses, as do graphing calculators. Results are shown only after pressing the [Enter] key. With some scientific calculators, the display shows only one number at a time, as illustrated here.

Key: → 3 [+] 2 [×] 7 [=]
Display → 3   2   7 17

Notice that the display does not change when [×] is pressed: A right parenthesis is never displayed. Instead, the expression that the right parenthesis encloses is calculated and that result displayed.

Key: → [(] 3 [+] 2 [)] [×] 7 [=]
Display → [3   2 [5]   7 35

The graphing calculator offers the best solution to these problems and at the same time provides other significant advantages, as noted in an earlier chapter. When the expression $3 + 2 \times (6^2 - 4)$ is keyed in, the display shows the full expression. Nothing is evaluated until you press [Enter] or [EXE]. Then the result appears on the next line to the right of the screen:

$$3 + 2 * (6^2 - 4)$$

67

Moreover, the last expression entered can be recalled and edited so that students can see how different expressions are evaluated. Only minimum key presses are required.

$3 + 2 * (6^2 - 4)$	67
$(3 + 2) * (6^2 - 4)$	160
$(3 + 2) * 6^2 - 4$	176
$3 + 2 * 6^2 - 4$	71

Nevertheless, the simple four-function calculator remains a powerful tool regardless of its limitations. For example, to evaluate 3^8, press 3 [×] [=] [=] [=] [=] [=] [=] [=]. (The first press of [×] will result in 9, or 3 × 3.) Students will be fascinated by how quickly numbers grow. Enter any number, press [×], and then repeatedly press [=]. Try two-digit numbers. Try 0.2.

Give students ample opportunity to explore expressions involving mixed operations and exponents, with only the conventions and the meaning of exponents to guide them. No rules for exponents should be promoted. When experience has provided a firm background, the rules of exponents will make sense and should not require rote memorization.

ACTIVITY 20.1

What's in an Expression?

Provide students with numerical expressions to evaluate with simple four-function calculators.

Here are some examples of the types of expressions that can be valuable:

$3 + 4 \times 8$ $4 \times 8 + 3$	$3^6 + 2^6$ $(3 + 2)^6$	$3^4 \times 7 - 5^2$ $(3 \times 7)^4 - 5 \times 2$	$3^4 \times 5^2$ $(3 \times 5)^6$

$\dfrac{5^3 \times 5^2}{5^6}$	$4 \times 3 - 2^3 \times 5 + 23 \times 9$	$\dfrac{4 \times 3^5}{2} \quad 4 + \dfrac{3^5}{2}$

When experiencing difficulty, students should write equivalent expressions without exponents or include parentheses and brackets to indicate explicit groupings. For example:

$$
\begin{aligned}
(7 \times 2^3 - 5)^3 &= (7 \times (2 \times 2 \times 2) - 5) \\
&\quad \times (7 \times (2 \times 2 \times 2) - 5) \\
&\quad \times (7 \times (2 \times 2 \times 2) - 5) \\
&= ((7 \times 8) - 5) \\
&\quad \times ((7 \times 8) - 5) \\
&\quad \times ((7 \times 8) - 5) \\
&= (56 - 5) \times (56 - 5) \times (56 - 5) \\
&= 51 \times 51 \times 51
\end{aligned}
$$

When discussing results, place all of the emphasis on the procedures rather than the answer. The fact that two groups achieved the same result does not help a group that achieved a different result. For many expressions, there is more than one way to proceed, and one may be easier to do or to understand than another.

Of course, calculators with algebraic logic will automatically produce correct results. Yet it remains important for students to know the correct order of operations. The calculator should not replace an understanding of the rules. The order-of-operation rules apply to symbolic manipulation in algebra and must also be understood if a calculator without algebraic logic is used.

The following activity involves exponents and estimation and is also a good problem-solving task.

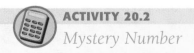

ACTIVITY 20.2
Mystery Number

Before class, write down any simple expression involving exponents, and evaluate it. Give the expression to the class with at least two of the numbers in the expression replaced by stars. Give students the value of the expression, and see which group, using calculators, can find correct values for the stars first. For example:
$(☆ + 7☆)^3 = 41\ 063\ 625$

The size of the result and the fact that it ends in 25 are clues that may help. There is more than one solution to this, so do not be too quick to tell students their answers are not correct.

Very Large Numbers

The real world is full of very large quantities and measures. We see references to huge numbers in the media all the time. Unfortunately, most of us have not developed an appreciation for extremely large numbers. Here are a few examples:

- The annual government expenditure this year in Canada is $219 billion.
- The GDP (gross domestic product), which represents the total goods produced in Canada for one year, is $1.17 trillion.
- A provincial lottery in which players pick 6 numbers out of 49 allows over 10 billion possible number combinations. There are $49 \times 48 \times 47 \times 46 \times 45 \times 44$ possible ways that the balls could come out of the hopper (10 068 347 520). But generally the order in which they are picked is not important. Since there are $6 \times 5 \times 4 \times 3 \times 2 \times 1 = 720$ different arrangements of 6 numbers, each collection appears 720 times. Therefore, there are *only* 10 068 347 520 divided by 720 possible lottery numbers, or in other words, 1 out of 13 983 816 chances to win.
- An estimate of the size of the universe is 40 billion light-years. One light-year is the number of kilometres light travels in *one year.* The speed of light is 298 050.7 kilometres per *second,* or 1 072 982 520 kilometres in an hour and 25 751 580 480 kilometres in a single day.
- The human body has about 100 billion cells.
- The distance to the sun is about 150 million kilometres.
- The population of the world has surpassed 6 billion.

In class, large numbers should be discussed in real contexts. Opportunities to explore such numbers can often be coordinated with teachers in social studies or science. Talk to teachers in the other disciplines, and design a joint exploration for your students to investigate large numbers related to their studies. Individuals or groups can select different facts to look up and discuss.

Representation of Large Numbers: Scientific Notation

The more common it becomes to find very large numbers in our daily lives, the more important it is to have convenient ways to represent them. One option is to say and write numbers in their common form. However, this practice can at times be cumbersome. Another option is to use exponential notation and our base-ten place-value system.

Students in elementary school learn how to multiply by 10, by 100, and by 1000 by simply adding the appropriate number of zeros. We can help students expand this idea by examining powers of 10 on a calculator that handles exponents. A graphing calculator is best, but is not the only option.

 ACTIVITY 20.3

Exploring Powers of 10

Have students use any calculator that permits entering exponents to explore some of the following:

a. **Explore 10^n for various values of n. What patterns do you notice? What does 1E15 mean? (1E15 is the TI-73 calculator form for 1×10^{15}.)**

b. **Find out the easiest expressions for one thousand, one million, one billion, one trillion. What patterns are there in these numbers?**

c. **Enter 45 followed by a string of zeros. How many will your calculator permit? What happens when you press** Enter**? What does 4.5E10 or 4.5×10^{10} mean?**

d. **What do 5.689E6 or 5.689×10^{10} mean? Can you enter this in another way?**

e. **Try sums like $(4.5 \times 10^n) + (27 \times 10^k)$ for different values of n and k. What can you find out?**

f. **What happens with products of numbers like those in item (e)?**

It is useful to become comfortable with the power-of-10 expressions in Activity 20.3. Students should eventually discover that when scientific or graphing calculators display numbers with more digits than the display will hold, they use *scientific notation*—a decimal number between 1 and 10 times a power of 10. For example, on the TI-73, the product of 45 000 000 × 8 000 000 is displayed as 3.6E14, meaning 3.6×10^{14}, or 360 000 000 000 000 (360 trillion).

Ask students why there are only 13 zeros. What happens when the numbers in the computation do not involve a lot of zeros? What if each factor in the product had been expressed in scientific notation: $(4.5 \times 10^7) \times (8 \times 10^6)$, or 4.5E7 × 8.0E6? Discuss the advantages of this latter notation, especially for multiplication and division. Here the significant digits can be multiplied mentally ($4.5 \times 8 = 36$) and the exponents added almost instantly to produce 36×10^{13} or 3.6×10^{14}.

Different notations have different purposes and values. Consider this fact: In 1990, the population of the world was more than 5 050 700 000 persons, about 1 billion fewer than in the year 2000. This can be expressed in various ways:

5 billion 50 million 700 thousand

5 050 700 000

5.0507×10^9

Less than 5.1 billion

A little more than 5 billion

Each way of stating the number has value and purpose in different contexts. Rather than spending time on exercises converting numbers from standard form to scientific notation, consider large numbers found in newspapers, magazines, and atlases. How are they written? How are they said aloud? When are they rounded? When are they not and why? What forms of the numbers seem best for what purposes?

Negative Exponents

When students have experienced negative integers and are beginning to explore exponents, it is interesting to consider what it might mean to raise a number to a negative power. For example, what does 2^{-4} mean, if anything? Two related options for exploring the possibilities of negative numbers seem reasonable. First, in the spirit of patterns in mathematics, examine a pattern of numbers, and see how it might best be expanded. As with large numbers, the powers of 10 seem the most profitable to explore because they are directly related to place value. Have students consider 10^n as follows:

$10^4 = 10\ 000$
$10^3 = 1000$
$10^2 = 100$
$10^1 = 10$
$10^0 = ?$
$10^{-1} = ?$

In this sequence, the most obvious entry for 10^0 is 1, and that is the *definition* of 10^0. That is, it is a convention that 10 or any other non-zero number raised to the power 0 is 1. So what is 10^{-1}? If the pattern is to continue, the 1 should move to the right of the decimal:

$10^0 = 1$
$10^{-1} = 0.1$
$10^{-2} = 0.01$
$10^{-3} = 0.001$

and so on. Notice how each of these numbers is written as a fraction:

$$10^{-3} = 0.001 = \frac{1}{1000} = \frac{1}{10^3}$$

Students should be encouraged to explore these numbers further.

Very Small Numbers

As with large numbers, it is extremely important to use real examples of very small numbers. Without real contexts, you may be tempted to resort to drill exercises that have little meaning for students. Here are a few examples of real-world values to explore:

- The length of a DNA strand in a cell is about 10^{-7} metres. This is also measured as 1000 *angstroms*. (Based on this information, how long is an angstrom?) How large is a cell?
- Human hair grows at the rate of 10^{-8} kilometres per hour.
- The chances of winning a lottery, based on selecting six numbers from a possible 44 (1 to 44), is 1 in 7.059 million. That is a probability of less than 1.4×10^{-10}.
- The mass of one atom of hydrogen is 0.000 000 000 000 000 000 001 675 grams.
- It takes sound 0.28 second (2.8×10^{-1}) to travel the length of a football field. In contrast, a TV signal travels 100 kilometres in about 0.000005368 second, or 5.3×10^{-6} second. A TV viewer at home hears the football being kicked before the receiver on the field does.

Integer Concepts (Signed Numbers)

Students almost daily have some interaction with negative numbers, or experience phenomena that negative numbers can model. Some examples:

A loss of money is a negative cash flow.

Slowing down the car is negative acceleration, and driving in reverse is negative velocity.

A countdown to blastoff is negative time.

Temperatures below zero and altitudes below ground level are negatives in relation to a scale.

In fact, almost any concept that is quantified and has direction probably has both a positive and a negative value.

Generally, negative values are introduced with *integers*—the whole numbers and their negatives or opposites—instead of with fractions or decimals.

Intuitive Models of Signed Quantities

As with any new types of numbers that students encounter, real models or examples are useful. Negative numbers or situations that model them do exist. It is a good idea to dis-

cuss some of these with your class before jumping directly into computation with these signed numbers.

Debits and Credits

Suppose that you are the bookkeeper for a small business. At any time, your records show how many dollars the company has in its account. There are always so many dollars in cash (credits or receipts) and so many dollars in accounts payable (debits). The difference between the debit and credit totals tells the value of the account. If there are more credits than debits, the account is positive, or "in the black." If there are more debits than credits, the account is in debt, shows a negative cash value, or is "in the red." Suppose further that all transactions are handled by mail. The letter carrier can bring mail, a positive action, or take mail away, a negative action.

With this scenario, it is easy to discuss addition and subtraction of signed quantities. An example is illustrated in Figure 20.1.

| Credits | | Debits | | Balance |
In	Out	In	Out	Begin 0
50				+50
		30		+20
	10			+10
		50		−40
25				−15
			20	+5

FIGURE 20.1 A ledger sheet model for integers.

Integer Hockey

A hockey player's plus/minus (+/-) rating is one of the statistics that contributes to an overall seasonal ranking. It comes into play when two teams are at even strength in a game (i.e., neither team has a penalty against them). If a player is on the ice when his team scores a goal he receives a plus (or +1) rating. If a goal is scored against the team, then a minus (or −1) is given. Plus/minus scores are calculated for every game and a single value assigned. This single value contributes to the player's overall seasonal rating, which is based on the total of every plus/minus game score. Similar to the debits and credits scenario, the plus/minus scores can be used for discussing positive and negative quantities. The chart in Figure 20.2 illustrates

Player	Team	Game 1	Game 2	Game 3	Game 4	Game 5
Peter Forseberg	Colorado Avalanche	$^-$2	$^-$1	E*	$^+$2	$^+$2
Milan Hejduk	Colorado Avalanche	$^+$2	$^+$2	$^-$1	E*	$^-$1
Nicklas Lidstrom	Detroit Red Wings	$^+$1	$^-$2	E*	$^+$1	$^+$1
Jere Lehtinen	Dallas Stars	$^-$2	$^+$1	$^+$2	$^-$1	E*
Derian Hatcher	Dallas Stars	$^+$1	$^-$3	E*	$^+$1	$^+$2

E* (even) represents a score of 0.

FIGURE 20.2 **Possible plus/minus scores for 5 games for the top 5 players in the plus/minus category for the National Hockey League 2002–2003 season.**

possible plus/minus scores for five games for the top five players in the plus/minus category for the National Hockey League 2002–2003 season.

Situations such as mailing debits and credits and the plus/ minus hockey scores are suggested as introductory discussion models. They can help students think intuitively about what happens to quantities when an action causes them to be less than 0. They also provide examples of a joining or positive action and a removal or negative action of both positive and negative quantities. With these models we can pose two specific types of questions for students:

1. Give students a beginning and an end value, and have them describe different ways that the change might have occurred. For example, how could Mats Sundin gone from a $^-$2 in game 1 to a $^+$3 in 4 games?
2. Give students either a beginning or an ending value and one or more actions, and have them determine the value not given. For example, if the company received $20 in credits and $35 in debits, resulting in a balance of negative $5, what did the company have to begin with?

 The calculator is another model that might be explored early in the discussion of signed numbers. It gives correct and immediate results that students seem to believe. The major drawback is that no rationale for the result is provided.

Have students explore subtraction problems such as 5 – 8 = ? and discuss the results. (Be aware that the negative sign appears in different places on different calculators.) Students can benefit by using the calculator along with the intuitive models and questions mentioned earlier. For example, how can you get from –5 to –17 by addition? 13 minus *what* is 15?

Mathematical Definition of Negative Numbers

Mathematicians define negative numbers in terms of whole numbers. Therefore, the definition of negative 3 is

the solution to the equation 3 + ? = 0. In general, the *opposite of n* is the solution to *n* + ? = 0. If *n* is a positive number, the *opposite of n* is a negative number. Therefore, the set of integers consists of the positive whole numbers, the opposites of the whole numbers, or negative numbers, and 0, which is neither positive nor negative. This is the definition found in student textbooks. Like many things in mathematics, abstract or symbolic definitions work best when there is some intuitive or conceptual framework with which to link the idea.

Operations with Integers

Until students encounter integers, the plus and minus signs are used only for the operations of addition and subtraction. Notation for signed numbers represents a real problem for many students. For example, the sum of 3 and negative 7 can be written as 3 + (–7) or as 3 + –7. The latter form might be clear in a printed book but obscure in handwritten form. The use of parentheses is awkward, especially in expressions already involving parentheses. On graphing calculators, the distinction is forced on the user: One key is used for subtraction and another for negatives. They do not work interchangeably.

Two Models for Integer Operations

Two models are popular for helping students understand how the four operations (+, –, ×, ÷) work with integers. One model uses counters in two different colours; one colour represents a positive count and the other a negative count. Thus, two different-coloured counters will cancel each other out. If yellow is positive and red is negative, then 5 yellows and 7 reds represent the same amount as 2 reds: –2 (see Figure 20.3). It is important with this model that students understand that it is always possible to add to or remove any number of pairs of counters, without changing the value of the grouping. But each pair must consist of one yellow, positive counter and one red, negative counter. (Intuitively, this is like adding equal quantities of debits and credits.) The actions of addition and subtraction are the same as for whole numbers; addition is

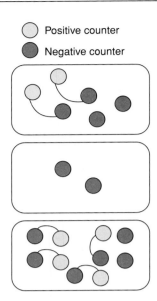

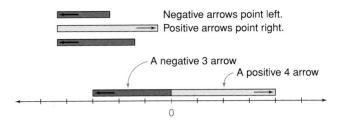

FIGURE 20.4 Number-line model for integers.

FIGURE 20.3 Each collection is a model of negative 2.

joining or adding counters, and subtraction is removing or taking away counters.

The other commonly used model is the number line and arrow. It is a bit more traditional and mathematical; however, many students find it confusing. On a number line, positive and negative numbers are measured distances to the right and left of 0. It is important to remember that signed values represent *directed distances,* not points on the number line. Moreover, the directed distances, not the points on the number line, are the models of the integers. To emphasize this idea for students, illustrate all directed distances with arrows, and avoid talking about number line coordinates as "numbers." Poster-board arrows representing different whole-number lengths can be made in two colours, yellow pointing to the right for positive quantities and red to the left for negative quantities (see Figure 20.4). The arrows help students think of integer quantities as directed distances. A positive arrow never points left, and a negative arrow never points right. Furthermore, each arrow is a quantity with both length (magnitude or absolute value) and direction (sign). These properties remain for each arrow regardless of its position on the number line. Small versions of the arrows, with which individual students can work, can easily be cut from poster board.

Note that it is generally easier to give students the rules (procedural knowledge) for integer operations than explanations with a model. The conceptual explanations do not make the rules easier to use, and it is not intended that students continue to rely on models as they practise integer arithmetic. It is important, though, that students not view the procedural rules for manipulating integers as

arbitrary and mysterious. Here is a case where we must make students responsible for the conceptual knowledge. If we emphasize only the procedural rules, there is little reason for students to attend to the conceptual justifications. Do not be content with right answers; always demand explanations.

Which Model to Use

Although the two models appear quite different, they are alike mathematically. Integers involve two concepts— *quantity* and *opposite*. The number of counters or the length of the arrows is a model for quantity. Opposite is represented as different colours or different directions.

Many teachers who have tried both models report that the counter model seems to be the favourite. It may be that students find the operations more difficult when they use the arrow model. Teachers are often tempted to use only the model that students like or understand better. This is a mistake! Remember that the dual concepts of integers are not in the models. They must be constructed by the students and imposed on the models. Students should experience both models and, perhaps even more importantly, discuss how the two are alike. A parallel development using both models at the same time may be the most appropriate conceptual approach.

A Problem-Solving Approach for Integers

The following discussion is more a quick explanation of how counters and arrows can be used to model operations with integers than a suggested pedagogical approach. Once your students understand how integers are represented by each of the models, you can present the operations for the integers in the form of problems. In other words, rather than explaining how addition of integers works and showing students how to solve exercises with the models, you pose an integer computation and let students use their models to find a solution. It may be useful to assign half of the class the number-line-and-arrow model and the other half the counters. When solutions have been reached, the groups can compare and justify their results. Many incorrect ideas will surface, but the learning that will come from the discussion and clarification will be far superior to an expository approach.

Addition and Subtraction

Adding or subtracting integers with the models is straight-forward and analogous to the corresponding debit-credit model or the hockey-score model. Since grade 7 or 8 students may not have used counters or number lines for a while, it would be good to begin working with either of these models using positive whole numbers. After a few examples to help students become familiar with the model for addition or subtraction with whole numbers, have them work through an example with integers using exactly the same reasoning. Remember, the emphasis should be on the rationale and not on how quickly students can get correct answers.

Several examples of addition are modelled in two ways in Figure 20.5: with positive and negative counters and with the number-line-and-arrow model. First examine the counter model. After the two quantities are joined, any pair of positive and negative counters can cancel each other out; then students can remove these, making it easier to see the result.

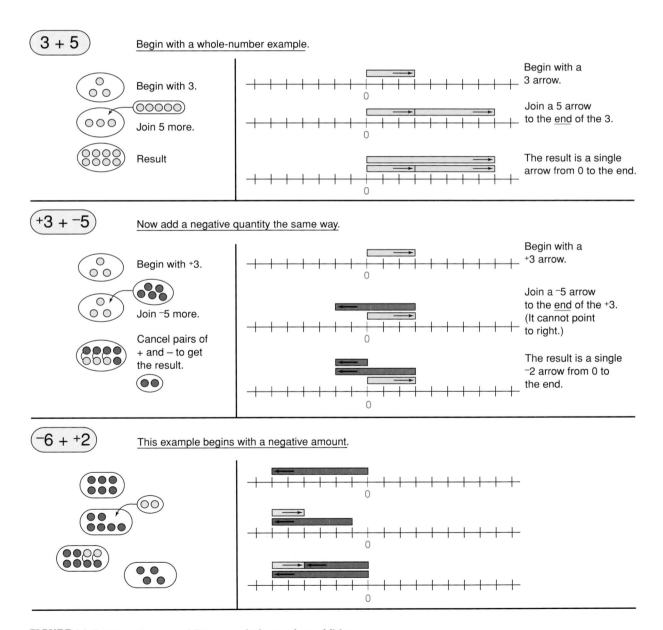

FIGURE 20.5 **Relate integer addition to whole-number addition.**

To add using the arrow model, note that each arrow that is added begins at the point where the previous arrow ends. In the ⁺3 + ⁻5 example, the positive arrow starts at 0 and ends at positive 3. From that point, the negative arrow begins and advances in the negative direction. The result of this action is an arrow which begins at 0 and ends where the second arrow ended. The same change of direction takes place in the ⁻6 + ⁺2 example. If a negative were added to a negative, the arrows would both go toward the left or negative; there would be no change of direction, just as in the 3 + 5 example.

Subtraction is represented as "remove" in terms of the counter model and "back up" in terms of the num-ber-line-and-arrow model. In Figure 20.6, for ⁻5 − ⁺2, both models begin with a representation of ⁻5. To remove two positive counters from a set that has none, a different representation of ⁻5 must first be made. Since any number of neutral pairs (one positive, one negative) can be added without changing the value of the set, two pairs are added so that two positive counters can be removed. The net effect is that there are more negative counters. This is like removing credits from your ledger if you are already in debt; you are left further in debt. A similar change in the representation of the beginning amount is always necessary when you need to subtract a quantity of a different sign.

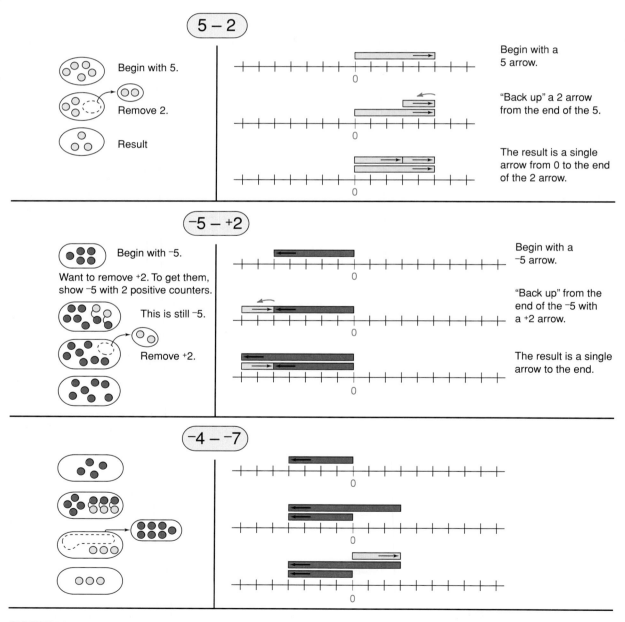

FIGURE 20.6 Integer subtraction is also related to whole numbers.

With the number-line-and-arrow model, subtraction means to back up or to move in the opposite direction. In the example of $^-5 - {}^+2$, the first arrow ends at $^-5$. Since a positive quantity is subtracted, use a positive arrow. To subtract, move the arrow in its opposite direction (left). The forward movement ends at $^-8$. The result of the operation is an arrow from 0 to the back end of the $^-2$ arrow. Have your students draw pictures to accompany integer computations. Set pictures are easy enough; they may consist of Xs and Os, for example. For the number-line-and-arrow model, there is no need for anything elaborate either. Figure 20.7 illustrates how a student might draw arrows for simple addition and subtraction exercises without even sketching the number line. Arrows show the direction, and magnitudes are written on the arrows. For your initial modelling, the poster-board arrows in two colours will help students see that negative arrows always point left, that addition is a forward movement, and that subtraction is a backward movement for either type of arrow.

It is important for students to see that $^+3 + {}^-5$ is the same as $^+3 - {}^-5$ and that $^+2 - {}^-6$ is the same as $^+2 + {}^+6$. With the method of modelling addition and subtraction described here, these expressions are quite discernible.

On graphing calculators, these expressions are entered using the "negative" key and the "subtraction" key. The difference is evident in the display, and the redundant superscript plus signs are not shown. Students can see that $^+3 + {}^-5$ and $3 - 5$ each results in $^-2$, and that $^+3 - {}^-5$ and $3 + 5$ are also alike.

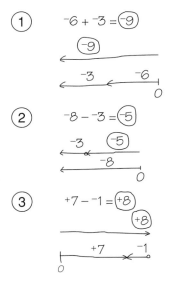

FIGURE 20.7 Students do not need elaborate drawings to think through the number-line model.

Multiplication and Division

Multiplication of integers should be treated as a direct extension of multiplication with whole numbers, just as addition and subtraction are connected to whole-number concepts. We frequently refer to whole-number multiplication as repeated addition. The first factor tells how many sets there are, or how many in all, beginning with zero, are added. This translates quite readily to integer multiplication when the first factor is positive, regardless of the sign of the second factor. The first example in Figure 20.8 illustrates a positive first factor and a negative second factor.

What could the meaning be when the first factor is negative, as in $^-2 \times {}^-3$? If a positive first factor means repeated addition (how many times added to 0), a negative first factor should mean repeated subtraction (how many times subtracted from 0). The second example in Figure 20.8 illustrates how multiplication, with the first factor negative, can be modelled. Students' understanding of multiplication of integers is dependent on how well they understood addition and subtraction of integers. There really are no new ideas, only an application of addition and subtraction concepts to multiplication.

The deceptively simple rules of "like signs yield positive products" and "unlike signs yield negative products" are quickly established. Once more, it is less important that your students be able to produce answers correctly and skillfully than that they be able to supply a rationale.

With division of integers, again explore the whole-number case first. Recall that 8 divided by 4 with whole numbers has two possible meanings that correspond to the following two missing-factor expressions: $4 \times ? = 8$ asks, "Four groups of *what* make eight?" whereas $? \times 4 = 8$ asks, "How many groups of four make eight?" Generally, it is the measurement model ($? \times 4$) that is used with integers, even though either model for division (measurement or sharing) can be used with both concepts. It is helpful to think of building the dividend by constructing sets starting from zero, using the divisor. This strategy is similar to measuring an amount by filling it with units.

The first example in Figure 20.9 illustrates how the two models work for whole numbers. Following that is an example where the divisor is positive but the dividend is negative. How many sets of $^+2$ will make $^-8$—in other words, $? \times {}^+2 = {}^-8$? If we try to add positive counters with the set model, the result will be positive, not negative. The only way to use sets of $^+2$ to make $^-8$ is to remove them from 0. This means that we must first change the representation of 0 as illustrated. For the number-line-and-arrow model, consider how arrows representing $^+2$ can be placed end to end so they result in a distance, which is 8 to the left of 0. The arrows must be placed on the number line so they are "backed up" from zero. They are repeatedly subtracted, or added a negative number of times. Try now to demonstrate $^+9$ divided by $^-3$ using both models.

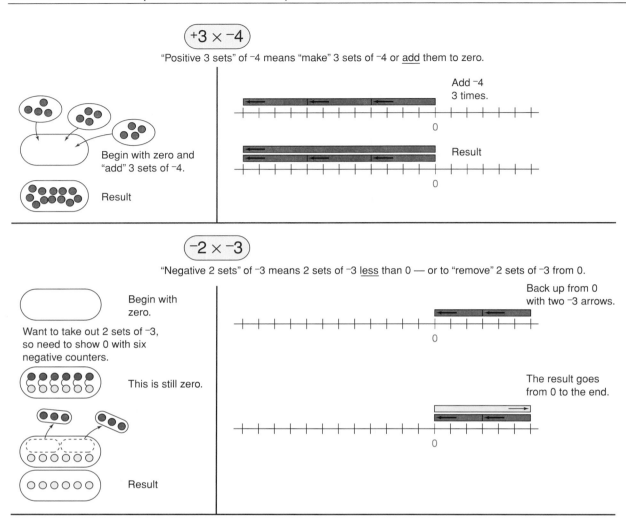

FIGURE 20.8 Multiplication by a positive first factor is repeated addition. Multiplication by a negative first factor is repeated subtraction.

The approach is very similar to this example. Then try a negative divided by a negative. That case is much easier to understand. However, the entire understanding of integer division rests on a good concept of a negative first factor for multiplication, and knowledge of the relationship between multiplication and division.

There is no need to rush your students to achieve mastery of the use of the models. It is much better if they first think about how to model the whole-number situation, then figure out how to deal with integers, with some guidance from you.

Rational Numbers

Several number ideas to which students have been exposed in the earlier grades, coupled with the ideas of the

integers, need to come together in grades 7 and 8. Students need to develop a complete understanding of rational numbers as numbers which can be expressed as $\frac{a}{b}$, where a and b are integers and b is not equal to 0. However, at this time their understanding should be limited to positive decimals and their fractional equivalents.

Fractions as Indicated Division

If four people were to share 12 candies, the number that each would get can be expressed by $12 \div 4$. If four people were to share three pizzas, the amount that each would get can be expressed similarly by $3 \div 4$; that is, three things divided four ways. In the pizza example, each person would receive three-fourths of a pizza. So $\frac{3}{4}$ and $3 \div 4$ are both expressions for the same idea: 3 things divided by 4. Similarly, in the candy example $\frac{12}{4}$ expresses the number

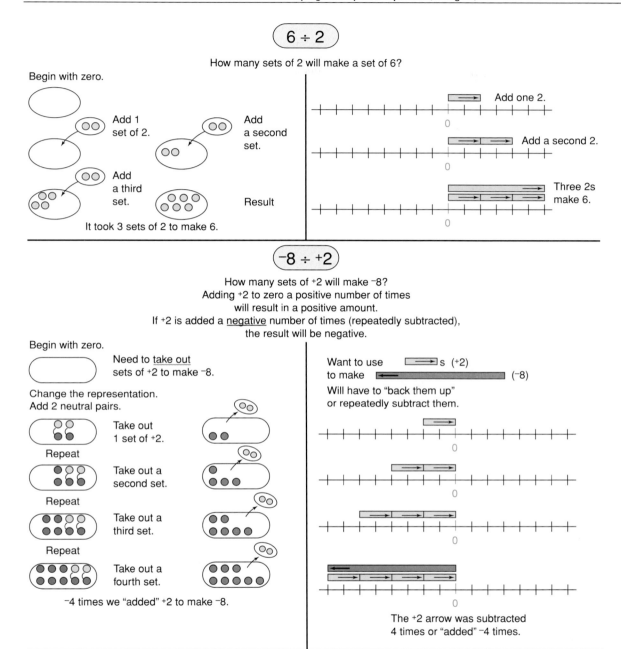

FIGURE 20.9 Division of integers following a measurement approach.

each will receive just as well as 12 ÷ 4. Put simply, a fraction $\frac{a}{b}$ is another way of writing $a \div b$.

Students find this meaning of fractions unusual. First, the indicated division is different from the meaning that has been carefully developed. Second, fractions are commonly thought of as amounts that are parts of wholes, not operations. Similarly, expressions such as 7 ÷ 3 are thought of as operations (things to be done), not numbers. In fact, however, 4, 2 + 2, 12 ÷ 3, and $\frac{8}{2}$ are all symbolic expressions for the same number. 12 ÷ 3 is not the ques-

tion and 4 the answer; both are expressions for 4. Likewise, 2 ÷ 3 and $\frac{2}{3}$ are both expressions for the quantity two-thirds. Do you find this a little hard to swallow? So do children. For the first time in seven or eight years of schooling, you are telling students that a symbol can represent two different things. This is a relatively sophisticated idea.

Here are some possible ways to help students develop the idea that a fraction is another way of expressing division.

ACTIVITY 20.4

How Do You Write It?

Present students with a simple word problem similar to the following: *Zach has 18 metres of rope. He cuts off one-fifth of the rope to make a leash for his dog, Sam. How much rope did he use for the leash?* **Three students have solved this problem.**

> **Student A: Zach cut off 3.6 metres because 18 ÷ 5 = 3.6.**
>
> **Student B: I did $\frac{1}{5} \times 18$ like this: $\frac{1}{5} \times \frac{18}{1} = \frac{18}{5} = 3\frac{3}{5}$. So the answer is 3 and $\frac{3}{5}$ metres.**
>
> **Student C: I did the same thing, but I just said the answer was $\frac{18}{5}$ metres.**

Which student is correct? Which is the "best" answer?

In the discussion of a problem situation like the one in Activity 20.4, you can lead students to see that $18 \div 5$ and $\frac{18}{5}$ mean exactly the same thing.

Similarly, discuss the difference between these three expressions:

$$\frac{1}{4} \text{ of } 24 \qquad \frac{24}{4} \qquad 24 \div 4$$

In the spirit of looking for patterns, here is a further idea:

ACTIVITY 20.5

Division Patterns

Have students do a series of divisions as follows: Begin with 18 and divide by 4. Record the result with a fraction remainder and as an improper fraction. Repeat with 17, then 16, and so on. What can you find out about these?

In "Division Patterns," students are thinking about division but are recording fractions. In the improper form, each fraction is written as equal to the corresponding division. This becomes more obvious when the dividend (resulting numerator) is less than 4 ($3 \div 4 = \frac{3}{4}$, $2 \div 4 = \frac{2}{4}$, $1 \div 4 = \frac{1}{4}$). Some children will explore $0 \div 4 = \frac{0}{4} = 0$ and continue to negative numbers: $^-1 \div 4 = \frac{^-1}{4}$. This gives rise to even further possibilities: What happens if you divide numbers by negative integers instead of positive numbers? Is $\frac{^-1}{4}$ the same as $\frac{1}{^-4}$? What about the fraction $\frac{^-2}{^-3}$?

Any or all of these discussions can lead to a general development of the idea that a fraction can be thought of as division of the numerator by the denominator, or that $\frac{a}{b}$ is the same as $a \div b$.

Fractions as Rational Numbers

In the early grades, children develop the idea that fractions are "things" such as parts of circular regions or shaded sections of rectangles. Even when fractions are seen as parts of sets, they remain, in the minds of children, more physical object than number. This is one reason that children have such a difficult time placing fractions on a number line. A significant leap toward thinking about fractions as numbers is made when students begin to understand that a decimal is a representation of a fraction. In Chapter 14, we explored the idea of the "friendly" fractions (halves, thirds, fourths, fifths, eighths) in terms of their decimal equivalents.

Students in grades 6, 7, and 8 need to know how to combine all of these ideas:

- $4\frac{3}{5}$ is 4.6 because $\frac{3}{5}$ is six-tenths of a whole, so 4 wholes and six-tenths is 4.6.
- $4\frac{3}{5}$ is $\frac{23}{5}$, and that is the same as $23 \div 5$, or 4.6 if I use decimals.
- 4.6 is read "four and six-tenths," so I can write that as $4\frac{6}{10} = 4\frac{3}{5}$.

What becomes clear in a discussion building on students' existing ideas is that any number, positive or negative, that can be written as a fraction can also be written as a decimal number. You can also reverse this idea and convert decimal numbers to fractions. Keep in mind that the purpose is to see that there are different symbolic notations for the same quantities—not to become skilled at conversions.

The result of this discussion is a reasonable definition of rational numbers: A *rational number* is any number that can be expressed as a fraction. Equivalently, a *rational number* is any number that can be written as either a terminating or repeating decimal number.

ACTIVITY 20.6

How Close Is Close?

Have students select any two fractions or any two decimal numbers that they think are "really close." It makes no difference what numbers students pick or even how close together they really are. Now challenge them to find at least 10 more numbers (fractions or decimals) that are between these two numbers. Do not be tempted to show students any clever methods for finding the numbers.

"How Close Is Close?" is an opportunity to find out how your students understand fractions and decimals. (The activity should be done in both forms eventually.) If students haven't been told a method, they must rely on their own ideas to come up with a solution. This activity offers a great opportunity for discussion, assessment of individual students' fraction and decimal concepts, and the introduction of perhaps the most interesting feature of the rational number system: density. The rational numbers are said to be *dense* because between any two rational numbers there exists an *infinite* number of other rational numbers. In other words, if you tried to plot all of the rationals between 0 and 1, you would have no gaps at all.

A true understanding of the density of rational numbers makes the irrationals even more amazing.

Real Numbers

As just noted, there are *irrational* numbers, numbers that are not rational. Although irrational numbers are not formally studied in grade 8, the distinction between irrational and rational numbers can still be mentioned (Saskatchewan Education, 1996). The irrationals together with the rational numbers make up the *real* numbers. The real numbers fill in all the holes on the number line, even though the holes are infinitesimally small. Students' first experience with irrational numbers typically occurs when exploring roots of whole numbers.

Introducing the Concept of Roots

The following activity provides a good introduction to square roots and cube roots. From this beginning, the notion of roots of any degree is easily developed.

ACTIVITY 20.7

Edges of Squares and Cubes

Show students pictures of three squares (or three cubes) as in Figure 20.10. The edges of the first and last figure are consecutive whole numbers. The areas (and volumes) of all three figures are provided. The students' task is to use a calculator to find the edge of the figure in the center. Use of the square root key is not permitted. Solutions will satisfy these equations:

$$\Box \times \Box = 45, \text{ or } \Box^2 = 45$$

and

$$\Box \times \Box \times \Box = 30, \text{ or } \Box^3 = 30$$

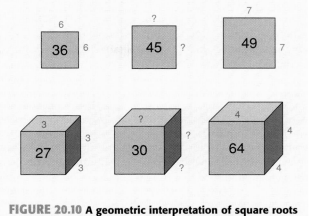

FIGURE 20.10 **A geometric interpretation of square roots and cube roots.**

In "Edges of Squares and Cubes," the calculator permits students to test a possible length of an edge to see if it is too long or too short. For example, to solve the cube problem, students might start with 3.5 and find that 3.5^3 is 42.875, much too large. Quickly, they will find that the solution is between 3.1 and 3.2. But where? Again, halfway is a good try: 3.15^3 is a bit more than 31.255. The next try should be lower. By continued guess and check, a simple calculator can get the result correct to six or more decimal places and a graphing calculator to as many as nine or more places.

From this simple introduction, students can be challenged to find solutions to equations such as $\Box^6 = 8$. These students are now prepared to understand the general definition of the *nth root* of a number N as the number which when raised to the *n*th power equals N. The *square* and *cube roots* are simply other names for the second and third roots. The notational convention of the radical sign comes last. It should then be clear that the $\sqrt{6}$ is a number and not an exercise to be done. The cube root of eight is the same as $\sqrt[3]{8}$, which is just another way of writing 2.

Irrational Numbers

One characterization of a rational number is that it can be written as a decimal where the decimal part is either finite or repeats infinitely. Thus both 3.45 and 87.19363636 ... are rational numbers and can each be converted to fractional form. But what about a decimal number that just goes on and on, with no repetition? Or what about the number 3.10100100010000100000 ...? These never repeat and are not finite and therefore are not rational. A real number that is not rational is called *irrational*.

The numbers π (pi) and $\sqrt{2}$ are both irrational numbers. The number π (pi) is a ratio of two measures in a circle, the circumference and the diameter. Although it is not possible to prove the irrationality of π (pi) at this level, the fact that it is irrational implies that it is impossible to have a circle with the lengths of both the circumference and the diameter rational. (Why?) A proof that $\sqrt{2}$ is irrational is generally explored at the high school level. The usual argument assumes that $\sqrt{2}$ *is* rational, which then leads to a contradiction.

Literature Connections

Some topics in this chapter present opportunities for "playing around" with ideas and numbers. Although teachers in grades 6, 7, and 8 do not always think of using literature as a springboard for mathematics, here are a few ideas that offer a change of pace in the upper grades.

The Phantom Tollbooth
(Juster, 1961)

Milo's remarkable journey through the lands beyond the magic toll booth are so full of wonderful words and ideas that the story is a must to read and discuss with adolescents regardless of the potential mathematical content. But the first page of Chapter 14, with its road sign indicating three directions to Digitopolis, is worthy of time in your mathematics class. You might want to convert measurements to metric prior to reading the story, as not all measurements will be listed in both imperial and metric formats as this is. The sign reads:

DIGITOPOLIS

5 Miles (8 kilometres)
1,600 Rods (8 kilometres)
8,800 Yards (7920 metres)
26,400 Feet (79 200 metres)
316,800 Inches (792 000 centimetres)
633,600 Half inches (792 000 centimetres)

AND THEN SOME

The discussion about which road is shorter or quicker is just great. Three pages later, Milo is told, "Why, did you know that if a beaver two feet long with a tail a foot and a half long can build a dam twelve feet high and six feet wide in two days, all you would need to build Boulder Dam is a beaver sixty-eight feet long with a fifty-one foot tail?" (p. 175). In the next chapter is an equally humorous discussion of infinity. That is followed by the chapter in which Milo meets the 0.58 boy.

Not only is this fine story filled with excellent language and fanciful ideas, but it provides many opportunities to wonder "what if?" or to create similar fantasies based on numbers. For example, students could write a new chapter for the book in which Milo journeys to a world in outer space, where the distances are enormous and everyone uses scientific notation.

The Guinness Book of World Records

Although it is not literature, *The Guinness Book of World Records* is an excellent source of amazing facts and interesting information that incorporates both large and small numbers. Using the information from the different categories in the book as a basis, students can create their own "world record" books, giving them practice with both large and small numbers. Sharing this book with the class is worth the time.

Math Curse
(Scieszka & Smith, 1995)

This book was an instant hit, probably because there are so many people out there who have math phobias. The first page sets the tone: "On Monday in math class Mrs. Fibonacci says, 'You know, you can think of almost everything as a math problem.' On Tuesday I start to have problems." Some may argue that this book is so anti-mathematics that it has no place in the elementary classroom. But it does provide an opportunity to show your human side as you discuss a wide range of mathematical ideas. ▪▪

Assessment Notes

Frequently, grade 6, 7, and 8 teachers get bogged down in the minutiae of their curriculum. Many books emphasize rules and exercises at the expense of opportunities for explorations. The content of this chapter focuses on your students' mathematical power rather than on the acquisition of skills.

For example, the discussion of exponents provides good opportunities to see how students reason, communicate ideas, go beyond the answer to generate their own ideas, and generally do mathematics. Once students have learned the relatively simple definition of what an exponent is, the search for easy tricks for multiplying and dividing should be left to them to discover, using their own reasoning. The discussions that ensue will be better than drilling rules about adding exponents when you multiply numbers with like bases. These are good opportunities to assess mathematical power.

With respect to integers, you have already been warned not to focus on the rules for operations. Certainly, the rules are important. However, if the rules for operating on the integers are developed by the students themselves, not only will students have a deeper understanding, you will have an opportunity to observe and assess their mathematical power.

Similar comments can be made about fraction and decimal relationships and rational numbers. The development of reasoning ability and students' belief that they can do mathematics is far more important than drilling rules. ▪▪

Reflections *on Chapter 20*

Writing to Learn

1. Explain the value of a graphing calculator's ability to display a complete arithmetic expression (with or without a variable) on a single line and to evaluate it on another line.
2. How can a calculator be used to explore the order-of-operations convention? Why is this rule something you must simply tell students?
3. Explain how powers of 10 are used to write very small and very large numbers. What is the particular form of the power-of-10 symbolism used in scientific notation and on the TI-73 calculator? What is the value of this notation?
4. Why is it probably better to use more than one model for integers, even if one seems to cause confusion for students?
5. Use both the arrow model and the counter model to demonstrate the following:

   $$^-10 + {}^+13 = {}^+3 \qquad ^-4 - {}^-9 = {}^+5 \qquad {}^+6 - {}^-7 = {}^+13$$
   $$^-4 \times {}^-3 = {}^+12 \qquad {}^+15 \div {}^-5 = {}^-3 \qquad ^-12 \div {}^-3 = {}^+4$$

6. How can you help students understand that a fraction such as $\frac{7}{8}$ means the same thing as $7 \div 8$?
7. How would you explain the difference between a rational and an irrational number to a grade 8 student?
8. What does $\sqrt{6}$ mean? How is $\sqrt{6}$ different from $\sqrt{4}$? How are they the same?
9. What does it mean to say that the rational numbers are dense?

For Discussion and Exploration

1. In *Principles and Standards for School Mathematics,* the authors of the 6–8 grade band apparently see the content of this chapter integrated with algebraic reasoning and functions, the content of the preceding chapters. Do you think it should be? What are some of the pros and cons of this approach?
2. Examine the table of contents in grade 6, 7, and 8 books from two or three different publishers. Using these books as a guide, how would you define "pre-algebra"? How much of the curriculum of these three grade levels seems repetitious? Is this the same for all publishers?
3. Use a calculator for the following exercises:
   a. Estimate the cube root of 10 to four decimal places.
   b. What do you think will happen if you enter 1000 in your calculator and then press ⊞ 2 ⊟ ⊟ …? Try it.
   c. What do you think will happen if you enter 1000 in your calculator and then repeatedly press the √ key? Before you try it, try to explain why you think it will happen.

Recommendations for Further Reading

Highly Recommended

Fitzgerald, W.M., Winter, M.J., Lappan, G., & Phillips, E. (1986). *Middle grades mathematics project: Factors and multiples.* Menlo Park, CA: AWL Supplemental.

This book is one in a series of five that has stood the test of time. The related topics of prime, factor, composite, prime factorization, divisor, multiple, common multiple, common factor, and relatively prime number are all developed in a succession of interesting games and activities for the middle grades. The focus is on pattern development and logical connections. This is an excellent way to involve students in good mathematics without overwhelming them with tedious algebraic ideas.

Graeber, A.O., & Baker, K.M. (1992). Little into big is the way it always is. *Arithmetic Teacher, 39*(8), 18–21.

This is one of the few articles to discuss fractions as indicated division. The authors look at practices in the elementary school that may lead to difficulty in this area and make practical suggestions for working with middle-school students.

Phillips, E., Gardella, T., Kelly, C., & Stewart, J. (1991). *Patterns and functions: Addenda series, grades 5–8.* Reston, VA: National Council of Teachers of Mathematics.

Again, the *Addenda* series is the place to go for excellent activities. In this volume, you will find sections on exponents and growth patterns, number theory and counting patterns, and rational number patterns. Other topics in the book are related more to the concepts of function and variable.

Other Suggestions

Borlaug, V. (1997). Building equations using M&M's. *Mathematics Teaching in the Middle School, 2,* 290–292.

Chalouh, L., & Herscovics, N. (1988). Teaching algebraic expression in a meaningful way. In A.F. Coxford (Ed.), *The ideas of algebra, K–12* (pp. 33–42). Reston, VA: National Council of Teachers of Mathematics.

Eisen, A.P. (1999). Exploring factor sets with a graphing calculator. *Mathematics Teaching in the Middle School, 5,* 78–82.

Kieran, C., & Chalouh, L. (1993). Prealgebra: The transition from arithmetic to algebra. In D.T. Owens (Ed.), *Research ideas for the classroom: Middle grades mathematics* (pp. 179–198). Old Tappan, NJ: Macmillan.

Patterson, A.C. (1997). Building algebraic expressions: A physical model. *Mathematics Teaching in the Middle School, 2,* 238–242.

Rubenstein, R.N. (1996). The function game. *Mathematics Teaching in the Middle School, 2,* 74–78.

Shilgalis, T.W. (1994). Are most fractions reduced? *Mathematics Teacher, 87,* 236–238.

Sobel, M.A., & Maletsky, E.M. (1995). *Teaching mathematics: A sourcebook of aids, activities, and strategies* (3rd ed.). Upper Saddle River, NJ: Prentice Hall.

Stacey, K., & MacGregor, M. (1997). Building foundations for algebra. *Mathematics Teaching in the Middle School, 2,* 253–260.

Section 3

Issues and Perspectives

The three chapters in this section provide practical suggestions for teaching mathematics at all grades levels. Even more importantly, these suggestions will help you develop a perspective on some major issues that pervade mathematics education.

Chapter 21 can be thought of as a companion to Chapter 4, where the basic structure for a problem-solving lesson was developed. Here you will find variations on implementing that structure, details of working with cooperative groups, tips for incorporating writing in mathematics, suggestions for homework, and perspectives on using your textbook.

Chapter 22 offers suggestions for and perspectives on reaching all children. Separate discussions deal with children with special learning problems, multicultural and gender issues, and the mathematically talented.

Although activities and suggestions for using calculators and computers are found throughout the book, Chapter 23 looks at these two forms of technology in a general way. It examines the frequently debated issue of calculator use and offers perspective on different ways to select and use software in your classroom.

Chapter 21

Planning for Effective Instruction

Natural learning ... doesn't happen on a time schedule and often requires more time than schools are organized to provide. Problem-solving experiences take time. It's essential that teachers provide the time that's needed for children to work through activities on their own and that teachers not slip into teaching-by-telling for the sake of efficiency.

Burns (1992, p. 30)

The three-part lesson format described in Chapter 4, p. 47, provides a basic structure for effective lessons. Even when a lesson does not seem to fit this design exactly, the basic idea for presenting a task *(introduction),* letting students work on the task *(development),* and discussing results and methods *(follow-up)* provides useful guidance in thinking about how lessons should be conducted.

This chapter describes some adaptations of the basic three-part format as well as some other instructional strategies: cooperative groups, writing in mathematics, homework, and the use of textbooks.

Adapting the Three-Part Lesson

The three-part lesson structure is built on the principle that mathematics can and should be taught through problem solving—that is, the mathematics on which students are working should be problematic. It should require them to be mentally active, to reason, to solve problems, to make sense of things, to conjecture, and to evaluate. Lessons that promote this mental engagement with con-cepts and ideas may not always appear to fit the intro-duction-development-follow-up structure described in Chapter 4.

Discourse

The value of classroom discussion of ideas cannot be overemphasized. As students make conjectures, describe and evaluate solutions to tasks, and share approaches as members of a community of learners, learning will occur in ways that otherwise would be impossible. Students then begin to take ownership of ideas and develop a sense of power as they make sense of mathematics.

When given a task, students should know that one of their responsibilities is to be able to discuss their ideas after they have had an opportunity to work on the problem. One grade 4 teacher discovered that she was too involved in her class discussions. The students tended to wait for her questions rather than tell about their solutions. To help her students be more personally responsible, she devised three posters, inscribed as follows:

How did you solve the problem?

Why did you solve it this way?

Why do you think your solution is correct and makes sense?

In the beginning, students referred to the posters as they made presentations to the class, but soon that was not required. They continued to refer to the posters as they wrote up the solutions to problems in the development portion of the lessons. During the follow-up part, students began to prompt presenters with comments such as: "You didn't answer the second question on the poster." One of the best results of these posters was that they helped remove the teacher from the content of the discussions. She no longer had to ask questions that made it seem to students that she had a single "best" answer in mind.

Regardless of the exact structure or time frame for a lesson, an opportunity for discourse should always be built in. After students have played a game, worked in a learning centre, completed a challenging worksheet, or engaged in a mental math activity with a full class, they can still discuss their activity: *What strategies worked well in the game? What did you find out in the learning centre? What are different ways to do this exercise?*

Written Work

The three-part format does not preclude students' completing a worksheet or writing explanations in the development portion of a lesson. In fact, a well-planned worksheet can be helpful in focusing attention. Tables, charts, graphs, drawings, and computations can all be part of the work students do, either in groups or independently. Written work in a fill-in-the-blanks format can place undue attention on getting answers. In contrast, a worksheet with questions and plenty of space to show work, answers, and rationale should promote student activity.

Some teachers give each group a transparency on which to record their solutions so they can share them with the class. Not only does the writing help students prepare their thoughts, but the transparency format adds to the perceived importance of the work and saves time in getting ideas to the class during discussions. For younger children it may be easier to prepare reports on large sheets of newsprint.

Mini-Lessons

Many tasks do not require the full period. The three-part format can be compressed into as little as 10 minutes. You might plan two or three cycles in a single lesson. For example, consider these tasks:

Grades K–1: Make up two questions that we can answer using the information in our graph.

Grade 2: Suppose you did not know the answer to problem 14. How could you start to figure it out?

Grades 4–5: On your geo-board, make a figure that illustrates the fraction $\frac{1}{4}$. Make a second figure that shows $\frac{1}{4}$ in another way.

Grades 6–7: Ammayya has this drawing of the first floor of her house. (Pass out drawing.) She wants to reduce it on the photocopy machine so that it will have a scale of 1 cm: 0.5 metres. By what percentage should she reduce it?

These are worthwhile tasks but probably would not require a full period to do and discuss.

A profitable strategy for short tasks is *think-pair-share*. Students are first directed to spend a minute developing their own thoughts and ideas on how to approach the task, or even coming up with what they think may be a good solution. Then they pair with a classmate and discuss each other's ideas. This provides an opportunity to test out ideas and to practice articulating them. The last step is to share the idea with the rest of the class. The pair may actually have two ideas, or they can be told to come to a single decision. The entire process, including some discussion, may take less than 15 minutes.

Worksheets with Manipulatives

Good activities can be built around a worksheet that requires the use of concrete models. Such worksheets guide the specifics of a manipulative activity. Students can draw simple pictures to show what they have done, or record numerical results of a manipulative activity.

Figure 21.1 is a worksheet of number combinations that might be used in grade 1. Counters are placed in the area at the top of the page and separated into two parts,

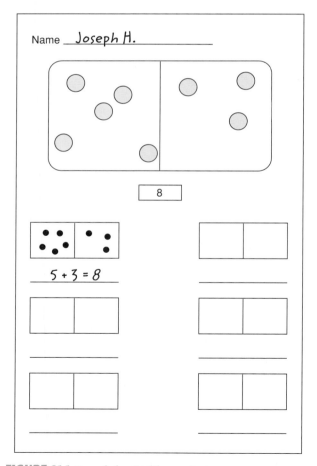

FIGURE 21.1 A worksheet with counters.

and dots are drawn in the small versions at the bottom. Many textbooks incorporate physical models into grade 1 and 2 lessons in this way.

The worksheet in Figure 21.2 is designed to follow a full-class discussion of trading with base-ten models. Students draw small dots, sticks, and squares to represent the base-ten materials with which they did the exercise.

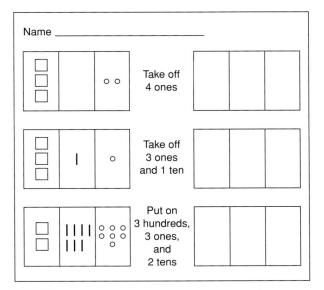

FIGURE 21.2 **A worksheet with base-ten materials.**

The grade 7 example in Figure 21.3 involves percentages approximated by familiar fractions. The students could use pie pieces and the hundredths disk (see Figure 14.1, p. 259) to determine the approximate equivalences without doing any computation.

Name _____

Which of these fractions is closest to the decimals below them? Use your pie pieces and hundredths disk to help you.

$\frac{3}{4}$ $\frac{1}{2}$ $\frac{5}{6}$

$\frac{2}{3}$ $\frac{1}{5}$ $\frac{3}{10}$

0.18 _____   0.45 _____

0.6 _____   0.81 _____

0.702 _____   0.285 _____

FIGURE 21.3 A worksheet for decimal-to-fraction estimation.

Worksheets such as these are appropriate when they are still problematic activities, not routine exercises. As with any task, they should be followed by discussion.

Workstations

A workstation approach is another alternative for carrying out student tasks. It can be adapted to any level. For a given topic, you might prepare as many as eight or 10 related activities to be placed in workstations. Materials are matched with particular activities and placed in separate tubs or boxes. These materials might include such things as scissors, paper, paste, special manipulatives, or worksheets to guide students as they work through the activity. Some activities may consist of games to be played by two or three children. The same type of activities may be used at more than one station, perhaps with slightly different levels of difficulty.

For children at the K–2 level, the activities must be modelled and practised in groups or with the full class before students begin working with them at stations. For older children activities can be explained orally, or written directions can serve as guides at the different stations.

The workstation approach is useful for all grade levels. The idea is simply to get all students working, either on their own or in small groups. For example, during a unit on percentage in grade 7, a number of different models and conceptual activities may be introduced during the first week. In the second week, the development portion of each period can involve activities using these models.

If you use workstations regularly, design an organizational scheme that will make using this format quick and easy. Use the same containers for activities throughout the year. In K–3 classrooms, label the containers, and assign each to a different area of the room: a space on a carpet, a table, or a collection of desks moved together. A sign or label at each area indicates which tubs belong there. Helpers can set out the tubs at the appropriate places in the room and return them at the end of the period. This procedure can be used all year. Only the activities in the tubs need to change to fit the concepts taught.

Whenever possible, some form of recording or writing should be included. This may involve drawing pictures, pasting down paper counters, or recording symbolically what was done with manipulatives. The recording represents accountability and suggests responsibility. The records provide a lasting opportunity for assessment. They can be displayed on bulletin boards, sent home for parents, or placed in students' portfolios.

Dealing with Diversity

Classrooms in school across Canada are increasingly heterogeneous. While the benefits of broadly inclusive classrooms far outweigh the negative aspects, there are difficulties. One of the major challenges that teachers face today is in trying to reach all of the students in their increasingly diverse classrooms.

Surprisingly for some, the problem-based approach is the best way both to teach mathematics and attend to the range of students. In the problem-based classroom, children are making sense of the mathematics in *their* way, bringing to the problem only the skills and ideas that they own. In contrast, in a highly teacher-directed lesson, it is assumed that all students will understand and use the same approach and the same ideas. Not all students are ready or able to tackle the same problem at the same level of sophistication at the same time. However, they must focus their attention on following the teacher's rules or directions in an instrumental manner. These demands often lead to much difficulty, and many students end up left behind or in need of serious remediation.

In addition to using a problem-based approach, there are specific things you can do to help attend to the diversity of learners in your classroom.

Involve Students in Collaborative Activities

Avoid ability groupings! Plan pairs and groups so that students with different abilities work together. Too often teachers feel that lower-skilled students are not able to do the regular work of the classroom. Students who have not mastered computational skills can nevertheless participate in projects that involve reasoning or creative ideas. In fact, the perspective of lower-skilled students can often be a positive factor in a mixed grouping. Expect students to have calculators available at all times, and help those with skill deficiencies become proficient with them.

Using a mixed-grouping approach will also accommodate students who perform above grade level. Although there are students at the extreme upper end of the spectrum who should be assigned projects and activities for the gifted (see Chapter 22), it is generally not advisable to separate them from the rest of the class. Highly skilled students are not necessarily the most creative or even those with the best conceptual backgrounds. Interaction in a mixed grouping is good for all.

Plan Differentiated Tasks

The ability level of many tasks can be modified by making small adjustments up or down in the numbers or the requirements involved. A general task can be discussed at the beginning of a lesson. This can be followed by a written task with numbers or other variations for two or three different levels.

For example, in one grade 2 class, the teacher regularly has students work on word problems that she pre-pares ahead of time. Two or three problems are on the page, with space for students to show their reasoning and their work. A problem may look like this:

Sanjay had _____ marbles. He gave Erica _____ marbles. How many marbles does Sanjay now have?

Before class, numbers are written in the blanks so that the same problem serves three different levels. For this example, Sanjay may have 121 marbles, 60 marbles, or 12 marbles, and correspondingly give Erica 46, 15, or 5. Thus, the same word problem involves 121–46, 60–15, and 12–5, all at the same time.

A similar approach is to put three sets of numbers or three variations of the same task on the board or on the worksheet. Rather than assign students a particular variation, allow them to select the numbers or variation with which they are comfortable. This approach empowers the students by putting some control in their hands. It also tells those at the lower levels that it is okay to work on easier problems, but also that they are free to challenge or stretch themselves. It is a form of student self-assessment in the sense that students are telling you with what they feel comfortable. You can compare a student's choice with your sense of his or her abilities. And finally, the idea that there are several alternatives provides a ready task for those who finish quickly.

Use Workstations

Another way to modify the level of a task is to create variations of the task at the different stations around the room. For example, if a grade 5 task involved equivalent fractions, a variety of related tasks could be selected and presented at the same time, then placed at different stations. Several stations could be created with different materials (pie pieces, paper for folding, counters, fraction pieces) to find common names for $\frac{2}{3}$. Of these, the pie piece approach is probably least challenging and the counters the most challenging. Another station might involve slicing squares to develop a procedure for finding equivalent fractions. Yet another station could have students trying to find different ways to compare two fractions, an activity that frequently has equivalent fractions embedded in it. (These activities are all discussed in Chapter 12.)

Students can be assigned to a station that best suits their needs. Students with different abilities can work together at a station that is challenging to the slower learners yet not demeaning to the more able. Each can write a separate report.

Avoid Skill-Oriented Tasks

Tasks that simply practise textbook skills need never be assigned uniformly to the entire class. Though skills are important, they should be practised at a level appropriate for the individual student. For those students who are beyond the need for practice in a particular skill, this kind of practice is boring busy work. For those students, on the other hand, who are not ready to practise that skill, the practice will only reinforce their sense of inadequacy. If a task involves a lot of computation, ensure that all students have calculators. Avoid tasks in which computational proficiency is the objective.

Cooperative Learning Groups

As noted, having students work in groups is an extremely effective technique for getting students actively involved in doing mathematics. Group work can be a regular feature of both student-centred and teacher-directed models of instruction. Here you will find some suggestions for establishing and working with effective groups.

Size and Composition

There is no magic number for the size of a group. However, the larger the group, the more skillful the group members must be in maintaining good working relations (Bennett, Rolheiser-Bennett, Stevahn, 1991). Johnson, Johnson, and Holubec (1993) point out that the more members in a group, the more possible interactions need to be accommodated. In a group of three, there are three possible student-student interactions. With four students, that number jumps to six. With five students, there are ten different pairs that must be able to interact, and the result is generally disappointing. It is generally recommended to begin with groups of two. In pairs, students can attend more easily to this new idea of working with someone. Also, it is somewhat more difficult to get left out of a pair (Bennett, Rolheiser-Bennett, Stevahn, 1991). Later, you will probably want to shift to groups of three or at most four.

For groups to function most effectively, they must view themselves as a unit, not as individuals sitting at the same table. Students must develop social skills of cooperation, sharing, listening, and responsibility. These skills are best developed by having groups remain intact for at least several weeks. If you use a fixed-group approach, spend considerable time determining the composition of the groups. Work on more than balance in abilities. Try also to mix boys and girls, to spread out both the leaders and the followers, to blend troublemakers with those who are cooperative. Avoid putting your problem children all in one group.

Developing Productive Group Behaviour

Working cooperatively and productively in groups is not something that children do automatically or easily. You cannot simply form groups and expect to see the benefits of group work happen magically. Students must be taught explicitly how to work cooperatively with their fellow students.

Specific Group Skills and Responsibilities

All students should understand which behaviour makes a group function effectively. The following are amongst the most important kinds of group behaviour.

1. *Share ideas and opinions.* Groups must learn to operate as a unit, not as a collection of individuals. Therefore, it is imperative that members all share their ideas and contribute their best thoughts to the task. Sharing is a two-way street. Each student is responsible for getting his or her ideas to the group and for listening to and accepting the ideas of other members. Sharing is not dominating.

2. *Ask and answer questions.* Each group member is responsible for his or her understanding of the ideas the group generates. If a student lacks some information or does not understand an idea being discussed, he or she has an obligation to ask other group members to explain the idea or task. All group members must be willing to help those who ask. Groups should come to realize that when they work together to share ideas and answer questions, they operate more effectively.

3. *Keep the group on task.* Group members need to learn to help each other attend to the job at hand. To achieve this goal, you will sometimes need to step in and restate the purpose of the activity, suggest a direction for the task, and remind students that there is only so much time. If students work without teacher direction, it is easy for them to stray from the task at hand and begin to play, argue, or discuss things unrelated to the task.

4. *Encourage participation.* Despite recommendations 1 and 2, there will be students who are reluctant to speak up in a group and who will sit and watch. Students in the group must not permit any member to be passive. When they notice a group member not participating, they need to bring him or her into the process: "What do you think, Nancy?" "Mark, do you think this is a good idea? What do you think we should try?"

These four specific group skills were taken from a much longer list suggested by Johnson, Johnson, and Holubec (1993). However, these four will go a long way towards getting your groups to work productively. If you decide to assign roles or have groups select roles for their members, it is important that roles reflect these group skills. For example, an "encourager" can be sure that all participate. A "director" can be assigned to keep the group on task. A "monitor" can be sure that all understand and are sharing ideas.

Teaching Group Social Skills

The first thing that must be done to establish effective groups is for students to understand and appreciate the values and benefits of working in a group:

- Everyone has two or three helpers.
- Everyone gets to talk and have his or her ideas heard.
- A collection of ideas is always better than just one idea.
- It is usually more fun to work with a partner than to work alone.

However, to reap these benefits, the group must learn how to work together.

Don't try to introduce all the group social skills at once. Select one or two ideas at a time, and discuss them with the class. Make a poster for the skill being discussed, with space to record students' ideas about what the skill looks and sounds like. Simply telling students to "share ideas" or to "encourage others" is generally a waste of time. Arrange students in temporary groups and have them model one skill, such as asking group members a question. Talk about how they sounded and discuss possible ways they could ask for information politely. Practise using materials, and talk about sharing.

Maintaining Group Skills

Each time you set students to work in groups, there should be two types of objectives that are understood by all groups. The first objective is the academic task or problem that is the goal of your lesson. The second objective will relate to social skills or general class behaviour. In the beginning, have students focus on one particular skill at a time. After assigning the group task for the day, you might say, "Today we are going to work especially hard at sharing with each other in our groups." You would write on the board, "Sharing with each other," then discuss and record what that would look and sound like. At the end of the period, each group would assess its performance at the designated skill, on an individual and/or group basis. Each student could respond to a statement such as, "Today I shared with my group: (a) not at all, (b) sometimes, (c) a lot." Also, the group could respond to a similar statement: "Today our group's members shared with each other: (a) really well, (b) sometimes, (c) not as well as we could have." Have the students add one or two sentences that describe their behaviour and what they will do to improve.

Continue throughout the year to have students work on their group skills. Like any other skill, these can be improved with practice and periodic evaluation, but can also deteriorate if students forget to work on them.

Group Recording and Reporting

Students should understand that when they report their group's work, they are sharing the ideas and the work of the group, not just their own ideas. Groups should always be prepared to share ideas orally or in written form. Preparing to make reports can also help groups work together more effectively.

Make it very clear that you may call on any member of the group to share or explain what the group did. In this way, students learn that they need to be sure that every group member understands the ideas developed in the group. You may find it useful to stop students just before your class discussion, and suggest that the groups make sure that each member understands what was done and is prepared to report if asked to do so.

If you use a record sheet or worksheet, it is better to have only one sheet per group, as this helps to create *positive interdependence*—a state where all group members perceive the need to work together to accomplish the same goal or common task (Bennett, Rolheiser-Bennett, Stevahn, 1991). Also, all group members should put their names at the top of the paper to emphasize that what is written on the page represents the ideas of the group. The person responsible for the writing or recording, the recorder, must be designated at the start of the activity. If you give each student a worksheet, cooperation in the group tends to break down as students become absorbed in completing their own papers.

Assessment of Group Work

The main reason for having students work in groups is to encourage interaction and promote learning. In this way, working cooperatively acts as a useful instructional tool. But many teachers are concerned that they do not know how to evaluate work done in groups. With the proper perspective, however, groups actually make assessment easier and more effective.

As noted in Chapter 5, much assessment data can and should be gathered through observation. Group work makes gathering information much easier and can ensure that data are gathered from all students, not just the vocal minority. If observation schemes are structured to accommodate groups, you will be able to focus your attention on the two or three groups you select each day. Over a few days, all groups, and thus all students, will have been observed.

A group-work approach will provide you with much more information in any given period than you could possibly gather without groups. When six or eight groups are working at the same time, you have six to eight times more student activity and talk to observe and listen to than you would in a classroom environment where children always work on their own to accomplish tasks. Also, it is easy to stand near as many as four groups at one time and listen in on all four conversations, or watch how all four groups are working.

Having each group submit a single written report substantially reduces the number of assignments you must assess. Moreover, it is considerably easier to make instructional decisions and provide feedback when you do not have to face a stack of papers submitted by all students individually.

Writing in the Mathematics Classroom

Writing in the mathematics classroom is an important instructional technique. It is entirely possible that you were never asked to write during your own mathematics learning, and so you may wonder why you should have children write and how to go about it. Here are some ideas to get you started.

The Value of Writing in Mathematics

When you write, you express your own ideas and use your own words and language. It is personal. In contrast, oral communication in the classroom is very public. Ideas "pop out" without editing or revision. Meaning is negotiated or interpreted by the class as a whole. When considering the value of writing in mathematics, the individual reflective quality of writing as compared to classroom discourse is an important factor. Writing in mathematics helps students become better mathematicians. It can also help them understand mathematical concepts more deeply, improve problem-solving strategies, and allow them to think of themselves as mathematical thinkers (Marks-Krpan, 2001).

Writing as a Learning Tool

The process of writing requires gathering, organizing, and clarifying thoughts. It demands that you find out what you know and don't know. It calls for thinking clearly. Similarly, doing mathematics depends on gathering, organizing, and clarifying thoughts, finding out what you know and don't know, and thinking clearly. Although the final representation of a mathematical pursuit looks very different from the final product of a writing effort, the mental journey is, at its base, the same—making sense of an idea and presenting it effectively (Burns, 1995b, p. 3).

When students write, they are able to stop first and think. They can incorporate drawings and symbolism to help convey their ideas. They can research an idea, or look back on related work to help put ideas together. All of this is very powerful, deliberate, reflective thinking. Writing is

much like teaching, in the sense that it requires collecting ideas and explaining them using only the tools you presently have. No doubt you have heard or even said, "I never really understood such-and-such until I taught it." In that sense, writing, like teaching, is very much like constructing ideas. It is a way to learning.

Because writing is such a powerful learning device, writing opportunities should be built into your lesson plans for mathematics whenever possible. Writing about the solution to a task, how it was done, and why it is correct is one of students' task responsibilities that should be explained in the introduction portion of the lesson. Be sure to provide time for writing in the development part of the lesson. A signal to the students indicating that it is time to begin their written report, if they haven't already done so, is helpful. Writing is excellent rehearsal for students as they prepare to share their ideas for class discussion. In the event that particular students or groups do not get the opportunity to present their ideas, the written report remains a record for your evaluation and feedback. This ensures that all voices are heard.

Writing time can also follow class discussion. When it does, it might be about summarizing what was learned during the lesson or unit, or it might give students the opportunity to tell you about ideas they still do not completely understand.

Writing as an Assessment Tool

Writing provides a unique window into students' thoughts and the way they understand ideas. Even a kindergarten child can express ideas in drawings or other markings on paper and begin to explain what he or she is thinking.

Oral communication, valuable as it may be, is gone at the end of the day. The notes you might take cannot account for all that is said in your class. When you are able to sit down with students' writing, you can reflect on each person individually, as well as on the class as a whole. Doing so enables you to gain an understanding of how they are progressing in the learning process (Marks-Krpan, 2001). You will then be able to target feedback and design special work for individual students. Written work also will help you assess the progress you are making with the current unit. Finally, student writing is an excellent tool for communicating with parents during conferences. It shows students' thinking, revealing much more than any grade or test score.

For writing to be effective, students need to feel free to tell you what they know and show you how they know it. Do not grade writing as you would a test—that will prevent the writing from being a learning opportunity for the students and a true assessment opportunity for you. Do, however, provide feedback to students—point out serious errors that need attention, comment on interesting ideas, and ask for further clarification. Not responding tells students you do not value what they have written. Help students see that their writing is important to you. Writing should never be busy work for students.

A particular writing task may on occasion be used for evaluation. You can have students do the same kind of writing on a test that they might do in their journals, or use other writing formats. Evaluation will be much more effective when students have had different writing experiences, because students will have had practice putting their ideas on paper.

Types of Writing Activities

Regardless of the specific form or label given to writing activities, the act of putting thoughts on paper can be a highly reflective activity that helps students clarify and organize their ideas.

Journal Writing

Journal writing has become the most popular form of writing in the mathematics classroom, and also the most loosely defined. Two teachers can have their students write in journals, and yet the kind of writing produced may be entirely different. Journals can be thought of as private, to be read only by you, the teacher, unless permission is granted to show a parent or to share with the class.

The journal can be used to have students explain a concept or an idea on which you have been working (*What does percent mean?*), to reflect on the day's lesson (*What did you learn today? What was easy to understand today? What was hard?*), or to show how a problem is solved. In fact, practically any writing activity can be done in a journal. It is the private communication format of a journal that makes it unique. (The format for journals and suggestions for writing prompts are discussed in Chapter 5.)

Problem Solving

When a problem is solved, students should learn to write much more than the answer. Written explanations of their reasoning and the processes they used should convey to others why the solution is correct. This means that students need to convince themselves that they are correct as well—an important part of doing mathematics. Encourage students to include drawings or any other explanation that would help the reader understand the solution.

Explaining an Idea

Somewhat different from solving a problem is the process of explaining an idea. This is prompted by straightforward requests such as, "Explain to me what three-fourths means" or "Show me what you know about the number 10" or "Why does the formula 'one-half base times height'

give the area of a triangle?" Usually, these writing tasks would closely follow the development of the idea in class.

Reflective Writing

Sometimes it is useful to get a general feel for students' perspective on a unit, how well they think they understand something, or what they like or dislike about mathematics or a topic in mathematics. You may want this type of writing to go into a journal, where the element of privacy encourages openness. If you make the writing task a little special, you are more likely to get true reflective thinking from your students. Here are a few suggestions for this type of assignment:

If mathematics were an animal, it would be....
The thing I like best about mathematics is....
The hardest part of this chapter on subtraction is....
I need help with _____ because....
To me, geometry means....

Practical Suggestions

Writing in mathematics is not easy for most students. Many will complain that they don't know what to write. Here are some tips that might help.

Help Students Get Started

Before offering a writing prompt, have a class discussion concerning the same topic as the prompt. As students suggest ideas, write them on the board in shortened phrases. Make lists of key words that are used in the students' discussion. Do not impose your language; record ideas using the students' words. To help with writing about a particular concept in mathematics, you might have students brainstorm and draw a "mind map" on the board showing how one idea is connected to another. Students can then use these notes, if they wish.

Nearly all of Marilyn Burns's books include examples of children's writing. She recommends the following formulation:

I (we) think the answer is _____.
I (we) think this because....

This simple formula can also be used in oral presentations. It is not necessary that children follow the exact wording, but these two lines are a nice way to suggest connecting an answer with its justification.

Cathy Marks-Krpan (2001) suggests using "thought starters" as writing prompts to help students with the beginning of an idea. A "thought starter" is an incomplete statement that students finish with their own thoughts. Here are some examples she provides:

I like....

I do not understand....

This concept map....

I feel that I know how to....

Measuring angles can be useful for....

Fractions are challenging when....

When children tell you they are stuck or don't know what to write, have them tell you about the problem or the question in the prompt. "Why do you think that is the answer? What did you do to get this? Tell me something you know about this shape you made (this measurement you did, this graph you made, this estimate you made)." Get the student thinking about several ideas, then ask him or her to repeat some of them. "What did you just tell me about how you got that answer?" Now he or she is ready to write. "What you just said to me are the same things you can write. Just pretend you are talking to me, and let those ideas go right through your hand onto the paper."

Huinker and Laughlin (1996) suggest changing the think-pair-share idea to think-talk-write. The "think" part is the same—a short time for students to get their thoughts together. The "talk" part is done with a partner or a small group. For the "write" part, students are told to use the same ideas and words they just talked about and heard in their conversation. They can add drawings or pictures to help. Think-talk-write can be a regular approach to writing in your classroom.

Write Often

One thing is certain: If your students write regularly—at least three times every week—they will get better at it. Try sharing some of the students' writing in your class, or with another class, so they will have some models. Soon they will become their own good models as writing becomes less of a chore and more of a learning experience.

For young students, the physical act of writing is difficult. If you have computers in your classroom, take advantage of word processing, and suggest to students that they leave blank spaces where necessary for any drawings. The big advantage of the computer is ease of revision.

Provide Purpose and Audience

All writers need to have a sense of their audience and know the purpose of their writing. Make these two points clear for every writing assignment or prompt. Often, you are the audience, so tell the students: "You are writing to me. Give me your best understanding about subtraction so what I read will tell me about what you know."

Other audiences might include class members (real or fictitious) who have missed a class. The purpose of the writing is to explain the ideas of the day's lesson. Or students can write to explain an idea for a student in a lower grade. This activity has the advantage of putting students in a position of confidence. Writing a letter to another class, to the principal, to parents, or to a public figure such as the mayor or the local Member of Parliament is useful when the purpose is to exhibit the results of a project.

Help the Pre-Writer and Early Writer

Children who do not yet have writing skills need to begin the process of recording and communicating their ideas. When we look at pictures and drawings made by young children, we should understand that they are most focused on themselves. They do not really have a sense of audience. Burns (1995b) suggests telling young children that what they put on their paper should remind them of what they are thinking. Suggest that they think about using words, numbers, and pictures to show their ideas. The result will not always make sense at first glance, so be sure to talk to the students about their writing and have them explain what they have written. At this early level, personal expression of ideas is most important.

When time permits, you can have students dictate what they want to write so that their words are on the paper. Be sensitive when using this technique; some children do not like having the teacher write for them.

In Chapter 5, there is an illustration of a large flipchart used by one kindergarten teacher as a "big journal." She writes ideas taken from the class during discussion. This is good modelling, but it does not replace students' formulation of ideas on paper or their own private writing.

Drill and Practice

Drill and practice, if not the mainstay of the mathematics classroom, is a strategy used regularly in nearly every classroom. This repetitive procedural work is supposed to cement ideas just learned. On the surface, it seems to make sense. But no new ideas are ever developed through drill.

Although drill does have its place, the traditional amount of drill needs to be drastically diminished. The key is for the practice to be effective and not the predominant feature of the instructional program.

What Should Be Practised

There are many procedural skills in mathematics that are worth practising. Once a skill is learned, it will become automatic through practice. A few examples may clarify this point.

Mastery of basic facts is as important today as ever, perhaps even more so. But mindless drill will do little to help students to this end. What needs to become automatic is the use of an effective strategy that facilitates mastery.

When a good way of thinking about a fact is used over and over, it soon becomes an unconscious process. Practice without an efficient strategy relies on rote memory and simply does not work very well.

Children who learn computational procedures without any understanding tend to practise what they think they should be doing. This inevitably means that it is their *errors* that are practised and strengthened. When students' practice focuses on their own invented strategies rather than on a collection of rules, they are free to invent short-cuts and other ideas. This is as true for the practice of flexible and conceptual approaches to proportion and percent problems as it is for computation. Proportion problems can be solved using a variety of algorithms. Effective strategies tend to vary from one problem to the next, depending on the numbers involved. Sometimes, all that is needed is a simple mental multiplication. Often a little sketch of the situation will help clarify what the two ratios are and indicate the necessary operation. Similarly, percent problems can often be solved in a variety of ways. What is most important in these instances is to be able to think about a situation meaningfully and not become totally absorbed with a prescribed procedural manoeuvre.

Practice should help students become comfortable with an idea. Lengthy drills of algorithmic skills tend to diminish flexibility and reflective thought. Frequently, teachers will drill skills in preparation for a standardized test. The result is that students respond as they have been drilled to do. Immediately, they begin to perform the drilled algorithm, when a mental computation, estimation, or a non-standard approach would be twice as fast, especially with a multiple-choice format. The distracter choices on standardized tests are designed to match the typical errors that students make in mindless application of the algorithms. Students who have had the opportunity to practise flexible conceptual approaches are much less likely to make these errors, and will actually be able to complete these tests more quickly.

Suggestions for Practice

The main suggestion for practice has already been made implicitly: Practise the use of flexible conceptual approaches, not isolated and meaningless procedures learned by rote. Here are some additional suggestions:

- Keep practice short. Fifteen minutes, three or four times per week, is much better than any full class period of practice.
- Individualize practice so that students are actually working on the things they need. Nothing is more pointless than repetitive drill of a mastered skill.
- Provide conceptual help. Students who are experiencing difficulty with practice are not going to be aided by more practice. A conceptual deficit is nearly always the root cause of a skill deficiency.

- Help students understand that the purpose of practice is to become quick, as well as flexible. Practice of meaningful skills allows students to use them with greater ease. With this in mind, avoid practice of things that students will not need to use, such as long division with three-digit divisors.

Homework

Homework can be a useful instructional tool. However, it must be coordinated with your instructional objectives and reflect what is happening in your classroom.

Conceptual Tasks for Homework

Traditionally, homework has been used as a means for providing extra drill and practice on the procedures taught that day. Drill-oriented homework is an obvious extension of lessons that end with a procedural "how-to" recipe. In a developmental approach, most lessons require reflection, with students justifying their results through the use of models or other methods. Drill-oriented homework is not an appropriate follow-up.

Does it follow that no homework should be assigned? Certainly not! Homework can serve the same purpose as working on a task or a new idea in class. A homework assignment may involve a task similar to one done in class that day, providing an opportunity for students to apply once more the ideas discussed in class. Completely new tasks can also be assigned as homework. Here, the *introduction* portion of a lesson occurs at the end of a class, homework supplies the *development* portion, and the next day begins with the *follow-up* discussion.

Homework is also an effective way to communicate to students and parents the importance of conceptual understanding and problem solving. When students take work home that involves problem solving, models, writing, or data gathering, parents can see that their children are doing more than drill. Homework is a parent's window to your classroom. Students may discuss homework with their parents, and most parents will ensure that their child's work is done.

Homework also builds self-reliance, as it obliges students to grapple with ideas without the teacher's guidance. In this sense, homework is a way of communicating to students, "I know you are able to do this on your own."

Homework Used for Drill

As already noted, practice does have a place. For activities from basic-fact drill to solving problems, homework can provide appropriate practice. Be sure to follow the suggestions in the preceding paragraphs. Keep drills short, and when possible, individualize them. Avoid giving drill-oriented homework just because you feel compelled to give a homework assignment.

One idea is to provide an answer key along with the drill. As part of the assignment, have students check their own drills against the key or have them use a calculator to check answers. Encourage them to note the ones that were wrong and redo these. Then they should write you a note about why they think they erred. Was it carelessness, or was it something with which they need help? If you let students see that the purpose of a drill is to improve their skill, they can participate in the assessment. With the offer of help when needed, the homework that is used for drill becomes an opportunity rather than an irksome chore.

Homework used for drill should never be graded, especially when students check their own work with an answer key. You can check that it was done, and you must respond to the self-assessments that students write. Do not penalize a student for wrong answers, especially if he or she knows why they are wrong or is asking for help.

Using Homework in the Classroom

How you attend, or fail to attend, to homework sends a clear value message to your students. However, checking homework in class can easily become a time-consuming burden. It is important to find ways of dealing with homework that are quick, yet effective.

First, confirm that assigned homework was done, and acknowledge the effort. This does not mean that you need to grade or evaluate it. Simply ask students to place it on their desks for you to see. Make it obvious that you do keep a daily record of whether homework was done or not.

Checking answers on homework is probably a waste of time. For drill and practice, the self-assessment approach is more effective and requires no class time. When homework is a task or problem, it should be followed up with a discussion, like the one in the follow-up portion of a lesson. Drawings and written explanations should be out on desks during the discussion. Instead of having all students share their work, look at one student's work, then ask students to compare it to what they did. "Beata, I see a different drawing on your paper. Can you tell us about that part?" "Pete, it looks like you may have done about the same thing. Is that right, or did you do something differently?" In this approach, homework is a continuation of the learning process. The responsibility for completing it is the same as the responsibility for completing work in class.

The Role of the Textbook

The textbook remains the most significant factor influencing instruction in the elementary classroom. When making decisions about the use of the textbook, it is good to have an objective view of textbooks and the role they can serve in instruction. You need to realize that the textbook is not necessarily your best guide to instruction. Your regional curriculum document is.

Textbooks are designed to meet the expectations of many different jurisdictions in order to fulfill the needs of the market. A textbook is restricted in what it can do by the limitations of the print medium. Pictures can be put on pages, but models cannot. For example, to illustrate movement and relationships, such as grouping 10 ones to make a single ten, requires a lot of page space. Young children have a great deal of difficulty following time-lapse sequence drawings that show materials in several stages of an activity. Using more pages simply creates a book that is too expensive and too heavy. Instead, ideas are frequently represented by a simple illustration followed by symbolic exercises that require less space.

For most of the market, the textbook is expected to teach, not simply pose tasks. As a result, the mainstream textbook is designed for the teacher who believes that the best teaching is done by following the text, and who values a high proportion of drill and practice. Most teachers have not yet adapted to the teaching-through-problem-solving approach described in this book, and feel somewhat challenged by textbooks that have done so. Remember, the textbook should be treated as one of the many resources you will use to support instruction and to help you achieve your objectives for mathematics. It is not meant to be followed page by page or to be used only for drill and practice.

How Are Textbooks Developed?

It is worthwhile to remember that publishing textbooks is a business. Most publishers enlist, as authors, mathematics educators and teachers who are quite knowledgeable about teaching mathematics. Publishers also do extensive market research to determine what teachers want in a book and what will sell. Often there is a gap between what the authors think would be good and what the publisher thinks will sell. Compromise between author and market becomes the rule. Rather than risk being too advanced with new pedagogical ideas, publishers try to offend no one. Consequently there is a gap between state-of-the-art mathematics education and what appears in textbooks.

Teacher's Editions

Authors have considerably more freedom in the teacher's editions. These editions are generally designed so the pages match those in the students' textbook. However, many publishers provide the teacher with two extra pages for each lesson. As well, there are additional pages with ideas, explanations, and hints in the front and back of each chapter. For the most part, the teacher's editions suggest some alternative and/or additional activities from those presented in the student textbook. Teachers should take advantage of this information. It is an excellent resource to help you with your planning. It is unfortunate that too many teachers view the textbook as the curriculum and feel compelled to "get students through every page," when in fact the real objective requires a much broader scope, as presented in the teacher's editions. The students' textbook is just one of many tools for instruction—not the objective, nor the curriculum.

Two-Page Lesson Format

The typical textbook lesson in the student book consists of a two-page presentation. A clear pattern to these lessons is observable in almost all popular textbook series. A portion of the first page consists of pictures and illustrations that depict the concepts for that lesson. It is intended that the teacher use this section of the page to discuss the concepts with the students. This section is followed by well-developed examples for the students to follow, or a guided exercise. Finally, the lesson has a series of exercises or practice activities. In this way, many lessons move quickly from conceptual development to symbolic or procedural activities.

(To a degree, this characterization of a textbook lesson is unfairly oversimplified. At the K–2 level, where children write directly in consumable workbooks, what the student writes for all or most of the two pages is usually tied to meaningful pictures or even simple hands-on models. As well, strict adherence to the two-page lesson is not always evident in grade 7 and grade 8 texts. There has been a definite movement in the textbook industry to develop pupil pages that require more use of hands-on models.)

The two-page format tends to send students the message that the pictures, concepts, and discussion part of a lesson can be ignored. As a result, many tune out until the teacher begins to explain how to do the exercises. Following page by page, and assigning only procedural exercises from a lesson, can easily negate all other efforts to communicate the importance of reasoning, of making and testing conjectures, of justifying results—in short, of doing mathematics.

Suggestions for Textbook Use

Our task as teachers is to help children construct relationships and ideas, not to get them to "do pages." The textbook is not the object of instruction.

With all of these warnings in mind, the textbook can be a source of ideas for designing lessons rather than prescriptions for what each lesson will be. Here are some suggestions:

- Teach to the big ideas or concepts, not the pages. Consider chapter objectives rather than lesson activities. The chapter or unit viewpoint will help focus on the big ideas rather than on the activity required to complete a page.
- Consider the conceptual portions of lessons as ideas or inspirations for planning more problematic activities. The students do not actually have to do the page. (Chapter 4 provides two examples.)
- Let the pace at which you work through a unit be determined by student performance and understanding, rather than the artificial norm of two pages per day.
- Use the ideas in the teacher's edition.
- Remember that there is no law saying every page must be done or every exercise completed. Select activities that suit your curriculum goals rather than designing instruction that fits the text. Feel free to omit pages and activities you believe are inappropriate for the needs of your students and your instructional goals.
- If the general approach in the text for a particular unit is not the same as the approach you prefer, omit its use for that unit altogether, or select only exercises that provide appropriate practice after you have developed the concepts with your method.
- When drill and practice at the symbolic level are desired, use the textbook as one source. Why write a drill if an acceptable one is there in the book?

Texts generally fit with your curriculum guidelines. So if tasks and activities are adapted from pages that match with the objectives you are teaching, you can be reasonably sure they will work well. It is not easy to make up good tasks for every lesson. Take advantage of the text.

Textbooks and other supplementary materials supplied by publishers usually include evaluation instruments that may be of use for diagnosis, for guiding the pace of your instruction, or for evaluation. Check to make sure that that the tests assess computational skills along with conceptual understanding, problem solving, or other process objectives. Today, there is a definite effort on the part of publishers to develop better assessments for higher-order skills.

Reflections *on* Chapter 21

Writing to Learn

1. Discussion or discourse is one of the most important components of a lesson. How can a teacher facilitate a discussion in the follow-up portion of a lesson without asking students specific task-oriented questions? What is the value of removing yourself from this leading role?
2. Describe at least three ways that the three-part lesson format can be modified or adapted.
3. How can differences in student abilities be dealt with in the classroom?
4. With respect to cooperative groups:
   a. Why are larger groups not likely to work as well as groups of two or three?
   b. What are some of the most important group skills needed for cooperative groups to work effectively? How can students be helped to learn them?
5. Describe several ways to include writing in mathematics.
6. Practice is not how skills are learned; rather it is how they become more automatic. What does this mean? Provide an example to explain your answer.
7. How can a task or problem be used as homework within the three-part lesson format? What are some of the advantages to assigning a task for homework?
8. Explain how to use a self-check method of practice for drill-oriented homework.
9. What is the major difference between the instructional method described in this book and the approach found in more traditional textbooks? Describe briefly what is meant by the "two-page lesson format" that is generally employed in popular basal textbooks. What is a serious drawback to lessons of this form?

For Discussion and Exploration

1. Examine a textbook for any grade level. Look at a whole chapter, and identify the two or three main objectives or big ideas covered in the chapter. Restrict yourself to no more than three, and be sure that nearly all topics in the chapter can be built into these big ideas. Now look at the individual lessons. Are the lessons really aimed at the big ideas you have identified? Will the lessons effectively develop the big ideas for this chapter? Try to find two or three tasks or explorations related to the big ideas you have described. If students work on these tasks, how many of the individual lesson objectives will be met?
2. Select a lesson or a short series of lessons from a traditional textbook. Using the ideas on the student pages, design a problematic task that addresses the same ideas. Will your task and follow-up discussion make an entire lesson? Are any ideas in the textbook lessons likely to be overlooked if your task is used instead? Now look at the teacher notes for these same lessons. What ideas can you find to help you develop a problematic lesson?

3. What homework would you assign for the lessons you described in question 2? What is the purpose of this homework? What would you do with this homework on the following day when it was due?

Recommendations for Further Reading

Highly Recommended

Dacey, L.S., & Eston, R. (1999). *Growing mathematical ideas in kindergarten*. Sausalito, CA: Math Solutions Publications.

Kindergarten teachers often find it difficult to put the practices discussed in a mathematics methods class into the kindergarten context. Dacey and Eston make the kindergarten classroom come alive in practical ways that encompass many of the general themes you have read about here: choosing tasks, teaching students to talk and listen, gathering assessment data, and much more. This is a must-have book for every kindergarten teacher.

Johnson, D.W., Johnson, R.T., & Holubec, E.J. (1993). *Circles of learning: Cooperation in the classroom* (4th ed.). Alexandria, VA: Association for Supervision and Curriculum Development.

This remains the best available guide for making cooperative learning work in your classroom.

Litton, N. (1998). *Getting your math message out to parents: A K–6 resource*. Sausalito, CA: Math Solutions Publications.

Well-meaning parents who remember mathematics as dominated by memorization and worksheets often challenge a constructivist, student-oriented approach to teaching. Litton is a classroom teacher who has practical suggestions for communicating with parents. The book includes chapters on parent conferences, newsletters, homework, and family math night.

Schroeder, M.L. (1996). Lesson design and reflection. *Mathematics Teaching in the Middle School, 1*, 649–652.

This article makes the suggestion that to become a better teacher, it is important to reflect on what you actually do as a teacher. It is recommended as a guide for looking at your own practice, whether you are a novice or an experienced teacher.

Thiessen, D., Matthias, M., & Smith, J. (1998). *The wonderful world of mathematics: A critically annotated list of children's books in mathematics* (2nd ed.). Reston, VA: National Council of Teachers of Mathematics.

In this second edition, Thiessen, Matthias, and Smith have compiled over 300 pages of children's books, each with annotation, rating, and suggested grade span. The book is structured by content area. It is a valuable resource.

Other Suggestions

Artzt, A.F. (1996). Developing problem-solving behaviors by assessing communication in cooperative learning groups. In P.C. Elliott (Ed.), *Communication in mathematics, K–12 and beyond* (pp. 116–125). Reston, VA: National Council of Teachers of Mathematics.

Artzt, A.F., & Newman, C.M. (1997). *How to use cooperative learning in the mathematics class* (2nd ed.). Reston, VA: National Council of Teachers of Mathematics.

Bennett, Rolheiser-Bennett, Stevahn. (1991). *Cooperative learning: Where hearts meet mind.* Toronto: Educational Connections.

Bickmore-Brand, J. (Ed.). (1990). *Language in mathematics.* Portsmouth, NH: Heinemann.

Borasi, R., Sheedy, J.R., & Siegel, M. (1990). The power of stories in learning mathematics. *Language Arts, 67,* 174–189.

Corwin, R.B., Storeygard, J., & Price, S.L. (1996). *Talking mathematics: Supporting children's voices.* Portsmouth, NH: Heinemann.

Davidson, N. (1990). Small-group cooperative learning in mathematics. In T.J. Cooney (Ed.), *Teaching and learning mathematics in the 1990s* (pp. 52–61). Reston, VA: National Council of Teachers of Mathematics.

Fitzgerald, W.M., & Bouck, M.K. (1993). Models of instruction. In D.T. Owens (Ed.), *Research ideas for the classroom: Middle grades mathematics* (pp. 244–258). Old Tappan NJ: Macmillan.

Griffiths, R., & Clyne, M. (1994). *Language in the mathematics classroom: Talking, representing, recording.* Portsmouth, NH: Heinemann.

Helton, S.M. (1995). I thik the citanre will hoder lase: Journal keeping in mathematics class. *Teaching Children Mathematics, 1,* 336–340.

Hill, S., & Hill, T. (1990). *The collaborative classroom: A guide to cooperative learning.* Portsmouth, NH: Heinemann.

Huinker, D.M., & Laughlin, C. (1996). Talk your way into writing. In P.C. Elliott (Ed.), *Communication in mathematics, K–12 and beyond* (pp. 81–88). Reston, VA: National Council of Teachers of Mathematics.

Johnson, D.W., & Johnson, R.T. (1989). Cooperative learning in mathematics education. In P.R. Trafton (Ed.), *New directions for elementary school mathematics* (pp. 234–245). Reston, VA: National Council of Teachers of Mathematics.

Johnson, D.W., Johnson, R.T., & Holubec, E.J. (1994). *Cooperative learning in the classroom.* Alexandria, VA: Association for Supervision and Curriculum Development.

Leinhardt, G. (1989). Math lessons: A contrast of novice and expert competence. *Journal for Research in Mathematics Education, 20,* 52–75.

Linchevski, L., & Kutscher, B. (1998). Tell me with whom you're learning, and I'll tell you how much you've learned: Mixed-ability versus same-ability grouping in mathematics. *Journal for Research in Mathematics Education, 29,* 533–554.

Madsen, A.L., & Baker, K. (1993). Planning and organizing the middle grades mathematics curriculum. In D.T. Owens (Ed.), *Research ideas for the classroom: Middle grades mathematics* (pp. 285–302). Old Tappan, NJ: Macmillan.

Marks-Krpan, C. (2001). *The write math: Writing in the math class.* New Jersey: Dale Seymour Publications.

McGrath, K.L. (1998). What is the score on scored discussions? *Mathematics Teaching in the Middle School, 4,* 50–58.

McIntosh, M.E. (1997). 500+ writing formats. *Mathematics Teaching in the Middle School, 2,* 354–358.

Mills, H., O'Keefe, T., & Whitin, D. (1996). *Mathematics in the making: Authoring ideas in primary classrooms.* Portsmouth, NH: Heinemann.

Mousley, J., & Sullivan, P. (Eds.). (1996). *Learning about teaching: An interactive tutorial program to facilitate the study of teaching.* The Australian Association of Mathematics Teachers. (Distributed by the National Council of Teachers of Mathematics.)

Newman, V. (1994). *Math journals: Tools for authentic assessment.* San Leandro, CA: Teaching Resource Center.

Norwood, K.S., & Carter, G. (1994). Journal writing: An insight into students' understanding. *Teaching Children Mathematics, 1,* 146–148.

Rowan, T.E., & Cetorelli, N.D. (1990). An eclectic model for teaching elementary school mathematics. In T. J. Cooney (Ed.), *Teaching and learning mathematics in the 1990s.* Reston, VA: National Council of Teachers of Mathematics.

Scheibelhut, C. (1994). I do and I understand, I reflect and I improve. *Teaching Children Mathematics, 1,* 242–246.

Thornton, C.A., & Wilson, S.J. (1993). Classroom organization and models of instruction. In R.J. Jensen (Ed.), *Research ideas for the classroom: Early childhood mathematics* (pp. 269–293). Old Tappan, NJ: Macmillan.

Whitin, D.J., & Whitin, P.E. (1996). Fostering metaphorical thinking through children's literature. In P.C. Elliott (Ed.), *Communication in mathematics, K–12 and beyond* (pp. 60–65). Reston, VA: National Council of Teachers of Mathematics.

Whitin, D.J., & Wilde, S. (1992). *Read any good math lately? Children's books for mathematical learning, K–6.* Portsmouth, NH: Heinemann.

Whitin, D.J., & Wilde, S. (1995). *It's the story that counts: More children's books for mathematical learning, K–6.* Portsmouth, NH: Heinemann.

Chapter 22

Teaching All Children Mathematics

A society can claim success in eradicating the malady of mathematics illiteracy if and only if all its progeny are able to develop to their fullest potential. If its offspring can become employable workers, wisely choosing consumers, and autonomously thinking citizens who can be contributors in the super symbolic quantitative world they will inherit, then society can say, "Victory is ours!"

Elliott and Garnett (1994, p. 15)

All of the NCTM *Standards* documents, beginning with the *Curriculum and Evaluation Standards for School Mathematics* in 1989 and including the *Principles and Standards for School Mathematics* in 2000, share a vision that *all* children can learn mathematics, not just the mathematically adept. For example, the 1989 *Standards* speaks of its goals for all students, the 1991 *Professional Standards* asserts that "all students can learn to think mathematically" (p. 21), and *Principles and Standards for School Mathematics* highlights mathematics learning by all students in its equity principle, one of the six principles on which it advises that mathematics instructional programs should be based.

Close examination of Canadian curricular documents reveals their alignment with views of the NCTM regarding children's learning of mathematics. For example, the *Ontario Curriculum Grades 1–8: Mathematics 1997*, states that "[the document] is intended for use with all students, including exceptional students" (*The Ontario Curriculum Grades 1–8 Mathematics*, p. 7). *Foundations for the Atlantic Canada Mathematics Curriculum* notes that "a teacher is

responsible for tailoring instruction to reach as many students of different cognitive levels as possible." In addition, it points out that "the mathematics curriculum and mathematics instruction must be designed to equally empower both male and female students, as well as members of all cultural backgrounds" (*Foundations for the Atlantic Canada Mathematics Curriculum*, p. 34).

To clarify what is meant by "all students," the NCTM Board of Directors in 1998 adopted its "Every Child" statement, which states:

> *By "every child," we mean every child—no exception.*
> *We are particularly concerned about students who have been denied access to education opportunities for any reason, such as language, ethnicity, physical impairment, gender, socioeconomic status, and so on. We emphasize that "every child" includes:*
>
> - *learners of English as a second language and speakers of English as a first language*
> - *members of underrepresented ethnic groups and members of well-represented groups*
> - *students who are physically challenged and those who are not*
> - *females and males*
> - *students who live in poverty and those who do not*
> - *students who have not been successful and those who have been successful in school and in mathematics (p. 11)*

Mathematics for All Children

Stop and think for a minute. Do you personally believe the quoted statement? Children with disabilities, children from impoverished homes, minority children—can all of these children learn to think mathematically? They certainly can. It is the responsibility of the classroom teacher to make that vision a reality. Teachers also need the support of the educational community including government, parents, and other stakeholders.

Diversity in Today's Classroom

It is no longer reasonable to talk about the "regular classroom." It is even difficult to talk about the "average child." The range of abilities, disabilities, and socioeconomic circumstances in classrooms today poses a significant challenge to teachers. Addressing the needs of *all* children means providing equal opportunities to any or all of the following:

- *Students with learning problems.* These may be students who are identified as having a specific learning disability, such as a problem with visual or auditory perception. The range and types of specific learning problems are quite varied. Other children have difficulties learning because they are slow learners or mildly handicapped.
- *Students from different cultural backgrounds.* Canada has become increasingly multi-ethnic and linguistically diverse, and this trend is continuing. Even though policymakers are working to assure high-quality education and equitable outcomes for all students, education still remains more oriented toward the white middle class, and is not necessarily congruent with other cultures and ethnic groups. Yet children of many backgrounds are in our classrooms and we must accommodate them in our teaching.
- *Students who are female.* Girls present caring teachers with another concern. Although the difference has decreased in recent years, after about grade 7, girls begin to fall behind boys in mathematics. Equally troubling is that girls exhibit more hesitancy about mathematics and have poorer self-concepts concerning mathematics than boys do.
- *Students who are mathematically promising.* Nearly every class has at least one child who finds the standard mathematics fairly trivial. These talented children are either bored or constantly providing the answers before others can think. A continued diet of mathematics instruction that is not sufficiently challenging for these students will not serve them well.

Challenging Traditional Beliefs

Meeting the needs of all children requires that we challenge and perhaps change many of our long-held assumptions about how mathematics should be taught, and about how children learn mathematics.

Change Beliefs about the Teaching of Mathematics

Our concept of mathematics as a rule-driven, computation-dominated discipline actually creates much of the difficulty we have in dealing with the range of children's talents and abilities. When every child is required to master each algorithm and memorize every basic fact before being permitted to move on to the next procedure or rule, the more able children in the room are quickly bored. Children at the other extreme begin to doubt that they have any mathematical ability.

Computation can be accomplished through the use of invented procedures or with the aid of technology. Geometry, measurement, probability, statistics, and algebra can all be accessed with minimal computational proficiency. There is neither evidence nor any logical argument to support the idea that computational proficiency is a prerequisite for meaningful mathematics. Furthermore, the computational expectations of the past are no longer necessary in the daily lives of citizens once they leave school. What is critically important, however, is the ability to reason and solve problems.

Change Beliefs about How Children Learn Mathematics

Traditionally, mathematics instruction has broken content into small, bite-sized increments. Each bit is explained, demonstrated, and then practised until mastery is achieved; then the next bit is introduced. The belief is that somehow the essentially passive students will put the bits together into some sort of cohesive whole. In classrooms for learning-disabled or low-average students, this approach has been even more pronounced and resistant to change. Unfortunately, much of the instruction for children experiencing mathematical difficulties is replete with worksheets and rote drill focused on "basic skills." What we know about how children learn would suggest a quite different approach.

There is no reason to believe that children with special needs, regardless of the nature of those needs, should learn any differently than other children (Andrews & Lupart, 2000; Baroody & Hume, 1991; Carey, Fennema, Carpenter, & Franke, 1995; Hutchinson, 2002; Poplin, 1988a, 1988b; Trafton & Claus, 1994, Winzer, 1996).

When skills rather than problem solving and concepts dominate, teachers find it useful to form ability groups. The results of creating ability groups are usually not as good as teachers believe. The degree of skill variability within each of two or three subgroups is not likely to be significantly less than that for the whole class. Furthermore, children in the lower groups are typically denied opportunities for interacting with their peers in situations involving higher-order thinking or reasoning. The mathematics to which children in the bottom group are generally relegated is skill remediation and isolated practice. There is little or no evidence to support the homogeneous grouping of children within classrooms or the creation of special homogeneous classes (Davidson & Hammerman, 1993; Oakes, 1990; Usiskin, 1993).

Inclusive Education

Canadian law guarantees "universal access" to schooling for all children. What this means is that every child, without exception for disability, has the right to free public schooling. The education act in each jurisdiction also guarantees this right. The trend today is towards a unified education system, where special and regular education are merged in order to meet the individual learning needs of all students (Andrews & Lupart, 2000). Across Canada, inclusion is the predominant approach, and inclusive schools are a natural part of our education system (Hutchinson, 2002).

Inclusion entitles exceptional students or students with special needs, the term used in British Columbia and Alberta, to have programs adapted to their needs. Exceptional includes giftedness and a wide range of disabilities, such as emotional, sensory, and physical disabilities.

Exceptionalities—Categories of Disabilities

Children bring to the classroom an enormous array of difficulties and differences rooted in both environmental and psychological factors. Each child is unique and should be regarded as such. It is incumbent upon the school to provide for the individual needs of children who are deemed exceptional.

Legal definitions for a wide range of exceptionalities are usually determined by the ministry of education of a provincial or territorial jurisdiction. Definitions include those for severe developmental disabilities (such as autism or Asperger syndrome), physical disabilities (such as hearing or vision impairment), and an array of other learning disabilities. These definitions, which are included in an Individual Education Plan (IEP), help to determine which children are eligible for special services and what type of services they will receive. The Individual Education Plan (IEP) describes in writing the adaptations, modifications, and services to be provided for the student deemed exceptional.

The Role of the Classroom Teacher

Although special educational services are available for eligible students, the "least restrictive environment" is increasingly "the regular classroom." It is likely that in any classroom a teacher will have a variety of children with special learning needs. However, as the inclusive classroom becomes more diversified, it also becomes more challenging for teachers to manage. This is not to say that help is not available.

Even though classroom teachers need not be experts in all of the potential disabilities with which they may be confronted, every teacher should become familiar with the special resources available. You can refer to the school's instructional support or consultation team for assistance and, more importantly, for information about the child. The more a teacher knows about the nature of a child's learning difficulties, the better prepared that teacher will be to provide tailored instruction that is directed to the learning needs of the student. The loud and clear message here is, "Get help!" Find out about how the special children in your classroom learn.

Rather than feeling defeated by the reality of a diverse class of children, consider the real benefits of an inclusion model (Borasi, 1994):

- Regular students serve as learning models for special students.
- Special students frequently offer unique alternative solutions to challenging problems encountered by the full class or in small cooperative groups.
- All students develop an awareness of and respect for individual differences.
- All students, not just the "regular" students, are exposed to good mathematics and challenging experiences.

Specific Learning Disabilities

The predominant instructional model for students with learning disabilities has historically viewed the learner as passive, with the mastery of skills taking precedence over understanding (Poplin, 1988a). It is this thinking that led to pull-out and self-contained-classroom approaches. As noted, these skills-oriented models have produced very limited results.

Poplin's conclusion is that constructivist theory provides the best directions for teachers of special students. That same suggestion is made either implicitly or explicitly by nearly every author in NCTM's excellent book *Windows of Opportunity: Mathematics for Students with Special Needs* (Thornton & Bley, 1994). Put simply, there is no need to change the content of the curriculum for students with learning disabilities. What must be done is what all good constructivist teachers do, and that is pay careful attention to the child and how he or she learns, and design instruction (not content) that maximizes the child's strengths while minimizing the impact of weaknesses.

A Perspective on Learning Disabilities

Students with learning disabilities have very specific problems with perceptual or cognitive processing. These problems may affect memory or the ability to speak or express ideas in writing, perceive auditory or written information, or integrate abstract ideas. The following insights offered by Borasi (1994) are an important point of departure for teachers who have children with learning disabilities in their classes:

- Students with learning disabilities are mentally capable; they are not slow or intellectually disabled.
- The classification of learning disabled is not useful to the classroom teacher without a clear understanding of the child's specific learning problem.
- Learning disabilities are not easily remediated and perhaps cannot be remediated at all.
- Learning disabilities should be compensated for by helping students use their strengths.
- Instructional accommodations and modifications will be needed to assist children with specific learning disabilities.

Borasi suggests that teachers accept the fact that learning disabilities are real, in the same sense that being blind or deaf is a real disability. You would not ask a blind person to "look more closely" or a deaf person to "listen more carefully." Hence we should never ask a child with a learning disability to do things that depend heavily on his or her area of deficit.

Adaptations for Specific Learning Difficulties

Table 22.1 identifies specific disabilities and gives a few examples of the mathematical problems that each might cause. Note that deficits or disabilities may be present as auditory problems, visual problems, or sometimes both. It is important that the teacher have as much detailed information as possible about children who have specific learning difficulties. If the child has already been evaluated by the school-based team, information will be available in an Individual Education Plan (IEP) to help identify specific weaknesses and strengths. The Plan will also describe ways to adapt instructional strategies to avoid weaknesses and capitalize on strengths.

Adaptations for Perceptual Deficits

There are many variations of perceptual problems; some are visual and others auditory. All involve confusion of input in one way or another. Children with *figure-ground* difficulties have trouble sorting out or recognizing component parts of what they see or hear. *Discrimination* difficulties involve the inability to discern differences in things seen or heard. Children with *reversal* problems have difficulty with left-right perceptions and tend to see things in mirror images of what they really are. *Spatial* organization deficits affect children's ability to interpret or implement the positions and arrangements of things. Spatially challenged children have difficulty not only with geometric models and drawings but also with organizing their own writing on paper.

The realm of perceptual problems is perhaps the area where the maxim "avoid weaknesses and capitalize on strengths" most clearly applies. Here are a few specific suggestions:

- Seat the child near you and the chalkboard.
- Keep the child's desk or workspace free of clutter.
- Maintain a moderate voice. Repeat main ideas.
- Structure text or worksheet pages for the child. Provide templates to block out all but one problem or exercise at a time. (Cut a rectangle in the centre of a half-sheet of tag-board. Make several templates with different-sized holes, and have the child keep them in her or his textbook.)
- Help the child design methods of organizing written work. Computations may be done on centimetre grid paper, with each number written in a separate square. Provide paper that has columns or templates drawn on it similar to those found in the Blackline Masters for traditional algorithms.
- Provide children with tape-recorded instructions that explain what may be difficult to discern from the available visual materials.
- Provide real geometric models whenever possible instead of relying on pictures in the text. Use geoboards, and materials such as pattern blocks for constructions, to keep drawing to a minimum.
- Assign a buddy to help read, explain, or repeat directions.

Adaptations for Memory Deficits

Memory deficits can also be specifically visual or auditory. Some children may have more difficulty recalling things seen than things heard, or vice versa. Children with *short-term memory* deficits can have trouble recalling things, even after a few seconds, when copying from the board or reading a word problem. Lengthy directions are also difficult. *Long-term memory* deficits are quite different. Children with this disability may show no difficulty with material when it is presented, but will appear to have learned nothing a day or a week later. Mastery of basic facts is a hallmark problem for children with this disability. *Sequential memory* problems result in the inability to retain the order of a sequence of events or a series of steps in directions or procedures. These children are likely to

Table 22.1: Examples of Specific Learning Disabilities and Their Possible Effects on Performance in Mathematics

Disability	Visual Deficit	Auditory Deficit
Perceptual		
Figure-ground	• May not finish page or loses place • Has difficulty reading multi-digit number	• Has trouble hearing patterns in counting • Has difficulty attending to classroom discourse
Discrimination	• Has difficulty differentiating coins • Has difficulty with numerical identification such as 2 for 5 or 3 for 8 • Mixes operation symbols	• Has trouble distinguishing between similar-sounding words, such as *thirty* and *thirteen*
Reversal	• Reverses digits in numbers • Has difficulty in regrouping	
Spatial	• Has trouble writing on lined paper • Fails to notice size differences in shapes (fractions or geometry) • Has difficulty writing numbers, especially fractions and decimals	
Memory		
Short-term	• Has difficulty retaining newly presented material • Has difficulty copying problems from the board • Has difficulty remembering facts in a word problem	• Has difficulty with oral drills • Has trouble with dictated assignments
Long-term	• Has difficulty retaining basic facts or procedures over long period • Has difficulty solving multi-operational computation (written or mental)	
Sequential	• Has difficulty following through a long or multi-step procedure such as computational algorithms • Has difficulty solving multi-step word problems	• Cannot retain story problems that are dictated
Integrative		
Closure	• Has difficulty visualizing groups • Has difficulty with missing addends and missing factors • Is unable to draw conclusions and so has trouble noticing and continuing patterns • Has difficulty with word problems • Has trouble continuing counting patterns from within a sequence	• Has difficulty counting on from within a sequence
Expressive language	• Finds rapid oral skills difficult	• Has difficulty counting on • Has difficulty with explanations
Receptive language	• Has difficulty relating words to meaning • Has difficulty with words having multiple meanings	• Has difficulty relating words to meanings • Has difficulty writing numbers from dictation
Abstract reasoning	• Is unable to solve word problems • Is unable to compare numbers in symbolic form • Cannot understand word problems	

Source: Adapted from *Teaching Mathematics to Students with Learning Disabilities* (3rd ed., pp. 8–9), by N. S. Bley & C. A. Thornton, 1995, Austin, TX: Pro-Ed. Copyright 1995. Reprinted by permission of Pro-Ed.

ask, "What do I do next?" when working on a computation or extending a pattern. It is important to distinguish this inability from a lack of understanding.

You can diminish the load on a student's short-term memory by breaking tasks and directions into small steps and providing a buddy to help with recall. Overcoming long-term memory problems requires over-learning, frequent practice, and as many associations with other ideas as possible. The following more specific suggestions may be useful:

- Rather than presenting a series of instructions, provide only one at a time. With good planning, sequenced instructions can be written out ahead of time.
- When teaching a specific procedure such as an algorithm, work with the student to create a model exercise showing each step. When possible, use the student's own invented strategies.
- For basic facts, use strategies and number relationships (see Chapter 8). Provide fact charts as shown in Figure 22.1, crossing out facts that are mastered.
- Allow use of a calculator at all times.

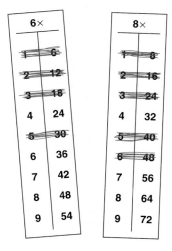

FIGURE 22.1 Permit the use of fact charts, but encourage memorization

Memory deficits tend to be exhibited in procedural work. Remember that no routine procedural knowledge, including mastery of basic facts, should prevent a student from making progress with mathematical ideas. Exploration of new concepts is never dependent on mastery of skills.

Adaptations for Integrative Deficits

Children with integrative problems seem to have difficulty with abstract ideas and conceptualization. These children are not slow or intellectually disabled—they have difficulty making the cognitive connections that others may find easy. Children with an integrative disorder may do quite well at rote procedures such as computational algorithms, even though these are no longer the focus of the mathematics curriculum. A general principle for helping these children integrate concepts and develop understanding is similar to a whole-language approach, and is not unlike the methods espoused for a good constructivist classroom. In short, help students use the experiences and ideas most familiar to them: their own invented procedures for solving problems, familiar models or personal drawings that make sense to them, and their own words in either written or oral form to express their ideas. Of course, these are good approaches for all children. The following more specific approaches may be helpful for children with integrative difficulties:

- Use familiar physical models for longer than the usual period of time.
- Have students articulate what they do as often as possible. Use both written and oral expression.
- Frequently require explanations and justifications. This self-monitoring can heighten the student's awareness of new ideas, and the verbalization can aid in making connections.
- Allow for repetition or practice of new conceptual ideas.

Adaptations for Attention Deficits

In many (not all) instances students with learning disabilities also are identified as having attention deficit disorder or attention deficit–hyperactivity disorder. These children have chronic difficulties with attention span, impulse control, and sometimes hyperactivity. Be careful to distinguish these true disorders from children who cause discipline problems for other reasons. The following strategies have proved useful:

- Establish clear routines, and discuss them with the child. Make expectations and consequences clear.
- Design learning activities that are active and engaging, rather than tedious or requiring long periods of silent seatwork.
- Plan for the child to do independent work in an environment free of visual and auditory distractions (for example, at a seat near a blank wall, away from classmates).
- Use highlighters to attract attention to important key ideas in textual material.
- Keep assignments short. Reduce exercise lists. Plan smaller subtasks within larger explorations or projects.
- Assign a buddy, and impress on both that the goal is to stay on task.

■ Instead of placing the child in a cooperative group of three or four, pair him or her with a buddy. Larger groups are more distracting and require more patience while others talk.

Mental Disabilities

All of us possess different mental capacities in addition to our individual strengths and weaknesses or learning styles. Children with intellectual disabilities (generally with IQ scores between 50 and 70) will be limited in the kind and degree of mathematical reasoning they can perform. Other children not as severely limited are sometimes labelled *slow learners*. Although severely disabled children are generally best served in a special classroom, there may be a wide range of intellectual disabilities in the regular classroom.

Modifications in Instruction

Limited cognitive abilities do not in any way alter the way that children learn. However, children with intellectual disabilities will learn much more slowly than those with normal intelligence and will reach a plateau much more quickly when it comes to the mathematical ideas with which they can work (Bley, 1994; Callahan & MacMillan, 1981). These children are likely to have limited memory, attention, and language abilities to assist them in the development of new ideas.

Though a fast-paced, highly interactive classroom may be somewhat overwhelming for children with intellectual disabilities, they can benefit from many of the same experiences as the rest of the class. They can and should participate in projects and hands-on activities with their peer group. They can participate in cooperative groups by taking on less demanding roles, such as materials organizer or encourager. They can learn to perform calculations on a calculator and can serve as the person in a group who performs this activity. Many children with disabilities are good at drawing or making graphs. Making expectations clear, simple, and appropriate for the child is another important consideration. For any activity planned for the class, find subtasks or related activities that are appropriate for the child. Clearly explain these expectations using simple directions; then have the child repeat the expectations in his or her own words.

Partner the child with different students periodically, and have the partner help the child with the same task or idea. This allows for necessary repeated exposure or "overlearning," and other students also will gain from serving as "the explainers." It is important for all children in the room to involve children with intellectual disabilities in activities and projects. The child gains from the richer ideas and interactions and will frequently contribute alternative solutions or ideas. All children gain an appreciation for and acceptance of human differences.

Modifications in Curriculum

Since children with intellectual disabilities learn much more slowly than other children, it follows that less content can be learned during the years they are in school. It makes sense to focus the available instructional time on those areas that are going to be of the most value to these students as adults. Computational skill is the most obvious area where changes in curricular expectations should be made. There is no reason to be obsessive about fact mastery. Traditional computational algorithms should be eliminated from their curriculum altogether.

Students should be taught to have a calculator handy for all mathematical work. The child with an intellectual disability should be given careful instruction and much practice using the calculator. A calculator with a printer is useful because it creates a printed record of work done. These students can use a calculator to do the same exercises that others are doing.

An area that should be stressed is the relationship of number to the real world. Whereas calculations can be mastered via the calculator, the meanings of numbers in the real world cannot. Do not confuse number meaning with place-value concepts. What is important here is to realize that the mass of a bag of flour is 2.5 kilograms, that $100 buys a pair of fancy sneakers, or that it takes about 20 minutes to walk about $1\frac{1}{2}$ kilometres. Numbers in the abstract will be of little use.

Multicultural and Social Equity

It may seem that mathematics, of all subjects in the curriculum, is culturally neutral. After all, 2 + 2 = 4 is a logical fact having little to do with ethnicity or poverty. Yet there is evidence (Hutchinson, 2002) that only some cultural groups are continually represented in science and mathematics, in schools and careers. There are also data that ESL students experience many learning difficulties in school. On the Education Quality and Accountability Office (EQAO) of Ontario's 1999 grade 3 tests for mathematics for three district school boards, the average percentage of students achieving at grade level or better was 43 percent for ESL students and 60 percent for non-ESL students. (It is important to note that Toronto, Ontario's largest city, has the biggest and most culturally diverse population in Canada.)

It is also known that poverty is associated with poor academic performance. According to Levin (1995), "Much Canadian research confirms poverty's negative influence on students' behaviour, achievement, and retention in school" (p. 212).

Do children from these groups not have the same mathematical or even general academic ability as their dominant group counterparts? There is no evidence to support such a view, yet discrepancies in achievement levels in mathematics remain a fact.

Access to Quality Teachers

At-risk students tend not to have access to high-quality, experienced teachers. It is well known that less-experienced, first-year teachers are placed in predominantly minority and multi-ethnic inner-city schools. These schools also experience high teacher turnover because of the many challenges they present. Nevertheless, teachers can help at-risk students achieve at the highest levels. In many schools across Canada, teachers are using multicultural perspectives in planning instruction, and fine-tuning programs as they struggle with problems relating to the ethnically diverse backgrounds of their students. Some have learned from colleagues, some from training, and all from personal insights.

School boards are supporting teachers and students through a number of different programs and policies. The Vancouver School Board offers staff development programs, such as assessment ESL software strategies for ESL/special needs learners, to teachers. The Calgary School Board clearly delineates responsibilities for the teacher, which include acquiring cross-cultural sensitivity, using diverse instructional strategies, and facilitating communication between school, parent, and student. The Winnipeg School Board, as part of its approach to strengthening ties between schools and families, has established a number of community liaison officer positions. These positions provide the kind of infrastructure support that minority students and parents find useful. The Peel Board of Education in Ontario has many programs supporting new immigrants and minority students. They vary from the educational use of videotape series produced by TVOntario, to curricula that enable students to see themselves reflected in their learning (Scott, 2001). The surprising reality is that at-risk students can change. Being exposed to regular high-quality instruction and appropriate programming, which many have not experienced before, can make a difference for these students.

Access to Curriculum

Evidence suggests that teachers who work with at-risk students tend to place less emphasis on curricular goals such as inquiry and problem solving. Differences occur in both pace and coverage of content. There is also a tendency to emphasize lower-level skills over higher-order thinking and engaging, meaningful explorations. These differences can be attributed to the curricular materials and resources teachers choose from among those available to enrich the curriculum.

Expectations

It is well known that teachers' beliefs have an impact on their students' outcomes and success. Concomitant with this view, it is also known that students will rise or fall to the level of teachers' expectations.

Teacher Expectations

There is a striking division among teachers of at-risk students. There are those who believe in the abilities of their students, and those who expect very little. The latter group will find it easy to blame the performance of their students on the myriad factors that exist outside the classroom. *It's the neighbourhood. They don't have two parents making them work. The parents are not educated. These kids come from an environment infested with drugs.* Teachers who voice such laments are using real facts as excuses for not making a difference (Ladson-Billings, 1997). If the excuses were valid, no teachers would believe in their students, yet many do—and achieve outstanding results.

Experts believe that one of the most important factors for success with disadvantaged or minority students is to develop in them a strong sense of self-esteem, helping children believe in themselves. This is an incredibly difficult task for the teacher whose expectations are low to begin with.

Examples of What Works

What we have learned is that narrow, skill-focused programs and highly prescriptive approaches do not work with students who belong to ethnic minorities. We have also seen that programs that target disadvantaged children by grouping them in special classrooms do not work. We *can* point to some recent examples of programs and the efforts of individual teachers that have worked exceptionally well with urban, minority, low-socioeconomic children. The common factors in these programs are not money, materials, or technology. What makes them succeed is a constructivist approach to instruction and a positive belief in the children.

The three examples described here are just that—examples. Many more success stories could be told, but most exhibit the same instructional characteristics as these cases.

Project IMPACT: CGI in an Urban Setting

Cognitively Guided Instruction (CGI) is a program developed at the University of Wisconsin in the mid-1980s. It is based on the belief that if "teachers had research-based knowledge about children's thinking in general, they would be more able to focus on individual children" (Carey et al., 1995, p. 101). The program is not a curriculum. It focuses on helping teachers listen to how children think and determine what they know and understand. Based on this knowledge of individual children, teachers try to build mathematics ideas on the considerable mathematical understanding that all children naturally bring to school.

Beginning in 1990, the CGI philosophy and approach were brought to three predominantly urban public schools outside of Washington, D.C. The schools were diverse in their ethnic makeup, with students speaking a variety of languages. Project IMPACT (Increasing the Mathematical Power of All Children and Teachers) began in grades K–3 and later extended to grade 5. The teachers were trained in CGI techniques during the summer and were supported by a specialist in the schools during the year. Teachers in the project came to recognize that every child, regardless of background or socioeconomic status, had mathematical knowledge.

The CGI method is essentially a constructivist approach based on the theory that ideas grow as children solve problems using their existing knowledge. IMPACT teachers would frequently propose a task, problem, or investigation; provide an opportunity on which to work or consider the task; and then ask questions: *What do you see? Tell us something else about this problem. What do you know? What else do you know? Tell us your thinking. What could we try? Does anyone have a different idea or notice something else about this problem?* All responses were valued by being listened to without judgment or evaluation. All children were expected to be active listeners, and all were called on to participate. When a child was reluctant, the other students and the teacher would be patient until a response was made. IMPACT schools used no tracking, and there was no grouping in the classrooms (Campbell, 1993).

Students in the IMPACT project were not taught traditional algorithms, nor were basic facts and skills stressed. On standardized tests, these children excelled at problem solving and understanding concepts, and were about average in skill development. A striking effect is the confidence that children displayed in being able to do mathematics. Teachers also became true believers that all children could do mathematics and could think mathematically (Campbell, 1996).

The QUASAR Project

QUASAR (Quantitative Understanding: Amplifying Student Achievement and Reasoning), begun in 1989, was a large reform project for middle schools in the United States. It focused on schools in economically disadvantaged communities and attempted to improve the participation and performance in mathematics of females, ethnic minorities, and the poor. The belief was that these groups have traditionally failed due primarily to a lack of "access to meaningful, high-quality experiences with mathematics

learning" (Silver Smith, & Nelson, 1995, p. 10). QUASAR believed that virtually all students could learn middle-school mathematics and move on to a challenging program at the secondary level.

The instruction in QUASAR schools was aimed at improving thinking, reasoning, and problem solving. Tasks were designed with multiple entry points and multiple paths to solutions, allowing for heterogeneous classrooms to participate fully in developing solutions. There was an emphasis on communication and discourse in the creation of classroom communities where thinking and reasoning are valued and risk takers are made to feel safe.

At each of its sites, QUASAR nearly eliminated the entrenched practice of academic tracking. A teacher at one site noted that "a lot of the kids that are classified as lost, or turned off, or unintelligent, or whatever, really have some powerful ideas and some powerful ways of thinking, and exposing the other kids to that and them to the ways the other kids think is just too powerful to overlook" (Silver et al., 1995, p. 28). To aid in handling the diversity of the classroom, many teachers used heterogeneous cooperative groups. In one classroom, test scores on a standardized test ranged from the 15th to the 98th percentile. Posters in the room suggested phrases that all students were to use: *Good answer. You can do it! You're on the right track. Give it a try. We'll help you through it.* Trust and mutual respect were key features of the program. Eventually, fear of giving wrong answers disappears in this kind of atmosphere, as students learn that there is no such thing as a "dumb question" or a "bad answer."

Teachers began to call the QUASAR project the "revolution of the possible."

Impact of a Single Teacher

For an individual teacher, there is comfort and value in being part of a project that promotes the kind of teaching described in the preceding examples. But the only projects most teachers are likely to be able to participate in will be the ones they initiate in their own rooms.

Ms. Hennessey is a veteran grade 5 teacher in a predominantly multi-ethnic Canadian school. She is an extremely effective teacher who has won awards for her work, particularly in literacy and language. She employs a technique called "writer's circle" in which children each have an opportunity to take centre stage and present their work, in a safe and nurturing environment, to the class for critiquing. Students give feedback to each other in a sensitive and thoughtful manner, as Ms. Hennessey listens. Students encourage one another and celebrate each other's work.

Ms. Hennessey also uses the same system in mathematics, where students share their solutions to investigations, writings, and reflections about mathematical ideas. The regular basal textbook is generally not used. Instead,

Ms. Hennessey incorporates investigations from Marilyn Burns and other authors with her own ideas to teach in a facilitative, supportive manner. The point is always that learning is not threatening and that the students are capable of good results and quality thinking.

Based on her studies of effective teachers, Ladson-Billings (1997) lists five guidelines or principles for the successful teaching of students who are traditionally at risk of failing:

1. *Have high expectations for all students, letting them know that you believe in them.* If you treat students as competent, they are likely to demonstrate competence.
2. *Use "instructional scaffolding."* Instead of worrying about what students do not know, work from what they do know toward what they do not know.
3. *Make instruction the focus of each class.* Avoid busy-work. Confront restlessness with an adjustment in instruction, rather than a focus on misbehaviour.
4. *Extend students' thinking and abilities beyond what they already know.* Provide challenging mathematics for all students, rather than attempting to maintain low levels of performance.
5. *Work at gaining in-depth knowledge of your students as well as knowledge of the subject matter.* Develop a positive identification with all students. Learn to see students of different ethnicities as being like you, rather than trying to make them "fit in."

Notice the principles of developmental or constructivist teaching, belief in students, and challenging curriculum. The fifth principle applies to multi-ethnic student populations. It dictates respect for culture, without which the other suggestions may well fail.

From Gender Bias to Gender Equity

Most elementary teachers are aware of few, if any, differences between boys and girls. Yet when careful comparisons were made over the years, real differences between boys and girls emerged. Elementary school girls have traditionally outperformed boys on standardized tests, although their lead disappears around grade 7. By the time of entry to university or college, many more boys than girls are entering fields of study that include heavy emphases on mathematics and science. Furthermore, there persists a common belief in our society that boys are better than girls at mathematics—what Damarin (1995) refers to as the "maleness of mathematics." In an age in which the ability to reason and solve problems, a knowledge of technology, and competence with general mathematical ideas are all demanded in the workplace, it is more vital than ever that teachers address the issues surrounding gender inequity in mathematics.

Defining the Problem of Gender Inequity

Three areas of inequity can be examined: differences in achievement, differences in beliefs and attitudes, and differences in representation in mathematics, science, and related careers.

Achievement

About 25 years ago, concern over differences in mathematics achievement between males and females led some observers to suggest that girls were perhaps not as capable of doing mathematics as boys. However, research indicated that girls tended to outperform boys until the junior high years, equalled them in early algebra, and began to lag well behind in geometry and beyond. When the range of performance was examined (instead of the average), the top and bottom levels were about the same for males and females. Thus it was not true that girls were outperformed, rather it was that more boys than girls did well (Burton, 1995).

Further study has indicated that a large part of the difference could be attributed to fewer girls taking mathematics courses in high school. When the criterion of courses taken is factored into the data, differences diminish. In recent years, gender differences in mathematics achievement have almost disappeared.

Despite the development, two facts remain. First, differences among girls are significantly greater than differences among boys. Many girls for one reason or another are still not achieving well. Hanrahan (2000) points out that teachers treat females differently than males, that there are major problems with role models for girls, and that there are boys' curricula and girls' curricula which are different. Second, the perception that boys are better at mathematics remains a seemingly intractable trait of our society. Yet there is no convincing evidence of a biological or genetic basis for gender differences in mathematics achievement.

Beliefs and Attitudes

The educational system does seem to have an effect on how girls view mathematics. As girls move into the upper grades, they report that they like mathematics less and have more self-doubts concerning their personal abilities than boys do. Self-doubts and poor self-concepts concerning mathematics lead to further problems. For example, girls are less likely to persist at challenging tasks than boys are. Weak self-concepts are likely to diminish participation in classroom interactions and group problem solving (Leder, 1995).

Societal norms of the past have another lingering negative effect. In a 1988 study of nine-year-olds, girls were just as likely as boys to say that they were good at mathematics. However, the girls were much less likely to say that mathematics would be useful in their future careers. In general, girls are much more ambivalent concerning the value of mathematics as an occupational prerequisite (Burton, 1995; Leder, 1995). If, as early as age nine, you regard the study of mathematics as irrelevant to your future, this will undoubtedly have an effect on your cognitive efforts and the courses you select at the secondary and post-secondary levels.

Underrepresentation

Choices that students make in terms of coursework and career decisions continue to reflect real differences between the sexes. While it is true girls are taking more mathematics courses than they have in the past, male enrolments continue to be higher in upper-level, more intensive mathematics courses, related applied fields, and occupations requiring mathematical sophistication (Leder, 1995). By opting out of advanced courses in high school, females are effectively excluded from a wide range of college options. Even when the actual mathematics knowledge is not the real issue, mathematics is often used as a filter for entrance into certain demanding career paths. "Equating intelligence with [mathematics] achievement keeps women out of well-paid, high-status fields which they would find interesting and exciting and for which they have the talent" (Tyrrell et al., 1994, p. 332). The result has been a substantially unequal distribution of the sexes across careers.

The serious gender gap in upper-level mathematics courses and in career patterns is perhaps the most serious issue in the entire gender equity discussion. With evidence ruling out a genetic difference or the existence of a "math gene," there are still not enough women embarking on career paths that are highly valued in society today.

Possible Causes of Gender Inequity

If the problem is not genetic, we should look to the educational system for the causes of gender inequity.

Teacher Interactions and Gender

Observations of teachers' gender-specific interactions in the classroom indicate that boys get more attention and different kinds of attention than girls do. Boys receive more criticism as well as more praise for correct answers. Boys also tend to be more involved in discipline-related attention and have their work monitored more carefully (Campbell, 1995; Leder, 1995). The increased attention, both positive and negative, that teachers unconsciously provide to males contributes to the impression of mathematics as a male domain. Attention is interpreted as value, with a predictable effect on both sexes.

Research has found that teachers wait longer for responses from boys than from girls (Leder, 1995). In one study, females received more wait time on low-level questions concerning facts and procedures, whereas males received longer wait times on more difficult, more challenging, and higher-cognitive questions. Over time, these subtle but real differences suggest to girls that they are not perceived as capable of quality thinking, and they eventually adopt this belief themselves.

Belief Systems Related to Gender

The belief that mathematics tends be a masculine field still persists. In adolescent years, when girls are significantly influenced by boys, many girls are afraid to act "too smart" for fear of alienating boys. Campbell (1995) points out that "unless boys as well as girls are convinced that 'real women do math,' efforts toward gender equity in mathematics will encounter obstacles based on stereotyped social roles" (p. 229).

There is evidence that teachers' and parents' erroneous belief that girls can't do math has a transfer effect on girls. It is easy for parents to reinforce this belief in their daughters and to suggest that it is not important to excel at mathematics "because you're a girl." Teachers and counsellors make similar subtle and sometimes not-so-subtle comments that cumulatively convince girls that they are not good at mathematics.

Working toward Gender Equity: What Can Be Done?

Campbell (1995) makes a compelling argument that we have tended to address gender inequity as a "girl problem." This places the focus of our efforts to solve the problem on girls—to make them somehow like mathematics more or take more courses in mathematics. This approach, she says, makes it seem that there really is something wrong with girls. "If you change a girl so that she 'loves math,' but then you put her back into the same environment and situations that caused her to hate mathematics in the first place, she will revert to hating mathematics" (p. 226). As already noted, the causes of girls' perceptions of themselves *vis-à-vis* mathematics are largely a function of the educational environment. That is where we should look for solutions.

Become Aware

Few teachers purposely take gender-specific actions that would have a negative effect on girls. Yet many teachers report that even as early as grade 1, if a boy is good at mathematics, it is taken as a reflection of mathematical ability, whereas if a girl excels, it is seen as the result of personal efforts. This differential belief system can be transmitted in the manner that praise is given: "Wow, Mark! You really are showing how smart you are" versus "Margie, I am glad to see how hard you worked on this problem" (Fennema, Peterson, Carpenter, & Lubinski, 1990).

As a teacher, you need to be aware of whether you are treating boys and girls differently. Work at ensuring equal treatment. Balance the number of questions and overall interactions between boys and girls. A simple approach is to keep a mental tally of questions asked of girls and boys. If discipline problems tend to draw more attention to boys, work at being less preoccupied with the boys' disturbances. Instead of reacting to the boys causing trouble, focus on the positive aspects of their behaviour and increase your attention to the girls.

Being aware of your gender-specific actions is more difficult than it may sound. To become more conscious of your behaviour, try tape-recording a class or two on a periodic basis. Tally the number of questions you ask boys and girls. Also note which students ask questions and what kind of questions they ask. At first, you will be surprised at how gender-biased your interaction is. Awareness takes effort.

Focus on Higher-Level Questioning

Shift from telling to asking. Focus your student interactions on higher-level questioning and problem-solving activities. Take equal interest in the ideas of all students. Especially at the upper grades, it requires extra time and consideration to ask more thought-provoking questions and de-emphasize telling. When teachers feel the pressure of time and the need to "cover the material," girls are more likely to sense this and avoid asking questions.

Be sure that you help all children understand, not just those (mostly males) who seek clarification. Instead of asking, "Are there any questions?" address individuals, especially girls: "Rachel, do you have any questions?" The latter approach shows interest in the individual and emphasizes that you value understanding over coverage. When boys and girls ask for help, provide equal treatment. Teachers almost inevitably will show a boy who asks for help how to perform the task. If a girl asks for assistance, the teacher will often complete the job for her (Hanrahan, 2000).

Involve All Students

Find ways to involve all students in your class, not just those who seem eager. Girls tend to shy away from involvement and are not as quick to seek help. The use of concrete materials can provide a way for all students to be active at the same time and for you to observe each student's thinking. Cooperative learning groups are another way to encourage involvement. Use mixed-gender groups to avoid gender-oriented competition between groups, and to

increase boy-girl interactions. Neither of these strategies is an automatic solution, however. With concrete materials, all students must be expected to be active. Similarly, cooperative groups must be continually monitored and evaluated to ensure that all students are participating.

Mathematics for the Gifted and Talented

Children who are typically known as "gifted" have special educational needs. In order to reach their potential, they require appropriate educational opportunities and challenges. Otherwise they are vulnerable to the same pitfalls that affect other children: becoming frustrated or bored in environments that are neither stimulating nor motivating (Winzer, 1996).

The lack of a universally agreed-upon definition of giftedness is one of the more enduring problems in the field of gifted education. Even though considerable research has been done on the education of the gifted, it offers little consensus. Alternative views have typically focused on two major questions: What does it mean to be gifted, and what practices and/or programs best cater to the needs of gifted children? There are also questions of time, teachers, funding, and materials.

Identification of "Giftedness"

Hutchinson (2002) defines students who are gifted or talented as "those who are advanced in one or many areas of development. They exceed teachers' and parents' expectations in specific areas of the school curriculum" (p. 66). In the past it was thought that gifted students were advanced in all areas. However, more recent research reveals that gifted learners usually are advanced in specific domains—a view that has been incorporated into provincial and territorial definitions. It is also important to be aware of other characteristics that will help to identify students who may be gifted or talented. Often their vocabulary is advanced for their age; they may show an unusual degree of curiosity and persistence with tasks they enjoy. It might also surprise you that their performance in subjects in which they do not excel will be ordinary. Indeed, there will be some children who are gifted or talented who will not exhibit any of these characteristics and might appear to be average or even below average (British Columbia Special Education Branch, 1995).

Mathematically Promising Students

Rather than *gifted* or *talented, promising* is the term used by the NCTM for students who are mathematically talented. The Task Force on the Mathematically Promising, convened in 1995 to prepare recommendations and draft a policy statement concerning the mathematically talented, preferred to use this term, because under common definitions of the gifted and talented, many mathematically adept students had been overlooked or excluded. The task force explained that mathematical promise was a function of *ability, motivation, belief,* and *experience or opportunity.* Usiskin (1999) suggests that the vast majority of the population has mathematical promise at birth. He argues that mathematical ability and talent can be nurtured in a large number of students if begun at an early age in school. Students require good teachers, quality curriculum, high expectations, and a supportive environment. With these factors in place, students who *work hard* have a high probability of developing special talents in mathematics. Of course, natural ability is a factor, but the argument is that substantially more people have the ability than make the effort to develop it.

The point that both the task force and Usiskin make is that we must come to understand that mathematical promise or talent is not a matter of heredity. A popular belief regarding mathematical ability is that children either "have it or they don't," that mathematical ability is a result of the roll of the genetic dice. In contrast, Asians generally believe that success in mathematics, as in any subject, is largely a function of individual effort.

The literature on mathematically promising students suggests that they may not be especially talented in other areas. Nor can mathematical promise be equated with general school achievement or facility with computational algorithms. Promising students generally have good verbal skills, curiosity, imagination, analytical thinking skills, and the ability to concentrate and work independently (House, 1999).

What all of this means for the identification of promising students is that simple criteria built on test scores, IQ, or high grades may exclude those who have a high probability of developing into exceptional mathematical students.

Teaching Gifted Students

You will find a number of approaches used for teaching gifted students. You will also find that more program options are available in urban than in rural centres. The three most common types of provision for promising students in Canada, as well as in the United States, are enrichment, ability groupings, and acceleration (Winzer, 1996). Each of these approaches is not without its proponents and detractors.

Acceleration

Acceleration is the practice of having students move faster than the normal level of instruction through academic content to meet their needs (British Columbia Special Education Branch, 1995, Winzer, 1996). What this means is that a classroom teacher provides a student with advanced curriculum when the student skips a grade, or a student takes a specific course at a higher level. Although many educators are opposed to acceleration, there is overwhelming research to support it. Daniel Keating, a world-renowned Canadian researcher in the field of children's cognitive and social development, notes that research studies unanimously support the benefits of this approach to working with gifted children. According to the document, *Gifted Education: A Resource Guide for Teachers* (British Columbia Special Education Branch, 1995), acceleration has been shown to be positive for gifted learners, both for achievers and those who are underachievers.

Yet acceleration can have the effect of developing a large array of meaningless skills, as students are pushed to learn more without exploring the ideas fully in a conceptual manner. Without adequate time, the guidance of a skilled teacher, and the benefit of directed discourse and exploration, students in acceleration programs will tend to focus on mechanical skills. This will also often happen when students are left to study independently.

Enrichment

Enrichment programs provide special activities in the regular classroom setting. Generally, classroom teachers provide these programs in consort with a resource teacher or other support personnel. The most popular of the three approaches to teaching gifted students, enrichment too has its critics. Proponents feel that it is beneficial because it allows the children to remain in the classroom and work with their peers. Too often, however, enrichment programs result in little more than "fun math time" with topics such as geometric puzzles, computer games, or the "problem of the day." Although good mathematics activities should be fun, they should accomplish much more. They should broaden students' mathematical horizons, require them to think deeply, make connections to earlier ideas and to real contexts, and challenge them to ask questions, make conjectures, and reason about important ideas.

Ability Grouping

Ability groupings, also known as "pull-out" programs, provide gifted students with an opportunity to work together with their true peers and intellectual and chronological equals. In this approach, students are removed from heterogeneous settings and placed in special groups. What this means is that students may go to special classrooms within their own school, they may work in an independent group at a different rate in their own classroom, they may attend class in a school nearby, or they may attend class in another district. The groups may meet on a full-time or a part-time basis, either during the school day or on an extracurricular basis (Winzer, 1996). In these programs, pacing of learning is matched to the needs of the student, the level of content is accelerated and more complex, and teachers are very skilled. Opponents of these programs claim that they foster elitism and limit contact between gifted and regular classroom children. They are not convinced that the curriculum expectations are always met in these programs. As expected, advocates argue that instruction for these students can only be effective when they are learning with their intellectual equals.

The Addition of Depth

To counteract some of the pitfalls of the enriched and accelerated approaches, Sheffield (1999) suggests that the benefits of both should be coupled with the opportunity for studying the complexities of new mathematical ideas, both in the regular curriculum and beyond it. Sheffield writes that promising students should be introduced to the "joys and frustrations of thinking deeply about a wide range of original, open-ended, or complex problems that encourage them to respond creatively in ways that are original, fluent, flexible, and elegant" (p. 46).

In the regular classroom, teachers often "reward" highly capable students for finishing routine tasks quickly by having them do more exercises or more tedious exercises than those required of the rest of the class. For example, if the full class is working on the multiplication algorithm for multi-digit numbers, there is no redeeming value in having promising students who complete their work quickly do more exercises, or exercises with more digits. However, they may be asked what would produce the largest or smallest products, given four distinct digits to make two factors. Is there a general rule? Why does the rule work? What if there were five digits?

Even more interesting than the max/min task is that for some products, interchanging the digits in each two-digit factor produces the same result:

$$\begin{array}{r} 24 \\ \times\,63 \\ \hline 1512 \end{array} \qquad \begin{array}{r} 42 \\ \times\,36 \\ \hline 1512 \end{array}$$

However, this obviously is not always the case, as a little experimentation will quickly show. When will this interchanging of the digits produce equal products and why? Students working on tasks such as these are engaged in a deeper exploration of the multiplication algorithm than simply learning how it works and how to use it.

The Open-Ended Approach

There is no simple formula for adding depth to mathematical explorations, but some valuable insights may be learned from the Japanese. According to Hashimoto and Becker (1999), the Japanese approach to mathematical problem solving involves making the problem open in one of three ways: the process is open (multiple paths to a solution are explored), the end product is open (there are multiple correct answers to be discovered), or the formulation of new problems is open (students explore new problems related to the one solved). Here is an example of each form of open problem:

OPEN PROCESS

Figure 22.2 shows a box of chocolates with some removed. How many chocolates are in the box?

Of course, the chocolates can be counted one by one. Another method is to note that there are three rows of six and two rows of three $(3 \times 6 + 2 \times 3)$. Can you find three or four additional ways to count the chocolates?

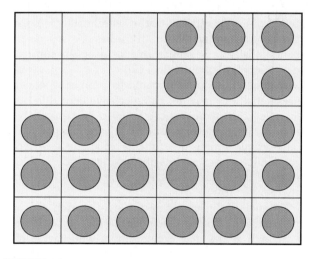

FIGURE 22.2 **This box of chocolates has some removed. How many chocolates remain in the box? How many ways can you find to get the answer?**

OPEN END PRODUCT

Given a collection of varied geometric shapes, select one. Describe a rule by which some of the other shapes are like the one you selected.

For example, if the figure selected were a trapezoid with two right angles, other shapes might be selected that had a pair of parallel sides. Another rule might be that the shape must have exactly two (or at least two) right angles. What other rules can you imagine for this shape?

OPEN QUESTION

There are four butterflies on the flower. If three more join them, how many butterflies are there altogether?

For this primary grade problem, Hashimoto and Becker suggest these possible ways to alter the question:

- Change the number of butterflies.
- Change the objects to something other than butterflies.
- Make the problem into a subtraction problem.

These three approaches to open-ended problem solving are explored in depth in *The Open-Ended Approach: A New Proposal for Teaching Mathematics* (Becker & Shimada, 1997). The authors are not at all suggesting that these methods are to be used only with promising students. On the contrary, these are good ways to challenge *all* students. In fact, many of the tasks found throughout this book either are already open-ended in one of these ways, or can be enriched in at least one of the ways suggested here. Application of the open-ended methods is an excellent way to add depth to both accelerated and enriched programs.

Reflections *on Chapter 22*

Writing to Learn

1. What traditional ideas about curriculum and teaching children must be changed so that the NCTM vision of all children learning mathematics can be realized?
2. How would you argue for the values of a diverse class that includes children with learning problems? That is, what are some of the benefits of including these students in the regular classroom?
3. Briefly describe each of the following specific learning disabilities, and give some indication of how the disability may affect mathematics learning or ability. For each disability, also list at least two ideas that can be used by the classroom teacher to help the child.
    a. Perceptual deficits (figure-ground, discrimination, reversal, spatial)
    b. Memory deficits (short-term and long-term)
    c. Integrative deficits
    d. Attention deficits
4. For children with intellectual disabilities (low-ability students, slow learners), how should content and instruction each be modified?
5. Describe, in general terms, one or more of the most significant ideas that should guide the teacher who is working with students from an ethnic minority group.
6. What are some factors that contribute to gender inequity, and what are the long-term effects of that inequity?
7. How can teachers in elementary school work to erase gender inequity?
8. Describe what is meant by enrichment, acceleration, and "pull-out" programming. What are the dangers of each of these approaches for mathematically promising students?
9. In the context of providing for the mathematically promising, what is meant by depth? How can the Japanese open-ended approaches help provide depth?

For Discussion and Exploration

1. Two common threads in this chapter are the beliefs that all children will benefit from a developmental or constructivist approach to teaching and that there is real value in teaching children in diverse, heterogeneous classrooms. Some teachers may argue with this position, contending that it is best for the majority of children if "special needs" students are isolated. Moreover, these students' needs are best met by special teachers in classes with fewer students. Pick a position in this argument, and articulate it in writing or in a classroom discussion.
2. In the discussion of multicultural equity, there was no mention of two ideas that are sometimes discussed in the literature. One is that students should be exposed to mathematical topics that reflect and honour the cultural heritage of ethnic students. This is a matter of *cultural infusion*. For example, examine the African strategy game of Kalah or the geometry in Islamic art and architecture. The other idea is that instruction needs to better reflect the indigenous knowledge and contributions of First Nations people (George Dei, 1996). How do you feel about either or both of these positions?
3. Based on your personal experiences, do you believe there is a gender problem in mathematics education? Cite some experiences that support your position. What do you think the situation is like today?
4. What would you do if you found yourself teaching a class with one exceptionally talented child who had no equal in the room? Assume that acceleration to the next grade has been ruled out due to social adjustment factors.

Recommendations for Further Reading
Highly Recommended

Andrews, J., & Lupart, J. (2000). *The inclusive classroom educating exceptional children*. Toronto: Nelson Thomson Learning.

   The editors of this book on special education, who are both from the University of Calgary, provide us with a comprehensive view of special education in Canada. They address many of the important topics, provide strategies for dealing with exceptional students, and also provide the reflections of key educators in the field. It will be a valuable reference for any classroom teacher.

Hutchinson, N.L. (2002). *Inclusion of exceptional learners in Canadian schools: a practical handbook for teachers*. Toronto: Prentice Hall.

This book really lives up to the word "practical" in its title. It is an extremely teacher-friendly resource that will assist you in your classroom work. It is up to date and easy to read, with excellent references. Hutchinson provides information regarding useful websites, identifies and describes key terms, and includes strategies for working with the varied exceptionalities.

Iseke-Barnes, J.M., & Wane, N.N. (Eds.). (2000). *Equity in schools and society*. Toronto: Scholars Choice.

The book effectively draws on history, sociology, literature, cultural expressions, films, and theory to examine equity issues that affect the teaching and learning process. The readings in this collection are intended to sensitize teachers to the restrictions race, class, and gender place on providing education that is fair and accessible to all students.

Journal of the Gifted and Talented Education Council of the Alberta Teachers' Association (AGATE)

This is a journal devoted exclusively to giftedness. The Special Millennium Issue (volume14, number 2) focuses on gifted education across Canada. Each article in the journal discusses aspects of gifted education in a particular province or territory, providing a valuable overview.

Secada, W.G., Fennema, E., & Adajian, L.B. (Eds.). (1995). *New directions for equity in mathematics education*. New York: Cambridge University Press.

The editors, long known for their research in this field, have assembled one of the best collections of essays to date on the issues of equity. An extremely readable book.

Sheffield, L.J. (Ed.). (1999). *Developing mathematically promising students*. Reston, VA: National Council of Teachers of Mathematics.

This book is the result of a recommendation to NCTM from the Task Force on Mathematically Promising Students. The book is a wealth of ideas and perspectives for working with our most talented students. Rather than the more simplistic approach of NCTM's earlier booklet on teaching the gifted, this book adds depth to any discussion of mathematics for the talented.

Thornton, C.A., & Bley, N.S. (Eds.). (1994). *Windows of opportunity: Mathematics for students with special needs*. Reston, VA: National Council of Teachers of Mathematics.

There are very few books that even attempt to address the issues of special-needs children and mathematics. (NCTM is working on a new book that should be out soon.) Thornton and Bley have put together an excellent book that could be a methods text or a resource for the classroom teacher, consisting of seven chapters on issues, eight that address content through perspective and vignettes, and six that look at promising practices. This book will remain a valuable resource even after the next special-needs book is published.

Trentacosta, J. (Ed.). (1997). *Multicultural and gender equity in the mathematics classroom: The gift of diversity*. Reston, VA: National Council of Teachers of Mathematics.

One of NCTM's finest yearbooks. Numerous articles address virtually every aspect of diversity, including various ethnicities, gender, and ethnomathematics.

Winzer, M.A. (1998). Inclusion practices in Canada: social, political, and educational influences. In S.J. Vitello & D.E. Mithaugh (Eds.), *Inclusive schooling national and international perspective (pp.132-150)*. Mahwah NJ :Lawrence Erlbaum Associates.

Winzer's chapter in this book offers a comprehensive and concise picture of inclusion practices in Canada. It is a quick and worthwhile read.

Other Suggestions

Bley, N.S., & Thornton, C.A. (1995). *Teaching mathematics to students with learning disabilities* (3rd ed.). Austin, TX: Pro-Ed.

British Columbia Special Education Branch. (1995). *Gifted education: a resource guide for teachers*. Victoria: Queen's Printer for British Columbia.

Campbell, P.F. (1996). Empowering children and teachers in the elementary mathematics classrooms of urban schools. *Urban Education, 30,* 449–475.

Cuevas, G., & Driscol, M. (Eds.). (1993). *Reaching all students with mathematics*. Reston, VA: National Council of Teachers of Mathematics.

Education Development Center. (1995). *Equity in education series: Gender-fair math*. Newton, MA: Author.

Garrison, L. (1997). Making the NCTM's standards work for emergent English speakers. *Teaching Children Mathematics, 4,* 132–138.

Griffiths, R., & Clyne, M. (1994). *Language in the mathematics classroom: Talking, representing, recording*. Portsmouth, NH: Heinemann.

Hanrahan, M. (2000). Producing the female reserve labour force: women and schooling. In J.M. Iseke-Barnes & N.N. Wane (Eds.), *Equity in schools and society* (pp. 227–238). Toronto: Canadian Scholars' Press Inc.

Karp, K., Allen, C., Allen, L.G., & Brown, E.T. (1998). Feisty females: Using children's literature with strong female characters. *Teaching Children Mathematics, 5,* 88–94.

Karp, K., Brown, E.T., Allen, L.G., & Allen, C. (1998). *Feisty females: Inspiring girls to think mathematically*. Portsmouth, NH: Heinemann.

Ladson-Billings, G. (1997). It doesn't add up: African-American students' mathematics achievement. *Journal for Research in Mathematics Education, 28,* 697–708.

Levin, B. (1995). Educational responses to poverty. *Canadian Journal of Education, 20* (2), 211–224.

Litton, N. (1998). *Getting your math message out to parents: A K–6 resource*. Sausalito, CA: Math Solutions Publications.

Mills, H., O'Keefe, T., & Whitin, D.J. (1996). *Mathematics in the making: Authoring ideas in primary classrooms*. Portsmouth, NH: Heinemann.

Rowser, J.F., & Koontz, T.Y. (1995). Inclusion of African-American students in mathematics classrooms: Issues of style, curriculum, and expectations. *Mathematics Teacher, 88,* 448–453.

Scott, F.B. (2001). *Teaching in a multicultural setting: A Canadian perspective*. Toronto: Prentice Hall.

Silver, E.A., & Stein, M.K. (1996). The QUASAR project: The "revolution of the possible" in mathematics instructional reform in urban middle schools. *Urban Education, 30,* 476–521.

Tate, W.F. (1997). Race-ethnicity, SES, gender, and language proficiency trends in mathematics achievement: An update. *Journal for Research in Mathematics Education, 28,* 652–679.

Tobias, R. (1992). *Nurturing at-risk youth in math and science: Curriculum and teaching considerations.* Bloomington, IN: National Education Service.

Toney, N.L. (1996). Facing racism in mathematics education. In D. Schifter (Ed.), *What's happening in math class? Reconstructing professional identities* (Vol. 2, pp. 26–36). New York: Teachers College Press.

Winzer, M. (1996). *Children with exceptionalities in Canadian classrooms.* Toronto: Allyn and Bacon.

Chapter 23

Technology and School Mathematics

Rapid developments in technology are changing (and ought to be changing) the way we teach mathematics, both because they modify our goals for the mathematics education of people and because they provide new tools with which we can better achieve our goals.

Willoughby (1990, p. 60)

The term *technology* in the context of school mathematics refers primarily to calculators of all sorts, and to computers, including access to the Internet and its available resources. Technology is so pervasive in our society that it is assumed that children will learn to use it in schools, and that it will be available there to help them learn better. But we should not let the attractiveness of technology blind us to the fact that the fundamental mathematics that students will need in tomorrow's society must be our foremost consideration. Technology must enhance the mathematics students learn. It should never be a replacement for good mathematics, nor should it become an end in itself.

To highlight its importance, the authors of *Principles and Standards for School Mathematics* made Technology one of its six principles (see Chapter 1). In 1998, NCTM issued a position statement on technology that begins: "The appropriate use of instructional technology tools is integral to the learning and teaching of mathematics and to the assessment of mathematics learning at all levels" (p. 17). Provincial and territorial curriculum documents well support these views of the NCTM, highlighting the importance of technology in students' learning of mathematics. The Saskatchewan Ministry of Education, as one example, discusses in detail the importance of calculator use in elementary and middle-grade students' learning of mathematics, "In elementary grades, students can use cal-

culators, along with manipulatives, to develop number concepts, counting skills and place value concepts." (*Mathematics 6–9: A Curriculum Guide for the Middle Level*, 1996) The use of calculators and computers is well supported in the Ontario government's recent mathematics initiative, the Early Math Strategy, developed to help primary students improve their basic mathematics understanding (Early Math Strategy, The Report of the Expert Panel on Early Math in Ontario, 2003).

Calculators and computer software are highlighted throughout Section 2 of this text, with references to specific activities and programs where they are appropriate. The purpose of this chapter is to examine technology and the teaching of mathematics in a more general way, so that you will be able to make informed judgments about the use of technology in your classroom.

Technology's Threefold Impact on Mathematics Education

Calculators and computers have had a profound impact on what mathematics is taught and how. First, some mathematics that we used to teach is now obsolete because of technology. Second, much of the mathematics that we teach can be taught better with technology. Third, many topics that we were unable to teach before can now be made accessible to students in meaningful ways.

Less Important or Obsolete Mathematics

Much of the mathematics that we used to teach has been supplanted by technology. The most obvious example is pencil-and-paper computation, whose importance has been diminished considerably by the wide availability of calculators. Even most critics of the reform movement would agree that there is no longer any need for drill involving tedious computations. These skills remain important, but they should be flexible and adaptable to the situation at hand.

Another area where less class time is needed is in techniques for the construction of graphs for data analysis. Thanks to computer graphing software and spreadsheets, tedious by-hand techniques for making charts and graphs have become extraneous, even in the lower grades. What this means is that the emphasis in the classroom can now be shifted to the question of which type of graph will best answer and communicate questions about the data. Multiple representations are quickly made, adjusted, and compared, with little or no class time wasted on thinking about scale or colour schemes.

In the upper elementary grades and high school, graphing calculators have de-emphasized the importance of learning to plot points and draw function graphs. Once students understand how graphs of functions come to be, technology is the best way to create those graphs.

Despite the obsolescence of a *mechanical* approach to doing mathematics, it is essential to recognize that mastery of basic facts and flexible methods of computation are just as important as ever, perhaps even more so. Computational fluency is a significant tool for making sense of the world and for mathematical problem solving. Tedious computational drills do not make for better mathematical thinking. Long division with a three-digit divisor should be left to the calculator.

Better-Taught Mathematics

Whenever technology is used, it should enhance the way that students interact with the mathematics involved. Avoid using technology to do something in mathematics just for the sake of saying you used technology. There are many worthwhile educational uses for technology that will dramatically improve students' understanding of underlying concepts.

One of the most striking examples of an area of mathematics that is better taught at the elementary level is the ability to examine real problems with real numbers. Doing so takes problem solving out of the realm of artificial constructs and into the real world. There is no need to use unrealistic numbers just to ensure that students can compute them, or to ensure that answers "come out even." In fact, problem solving is further enhanced by removing the distractions of tedious computations, which in the past were so laborious that students often lost sight of the essential features of the problems or the reasons for computing them in the first place.

Calculators help very young children learn to count, to skip-count, to practise mental math, and to search for patterns. Connections between decimals and common fractions are clearly enhanced by calculators that permit conversions between these forms.

Geometry is an area where technology has had a dramatic impact. Students with poor motor skills can now assemble beautiful patterns with colourful tiles. Rotation and reflection transformations are easily made, modified, and explored. Dynamic geometry programs such as *The Geometer's Sketchpad,* once used exclusively for high school, are now finding increased use in grades 7 and 8. These programs allow students to explore geometric ideas rather than relying on static drawings and memorizing definitions.

Computer versions of some manipulative materials such as base-ten blocks, fractional pie pieces, or fraction pieces have the potential for enhancing what these same materials can do in their concrete form. Care must be taken to ensure that the slick presentations on the computer screen are really augmenting the opportunity to learn. Many programs do an excellent job of "showing" conceptual ideas, while offering little that is problematic for students. As a teaching technique, "show and tell" is no more effective when done by a computer than when done by a teacher.

More Accessible Mathematics

Perhaps the most dramatic examples of technology opening mathematical doors for students are found at the high school level. There, technology has the potential of radically altering the curriculum to include many topics that were simply not available to students without it. For example, with only a graphing calculator, polynomials and rational functions of any degree can be explored as easily as a simple quadratic. Computer algebra systems—now found on graphing calculators such as the TI-92—perform complex symbolic manipulations instantly, meaning that concepts that were once difficult to work with at the university level are now accessible in high school.

At the K–5 level, some topics have been enhanced dramatically as a result of technology. We have already discussed the improvement in data analysis, which permits students to explore how a graph helps makes sense of data, rather than simply learning how to make the graph. Probability experiments can now be done with thousands of trials, making it possible for students to understand how, in the long run, chance occurrences will approach theoretical values.

The graphing calculator makes it possible for students to explore a wide variety of functions and their corresponding graphical representations. It is as easy to graph $y = 345.39x^2 - 72.3$ as it is to graph $y = 3x + 2$. Calculators and computers can be used to find equations of functions that approximate scatter plots of real data. The wealth of geometric relationships that students can explore with dynamic geometry software is amazing.

Calculators in the Mathematics Classroom

Mathematics educators have long understood the value of calculators in the study of mathematics. In 1976, the NCTM published a special issue of *The Arithmetic Teacher* devoted to the use of calculators. Since then, there have been other focus issues, a series of position statements, the 1989 *Curriculum and Evaluation Standards,* an NCTM yearbook (Fey, 1992), and now *Principles and Standards for School Mathematics,* as well as regional curricular documents in Canada, all advocating the regular use of calculators in the teaching of mathematics at all grade levels.

The everyday use of calculators in society, coupled with professional support of calculators in schools, has had a muted impact on the mathematics classroom, especially at the elementary level. Resistance to the use of calculators has diminished but not disappeared. The vocal minority of detractors of the reform movement often assail the use of calculators as "dumbing down" the curriculum or as a "crutch." Their inflammatory rhetoric often resonates with parents, who want what is best for their children. Parents must be made aware of the fact that calculator use will in no way prevent Jeremy or Jenny from learning mathematics; in fact, calculators make *learning* much easier.

Benefits of Calculator Use

Rather than fearing the potential dangers of calculators, it is important to understand how they can contribute to the learning of mathematics. In this section, we focus on simple calculators, and reserve discussion of the graphing calculator for later.

Calculators Can Be Used to Develop Concepts

The calculator can be much more than a device for calculation. It can be used effectively to develop concepts. *Adding It Up: Helping Children Learn Mathematics* (National Research Council, 2001) cites long-term studies that have shown that students in grades 4–6 who used calculators improved their conceptual understanding. Activities for developing concepts with the calculator have been suggested throughout this book, especially in the areas of numeration and computation. Here are a few more activities that illustrate this point.

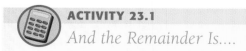

ACTIVITY 23.1
And the Remainder Is....

Consider the fact that 796 ÷ 42 = 18.95238. The students' task is to find a method for determining the whole-number remainder with a simple four-function calculator. (Some calculators have an integer division key that provides the remainder.)

In Chapter 7, Activity 7.6 (p. 130) asked students to find the quotient without using the division key. A repeated subtraction or repeated addition method provides possible solutions to that task, and each will give the remainder. In Activity 23.1, the challenge is to use the result in some way to determine the remainder. One solution uses the whole-number part, 18. The other uses the decimal part (0.95238). In discussions where students invent and defend these solutions, a greater understanding of division will certainly result.

ACTIVITY 23.2
Too Hard for the Calculator?

Find a way to use the calculator to compute the product of two numbers such as 3456 and 88 888. When this product is entered on a simple calculator, the result is too large and results in an overload.

Finding solutions to Activity 23.2 requires students to use place-value concepts and take numbers apart in creative ways. Not only does this help students explore number concepts, the methods of taking numbers apart and recombining them are also fundamental to mental computation.

ACTIVITY 23.3
Numbers in Between

Quickly review with students the fact that a number can be multiplied by itself by pressing the number followed by ⊠ ▤ . For example, 4 ⊠ ▤ produces 16. The task is to determine what number multiplied by itself will give 43. Students in about grade 4 or 5 will quickly discover that 6 is too small and 7 is too large. What is needed is a number *between* 6 and 7. For students who have not yet experienced decimal numbers or are just learning about them, suggest numbers such as 6.1, 6.2, ..., 6.9, explaining that these numbers are between 6 and 7.

Students exploring with "Numbers in Between" will begin to think of decimals in the same way they think of fractions. Further, the activity helps students understand that each successive decimal place is a subdivision of the preceding position value.

Algebraic reasoning involves searching for and describing patterns in all types of situations. The following activity provides an open-ended search for patterns. There are numerous interesting patterns to be found.

ACTIVITY 23.4
Keypad Partner Numbers

Define a *keypad partner number* (KPN) as a two-digit number than can be entered on a calculator by pressing two keys that are adjacent either vertically, horizontally, or diagonally in any direction. Examples of KPNs are 63, 12, 21, and 48. The numbers 73 and 28 are not KPNs. The initial task is to find two different pairs of KPNs that have the same sum (for example, 32 + 65 = 62 + 35). After some pairs with the same sum are found, try to find some pattern or generalization about KPNs with like sums. Challenge students to explain why their patterns work. Instead of sums, look for common differences.

It is surprising how many different ideas students can discover with patterns on the calculator, especially if they work in groups. Ideas that rely on place value can be found by looking at the sum of the digits and examination of the addition algorithm. Sometimes students draw pictures of the keypad and discover relationships involving the spatial configurations of the keys.

Calculators Can Be Used for Drill and Practice

The calculator is an excellent drill-and-practice device that requires no computer or software. For example, students who want to practise the multiples of 7 can press 7 ⊠ 3 and delay pressing the ⊟ . The challenge is to answer the fact by themselves before pressing the ⊟ key. Subsequent multiples of 7 can be checked by simply pressing the second factor and the ⊟ . In Chapter 11, activities with the calculator were suggested for developing mental computation and estimation skills.

A class can be split in half, with one half required to use a calculator and the other required to do the computations mentally. Have the two groups try and see who solves problems faster. For 3000 + 1765, the mental group wins every time. It will also win for simple facts and numerous problems that lend themselves to mental computation. Of course, there are many computations, such as 537 × 32, where the calculator is preferred and that side will win. Not only does this simple exercise provide prac-

tice with mental math, but it also demonstrates to students that it is not always appropriate to reach for the calculator.

Calculators Enhance Problem Solving

Several research studies have found that calculator use improved the problem-solving abilities of learners at all grade levels (NRC, 2001). The mechanics of computation can often distract students' attention from the meaning of the problem on which they are working. As students come to understand the meanings of the operations, they should be exposed to realistic problems with realistic numbers. The numbers to compute may be beyond their abilities, but the calculator will make these realistic problems accessible.

Calculators Help Improve Student Attitudes

The overwhelming conclusion of numerous research studies is that students' attitudes toward mathematics are better in classrooms where calculators are used than where they are not (Hembree & Dessart, 1986; Reys & Reys, 1987, NRC, 2001). Students using calculators tend to be confident and persistent in solving problems. Although some of these studies are old, there is no reason to believe they are less valid today.

Calculators Save Time

By-hand computation is time-consuming, especially for young students who have not developed a high degree of mastery. Why should time be wasted having students add numbers to find the perimeter of a polygon? Why compute averages, find percents, convert fractions to decimals, or solve problems of any sort with pencil-and-paper methods when computational skills are not the objective of the lesson?

Calculators Are Commonly Used in Society

Nowadays, almost everyone uses calculators in every facet of life that involves any sort of exact computation—everyone except schoolchildren. It is only logical that students be taught how to use this commonplace tool effectively. Many adults have not learned how to use the automatic constant feature of a calculator and are not practised in recognizing gross errors that are often made on calculators. Effective use of calculators is an important skill that is best learned by using them regularly in a meaningful way.

Addressing Myths and Fears about Using Calculators

The lingering opposition to calculators is largely based on misinformation. Myths and fears about students not learning because they use calculators still persist, even in the face of evidence to the contrary.

Myth: If Kids Use Calculators, They Won't Learn the "Basics"

Every advocate of calculator use must make it clear to parents that basic fact mastery and flexible computational skills, including mental computation, remain important goals of the curriculum. Research has demonstrated that the availability of calculators has no negative effect on traditional skills (NRC, 2001). Most importantly, the ability to perform tedious by-hand computations does not involve thinking or reasoning or solving problems. Employers want employees who can think and solve novel problems.

Myth: Calculators Make Students Lazy

Almost no mathematical thinking is involved in doing routine computations by hand. People who use calculators when solving problems are therefore using their intellect in more important ways—reasoning, conjecturing, and testing ideas. When used appropriately, calculators enhance learning; they do not get in the way of learning.

Myth: Students Should Learn the "Real Way" before Using Calculators

Following rules for pencil-and-paper computation does little to help students understand the reasoning behind them. A glaring example is the invert-and-multiply method for division of fractions. Few parents, and only some elementary teachers, can explain why this method makes sense. Yet they all have had extensive practice with that technique. The same is true, to one degree or another, of nearly all computational procedures.

It is essential to point out that by-hand techniques are not to be totally abandoned and that introductory explorations are often best done without a calculator. The teacher must play a role in setting the necessary explorations in the classroom. The calculator should never replace understanding!

Myth: Students Will Become Overly Dependent on Calculators

Calculators kept from students are like forbidden fruit. When finally allowed to use them, students often use them for the simplest of tasks. Teachers in the upper grades often complain that students are using their calculators all the time.

It is essential that mastery of basic facts, mental computation, and some attention to by-hand techniques continue to be requirements for all students. In lessons where these skills are the objective, the calculator should simply be off limits. Once students have learned these essential non-calculator skills, they rarely use the calculator inappropriately. Further, if the calculator is always available for appropriate uses, students learn when and how to use it wisely.

Calculators for Every Student, Every Day

Calculators should be in or on student's desks at all times from kindergarten through high school. This position may seem radical to some people, but we should give it serious consideration. In addition to the benefits already described, here are a few arguments in favour of calculator access at all times:

- First and foremost, it does no harm. Any teacher can conduct an activity or pose tasks in which calculators are set off limits. Availability of calculators does not detract from the development of basic skills.
- Many excellent explorations that happen spontaneously in a problem-solving environment will be enhanced by the use of calculators. Students should not have to leave their desks or ask permission to use a calculator when solving a problem. Stopping the flow of a lesson to pass out calculators detracts from the learning process.
- When calculators are kept from students, they tend to be used for special "calculator lessons," promoting the students' belief that calculators are not common tools for solving problems.
- Students must learn to make wise choices about when to use calculators—for tedious computations—and when to use mental math—for simple computations and estimations. They learn this only by making such choices independently and on a regular basis.

Graphing Calculators

The graphing calculator, once thought useful only in high school but now important to grade 7 and 8 mathematics, deserves some special attention. Today, a graphing calculator makes sense for students in these grades. However, cost is still a possible deterrent. Several models are available for under $75, less than the cost of a pair of sneakers or a few CDs. A calculator purchased in grade 7 or 8 may be the only one the student will need throughout high school. A school can purchase a classroom set for less than the price of a single computer.

What the Graphing Calculator Offers

It is a mistake to think that graphing calculators are used only for doing "high-powered" mathematics of the kind studied by honours students in high school. Here is a list of some features of the graphing calculator that can be useful with a standard grade 7 or 8 curriculum.

- ■ The display window permits compound expressions such as 3 + 4(5 − 6/7) to be shown completely before being evaluated. Further, once evaluated, previous expressions can be recalled and modified. This promotes an understanding of notation and order of operations. The device is also a significant tool for exploring patterns and solving problems. Expressions can include exponents, absolute values, and negation signs, with no restrictions on the values used.
- ■ Even without using function definition capability, students can insert values into expressions or formulas without having to enter the entire formula for each new value. The results can be entered into a list or table of values and stored directly on the calculator for further analysis.
- ■ Variables can be used in expressions and then assigned different values to see the effect on expressions. This simple method helps with the idea of a variable as something that varies.
- ■ The distinction between "negative" and "minus" is clear and very useful. A separate key is used to enter the negative of a quantity. The display shows the negative sign as a superscript. If $^-5$ is stored in the variable b, then the expression $^-2 - b$ will be evaluated correctly as 3. This feature is a significant aid in the study of integers and variables.
- ■ Points can be plotted on a coordinate screen either by entering coordinates and seeing the result or by moving the cursor to a particular coordinate on the screen.
- ■ Very large and very small numbers are managed without error. Graphing calculators use scientific notation so that large and small numbers do not result in error statements. For example, $23! = 1.033314797 \times 10^{40}$.
- ■ Built-in statistical functions allow students to examine the means and medians of large sets of realistic data without a computer. Data are entered, ordered, added to, or changed almost as easily as on a spreadsheet.
- ■ Graphs for data analysis are available, including box-and-whisker plots, histograms, and, on some calculators, pie charts, bar graphs, and pictographs.
- ■ Random number generators allow for the simulation of a variety of probability experiments that would be difficult without such a device.
- ■ Functions can be explored in three of the five modes discussed in Chapter 19: equation, table, and graph. Because the calculator easily switches from one to the other, and because of the trace feature, the connections between these modes become quite clear. Even grade 7 students can explore a variety of types of functions along with their graphs and function tables.
- ■ The graphing calculator is programmable. Programs are very easily written and understood. For example, a program involving the Pythagorean theorem can be used to find the length of sides of right triangles.
- ■ Data, programs, and functions can be shared from one graphing calculator to another—even to the display calculator for the overhead or TV monitor. This permits students to share and discuss their work with the rest of the class. Calculators also connect to computers to store data and programs and to print out anything that can be seen on the calculator screen.

Most of the ideas on this list have been explored briefly in appropriate chapters in this book.

Arguments against graphing calculators are similar to those for other calculators—and are equally hollow and unsubstantiated. These amazing tools have the potential to significantly open up real mathematics for students. It is time that graphing calculators were used more regularly.

The Computer as a Tool in Mathematics

Tool software is a generic term for software that performs a function that makes doing something easier. The most common tool software is the word processor. Other popular tools include spreadsheets, databases, and presentation software such as *PowerPoint*. A number of powerful tools have been created for use in the mathematics classroom. These exist in two formats: as stand-alone programs that can be purchased from software publishers, and as Internet-based applications or *applets* (little applications) accessible through web browsers such as Netscape Navigator and Microsoft Internet Explorer. Applets are always much smaller, more targeted programs than commercial software. A significant advantage is that they can be freely accessed on the Internet. Many can also be downloaded, so that a continuous Internet connection is not required.

A mathematical software tool is somewhat like a physical manipulative; by itself, it does not teach. However, the user of a well-designed tool software package has an electronic "thinker toy" with which to explore mathematical ideas.

The sections that follow each describe, in general terms, types of tool software that now exist. No attempt is made to describe specific software titles in any detail. Representative programs are mentioned.

Electronic Manipulatives for Numeration

Most tool software for grades K–4 falls in this category. In these programs, screen versions of popular manipulative models are available for students to work with freely, without the computer posing problems, evaluating results, or telling the students what to do.

At the earliest level, there are programs that provide "counters" such as coloured tiles, pictures of assorted objects, or in one specific case, Unifix cubes. (Unifix cubes are interlocking coloured plastic cubes that are about 2 centimetres in width.) Typically, students can drag counters to any place on the screen, change the colours, and put them in groupings. Some programs have options that turn on counters for the screen or subsets of the screen. In *Unifix Software* (Hickey, 1996), each bar of cubes can have a label indicating the number of cubes in the bar. Another option is for the screen or sections of the screen to indicate the total number of cubes in that section. Non-mathematical programs such as *Kid Pix* (Learning Company, 1999) can also be used to "stamp" discrete objects on the screen.

Base-ten blocks and assorted fraction pieces are available in some software packages. Usually these are not pure tool programs, but have other components that would fall into the category of instructional software— programs that attempt to teach or tutor. Some fraction models are more flexible than the concrete models. For example, a circular region might be subdivided into many more fractional parts than is reasonable with concrete models. When the models are connected with on-screen counters, it is possible with some programs to have fraction or decimal representations shown so that connections between fractions and decimals can be illustrated. So far, no tools for base-ten models or fraction models have been produced that are completely open to student use without some constraints. For example, in *MathKeys: Unlocking Whole Numbers, Grades 3–5* (MECC, 1995b), pieces can be combined or taken apart only by adding or subtracting two quantities. Other programs impose similar constraints.

Another tool in some programs in which number is combined with other features is a hundreds board. Students can colour in squares with the click of a mouse and search for patterns.

The obvious question is, "Why not simply use the actual concrete models?" When selecting these tools, there should always be some clear advantage to using the computer versions. The following are features or characteristics that may make these programs a worthwhile addition to your classroom. Not every program offers all of these features.

■ *Freedom of manipulation.* Is it at least as easy to use the screen version of the manipulative as it would be to use the concrete version? Students should be allowed to use the models in their own way without undue guidance or feedback from the computer.

■ *Connection with symbolism.* In what way are symbols attached to the models? Can the symbolism be turned on and off? Is there a variety of options?

■ *Journal capability.* Many programs offer a space at the bottom of the screen where students can write about their work. Teachers may be able to use this same space to present problems that students then solve.

■ *Print and save capabilities.* How easy is it for students to print a picture of their work? Can they easily save their work and return to it later? (This is unusual in most programs of this type.)

Geometry Tools

Computer tools for geometric exploration are much closer to pure tools than those just described for number and numeration. That is, students can use most of these tools without any constraints. They typically offer some significant advantages over concrete models; however, the computerized tools should never replace the concrete ones.

Blocks and Tiles

Programs that allow students to "stamp" geometric tiles or blocks on the screen are quite common. Typically, there is a palette of blocks, often the same as pattern blocks or tangrams, from which students can choose by clicking the mouse. Often the blocks can be made "magnetic" so that when one is released close to another block, the two will snap together, matching like sides. Blocks can usually be rotated, either freely or in set increments. Different programs offer different variations and features. You may find the following:

■ The ability to enlarge or reduce the size of blocks, usually by set increments
■ The ability to "glue" blocks together to make new blocks
■ The ability to reflect one or more blocks across a mirror line or to rotate them about a point
■ Puzzle tasks built into the program
■ The ability to measure area or perimeter
■ The ability to select polygons with a varying number of sides
■ The possibility of creating three-dimensional shapes and rotating them in space

In addition to these features, the presence of a journal or other space for writing is worth looking for, as with other tools. Print and save options are also important. With real blocks, the design is gone when the blocks are returned to the bucket. For students who have poor motor coordination or a physical disability that makes block manipulation difficult, the computer versions of blocks are a real plus. Colourful printouts can be displayed, discussed, and taken home.

Drawing Programs

For younger students, drawing shapes on a grid is much easier and more useful for geometric exploration than free-form drawing. Several programs offer electronic geo-boards on which lines can be drawn between points on a grid. When a shape such as a triangle is formed, it can typically be altered, just as you would move a rubber band on a geo-board. The electronic geo-board programs offer ease of use, a larger grid on which to draw, and the ability to save and print. Some have measuring capabilities as well as the capacity to reflect and rotate shapes—things that are difficult or impossible to do on a physical geo-board.

Dynamic Geometry Software

Dynamic geometry programs are much more than simple drawing packages. These exciting programs allow students to create shapes on the computer screen and then manipulate and measure them by dragging vertices. Relationships between lines and shapes, once created, are always preserved. Although they were originally designed for high school, there is now good reason for these programs to be a part of the classroom at least by grade 7. More detailed discussion of these programs can be found in Chapter 17. An example of a dynamic geometry exploration is shown in Figure 23.1. There, the midpoints of a freely formed quadrilateral are joined. Subsequent drawings show the same figure after the vertices have been dragged to different positions. The midpoints remain as midpoints no matter how the shape is altered.

Probability and Data Analysis Tools

These computer tools allow students to enter data and then use it to create a wide choice of graphs. In addition, most programs will produce typical statistics such as mean, median, and range. Some programs are designed for students in the primary grades. Others are more sophisticated and can be used through the middle grades. These tools make it possible to change the emphasis in data analysis from "how to construct graphs" to "how to judge which graph best tells the story."

It should be noted that the spreadsheet and the graphing calculator provide much the same capabilities as dedicated data graphing software. Generally, data programs offer more graphing options and easier use than a spreadsheet, since they are designed to assist in the development of data analysis concepts.

Probability Tools

These programs, some of which are described in Chapter 18, make it easy to conduct controlled probability experiments and see graphical representations of the results.

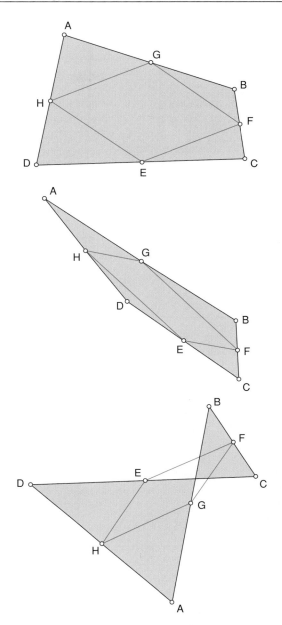

FIGURE 23.1 The original quadrilateral with midpoints joined can be pulled and stretched into any configuration, and the midpoints remain joined. Students can examine the results and form conjectures concerning observed relationships. What do you see in these screens produced by *The Geometer's Sketchpad?*

Students using these programs must accept that when the computer "flips a coin" or "spins a spinner," the results are just as random and have the same probabilities as if done with real coins or spinners. The value of these programs is found in the ease with which experiments can be designed and large numbers of trials conducted.

Spreadsheets

Spreadsheets are programs that can manipulate rows and columns of numerical data. Values taken from one position in the spreadsheet can be used in formulas to determine the value of entries elsewhere in the spreadsheet. When an entry is changed, the spreadsheet updates all values immediately. Words can also be written into spreadsheets as labels for columns or rows.

Because the spreadsheet is among the most popular pieces of standard tool software outside of schools, it is often available in integrated packages you may already have on your computer. There are spreadsheets in *Microsoft Works, Claris Works,* and *Microsoft Office.* The program *Cruncher* (SRA/McGraw-Hill, 1996) is an example of a slightly simplified spreadsheet designed for use by stu-

dents in grades 3 and up. It includes colourful graphing capability, a clip-art component, and a place in each file where students can add notes in text form. Standard spreadsheets also provide graphing capabilities. Figure 23.2 was created with *Cruncher* and shows how the spreadsheet can be used as a data analysis tool.

Instructional Software

Students are meant to interact with instructional software as they would with a textbook or a tutor. These programs are designed to teach. The distinction between tool and instructional software is not always clear, since some packages include a tool-only component. Nor is it always clear how to categorize particular instructional programs. In the

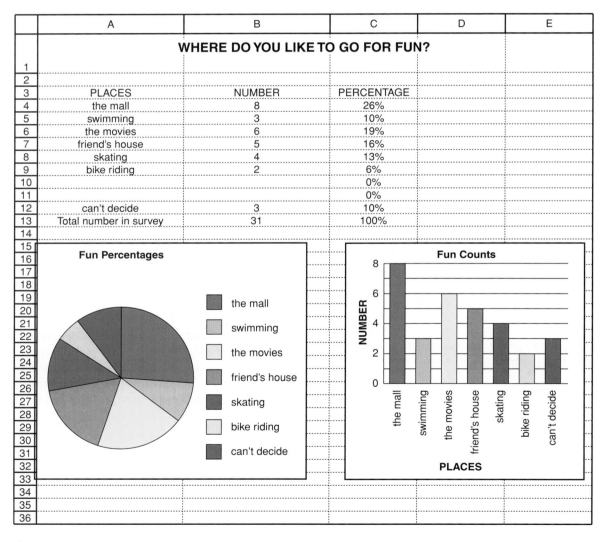

	A	B	C	D	E
	WHERE DO YOU LIKE TO GO FOR FUN?				
1					
2					
3	PLACES	NUMBER	PERCENTAGE		
4	the mall	8	26%		
5	swimming	3	10%		
6	the movies	6	19%		
7	friend's house	5	16%		
8	skating	4	13%		
9	bike riding	2	6%		
10			0%		
11			0%		
12	can't decide	3	10%		
13	Total number in survey	31	100%		
14					

Fun Percentages

- the mall
- swimming
- the movies
- friend's house
- skating
- bike riding
- can't decide

Fun Counts

NUMBER

PLACES

FIGURE 23.2 A simple spreadsheet, *Cruncher*, can be used by elementary school students to investigate data and prepare appropriate graphs.

following discussion, the intent is to provide some perspective on the different kinds of input to your mathematics program that instructional software might offer.

Concept Instruction

A growing number of programs make an effort to offer conceptual instruction. Some, like *Mathville* (Courseware Solutions, 2000), the *Fizz & Martina's Math Adventures* series of programs (Tom Snyder Productions, 1998), and the *Prime Time Math* series (Tom Snyder Productions, 1999), rely on real-world contexts to illustrate mathematical ideas. These are problem-solving situations in which specific concepts are developed in a guided manner to solve the problem.

More common in this category is the use of a visual model and much more directed instruction. *Math Trek* (The Nectar Foundation, 2000), MECC's *MathKeys* programs (MECC, 1995a, 1995b, 1995c, 1996a, 1996b), *CampOS Math* (Pierian Spring Software, 1996), and the Tenth Planet series (1998a, 1998b) use this approach. In *MathKeys,* the models are set up in a non-contextual manner. *CampOS Math* and the Tenth Planet packages embed models into a contextual format, but these stop short of being real-world.

CD-ROM technology gives authors the chance to create highly interactive models that are mathematically correct and inviting. What is most often missing is a way to make the mathematics problematic or to connect the conceptual activity with the symbolic techniques. Further, when students work on a computer, there is little opportunity for discourse, conjecture, or original ideas. In some instances, the best approach might be for the teacher to control the program on a large display screen in front of the class. In this way, the teacher can pose questions and entertain discussion that is simply not possible with one student on a computer.

Problem Solving

With the current focus on problem solving, more software publishers purport to teach students to solve problems. The Fizz & Martina and Prime Time Math series can be included in the problem-solving category. Here the problems are not typical story problems awaiting a computation, but more thoughtful stories set in real contexts. Another example is *The New Adventures of Jasper Woodbury* (Learning Company, 1996). Designed for students in middle school, these video episodes are on videodisk. Bar codes included with the print material make it easy to jump to appropriate sections of the extended problems. A single unit may take as many as five days to complete.

At the other end of the spectrum are programs that offer little more than a large library of typical story problems. Usually, the teacher can control the problem diffi-culty and the operations to be used. These programs would be more valuable if they were to offer some conceptual assistance when the student gets a problem incorrect. However, this is rarely the case.

Logic problem solving is another variant of problem-solving software. This category includes attribute activities, as in *Logical Journey of the Zoombinis* (Brøderbund, 1996b), spatial reasoning, as in *Super Factory* (Sunburst Communications), and number patterns, as in *The King's Rule* (Sunburst Communications).

Drill and Practice

Drill-and-practice programs give students practice with skills presumably taught prior to using the programs. In general, a drill program poses questions that are answered directly or by selecting from a multiple-choice list. Many of these programs are set in arcade formats that make them exciting for students who like that sort of video game. But the format has nothing to do with the practice involved.

Drill programs evaluate responses immediately. The manner in which they respond to the first or second incorrect answer is an important distinguishing feature. At one extreme, the answer is simply recorded as wrong. There may be a second or third chance to correct it. At the other extreme, the program will branch to an explanation of the correct response. Somewhere in the middle are programs that will provide a useful hint or supply a visual model to help with the task. Some programs offer record-keeping features so the teacher can keep track of individual students' progress.

Although computer drill is convenient, there is little evidence to suggest that it is any more effective than non-computer drills. A major advantage is in the formats, which can add motivation to an otherwise boring activity. Drill programs are plentiful. They tend to be cheap, and their publishers promise extravagant and unlikely results. Some drill is important, but drill is not how students learn mathematics.

Guidelines for Selecting Software

There is so much software for mathematics today, and it is so expensive that it is important to make informed decisions when investing limited resources. The most important thing to do before purchasing software is to be well informed about the product and to evaluate its merits in an objective manner.

Gathering Information

Some of the best sources of information concerning new software are provincial or territorial ministry documents and the review section of the NCTM journals or other journals that you respect. Typically, two or three pieces of software are reviewed in each issue of a journal, approximately 20 titles per year. Search through two or three years of back issues to find software that appeals. Many web sites offer reviews on both commercially available software and Internet-based applets. The Illuminations website by NCTM (http://illuminations.nctm.org) is one such site. When selecting any computer-based tool or instructional software, it is important to evaluate it appropriately.

Once you have selected some software, try to get a preview copy or at least a demonstration version. The latter may not let you actually interact with the software, but rather view a sort of commercial on your computer. Many distributors will send their software to you for 30-day approval. If this option is available, take advantage of it. Before purchasing, try the software with children in the grade that will be using it.

Catalogues are useful for finding prices and titles. They are of limited value for understanding how the software works or even what the content is. A title that says it explores "addition and subtraction" does not tell you if it involves basic facts, concepts, contextual problems, or multi-digit computation. Drill-and-practice software is rarely distinguished from concept software. Remember, it is the content in which you are interested, not the game the students will be playing.

Criteria

Here are some things to think about as you review software before purchasing it or using it in your classroom:

- What does this software do better than comparable non-computer-based activities? Don't select or use software just so your students will have an opportunity to use the computer. Be sure to get past the clever graphics and the games. Focus on what students will be learning.
- How are students likely to be engaged with the *content* (not the bells and whistles)? Remember that students' reflective thought is the most significant factor in effective instruction. Is the mathematics presented so that it is problematic for the student?
- How easy is the program to use? It is not necessary for students to be able to learn the program on their own; you can teach them to use it. But there should not be so much tedium in using the program that attention is diverted from the content. This will cause students to become frustrated.
- What sort of conceptual information is provided? In drill programs, how are wrong answers handled? Will the models or explanations aid student understanding?
- What controls are provided for the teacher? Are there options that can be turned on and off (e.g., sound, types of feedback or help, levels of difficulty)? Is there

a provision for record keeping so that you will know what progress individual students have made?
- What is the nature and quality of the print material and the manual? Minimally, the manual should make it clear how the program is to operate and should provide assistance for troubleshooting. Many programs come with extensive off-computer activities, lesson plans, Blackline Masters, and suggestions for ways to use the program with your class.
- Is a site licence or network licence available? If you purchase a single-user package, it is not legal to install the software on multiple computers. Also, note that many programs that come on a CD must be used with the CD in the computer in order to run the program. Does this constraint fit with your school situation?

Guidelines for Using Software

How software is used in mathematics instruction will vary considerably with the topic, grade level, and the software itself. The following are considerations that you should keep in mind.

- Software should contribute to the objectives of the lesson or unit. It should not be used as an add-on or substitute for more accessible approaches. It should take advantage of what technology can do efficiently and well.
- For individualized or small-group use, plan to provide specific instructions for how the software is used, and plan to provide time for students to freely explore or practice using the software.
- Combine software activities with activities off the computer (e.g., collect measurement data in the classroom to enter in a spreadsheet).
- Create a management plan for using the software. This could include a schedule for when the software is used (e.g., during centres, during small-group work) and a way to assess the effectiveness of the software use. Although some software programs include a way to keep track of student performance, you may need to rely on other assessment strategies to determine whether the software is effectively meeting your lesson or unit objectives.

Mathematics Education Resources on the Internet

In addition to providing access to Internet-based software applications or applets, the World Wide Web is a wellspring of information and resources for both teachers and students interested in mathematics and teaching mathematics.

Instead of using a standard search engine to find mathematics-related information, it is better to have some places to begin. Several good websites in different categories will usually provide you with more links to other sites. One place to get good websites is the NCTM's *News Bulletin,* a newsletter sent free to all members nine times each year. For several years, the *Bulletin* has featured information about useful websites. Make it a habit to check these out in each issue.

Professional Information

Most professional organizations have established websites on which they provide information about their organizations, conferences, current issues and events, publications, and other matters. Often these sites provide useful links to related resources or information. Periodically visiting these sites is a good way to stay current with what is going on. Most provinces and territories have a professional mathematics organization whose website you can readily access through Math Central, an Internet service for mathematics teachers and students developed and hosted by the University of Regina. The list of professional organizations can be found by accessing The Bulletin Board http://math-central.uregina.ca/BB/. The following are some other well-used websites.

National Council of Teachers of Mathematics
http://www.nctm.org

> NCTM's home page is growing and changing every month. There is up-to-date information about issues in mathematics education, including all NCTM position statements and a list of short papers that can be faxed to you free. There is conference information, including the ability to register for conferences and submit topics you may wish to present. Each of the journals has a separate page with information about the current issue. The full publications and materials catalogue is available, and purchases can be made online. Plus there are links to numerous organizations and sites of interest to the membership.

Eisenhower National Clearinghouse
http://www.enc.org

> This is a site of links. There are links to information about reform curriculum materials for K–12 mathematics and science, information and articles on reform issues, information about TIMSS, and ideas for classroom use.

Association for Supervision and Curriculum Development
http://www.ascd.org

> ASCD is an international nonprofit educational association that is committed to successful teaching and learning for all.

EQUALS and Family Math
http://equals.lhs.berkeley.edu/Eqhome2htm

> The EQUALS program is dedicated to equal opportunity for females in mathematics and science. It publishes *Family Math* and other valuable resources. For those interested in issues surrounding gender equity and parent involvement, this is a good place to begin.

Mathematically Sane
www.mathematicallysane.com

> This is an important and unique website that provides evidence for, and discussion of the success of, reform initiatives in mathematics education. Its mission statement identifies the site as created by a "grassroots organization of teachers, administrators, teacher educators, parents, and mathematicians concerned about the future of mathematics education." It is well worth visiting and exploring this website. Although it is based in the United States, you can find commentaries written by Canadian mathematics educators.

Teacher Resources

The Internet is a wonderful source of creative and useful lesson ideas. It is also a good way to find out about materials and software. The sites listed here were selected because of the quantity of information that is available on them and because the site addresses are not likely to change or disappear quickly. However, these few suggestions only scratch the surface. A large number of other resources are accessible through these sites.

Math Central
http://mathcentral.uregina.ca/

> Math Central is an Internet service provided by the Department of Mathematics and Statistics and the Faculty of Education at the University of Regina. There are different components to this site, offered in both French and English. The Resource Room is a place where mathematics educators can share resources, teaching ideas, lesson plans, etc. Other components include Quandaries and Queries, Teacher Talk, and Monthly Problems (offered in English, French and Spanish).

The Math Forum
http://forum.swarthmore.edu

> Along with the NCTM site, this may be your most important source of information and links to useful sites. The Forum has resources for both teachers and students. There are suggestions for lessons, puzzles, and activities, plus links to other sites with similar information. There are forums where teachers can talk with other teachers. Two pages accept questions about mathematics from students or teachers (Ask Dr. Math) and about teaching mathematics from teachers (Teacher 2 Teacher). Problems are regularly posted, and solutions can be entered via the Internet. Information is available about software, and some can be downloaded free, including demo versions of *The Geometer's Sketchpad.*

The Lesson Plans Page
http://www.lessonplanspage.com/

> This is an excellent site for accessing lesson plans for mathematics, among other subject areas. It is home to

over 900 lesson plans, and growing. Lesson plans are not only organized by subject area, they are also grouped by grade level. The lesson plans are detailed and complete and mostly of high quality.

Mathematics Archives: K12 Internet Sites

http://archives.math.utk.edu/k12.html

This page contains a very large collection of links to lessons, software, information (both public domain and commercial), and curriculum materials. Each of the hundreds of sites has a brief description. If you want to find an Internet address for a mathematics resource, this may be a good place to look.

School Net

http://www.schoolnet.ca/home/e/

Canada's School Net is one of the best educational web sites, with over 7000 learning resources. @SchoolNet Today is a daily information news service on the world of e-learning. The School Net service is offered in French and English. Features available are Degrassi Homework Helper for students and Helpful Sites by Subjects, which links teachers to online resources by subjects, organized by grade level, etc.

Homepage for New Math Teachers

http://www.clarityconnect.com/webpages/terri/terri.html

A veteran teacher, Terri Santi offers advice on a list of subjects challenging the new teacher. In addition, she provides clever problems to pose to students, links to a huge number of useful sites, and much more.

Annenberg/CPB Projects

http://www.learner.org

The site lists free on-line learning activities, including information about all sorts of interesting uses of mathematics and science in the real world, resources for free and inexpensive materials from Annenberg, and information about funding opportunities. It is a tremendous resource. Be sure to check the SAMI page.

Data and Resources for Students

On many of the sites just listed, there is information designed for students as well as teachers. In addition to things such as games and activities, the web is a bountiful source of data that may be used in various projects, such as comparing the population of your city to those in other parts of the world, or researching economics or geography nationwide or around the world. Here are just a few sites that fall into this category of data resources.

Environment Canada

www.ec.gc.ca

This site provides a wide source of information on weather and environmental information for Canada. All data are available in French and English.

Stock Market Information

www.globeinvestor.com

This site provides up-to-the-minute Canadian stock market research and information.

Statistics Canada

http://www.statcan.ca

This site offers valuable statistical data on a variety of topics. The site is also useful for teachers.

The World Fact Book

http://www.odci.gov/cia/publications/factbook/index.html

This page provides demographic information for every nation in the world, including population, age distributions, death and birth rates, and information on the economy, government, transportation, and geography. Maps are included as well.

The Canadian Encyclopedia

www.thecanadianencyclopedia.com

This interactive website offers extensive information on a variety of topics ranging from Canadian history to mathematics. There are French, English and Junior Edition versions as well as a student guide.

Reflections **on Chapter 23**

Writing to Learn

1. Technology has affected the mathematics curriculum and how it is taught in three ways. Explain each, and give an example to support your explanation. Can you think of examples that are not included in this chapter?

2. Describe some of the benefits of using calculators regularly in the mathematics classroom. Which of these seem to you to be the most compelling? What are some of the arguments against using calculators? Answer each of the arguments against calculators as if you were giving a speech at your Parent Council meeting or arguing for regular use of calculators before your principal.

3. Aside from the special features of graphing calculators, what are some of the benefits that come simply from having a large display screen and the ability to recall prior statements?

4. What are at least three features of graphing calculators that truly improve the learning of mathematics in grades 7 and 8?

5. Describe what is meant by tool software in mathematics. Describe several types.

6. Describe the three categories of computer instructional software. If you have seen or used examples from these categories, use those in your descriptions.
7. What are some criteria that seem most important to you when selecting software?
8. What kind of information can you expect to find on the Internet?

For Discussion and Exploration

1. Talk with some teachers about their use or non-use of calculators in the classroom. How do the teachers who use them go about doing so? What are the main reasons for not using them? Read the position statements on calculators in your regional mathematics curriculum document. How do the reasons of the teachers with whom you talked compare with these statements?
2. Among the software kept at your school, find one example of drill-and-practice and one other form of instructional software for mathematics. Try each, and decide how it would be used in your classroom (if at all). Be sure to check the documentation for suggested grade levels.
3. Check out at least three of the websites suggested for teacher resources. Be sure to follow some of the links to other sites. Share at least two good ideas with a friend. Get the friend to do the same.

Recommendations for Further Reading

Highly Recommended

Calvert, L.M.G. (1999). A dependence on technology and algorithms or a lack of number sense? *Teaching Children Mathematics, 6,* 6–7.

Calvert offers simple but convincing answers to individuals, including teachers, who believe that calculators stop children from thinking. This two-page article is well worth looking up.

Clements, D.H. (1999). The effective use of computers with young children. In J.V. Copley (Ed.), *Mathematics in the early years* (pp. 119–128). Reston, VA: National Council of Teachers of Mathematics.

Clements is a well-known researcher in the area of computer use for young children. In this article, he offers guidance on the use of computers with young children, provides numerous examples of different types of programs for the young, and offers cautions about casually believing that all computer activities are good. There is an extensive bibliography.

Dockterman, D.A. (1991). *Great teaching in the one-computer classroom* (3rd ed.). Watertown, MA: Tom Snyder Productions.

Though not about teaching mathematics, this little book, written in a teacher-friendly style, is about practical uses of a single computer in the classroom. Topics include cooperative learning, interactive video, and using the computer to make classroom life easier.

Heide, A. & Henderson, D. (2001). *Active learning in the digital age classroom.* Toronto: Trifolium Books Inc.

This book is the essential "how-to" technology integration resource for teachers. In the book, the authors examine the revolutionary effects of Information and Communication Technologies (ICT) on the environment of education, and offer a broad range of suggestions, ideas, and advice on their use in classroom settings.

Schwartz, L.M., Willing, K.R. (2001). *Computer activities for the cooperative classroom.* Markham, Ontario: Pembroke Publishers.

This practical book, on integrating computers effectively into your classroom program, was developed by two classroom teachers. The authors offer strategies for doing so, including the most up-to-date assessment and evaluation techniques, a list of online and paper-based resources, etc. A "must have" that will be well used.

Other Suggestions

Andrew, C. (2002). Ken Dryden: learning sport and learning from sport [www.leafsatschool.com] *Education Today, 14* (1).

Barron, A.E., & Hynes, M.C. (1996). Using technology to enhance communication in mathematics. In P.C. Elliott (Ed.), *Communication in mathematics, K–12 and beyond* (pp. 126–136). Reston, VA: National Council of Teachers of Mathematics.

Battista, M.T. (1998). *Shape makers: Developing geometric reasoning with the Geometer's Sketchpad.* Emeryville, CA: Key Curriculum Press.

Bayliffe, J., Brie, R., & Oliver, B. (1994). Using technology to enhance "My travels with Gulliver." *Teaching Children Mathematics, 1,* 188–191.

Bitter, G.G., & Hatfield, M.M. (1998). The role of technology in the middle grades. In L.P. Leutzinger (Ed.), *Mathematics in the middle* (pp. 36–41). Reston, VA: National Council of Teachers of Mathematics.

Blades, D. (2002). Statistics Canada supports science, mathematics and technology education. *Canadian Journal Science Mathematics and Technology Education, 2* (4) 576-577.

Calculator-Enhanced Mathematics Instruction Steering Committee. (1992). *Calculators for classrooms* [Video and guidebook]. Reston, VA: National Council of Teachers of Mathematics.

Campbell, P.F., & Clements, D.H. (1990). Using microcomputers for mathematics learning. In J.N. Payne (Ed.), *Mathematics for the young child* (pp. 265–283). Reston, VA: National Council of Teachers of Mathematics.

Drier, H.S., Dawson, K.M., & Garofalo, J. (1999). Not your typical math class. *Educational Leadership, 56*(5), 21–25.

Drosdeck, C.C. (1995). Promoting calculator use in elementary classrooms. *Teaching Children Mathematics, 1,* 300–305.

Eisenhower National Clearinghouse for Mathematics and Science Education. (1999). Integrating technology in the classroom. [Theme issue]. *ENC Focus, 6*(3).

Fey, J.T. (Ed.). (1992). *Calculators in mathematics education.* Reston, VA: National Council of Teachers of Mathematics.

Higginson, W., Sinclair, N., Jackiw, N. (2000). The sketchmad collaborative: a project to support Ontario teachers using

"The Geometer's Sketchpad." *Gazette Ontario Association for Mathematics Education, 39* (2) 25-27.

Jensen, R.J., & Williams, B.S. (1993). Technology: Implications for the middle grades. In D.T. Owens (Ed.), *Research ideas for the classroom: Middle grades mathematics* (pp. 225–243). Old Tappan, NJ: Macmillan.

McFarlane, K. (2001). Just another electric circus? Meeting standards for k–12 e-learning classroom resources. *Education Canada,* 41(3) pp. 25-27.

Murray, M., Mokros, J., & Rubin, R.A. (1999). Mathematically rich, equitable game software. *Mathematics Teaching in the Middle School, 5,* 180–186.

Owens, J.E. (1995). Playing green globs on a TI-81. *Mathematics Teaching in the Middle School, 1,* 370–374.

Russell, J.C. (1998). *Spreadsheet activities in middle school mathematics* (2nd ed.). Reston, VA: National Council of Teachers of Mathematics.

Schielack, J.F., & Chancellor, D. (1995). *Uncovering mathematics with manipulatives and calculators: Level 1.* Dallas: Texas Instruments.

Schielack, J.F., & Chancellor, D. (1995). *Uncovering mathematics with manipulatives and calculators: Levels 2 and 3.* Dallas: Texas Instruments.

Taylor, L.J.C., & Nichols, J.A. (1994). Graphing calculators aren't just for high school students. *Mathematics Teaching in the Middle School, 1,* 190–196.

Troutner, J. (2002). Web wonders: mathematics. *Teacher Librarian,* 29 (3) pp. 40–41.

Zech, L., Vye, N.J., Bransford, J.D., Swink, J., Mayfield-Stewart, C., Goldman, S.R., & the Cognition and Technology Group at Vanderbilt. (1994). Bringing geometry into the classroom with videodisc technology. *Mathematics Teaching in the Middle School, 1,* 228–233.

Principles and Standards for School Mathematics

Content Standards and Grade Level Expectations

Number and Operations

STANDARD

Instructional programs from prekindergarten through grade 12 should enable all students to

Pre K–2
Expectations
In prekindergarten through grade 2, all students should—

Grades 3–5
Expectations
In grades 3-5, all students should—

STANDARD	Pre K–2 Expectations	Grades 3–5 Expectations
Understand numbers, ways of representing numbers, relationships among numbers, and number systems	• count with understanding and recognize "how many" in sets of objects; • use multiple models to develop initial understandings of place value and the base-ten number system; • develop understanding of the relative position and magnitude of whole numbers and of ordinal and cardinal numbers and their connections; • develop a sense of whole numbers and represent and use them in flexible ways, including relating, composing, and decomposing numbers; • connect number words and numerals to the quantities they represent, using various physical models and representations; • understand and represent commonly used fractions, such as $\frac{1}{4}$, $\frac{1}{3}$, and $\frac{1}{2}$.	• understand the place-value structure of the base-ten number system and be able to represent and compare whole numbers and decimals; • recognize equivalent representations for the same number and generate them by decomposing and composing numbers; • develop understanding of fractions as parts of unit wholes, as parts of a collection, as locations on number lines, and as divisions of whole numbers; • use models, benchmarks, and equivalent forms to judge the size of fractions; • recognize and generate equivalent forms of commonly used fractions, decimals, and percents; • explore numbers less than 0 by extending the number line and through familiar applications; • describe classes of numbers according to characteristics such as the nature of their factors.
Understand meanings of operations and how they relate to one another	• understand various meanings of addition and subtraction of whole numbers and the relationship between the two operations; • understand the effects of adding and subtracting whole numbers; • understand situations that entail multiplication and division, such as equal groupings of objects and sharing equally.	• understand various meanings of multiplication and division; • understand the effects of multiplying and dividing whole numbers; • identify and use relationships between operations, such as division as the inverse of multiplication, to solve problems; • understand and use properties of operations, such as the distributivity of multiplication over addition.
Compute fluently and make reasonable estimates	• develop and use strategies for whole-number computations, with a focus on addition and subtraction; • develop fluency with basic number combinations for addition and subtraction; • use a variety of methods and tools to compute, including objects, mental computation, estimation, paper and pencil, and calculators.	• develop fluency with basic number combinations for multiplication and division and use these combinations to mentally compute related problems, such as 30×50; • develop fluency in adding, subtracting, multiplying, and dividing whole numbers; • develop and use strategies to estimate the results of whole-number computations and to judge the reasonableness of such results; • develop and use strategies to estimate computations involving fractions and decimals in situations relevant to students' experience; • use visual models, benchmarks, and equivalent forms to add and subtract commonly used fractions and decimals; • select appropriate methods and tools for computing with whole numbers from among mental computation, estimation, calculators, and paper and pencil according to the context and nature of the computation and use the selected method or tool.

Number and Operations

STANDARD

Instructional programs from prekindergarten through grade 12 should enable all students to

STANDARD	Grades 6–8 Expectations In grades 6–8 all students should—	Grades 9–12 Expectations In grades 9–12 all students should—
Understand numbers, ways of representing numbers, relationships among numbers, and number systems	• work flexibly with fractions, decimals, and percents to solve problems; • compare and order fractions, decimals, and percents efficiently and find their approximate locations on a number line; • develop meaning for percents greater than 100 and less than 1; • understand and use ratios and proportions to represent quantitative relationships; • develop an understanding of large numbers and recognize and appropriately use exponential, scientific, and calculator notation; • use factors, multiples, prime factorization, and relatively prime numbers to solve problems; • develop meaning for integers and represent and compare quantities with them.	• develop a deeper understanding of very large and very small numbers and of various representations of them; • compare and contrast the properties of numbers and number systems, including the rational and real numbers, and understand complex numbers as solutions to quadratic equations that do not have real solutions; • understand vectors and matrices as systems that have some of the properties of the real-number system; • use number-theory arguments to justify relationships involving whole numbers.
Understand meanings of operations and how they relate to one another	• understand the meaning and effects of arithmetic operations with fractions, decimals, and integers; • use the associative and commutative properties of addition and multiplication and the distributive property of multiplication over addition to simplify computations with integers, fractions, and decimals; • understand and use the inverse relationships of addition and subtraction, multiplication and division, and squaring and finding square roots to simplify computations and solve problems.	• judge the effects of such operations as multiplication, division, and computing powers and roots on the magnitudes of quantities; • develop an understanding of properties of, and representations for, the addition and multiplication of vectors and matrices; • develop an understanding of permutations and combinations as counting techniques.
Compute fluently and make reasonable estimates	• select appropriate methods and tools for computing with fractions and decimals from among mental computation, estimation, calculators or computers, and paper and pencil, depending on the situation, and apply the selected methods; • develop and analyze algorithms for computing with fractions, decimals, and integers and develop fluency in their use; • develop and use strategies to estimate the results of rational-number computations and judge the reasonableness of the results; • develop, analyze, and explain methods for solving problems involving proportions, such as scaling and finding equivalent ratios.	• develop fluency in operations with real numbers, vectors, and matrices, using mental computation or paper-and-pencil calculations for simple cases and technology for more-complicated cases; • judge the reasonableness of numerical computations and their results.

Algebra
STANDARD

Instructional programs from prekindergarten through grade 12 should enable all students to—

	Pre-K–2 **Expectations** In prekindergarten through grade 2 all students should—	Grades 3–5 **Expectations** In grades 3–5 all students should—
Understand patterns, relations, and functions	• sort, classify, and order objects by size, number, and other properties; • recognize, describe, and extend patterns such as sequences of sounds and shapes or simple numeric patterns and translate from one representation to another; • analyze how both repeating and growing patterns are generated.	• describe, extend, and make generalizations about geometric and numeric patterns; • represent and analyze patterns and functions, using words, tables, and graphs.
Represent and analyze mathematical situations and structures using algebraic symbols	• illustrate general principles and properties of operations, such as commutativity, using specific numbers; • use concrete, pictorial, and verbal representations to develop an understanding of invented and conventional symbolic notations.	• identify such properties as commutativity, associativity, and distributivity and use them to compute with whole numbers; • represent the idea of a variable as an unknown quantity using a letter or a symbol; • express mathematical relationships using equations.
Use mathematical models to represent and understand quantitative relationships	• model situations that involve the addition and subtraction of whole numbers, using objects, pictures, and symbols.	• model problem situations with objects and use representations such as graphs, tables, and equations to draw conclusions.
Analyze change in various contexts	• describe qualitative change, such as a student's growing taller; • describe quantitative change, such as a student's growing two inches in one year.	• investigate how a change in one variable relates to a change in a second variable; • identify and describe situations with constant or varying rates of change and compare them.

Algebra
STANDARD

Instructional programs from prekindergarten through grade 12 should enable all students to—

	Grades 6–8 Expectations — In grades 6–8 all students should—	Grades 9–12 Expectations — In grades 9–12 all students should—
Understand patterns, relations, and functions	• represent, analyze, and generalize a variety of patterns with tables, graphs, words, and, when possible, symbolic rules; • relate and compare different forms of representation for a relationship; • identify functions as linear or nonlinear and contrast their properties from tables, graphs, or equations.	• generalize patterns using explicitly defined and recursively defined functions; • understand relations and functions and select, convert flexibly among, and use various representations for them; • analyze functions of one variable by investigating rates of change, intercepts, zeros, asymptotes, and local and global behaviour; • understand and perform transformations such as arithmetically combining, composing, and inverting commonly used functions, using technology to perform such operations on more-complicated symbolic expressions; • understand and compare the properties of classes of functions, including exponential, polynomial, rational, logarithmic, and periodic functions; • interpret representations of functions of two variables.
Represent and analyze mathematical situations and structures using algebraic symbols	• develop an initial conceptual understanding of different uses of variables; • explore relationships between symbolic expressions and graphs of lines, paying particular attention to the meaning of intercept and slope; • use symbolic algebra to represent situations and to solve problems, especially those that involve linear relationships; • recognize and generate equivalent forms for simple algebraic expressions and solve linear equations.	• understand the meaning of equivalent forms of expressions, equations, inequalities, and relations; • write equivalent forms of equations, inequalities, and systems of equations and solve them with fluency—mentally or with paper and pencil in simple cases and using technology in all cases; • use symbolic algebra to represent and explain mathematical relationships; • use a variety of symbolic representations, including recursive and parametric equations, for functions and relations; • judge the meaning, utility, and reasonableness of the results of symbol manipulations, including those carried out by technology.
Use mathematical models to represent and understand quantitative relationships	• model and solve contextualized problems using various representations, such as graphs, tables, and equations.	• identify essential quantitative relationships in a situation and determine the class or classes of functions that might model the relationships; • use symbolic expressions, including iterative and recursive forms, to represent relationships arising from various contexts; • draw reasonable conclusions about a situation being modelled.
Analyze change in various contexts	• use graphs to analyze the nature of changes in quantities in linear relationships.	• approximate and interpret rates of change from graphical and numerical data.

Geometry
STANDARD

Instructional programs from prekindergarten through grade 12 should enable all students to—

	Pre-K–2 Expectations	Grades 3–5 Expectations
	In prekindergarten through grade 2 all students should—	In grades 3–5 all students should—
Analyze characteristics and properties of two- and three-dimensional geometric shapes and develop mathematical arguments about geometric relationships	• recognize, name, build, draw, compare, and sort two- and three-dimensional shapes; • describe attributes and parts of two- and three-dimensional shapes; • investigate and predict the results of putting together and taking apart two- and three-dimensional shapes.	• identify, compare, and analyze attributes of two- and three-dimensional shapes and develop vocabulary to describe the attributes; • classify two- and three-dimensional shapes according to their properties and develop definitions of classes of shapes such as triangles and pyramids; • investigate, describe, and reason about the results of subdividing, combining, and transforming shapes; • explore congruence and similarity; • make and test conjectures about geometric properties and relationships and develop logical arguments to justify conclusions.
Specify locations and describe spatial relationships using coordinate geometry and other representational systems	• describe, name, and interpret relative positions in space and apply ideas about relative position; • describe, name, and interpret direction and distance in navigating space and apply ideas about direction and distance; • find and name locations with simple relationships such as "near to" and in coordinate systems such as maps.	• describe location and movement using common language and geometric vocabulary; • make and use coordinate systems to specify locations and to describe paths; • find the distance between points along horizontal and vertical lines of a coordinate system.
Apply transformations and use symmetry to analyze mathematical situations	• recognize and apply slides, flips, and turns; • recognize and create shapes that have symmetry.	• predict and describe the results of sliding, flipping, and turning two-dimensional shapes; • describe a motion or a series of motions that will show that two shapes are congruent; • identify and describe line and rotational symmetry in two- and three-dimensional shapes and designs.
Use visualization, spatial reasoning, and geometric modelling to solve problems	• create mental images of geometric shapes using spatial memory and spatial visualization; • recognize and represent shapes from different perspectives; • relate ideas in geometry to ideas in number and measurement; • recognize geometric shapes and structures in the environment and specify their location.	• build and draw geometric objects; • create and describe mental images of objects, patterns, and paths; • identify and build a three-dimensional object from two-dimensional representations of that object; • identify and build a two-dimensional representation of a three-dimensional object; • use geometric models to solve problems in other areas of mathematics, such as number and measurement; • recognize geometric ideas and relationships and apply them to other disciplines and to problems that arise in the classroom or in everyday life.

Geometry

STANDARD

Instructional programs from prekindergarten through grade 12 should enable all students to—

	Grades 6–8 **Expectations** In grades 6–8 all students should—	**Grades 9–12** **Expectations** In grades 9–12 all students should—
Analyze characteristics and properties of two- and three-dimensional geometric shapes and develop mathematical arguments about geometric relationships	• precisely describe, classify, and understand relationships among types of two- and three-dimensional objects using their defining properties; • understand relationships among the angles, side lengths, perimeters, areas, and volumes of similar objects; • create and critique inductive and deductive arguments concerning geometric ideas and relationships, such as congruence, similarity, and the Pythagorean relationship.	• analyze properties and determine attributes of two- and three-dimensional objects; • explore relationships (including congruence and similarity) among classes of two- and three-dimensional geometric objects, make and test conjectures about them, and solve problems involving them; • establish the validity of geometric conjectures using deduction, prove theorems, and critique arguments made by others; • use trigonometric relationships to determine lengths and angle measures.
Specify locations and describe spatial relationships using coordinate geometry and other representational systems	• use coordinate geometry to represent and examine the properties of geometric shapes; • use coordinate geometry to examine special geometric shapes, such as regular polygons or those with pairs of parallel or perpendicular sides.	• use Cartesian coordinates and other coordinate systems, such as navigational, polar, or spherical systems, to analyze geometric situations; • investigate conjectures and solve problems involving two- and three-dimensional objects represented with Cartesian coordinates.
Apply transformations and use symmetry to analyze mathematical situations	• describe sizes, positions, and orientations of shapes under informal transformations such as flips, turns, slides, and scaling; • examine the congruence, similarity, and line or rotational symmetry of objects using transformations.	• understand and represent translations, reflections, rotations, and dilations of objects in the plane by using sketches, coordinates, vectors, function notation, and matrices; • use various representations to help understand the effects of simple transformations and their compositions.
Use visualization, spatial reasoning, and geometric modelling to solve problems	• draw geometric objects with specified properties, such as side lengths or angle measures; • use two-dimensional representations of three-dimensional objects to visualize and solve problems such as those involving surface area and volume; • use visual tools such as networks to represent and solve problems; • use geometric models to represent and explain numerical and algebraic relationships; • recognize and apply geometric ideas and relationships in areas outside the mathematics classroom, such as art, science, and everyday life.	• draw and construct representations of two- and three-dimensional geometric objects using a variety of tools; • visualize three-dimensional objects from different perspectives and analyze their cross sections; • use vertex-edge graphs to model and solve problems; • use geometric models to gain insights into, and answer questions in, other areas of mathematics; • use geometric ideas to solve problems in, and gain insights into, other disciplines and other areas of interest such as art and architecture.

Measurement

Instructional programs from prekindergarten through grade 12 should enable all students to—

	Pre-K–2 Expectations	Grades 3–5 Expectations
	In prekindergarten through grade 2 all students should—	In grades 3-5 all students should—
Understand measurable attributes of objects and the units, systems, and processes of measurement	• recognize the attributes of length, volume, mass, area, and time; • compare and order objects according to these attributes; • understand how to measure using nonstandard and standard units; • select an appropriate unit and tool for the attribute being measured.	• understand such attributes as length, area, mass, volume, and size of angle and select the appropriate type of unit for measuring each attribute; • understand the need for measuring with standard units and become familiar with standard units in the customary and metric systems; • carry out simple unit conversions, such as from centimetres to metres, within a system of measurement; • understand that measurements are approximations and understand how differences in units affect precision; • explore what happens to measurements of a two-dimensional shape such as its perimeter and area when the shape is changed in some way.
Apply appropriate techniques, tools, and formulas to determine measurements	• measure with multiple copies of units of the same size, such as paper clips laid end to end; • use repetition of a single unit to measure something larger than the unit, for instance, measuring the length of a room with a single metrestick; • use tools to measure; • develop common referents for measures to make comparisons and estimates.	• develop strategies for estimating the perimeters, areas, and volumes of irregular shapes; • select and apply appropriate standard units and tools to measure length, area, volume, mass, time, temperature, and the size of angles; • select and use benchmarks to estimate measurements; • develop, understand, and use formulas to find the area of rectangles and related triangles and parallelograms; • develop strategies to determine the surface areas and volumes of rectangular solids.

Measurement

STANDARD

Instructional programs from prekindergarten through grade 12 should enable all students to—

	Grades 6–8 **Expectations** In grades 6–8 all students should—	Grades 9–12 **Expectations** In grades 9–12 all students should—
Understand measurable attributes of objects and the units, systems, and processes of measurement	• understand both metric and customary systems of measurement; • understand relationships among units and convert from one unit to another within the same system; • understand, select, and use units of appropriate size and type to measure angles, perimeter, area, surface area, and volume.	• make decisions about units and scales that are appropriate for problem situations involving measurement.
Apply appropriate techniques, tools, and formulas to determine measurements	• use common benchmarks to select appropriate methods for estimating measurements; • select and apply techniques and tools to accurately find length, area, volume, and angle measures to appropriate levels of precision; • develop and use formulas to determine the circumference of circles and the area of triangles, parallelograms, trapezoids, and circles and develop strategies to find the area of more-complex shapes; • develop strategies to determine the surface area and volume of selected prisms, pyramids, and cylinders; • solve problems involving scale factors, using ratio and proportion; • solve simple problems involving rates and derived measurements for such attributes as velocity and density.	• analyze precision, accuracy, and approximate error in measurement situations; • understand and use formulas for the area, surface area, and volume of geometric figures, including cones, spheres, and cylinders; • apply informal concepts of successive approximation, upper and lower bounds, and limit in measurement situations; • use unit analysis to check measurement computations.

Data Analysis and Probability

STANDARD

Instructional programs from prekindergarten through grade 12 should enable all students to—

STANDARD	Pre-K–2 Expectations In prekindergarten through grade 2 all students should—	Grades 3–5 Expectations In grades 3–5 all students should—
Formulate questions that can be addressed with data and collect, organize, and display relevant data to answer them	• pose questions and gather data about themselves and their surroundings; • sort and classify objects according to their attributes and organize data about the objects; • represent data using concrete objects, pictures, and graphs.	• design investigations to address a question and consider how data-collection methods affect the nature of the data set; • collect data using observations, surveys, and experiments; • represent data using tables and graphs such as line plots, bar graphs, and line graphs; • recognize the differences in representing categorical and numerical data.
Select and use appropriate statistical methods to analyze data	• describe parts of the data and the set of data as a whole to determine what the data show.	• describe the shape and important features of a set of data and compare related data sets, with an emphasis on how the data are distributed; • use measures of centre, focusing on the median, and understand what each does and does not indicate about the data set; • compare different representations of the same data and evaluate how well each representation shows important aspects of the data.
Develop and evaluate inferences and predictions that are based on data	• discuss events related to students' experiences as likely or unlikely.	• propose and justify conclusions and predictions that are based on data and design studies to further investigate the conclusions or predictions.
Understand and apply basic concepts of probability		• describe events as likely or unlikely and discuss the degree of likelihood using such words as certain, equally likely, and impossible; • predict the probability of outcomes of simple experiments and test the predictions; • understand that the measure of the likelihood of an event can be represented by a number from 0 to 1.

Data Analysis and Probability

STANDARD	Grades 6–8 Expectations	Grades 9–12 Expectations
Instructional programs from prekindergarten through grade 12 should enable all students to—	In grades 6–8 all students should—	In grades 9–12 all students should—
Formulate questions that can be addressed with data and collect, organize, and display relevant data to answer them	• formulate questions, design studies, and collect data about a characteristic shared by two populations or different characteristics within one population; • select, create, and use appropriate graphical representations of data, including histograms, box plots, and scatterplots.	• understand the differences among various kinds of studies and which types of inferences can legitimately be drawn from each; • know the characteristics of well-designed studies, including the role of randomization in surveys and experiments; • understand the meaning of measurement data and categorical data, of univariate and bivariate data, and of the term variable; • understand histograms, parallel box plots, and scatterplots and use them to display data; • compute basic statistics and understand the distinction between a statistic and a parameter.
Select and use appropriate statistical methods to analyze data	• find, use, and interpret measures of centre and spread, including mean and interquartile range; • discuss and understand the correspondence between data sets and their graphical representations, especially histograms, stem-and-leaf plots, box plots, and scatterplots.	• for univariate measurement data, be able to display the distribution, describe its shape, and select and calculate summary statistics; • for bivariate measurement data, be able to display a scatterplot, describe its shape, and determine regression coefficients, regression equations, and correlation coefficients using technological tools; • display and discuss bivariate data where at least one variable is categorical; • recognize how linear transformations of univariate data affect shape, centre, and spread; • identify trends in bivariate data and find functions that model the data or transform the data so that they can be modelled.
Develop and evaluate inferences and predictions that are based on data	• use observations about differences between two or more samples to make conjectures about the populations from which the samples were taken; • make conjectures about possible relationships between two characteristics of a sample on the basis of scatterplots of the data and approximate lines of fit; • use conjectures to formulate new questions and plan new studies to answer them.	• use simulations to explore the variability of sample statistics from a known population and to construct sampling distributions; • understand how sample statistics reflect the values of population parameters and use sampling distributions as the basis for informal inference; • evaluate published reports that are based on data by examining the design of the study, the appropriateness of the data analysis, and the validity of conclusions; • understand how basic statistical techniques are used to monitor process characteristics in the workplace.
Understand and apply basic concepts of probability	• understand and use appropriate terminology to describe complementary and mutually exclusive events; • use proportionality and a basic understanding of probability to make and test conjectures about the results of experiments and simulations; • compute probabilities for simple compound events, using such methods as organized lists, tree diagrams, and area models.	• understand the concepts of sample space and probability distribution and construct sample spaces and distributions in simple cases; • use simulations to construct empirical probability distributions; • compute and interpret the expected value of random variables in simple cases; • understand the concepts of conditional probability and independent events; • understand how to compute the probability of a compound event.

Appendix B

Professional Standards for Teaching Mathematics

Teaching Standards

Teaching Standards

1. Worthwhile Mathematical Tasks

The teacher of mathematics should pose tasks that are based on

- Sound and significant mathematics
- Knowledge of students' understandings, interests, and experiences
- Knowledge of the range of ways that diverse students learn mathematics

and that

- Engage students' intellect
- Develop students' mathematical understandings and skills
- Stimulate students to make connections and develop a coherent framework for mathematical ideas
- Call for problem formulation, problem solving, and mathematical reasoning
- Promote communication about mathematics
- Represent mathematics as an ongoing human activity
- Display sensitivity to, and draw on, students' diverse background experiences and dispositions
- Promote the development of all students' dispositions to do mathematics

2. Teacher's Role in Discourse

The teacher of mathematics should orchestrate discourse by

- Posing questions and tasks that elicit, engage, and challenge each student's thinking
- Listening carefully to students' ideas
- Asking students to clarify and justify their ideas orally and in writing
- Deciding what to pursue in depth from among the ideas that students bring up during a discussion
- Deciding when and how to attach mathematical notation and language to students' ideas
- Deciding when to provide information, when to clarify an issue, when to model, when to lead, and when to let a student struggle with a difficulty
- Monitoring students' participation in discussions and deciding when and how to encourage each student to participate

3. Students' Role in Discourse

The teacher of mathematics should promote classroom discourse in which students

- Listen to, respond to, and question the teacher and one another
- Use a variety of tools to reason, make connections, solve problems, and communicate
- Initiate problems and questions
- Make conjectures and present solutions
- Explore examples and counterexamples to investigate a conjecture
- Try to convince themselves and one another of the validity of particular representations, solutions, conjectures, and answers
- Rely on mathematical evidence and argument to determine validity

4. Tools for Enhancing Discourse

The teacher of mathematics, in order to enhance discourse, should encourage and accept the use of

- Computers, calculators, and other technology
- Concrete materials used as models
- Pictures, diagrams, tables, and graphs
- Invented and conventional terms and symbols
- Metaphors, analogies, and stories
- Written hypotheses, explanations, and arguments
- Oral presentations and dramatizations

5. Learning Environment

The teacher of mathematics should create a learning environment that fosters the development of each student's mathematical power by

- Providing and structuring the time necessary to explore sound mathematics and grapple with significant ideas and problems
- Using the physical space and materials in ways that facilitate students' learning of mathematics
- Providing a context that encourages the development of mathematical skill and proficiency
- Respecting and valuing students' ideas, ways of thinking, and mathematical dispositions and by consistently expecting and encouraging students to
- Work independently or collaboratively to make sense of mathematics
- Take intellectual risks by raising questions and formulating conjectures
- Display a sense of mathematical competence by validating and supporting ideas with mathematical argument

6. Analysis of Teaching and Learning

The teacher of mathematics should engage in ongoing analysis of teaching and learning by

- Observing, listening to, and gathering other information about students to assess what they are learning
- Examining effects of the tasks, discourse, and learning environment on students' mathematical knowledge, skills, and dispositions in order to
- Ensure that every student is learning sound and significant mathematics and is developing a positive disposition toward mathematics
- Challenge and extend students' ideas
- Adapt or change activities while teaching
- Make plans, both short- and long-range
- Describe and comment on each student's learning to parents and administrators, as well as to the students themselves

REFERENCES

Alcaro, P., Alston, A., & Katims, N. (2000). Fractions attack! Children thinking and talking mathematically. *Teaching Children Mathematics*, 6, 562–565.

Anderson, A., & Poirier, L. (1999). Elementary mathematics. In J. Grant McLoughlin (Ed.), *Proceedings of the Canadian Mathematics Education Study Group*, 91–95.

Andrew, C. (2002). Ken Dryden learning sport and learning from sport [www.leafsatschool.com] *Education Today, 14* (1).

Ann Arbor Public Schools. (1993). *Alternative assessment: Evaluating student performance in elementary mathematics*. White Plains, NY: Cuisenaire-Dale Seymour.

Artuso, M. (1993). *Children's understanding of place value in mathematics: a cognitive developmental view*, Unpublished master's thesis, York University, Toronto, Ontario.

Ashcraft, M. H., & Christy, K. S. (1995). The frequency of arithmetic facts in elementary texts: Addition and multiplication in grades 16. *Journal for Research in Mathematics Education, 26*, 396–421.

Atlantic Provinces Education Foundation. (1993). *Foundations for the Atlantic Canada mathematics curriculum*. Halifax, NS: Atlantic Provinces Education Foundation.

Austin, R., & Thompson, D. (1997). Exploring algebraic patterns through literature. *Mathematics Teaching in the Middle School, 2*, 274–281.

Babcock, J. E. (1998). *U.S. TIMSS Report No. 8*. East Lansing: TIMSS National Research Center, Michigan State University.

Backhouse, J., Haggarty, L., Pine, S., & Stratton, J. (1992). *Improving the learning of mathematics*. Portsmouth, NH: Heinemann.

Baek, J. (1998). Children's invented algorithms for multidigit multiplication problems. In L. J. Morrow (Ed.), *The teaching and learning of algorithms in school mathematics* (pp. 151–160). Reston, VA: National Council of Teachers of Mathematics.

Baker, A., & Baker, J. (1991). *Maths in the mind: A process approach to mental strategies*. Portsmouth, NH: Heinemann.

Baker, J., & Baker, A. (1990). *Mathematics in process*. Portsmouth, NH: Heinemann.

Ball, D. L. (1992). Magical hopes: Manipulatives and the reform of math education. *American Educator, 16*(2), 14–18, 46–47.

Baratta-Lorton, M. (1976). *Mathematics their way*. Memo Park, CA: AWL Supplemental.

Barb, C., & Larson-Quinn, A. (1997). Problem solving does not have to be a problem. *The Mathematics Teacher, 90* (7), 536–542.

Baroody, A. J. (1985). Mastery of the basic number combinations: Internalization of relationships or facts? *Journal for Research in Mathematics Education, 16*, 83–98.

Baroody, A. J. (1987). *Children's mathematical thinking: A developmental framework for preschool, primary, and special education teachers*. New York: Teachers College Press.

Baroody, A. J., & Hume, J. (1991). Meaningful mathematics instruction: The case of fractions. *Remedial and Special Education, 12*, 54–68.

Battista, M. T. (1998). *Shape makers: Developing geometric reasoning with the Geometer's Sketchpad*. Emeryville, CA: Key Curriculum Press.

Battista, M. T. (1999). The mathematical miseducation of America's youth: Ignoring research and scientific study in education. *Phi Delta Kappan, 80*, 424–433.

Becker, J. P., & Shimada, S. (Eds.). (1997). *The open-ended approach: A new proposal for teaching mathematics*. Reston, VA: National Council of Teachers of Mathematics.

Bell, M. (1998, Winter). Problems with implementing new curricula: The example of the K–6 Everyday Mathematics Curriculum. *UCSMP Newsletter, 24*, 1–2.

Bennett, B., Rolheiser-Bennett, C., & Stevahn, L. (1991). *Cooperative learning where heart meets mind*. Toronto, Ontario: Educational Connections.

Bennett, D. (1992). *Exploring geometry with the Geometer's Sketchpad*. Emeryville, CA: Key Curriculum Press.

Bialystok, E., & Codd, J. (2000). Representing quantity beyond whole numbers: some, none and part. *Canadian Journal of Experimental Psychology*, 54 (2), 117–128.

Blades, D. (2002). Statistics Canada supports science, mathematics and technology education. *Canadian Journal Science Mathematics and Technology Education, 2* (4) 576–577.

Bley, N. S. (1994). Accommodating special needs. In C. A. Thornton & N. S. Bley (Eds.), *Windows of opportunity: Mathematics for students with special needs* (pp. 137–163). Reston, VA: National Council of Teachers of Mathematics.

Bley, N. S., & Thornton, C. A. (1995). *Teaching mathematics to students with learning disabilities* (3rd ed.). Austin, TX: Pro-Ed.

Boater, J. (1998). Open and closed mathematics: Student experiences and understandings. *Journal for Research in Mathematics Education, 29*, 41–62.

Booth, L. R. (1988). Children's difficulties in beginning algebra. In A. E Coxford (Ed.), *The ideas of algebra, K–12* (pp. 20–32). Reston, VA: National Council of Teachers of Mathematics.

Borasi, R. (1994, April). *Implementing the NCTM Standards in "inclusive" mainstream classrooms*. Paper presented at the annual meeting of the National Council of Teachers of Mathematics, Indianapolis, IN.

Bresser, R. (1995). *Math and literature (grades 4–6)*. Sausalito, CA: Math Solutions Publications.

Bright, G. W., Behr, M. J., Post, T. R., & Wachsmuth, I. (1988). Identifying fractions on number lines. *Journal for Research in Mathematics Education, 19*, 215–232.

Brooks, J. G., & Brooks, M. G. (1993). *In search of understanding: The case for the constructivist classroom*. Alexandria, VA: Association for Supervision and Curriculum Development.

Brownell, W. A., & Chazal, C. B. (1935). The effects of premature drill in third-grade arithmetic. *Journal of Educational Research, 29*, 17–28.

Brueningsen, C., Bower, B., Antinone, L., & Brueningsen, E. (1994). *Real-world math with the CBL system: 25 activities using the CBL and TI–82*. Dallas: Texas Instruments.

Burger, W. E. (1985). Geometry. *Arithmetic Teacher, 32*(6), 52–56.

Burger, W. E., & Shaughnessy, J. M. (1986). Characterizing the van Hiele levels of development in geometry. *Journal for Research in Mathematics Education, 17*, 13–48.

Burns, M. (1982). *Math for smarty pants*. New York: Little, Brown.

Burns, M. (1987). *A collection of math lessons from grades 3 through 6*. Sausalito, CA: Math Solutions Publications.

Burns, M. (1992a). *About teaching mathematics: A K–8 resource*. Sausalito, CA: Math Solutions Publications.

Burns, M. (1992b). *Math and literature (K–3)*. Sausalito, CA: Math Solutions Publications.

Burns, M. (1995a). *Timed tests. Teaching Children Mathematics, 1*, 408–409.

Burns, M. (1995b). *Writing in math class*. Sausalito, CA: Math Solutions Publications.

Burns, M. (1996). *50 problem-solving lessons: Grades 1–6*. Sausalito, CA: Math Solutions Publications.

Burns, M. (1998). *Math: Facing an American phobia*. Sausalito, CA: Math Solutions Publications.

Burns, M. (1999, April). *Making sense of mathematics: A look toward the twenty-first century*. Paper presented at the annual meeting of the National Council of Teachers of Mathematics, San Francisco.

Burton, N. (1995). Trends in mathematics achievement for young men and women. In I. M. Carl (Ed.), *Prospects for school mathematics* (pp. 115–130). Reston, VA: National Council of Teachers of Mathematics.

Callahan, L. G., & MacMillan, D. L. (1981). Teaching mathematics to slow-learning and mentally retarded children. In V J. Glennon (Ed.), *The mathematical education of exceptional children and youth: An interdisciplinary approach* (pp. 146–190). Reston, VA: National Council of Teachers of Mathematics.

Campbell, P. B. (1995). Redefining the "girl problem in mathematics." In W. G. Secada, E. Fennema, & L. B. Adajian (Eds.), *New directions for equity in mathematics education* (pp. 225–241). New York: Cambridge University Press.

Campbell, P. E.(1993). Making equity a reality in classrooms. *Arithmetic Teacher, 41*, 110–113.

Campbell, P. E. (1996). Empowering children and teachers in the elementary mathematics classrooms of urban schools. *Urban Education, 30,* 449–475.

Campbell, P. E. (1997, April). *Children's invented algorithms: Their meaning and place in instruction.* Paper presented at the annual meeting of the National Council of Teachers of Mathematics, Minneapolis, MN.

Campbell, P. E., & Johnson, M. L. (1995). How primary students think and learn. In I. M. Carl (Ed.), *Prospects for school mathematics* (pp. 21–42). Reston, VA: National Council of Teachers of Mathematics.

Campbell, P. E., Rowan, T. E., & Suarez, A. R. (1998). What criteria for student-invented algorithms? In L. J. Morrow (Ed.), *The teaching and learning of algorithms in school mathematics* (pp. 49–55). Reston, VA: National Council of Teachers of Mathematics.

Campione, J. C., Brown, A. L., & Connell, M. L. (1989). Metacognition: On the importance of understanding what you are doing. In R. I. Charles & E. A. Silver (Eds.), *The teaching and assessing of mathematical problem solving* (pp. 93–114). Reston, VA: National Council of Teachers of Mathematics.

Carey, D. A., Fennema, E., Carpenter, T. P., & Franke, M. L. (1995). Equity and mathematics education. In W. G. Secada, E. Fennema, & L. B. Adajian (Eds.), *New directions for equity in mathematics education* (pp. 93–125). New York: Cambridge University Press.

Carpenter, P. E., Carey, D. A., & Kouba, V. L. (1990). A problem-solving approach to the operations. In J. N. Payne (Ed.), *Mathematics for the young child* (pp. 111–131). Reston, VA: National Council of Teachers of Mathematics.

Carpenter, P. E., Franke, M. L., Jacobs, V. R., Fennema, E., & Empson, S. B. (1998). A longitudinal study of invention and understanding in children's multidigit addition and subtraction. *Journal for Research in Mathematics Education, 29,* 3–20.

Carpenter, T. E., & Moser, J. M. (1983). The acquisition of addition and subtraction concepts. In R. A. Lesh & M. Landau (Eds.), *Acquisition of mathematics concepts and processes* (pp. 7–44). Orlando, FL: Academic Press.

Carpenter, T. P., Ansell, E., Franke, M. L., Fennema, E., & Weisbeck, L. (1993). A study of kindergarten children's problem-solving processes. *Journal for Research in Mathematics Education, 24,* 428–441.

Carpenter, T. P., Fennema, E., Franke, M. L., Levi, L., & Empson, S. B., (1996). Cognitively guided instruction: a knowledge base for reform in primary mathematics instruction. *Elementary School Journal, 97* (1), 3-20.

Carroll, W. M. (1988). Cross sections of clay solids. *Arithmetic Teacher, 35*(7), 6–11.

Carroll, W. M. (1996). Use of invented algorithms by second graders in a reform mathematics curriculum. *Journal of Mathematical Behavior, 15,* 137–150.

Carroll, W. M. (1997). Results of third-grade students in a reform curriculum on the Illinois State Mathematics Test. *Journal for Research in Mathematics Education, 28,* 237–242.

Carroll, W. M., & Porter, D. (1997). Invented strategies can develop meaningful mathematical procedures. *Teaching Children Mathematics, 3,* 370–374.

Chalouh, L., & Herscovics, N. (1988). Teaching algebraic expressions in a meaningful way. In A. F. Coxford (Ed.), *The ideas of algebra, K–12* (pp. 33–42). Reston, VA: National Council of Teachers of Mathematics.

Chambers, D. L. (1994). Cognitively guided instruction. *Teaching Children Mathematics, 1,* 116.

Chambers, D. L. (1996). Direct modeling and invented procedures: Building on students' informal strategies. *Teaching Children Mathematics, 3,* 92–95.

Charles, R. I., Lester, F. K., Jr., & O'Daffer, P. (1987). *How to evaluate progress in. problem solving.* Reston, VA: National Council of Teachers of Mathematics.

Charles, R. L., Chancellor, D., Harcourt, L., Moore, D., Schielack, J. F, Van de Walle, J. A., & Wortzman, R. (1998). *Scott Foresman-Addison Wesley MATH (Grades K to 5).* Glenview, IL: Scott Foresman-Addison Wesley.

Clark, E. B., & Kamii, C. K. (1996). Identification of multiplicative thinking in children in grades 1–5. *Journal for Research in Mathematics Education, 27,* 41–51.

Clarke, C. (1992). Quick and easy math centers, *Prime Areas, 35* (3), 5–7.

Clements, D. H., & Battista, M. T. (1990). Constructivist learning and teaching. *Arithmetic Teacher, 38*(1), 34–35.

Cobb, P. (1988). The tension between theories of learning and instruction in mathematics education. *Educational Psychologist, 23,* 87–103.

Cobb, P. (1995). Cultural tools and mathematical learning: A case study. *Journal for Research in Mathematics Education, 26,* 362–385.

Colgan, L. E. (2000). Testing the big ideas in mathematics. *Orbit, 30* (4), 54–57.

Corwin, R. B. (1996). *Talking mathematics: Supporting children's voices.* Portsmouth, NH: Heinemann.

Council of Ministers of Education (2001). *School Achievement Indicators program SAIP mathematics III 2001.* Toronto: Council of Ministers of Education.

Countryman, J. (1992). *Writing to learn mathematics: Strategies that work, K–12.* Portsmouth, NH: Heinemann.

Cramer, K. & Henry, A. (2002). Using manipulative models to build number sense for addition of fractions. In B. Litwiller, (Ed.), *Making sense of fractions, ratios, and proportions* (pp. 41–48). Reston, VA: National Council of Teachers of Mathematics.

Cuisenaire-Dale Seymour Publications. (1995). *Investigations in number data and space.* White Plains, NY: Author.

Curcio, E. R., & Bezuk, N. S. (1994). *Understanding rational numbers and proportions: Addenda series, grades 5–8.* Reston, VA: National Council of Teachers of Mathematics.

Damarin, S. K. (1995). Gender and mathematics from a feminist standpoint. In W. G. Secada, E. Fennema, & L. B. Adajian (Eds.), *New directions for equity in mathematics education* (pp. 242–257). New York: Cambridge University Press.

Davidson, E., & Hammerman, J. (1993). Homogenized is only better for milk. In G. Cuevas & M. Driscol (Eds.), *Reaching all students with mathematics* (pp. 197–212). Reston, VA: National Council of Teachers of Mathematics.

Davis, R. B. (1986). *Learning mathematics: The cognitive science approach to mathematics education.* Norwood, NJ: Ablex.

de Villiers, M. D. (1999). *Rethinking proof with the Geometer's Sketchpad.* Emeryville, CA: Key Curriculum Press.

Dei, G. J. S. (1996). *Anti-racism education theory and practice.* Halifax: Fernwood Publishing.

Downs, R. E., Mathew, J. L., & McKinney, M. L. (1994). Issues of identification. In C. A. Thornton & N. S. Bley (Eds.), *Windows of opportunity: Mathematics for students with special needs* (pp. 61–81). Reston, VA: National Council of Teachers of Mathematics.

Earl, L., & Katz, S. (2000). The paradox of classroom assessment. *Orbit, 30* (4) 8–10.

Early math strategy the report of the expert panel on early math in Ontario (2003). Ministry of Education and Training, Queen's Printer for Ontario.

Early numeracy project, (2003). British Columbia: Ministry of Education, British Columbia.

Elliott, P. C., & Garnets, C. (1994). Mathematics power for all. In C. A. Thornton, & N. S. Bley (Eds.), *Windows of opportunity: Mathematics for students with special needs* (pp. 3–17). Reston, VA: National Council of Teachers of Mathematics.

Fennema, E., Carpenter, T. E., Franke, M. L., & Carey, D. A. (1993). Learning to use children's mathematics thinking: A case study. In R. B. Davis & C. A. Maher (Eds.), *School, mathematics, and the world of reality* (pp. 93–117). Needham Heights, MA: Allyn & Bacon.

Fennema, E., Carpenter, T. E., Levi, L., Franke, M. L., & Empson, S. (1997). *Cognitively guided instruction: Professional development in primary mathematics.* Madison: Wisconsin Center for Education Research.

Fennema, E., Peterson, E. L., Carpenter, T. P, & Lubinski, C. (1990). Teacher attributes and beliefs about girls, boys, and mathematics. *Educational Studies in Mathematics, 21,* 55–69.

Fey, J. T. (Ed.). (1992). *Calculators in mathematics education.* Reston, VA: National Council of Teachers of Mathematics.

Fischer, E. E. (1990). A part-part-whole curriculum for teaching number in the kindergarten. *Journal for Research in Mathematics Education, 21,* 207–215.

Flewelling, G., & Higginson, W. (2000). *Realizing a vision of tomorrow's mathematics classroom, a handbook on rich learning tasks.* Kingston, ON: Centre for Mathematics, Science and Technology Education, Queen's University.

Flewelling, G., Higginson, W., Roulet, G., & Taylor, P. (1997). Tomorrow's mathematics classroom: a vision of mathematics education, In Y. M.

Pothier (Ed.), *Proceedings of the Canadian Mathematics Education Study Group*, 151–152.

Flewelling, G. Lind, S., & Sauer, R. (1999) *Mathematics assessment activities 3. Teacher's resource book*. Vancouver: Gage Educational Publishing Company. Note: Resource books in this series are available for the different elementary grades.

Fosnaugh, L. S., & Harrell, M. E. (1996). Covering the plane with reptiles. *Mathematics Teaching in the Middle School, 1*, 666–670.

Fosnot, C. T. & Dolk, M. (2001). *Young mathematicians at work: Constructing multiplication and division*. Portsmouth, NH: Heinemann.

Fosnot, C. T. & Dolk, M. (2001). *Young mathematicians at work: Constructing number sense, addition, and subtraction*. Portsmouth, NH: Heinemann.

Foundations for the Atlantic Canada Mathematics Curriculum (1995). Halifax, Nova Scotia: Nova Scotia Department of Education and Culture English Program Services.

Friel, S. N., Mokros, J. R., & Russell, S. J. (1992). *Statistics: Middles, means, and in–betweens*. A unit of study for grades 5–6 from *Used numbers: Real data in the classroom*. White Plains, NY: Cuisenaire-Dale Seymour.

Frketich, D., & Tomlinson, M. (1996-97). Problem solving + communication = successful, confident math students. *Prime Areas, 39* (1), 18-23.

Fuson, K. C. (1984). More complexities in subtraction. *Journal for Research in Mathematics Education, 15*, 214–225.

Fuson, K. C. (1992). Research on whole number addition and subtraction. In D. A. Grouws (Ed.), *Handbook of research on teaching and learning* (pp. 243–275). Old Tappan, NJ: Macmillan.

Fuson, K. C., & Hall, J. W. (1983). The acquisition of early number word meanings: A conceptual analysis and review. In H. P. Ginsburg (Ed.), *The development of mathematical thinking* (pp. 49–107). Orlando, FL: Academic Press.

Fuson, K. C., Wearne, D., Hiebert, J. C., Murray, H. G., Human, P. G., Olivier, A. L, Carpenter, T. P., & Fennema, E. (1997). Children's conceptual structures for multidigit numbers and methods of multidigit addition and subtraction. *Journal for Research in Mathematics Education, 28*, 130–162.

Fuys, D., Geddes, D., & Tischler, R. (1988). *The van Hiele model of thinking in geometry among adolescents* (Journal for Research in Mathematics Education Monograph No. 3). Reston, VA: National Council of Teachers of Mathematics.

Garland, T. H. (1987). *Fascinating Fibonaccis: Mystery and magic in numbers*. White Plains, NY: Cuisenaire–Dale Seymour.

Garofalo, J. (1987). Metacognition and school mathematics. *Arithmetic Teacher, 34*(9), 22–23.

Geddes, D., & Fortunato, I. (1993). Geometry: Research and classroom activities. In D. T. Owens (Ed.), *Research ideas for the classroom: Middle grades mathematics* (pp. 199–222). Old Tappan, NJ: Macmillan.

Gelman, R., & Gallistel, C. R. (1978). *The child's understanding of number*. Cambridge, MA: Harvard University Press.

Gelman, R., & Meck, E. (1986). The notion of principle: The case of counting. In J. C. Hiebert (Ed.), *Conceptual and procedural knowledge: The case of mathematics* (pp. 29–57). Mahwah, NJ: Erlbaum.

Ginsburg, H. P (1977). *Children's arithmetic: The learning process*. New York: Van Nostrand.

Gnanadesikan, M., Schaeffer, R. L., & Swift, J. (1987). *The art and techniques of simulation: Quantitative literacy series*. White Plains, NY: Cuisenaire-Dale Seymour.

Greenes, C., Garfunkel, E., & De Bussey, M. (1994). Planning for instruction: The individualized education plan and the mathematics individualized learning plan. In C. A. Thornton & N. S. Bley (Eds.), *Windows of opportunity: Mathematics for students with special needs* (pp. 115–135). Reston, VA: National Council of Teachers of Mathematics.

Green, B. (1992). Multiplication and division as models of situations. In D. A. Grouws (Ed.), *Handbook of research on mathematics teaching and learning* (pp. 276–295). Old Tappan, NJ: Macmillan.

Groff, P. (1996). It is time to question fraction teaching. *Mathematics Teaching in the Middle School, 1*, 604–607.

Gutstein, E., & Romberg, T. A. (1995). Teaching children to add and subtract. *Journal of Mathematical Behavior, 14*, 283–324.

Hankes, J. E. (1996). An alternative to basic-skills remediation. *Teaching Children Mathematics, 2*, 452–457.

Hashimoto, Y., & Becker, J. (1999). The open approach to teaching mathematics: Creating a culture of mathematics in the classroom: Japan. In L.

J. Sheffield (Ed.), *Developing mathematically promising students* (pp. 101–119). Reston, VA: National Council of Teachers of Mathematics.

Heide, A., & Henderson, D. (2001). *Active learning in the digital age classroom*. Toronto: Trifolium Books Inc.

Hembree, R., & Dessart, D. D. (1986). Effects of hand-held calculators in pre-college mathematics education: A meta-analysis. *Journal for Research in Mathematics Education, 17*, 83–99.

Hiebert, J. C. (1990). The role of routine procedures in the development of mathematical competence. In T. J. Cooney (Ed.), *Teaching and learning mathematics in the 1990s* (pp. 31–40). Reston, VA: National Council of Teachers of Mathematics.

Hiebert, J. C., & Carpenter, T. P. (1992). Learning and teaching with understanding. In D. A. Grouws (Ed.), *Handbook of research on mathematics teaching and learning* (pp. 65–97). Old Tappan, NJ: Macmillan.

Hiebert, J. C., Carpenter, T. P., Fennema, E., Fuson, K. C., Human, P. G., Murray, H. G., Olivier, A. L., & Wearne, D. (1996). Problem solving as a basis for reform in curriculum and instruction: The case of mathematics. *Educational Researcher, 25*, 12–21.

Hiebert, J. C., Carpenter, T. P, Fennema, E., Fuson, K. C., Wearne, D., Murray, H. G., Olivier, A. I., & Human, P. G. (1997). *Making sense: Teaching and learning mathematics with understanding*. Portsmouth, NH: Heinemann.

Hiebert, J. C., & Lindquist, M. M. (1990). Developing mathematical knowledge in the young child. In J. N. Payne (Ed.), *Mathematics for the young child* (pp. 17–36). Reston, VA: National Council of Teachers of Mathematics.

Hiebert, J. C., & Wearne, D. (1996). Instruction, understanding, and skill in multidigit addition and subtraction. *Cognition and Instruction, 14*, 251–283.

Higginson, W., Sinclair, N., & Jackiw, N. (2000). The sketchmad collaborative: a project to support Ontario teachers using "the geometer's sketchpad." *Gazette Ontario Association for Mathematics Education, 39* (2) 25-27.

Hilliard, A. G., III. (1995). Mathematics excellence for cultural "minority" students: What is the problem? In I. M. Carl (Ed.), *Seventy five years of progress: Prospects for school mathematics* (pp. 99–114). Reston, VA: National Council of Teachers of Mathematics.

Hoffer, A. R. (1983). Van Hiele-based research. In R. A. Lesh & M. Landau (Eds.), *Acquisition of mathematics concepts and processes* (pp. 205–227). Orlando, FL: Academic Press.

Hoffer A. R., & Hoffer, S. A. K. (1992). Ratios and proportional thinking. In T. R. Post (Ed.), *Teaching mathematics in grades K–8: Research-based methods* (2nd ed., pp. 303–330). Needham Heights, MA: Allyn & Bacon.

Hope, J. A., Leutzinger, L. P., Reys, B. J., & Reys, R. E. (1988). *Mental math in the primary grades*. White Plains, NY: Cuisenaire-Dale Seymour.

Hope, J. A., Reys, B. J., & Reys, R. E. (1987). *Mental math in the middle grades*. White Plains, NY: Cuisenaire–Dale Seymour.

Hope, J. A., Reys, B. J., & Reys, R. E. (1988). *Mental math in the junior high school*. White Plains, NY: Cuisenaire–Dale Seymour.

House, P A. (1999). Promises, promises, promises. In L. J. Sheffield (Ed.), *Developing mathematically promising students* (pp. 1–7). Reston, VA: National Council of Teachers of Mathematics.

Howden, H. (1989). Teaching number sense. *Arithmetic Teacher, 36*(6), 6–11.

Huinker, D. M. (1994, April). *Multistep word problems: A strategy for empowering students*. Paper presented at the annual meeting of the National Council of Teachers of Mathematics, Indianapolis, IN.

Huinker, D. M. (1998). Letting fraction algorithms emerge through problem solving. In L. J. Morrow (Ed.), *The teaching and learning of algorithms in school mathematics* (pp. 170–182). Reston, VA: National Council of Teachers of Mathematics.

Huinker, D. M., & Laughlin, C. (1996). Talk your way into writing. In P C. Elliott (Ed.), *Communication in mathematics, K–12 and beyond* (pp. 81–88). Reston, VA: National Council of Teachers of Mathematics.

Irvine, R., & Walker, K. (1996a). *Smart arithmetic: A thinking approach to computation, grades 1–3*. Chicago: Creative Publications.

Irvine, R., & Walker, K. (1996b). Smart arithmetic: A thinking approach to computation, grades 4–6. Chicago: Creative Publications.

James, G. (1976). *Mathematics dictionary*. Fourth edition. New York: Van Nostrand Reinhold Company.

Janvier, C. (Ed.). (1987). *Problems of representation in the teaching and learning of mathematics*. Mahwah, NJ: Erlbaum.

Johnson, D. W., Johnson, R. T., & Holubec, E. J. (1993). *Circles of learning: Cooperation in the classroom* (4th ed.). Alexandria, VA: Association for Supervision and Curriculum Development.

Kamii, C. K. (1985). *Young children reinvent arithmetic.* New York: Teachers College Press.

Kamii, C. K. (1989). *Young children continue to reinvent arithmetic: 2nd grade.* New York: Teachers College Press.

Kamii, C. K., & Clark, E. B. (1995). Equivalent fractions: Their difficulty and educational implications. *Journal of Mathematical Behavior 14,* 365–378.

Kamii, C. K., & Dominick, A. (1997). To teach or not to teach the algorithms. *Journal of Mathematical Behavior, 16,* 51–62.

Kamii, C. K., & Dominick, A. (1998). The harmful effects of algorithms in grades 1–4. In L. J. Morrow (Ed.), *The teaching and learning of algorithms in school mathematics* (pp. 130–140). Reston, VA: National Council of Teachers of Mathematics.

Kaput, J. J. (1998). Transforming algebra from an engine of inequity to an engine of mathematical power by "algebrafying" the K–12 curriculum. In *The nature and role of algebra in the K–14 curriculum: Proceedings of a national symposium* (pp. 25–26). Washington, DC: National Academy Press.

Karplus, R., Pulos, S., & Stage, E. K. (1983). Proportional reasoning of early adolescents. In R. A. Lesh & M. Landau (Eds.), *Acquisition of mathematics concepts and processes* (pp: 45–90). Orlando, FL: Academic Press.

Kelleher, H., Nicol, C., Anderson,A., Martin, L., & Ercikan, K. (2000). *Early Numeracy Project,* Ministry of Education, British Columbia.

Kenney, E. A., & Silver, E. A. (Eds.) (1997). *Results from the sixth mathematics assessment of the National Assessment of Educational Progress.* Reston, VA: National Council of Teachers of Mathematics.

Kenney, P. A., & Kouba, V. L. (1997). What do students know about measurement? In P. A. Kenney & E. A. Silver (Eds.), *Results from the sixth mathematics assessment of the National Assessment of Educational Progress* (pp. 141–163). Reston, VA: National Council of Teachers of Mathematics.

Kenney, P. A., Lindquist, M. M., & Hefferman, C.L. (2002). Butterflies and caterpillars: Multiplicative and proportional reasoning in the early grades. In B. Litwiller (Ed.), *Making sense of fractions, ratios, and proportions* (pp. 87–99). Reston, VA: National Council of Teachers of Mathematics.

Kieren, T. (1984). Helping children understand rational numbers. *Arithmetic Teacher, 31*(6), 3.

Kouba, V. L. (1989). Children's solution strategies for equivalent set multiplication and division word problems. *Journal for Research in Mathematics Education, 20,* 147–158.

Kouba, V. L., Brown, C. A., Carpenter, T. P., Lindquist, M. M., Silver, E. A., & Swafford, J. O. (1988a). Results of the fourth NAEP assessment of mathematics: Number, operations, and word problems. *Arithmetic Teacher, 35*(8), 14–19.

Kouba, V. L., Brown, C. A., Carpenter, T. P., Lindquist, M. M., Silver, E. A., & Swafford, J. O. (1988b). Results of the fourth NAEP assessment of mathematics: Measurement, geometry, data interpretation, attitudes, and other topics. *Arithmetic Teacher, 35*(9), 10–16.

Kouba, V. L., Zawojewski, J. S., & Strutchens, M. E. (1997). What do students know about numbers and operations? In P A. Kenney & E. A. Silver (Eds.), *Results from the sixth mathematics assessment of the National Assessment of Educational Progress* (pp. 87–140). Reston, VA: National Council of Teachers of Mathematics.

Kroll, D. L., Masingila, J. O., & Mau, S. T. (1992). Cooperative problem solving: But what about grades? *Arithmetic Teacher, 39*(6), 17–23.

Kuhn, G. (1994). *Mathematics assessment: What works in the classroom.* San Francisco: Jossey-Bass.

Labinowicz, E. (1985). *Learning from children: New beginnings for teaching numerical thinking.* Menlo Park, CA: AWL Supplemental.

Labinowicz, E. (1987). Assessing for learning: The interview method. *Arithmetic Teacher, 35*(3), 22–24.

Ladson-Billings, G. (1995). Making mathematics meaningful in multicultural contexts. In W. G. Secada, E. Fennema, & L. B. Adajian (Eds.), *New directions for equity in mathematics education* (pp. 126–145). New York: Cambridge University Press.

Lamon, S. J. (1993). Ratio and proportion: Connecting content and children's thinking. *Journal for Research in Mathematics Education, 24,* 41–61.

Lamon, S. J. (1999). *Teaching fractions and ratios for understanding: essential content knowledge and instructional strategies for teachers.* Mahwah, NJ: Lawrence Erlbaum.

Lampert, M. (1990). When the problem is not the question and the solution is not the answer: Mathematical knowing and teaching. *American Educational Research journal, 27,* 29–63.

Landwehr, J. M., & Watkins, A. E. (1987). *Exploring data: Quantitative literacy series.* White Plains, NY: Cuisenaire-Dale Seymour.

Lappan, G. (1998). Capturing patterns and functions: Variables and joint variation. In *The nature and role of algebra in the K–14 curriculum: Proceedings of a national symposium* (pp. 57–59). Washington, DC: National Academy Press.

Lappan, G., & Briars, D. (1995). How should mathematics be taught? In I. M. Carl (Ed.), *Seventy-five years of progress: Prospects for school mathematics* (pp. 115–156). Reston, VA: National Council of Teachers of Mathematics.

Lappan, G., & Even, R. (1989). *Learning to teach: Constructing meaningful understanding of mathematical content* (Craft Paper No. 89–3). East Lansing: Michigan State University.

Lappan, G., & Mouck, M. K. (1998). Developing algorithms for adding and subtracting fractions. In L. J. Morrow (Ed.), *The teaching and learning of algorithms in school mathematics* (pp. 183–197). Reston, VA: National Council of Teachers of Mathematics.

Leder, G. C. (1995). Equity inside the mathematics classroom: Fact or artifact? In W. G. Secada, E. Fennema, & L. B. Adajian (Eds.), *New directions for equity in mathematics education* (pp. 209–224). New York: Cambridge University Press.

Lemaire, P., Lechacheur, M. & Farioli, F. (2000). Children's strategy use in computational estimation. *Canadian Journal of Experimental Psychology, 54*(2), 141–148.

Lesh, R. A., Post, T. R., & Behr, M. J. (1987). Representations and translations among representations in mathematics learning and problem solving. In C. Janvier (Ed.), *Problems of representation in the teaching and learning of mathematics* (pp. 33–40). Mahwah, NJ: Erlbaum.

Lesh, R. A., Post, T. R., & Behr, M. J. (1988). Proportional reasoning. In J. C. Hiebert & M. J. Behr (Eds.), *Number concepts and operation in the middle grades* (pp. 93–118). Reston, VA: National Council of Teachers of Mathematics.

Lester, E. K., Jr. (1989). Reflections about mathematical problem-solving research. In R.I. Charles & E. A. Silver (Eds.), *The teaching and assessing of mathematical problem solving* (pp. 115–124). Reston, VA: National Council of Teachers of Mathematics.

Lester, F. K., Jr. (1994). Musings about mathematical problem-solving research, 1970–1994. *Journal for Research in Mathematics Education, 25,* 660–675.

Lester, J. B. (1996). Establishing a community of mathematics learners. In D. Schifter (Ed.), *What's happening in math class? Envisioning new practices through teacher narratives* (pp. 88–102). New York: Teachers College Press.

Liedtke, W. (1996–97). Fostering the development of conceptual knowledge: The basic addition facts. *Prime Areas, 93*(1), 42–51).

Liedtke, W. (1999). *Teacher-centred projects: Risk taking and flexible thinking.* Proceedings of a faculty conference, Connections '98, Victoria, British Columbia.

Liedtke, W., & Kallio, P. (1992-93). Promoting the development of number sense in the early years. *Prime Areas, 35*(1), 43–45.

Liedtke, W. W. (1988). Diagnosis in mathematics: The advantages of an interview. *Arithmetic Teacher, 36*(3), 26–29.

Lindquist, M. M. (1987a). Estimation and mental computation: Measurement. *Arithmetic Teacher, 34*(5), 16–17.

Lindquist, M. M. (1987b). Problem solving with five easy pieces. In J. M. Hill (Ed.), *Geometry for grades K–6: Readings from The Arithmetic Teacher* (pp. 152–156). Reston, VA: National Council of Teachers of Mathematics.

Lo, J., & Watanabe, T. (1997). Developing ratio and proportion schemes: A story of a fifth grader. *Journal for Research in Mathematics Education, 28,* 216–236.

Lodholz, R. D. (1990). The transition from arithmetic to algebra. In E. L. Edwards Jr. (Ed.), *Algebra for everyone* (pp. 24–33). Reston, VA: National Council of Teachers of Mathematics.

Lubinski, C. A., & Thiessen, D. (1996). Exploring measurement through literature. *Teaching Children Mathematics, 2,* 260–263.

Mack, N. K. (1995). Confounding whole-number and fraction concepts when building on informal knowledge. *Journal for Research in Mathematics Education, 26,* 422–441.

Madell, R. (1985). Children's natural processes. *Arithmetic Teacher, 32*(7), 20–22.

Marks-Krpan, K. (2001). *The write math writing about math in the classroom.* Parsippany, NJ: Dale Seymour Publications.

Marolda, M. R., & Davidson, P. S. (1994). Assessing mathematical abilities and learning approaches. In C. A. Thornton & N. S. Bley (Eds.), *Windows of opportunity: Mathematics for students with special needs* (pp. 83–113). Reston, VA: National Council of Teachers of Mathematics.

Martin, G., & Strutchens, M.E. (2000). Geometry and measurement. In E.A. Silver & P.A. Kenney (Eds.), *Results from the seventh mathematics assessment of the National Assessment of Educational Progress* (pp. 193–234). Reston VA: National Council of Teachers of Mathematics.

Mathematical Sciences Education Board, National Research Council. (1989). *Everybody counts: A report to the nation on the future of mathematics education.* Washington, DC: National Academy Press.

McCoy, L. P. (1997). Algebra: Real-life investigations in a lab setting. *Mathematics Teaching in the Middle School, 2,* 220–224.

McFarlane, K. (2001). Just another electric circus? Meeting standards for k–12 e-learning classroom resources. *Education Canada, 41*(3), 25–27.

Milauskas, G. A. (1987). Creative geometry problems can lead to creative problem solvers. In M. M. Lindquist (Ed.), *Learning and teaching geometry, K–12* (pp. 69–84). Reston, VA: National Council of Teachers of Mathematics.

Mokros, J., Russell, S. J., & Economopoulos, K. (1995). *Beyond arithmetic: Changing mathematics in the elementary classroom.* White Plains, NY: Cuisenaire-Dale Seymour.

Moss, J. (2002). Percents and proportions in the center: Altering the teaching sequence for rational number. In B. Litwiller (Ed.), *Making sense of fractions, ratios, and proportions* (pp. 109–120). Reston, VA: National Council of Teachers of Mathematics.

Mulligan, J. T., & Mitchelmore, M. C. (1997). Young children's intuitive models of multiplication and division. *Journal for Research in Mathematics Education, 28,* 309–330.

Munby, H., Locke, C. L. (2000). Changing assessment practices in the classroom: a study of one teacher's challenge. *Alberta Journal of Educational Research, 46*(3), 267–279.

Myers, John, J. (1995). Promoting purposeful talk in the cooperative language arts classroom. In R.J. Stahl (Ed.). *Cooperative learning in language arts a handbook for teachers* (pp. 407–422), CA: Addison Wesley Publishing Co. Inc.

National Council of Teachers of Mathematics. (1989). *Curriculum and evaluation standards for school mathematics.* Reston, VA: Author.

National Council of Teachers of Mathematics. (1991). *Professional standards for teaching mathematics.* Reston, VA: Author.

National Council of Teachers of Mathematics. (1995). *Assessment standards for school mathematics.* Reston, VA: Author.

National Council of Teachers of Mathematics. (1998). *1998–1999 NCTM member handbook: NCTM goals, leaders, and position statements.* Reston, VA: Author.

National Council of Teachers of Mathematics. (2000). *Principles and standards for school mathematics.* Reston, VA: Author.

National Research Council. (2001). *Adding it up: Helping children learn mathematics.* J. Kilpatrick, J. Swafford, & B. Findell (Eds.). Mathematics Learning Study Committee, Center for Education Division of Behavioral and Social Sciences and Education. Washington, DC: National Academy Press.

Noddings, N. (1993). Constructivism and caring. In R. B. Davis & C. A. Maher (Eds.), *School, mathematics, and the world of reality* (pp. 35–50). Needham Heights, MA: Allyn & Bacon.

Noelting, G. (1980). The development of proportional reasoning and the ratio concept: 1. Differentiation of stages. *Educational Studies in Mathematics, 11,* 217–253.

Oakes, J. (1990). *Multiplying inequalities: The effects of race, social class, and tracking opportunities to learn mathematics and science.* Santa Monica, CA: Rand.

Oakes, J. (1995). Opportunity to learn: Can standards-based reform be equity–based reform? In I. M. Carl (Ed.), *Seventy-five years of progress: Prospects for school mathematics* (pp. 78–98). Reston, VA: National Council of Teachers of Mathematics.

O'Brien, T. C. (1999). Parrot math. *Phi Delta Kappan, 80,* 434–438.

The Ontario Curriculum Grades 1–8 Mathematics (1997). Ontario: Ministry of Education and Training.

Oppedal, D. C. (1995). Mathematics is something good. *Teaching Children Mathematics, 2,* 36–40.

Papert, S. (1980). *Mindstorms: Children, computers, and powerful ideas.* New York: Basic Books.

Payne, W. (1992-93). Whole math and the computer beyond drill and practice. *Prime Areas, 35*(3), 71–72.

Phillips, E. (1992-93). A selection of math games and activities for early primary. *Prime Areas, 35*(3), 8–10.

Pirie, S., & Kieren, T. (1992). Creating constructivist environments and constructing creative mathematics. *Educational Studies in Mathematics, 23,* 505–528.

Pirie, S., & Kieren, T. (1994). Growth in mathematical understanding: how can we characterize it and how can we represent it? *Educational Studies in Mathematics, 26,* 165–190.

Polya, G. (1957). *How to solve it.* Princeton, NJ: Princeton University Press.

Poplin, M. S. (1988a). Holistic/constructivist principles of the teaching/learning process: Implications for the field of learning disabilities. *Journal of Learning Disabilities, 21,* 401–416.

Poplin, M. S. (1988b). The reductionistic fallacy in teaming disabilities: Replicating the past by reducing the present. *Journal of Learning Disabilities, 21,* 389–398.

Post, T. R. (1981). Fractions: Results and implications from the National Assessment. *Arithmetic Teacher, 28*(9), 26–31.

Post, T. R., Behr, M. J., & Lesh, R. A. (1988). Proportionality and the development of prealgebra understandings. In A. E Coxford (Ed.), *The ideas of algebra, K–12* (pp. 78–90). Reston, VA: National Council of Teachers of Mathematics.

Post, T. R., Wachsmuth, I., Lesh, R. A., & Behr, M. J. (1985). Order and equivalence of rational numbers: A cognitive analysis. *Journal for Research in Mathematics Education, 16,* 18–36.

Raimi, R. A., & Braden, L. S. (1998). *State mathematics: An appraisal of math standards in 46 states, the District of Columbia, and Japan.* Washington, DC: Thomas B. Fordham Foundation.

Rathmell, E. C. (1978). Using thinking strategies to teach the basic skills. In M. N. Suydam (Ed.), *Developing computational skills* (pp. 13–38). Reston, VA: National Council of Teachers of Mathematics.

Reese, C. M., Miller, K. E., Mazzeo, J., & Dossey, J. A. (1997). *NAEP 1996 mathematics report card for the nation and the states: Findings from the National Assessment of Educational Progress.* Washington, DC: National Center for Education Statistics.

Resnick, L. B. (1983). A developmental theory of number understanding. In H. P Ginsburg (Ed.), *The development of mathematical thinking* (pp. 109–151). Orlando, FL: Academic Press.

Reys, B. J., & Reys, R. E. (1987). Calculators in the classroom: How can we make it happen? *Arithmetic Teacher, 34*(6), 12–14.

Reys, B. J., & Reys, R. E. (1995). Japanese mathematics education: What makes it work. *Teaching Children Mathematics, 1,* 474–475.

Reys, B. J., Robinson, E., Sconiers, S., & Mark, J. (1999). Mathematics curricula based on rigorous national standards: What, why, and how? *Phi Delta Kappan, 80,* 454–456.

Reys, R. E., & Reys, B. J. (1983). *Guide to using estimation skills and strategies (GUESS)* (Boxes I and II). White Plains, NY: Cuisenaire-Dale Seymour.

Robitaille, D. F., Beaton, A. E., & Plomp, T. (Eds.) (2000). *The impact of TIMSS on the teaching and learning of mathematics and science.* Vancouver: Pacific Educational Press.

Robitaille, D. F., Taylor, A. R., & Orpwood, G. (1996). *The TIMMS-Canada report Volume 1: grade 8.* Vancouver, Canada: University of British Columbia.

Robitaille, D. F., Taylor, A. R., & Orpwood, G. (1996). *The TIMMS-Canada report Volume 2: grade 4.* Vancouver, Canada: University of British Columbia.

Rolheiser, C., Bower, B. & Stevahn, L. (2000). *The Portfolio Organizer.* Alexandria, VA: Association for Supervision and Curriculum Development.

Ross, S. H. (1986). *The development of children's place–value numeration concepts in grades two through five.* Paper presented at the annual meeting of the American Educational Research Association, San Francisco. (ERIC Document Reproduction Service No. ED 2773 482)

Ross, S. H. (1989). Parts, wholes, and place value: A developmental perspective. *Arithmetic Teacher, 36*(6), 47–51.

Rowan, T. E. (1995, March). *Helping children construct mathematical understanding with IMPACT.* Paper presented at the regional meeting of the National Council of Teachers of Mathematics, Chicago.

Rowan, T. E., & Bourne, B. (1994). *Thinking like mathematicians: Putting the K–4 Standards into practice.* Portsmouth, NH: Heinemann.

Runion, G. E. (1990). *The golden section.* White Plains, NY: Cuisenaire-Dale Seymour.

Russell, S. J. (1997, April). *Using video to study students' strategies for whole-number operations.* Paper presented at the annual meeting of the National Council of Teachers of Mathematics, Minneapolis, MN.

Russell, S. J., & Corwin, R. B. (1990). *Sorting: Groups and graphs.* A unit of study for grades 2–3 from *Used numbers: Real data in the classroom.* White Plains, NY: Cuisenaire-Dale Seymour.

Saskatchewan Education. (1996). *Mathematics 6-9: A Curriculum Guide for the Middle Level.* Saskatchewan: Saskatchewan Education.

Scheer, J. K. (1980). The etiquette of diagnosis. *Arithmetic Teacher, 27*(9), 18–19.

Schifter, D., Bastable, V., & Russell, S. J. (1999a). *Developing mathematical ideas: Numbers and operations, Part 1: Building a system of tens* (Casebook). White Plains, NY: Cuisenaire-Dale Seymour.

Schifter, D., Bastable, V., & Russell, S. J. (1999b). *Developing mathematical ideas: Numbers and operations, Part 2: Making meaning for operations* (Casebook). White Plains, NY: Cuisenaire-Dale Seymour.

Schifter, D., Bastable, V., & Russell, S. J. (1999c). *Developing mathematical ideas: Numbers and operations, Part 2: Making meaning for operations* (Facilitator's guide). White Plains, NY: Cuisenaire-Dale Seymour.

Schifter, D., & Fosnot, C. T. (1993). *Reconstructing mathematics education: Stories of teachers meeting the challenge of reform.* New York: Teachers College Press.

Schmidt, W. H., McKnight, C. C., & Raizen, S. A. (1996). *Executive summary of a splintered vision: An investigation of U.S. science and mathematics education.* Boston: Kluwer.

Schoenfeld, A. H. (1988). What's all the fuss about metacognition? In A. H. Schoenfeld (Ed.), *Cognitive science and mathematics education* (pp. 189–215). Mahwah, NJ: Erlbaum.

Schoenfeld, A. H. (1992). Learning to think mathematically: Problem solving, metacognition, and sense making in mathematics. In D. A. Grouws (Ed.), *Handbook of research on teaching and learning* (pp. 334–370). Old Tappan, NJ: Macmillan.

Schoenfeld, A. H. (1994). Reflections on doing and teaching mathematics. In A. H. Schoenfeld (Ed.), *Mathematical thinking and problem solving* (pp. 53–70). Mahwah, NJ: Erlbaum.

Schroeder, T. L., & Lester, E. K., Jr. (1989). Developing understanding in mathematics via problem solving. In P. R. Trafton (Ed.), *New directions for elementary school mathematics* (pp. 31–42). Reston, VA: National Council of Teachers of Mathematics.

Schwartz, L. M., & Willing, K. R. (2001). *Computer activities for the cooperative classroom.* Markham, Ontario: Pembroke Publishers.

Schwartz, S. L. (1996). Hidden messages in teacher talk: Praise and empowerment. *Teaching Children Mathematics, 2,* 396–401.

Sconyers, J. M. (1995). Proof and the middle school mathematics student. *Mathematics Teaching in the Middle School, 1,* 516–518.

Seymour, D. (1971). *Tangramath.* Chicago: Creative Publications.

Sheffield, L. J. (1999). Serving the needs of the mathematically promising. In L. J. Sheffield (Ed.), *Developing mathematically promising students* (pp. 43–55). Reston, VA: National Council of Teachers of Mathematics.

Sheffield, S. (1995). *Math and literature, K–3* (Vol. 2). Sausalito, CA: Math Solutions Publications.

Silver, E. A., Smith, M. S., & Nelson, B. S. (1995). The QUASAR project: Equity concerns meet mathematics education reform in the middle school. In W. G. Secada, E. Fennema, & L. B. Adajian (Eds.), *New directions for equity in mathematics education* (pp. 9–56). New York: Cambridge University Press.

Silver, E. A., & Stein, M. K. (1996). The QUASAR project: The "revolution of the possible" in mathematics instructional reform in urban middle schools. *Urban Education, 30,* 476–521.

Simmt, E. (1996). {Parents} (children} {mathematics}: researching the intersection. In Y.M. Pothier (Ed.), *Proceedings of the Canadian Mathematics Educational Study Group,* 99–109.

Simmt, E. (1998). Reflections on an extracurricular parent-child mathematics program. *delta-K, 35*(1), 56–60.

Simon, M. A. (1995). Reconstructing mathematics pedagogy from a constructivist perspective. *Journal for Research in School Mathematics, 26,* 114–145.

Skemp, R. (1978). Relational understanding and instrumental understanding. *Arithmetic Teacher, 26*(3), 9–15.

Smith, J. P., III. (1996). Efficacy and teaching mathematics by telling: A challenge for reform. *Journal for Research in Mathematics Education, 27,* 387–402.

Smith, J. P., III. (2002). The development of students' knowledge of fractions and ratios. In B. Litwiller (Ed.), *Making sense of fractions, ratios, and proportions* (pp. 3–17). Reston, VA: National Council of Teachers of Mathematics.

Steffe, L. (1988). Children's construction of number sequences and multiplying schemes. In J. C. Hiebert & M. J. Behr (Eds.), *Number concepts and operations in the middle grades* (pp. 119–140). Mahwah, NJ: Erlbaum.

Stein, M. K., Grover, B. W., & Henningsen, M. (1996). Building student capacity for mathematical thinking and reasoning: An analysis of mathematical tasks used in reform classrooms. *American Educational Research journal, 33,* 455–488.

Stein, M. K., & Lane, S. (1996). Instructional tasks and the development of student capacity to think and reason: An analysis of the relationship between teaching and learning in a reform mathematics project. *Educational Research and Evaluation, 2,* 50–58.

Steinberg, R. M. (1985). Instruction on derived facts strategies in addition and subtraction. *Journal for Research in Mathematics Education, 16,* 337–355.

Stenmark, J. K. (1989). *Assessment alternatives in mathematics: An overview of assessment techniques that promote learning.* Berkeley: EQUALS, University of California.

Stenmark, J. K. (Ed.). (1991). *Mathematics assessment: Myths, models, good questions, and practical suggestions.* Reston, VA: National Council of Teachers of Mathematics.

Stiles, C. (1992). Journals as a tool for assessment. *Research Forum, 9,* 20–22.

Stoessiger, R., & Edmunds, J. (1992). *Natural learning and mathematics.* Portsmouth, NH: Heinemann.

Strutchens, M. E., & Blume, G. W. (1997). What do students know about geometry? In P. A. Kenney & E. A. Silver (Eds.), *Results from the sixth mathematics assessment of the National Assessment of Educational Progress* (pp. 165–193). Reston, VA: National Council of Teachers of Mathematics.

Taylor, A. R. & Tubianosa, T. S. (2001). *Student assessment in Canada.* Kelowna, BC: Society For The Advancement of Excellence in Education.

Teach Magazine, (2002). Curricula: the math-art project [Incorporating nautilus fossils] [Pines Senior Public School, Clarke Township], *Teach Magazine.*

Theissen, D., Matthias, M., & Smith, J. (1998). *The wonderful world of mathematics: A critically annotated list of childrens' books in mathematics* (2nd ed.). Reston, VA: National Council of Teachers of Mathematics.

Thompson, C. S. (1990). Place value and larger numbers. In J. N. Payne (Ed.), *Mathematics for the young child* (pp. 89–108). Reston, VA: National Council of Teachers of Mathematics.

Thompson, C. S., & Hendrickson, A. D. (1986). Verbal addition and subtraction problems: Some difficulties and some solutions. *Arithmetic Teacher, 33*(7), 21–25.

Thompson, C. S., & Van de Walle, J. A. (1984). The power of 10. *Arithmetic Teacher, 32*(3), 6–11.

Thompson, D. R., Austin, R. A., & Beckmann, C. E. (2002). Using literature as a vehicle to explore proportional reasoning. In B. Litwiller (Ed.), *Making sense of fractions, ratios, and proportions* (pp.130–137). Reston, VA: National Council of Teachers of Mathematics.

Thompson, E. W. (1994). Concrete materials and teaching for mathematical understanding. *Arithmetic Teacher, 41,* 556–558.

Thompson, P. W., & Thompson, A. G. (1994). Talking about rates conceptually, Part 1: A teacher's struggle. *Journal for Research in Mathematics Education, 25,* 279–303.

Thornton, C. A. (1982). Doubles up—easy! *Arithmetic Teacher, 29*(8), 20.

Thornton C. A. (1990). Strategies for the basic facts. In J. N. Payne (Ed.), *Mathematics for the young child* (pp. 133–151). Reston, VA: National Council of Teachers of Mathematics.

Thornton, C. A., & Bley, N. S. (Eds.). (1994). *Windows of opportunity: Mathematics for students with special needs* (pp. 19–39). Reston, VA: National Council of Teachers of Mathematics.

Thornton, C. A., & Noxon, C. (1977). *Look into the facts* (4 vols.). Chicago: Creative Publications.

Thornton, C. A., & Toohey, M. A. (1984). *A matter of facts* (4 vols.). Chicago: Creative Publications.

Trafton, P. R., & Claus, A. S. (1994). A changing curriculum for a changing age. In C. A. Thornton, & N. S. Bley (Eds.), *Windows of opportunity: Mathematics for students with special needs* (pp. 19–39). Reston, VA: National Council of Teachers of Mathematics.

Troutner, J. (2002). Web wonders: mathematics. *Teacher Librarian, 29* (3) pp. 40–41.

Tsuruda, G. (1994). *Putting it together: Middle school math in transition.* Portsmouth, NH: Heinemann.

Tyrrell, J., Brown, C., Ellis, J., Fox, R., Kinley, R., & Reilly, B. (1994). Gender and mathematics: Equal access to successful learning. In J. Neyland (Ed.), *Mathematics education: A handbook for teachers* (Vol. 1, pp. 330–347). Wellington, New Zealand: Wellington College of Education.

Tzur, R. (1999). An integrated study of children's construction of improper fractions and the teacher's role in promoting learning. *Journal for Research in Mathematics Education, 30,* 390–416.

University of Chicago School Mathematics Project. (1999, Spring). Frequently asked questions about our materials. *UCSMP Newsletter, 25,* 2–3.

U.S. Department of Education, Office of Educational Research and Improvement. (1996). *Pursuing excellence: A study of U.S. eighth grade mathematics and science teaching, learning, curriculum, and achievement in international context.* LACES 97–198. Washington, DC: U.S. Government Printing Office.

U.S. Department of Education, Office of Educational Research and Improvement. (1997a). *Introduction to TIMSS.* Washington, DC: U.S. Government Printing Office.

U.S. Department of Education, Office of Educational Research and Improvement. (1997b). *Moderator's guide to eighth grade mathematics lessons: United States, Japan, and Germany.* Washington, DC: U.S. Government Printing Office.

U.S. Department of Education, Office of Educational Research and Improvement. (1997c). *Pursuing excellence: A study of U.S. fourth-grade mathematics and science achievement in international context.* LACES 97–255. Washington, DC: U.S, Government Printing Office.

Usiskin, Z. (1988). Conceptions of school algebra and uses of variables. In A. F Coxford (Ed.), *The ideas of algebra, K–12* (pp. 8–19). Reston, VA: National Council of Teachers of Mathematics.

Usiskin, Z. (1993). If everybody counts, why do so few survive? In G. Cuevas & M. Driscol (Eds.), *Reaching all students with mathematics* (pp. 7–22). Reston, VA: National Council of Teachers of Mathematics.

Usiskin, Z. (1999). The mathematically promising and the mathematically gifted. In L. J. Sheffield (Ed.), *Developing mathematically promising students* (pp. 57–69). Reston, VA: National Council of Teachers of Mathematics.

Varney, S. (1992-93). Using calculators in the early primary classroom. *Prime Areas, 35*(3), 17–21.

von Glasersfeld, E., (1990). An exposition of constructivism: Why some like it radical. In R. B. Davis, C. A. Maher, & N. Noddings (Eds.), *Constructivist views on the teaching and learning of mathematics* (pp. 19–29). Reston, VA: National Council of Teachers of Mathematics.

Weininger, O. (1991). *Third-R structures: the math research program in primary grades.* Toronto: Ontario Institute for Studies in Education.

Welchman-Tischler, R. (1992). *How to use children's literature to teach mathematics.* Reston, VA: National Council of Teachers of Mathematics.

Wheatley, G. H., & Hersberger, J. (1986). A calculator estimation activity In H. Schoen (Ed.), *Estimation and mental computation* (pp. 182–185). Reston, VA: National Council of Teachers of Mathematics.

Whiteley, W. (1999). Mathematics Lecture II: The decline and rise of geometry in 20th century north america. In J. Grant McLoughlin (Ed.), *Proceedings of the Canadian Mathematics Education Study Group,* (7–21).

Whitin, D. J., & Whitin, P. E. (1998). The "write" way to mathematical understanding. In L. J. Morrow (Ed.), *The teaching and learning of algorithms in*

school mathematics (pp. 161–169). Reston, VA: National Council of Teachers of Mathematics.

Whitin, D. J., & Wilde, S. (1992). *Read any good math lately? Children's books for mathematical learning, K–6.* Portsmouth, NH: Heinemann.

Whitin, D. J., & Wilde, S. (1995). *It's the story that counts: More children's books for mathematical learning, K–6.* Portsmouth, NH: Heinemann.

Williamson, M. E. (1991). *Implementing metacognitive processing in the mathematics classroom.* Unpublished master's thesis, University of British Columbia Vancouver, Canada.

Willoughby, S. S. (1990). *Mathematics education in a changing world.* Alexandria, VA: Association for Supervision and Curriculum Development.

Winter, M. J., Lappan, G., Phillips, E., & Fitzgerald, W. (1986). *Middle grades mathematics project: Spatial visualization.* Menlo Park, CA: AWL Supplemental.

Wirtz, R. (1974). *Mathematics for everyone.* Washington, DC: Curriculum Development Associates.

Wisnia, L., & Rutherford, S. (1993-94). Whole math: exploring the possibilities. *Prime Areas, 36* (1), 76–82.

Wood, T., Cobb, E., Yackel, E., & Dillon, D. (Eds.). (1993). *Rethinking elementary school mathematics: Insights and issues (Journal for Research in Mathematics Education* Monograph No. 6). Reston, VA: National Council of Teachers of Mathematics.

Wood, T., & Setters, P. (1996). Assessment of a problem-centered mathematics program: Third grade. *Journal for Research in Mathematics Education, 27,* 337–353.

Wood, T., & Setters, P. (1997). Deepening the analysis: Longitudinal assessment of a problem–centered mathematics program. *Journal for Research in Mathematics Education, 28,* 163–168.

Yackel, E., Cobb, P., Wood, T., Wheatley, G. H., & Merkel, G. (1990). The importance of social interaction in children's construction of mathematical knowledge. In T. J. Cooney (Ed.), *Teaching and learning mathematics in the 1990s* (pp. 12–21). Reston, VA: National Council of Teachers of Mathematics.

Children's Literature

Anno, M. (1982). *Anno's counting house.* New York: Philomel Books.

Anno, M. (1994). *Anno's magic seeds.* New York: Philomel Books.

Anno, M., & Anno, M. (1983). *Anno's mysterious multiplying jar.* New York: Philomel Books.

Ash, R. (1996). *Incredible comparisons.* New York: Dorling Kindersley.

Briggs, R. (1970). *Jim and the beanstalk.* New York: Coward–McCann.

Carle, E. (1969). *The very hungry caterpillar.* New York: Putnam.

Chalmers, M. (1986). *Six dogs, twenty-three cats, forty-five mice, and one hundred sixteen spiders.* New York: HarperCollins.

Chwast, S. (1993). *The twelve circus rings.* San Diego, CA: Gulliver Books.

Clement, R. (1991). *Counting on Frank.* Milwaukee: Gareth Stevens.

Cushman, R. (1991). *Do you wanna bet? Your chance to find out about probability.* New York: Clarion Books.

Dee, R. (1988). *Two ways to count to ten.* New York: Holt.

Friedman, A. (1994). *The king's commissioners.* New York: Scholastic.

Gag, W. (1928). *Millions of cats.* New York: Coward–McCann.

Giganti, P. (1988). *How many snails? A counting book.* New York: Greenwillow.

Giganti, P. (1992). *Each orange had 8 slices.* New York: Greenwillow.

Hoban, T. (1981). *More than one.* New York: Greenwillow.

Hutchins, P. (1986). *The doorbell rang.* New York: Greenwillow.

Jaspersohn, W. (1993). *Cookies.* Old Tappan, NJ: Macmillan.

Juster, N. (1961). *The phantom tollbooth.* New York: Random House.

Lobal, A. (1970). *Frog and Toad are friends.* New York: HarperCollins.

Mathews, L. (1979). *Gator pie.* New York: Dodd, Mead.

McKissack, P. C. (1992). *A million fish ... more or less.* New York: Knopf.

Munsch, R. (1987). *Moira's birthday.* Toronto: Annick Press.

Myller, R. (1990). *How big is a foot?* New York: Dell.

Norton, M. (1953). *The borrowers.* Orlando, FL: Harcourt Brace.

Parker, T. (1984). *In one day.* Boston: Houghton Mifflin.

Pluckrose, H. (1988). *Pattern.* New York: Franklin Watts.

St. John, G. (1975). *How to count like a Martian.* New York: Walck.

Schwartz, D. M. (1985). *How much is a million?* New York: Lothrop, Lee & Shepard.

Schwartz, D. M. (1989). *If you made a million.* New York: Lothrop, Lee & Shepard.

Schwartz, D. M. (1999). *If you hopped like a frog.* New York: Scholastic.

Scieszka, J., & Smith, L. (1995). *Math curse.* New York: Viking Penguin.

Shannat, M. W. (1979). *The 329th friend.* New York: Four Winds Press.

Silverstein, S. (1974). One inch tall. In *Where the sidewalk ends* (p. 55). New York: HarperCollins.

Tahan, M. (1993). *The man who counted: A collection of mathematical adventures.* (Trans. L. Clark & A. Reid). New York: Norton.

Wells, R. E. (1993). *Is a blue whale the biggest thing there is?* Morton Grove, IL: Whitman.

Wolkstein, D. (1972). *8,000 stones.* New York: Doubleday.

Computer Software

Broderbund. (1995a). *James discovers math.* Novato, CA: Author.

Broderbund. (1995b). *Tabletop, Jr.* Novato, CA: Author.

Broderbund. (1996a). *Kid pix.* Novato, CA: Author.

Broderbund. (1996b). *Logical journey of the Zoombinis.* Novato, CA: Author.

Clements, D. H., & Meredith, J. S. (1994). *Turtle math.* Highgate Springs, VT: Logo Computer Systems.

Clements, D. H., & Sarama, J. (1995). *Shapes: Mathematical thinking.* Highgate Springs, VT: Logo Computer Systems.

Davidson & Associates. (n.d.). *Math for the real world.* Torrence, CA: Author.

Davidson & Associates. (n.d.). *Mega math blaster.* Torrence, CA: Author.

Edmark Corp. (1993). *Millie's math house.* Redmond, WA: Author.

Edmark Corp. (1996). *GeoComputer.* Redmond, WA: Author.

Education Development Center. (1991). *My travels with Gulliver.* Scotts Valley, CA: Wings for Learning.

EduQuest. (1994). *Math and more 3: Patterns on lattices.* Atlanta: IBM Corp.

EdVenture Software. (1997). *Gold medal mathematics.* Norwalk, CT: Author.

Gamco Education Software. (1994). *Word problem square off.* Clayton, MO: Siboney Learning Group.

Hickey, A. (1996). *Unifix software.* Rowley, MA: Didax Educational Resources.

Jazz Interactive. (n.d.). *Performance math.* Glenview, IL: Scott Foresman-Addison Wesley

Key Curriculum Press. (1995). *The geometer's sketchpad* (Version 3.0). Emeryville, CA: Author.

Learning Co. (1996). *The new adventures of Jasper Woodbury.* Mahwah, NJ: Author.

Learning Co. (1999). *Kid pix 2.* Mahwah, NJ: Author.

LOGAL Educational Software and Systems. (1994a). *Geometry. inventor.* Cambridge, MA: Author.

LOGAL Educational Software and Systems. (1994b). *The probability constructor.* Cambridge, MA: Author.

MacWarehouse. (1996). *Power Rangers ZEO: Power active math.* Lakewood, NJ: Author.

MECC. (1994). *TesselMania!* Minneapolis, MN: Author.

MECC. (1995a). *MathKeys: Geometry, Vol. 1.* Minneapolis, MN: Author.

MECC. (1995b). *MathKeys: Unlocking whole numbers, grades 3–5.* Minneapolis, MN: Author.

MECC. (1995c). *MathKeys: Unlocking probability (Vols. 1 & 2).* Minneapolis, MN: Author.

MECC. (1995d). *Math munchers deluxe.* Minneapolis, MN: Author.

MECC. (1995e). *TesselMania! Deluxe.* Minneapolis, MN: Author.

MECC. (1996a). *MathKeys: Unlocking fractions and decimals, grades 3–5.* Minneapolis, MN: Author.

MECC. (1996b). *MathKeys: Unlocking whole numbers, grades K–2.* Minneapolis, MN: Author.

O'Brien, T. C. (n.d.). *Teasers by Tobbs: Numbers and operations.* Pleasantville, NY: Sunburst Communications.

Pierian Spring Software. (1996). *CampOS math.* Portland, OR: Author.

SkillsBank Corp. (1996). *CornerStone mathematics, grades 3–8.* Baltimore, MD: Author.

SRA/McGraw-Hill. (1996). *The SRA crunches.* Columbus, OH: Author.

Sunburst Communications. (1995). *Shape up.* Pleasantville, NY: Author.

Sunburst Communications. (n.d.). *The king's rule.* Pleasantville, NY: Author.

Sunburst Communications. (n.d.). *Super factory.* Pleasantville, NY: Author.

Tenth Planet. (1997). *Grouping and place value.* Pleasantville, NY: Sunburst Communications.

Tenth Planet. (1998a). *Combining and breaking apart numbers.* Pleasantville, NY: Sunburst Communications.

Tenth Planet. (1998b). *Fraction operations.* Pleasantville, NY: Sunburst Communications.

Tenth Planet. (1998c). *Number meanings and counting.* Pleasantville, NY: Sunburst Communications.

Tenth Planet. (1998d). *Representing fractions.* Pleasantville, NY: Sunburst Communications.

Texas Instruments. (1994). *Cabri geometry II.* Dallas: Author.

Tom Snyder Productions. (1993). *The graph club.* Watertown, MA: Author.

Tom Snyder Productions. (1998). *Fizz & Martina's math adventures: Lights, camera, fractions.* Watertown, MA: Author.

Tom Snyder Productions. (1999). *Prime time math.* Watertown, MA: Author.

Index

Blackline Masters and Materials Construction Tips

Permission is given to reproduce any of the Blackline Masters for classroom use. Pages are perforated.

Suggestions for Use and Construction of Materials

Card Stock Materials

A good way to have many materials made quickly and easily for students is to have them duplicated on card stock at a photocopy store. Card stock is a heavy paper that comes in a variety of colours. It is also called *cover stock* or *index stock*. The price is about twice that of paper.

Card stock can be laminated and then cut into smaller pieces if desired. The laminate adheres very well. Laminate first, and then cut into pieces afterward. Otherwise you will need to cut each piece twice.

Materials are best kept in plastic bags with zip-type closures. Freezer bags are recommended for durability. Punch a hole near the top of the bag so that you do not store air. Lots of small bags can be stuffed into the largest bags. You can always see what you have stored in the bags.

The following list is a suggestion for materials that can be made from card stock using the masters in this section. Quantity suggestions are also given.

Dot Cards

One complete set of cards will serve four to six children. Duplicate each set in a different colour so that mixed sets can be separated easily. Laminate and then cut with a paper cutter.

Five-Frames and Ten-Frames

Five-frames and ten-frames are best duplicated on light-coloured card stock. Do not laminate; if you do, the mats will curl and counters will slide around.

10 × 10 Multiplication Array

Make one per student in any colour. Lamination is suggested. Provide each student with an L-shaped piece of tagboard.

Base-Ten Pieces (Centimetre Grid)

Use the grid (number 11) to make a master as directed. Run copies on white card stock. One sheet will make 4 hundreds and 10 tens or 4 hundreds and a lot of ones. Mount the printed card stock on white poster board using either a dry-mount press or permanent spray adhesive. (Spray adhesive can be purchased in art supply stores. It is very effective but messy to handle.) Cut into pieces with a paper cutter. For the tens and ones pieces, it is recommended that you mount the index stock onto *mount board* or *illustration board,* also available in art supply stores. This material is thicker and will make the pieces easier to handle. It is recommended that you *not* laminate the base-ten pieces. A kit consisting of 10 hundreds, 30 tens, and 30 ones is adequate for each student or pair of students.

Bean Stick Base-Ten Pieces

Use dried beans (great northern, pinto, etc.) to make bean sticks. Craft sticks can be purchased in craft stores in boxes of 500. Use white glue (such as Elmer's) or a glue gun. Also dribble a row of glue over the beans to keep them from splitting off the sticks. (The white glue dries clear.) For hundreds, use the master mounted on poster board.

Little Ten-Frames

There are two masters for these materials. One has full ten-frames and the other has 1 to 9 dots, including two with 5 dots. Copy the 1-to-9 master on one colour of card stock and the full ten-frames on another. Cut off most of the excess stock (do not trim) and then laminate. Cut into little ten-frames. Each set consists of 20 pieces: 10 full ten-frames and 10 of the 1-to-9 pieces, including 2 fives. Make a set for each child.

Place-Value Mat (with Ten-Frames)

Mats can be duplicated on any pastel card stock. It is recommended that you not laminate these because they tend to curl and counters slide around too much. Make one for every child.

One way to make a three-place place-value mat is simply to tape a half-sheet of blank card stock to the left edge of a two-place mat. Use strapping tape (filament tape used for packages). The tape will act as a hinge and permit the extra piece to be folded under for storage.

Circular Fraction Pieces

First make three copies of each page of the master. Cut the disks apart and tape onto blank pages with three of the same type on a page. You will then have a separate master for each size with three full circles per master. Duplicate each master on a different colour card stock. Laminate and then cut the circles out. A kit for one or two students should have two circles of each size piece.

Hundredths Disk

These disks can be made on paper but are much more satisfying on card stock. Duplicate the master on two contrasting colours. Laminate and cut the circles and also the slot on the dotted line. The smiley face is used as a decimal point on the desktop. Make a set for each student. It's easy and worthwhile.

Tangrams and Five Easy Pieces

Both tangrams and Five Easy Pieces should be copied on card stock and then laminated. Especially for younger children, the card stock should first be mounted on poster board to make the pieces a bit thicker and easier to put together in puzzles. You will want one set of each per student. Keep individual sets in plastic bags.

Woozle Cards

Copy the Woozle Card master on white or off-white card stock. You need two copies per set. Before laminating, colour one set one colour and the other a different colour. An easy way to colour the cards is to make one pass around the inside of each Woozle, leaving the rest of the creature white. If you colour the entire Woozle, the dots may not show up. Make one set for every four students.

Transparencies and Overhead Models

A copy of any page can be made into a transparency with thermal transparency masters and a transparency machine. (Check with your media specialist.) Photocopiers can also be used to make transparencies.

Some masters make fine transparency mats to use for demonstration purposes on the overhead. The 10×10 array, the blank hundreds board, and the large geo-board are examples. The five-frame and ten-frame work well with counters. The place-value mat can be used with strips and squares or with counters and cups directly on the overhead. The missing-part blank and the record blanks for the four algorithms are pages that you may wish to use as write-on transparencies. Of course, you will want to copy these and many other pages on paper for your students to write on.

A transparency of the 10 000 grid is the easiest way there is to show 10 000 or to model four-place decimal numbers. You will need to be careful in making the transparency. If too dark, the squares run together, and if too light, you will find that some squares do not reproduce. It can be done! If you pull the overhead away from the screen until the square is as large as possible, each tiny square can be seen across the average room and individual squares or strips of squares can be coloured with a pen.

All of the line and dot grids are useful to have available as transparencies. You may find it a good idea to make several copies of each and keep them in a folder where you can get to them easily.

For the Woozle Cards, dot cards, and little ten-frames, make a reduction of the master on a photocopy machine. Then make transparencies of the small cards, cut them apart, and use them on the overhead. The dot cards and little ten-frames are best on a coloured transparency. Use two colours for the little ten-frames. The Woozle Cards are best on a clear transparency. Colour them with a permanent transparency marker.

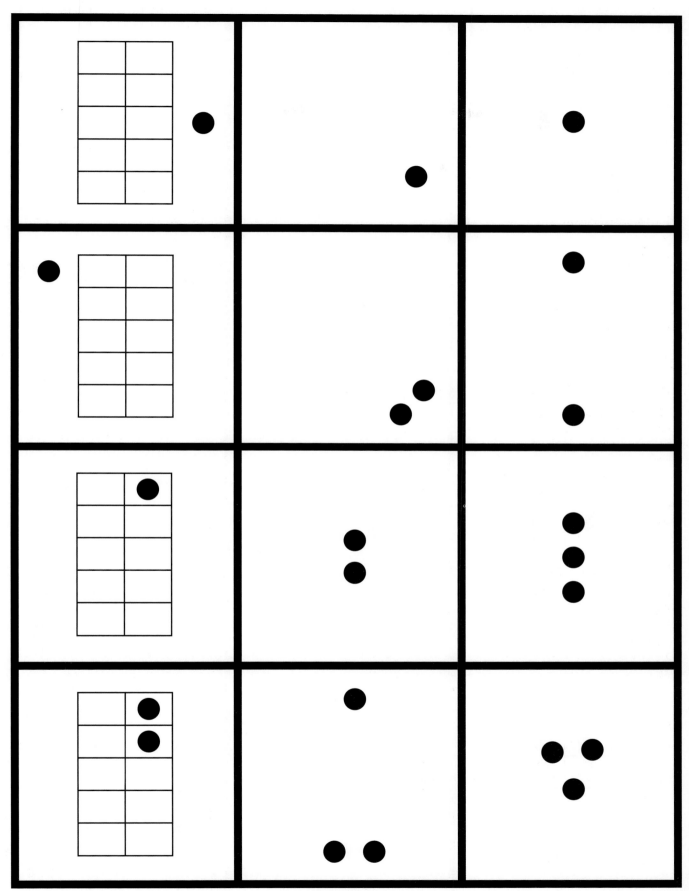

Dot cards— 1

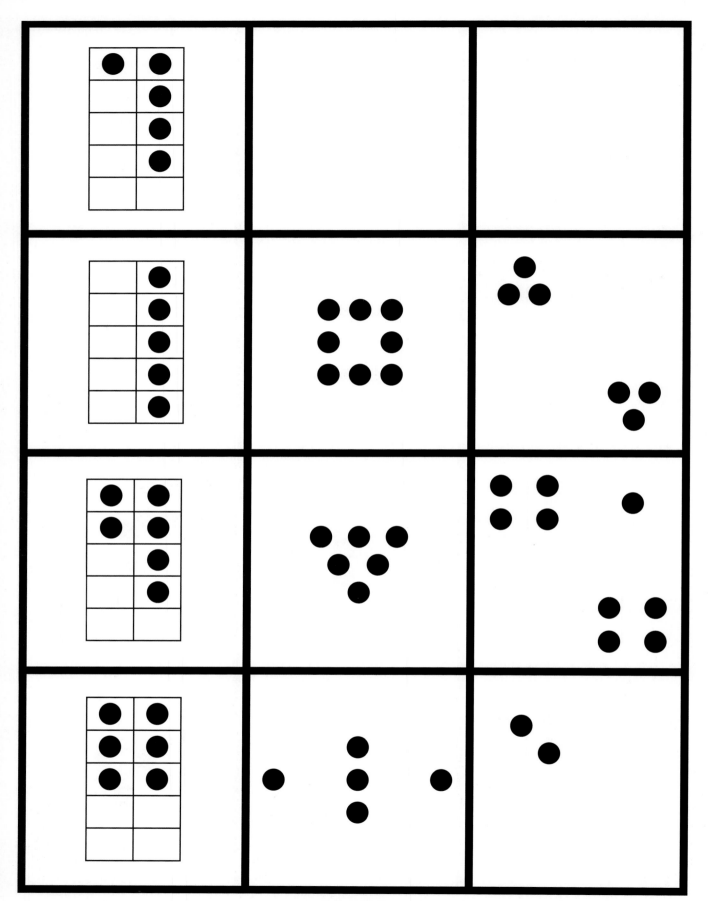

Dot cards—2

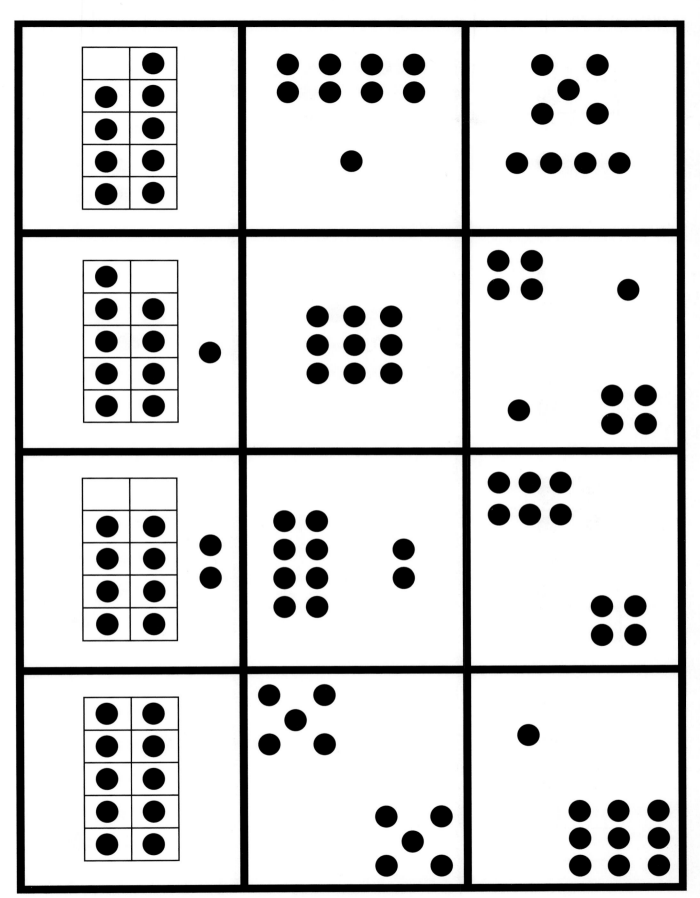

Dot cards—3

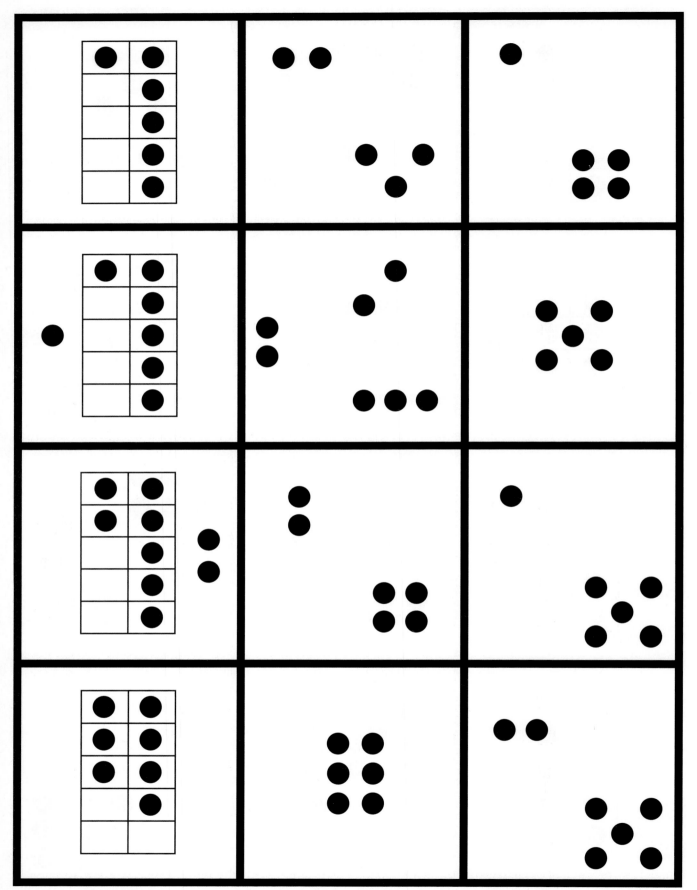

Dot cards—4

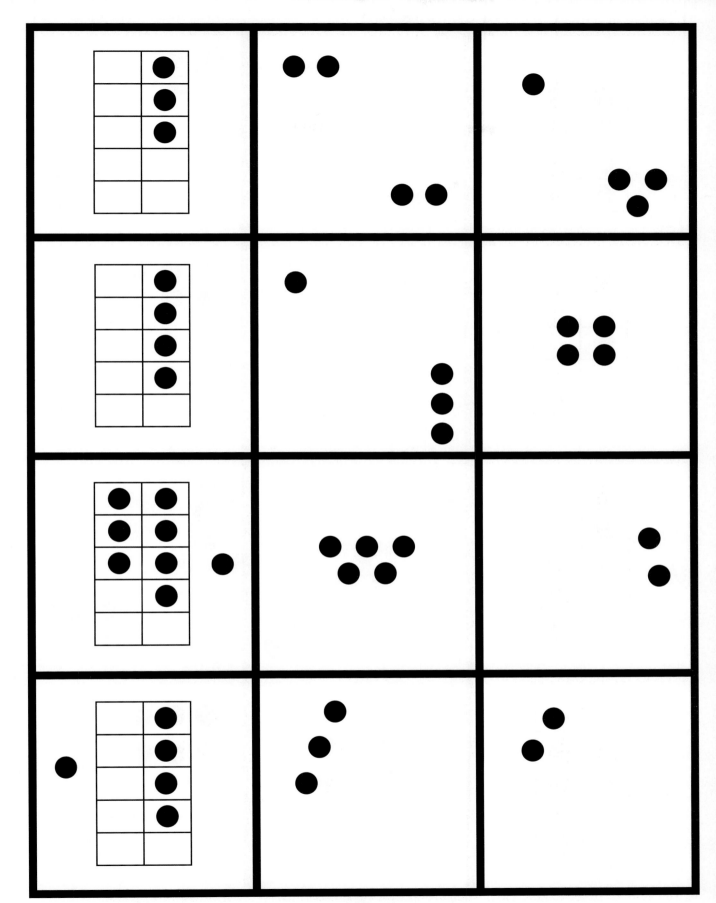

Dot cards—5

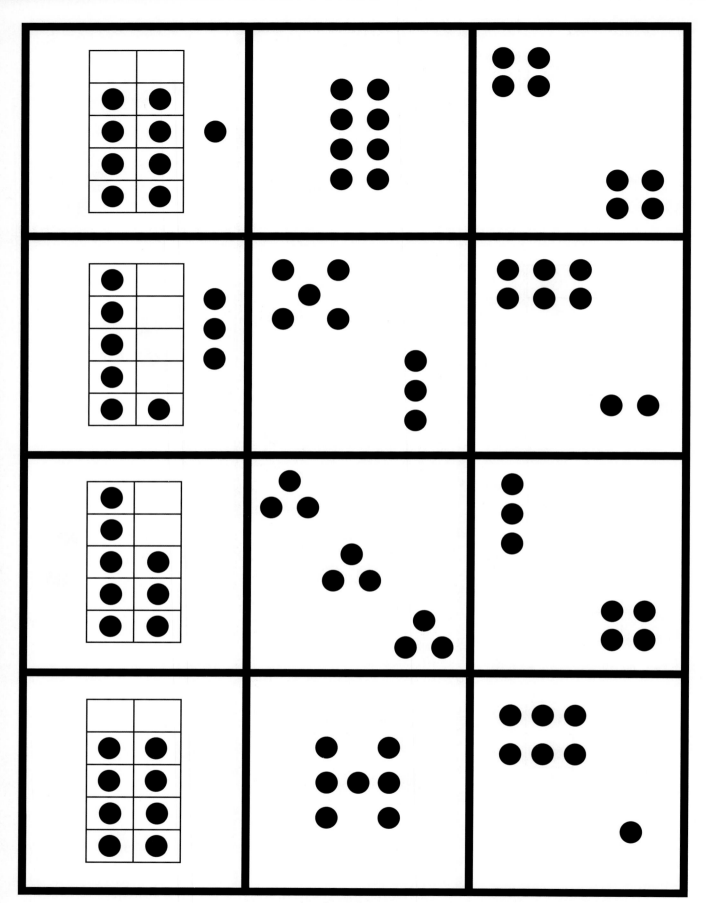

Dot cards—6

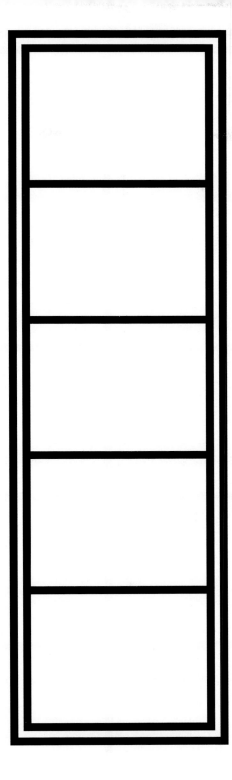

Five-frame—7

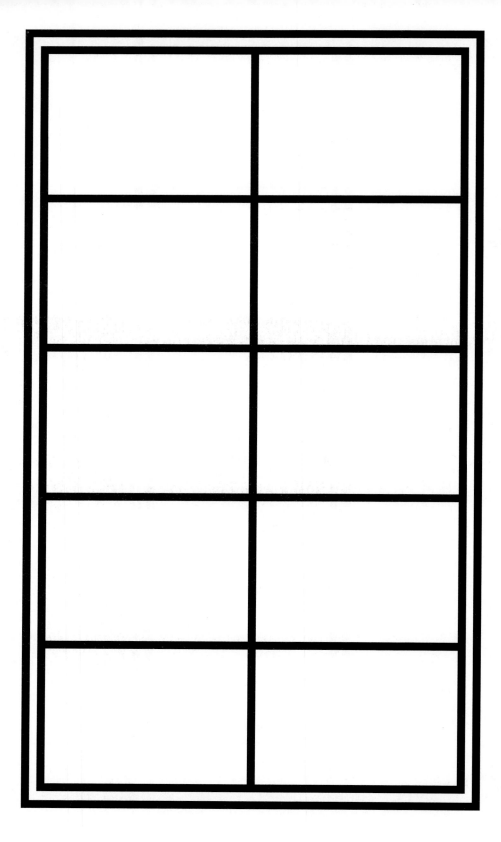

Ten-frame—8

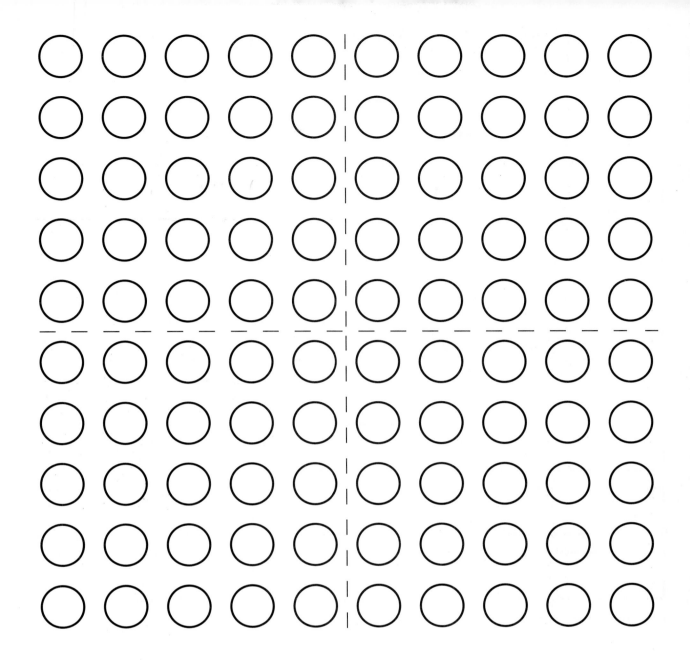

10 x 10 multiplication array—9

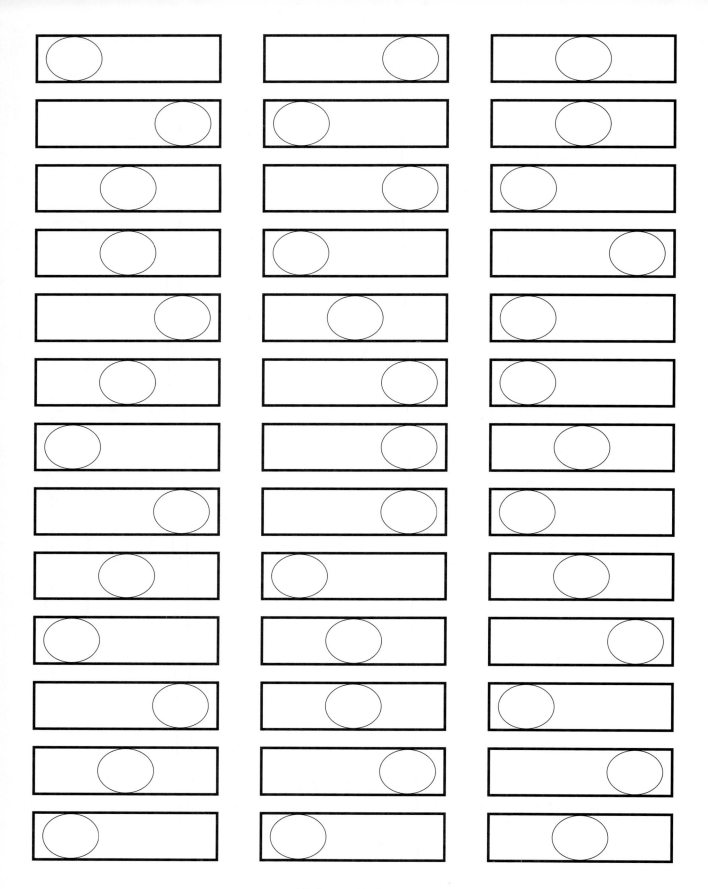

Missing-part blanks—10

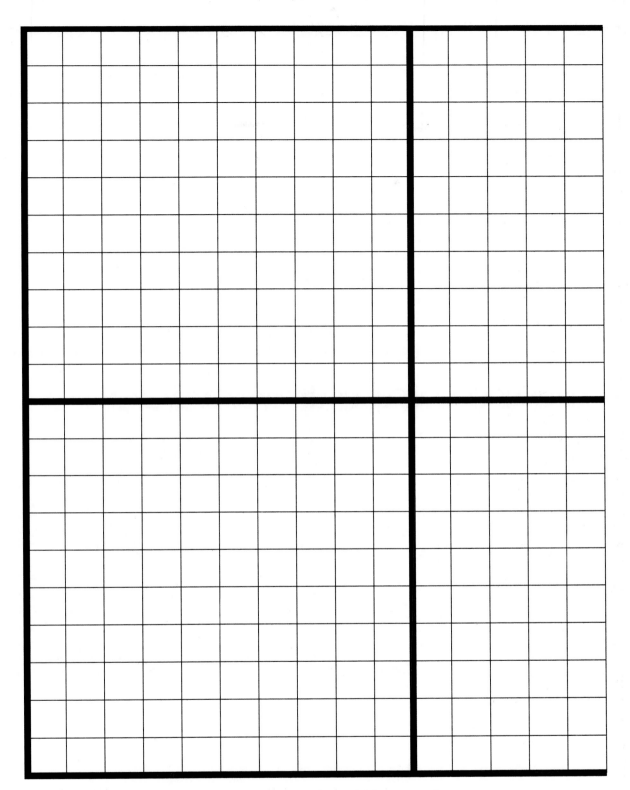

1. Make two copies of this page. Cut out the grid from each copy.
2. Overlap the two grids, and tape onto a blank sheet to form a 20-by-25-cm grid with 4 complete hundreds squares and 2 rows of 5 tens each.
3. Use this as a master to make copies on card stock.

Base-ten materials grid—11

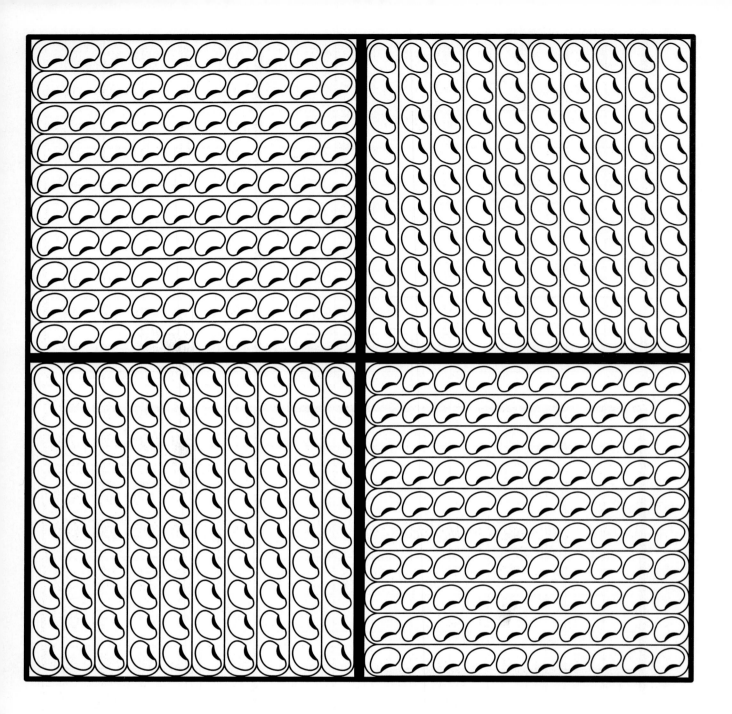

Hundreds master for bean stick base-ten pieces—12

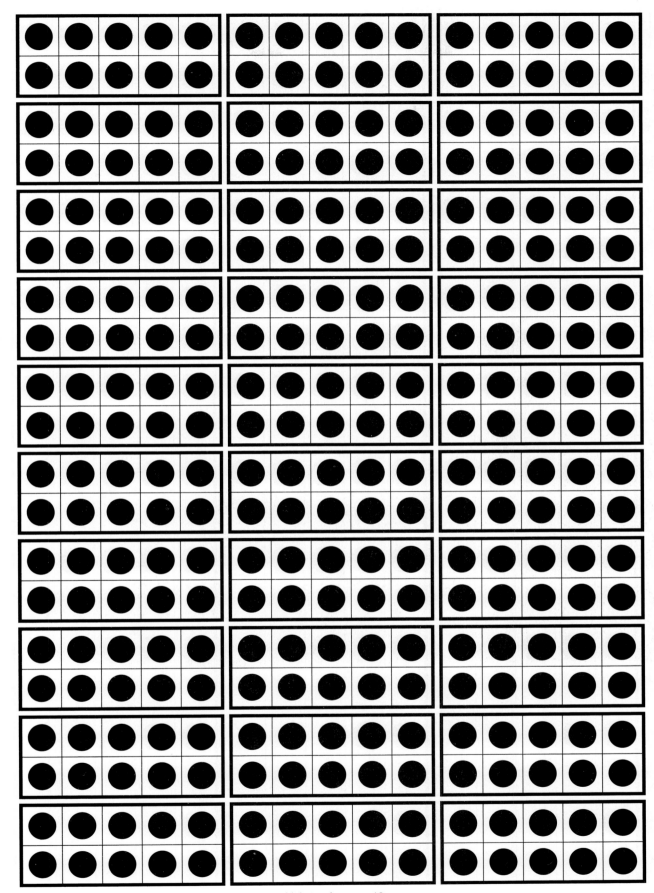

Little ten-frames—13

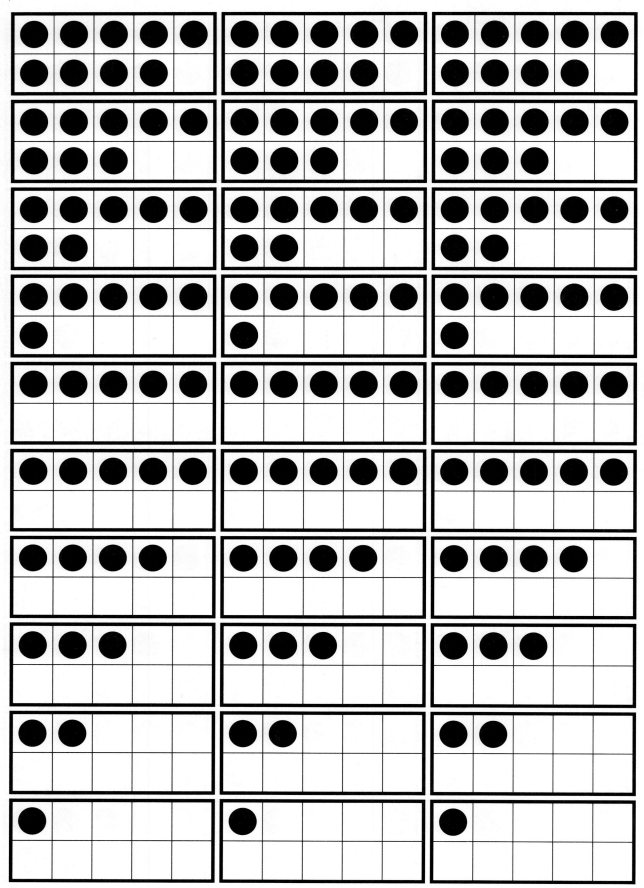

Little ten-frames—14

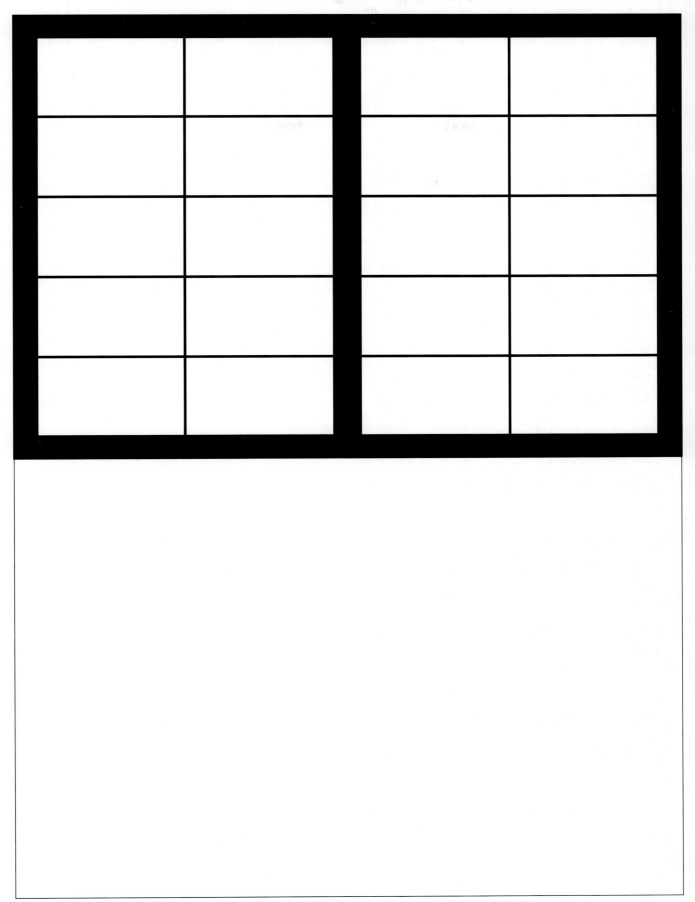

Place-value mat (with ten-frames)—15

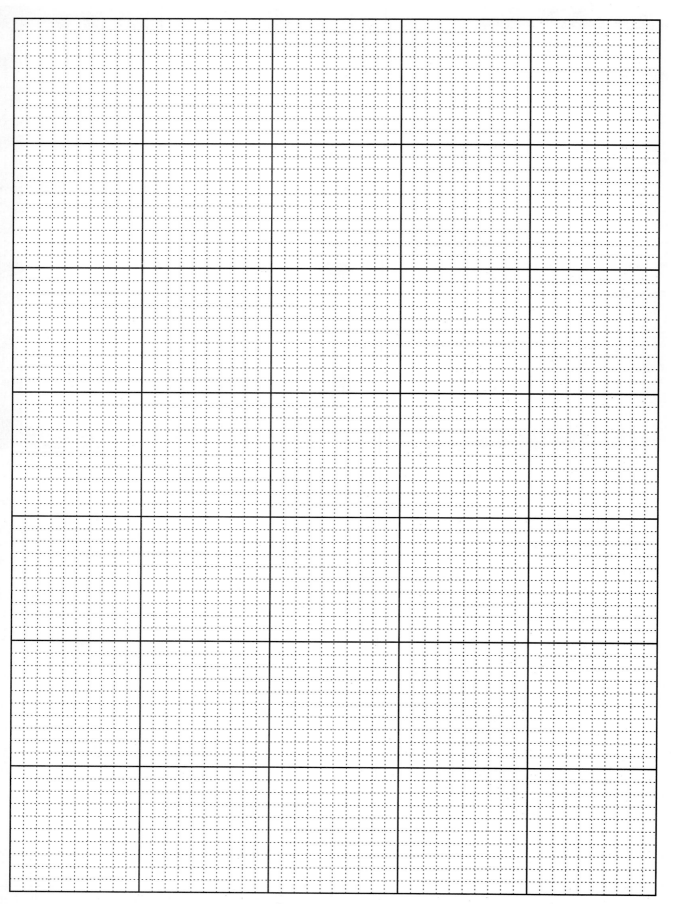

Base-ten grid paper—16

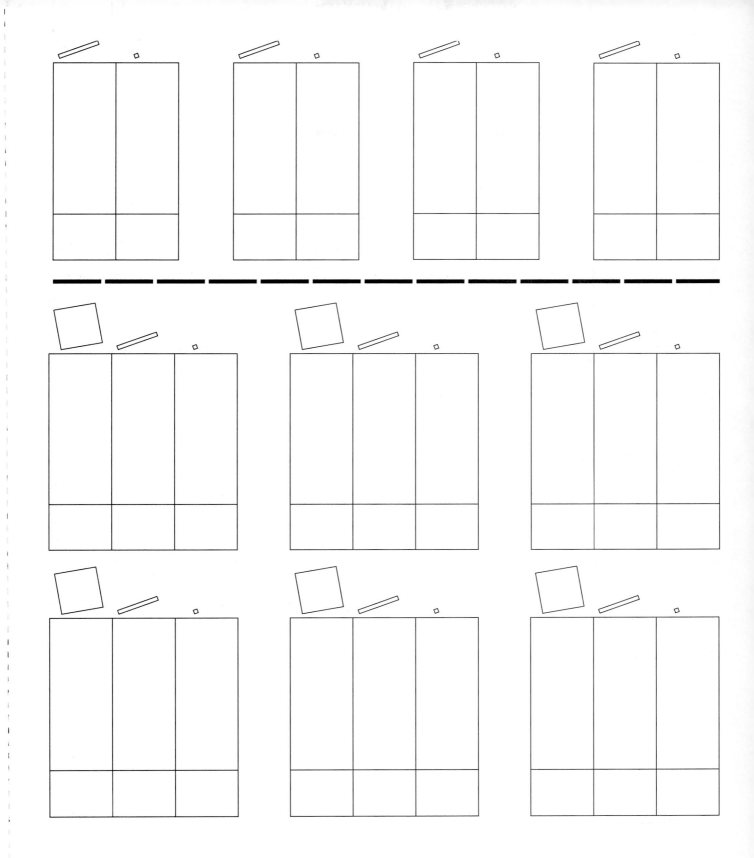

Addition and subtraction record blanks—17

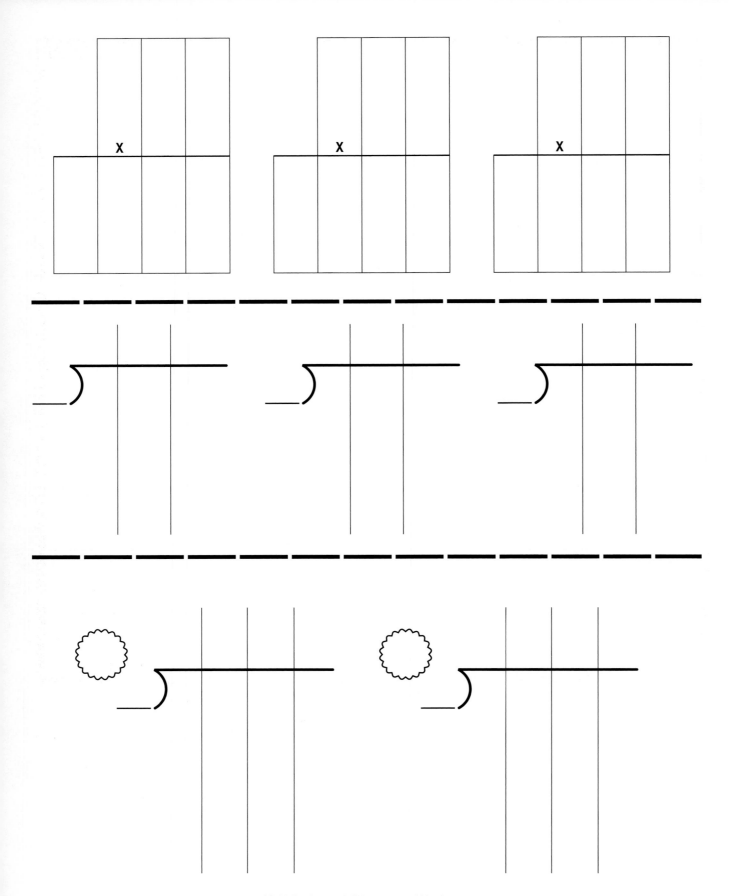

Multiplication and division record blanks—18

Blank 100 chart (10 × 10 square)—19

1	2	3	4	5	6	7	8	9	10
11	12	13	14	15	16	17	18	19	20
21	22	23	24	25	26	27	28	29	30
31	32	33	34	35	36	37	38	39	40
41	42	43	44	45	46	47	48	49	50
51	52	53	54	55	56	57	58	59	60
61	62	63	64	65	66	67	68	69	70
71	72	73	74	75	76	77	78	79	80
81	82	83	84	85	86	87	88	89	90
91	92	93	94	95	96	97	98	99	100

100 chart—20

1	2	3	4	5	6	7	8	9	10
11	12	13	14	15	16	17	18	19	20
21	22	23	24	25	26	27	28	29	30
31	32	33	34	35	36	37	38	39	40
41	42	43	44	45	46	47	48	49	50
51	52	53	54	55	56	57	58	59	60
61	62	63	64	65	66	67	68	69	70
71	72	73	74	75	76	77	78	79	80
81	82	83	84	85	86	87	88	89	90
91	92	93	94	95	96	97	98	99	100

1	2	3	4	5	6	7	8	9	10
11	12	13	14	15	16	17	18	19	20
21	22	23	24	25	26	27	28	29	30
31	32	33	34	35	36	37	38	39	40
41	42	43	44	45	46	47	48	49	50
51	52	53	54	55	56	57	58	59	60
61	62	63	64	65	66	67	68	69	70
71	72	73	74	75	76	77	78	79	80
81	82	83	84	85	86	87	88	89	90
91	92	93	94	95	96	97	98	99	100

1	2	3	4	5	6	7	8	9	10
11	12	13	14	15	16	17	18	19	20
21	22	23	24	25	26	27	28	29	30
31	32	33	34	35	36	37	38	39	40
41	42	43	44	45	46	47	48	49	50
51	52	53	54	55	56	57	58	59	60
61	62	63	64	65	66	67	68	69	70
71	72	73	74	75	76	77	78	79	80
81	82	83	84	85	86	87	88	89	90
91	92	93	94	95	96	97	98	99	100

1	2	3	4	5	6	7	8	9	10
11	12	13	14	15	16	17	18	19	20
21	22	23	24	25	26	27	28	29	30
31	32	33	34	35	36	37	38	39	40
41	42	43	44	45	46	47	48	49	50
51	52	53	54	55	56	57	58	59	60
61	62	63	64	65	66	67	68	69	70
71	72	73	74	75	76	77	78	79	80
81	82	83	84	85	86	87	88	89	90
91	92	93	94	95	96	97	98	99	100

Four 100 charts—21

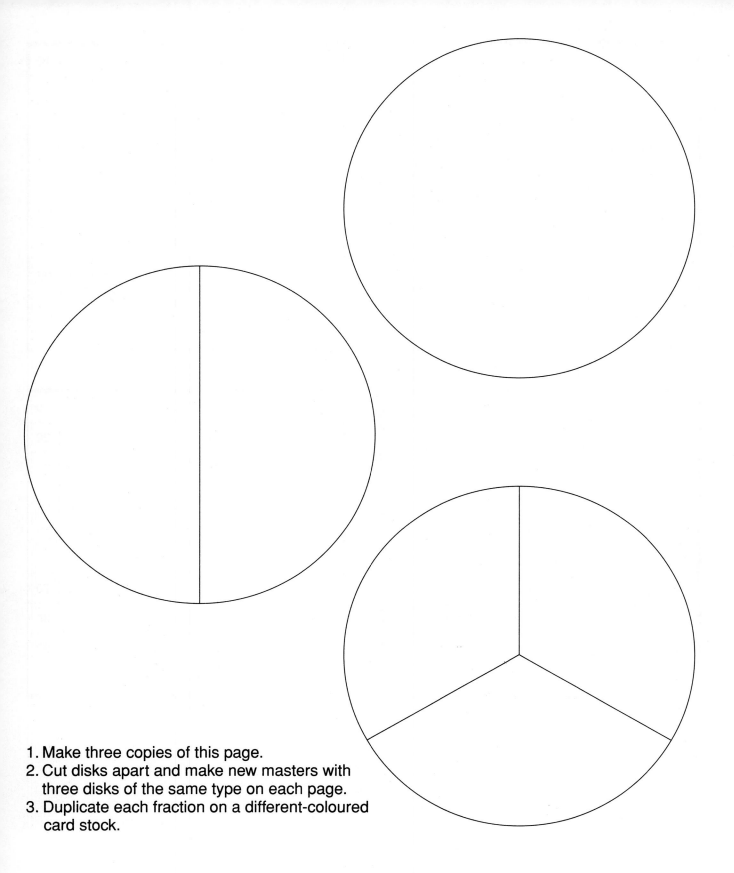

1. Make three copies of this page.
2. Cut disks apart and make new masters with three disks of the same type on each page.
3. Duplicate each fraction on a different-coloured card stock.

Circular fraction pieces—22

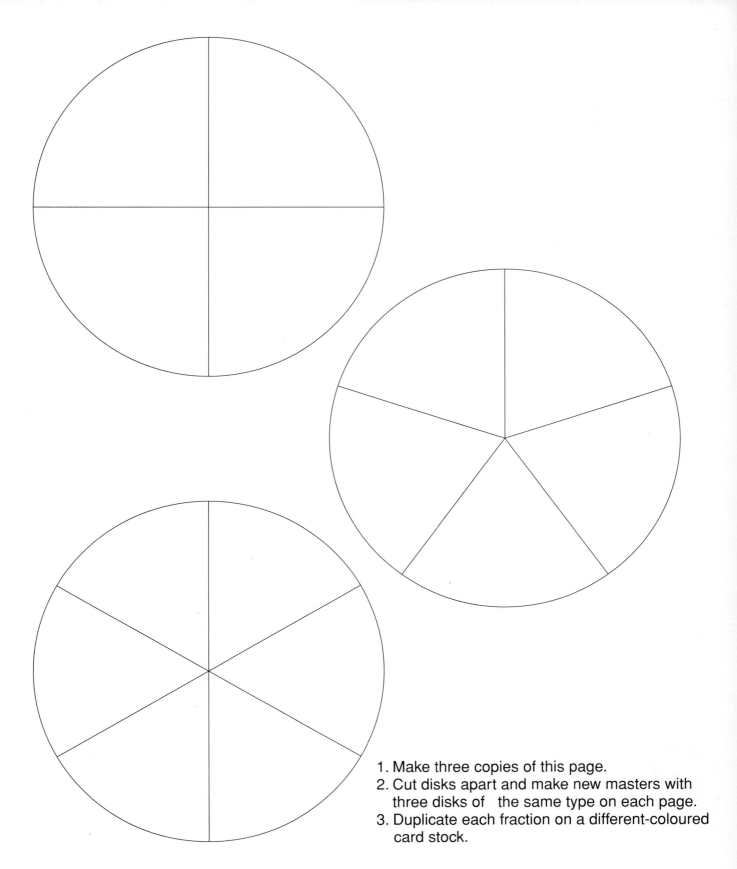

1. Make three copies of this page.
2. Cut disks apart and make new masters with three disks of the same type on each page.
3. Duplicate each fraction on a different-coloured card stock.

Circular fraction pieces—23

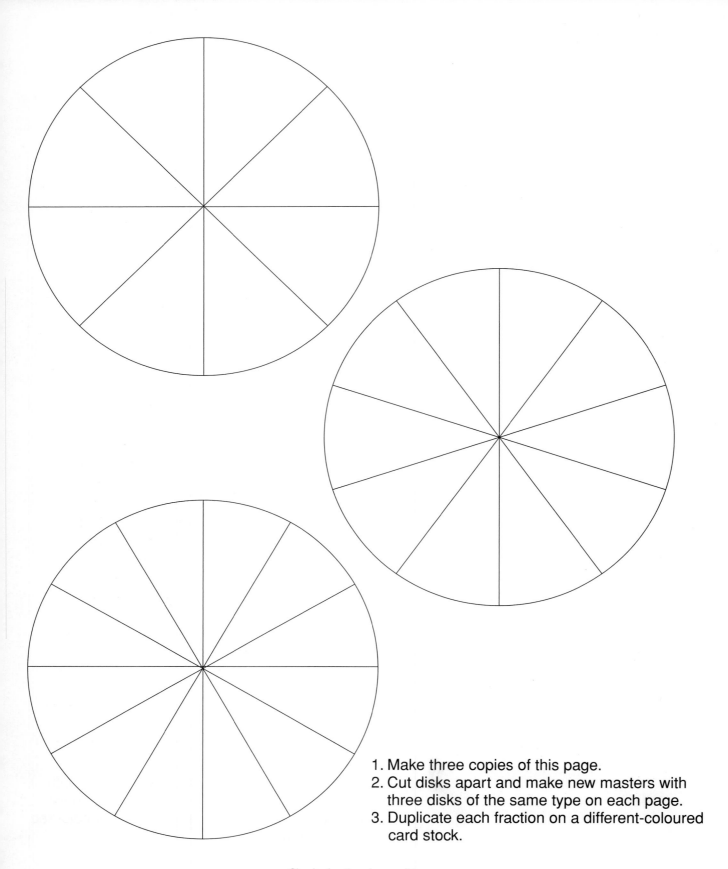

1. Make three copies of this page.
2. Cut disks apart and make new masters with three disks of the same type on each page.
3. Duplicate each fraction on a different-coloured card stock.

Circular fraction pieces—24

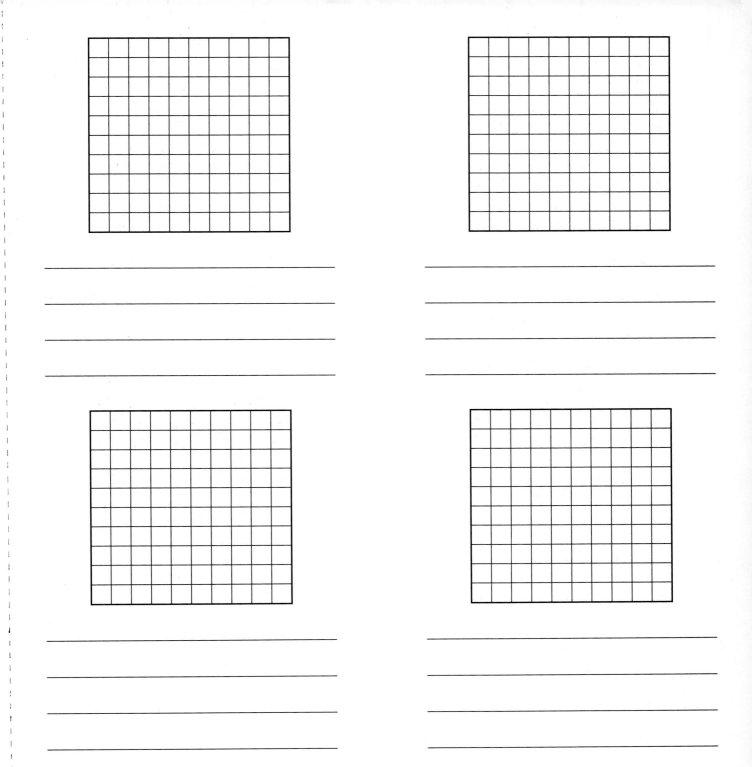

10 × 10 grids—25

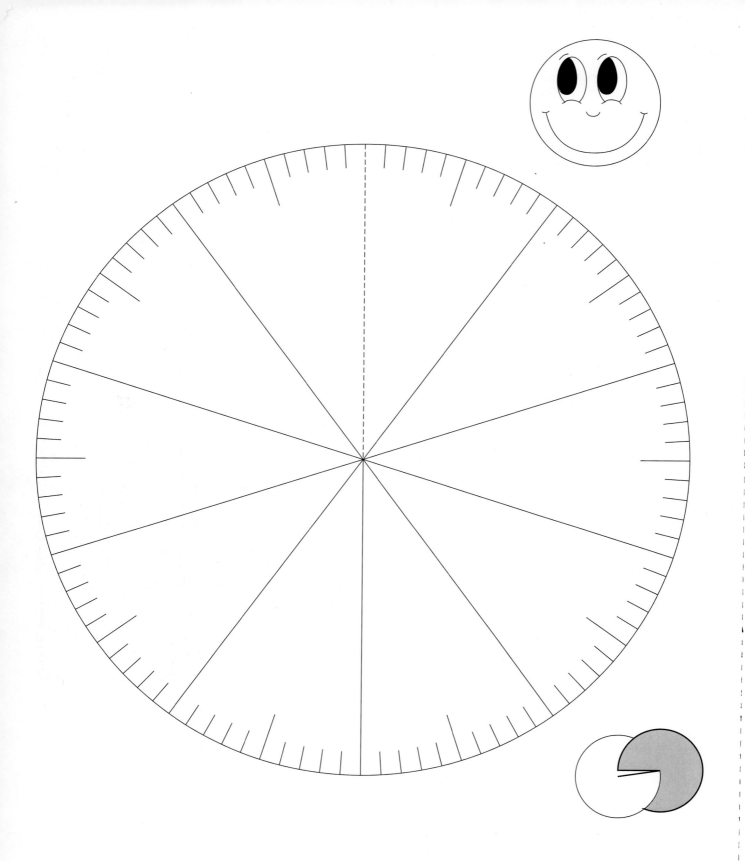

Hundredths disk—26

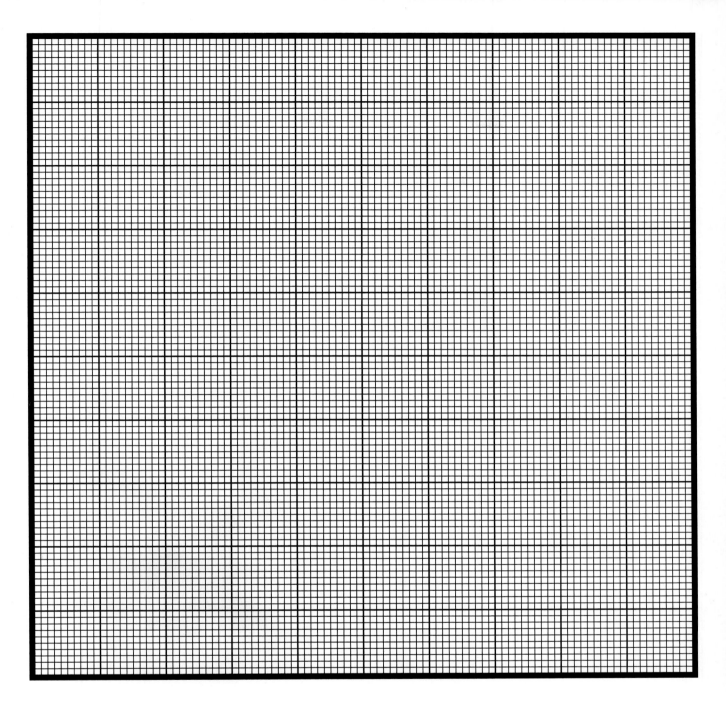

10 000 grid—27

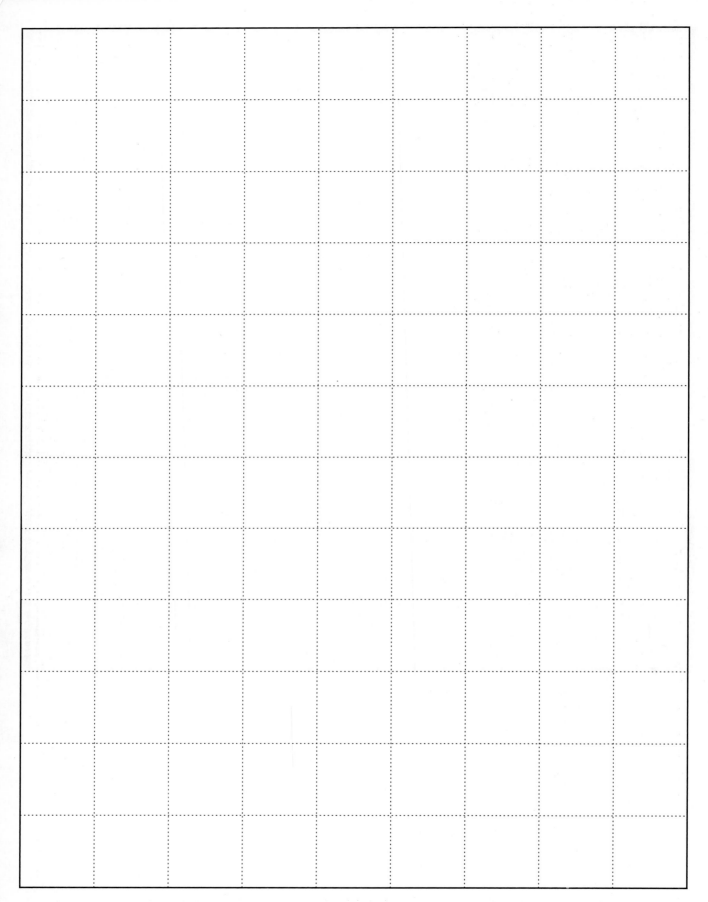

2-cm square grid—28

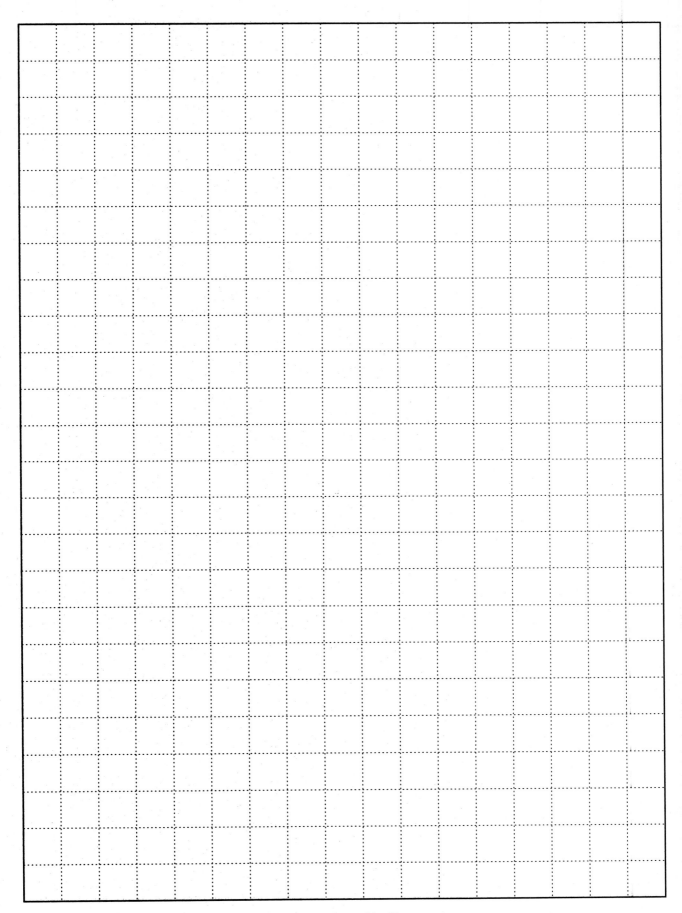

1-cm square grid—29

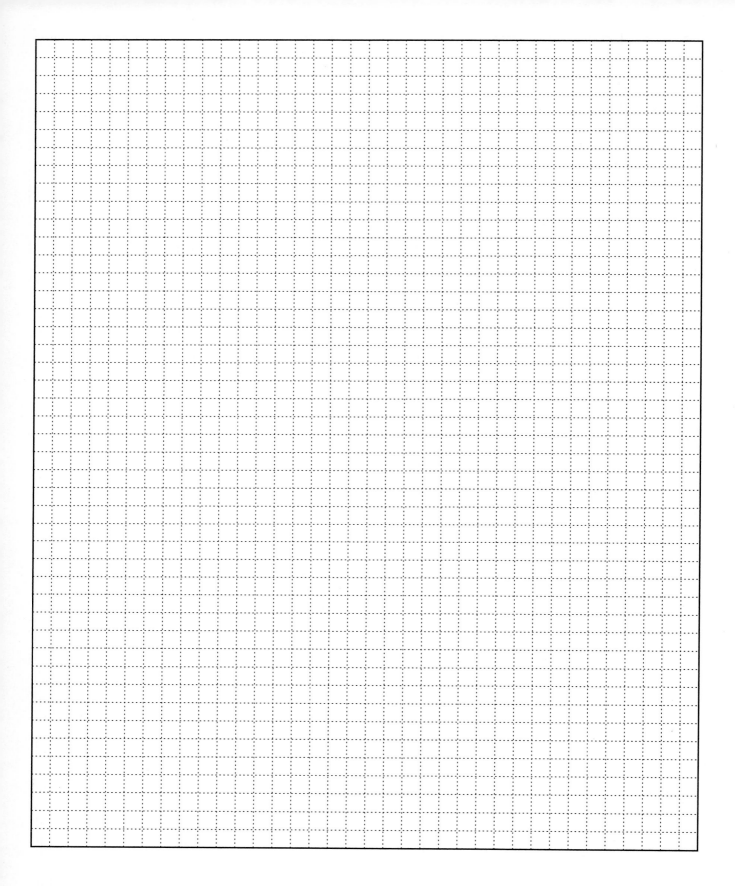

0.5-cm square grid—30

1-cm square dot grid—31

2-cm isometric grid—32

1-cm isometric dot grid—33

1-cm square/diagonal grid—34

1-cm hex grid—35

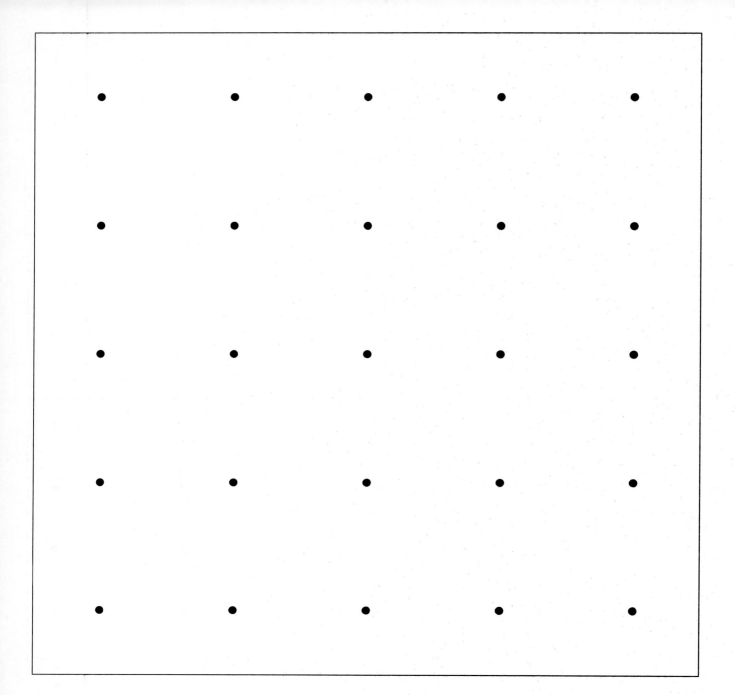

Geo-board pattern—36

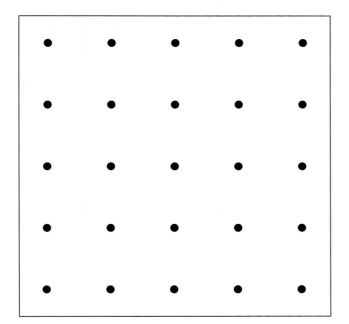

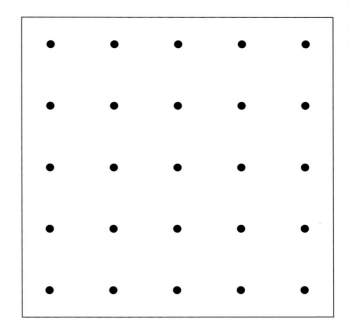

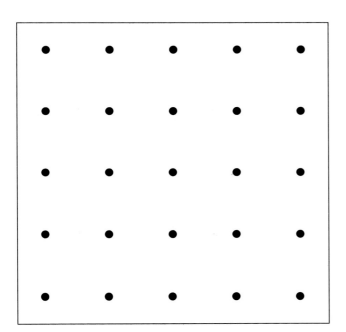

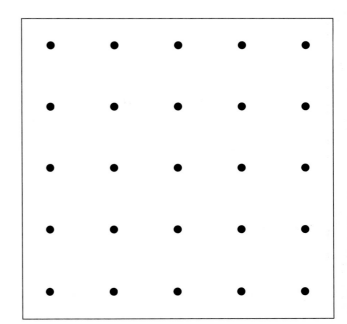

Geo-board recording sheets—37

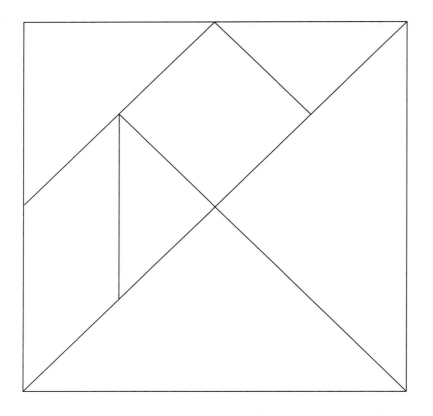

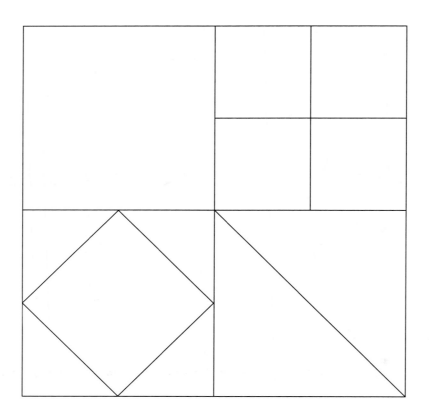

Tangrams and Five Easy Pieces—38

Woozle Cards—39